AutoCAD LT 2020

for Designers

(13th Edition)

CADCIM Technologies
525 St. Andrews Drive
Schererville, IN 46375, USA
(www.cadcim.com)

Contributing Author
Sham Tickoo
Purdue University Northwest
Department of Mechanical Engineering Technology
Hammond, Indiana, USA

CADCIM Technologies

AutoCAD LT 2020 for Designers
Sham Tickoo

CADCIM Technologies
525 St Andrews Drive
Schererville, Indiana 46375, USA
www.cadcim.com

ISBN 978-1-64057-066-5

www.cadcim.com

DEDICATION

*To teachers, who make it possible to disseminate knowledge
to enlighten the young and curious minds
of our future generations*

*To students, who are dedicated to learning new technologies
and making the world a better place to live in*

SPECIAL RECOGNITION

*A special thanks to Mr. Denis Cadu and the ADN team of Autodesk Inc.
for their valuable support and professional guidance to
procure the software for writing this textbook*

THANKS

*To the faculty and students of the MET department of
Purdue University Northwest for their cooperation*

To employees of CADCIM Technologies for their valuable help

Online Training Program Offered by CADCIM Technologies

CADCIM Technologies provides effective and affordable virtual online training on various software packages including Computer Aided Design, Manufacturing, Engineering (CAD/CAM/CAE), computer programming languages, animation, architecture, and GIS. The training is delivered 'live' via Internet at any time, any place, and at any pace to individuals as well as the students of colleges, universities, and CAD/CAM training centers. The main features of this program are:

Training for Students and Companies in a Classroom Setting

Highly experienced instructors and qualified engineers at CADCIM Technologies conduct the classes under the guidance of Prof. Sham Tickoo of Purdue University Northwest, USA. This team has authored several textbooks that are rated "one of the best" in their categories and are used in various colleges, universities, and training centers in North America, Europe, and in other parts of the world.

Training for Individuals

CADCIM Technologies with its cost effective and time saving initiative strives to deliver the training in the comfort of your home or work place, thereby relieving you from the hassles of traveling to training centers.

Training Offered on Software Packages

CADCIM provides basic and advanced training on the following software packages:

***CAD/CAM/CAE**: CATIA, Pro/ENGINEER Wildfire, PTC Creo Parametric, Creo Direct, SOLIDWORKS, Autodesk Inventor, Solid Edge, NX, AutoCAD, AutoCAD LT, AutoCAD Plant 3D, Customizing AutoCAD, EdgeCAM, and ANSYS*

***Architecture and GIS**: Autodesk Revit Architecture, AutoCAD Civil 3D, Autodesk Revit Structure, AutoCAD Map 3D, Revit MEP, Navisworks, Primavera, and Bentley STAAD Pro*

***Animation and Styling**: Autodesk 3ds Max, Autodesk 3ds Max Design, Autodesk Maya, Autodesk Alias, Foundry NukeX, and MAXON CINEMA 4D, Adobe Flash, and Adobe Premiere*

***Computer Programming**: C++, VB.NET, Oracle, AJAX, and Java*

For more information, please visit the following link: ***https://www.cadcim.com***

Note

If you are a faculty member, you can register by clicking on the following link to access the teaching resources: ***https://www.cadcim.com/Registration.aspx***. The student resources are available at ***https://www.cadcim.com***. We also provide **Live Virtual Online Training** on various software packages. For more information, write us at ***sales@cadcim.com***.

Table of Contents

Chapter 2: Getting Started with AutoCAD LT

Chapter 3: Getting Started with Advanced Sketching

Chapter 4: Working with Drawing Aids

Chapter 7: Creating Texts and Tables

Chapter 8: Basic Dimensioning, Geometric Dimensioning, and Tolerancing

Chapter 9: Editing Dimensions

Chapter 10: Dimension Styles, Multileader Styles, and System Variables

Chapter 11: Hatching Drawings

Chapter 12: Model Space Viewports, Paper Space Viewports, and Layouts

Chapter 13: Plotting Drawings

Chapter 14: Template Drawings

Chapter 15: Working with Blocks

Chapter 16: Defining Block Attributes

Chapter 17: Understanding External References

CHAPTERS AVAILABLE FOR FREE DOWNLOAD

In this textbook six chapters have been given for free download. You can download these chapters from our website *www.cadcim.com*. To download these chapters follow the given path: *Textbooks > CAD/CAM > AutoCAD LT > AutoCAD LT 2020 for Designers, 13th Edition > Chapters for Free Download* and then select the chapter name from the **Chapters for Free Download** drop-down. Click the **Download** button to download the chapter in the PDF format.

Chapter 18: Working with Advanced Drawing Options

Chapter 19: Grouping and Advanced Editing of Sketched Objects

Chapter 20: Working with Data Exchange & Object Linking and Embedding

Chapter 21: Conventional Dimensioning and Projection Theory Using AutoCAD LT

Chapter 22: Concepts of Geometric Dimensioning and Tolerancing

Chapter 23: Isometric Drawings

This page is intentionally left blank

Preface

AutoCAD LT 2020

AutoCAD LT, developed by Autodesk Inc., is the most popular PC-CAD system available in the market. Today, over 7 million people use AutoCAD LT and other AutoCAD-based design products. 100% of the Fortune 100 firms and 98% of the Fortune 500 firms are Autodesk customers. AutoCAD LT's open architecture allows third-party developers to write application software that has significantly added to its popularity. For example, the author of this book has developed a software package "**SMLayout**" for sheet metal products that generates a flat layout of various geometrical shapes such as transitions, intersections, cones, elbows, tank heads, and so on. Several companies in Canada and United States are using this software package with AutoCAD LT to design and manufacture various products. AutoCAD LT also facilitates customization that enables the users to increase their efficiency and improve their productivity.

The **AutoCAD LT 2020 for Designers** textbook contains detailed explanation of AutoCAD LT commands and their applications to solve drafting and design problems. Every AutoCAD LT command is thoroughly explained with the help of examples and illustrations. This makes it easy for the users to understand the functions and applications in the drawing. After reading this textbook, you will be able to use AutoCAD LT commands to make drawings, dimension drawings, apply constraints to sketches, insert symbols as well as create text, blocks, and dynamic blocks.

The book also covers basic drafting and design concepts that provide you with the essential drafting skills to solve the drawing problems in AutoCAD LT. These concepts include dimensioning principles and assembly drawings. While going through this textbook, you will discover some new unique applications of AutoCAD LT that will have a significant effect on your drawings. In addition, you will be able to understand why AutoCAD LT has become such a popular software package and an international standard in PC-CAD.

Symbols Used in the Textbook

Note

The author has provided additional information to the users about the topic being discussed in the form of notes.

Tip

Special information and techniques are provided in the form of tips that will increase the efficiency of the users.

New

This symbol indicates that the command or tool being discussed is new.

Enhanced

This symbol indicates that the command or tool being discussed has been enhanced in AutoCAD LT 2020.

Formatting Conventions Used in the Textbook

Refer to the following list for the formatting conventions used in this textbook.

• Command names are capitalized and written in boldface letters.	Example: The **MOVE** command
• A key icon appears when you have to respond by pressing the ENTER or the RETURN key.	Enter
• Command sequences are indented. The responses are indicated in boldface. The directions are indicated in italics and the comments are enclosed in parentheses.	Command: **MOVE** Select object: **G** Enter group name: *Enter a group name (the group name is group1)*
• The methods of invoking a tool/option from the **Ribbon**, **Menu Bar**, **Quick Access Toolbar**, **TOOL PALETTES**, **Application menu**, toolbars, Status Bar, and Command prompt are enclosed in a shaded box.	**Ribbon:** Draw > Line **Menu Bar:** Draw > Line **Tool Palettes:** Draw > Line **Toolbar:** Draw > Line **Command:** LINE or L

Naming Conventions Used in the Textbook

Tool

If you click on an item in a toolbar or a panel of the **Ribbon** and a command is invoked to create/edit an object or perform some action, then that item is termed as **tool**.

For example:
To Create: **Line** tool, **Circle** tool
To Edit: **Fillet** tool, **Array** tool, **Stretch** tool
Action: **Zoom** tool, **Move** tool, **Copy** tool

If you click on an item in a toolbar or a panel of the **Ribbon** and a dialog box is invoked wherein you can set the properties to create/edit an object, then that item is also termed as **tool**, refer to Figure 1.

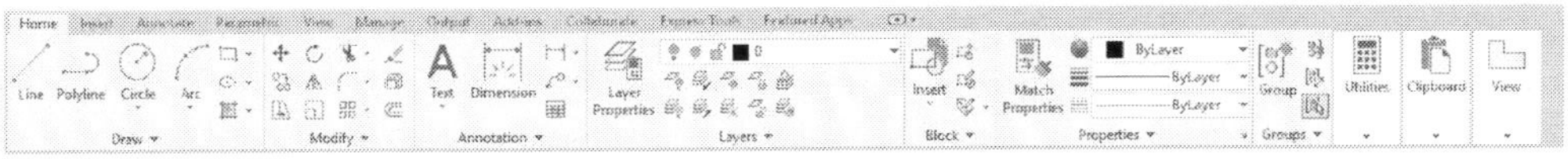

Figure 1 *Various tools in the* ***Ribbon***

For example:
To Create: **Define Attributes** tool, **Create** tool, **Insert** tool
To Edit: **Edit Attributes** tool, **Block Editor** tool

Button

If you click on an item in a toolbar or a panel of the **Ribbon** and the display of the corresponding object is toggled on/off, then that item is termed as **Button**. For example, **Grid** button, **Snap** button, **Ortho** button, **Properties** button, **Tool Palettes** button, and so on; refer to Figure 2.

Figure 2 *Various buttons displayed in the* ***Status Bar*** *and* ***Ribbon***

The item in a dialog box that has a 3d shape is also termed as **Button**. For example, **OK** button, **Cancel** button, **Apply** button, and so on.

Dialog Box

The naming conventions used for the components in a dialog box are mentioned in Figure 3.

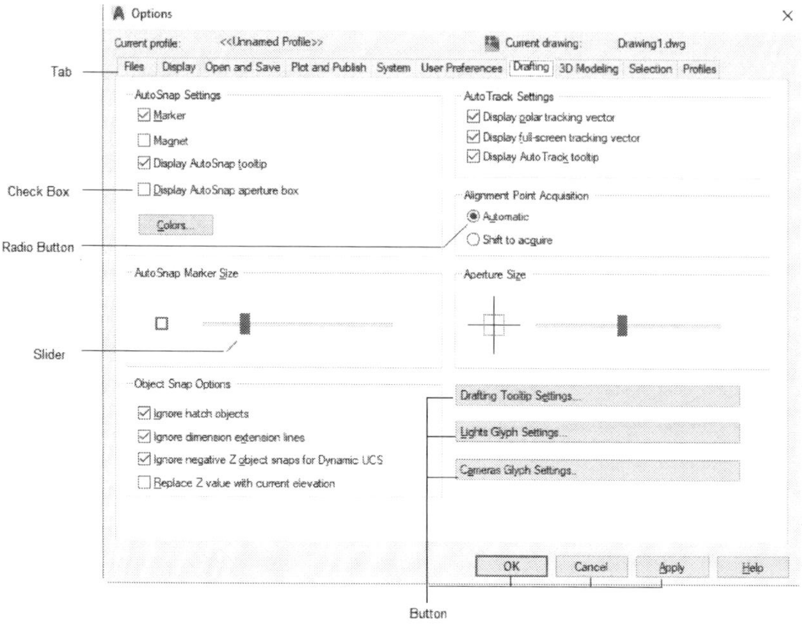

Figure 3 *The components of a dialog box*

Drop-down

A drop-down is the one in which a set of common tools are grouped together. You can identify a drop-down with a down arrow on it. These drop-downs are given a name based on the tools grouped in them. For example, **Circle** drop-down, **Fillet/Chamfer** drop-down, and so on; refer to Figure 4.

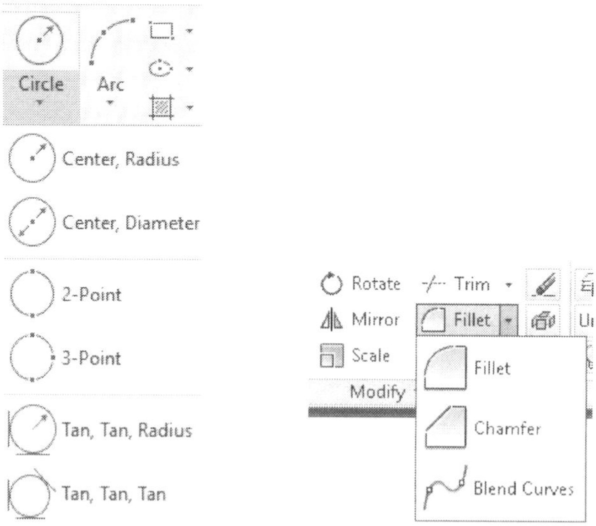

Figure 4 *The **Circle** and **Fillet** drop-downs*

Drop-down List

A drop-down list is the one in which a set of options are grouped together. You can set various parameters using these options. You can identify a drop-down list with a down arrow on it. To know the name of a drop-down list, move the cursor over it; its name will be displayed in a tool tip. For example, **Lineweight** drop-down list, **Linetype** drop-down list, **Object Color** drop-down list, **Visual Styles** drop-down list, and so on; refer to Figure 5.

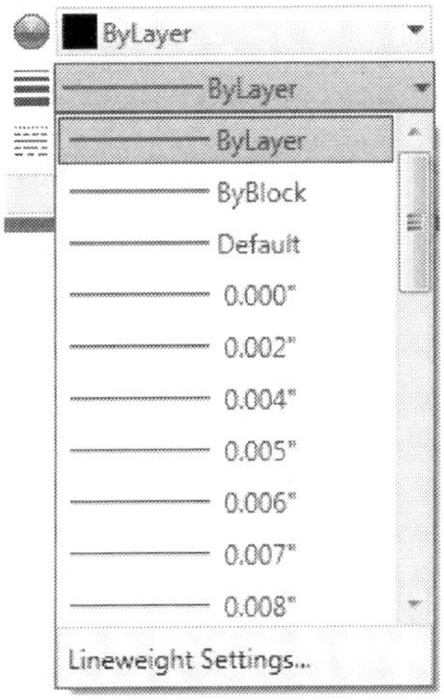

Figure 5 *The* ***Lineweight*** *drop-down list*

Options

The options are the items that are available in shortcut menu, drop-down list, Command prompt, **Properties** panel, and so on. For example, choose the **Properties** option from the shortcut menu displayed on right-clicking in the drawing area, refer to Figure 6.

Tools and Options in Menu Bar

A menu bar consists of both tools and options. As mentioned earlier, the term **tool** is used to create/edit something or to perform some action. For example, in this textbook, the item **3Points** has been used to create an arc using three points; therefore it will be referred as a tool, refer to Figure 7.

Similarly, an option in the menu bar is the one that is used to set some parameters. For example, in Figure 7, the item **Linetype** has been used to set/load the linetype; therefore it will be referred to as an option.

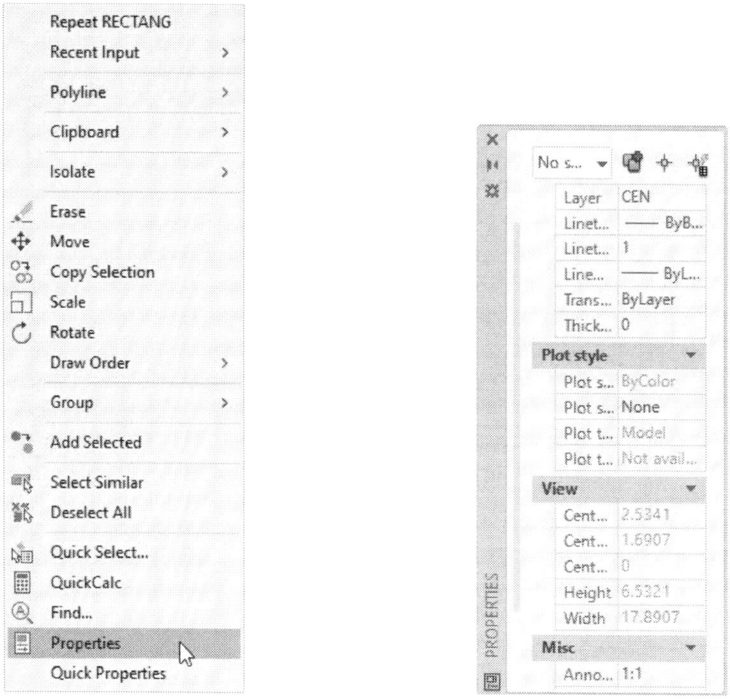

Figure 6 *Options in the shortcut menu and the **Properties** palette*

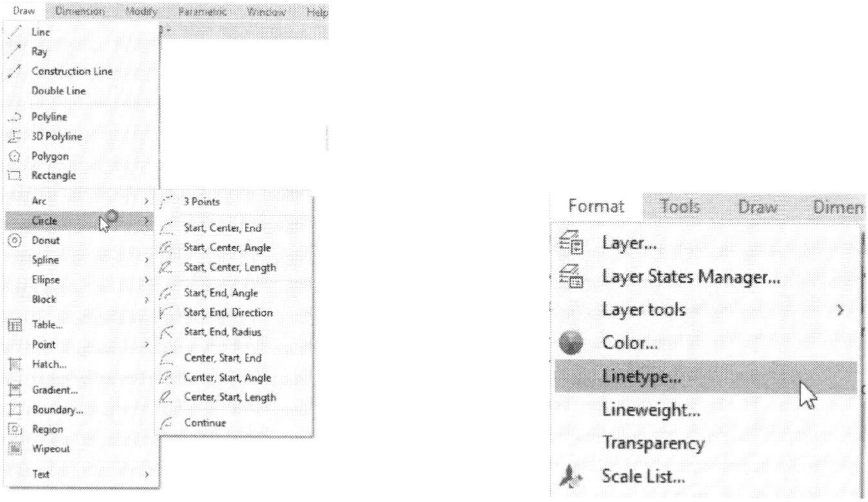

Figure 7 *Tools and options in the menu bar*

Free Companion Website

It has been our constant endeavor to provide you the best textbooks and services at affordable price. In this endeavor, we have come out with a Free Companion website that will facilitate the process of teaching and learning of AutoCAD LT 2020. If you purchase this textbook, you will get access to the files on the Companion website.

The following resources are available for the faculty and students in this website:

Faculty Resources

- **Technical Support**
  You can get online technical support by contacting ***techsupport@cadcim.com***.

- **Instructor Guide**
  Solutions to all review questions and exercises in the textbook are provided in this link to help the faculty members test the skills of the students.

- **Drawing Files**
  The drawing files used in examples and exercises are available for free download.

Student Resources

- **Technical Support**
  You can get online technical support by contacting ***techsupport@cadcim.com***.

- **Part Files**
  The part files used in illustrations and examples are available for free download.

You can access additional learning resources by visiting ***https://allaboutcadcam.blogspot.com***.

If you face any problem in accessing these files, please contact the publisher at ***sales@cadcim.com*** or the author at ***stickoo@pnw.edu*** or ***tickoo525@gmail.com***.

Stay Connected

You can now stay connected with us through Facebook and Twitter to get the latest information about our textbooks, videos, and teaching/learning resources. To stay informed of such updates, follow us on Facebook (***www.facebook.com/cadcim***) and Twitter (**@cadcimtech**). You can also subscribe to our YouTube channel (***www.youtube.com/cadcimtech***) to get the information about our latest video tutorials.

This page is intentionally left blank

Chapter 1

Introduction to AutoCAD LT

Learning Objectives

After completing this chapter, you will be able to:

- *Start AutoCAD LT*
- *Understand the usage of the components of the initial AutoCAD LT screen*
- *Invoke AutoCAD LT commands from the keyboard, menus, toolbars, shortcut menus, Tool Palettes, and Ribbon*
- *Work with File Tabs*
- *Understand the usage of components of dialog boxes in AutoCAD LT*
- *Start a new drawing using the New tool, File tabs, and Startup dialog box*
- *Save the work using various file-saving commands*
- *Close a drawing*
- *Open an existing drawing*
- *Quit AutoCAD LT*
- *Understand various options of AutoCAD LT help*
- *Understand the use of Active Assistance, Learning Assistance, and other interactive help options*
- *Understand the concept of Design Feed*

Key Terms

- *Initial Setup*
- *AutoCAD LT Screen Components*
- *Ribbon*
- *Application Menu*
- *Tool Palettes*
- *Menu Bar*
- *Toolbar*
- *New*
- *Save*
- *Save As*
- *Close*
- *STARTUP*
- *Open*
- *Partial open*
- *Drawing Recovery Manager*
- *Workspaces*
- *Help*
- *A360*
- *Autodesk Cloud*
- *Design Feed*
- *File Tabs*

AutoCAD LT SCREEN COMPONENTS

The initial AutoCAD LT screen comprises of drawing area, command window, menu bar, several toolbars, Model and Layout tabs, and Status Bar, as shown in Figure 1-1. A title bar that has AutoCAD LT symbol and the current drawing name is displayed on top of the screen.

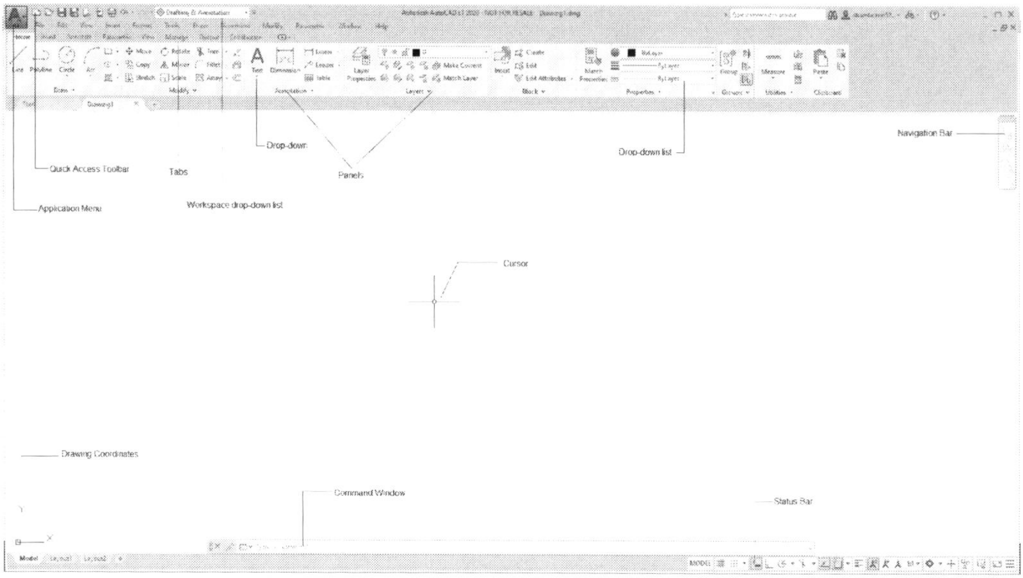

Figure 1-1 *Screen components in the* ***Drafting*** *&* ***Annotation*** *workspace of AutoCAD LT*

Start Tab

In AutoCAD LT, the **Start** tab is displayed in the AutoCAD LT environment when you close all the drawing templates or when there are no drawings open. The **Start** tab contains two sliding pages, **CREATE** and **LEARN**, refer to Figure 1-2. These frames are discussed next.

CREATE

When you click on **CREATE**, the **CREATE** page is displayed. In the **CREATE** page, you can access sample file, recent files, templates, product updates, as well as connect with the online community. The **CREATE** page is divided into three columns: **Get Started, Recent Documents**, and **Notifications/Connect**.

LEARN

When you click on **LEARN**, the **LEARN** page is displayed. The **LEARN** page provides tools to help you learn AutoCAD LT 2020. You slide to the **LEARN** page from the **CREATE** page by clicking on **LEARN** at the bottom of the page. This page is divided into three columns: **What's New**, **Getting Started Videos for AutoCAD LT**, and **Learning Tips/Online Resources** with **Security Updates**.

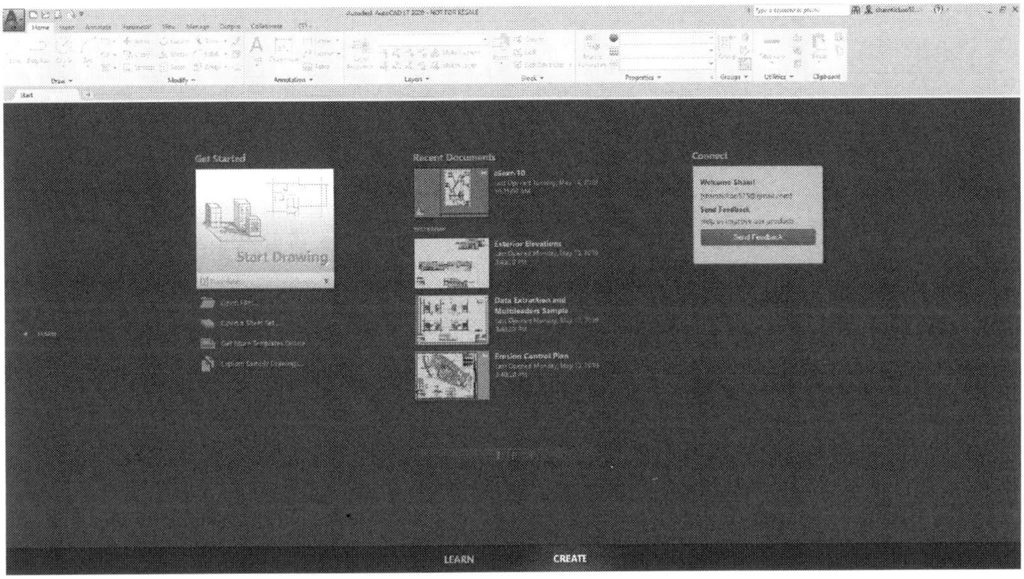

*Figure 1-2 The **Start** tab in AutoCAD LT*

Drawing Area

The drawing area covers the major portion of the screen. In this area, you can draw the objects and use the commands. To draw the objects, you need to define the coordinate points, which can be selected by using your pointing device. The position of the pointing device is represented on the screen by the cursor. The window also has the standard Windows buttons such as close, minimize, and so on, on the top right corner. These buttons have the same functions as for any other standard window.

Command Window

The command window at the bottom of the drawing area has the Command prompt where you can enter the commands. It also displays the subsequent prompt sequences and the messages. You can change the size of the window by placing the cursor on the top edge (double line bar known as the grab bar) and then dragging it. This way you can increase its size to see all the previous commands you have used. By default, the command window displays only three lines. You can also press the F2 key to display **AutoCAD LT Text Window**, which displays the previous commands and prompts.

Tip

*You can hide all toolbars displayed on the screen by pressing the CTRL+0 keys or by choosing **View > Clean Screen** from the menu bar. To turn on the display of the toolbars again, press the CTRL+0 keys. You can also choose the **Clean Screen** button in the Status Bar to hide all toolbars.*

Auto Correct the Command Name

In AutoCAD LT, if you type a wrong command name in the Command prompt, a suggestion list with most relevant commands will be displayed, refer to Figure 1-3. You can invoke the desired command by selecting the required option from this list.

Auto Complete the Command Name

When you start typing a command name in the Command prompt, the complete name of the command will be displayed automatically. Also, a list of corresponding commands will be displayed, as shown in Figure 1-4. The commands that have not been used for a long time will be grouped in folders at the bottom of the list.

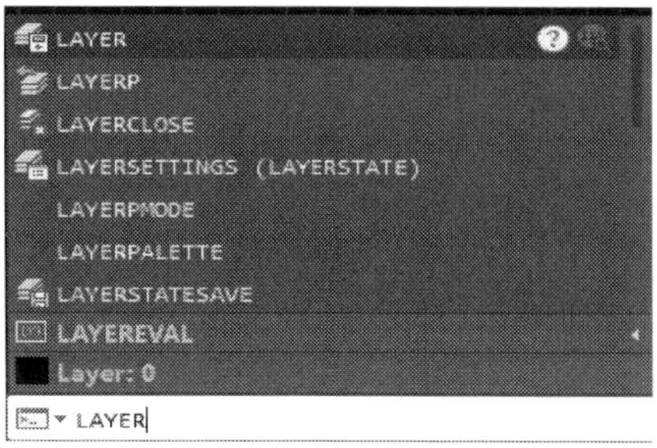

Figure 1-3 *Suggestion list with relevant commands*

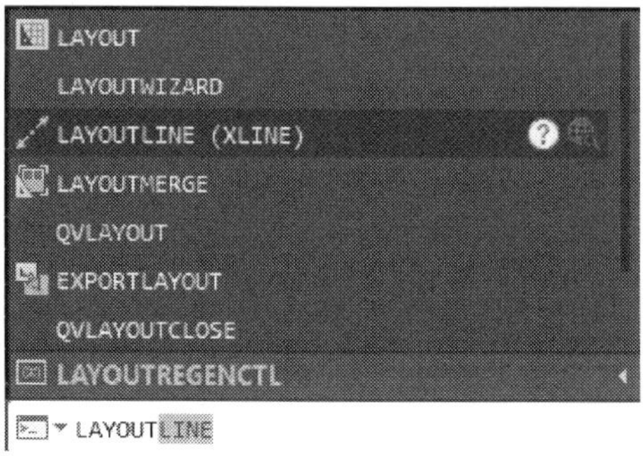

Figure 1-4 *Command bar displaying complete command name automatically*

Internet Search

You can get more information about a command by using the **Search in Help** and **Search on Internet** buttons available adjacent to the command name in the Command line, refer to Figure 1-5. If you choose the **Search in Help** button, the **Autodesk AutoCAD LT 2020 -Help** dialog box will be displayed. In this dialog box, you can find information about the command. By using the **Search on Internet** button, you can find information about the command on internet. Note that these buttons will be available adjacent to the selected command name in the suggestion list.

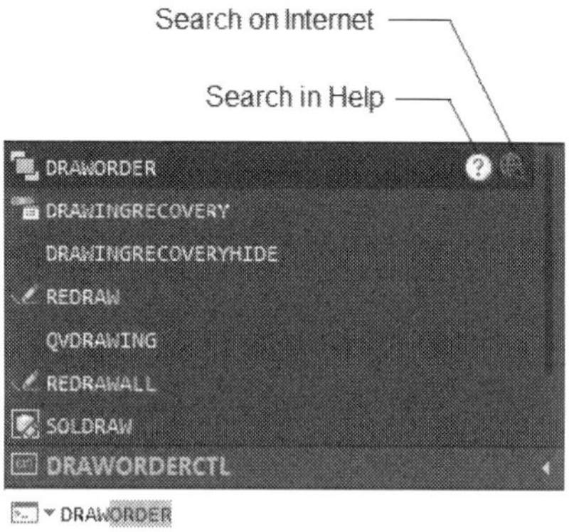

Figure 1-5 *The **Search in Help** and **Search on Internet** buttons displayed in the suggestion list*

Synonym Suggestions

In AutoCAD LT, you can invoke a command by entering synonyms of the command name. By entering the synonym in the Command prompt, the command related to the synonym entered will be displayed. For example, if you enter **ROUND** in the Command prompt, then the **FILLET** command will be displayed, as shown in Figure 1-6.

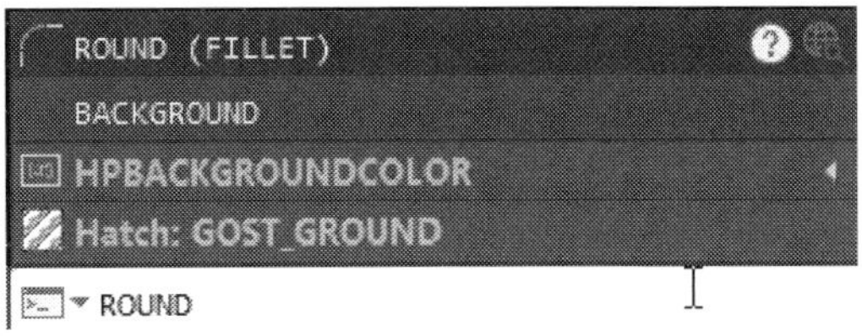

***Figure 1-6** Suggestion list displayed after entering a synonym of command name in the Command prompt*

Input Search Options

In AutoCAD LT, you can enable or disable the functions such as Auto Complete and Auto Correct by using the options available in the **Input Search Options** dialog box. To invoke this dialog box, right-click on the Command prompt; a shortcut menu will be displayed. Next, choose **Input Search Options** from the shortcut menu; the **Input Search Options** dialog box will be displayed, refer to Figure 1-7. You can now enable or disable the required functions by using this dialog box.

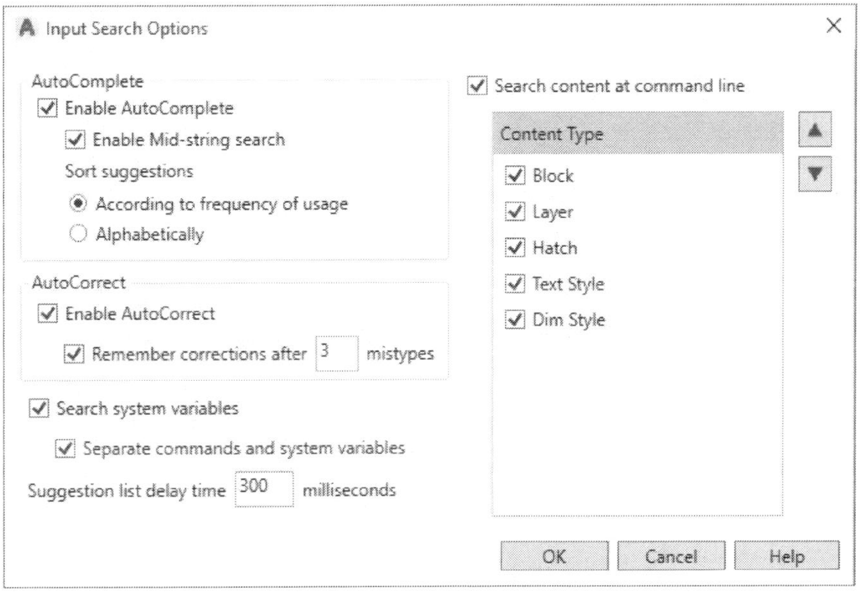

***Figure 1-7** The **Input Search Options** dialog box*

Navigation Bar

The **Navigation Bar** is displayed in the drawing area and contains navigation tools. These tools are grouped together, refer to Figure 1-8. The tools in the navigation bar are discussed next.

2D wheel (SteeringWheels)

The **2D wheel (SteeringWheels)** has a set of navigation tools such as pan, zoom, and so on. You will learn more about the **2D wheel (SteeringWheel**) in the later chapters.

Pan

This tool allows you to view the portion of the drawing that is outside the current display area. To do so, choose this tool, press and hold the left mouse button, and then drag the drawing area. Press ESC to exit this command.

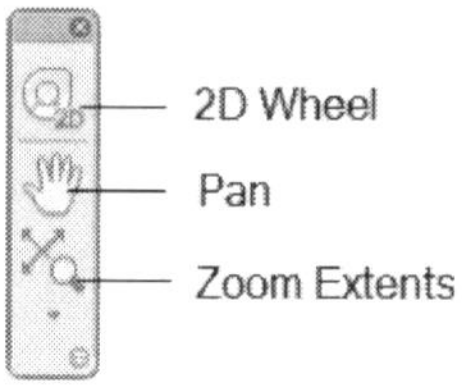

Figure 1-8** Tools in the **Navigation Bar

Zoom

The tools to enlarge the view of the drawing on the screen without affecting the actual size of the objects are grouped together. You will learn more about zoom tools in later chapters.

Status Bar

The Status Bar is displayed at the bottom of the screen and is also called the Application Status Bar. It contains some useful information and buttons that make it easy to change the status of some AutoCAD LT functions, refer to Figure 1-9. You can toggle between the on and off states of most of these functions by choosing them. You can add or remove these buttons in the Status Bar by selecting respective options from the **Customization** flyout.

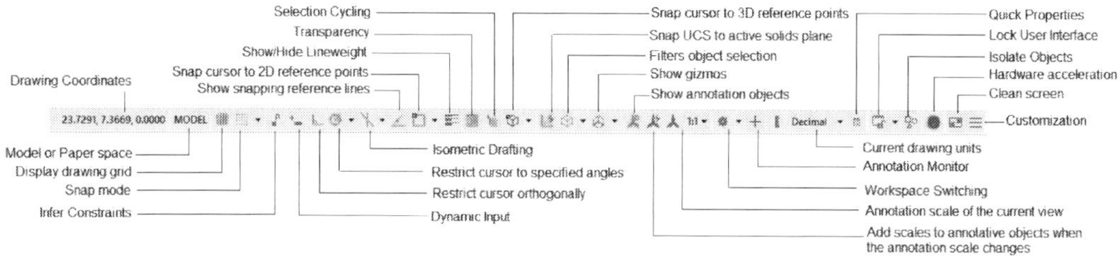

***Figure 1-9** The Status Bar displayed in the **Drafting & Annotation** workspace*

Coordinates

The information about the coordinates is displayed at the left corner of the Status Bar near the **Model** and **Layout** tabs. You can choose the **coordinates** button to toggle between the on and off states. The **COORDS** system variable controls the type of display of the coordinates. If the value of the **COORDS** variable is set to 0, the coordinate display is static, that is, the coordinate values displayed in the Status Bar change only when you specify a point. If the value of the **COORDS** variable is set to 1, 2, or 3, the coordinate display is dynamic. When the variable is set to 1, AutoCAD LT constantly displays the absolute coordinates of the graphics cursor with respect to the UCS origin. The polar coordinates (length<angle) are displayed if you are in an AutoCAD LT command and the **COORDS** variable is set to 2. By default, the **COORDS** variable is set to 1. You can also click on the **Drawing Coordinates** area to change the coordinate status from on to off and vice-versa.

MODEL

The **MODEL** button is chosen by default because you will be working in the model space to create drawings. You will learn more about the model space in later chapters.

GRIDMODE

In AutoCAD LT, the grid lines are used as reference lines to draw objects. If the **GRIDMODE** button is chosen, the Display drawing grid is on and the grid lines are displayed on the screen. The F7 function key can be used to turn the grid display on or off.

SNAPMODE

If the **SNAPMODE** button is chosen, the snap mode is on. So, you can move the cursor in fixed increments. The F9 key acts as a toggle key to turn the snap off or on.

Dynamic Input

The **Dynamic Input** button is used to turn the **Dynamic Input** mode on or off. Turning it on facilitates the heads-up design approach because all commands, prompts, and dimensional inputs will now be displayed in the drawing area and you do not need to look at the Command prompt all the time. This saves the design time and also increases the efficiency of the user. If the **Dynamic Input** mode is turned on, you will be allowed to enter the commands through the **Pointer Input** boxes, and the numerical values through the **Dimensional Input** boxes. You will also be allowed to select the command options through the **Dynamic Prompt** options in the graphics window. To turn the **Dynamic Input** on or off, use the F12 key.

ORTHOMODE

If the **ORTHOMODE** button is chosen, you can draw lines at right angles only. You can use the F8 function key to turn ortho on or off.

Polar Tracking

If you turn the polar tracking on, the movement of the cursor is restricted along a path based on the angle set as the polar angle. Choose the **Polar Tracking** button to turn the polar tracking on. You can also use the F10 function key to turn on this option. Note that turning the polar tracking on, automatically turns off the ortho mode.

Isometric Drafting

In AutoCAD LT, you can activate the required working plane. To activate the required working plane, choose the **Isometric Drafting** button from the Status Bar. On choosing this button, a flyout is displayed with the **isoplane Left**, **isoplane Top**, and **isoplane Right** options. You can choose the required option from this flyout to activate the respective work plane.

Object Snap Tracking

When you choose this button, the inferencing lines will be displayed. Inferencing lines are dashed lines that are displayed automatically when you select a sketching tool and track a particular keypoint on the screen. Choosing this button turns the object snap tracking on or off. You can also use the F11 function key to turn the object snap tracking on or off.

Object Snap

When the **Object Snap** button is chosen, you can use the running object snaps to snap on to a point. You can also use the F3 function key to turn the object snap on or off. The status of **OSNAP** (off or on) does not prevent you from using the immediate mode object snaps.

Show/Hide Lineweight

Choose this button in the Status Bar to turn on or off the display of lineweights in the drawing.

Transparency

This button is available in the Status Bar and is chosen to turn on or off the transparency set for a drawing. You can set the transparency in the **Properties** panel or in the layer in which the sketch is drawn.

Selection Cycling

When this button is chosen, you can cycle through the objects to be selected, if they are overlapping or close to other entities. On selecting an entity when this button is chosen, the **Selection** list box with a list of the entities that can be selected will be displayed. You can use CTRL+W as a shortcut key to toggle this button.

Show annotation objects

This button is used to control the visibility of the annotative objects that do not support the current annotation scale in the drawing area.

Add Scales to annotative objects when the annotative scale changes

This button, if chosen, automatically adds all the annotation scales that are set current to all the annotative objects present in the drawing.

Annotation Scale of the current view

The annotation scale controls the size and display of the annotative objects in the model space. The **Annotation Scale** button has a flyout that displays all the annotation scales available for the current drawing.

Workspace Switching

In AutoCAD LT, you can switch between different environments or workspaces, by using the **Workspace Switching** button that is available at the right of the Status Bar. On clicking the **Workspace Switching** button, a flyout will be displayed with the list of all available workspace. You can select the required workspace to invoke. You will learn more about workspaces later in this chapter.

Annotation Monitor

The **Annotation Monitor** button is used to turn the **Annotation Monitor** on or off. If it is turned on, all the non-associative annotations will get highlighted by placing a badge on them, as shown in Figure 1-10. In this figure, the Line leader is not associated with line.

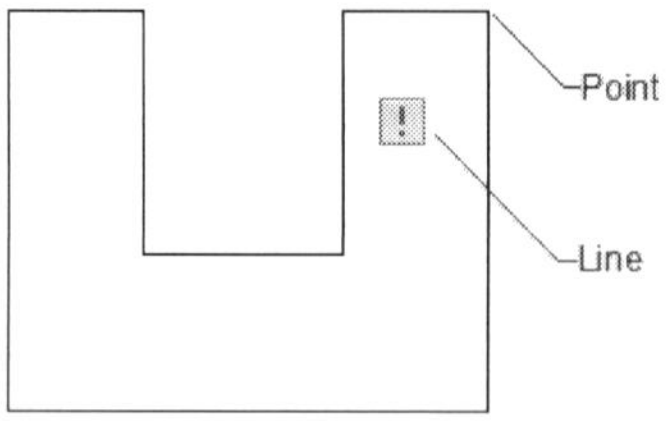

Figure 1-10 The non-associative annotation

Current drawing units

The **Current drawing units** button displays and controls the units of drawing. It has a flyout that displays all the unit systems available for drawing.

Quick Properties
If you select a sketched entity with this button is chosen in the Status Bar, the properties of the selected entity will be displayed in a panel. You can use CTRL+SHIFT+P as a shortcut key to toggle this button.

Lock UI
This button is used to lock/unlock the toolbars/pannels.

Graphics Performance
This button is used to set the performance of the software to an acceptable level.

Isolate Objects
This button is used to hide or isolate objects from the drawing area. On choosing this button, a flyout will be displayed with two options. Choose the **Isolate Objects** option from this flyout and then select the objects to hide or isolate. To end isolation or display a hidden object, click on this button again and choose the **End Object Isolation** option.

Clean Screen
The **Clean Screen** button is available at the lower right corner of the screen. This button, when chosen, displays an expanded view of the drawing area by hiding all the toolbars except the command window, Status Bar, and menu bar. The expanded view of the drawing area can also be displayed by choosing **View > Clean Screen** from the menu bar or by using the CTRL+0 keys. Choose the **Clean Screen** button again to restore the previous display state.

Customization
The **Customization** button is available at right corner of the Status Bar. Using this button, you can customize to add or remove tools in the Status Bar.

Plot/Publish Details Report Available

This icon is displayed in the Status Bar when some plotting or publishing activity is performed in the background. When you click on this icon, the **Plot and Publish Details** dialog box, which provides the details about the plotting and publishing activity, will be displayed. You can copy this report to the clipboard by choosing the **Copy to Clipboard** button from the dialog box.

Manage Xrefs

The **Manage Xrefs** icon is displayed in the Status Bar whenever an external reference drawing is attached to the selected drawing. This icon displays a message and an alert whenever the Xreffed drawing needs to be reloaded. To find detailed information regarding the status of each Xref in the drawing and the relation between the various Xrefs, click on the **Manage Xrefs** icon; the **External References Palette** will be displayed. The Xrefs are discussed in detail in Chapter 17, understanding External References.

INVOKING TOOLS IN AutoCAD LT
On starting AutoCAD LT, when you are in the drawing area, you need to invoke AutoCAD LT tools to perform an operation. For example, to draw a line, first you need to invoke the **Line**

tool and then define the start point and the endpoint of the line. Similarly, if you want to erase objects, you must invoke the **Erase** tool and then select the objects for erasing. AutoCAD LT has provided the following methods to invoke the commands:

Keyboard

You can invoke any AutoCAD LT command from the keyboard by typing the command name and then pressing the ENTER key. As you type the first letter of command, AutoCAD LT displays all available commands starting with the letter typed. If the **Dynamic Input** is on and the cursor is in the drawing area, by default, the command will be entered through the **Pointer Input** box. The **Pointer Input** box is a small box displayed on the right of the cursor, as shown in Figure 1-11. However, if the cursor is currently placed on any toolbar or menu bar, or if the **Dynamic Input** is turned off, the command will be entered through the Command prompt. Before you enter a command, the Command prompt is displayed as the last line in the command window area. If it is not displayed, you must cancel the existing command by pressing the ESC (Escape) key.

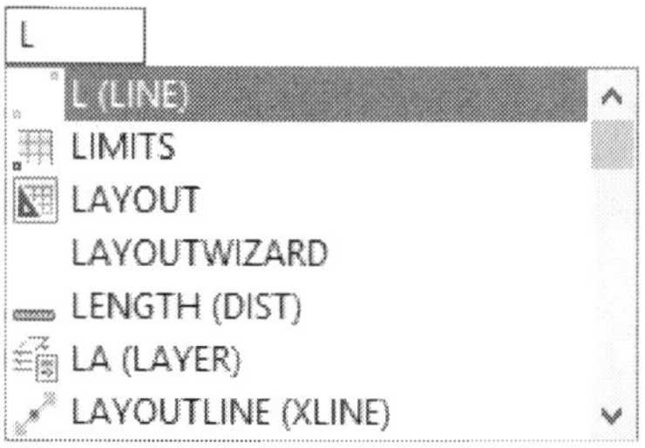

***Figure 1-11** The **Pointer Input** box displayed when the **Dynamic Input** is on*

The following example shows how to invoke the **LINE** command using the keyboard:

Command: **LINE** or **L** [Enter] (L is command alias)

Ribbon

In AutoCAD LT, you can also invoke a tool from the **Ribbon**. The tools for creating, modifying, and annotating the 2D designs are available in the panels instead of being spread out in the entire drawing area in different toolbars and menus, refer to Figure 1-12.

***Figure 1-12** The **Ribbon** for the **Drafting & Annotation** workspace*

When you start the AutoCAD LT session for the first time, by default the **Ribbon** is displayed horizontally below the **Quick Access Toolbar**. The **Ribbon** consists of various tabs. The tabs have different panels, which in turn, have tools arranged in rows. Some of the tools have small black down arrow. This indicates that the tools having similar functions are grouped together. To choose a tool, click on the down arrow; a drop-down will be displayed. Choose the required tool from the drop-down displayed. Note that if you choose a tool from the drop-down, the corresponding command will be invoked and the tool that you have chosen will be displayed in the panel. For example, to draw a circle using the **2-Point** option, click on the down arrow next to the **Center, Radius** tool in the **Draw** panel of the **Home** tab; a flyout will be displayed. Choose the **2-Point** tool from the flyout and then draw the circle. You will notice that the **2-Point** tool is displayed in place of the **Center, Radius** tool.

Choose the down arrow to expand the panel. You will notice that a push pin is available at the left end of the panel. Click on the push pin to keep the panel in the expanded state. Also, some of the panels have an inclined arrow at the lower-right corner. When you left click on an inclined arrow, a dialog box is displayed. You can define the setting of the corresponding panel in the dialog box.

You can reorder the panels in the tab. To do so, press and hold the left mouse button on the panel to be moved and drag it to the required position. To undock the **Ribbon**, right-click on the blank space in the **Ribbon** and choose the **Undock** option. You can move, resize, anchor, and auto-hide the **Ribbon** using the shortcut menu that will be displayed when you right-click on the heading strip. To anchor the floating **Ribbon** to the left or right of the drawing area in the vertical position, right-click on the heading strip of the floating **Ribbon**; the shortcut menu is displayed. Choose the corresponding option from this shortcut menu. The **Auto-hide** option will hide the **Ribbon** into the heading strip and will display it only when you move the cursor over this strip.

You can customize the display of tabs and panels in the **Ribbon**. To customize the **Ribbon**, right-click on any one of the tools in it; a shortcut menu will be displayed. On moving the cursor over one of the options, a flyout will be displayed with a tick mark before all options and the corresponding tab or panel will be displayed in the **Ribbon**. Select/clear appropriate option to display/hide a particular tab or panel.

Application Menu

The **Application Menu** is available at the top-left of the AutoCAD LT window. It contains some of the tools that are available in the **Standard** toolbar. Click the down arrow on the **Application Menu** to display the tools, refer to Figure 1-13. You can search for tools or commands by using the search field on the top of the **Application Menu**. To search a tool or command, enter its complete or partial name in the search field; the list of related tools and commands will be displayed. If you click on a tool from the list, the corresponding command will get activated.

By default, the **Recent Document** button is chosen in the **Application Menu**. Therefore, the recently opened drawings will be listed. If you have opened multiple drawing files, choose the **Open Documents** button; the documents that are opened will be listed in the **Application Menu**. To set the preferences of the file, choose the **Options** button available at the bottom-right of the **Application Menu**. To exit AutoCAD LT, choose the **Exit Autodesk AutoCAD LT 2020** button next to the **Options** button.

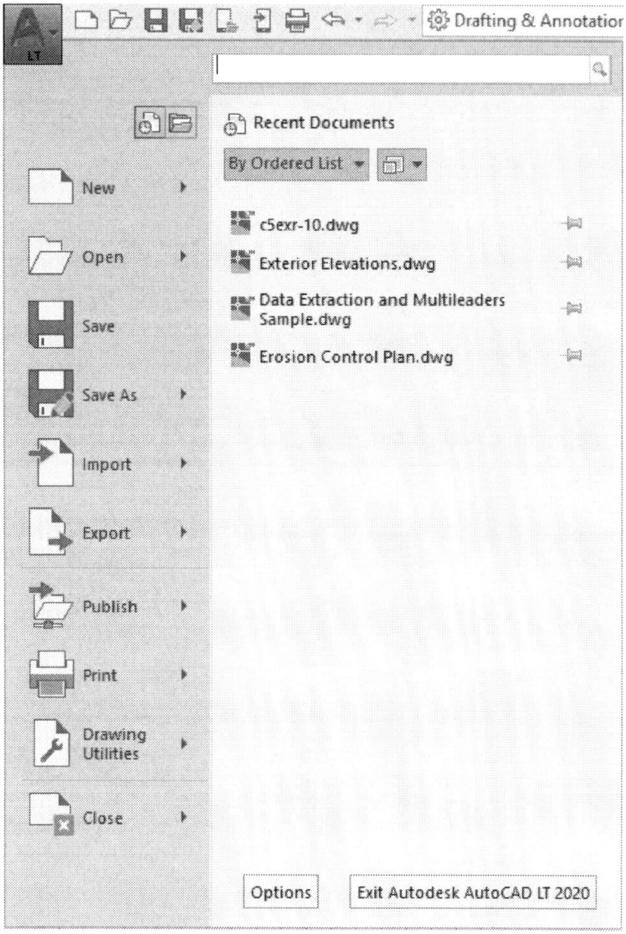

Figure 1-13 The ***Application Menu***

Tool Palettes

AutoCAD LT has provided **Tool Palettes** as an easy and convenient way of placing and sharing hatch patterns and blocks in the current drawing. By default, the **Tool Palettes** are not displayed. Choose the **Tool Palettes** button from the **Palettes** panel in the **View** tab or choose the CTRL+3 keys to display the **Tool Palettes** as a window in the drawing area. You can resize the **Tool Palettes** using the resizing cursor that is displayed when you place the cursor on the top or bottom extremity of the **Tool Palettes**. The **Tool Palettes** are discussed in detail in Chapter 11, Hatching Drawings.

Menu Bar

You can also select commands from the menu bar. Menu Bar is not displayed by default. To display the menu bar, click on the down arrow in the **Quick Access Toolbar**; a flyout is displayed. Choose the **Show Menu Bar** option from it; the menu bar will be displayed. As you move the cursor over the menu bar, different tabs are highlighted. You can choose the desired item by left-clicking on it; the corresponding menu is displayed directly under the title. For example, to draw an ellipse using the **Center** option, choose the **Draw** menu and then choose the **Ellipse** option; a cascading menu will be displayed. From the cascading menu, choose the

Center option. In this text, this command selection sequence will be referenced as choosing **Draw > Ellipse > Center** from the menu bar.

Toolbar

In AutoCAD LT, toolbars are not displayed by default. To display a toolbar, choose **Tools > Toolbars > AutoCAD LT** from the **Menu Bar**; a list of toolbars will be displayed. Select the required toolbar. Figure 1-14 shows the **Draw** toolbar.

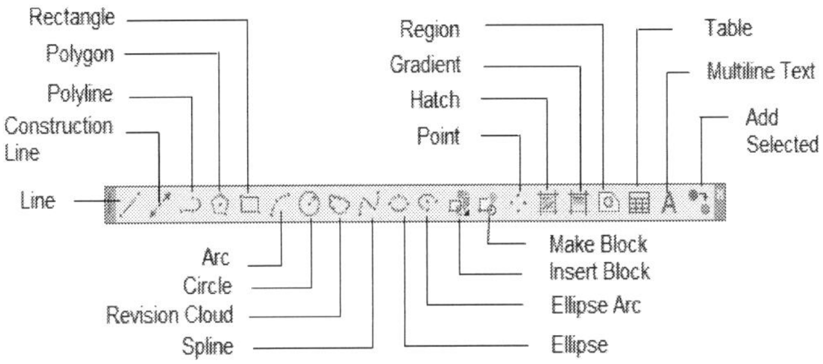

*Figure 1-14 The **Draw** toolbar*

Shortcut Menu

AutoCAD LT has provided shortcut menus as an easy and convenient way of invoking the recently used tools. These shortcut menus are context-sensitive, which means that the tools present in them are dependent on the place/object for which they are displayed. A shortcut menu is invoked by right-clicking and is displayed at the cursor location. You can right-click anywhere in the drawing area to display the general shortcut menu. It generally contains an option to select the previously invoked tool again, apart from the common tools for Windows, refer to Figure 1-15.

If you right-click in the drawing area while a command is active, a shortcut menu is displayed, containing the options of that particular command. Figure 1-16 shows the shortcut menu when the **Polyline** tool is active.

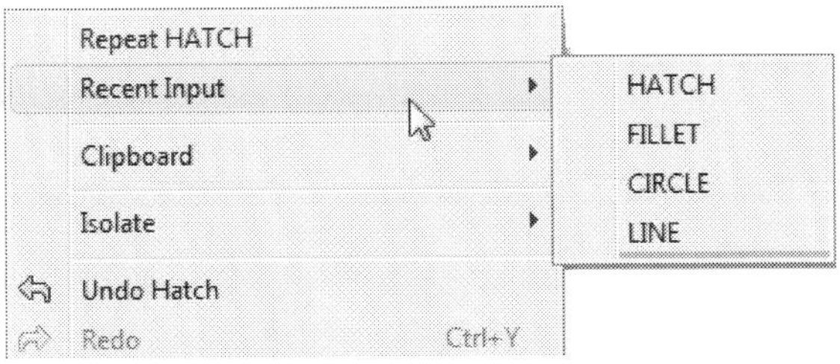

Figure 1-15 Partial view of the shortcut menu with the recently used tools

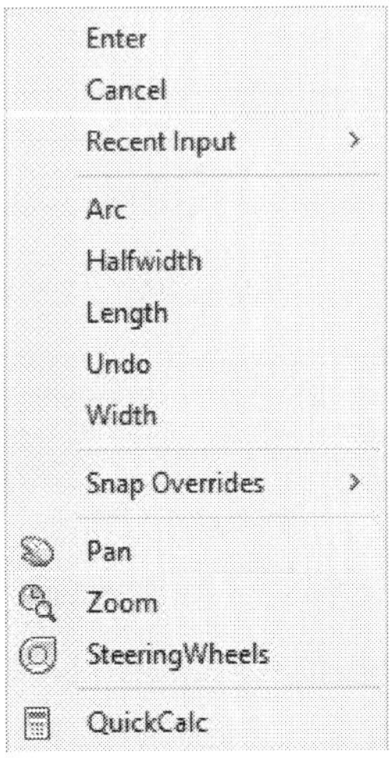

*Figure 1-16 Shortcut menu displayed when the **Polyline** tool is active*

File Tabs

The **File Tabs** button is available in the **Interface** panel of the **View** tab. It is used to toggle the display of the **File tab** bar which displays all opened files. You can easily switch between multiple opened drawings by clicking on them.

You can also create a new drawing file by clicking on the (+) sign available at the end of the File tab bars. When you click on the (+) sign, the **New Tab** will be displayed. You can create a new drawing by clicking on the **Start Drawing** icon on the left side of the **New Tab** in the **Get Started** area. Figure 1-17 shows the **File Tabs** button chosen in the **Ribbon**.

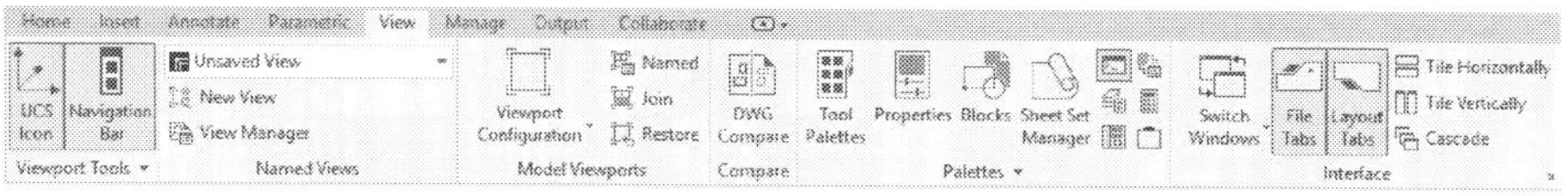

*Figure 1-17 The **File Tabs** button chosen in the **Ribbon***

In the File tab bar, all the tabs added get arranged in the sequence in which the respective drawings are opened or created. You can change the sequence of tabs in the File tab bar by using the left mouse button. To do so, press and hold the left mouse button on any tab and drag it to the desired location, refer to Figure 1-18.

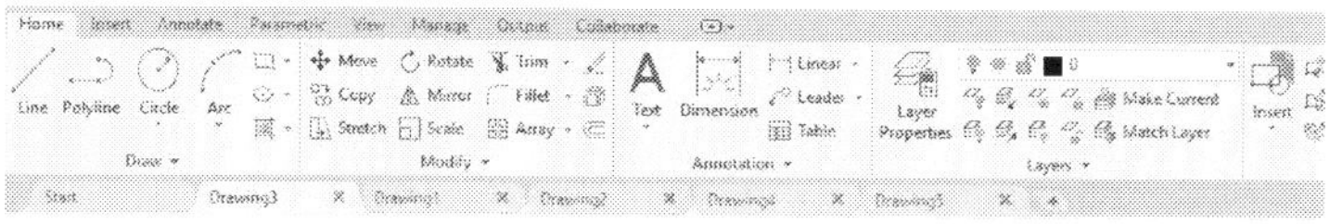

Figure 1-18 Tab dragged in the File tab bar

In AutoCAD LT, if a large number of files are opened, some of the files will not be visible in the File tab bar and therefore an overflow symbol will be displayed on the right end of the File tab bar. To open any tab which is not visible in the File tab bar, click on the overflow symbol; the names of all the tabs will be displayed in a flyout. Also, when you move the cursor on a tab name, previews of the Model, Layout1, Layout2, and so on will be displayed, refer to Figure 1-19. You can open the desired environment by clicking on its preview.

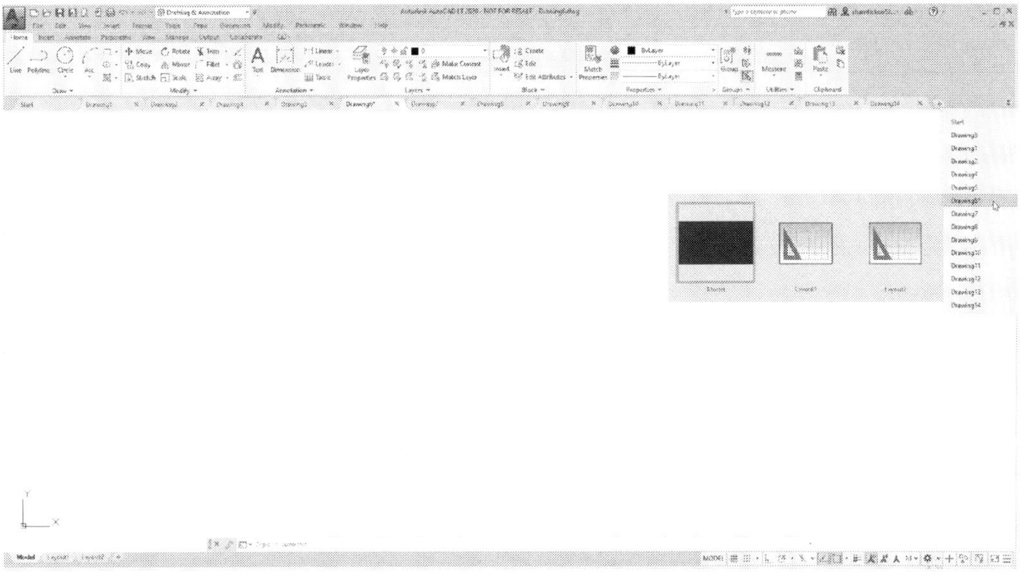

Figure 1-19 *Flyout with file tab names and preview of their respective drawings*

If you move the cursor over a file tab, the preview of the model and layouts will be displayed. When you move the cursor over any preview, the corresponding preview will be displayed in the drawing area, refer to Figure 1-20.

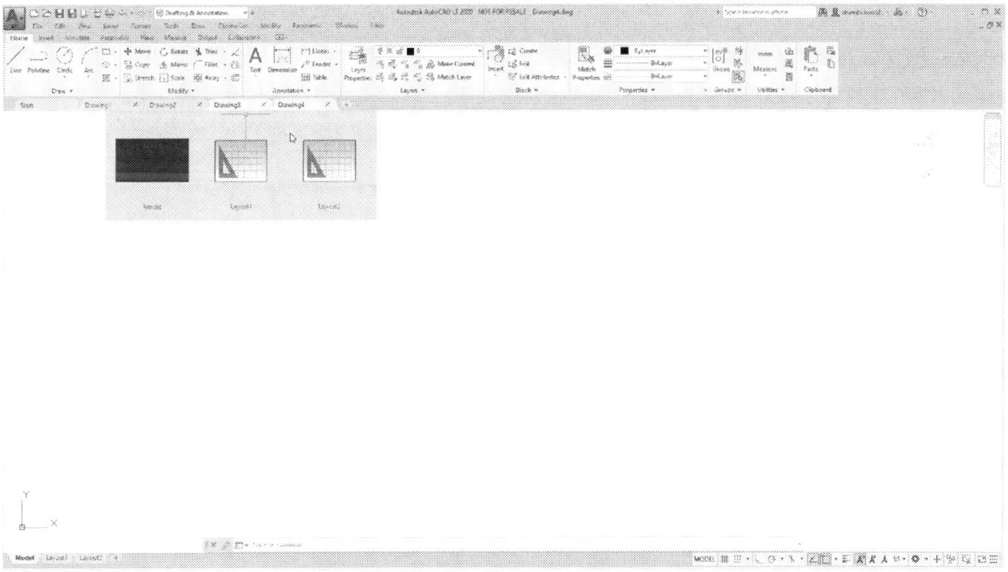

Figure 1-20 *Previews of model and layouts*

There are two buttons available at the top of preview window: **Plot** and **Publish**. By using **Plot**, you can plot the drawing and by using **Publish,** you can publish the drawing. When you right-click on a file tab, a shortcut menu containing various options such as **New**, **Open**, **Save**, **Save As**, **Close**, and so on will be displayed, refer to Figure 1-21. You can choose the option from the shortcut menu as per your requirement.

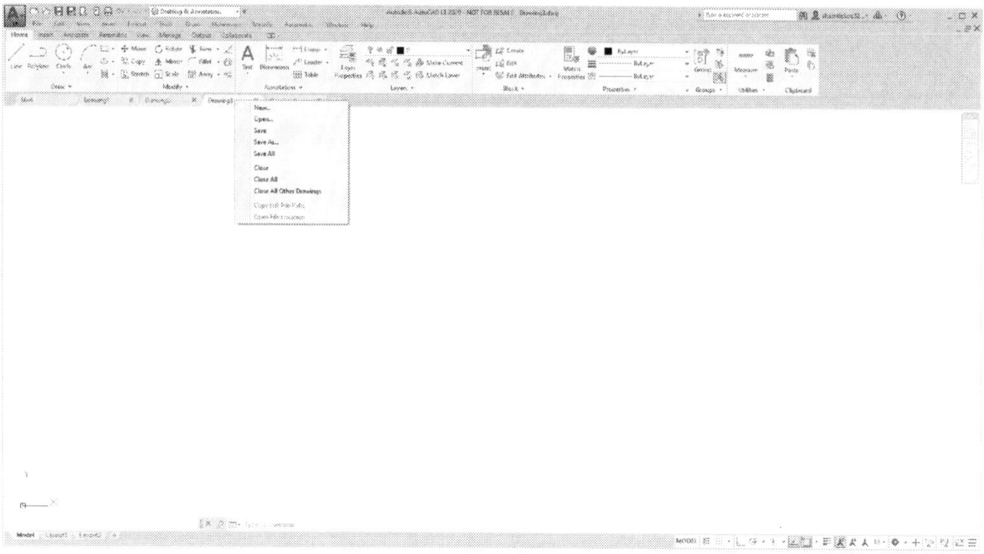

***Figure 1-21** Shortcut menu displayed on right-clicking on the File tab bar*

There are two icons displayed on the file tab: Asterisk icon and Lock icon. The Asterisk icon indicates that the file is modified but not saved. The Lock icon indicates that the file is locked and the changes cannot be saved with the original file name, although you can use the **SaveAs** tool to create another copy.

To open a drawing as a locked file, first select the **Open** option from the shortcut menu displayed on right-clicking over the file tab; the **Select File** dialog box will be displayed. Select the desired file and then select the **Open Read-Only** option from the **Open** drop-down list, as shown in Figure 1-22. On doing so, the file will be opened as a locked file in the drawing area. You can also open the file as a locked file by using the **Open** button from the Quick Access Bar.

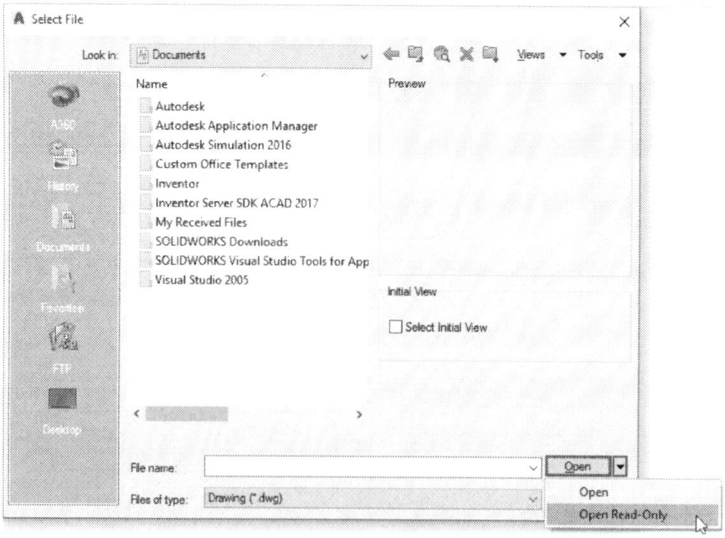

***Figure 1-22** Selecting the **Open Read-Only** option*

AutoCAD LT DIALOG BOXES

There are certain commands, which when invoked, display a dialog box. A dialog box is a convenient method of a user interface. When you choose an item in the menu bar with the ellipses [...], it displays the dialog box. For example, **Options** in the **Tools** menu displays the **Options** dialog box. A dialog box contains a number of parts like the dialog label, radio buttons, text or edit boxes, check boxes, slider bars, image boxes, and command buttons. These components are also referred to as tiles. Some of the components of a dialog box are shown in Figure 1-23.

You can select the desired tile of the dialog box by using the pointing device, which is represented by an arrow when a dialog box is invoked. The titlebar displays the name of the dialog box. The tabs specify the various sections with a group of related options under them. The check boxes are toggle options for making the particular option available or unavailable. The drop-down list displays an item and an arrow on the right which when selected displays a list of items to choose from.

You can make a selection in the radio buttons. Only one can be selected at a time. The image displays the preview image of the item selected. The text box is an area where you can enter a text such as a file name. It is also called an edit box, because you can make changes to the text entered. In some dialog boxes, there is the [...] button, which displays another related dialog box. There are certain buttons (**OK**, **Cancel**, **Help**) at the bottom of the dialog box. The name implies their functions. The button with a dark border is the default button. The dialog box has the **Help** button for getting help on the various features of the dialog box.

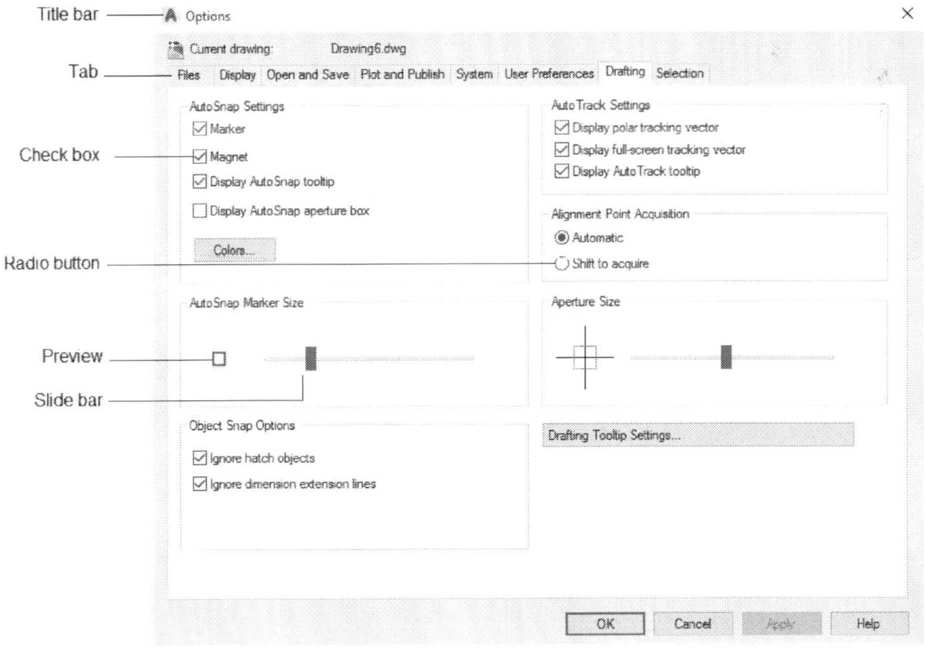

Figure 1-23 *Components of a dialog box*

STARTING A NEW DRAWING

Application Menu: New > Drawing	**Menu Bar:** File > New
Quick Access Toolbar: New	**Command:** NEW or QNEW

You can open a new drawing using the **New** tool in the Quick Access Toolbar. When you invoke the **New** tool, by default AutoCAD LT will display the **Select template** dialog box, as shown in Figure 1-24. This dialog box displays a list of default templates available in AutoCAD LT. The default selected template is acadlt.dwt, which starts the 2D drawing environment. You can select the acadlt.dwt template to start the drawing environment. Alternatively, you can select any other template to start a new drawing that will use the settings of the selected template. You can also open any drawing without using any template either in metric or imperial system. To do so, choose the down arrow on the right of the **Open** button and choose the **Open with no Template-Metric** option or the **Open with no Template-Imperial** option from the flyout.

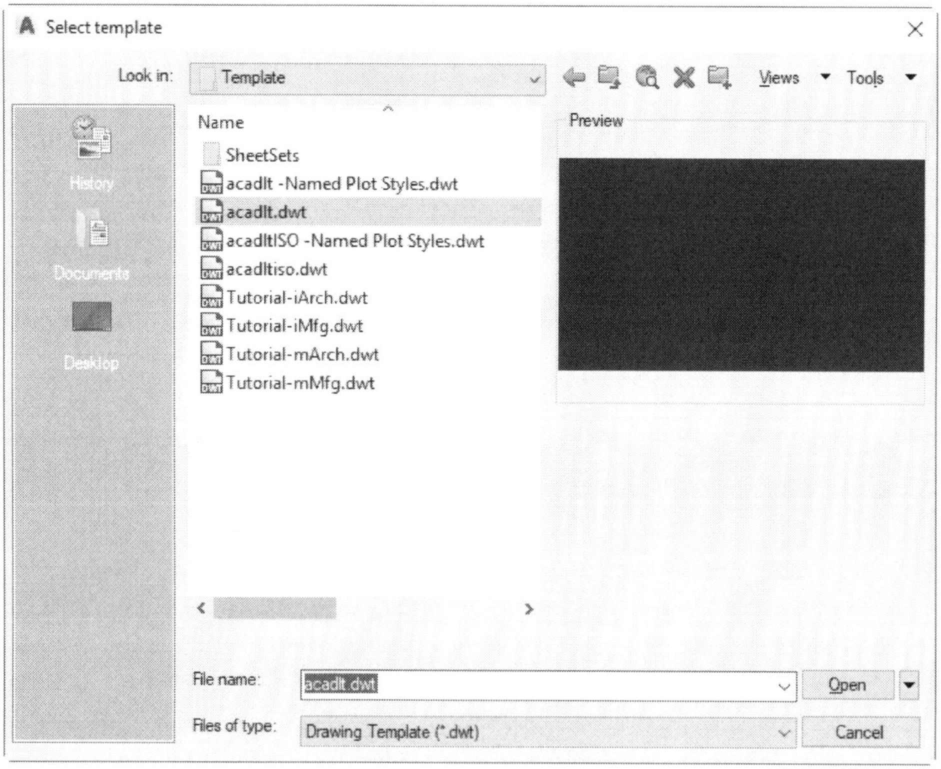

***Figure 1-24** The **Select template** dialog box*

You can also open a new drawing using the **Start from Scratch**, **Use a Template**, or **Use a Wizard** option from the **Create New Drawing** dialog box. To invoke the **Create New Drawing** dialog box, enter **STARTUP** in the command window and then enter **1** as the new value for this system variable. After setting **1** as the new value for the system variable, whenever you invoke the **New** tool, the **Create New Drawing** dialog box will be displayed, as shown in Figure 1-25. The options in this dialog box are discussed next.

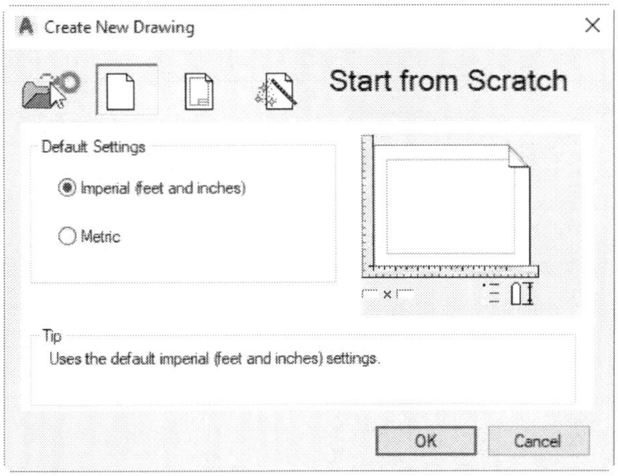

***Figure 1-25** The **Create New Drawing** dialog box*

Open a Drawing

By default, this option is not available. This option will be available when you start a new session of AutoCAD LT. This option will be discussed later in this chapter.

Start from Scratch

When you choose the **Start from Scratch** button, refer to Figure 1-25. AutoCAD LT provides you with options to start a new drawing that contains the default AutoCAD LT setup for Imperial (*Acadlt.dwt*) or Metric drawings (*Acadltiso.dwt*). If you select the Imperial default setting, the limits are 12X9, text height is 0.20, and dimensions and linetype scale factors are 1.

Use a Template

When you choose the **Use a Template** button in the **Create New Drawing** dialog box, AutoCAD LT displays a list of templates, refer to Figure 1-26. The default template file is *acadlt.dwt* or *acadltiso.dwt*, depending on the installation. You can directly start a new file in the 2D sketching environment by selecting the *acadlt.dwt* or *acadltiso.dwt* template. If you use a template file, the new drawing will have the same settings as specified in the template file. All the drawing parameters of the new drawing such as units, limits, and other settings are already set according to the template file used. The preview of the template file selected is displayed in the dialog box. You can also define your own template files that are customized to your requirements (see Chapter 14, Template Drawings). To differentiate the template files from the drawing files, the template files have a *.dwt* extension whereas the drawing files have a *.dwg* extension. Any drawing file can be saved as a template file. You can use the **Browse** button to select other template files. When you choose the **Browse** button, the **Select a template file** dialog box is displayed with the **Template** folder open, displaying all the template files.

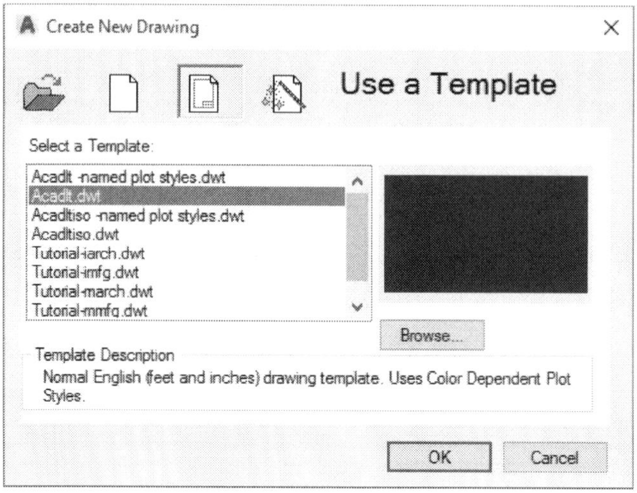

*Figure 1-26 The default templates displayed on choosing the **Use a Template** button*

Use a Wizard

The **Use a Wizard** option allows you to set the initial drawing settings before actually starting a new drawing. When you choose the **Use a Wizard** button, AutoCAD LT provides you with the option for using the **Advanced Setup** or **Quick Setup**, refer to Figure 1-27. In the **Advanced Setup**, you can set the units, limits, and the different types of settings for a drawing. In the **Quick Setup**, you can specify the units and the limits of the work area.

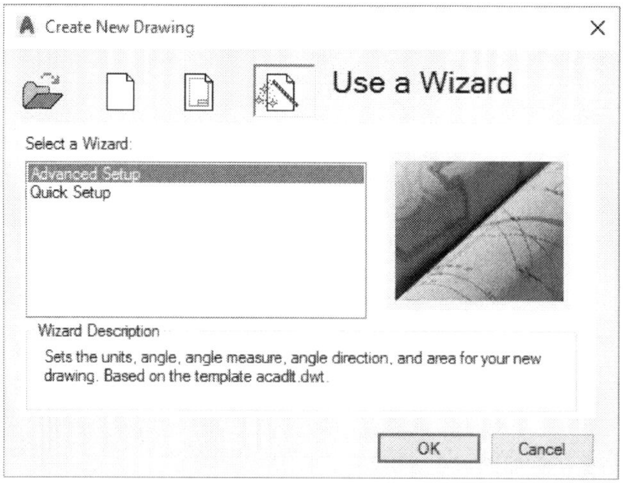

*Figure 1-27 The wizard options displayed on choosing the **Use a Wizard** button*

Advanced Setup

This option allows you to preselect the parameters of a new drawing such as the units of linear and angular measurements, type and direction of angular measurements, approximate area desired for the drawing, precision for displaying the units after decimal, and so on. When you select the **Advanced Setup** wizard option from the **Create New Drawing** dialog box and choose the **OK** button, the **Advanced Setup** wizard is displayed. In this wizard, the **Units** page is displayed by default, as shown in Figure 1-28.

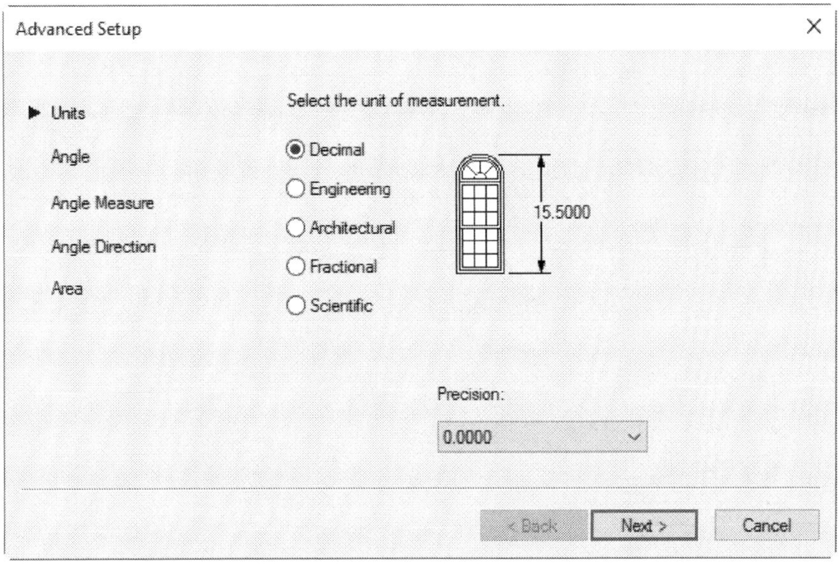

***Figure 1-28** The **Units** page of the **Advanced Setup** wizard*

This page is used to set the units for measurement in the current drawing. You can select the required unit of measurement by selecting the respective radio button. You will notice that the preview image is modified accordingly. The different units of measurement you can choose from are Decimal, Engineering, Architectural, Fractional, and Scientific. You can also set the precision for the measurement units by selecting it from the **Precision** drop-down list.

Choose the **Next** button to open the **Angle** page, as shown in Figure 1-29. You will notice that an arrow appears on the left of **Angle** in the **Advanced Setup** wizard. This implies that this page is current.

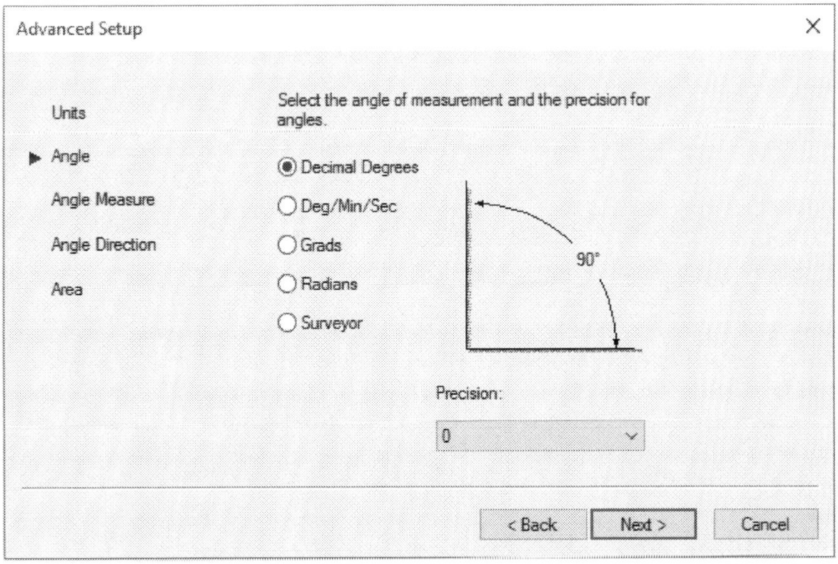

***Figure 1-29** The **Angle** page of the **Advanced Setup** wizard*

This page is used to set the units for angular measurements and its precision. The units for angle measurement are Decimal Degrees, Deg/Min/Sec, Grads, Radians, and Surveyor. The units for angle measurement can be set by selecting any one of these radio buttons as required. The preview of the selected angular unit is displayed on the right of the radio buttons. The precision format changes automatically in the **Precision** drop-down list depending on the angle measuring system selected. You can then select the precision from the drop-down list.

The next page is the **Angle Measure** page, as shown in Figure 1-30. This page is used to select the direction of the baseline from which the angles will be measured. You can also set your own direction by selecting the **Other** radio button and then entering the value in its edit box. This edit box is available when you select the **Other** radio button.

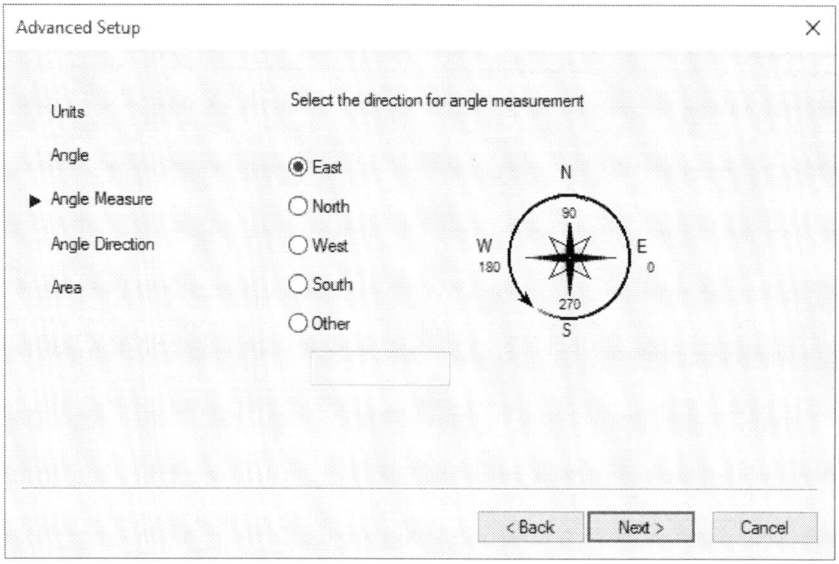

***Figure 1-30** The **Angle Measure** page of the **Advanced Setup** wizard*

Choose **Next** to display the **Angle Direction** page, refer to Figure 1-31 to set the orientation for the angle measurement. By default, the angles are positive, if measured in a counterclockwise direction. This is because the **Counter-Clockwise** radio button is selected. If you select the **Clockwise** radio button, the angles will be considered positive when measured in the clockwise direction.

To set the limits of the drawing, choose the **Next** button; the **Area** page will be displayed, as shown in Figure 1-32. You can enter the width and length of the drawing area in the respective edit boxes.

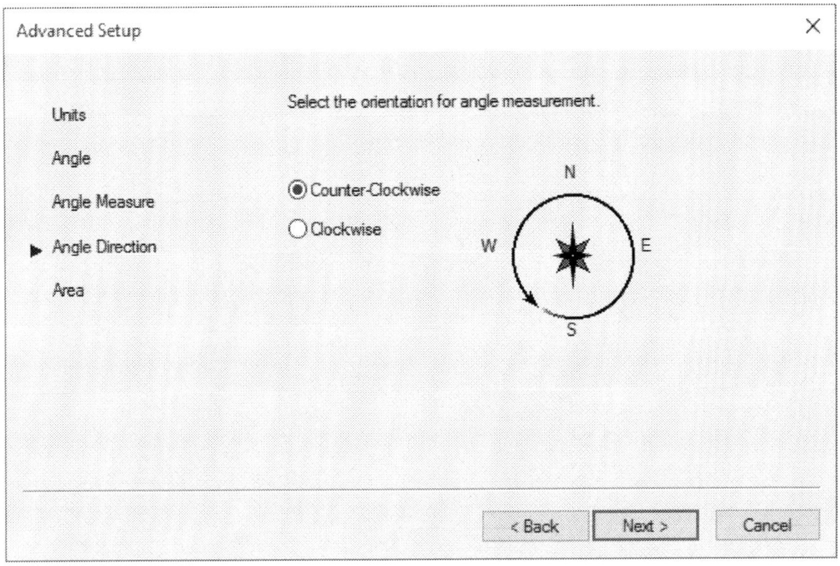

Figure 1-31 The ***Angle Direction*** *page of the* ***Advanced Setup*** *wizard*

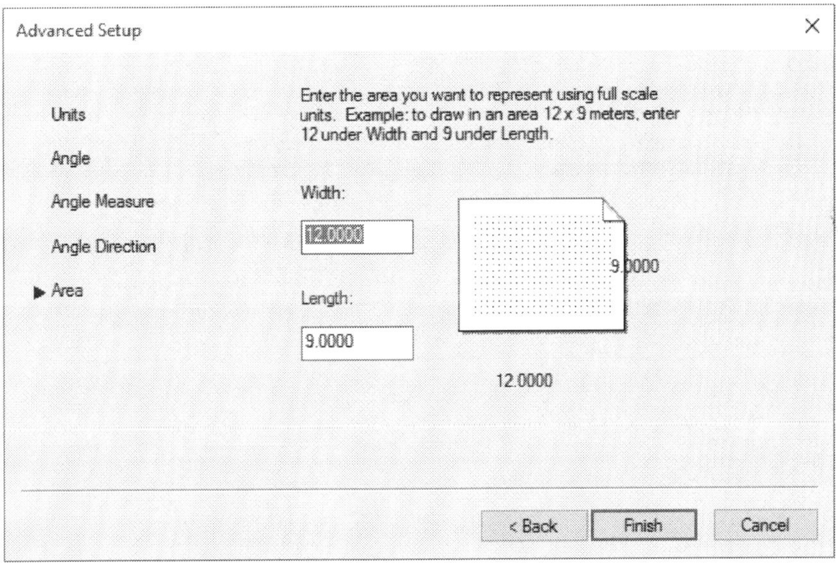

Figure 1-32 The ***Area*** *page of the* ***Advanced Setup*** *wizard*

Note

Even after you increase the limits of the drawing, the drawing display area is not increased. You need to invoke the ***Zoom All*** *tool from the Navigation Bar to increase the drawing display area.*

Quick Setup

When you choose the **Quick Setup** option and then choose the **OK** button, the **Quick Setup** wizard is displayed. This wizard has two pages: **Units** and **Area**. The **Units** page is opened by default, as shown in Figure 1-33. The options in the **Units** page are similar to those in the **Units** page of the **Advanced Setup** wizard. The only difference is that you cannot set the precision for the units in this wizard.

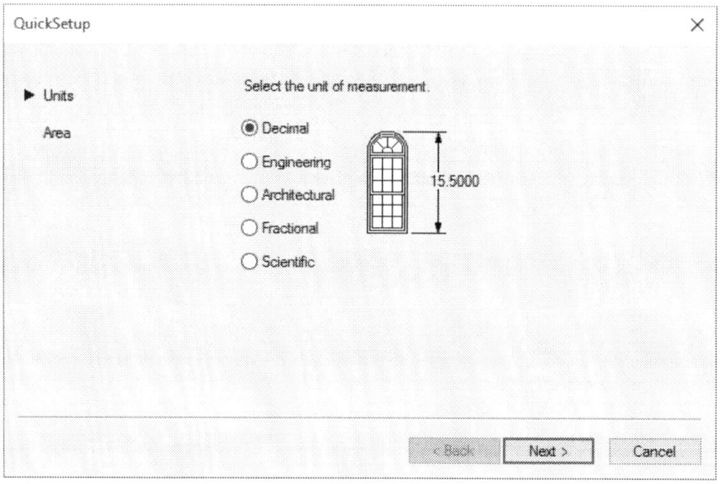

***Figure 1-33** The **Units** page of the **QuickSetup** wizard*

Choose **Next** to display the **Area** page, as shown in Figure 1-34. The **Area** page of the **Quick Setup** is similar to that of the **Advanced Setup** wizard. In this page, you can set the drawing limits.

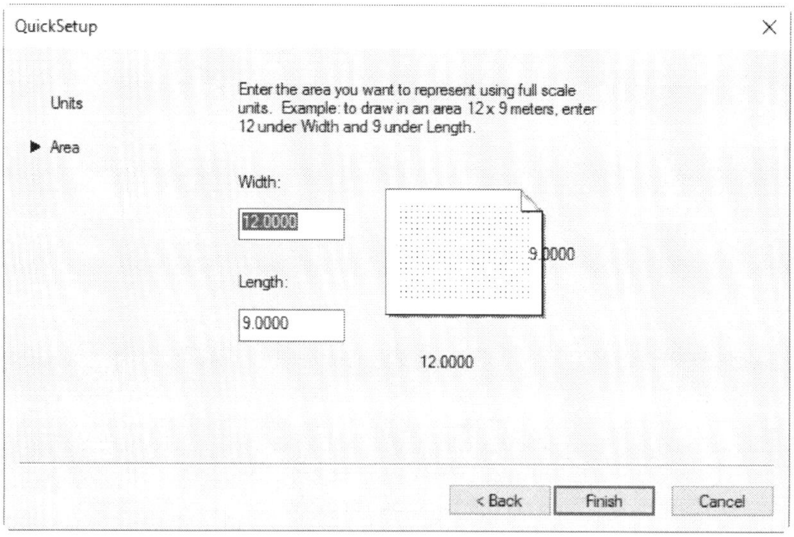

***Figure 1-34** The **Area** page of the **QuickSetup** wizard*

Tip
*When you open an AutoCAD LT session, a drawing opens automatically. But you can open a new drawing using options such as **Start from Scratch** and **Use a Wizard** before entering into AutoCAD LT environment using the **Startup** dialog box. As mentioned earlier, the display of the **Startup** dialog box is turned off by default. Refer to the section **Starting a New Drawing** to know how to turn on the display of this dialog box.*

SAVING YOUR WORK

Application Menu: SAVE AS, SAVE **Menu Bar:** File > Save or Save As
Quick Access Toolbar: Save or Save As **Command:** QSAVE, SAVEAS, SAVE

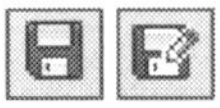

You must save your work before you exit the drawing editor or turn off your system. Also, it is recommended that you save your drawings at regular intervals, so that in the event of a power failure or an editing error, the work will be retained.

AutoCAD LT has provided the **QSAVE**, **SAVEAS**, and **SAVE** commands that allow you to save your work. These commands allow you to save your drawing by writing it to a permanent storage device, such as a hard drive or in any removable drive.

When you choose the **Save** tool from the **Quick Access Toolbar** or the **Application Menu**, the **QSAVE** command is invoked. If the current drawing is unnamed and you save the drawing for the first time in the current session, the **SAVEAS** command will be invoked and you will be prompted to enter the file name in the **Save Drawing As** dialog box, as shown in Figure 1-35. You can enter the name for the drawing and then choose the **Save** button. If you have saved a drawing file once and then edited it, you can use the **Save** tool to save it, without the system prompting you to enter a file name. This allows you to do a quick save.

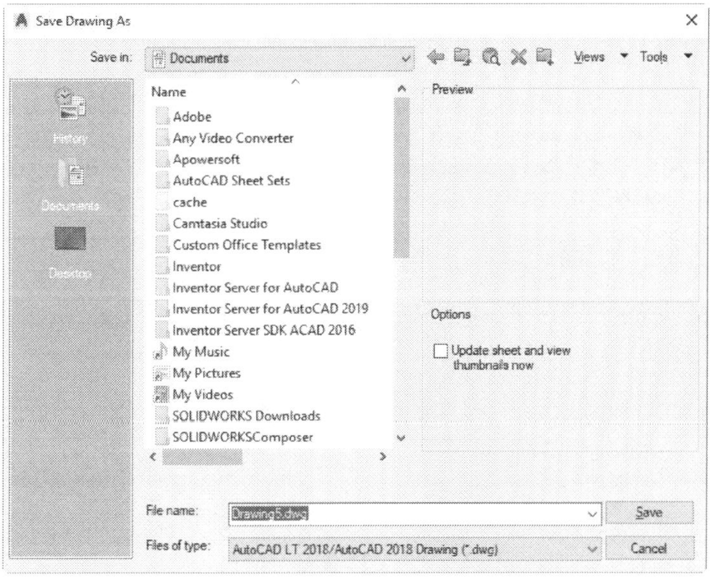

Figure 1-35 *The* ***Save Drawing As*** *dialog box*

When you choose **SaveAs** from the **Application Menu** or choose the **Save As** tool from the **Quick Access Toolbar**, the **Save Drawing As** dialog box is displayed, similar to that shown in Figure 1-35. Even if the drawing has been saved with a file name, this tool gives you an option to save it with a different file name. In addition to saving the drawing, it sets the name of the current drawing to the file name you specify, which is displayed in the title bar. This tool is used when you want to save a previously saved drawing with a different file name. You can also use this tool when you make certain changes to a template and want to save the changed template drawing but leave the original template unchanged.

Save Drawing As Dialog Box

The **Save Drawing As** dialog box displays the information related to the drawing files on your system. The various components of the dialog box are discussed next.

Places List

A column of icons is displayed on the left side of the dialog box. These icons contain the shortcuts to the folders that are frequently used. You can quickly save your drawings in one of these folders. The **History** folder displays the list of the most recently saved drawings. You can save your personal drawings in the **Documents** or the **Favorites** folder. The **FTP** folder displays the list of the various FTP sites that are available for saving the drawing. By default, no FTP sites are shown in the dialog box. To add a FTP site to the dialog box, choose the **Tools** button on the upper-right corner of the dialog box to display a shortcut menu and select **Add/Modify FTP Locations**. The **Desktop** folder displays the list of contents on the desktop. You can add a new folder in this list for an easy access by simply dragging the folder on to the **Places** list area. You can rearrange all these folders by dragging them and then placing them at the desired locations. It is also possible to remove the folders, which are not in frequent use. Right-click on the particular folder and then select **Remove** from the shortcut menu. Now, you can also save the document to new location of Autodesk Cloud. The option for saving the document is discussed next.

File name Edit Box

To save your work, enter the name of the drawing in the **File name** edit box by typing the file name or selecting it from the drop-down list. If you select the file name, it automatically appears in the **File name** edit box. If you have already assigned a name to the drawing, the current drawing name is taken as the default name. If the drawing is unnamed, the default name *Drawing1* is displayed in the **File name** edit box. You can also choose the down arrow located on the right of the edit box to display the names of the previously saved drawings and choose a name here.

Files of type Drop-down List

The **Files of type** drop-down list, refer to Figure 1-36 is used to specify the drawing format in which you want to save the file. For example, to save the file as an AutoCAD LT 2004 drawing file, select **AutoCAD LT 2004/LT2004 Drawing (*.dwg)** from the drop-down list.

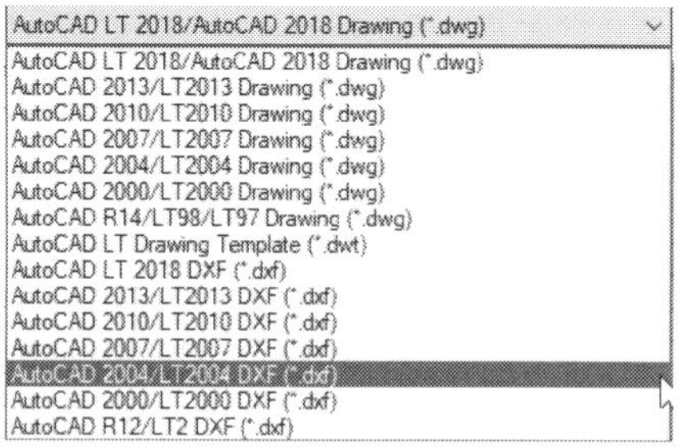

***Figure 1-36** The **Files of type** drop-down list*

Save in Drop-down List

The current drive and path information is listed in the **Save in** drop-down list. AutoCAD LT will initially save the drawing in the default folder, but if you want to save the drawing in a different folder, you have to specify the path. For example, to save the present drawing as *house* in the *C1* folder, choose the arrow button in the **Save in** drop-down list to display the drop-down list. Select **C**: from the drop-down list; all folders in the C drive will be listed in the **File** list box. Double-click on the **C1** folder, if it is already listed there or create a folder C1 by choosing the **Create New Folder** button. Select *house* from the list, if it is already listed there, or enter it in the **File name** edit box and then choose the **Save** button. Your drawing (*house*) will be saved in the *C1* folder (*C:\C1\house.dwg*). Similarly, to save the drawing in the D drive, select **D:** in the **Save in** drop-down list.

Tip

The file name you enter to save a drawing should match its contents. This helps you to remember the drawing details and make it easier to refer to them later. Also, the file name can be 255 characters long and can contain spaces and punctuation marks.

Views drop-down list

The **Views** drop-down list has the options for the type of listing of files and displaying the preview images, refer to Figure 1-37.

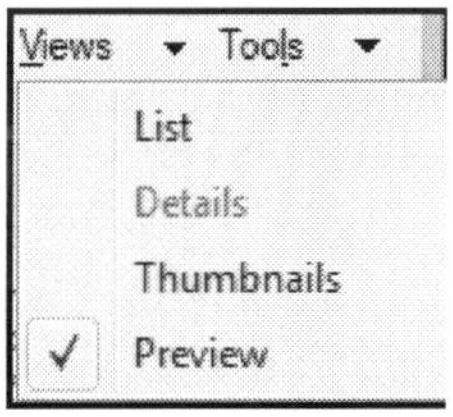

***Figure 1-37** The Views drop-down list*

List, Details, and Thumbnails Options

If you choose the **Details** option, it will display the detailed information about the files (size, type, date, and time of modification) in the **Name** list box. In the detailed information, if you click on the **Name** label, the files are listed with the names in alphabetical order. If you double-click on the **Name** label, the files will be listed in reverse order. Similarly, if you click on the **Size** label, the files are listed according to their size in ascending order. Double-clicking on the **Size** label will list the files in descending order of size. Similarly, you can click on the **Type** label or the **Date Modified** label to list the files accordingly. If you choose the **List** option, all files present in the current folder will be listed in the **File** list box. If you choose the **Thumbnails** option, the list box displays the preview of all the drawings, along with their names displayed at the bottom of the drawing preview.

Create New Folder Button

If you choose the **Create New Folder** button, AutoCAD LT creates a new folder under the name **New Folder**. The new folder is displayed in the **File** list box. You can accept the name or change it to your requirement. You can also use the ALT+5 keys to create a new folder.

Up one level Button

The **Up one level** button displays the folders that are up by one level. For example, if you are in the *Sample* subfolder of the *AutoCAD LT 2020* folder, then choosing the **Up one level** button will take you to the *AutoCAD LT 2020* folder. You can also use the ALT+2 keys to do the same.

Search the Web

When you choose this button, the Browse the Web - Save dialog box is displayed that enables you to access and store AutoCAD LT files on the Internet. You can also use the ALT+3 keys to browse the Web when this dialog box is available on the screen.

Tools drop-down List

The **Tools** drop-down list, refer to Figure 1-38 has an option for adding or modifying the FTP sites. These sites can then be browsed from the FTP shortcut in the **Places** list. The **Add Current Folder to Places** and **Add to Favorites** options are used to add the folder displayed in the **Save in** edit box to the **Places** or the **Favorites** folder. The **Options** button is used for invoking **Saveas Options** dialog box where you can save the proxy images of the custom objects. It has the **DWG Options** and **DXF Options** tabs. The **Digital Signature** button is used to invoke the **Digital Signatures** dialog box, which is used to configure the security options of the drawing.

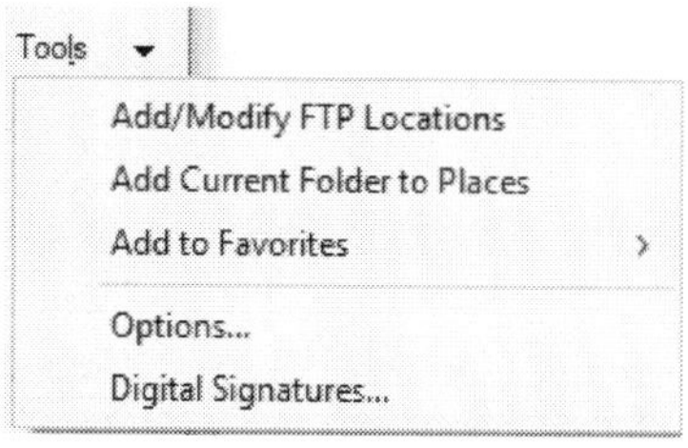

***Figure 1-38** The **Tools** drop-down list*

AUTOMATIC TIMED SAVE

AutoCAD LT allows you to save your work automatically at specific intervals. To change the time intervals, you can specify the intervals duration in minutes in the **Minutes between saves** text box in the **File Safety Precautions** area in the **Options** dialog box (**Open and Save** tab). This dialog box can be invoked by choosing the **Options** button from the **Application Menu**. Depending on the power supply, hardware, and type of drawings, you should decide on an appropriate time and assign it to this variable. AutoCAD LT saves the drawing with the file extension *.sv$*. You can also change the time interval by using the **SAVETIME** system variable.

> **Tip**
> *Although the automatic save feature saves your drawing after a certain time interval, you should not completely depend on it because the procedure for converting the ac$ file into a drawing file is cumbersome. Therefore, it is recommended that you save your files regularly using the **QSAVE** or **SAVEAS** command.*

CREATING BACKUP FILES

If the drawing file already exists and you use **Save** or **Save As** tool to update the current drawing, AutoCAD LT creates a backup file. AutoCAD LT takes the previous copy of the drawing and changes it from a file type *.dwg* to *.bak*, and the updated drawing is saved as a drawing file with the *.dwg* extension. For example, if the name of the drawing is *myproj.dwg*, AutoCAD LT will change it to *myproj.bak* and save the current drawing as *myproj.dwg*.

Changing Automatic Timed Saved and Backup Files into AutoCAD LT Format

Sometimes, you may need to change the automatic timed saved and backup files into AutoCAD LT format. To change a backup file into AutoCAD LT format, open the folder, in which you have saved the backup or the automatic timed saved drawing. Now, choose the **View** tab and select the **File name extensions** check box from the **Show/hide** area. Rename the automatic saved drawing or the backup file with a different name and also, change the extension of the drawing from .sv$ or .bak to .dwg.

Using the Drawing Recovery Manager to Recover Files

The files that are saved automatically can also be retrieved by using the **DRAWING RECOVERY MANAGER**. You can open the **DRAWING RECOVERY MANAGER** by entering **DRAWINGRECOVERY** at the Command prompt.

If the automatic save operation is performed in a drawing and the system crashes accidentally, the next time you run AutoCAD LT, the **Drawing Recovery** message box will be displayed, as shown in Figure 1-39. The message box informs you that the program unexpectedly failed and you can open the most suitable among the backup files created by AutoCAD LT. Choose the **Close** button from the **Drawing Recovery** message box; the **DRAWING RECOVERY MANAGER** is displayed on the left of the drawing area, as shown in Figure 1-40.

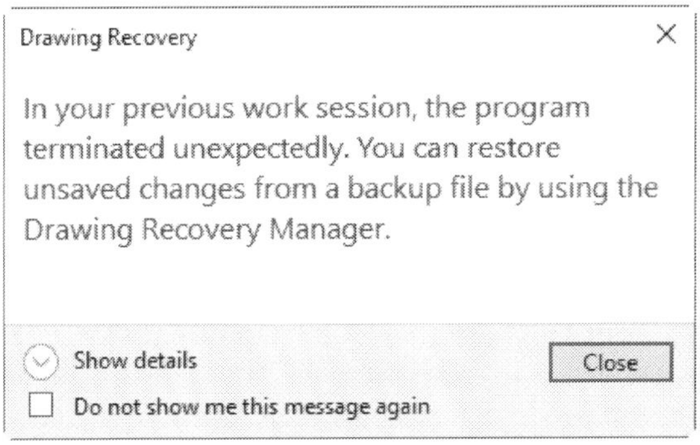

*Figure 1-39 The **Drawing Recovery** message box*

The **Backup Files** rollout lists the original files, the backup files, and the automatically saved files. Select a file; its preview will be displayed in the **Preview** rollout. Also, the information corresponding to the selected file will be displayed in the **Details** rollout. To open a backup file, double-click on its name in the **Backup Files** rollout. Alternatively, right-click on the file name and then choose **Open** from the shortcut menu. It is recommended that you save the backup file at the desired location before you start working on it.

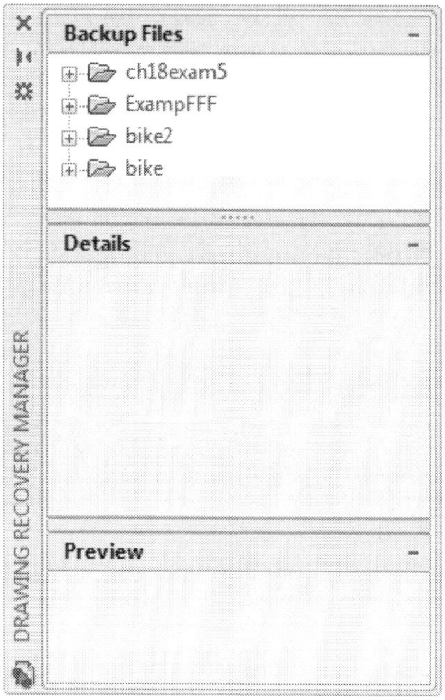

Figure 1-40 The DRAWING RECOVERY MANAGER

CLOSING A DRAWING

You can close the current drawing file without actually quitting AutoCAD LT by choosing **Close > Current Drawing** from the **Application Menu** or by entering **CLOSE** in the Command prompt. If multiple drawing files are opened, choose **Close > All Drawings** from the **Application Menu**. If you have not saved the drawing after making the last changes to it and you invoke the **CLOSE** command, AutoCAD LT displays a dialog box that allows you to save the drawing before closing. This box gives you an option to discard the current drawing or the changes made to it. It also gives you an option to cancel the command. After closing the drawing, you are still in AutoCAD LT from where you can open a new or an already saved drawing file. You can also use the close button (**X**) of the drawing area to close the drawing.

OPENING AN EXISTING DRAWING

Application Menu: Open > Drawing	**Quick Access Toolbar:** Open
Menu Bar: File > Open	**Command:** OPEN

You can open an existing drawing file that has been saved previously. There are three methods that can be used to open a drawing file: by using the **Select File** dialog box, by using the **Create New Drawing** dialog box, and by dragging and dropping.

Opening an Existing Drawing Using the Select File Dialog Box

If you are already in the drawing editor and you want to open a drawing file, choose the **Open** tool from the **Quick Access Toolbar**; the **Select File** dialog box will be displayed, as shown in Figure 1-41. You can select the drawing to be opened using this dialog box.

This dialog box is similar to the standard dialog boxes. You can choose the file you want to open from the folder in which it is stored. You can change the folder from the **Look in** drop-down list. You can then select the name of the drawing from the list box or you can enter the name of the drawing file you want to open in the **File name** edit box. After selecting the drawing file, you can choose the **Open** button to open the file. Here, you can choose *Drawing1* from the list and then choose the **Open** button to open the drawing.

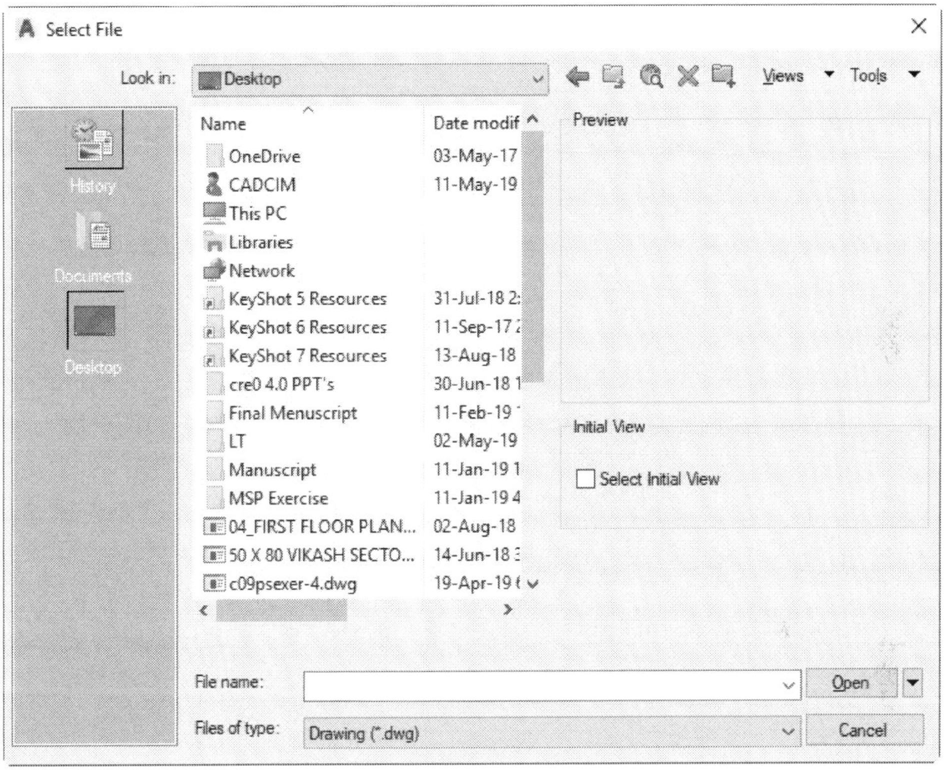

*Figure 1-41 The **Select File** dialog box*

When you select a file name, its image is displayed in the **Preview** box. If you are not sure about the file name of a particular drawing but know the contents, you can select the file names and look for the particular drawing in the **Preview** box. You can also change the file type by selecting it in the **Files of type** drop-down list. Apart from the *dwg* files, you can open the *dwt* (template) files or the *dxf* files. You have all the standard icons in the Places list that can be used to open drawing files from different locations. The **Open** button has a drop-down list, as shown in Figure 1-42. You can choose a method for opening the file using this drop-down list. These methods are discussed next.

*Figure 1-42 The **Open** drop-down list*

Open Read-Only

To view a drawing without altering it, you must select the **Open Read-Only** option from the drop-down list. In other words, **Open Read-Only** option protects the drawing file from changes. AutoCAD LT does not prevent you from editing the drawing, but if you try to save the opened drawing with the original file name, AutoCAD LT warns you that the drawing file is write protected. However, you can save the edited drawing to a file with a different file name using the **Save Drawing As** dialog box. This way you can preserve your drawing.

Select Initial View

A view is defined as the way you look at an object. Select the **Select Initial View** check box if you want to load a specific view initially when AutoCAD LT loads the drawing. This option will work, if the drawing has saved views. This is generally used while working on a large complicated drawing, in which you want to work on a particular portion of the drawing. You can save that particular portion as a view and then select it to open the drawing next time. You can save a desired view, by using AutoCAD LT's **VIEW** command (see "Creating Views" topic, Chapter 6). If the drawing has no saved views, selecting this option will load the last view. If you select the **Select Initial View** check box and then choose the **OK** button, AutoCAD LT will display the **Select Initial View** dialog box. You can select the view name from this dialog box, and AutoCAD LT will load the drawing with the selected view displayed.

Tip

*1. Apart from opening a drawing from the **Startup** dialog box or the **Select File** dialog box, you can also open a drawing from the **Application Menu**. By default, the **Recent Documents** option is chosen in the **Application Menu**. As a result, the most recently opened drawings will be displayed and you can open the required file from it.*

2. It is possible to open an AutoCAD LT 2000 drawing in AutoCAD LT 2020. However, when you save this drawing, it is automatically converted and saved as an AutoCAD LT 2020 drawing file.

Opening an Existing Drawing Using the Startup Dialog Box

If you have configured the settings to show the **Startup** dialog box by setting the **STARTUP** system variable value as **1**, the **Startup** dialog box will be displayed every time you start a new AutoCAD LT session. The first button in this dialog box is the **Open a Drawing** button. When you choose this button, a list of the recently opened drawings will be displayed for you to select from, refer to Figure 1-43. Note that this button is activated only when this dialog box is displayed by default on starting a new session of AutoCAD LT. The **Browse** button displays the **Select File** dialog box, which allows you to browse to another file.

Note

*The display of the dialog boxes related to opening and saving drawings will be disabled, if the **STARTUP** and **FILEDIA** system variables are set to 0. The initial value of these variables is 1.*

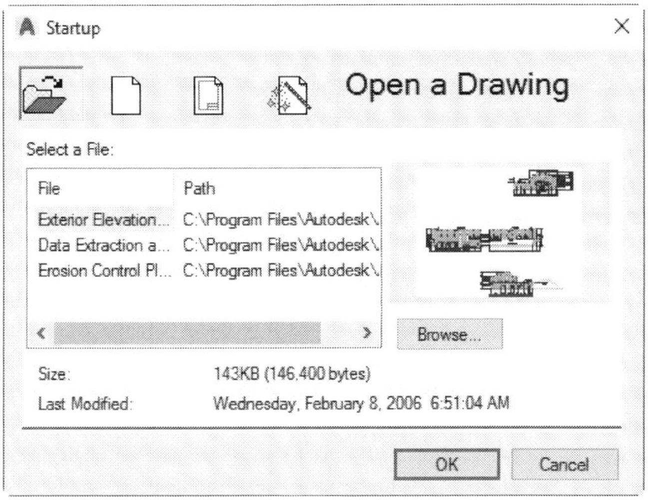

Figure 1-43 *List of the recently opened drawings*

Opening an Existing Drawing Using the Drag and Drop Method

You can also open an existing drawing in AutoCAD LT by dragging it from the Window Explorer and dropping it into AutoCAD LT. If you drop the selected drawing in the drawing area, the drawing will be inserted as a block and as a result, you cannot modify it. But, if you drag the drawing from the Window Explorer and drop it anywhere other than the drawing area, AutoCAD LT opens the selected drawing.

QUITTING AutoCAD LT

You can exit the AutoCAD LT program by using the **EXIT** or **QUIT** command. Even if you have an active command, you can choose **Exit Autodesk AutoCAD LT 2020** from the **Application Menu** to quit the AutoCAD LT program. In case the drawing has not been saved, it allows you to save the work first through a dialog box. Note that if you choose **No** in this dialog box, all the changes made in the current list till the last save will be lost. You can also choose the **Close** button (**X**) of the main AutoCAD LT window (present in the title bar) to end the AutoCAD LT session.

CREATING AND MANAGING WORKSPACES

A workspace is defined as a customized arrangement of **Ribbon**, toolbars, menus, and window palettes in the AutoCAD LT environment. You can create your own workspaces, in which only specified toolbars, menus, and palettes are available. When you start AutoCAD LT, by default, the **Drafting & Annotation** workspace is the current workspace. You can select any other predefined workspace from the **Workspace** drop-down list available in the title bar, next to the **Quick Access Toolbar**, refer to Figure 1-44. You can also set the workspace from the flyout that will be displayed on choosing the **Workspace Switching** button on the Status Bar or by choosing the required workspace from the **Quick Access Toolbar**.

***Figure 1-44** The predefined workspaces*

Creating a New Workspace

To create a new workspace, customize the **Ribbon** and invoke the palettes to be displayed in the new workspace. Next, select the **Save Current As** option from the **Workspace** drop-down list in the titlebar; the **Save Workspace** dialog box will be displayed, as shown in Figure 1-45. Enter the name of the new workspace in the **Name** edit box and choose the **Save** button.

The new workspace is now the current workspace and is added to the **Workspace** drop-down list in the **Quick Access Toolbar**. Likewise, you can create workspaces based on your requirement and switch from one workspace to the other by selecting the name from the drop-down list in the **Workspaces** toolbar or the drop-down list in the **Quick Access Toolbar**.

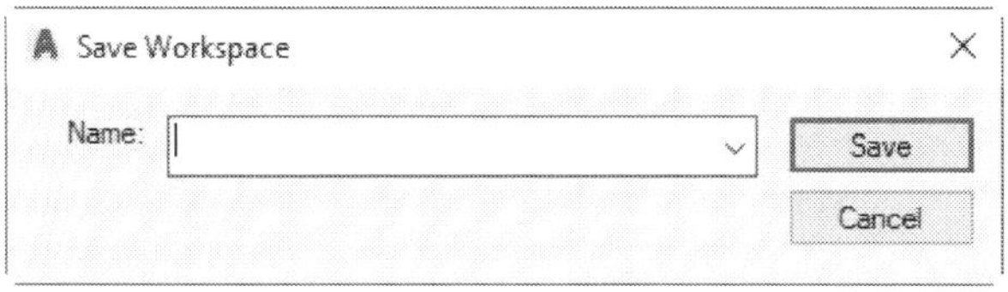

***Figure 1-45** The **Save Workspace** dialog box*

Modifying the Workspace Settings

AutoCAD LT allows you to modify the workspace settings. To do so, select the **Workspace Settings** option in the **Workspace** drop-down list in the title bar; the **Workspace Settings** dialog box will be displayed, as shown in Figure 1-46. All workspaces are listed in the **My Workspace** drop-down list. You can make any workspace as My Workspace by selecting it from the **My Workspace** drop-down list. You can also choose the **My Workspace** button from the **Workspaces** toolbar to change the current workspace to the one that was set as My Workspace in the **Workspace Settings** dialog box. The other options in this dialog box are discussed next.

Menu Display and Order Area

The options in this area are used to control the display and the order of display of workspaces in the **Workspace** drop-down list. By default, workspaces are listed in the sequence of their creation. To change the order, select a workspace and choose the **Move Up** or **Move Down** button. To control the display of the workspaces, you can select or clear the check boxes. You can also add a separator between workspaces by choosing the **Add Separator** button. A separator is a line that is placed between two workspaces in the **Workspace** drop-down list in the title bar, as shown in Figure 1-47.

When Switching Workspaces Area

By default, the **Do not save changes to workspace** radio button is selected in this area. This ensures that while switching the workspaces, the changes made in the current workspace will not be saved. If you select the **Automatically save workspace changes** radio button, the changes made in the current workspace will be automatically saved when you switch to the other workspace.

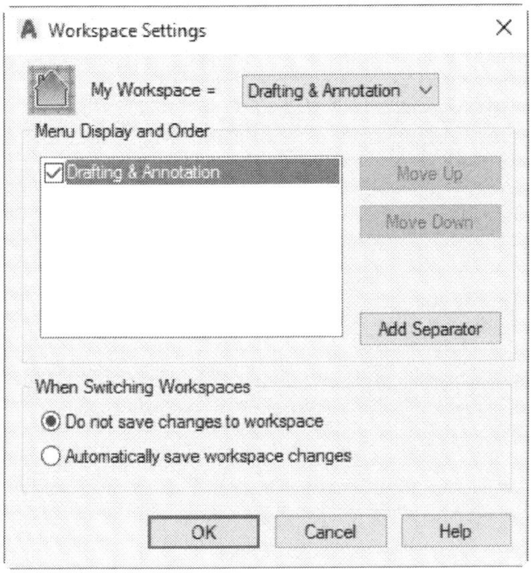

Figure 1-46 The ***Workspace Settings*** *dialog box*

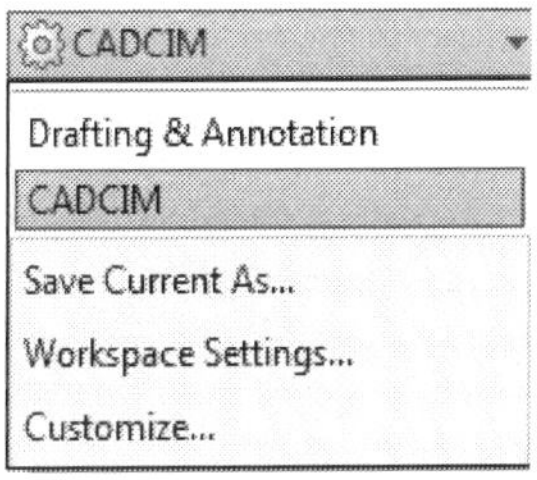

Figure 1-47 The ***Workspace*** *drop-down list after adding separators*

AutoCAD LT HELP

Titlebar: ? > Help **Shortcut Key:** F1 **Command:** HELP or ?

You can get the on-line help and documentation about the working of AutoCAD LT 2020 commands from the **Help** menu in the title bar, refer to Figure 1-48. You can also access the **Help** menu by pressing the F1 function key. An **InfoCenter** bar is displayed at the top right corner in the title bar that will help you sign in to the Autodesk Online services, refer to Figure 1-49. You can also access AutoCAD LT community by using certain keywords. Some important options in the **Help** menu are discussed next.

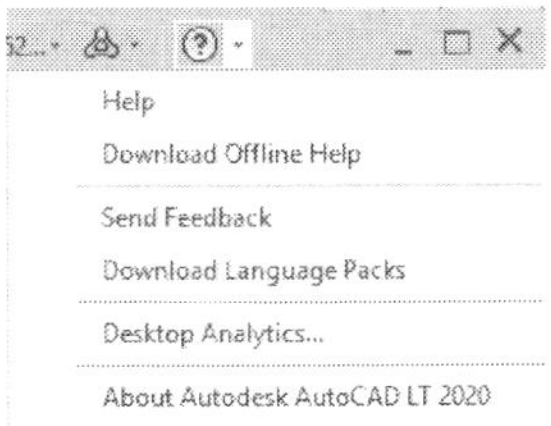

Figure 1-48 The ***Help*** *menu*

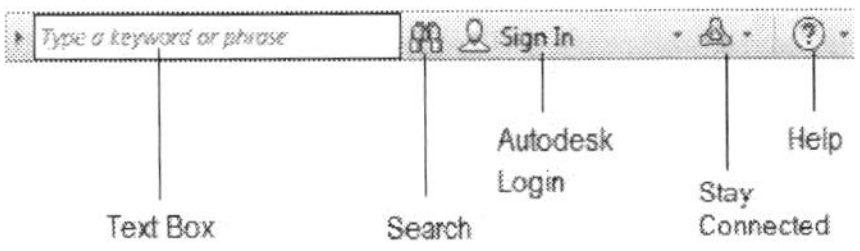

Figure 1-49 The ***InfoCenter*** *bar*

In **Autodesk AutoCAD LT 2020 - Help** window, as shown in Figure 1-50, you can browse videos, tutorials, and documentation for beginners and advanced users in the **Learn** and **Resources** sections. You can download sample files and offline help database from the **Downloads** section. You can also connect to other users of Autodesk community and discussion groups using the **Connect** section.

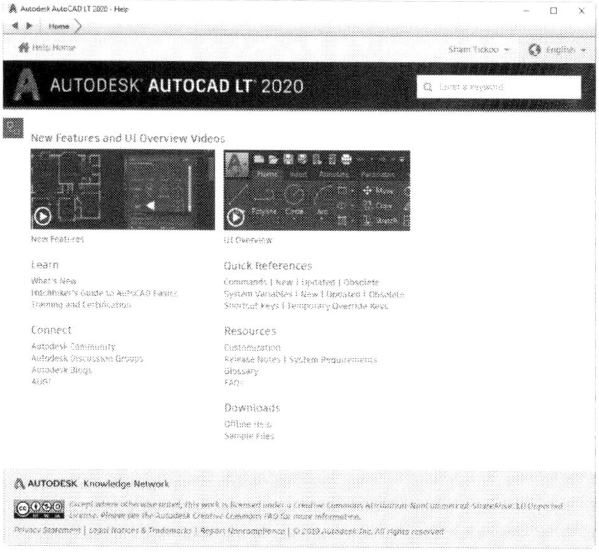

Figure 1-50 *The* ***Autodesk AutoCAD LT 2020 - Help*** *window*

Download Offline Help

This option is used to read the help contents and topics, when the user has no internet access. (AutoCAD LT prompts you to download 120 MB File, user can save this file and then use it later on.)

Send Feedback

You can also directly contact Autodesk regarding support, discussion, or any consulting work. When you click on this option, a page will be displayed asking for the required queries and contact details. After entering the contact details, you can press **Submit** to exit.

Download Language Packs

Once AutoCAD LT is installed, you can install the **AutoCAD LT language pack** to run AutoCAD LT in your preferred language by choosing this option.

Customer Involvement Program

This option is used to share your configuration information and uses of Autodesk products with Autodesk. The collected information is used by Autodesk for the improvement of Autodesk softwares.

Desktop Analytics

When you choose this option, the **Desktop Analytics Program** dialog box will be displayed. In the dialog box, Autodesk will prompt you to participate in a programme to simply collect nonpersonal product usage information from the Autodesk software.

About Autodesk AutoCAD LT 2020

This option gives you information about the Release, Serial number, Licensed to, and also the legal description about AutoCAD LT.

SAVE TO WEB & MOBILE

Application Menu: Save As > Drawing to AutoCAD Web & Mobile
Quick Access Toolbar: Save to Web & Mobile **Command:** SAVETOWEBMOBILE

Using the **Save to Web & Mobile** tool, you can save copy of your drawings in your Autodesk web & mobile account from any remote location in the world using any device such as desktop or mobile having internet access. You can access this tool from the **Quick Access Toolbar** or **Application Menu**. When you choose this tool, the **Save in AutoCAD Web & Mobile Cloud Files** dialog box will be displayed, refer to Figure 1-51.

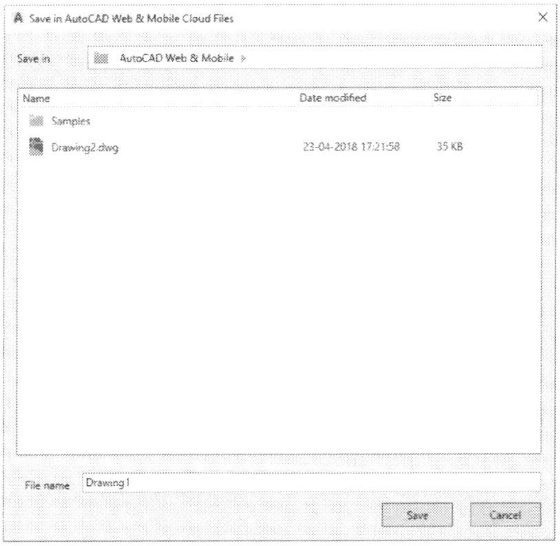

*Figure 1-51 The **Save in AutoCAD Web & Mobile Cloud Files** dialog box*

Enter the name of the file to be saved in the **File name** edit box. Next, choose the **Save** button.

Note

*1. The name of the saved files appear in the **Name** column of the list box available in the **Save in AutoCAD Web & Mobile Cloud Files** dialog box when you invoke this dialog box again.*
2. You need to first sign in to your Autodesk account to use this tool. If you are not signed in and choose this tool, the Autodesk sign-in window will appear and will prompt you to sign in first.
*3. The drawing files saved in your web and mobile account are saved to the cloud and utilise the cloud space. You can save them to your device by using the **Save As** tool.*
4. You can also share the saved files with any of the co-workers or clients across the world. They can review or edit the drawing file depending upon the permissions you grant them.

After saving the file to your web and mobile account, you can access it from anywhere across the world using any device (mobile, tablet, etc.) with a Wi-fi or internet connection.

Note

You can access the saved web and mobile files using the ***Open from Web & Mobile*** *tool available in the* ***Quick Access Toolbar****.*

ADDITIONAL HELP RESOURCES

1. You can get help for a command while working by pressing the F1 key. The help html containing information about the command is displayed. You can exit the dialog box and continue with the command.

2. You can get help about a dialog box by choosing the **Help** button in that dialog box.

3. Autodesk has provided several resources that you can use to get assistance with your AutoCAD LT questions. The following is a list of some of the resources:

   a. Autodesk web site *https://www.autodesk.com*
   b. AutoCAD LT Technical Assistance website *https://www.autodesk.com/support*
   c. AutoCAD LT Discussion Groups website *https://discussion.autodesk.com/index.jspa*

4. You can also get help by contacting us at *techsupport@cadcim.com* and *sales@cadcim.com*.

5. You can download AutoCAD LT drawings, programs, and special topics by registering yourself as faculty at: *https://cadcim.com/Registration.aspx*

Self-Evaluation Test

Answer the following questions and then compare them to those given at the end of this chapter:

1. The ________ button is used to set the performance of the software at an acceptable level.

2. If the __________ variable is set to 1 and you invoke the **New** tool, the **Create New Drawing** dialog box will be displayed.

3. If you want to work on a drawing without altering the original drawing, you must select the __________ option from the **Open** drop-down list in the **Select File** dialog box.

4. The __________ option enables you to open only a selected view or a selected layer of the current drawing.

5. You can use the __________ command to close the current drawing file without actually quitting AutoCAD LT.

6. The __________ system variable can be used to change the time interval for automatic save.

7. By using the__________ button, you can find information about a command on internet.

8. You can enable or disable the functions such as AutoComplete, AutoCorrect, and so on by using the options available in the__________ dialog box.

9. The__________ button is used to toggle the display of the File tab bar which displays all opened files.

10. The __________ palette is used to share a document with the people who have A360 account.

11. You can press the F3 key to display the **AutoCAD LT** text window, which displays the previous commands and prompts. (T/F)

12. If you do not have internet connection, you cannot access the Help files. (T/F)

13. If a drawing was partially opened and saved previously, it is not possible to open it again with the same layers and views. (T/F)

14. If the current drawing is unnamed and you save the drawing for the first time, the **Save** tool will prompt you to enter the file name in the **Save Drawing As** dialog box. (T/F)

Review Questions

Answer the following questions:

1. Which of the following combination of keys should be pressed to hide all toolbars displayed on the screen?

   (a) CTRL+3 (b) CTRL+0
   (c) CTRL+5 (d) CTRL+2

2. Which of the following combination of keys should be pressed to turn on or off the display of the **TOOL PALETTES** window?

   (a) CTRL+3 (b) CTRL+0
   (c) CTRL+5 (d) CTRL+2

3. Which of the following commands is used to exit the AutoCAD LT program?

   (a) **QUIT** (b) **END**
   (c) **CLOSE** (d) None of these

4. Which of the following options in the **Startup** dialog box is used to set the initial drawing settings before actually starting a new drawing?

   (a) **Start from Scratch** (b) **Use a Template**
   (c) **Use a Wizard** (d) None of these

5. Which of the following commands is invoked when you choose **Save** from the **File** menu or the **Save** tool from the Quick Access Toolbar?

    (a) **SAVE** (b) **LSAVE**
    (c) **QSAVE** (d) **SAVEAS**

6. AutoCAD LT has provided __________ as an easy and convenient way of placing and sharing hatch patterns and blocks in the current drawing.

7. By default, the angles are positive if measured in the __________ direction.

8. The __________check box is used to toggle the display of resolved posts.

9. The shortcut menu invoked by right-clicking on the command window displays the most recently used commands and some of the window options such as **Copy**, **Paste**, and so on. (T/F)

10. You can open an AutoCAD LT 2002 drawing in AutoCAD LT 2020. (T/F)

11. The file name that you enter to save a drawing in the **Save Drawing As** dialog box can be 255 characters long but cannot contain spaces and punctuation marks. (T/F)

12. You can close a drawing in AutoCAD LT even if a command is active. (T/F)

Answers to Self-Evaluation Test

1. Hardware Acceleration, 2. STARTUP, 3. Open Read-Only, 4. Partial Open, 5. CLOSE, 6. SAVETIME, 7. Search on Internet, 8. Input Search Options, 9. File Tabs, 10. Design Feed, 11. F, **12.** F, **13.** F, **14.** T

Chapter 2

Getting Started with AutoCAD LT

Learning Objectives

After completing this chapter, you will be able to:

- *Draw lines by using the Line tool*
- *Understand the coordinate systems used in AutoCAD LT*
- *Clear the drawing area by using the Erase tool*
- *Understand two basic object selection methods: Window and Window Crossing methods*
- *Draw circles by using various tools*
- *Use the Zoom and Pan tools*
- *Set up units by using the Units tool*
- *Set up and determine limits for a given drawing*
- *Plot drawings by using the basic plotting options*
- *Use the Options dialog box and specify settings*

Key Terms

- *Dynamic Input*
- *Line*
- *Coordinate Systems*
- *Absolute Coordinate System*
- *Relative Coordinate System*
- *Direct Distance Entry*
- *Erase*
- *Object Selection*
- *Circle*
- *Zoom*
- *Pan*
- *Units Format*
- *Limits*
- *Plot*
- *Options*

DYNAMIC INPUT MODE

In AutoCAD LT, the Dynamic Input mode allows you to enter the commands through the pointer input and the dimensions using the dimensional input. When this mode is turned on, all prompts are available at the tooltip as dynamic prompts and you can select the command options through the dynamic prompt. To enter the Dynamic Input mode, Choose the **Dynamic Input** option in the Status Bar.

Note

*If the **Dynamic Input** option is not displayed in the Status Bar, click on **Customization** in the Status Bar and turn on the **Dynamic Input** option in the Flyout.*

The settings for the Dynamic Input mode are done through the **Dynamic Input** tab of the **Drafting Settings** dialog box. To invoke the **Drafting Settings** dialog box, right-click on the **Dynamic Input** button in the Status Bar; a shortcut menu will be displayed. Choose the **Dynamic Input Settings** option from the shortcut menu; the **Drafting Settings** dialog box will be displayed, as shown in Figure 2-1. The options in the **Dynamic Input** tab are discussed next.

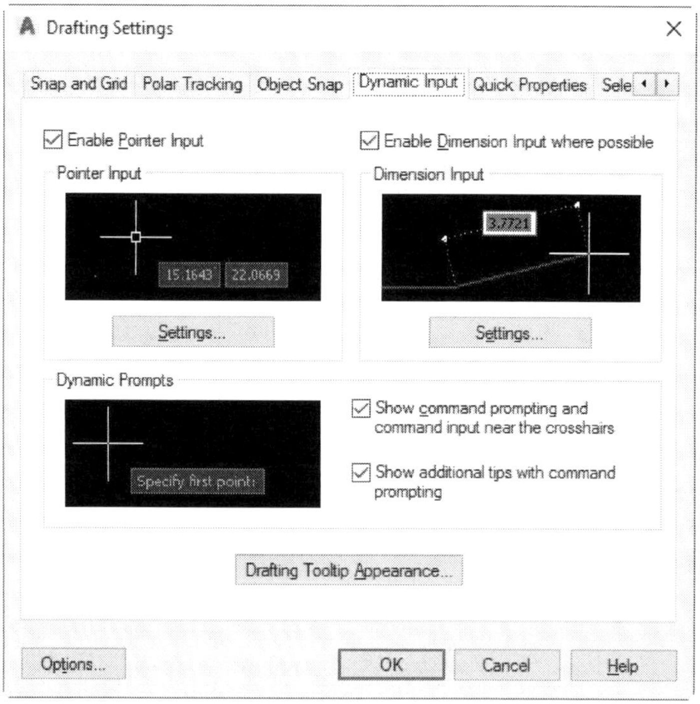

***Figure 2-1** The **Dynamic Input** tab of the **Drafting Settings** dialog box*

Enable Pointer Input

If the **Enable Pointer Input** check box is selected, you can enter the commands through the pointer input. Figure 2-2 shows the **CIRCLE** command entered through the pointer input. If this check box is cleared, the **Dynamic Input** option will be turned off and the commands have to be entered through the Command prompt. If you enter any alphabet at the **Pointer Input** tab all the tools whose names start with the entered alphabet will be displayed in a list at the **Dynamic Input**, see Figure 2-2.

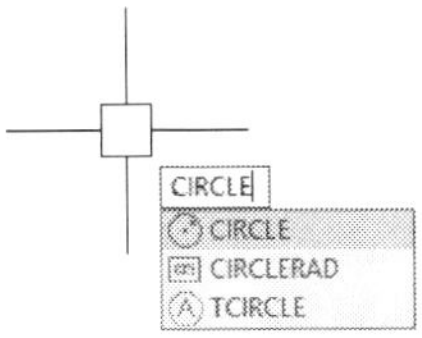

***Figure 2-2** Entering a command using the pointer input*

If you choose the **Settings** button from the **Pointer Input** area, the **Pointer Input Settings** dialog box will be displayed, as shown in Figure 2-3. The radio buttons in the **Format** area of this dialog box are used to set the default settings in either Polar or Cartesian format for specifying the second or next points for the entities. By default, the **Polar format** and **Relative coordinates** radio buttons are selected. As a result, the coordinates will be specified in the polar form and with respect to the relative coordinates system. You can select the **Cartesian format** radio button to enter the coordinates in Cartesian form. Similarly, if you select the **Absolute coordinates** radio button, the numerical entries will be measured with respect to the absolute coordinate system.

The options in the **Visibility** area of the **Pointer Input Settings** dialog box are used to set the visibility of the coordinates tool tips. By default, the **When a command asks for a point** radio button is selected. You can select the other radio buttons to modify this display.

Enable Dimension Input where possible

The **Enable Dimension Input where possible** check box is selected by default. As a result, the dimension input field is displayed in the graphics area showing the preview of that dimension. Figure 2-4 displays the dimension input fields. The options under the Dynamic prompt will be available when you press the down arrow key from the keyboard. The dotted lines show the geometric parameters like length, radius, or diameter corresponding to that dimension. Figure 2-4 shows a line being drawn using the **Pline** command. The two dimension inputs shown are for the length of the line and the angle with positive direction of the X axis.

Using the TAB key, you can toggle between the dimension input fields. As soon as you specify one dimension and move to the other, the previous dimension will be locked. If the **Enable Dimension Input where possible** check box is cleared, the preview of dimensions will not be displayed. You can only enter the dimensions in the dimension input fields below the cursor, as shown in Figure 2-5. Choose the **Settings** button from the **Dimension Input** area to display the **Dimension Input Settings** dialog box, as shown in Figure 2-6.

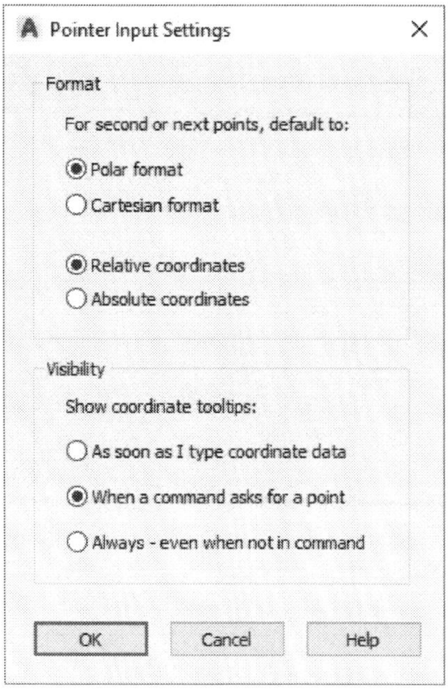

***Figure 2-3** The **Pointer Input Settings** dialog box*

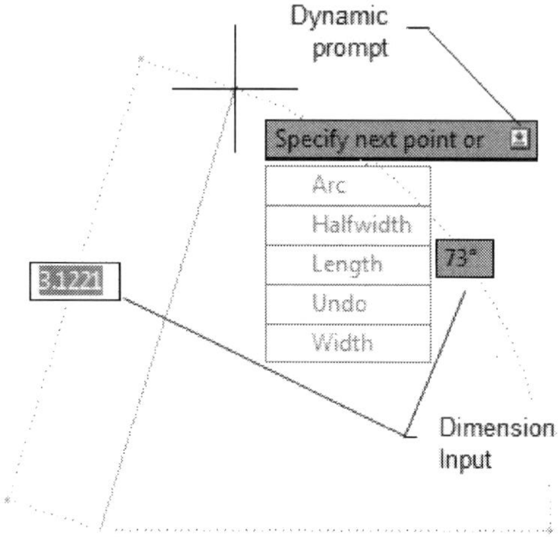

***Figure 2-4** Input fields displayed when the **Enable Dimension Input where possible** check box is selected*

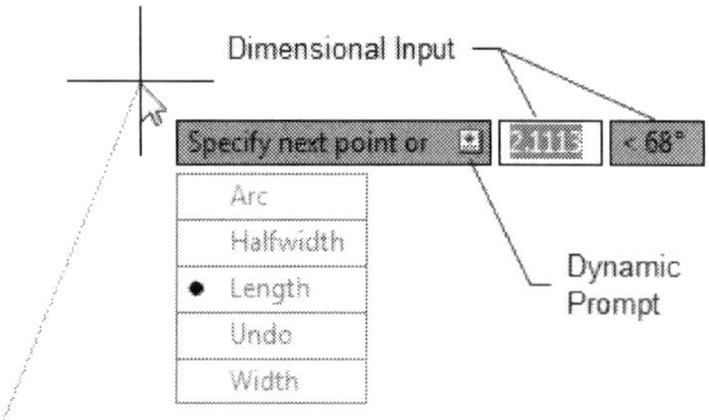

***Figure 2-5** Input fields displayed when the **Enable Dimension Input where possible** check box is cleared*

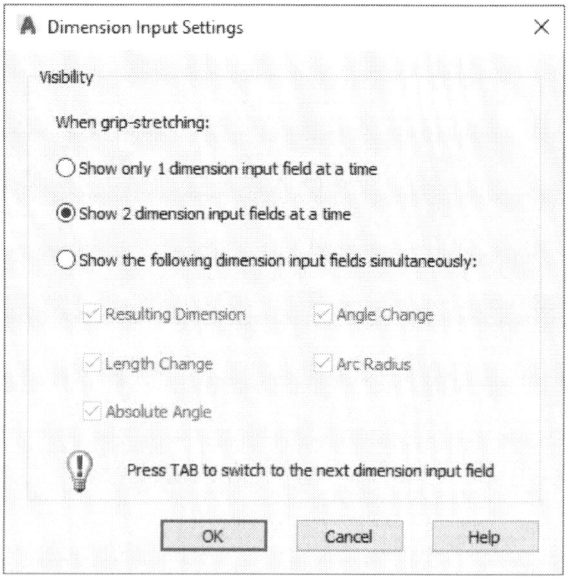

***Figure 2-6** The **Dimension Input Settings** dialog box*

By default, the **Show 2 dimension input fields at a time** radio button is selected. As a result, two dimension input fields will be displayed in the drawing area while stretching a sketched entity. The two input fields will depend on the entity that is being stretched. For example, if you stretch a line using one of its endpoints, the input field will show the total length of the line and the change in its length. Similarly, while stretching a circle using the grip on its circumference, the input fields will show the total radius and the change in the radius. You can set the priority to display only one input field or various input fields, simultaneously, by selecting their respective check boxes.

Tip
If multiple dimension input fields are available, use the TAB key to switch between the dimension input fields.

Show command prompting and command input near the crosshairs

If this check box is selected, the prompt sequences will be dynamically displayed near the crosshairs. Whenever a blue arrow appears at the pointer input, it suggests that the access options are available. To access these options, press the down arrow key to see the dynamic prompt listing all options. In the dynamic prompt, you can use the cursor or the down arrow key to jog through the options. A black dot will appear before the option that is currently active. In Figure 2-5, the **Length** option is currently active. Press ENTER to confirm the polyline creation with the **Length** option.

Show additional tips with command prompting

In AutoCAD LT, on selecting the **Show additional tips with command prompting** check box available in the **Dynamic Input** tab of the **Drafting Settings** dialog box, refer to Figure 2-1, the display of tips for the grip manipulation will be turned on.

Drafting Tooltip Appearance

When you choose the **Drafting Tooltip Appearance** button, the **Tooltip Appearance** dialog box will be displayed, as shown in Figure 2-7. This dialog box contains the options to customize the tooltip appearance.

The **Colors** button is chosen to change the color of the tooltip in the model space or layouts. The edit box in the **Size** area is used to specify the size of the tooltip. You can also use the slider to control the size of the tool tip. The preview is displayed in the **Model Preview** area and the **Layout Preview** area as soon as the value is changed in the **Size** edit box.

Similarly, the transparency of the tooltip can be controlled using the edit box or the slider in the **Transparency** area. Selecting the **Override OS settings for all drafting tooltips** radio button in the **Apply to** area ensures that changes made in the **Tooltip Appearance** dialog box will be applied to all drafting tooltips. If you select the **Use settings only for Dynamic Input tooltips** radio button, the changes will be applied only to the **Dynamic Input** tooltips. For example, if you change any of the parameters using the **Tooltip Appearance** dialog box and select the **Use settings only for Dynamic Input tooltips** radio button, the tooltips for the dynamic input will be modified but for the polar tracking it will consider the original values.

On the other hand, if you select the **Override OS settings for all drafting tooltips** radio button, the tooltips displayed for the polar tracking will also be modified based on the values in the **Tooltip Appearance** dialog box.

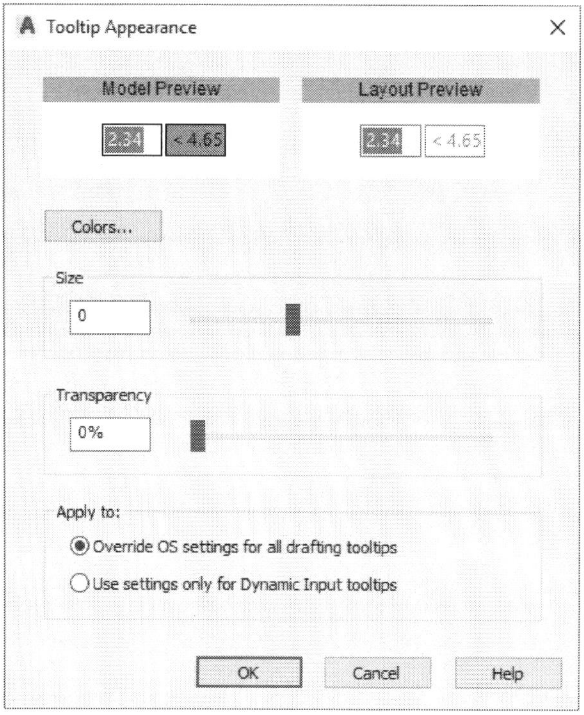

*Figure 2-7 The **Tooltip Appearance** dialog box*

DRAWING LINES IN AutoCAD LT

Ribbon: Home > Draw > Line **Toolbar:** Draw > Line
Menu Bar: Draw > Line **Command:** LINE or L

The most commonly used fundamental object in a drawing is line. In AutoCAD LT, a line is drawn between two points by using the **Line** tool. You can invoke the **Line** tool from the **Draw** panel of the **Home** tab in the **Ribbon**, refer to Figure 2-8. Alternatively, you can invoke the **Line** tool from the **Draw** toolbar, as shown in Figure 2-9. However, the **Draw** toolbar is not displayed by default. To invoke this toolbar, choose **Tools > Toolbars > AutoCAD LT > Draw** from the Menu Bar.

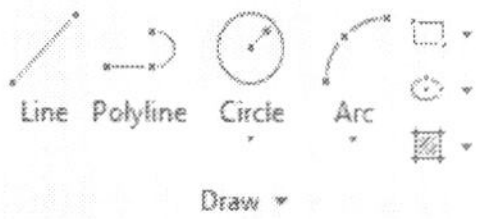

*Figure 2-8 The **Line** tool in the **Draw** panel*

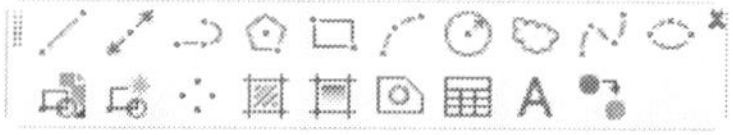

*Figure 2-9 The **Line** tool in the **Draw** toolbar*

You can also invoke the **Line** tool by entering **LINE** or **L** (L is the alias for the **LINE** command) at the Command prompt. On invoking the **Line** tool, you will be prompted to specify the starting point of the line. Specify a point by clicking the left mouse button in the drawing area or by entering its coordinates in the Dynamic Input fields or the command prompt. After specifying the first point, you will be prompted to specify the second point. Specify the second point; a line will be drawn, refer to Figure 2-10. You may continue specifying points and draw lines or terminate the **Line** tool by pressing ENTER, ESC, or SPACEBAR. You can also right-click to display the shortcut menu and then choose the **Enter** or **Cancel** option from it to exit the **Line** tool.

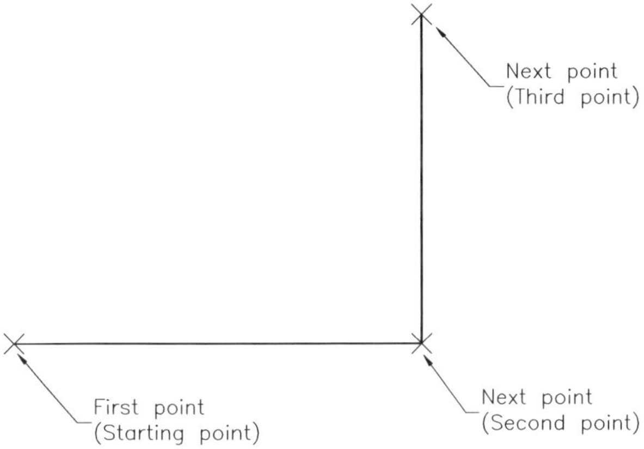

Figure 2-10 *Drawing lines using the **Line** tool*

Start a new file with the ***acadlt.dwt*** template in the **Drafting & Annotation** workspace. The prompt sequence for drawing the sketch shown in Figure 2-10 is given next.

*Choose the **Line** tool*

Specify first point: *Move the cursor (mouse) and left-click to specify the first point.*

Specify next point or [Undo]: *Move the cursor horizontal towards the right and left-click to specify the second point.*

Specify next point or [Undo]: *Specify the third point.*

Specify next point or [Close/Undo]: Enter *(Press ENTER to exit the **Line** tool.)*

Note

When you specify the start point of a line by pressing the left mouse button, a rubber band line stretches between the selected point and the current position of the cursor. This line is sensitive to the movement of the cursor and helps you select the direction and the placement for the next point for the line.

Note that in the Command prompt the **Close**, **Undo**, and **Exit** options will be displayed when the lines are created using the **Line** tool. All these options are discussed next.

The Close Option

After drawing two continuous lines by using the **Line** tool, you will notice that the **Close** option is displayed at the Command prompt. The **Close** option is used to join the current point with the start point of the first line when two or more continuous lines are drawn or enter **C** at the Command prompt as given in the Command prompt below.

*Choose the **Line** tool.*

LINE Specify first point: *Pick the first point.*

Specify next point or [Undo]: *Pick the second point.*

Specify next point or [eXit/Undo]: *Pick the third point.*

Specify next point or [Close/eXit/Undo]: *Pick the fourth point.*

Specify next point or [Close/eXit/Undo]: **C** Enter or *(Pick the first point again)*. Refer to Figure 2-11.

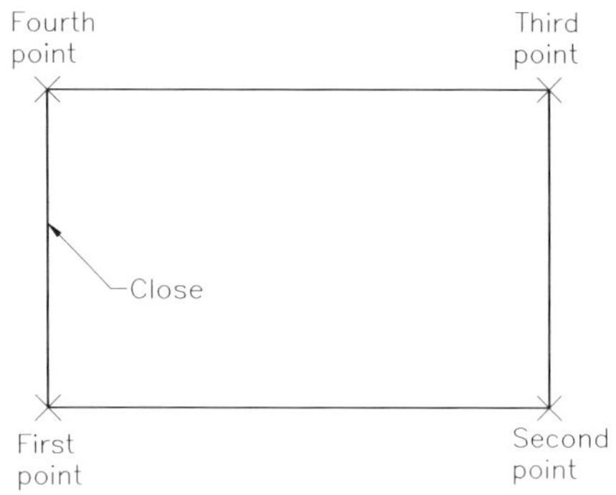

Figure 2-11 *Using the **Close** option with the **Line** tool*

You can also choose the **Close** option from the shortcut menu which appears when you right-click in the drawing area.

Tip

*After exiting the **Line** tool, to draw another line starting from the endpoint of the previous line, press ENTER twice; a new line will start from the endpoint of the previous line. Alternatively, you can choose the **Line** tool and then type the @ symbol, a new line will start from the end point of the previous line. For example, after drawing a circle if you invoke the **Line** tool, the @ symbol will snap to the center point of the circle.*

The Undo Option

While drawing a line, if you specify a wrong endpoint, then you can undo the last specified point and go back to the previous stage by using the **Undo** option of the **Line** tool. You can use this option multiple times. To use this option, type **Undo** (or just **U**) at the **Specify next point or [Undo]** prompt. You can also right-click to display the shortcut menu and then choose the **Undo** option.

The Exit Option

While drawing a line, if you want to exit the line tool then you can do so by using the **eXit** option of the **Line** tool. To use this option, type **Exit** (or just **X**) at the **Specify next point or [eXit/Undo]** prompt. You can also right-click and choose the **eXit** option from the shortcut menu.

Note

By default, whenever you open a new drawing, you need to modify the drawing display area. To modify the display area, select the required tool from the ***Zoom*** *drop-down in the* ***Navigator*** *bar; the drawing display gets modified. You will learn more about the Zoom tools later in this chapter.*

INVOKING TOOLS USING DYNAMIC INPUT/COMMAND PROMPT

In AutoCAD LT, if you enter any alphabet at the Command prompt or Dynamic Input, all the tools whose name start with the entered alphabet will be displayed in a list at the Command prompt or Dynamic Input. For example, if you enter **L** at the Command prompt or Dynamic Input, all the tools whose names start with the alphabet L will be displayed, refer to Figure 2-12. In this way, you can view all the tool names starting with a particular alphabet and select the required tool.

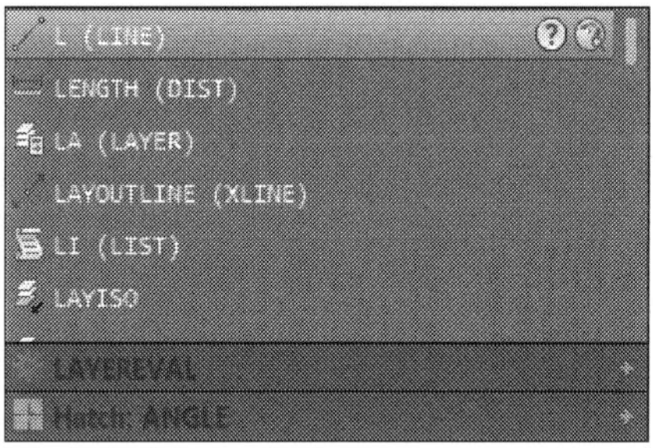

Figure 2-12 *List displayed after typing L at the Command prompt*

COORDINATE SYSTEMS

In AutoCAD LT, the location of a point is specified in terms of Cartesian coordinates. In this system, each point in a plane is specified by a pair of numerical coordinates. To specify a point in a plane, take two mutually perpendicular lines as references. The horizontal line is called the *X* axis, and the vertical line is called the *Y* axis. The *X* and *Y* axes divide the *XY* plane into four parts, generally known as quadrants. The point of intersection of these two axes is called the origin and the plane is called the XY plane. The origin has the coordinate values of X = 0, Y = 0. The origin is taken as the reference for locating a point on the *XY* plane. Now, to locate a point, say P, draw a vertical line intersecting the X axis. The horizontal distance between the origin and the intersection point will be called the X coordinate of P. It will be denoted as P(x). The *X* coordinate specifies how far the point is to the left or right from the origin along the *X* axis. Now, draw a horizontal line intersecting the Y axis. The vertical distance between the origin and the intersection point will be the Y coordinate of P. It will be denoted as P(y). The *Y* coordinate specifies how far the point is to the top or bottom from the origin along the *Y* axis. The intersection point of the horizontal and vertical lines is the coordinate of the point and is denoted as P(x,y). The *X* coordinate is positive, if measured from the right of the origin and is negative, if measured from the left of the origin. The *Y* coordinate is positive if measured above the origin and is negative if measured below the origin, refer to Figure 2-13.

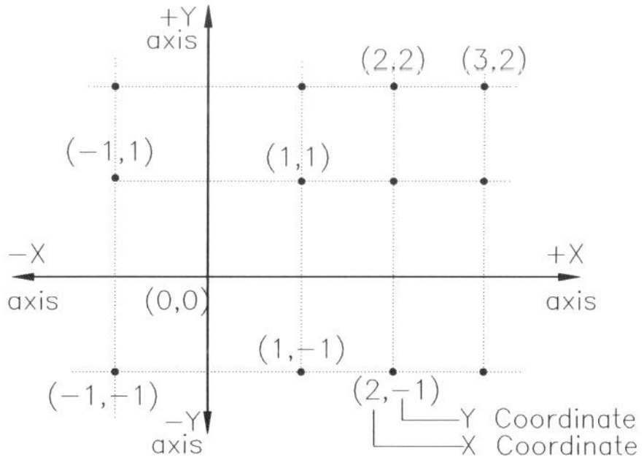

Figure 2-13 *Cartesian coordinate system*

In AutoCAD LT, the default origin is located at the lower left corner of the drawing area. AutoCAD LT uses the following coordinate systems to locate a point in the XY plane.

1. Absolute coordinates
2. Relative coordinates
    a. Relative rectangular coordinates
    b. Relative polar coordinates
3. Direct distance entry

If you are specifying a point by entering its location at the Command prompt then you need to use any one of the coordinate systems.

Absolute Coordinate System

In the Absolute Coordinate System, points are located with respect to the origin (0,0). For example, a point with X = 4 and Y = 3 is measured 4 units horizontally (distance along the *X* axis) and 3 units vertically (distance along the *Y* axis) from the origin, as shown in Figure 2-14. In AutoCAD LT, the absolute coordinates are specified at the Command prompt by entering *X* and *Y* coordinates separated by a comma. However, remember that if you are specifying the coordinates by using the **Dynamic Input** mode, you need to add # as the prefix to the X coordinate value. For example, enter #1,1 in the dynamic input boxes to use the Absolute Coordinate System. The following example illustrates the use of absolute coordinates at the Command prompt to draw the rectangle shown in Figure 2-15.

Choose the ***Line*** *tool (Ensure that the* ***Dynamic Input*** *button is not chosen)*

LINE Specify first point: **1,1** Enter *(X = 1 and Y = 1.)*

Specify next point or [Undo]: **4,1** Enter *(X = 4 and Y = 1.)*

Specify next point or [Undo]: **4,3** Enter

Specify next point or [Close /eXit/Undo]: **1,3** Enter

Specify next point or [Close/eXit/Undo]: **C** Enter

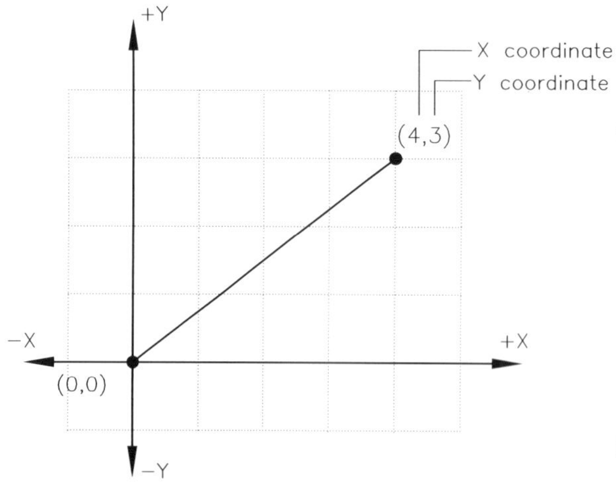

Figure 2-14 *Absolute Coordinate System*

Figure 2-15 *Rectangle created by using absolute coordinates*

Example 1 Absolute Coordinate System

Draw the profile shown in Figure 2-16 by using the Absolute Coordinate system. The absolute coordinates of the points are given in the following table. Save the drawing with the name *Exam1.dwg*.

Point	Coordinates	Point	Coordinates
1	3,1	5	5,2
2	3,6	6	6,3
3	4,6	7	7,3
4	4,2	8	7,1

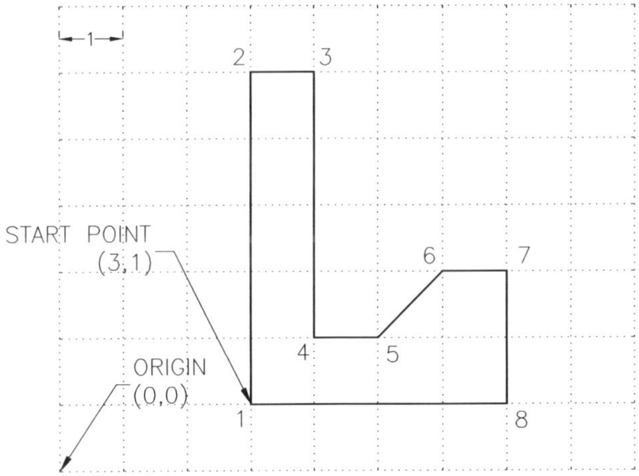

***Figure 2-16** Drawing a figure using the absolute coordinates*

Start a new file with the ***acadlt.dwt*** template in the **Drafting & Annotation** workspace. Once you know the coordinates of the points, you can draw the sketch by using the **Line** tool. The prompt sequence is given next.

*Choose the **Zoom All** tool*

*Choose the **Line** tool*

LINE Specify first point: **3,1** Enter *(Start point.)*

Specify next point or [Undo]: **3,6** Enter

Specify next point or [eXit/Undo]: **4,6** Enter

Specify next point or [Close/eXit/Undo]: **4,2** Enter

Specify next point or [Close/eXit/Undo]: **5,2** Enter

Specify next point or [Close/eXit/Undo]: **6,3** Enter

Specify next point or [Close/eXit/Undo]: **7,3** Enter

Specify next point or [Close/eXit/Undo]: **7,1** Enter

Specify next point or [Close/eXit/Undo]: **C** Enter

Choose the **Save** tool from the **Quick Access** Toolbar to display the **Save Drawing As** dialog box. Enter **Exam1** in the **File name** edit box and then choose the **Save** button. The drawing will be saved with the specified name in the default *Documents* folder.

Exercise 1 Absolute Coordinate System

Draw the profile shown in Figure 2-17. The distance between the dotted lines is 1 unit. Enter the absolute coordinates for the points given in the following table. Then, use these coordinates to draw the given figure.

Point	Coordinates	Point	Coordinates
1	2, 1	6	______
2	______	7	______
3	______	8	______
4	______	9	______
5	______		

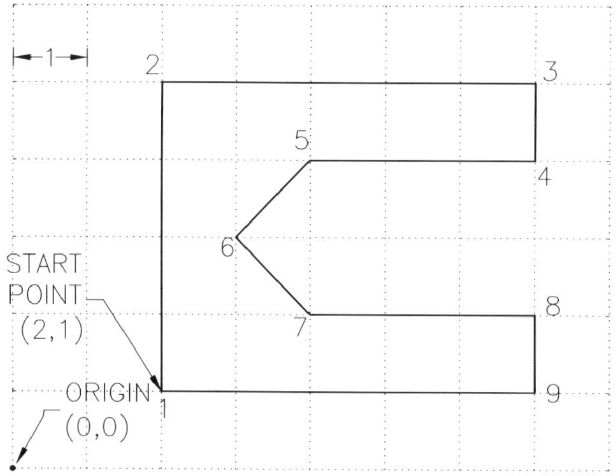

Figure 2-17 *Drawing for Exercise 1*

Relative Coordinate System

There are two types of relative coordinates: relative rectangular and relative polar.

Relative Rectangular Coordinates

In the Relative Rectangular Coordinate system, the location of a point is specified with respect to the previous point and not with respect to the origin. To enter coordinate values in terms of the Relative Rectangular Coordinate system, check whether the **Dynamic Input** is on or not. If the **Dynamic Input** is turned on, then by default the profile will be drawn using the Relative Rectangular Coordinate system. Therefore, in this case, enter the X coordinate, type comma (,), and then enter the Y coordinate. However, if the **Dynamic Input** is turned off, the coordinate values have to be prefixed by the @ symbol, so that the profile will be drawn using the Relative Rectangular Coordinate system. For example, to draw a rectangle, refer to Figure 2-18, using the Relative Rectangular Coordinate system, you need to use the following prompt sequence:

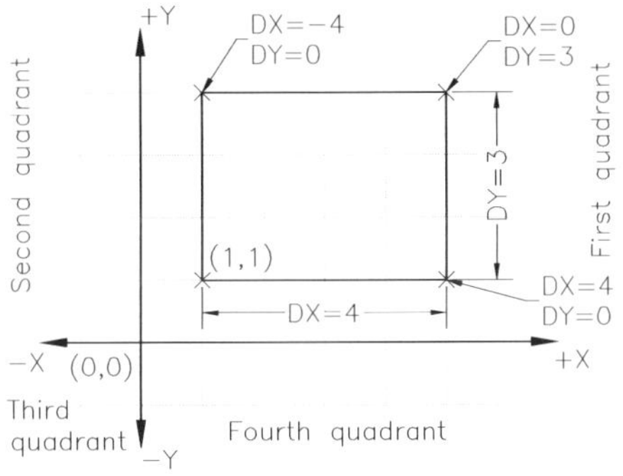

Figure 2-18 Drawing lines using the relative rectangular coordinates

*Choose the **Line** tool*

LINE Specify first point: **1,1** [Enter] *(Start point)*

Specify next point or [Undo]: **@4,0** [Enter]

Specify next point or [eXit/Undo]: **@0,3** [Enter]

Specify next point or [Close/eXit/Undo]:**@-4,0** [Enter]

Specify next point or [Close/eXit/Undo]: **@0,-3** [Enter]

Specify next point or [Close/eXit/Undo]: [Enter]

Remember that if the **Dynamic Input** is on, you need to use a comma (,) after entering the first value in the Dynamic Input boxes, otherwise AutoCAD LT will take coordinates in relative polar form.

Sign Convention. As mentioned, in the Relative Rectangular Coordinate system, the distance along the X and Y axes is measured with respect to the previous point. To understand the sign convention, imagine a horizontal line and a vertical line passing through the previous points so that you get four quadrants. If the new point is located in the first quadrant, then both the distances (DX and DY) will be specified as positive values. If the new point is located in the third quadrant, then both the distances (DX and DY) will be specified as negative values. In other words, the point will have a positive coordinate values, if it is located above or on the right of an axis. Similarly, the point will have a negative coordinate value, if it is located below or on the left of the axis.

Example 2 Relative Rectangular Coordinates

Draw the profile shown in Figure 2-19 using Relative Rectangular Coordinates. The coordinates for the points are given in the table below.

Point	Coordinates
1	3,1
2	@4,0
3	@0,1
4	@-1,0
5	@1,1
6	@0,2
7	@-1,0

Point	Coordinates
8	@-1,-1
9	@-1,1
10	@-1,0
11	@0,-2
12	@1,-1
13	@-1,0
14	@0,-1

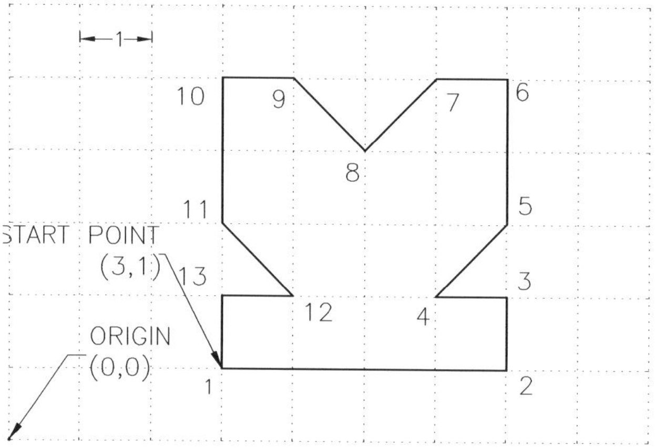

Figure 2-19 *Profile for Example 2*

Start a new file with the *acadlt.dwt* template in the **Drafting & Annotation** workspace. Before you proceed, you need to make sure that the **Dynamic Input** is turned on.

Choose the ***Zoom All*** tool

*Choose the **Line** tool*

LINE Specify first point: *Type* **3,1** *in the dynamic input boxes and press* Enter *(Start point)*

Specify next point or [Undo]: *Type* **4,0** *in the dynamic input boxes and press* Enter

Specify next point or [eXit/Undo]: *Type* **0,1** *in the dynamic input boxes and press* Enter

Specify next point or [Close/eXit/Undo]: *Type* **-1,0** *in the dynamic input boxes and press* Enter

Specify next point or [Close/eXit/Undo]: *Type* **1,1** *in the dynamic input boxes and press* Enter

Specify next point or [Close/eXit/Undo]: *Type* **0,2** *in the dynamic input boxes and press* Enter

Specify next point or [Close/eXit/Undo]: **-1,0** *and press* Enter

Specify next point or [Close/eXit/Undo]: **-1,-1** *and press* Enter

Specify next point or [Close/eXit/Undo]: **-1,1** *and press* Enter

Specify next point or [Close/eXit/Undo]: **-1,0** *and press* Enter

Specify next point or [Close/eXit/Undo]: **0,-2** *and press* Enter

Specify next point or [Close/eXit/Undo]: **1,-1** *and press* Enter

Specify next point or [Close/eXit/Undo]: **-1,0** *and press* Enter

Specify next point or [Close/eXit/Undo]: **0,-1** *and press* Enter

Specify next point or [Close/eXit/Undo]: Enter

Exercise 2 Relative Rectangular Coordinates

For Figure 2-20, enter the relative rectangular coordinates of the points given in the following table. Then, use these coordinates to draw the figure. The distance between the dotted lines is 1 unit.

Point	Coordinates
1	2, 1
2	______
3	______
4	______
5	______
6	______
7	______
8	______
9	______
10	______
11	______

Point	Coordinates
12	______
13	______
14	______
15	______
16	______
17	______
18	______
19	______
20	______
21	______
22	______

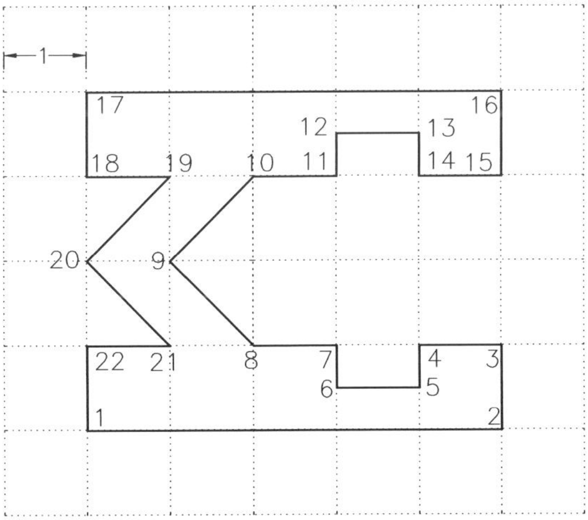

Figure 2-20 Drawing for Exercise 2

Relative Polar Coordinates

In the Relative Polar Coordinate system, the location of a point is specified by defining the distance of the point from the current point and the angle between the two points with respect to the positive *X* axis. The prompt sequence to draw a line of length 5 units whose start point is at 1,1 and inclined at an angle of 30 degrees to the *X* axis, as shown in Figure 2-21, is given next.

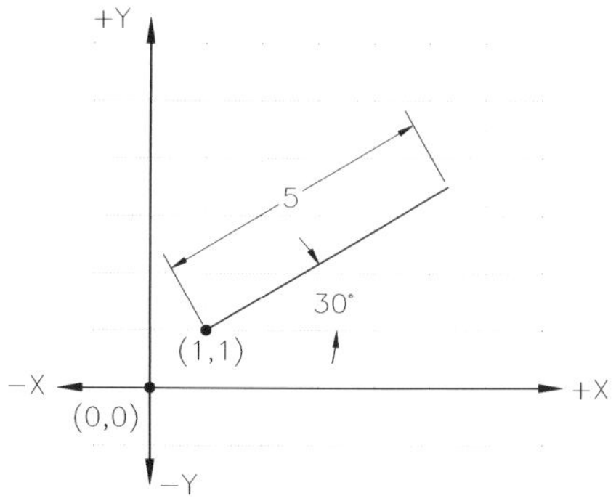

Figure 2-21 *Drawing a line by using relative polar coordinates*

Choose the ***Line*** *tool*
Specify first point: **1,1** Enter
Specify next point or [Undo]: **@5<30** Enter

If the **Dynamic Input** is on, by default the relative polar coordinate mode will be activated. Therefore, when you invoke the **Line** tool and specify the start point, two input boxes will be displayed. The second input box shows the angle value, preceded by the **<** symbol. Now, enter the distance value and press the TAB key to shift to the second input box, and then enter the angle value.

Sign Convention. By default, in the relative polar coordinate system, the angle is measured from the horizontal axis as the zero degree. Also, the angle is positive if measured in counter clockwise direction and is negative if measured in clockwise direction. Here, it is assumed that the default setup of the angle measurement has not been changed.

Note

You can modify the default settings of the angle measurement direction by using the ***Units*** *tool from the* ***Format*** *tab of the Menu Bar which is discussed later in this chapter.*

Example 3 — Relative Polar Coordinates

Draw the profile shown in Figure 2-22 by using the Relative Polar Coordinates. The relative coordinate values of each point are given in the table. The start point is located at 1.5, 1.75. Save this drawing with the name *Exam3.dwg*. The dimensions and the numbering are for reference only.

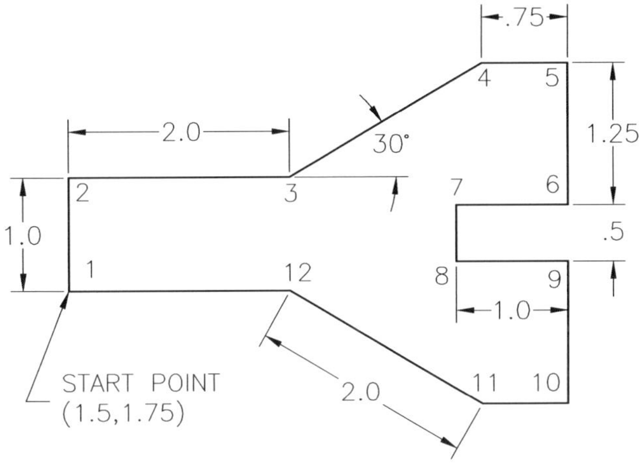

Figure 2-22 *Drawing for Example 3*

Point	Coordinates
1	1.5,1.75
2	@1.0<90
3	@2.0<0
4	@2.0<30
5	@0.75<0
6	@1.25<-90 (or <270)

Point	Coordinates
7	@1.0<180
8	@0.5<270
9	@1.0<0
10	@1.25<270
11	@0.75<180
12	@2.0<150

Start a new file with the ***acadlt.dwt*** template in the **Drafting & Annotation** workspace. Next, you need to modify the drawing display area. To do so, choose the **Zoom Extents** tool from the **Navigation bar**. Next, turn off the **Dynamic Input** option by choosing the **Dynamic Input** button from the Status Bar.

*Choose the **Line** tool*

LINE Specify first point: **1.5,1.75** Enter *(Start point)*

Specify next point or [Undo]: **@1<90** Enter

Specify next point or [eXit/Undo]: **@2.0<0** Enter

Specify next point or [Close/eXit/Undo]: **@2<30** Enter

Specify next point or [Close/eXit/Undo]: **@0.75<0** Enter

Specify next point or [Close/eXit/Undo]: **@1.25<-90** Enter

Specify next point or [Close/eXit/Undo]: **@1.0<180** Enter

Specify next point or [Close/eXit/Undo]: **@0.5<270** Enter

Specify next point or [Close/eXit/Undo]: **@1.0<0** Enter

Specify next point or [Close/eXit/Undo]: **@1.25<270** Enter

Specify next point or [Close/eXit/Undo]: **@0.75<180** Enter

Specify next point or [Close/eXit/Undo]: **@2.0<150** Enter

Specify next point or [Close/eXit/Undo]: **C** Enter *(The last point joins with the first point)*

To save this drawing, choose the **Save** tool from the **Quick Access** Toolbar; the **Save Drawing As** dialog box will be displayed. Enter **Exam3** in the **File name** edit box and then choose the **Save** button; the drawing will be saved with the specified name in the **My Documents** folder.

Exercise 3 Specifying Points using Coordinates

Draw the profile shown in Figure 2-23 by specifying points using the absolute, relative rectangular, and relative polar coordinate systems. Do not dimension the profile. They are given for reference only.

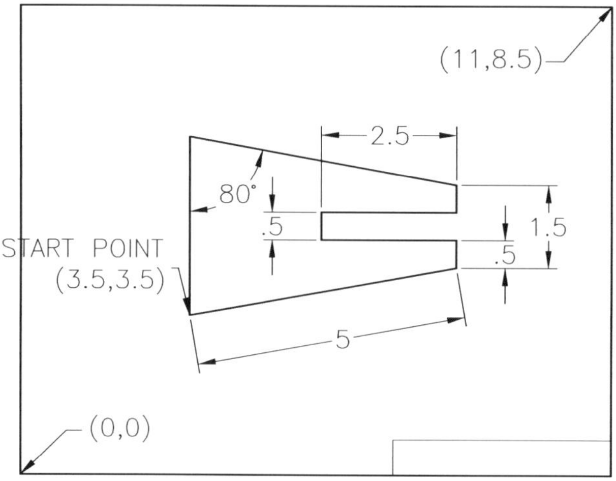

***Figure 2-23** Drawing for Exercise 3*

Direct Distance Entry

The easiest way to draw a line in AutoCAD LT is by using the Direct Distance Entry method. Before drawing a line by using this method, ensure that the **Dynamic Input** button is chosen in the Status Bar. Next, choose the **Line** tool; you will be prompted to specify the start point. Enter the coordinate values in the text box and press ENTER; you will be prompted to specify the next point. Now, enter the absolute length of the line and its angle with respect to the current position of the cursor in the corresponding text boxes, as shown in Figure 2-24. Note that you can use the TAB key to toggle between the text boxes. If the **Ortho** mode is on while drawing lines using this method, you can position the cursor only along the *X* or *Y* axis. If the **Dynamic Input** button is not chosen, then you need to enter the length of the line at the Command prompt. Therefore, position the cursor at the desired angle, type the length at the Command prompt, and then press ENTER, refer to Figure 2-24.

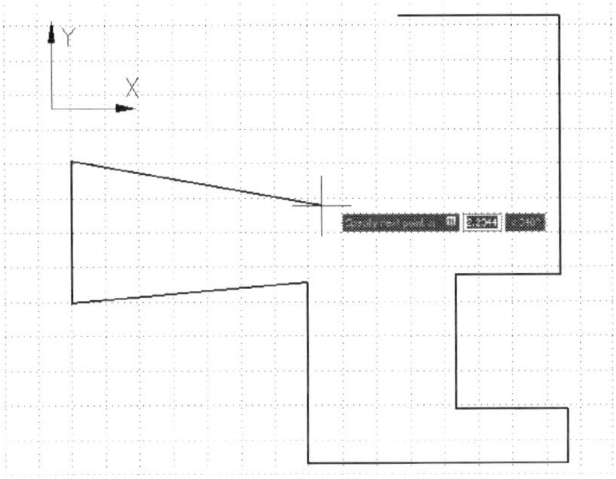

Figure 2-24 *Drawing lines using the Direct Distance Entry method*

Choose the ***Line*** *tool*

LINE Specify first point: *Start point.*

Specify next point or [Undo]: *Position the cursor and then enter distance.*

Specify next point or [eXit/Undo]: *Position the cursor and then enter distance.*

Example 4 Direct Distance Entry

In this example, you will draw the profile shown in Figure 2-25, by using the Direct Distance Entry method. The start point is 2,2.

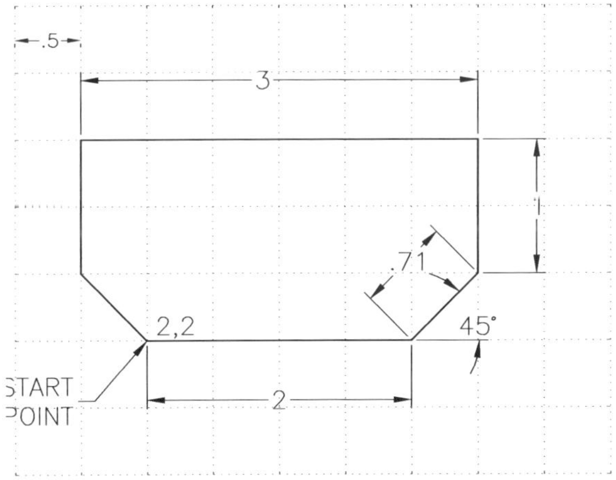

Figure 2-25 *Drawing for Example 4*

Also, you can use the Polar Tracking option to draw lines. The Polar Tracking option allows you to track the lines that are drawn at specified angles. The default angle specified for polar tracking is 90 degrees. Therefore, by default, you can track lines at an angle that is multiple of 90 degrees, such as 90, 180, 270, and 360. In this example, you need to draw lines at the angles that are multiples of 45 degrees such as 45, 90, 135, and so on. Therefore, first you need to set the polar tracking angle as 45 degrees.

Note
You will learn more about polar tracking in Chapter 4

1. Start a new file with the ***acadlt.dwt*** template in the **Drafting & Annotation** workspace.

2. To add a 45-degree angle to polar tracking, right-click on the **Polar Tracking** button on the Status Bar and then choose **45** from the shortcut menu displayed. Again, choose the **Polar Tracking** button in the Status Bar to turn polar tracking on.

3. Choose the **Line** tool from the **Draw** panel of the **Home** tab; you are prompted to specify the start point.

4. Enter **2,2** at the Command prompt and press ENTER; you are prompted to specify the next point.

5. Move the cursor horizontally toward the right and when the tooltip displays 0 as polar angle, type **2** and press ENTER; you are prompted to specify the next point.

6. Move the cursor at an angle close to 45 degrees and when the tooltip displays 45 as the value of polar angle, type **0.71** and press ENTER; you are prompted to specify next point.

7. Move the cursor vertically upward and when the tooltip displays 90 as the value of polar angle, type **1** and press ENTER; you are prompted to specify the next point.

8. Move the cursor horizontally toward the left and when the tooltip displays 180 as the value of polar angle, type **3** and press ENTER; you are prompted to specify the next point.

9. Move the cursor vertically downward and when the tooltip displays 90 the value of polar angle, type **1** and press ENTER; you are prompted to specify the next point.

10. Type **C** and press ENTER.

Tip
*You can add more angular values to the shortcut menu that is displayed on clicking the **Polar Tracking** in the Status Bar. To do so, choose the **Tracking Settings** option from the shortcut menu; the **Drafting Setting** dialog box will be displayed. Next, in the **Polar angle settings** area choose the **New** button and then enter the new angle value in the edit field that appears in the Additional angles box of the dialog box. Similarly, you can specify multiple angle values. Once you are done, choose the **OK** button.*

EXERCISE 4 Direct Distance Entry

Use the Direct Distance Entry method to draw a parallelogram. The base of the parallelogram equals 4 units, the side equals 2.25 units, and the angle equals 45 degrees. Draw the same parallelogram using the absolute, relative, and polar coordinates. Note the differences and the advantages of using this method over Relative and Absolute Coordinate methods.

ERASING OBJECTS

Ribbon: Home > Modify > Erase **Toolbar:** Modify > Erase
Menu Bar: Modify > Erase
Command: ERASE or E

Sometimes, you may need to erase the unwanted objects from the objects drawn. You can do so by using the **Erase** tool. This tool is used exactly the same way as an eraser is used in manual drafting to delete the unwanted lines. To erase an object, choose the **Erase** tool from the **Modify** panel, refer to Figure 2-26.

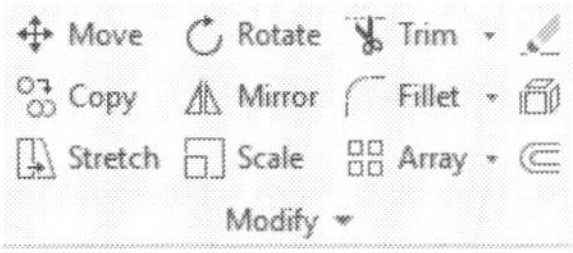

*Figure 2-26 The **Erase** tool in the **Modify** panel*

You can also choose the **Erase** tool from the Modify toolbar, as shown in Figure 2-27. To invoke the **Modify** toolbar, choose **Tools > Toolbars > AutoCAD LT > Modify** from the Menu Bar. On invoking the **Erase** tool a small box, known as pick box, replaces the screen cursor. To erase the object, select it by using the pick box, refer to Figure 2-28; the selected object will be displayed in transparent lines and the **Select objects** prompt will be displayed again. You can either continue selecting the objects or press ENTER to terminate the object selection process and erase the selected objects. The prompt sequence is given next.

*Figure 2-27 The **Erase** tool in the **Modify** toolbar*

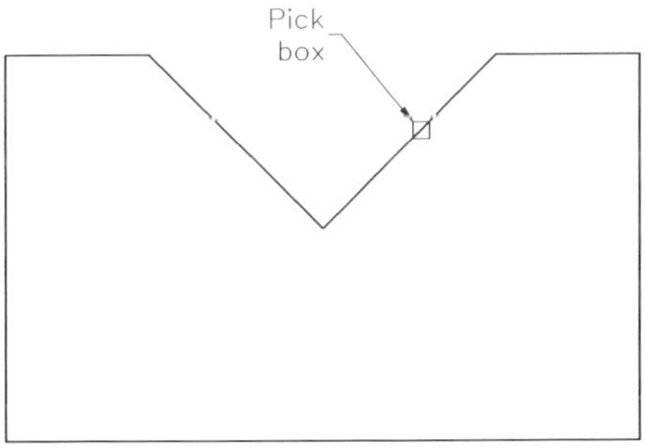

Figure 2-28 Selecting the object by positioning the pick box at the top of the object

*Choose the **Erase** tool*

Select objects: *Select the first object.*

Select objects: *Select the second object.*

Select objects:

If you enter **ALL** at the **Select objects** prompt, all the objects in the drawing area will get selected even if they are outside the display area. Now, if you press ENTER, all the selected objects will be erased. To erase the objects, you can also first select the objects to be erased from the drawing and then choose the **Erase** option from this shortcut menu that is displayed on right-clicking in the drawing area.

CANCELING AND UNDOING OPERATIONS

If you have erased an object unintentionally, then to restore the erased object, enter the **OOPS** or **UNDO** command. The **OOPS** command is used to restore the last erased object from the drawing area. The **UNDO** command is used to undo the action of the previously performed command. You can also choose the **Undo** tool from the **Quick Access** Toolbar. To cancel or exit a command, press the ESC (Escape) key on the keyboard.

OBJECT SELECTION METHODS

The usual method to select objects is by selecting them individually. But it will be time-consuming, if you have a number of objects to select. This problem can be solved by creating a selection set that enables you to select several objects at a time. The selection set options can be used with those tools that require object selection, such as **Erase** and **Move**. There are many object selection methods, such as **Window**, **Crossing**, and so on. In this chapter, you will learn two methods: **Window** and **Crossing**. The remaining options are discussed in Chapter 5.

Window Selection Method

The window selection is one of the selection methods in which an object or a group of objects is selected by drawing a window. The objects that are completely enclosed within the window are selected and the objects that lie partially inside the boundaries of the window are not selected. To select the objects by using the **Window** option, specify first corner point for the polygon and then type **WP** at the **Command** prompt. Next, draw a polygon to select object and then press ENTER. As you move the cursor, a blue color window of continuous line will be displayed. The size of this window changes as you move the cursor. Figure 2-29 shows the window drawn to select the objects by using the **Window** option. The objects that will be selected are shown in light blue shaded lines.

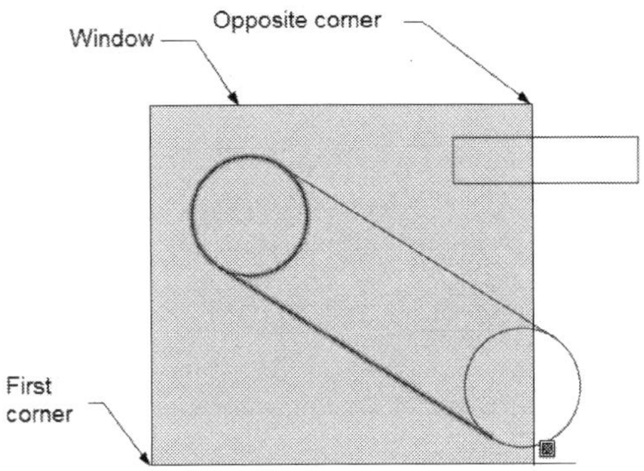

Figure 2-29 *Selecting objects using the* ***Window*** *option*

You can also invoke the **Window** option without entering **WP** at the Command prompt. To do so, specify a point on the screen. This is considered as the first corner of the window. Moving the cursor to the right will display a blue-shaded window. After enclosing the required objects, specify the other corner of the window. The objects that are completely enclosed within the window will be selected and displayed in shaded blue lines. The following is the prompt sequence for displaying automatic window after the **Erase** tool.

Select objects: *Select a blank point as the first corner of the window*

Specify opposite corner: *Drag the cursor to the right to select the other corner of the window*

Select objects: Enter

Crossing Selection Method

In the Crossing selection method, both partially as well as completely enclosed object or group of objects get selected. The objects to be selected can be touching the window boundaries or be completely enclosed within it. To select the objects by using the Crossing selection method, specify the first corner point of a polygon and then type **CP** at the Command prompt and draw a polygon to select the objects and then press ENTER. As you move the cursor, a green color window with dashed outline is displayed. Figure 2-30 shows a window drawn to select objects by using the Crossing selection method. The objects that need to be selected are shown in shaded blue lines.

You can also invoke the Crossing selection method without entering **CP** at the Command prompt. To do so, specify a point in the drawing area and move the cursor to the left. As you move the cursor, a green colored window with dashed outline will be displayed. Specify the opposite corner of the window; the objects touching the window boundary and that are enclosed within this window get selected and are displayed as shaded green lines. The prompt sequence for the crossing selection method when you choose the **Erase** tool is given next.

Select objects: *Select a blank point as the first corner of the crossing window*

Specify opposite corner: *Drag the cursor to the left to select the other corner of the crossing window*

Select objects: Enter

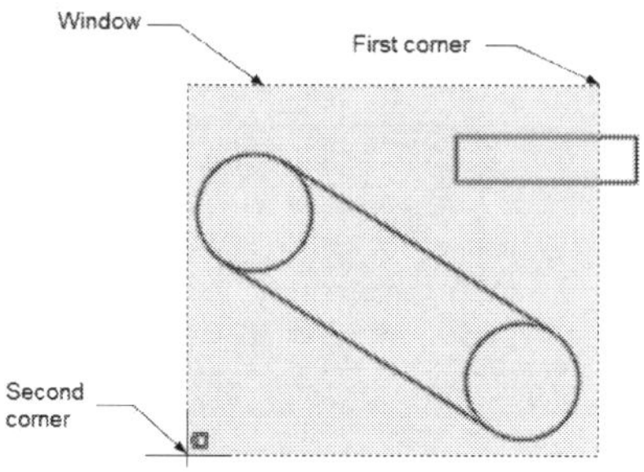

Figure 2-30 *Selecting objects using the Crossing Selection method*

Tip

You can also select the objects by using the Window or Window Crossing methods without invoking a command. To do so, specify the start point of the selection window and then drag the cursor to enclose the objects in a window. If you move the cursor to the left of the start point, the Crossing Selection method will be activated. But, if you move the cursor to the right of the start point, the Window selection method will be activated.

If you do not invoke any tool and click to specify the first corner of the window for window selection or window crossing , the Command prompt provides you with three selection options: **Fence**, **WPolygon**, and **CPolygon**. If you enter **FENCE** or **F** at the Command prompt, you can select objects by drawing a fence around them. If you enter **WP** at the Command prompt, you can select objects by drawing a polygon around them. If you enter **CP** at the Command prompt, you can select objects by drawing a polygon around them. These options will be discussed in detail in Chapter 5.

Lasso Selection Method

The Lasso's selection is one of the selection methods in which an object or group of objects which are completely or partially enclosed by the selection area are selected. The objects to be selected can touch the window boundaries or can be completely enclosed within it. To select the objects by using the Lasso method, press and hold the left mouse button and drag the cursor; a selection area will be displayed, as shown in Figure 2-31.

Note that if you drag the cursor from left to right, only the objects enclosed in the area will be selected. And, if you drag the cursor from right to left, the objects touching the boundary of the Lasso Selection Area will also be selected.

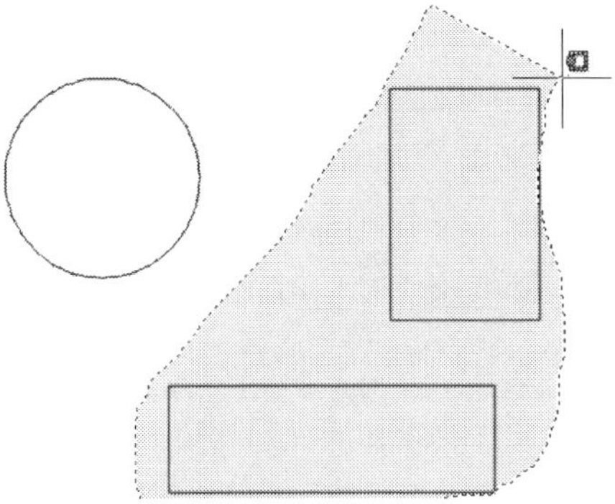

Figure 2-31 Selecting objects using the Lasso selection method

To activate the Lasso selection method, invoke the **Options** dialog box and choose the **Selection** tab; the options available in the **Selection** tab will be displayed. Select the **Allow press and drag for Lasso** check box available in the **Selection modes** area of the dialog box; the Lasso selection will be activated, if not already activated by default, refer Figure 2-32.

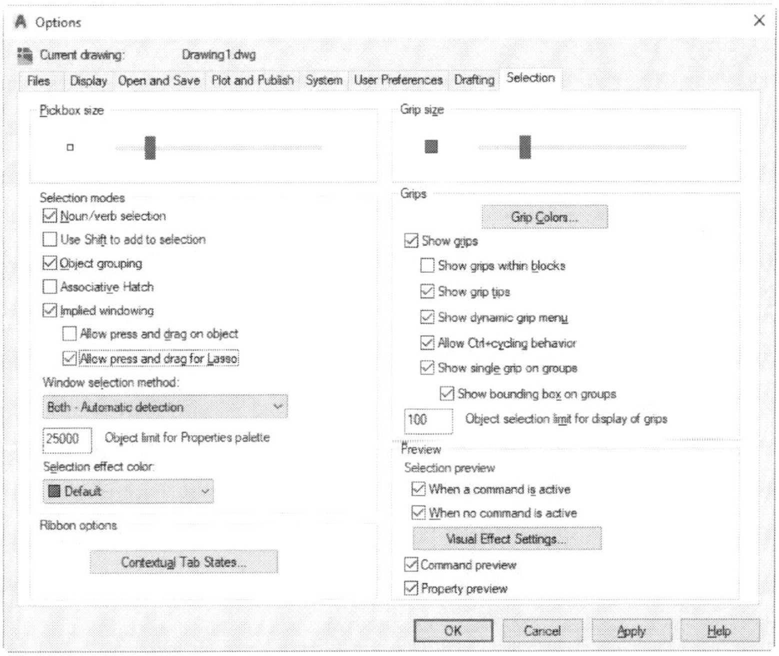

Figure 2-32 Selecting the ***Allow press and drag for Lasso*** *check box from the* ***Options*** *dialog box*

DRAWING A CIRCLE

Ribbon: Home > Draw > Circle drop-down > Center, Radius
Toolbar: Draw > Circle **Menu Bar:** Draw > Circle
Command: CIRCLE or C

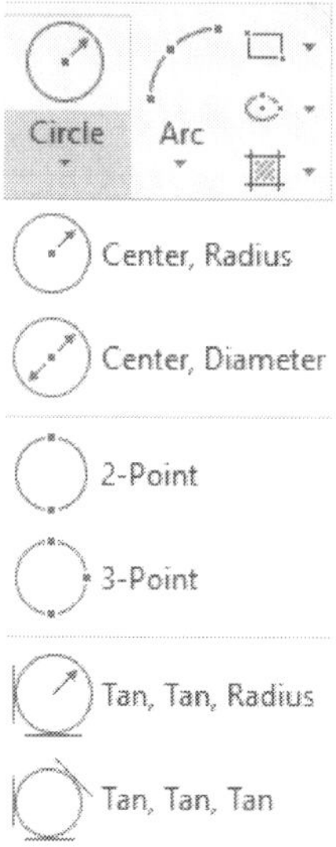

***Figure 2-33** Tools in the **Circle** drop-down*

A circle is drawn by using the **Circle** tool. In AutoCAD LT, you can draw a circle by using six different tools. All these tools are grouped together in the **Draw** panel of the **Ribbon**. To view these tools, choose the down arrow next to the **circle** tool in the **Draw** panel, as shown in Figure 2-33; all the tools will be listed in the drop-down. Note that the name of the tool chosen last will be displayed in the **Draw** panel. You can also invoke the **Circle** tool from the **Draw** toolbar, or by entering **C** in the command prompt. The different methods to draw a circle are discussed next.

Drawing a Circle by Specifying Center and Radius

Ribbon: Home > Draw > Circle drop-down > Center, Radius

To draw a circle by specifying the center and the radius and with the **Dynamic Input** button chosen, choose the **Center, Radius** tool from the **Draw** panel; you will be prompted to specify the center of the circle. Type the coordinates and press ENTER or specify the center by using the left mouse button. After specifying the center of the circle, move the cursor to define its radius; the current radius of the circle will be displayed in the dimension input box, as shown in Figure 2-34. This radius value will change as you move the cursor. Type a radius value in the dimension input box or click to define the radius; a circle of the specified radius value will be drawn. If the **Dynamic Input** is not chosen, you need to specify the input values in the Command prompt.

Drawing a Circle by Specifying Center and Diameter

Ribbon: Home > Draw > Circle drop-down > Center, Diameter

To draw a circle by specifying center and diameter, when the **Dynamic Input** button is chosen, choose the **Center, Diameter** tool from the **Draw** panel; you will be prompted to specify the center. Type the coordinates and press ENTER or specify the center by using the left mouse button. After specifying the center of the circle, move the cursor to define its diameter; the current diameter of the circle will be displayed in the dimension input box, as shown in Figure 2-35. This diameter value will change as you move the cursor. Type a diameter value in the dimension input box or click to define the diameter; a circle of the specified diameter value will be drawn. If the **Dynamic Input** is not chosen, you need to specify the input values in the Command prompt.

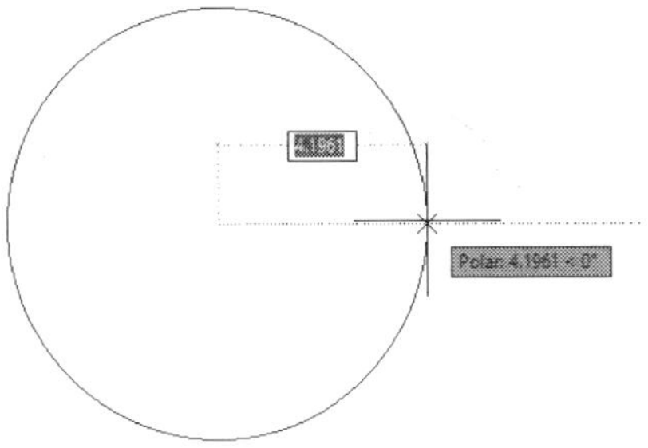

Figure 2-34 Drawing a circle by specifying the center and the radius

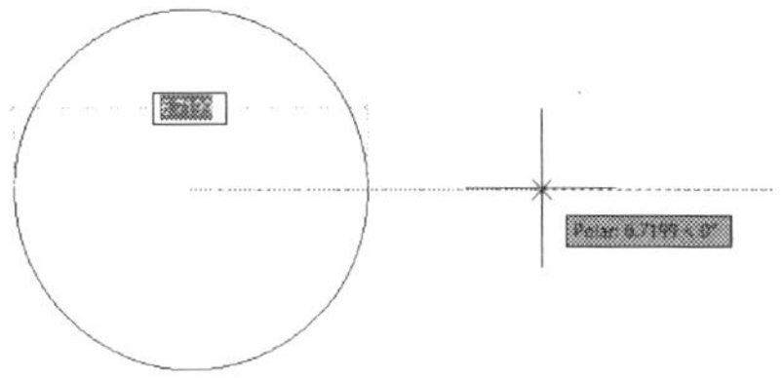

Figure 2-35 Drawing a circle by specifying the center and the diameter

Drawing a Circle by Specifying Two Diametrical Ends

Ribbon: Home > Draw > Circle drop-down > 2-Point
Command: CIRCLE or C > 2P

You can also draw a circle by specifying its two diametrical ends, refer to Figure 2-36. To do so, choose the **2-Point** tool from the **Draw** panel; you will be prompted to specify the first end of the diameter. Type the coordinates and press ENTER. After specifying the first end point of the diameter of the circle, move the cursor to define the second end point of its diameter.

Drawing a Circle by Specifying Three Points on a Circle

Ribbon: Home > Draw > Circle drop-down > 3-Point
Command: CIRCLE or C > 3P

To draw a circle by specifying three points on its periphery, choose the **3-Point** tool from the **Draw** panel and specify the three points in succession. You can type the coordinates of the points or specify them by using the left mouse button.

The prompt sequence to type the three coordinates on choosing the **3-Point** tool is given below.

Specify center point for circle or [3P/2P/Ttr(tan tan radius)]: _3p

Specify first point on circle: **3,3**

Specify second point on circle: **3,1**

Specify third point on circle: **4,2** *(refer to Figure 2-37)*

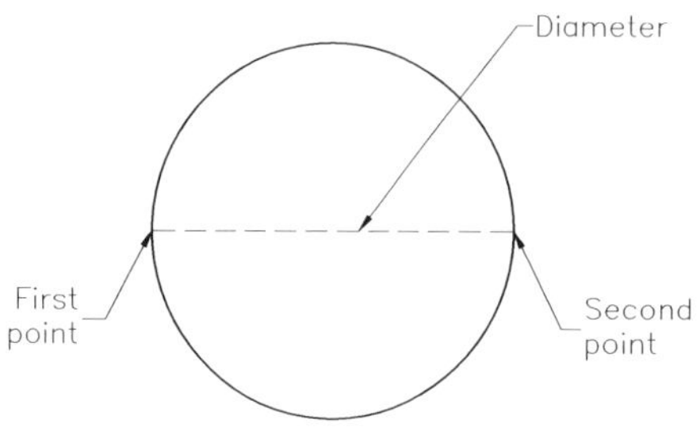

Figure 2-36 *A circle drawn by using the **2-Point** tool*

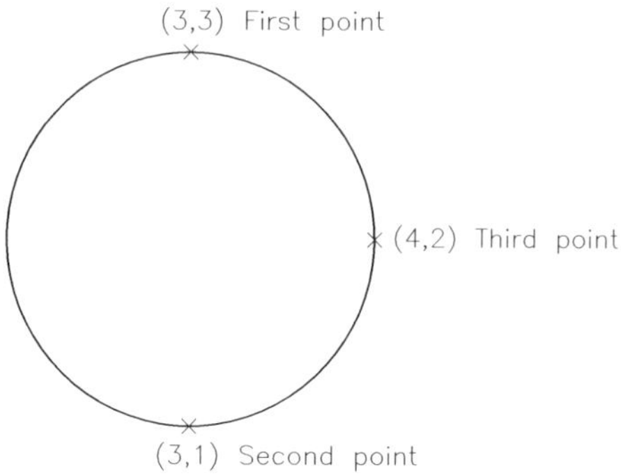

Figure 2-37 *A circle drawn by using the **3-Point** tool*

You can also use the relative rectangular coordinates to define the points.

Drawing a Circle Tangent to Two Objects

Ribbon: Home > Draw > Circle drop-down > Tan, Tan, Radius
Command: CIRCLE or C > Ttr

An object (line, circle, or arc) is said to be tangent to a circle or an arc if it touches the circumference of the circle or the arc at only one point. To draw a circle that has specified radius and is tangent to two objects, choose the **Tan, Tan, Radius** tool from the **Draw** panel; you will be prompted to specify a point on the first object to be tangent to the circle. Move the cursor near the object to be made tangent to the circle; a tangent symbol will be displayed. Specify the first point; you will be prompted to specify a point on the second object for second tangent of circle. Move the cursor near the second object that is to be tangent to the circle; a tangent symbol will be displayed. Specify the second point; you will be prompted to specify the radius. Type the radius value in the dimension input box and press ENTER; a circle of the specified radius and tangent to two specified objects will be drawn.

In Figures 2-38 through 2-41, the dotted circle represents the circle that is tangent to two objects. The circle actually drawn depends on how you select the objects to be made tangent to the new circle. The figures show the effect of selecting different points on the objects. If you specify too small or large radius, you may get unexpected results or the "**Circle does not exist**" prompt.

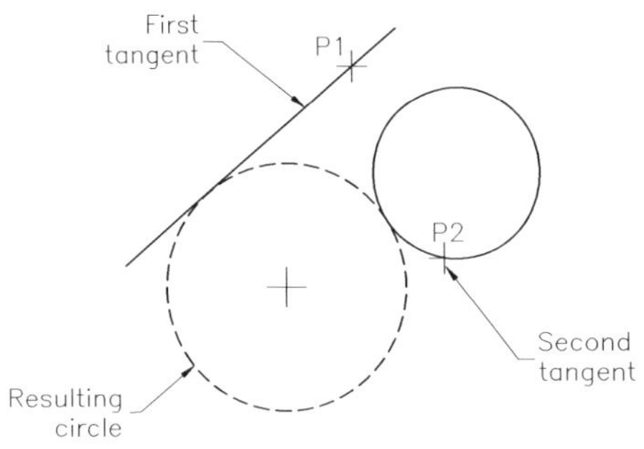

Figure 2-38 *Drawing a circle tangent to two objects*

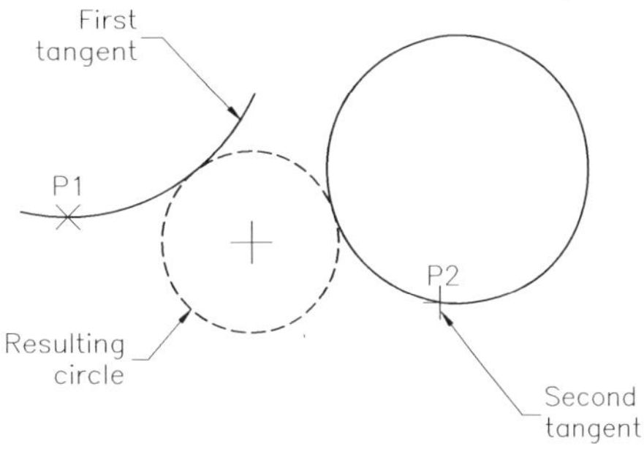

Figure 2-39 *Drawing a circle tangent to two objects*

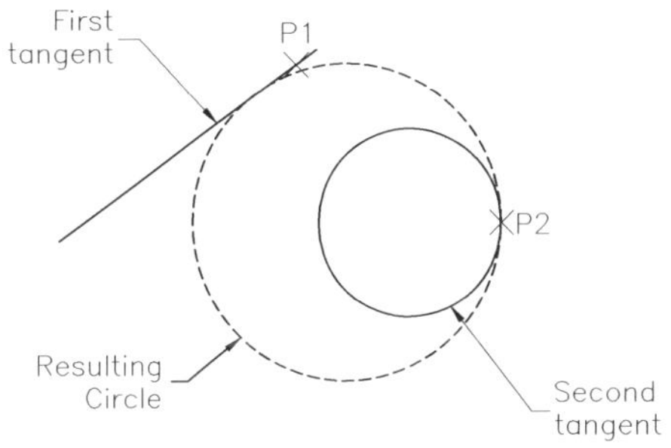

Figure 2-40 *Drawing a circle tangent to two objects*

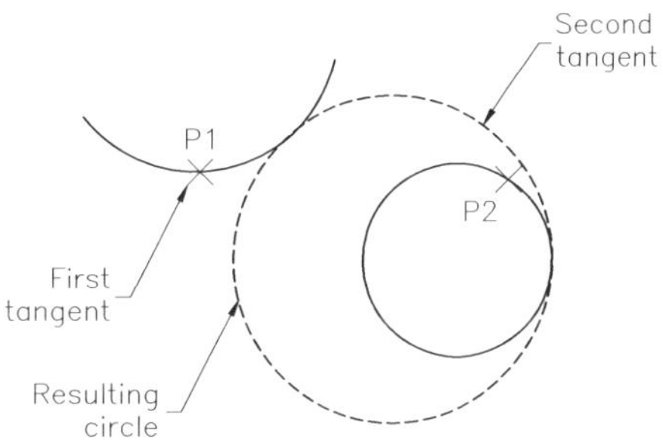

Figure 2-41 *Drawing a circle tangent to two objects*

Drawing a Circle Tangent to Three Objects

Ribbon: Home > Draw > Circle drop-down > Tan, Tan, Tan

You can also draw a circle that is tangent to three objects. To do so, choose the **Tan, Tan, Tan** tool from the **circle** drop-down from the **Draw** panel and select the three objects in succession to which the resulting circle is to be tangent; the circle will be drawn, as shown in Figure 2-42.

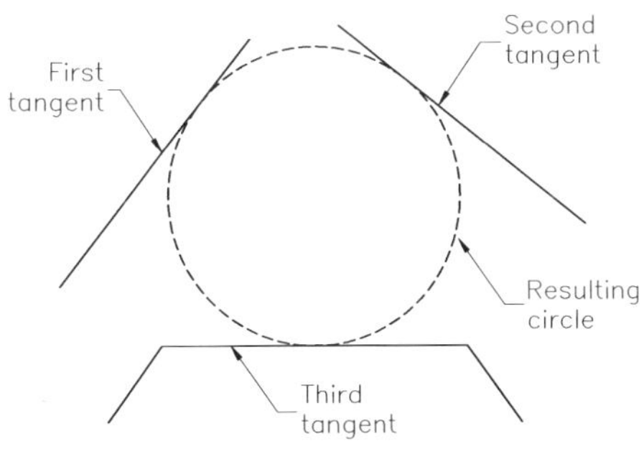

Figure 2-42 *Drawing a circle tangent to three objects*

Exercise 5 Line and Circle

Draw the profile shown in Figure 2-43 using various options of the **Line** and **Circle** tools. Use the absolute, relative rectangular, or relative polar coordinates for drawing the triangle. The vertices of the triangle will be used as the center of the circles. The circles can be drawn by using the **Center, Radius**, or **Center, Diameter**, or **Tan, Tan, Tan** tools. Do not apply dimensions, they are for reference only.

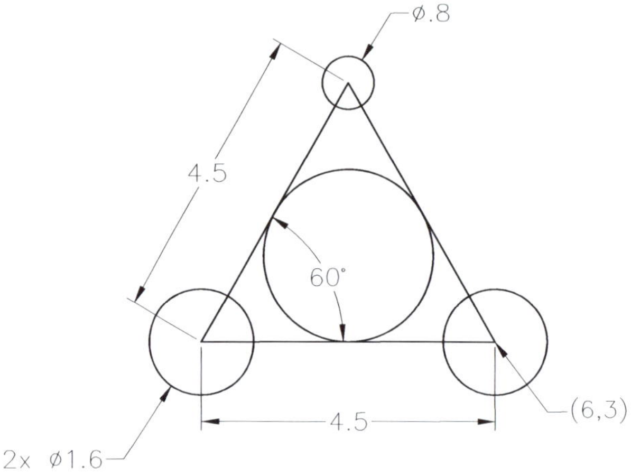

Figure 2-43 *Drawing for Exercise 5*

BASIC DISPLAY COMMANDS

Sometimes while drawing a sketch, it may be very difficult to view and alter minute details. You can overcome this problem by viewing only a specific portion of the drawing. This is done by using the **Zoom** tools. These tools let you enlarge or reduce the size of the drawing displayed on the screen. Similarly, you may need to slide the drawing view. This can be done by using the **Pan** tool. These are called display commands and are discussed next.

Zooming Drawings

The **Zoom** tools are used to enlarge or reduce the view of a drawing on the screen without affecting the actual size of entities. These tools are grouped together and are available in the Navigator Bar. To invoke different Zoom tools, click on the down arrow next to the **Zoom Extents** tool in the Navigator Bar; the **Zoom** drop-down will be displayed with different Zoom tools, as shown in Figure 2-44. You can also invoke the Zoom tools by choosing **View > Zoom** from the Menu Bar. To display the Menu Bar, left-click on the arrow in the **Quick Access** Toolbar and then select **Show Menu Bar**. Some Zoom tools are also available in the **Standard** toolbar. These tools are discussed next.

Zoom Extents

Choose the **Zoom Extents** tool to increase or decrease the drawing display area so that all sketched entities or dimensions fit inside the current view.

Zoom Window

This is the most commonly used tool of the **Zoom** drop-down. On choosing this tool, you need to draw a window by specifying its two opposite corners. The center of the zoom window becomes the center of the new display area and the objects in this window are magnified.

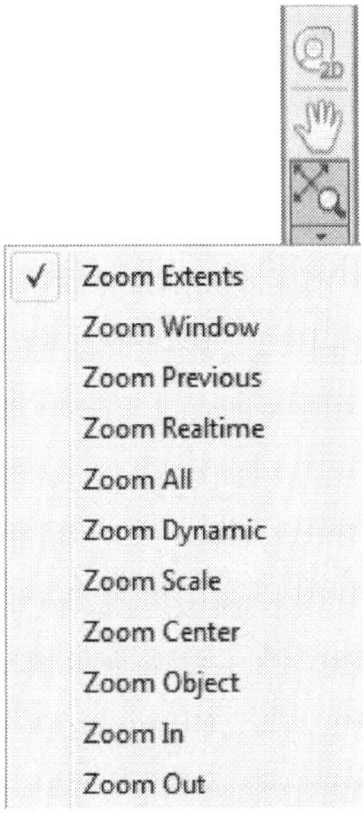

Figure 2-44 *Zoom tools in the* ***Navigator Bar***

Zoom Previous

While working on a complex drawing, you may need to zoom in a drawing multiple times to edit some minute details. After completing the editing, if you want to view the previous views, choose the **Zoom Previous** tool. You can view up to the last ten views by using the **Zoom Previous** tool.

Zoom Realtime

The **Zoom Realtime** tool is used to dynamically zoom in or out of a drawing. When you choose this tool, the cursor will be replaced by the zoom cursor. To zoom out a drawing, press and hold the left mouse button and drag the cursor downward. Similarly, to zoom in a drawing, press and hold the left mouse button and drag the cursor upward. As you drag the cursor, the drawing display changes dynamically. After you get the desired view, exit this tool by right-clicking and then choosing **Exit** from the shortcut menu displayed. On exiting this tool, the zoom cursor will change into cross hairs. Next, press the ESC key. You can also exit the **Zoom Realtime** tool by pressing the ESC key. If you have a mouse with scroll wheel, then scroll the wheel to zoom in/out the drawing.

Zoom In / Zoom Out

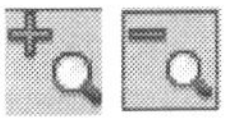

Choose the **Zoom In / Zoom Out** tool to increase/decrease the size of the drawing view twice/half of the original drawing size, respectively.

Note

You will learn about other Zoom tools in detail in Chapter 6.

Moving the View

You can use the **Pan** tool to move a view by sliding and placing it at the required position. To pan a drawing view, invoke the **Pan** tool from the Navigator Bar; a hand cursor will be displayed. Click and drag the cursor in any direction to move the drawing. To exit the **Pan** tool, right-click and then choose **Exit** from the shortcut menu. You can also press the ESC or ENTER key to exit the tool.

SETTING UNIT TYPE AND PRECISION

Application Menu: Drawing Utilities > Units **Command:** UN/UNITS

In the previous chapter, you learned to set units while starting a drawing by using the **Use a Wizard** option in the **Startup** dialog box. But, if you are drawing a sketch in an existing template or in a new template, you need to change the format of the units for distance and angle measurements. To do so, choose **Format > Units** from the Menu Bar; the **Drawing Units** dialog box will be displayed, as shown in Figure 2-45. You can also invoke this dialog box by choosing **Drawing Utilities > Units** from the **Application Menu**. The procedure to change the units format is discussed next.

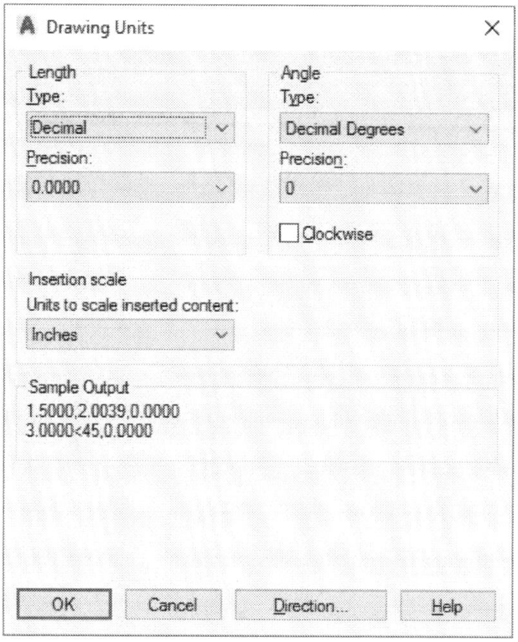

Figure 2-45 *The **Drawing Units** dialog box*

Specifying the Format

In the **Drawing Units** dialog box, you can select the desired format of units from the **Type** drop-down list. You can select any one of the five formats given next.

Architectural (0'-01/16") Decimal (0.00) Engineering (0'-0.00")
Fractional (0 1/16) Scientific (0.00E+01)

If you select the scientific, decimal, or fractional format, you can enter distance or coordinate values in any of these three formats, but not in engineering or architectural units. If you select the engineering or architectural format, you can enter distances or coordinates in any of the five formats.

Note

The inch symbol (") is optional. For example, 1'1-3/4" is same as 1'1-3/4 and 3/4" is same as 3/4.

Specifying the Angle Format

You can select any one of the following five angle measuring formats:

1. Decimal Degrees (0)
2. Deg/min/sec (0d)
3. Grads (0g)
4. Radians (0r)
5. Surveyor's Units (N 0d E)

If you select any one of the first four measuring formats, you can specify the angle in the Decimal, Degrees/minutes/seconds, Grads, or Radians system, but you cannot enter the angle in the Surveyor's Units system. However, if you select the Surveyor's Units system, you can enter angle values in any of the five systems. To enter a value in another system, use the appropriate suffixes and symbols, such as r (Radians), d (Degrees), or g (Grads). If you enter an angle value without indicating the symbol of a measuring system, it is taken in the current system.

In Surveyor's Units, you must specify the angle that the line makes with respect to the north-south direction, as shown in Figure 2-46. For example, if you want to define an angle of 60-degree with north, in the Surveyor's Units the angle will be specified as N 60d E. Similarly, you can specify angles such as S 50d E, S 50d W, and N 75d W, refer to Figure 2-46. You cannot specify an angle that exceeds 90-degree (N 120 E). Angles can also be specified in radians or grads; for example, 180-degree is equal to π(3.14159) radians. You can convert degrees into radians, or radians into degrees by using the equations given below.

radians = degrees x 3.14159/180;
degrees = radians x 180/3.14159

Grads are generally used in land surveys. There are 400 grads or 360 degree in a circle. 90 degree angle is equal to 100 grads.

In AutoCAD LT, if an angle is measured in the counter-clockwise direction, then it is positive. Also, the angles are measured about the positive X axis, refer to Figure 2-47. If you want the angles to be measured as positive in the clockwise direction, select the **Clockwise** check box from the **Angle** area. You can specify the precision for the length and angle in the respective **Precision** drop-down lists in this dialog box.

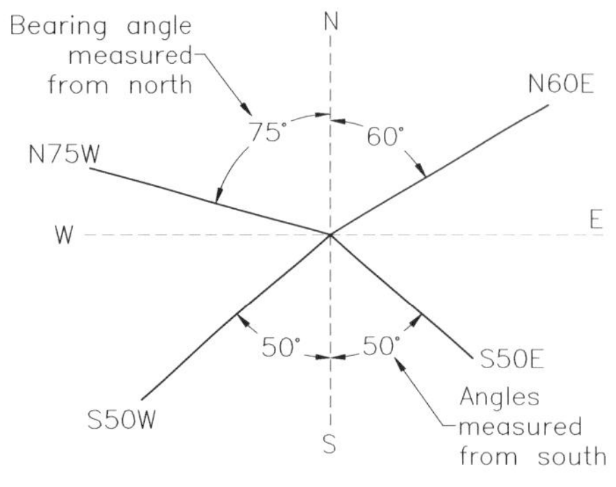

Figure 2-46 Specifying angles in Surveyor's Units

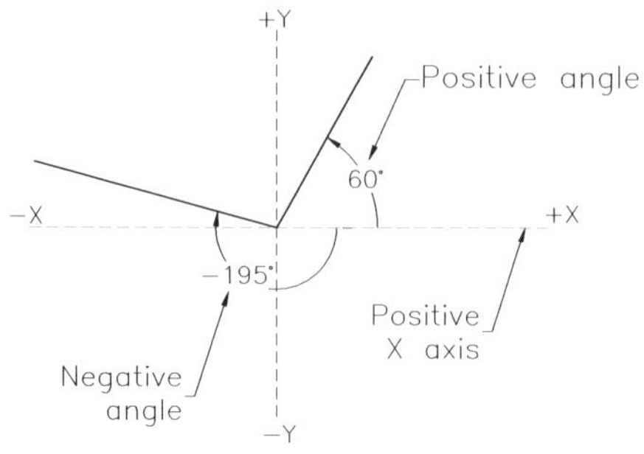

***Figure 2-47** Measuring angles*

Setting the Direction for Angle Measurement

As mentioned above, angles are measured about the positive X axis. This means the base angle (0-degree) is set along the east direction, refer to Figure 2-48. To change this base angle, choose the **Direction** button in the **Drawing Units** dialog box; the **Direction Control** dialog box will be displayed, as shown in Figure 2-49. Select the appropriate radio button to specify the direction for the base angle (0-degree).

If you select the **Other** option, you can set the direction of your choice for the base angle (0-degree) by entering a value in the **Angle** edit box or by choosing the **Pick an angle** button and picking two points to specify the angle. After specifying the base angle direction, choose the **OK** button to apply the settings.

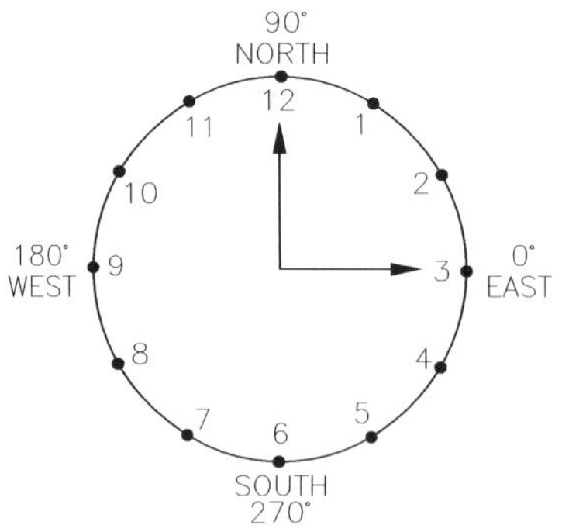

***Figure 2-48** North, South, East, and West directions*

***Figure 2-49** The **Direction Control** dialog box*

Tip

*If you are entering values by using the dimension input boxes that are displayed when the **Dynamic Input** option is on, then you are not required to set the base angle.*

Specifying Units for the Drawing or Block to be Inserted

To set units for a block or a drawing to be inserted, select a unit from the **Units to scale inserted content** drop-down list. Now, if you insert a block or a drawing from the **DesignCenter**, the specified unit will be applied to the block. Even if the block was created using a different measuring unit, AutoCAD LT scales it and inserts it using the specified measuring unit. If you select **Unit less** from the drop-down list, then the units specified in the **Insertion Scale** area of the **User Preferences** tab in the **Options** dialog box will be used.

Note

Inserting blocks in a drawing is discussed in detail in Chapter 15.

Sample Output

The **Sample Output** area in this dialog box shows the example of the current format used for specifying units and angles. When you change the type of length and angle measure in the **Length** and **Angle** areas of the **Drawing Units** dialog box, the corresponding example is displayed in the **Sample Output** area.

Example 5 — Setting Units

In this example, you will set the units and draw the profile with specifications shown in Figure 2-50.

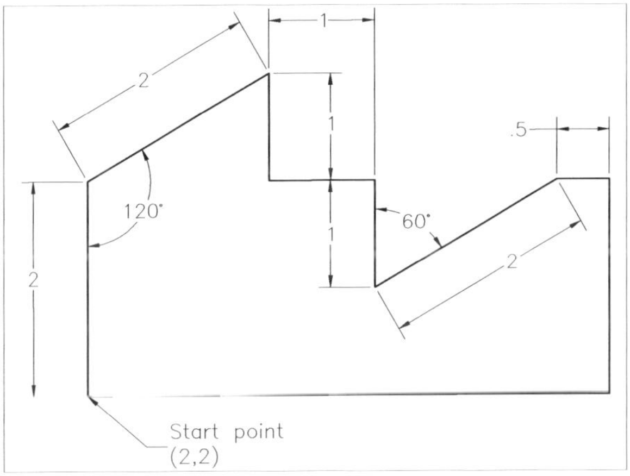

Figure 2-50 *Drawing for Example 5*

a. Set the units of length to fractional with the denominator of the smallest fraction equal to 32.
b. Set the angular measurement to Surveyor's Units with the number of fractional places for display of angles equal to zero.
c. Set the base angle (0-degree) to North and the direction of measurement of angles to clockwise.

The following steps are required to complete this example:

1. Start a new file with the acadlt.dwt template in the **Drafting & Annotation** workspace and invoke the **Drawing Units** dialog box by choosing **Drawing Utilities > Units** from the **Application Menu**. You can also invoke this dialog box by choosing **Format > Units** from the Menu Bar.

2. In the **Length** area of this dialog box, select **Fractional** from the **Type** drop-down list. Select **0 1/32** from the **Precision** drop-down list.

3. In the **Angle** area of this dialog box, select **Surveyor's Units** from the **Type** drop-down list. From the **Precision** drop-down list, select **N 0d E**, if it has not been already selected. Also, select the **Clockwise** check box to set the clockwise angle measurement to positive.

4. Choose the **Direction** button to display the **Direction Control** dialog box. Next, select the **North** radio button. Choose the **OK** button to exit the **Direction Control** dialog box.

5. Choose the **OK** button to exit the **Drawing Units** dialog box.

6. With the units set, you need to draw Figure 2-50 using the relative polar coordinates. Turn off the dynamic input. The prompt sequence to complete the sketch is as follows:

   *Choose the **Line** tool*
   LINE Specify first point: ***2,2*** Enter
   Specify next point or [Undo]: ***@2.0<0*** Enter
   Specify next point or [eXit/Undo]: ***@2.0<60*** Enter
   Specify next point or [Close/eXit/Undo]: ***@1<180*** Enter
   Specify next point or [Close/eXit/Undo]: ***@1<90*** Enter
   Specify next point or [Close/eXit/Undo]: ***@1<180*** Enter
   Specify next point or [Close/eXit/Undo]: ***@2.0<60*** Enter
   Specify next point or [Close/eXit/Undo]: ***@0.5<90*** Enter
   Specify next point or [Close/eXit/Undo]: ***@2.0<180*** Enter
   Specify next point or [Close/eXit/Undo]: ***C*** Enter

   Here, the units are fractional and the angles are measured from north (90-degree axis). Also, the angles are measured as positive in the clockwise direction and negative in the counterclockwise direction.

7. To modify the drawing display area, choose the **Zoom All** tool from the Navigator Bar.

SETTING THE LIMITS OF A DRAWING

Menu Bar: Format > Drawing Limits **Command:** LIMITS

In AutoCAD LT, limits represent the drawing area and it is endless. Therefore, you need to define the drawing area before starting the drawing. In the previous chapter, you learned to set limits while starting a drawing by using the **Use a Wizard** option in the **Startup** dialog box.

If you are working in a drawing by using the default template, you need to change the limits. For example, the *acadlt.dwt* template has the default limits set to 12,9. To draw a rectangle of dimension 15x10 in this template, you need to change its limits to 24x18. To do so, choose **Format > Drawing Limits** from the Menu Bar; you will be prompted to specify the lower left corner. The following is the prompt sequence of this tool for setting the limits to 24,18 for the *acadlt.dwt* template which has the default limit 12,9.

*Choose the **Drawing Limits** tool*
Reset Model space limits:
Specify lower left corner or [ON/OFF]<0.0000,0.0000>: **0,0** Enter
Specify upper right corner <12.0000,9.0000>: **24,18** Enter

Tip
*Whenever you reset the drawing limits, the display area does not change automatically. You need to use the **Zoom All** tool chosen from the **Zoom** drop-down to display the complete drawing area.*

The limits of the drawing area are usually determined by the following factors:

1. The actual size of drawing.
2. The space needed for adding dimensions, notes, bill of materials, and other necessary details.
3. The space between various views so that the drawing does not look cluttered.
4. The space for the border and title block, if any.

Setting Limits

To get a good idea of how to set up limits, it is better to draw a rough sketch of a drawing. This will help in calculating the required drawing area. For example, if an object has a front view size of 5 x 5, a side view size of 3 x 5, and a top view size of 5 x 3, the limits should be set so that the drawing and everything associated with it can be easily accommodated within the set limit. In Figure 2-51, the space between the front and side views is 4 units and between the front and top views is 3 units. Also, the space between the border and the drawing is 5 units on the left, 5 units on the right, 3 units at the bottom, and 2 units at the top. (The space between the views and between the borderline and the drawing depends on the drawing.)

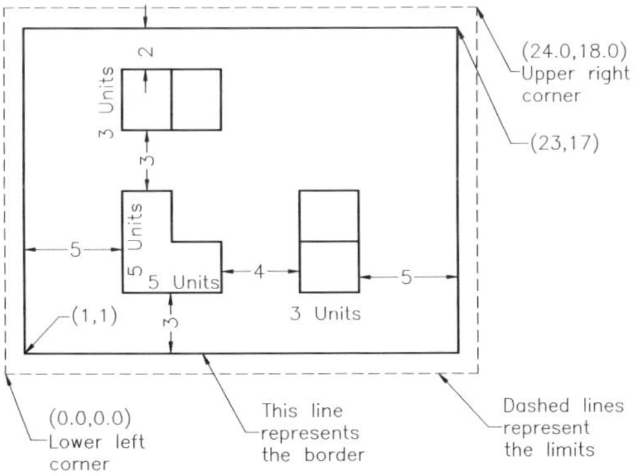

***Figure 2-51** Setting limits in a drawing*

After knowing the size of different views, the space required between views, the space between the border and the drawing, and the space required between the borderline and the edges of the paper, you can calculate the space in the following way:

Space along (*X* axis) = 1 + 5 + 5 + 4 + 3 + 5 + 1 = 24
Space along (*Y* axis) = 1 + 3 + 5 + 3 + 3 + 2 + 1 = 18

This shows that the limits you need to set for this drawing is 24 x 18. Once you have determined the space, select the sheet size that can accommodate your drawing. In the case just explained, you will select a D size (34 x 22) sheet. Therefore, the actual drawing limits will be 34,22.

Tip
*To display the grid, choose the **Display drawing grid** button from the Status Bar. By default, the grid will be displayed beyond the limits. To display the grid up to the limits, use the **Limits** option of the **GRID** command and set the **Display grid beyond Limits [Yes/No] <Yes>:** option to **No**; the grids will be displayed only up to the limits set.*

Limits for Architectural Drawings

Most architectural drawings are drawn at the scale of 1/4" = 1', 1/8" = 1', or 1/16" = 1'. You must set the limits accordingly. The following example illustrates how to calculate the limits of an architectural drawings.

Given

Sheet size = 24" x 18"
Scale is 1/4" = 1'

Calculate limits

Scale is 1/4" = 1'
or 1/4" = 12"
or 1" = 48"
X limit = 24" x 48"
= 1152" or 1152 Units
= 96'
Y limit = 18" x 48"
= 864" or 864 Units
= 72'

Thus, the scale factor is 48 and the limits are 1152",864" or 96',72'.

Example 6 Setting Limits

In this example, you will calculate the limits and determine an appropriate drawing scale factor for the drawing shown in Figure 2-52. You will plot the drawing on a 12" x 9" sheet. Assume the missing dimensions.

The calculation for the scale factor is given next.

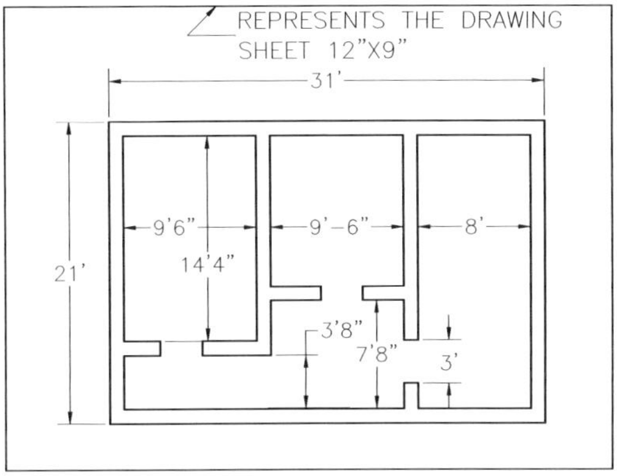

Figure 2-52 *Drawing for Example 6*

Given or known

Overall length of the drawing = 31'
Length of the sheet = 12"
Approximate space between the drawing and the edges of the paper = 2"

Calculate the scale factor

To calculate the scale factor, you have to try various scales until you find the one that satisfies the given conditions. After some experience, you will find this fairly easy to do. For this example, assume a scale factor of 1/4" = 1'.

Scale factor 1/4" = 1' or 1" = 4'

Thus, a line 31' long will be = 31'/4' = 7.75" on paper. Similarly, a line 21' long = 21'/4' = 5.25". Approximate space between the drawing and the edges of paper = 2".

Therefore, the total length of the sheet = 7.75 + 2 + 2 = 11.75"

Similarly, the total width of the sheet = 5.25 + 2 + 2 = 9.25"
Because you selected the scale 1/4" = 1', the drawing will definitely fit in the given sheet of paper (12" x 9"). Therefore, the scale for this drawing is 1/4" = 1'.

Calculate limits

Scale factor = 1" = 48" or 1" = 4'
The length of the sheet is 12"
Therefore, X limit = 12 x 4' = 48' and Y limit = 9 x 4' = 36'

Limits for Metric Drawings

When the drawing units are in metric, you must use the standard metric size sheets or calculate limits in millimeters (mm). For example, if the sheet size is 24 X 18, the limits, after conversion to the metric system, will be 609.6,457.2 (multiplying length and width by 25.4). You can round these numbers to the nearest whole numbers 610,457. Note that the metric drawings do not require any special setup, except for the limits. Metric drawings are like any other drawings that use decimal units. Similar to architectural drawings, you can draw metric drawings to a scale. For example, if the scale is 1:20, you must calculate the limits accordingly. The following example illustrates how to calculate limits for metric drawings:

Given

Sheet size = 24" x 18"
Scale = 1:20

Calculate limits

Scale is 1:20
Therefore, scale factor = 20
X limit = 24 x 25.4 x 20 = 12192 units
Y limit = 18 x 25.4 x 20 = 9144 units

Exercise 6 Setting Units and Limits

Set the units of the drawing according to the specifications given below and then make the drawing shown in Figure 2-53 (leave a space of 3 to 5 units around the drawing for dimensioning and title block). The space between the dotted lines is 1 unit.

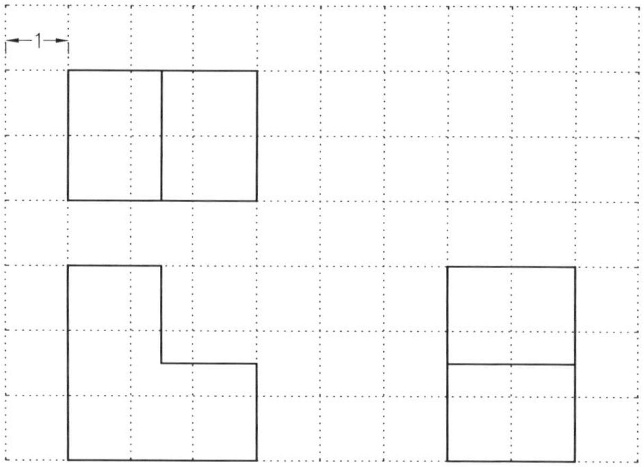

Figure 2-53 *Drawing for Exercise 6*

1. Set UNITS to decimal units with two digits to the right of the decimal point.
2. Set the angular measurement to decimal degrees with the number of decimal places for display of angles equal to 1.
3. Set the direction to 0-degree (east) and the direction of measurement of angles to counterclockwise (angles measured positive in a counterclockwise direction).
4. Set the limits leaving a space of 3 to 5 units around the drawing for dimensioning and title block.

INTRODUCTION TO PLOTTING DRAWINGS

Ribbon: Output > Plot > Plot	**Quick Access Toolbar:** Plot
Application Menu: Print > Plot	**Command:** PLOT or PRINT

After creating a drawing of an architectural plan or a mechanical component, you may need to send it to the client or have a hard copy for reference. To do so, you need to plot the drawing. To plot the drawing, choose **Plot** from the **Quick Access** Toolbar; the **Plot - Model** dialog box will be displayed. If the dialog box is not expanded by default, choose the **More Options** button at the lower right corner of the dialog box, refer to Figure 2-54.

Basic Plotting

Basic plotting involves selecting the correct output device (plotter), specifying the area to plot, selecting the paper size, specifying the plot origin, orientation, and the plot scale.

To learn the basic plotting, you will plot the drawing drawn in Example 3 of this chapter. It is assumed that AutoCAD LT is configured for two output devices: Default Windows System Printer and 53436DrawingMaster DM800.

1. Invoke the **Plot** dialog box by choosing the **Plot** tool in the **Quick Access** Toolbar.

2. The name of the default system printer is displayed in the **Name** drop-down list in the **Printer/plotter** area. Select the printer to be used from the **Name** drop-down list.

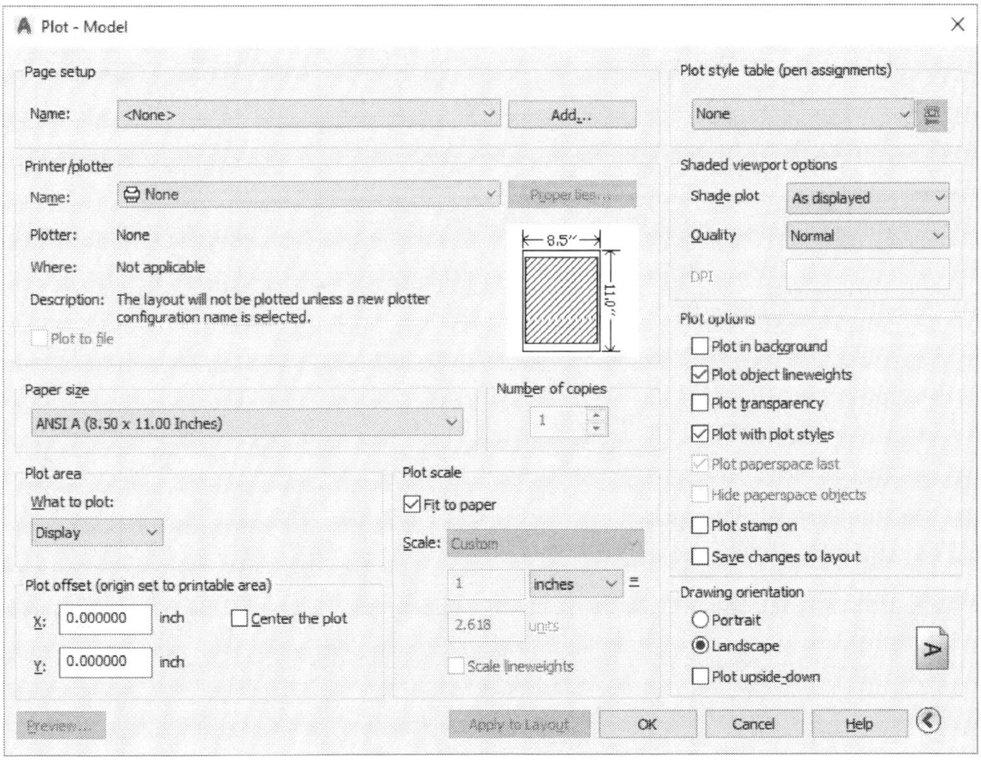

*Figure 2-54 The **Plot-Model** dialog box*

3. Select the **Window** option from the **What to plot** drop-down list in the **Plot area**. The dialog box will close temporarily and the drawing area will appear. Next, select two opposite corners to define a window that can enclose the entire area you want to plot. Note that the complete drawing along with the dimensions should be enclosed in the window. Once you have defined the two corners, the **Plot** dialog box will reappear.

4. To set the size of the plot, you need to select a paper size from the drop-down list in the **Paper size** area. After selecting the paper size, you need to set the orientation of the paper. To set the orientation, expand the **Plot** dialog box by choosing the **More Options** button at the lower right corner of the dialog box. You can set the orientation as **Landscape** or **Portrait** by selecting the appropriate radio button from the **Drawing orientation** area. The sections in the **Plot** dialog box related to the paper size and orientation are automatically revised to reflect the new paper size and orientation. For this example, you will specify the **A4** paper size and the **Portrait** orientation.

5. You can also modify values for the plot offset in the **Plot offset (origin set to printable area)** area; the default value for X and Y is 0. For this example, you can select the **Center the plot** check box to get the drawing at the center of the paper.

6. In AutoCAD LT, you can enter values for the plot scale in the **Plot scale** area. Clear the **Fit to paper** check box if it is selected and then click on the **Scale** drop-down list in the **Plot scale** area to display various scale factors. From this list, you can select a scale factor based on your requirement. For example, if you select the scale factor **1/4" = 1'-0"**, the edit boxes below the drop-down list will show 0.25 inches = 12 units. If you want the drawing to be plotted so that it fits on the specified sheet of paper, select the **Fit to paper** check box. On selecting this check box, AutoCAD LT will determine the scale factor and display it in the edit boxes. For this example, you will plot the drawing so that it scales to fit the paper. Therefore, select the **Fit to paper** check box and notice the change in the edit boxes. You can also enter arbitrary values in the edit boxes.

7. To preview a plot, choose the **Preview** button. You can preview the plot on the specified paper size. In the preview window, the realtime zoom icon will be displayed. If needed, you can zoom in or zoom out the preview image for better visualization.

8. If the plot preview is satisfactory, you can plot your drawing by right-clicking and then choosing **Plot** from the shortcut menu displayed. If you want to make some changes in the settings, choose **Exit** in the shortcut menu or press the ESC or ENTER key to get back to the dialog box. Change the parameters and choose the **OK** button in the dialog box to plot the drawing.

MODIFYING AutoCAD LT SETTINGS BY USING THE OPTIONS DIALOG BOX

Application Menu: Options **Command:** OP/OPTIONS

You can use the **Options** dialog box to change the default settings and customize them to your requirements. For example, you can use this dialog box to turn off the settings that are used to display the shortcut menu, change the display color of the objects, or specify the support directories containing the files you need.

To invoke the **Options** dialog box, right-click at the Command prompt or in the drawing area when no command is active or no object is selected and then choose **Options** from the shortcut menu; the **Options** dialog box will be displayed, as shown in Figure 2-55. The name of the current profile and the current drawing names will be displayed below the title bar. You can save a set of custom settings in a profile to be used later for other drawings. The different tabs in the **Options** dialog box are discussed next.

Files

This tab stores the directories in which AutoCAD LT looks for the driver, support, menu, project, template, and other files. It uses three icons: folder, paper stack, and file cabinet. The folder icon is for a search path, the paper stack icon is for files, and the file cabinet icon is for a specific folder. Suppose you want to know the path of the font mapping file. To do so, you need to click on the + symbol with the **Text Editor**, **Dictionary**, and **Font File Names** folders and then select the **Font Mapping File** node, refer to Figure 2-55. Similarly, you can define a custom hatch pattern file and then add its search path.

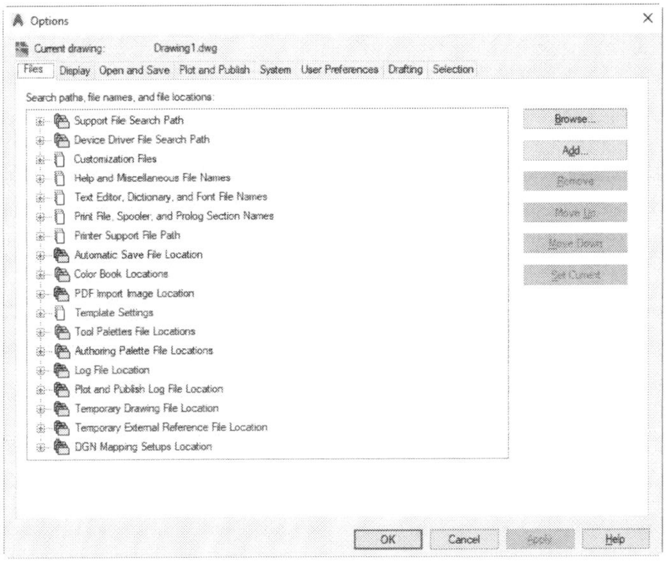

*Figure 2-55 The **Options** dialog box*

Display

This tab is used to control the drawing and window settings like screen menu display and scroll bar. For example, to display the scroll bars in the drawing window to scroll up and down, select the **Display scroll bars in the drawing window** check box from the **Window Elements** area. You can change the background color of the graphics window, layout window, and command line as well as the color of the command line text by using the **Drawing Window Colors** dialog box that is displayed on choosing the **Colors** button. In the **Display** tab, you can specify the parameters to set the display resolution and display performance. You can also set the smoothness and resolutions of certain objects such as circle, arc, and polyline curve.

You can also, apply the solid fills, and so on. In this tab, you can toggle on and off the various layout elements such as the layout tabs on the screen, margins, paper background, and so on.

Open and Save

This tab is used to control the parameters related to the opening and saving of files in AutoCAD LT. You can specify the file type while saving using the **SAVEAS** command. The various formats available are **AutoCAD 2018 Drawing (*.dwg)**, **AutoCAD LT 2013 Drawing (*.dwg)**, **AutoCAD 2010/LT 2,010 Drawing (*.dwg)**, **AutoCAD 2007/LT 2007 Drawing (*.dwg)**, **AutoCAD 2004/LT 2004 Drawing (*.dwg)**, **AutoCAD 2000/LT 2000 Drawing (*.dwg)**, **AutoCAD R14/LT98/LT97 Drawing (*.dwg)**, **AutoCAD LT Drawing Template(*.dwt)**, **AutoCAD LT 2013 DXF(*.dxf)**, **AutoCAD 2010/LT 2010 DXF (*.dxf)**, **AutoCAD 2007/LT 2007 DXF (*.dxf)**, **AutoCAD 2004/LT 2004 DXF (*.dxf)**, **AutoCAD 2000/LT 2000 DXF(*.dxf)**, and **AutoCAD R12/LT2 DXF (*.dxf)**. You can also set various file safety precautions such as the Automatic Save feature or the creation of a backup copy. On selecting the **Display digital signature information** check box, you can view the digital signature information when a file with a valid digital signature is opened. You can change the number of the recently saved files to be displayed in the **File Open** area. You can also set the various parameters for external references.

Plot and Publish

The options in this tab are used to control the parameters related to the plotting and publishing of the drawings in AutoCAD LT. You can set the default output device and also add a new plotter. You can set the general parameters such as the layout or plot device paper size and the background processing options while plotting or publishing. It is possible to select the spool alert for the system printer and also the OLE plot quality. You can also set the parameters for the plot style such as the color-dependent plot styles or the named plot styles.

System

This tab contains AutoCAD LT system settings options such as the adjusting graphic performance and pointing device settings options where you can choose the pointing device driver. Here you can also set, the display of the Startup option while opening a new session of AutoCAD LT and the **OLE Properties** dialog box, and beep for wrong user input. You also have options to set the parameters for database connectivity.

User Preferences

The parameters in this tab are used to control the settings such as the right-click customization to change the shortcut menus according to the user's preferences. You can set the units parameters for the blocks or drawings that are inserted as well as the priorities for various coordinate data entry methods. You can also set the order of object sorting methods and also set the lineweight options.

Drafting

The options in this tab are used to control the settings such as autosnap settings and aperture size. Here you can also set the toggles on and off for the various autotracking settings. Using this tab, you can also set the tool tip appearance of **Dynamic Input** mode in the Model and Paper space.

Selection

This tab is used to control the methods of object selection, grips, grip colors, and the grip size. You can also set the toggles on or off for various selection modes.

Note

The options in various tabs of the ***Options*** *dialog box have been discussed throughout the book wherever applicable.*

Tip

Some options in the ***Options*** *dialog box have drawing file icon on their Left. For example, the options in the* ***Display resolution*** *area of the* ***Display*** *tab have drawing file icons. This specifies that these parameters are saved with the current drawing only; therefore, it affects only that drawing. The options without the drawing file icon are saved with the current profile and affect all drawings present in that AutoCAD LT session or future sessions.*

Example 7 Modifying the Default Options

In this example, you will create a profile with specific settings by using the **Options** dialog box.

1. Choose **Options** from the **Application Menu** to invoke the **Options** dialog box. Alternatively, right-click in the drawing area to display the shortcut menu, and then choose **Options** to invoke this dialog box.

2. Choose the **Display** tab and then choose the **Colors** button; the **Drawing Window Colors** dialog box is displayed. Select **2D model space** in the **Context** area and **Background** in the **Interface element** area. Select **White** from the **Color** drop-down list; the background color of the model tab will turn white. Choose the **Apply & Close** button to return to the **Options** dialog box.

3. Choose the **Drafting** tab and then change **AutoSnap Marker Size** to the maximum using the slider bar. Choose the **Apply** button and then the **OK** button to exit the dialog box.

4. Draw a line and then choose the **Object Snap** button from the Status Bar. Again, invoke the **Line** tool and move the cursor on the previously drawn line; a marker will be displayed at the endpoint. Notice the size of the marker now.

Self-Evaluation Test

Answer the following questions and then compare them to those given at the end of this chapter:

1. You can erase a line drawn by using the __________ option of the **Line** tool.

2. Choose the __________tool from the **Circle** drop-down to draw a circle that is tangent to the two previously drawn objects.

3. The __________ tool is used to enlarge or reduce the view of a drawing without affecting the actual size of the entities.

4. After increasing the drawing limits, you need to choose the __________ tool from the Navigator Bar to display the complete area inside the drawing area.

5. In __________ units, you must specify the bearing angle that a line makes with the north-south direction.

6. You can preview a plot before actually plotting it by using the __________ button in the **Plot** dialog box.

7. You can draw a line by specifying the length and direction of the line using the Direct Distance Entry method. (T/F)

8. In the Window Crossing object selection method, only those objects that are completely enclosed within the boundaries of the crossing box are selected. (T/F)

9. Choose the **3-Point** tool from the **Circle** drop-down to draw a circle by specifying two endpoints of the circle's diameter. (T/F)

10. If you choose the engineering or architectural format for units in the **Drawing Units** dialog box, you can enter distances or coordinates in any of the five formats. (T/F)

Review Questions

Answer the following questions:

1. Which of the following keys is not used to terminate the **Line** tool at the **Specify next point or [Close/Undo]:** prompt?

   (a) SPACEBAR (b) BACKSPACE
   (c) ENTER (d) ESC

2. Which of the following tools is used to zoom a drawing up to the limits or the extents, whichever is greater?

   (a) **Zoom Previous** (b) **Zoom Window**
   (c) **Zoom All** (d) **Zoom Realtime**

3. How many formats of units can be chosen from the **Drawing Units** dialog box?

   (a) Three (b) Five
   (c) Six (d) Seven

4. Which of the following input methods cannot be used to invoke the **Options** tool for displaying the **Options** dialog box?

   (a) Menu (b) Toolbar
   (c) Shortcut menu (d) Command prompt

5. When you define direction by specifying angle, the output of the angle does not depend on which one of the following factors?

   (a) Angular units (b) Angle value
   (c) Angle direction (d) Angle base

6. The __________ option of the **Line** tool can be used to join the current point with the initial point of the first line when two or more lines are drawn in succession.

7. The __________ option of drawing a circle cannot be invoked by entering the command at the Command prompt.

8. When you select any type of unit and angle in the **Length** or **Angle** area of the **Drawing Units** dialog box, the corresponding example is displayed in the __________ area of the dialog box.

9. If you want a drawing to be plotted so that it fits on the specified sheet of paper, select the __________ option in the **Plot** dialog box.

10. The __________ tab in the **Options** dialog box is used to store the details of all the profiles available in the current drawing.

11. You can use the __________ command to change the settings that affect the drawing environment or the AutoCAD LT interface.

12. In the relative rectangular coordinate system, the displacements along the X and Y axes (DX and DY) are measured with respect to the previous point and not with respect to the origin. (T/F)

13. In AutoCAD LT, by default angles are measured along the positive X axis and it will be positive if measured in the counterclockwise direction. (T/F)

14. You can also invoke the **Plot** dialog box by choosing the **Plot** option from the shortcut menu displayed on right-clicking in the Command window. (T/F)

15. The **Files** tab of the **Options** dialog box is used to store the directories in which AutoCAD LT looks for the driver, support, menu, project, template, and other files. (T/F)

Exercise 7 Relative Rectangular & Absolute Coordinates

Invoke the **Line** tool and draw an object using the following relative rectangular and absolute coordinate values to draw the object.

Point	Coordinates
1	3.0, 3.0
2	@3,0
3	@-1.5,3.0
4	@-1.5,-3.0
5	@3.0,5.0
6	@3,0
7	@-1.5,-3
8	@-1.5,3

Exercise 8 Relative Rectangular & Polar Coordinates

Draw the profile shown in Figure 2-56 by using the relative rectangular and relative polar coordinates of the points given in the following table. The distance between the dotted lines is 1 unit. Save this drawing with the name *C02_Exer8.dwg*.

Point	Coordinates	Point	Coordinates
1	3.0, 1.0	9	________
2	________	10	________
3	________	11	________
4	________	12	________
5	________	13	________
6	________	14	________
7	________	15	________
8	________	16	________

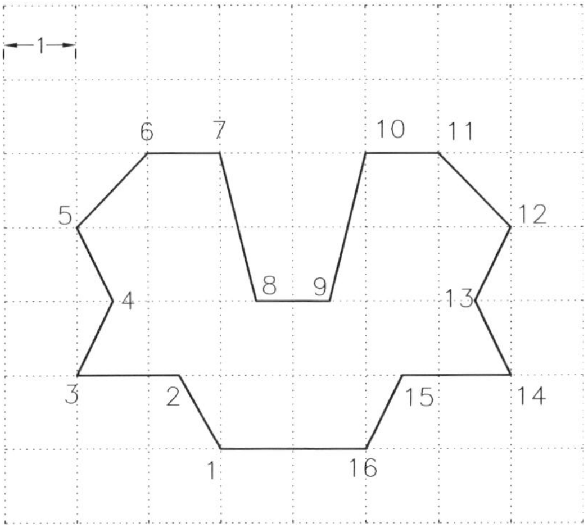

Figure 2-56 Drawing for Exercise 8

Exercise 9 Relative Polar Coordinates

For the drawing shown in Figure 2-57, enter the relative polar coordinates of the points in the following table. Next, use these coordinates to create the drawing. Do not dimension the drawing.

Point	Coordinates	Point	Coordinates
1	1.0, 1.0	6	______
2	______	7	______
3	______	8	______
4	______	9	______
5	______		

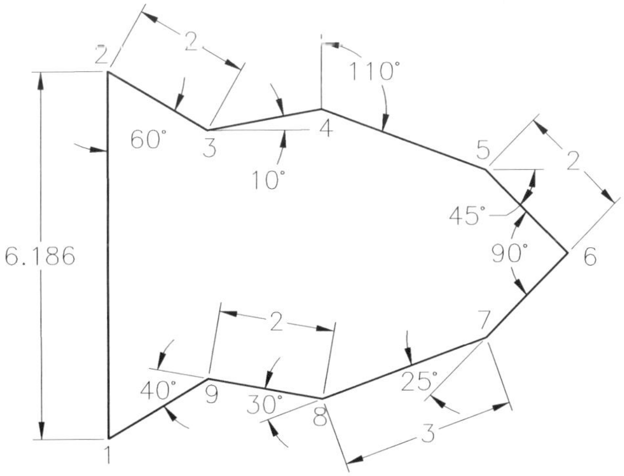

Figure 2-57 Drawing for Exercise 9

Exercise 10 *Line and Circle*

Draw the sketch shown in Figure 2-58 by using the **Line** and **Center, Radius** tools. The distance between the dotted lines is 1.0 unit.

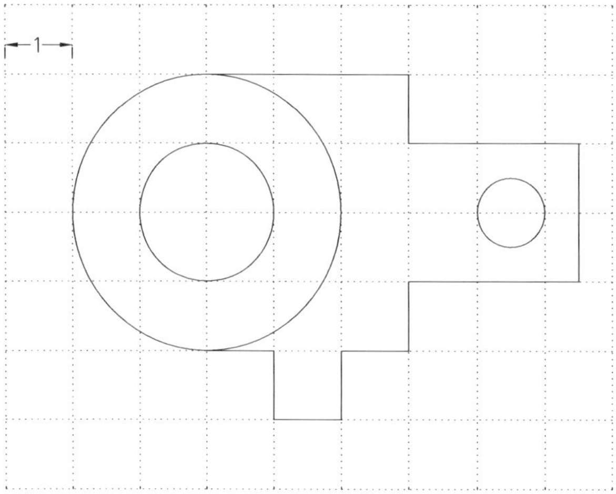

Figure 2-58 *Drawing for Exercise 10*

Exercise 11 *Line and Circle Tangent to Two objects*

Draw the sketch shown in Figure 2-59 using the **Line** and **Tan, Tan, Radius** tools.

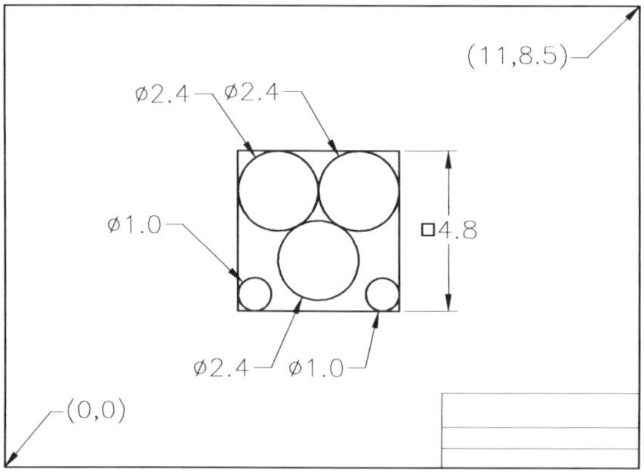

Figure 2-59 *Drawing for Exercise 11*

Exercise 12 — Setting Units

Set the units for a drawing based on the following specifications.

1. Set the units to architectural with the denominator of the smallest fraction equal to 16.
2. Set the angular measurement to degrees/minutes/seconds with the number of fractional places for the display of angles equal to 0d00'.
3. Set the direction to 0-degree (east) and the direction of measurement of angles to counterclockwise (angles measured positive in counterclockwise direction).

Based on Figure 2-60, determine and set the limits for the drawing. The scale for this drawing is 1/4" = 1'. Leave enough space around the drawing for dimensioning and title block. (HINT: Scale factor = 48 sheet size required is 12 x 9; therefore, the limits are 12 X 48, 9 X 48 = 576, 432. Expand the **Zoom** drop-down and then select the **Zoom All** tool to display the new limits.)

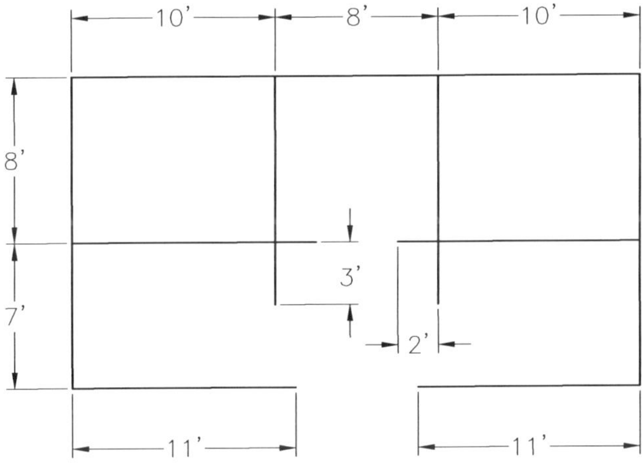

Figure 2-60 *Drawing for Exercise 12*

Exercise 13

Draw the object shown in Figure 2-61. The distance between the dotted lines is 1 unit. Determine the limits for this drawing and use the Decimal units with 0.00 precision.

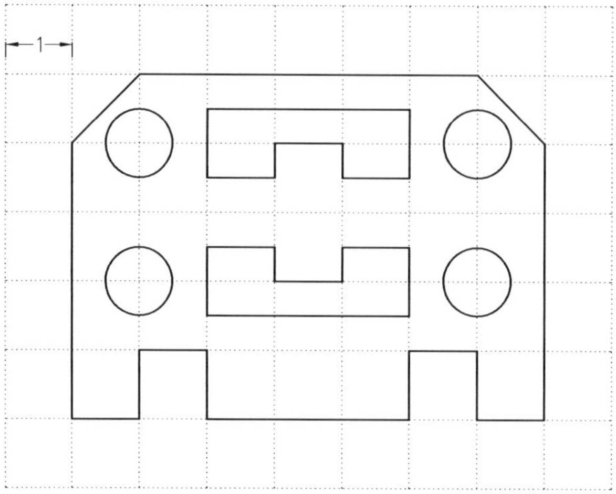

Figure 2-61 *Drawing for Exercise 13*

Exercise 14

Draw the object shown in Figure 2-62. The distance between the dotted lines is 10 feet. Determine the limits for this drawing and use the Engineering units with 0'0.00" precision.

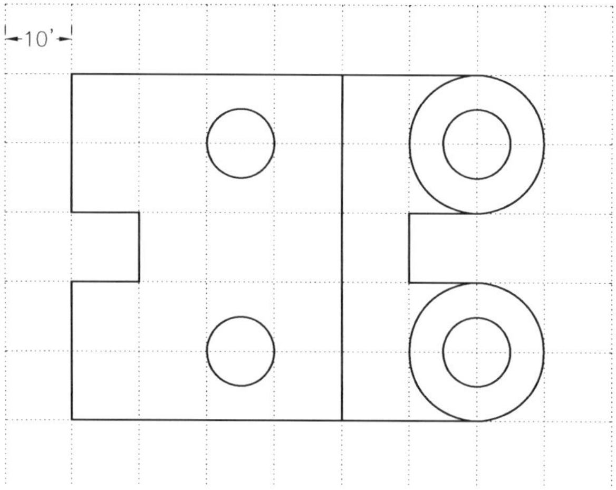

Figure 2-62 *Drawing for Exercise 14*

Problem-Solving Exercise 1

Draw the object shown in Figure 2-63, using the **Line** and **Center, Diameter** tools. In this exercise only the diameters of the circles are given. To draw the lines and small circles (Dia 0.6), you need to find the coordinate points for the lines and the center points of the circles. For example, if the center of concentric circles is at 5,3.5, then the *X* coordinate of the lower left corner of the rectangle will be 5.0 - 2.4 = 2.6.

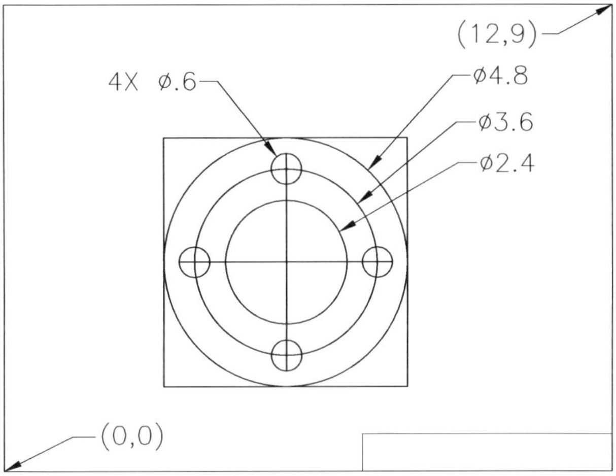

Figure 2-63 *Drawing for Problem-Solving Exercise 1*

Answers to Self-Evaluation Test

1. Undo, **2. Tan, Tan, Radius**, 3. **ZOOM**, 4. **Zoom All**, 5. Surveyor's, **6. Preview 7**. T, **8**. F, **9**. F, **10**. T

Chapter 3

Getting Started with Advanced Sketching

Learning Objectives

After completing this chapter, you will be able to:

- *Draw arcs using various options*
- *Draw rectangles, ellipses, elliptical arcs, and polygons*
- *Draw polylines and donuts*
- *Place points and change their style and size*
- *Create simple text*
- *Draw infinite lines*
- *Write simple text*

Key Terms

- *Arc*
- *Rectangles*
- *Explode*
- *Ellipse*
- *Elliptical Arc*
- *Polygon*
- *Polylines*
- *Donut*
- *Points*
- *Construction Line*
- *Text*
- *Ray*
- *FILLMODE*
- *PDMODE*
- *DDPTYPE*

DRAWING ARCS

Ribbon: Home > Draw > Arc drop-down **Toolbar:** Draw > Arc
Menu Bar: Draw > Arc **Command:** ARC or A

An arc is defined as a segment of a circle. In AutoCAD LT, an arc is drawn by using the tools available in the **Arc** drop-down. There are eleven different tools to draw an arc. The tools to draw an arc are grouped together in the **Arc** drop-down of the **Draw** panel in the **Ribbon**, see Figure 3-1. You can choose the appropriate tool depending upon the parameters known and then draw the arc. Remember that the tool that was used last to create an arc will be displayed in the **Draw** panel. The different methods to draw an arc are discussed next.

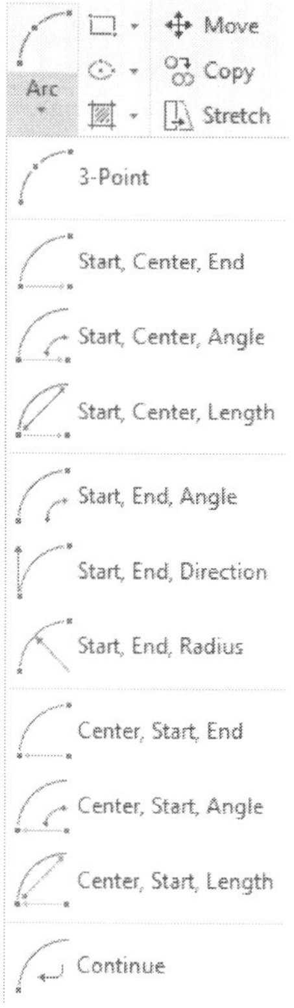

***Figure 3-1** The tools in the **Arc** drop-down*

Drawing an Arc by Specifying Three Points

To draw an arc by specifying the start point, endpoint, and another point on its periphery, choose the **3-Point** tool from the **Draw** panel (see Figure 3-1). On doing so, you will be prompted to specify the start point. Specify the first point or enter coordinates. Then, specify the second point and the endpoint of the arc, see Figure 3-2.

Following is the prompt sequence to draw an arc by specifying three points (You can also specify the points by using the mouse).

*Choose the **3-Point** tool from the **Arc** drop-down in the **Draw** panel (Ensure that dynamic input is off)*
Specify start point of arc or [Center]: **2,2** Enter
Specify second point of arc or [Center/End]: **3,3** Enter
Specify end point of arc: **3,4** Enter

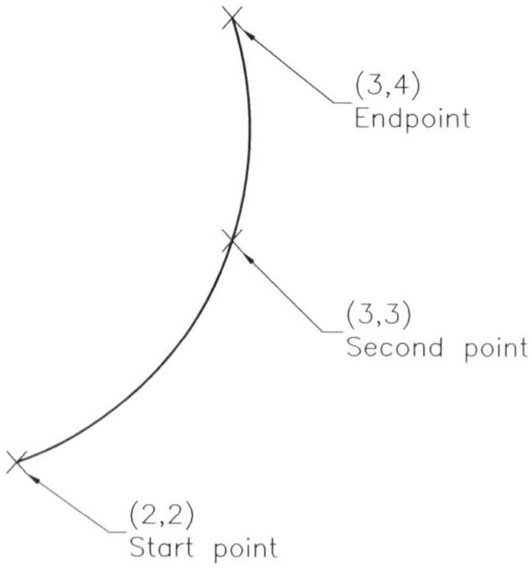

***Figure 3-2** Drawing an arc using the **3-Point** tool*

Exercise 1 — 3-Point

Draw several arcs by using the **3-Point** tool. The points can be selected by entering coordinates or by specifying points on the screen. Also, try to create a circle by drawing two separate arcs and a single arc and notice the limitations of the **Arc** tools.

Drawing an Arc by Specifying its Start Point, Center Point, and Endpoint

If you know the start point, endpoint, and center point of an arc, choose the **Start, Center, End** tool from the **Arc** drop-down in the **Draw** panel and then specify the start, center, and end points in succession; the arc will be drawn. The radius of the arc is determined by the distance between the center point and the start point. Therefore, the endpoint is used to calculate the angle at which the arc ends. Note that in this case, the arc will be drawn in counterclockwise direction from the start point to the endpoint around the specified center, as shown in Figure 3-3.

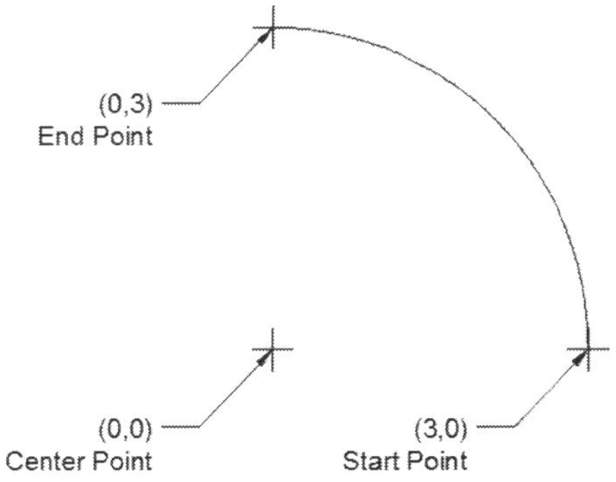

*Figure 3-3 Drawing an arc using the **Start, Center, End** tool*

Drawing an Arc by Specifying its Start Point, Center Point, and Included Angle

Included angle is the angle between the start and end points of an arc about the specified center. If you know the location of the start point, center point, and included angle of an arc, choose the **Start, Center, Angle** tool from the **Arc** drop-down in the **Draw** panel and specify the start point, center point, and included angle; the arc will be drawn in a counterclockwise direction with respect to the specified center and start point, see Figure 3-4.

If you enter a negative angle value, the arc will be drawn in a clockwise direction, see Figure 3-5. Following is the prompt sequence to draw an arc by specifying the center point at (2,2), start point at (3,2), and an included angle of -60 degrees:

*Choose the **Start, Center, Angle** tool from the **Draw** panel (Ensure that dynamic input is off)*
Specify start point of arc or [Center]: **3,2** Enter
Specify second point of arc or [Center/End]: _c
Specify center point of arc: **2,2** Enter
Specify end point of arc (hold Ctrl to switch direction) or [Angle/chord Length]: _a
Specify included angle (hold Ctrl to switch direction): **-60** Enter See Figure 3-5.

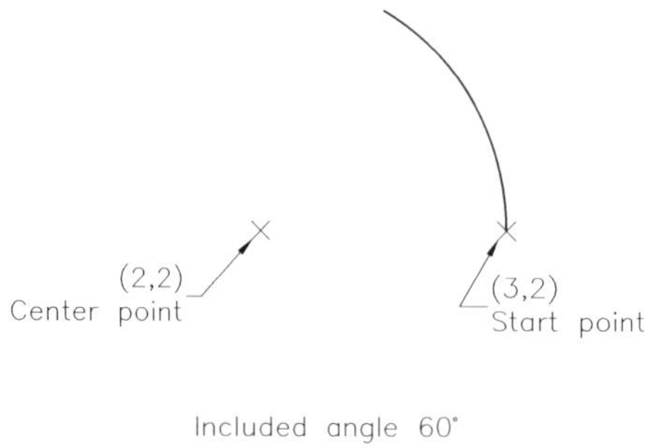

Figure 3-4 *Drawing an arc using the* ***Start, Center, Angle*** *tool*

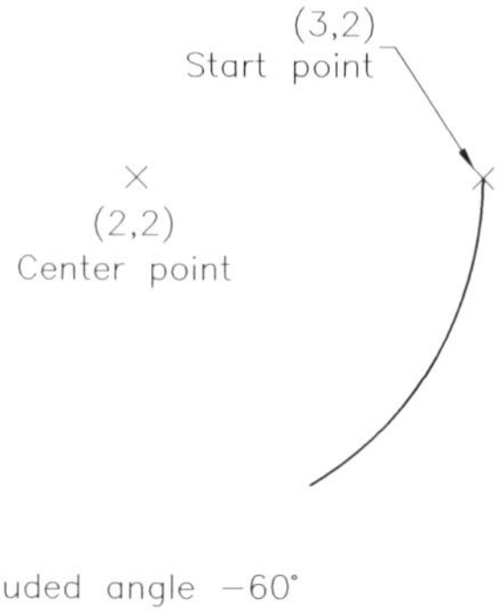

Figure 3-5 *Drawing an arc by specifying a negative angle using the* ***Start, Center, Angle*** *tool*

In AutoCAD LT, while creating an arc, you can flip the direction of the arc for specifying a point on the arc circumference using the CTRL key. To do so, while creating the arc, if you press and hold the CTRL key and move the cursor, you will notice that the direction of arc has been flipped. Now, you can specify the parameters of the arc in different direction. Note that if you release the CTRL key, the direction of arc creation will switch back to the previous direction.

Exercise 2 — *Start, Center, Angle*

a. Draw an arc whose start point is at 6,3, center point is at 3,3, and the included angle is 240 degrees.

b. Draw the profile shown in Figure 3-6. The distance between the dotted lines is 1.0 unit. Create the arcs by using different arc command options as indicated in the figure.

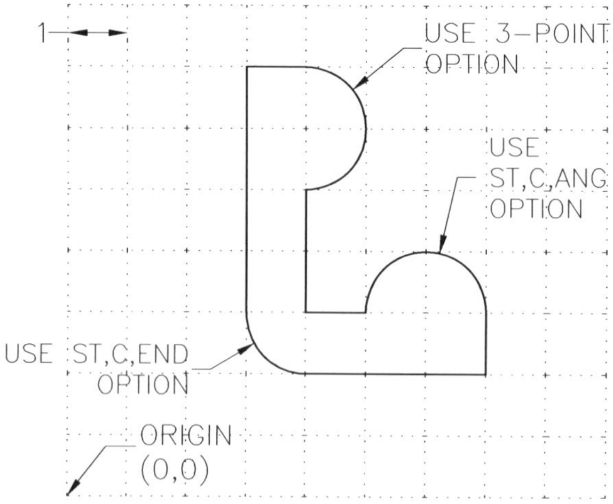

Figure 3-6 *Drawing for Exercise 2*

Drawing an Arc by Specifying the Start Point, Center Point, and Chord Length

A chord is defined as a straight line connecting the start point and endpoint of an arc. To draw an arc by specifying its chord length, choose the **Start, Center, Length** tool from the **Arc** drop-down in the **Draw** panel and specify the start point, center point, and length of the chord in succession. On specifying the chord length, AutoCAD LT will calculate the included angle and an arc will be drawn in the counterclockwise direction from the start point. A positive chord length gives the smallest possible arc with that length, as shown in Figure 3-7. This arc is known as minor arc. The included angle in a minor arc is less than 180 degrees. A negative value for the chord length results in the largest possible arc also known as major arc, as shown in Figure 3-8.

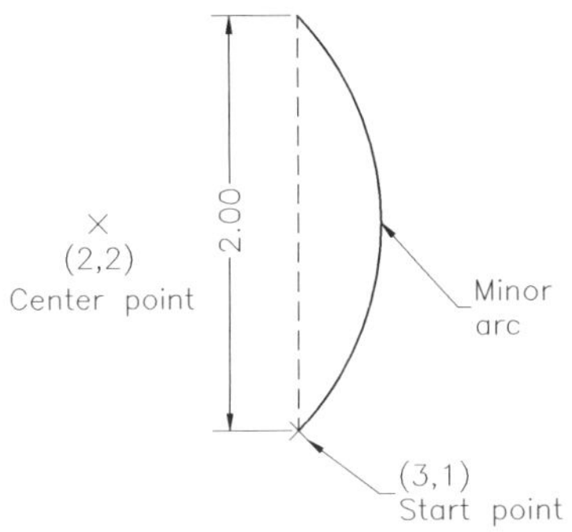

*Figure 3-7 Drawing a minor arc by specifying a positive chord length using the **Start, Center, Length** tool*

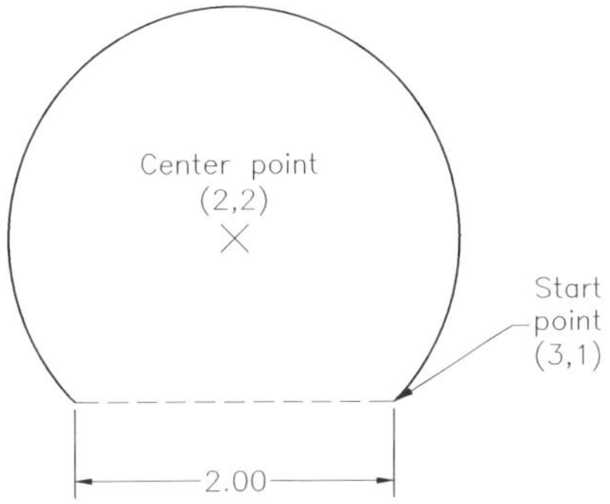

*Figure 3-8 Drawing a major arc by specifying a negative chord length using the **Start, Center, Length** tool*

Drawing an Arc by Specifying its Start Point, Endpoint, and Included Angle

To draw an arc by specifying its start point, endpoint, and the included angle, choose the **Start, End, Angle** tool from the **Arc** drop-down in the **Draw** panel and specify the start point, endpoint, and the included angle in succession; the arc will be drawn. A positive included angle value draws an arc in a counterclockwise direction from the start point to the endpoint, as shown in Figure 3-9. Similarly, a negative included angle value draws the arc in a clockwise direction.

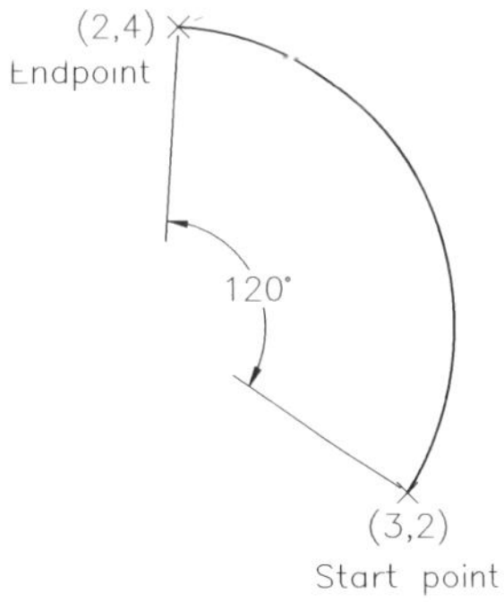

*Figure 3-9 Drawing an arc using the **Start, End, Angle** tool*

Drawing an Arc by Specifying its Start Point, Endpoint, and Direction

This option is used to draw a major or minor arc whose size and position are determined by the distance between the start point and endpoint and the direction specified. You can specify the direction by selecting a point on a line that is tangent to the start point or by entering an angle between the start point of the arc and the end point of the tangent line.

To draw an arc by specifying its direction, choose the **Start, End, Direction** tool from the **Arc** drop-down in the **Draw** panel and specify the start and end points in succession; you will be prompted to specify the direction. Specify a point on the line that is tangent to the start point or enter an angle between the start point of the arc and the end point of the tangent line; an arc will be drawn.

In other words, on using this option, the arc will start in the direction you specify (the start of the arc is established tangent to the direction you specify). The prompt sequence to draw an arc, whose start point is at 3,6, endpoint is at 4.5,3, and direction of -40 degrees is given next.

Choose the ***Start, End, Direction*** *tool from the* ***Arc*** *drop-down in the* ***Draw*** *panel (Ensure that dynamic input is off)*
Specify start point of arc or [Center]: **3,6** Enter
Specify second point of arc or [Center/End]: _e
Specify end point of arc: **4.5,3** Enter
Specify center point of arc (hold Ctrl to switch direction) or [Angle/Direction/Radius]: _d
Specify tangent direction for the start point of arc (hold Ctrl to switch direction): **-40** Enter, see Figure 3-10.

The prompt sequence to draw an arc whose start point is at 4,3, endpoint is at 3,5, and direction of 90 degrees, is given next.

Choose the ***Start, End, Direction*** *tool from the* ***Arc*** *drop-down in the* ***Draw*** *panel (Ensure that dynamic input is off)*
Specify start point of arc or [Center]: **4,3** Enter
Specify second point of arc or [Center/End]: _e
Specify end point of arc: **3,5** Enter
Specify center point of arc (hold Ctrl to switch direction) or [Angle/Direction/Radius]: _d
Specify tangent direction for the start point of arc (hold Ctrl to switch direction): **90** Enter
See Figure 3-11.

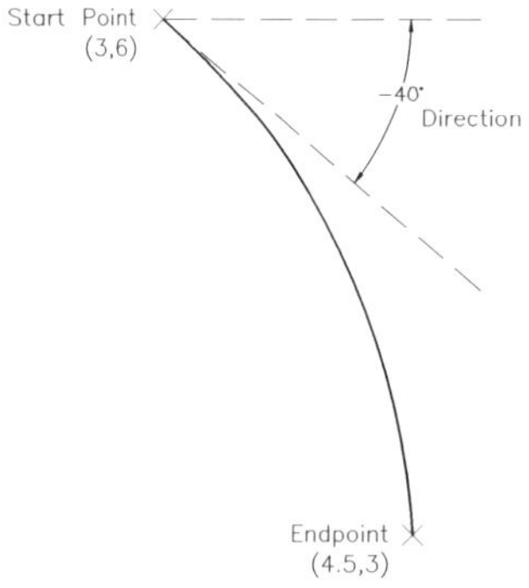

Figure 3-10 *Drawing an arc in the negative direction using the* ***Start, End, Direction*** *tool*

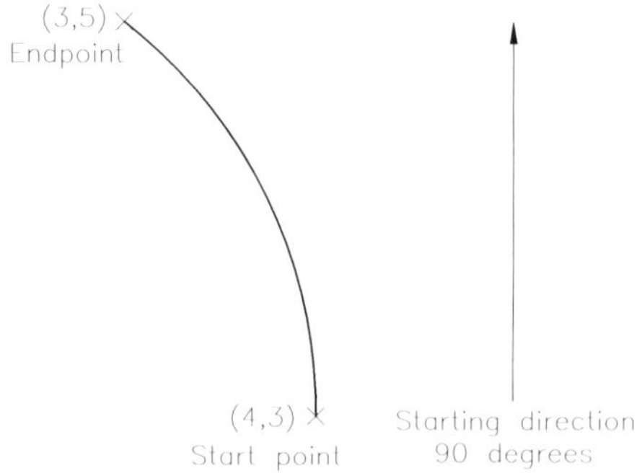

Figure 3-11 *Drawing an arc using the* ***Start, End, Direction*** *tool*

Exercise 3 — Start, End, Direction

a. Specify the directions and coordinates of two arcs in such a way that they form a circular figure.

b. Draw the profile shown in Figure 3-12. Create the curves by using the **Start, End, Direction** tool. The distance between the dotted lines is 1.0 unit and the diameter of the circles is 1 unit.

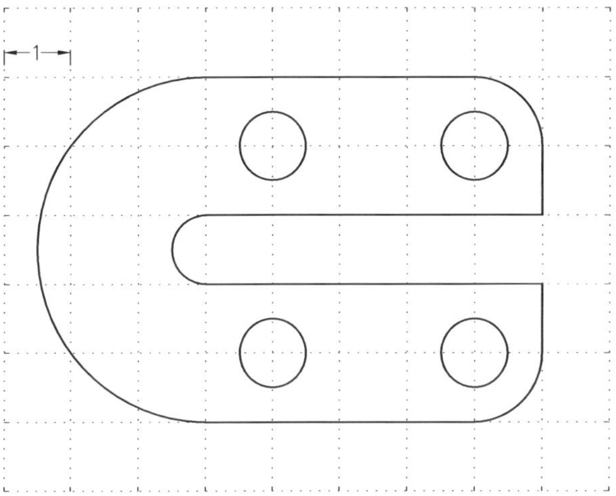

Figure 3-12 *Drawing for Exercise 3*

Drawing an Arc by Specifying its Start Point, Endpoint, and Radius

If you know the location of the start point, endpoint, and radius of an arc, choose the **Start, End, Radius** tool from the **Draw** panel and specify the start and end points; you will be prompted to specify the radius. Enter the radius value; the arc will be drawn. In this case, the arc will be drawn in counterclockwise direction from the start point. This means that a negative radius value results in a major arc (the largest arc between the two endpoints), see Figure 3-13(a) whereas a positive radius value results in a minor arc (smallest arc between the start point and the endpoint), see Figure 3-13(b).

Drawing an Arc by Specifying its Center Point, Start Point, and Endpoint

The **Center, Start, End** tool is the modification of the **Start, Center, End** tool. Use this tool whenever it is easier to start drawing an arc by establishing the center first. Here, the arc is always drawn in a counterclockwise direction from the start point to the endpoint around the specified center. The prompt sequence for drawing the arc shown in Figure 3-14, which has a center point at (3,3), start point at (5,3), and endpoint at (3,5) is given next.

*Choose the **Center, Start, End** tool from the **Arc** drop-down in the **Draw** panel.*
Specify center point of arc: **3,3** Enter
Specify start point of arc: **5,3** Enter
Specify end point of arc (hold Ctrl to switch direction) or [Angle/chord Length]: **3,5** Enter

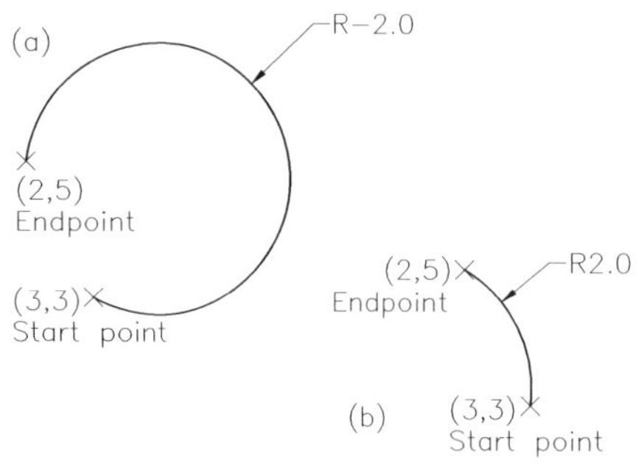

***Figure 3-13** Drawing an arc using the **Start, End, Radius** tool*

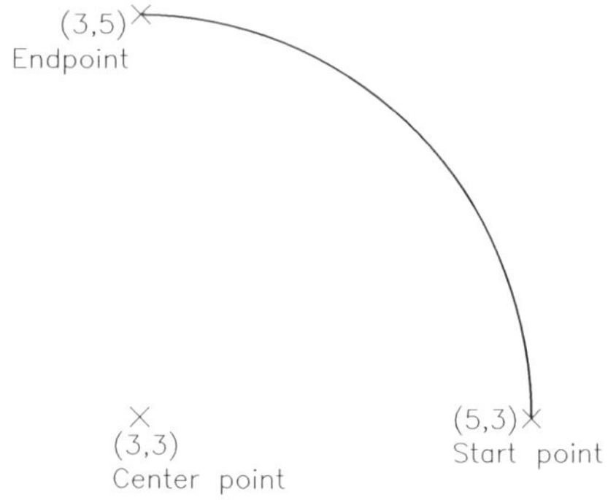

***Figure 3-14** Drawing an arc using the **Center, Start, End** tool*

Drawing an Arc by Specifying its Center Point, Start Point, and Angle

You can use the **Center, Start, Angle** tool if you need to draw an arc by specifying the center first. The prompt sequence for drawing the arc shown in Figure 3-15, which has a center point at (4,5), start point at (5,4), and included angle of 120 degrees is given next.

*Choose the **Center, Start, Angle** tool from the **Arc** drop-down in the **Draw** panel (Ensure that dynamic input is off)*
Specify center point of arc: **4,5** Enter
Specify start point of arc: **5,4** Enter
Specify included angle (hold Ctrl to switch direction): **120** Enter, see Figure 3-15.

Drawing an Arc by Specifying the Center Point, Start Point, and Chord Length

The **Center, Start, Length** tool is used whenever it is easier to draw an arc by establishing the center first. The prompt sequence for drawing the arc shown in Figure 3-16, which has a center point at (2,2), start point at (4,3), and length of chord as 3 is given next.

*Choose the **Center, Start, Length** tool from the **Arc** drop-down in the **Draw** panel (Ensure that dynamic input is off)*
Specify center point of arc: **2,2** Enter
Specify start point of arc: **4,3** Enter
Specify length of chord (hold Ctrl to switch direction): **3** Enter, see Figure 3-16.

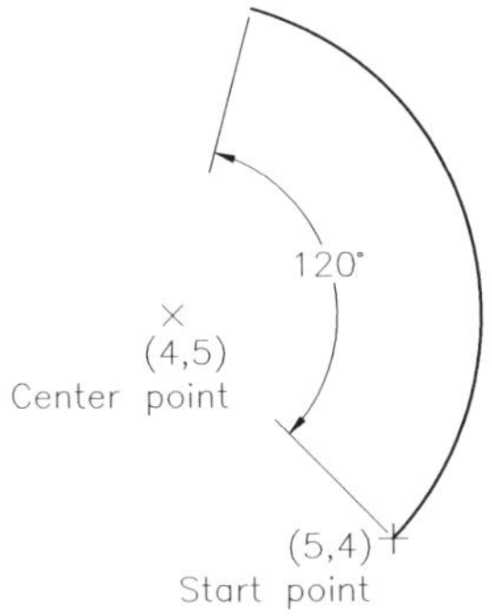

Figure 3-15 *Drawing an arc using the* ***Center, Start, Angle*** *tool*

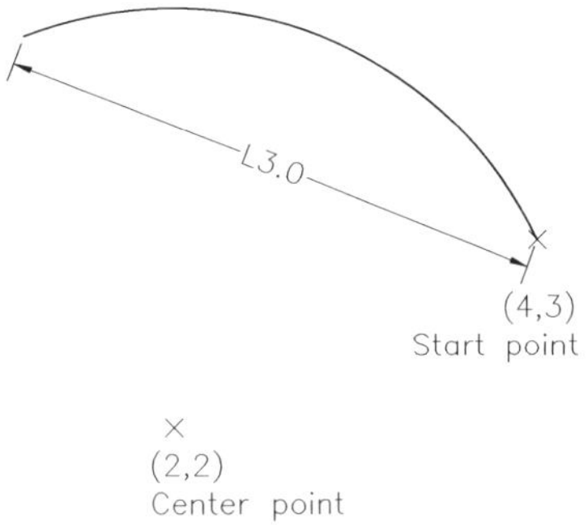

Figure 3-16 *Drawing an arc using the* ***Center, Start, Length*** *tool*

Exercise 4 Center, Start, Length

Draw a minor arc with the center point at (3,4), start point at (4,2), and chord length of 4 units.

Drawing an Arc by Using the Continue Tool

To continue drawing an arc from a previously drawn arc or line, choose the **Continue** tool from the **Arc** drop-down in the **Draw** panel; the start point and the direction of the arc will be taken from the endpoint and the ending direction of the previous line or arc. Specify the endpoint to draw an arc. If this option is used to draw arcs, each successive arc will be tangent to the previous one. This option is used to draw arcs that are tangent to the previously drawn line.

Tip

The ***Continue*** *tool can also be invoked automatically by first drawing a line or an arc, then choosing a tool from the* ***Arc*** *drop-down in the* ***Draw*** *panel, and finally pressing ENTER at the* ***Specify start point of arc or [Center]*** *prompt.*

Exercise 5

a. Use the **Center**, **Start**, **Angle**, and **Continue** tools to draw the profiles shown in Figure 3-17.

b. Draw the profile shown in Figure 3-18. The distance between the dotted lines is 1.0 unit. Create the radii as indicated in the drawing by using the **Arc** tools.

Figure 3-17 Drawing for Exercise 5(a)

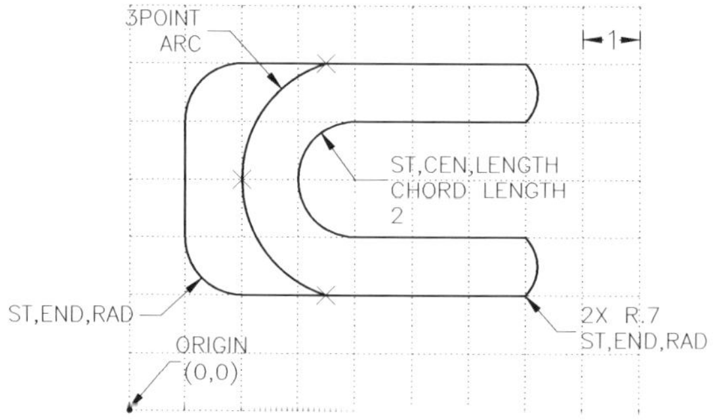

Figure 3-18 Drawing for Exercise 5(b)

DRAWING RECTANGLES

Ribbon: Home > Draw > Rectangle **Toolbar:** Draw > Rectangle
Command: RECTANG

A rectangle is drawn by choosing the **Rectangle** tool (see Figure 3-19) from the **Draw** panel. In AutoCAD LT, you can draw rectangles by specifying two opposite corners of the rectangle, by specifying the area and the size of one of the sides, or by specifying the dimensions of the rectangle. All these methods of drawing rectangles are discussed next.

Drawing Rectangles by Specifying Two Opposite Corners

On invoking the **Rectangle** tool, you will be prompted to specify the first corner of the rectangle. Enter the coordinates of the first corner or specify the start point by using the mouse; you will be prompted to specify the other corner. The first corner can be any one of the four corners. Specify the diagonally opposite corner by entering the coordinates or by using the left mouse button, as shown in Figure 3-20.

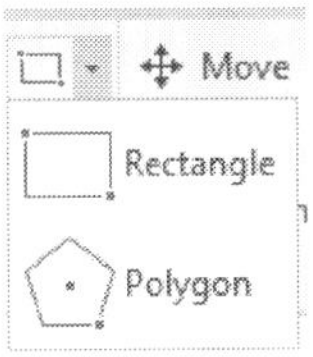

*Figure 3-19 Invoking the **Rectangle** tool from the **Draw** panel*

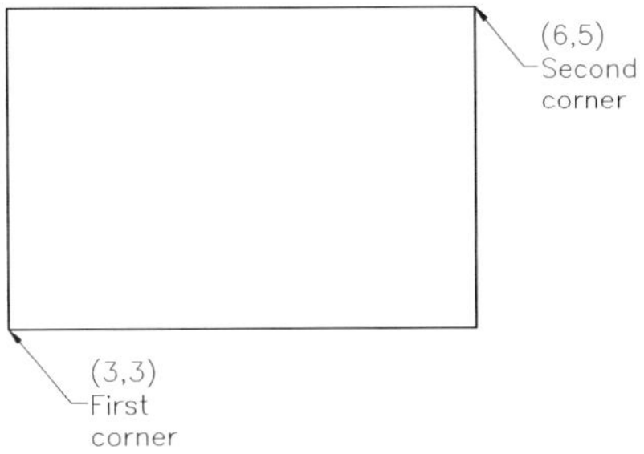

Figure 3-20 Drawing a rectangle by specifying two opposite corners

Drawing Rectangles by Specifying its Area and One Side

To draw a rectangle by specifying its area and the length of one of the sides, first specify the start point. Next, invoke the shortcut menu by right-clicking and then choose the **Area** option. Next, specify the parameters; the rectangle is drawn. Following is the prompt sequence to draw a rectangle whose start point is at 3,3, has area 15 units, and length 5 units:

*Choose the **Rectangle** tool from the **Draw** panel*
Specify first corner point or [Chamfer/Elevation/Fillet/Thickness/Width]: **3,3** Enter
Specify other corner point or [Area/Dimensions/Rotation]: **A** Enter
Enter area of rectangle in current units <100.000>: **15** Enter
Calculate rectangle dimensions based on [Length/Width] <Length>: **L** Enter
Enter rectangle length <10.0000>: **5** Enter

In the above case, the area and length of the rectangle were entered. The system automatically calculates the width of the rectangle by using the following formula:

Area of rectangle = Length x Width
Width = Area of rectangle/Length
Width =15/5
Width =3 units

Drawing Rectangles by Specifying their Dimensions

You can also draw a rectangle by specifying its dimensions. This can be done by choosing the **Dimensions** option from the shortcut menu at the **Specify other corner point or [Area/Dimensions/Rotation]** prompt and entering the length and width of the rectangle. The prompt sequence for drawing a rectangle at 3,3 with a length of **5** units and width of **3** units is given next.

*Choose the **Rectangle** tool from the **Draw** panel*
Specify first corner point or [Chamfer/Elevation/Fillet/Thickness/Width]: **3,3** Enter
Specify other corner point or [Area/Dimensions/Rotation]: **D** Enter
Specify length for rectangles <0.0000>: **5** Enter
Specify width for rectangles <0.0000>: **3** Enter

Specify other corner point or [Area/Dimensions/Rotation]: *Click on the screen to specify the orientation of rectangle.*

Here, you are allowed to choose any one of the four locations for placing the rectangle. You can move the cursor to see the four quadrants. Depending on the location of the cursor, the corner point that is specified first holds the position of either the lower left corner, the lower right corner, the upper right corner, or the upper left corner. After deciding the position, you can click to place the rectangle.

Drawing Rectangle at an Angle

You can also draw a rectangle at an angle. This can be done by choosing the **Rotation** option from the shortcut menu, at the **Specify other corner point or [Area/Dimensions/Rotation]** prompt and entering the rotation angle. After entering the rotation angle, you can continue sizing the rectangle using any one of the above discussed methods. The prompt sequence for drawing a rectangle at an angle of 45-degree is:

*Choose the **Rectangle** tool from the **Draw** panel*
Specify first corner point or [Chamfer/Elevation/Fillet/Thickness/Width]: *Select a point as lower left corner location.*
Specify other corner point or [Area/Dimensions/Rotation]: **R** Enter
Specify rotation angle or [Pick points] <current>: **45** Enter
Specify other corner point or [Area/Dimensions/Rotation]: *Select a diagonally opposite point.*

While specifying the other corner point, you can place the rectangle in any of the four quadrants. Move the cursor in different quadrants and then select a point in the quadrant in which you need to draw the rectangle. Figure 3-21 shows a rectangle drawn at an angle of 45-degree.

Note
Once the rotation angle has been specified, the subsequent rectangles will be drawn at an angle as specified. If you do not want to draw the subsequent rectangles at an angle, you need to set the rotation angle to zero.

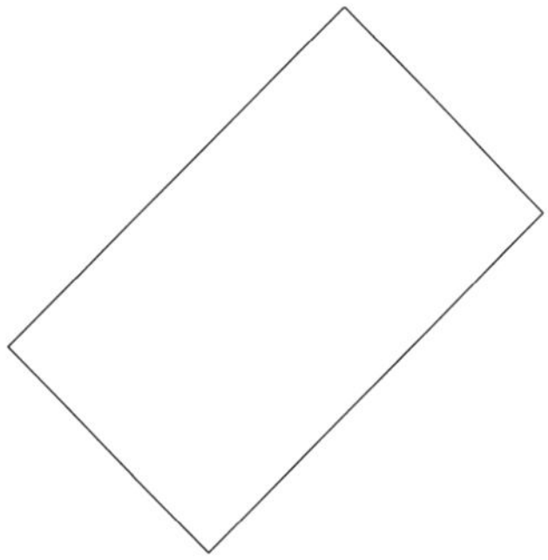

Figure 3-21 *Rectangle drawn at an angle*

You can also set some of the parameters of a rectangle before specifying the start point. These parameters are the options in the Command Prompt and are discussed next.

Chamfer

The **Chamfer** option is used to create a chamfer, which is an angled corner, by specifying the chamfer distances, see Figure 3-22. The chamfer is created at all four corners. You can give two different chamfer values to create an unequal chamfer.

*Choose the **Rectangle** tool from the **Draw** panel*
Specify first corner point or [Chamfer/Elevation/Fillet/Thickness/Width]: **C** Enter
Specify first chamfer distance for rectangles <0.0000>: *Enter a value, d1.*
Specify second chamfer distance for rectangles <0.0000>: *Enter a value, d2.*
Specify first corner point or [Chamfer/Elevation/Fillet/Thickness/Width]: *Select a point as lower left corner.*
Specify other corner point or [Area/Dimensions/Rotation]: *Select a point as upper right corner.*

Fillet

The **Fillet** option is used to create a filleted rectangle, see Figure 3-23. You can specify the required fillet radius. The following is the prompt sequence for specifying the fillet:

*Choose the **Rectangle** tool from the **Draw** panel*
Specify first corner point or [Chamfer/Elevation/Fillet/Thickness/Width]: **F** Enter
Specify fillet radius for rectangles <0.0000>: *Enter a value.*
Specify first corner point or [Chamfer/Elevation/Fillet/Thickness/Width]: *Select a point as lower left corner.*
Specify other corner point or [Area/Dimensions/Rotation]: *Select a point as upper right corner.*

Note that the rectangle will be filleted only if the length and width of the rectangle are equal to or greater than twice the value of the specified fillet. Otherwise, AutoCAD LT will draw a rectangle without fillets.

Note
You can draw a rectangle with chamfers or fillets. If you specify the chamfer distances first and then specify the fillet radius in the same rectangle, the rectangle will be drawn with fillets only.

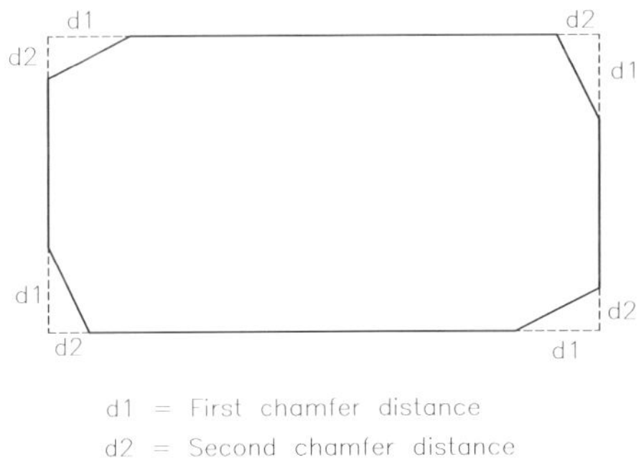

Figure 3-22 *Drawing a rectangle with chamfers*

Figure 3-23 *Drawing a rectangle with fillets*

Width

The **Width** option is used to create a rectangle whose line segments have some specified width, as shown in Figure 3-24.

Specify first corner point or [Chamfer/Elevation/Fillet/Thickness/Width]: **W** Enter
Specify line width for rectangles <0.0000>: *Enter a value.*

Thickness

The **Thickness** option is used to draw a rectangle that is extruded in the Z direction by a specified value of thickness. For example, if you draw a rectangle with thickness of 2 units, you will get a cuboid whose height is 2 units. To view the cuboid, choose **SE Isometric** from **View > Views** panel. To restore the view to the plan view, choose **Top** from **View > Views** panel.

Specify first corner point or [Chamfer/Elevation/Fillet/Thickness/Width]: **T** Enter
Specify thickness for rectangles <0.0000>: *Enter a value.*

Elevation

The **Elevation** option is used to draw a rectangle at a specified distance from the *XY* plane along the *Z* axis. For example, if the elevation is 2 units, the rectangle will be drawn two units above the *XY* plane. If the thickness of the rectangle is 1 unit, you will get a rectangular box of 1 unit height located 2 units above the *XY* plane, see Figure 3-25.

Specify first corner point or [Chamfer/Elevation/Fillet/Thickness/Width]: **E** Enter
Specify elevation for rectangles <0.0000>: *Enter a value.*

To view the rectangle in 3D space, choose **SE Isometric** from **View > Views** panel. To restore the view to the plan view, choose **Top** from **View > Views** panel.

Figure 3-24 *Drawing a rectangle of specified width*

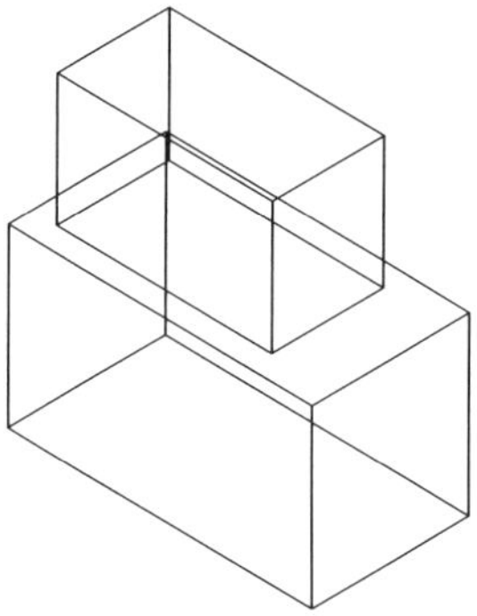

Figure 3-25 *Drawing rectangles with thickness and elevation specified*

Note

1. The values you enter for fillet, width, elevation, and thickness become the current values for the rectangles drawn subsequently. Therefore, you need to reset the values based on the requirement.

2. A rectangle generated by using the ***Rectangle*** *tool is treated as a single object. To edit individual lines of the rectangle, you need to explode the rectangle by using the* ***Explode*** *tool from the* ***Modify*** *panel of the* ***Home*** *tab and then edit them.*

Exercise 6 Rectangle

Draw a rectangle of length 4 units, width 3 units, and start point at (1,1). Draw another rectangle of length 2 units and width 1 units, with its first corner at 1.5,1.5, and which is at an angle of 65-degree.

DRAWING ELLIPSES

Ribbon: Home > Draw > Ellipse drop-down **Toolbar:** Draw > Ellipse
Command: ELLIPSE

If you cut a cone by a cutting plane at an angle and view the cone perpendicular to the cutting plane, the shape created is called an ellipse. An ellipse can be created by using different tools available in the **Ellipse** drop-down of the **Draw** panel, refer to Figure 3-26. In AutoCAD LT, you can create a true ellipse, also known as a NURBS-based (Non-Uniform Rational Bezier Spline) ellipse. A true ellipse has center and quadrant points. If you select it, grips (small blue squares) will be displayed at the center and quadrant points of the ellipse. If you move one of the grips located on the perimeter of the ellipse, the size of the ellipse will change.

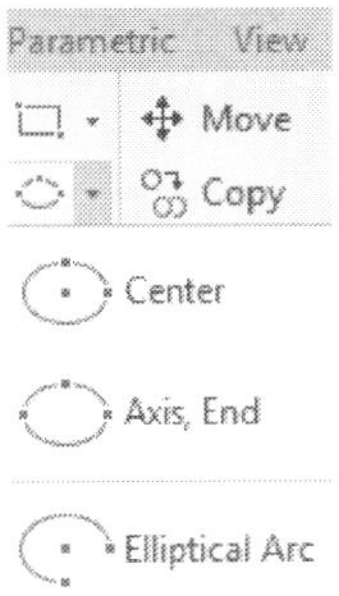

***Figure 3-26** Tools in the **Ellipse** drop-down of the **Draw** panel*

Once you invoke the **Ellipse** tool, the **Specify axis endpoint of ellipse or [Arc/Center]** or **Specify axis endpoint of ellipse or [Arc/Center/Isocircle]** (if isometric snap is ON) prompt will be displayed. The response to this prompt depends on the option you choose. The various options are explained next.

Note

*By default, the **Isocircle** option is not available for the **Ellipse** tool. To display this option, you have to select the **Isometric snap** radio button in the **Snap and Grid** tab of the **Drafting Settings** dialog box.*

Drawing Ellipse Using the Center Option

To draw an ellipse by specifying center point, endpoint of one axis, and length of the other axis, choose the **Center** tool from the **Ellipse** drop-down in the **Draw** panel; you will be prompted to specify the center of the ellipse. The center of an ellipse is defined as the point of intersection of the major and minor axes. Specify the center point or enter coordinates; you will be prompted to specify the endpoint. Specify the endpoint of the major or minor axis; you will be prompted to specify the distance of the other axis. Specify the distance; the ellipse will be drawn.

After specifying the endpoint of one axis, you can enter **R** at the **Specify distance to other axis or [Rotation]** prompt to specify the rotation angle around the major axis. In this case, the first axis specified is considered as the major axis. On specifying the rotation angle, the ellipse will be drawn at an angle with respect to the major axis. Note that the rotation angle should not be given in the range from 89.4 degrees to 90.6 degrees because it will appear as a straight line. Figure 3-27 shows the ellipse created at different rotation angles.

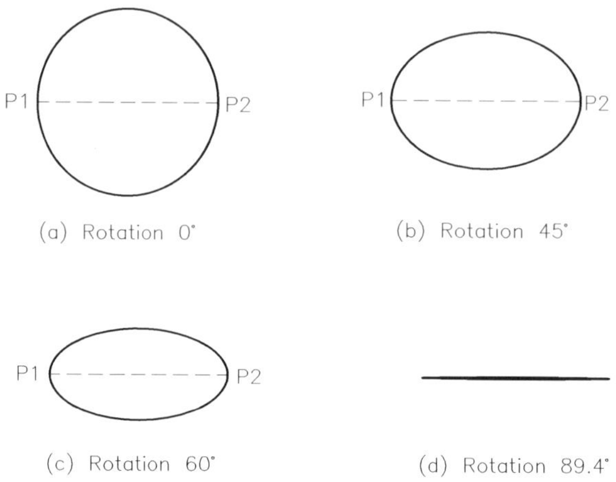

Figure 3-27 *Rotation about the major axis*

Drawing an Ellipse by Specifying its Axis and Endpoint

To draw an ellipse by specifying one of its axes and the endpoint of the other axis, choose the **Axis, End** tool from the **Ellipse** drop-down in the **Draw** panel; you will be prompted to specify the axis end point. Specify the first endpoint of one of the axis of the ellipse; you will be prompted to specify the other endpoint of the axis. Specify the other endpoint of the axis. Now, you can specify the distance to other axis from the center or specify the rotation angle around the specified axis.

Figure 3-28 shows an ellipse with one endpoint of the axis located at (3,3), the other at (6,3), and the distance to the other axis as 1 unit. Figure 3-29 shows an ellipse with one endpoint of the axis located at (3,3), the other at (4,2), and the distance to the other axis as 2 units.

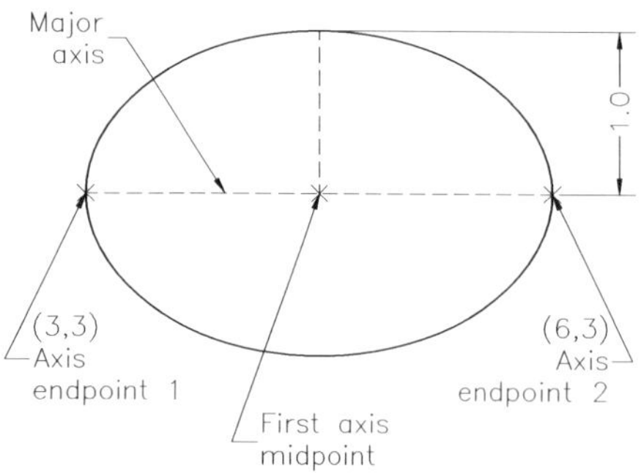

Figure 3-28 *Drawing an ellipse using the Minor axis and end points on the Major Axis*

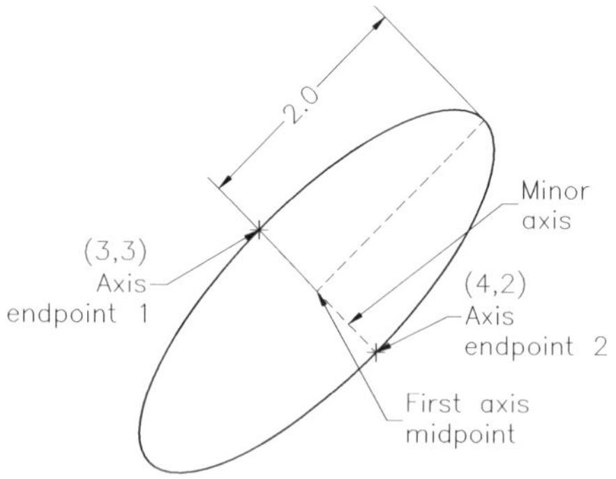

Figure 3-29 *Drawing an ellipse using the Major axis and end points on the Minor Axis*

Exercise 7 *Ellipse*

Draw an ellipse whose major axis is 4 units and the rotation around this axis is 60 degrees. Draw another ellipse whose rotation around the major axis is 15 degrees.

Drawing Elliptical Arcs

Ribbon: Home > Draw > Ellipse drop-down > Elliptical Arc
Command: ELLIPSE > Arc

In AutoCAD LT, you can draw an elliptical arc by choosing the **Elliptical Arc** tool from the **Ellipse** drop-down in the **Draw** panel. On choosing this tool, you can specify the endpoints of one of the axes, the distance to other axis from the center, and any one of the following information:

1. Start and End angles of the arc.
2. Start and Included angles of the arc.
3. Start and End parameters.

Remember that in case of elliptical arcs, angles are measured from the first point and in counterclockwise direction.

In this section, you will draw an elliptical arc by using the information given below.

a. Start angle = -45, end angle = 135
b. Start angle = -45, included angle = 225
c. Start parameter = @1,0, end parameter = @1<225

Specifying the Start and End Angles of the Elliptical Arc [Figure 3-30(a)]

*Choose the **Elliptical Arc** tool from the **Draw** panel*
Specify axis endpoint of elliptical arc or [Center]: *Select the first endpoint*
Switch on the Ortho mode by pressing F8, if it is not already chosen
Specify other endpoint of axis: *Select the second point to the left of the first point*
Specify distance to other axis or [Rotation]: *Select a point or enter a distance*
Specify start angle or [Parameter]: **-45** Enter
Specify end angle or [Parameter/Included angle]: **135** Enter *(Angle where arc ends)*

Specifying the Start and Included Angles of the Elliptical Arc [Figure 3-30(b)]

*Choose the **Elliptical Arc** tool from the **Draw** panel*
Specify axis endpoint of elliptical arc or [Center]: *Select the first endpoint*
Specify other endpoint of axis: *Select the second point*
Specify distance to other axis or [Rotation]: *Select a point or enter a distance*
Specify start angle or [Parameter]: **-45** Enter
Specify end angle or [Parameter/Included angle]: **I** Enter
Specify included angle for arc<current>: **225** Enter *(Included angle)*

Specifying the Start and End Parameters [Figure 3-30(c)]

Choose the ***Elliptical Arc*** *tool from the* ***Draw*** *panel*
Specify axis endpoint of elliptical arc or [Center]: *Select the first endpoint*
Specify other endpoint of axis: *Select the second endpoint*
Specify distance to other axis or [Rotation]: *Select a point or enter a distance*
Specify start angle or [Parameter]: **P**
Specify start parameter or [Angle]: **@1,0**
Specify end parameter or [Angle/ Included angle]: **@1<225**

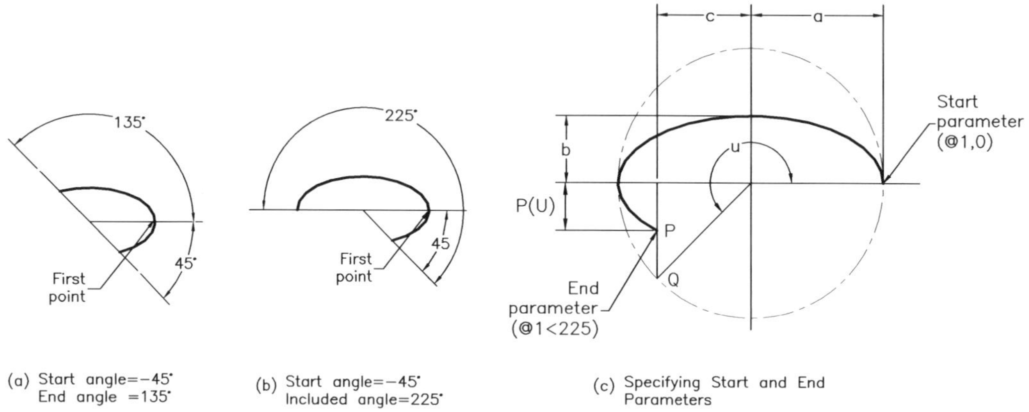

Figure 3-30 *Drawing elliptical arcs*

Exercise 8 — *Elliptical Arc*

a. Construct an ellipse with center at (2,3), axis endpoint at (4,6), and the other axis endpoint at a distance of 0.75 unit from the midpoint of the first axis.

b. Draw the profile shown in Figure 3-31. The distance between the dotted lines is 1.0 unit.

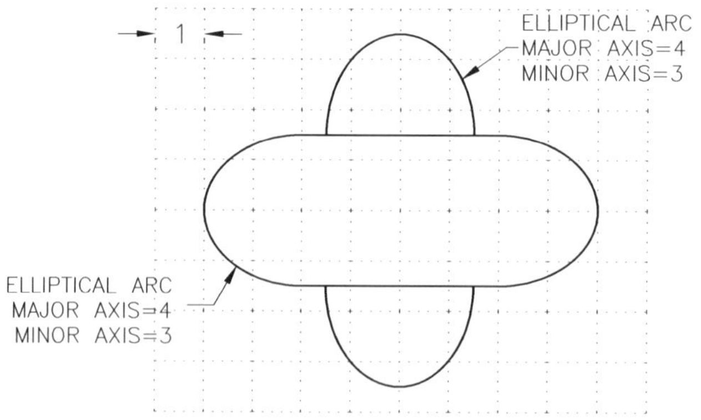

Figure 3-31 *Drawing for Exercise 8*

DRAWING REGULAR POLYGONS

Ribbon: Home > Draw > Polygon **Toolbar:** Draw > Polygon
Command: POLYGON

A regular polygon is a closed geometric entity with equal sides. The number of sides of a polygon vary from 3 to 1024. For example, a triangle is a three-sided polygon and a pentagon is a five-sided polygon. To draw a regular 2D polygon, choose the **Polygon** tool from the **Draw** panel; you will be prompted to specify the number of sides. Type the number of sides and press ENTER. Now, you can draw the polygon by specifying the length of an edge or by specifying the center of the polygon. Both these methods are discussed next.

Drawing a Polygon by Specifying the Center of Polygon

After you specify the number of sides and press ENTER, you will be prompted to specify the center of polygon. Specify the center point; you will be prompted to specify whether the polygon to be drawn is inscribed in a circle or circumscribed about an imaginary circle. A polygon is said to be inscribed when it is drawn inside an imaginary circle such that the vertices of the polygon touch the circle, see Figure 3-32, whereas a polygon is said to be circumscribed when it is drawn outside the imaginary circle such that the sides of the polygon are tangent to the circle, see Figure 3-33. Type **I** or **C** to draw an inscribed or a circumscribed polygon respectively, and press ENTER; you will be prompted to specify the radius. Specify the radius and press ENTER; a polygon will be created.

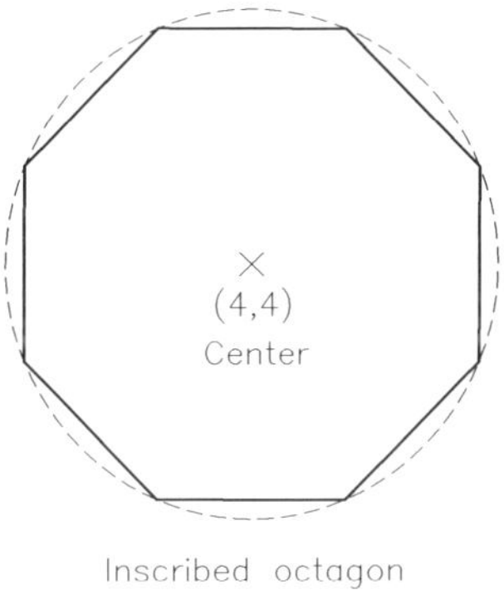

Figure 3-32 *Drawing an inscribed polygon using the* ***Center of Polygon*** *option*

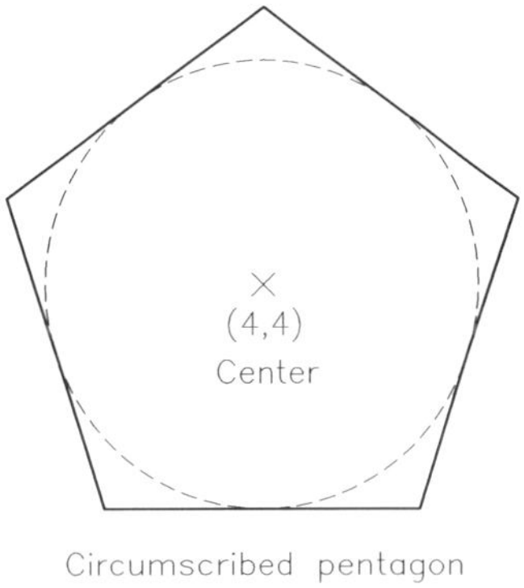

Figure 3-33 *Drawing a circumscribed polygon using the* ***Center of Polygon*** *option*

Drawing a Polygon by Specifying an Edge

To draw a polygon by specifying the length of an edge, you need to type **E** at the **Specify center of polygon or [Edge]** Command prompt and press ENTER. Next, specify the first and second endpoints of the edge in succession; the polygon will be drawn in counterclockwise direction, as shown in Figure 3-34.

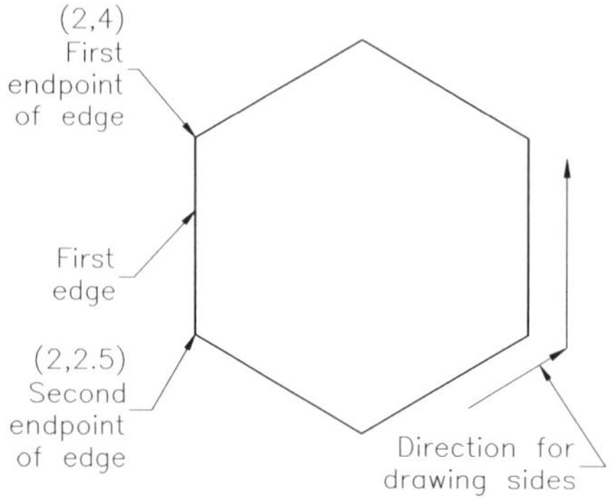

***Figure 3-34** Drawing a polygon (hexagon) using the **Edge** option*

Exercise 9

Draw a circumscribed polygon of eight sides by using the **Center of Polygon** method.

Exercise 10

Draw a polygon of ten sides by using the **Edge** option and an elliptical arc, as shown in Figure 3-35. Let the first endpoint of the edge be at (7,1) and the second endpoint be at (8,2).

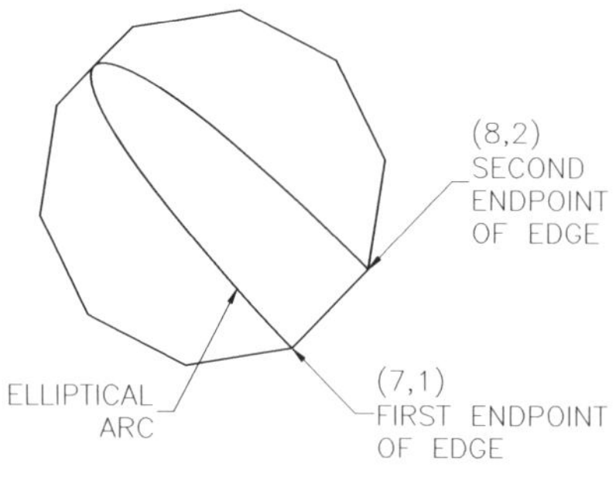

***Figure 3-35** Polygon and elliptical arc for Exercise 10*

DRAWING POLYLINES

Ribbon: Home > Draw > Polyline **Toolbar:** Draw > Polyline
Command: PLINE or PL

Etymologically, polylines means many lines. Some of the features of a polyline are listed below.

1. Polylines can be constructed with desired width. They are very flexible and can be used to draw any shape, such as a filled circle or a donut.
2. Polylines can be used to draw objects in any linetype (for example, hidden linetype).
3. Polylines are edited by using the advanced editing tools such as the **Edit Polyline** tool from the **Modify** panel of the **Home** tab.

4. A single polyline object can be formed by joining polylines and polyarcs of different thickness.
5. It is easy to determine the area or perimeter of a polyline feature.

To draw a polyline, choose the **Polyline** tool from the **Draw** panel, see Figure 3-36. The **Polyline** tool functions fundamentally like the **Line** tool except that some additional options are provided and all the segments of the polyline form a single object. After invoking the **Polyline** tool and specifying the start point, the following prompt is displayed.

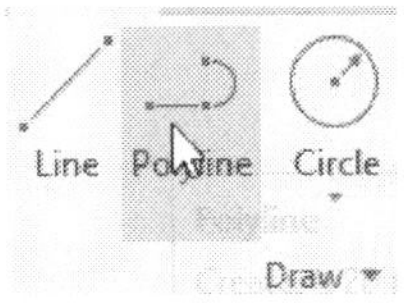

***Figure 3-36** Choosing the **Polyline** tool from the **Draw** panel*

Specify start point: *Specify the starting point or enter its coordinates.*
Current line-width is 0.0000
Specify next point or [Arc/Halfwidth/Length/Undo/Width]:

Note that the message **Current line-width is 0.0000** is displayed automatically indicating that the polyline drawn will have 0.0000 width.

When you are prompted to specify the next point, you can continue specifying the next point and draw a polyline, or depending on your requirements, the other options can be invoked. All these options are discussed next.

Next Point of Line

This is the default option that is displayed after specifying the start point and is used to specify the next point of the current polyline segment. If additional polyline segments are added to the first polyline, AutoCAD LT automatically makes the endpoint of the previous polyline segment as the start point of the next polyline segment. The prompt sequence is given next.

*Choose the **Polyline** tool from the **Draw** panel*
Specify start point: *Specify the start point of the polyline.*
Current line-width is 0.0000.
Specify next point or [Arc/Halfwidth/Length/Undo/Width]: *Specify the endpoint of the first polyline segment.*
Specify next point or [Arc/Close/Halfwidth/Length/Undo/Width]: *Specify the endpoint of the second polyline segment, or press ENTER to exit the tool.*

Width

To change the current width of a polyline, enter **W** (width option) at the last prompt. You can also right-click and choose the **Width** option from the shortcut menu. On doing so, you will be prompted to specify the width at the start and end of the polyline. Specify the widths of the polyline and press ENTER; the polyline of specified width will be drawn.

The starting width value is taken as the ending width value by default. Therefore, to have a uniform polyline, you need to press ENTER at the **Specify ending width <>** prompt. However, if you specify a different value for the ending width, the resulting polyline will be tapered.

For example, to draw a polyline of uniform width 0.25 unit, start point at (4,5), endpoint at (5,5), and the next endpoint at (3,3), use the following prompt sequence:

Choose the ***Polyline*** *tool from the* ***Draw*** *panel*
Specify start point: **4,5** Enter
Current line-width is 0.0000
Specify next point or [Arc/Halfwidth/Length/Undo/Width]: **W** Enter
Specify starting width <current>: **0.25** Enter
Specify ending width <0.25>: Enter
Specify next point or [Arc/Halfwidth/Length/Undo/Width]: **5,5** Enter
Specify next point or [Arc/Close/Halfwidth/Length/Undo/Width]: **3,3** Enter
Specify next point or [Arc/Close/Halfwidth/Length/Undo/Width]: Enter, *See Figure 3-37.*

Similarly, to draw a tapered polyline of starting width 0.5 units and an ending width 0.15 units, a start point at (2,4), and an endpoint at (5,4), use the prompt sequence given next.

Choose the ***Polyline*** *tool from the* ***Draw*** *panel*
Specify start point: **2,4** Enter
Current line-width is 0.0000
Specify next point or [Arc/Halfwidth/Length/Undo/Width]: **W** Enter
Specify starting width <0.0000>: **0.50** Enter, *See Figure 3-38.*
Specify ending width <0.50>: **0.15** Enter
Specify next point or [Arc/Halfwidth/Length/Undo/Width]: **5,4** Enter
Specify next point or [Arc/Close/Halfwidth/Length/Undo/Width]: Enter

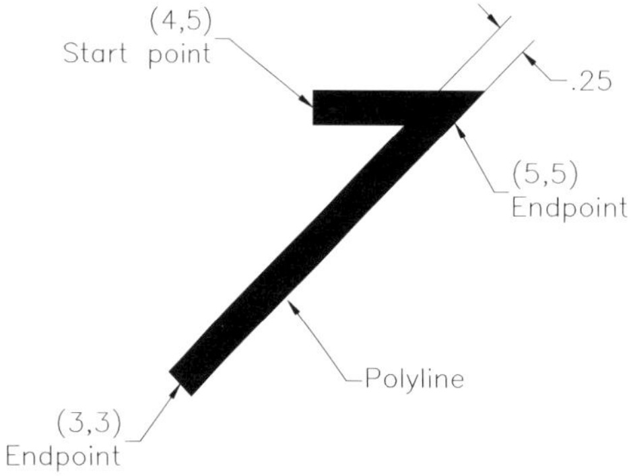

Figure 3-37 *Drawing a uniform polyline using the* ***Polyline*** *tool*

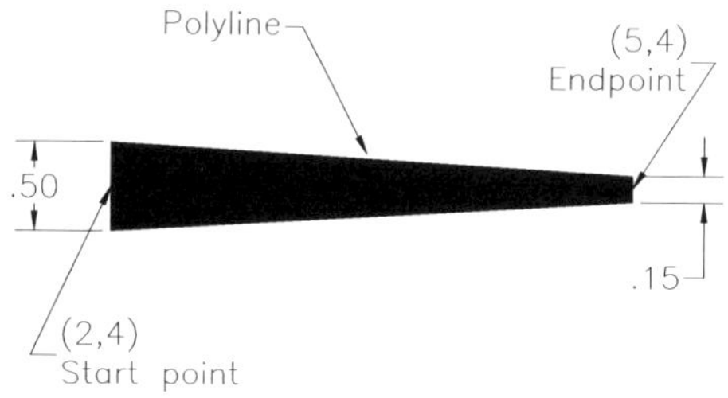

Figure 3-38 *Drawing a tapered polyline using the* ***Polyline*** *tool*

Halfwidth

The halfwidth distance is equal to the half of the actual width of a polyline. This option is invoked by entering **H** or choosing **Halfwidth** from the shortcut menu. The prompt sequence to specify the starting and ending halfwidths of a polyline is given next.

Specify next point or [Arc/Halfwidth/Length/Undo/Width]: **H** Enter
Specify starting half-width <0.0000>: **0.12** Enter *(Specify the desired starting halfwidth)*
Specify ending half-width <0.1200>: **0.05** Enter *(Specify the desired ending halfwidth)*

Length

The **Length** option is used to draw a new polyline segment of specified length and at the same angle as the last polyline segment or tangent to the previous polyarc segment. This option is invoked by entering **L** at the following prompt or by choosing **Length** from the shortcut menu.

Specify next point or [Arc/Close/Halfwidth/Length/Undo/Width]: **L** Enter
Specify length of line: *Specify the desired length of the Pline*

Undo

This option erases the most recently drawn polyline segment. It can be invoked by entering **U** at the **Specify next point or [Arc/Close/Halfwidth/Length/Undo/Width]** prompt. You can use this option repeatedly until you reach the start point of the first polyline segment. If you use this option again, the message **All segments already undone** will be displayed.

Close

This option will be available only when at least one segment of a polyline is drawn. It closes the polyline by drawing a polyline segment from the most recent endpoint to the initial start point. After that exit from the **Polyline** tool.

Arc

This option is used to switch from polylines to polyarcs. You can also set the parameters associated with polyarcs. By default, the arc segment is drawn tangent to the previous segment of the polyline. The direction of the previous line, arc, or polyline segment is the default direction for the polyarc. On invoking the arc option, you need to choose the sub-options to draw the polyarc. Some of the sub-options to draw a polyarc are similar to that of drawing an arc. The sub-options that are different are discussed next.

CLose

This option will be available only when you specify two or more than two points for creating the polyline segments. To join the start and last points of a polyline in the form of an arc, type **CL** at the **Specify endpoint of arc or [Angle/CEnter/CLose/Direction/Halfwidth/Line/Radius/Second pt/Undo/Width]** Command prompt and press ENTER; an arc will be created that will close the loop.

Direction

Usually, the arc drawn by using the **Arc** option of the **Polyline** tool is tangent to the previously drawn polyline segment. In other words, the starting direction of the arc depends upon the ending direction of the previous segment. The **Direction** option is used to specify the direction of the tangent for the arc segment to be drawn. You need to specify the direction by specifying a point. The prompts are given next.

Specify tangent direction for the start point of arc: *Specify the direction.*
Specify endpoint of arc (hold CTRL to switch direction): *Specify the endpoint of arc.*

Halfwidth
The use of this option is similar to the option used for the polyline segment. It is used to specify the starting and ending halfwidths of an arc segment.

Line
This option is used to invoke the **Line** mode again.

Radius
This option is used to specify the radius of the arc segment. The prompt sequence for specifying the radius is given next.

Specify endpoint of arc or [Angle/CEnter/CLose/Direction/Halfwidth/Line/Radius/
Second pt/Undo/Width]: **R**
Specify radius of arc: *Specify the radius of the arc segment.*
Specify endpoint of arc (hold Ctrl to switch direction) or [Angle]: *Specify the endpoint of arc or choose an option.*

If you specify a point, the arc segment will be drawn. If you enter an angle, you will have to specify the angle and the direction of the chord at the **Specify included angle** and **Specify direction of chord for arc (hold Ctrl to switch direction) <current>** prompts, respectively.

Second pt
This option is used to select the second point of an arc in the **3-Point arc** option. The prompt sequence is given next.

Specify second point of arc: *Specify the second point on the arc*
Specify endpoint of arc: *Specify the third point on the arc*

Width
This option is used to enter the width of the arc segment. The prompt sequence for specifying the width is the same as that of the polyline. To draw a tapered arc segment, as shown in Figure 3-39, you need to enter different values at the starting width and ending width prompts.

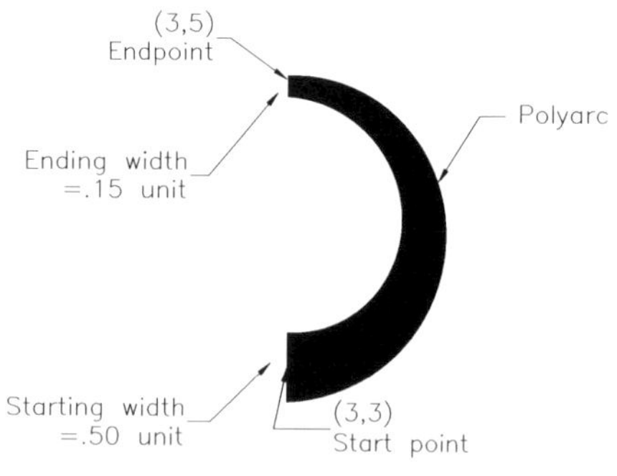

Figure 3-39 *Drawing a polyarc*

The prompt sequence to draw an arc, whose start point is at (3,3), endpoint is at (3,5), starting width is 0.50 unit, and ending width is 0.15 unit, is given next.

*Choose the **Polyline** tool from the **Draw** panel*
Specify start point: **3,3** Enter
Current line-width is 0.0000
Specify next point or [Arc/Halfwidth/Length/Undo/Width]: **A** Enter
Specify endpoint of arc (hold Ctrl to switch direction) or [Angle/CEnter/Direction/Halfwidth/

Line/Radius/Second pt/Undo/Width]: **W** Enter
Specify starting width <current>: **0.50** Enter
Specify ending width <0.50>: **0.15** Enter
Specify endpoint of arc (hold Ctrl to switch direction) or [Angle/CEnter/Direction/Halfwidth/Line/Radius/Second pt/Undo/Width]: **3,5** Enter
Specify endpoint of arc (hold Ctrl to switch direction) or [Angle/CEnter/CLose/Direction/Halfwidth/Line/Radius/Second pt/Undo/Width]: Enter

Tip

*In AutoCAD LT, you can close an open polyline using the **Fillet** tool (by defining radius as zero). To do so, choose the **Fillet** tool from the **Modify** panel of the **Home** tab and select the two openends of the polyline. Figure 3-40 shows an open polyline and Figure 3-41 shows closed polyline after selecting both ends.*

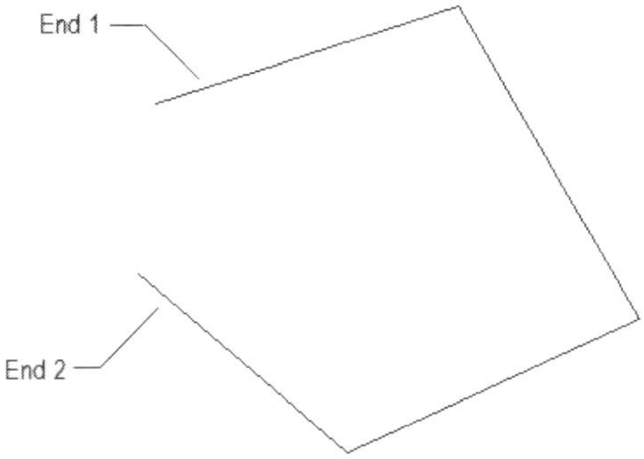

Figure 3-40 *Open polyline with two ends*

Figure 3-41 *Final closed polyline*

Exercise 11

Draw the objects shown in Figures 3-42 and 3-43 by using the polylines of different width.

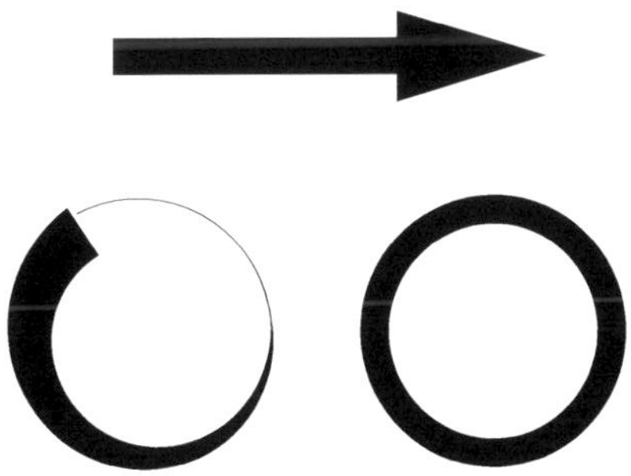

Figure 3-42 *Drawing for Exercise 11*

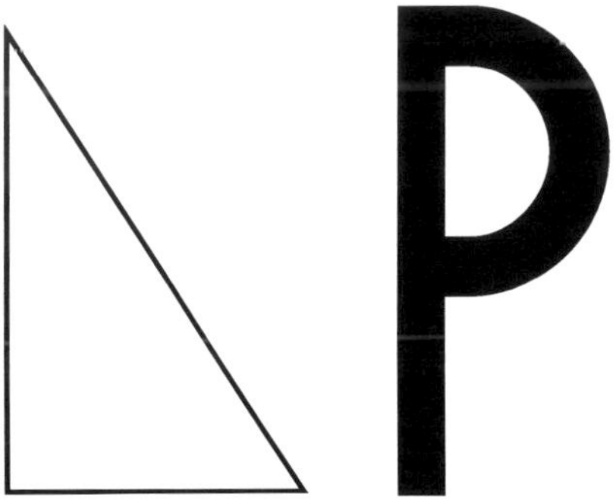

Figure 3-43 *Drawing for Exercise 11*

DRAWING DONUTS

Ribbon: Home > Draw > Donut **Command:** DONUT or DOUGHNUT

In AutoCAD LT, the **Donut** tool is used to draw an object that looks like a filled circle ring called donut. AutoCAD LT'S donuts are made of two semicircular polyarcs with a certain width. Therefore, the **Donut** tool allows you to draw a thick circle. The donuts can have any inside and outside diameters. If **FILLMODE** is off, a donut will look like a circle (if the inside diameter is zero) or a concentric circle (if the inside diameter is not zero). On invoking the **Donut** tool, you will be prompted to specify the diameters. After specifying the two diameters, the donut gets attached to the crosshairs. Specify a point for the center of the donut in the drawing area to place the donut. In this way, you can place as many donuts as required without exiting the tool. Press ENTER to exit the tool.

The default values for the inside and outside diameters of donuts are saved in the **DONUTID** and **DONUTOD** system variables. A solid-filled circle is drawn by specifying the inside diameter as zero, if **FILLMODE** is on.

Example 1 — Donut

You will draw an unfilled donut shown in Figure 3-44 with an inside diameter of 0.75 unit, an outside diameter of 2.0 units, and centered at (2,2). You will also draw a filled donut and a solid-filled donut with the given specifications.

The following is the prompt sequence to draw an unfilled donut shown in Figure 3-44.

Command: **FILLMODE** Enter
New value for FILLMODE <1>: **0** Enter
Command: *Choose the **Donut** tool from the **Draw** panel*
Specify inside diameter of donut<0.5000>: **0.75** Enter
Specify outside diameter of donut <1.000>: **2** Enter
Specify center of donut or <exit>: **2,2** Enter
Specify center of donut or <exit>: Enter

The prompt sequence for drawing a filled donut with an inside diameter of 0.5 unit, outside diameter of 2.0 units, and centre at some specified point is given below:

Command: **FILLMODE** Enter
Enter new value for FILLMODE <0>: **1** Enter
Command: *Choose the **Donut** tool from the **Draw** panel*
Specify inside diameter of donut<0.5000>: **0.50** Enter
Specify outside diameter of donut <1.000>: **2** Enter
Specify center of donut or <exit>: *Specify a point*
Specify center of donut or <exit>: Enter, *See Figure 3-45*

To draw a solid-filled donut with an outside diameter of 2.0 units, use the following prompt sequence:

*Choose the **Donut** tool from the **Draw** panel*
Specify inside diameter of donut <0.50>: **0** Enter
Specify outside diameter of donut <1.0>: **2** Enter
Specify center of donut or <exit>: *Specify a point*
Specify center of donut or <exit>: Enter, *See Figure 3-46*

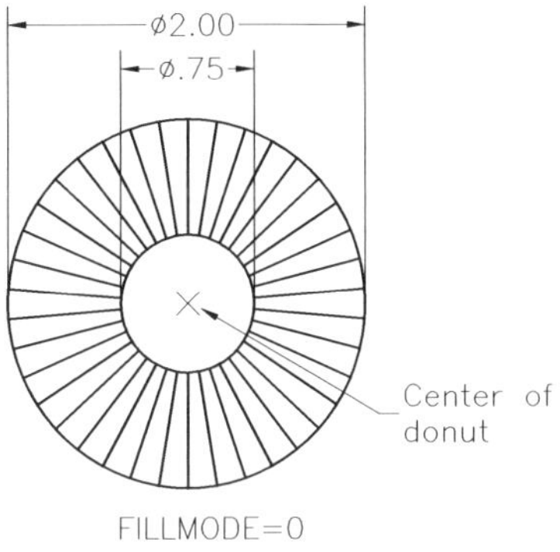

Figure 3-44 *Unfilled donut*

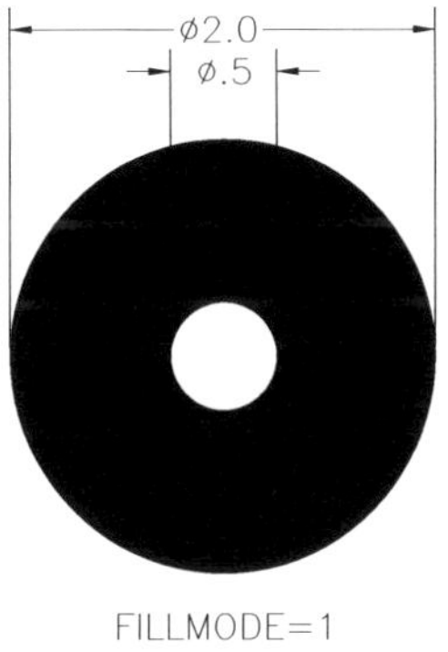

Figure 3-45 *Filled donut*

Figure 3-46 *Solid-filled donut*

PLACING POINTS

A point is one of the basic drawing objects and is specified as a dot (a period). A point is defined as a geometric object that has no dimension and properties except location. However, in AutoCAD LT, you can control the size and appearance (style) of a point. You will first learn to change the point style and size and then about various methods to place a point.

Changing the Point Style and Size

Ribbon: Home > Utilities > Point Style **Command:** DDPTYPE or PTYPE

To change the style and size of a point, choose the **Point Style** tool from the **Utilities** panel in the **Draw** tab; the **Point Style** dialog box will be displayed, as shown in Figure 3-47. Select any one of the twenty point styles in the **Point Style** dialog box. You can specify the point size as a specified percentage of the drawing area or as an absolute size by selecting the **Set Size Relative to Screen** or **Set Size in Absolute Units** radio button respectively. After selecting the appropriate radio button, enter the point size in the **Point Size** edit box. Choose the **OK** button after specifying the parameters. Now, the points will be drawn according to the selected style and size, until you change the style and size. You can also change the point style and the point size by using the **PDMODE** and **PDSIZE** system variables, respectively. The different values of **PDMODE** and the resulting style are shown in Figure 3-48.

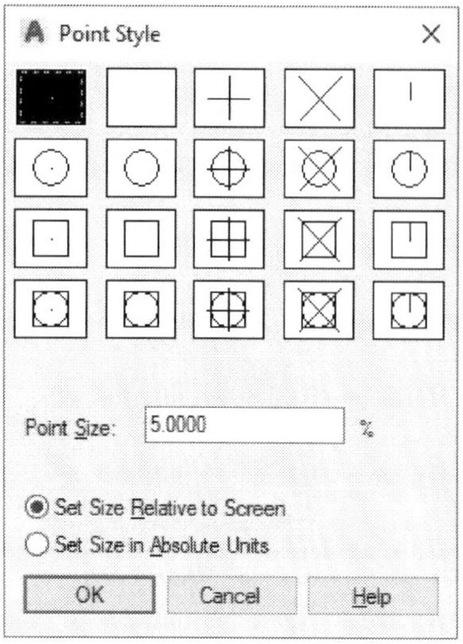

*Figure 3-47 The **Point Style** dialog box*

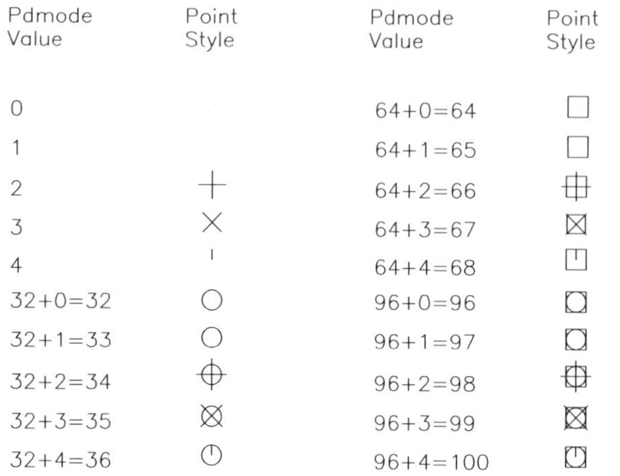

*Figure 3-48 Different point styles for **PDMODE** values*

Note

*On selecting the **Set Size Relative to Screen** radio button, the point size will not change when you zoom in or zoom out the drawing. However, on selecting the **Set Size in Absolute Units** radio button, the size of the point will change when you zoom the drawing in or out.*

Placing Multiple Points

Ribbon: Home > Draw > Multiple Points **Toolbar:** Draw > Point
Menu Bar: Draw > Point > Multiple Point

To place points, choose the **Multiple Points** tool from the **Draw** panel (see Figure 3-49); the current **PDMODE** and **PDSIZE** values will be displayed and you will be prompted to specify a point. Left-click to place a point.

Next, continue placing as many points as needed and then press ESC to exit the command. You can also enter the coordinate value and place a point at a particular location.

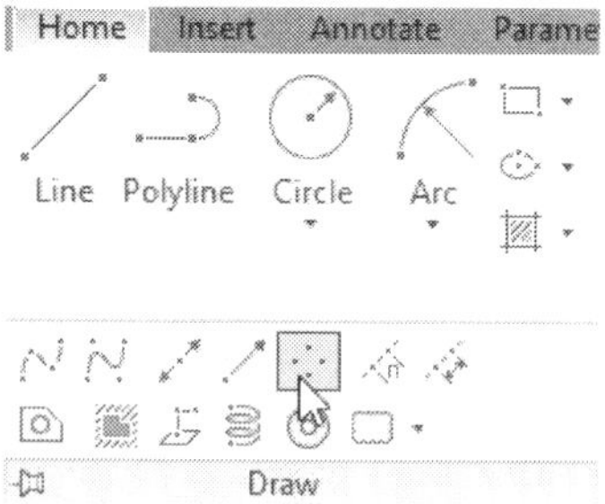

*Figure 3-49 Choosing the **Multiple Points** tool from the **Draw** panel*

Placing Points at Equal Distance

Ribbon: Home > Draw > Divide **Command:** DIV or DIVIDE

To place points at equal an distance on an object, choose the **Divide** tool from the **Draw** panel; you will be prompted to select an object. Select an object; you will be prompted to specify the number of segments. Enter the number of segments; the points will be placed on the object.

Placing Points at Specified Intervals

Ribbon: Home > Draw > Measure **Command:** MEASURE

You can place points at specified intervals on an object by selecting the object and specifying the length of the segment between two points. To do so, choose the **Measure** tool from the **Draw** panel; you will be prompted to select the object to measure. Select the object; you will be prompted to specify the length of the segment. Specify the length of the segment; the points will be placed at specified intervals.

Exercise 12 ***PDMODE and PDSIZE***

a. Try various combinations of the **PDMODE** and **PDSIZE** variables.

b. Check the difference between the points generated by using the negative values of **PDSIZE** and the points generated by using the positive values of **PDSIZE**.

DRAWING INFINITE LINES

In AutoCAD LT, you can draw a construction line or a ray that aids in construction or projection. A construction line (xline) is a 3D line that extends to infinity from both the ends. As the line is infinite in length, it does not have any endpoint, whereas, a ray is a 3D line that extends to infinity from one end. The other end of the ray is a finite endpoint. The xlines and rays have zero extents. This means that the extents of the drawing will not change, if you use the **Zoom All** tool. Most of the object snap modes work with both xlines and rays with some limitations. You cannot use the **Endpoint** object snap with the xline because by definition an xline does not have any endpoints. However, for rays, you can use the **Endpoint** snap on one end only. Also, xlines and rays take the properties of the layer, in which they are drawn.

Tip
Sometimes, Xlines and rays when plotted like any other object may create confusion. Therefore, it is recommended to create the construction lines in a different layer altogether such that you can recognize them easily. You will learn about layers in the later chapters.

Drawing Construction Lines

Ribbon: Home > Draw > Construction Line **Toolbar:** Draw > Construction Line
Command: XLINE

To draw a construction line that extends to infinity from both sides, invoke the **Construction Line** tool from the **Draw** panel. The prompt sequence that is displayed on choosing this tool is as follows:

Specify a point or [Hor/Ver/Ang/Bisect/Offset]: *Specify an option or select a point through which the xline will pass.*

The various options displayed on invoking the **Construction Line** tool are discussed next.

Point

If you use the default option, you need to specify two points through which the xline will pass. After specifying the first point, move the cursor; a line will get attached to the cursor. On specifying the second point, an xline will be created that passes through the first and second points (Figure 3-50).

Specify a point or [Hor/Ver/Ang/Bisect/Offset]: *Specify a point.*
Specify through point: *Specify the second point.*

You can continue to select more points to create more xlines. All these xlines will pass through the first point you had selected at the **Specify a point** prompt. This point is also called the root point. Right-click or press ENTER to exit the tool.

Horizontal

This option is used to create horizontal xlines of infinite length that pass through the selected points. The xlines will be parallel to the *X* axis of the current UCS, see Figure 3-51. On invoking this option, a horizontal xline will be attached to the cursor and you will be prompted to select a point through which the horizontal xline will pass. Specify a point. You can continue specifying more points to draw more horizontal xlines. To exit the tool, right-click or press ENTER.

Vertical

This option is used to create vertical xlines of infinite length that pass through the selected points. The xlines will be parallel to the *Y* axis of the current UCS, see Figure 3-51.

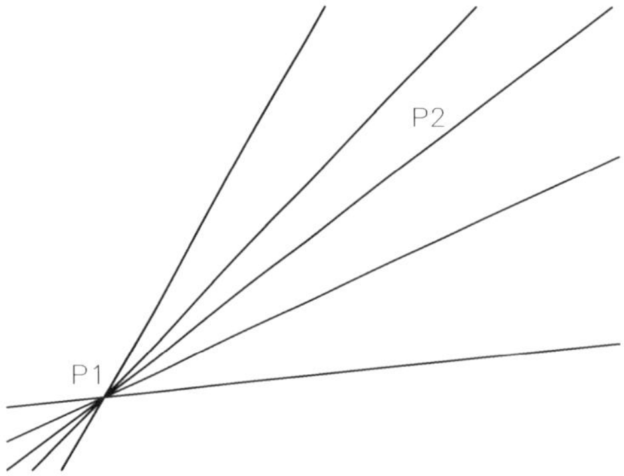

Figure 3-50 *Drawing the xlines*

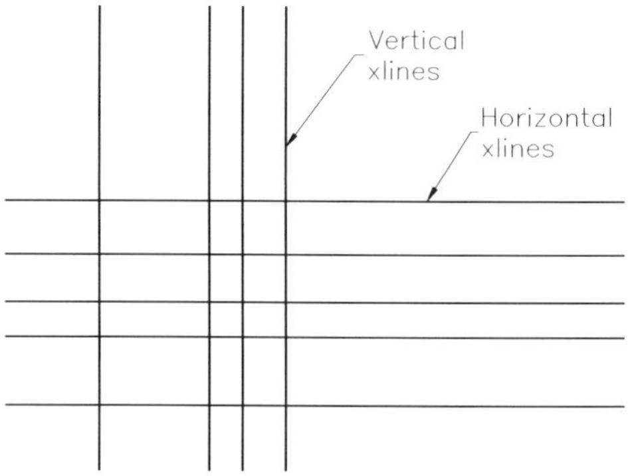

Figure 3-51 *Horizontal and vertical xlines*

Angular

This option is used to create xlines of infinite length that pass through the selected point at same specified angle (see Figure 3-52). The angle can be specified by entering a value. You can also invoke the **Reference** option by selecting an object and then specifying an angle relative to it. The **Reference** option is useful when the actual angle is not known, but the angle relative to an existing object can be specified.

*Choose the **Construction Line** tool from the **Draw** panel*
Enter angle of xline (0) or [Reference]: **R** Enter *(Use the **Reference** method to specify the angle)*

Select a line object: *Select a line.*
Enter angle of xline <0>: *Enter angle (the angle will be measured counterclockwise with respect to the selected line)*
Specify through point: *Specify the second point.*

Bisect

This option is used to create an xline that bisects an angle. In this case, you need to specify the vertex, start point, and endpoint of the angle. The xline will pass through the vertex and bisect the angle specified by selecting two points. The xline created using this option will lie on the plane defined by the selected points. The following is the prompt sequence for this option, refer to Figure 3-53.

*Choose the **Construction Line** tool from the **Draw** panel*
XLINE Specify a point or [Hor/Ver/Ang/Bisect/Offset]: **B** Enter
Specify angle vertex point: *Enter a point (P1).*
Specify angle start point: *Enter a point (P2).*
Specify angle end point: *Enter a point (P3).*
Specify angle end point: *Select more points or press ENTER or right-click to end the tool.*

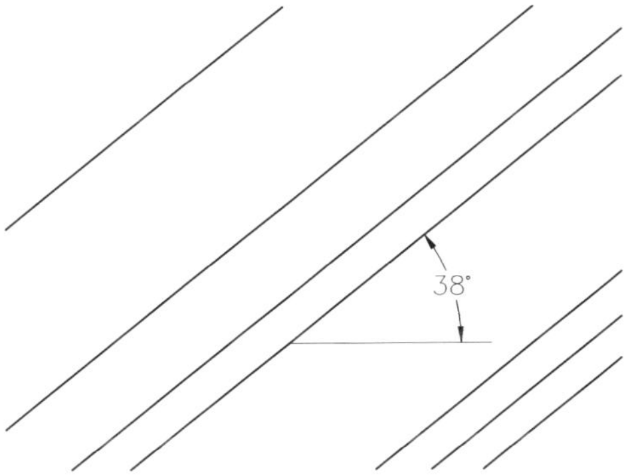

Figure 3-52 *The angular xlines*

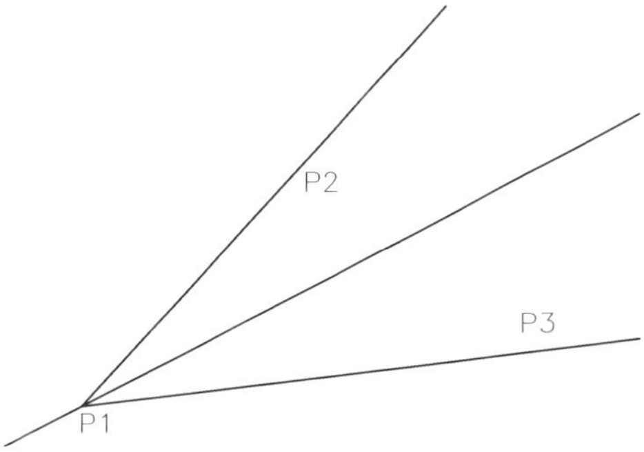

Figure 3-53 *Using the **Bisect** option to draw xlines*

Offset

The **Offset** option is used to create xlines that are parallel to a selected line/xline at a specified offset distance. You can specify the offset distance by entering a numerical value or by selecting two points on the screen. If you choose the **Through** option, the offset line will pass through the selected point. The following is the prompt sequence for this option:

*Choose the **Construction Line** tool from the **Draw** panel*
XLINE Specify a point or [Hor/Ver/Ang/Bisect/Offset]: **O** Enter
Specify offset distance or [Through] <Through>: *Press ENTER to accept the **Through** option or specify a distance from the selected line object at which the xline shall be drawn.*
Select a line object: *Select the object to which the xline is drawn parallel and at a specified distance.*
Specify through point: *Select a point through which the xline should pass.*

After specifying the offset distance and selecting a line object, you need to specify the direction in which the xline has to be offset. You can continue drawing construction lines or right-click or press ENTER to exit the tool.

Drawing Ray

Ribbon: Home > Draw > Ray **Command:** RAY

A ray is a 3D line similar to the xline construction line with the difference being that it extends to infinity only in one direction. It starts from a specified point and extends to infinity through the specified point. The prompt sequence is given next.

Specify start point: *Select the start point for the ray.*
Specify through point: *Specify the second point.*

Press ENTER or right-click to exit the tool.

WRITING A SINGLE LINE TEXT

Ribbon: Home > Annotation > Text drop-down > Single Line **Command:** TEXT

The **Single Line** tool is used to write a single line text. Although you can write more than one line of text using this command, but each line will be a separate text entity. To write text, choose the **Single Line** tool from **Home > Annotation > Multiline Text** drop-down. This tool is also available in the **Multiline Text** drop-down available in the **Text** panel of the **Annotate** tab. After invoking this tool, you need to specify the start point for the text. Next, you need to specify the text height and the rotation angle. As you enter the characters, they start appearing on the screen. After typing a line if you press ENTER, the cursor will be automatically placed at the start of the next line and the prompt for entering another line will be repeated. Type another line or press ENTER again to exit the tool. You can use the BACKSPACE key to edit the text on the screen while writing it. The prompt sequence is given next.

*Choose the **Single Line** tool from the **Annotation** panel*
Current text style: "Standard" Text height: 0.2000 Annotative: No Justify: Left
Specify start point of text or [Justify/Style]: *Specify the starting point of the text.*
Specify height<current>: *Enter the text height.*
Specify rotation angle of text <0>: Enter
Enter the first line of the text in the text box displayed in the drawing window.
Enter the second line of the text in the text box displayed in the drawing window.
Press ENTER twice to exit.

Note

The other tools to enter text are discussed in detail in Chapter 7.

Self-Evaluation Test

Answer the following questions and then compare them to those given at the end of this chapter:

1. The __________ option of the **Rectangle** tool is used to draw a rectangle at a specified distance from the XY plane along the Z axis.

2. If the **FILLMODE** is set to __________, only the outlines for the new polyline will be drawn.

3. You can get a __________ polyline by entering two different values at the starting width and ending width prompts.

4. Choose the __________ tool from the **Draw** panel to place points at specified intervals on an object.

5. Choose the __________ tool from the **Draw** panel to draw as many points as you want in a single command.

6. The size of a point will be taken as a percentage of the viewport size if you enter a __________ value for the **PDSIZE** variable.

7. While drawing an arc by choosing the **Start, Center, Angle** tool, if you enter the included angle with a negative value, an arc will be drawn in a clockwise direction. (T/F)

8. After choosing the **Arc** tool, if you press ENTER instead of specifying the start point, the start point and direction of the arc will be taken from the endpoint and ending direction of the previous line or the arc drawn. (T/F)

9. A rectangle can be drawn by specifying the dimension using the **Dimension** option. (T/F)

10. The start and end parameters of an elliptical arc are determined by specifying a point on the circle whose diameter is equal to the minor diameter of an ellipse. (T/F)

Review Questions

Answer the following questions:

1. On drawing an arc by choosing the **Start, Center, Length** tool, a positive chord length generates the smallest possible arc (minor arc), and the arc is always less than:

   (a) 90 degree (b) 180 degree
   (c) 270 degree (d) 360 degree

2. Which one of the following options of the **Rectangle** tool is used to draw a rectangle that is extruded in the Z direction by a specified value?

   (a) **Elevation** (b) **Thickness**
   (c) **Extrude** (d) **Width**

3. Which of the following tools should be used to draw a line in 3D space that starts from a specified start point and the other end extends to infinity?

   (a) **Polyline** (b) **Ray**
   (c) **Construction Line** (d) **Multiline Text**

4. A polygon is said to be __________ when it is drawn inside an imaginary circle and its vertices touch the circle.

5. If additional polyline segments are added to the first polyline, the __________ of the first polyline segment becomes the start point of the next polyline segment.

6. To create a solid-filled circle by using the **Donut** tool, the value of the inside diameter of the circle should be __________.

7. By using the **Donut** tool, you can draw a solid-filled circle by specifying the inside diameter as __________ and keeping the **FILLMODE** on.

8. The __________ option of the **Construction Line** tool is used to create construction lines of infinite length that are parallel to the *Y* axis of the current UCS.

9. You can use the __________ key to edit text on the screen while writing it using the **Single Line** tool.

10. While drawing an arc by choosing the **Start, End, Angle** tool, a negative included angle value draws the arc in clockwise direction. (T/F)

11. When the **Continue** option of the **Arc** tool is used to draw arcs, each successive arc is perpendicular to the previous one. (T/F)

12. If you first specify the chamfer distances first and then specify the fillet radius of the same **Rectangle** tool, the rectangle will be drawn with chamfers only. (T/F)

13. A rectangle drawn using the **Rectangle** tool is treated as a combination of different objects; therefore individual sides can be edited independently. (T/F)

Exercise 13 *Arc*

Draw the sketch shown in Figure 3-54. The distance between the dotted lines is 1.0 unit. Create arcs by choosing appropriate tools from the **Arc** drop-down.

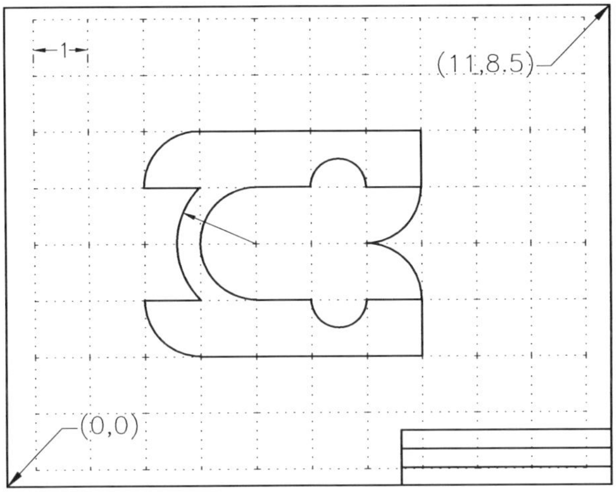

Figure 3-54 Drawing for Exercise 13

Exercise 14 Ellipse

Draw the sketch shown in Figure 3-55. The distance between the dotted lines is 0.5 unit. Create ellipses using the tools in the **Ellipse** drop-down.

Figure 3-55 Drawing for Exercise 14

Exercise 15

Draw the sketch shown in Figure 3-56 using the **Line**, **Circle**, and **Arc** tools. The distance between the dotted lines is 1.0 unit and the diameter of the circles is 1.0 unit.

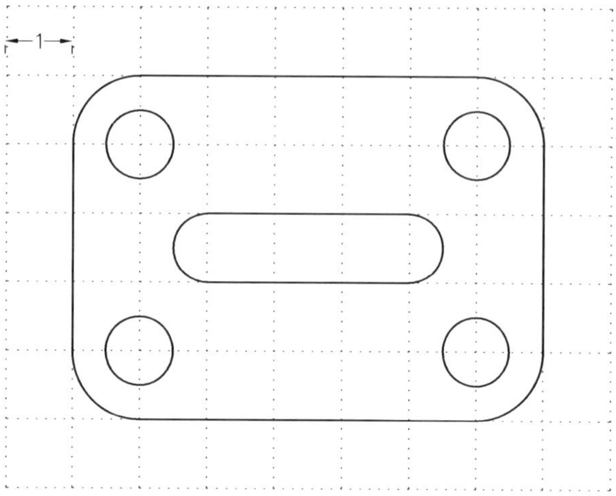

Figure 3-56 Drawing for Exercise 15

Exercise 16

Draw the sketch shown in Figure 3-57 using the **Line**, **Circle**, and **Arc** tools or their options. The distance between the grid lines is 1.0 unit and the diameter of the circle is 1.0 unit.

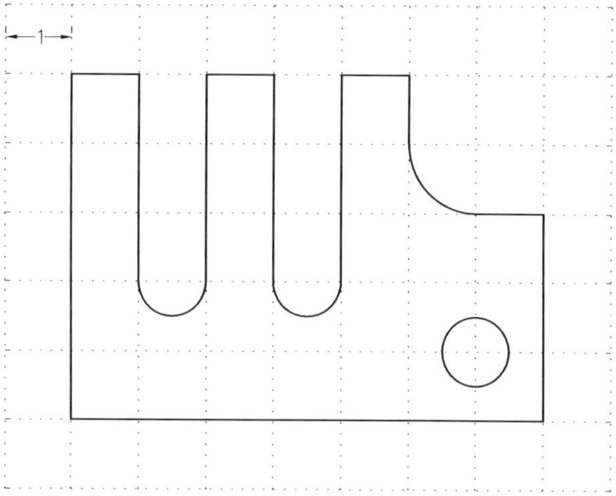

Figure 3-57 Drawing for Exercise 16

Exercise 17

Draw the object shown in Figure 3-58. The distance between the dotted lines is 5 inches. Determine the limits for this drawing and use the Fractional units with 0 1/16 precision.

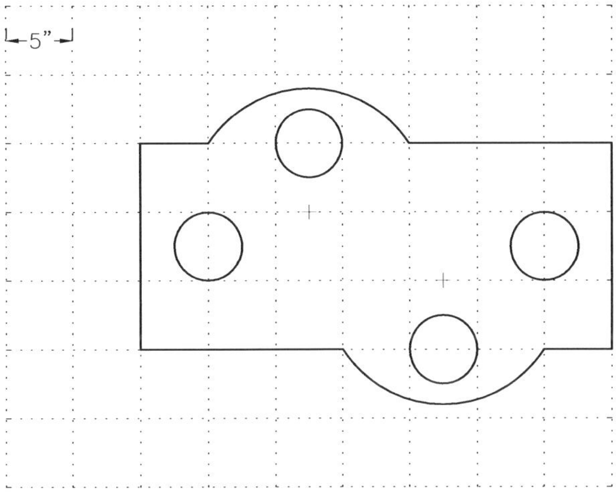

Figure 3-58 *Drawing for Exercise 17*

Problem-Solving Exercise 1 — Arc

Draw the sketch shown in Figure 3-59. Next, create arcs by using the **Arc** tools, indicated in the drawing. (Use the @ symbol to snap to the previous point. Example: Specify start point of arc or [Center]: @)

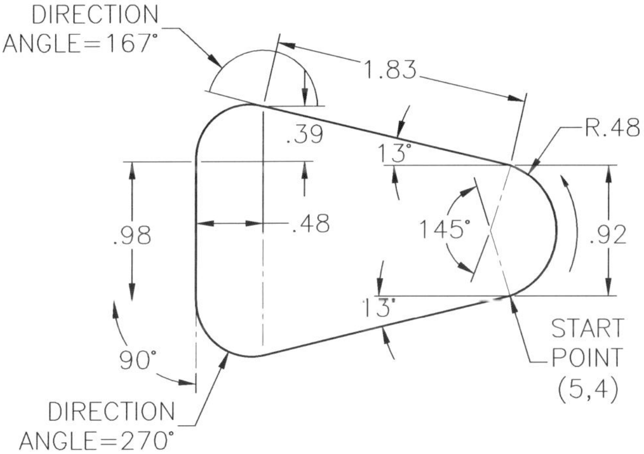

Figure 3-59 *Drawing for Problem-Solving Exercise 1*

Problem-Solving Exercise 2 Arc

Draw the sketch shown in Figure 3-60. Create arcs by using the **Arc** tools. The distance between the dotted lines is 0.5 unit.

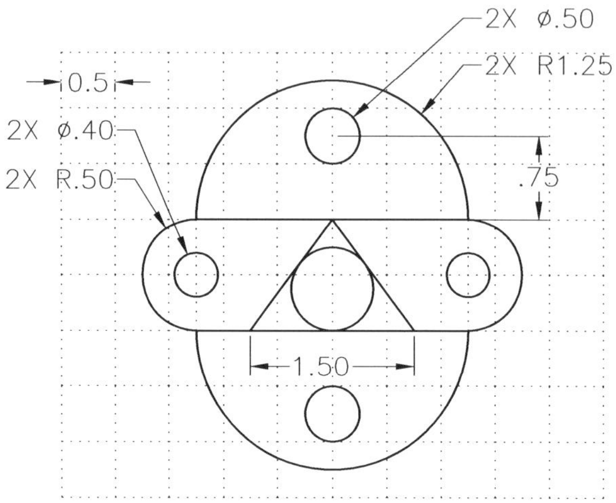

Figure 3-60 *Drawing for Problem-Solving Exercise 2*

Problem-Solving Exercise 3 Arc

Draw the sketch shown in Figure 3-61 by using different tools in the **Draw** panel. Note, Sin30=0.5 and Sin60=0.866. The distance between the dotted lines is 1 unit.

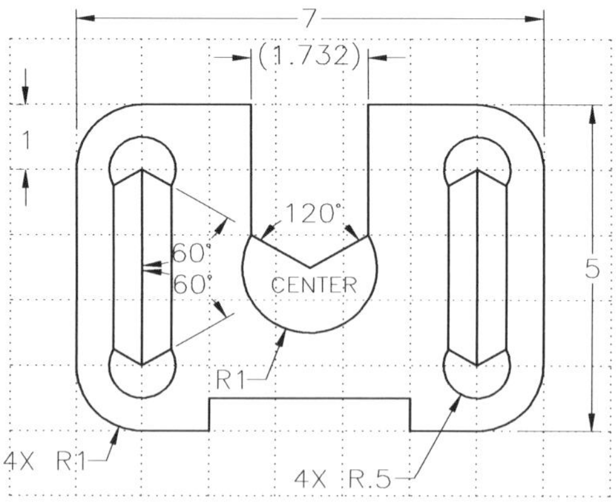

Figure 3-61 *Drawing for Problem-Solving Exercise 3*

Problem-Solving Exercise 4

Draw the sketch shown in Figure 3-62 using the **Polygon**, **Circle**, and **Line** tools.

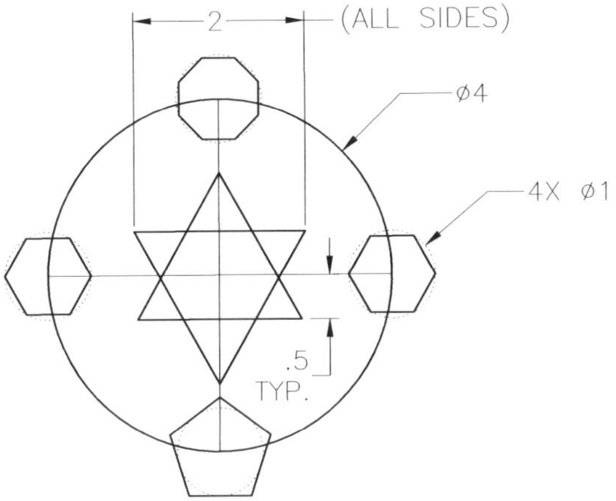

Figure 3-62 *Drawing for Problem-Solving Exercise 4*

Problem-Solving Exercise 5

Draw the sketch shown in Figure 3-63 by using different tools in the **Draw** panel. Also, draw the hidden lines and center lines as continuous lines. Note that the dimensions are given only for your reference.

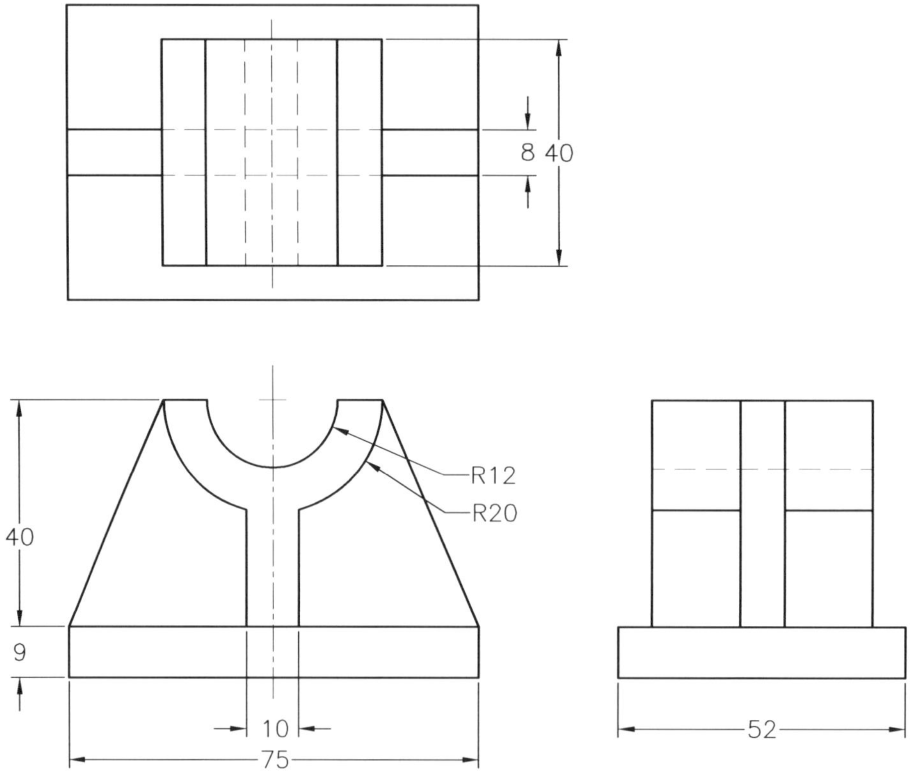

Figure 3-63 *Drawing for the Problem-Solving Exercise 5*

Answers to Self-Evaluation Test

1. Elevation, **2.** 0, **3.** tapered, **4. Measure**, **5. Multiple Point**, **6.** Negative, **7.** T, **8.** T, **9.** T, **10.** F

Chapter 4

Working with Drawing Aids

Learning Objectives

After completing this chapter, you will be able to:

- *Set up layers, and assign colors and line type to them*
- *Change general object properties using the Properties toolbar*
- *Change object properties using the Properties tool*
- *Determine the line type scaling and the LTSCALE factor for plotting*
- *Set up Grid, Snap, and Ortho modes*
- *Use the object snaps and run the Object Snap modes*
- *Use AutoTracking to locate keypoints in a drawing*

Key Terms

- *Layer*
- *Freeze*
- *Thaw*
- *Plot Style*
- *Reconciling Layers*
- *Isolating Layers*
- *Quick Properties*
- *Global Linetype scaling*
- *Current Linetype scaling*
- *DesignCenter*
- *DSETTINGS*
- *OSNAP*

INTRODUCTION

In this chapter, you will learn about the drawing setup and the factors that affect the quality and accuracy of a drawing. This chapter contains a detailed description of the procedure of setting up a layer. You will also learn about some other drawing aids, such as Grid, Snap, and Ortho. These aids will help you create drawings accurately and quickly.

UNDERSTANDING THE CONCEPT AND USE OF LAYERS

The concept of layers can be best explained by using the concept of overlays in manual drafting. In manual drafting, different details of a drawing can be drawn on different sheets of paper or overlays. Each overlay is perfectly aligned with the others. Once all of them are placed on top of each other, you can reproduce the entire drawing. For example, in Figure 4-1, the object lines are drawn in the first overlay and the dimensions in the second overlay. You can place these overlays on top of each other and get a combined look of the drawing.

In AutoCAD LT, instead of using overlays, you can use layers. Each layer is assigned a name. You can also assign a color and a line type to a layer. For example, in Figure 4-2, the object lines are drawn in the OBJECT layer and the dimensions are drawn in the DIM layer. The object lines will be red because red has been assigned to the OBJECT layer. Similarly, the dimension lines will be green because green has been assigned to the DIM layer. You can display the layers together, individually, or in any combination.

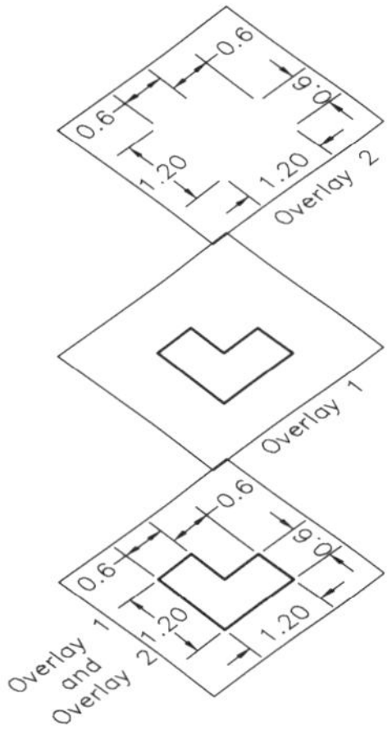

Figure 4-1 Drawing lines and dimensions in different overlays

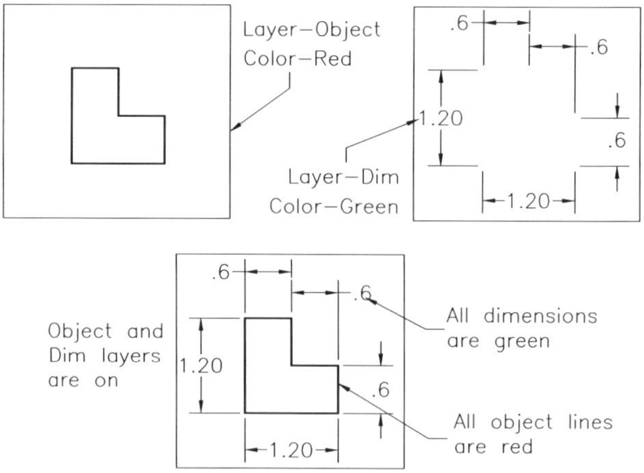

Figure 4-2 Drawing lines and dimensions in different layers

Advantages of Using Layers

1. Each layer can be assigned a different color. Assigning a particular color to a group of objects is very important for plotting. For example, if all object lines are red, then at the time of plotting, you can assign the red color to a slot (pen) that has the desired tip width. Similarly, if the dimensions are green, you can assign the green color to another slot (pen) that has a thin tip. By assigning different colors to different layers, you can control the width of lines while plotting the drawing. You can also make a layer plotable or non-plotable.

2. Layers are also useful for performing some editing operations. For example, to erase all dimensions in a drawing, you can freeze or lock all layers except the dimension layer, then select all objects by using the Window Crossing option and erase all dimensions.
3. You can turn off a layer or freeze a layer that you do not want to be displayed or plotted.
4. You can lock a layer to prevent the user from accidentally editing the objects in it.
5. Colors also help you distinguish different groups of objects. For example, in architectural drafting, the plans for foundation, floors, plumbing, electrical work, and heating systems may be made in different layers. In electronic drafting and in PCB (printed circuit board), the design of each level of a multilevel circuit board can be drawn on a separate layer. Similarly, in mechanical engineering, the main components of an assembly can be made in one layer, other components such as nuts, bolts, keys, and washers can be made in another layer, and the annotations such as datum symbols and identifiers, texture symbols, Balloons, and Bill of Materials can be made in yet another layer.

WORKING WITH LAYERS

Ribbon: Home > Layers > Layer Properties **Command:** LAYER or LA
Toolbar: Layers > Layer Properties Manager

You can freeze, thaw, lock, unlock layers using the **Layers** panel in the **Ribbon** (see Figure 4-3). However, to add new layers, to delete the existing layers, or to assign colors and linetypes to layers, you need to invoke the **LAYER PROPERTIES MANAGER.**

To invoke the **LAYER PROPERTIES MANAGER**, choose the **Layer Properties** button from the **Layers** panel in the **Home** tab, or invoke it from the **Layers** toolbar, (see Figure 4-4).

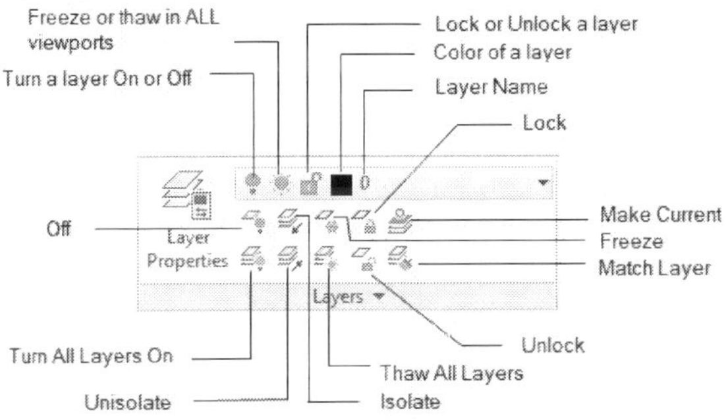

Figure 4-3 *The **Layers** panel*

Figure 4-4 *The **Layers** toolbar*

On invoking the **LAYER PROPERTIES MANAGER**, a default layer with the name 0 is displayed. It is the current layer and any object you draw is created in it. The current layer can be recognized by the green colored tick mark in the **Status** column. There are certain features such as color, linetype, and lineweight that are associated with each layer. The **0** layer has the default color as white, linetype as continuous, and lineweight as default.

Creating New Layers

To create new layers, choose the **New Layer** button in the **LAYER PROPERTIES MANAGER**; a new layer, named Layer1, with the same properties as that of the current layer will be created and listed, as shown in Figure 4-5. Alternatively, right-click anywhere in the **Layers** list area of the **LAYER PROPERTIES MANAGER** and then choose the **New Layer** option from the shortcut menu to create a new layer. If there are more layers and you right-click on a layer other than the current layer and then choose **New Layer** from the shortcut menu, a new layer will be created with the properties similar to the layer on which you right-clicked. To create a new layer that is automatically frozen in all viewports, choose the **New Layer VP Frozen in All Viewports** button.

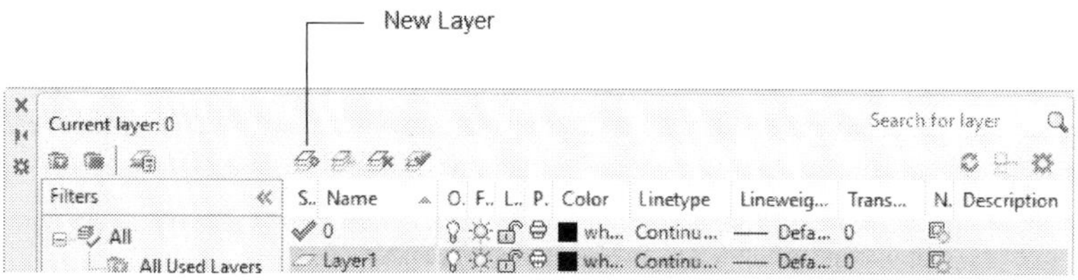

***Figure 4-5** Partial view of the **LAYER PROPERTIES MANAGER** with the new layer created*

Naming a New Layer

New layers are created with the name layer 1, layer 2, and so on. To change or edit the name of a layer, select it, then click once in the field corresponding to the **Name** column, and enter a new name. Some of the points to be remembered while naming a layer are given below.

1. A layer name can be up to 255 characters long, including letters (a-z), numbers (0-9), special characters ($ _ -), and spaces. Any combination of lower and uppercase letters can be used while naming a layer. However, characters such as <>/\;:,’?*|”=, and so on are not valid characters while naming a layer.
2. Layers should be named to help the user identify the contents of the layer. For example, if a layer name is HATCH, a user can easily identify it and its contents. On the other hand, if a layer's name is X261, it is hard to identify its contents.
3. Layer names should be short, but should also convey the meaning.

Tip

If you exchange drawings or provide drawings to consultants or others, it is very important that you standardize and coordinate layer names and other layer settings.

Making a Layer Current

To draw an object in a particular layer, you need to make it the current layer. There are different methods to make a layer current and these are listed below.

1. Double-click on the name of a layer in the list box in the **LAYER PROPERTIES MANAGER**; the selected layer is made current.
2. Select the name of the layer in the **LAYER PROPERTIES MANAGER** and then choose the **Set Current** button in the **LAYER PROPERTIES MANAGER**.
3. Right-click on a layer in the **Layer** list box in the **LAYER PROPERTIES MANAGER** and choose the **Set current** option from the shortcut menu displayed, see Figure 4-6.
4. Select a layer from the **Layer** drop-down list in the **Layers** toolbar or from the **Layers** panel. Choose the **Make Current** button from the **Layers** panel; you will be prompted to select the object whose layer you want to make current. Select the required object; the layer associated with that object will become current.

On making a layer as the current layer, a green color tick mark will be displayed in the **Status** column of that layer. The name and properties of the current layer will be displayed in the **Layers** toolbar and the name of the current layer will be displayed at the upper-left corner of the **LAYER PROPERTIES MANAGER**.

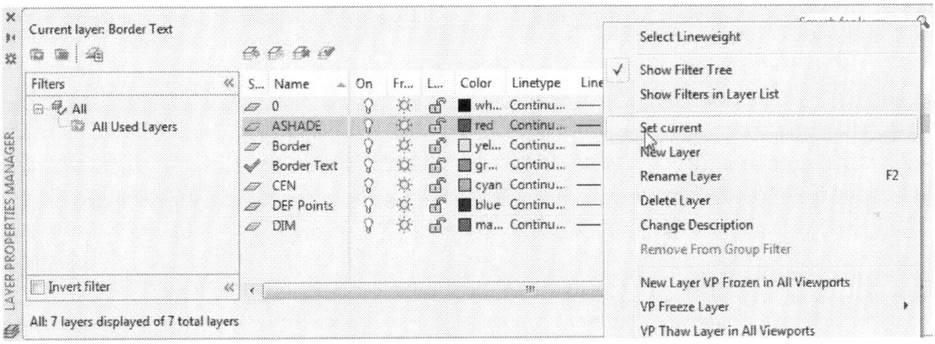

***Figure 4-6** The **LAYER PROPERTIES MANAGER** with the shortcut menu*

Note

*If you select more than one layer at a time using the SHIFT or CTRL key, the **Set Current** option does not appear in the shortcut menu in the **LAYER PROPERTIES MANAGER**. This is because only one layer can be made current at a time.*

Controlling the Display of Layers

You can control the display of layers by using the display options from the **LAYER PROPERTIES MANAGER**. These options are discussed next.

Turn a layer On or Off

Choose the **Turn a layer On or Off** toggle icon (bulb) to turn a layer on or off. You can also turn the layer on or off by clicking on the **On/Off** toggle icon located in the **Layer** drop-down list in the **Layers** toolbar or the **Layers** panel, as shown in Figure 4-7. The objects in the layers that are turned on are displayed and can be plotted, while the objects in the layers that are turned off are not displayed and cannot be plotted. However, you can perform the operations such as drawing and editing of the objects in the layer that has been turned off. You can turn the current layer off, but AutoCAD LT will display a message box informing you that the current drawing layer has been turned off.

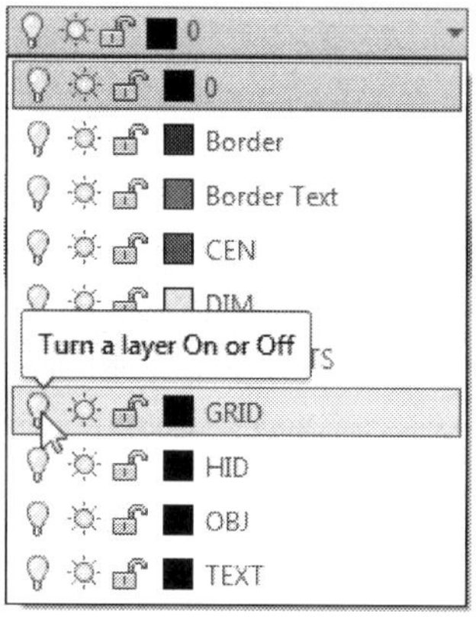

***Figure 4-7** Turning off the **GRID** layer*

Freeze or thaw in ALL Viewports

Sometimes, in an architectural drawing, you may not need the door tag, window tag, or surveyor data to be displayed, so that they are not changed. These types of information or entities can be placed in a particular layer and that layer can be frozen. You cannot edit the entities in the frozen layer. Also, frozen layers are invisible and cannot be plotted. To freeze a layer, select it and choose the **Freeze or thaw in ALL viewports** toggle icon (sun/snowflakes) in the **LAYER PROPERTIES MANAGER**. Note that the current layer cannot be frozen. You can also choose the **Freeze or thaw in ALL viewports** toggle icon in the **Layers** panel of the **Ribbon** or in the **Layers** toolbar to freeze or thaw a layer. The **Thaw** option negates the effect of the **Freeze** option, and the frozen layers are restored to normal. The difference between the usage of the **Off** option and the **Freeze** option is that in using the **Freeze** option, the layer is frozen and the entities in the frozen layer are not regenerated and thus save time.

New VP Freeze

On choosing the **Layout** tab, you will observe that a default viewport is displayed in the drawing area. You can also create new viewports anytime during the design. If you want to freeze some layers in all the subsequent new viewports, select the layers, and then choose the **New VP Freeze** toggle icon. The selected layers will be frozen in all the subsequently created viewports, without affecting the existing viewports.

VP Freeze

This icon will be available only if you invoke the **LAYER PROPERTIES MANAGER** in the **Layout** tab, see Figure 4-8. The **Freeze or thaw in current viewport** icon will also be available in the **Layer** drop-down list in the **Layers** panel of the **Ribbon** or in the **Layers** toolbar. If there are multiple viewports, make a viewport as the current viewport by double-clicking in it and freeze or thaw the selected layer in it by choosing the **VP Freeze** icon in the **LAYER PROPERTIES**

MANAGER. However, a layer that is frozen in the model space cannot be thawed in the current viewport.

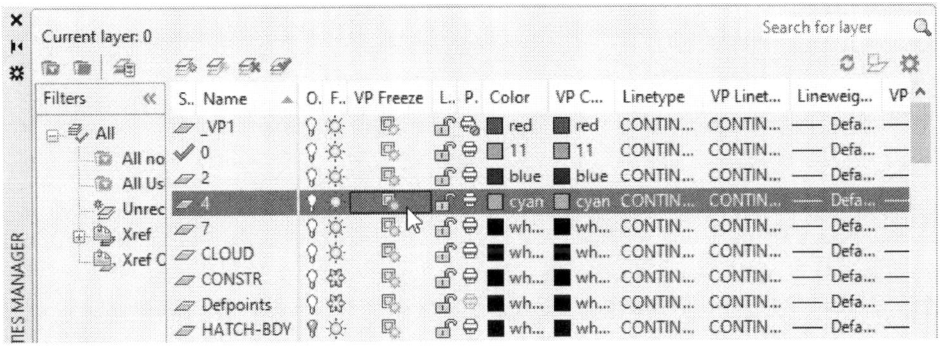

*Figure 4-8 Partial view of the **LAYER PROPERTIES MANAGER** with the **VP Freeze** icon*

Lock or Unlock a Layer

While working on a drawing, if you want to avoid editing some objects on a particular layer but still need to have them visible, use the **Lock/Unlock** toggle icon to lock the layer. However, you can still use the objects in the locked layer for **Object Snaps** and inquiry tools such as **List**. You can also make the locked layer as the current layer and draw objects on it. Note that you can also plot a locked layer. The **Unlock** option negates the **Lock** option and allows you to edit objects on the layers that were previously locked.

Make a Layer Plotable or Non plotable

By default, you can plot all layers, except the layers that are turned off or frozen. If you do not want to plot a layer that is not turned off or frozen, select the layer and choose the **Plot** icon (printer). This is a toggle icon, therefore you can choose this icon again to plot the layer.

Assigning Linetype to a Layer

By default, continuous linetypes are assigned to a layer, if no layer is selected while creating a new layer. Otherwise, new layer takes the properties of the selected layer. To assign a new linetype to a layer, click on the field under the **Linetype** column of that layer in the **LAYER PROPERTIES MANAGER**; the **Select Linetype** dialog box showing the linetypes loaded on your computer will be displayed. Select the new linetype and then choose the **OK** button; the selected linetype will be assigned to the layer. If you are opening the **Select Linetype** dialog box for the first time, only the **Continuous** linetype will be displayed, as shown in Figure 4-9.

You need to load linetypes and then assign them to layers. To load linetypes, choose the **Load** button in the **Select Linetype** dialog box; the **Load or Reload Linetypes** dialog box will be displayed, see Figure 4-10. This dialog box displays all linetypes in the *acadlt.in* or *acadltiso.lin* file. In this dialog box, you can select a single linetype, or a number of linetypes by pressing and holding the SHIFT or CTRL key and then selecting the linetypes. After selecting the linetypes, choose the **OK** button; the selected linetypes are loaded in the **Select Linetype** dialog box. Now, select the desired linetype and choose **OK**; the selected linetype is assigned to the selected layer.

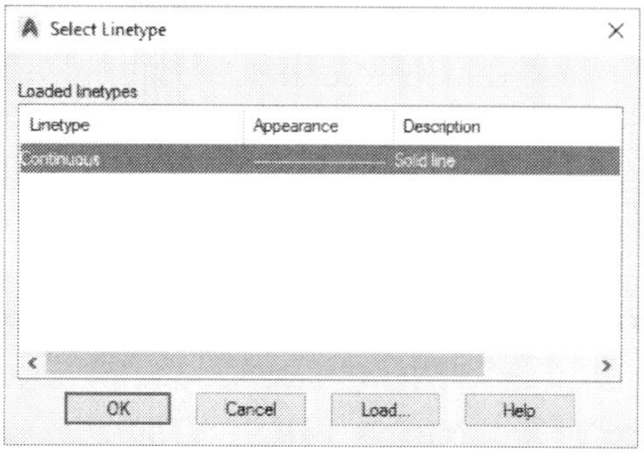

Figure 4-9 *The* ***Select Linetype*** *dialog box*

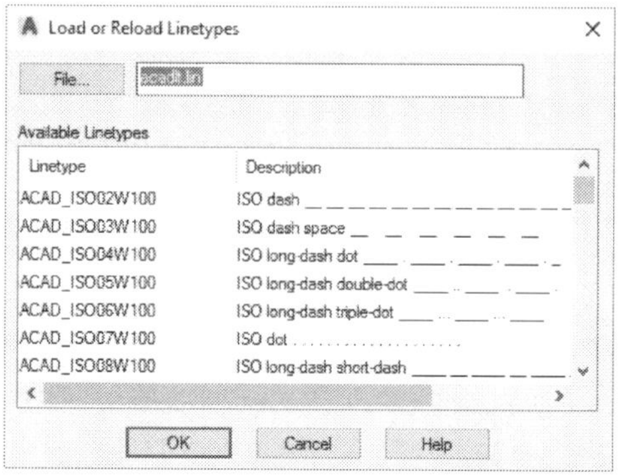

Figure 4-10 *The* ***Load or Reload Linetypes*** *dialog box*

Assigning Transparency to a Layer

By default, no transparency is assigned to a layer, if **Layer 0** is selected while creating that layer. Otherwise, new layer takes the transparency of the selected layer. To assign transparency to a layer, click on the **Transparency** field of that layer; the **Layer Transparency** dialog box will be displayed. Select the required transparency level from the **Transparency value (0-90)** drop-down list and choose **OK**. You can also enter a value in this drop-down list. Now, if you place an object on this layer, the object will have a faded color according to the specified transparency value.

Assigning Color to a Layer

To assign a color to a layer, select the color swatch in that layer in the **LAYER PROPERTIES MANAGER**; the **Select Color** dialog box will be displayed. Select the desired color and then choose the **OK** button; the selected color will be assigned to the layer.

Assigning Lineweight to a Layer

Lineweight is used to give thickness to objects in a layer. For example, if you create a sectional plan, you can assign a layer with a larger value of lineweight to create the objects through which the section is made. Another layer with a lesser lineweight can be used to show the objects through which the section does not pass. This thickness is displayed on the screen if the display of the lineweight is on. The lineweight assigned to an object can also be plotted. To assign a lineweight to a layer, select the layer and then click on the lineweight associated with it; the **Lineweight** dialog box will be displayed, see Figure 4-11. Select a lineweight and then choose **OK** from this dialog box to return to the **LAYER PROPERTIES MANAGER**.

Tip

Remember that the ***Linetype Control, Lineweight Control, Color Control,*** *and* ***Plot Style Control*** *list boxes in the* ***Properties*** *panel should display* ***ByLayer*** *as the current property of objects. This is to ensure that the objects drawn in a layer take the properties assigned to the layer in which they are drawn.*

Assigning Plot Style to a Layer

The plot style is a group of property settings such as color, linetype, and lineweight that can be assigned to a layer. The assigned plot style affects the drawings while plotting only. The drawing, in which you are working, should be in the named plot style mode (*.stb*) to make the plot style available in the **LAYER PROPERTIES MANAGER**. If the **Plot Style** icon in the dialog box is not available, then you are in a color-dependent mode (*.ctb*). To make this icon available, choose the **Options** button from the **Application Menu**; the **Options** dialog box will be displayed. Choose the **Plot and Publish** tab from this dialog box. Next, choose the **Plot Style Table Settings** button to invoke the **Plot Style Table Settings** dialog box. In this dialog box, select the **Use named plot styles** radio button from the **Default plot style behavior for new drawings** area and then exit both the dialog boxes. After changing the plot style to named plot style dependent, you have to start a new AutoCAD LT session to apply this setting. Start a new AutoCAD LT session with templates like *acadlt -Named Plot Styles* and invoke the **LAYER PROPERTIES MANAGER** . You will notice that the default plot style is **Normal**, in which the color, linetype, and lineweight are BYLAYER. To assign a plot style to a layer, select the layer and then click on its plot style; the **Select Plot Style** dialog box will be displayed, as shown in Figure 4-12. In this dialog box, you can select a specific plot style from the **Plot styles** list of available plot styles. Plot styles need to be created before you can use them (see Chapter 13, *Plotting Drawings*). Choose **OK** to return to the **LAYER PROPERTIES MANAGER** .

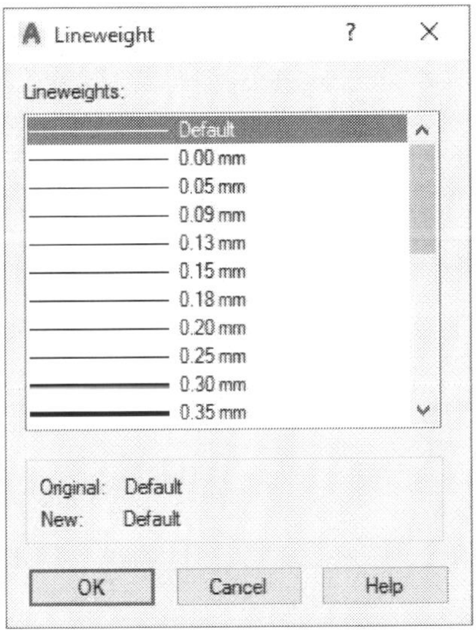

***Figure 4-11** The **Lineweight** dialog box*

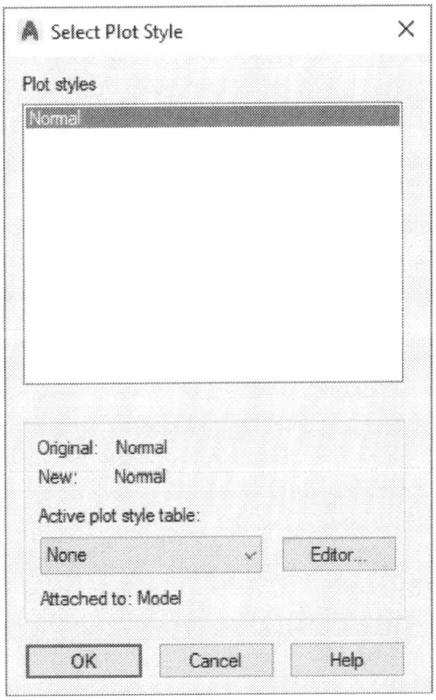

***Figure 4-12** The **Select Plot Style** dialog box*

Tip

*You can also change the plot style mode from the command line by using the **PSTYLEPOLICY** system variable. A value of 0 sets it to the color-dependent mode and a value of 1 sets it to the named mode.*

Note

When you are in a viewport, you can override the color, linetype, lineweight, and plot style settings assigned to a selected layer for the particular viewport (current viewport). These settings for all other viewports and model space will remain unaffected. All these overrides are highlighted in different background colors. Also, the icon of the selected layer under the ***Status*** *column will change indicating that some of the properties of the selected layer have been overridden by the new ones (see Chapter 12, for Model Space Viewports, Paper Space Viewports, and Layouts).*

Arranging Layers in Increasing Order

In AutoCAD LT, the layers in the **LAYER PROPERTIES MANAGER** get arranged automatically in the numerical and alphabetical order. For example, if the layers created are in numeric form 0, 1, 3, 2, 20, 25, 17, then they will be automatically arranged as 0, 1, 2, 3, 17, 20, 25, refer to Figure 4-13. Similarly, if the layers are created in the form of 0, 4, 2, 1, 3, A, C, D, B, then the numerical values will take precedence over the alphabetical values and the layers will be arranged as 0, 1, 2, 3, 4, A, B, C, D, refer to Figure 4-14. Note that, if the layers are not arranged in an order, then you need to choose the **Refresh** button available on the top right corner of the **LAYER PROPERTIES MANAGER** to get them arranged.

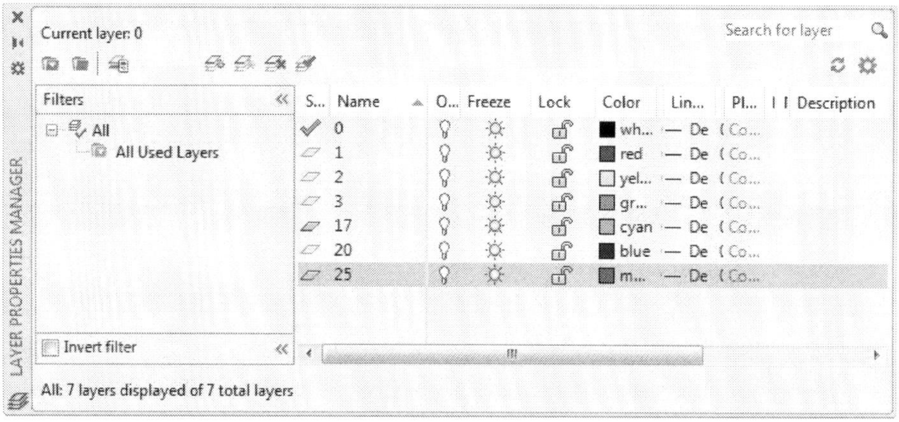

Figure 4-13 *The layers arranged in increasing order in the* ***LAYER PROPERTIES MANAGER***

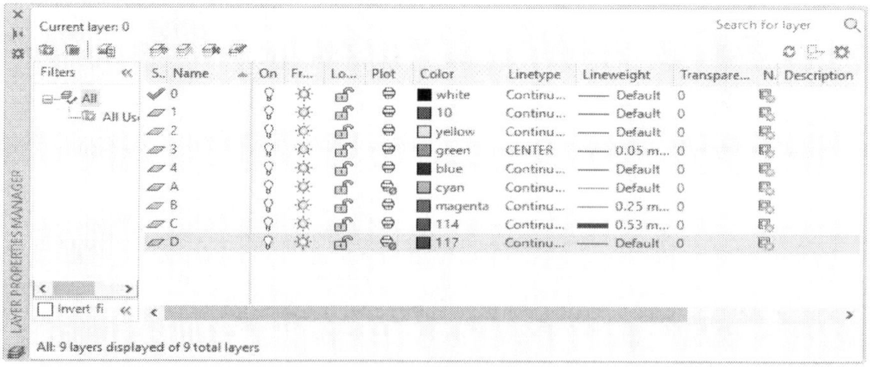

Figure 4-14 *The layers arranged automatically in the* ***LAYER PROPERTIES MANAGER***

Note

You can reverse the order of layers by clicking on the ***Name*** *column in the* ***LAYER PROPERTIES MANAGER****.*

Arranging Layers in Increasing Order with Respect to First Digit

The layers in the **LAYER PROPERTIES MANAGER** can be assigned numeric names. In AutoCAD LT, you can assign numeric name to layers in **LAYER PROPERTIES MANAGER** and then arrange them in increasing order on the basis of the first digit of the numeric names assigned. For example, if there are layers in the **LAYER PROPERTIES MANAGER** with the name 1, 4, 10, 12, and 50, then these layers will be arranged in increasing order with respect to their values. To arrange the names of layers in increasing order with respect to their first digits, specify the value of SORTORDER system variable at the Command prompt. Figures 4-15 and 4-16 show the layers arranged with the SORTORDER value as 1 and 0 respectively.

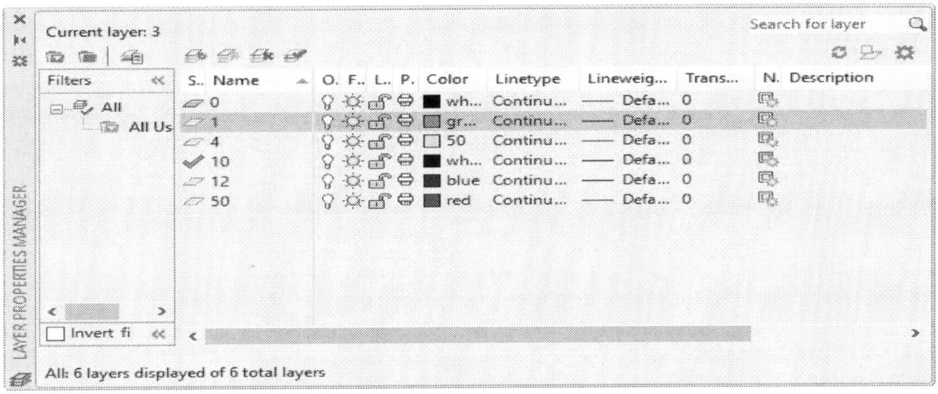

Figure 4-15 *The layers arranged with the value of SORTORDER system variable as 1*

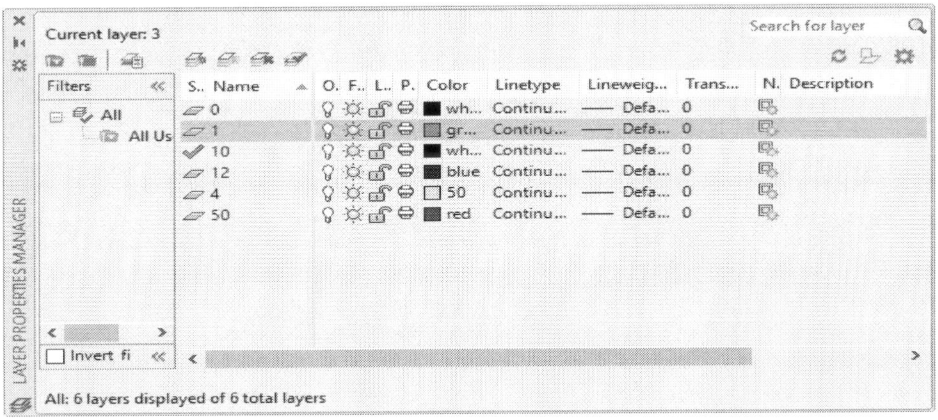

Figure 4-16 *The layers arranged with the value of SORTORDER system variable as 0*

Merging Layers

Ribbon: Home > Layers > Merge **Command:** LAYMRG

In AutoCAD LT, you can merge objects of different layers to a specific layer. On doing so, the layers of the objects to be merged will be deleted and properties of the objects to be merged will be modified as per the newly specified layer. To merge objects of different layers to a specific layer, choose the **Merge** tool from the **Layers** panel of the **Home** tab; you will be prompted to select objects of different layers that are to be merged. The following is the prompt sequence displayed on invoking this tool.

Select object on layer to merge or [Name] : Select objects whose layer you want to merge Enter
Select object on target layer or [Name] : Select the target object with which you want to merge the layers Enter
Do you wish to continue? [Yes/No] <No>: Enter the required option or press Enter

You can also merge the layers using the **LAYER PROPERTIES MANAGER**. To do so, invoke the **LAYER PROPERTIES MANAGER** and then select the layers to be merged. You can select multiple layers by using the CTRL key. After selecting the layers to be merged, right click; a shortcut menu will be displayed, refer to Figure 4-17. Now, choose the **Merge selected layer(s) to** option; the **Merge to Layer** dialog box will be displayed, refer to Figure 4-18. In this dialog box, select the required layer with which you want to merge the selected layers. Next, choose the **OK** button from **Merge to Layer** dialog box; the **Merge to Layer** message box will be displayed, refer to Figure 4-19. Choose the **Yes** button from the message box; the selected layers will be merged with the layer selected from the **Merge to Layer** dialog box.

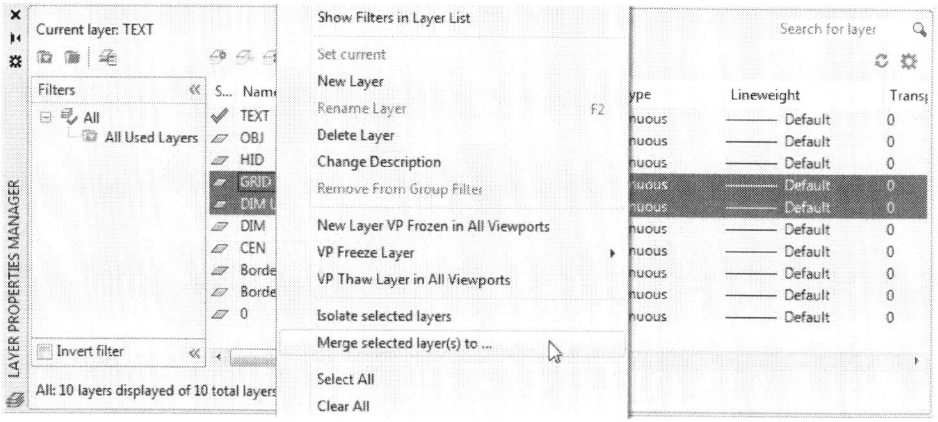

Figure 4-17 The shortcut menu displayed on right-clicking on the layers

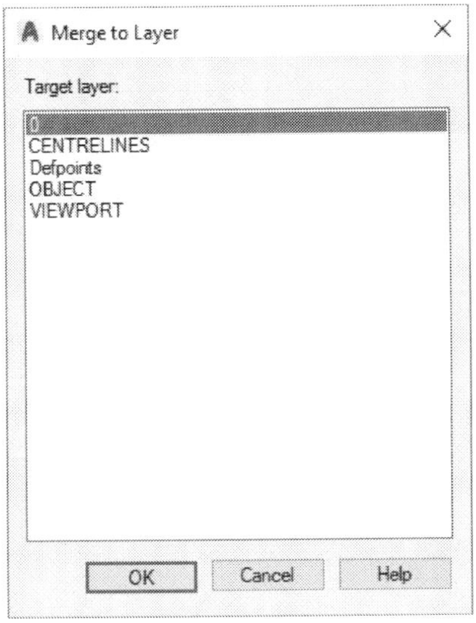

*Figure 4-18 The **Merge to Layer** dialog box*

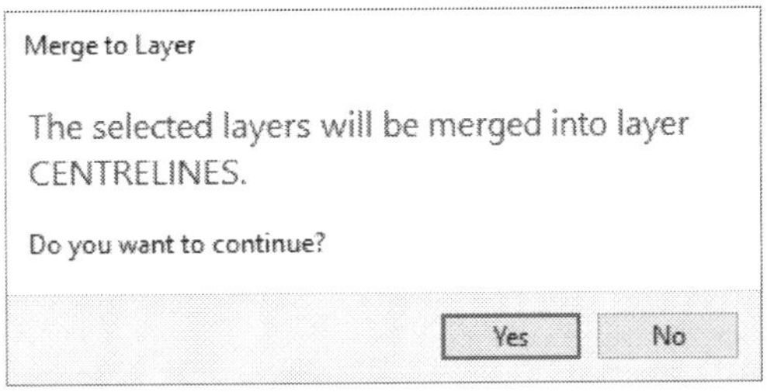

*Figure 4-19 The **Merge to Layer** message box*

Deleting Layers

To delete a layer, select it and then choose the **Delete Layer** button from the **LAYER PROPERTIES MANAGER**. Note that you cannot delete these layers: 0, Defpoints (created while dimensioning), Ashade (created while rendering), current layer, definition blocks, and an Xref-dependent layer.

Managing the Display of Columns

You can change the display order of columns in the **LAYER PROPERTIES MANAGER**. To do so, drag and drop the desired column head to the desired location. You can also change the display order by right-clicking on the column head and choosing the **Customize** option from the shortcut menu, as shown in Figure 4-20. On choosing this option, the **Customize Layer Columns** dialog box will be displayed, as shown in Figure 4-21. Select the desired column from the list and then choose the **Move Up** or **Move Down** button to change the display order.

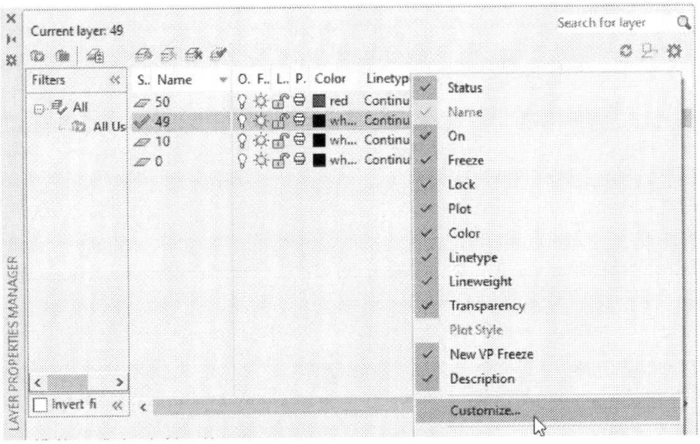

Figure 4-20 The shortcut menu to manage column heads

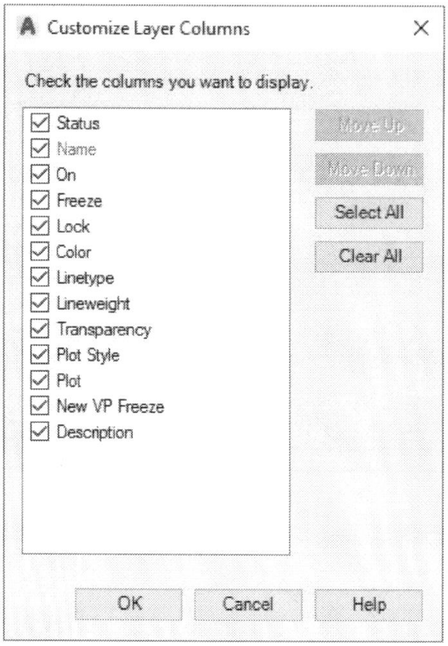

Figure 4-21 *The* ***Customize Layer Columns*** *dialog box*

You can also control the column heads to be displayed in the **LAYER PROPERTIES MANAGER** by using the shortcut menu shown in Figure 4-20. The tick marked entries in the shortcut menu will be displayed in the list. Choose the entry that you want to display in the **LAYER PROPERTIES MANAGER** from the shortcut menu.

Selective Display of Layers

If a drawing has a limited number of layers, it is easy to scan through them. However, if the drawing has a large number of layers, it is sometimes difficult to search through the layers. To solve this problem, you can use layer filters. By defining filters, you can specify the properties and display only those layers in the **LAYER PROPERTIES MANAGER** that match the properties in the filter. By default, the **All** and **All Used Layers** filters are created. The **All** filter is selected by default, and therefore, all layers are displayed. If you select the **All Used Layers** filter, only the layers that are used in the drawing will be displayed.

AutoCAD LT allows you to create a layer property filter or a layer group filter. A layer group filter can have additional layer property filters. To create a filter, choose the **New Property Filter** button, which is the first button on the top left corner of the dialog box. When you choose this button, a new property filter will be added to the list and the **Layer Filter Properties** dialog box will be displayed, as shown in Figure 4-22.

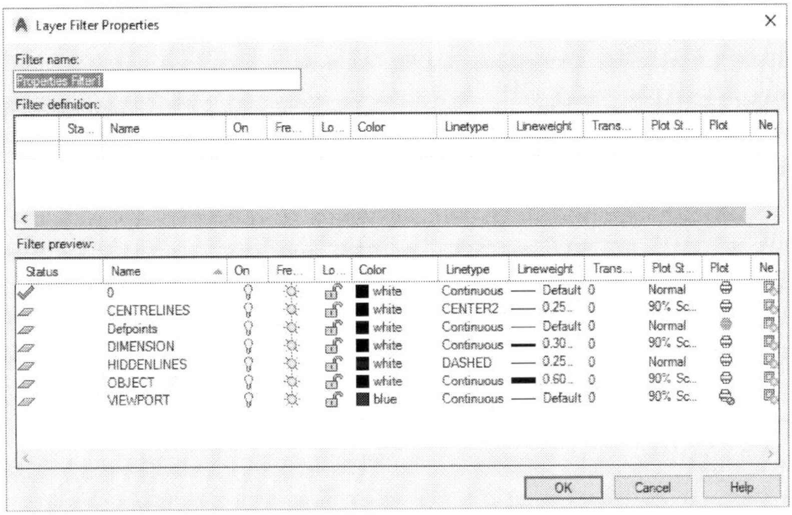

Figure 4-22 The ***Layer Filter Properties*** *dialog box*

The default name of the filter is displayed in the **Filter name** edit box. You can enter a new name for the filter in this edit box. Using the **Layer Filter Properties** dialog box, you can create filters based on any property column in the **Filter definition** area. The layers that will be actually displayed in the **LAYER PROPERTIES MANAGER** based on the filter that you create will be displayed in the **Filter preview** area. For example, to list only those layers that are red in color, click on the field under the **Color** column; a swatch **[...]** button will be displayed in this field. Choose this button to display the **Select Color** dialog box. Select **Red** from this dialog box and then exit it. You will notice that the filter row color has changed to red and the display of layers in the **Filter preview** has been modified such that only the red layers are displayed.

After creating the filter, exit the **Layer Filter Properties** dialog box. The layer filter is selected automatically in the **LAYER PROPERTIES MANAGER** and only the layers that satisfy the filter properties are displayed. You can restore the display of all layers again by clicking on the **All** filter.

Choose the **New Group Filter** button (second button on the top left corner of the dialog box) to group all filters under a common group name. You can create groups and subgroups of filters to categorize the filters with similar criteria.

Note

To modify a layer filter, double-click on it; the ***Layer Filter Properties*** *dialog box will be displayed. Modify the filter and then exit the dialog box.*

In the **LAYER PROPERTIES MANAGER**, when you select the **Invert filter** check box, the selected filter parameters are inverted. For example, if you have selected a filter to show all layers, none of the layers will be displayed. Note that in the **LAYER PROPERTIES MANAGER**, the current layer is not displayed in the list box if it is not among the filtered layers.

Layer States

While working in a drawing, you can save the properties of all layers under one name and restore the properties later. The properties thus saved can also be imported to other drawings. This saves time in setting the layer properties again in a new drawing. To save the properties of all layers in a drawing, choose the **Layer States Manager** button in the **LAYER PROPERTIES MANAGER**; the **Layer States Manager** dialog box will be displayed, as shown in Figure 4-23.

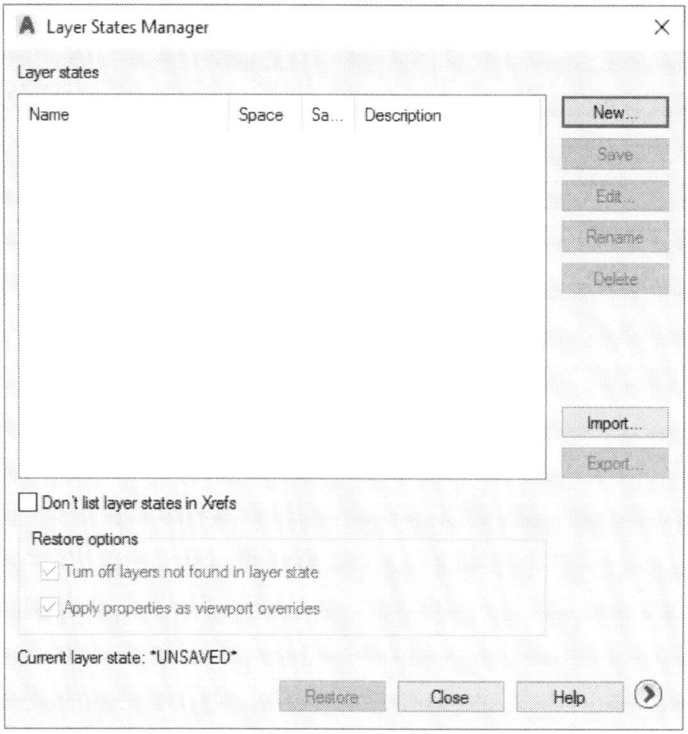

***Figure 4-23** The **Layer States Manager** dialog box*

Choose the **New** button to invoke the **New Layer State to Save** dialog box. Specify the name and description related to the state of a layer in the **New layer state name** and **Description** edit boxes respectively, and then choose the **OK** button. Choose the **More Restore Options (Alt+>)** button next to the **Help** button; the dialog box will expand. Specify different states and properties of the layers by selecting the corresponding check boxes in the **Layers properties to restore** area. Choose the **Restore** button to save the layer state. However, this layer state is saved only for the current file. If you want to use the current layer state in other files also, you need to save them. To do so, choose the **Export** button; the **Export layer state** dialog box will be invoked. Enter a name for the layer state. The layer state will be exported with the *.las* extension.

You can also import a layer state later in any other file by using the **Layer States Manager** dialog box. On importing a layer state, you can edit the states and properties of the imported layer state. You can also rename and delete a layer state.

Select the **Don't list layer states in Xrefs** check box; the layer states that are defined in an externally referenced drawing will be referenced from the **Layer states** list box. Select the **Turn off layers not found in layer state** check box to turn off the newly created layers (that were created after defining the layer state) so that the drawing appears the same as it was when the layer state was saved. The **Apply properties as viewport overrides** check box is used to apply the layer property overrides to the current viewport. This check box is selected by default and is available only when a viewport is active.

Note

*1. Select the **New Layer State** option from the **Layer State** drop-down list in the **Layers** panel of the **Home** tab to invoke the **New Layer State to Save** dialog box and save the new layer state. Similarly, select the **Manage Layer States** option from the **Layer State** drop-down list to invoke the **Layer States Manager** dialog box.*

*2. The linetypes will be restored with the layer state in a new drawing file only if the linetypes are already loaded using the **Select Linetype** dialog box.*

Reconciling New Layers

When you save or plot a drawing for the first time, AutoCAD LT compiles a list of existing layers. These layers are known as reconciled layers. When new layers are inserted or an external reference is attached to the current drawing, AutoCAD LT compares these new layers (unreconciled layers) with the previously created list. This helps prevent any new layers from being added to the current drawing without user's permission.

If you need AutoCAD LT to notify the unreconciled layer, choose the **Settings** button from the **LAYER PROPERTIES MANAGER**; the **Layer Settings** dialog box will be displayed. Select the **Evaluate all new layers added to drawing** check box and then select the **Evaluate all new layers** radio button. Next, select the **Notify when new layers are present** check box from the **Layer Settings** dialog box. You can also choose the options under this check box based on your requirements.

After selecting the **Notify when new layers are present** check box and the corresponding options, AutoCAD LT displays the **Unreconciled New Layers** information bubble by default, as shown in Figure 4-24, whenever new unreconciled layers are found in the current drawing or in the externally referenced drawings. As soon as the unreconciled layers are found in the drawing, an **Unreconciled New Layers** filter is automatically created in the **LAYER PROPERTIES MANAGER**. Click on the blue link in the information bubble or open the **LAYER PROPERTIES MANAGER** to view the unreconciled layers. To reconcile the layers, select all the unreconciled layers in the **LAYER PROPERTIES MANAGER**, right-click on them, and choose the **Reconcile Layer** option from the shortcut menu displayed.

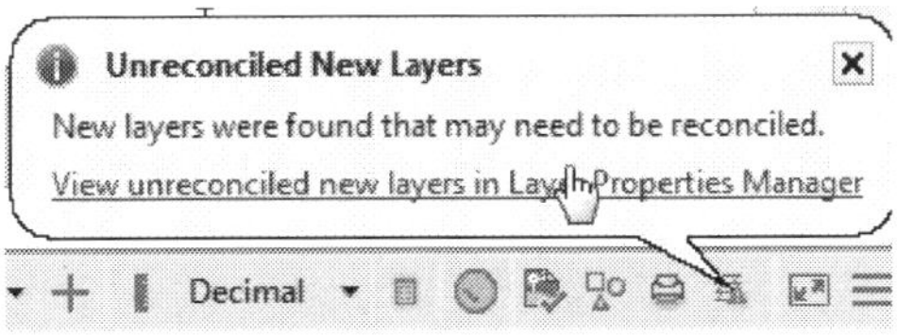

***Figure 4-24** The information bubble for unreconciled layers*

Isolating and Unisolating Layers

Ribbon: Home > Layers > Isolate/Unisolate **Command:** LAYISO/LAYUNISO
Toolbar: Layers II > Layer Isolate/Layer Unisolate

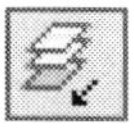

The isolate and unisolate options are used to lock or turn off all layers except the layers of the selected objects. To isolate a layer, choose the **Isolate** tool from the **Layers** panel; you will be prompted to select the objects. Select one or more objects and press the ENTER key; the layers corresponding to the selected objects will get isolated and unlocked. All other layers will be turned off or frozen in the current viewport or locked depending on the current settings. The unisolated layers (locked) will appear faded. This will help you to differentiate between the isolated and unisolated layers. You can change the settings by choosing the **Settings** option from the shortcut menu at the **Select objects on the layer(s) to be isolated or [Settings]** prompt. The options at the **Settings** prompt are discussed next.

Off

This option is used to turn off or freeze all layers except the selected layers. Choose the **Off** sub option to turn off all layers, except the selected one in all viewports, and choose the **Vpfreeze** sub option to freeze all layers, except the selected one only in the current floating viewport.

Lock and fade

This option is used to lock all layers except the selected one and prompts you to enter the fade value to specify the fading intensity. You can also control the fading intensity by dragging the **Locked layer fading** sliding bar in the **Layers** panel. You can also turn off or on the fading effect by choosing the **Locked Layer Fading** button from the **Layers** panel.

To unisolate the previously isolated layer, choose the **Unisolate** tool from the **Layers** panel.

Controlling the Layer Settings

The **Settings** button in the **LAYER PROPERTIES MANAGER** is used to control the new layer notification settings. You can also change the background color used to highlight the layer properties that are overridden in the current viewport. Choose the **Settings** button in the **LAYER PROPERTIES MANAGER**; the **Layer Settings** dialog box will be displayed (see Figure 4-25). The options in the **Layer Settings** dialog box are discussed next.

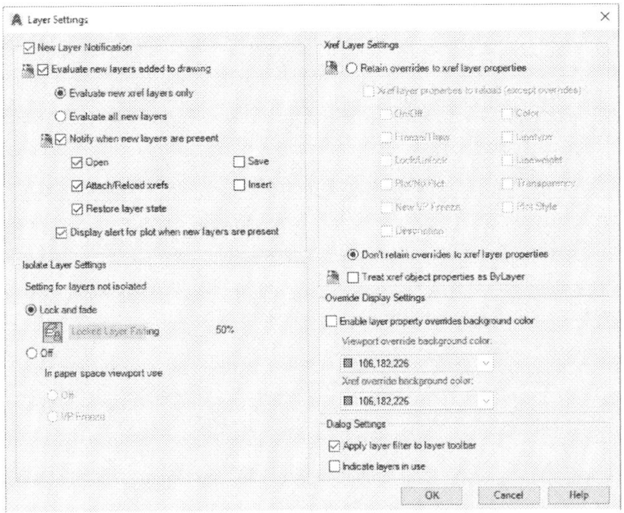

*Figure 4-25 The **Layer Settings** dialog box*

New Layer Notification Area

By default, the **Evaluate new layers added to drawing** check box is cleared. Therefore, the new layers will not be evaluated. Also, the user will not be informed about the unreconciled layers. Select the **Evaluate new layers added to drawing** check box; all other options in this area will be available. The **Evaluate new xref layers only** radio button is selected by default and allows AutoCAD LT to evaluate the new layers added only to the externally referenced drawings. Select the **Evaluate all new layers** radio button to evaluate all the layers in the drawing, including the unreconciled layers of the externally referenced drawings. This setting can also be controlled by setting the **LAYEREVAL** system variable to 2.

The **Notify when new layers are present** check box is selected by default and is used to specify the operations after which AutoCAD LT will evaluate the unreconciled files. These operations include open, save, attach/reload xrefs, insert, restore layer states, and plot. Select the respective check boxes to specify your preferences. These settings can also be specified by using the **LAYERNOTIFY** system variable. The values for this system variable are 0, 1, 2, 4, 8, 16, and 32. The respective operations after which an information bubble will be displayed are Off, Plot, Open, Load/Reload/Attach for xrefs, Restore layer state, Save, and Insert.

Isolate Layer Settings Area

The options in this area are used to set the display state of the unisolated layers. If you need to display a locked layer in a faded mode, select the **Lock and fade** radio button and set the intensity of fading by using the slider. Similarly, you can make the unisolated layers turned off or VP Freeze in the viewport by selecting the **Off** radio button and the corresponding option.

Dialog Settings Area

You can apply the current layer filter to the **Filter applied** drop-down list in the **Layers** toolbar. To do so, invoke the **Layer Filter Properties** dialog box by choosing the **New Property Filter** button from the **LAYER PROPERTIES MANAGER**. Select the layer state or property from the **Filter definition** list box and choose the **OK** button. Only the filtered layers will be displayed in the **Filter applied** drop-down list of the **Layers** toolbar.

Example 1 — Layers

Set up three layers with the following linetypes and colors. Then, create the drawing shown in Figure 4-26 (without dimensions).

Layer Name	Color	Linetype	Lineweight
Obj	Red	Continuous	0.012"
Hid	Yellow	Hidden	0.008"
Cen	Green	Center	0.006"

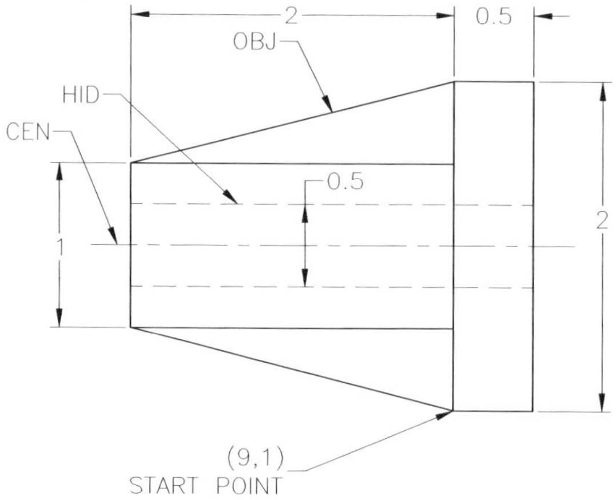

Figure 4-26 *Drawing for Example 1*

In this example, assume that the limits and units are already set. Before drawing the lines, you need to create layers and assign colors, linetypes, and lineweights to them. Also, depending on the objects that you want to draw, you need to set a layer as the current layer. In this example, you will create layers by using the **LAYER PROPERTIES MANAGER**. You will use the **Layer** drop-down list in the **Layers** panel to set a layer as the current layer and then draw the figure.

1. As the lineweights specified are given in inches, first you need to change their units, if they are in millimeters. To do so, invoke the **Lineweight Settings** dialog box by right-clicking on the **Show/Hide Lineweight** button in the Status Bar and then choose the **Lineweight Settings** option from the shortcut menu. Select the **Inches (in)** radio button in the **Units for Listing** area of the dialog box and then choose the **OK** button.

2. Choose the **Layer Properties** button from the **Layers** panel in the **Home** tab of the **Ribbon** to display the **LAYER PROPERTIES MANAGER**. The layer **0** with default properties is displayed in the list box.

3. Choose the **New Layer** button; a new layer (Layer1) with the default properties is displayed in the list box. Change the default name, **Layer1** to **Obj**.

4. Left-click on the **Color** field of this layer; the **Select Color** dialog box is displayed. Select the **Red** color and then choose **OK**; red color is assigned to the **Obj** layer.

5. Left-click on the **Lineweight** field of the **Obj** layer; the **Lineweight** dialog box is displayed. Select **0.012"** and then choose **OK**; the selected lineweight is assigned to the **Obj** layer.

6. Again, choose the **New Layer** button; a new layer (Layer1) with properties similar to that of the **Obj** layer is created. Change the default name to **Hid**.

7. Left-click on the **Color** field of this layer; the **Select Color** dialog box is displayed. Select the **Yellow** color and then choose **OK**.

8. Left-click on the **Linetype** field of the **Hid** layer; the **Select Linetype** dialog box is displayed. If the **HIDDEN** linetype is not displayed in the dialog box, choose the **Load** button; the **Load or Reload Linetypes** dialog box is displayed. Select **HIDDEN** from the list and choose the **OK** button from the **Load or Reload Linetypes** dialog box. Next, select **HIDDEN** from the **Select Linetype** dialog box and then choose the **OK** button.

9. Left-click on the **Lineweight** field of the **Hid** layer; the **Lineweight** dialog box is displayed. Select **0.008"** and then choose **OK**; the selected lineweight is assigned to the **Hid** layer.

10. Similarly, create the new layer **Cen** and assign the color **Green**, linetype **CENTER**, and lineweight **0.006"** to it.

11. Select the **Obj** layer and then choose the **Set Current** button to make the **Obj** layer current, see Figure 4-27. Choose the **Close** button to exit the **LAYER PROPERTIES MANAGER**.

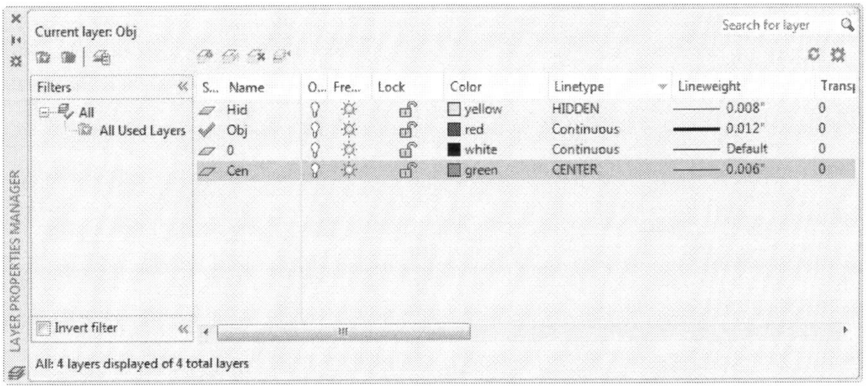

Figure 4-27 *Layers created for Example 1*

12. Choose the **Show/Hide Lineweight** button from the Status Bar to turn on the display of the lineweights of the lines to be drawn.

13. Choose the **Dynamic Input** button from the Status Bar to turn it on.

14. Choose the **Line** tool from the **Draw** panel and draw solid lines in the drawing, refer to Figure 4-26. Make sure that the start point of the line is at 9,1. You will notice that a continuous

line is drawn in red color. This is because the **Obj** layer is the current layer and red color is assigned to it.

15. Click the down arrow in the **Layer** drop-down list available in the **Layers** panel to display the list of layers and then select the **Hid** layer from the list to make it current, as shown in Figure 4-28.

16. Draw two hidden lines; the lines are displayed in yellow color with hidden linetype.

17. Draw the center line; the centerline is displayed in yellow color with hidden linetype. This is because the **Hid** layer is the current layer.

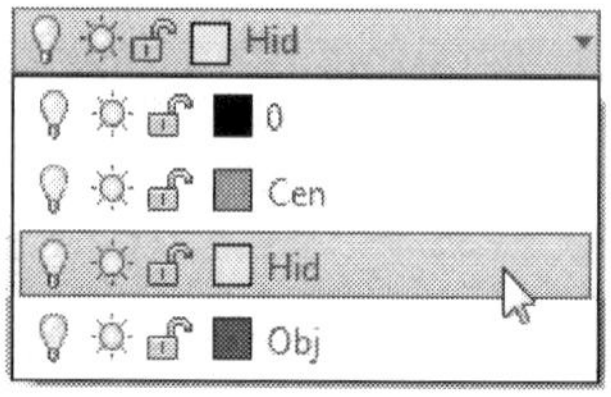

***Figure 4-28** Selecting the **Hid** layer from the **Layers** panel to set it as the current layer*

18. Now, select the centerline and then select the **Cen** layer from the **Layer** drop-down list available in the **Layers** panel; the color and linetype of the centerline is changed.

Exercise 1 Layers

Set up layers with the following linetypes and colors. Then make the drawing (without dimensions), as shown in Figure 4-29. The distance between the dotted lines is 1.0 unit.

Layer Name	Color	Linetype
Object	Red	Continuous
Hidden	Yellow	Hidden
Center	Green	Center
Dimension	Blue	Continuous

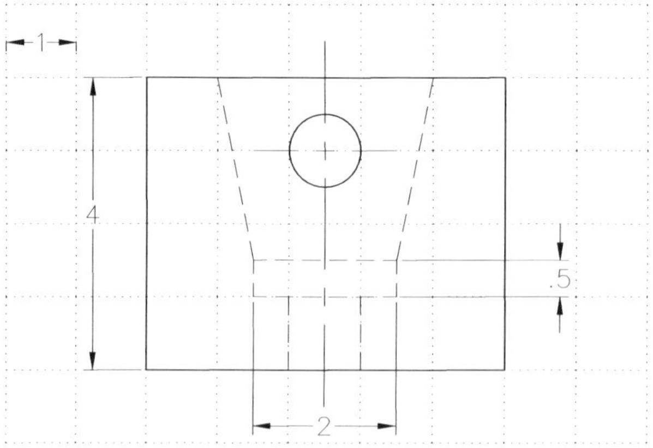

***Figure 4-29** Drawing for Exercise 1*

OBJECT PROPERTIES

Drawing entities have properties such as color, linetype, lineweight, and plot style based on the layer it is associated with. However, you can change these properties by using the **PROPERTIES** palette or the **Properties** panel in the **Home** tab of the **Ribbon**. By default, the **By Layer** option will be selected in the **Object Color**, **Lineweight**, and **Linetype** drop-down lists of the **Properties** panel in the **Ribbon**. Therefore, the properties set in the current layer will be applied to the entities in it. The procedure to change the properties of the selected objects is discussed next.

Changing the Color

Select the object whose color you want to change; the current color of the object will be displayed in the **Object Color** drop-down list. To change this color, click on the down arrow in the **Object Color** drop-down list, refer to Figure 4-30, and select a new color; the selected color will be applied to the object. If you want to assign a color that is not displayed in the list, select the **More Colors** option; the **Select Color** dialog box will be displayed. You can select the desired color in this dialog box, and then choose the **OK** button.

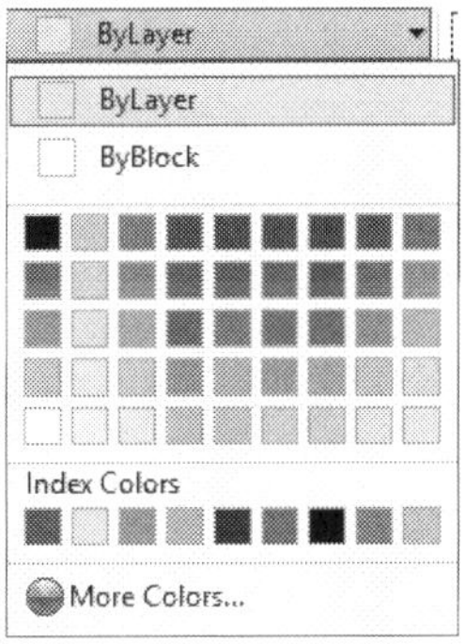

***Figure 4-30** Different colors in the*
***Object Color** drop-down list*

To set a color other than the one set in the current layer as the current color, choose a color from the **Object Color** drop-down list without selecting an object. Now, all new objects will be drawn in this color.

Changing the Linetype

To set a linetype other than the one set in the current layer as the current linetype, select a linetype from the **Linetype** drop-down list in the **Properties** panel from the **Home** tab, as shown in Figure 4-31. Now, all objects will be drawn in this linetype.

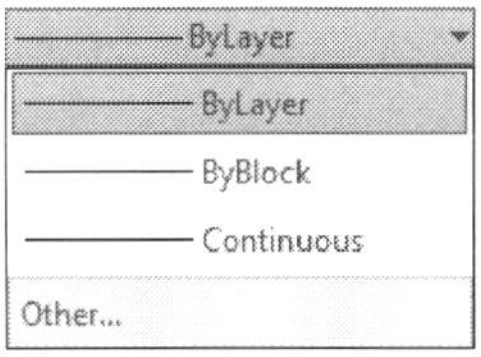

***Figure 4-31** The **Linetype** drop-down list*

To assign a linetype that is not displayed in the list, choose the **Other** option; the **Linetype Manager** dialog box will be displayed, as shown in Figure 4-32. By default, the **ByLayer**, **ByBlock**, and **Continuous** linetypes will be listed in this dialog box. To load other linetypes, choose the **Load** button; the **Load or Reload Linetypes** dialog box will be displayed. Select a linetype in this dialog box; they will be displayed in the **Linetype Manager** dialog box. Next, select the required linetype from this dialog box and choose **OK**. You can also make a linetype current by using the **Current** button in the **Linetype Manager** dialog box.

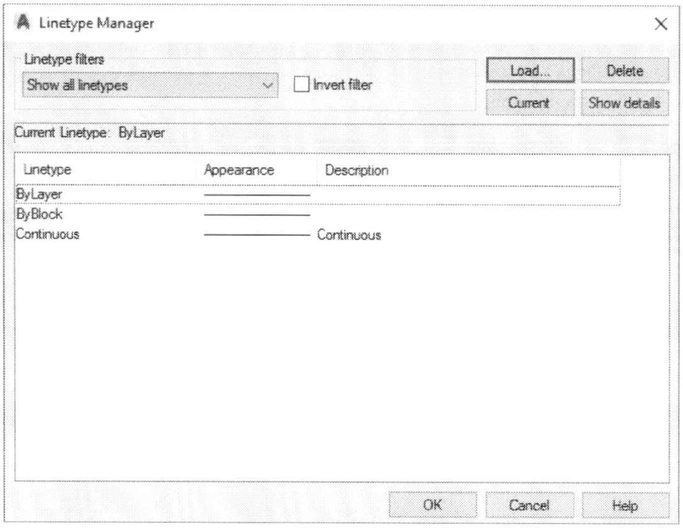

***Figure 4-32** The **Linetype Manager** dialog box*

Changing the Lineweight

To change the lineweight of a selected object, select a different lineweight value from the **Lineweight** drop-down list in the **Properties** panel. Also, you can set a new lineweight as current by selecting it from the list. To assign a lineweight value that is not listed in the drop-down list, select the **Lineweight Settings** option from the **Lineweight** drop-down list; the **Lineweight Settings** dialog box will be displayed, as shown in Figure 4-33. You can also invoke this dialog box by choosing the **Lineweight Settings** option from the shortcut menu that is displayed on right-clicking on the **Show/Hide Lineweight** button in the Status Bar. In this dialog box, set the current lineweight for the objects. You can change the units for the lineweight and also the display of lineweights for the current drawing. Lineweights are displayed in pixel widths and depending on the lineweight value chosen, the lineweights are displayed if the **Display Lineweight** check box is selected. For a large drawing, displaying lineweight increases the regeneration time, and therefore the corresponding check box should be cleared. As mentioned earlier, you can also turn the display of lineweights to on or off directly from the Status Bar by choosing the **Show/ Hide Lineweight** button. The value set in the **Adjust Display Scale** slider bar also affects the regeneration time. You can keep the slider bar at **Max** for getting a good display of different lineweights on the screen in the Model space; otherwise keep it at **Min** for a faster regeneration.

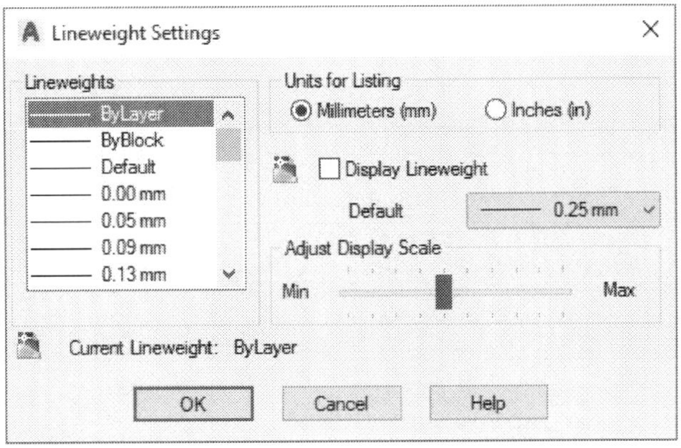

Figure 4-33 *The* ***Lineweight Settings*** *dialog box*

Changing the Plot Style

The options in this drop-down list will be available only if you are using the named plot style modes. To change the plot style, select a plot style from the **Plot Style** drop-down list in the **Properties** panel. Also, you can set a new plot style as current by selecting it from the drop-down list.

Changing Object Properties using the Properties Palette

Ribbon: View > Palettes > Properties **Command:** PROPERTIES/CH/MO/PR
Toolbar: Standard > Properties

The **PROPERTIES** palette is used to set the current properties and to change the general properties of the selected objects. The **PROPERTIES** palette (see Figure 4-34) is displayed on choosing the **Properties** tool from the **Palettes** panel of the **View** tab. It can also be invoked by right-clicking on an object and then choosing the **Properties** option from the shortcut menu. On right-clicking in the **PROPERTIES** palette, a shortcut menu will be displayed from where you can choose **Allow Docking** or **Auto-Hide** to dock or hide the palette.

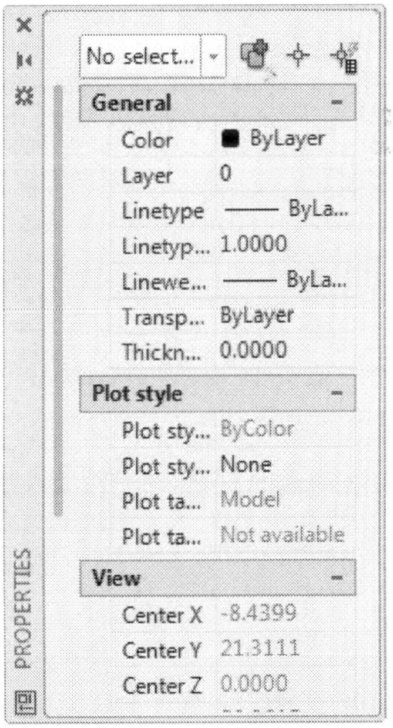

Figure 4-34 *The* ***PROPERTIES*** *palette*

When you select an object, the palette displays the properties of the selected object. Depending on the object selected, the properties differ. If you change the properties in the **PROPERTIES** palette without selecting any object, the current properties will be changed in the **Properties** panel in the **Home** tab. Now, if you draw an object, it will have the properties set in the **PROPERTIES** palette.

When you select **Color** from the **General** list, the color of the selected object is displayed, along with a down arrow. Click the down arrow and select a color from the list to assign to the selected object. If you want to assign a color that is not displayed in the list, choose the **Select Color** option to display the **Select Color** dialog box. You can select the desired color in this dialog box, and then choose the **OK** button.

Similarly, you can set current the linetype, lineweight, linetype scale, and other properties for the other objects individually. You can also assign a hyperlink to an object. The **Hyperlink** field in this window displays the name and description of the hyperlink, if any, assigned to the object. If there is no hyperlink attached to the object, this field will be blank. To add a hyperlink to a selected object, click on this field; the button will be displayed in this field. Choose the button; the **Insert Hyper link** dialog box will be displayed where you can enter the path of the URL or the file that you want to link to the selected object.

Exercise 2 — *Object Properties*

Draw a hexagon on the **Obj** layer in red. Keep the linetype hidden. Now, use the **PROPERTIES** palette to change the layer, the color to yellow, and the linetype to continuous.

Changing Object Properties using the Quick Properties Palette

Status Bar: Quick Properties

In AutoCAD LT, you can view some of the properties of the selected entity in the **Quick Properties** palette or in the **Properties** palette. To view the properties, keep the **Quick Properties** button chosen in the Status Bar and then select an entity; some of the properties of the selected entity will be displayed in the **Quick Properties** palette. Alternatively, enter **QP** at the Command prompt invoke the **Quick Properties** palette. You can change the properties that are displayed in the **Quick Properties** palette. Figure 4-35 shows the **Quick Properties** palette that is displayed on selecting a line.

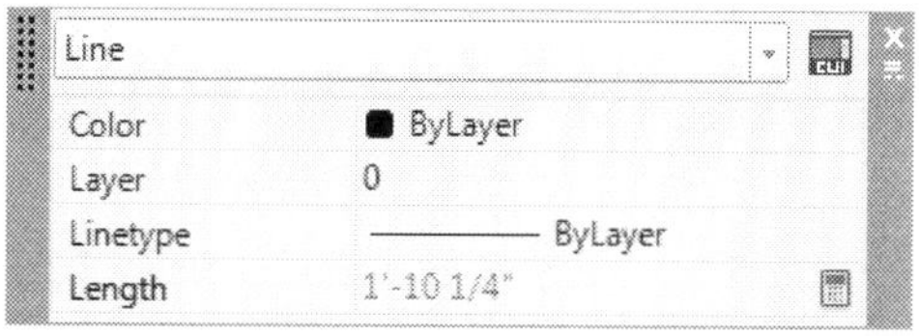

***Figure 4-35** The **Quick Properties** palette*

If you select multiple objects of different types, then in the drop-down list available in the **Quick Properties** palette, the name of the objects will be defined as **All** and the number of selected entities will be displayed in parenthesis. After selecting multiple entities, you can also select a particular type of object from the drop-down list to view the properties of the particular object type.

To set the properties displayed in the **Quick Properties** palette, right-click on the **Quick Properties** button in the Status Bar and choose the **Quick Properties Settings** option; the **Drafting Settings** dialog box will be displayed with the **Quick Properties** tab chosen. You can specify the display of the object type, the position of palette on invoking, and the height of palette by selecting a suitable option in this dialog box.

You can customize the **Quick Properties** palette such that it displays the required properties of a selected entity. To do so, choose the **Customize** button available next to the drop-down list; the **Customize User Interface** dialog box will be displayed. In the dialog box, different object types and their corresponding properties will be displayed on the right. If you select an object type, you will notice that the check boxes of some of the properties are selected. The properties, whose check boxes are selected, will be listed in the **Quick Properties** palette. You can also select the check boxes of the properties that you want to be displayed in the **Quick Properties** palette. If you place the cursor over an entity and pause, a tooltip, called the rollover tooltip, will be displayed. You can synchronize the properties displayed in the rollover tooltip and the **Quick Properties** panel. To do so, invoke the **Customize User Interface** dialog box, right-click on the **Rollover Tooltips** sub node in it, and choose the **Synchronize with Quick Properties** option from the shortcut menu.

GLOBAL AND CURRENT LINETYPE SCALING

The **LTSCALE** system variable controls the global scale factor of the lines in a drawing. For example, if **LTSCALE** is set to 2, all lines in the drawing will be affected by a factor of 2. Like **LTSCALE**, the **CELTSCALE** system variable controls the linetype scaling with the only difference that **CELTSCALE** determines the current linetype scaling. For example, if you set **CELTSCALE** to 0.5, all lines drawn after setting the new value for **CELTSCALE** will have the linetype scaling factor of 0.5. The value is retained in the **CELTSCALE** system variable. For example, line (a) in Figure 4-36 is drawn with a **CELTSCALE** factor of 1 and line (b) is drawn with a **CELTSCALE** factor of 0.5. The length of the dash is reduced by a factor of 0.5 when **CELTSCALE** is 0.5. The net scale factor is equal to the product of **CELTSCALE** and **LTSCALE**. Figure 4-36(c) shows a line that is drawn with **LTSCALE** of 2 and **CELTSCALE** of 0.25. The net scale factor = **LTSCALE** X **CELTSCALE** = 2 X 0.25 = 0.5. You can also change the global and current scale factors by entering a desired value in the **Linetype Manager** dialog box. If you choose the **Show details** button, the properties associated with the selected linetype will be displayed, as shown in Figure 4-37. You can change the values according to your drawing requirements.

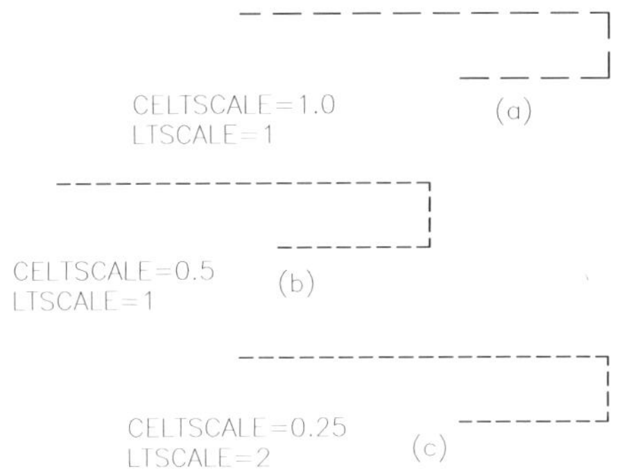

***Figure 4-36** Using **CELTSCALE** to control current linetype scaling*

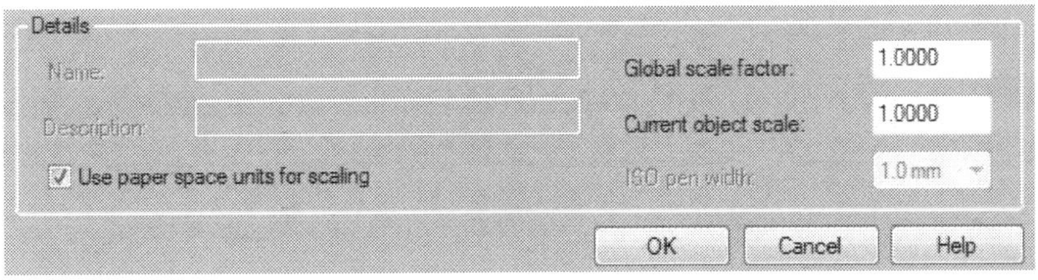

***Figure 4-37** The **Details** area of the **Linetype Manager** dialog box*

LTSCALE FACTOR FOR PLOTTING

The **LTSCALE** factor for plotting depends on the size of the sheet you use to plot the drawing. For example, if the limits are 48 by 36, the drawing scale is 1:1, and to plot the drawing on a 48" by 36" size sheet, then the **LTSCALE** factor is 1. If you check the specification of the **Hidden** linetype in the *acad.lin* file, the length of each dash is 0.25. Hence, when you plot a drawing with 1:1 scale, the length of each dash in a hidden line will be 0.25.

However, if the drawing scale is 1/8" = 1' and you want to plot the drawing on 48" by 36" paper, the **LTSCALE** factor must be 8 x 12 = 96. The length of each dash in the hidden line will increase by a factor of 96, because the **LTSCALE** factor is 96. Therefore, the length of each dash will be (0.25 x 96 = 24) units. At the time of plotting, the scale factor must be 1:96 to plot the 384' by 288' drawing on 48" by 36" paper. Each dash of the hidden line that was 24" long on the drawing will be 24/96 = 0.25" long when plotted. Similarly, if the desired text size on the paper is 1/8", the text height in the drawing must be 1/8 x 96 = 12".

LTSCALE factor for PLOTTING = Drawing Scale

Sometimes your plotter may not be able to plot a 48" by 36" drawing, or you might like to decrease the size of the plot so that the drawing fits within the specified area. To get the correct dash length for hidden, center, or other lines, you must adjust the **LTSCALE** factor. For example, if you want to plot the previously mentioned drawing in a 45" by 34" area, the correction factor is:

Correction factor = 48/45
= 1.0666

New **LTSCALE** factor = **LTSCALE** factor x Correction factor
= 96 x 1.0666
= 102.4

New **LTSCALE** factor for PLOTTING = Drawing Scale x Correction Factor

Note

*If you change the **LTSCALE** factor, all lines in the drawing will be affected by the new ratio.*

Changing the Linetype Scale Using the PROPERTIES Palette

You can also change the linetype scale of an object by using the **PROPERTIES** palette. To do so, select the object and then invoke the **Properties** tool; the **PROPERTIES** palette will be displayed. Next, locate the **Linetype scale** edit box in the **General** list and enter a new linetype scale value in the edit box. The linetype scale of the selected objects is changed as specified.

WORKING WITH THE DesignCenter

Ribbon: View > Palettes > DesignCenter **Command:** ADC/ADCENTER
Toolbar: Standard > DesignCenter

The **DesignCenter** allows you to reuse and share contents in different drawings. You can use this palette to locate the drawing data with the help of search tools and then use it in your drawing. You can insert layers, linetypes, blocks, layouts, external references, and other drawing content in any number of drawings. Hence, if a layer is created once, it can be used repeatedly any number of times.

Open the **DESIGN CENTER** palette and then choose the **Tree View Toggle** button to display the **Tree pane** and the **Palette** side by side (if they are not already displayed). Open the folder that contains the drawing having the required layers and linetypes to be inserted. You can use the **Load** and **Up** buttons to open the folder. For example, to insert some layers and linetypes from the drawing *c4d1* saved at the *C:\AutoCAD LT 2020\c04_ACAD LT_2020*, browse to the folder and open *c4d1* to display its contents. Select **Layers**; the layers created in *c4d1* will be displayed in the **Palette**. Press and hold the CTRL key and select the **Border** and **CEN** layers. Right-click to display the shortcut menu and choose **Add Layer(s)**, as shown in Figure 4-38; the two layers are added to the current drawing. You can also drag and drop the desired layers into the current drawing. If you open the drop-down list in the **Layers** toolbar, you will notice that the two layers are listed there. Similarly, you can insert the other elements such as linetypes, blocks, dimension styles, and so on. You will learn more about **DesignCenter** in later chapters.

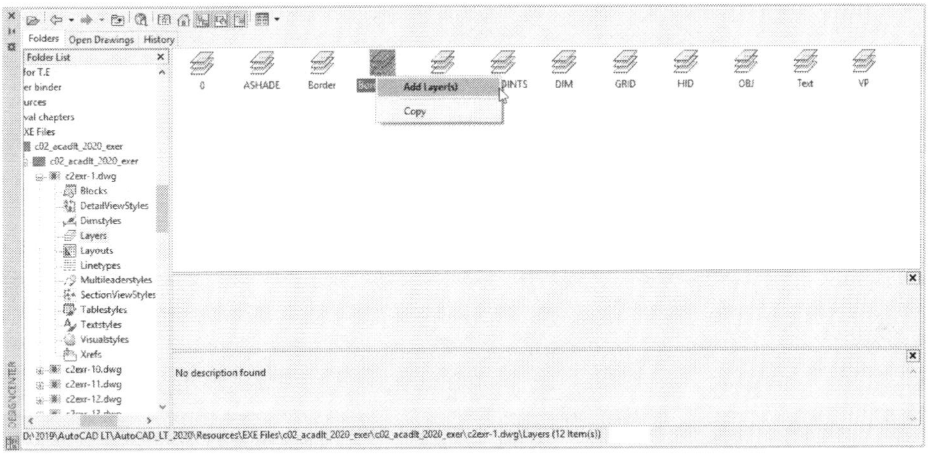

*Figure 4-38 The partial view of **DesignCenter** with the shortcut menu*

DRAFTING SETTINGS DIALOG BOX

Command: DSETTINGS

You can use the **Drafting Settings** dialog box to set the drawing modes such as Grid, Snap, Object Snap, Polar, Object Snap tracking, and Dynamic Input. All these modes help you draw accurately and also increase the drawing speed. You can right-click on the **Snap Mode**, **Display drawing grid**, **Ortho Mode**, **Polar Tracking**, **Object Snap**, **Object Snap Tracking**, **Dynamic Input**, **Quick Properties**, or **Selection Cycling** button in the Status Bar to display a shortcut menu. In this shortcut menu, choose **Settings** to display the **Drafting Settings** dialog box, as shown in Figure 4-39. This dialog box has six tabs: **Snap and Grid**, **Polar Tracking**, **Object Snap**, **Dynamic Input**, **Quick Properties**, and **Selection Cycling**. On starting AutoCAD LT, these tabs have default settings. You can change them according to your requirements.

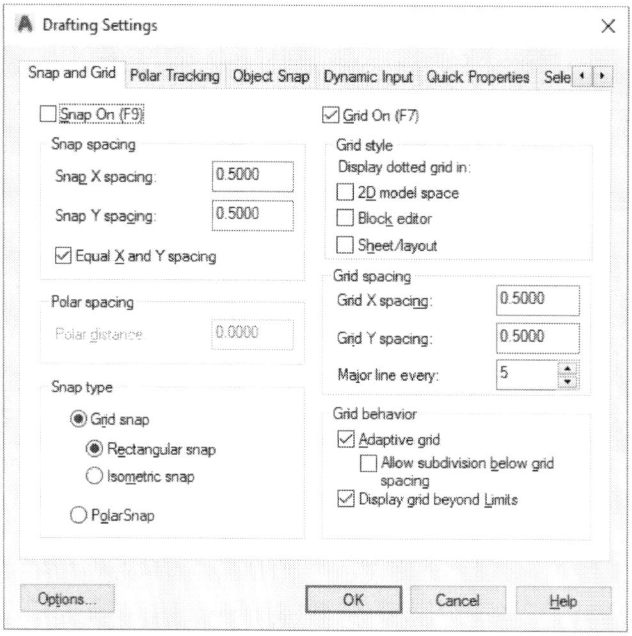

Figure 4-39 *The* ***Drafting Settings*** *dialog box*

Setting Grid

Grid lines are the checked lines on the screen at predefined spacing, see Figure 4-40. In AutoCAD LT, by default, the grids are displayed as checked lines. You can also display the grids as dotted lines, refer to Figure 4-41. To do so, set the **2D model space** check box in the **Grid style** area of the **Snap and Grid** tab of the **Drafting Settings** dialog box. These dotted lines act as a graph that can be used as reference lines in a drawing. You can change the distance between grid lines as per your requirement. If grid lines are displayed within the drawing limits, it helps to define the working area. The grid also gives you an idea about the size of the drawing objects. By default, the grid will be displayed beyond the limits. To display the grid up to the limits, right-click on the **Display drawing grid** button in the Status Bar and then choose the **Settings** option from the shorcut-menu displayed; the **Drafting Settings** dialog box will be displayed. In this dialog box, clear the **Display grid beyond Limits** check box from the **Grid behavior** area. Now, the grids will be displayed only up to the limits set.

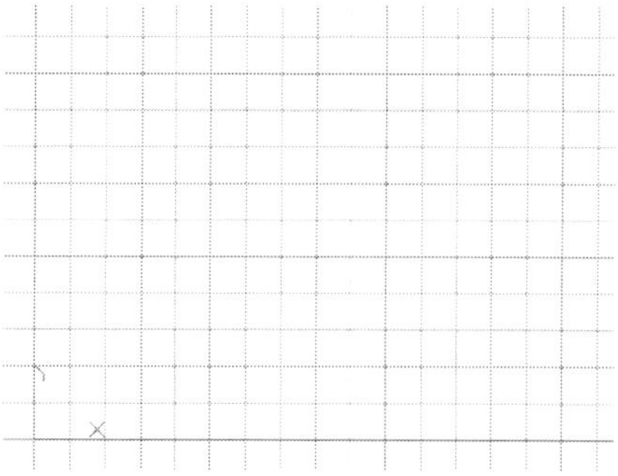

Figure 4-40 *Grid as checked lines*

Figure 4-41 *Grid as dots*

Grid On (F7): Turning the Grid On or Off

You can turn the grid display on/off by using the **Grid On** check box in the **Drafting Settings** dialog box. You can also turn the grid display on/off by choosing the **Display drawing grid** button in the Status Bar or by using the F7 key. **Display drawing grid** is a toggle button. When the grid display is turned on after it has been turned off, the grid is set to the previous grid spacing.

Grid X Spacing and Grid Y Spacing

The **Grid X spacing** and **Grid Y spacing** edit boxes in the **Drafting Settings** dialog box are used to define the desired grid spacing along the X and Y axes. For example, to set the grid spacing to 0.5 units, enter **0.5** in the **Grid X spacing** and **Grid Y spacing** edit boxes. You can also enter different values for the horizontal and vertical grid spacing, see Figure 4-42. If you specify only the grid X spacing value and then choose the **OK** button in the dialog box, the corresponding Y spacing value will automatically be set to match the X spacing value, as shown in Figure 4-42. Therefore, if you want different X and Y spacing values, clear the **Equal X and Y spacing** check box in the **Snap spacing** area, and enter different X and Y spacing values to create unequal Grid Spacing, as shown in Figure 4-43.

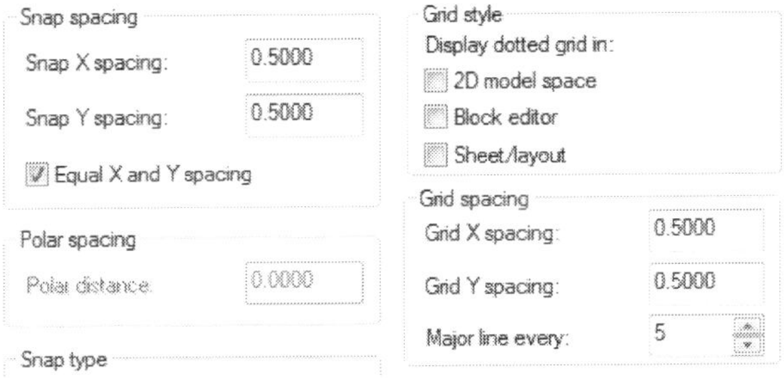

***Figure 4-42** The **Grid Spacing** area of the **Drafting Settings** dialog box*

Note

Grids are especially effective in drawing when the objects in the drawing are placed at regular intervals.

Setting Snap

After displaying the grid, you need to switch on the snap mode so that the cursor snaps to the snap point. The snap points are invisible points (see Figure 4-44) that are created at the intersection of invisible horizontal and vertical lines. A snap point is independent of the grid spacing and the two can have equal or different values. Therefore, when the snap mode is on, the cursor moves in specified intervals from one point to another. You can turn on the snap mode even when the grid lines are invisible. To set snap spacing, enter the X and Y values in the corresponding edit boxes in the **Snap spacing** area of the **Snap and Grid** tab in the **Drafting Settings** dialog box, refer to Figure 4-42. You can turn the snap mode on/off by selecting the **Snap On** check box from the **Drafting Settings** dialog box. You can also turn the snap on or off by choosing the **Snap Mode** button in the Status Bar, or from the shortcut menu

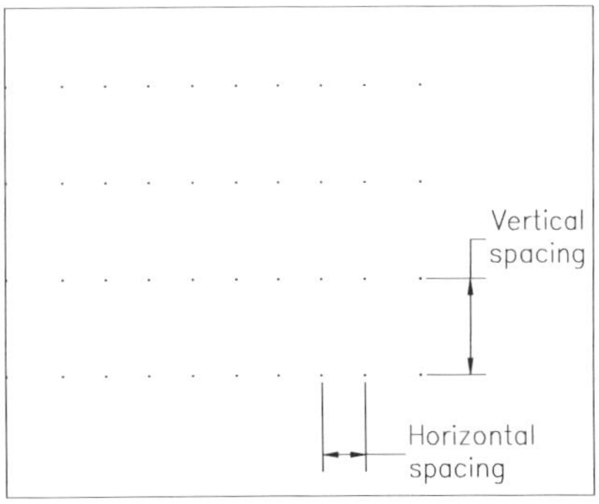

***Figure 4-43** Creating unequal grid spacing*

displayed by right-clicking on the **Snap Mode** button in the Status Bar, or by using the function key F9 as a toggle key.

Snap Type

There are two snap types, **PolarSnap** and **Grid snap**. On selecting **Grid snap**, the cursor snaps along the grid. The **Grid snap** is either of the **Rectangular snap** type or of the **Isometric snap** type. Rectangular snap is the default snap and has been discussed earlier. The other types are discussed next.

Isometric Snap

The isometric mode is used to make isometric drawings. In isometric drawings, the isometric axes are at angle of 30, 90, and 150 degrees. The isometric snap/grid enables you to display the grid lines along these axes, see Figure 4-45. Select the **Isometric snap** radio button in the **Snap type** area of the **Drafting Settings** dialog box to set the snap grid to the isometric mode. The default mode is off (standard). Once you select the **Isometric snap** radio button and choose **OK** in the dialog box, the cursor aligns with the isometric axis. You will notice that the X spacing is not available for this option. You can change the vertical snap and grid spacing by entering values in the **Snap Y spacing** and **Grid Y spacing** edit boxes. While drawing in isometric mode, you can adjust the cursor orientation to the left, top, or right plane of the drawing by using the F5 key. The procedure to create drawings using the **Isometric snap** option is discussed in later chapters.

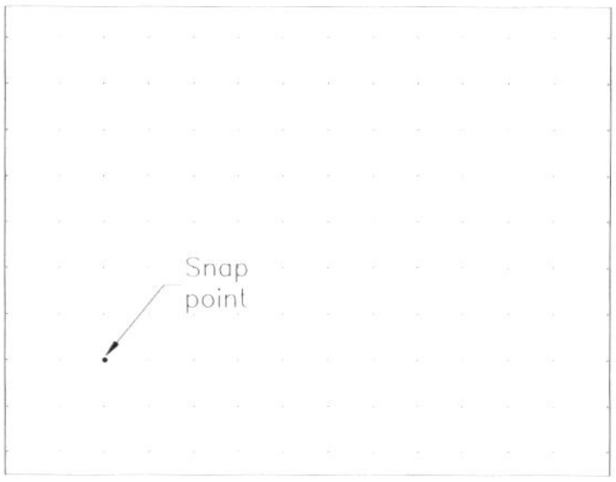

Figure 4-44 *Invisible Snap grid*

Figure 4-45 *Isometric Snap grid*

PolarSnap

The polar snap is used to snap points at a specified distance along the polar alignment angles. To set the snap mode as polar, select the **PolarSnap** radio button in the **Snap type** area; the **Polar distance** edit box will be enabled and the snap spacing options will be disabled. Enter a value for the distance in the **Polar distance** edit box and choose the **OK** button. If this value is zero, AutoCAD LT takes the same value as specified for Snap X spacing earlier. Now, if you draw a line, the cursor snaps along an imaginary line according to the Polar tracking angles that are relative to the last point selected. The polar tracking angle can be set in the **Polar Tracking** tab of the **Drafting Settings** dialog box (discussed later in this chapter).

For example, select the **PolarSnap** radio button and enter **0.5** in the **Polar distance** edit box. Choose the **Polar Tracking** tab and enter **30** in the **Increment angle** drop-down list and then choose the **OK** button. Choose the **Snap Mode** and **Polar Tracking** buttons in the Status Bar. Invoke the **Line** tool and select the start point anywhere on the screen. Now, if you move the cursor at angles in multiples of 30-degree, a dotted line will be displayed and if you move the cursor along this dotted line, a small cross mark will be displayed at a distance of 0.5 (polar snap).

DRAWING STRAIGHT LINES USING THE ORTHOMODE

The **ORTHOMODE** is used to draw lines at right angles only. You can turn the **Ortho** mode on or off by choosing the **ORTHOMODE** button in the Status Bar, by using the function key F8, or by using the **ORTHO** command. When the **ORTHOMODE** mode is on and you move the cursor to specify the next point, a rubber-band line is connected to the cursor in horizontal (parallel to the *X* axis) or vertical (parallel to the *Y* axis) direction. To draw a line in the Ortho mode, specify the start point at the **Specify first point** prompt. To specify the second point, move the cursor and specify a desired point. The line drawn will be either vertical or horizontal, depending on the direction in which you move the cursor, see Figures 4-46 and 4-47.

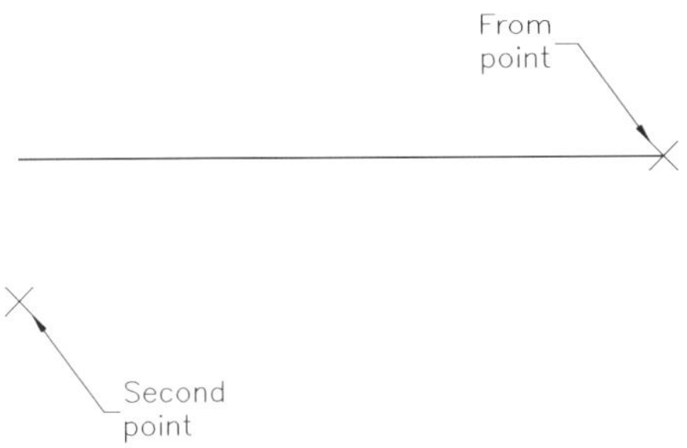

*Figure 4-46 Drawing a horizontal line using the **Ortho** mode*

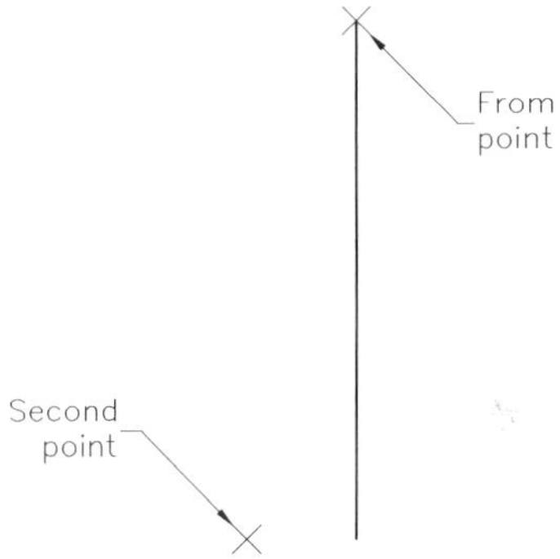

*Figure 4-47 Drawing a vertical line using the **Ortho** mode*

Tip

*You can use the buttons in the Status Bar (at the bottom of the graphics area) to toggle between on or off for different drafting functions like **Snap**, **Grid**, and **Ortho**.*

WORKING WITH OBJECT SNAPS

Toolbar: Object Snap

The term object snap refers to the cursor's ability to snap exactly to a geometric point on an object. The advantage of using object snaps is that you do not have to specify an exact point. For example, to snap the midpoint of a line, use the **Midpoint** object snap and move the cursor closer to the object; a marker (in the form of a geometric shape, a triangle for Midpoint) will automatically be displayed at the mid point. Click to snap the mid point.

Object snaps recognize only the objects that are visible on the screen, which include the objects on the locked layers. The objects on the layers that are turned off or frozen are not visible, and they cannot be used for object snaps.

Object snapping can be done by using the **Object Snap modes** shortcut menu. To invoke this shortcut menu, choose a tool, press and hold the SHIFT key, and then right-click, see Figure 4-48. You can also do object snapping by using the **Object Snap** toolbar shown in Figure 4-49. Alternatively, you can invoke the **Object Snap modes** shortcut menu when you are inside any other sketching tool. For example, invoke the **Center, Radius** tool from the **Draw** panel and then right-click to invoke the shortcut menu. From the shortcut menu, choose the **Snap Overrides** option to display the **Object Snaps** shortcut menu. The following are the object snap modes in AutoCAD LT.

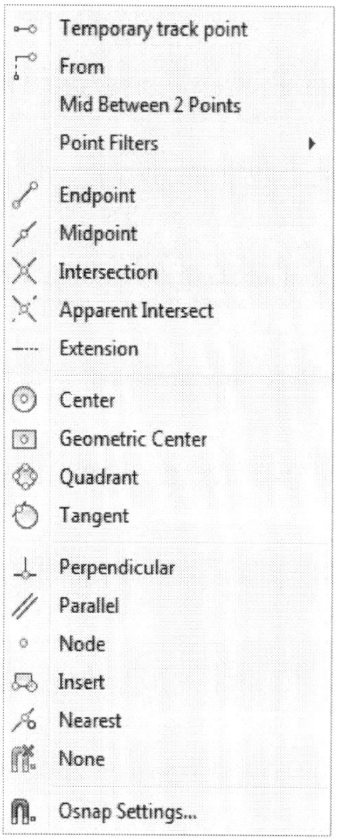

***Figure 4-48** The **Object Snap modes** shortcut menu*

Endpoint
Perpendicular
Midpoint
Parallel
Intersection
Insert
Apparent Intersect Extension
Geometric center
Node
Midpoint Between two points

Center
Nearest
Quadrant
None
Tangent
From

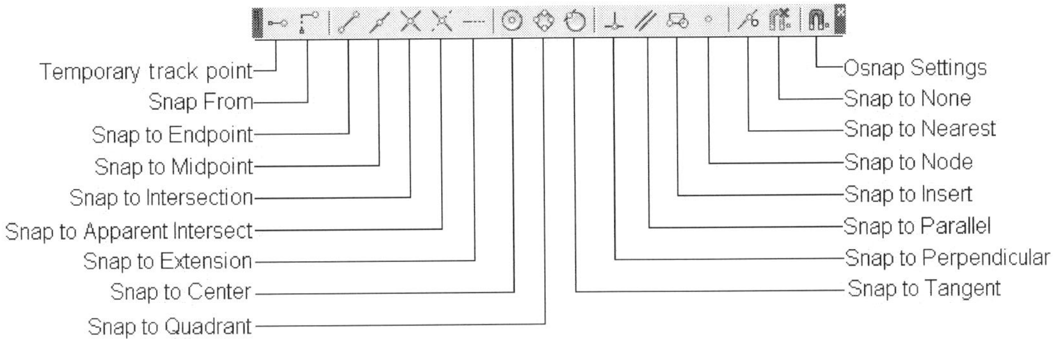

Figure 4-49 *The* ***Object Snap*** *toolbar*

AutoSnap

The AutoSnap feature controls various characteristics for the object snap. As you move the target box over the object, AutoCAD LT displays the geometric marker corresponding to the shapes shown in the **Object Snap** tab of the **Drafting Settings** dialog box. You can change different AutoSnap settings such as attaching a target box to the cursor when you invoke any object snap, or change the size and color of the marker. These settings can be changed from the **Options** dialog box (**Drafting** tab). You can invoke the **Options** dialog box from the **Application Menu**, or by choosing the **Options** button in the **Drafting Settings** dialog box. After invoking the **Options** dialog box, choose the **Drafting** tab in this dialog box; the **AutoSnap Settings** area will be displayed, see Figure 4-50. Select the **Marker** check box to toggle the display of the marker. Select the **Magnet** check box to toggle the magnet that snaps the crosshairs to the particular point of the object for that object snap.

You can use the **Display AutoSnap tooltip** and **Display AutoSnap aperture box** check boxes to toggle the display of the tooltip and the aperture box. Note that if the **Display AutoSnap tooltip** check box is selected in the **Options** dialog box and you move the cursor over an entity, after invoking a tool, the autosnap marker will be displayed. Now, do not move the cursor; the name of the object snap will be displayed. You can change the size of the marker and the aperture box by moving the **AutoSnap Marker Size** and **Aperture Size** slider bars, respectively. You can also change the color of the markers by choosing the **Colors** button. The size of the aperture is measured in pixels (short form of picture elements). Picture elements are dots that make up the screen picture. The aperture size can also be changed by using the **APERTURE** command. The default value for the aperture size is 10 pixels. The display of the marker and the tooltip is controlled by the **AUTOSNAP** system variable. The following are the bit values for **AUTOSNAP**.

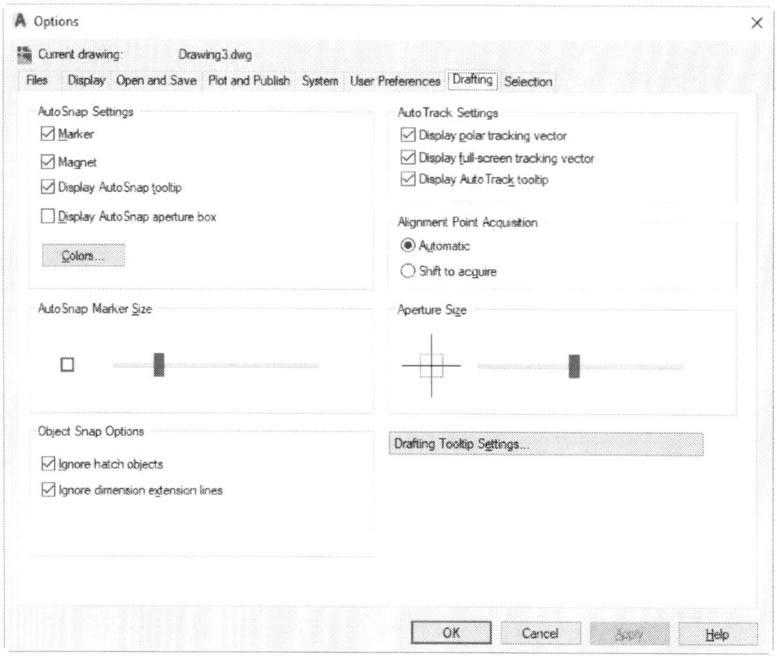

*Figure 4-50 The **Drafting** tab in the **Options** dialog box*

Bit Values	**Functions**
0	Turns off the Marker, AutoSnap Tooltip, and Magnet
1	Turns on the AutoSnap marker
2	Turns on the AutoSnap tooltips
4	Turns on the AutoSnap magnet
8	Turns on polar tracking
16	Turns on object snap tracking
32	Turns on tooltips for polar tracking, object snap tracking, and Ortho mode

The basic functionality of Object Snap modes is discussed next.

Endpoint

The **Endpoint** Object Snap mode is used to snap the cursor to the closest endpoint of a line or an arc. To use this Object Snap mode, invoke a draw tool such as **Line** and choose the **Snap to Endpoint** button and move the cursor (crosshairs) anywhere close to the endpoint of the object; a marker will be displayed at the endpoint. Click to select that point; the endpoint of the object will be snapped. If there are several objects near the cursor crosshairs, the endpoint of the object that is closest to the crosshairs will be snapped. However, if the **Magnet** is on, you can move to grab the desired endpoint. Figure 4-51 shows the cursor snapping the end point of a circle. The dotted line is the proposed line to be drawn.

Midpoint

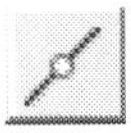

The **Midpoint** Object Snap mode is used to snap the midpoint of a line or an arc. To use this Object Snap mode, choose the **Snap to Midpoint** button and select an object anywhere; the midpoint of the object will be snapped. Figure 4-52 shows the cursor snapping to the midpoint of a line. The dotted line is the proposed line to be drawn.

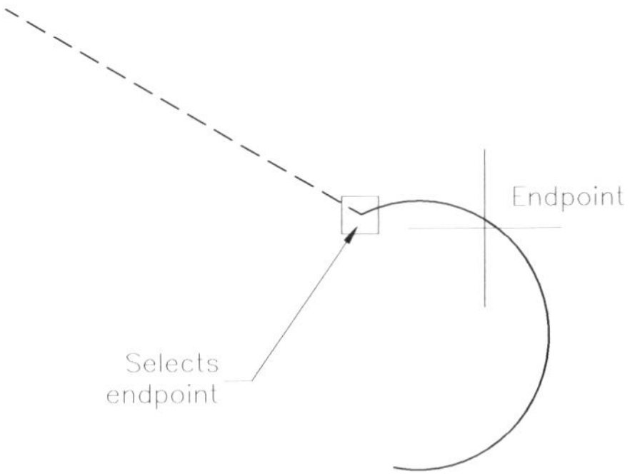

Figure 4-51 The ***Endpoint*** *Object Snap mode*

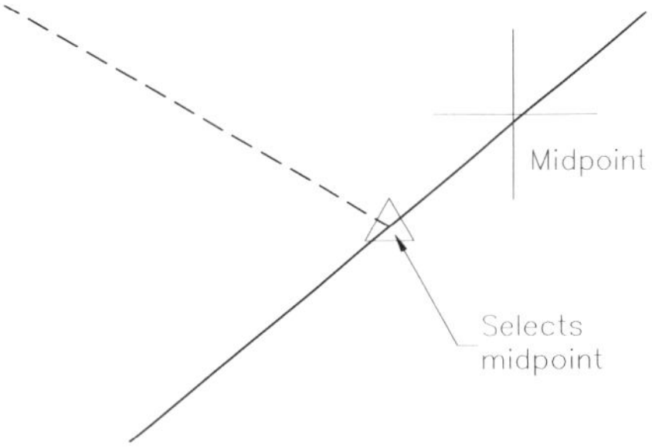

Figure 4-52 The ***Midpoint*** *Object Snap mode*

Nearest

The **Nearest** Object Snap mode is used to select a point on an object (line, arc, circle, or ellipse) that is visually closest to the crosshairs. To use this mode, invoke a tool, choose the **Nearest** object snap, and then move the crosshairs near the intended point on the object; a marker will be displayed. Left-click to snap that point. Figure 4-53 shows the cursor snapping the point in a line. The dotted line is the proposed line to be drawn.

Center

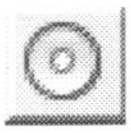

The **Center** Object Snap mode is used to snap the cursor to the center point of an ellipse, circle, or arc. After choosing this option, move the cursor on the circumference of a circle or an arc; a marker will be displayed at the center of the circle. Left-click to snap the center of the circle. Figure 4-54 shows the cursor snapping the center point of a circle. The dotted line is the proposed line to be drawn.

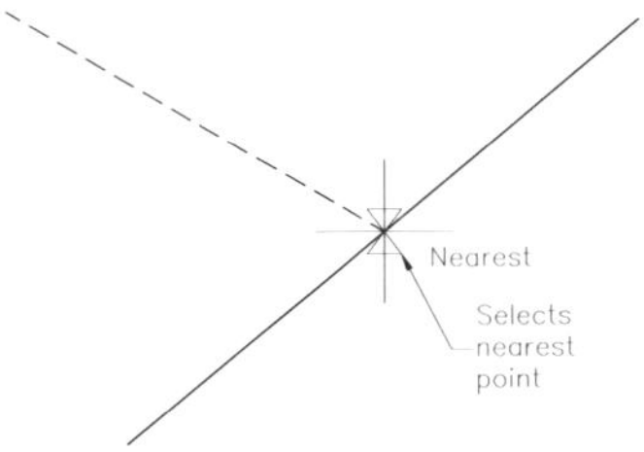

Figure 4-53 The ***Nearest*** *Object Snap mode*

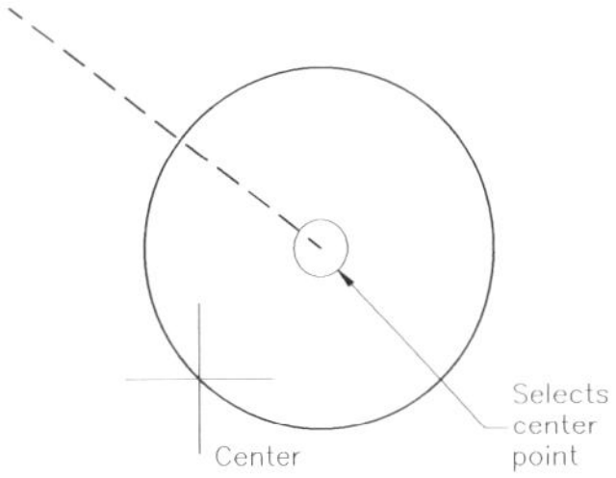

Figure 4-54 The ***Center*** *Object Snap mode*

Tangent

The **Tangent** Object Snap mode is used to snap the cursor to the tangent point of an existing ellipse, circle, or arc. To use this mode, invoke the **Line** tool and choose the **Tangent** Object snap. Now, place the cursor on the circumference of the circle or arc and click on the circumference of the circle when the Tangent icon is displayed. Figure 4-55 shows the cursor placed on the circumference of the circle. The dashed line is the proposed tangential line.

Note

*If the start point of a line is defined by using the **Tangent** Object Snap, the tip shows **Deferred Tangent**. However, if you end the line using this Object Snap, the tip shows **Tangent**.*

Figure 4-56 shows the use of the **Nearest**, **Endpoint**, **Midpoint**, and **Tangent** Object Snap modes.

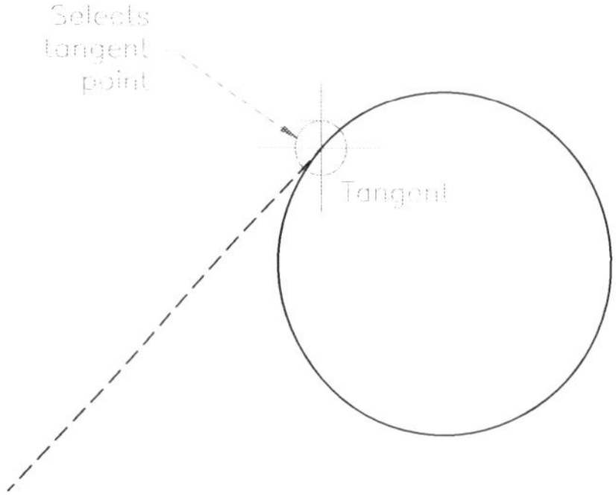

*Figure 4-55 The **Tangent** Object Snap mode*

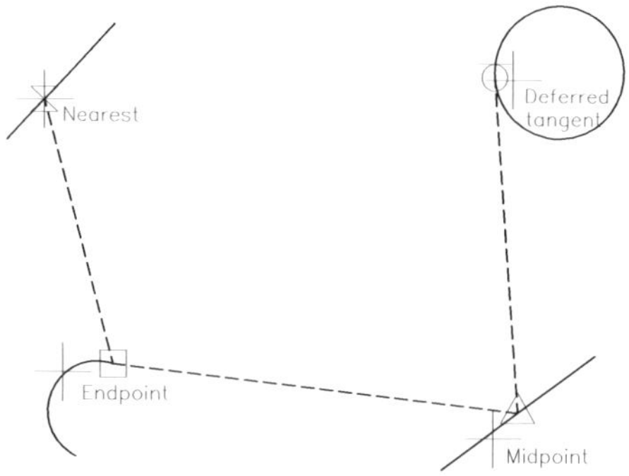

*Figure 4-56 Using the **Nearest**, **Endpoint**, **Midpoint**, and **Tangent** Object Snap modes*

Quadrant

The **Quadrant** Object Snap mode is used to snap the cursor to the quadrant point of an ellipse, an arc, or a circle. A circle has four quadrants, and each quadrant subtends an angle of 90 degrees. Therefore, the quadrant points are located at **0**, **90**, **180**, and **270**-degree positions. If the circle is inserted as a block (see Chapter 15) and rotated, the quadrant points will also be rotated by the same degree, see Figures 4-57 and 4-58.

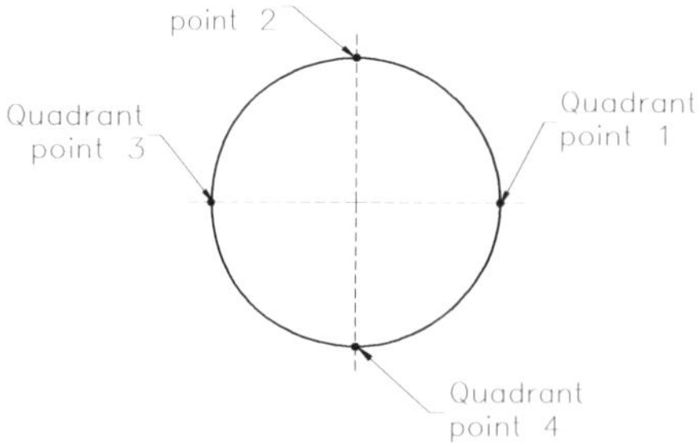

Figure 4-57 Location of the circle quadrants

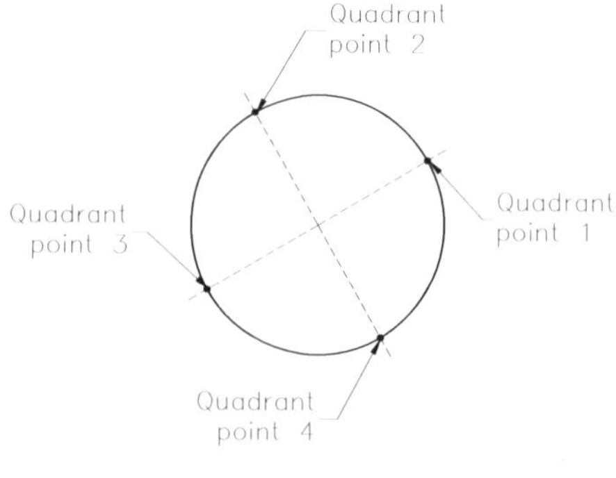

Figure 4-58 Quadrants in a rotated circle

To use this object snap, position the cursor on the circle or arc closest to the desired quadrant and click when the marker is displayed. Figure 4-59 shows the cursor selecting the third quadrant and the proposed line.

Intersection

The **Intersection** Object Snap mode is used to snap the cursor to a point where two or more lines, circles, ellipses, or arcs intersect. To use this object snap, move the cursor to the desired intersection point such that the intersection is within the target box and click when the intersection marker is displayed. Figure 4-60 shows the cursor selecting the intersection point and the proposed line is in dotted line.

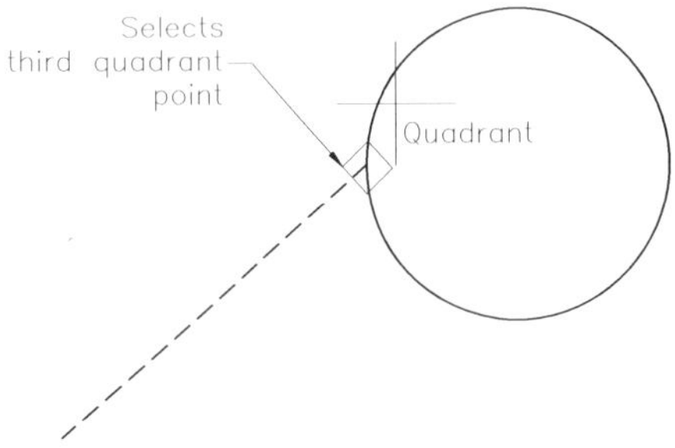

Figure 4-59 *The **Quadrant** Object Snap mode*

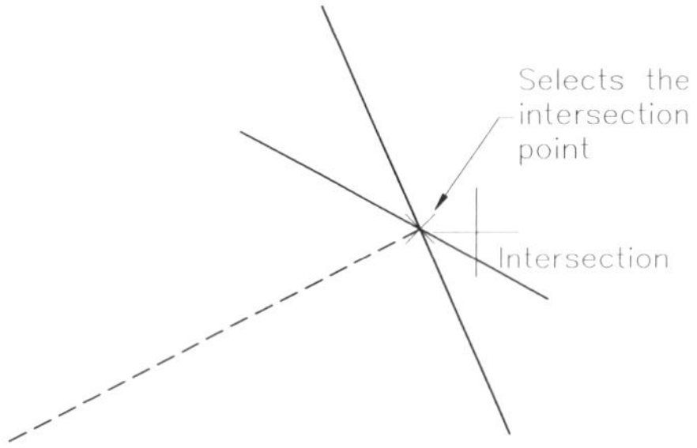

Figure 4-60 *The **Intersection** Object Snap mode*

After setting the **Intersection** Object Snap mode, if the cursor is close to an object and not close to actual intersection, the **Extended Intersection** tooltip will be displayed. If you select this object, you need to select another object. Move the cursor close to another object; the intersection point will be snapped. Left-click to select the intersection point. But if the object selected second does not intersect with the object selected first, then the cursor will snap to the extended intersection point, as shown in Figure 4-61. The extended intersections are the intersections that do not exist, but are imaginary and formed if a line or an arc is extended.

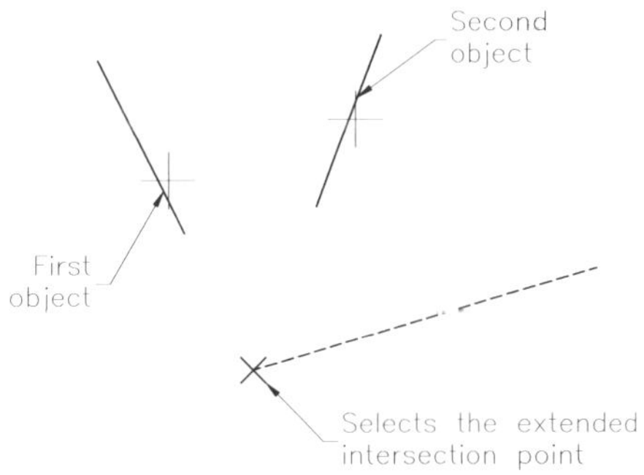

Figure 4-61 *The **Extended Intersection** Object Snap mode*

Apparent Intersection

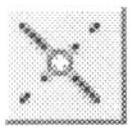

The **Apparent Intersection** Object Snap mode is used to select the projected intersections of two objects in 3D space. Sometimes, two objects appear to intersect one another in the current view, but in 3D space they do not actually intersect. The **Apparent Intersection** snap mode is used to select such intersections. This mode works on wireframes in 3D space. If you use this object snap mode in 2D, it works like an extended intersection.

Perpendicular

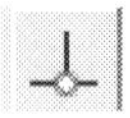

The **Perpendicular** Object Snap mode is used to draw a line perpendicular to or from another line, or normal to or from an arc or a circle, or to an ellipse. After invoking the **Line** tool, if you invoke this mode and then select an object, a perpendicular line will be attached to the cursor. Move the cursor and place the line, as shown in Figure 4-62. But after invoking the **Line** tool, if you select the start point of the line first and then invoke the **Perpendicular** Object Snap mode, you need to select an object. On doing so, AutoCAD LT selects a point such that the resulting line is perpendicular to the selected object, as shown in Figure 4-63.

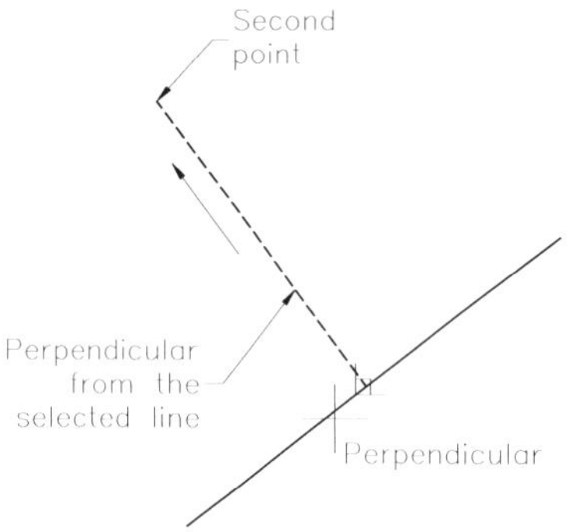

***Figure 4-62** Selecting the perpendicular snap first*

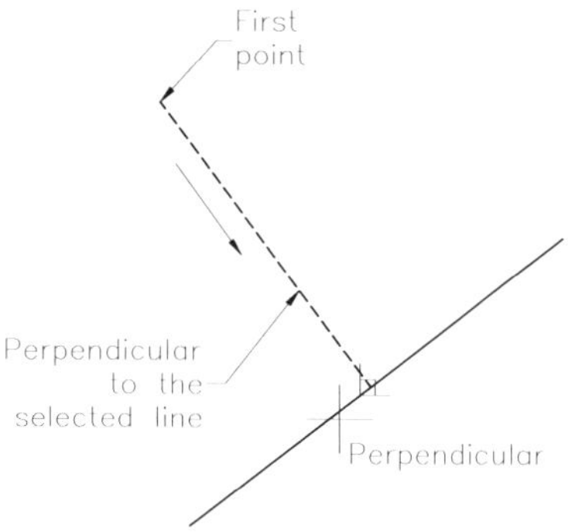

***Figure 4-63** Selecting the start point and then the perpendicular snap*

Figure 4-64 shows the use of various object snap modes.

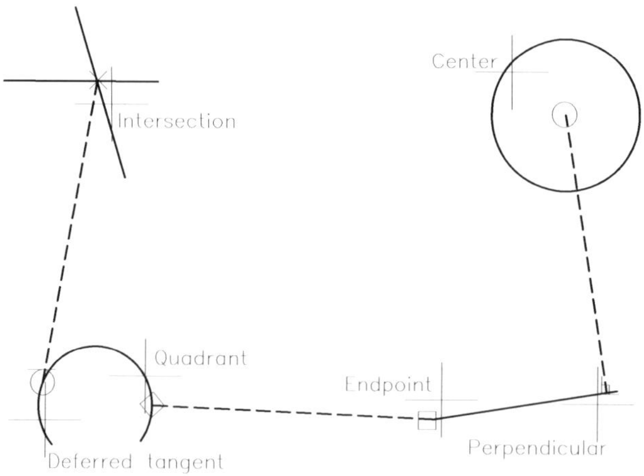

***Figure 4-64** Using various object snap modes to locate points*

Exercise 3 — Quadrant & Tangent

Draw the sketch shown in Figure 4-65. P1 and P2 are the center points of the top and bottom arcs. The space between the dotted lines is 1 unit.

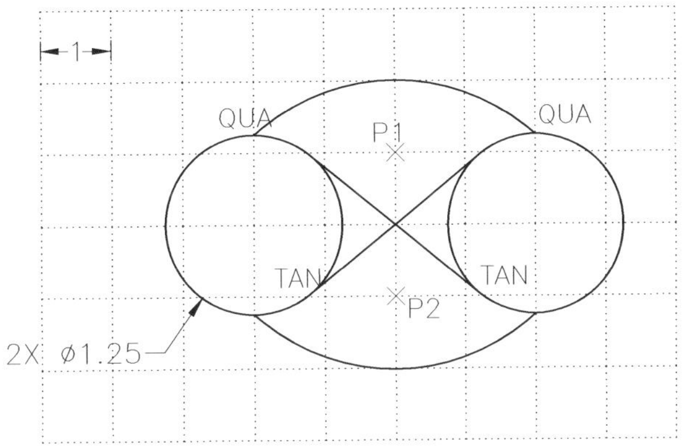

Figure 4-65 Drawing for Exercise 3

Node

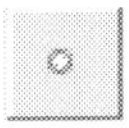

You can use the **Node** Object Snap mode to snap the points placed by using the **Multiple Points**, **Divide**, or **Measure** tools. Figure 4-66 shows the three points placed by using the **Multiple Points** tool. The dotted line indicates the proposed line to be drawn, and the **Node** tooltip displayed on moving the cursor close to a point.

Insertion

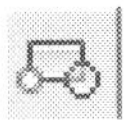

The **Insertion** Object Snap mode is used to snap to the insertion point of a text, shape, block, attribute, or attribute definition. The insertion point is the point with respect to which a text, shape, or a block is inserted. Figure 4-67 shows the insertion point of the text and the block. The dotted line is the proposed line to be drawn.

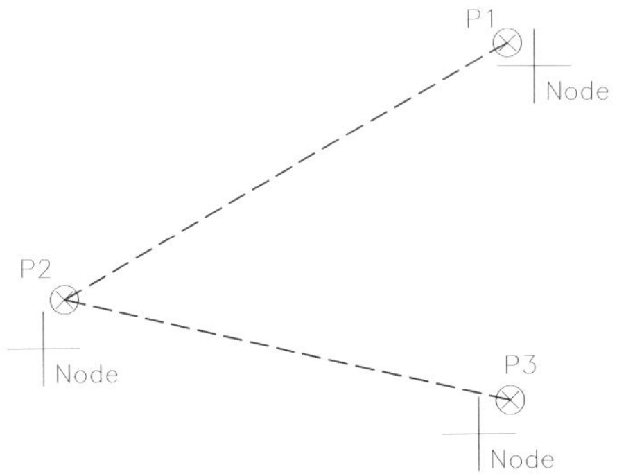

*Figure 4-66 Using the **Node** Object Snap*

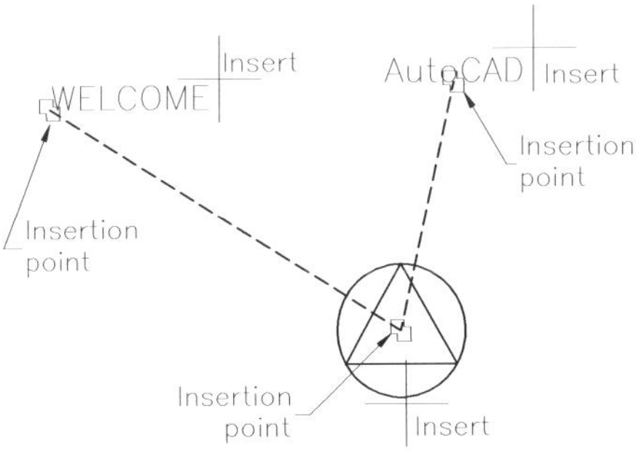

*Figure 4-67 The **Insertion** Object Snap*

Snap to None

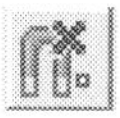

The **Snap to None** Object Snap mode is used to turn off any running object snap (see the section "Running Object Snap Mode" that follows) for one point only. The following example illustrates the use of this Object Snap mode.

Invoke the **Drafting Settings** dialog box and choose the **Object Snap** tab. Select the **Midpoint** and **Center** check boxes. This sets the object snap to midpoint and center. Now, to draw a line whose start point is closer to the endpoint of another line, invoke the **Line** tool and move the cursor to the desired position on the previous line. The cursor automatically snaps to the midpoint of the line. You can disable this automatic snap by choosing the **Snap to None** object snap from the **Object Snap** toolbar.

Parallel

When you need to draw a line parallel to a line or a polyline, use the **Parallel** Object Snap. For example, when you are in the middle of the **Line** tool, and you have to draw a line parallel to the one already drawn, you can use the **Parallel** object snap mode as discussed next.

1. Choose **Line** from the **Draw** toolbar.
2. Select a point on the screen.
3. Choose the **Parallel** button from the **Object Snap** toolbar.
4. Move the cursor close to the reference object and pause for a while; the parallel tooltip appears on it, indicating that the line has been selected.
5. Now, move the cursor at an angle parallel to the line; an imaginary parallel line (construction line) appears, on which you can select the next point. As you move the cursor on the construction line, a tooltip with relative polar coordinates is displayed near the cursor. This helps you to select the next point. The line thus drawn is parallel to the selected object, as shown in Figure 4-68.

Extension

The **Extension** Object Snap mode is used to locate a point on the proposed extension path of a line or an arc (Figure 4-69). It can also be used with intersection to determine the extended intersection point. To snap a point by using this snap mode, choose the **Line** tool from the **Draw** toolbar, and then choose the **Snap to Extension** button from the **Object Snap** toolbar. Briefly pause at the end of the line or the arc; a small plus sign (+) or a tooltip will appear at the end of the line or the arc, indicating that it has been selected. If you move the cursor along the line, a temporary extension path will be displayed and the tooltip displays the relative polar coordinates from the end of the line. Select a point or enter a distance to begin a line and then select another point to finish the line.

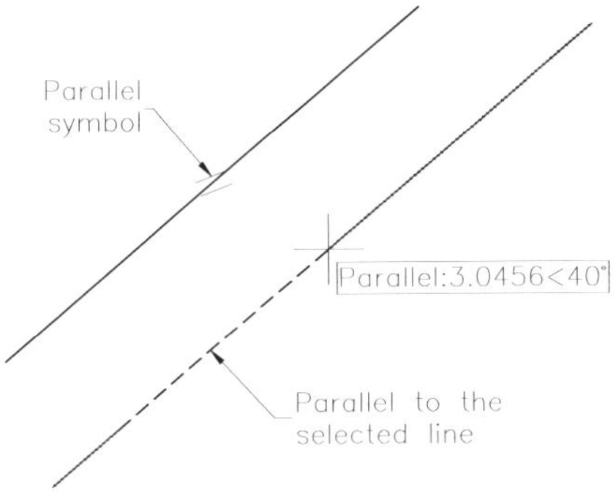

Figure 4-68 *The **Parallel** Object Snap mode*

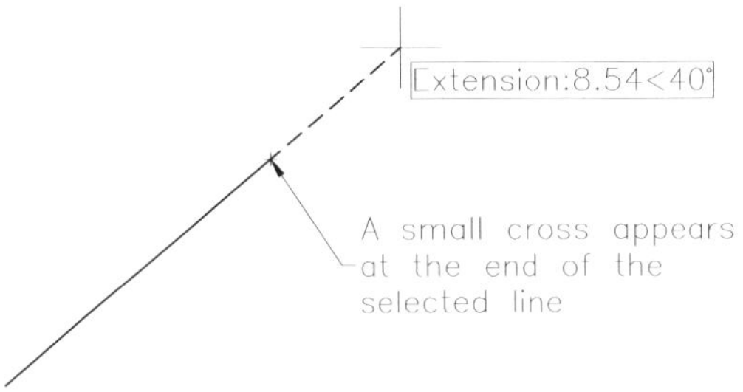

Figure 4-69 *The **Extension** Object Snap mode*

Tip

*While using the **Parallel** object snap mode, you can choose more than one line as reference line which is indicated by a plus sign. Depending upon the direction in which you move the cursor, AutoCAD LT will choose any one of these reference lines and the chosen line will be marked with the parallel symbol in place of the plus sign.*

*Similarly, while using the **Extension** object snap mode, you can choose more than one endpoint as the reference.*

From

The **From** Object Snap mode is used to locate a point relative to a given point (Figure 4-70). For example, to locate a point that is 2.5 units up and 1.5 units right from the endpoint of a given line, you can use the **From** Object Snap mode as follows:

*Choose the **Line** tool.*
Specify first point: *Choose the **Snap From** button from the **Object Snap** toolbar.*
Specify first point: _from Base point: *Specify the base point.*
Specify first point: _from Base point: <Offset>: **@1.5,2.5**

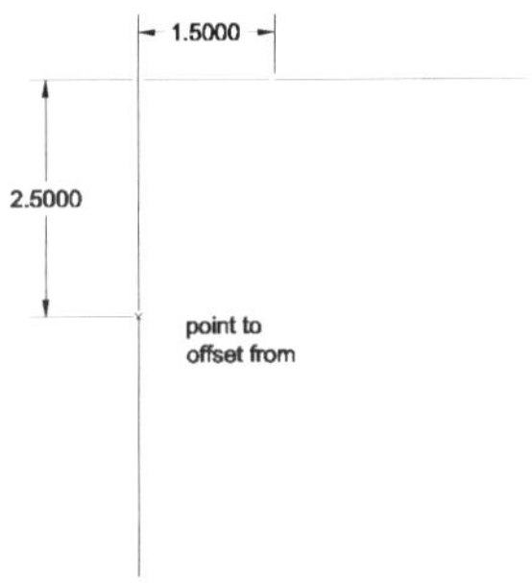

Figure 4-70 *Using the **From** Object Snap mode to locate a point*

Note

*The **From** Object Snap mode cannot be used as the running object snap.*

Geometric Center

The **Geometric Center** Object Snap mode is used to snap the cursor to the Geometric center point of the Geometric entities. After choosing this option, move the cursor on the Geometric entity; a marker will be displayed at the Geometric center of the entity. Figure 4-71 shows the cursor snapping the Geometric center of a rectangle.

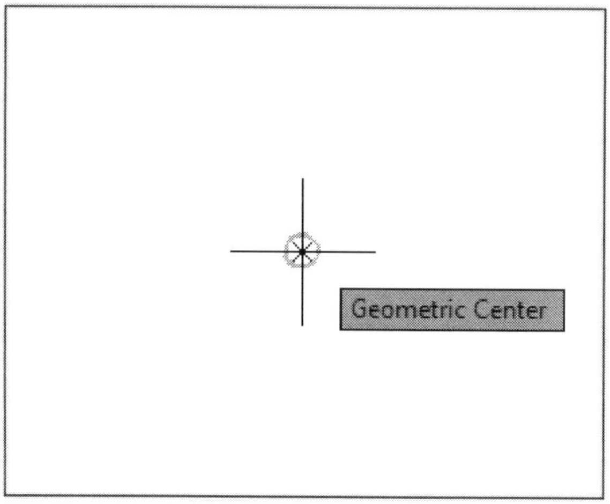

Figure 4-71 *The* ***Geometric Center*** *Object Snap mode*

Mid Between 2 Points

This Object Snap mode is used to select the midpoint of an imaginary line drawn between two selected points. Note that this Object Snap mode can only be invoked from the shortcut menu. To understand the working of this Object Snap mode, refer to the sketch shown in Figure 4-72. In this sketch, there are two circles and you need to draw another circle with the center point at the midpoint of an imaginary line drawn between the center points of two existing circles. The following is the prompt sequence:

Choose the ***Center, Radius*** *tool*
Specify center point for circle or [3P/2P/Ttr (tan tan radius)]: *Right-click and choose* ***Mid Between 2 Points*** *from the* ***Snap Overrides*** *cascading menu*
_m2p First point of mid: *Snap the center of the left circle*
Second point of mid: *Snap the center of the right circle*
Specify radius of circle or [Diameter] <current>: *Specify the radius of the new circle*

Temporary Track Point

The **Temporary track point** is used to locate a point with respect to two different points. If you choose this button and then select a point and move the cursor, an orthogonal imaginary line will be displayed either horizontally or vertically. Then, you need to select another point to display another orthogonal imaginary line in the other direction. The required point will be located where these two imaginary lines intersect. You can also use this option along with the other Object Snap modes. To locate a point, invoke the **Line** tool from the **Draw** toolbar and then use the temporary tracking as follows.

Specify first point: *Choose the* ***Temporary track point*** *button from the* ***Object Snap*** *toolbar.*
Specify temporary OTRACK point: *Choose the* ***Snap to Midpoint*** *button from the* ***Object Snap*** *toolbar.*
Select the midpoint of the line and move the cursor horizontally toward the right.
Specify first point: *Choose the* ***Temporary Tracking Point*** *button from the* ***Object Snap*** *toolbar.*

Specify temporary OTRACK point: *Choose the **Snap to Endpoint** button from the **Object Snap** toolbar.*
Select the upper endpoint of the line and move the cursor vertically down.

As you move the cursor down, both the horizontal and vertical imaginary lines will be displayed, as shown in Figure 4-73. Select their intersection point and then draw the line.

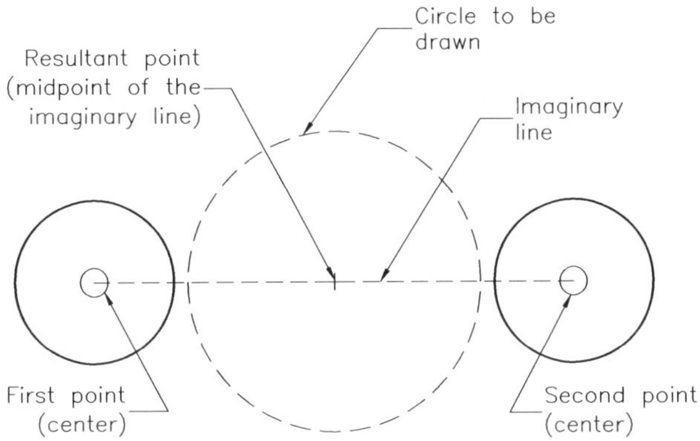

*Figure 4-72 Using the **Midpoint Between 2 Points** Object Snap mode to locate a point*

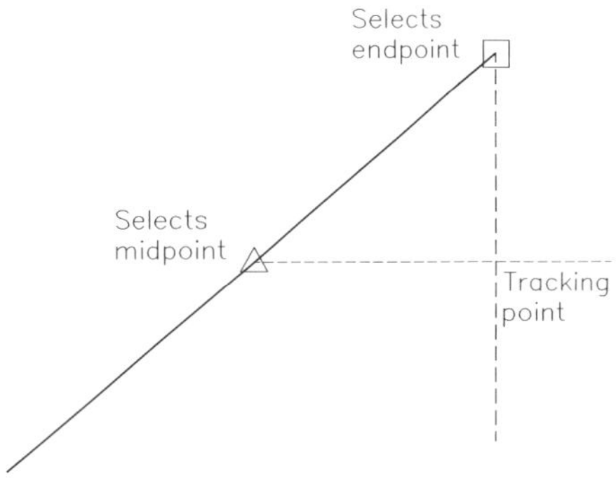

Figure 4-73 Using temporary tracking point

Combining Object Snap Modes

You can also combine the snaps from the command line by separating the snap modes with a comma. In this case, AutoCAD LT searches for the specified modes and grabs the point on the object that is closest to the point where the object is selected. The prompt sequence for using the **Midpoint** and **Endpoint** object snaps is given next.

*Choose the **Line** tool*
_line Specify first point: **MID, END** Enter *(MIDpoint or ENDpoint object snap.)*
Of: *Select the object*

Note
In reference to object snaps, "line" generally includes xlines, rays, and polyline segments, and "arc" generally includes polyarc segments.

Exercise 4

Draw the sketch shown in Figure 4-74. The space between the dotted lines is 1 unit.

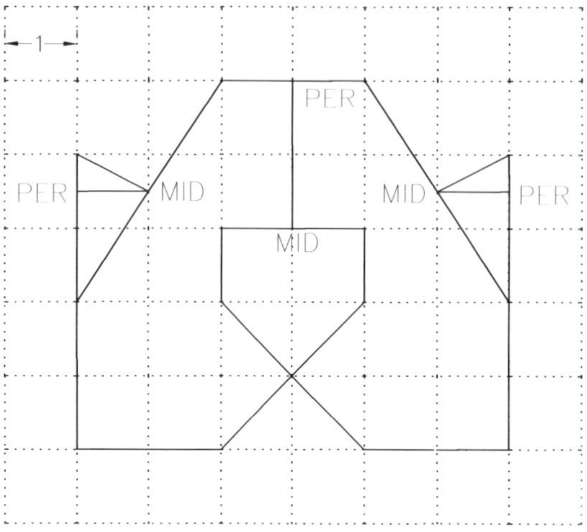

Figure 4-74 Drawing for Exercise 4

Using Coordinate Filters

Coordinate filters are also known as Point filters and they allow you to align objects by filtering the coordinate of the existing geometries.

To invoke the point/coordinate filters (.X, .Y, .Z, XY, .XZ, and .YZ filters), press the SHIFT key and then right click; a shortcut menu will be invoked. Next, move the cursor over the **Point Filters** option; a cascading menu will be displayed. In this cascading menu, you can select the required type of filter. On invoking **.X** point filter, you can click on a point in the drawing area whose X coordinate needs to be defined. After defining the X coordinate, you will be prompted to define Y or Z coordinate. Click on another point in the drawing area to define the Y or Z coordinate.

For example, if you want to draw a circle at the center of a rectangle, you can use the point filters. To do so, invoke the **Circle**, **Radius** tool and then press the SHIFT key and right-click to invoke the shortcut menu. Next, move the cursor over the **Point Filter** option; a cascading menu appears. Select the **.X** option; you will be prompted to specify the X coordinate (**.X** of). Click on the midpoint of a horizontal line; you will be prompted to specify the y coordinate [**.X** of (need **YZ**)]. Click on the midpoint of a vertical line; the center point of the circle is specified. Next, specify the radius or diameter of the circle by entering a value at the Command prompt; the circle will be created.

RUNNING OBJECT SNAP MODE

Toolbar: Object Snap > Osnap Settings **Command:** OS/OSNAP

In the previous sections, you have learned to use object snaps to snap to different points of an object. The object snaps are to be selected from the toolbar or from the shortcut menu. One of the drawbacks of this method is that you have to select them every time, even if you are using the same snap mode again. This problem can be resolved by using Running Osnap. The Running Osnap can be invoked by using the **Object Snap** tab of the **Drafting Settings** dialog box (Figure 4-75). If you choose the **Osnap Settings** button from the toolbar, or enter **OSNAP** at the Command prompt, or choose **Settings** from the shortcut menu displayed on right-clicking on the **OSNAP** button in the Status Bar, then the **Object Snap** tab will be displayed in the **Drafting Settings** dialog box. In this tab, you can set the running object snap modes by selecting the check boxes next to the snap modes. For example, to set **Endpoint** as the running Object Snap mode, select the **Endpoint** check box and then the **OK** button in the dialog box.

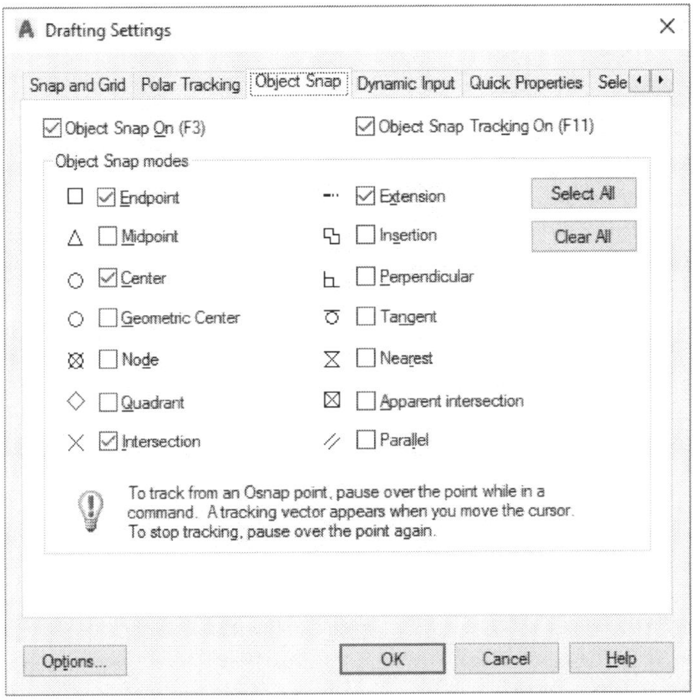

*Figure 4-75 The **Drafting Settings** dialog box (**Object Snap** tab)*

Once you set the running Object Snap mode, a marker will be displayed when you move the crosshairs over the key points. If you have selected a combination of modes, AutoCAD LT selects the mode that is closest to the crosshairs. For example, if you have selected the **Endpoint**, **Midpoint**, and **Center** check boxes in the dialog box and move the cursor over a line, the endpoint or the midpoint will be displayed, depending upon the position of the crosshair. Similarly, if you place the cursor over the circumference of a circle, the center will be displayed. The running Object Snap mode can be turned on or off without losing the object snap settings by choosing the **OSNAP** button in the Status Bar. You can also accomplish this by pressing the function key F3 or CTRL+F keys.

Overriding the Running Snap

When you select the running object snaps, all other Object Snap modes are ignored unless you select another Object Snap mode. Once you select a different osnap mode, the running OSNAP mode is temporarily overruled. After the operation has been performed, the running OSNAP mode becomes active again. If you want to discontinue the current running Object Snap mode completely, choose the **Clear All** button in the **Drafting Settings** dialog box. If you want to temporarily disable the running object snap, choose the **OSNAP** button (off position) in the Status Bar.

If you override the running object snap modes for a point selection and do not find a point to satisfy the override Object Snap mode, AutoCAD LT displays a message to this effect. For example, if you specify an override Object Snap mode of center and no circle, ellipse, or arc is found at that location, AutoCAD LT will display the message "**Point or option keyword required**".

Cycling through Snaps

AutoCAD LT displays the geometric marker corresponding to the shapes shown in the **Object Snap** tab of the **Drafting Settings** dialog box. You can use the TAB key to cycle through the snaps. For example, if you have a circle with an intersecting rectangle, as shown in Figure 4-76 and you want to snap to one of the geometric points on the circle, you can use the TAB key to cycle through geometric points. The geometric points for a circle are the center point, quadrant points, and intersecting points with the rectangle. To snap to one of these points, first you need to set the running object snaps (center, quadrant, and intersection object snaps) in the **Drafting Settings** dialog box. Then, invoke a tool and move the cursor over the objects; AutoSnap displays a marker and a tooltip. You can cycle through the snap points by pressing the TAB key. For example, if you press the TAB key while the aperture box is on the circle and the rectangle (near the lower left intersection point), the intersection, center, and quadrant points will be displayed one by one. Left-click to select the required key point.

Setting the Priority for Coordinate Entry

Sometimes you may want the keyboard entry to take precedence over the running Object Snap modes. This is useful when you want to locate a point that is close to the running osnap. By default, when you specify the coordinates (by using the keyboard) of a point located near a running osnap, AutoCAD LT ignores the point and snaps to the running osnap. For example, if you have selected the **Intersection** object snap in the **Object Snap** tab of the **Drafting Settings** dialog box and if you enter the coordinates of the endpoint of a line very close to the intersection point (Figure 4-77 a), the line will snap to the intersection point and ignore the keyboard entry point.

Therefore, to set the priority between the keyboard entry and the object snap, select the **Keyboard entry** radio button in the **User Preferences** tab of the **Options** dialog box, see Figure 4-78, and then choose **OK**. Now, if you enter the coordinates of the endpoint of a line very close to the intersection point (Figure 4-77 b), the start point will snap to the coordinates specified and the running osnap (intersection) is ignored. This setting is stored in the **OSNAPCORD** system variable and you can also set the priority through this variable. A value **0** gives priority to running osnap, value **1** gives priority to the keyboard entry, and value **2** gives priority to the keyboard entry except scripts.

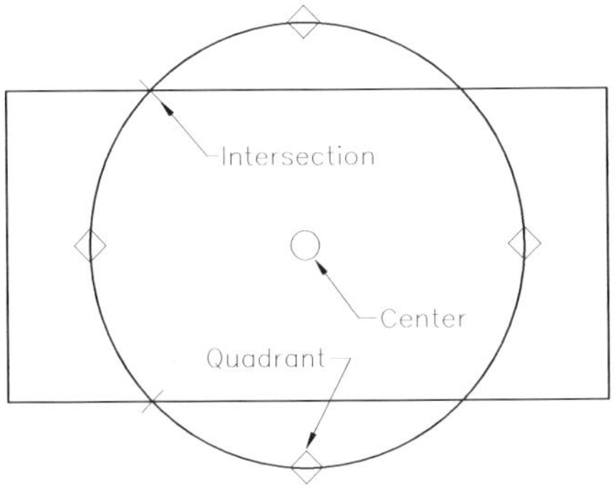

Figure 4-76 *Using the TAB key to cycle through the snaps*

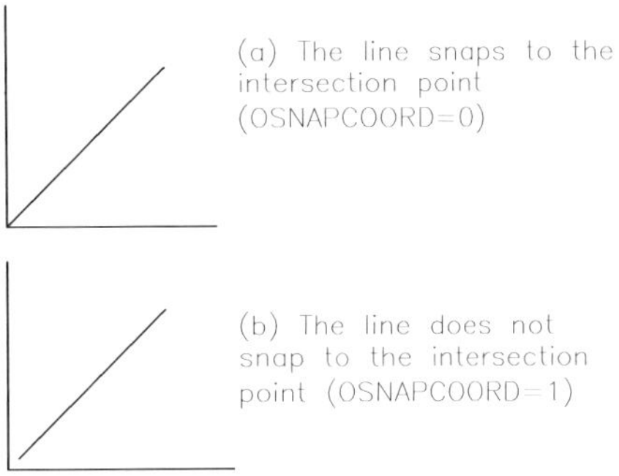

Figure 4-77 *Setting the coordinate entry priority*

> **Tip**
> *If you do not want the running osnap to take precedence over the keyboard entry, you can simply disable the running osnap temporarily by choosing the **OSNAP** button in the Status Bar to disable it. This lets you specify a point close to a running osnap. This way you do not have to change the settings for coordinate entry in the **Options** dialog box.*

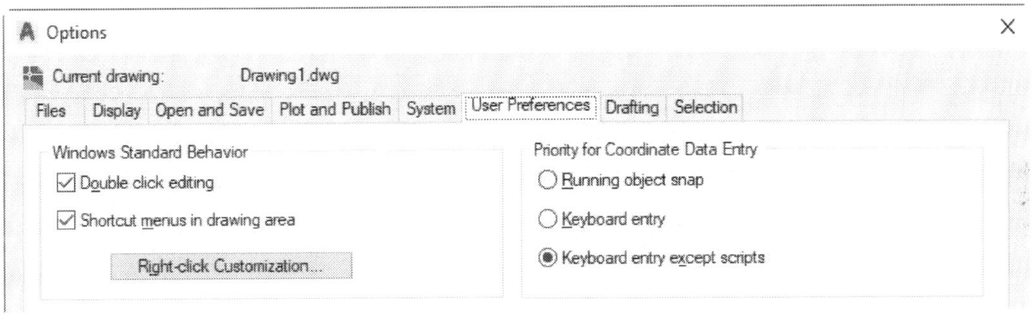

Figure 4-78 *Setting priority for coordinate data entry in the **Options** dialog box*

USING AUTOTRACKING

While using AutoTracking, the cursor moves along temporary paths to locate key points in a drawing. It can be used to locate points with respect to other points or objects in the drawing. There are two types of AutoTracking options: Object Snap Tracking and Polar Tracking.

Object Snap Tracking

Object Snap Tracking is used to track the movement of the cursor along the alignment paths, based on the Object Snap points (running osnaps) selected in the **Object Snap** tab of the **Drafting Settings** dialog box. You can set the object snap tracking on by selecting the **Object Snap Tracking On (F11)** check box in the **Object Snap** tab of the **Drafting Settings** dialog box or by choosing the **Object Snap Tracking** button in the Status Bar, or by using the function key F11.

The direction of a path is determined by the motion of the cursor or the point you select on an object. For example, to draw a circle whose center is located at the intersection of the imaginary lines passing through the center of two existing circles (Figure 4-79), you can use AutoTracking. To do so, choose **Center** in the **Object Snap** tab of the **Drafting Settings** dialog box and turn on the **Object Snap** button in the Status Bar. Now, activate the object tracking by choosing the **Object Snap Tracking** button in the Status Bar. Choose the **Center, Radius** button from the **Draw** toolbar and pause the cursor at the center of the first circle till the marker or a plus sign is displayed. Then, move it horizontally to get the imaginary horizontal line. Move the cursor toward the second circle; the horizontal path disappears. Now, place the cursor for a while at the center of the second circle and move it vertically to get the imaginary vertical line. Move the cursor along the vertical alignment path and when you are in line with the other circle, the horizontal path will also be displayed. Select the intersection of the two alignment paths. The selected point becomes the center of the circle. Then, enter radius or specify a point.

Similarly, you can use AutoTracking in combination with the **Midpoint** object snap to locate the center of the rectangle and then draw a circle (Figure 4-80).

Note

*Object tracking works only when **OSNAP** is on and some running object snaps have been set.*

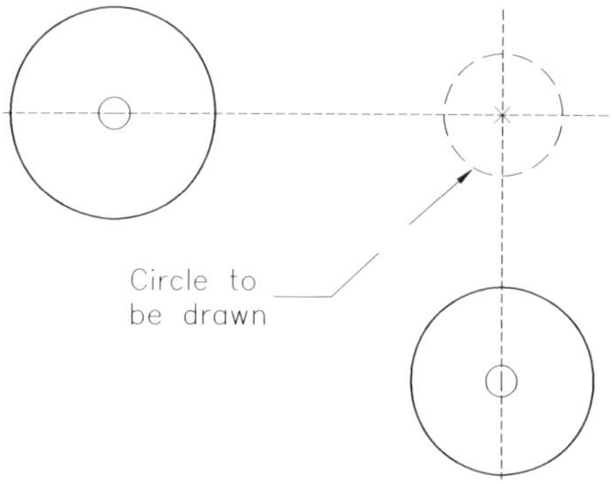

Figure 4-79 *Using **AutoTracking** to locate a point (center of circle)*

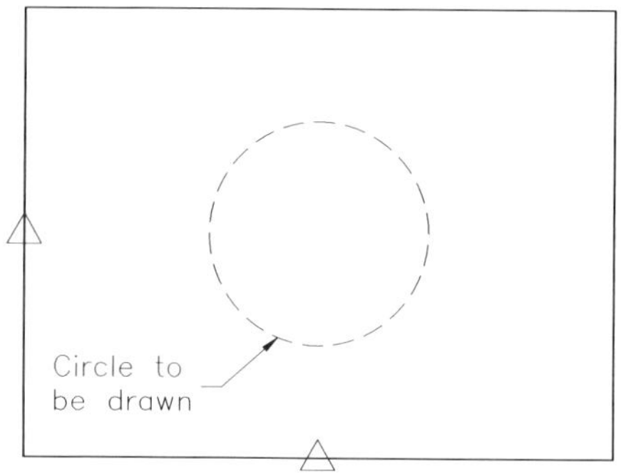

Figure 4-80 *Using **AutoTracking** to locate a point (midpoint of rectangle)*

Polar Tracking

Polar Tracking is used to locate points on an angular alignment path. Polar tracking can be selected by choosing the **Polar Tracking** button in the Status Bar, by using the function key F10, or by selecting the **Polar Tracking On (F10)** check box in the **Polar Tracking** tab of the **Drafting Settings** dialog box (Figure 4-81). Polar Tracking constrains the movement of the cursor along a path that is based on the polar angle settings. For example, if the **Increment angle** list box value is set to 15-degree in the **Polar Angle Settings** area, the cursor will move along the alignment paths that are multiples of 15-degree (0, 15, 30, 45, 60, and so on) and a tooltip will also display the distance and angle. Selecting the **Additional angles** check box and choosing the **New** button allows you to add an additional angle value. The imaginary path will also be displayed at these new angles, apart from the increments of the increment angle selected.

For example, if the increment angle is set to **15** and you add an additional angle of **22**, the imaginary path will be displayed at 0, 15, 22, 30, 45, and the increments of 15. Polar tracking is used only when the Ortho mode is off.

In the **Drafting Settings** dialog box (**Polar Tracking** tab), you can set the polar tracking to absolute or relative to the last segment. If you select the **Absolute** radio button, the base angle is taken from 0. If you select the **Relative to last segment** radio button, the base angle for the increments is set to the last segment drawn. You can also use Polar tracking together with Object tracking. You can select the **Track using all polar angle settings** radio button in the dialog box.

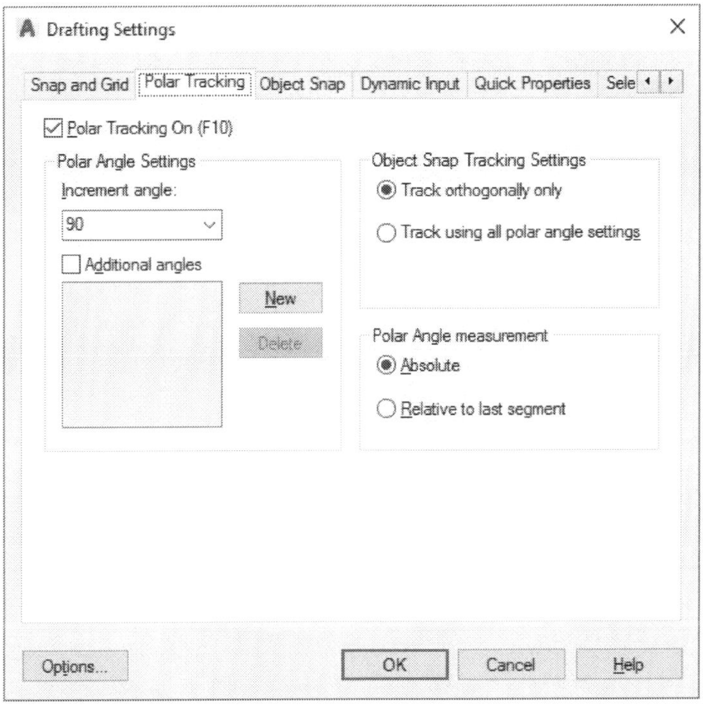

Figure 4-81 *The **Polar Tracking** tab in the **Drafting Settings** dialog box*

AutoTrack Settings

You have different settings while working with autotracking. These settings can be specified in the **Drafting** tab of the **Options** dialog box (Figure 4-82). If you choose the **Options** button in the **Polar Tracking** tab of the **Drafting Settings** dialog box, the **Options** dialog box with the **Drafting** tab chosen will be displayed. You can use the **Display polar tracking vector** check box to toggle the display of the angle alignment path for Polar tracking. You can also use the **Display full-screen tracking vector** check box to toggle the display of a full-screen construction line for Otrack. You can use the **Display Auto Track tooltip** check box to toggle the display of tooltips with the paths. You can also use the **TRACKPATH** system variable to set the path display settings.

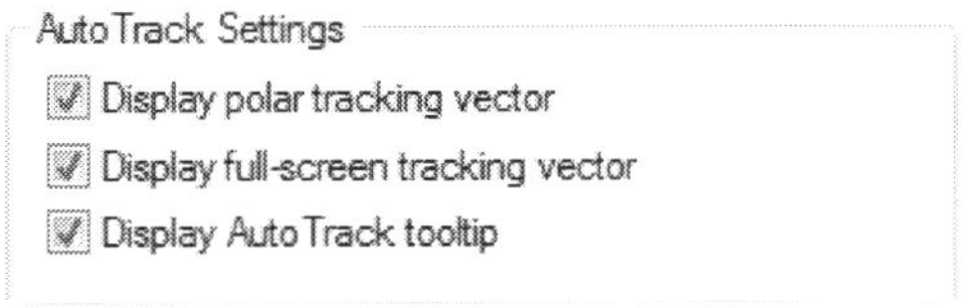

Figure 4-82 *The **AutoTrack Settings** area in the **Options** dialog box (**Drafting** tab)*

Tip

*You need the **Options** dialog box quite frequently to change different drafting settings. When you choose the **Options** button from the **Drafting Settings** dialog box, it directly opens the required tab. After making changes in the dialog box, choose the **OK** button to get back to the **Drafting Settings** dialog box. The **Options** button is available in all the three tabs of the **Drafting Settings** dialog box.*

FUNCTION AND CONTROL KEYS

You can also use the function and control keys to change the status of the coordinate display, Snap, Ortho, Osnap, tablet, screen, isometric planes, running Object Snap, Grid, Polar, and Object tracking. The following is a list of functions and their control keys.

F1 Help
F2 Graphics Screen/AutoCAD Text Window
F3 Osnap On/Off (CTRL+F)
F5 Isoplane top/right/left (CTRL+E)
F7 Grid On/Off (CTRL+G)
F8 Ortho On/Off (CTRL+L)
F9 Snap On/Off (CTRL+B)
F10 Polar tracking On/Off
F11 Object Snap tracking
F12 Dynamic Input On/Off

Self-Evaluation Test

Answer the following questions and then compare them to those given at the end of this chapter:

1. You can change the plot style mode from the Command prompt by using the _________ system variable.

2. The _________ button enables you to set up an invisible grid that allows the cursor to move in fixed increments from one snap point to another.

3. The _________ snap works along with polar and object tracking only.

4. The _________ Object Snap mode is used to select the projected or visual intersections of two objects in 3D space.

5. The _________ can be used to locate a point with respect to two different points.

6. You can set the priority between the keyboard entry and the object snap through the _________ tab of the **Options** dialog box.

7. The layers that are turned off are displayed on the screen but cannot be plotted. (T/F)

8. The drawing, in which you are working, should be in the named plot style mode (*.stb*) to make the plot style available in the **LAYER PROPERTIES MANAGER**. (T/F)

9. The grid pattern appears within the drawing limits which helps define the working area. (T/F)

10. If a circle is inserted as a rotated block, the quadrant points are not rotated by the same amount. (T/F)

Review Questions

Answer the following questions:

1. Which of the following options is not displayed in the shortcut menu displayed on right-clicking on a layer in the **LAYER PROPERTIES MANAGER** when you select more than one layer by using the SHIFT key?

   (a) **New Layer** (b) **Select All**
   (c) **Make Current** (d) **Clear All**

2. Which of the following function keys acts as a toggle key for turning the grid display on or off?

   (a) F5 (b) F6
   (c) F7 (d) F8

3. Which one of the following object snap modes is used to turn off any running object snap for one point only?

   (a) **NODE** (b) **NONE**
   (c) **FROM** (d) **NEAREST**

4. Which of the following object snap modes cannot be used as the running object snap?

   (a) **EXTENSION** (b) **PARALLEL**
   (c) **FROM** (d) **NODE**

5. Which of the following keys can be used to cycle through different running object snaps?

   (a) ENTER (b) SHIFT
   (c) CTRL (d) TAB

6. While working on a drawing, you can save all layers with their current properties settings anytime under one name and then restore them later using the __________ button in the **LAYER PROPERTIES MANAGER**.

7. You can use the __________ window to locate the drawing data with the help of the search tools and then use it in your drawing.

8. The __________ function key is used to turn on/off the Osnap.

9. The difference between the usage of the **Off** option and the **Freeze** option is that in the **Freeze** option, the frozen layers are not __________ by the computer while regenerating the drawing.

10. The size of the aperture is measured in __________.

11. In the **Extension** object snap mode, when you move the cursor along a path, a temporary extension path and the tooltip are displayed with the cursor. The tooltip displays __________ coordinates from the end of the line.

12. You cannot enter different values for the horizontal and vertical grid spacing. (T/F)

13. You can lock a layer to prevent a user from accidentally editing the objects in it. (T/F)

14. When a layer is locked, you cannot use the objects in it for object Snapping. (T/F)

15. The thickness given to the objects in a layer, by using the **Lineweight** option, is displayed on the screen and can be plotted. (T/F)

Exercise 5 — Line type and Object Color

Set up layers with the following linetypes and colors. Then make the drawing, as shown in Figure 4-83. The distance between the dotted lines is 1.0 unit.

Layer name	Color	Linetype
Object	Red	Continuous
Hidden	Yellow	Hidden
Center	Green	Center

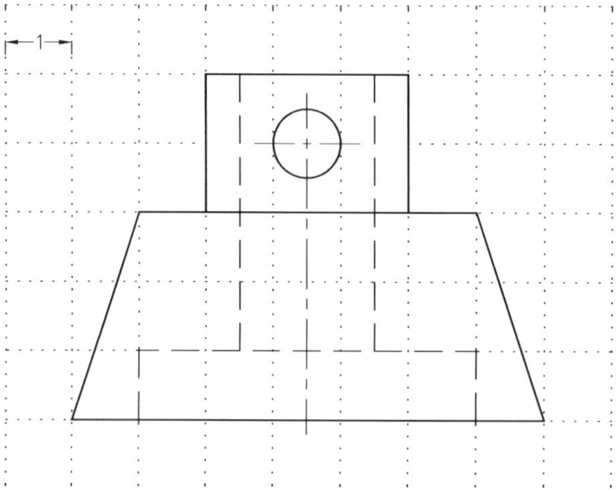

Figure 4-83 *Drawing for Exercise 5*

Exercise 6 Line type and Object Color

Set up layers, linetypes, and colors and then make the drawing shown in Figure 4-84. The distance between the dotted lines is 1.0 unit.

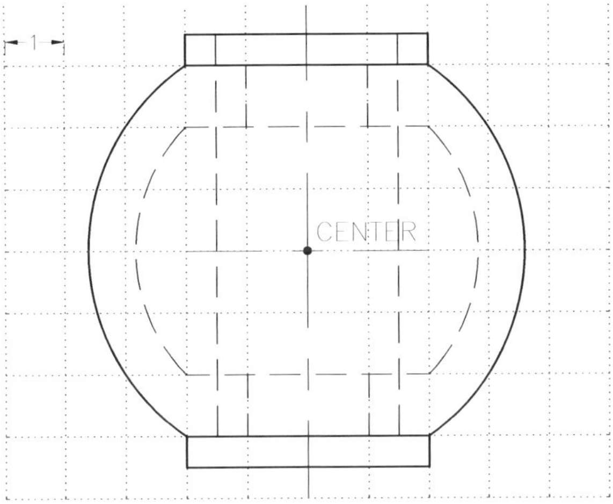

Figure 4-84 *Drawing for Exercise 6*

Exercise 7 Line type and Object Color

Set up layers, linetypes, and colors and then make the drawing shown in Figure 4-85. Use the object snaps as indicated.

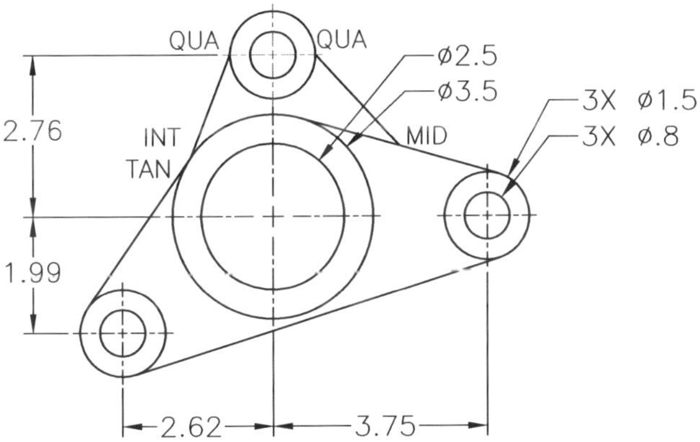

Figure 4-85 *Drawing for Exercise 7*

Problem-Solving Exercise 1

Draw the object shown in Figure 4-86. First draw the lines and then draw the arcs using the appropriate Arc tools.

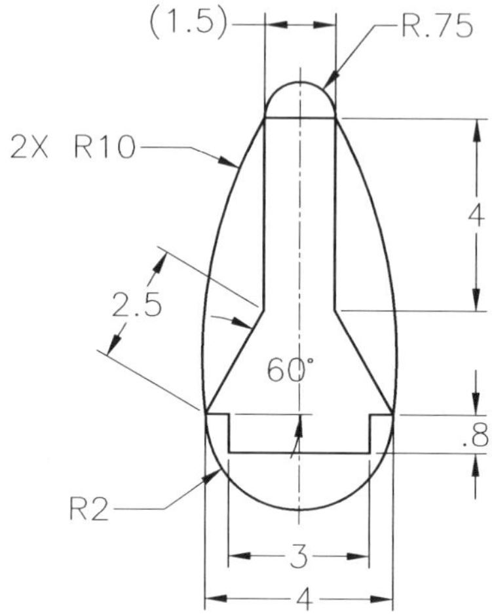

Figure 4-86 Drawing for Problem-Solving Exercise 1

Problem-Solving Exercise 2

Draw the object shown in Figure 4-87. First draw the front view (bottom left) and then the side and top views.

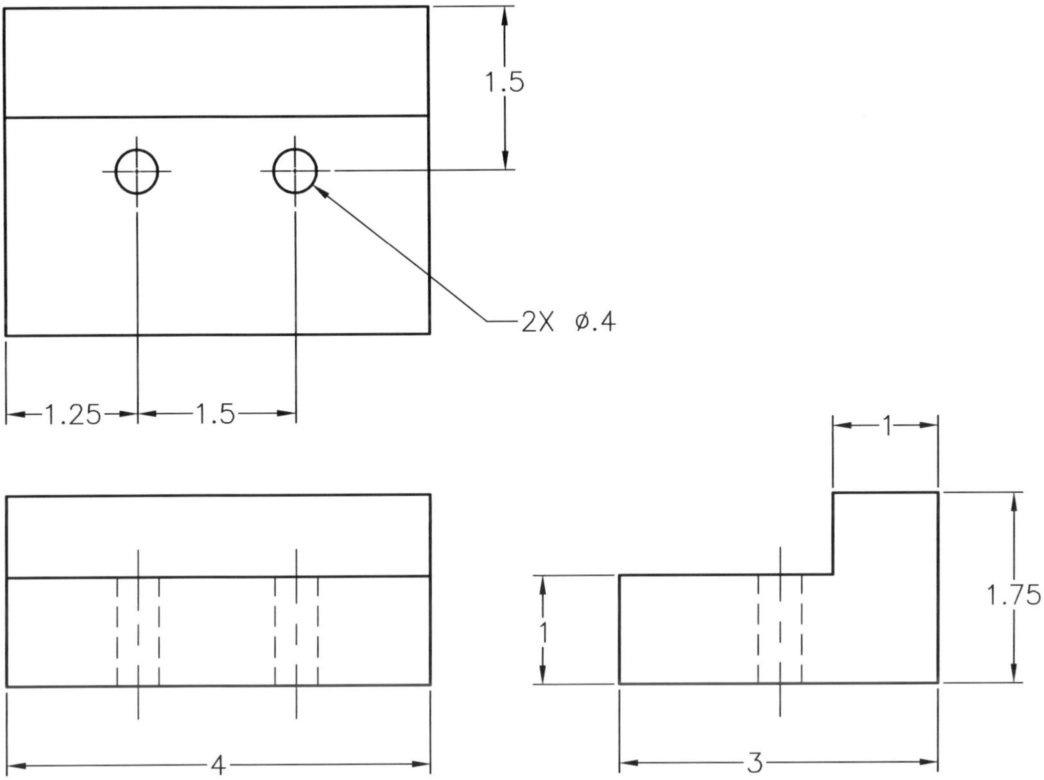

Figure 4-87 *Drawing for Problem-Solving Exercise 2*

Answers to Self-Evaluation Test

1. **PSTYLEPOLICY**, **2.** **SNAP**, **3.** Polar, **4.** **Apparent Intersection**, **5.** **Temporary Tracking**, **6.** **User Preferences**, **7.** F, **8.** T, **9.** T, **10.** F

Chapter 5

Editing Sketched Objects-I

Learning Objectives

After completing this chapter, you will be able to:

- *Create selection sets using various object selection options*
- *Use the Move and Copy tools*
- *Copy objects using the Array tool*
- *Understand various editing and measuring tools*

Key Terms

• *Move*	• *Chamfer*	• *Array*	• *Lengthen*
• *Copy*	• *Trim*	• *Rotate*	• *Measure*
• *Break*	• *Extend*	• *Mirror*	• *Divide*
• *Offset*	• *Stretch*	• *Scale*	• *Blend*

CREATING A SELECTION SET

For most of the tools, the default object selection method is to use the pick box (cursor) and select one entity at a time. You can also click in blank area and select objects by using the **Window** option or the **Crossing** option. In Chapter 2, these two options were discussed. The other options used for selection are listed below and are discussed in this chapter.

Last	CPolygon	Add	Undo	Previous	Fence
Box	SIngle	ALL	Group	AUto	Remove
WPolygon	Multiple				

Last

This option is used to select the last drawn object, which is partially or fully visible in the current display. This is the most suitable option to select the last drawn object while editing it. Keep in mind that if the last drawn object is not in the current display, the last drawn object in the current display will be selected. Although a selection can be formed using the **Last** option, only one object is selected at a time. However, you can use the **Last** option a number of times but it will require you to start the command again. You can use the **Last** selection option with any tool that requires the selection of multiple objects (for example, **Copy**, **Move**, and **Erase**). To select the last drawn object by using this option, invoke a particular tool, and then enter **LAST** or **L** at the **Select objects** prompt to use this object selection method.

Exercise 1 — *Erase*

Draw the profile shown in Figure 5-1(a) by using the **Line** tool. Then, use the **Last** option of the **Erase** tool to erase the three most recently drawn lines to obtain Figure 5-1(d).

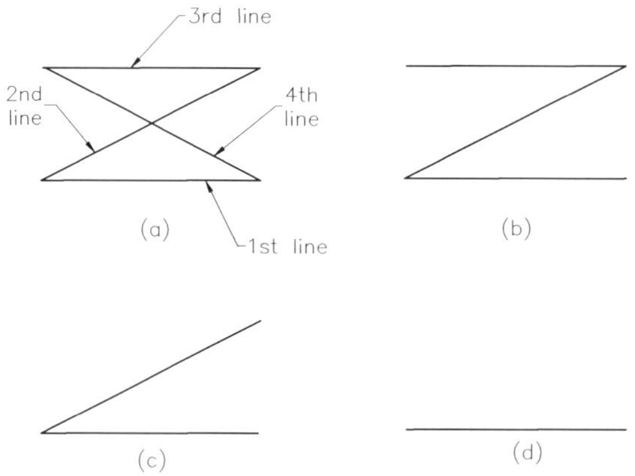

Figure 5-1 *The initial and final profiles for Exercise 1*

Previous

The **Previous** option is used to select the objects that were selected in the previous selection set. Generally, AutoCAD LT saves the previous selection set; therefore, you can select those objects again by using the **Previous** option, instead of invoking the same selection method. In other words, with the help of the **Previous** option, you can select the previous set without selecting the objects individually. The prompt sequence for doing so is given next.

*Choose the **Copy** tool from the **Modify** panel*
Select objects: *Select the objects*
Select objects: Enter
Specify base point or [Displacement mOde] <Displacement>: *Specify the base point*
Specify second point of displacement or <use first point as displacement>: *Specify the point for displacement*
*Choose the **Move** tool from the **Modify** panel*
Select objects: **P** Enter
found

You cannot select objects in the model space and then use the same selection set in the paper space, or vice versa. This is because AutoCAD LT keeps the record of the space (paper space or model space), in which the individual selection set is created.

WPolygon

This option is similar to the **Window** option with the only difference that by using this option, you can define a window consisting of an irregular polygon. You can specify the selection area by specifying points around the object that you want to select (Figure 5-2). Similar to the window method, the objects to be selected by using this method should be completely enclosed within the polygon. The polygon is formed as you specify points and can take any shape except a self-intersecting profile. The last segment of the polygon is automatically drawn to close the polygon. The polygon can be created by specifying the coordinates of the points or by specifying the points with the help of a pointing device. With the **Undo** option, the most recently specified WPolygon point can be undone. To use the **WPolygon** option with the object selection tools such as **Erase**, **Move**, **Copy**, invoke a tool, enter **WP** at the **Select objects** prompt, and then select the vertices of the polygon.

Exercise 2 — *WPolygon*

Draw several objects, select some of them using the **WPolygon** option and then erase them.

CPolygon

This option is similar to the **Window** option with the only difference that by using this option you can define a window consisting of an irregular polygon. The procedure to create a polygon is the same as that of **WPolygon**. In this option, in addition to the objects that are completely enclosed within the polygon, an object lying partially inside the polygon or even touching it is also selected (Figure 5-3).

CPolygon is formed as you specify the points. The points can be specified at the Command line or by specifying points using the mouse. Just as in the **WPolygon** option, the crossing polygon can take any shape except a self-intersecting profile. As the last segment of the polygon is drawn automatically, the CPolygon is closed at all times.

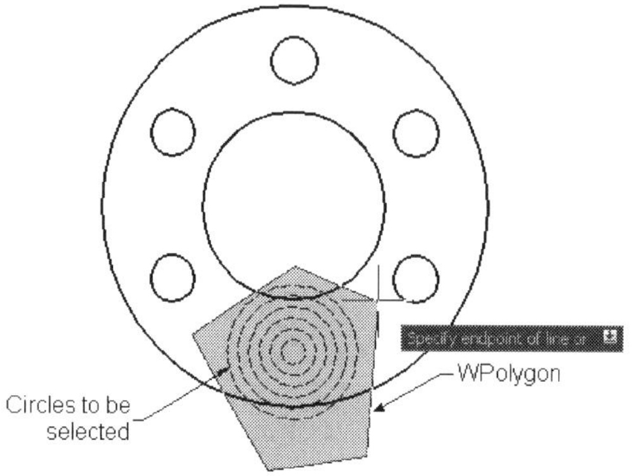

*Figure 5-2 Selecting objects using the **WPolygon** option*

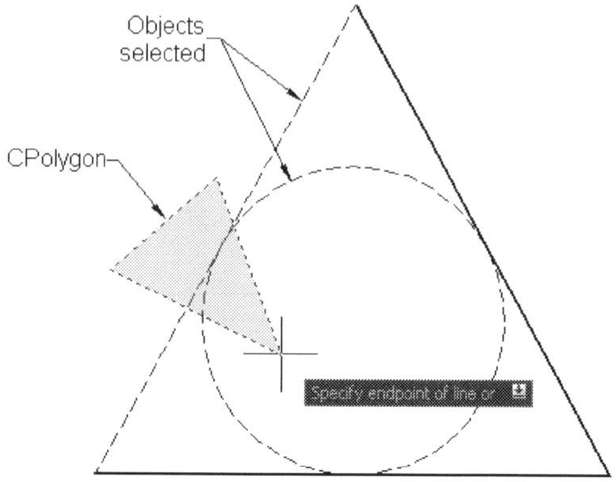

*Figure 5-3 Selecting objects using the **CPolygon** option*

Remove

The **Remove** option is used to remove the objects from a selection set, but not from the drawing. The following is the prompt sequence used for removing the objects from the selection set shown in Figure 5-4.

> *Choose the **Erase** tool from the **Modify** panel of the **Home** tab*
> Select objects: *Select objects (a), (b), and (c)*
> Select objects: **R** Enter
> Remove objects: *Select object (a)*
> 1 found, 1 removed, 2 total
> Remove objects: Enter

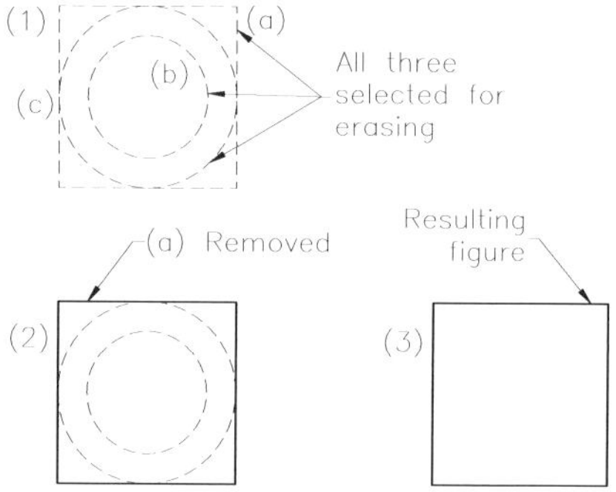

Figure 5-4 Removing objects using the Remove option

> **Tip**
> *Objects can also be removed from a selection set by using the SHIFT key. For example, pressing the SHIFT key and selecting an object (a) with the pointing device will remove the object from the selection set. On doing so, the message: **1 found, 1 removed, 2 total** will be displayed.*

Add

You can use the **Add** option to add objects to a selection set. When you start creating a selection set, you are in the **Add** mode. Once you create a selection set by using any selection method, you can add more objects by simply selecting them with the pointing device, if the system variable **PICKADD** is set to 2 (default). If it is set to 0, you need to press the SHIFT key and then select the objects to add objects to the selection set.

ALL

The **ALL** selection option is used to select all objects in the current working environment of the current drawing. Note that the objects in the "OFF" layers can also be selected by using the

ALL option. However, you cannot select the objects that are in the frozen layers by using this method. You can use this selection option with only those tools that require object selection. After invoking a tool, enter **ALL** at the **Select objects** prompt. Once you enter this option, all the objects drawn on the screen will be highlighted. For example, if there are four objects on the screen and you want to erase all of them, follow the prompt sequence given next.

*Choose the **Erase** tool from the **Modify** panel of the **Home** tab*
Select objects: **ALL** Enter
4 found
Select objects: Enter

You can also use this option in combination with the other selection options. For example, consider that there are five objects on the drawing screen and you want to erase three of them. To do so, invoke the **Erase** tool, enter **ALL** at the **Select objects** prompt. Then, press the SHIFT key and select the two objects that you want to remove from the selection set. Next, press ENTER; the remaining three objects will be erased.

Fence

In the **Fence** option, a selection set is created by drawing an open polyline through the objects to be selected. In such a case, any object touched by the polyline is selected (Figure 5-5). The selection fence can be created by entering the coordinates at the Command line or by specifying the points with the pointing device. With this option, more flexibility of selection is provided because a fence can intersect itself. The **Undo** option can be used to undo the most recently selected fence point. Like the other selection options, this option is also used with the tools that need an object selection. The prompt sequence to use the **Fence** option after choosing the **Erase** tool is given next.

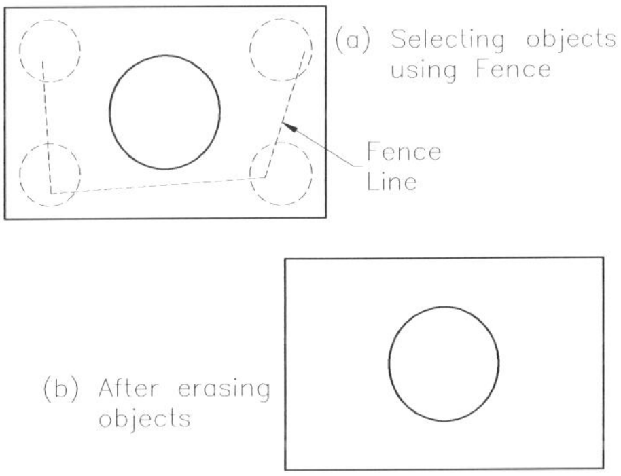

Figure 5-5 *Erasing objects using the **Fence** option*

Select objects: **F** Enter
Specify first fence point or pick/drag cursor: *Specify the first point*
Specify next fence point or [Undo]: *Specify the second point*
Specify next fence point or [Undo]: *Specify the third point*
Specify next fence point or [Undo]: *Specify the fourth point*
Specify next fence point or [Undo]: Enter
Select object: Enter

Group

The **Group** option enables you to select a group of objects by their group name. You can create a group and assign a name to it with the help of the **Group** tool in the **Groups** panel of the **Home** tab (see Chapter 19, *Grouping and Advanced Editing of Sketched Objects*). Once a group has been created, you can select it by using the **Group** option for editing. This makes the object selection process easier and faster, since a set of objects can be selected by just entering the name of their group. The prompt sequence to use the **Group** option is given next.

Choose the ***Move*** *tool*
Select objects: **G** [Enter]
Enter group name: *Enter the name of the predefined group you want to select*
4 found
Select objects: [Enter]

Exercise 3 *Erase*

Draw six circles and then erase all of them by using the **ALL** option of the **Erase** tool. Next, use undo command so that all the circles are displayed in the drawing area. Now use the **Fence** selection set option of the **Erase** tool, and remove alternate circles.

Box

If the system variable **PICKAUTO** is set to 1 (default), the **Box** selection option is used to select the objects inside a rectangle. After you have entered **Box** at the **Select objects** prompt, you need to specify the two corners of a rectangle at the **Specify first corner** and **Specify opposite corner** prompts. If you define the box from right to left, it will be equivalent to the **Crossing** option. Therefore, it also selects the objects that touch the rectangle boundaries, in addition to the ones that are completely enclosed within the rectangle. If you define the box from left to right, this option will be equivalent to the **Window** option and select only the objects that are completely enclosed within the rectangle.

The prompt sequence after choosing the **Box** option is given next.

Specify first corner: *Specify a point*
Specify opposite corner: *Specify the opposite corner point of the box*
Select objects: [Enter]

AUto

The **AUto** option is used for automatic selection. Using this option, you can select either a single object or a number of objects by creating a window or a crossing. If you select a single object, it will be selected. If you specify a point in the blank area, you are automatically in the **Box** selection option, and the point you have specified becomes the first corner of the box. **AUto** and **Add** are the default selection methods in such cases.

Multiple

On entering **M** (Multiple) at the **Select objects** prompt, you can select multiple objects at a single **Select objects** prompt. In this case, the selected objects will not be highlighted. Once you give a null response to the **Select objects** prompt, all selected objects will be highlighted together.

Undo

This option removes the most recently selected object from the selection set.

SIngle

When you enter **SI** (SIngle) at the **Select objects** prompt, the selection takes place in the **SIngle** selection mode. Once you select an object or a number of objects using the **Window** or **Crossing** option, the **Select objects** prompt does not repeat. AutoCAD LT proceeds with the tool for which the selection has been made.

*Choose the **Erase** tool*
Select objects: **SI** [Enter]
Select objects: *Select the object to erase; the selected object is erased*

You can also create a selection set by using the **SELECT** command. The prompt sequence to do so is given next.

Command: **SELECT** [Enter]
Select objects: *Use any selection method*

EDITING SKETCHES

To use AutoCAD LT efficiently, you need to know the editing tools and how to use them. In this section, you will learn about the editing tools. These tools can be invoked from the **Ribbon**, or toolbar, or through the Command prompt. Some of the editing tools or commands such as **ERASE** and **OOPS** have been discussed in Chapter 2 (*Getting Started with AutoCAD LT*).

MOVING SKETCHED OBJECTS

Ribbon: Home > Modify > Move **Toolbar:** Modify > Move
Command: MOVE (M)

The **Move** tool is used to move one or more objects from their current location to a new location without changing their size or orientation. On choosing this tool from the **Modify** panel, refer to Figure 5-6, you will be prompted to select the objects to be moved. Select the object by using any one of the selection techniques discussed earlier; you will be prompted to specify the base point. The base point is the reference point with respect to which the object will be picked and moved. It is recommended to select the base point on the object selected to be moved. On specifying the base point, you will be prompted to specify the second point of displacement. This is the new location where you want to move the object. On specifying this point, the selected objects will move to this point. Figure 5-7 shows objects moved by using the **Move** tool. The prompt sequence that will be followed on choosing the **Move** tool from the **Modify** panel is given next.

Select objects: *Select the objects to be moved* [Enter]
Specify base point or [Displacement] <Displacement>: *Specify the base point to move the selected object(s)*
Specify second point or <use first point as displacement>: *Specify the second point or press ENTER to use the first point*

If you press ENTER at the **Specify second point of displacement or <use first point as displacement>** prompt, AutoCAD LT interprets the first point as the relative value of the displacement in the *X* axis and *Y* axis directions. This value will be added in the *X* and *Y* axis coordinates and the object will be automatically moved to the resultant location. For example, draw a circle with its center at (3,3) and then select the center point of the circle as the base point. Now, at the **Specify second point of displacement or <use first point as displacement>** prompt, press ENTER. You will notice that the circle is moved such that its center is now placed at 6,6. This is because 3 units (initial coordinates) are added along both the X and Y directions.

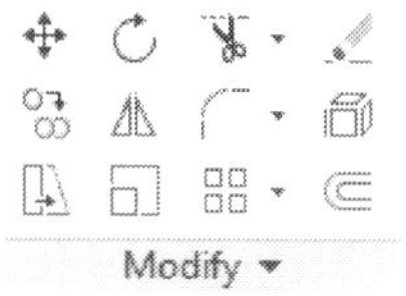

*Figure 5-6 The **Modify** panel*

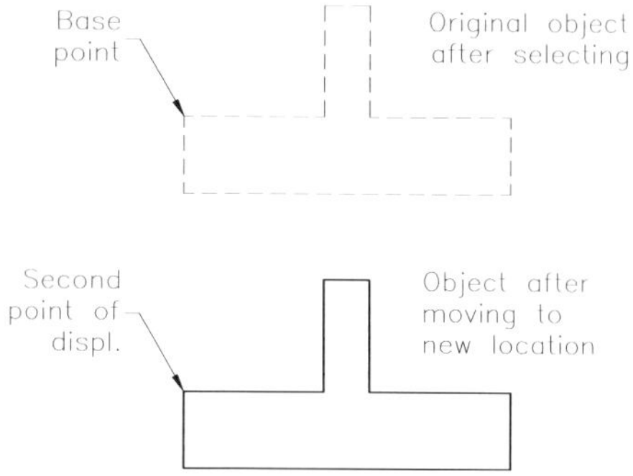

Figure 5-7 Moving the object to a new location

COPYING SKETCHED OBJECTS

Ribbon: Home > Modify > Copy **Toolbar:** Modify > Copy
Command: COPY (CO)

The **Copy** tool is used to copy any existing objects. This tool is used to make the copies of the selected objects and place them at the specified location. To copy the objects, you need to invoke this tool, select the objects and then specify the base point. Next, you need to specify the second point where the copied objects have to be placed. Figure 5-8 shows the objects copied by using this tool. The prompt sequence that will be followed when you choose the **Copy** tool from the **Modify** panel is given next.

Select objects: *Select the objects to copy* Enter
Specify base point or [Displacement/mOde]<Displacement>: *Specify the base point*
Specify second point or [Array] <use first point as displacement>: *Specify a new position on the screen using the pointing device or by entering coordinates*
Specify second point or [Array/Exit/Undo] <Exit>: Enter

Creating Multiple Copies

On specifying the second point, the copy of the selected objects will be created and you will be prompted again to specify the second point. You can continue specifying the second point for creating multiple copies of the selected entities, as shown in Figure 5-9. You can use **U (Undo)** option to undo the last copied instance at any stage of the **Copy** tool. After entering **U**, you can again specify the position of the last instance.

The prompt sequence for creating multiple copies of an object by using the **Copy** tool is given next.

Select objects: *Select the objects to copy* Enter
Specify base point or [Displacement/mOde]<Displacement>: **O** Enter
Enter a copy mode option [Single/Multiple]<current>: **M** Enter

Specify base point or [Displacement/mOde]<Displacement>: *Specify the base point*
Specify second point or [Array] <use first point as displacement>: *Specify a point for placement*
Specify second point or [Array/Exit/Undo] <Exit>: *Specify another point for placement*
Specify second point or [Array/Exit/Undo] <Exit>: *Specify another point for placement*
Specify second point or [Array/Exit/Undo] <Exit>: Enter

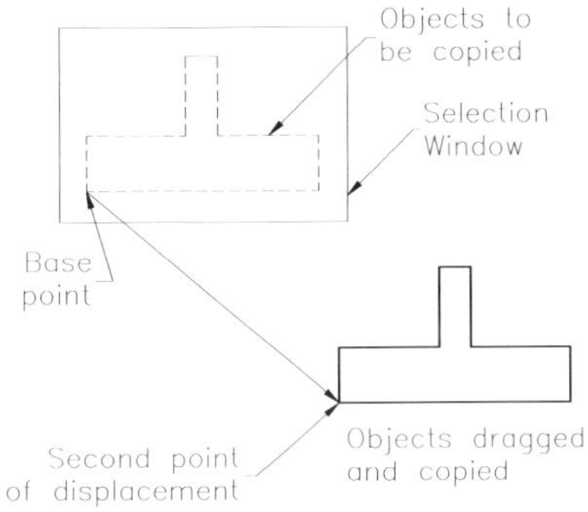

Figure 5-8 *The objects copied by using the **COPY** tool*

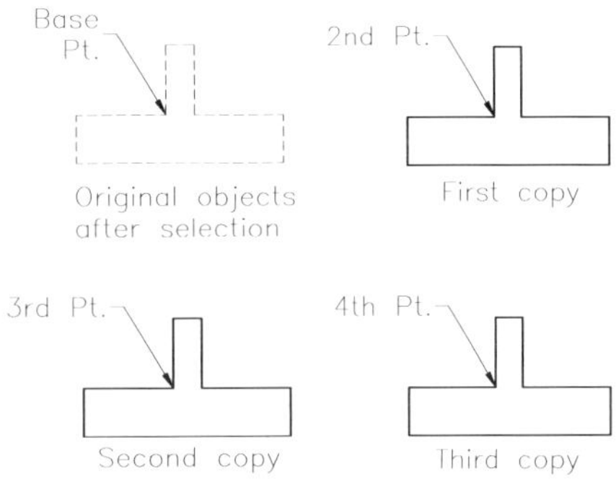

Figure 5-9 *Making multiple copies*

Creating an Array of Selected Objects

After specifying the base point, you will be prompted to specify the second point (where the copied object will be placed). You can create an array (multiple copies arranged in linear manner) of the selected objects by entering **ARRAY** or **A** at the **Specify second point or [Array] <use first point as displacement>:** command prompt. On entering the required command at the Command prompt, you will be prompted to specify the number of items to array. Enter the number of items and press ENTER; you will be prompted to specify the second point and the preview of the array of selected items will be displayed attached to the cursor. Click to specify the second point; the linear array of selected object will be created, refer to Figure 5-10. In this array, the distance between any two consecutive items will be equal to the distance specified between the first and second points. If you enter **FIT** at the **Specify second point or [Fit]** command prompt, all array items will fit inside the first and second points, refer to Figure 5-11.

The prompt sequence for creating a linear array of a rectangle with the second point option of the **Copy** tool is given next, refer to Figure 5-10.

*Choose the **Copy** tool from the **Modify** panel of the **Home** tab*
Select objects: 1 found
Select objects: Enter
Current settings: Copy mode = Multiple
Specify base point or [Displacement/mOde] <Displacement>: *Specify the base point*
Specify second point or [Array] <use first point as displacement>: **A** or **ARRAY**
Enter number of items to array: **3**
Specify second point or [Fit]: *Specify another point for placement*

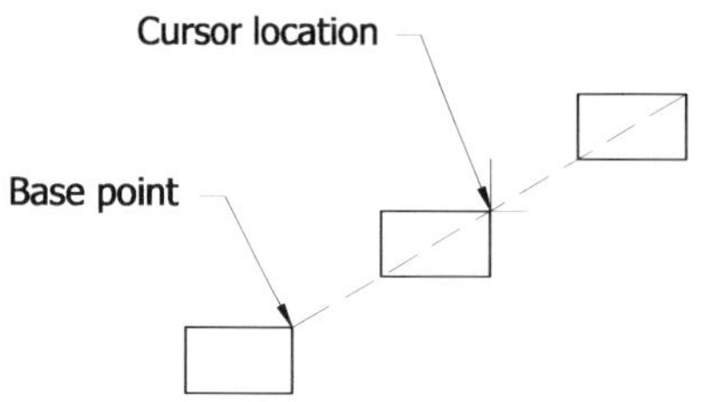

*Figure 5-10 Linear array created by using the **Copy** tool*

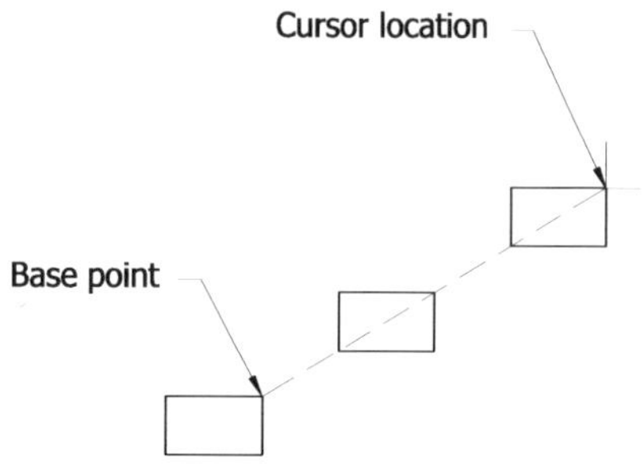

*Figure 5-11 Array created by using the **Fit** option of the **Copy** tool*

The prompt sequence for creating the linear array of a rectangle by using the **Fit** option of the **Copy** tool is given next, refer to Figure 5-11.

*Choose the **Copy** tool*
Select objects: 1 found
Select objects: Enter
Current settings: Copy mode = Multiple
Specify base point or [Displacement/mOde] <Displacement>: *Specify the base point*
Specify second point or [Array] <use first point as displacement>: **A** or **ARRAY**
Enter number of items to array: **3**
Specify second point or [Fit]: **F** or **FIT**
Specify second point or [Array]: *Specify another point for placement*

Creating a Single Copy

By default, AutoCAD LT creates multiple copies of the selected objects. However, you can also create a single copy of the selected object. To create a single copy of the selected object, choose the **mode** option from the shortcut menu at the **Specify base point or [Displacement/mOde]** <current> prompt. Next, choose the **Single** option from the shortcut menu at the **Enter a copy mode option [Single/Multiple] <current>** prompt. On specifying the second point of displacement, a copy will be placed at that point. Now, you can exit the **Copy** tool.

Note
You can also copy an object by using CTRL+C. The copied content will be stored in the clipboard.

Exercise 4 — Copy

In this exercise, you will create the drawing shown in Figure 5-12. Use the **Copy** tool for creating the drawing.

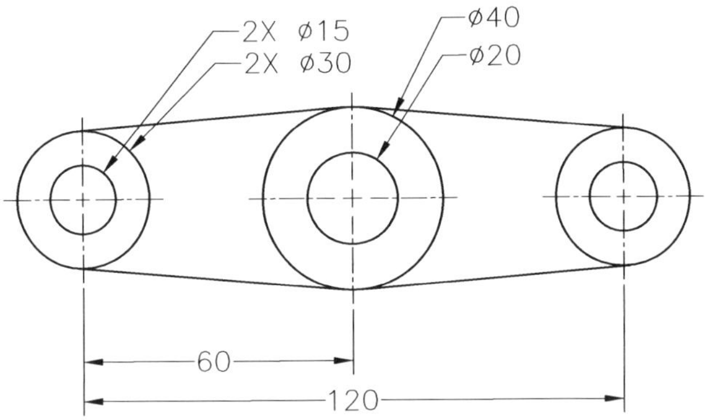

Figure 5-12 *Drawing for Exercise 4*

PASTING CONTENTS FROM THE CLIPBOARD

Ribbon: Home > Clipboard > Paste > Paste as Block **Command:** PASTEBLOCK

The **Paste as Block** tool is used to paste the contents of the Clipboard into a new drawing or in the same drawing at a new location. You can also invoke the **PASTEBLOCK** command from the shortcut menu by right-clicking in the drawing area and then choosing **Clipboard > Paste as Block**.

PASTING CONTENTS USING THE ORIGINAL COORDINATES

Ribbon: Home > Clipboard > Paste > Paste to Original Coordinates
Command: PASTEORIG

The **Paste to Original Coordinates** tool is used to paste the contents of the Clipboard into a new drawing by using coordinates from the original drawing. You can invoke the **PASTEORIG** command from the shortcut menu by right-clicking in the drawing area and then choosing **Clipboard > Paste to Original Coordinates**. Note that this command will be available only when the Clipboard contains AutoCAD LT data from a drawing other than the current drawing.

OFFSETTING SKETCHED OBJECTS

Ribbon: Home > Modify > Offset **Toolbar:** Modify > Offset
Command: OFFSET (O)

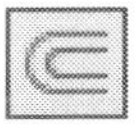

You can use the **Offset** tool to draw parallel lines, polylines, concentric circles, arcs, curves, and so on (Figure 5-13). However, you can offset only one entity at a time. While offsetting an object, you need to specify the offset distance and the side to offset, or specify the distance by which the selected object has to be offset. Depending on the side to offset, the resulting object will be smaller or larger than the original object. For example, while offsetting a circle if the offset side is toward the inner side of the perimeter, the resulting circle will be smaller than the original one.

The prompt sequence that will follow when you choose the **Offset** tool from the **Modify** panel is given next.

Current settings: Erase source=No Layer=Source OFFSETGAPTYPE=0
Specify offset distance or [Through/Erase/Layer] <Through>: *Specify the offset distance*
Select object to offset or [Exit/Undo]<Exit>: *Select the object to offset*
Specify point on side to offset or [Exit/Multiple/Undo] <Exit>: *Specify a point on the side to offset*
Select object to offset or [Exit/Undo]<Exit>: *Select another object to offset or press* Enter

Through Option

While offsetting the entities, the offset distance can be specified by entering a value or by specifying two points. The distance between these two points will be used as the offset distance. The **Through** option is generally used to create orthographic views. In this case, you do not need to specify a distance; you need to specify an offset point, see Figure 5-14. The offset distance is stored in the **OFFSETDIST** system variable. A negative value indicates that the offset value is set to the **Through** option. Using this option, you can offset lines, arcs, 2D polylines, xlines, circles, ellipses, elliptical arcs, rays, and planar splines. If you try to offset objects other than these, the message **Cannot offset that object** is displayed.

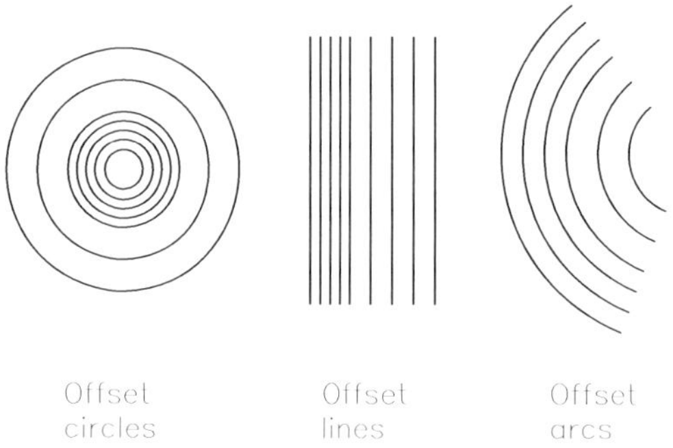

***Figure 5-13** Using the **Offset** tool to create multiple offset entities*

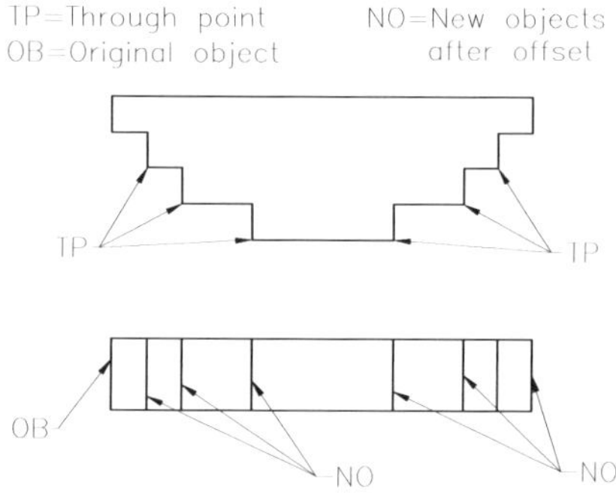

***Figure 5-14** Using the **Through** option*

Erase Option

The **Erase** option is used to specify whether the source object has to be deleted or not. Enter **Yes** at the **Erase source object after offsetting** prompt to delete the source object after creating the offset. The prompt sequence that will follow when you choose the **Erase** option is given next.

Current settings: Erase source=No Layer=Source OFFSETGAPTYPE=0
Specify offset distance or [Through/Erase/Layer] <current>: **E**
Erase source object after offsetting? [Yes/No] <No>: **Y**
Specify offset distance or [Through/Erase/Layer] <current>:

Layer Option

The **Layer** option is used to specify whether the offset entity will be placed in the current layer or the layer of the source object. The prompt sequence to offset the entity in the **Source** layer is given next.

Current settings: Erase source=Yes Layer=Current OFFSETGAPTYPE=0
Specify offset distance or [Through/Erase/Layer] <current>: **L**
Enter layer option for offset objects [Current/Source] <Current>: **S**
Specify offset distance or [Through/Erase/Layer] <current>:

Exercise 5 — *Offset*

Use the **Offset** tool to draw the drawings for the exercise 5(a) and exercise 5(b) shown in Figures 5-15 and 5-16, respectively.

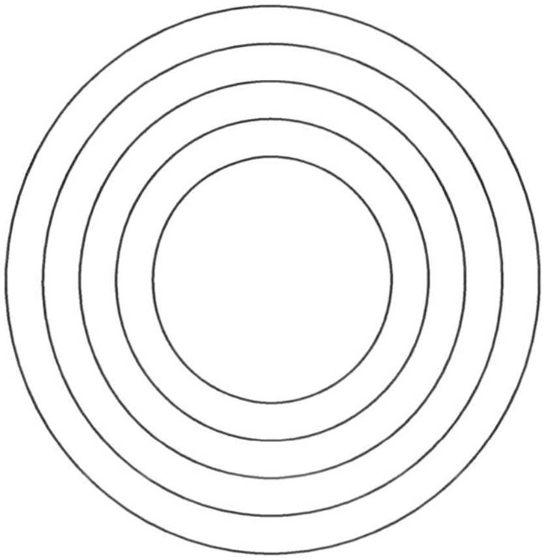

Figure 5-15 *Drawing for Exercise 5 (a)*

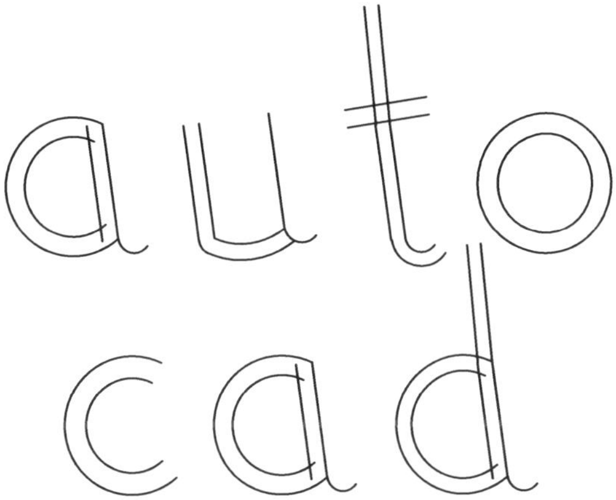

Figure 5-16 *Drawing for Exercise 5 (b)*

ROTATING SKETCHED OBJECTS

Ribbon: Home > Modify > Rotate **Toolbar:** Modify > Rotate
Command: ROTATE/RO

While creating designs, sometimes you have to rotate an object or a group of objects. You can accomplish this by using the **Rotate** tool. On invoking this tool, you will be prompted to select the objects and the base point about which the selected objects will be rotated. You should be careful in selecting the base point if the base point is not located on the known object. After you specify the base point, you need to enter the rotation angle. By default, a positive angle value results in a counterclockwise rotation, whereas a negative angle value results in a clockwise rotation (Figure 5-17). The **Rotate** tool can also be invoked from the shortcut menu by selecting an object and right-clicking in the drawing area and choosing the **Rotate** option from the shortcut menu.

If you need to rotate objects with respect to a known angle, you can do so by using the **Reference** option in two different ways. The first way is to specify the known angle as the reference angle, followed by the proposed angle by which the objects will be rotated (Figure 5-18). Here the object is first rotated clockwise from the *X* axis, through the reference angle. Then the object is rotated through the new angle from this reference position in a counterclockwise direction. The prompt sequence after choosing **Rotate** tool is given next.

Current positive angle in UCS: ANGDIR=*current* ANGBASE=*current*
Select objects: *Select the objects for rotation* Enter
Specify base point: *Specify the base point*
Specify rotation angle or [Copy/Reference]<current>: **R** Enter
Specify the reference angle <0>: *Enter reference angle* Enter
Specify the new angle or [Points]: *Enter new angle or enter **P** to select two points for specifying the angle value* Enter

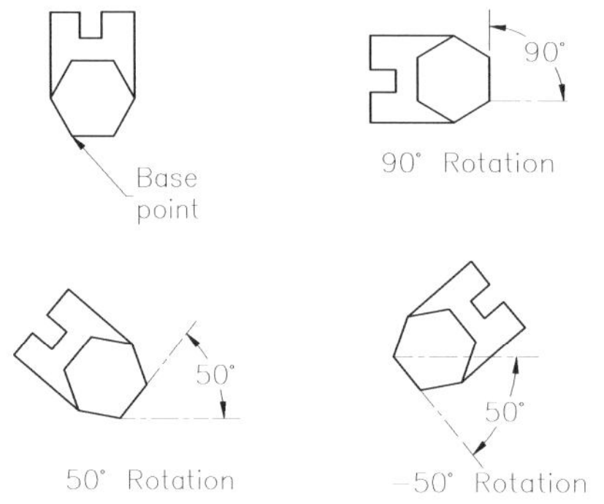

***Figure 5-17** Rotation of objects in different rotation angles*

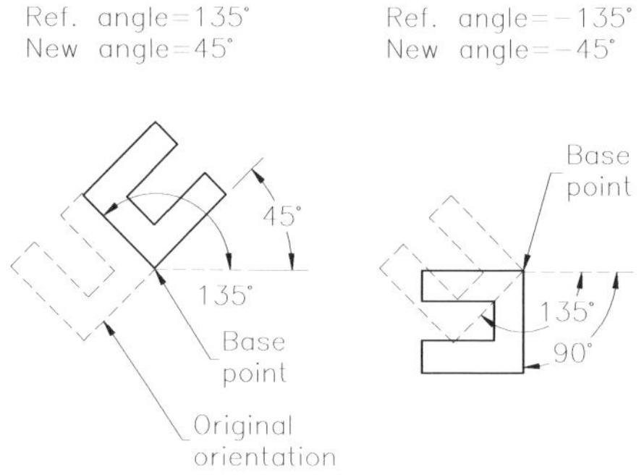

***Figure 5-18** Rotation using the **Reference** option*

The other method is used when the reference angle and the new angle are not known. In this case, you can use the edges of the original object and the reference object to specify the original object and the reference angle, respectively. Figure 5-19 shows a model and a line created at an unknown angle. In this case, this line will be used as a reference object for rotating the object. In such cases, remember that the base point should be taken on the reference object. This is because you cannot define two points for specifying the new angle. You have to directly enter the angle value or specify only one point. Therefore, the base point will be taken as the first point and the second point can be defined for a new angle. Figure 5-20 shows the model after rotating it with reference to the line such that the line and the model are inclined at similar angles. The prompt sequence to rotate the model shown in Figure 5-19 is given next.

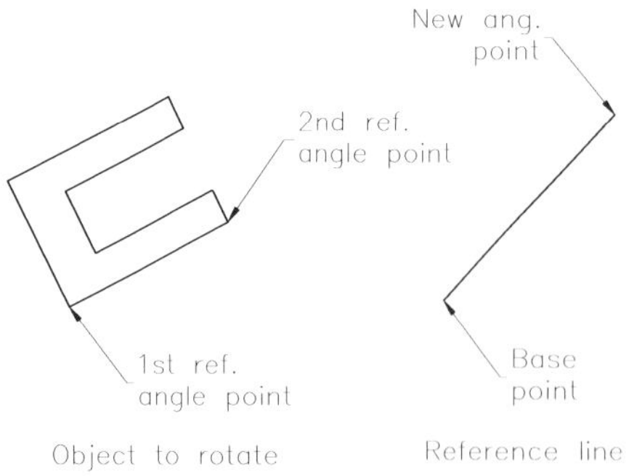

***Figure 5-19** Rotating the model using a reference line*

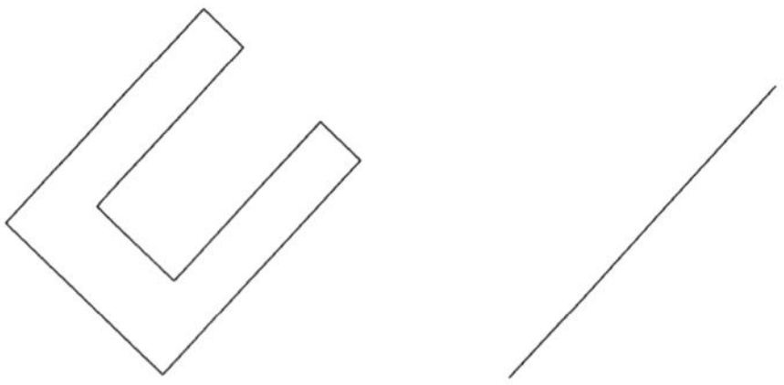

***Figure 5-20** The model after rotating with reference to the line*

Current positive angle in UCS: ANGDIR=*current* ANGBASE=*current*
Select objects: *Select the object for rotation* Enter
Specify base point: *Specify the base point as the lower endpoint of the line, refer to Figure 5-19*
Specify rotation angle or [Copy/Reference]<current>: **R** Enter
Specify the reference angle <current>: *Specify the first point on the edge of the model, refer to Figure 5-19*
Specify the reference angle <current>: Specify second point: *Specify the second point on the same edge of the model, refer to Figure 5-19*
Specify the new angle or [Points]<current>: *Select the other endpoint of the reference line, refer to Figure 5-19*

You can also specify a new angle by entering a numeric value at the **Specify the new angle or [Points]<current>** prompt.

If you want to retain the original object and create a copy while rotating, use the **Copy** option of the **Rotate** tool. The source entity is retained in its original orientation and a new instance is created and rotated through the specified angle. The prompt sequence for the **Copy** option is given next.

Current positive angle in UCS: ANGDIR=counterclockwise ANGBASE=0
Select objects: *Select the object for rotation* Enter
Specify base point: *Specify a base point about which the selected objects will be rotated*
Specify rotation angle or [Copy/Reference] <current>: **C** Enter
Rotating a copy of the selected objects
Specify rotation angle or [Copy/Reference] <current>: *Enter a positive or negative rotation angle, or specify a point*

SCALING THE SKETCHED OBJECTS

Ribbon: Home > Modify > Scale **Toolbar:** Modify > Scale
Command: SCALE/SC

Sometimes you need to change the size of objects in a drawing. You can do so by using the **Scale** tool. This tool dynamically enlarges or shrinks a selected object about a base point keeping the aspect ratio of the object constant. This means that the size of the object will increase or decrease equally in the X, Y, and Z directions. The dynamic scaling property allows you to view the object as it is being scaled. Another advantage of this tool is that if you have dimensioned the drawing, they will also change accordingly. You can also invoke the **Scale** tool from the shortcut menu by right-clicking in the drawing area and choosing the **Scale** tool. The prompt sequence that will follow when you choose the **Scale** tool is given next.

Select objects: *Select the objects to be scaled* Enter
Specify base point: *Specify the base point, preferably a known point*
Specify scale factor or [Copy/Reference]: *Specify the scale factor*

The base point will not move from its position and the selected object(s) will be scaled with respect to the base point, refer to Figures 5-21 and 5-22. To reduce the size of an object, the scale factor should be less than 1 and to increase its size, the scale factor should be greater than 1.

You can enter a scale factor or select two points to specify a distance as a factor. When you select two points to specify a distance as a factor, the first point should be on the referenced object.

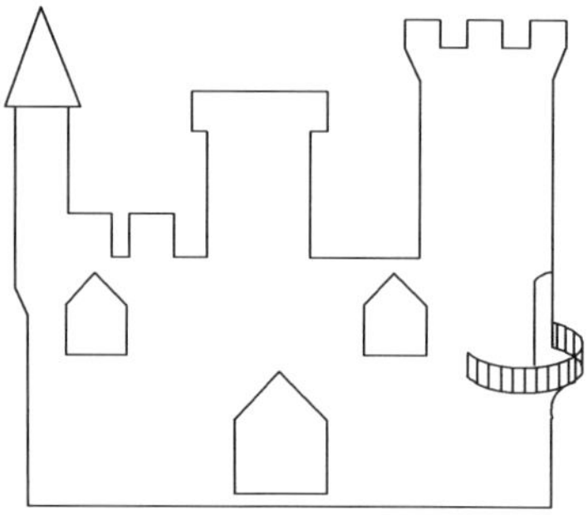

Figure 5-21 *Original object*

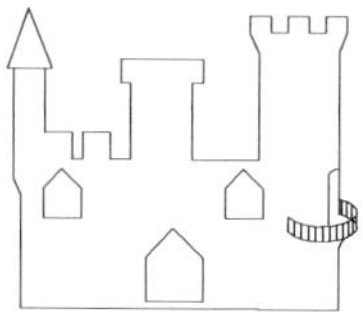

Figure 5-22 *Object after scaling to 0.5 of the actual size*

Sometimes, it is time-consuming to calculate the relative scale factor. In such cases, you can scale the object by specifying a desired size in relation to the existing size (a known dimension). In other words, you can use a reference length. This can be done by entering **R** at the **Specify scale factor or [Copy/Reference]** prompt. Then, you can either specify two points to specify the length or enter a length. At the next prompt, enter the length relative to the reference length. For example, if a line is 2.5 units long and you want its length to be 1.00 unit, then instead of calculating the relative scale factor, you can use the **Reference** option. The prompt sequence for using the **Reference** option is given next.

Select objects: *Select the object to scale* Enter
Specify base point: *Specify the base point*
Specify scale factor or [Copy/Reference]<current>: **R** Enter
Specify reference length <current>: *Specify the reference length*
Specify new length [Point]: *Specify the new length or enter **P** to select two points for specifying the angle value*

Similar to the **Rotate** tool, you can also scale one object by using the reference of another object. Again, in this case also, the base point has to be taken on the reference object as you can define only one point for the new length.

You can use the **Copy** option to retain the source object and scale the copied instance of the source object. The prompt sequence for using the **Copy** option is given next.

Select objects: *Select the object to scale* Enter
Specify base point: *Specify the base point*
Specify scale factor or [Copy/Reference]: **C** Enter
Scaling a copy of the selected objects
Specify scale factor or [Copy/Reference]: *Specify the scale factor*

> **Tip**
> *If you need to change the dimensions of all the objects with respect to other units, you can use the* ***Reference*** *option of the* ***Scale*** *tool to correct the error. To do so, select the entire drawing by using the* ***ALL*** *selection option. Next, specify the* ***Reference*** *option, and then select the endpoints of the object whose desired length is known. Specify the new length; all the objects in the drawing will be scaled automatically to the desired size.*

FILLETING THE SKETCHES

Ribbon: Home > Modify > Fillet drop-down > Fillet
Toolbar: Modify > Fillet **Command:** FILLET/F

The edges in a model are generally filleted to reduce the area of stress concentration. The **Fillet** tool helps you form round corners between two entities that form a sharp vertex. As a result, a smooth round arc is created that connects the two objects. A fillet can also be created between two intersecting or parallel lines as well as non-intersecting and nonparallel lines, arcs, polylines, xlines, rays, splines, circles, and true ellipses. The fillet arc created will be tangent to both the selected entities. The default fillet radius is 0.0000. Therefore, after invoking this tool, you first need to specify the radius value. The prompt sequence displayed on choosing the **Fillet** tool from the **Fillet** drop-down in the **Modify** panel (Figure 5-23) is given next.

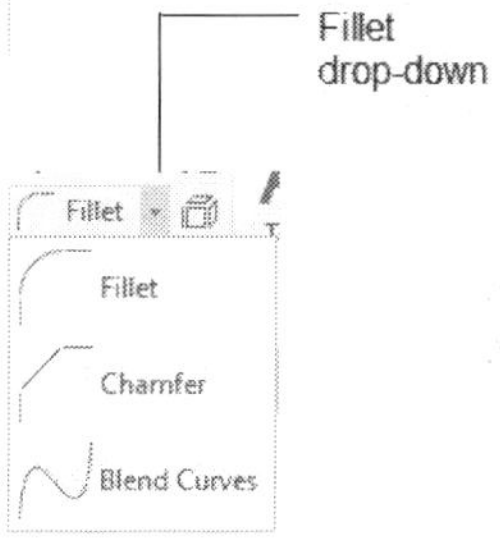

Figure 5-23 *Tools in the* ***Fillet*** *drop-down*

Current Settings: Mode= TRIM, Radius= 0.0000
Select first object or [Undo/Polyline/Radius/Trim/Multiple]:

Creating Fillets Using the Radius Option

The fillet you create depends on the radius distance specified. The default radius is 0.0000. You can enter a distance or specify two points. The new radius you enter becomes the default radius and remains in effect until changed. Note that the **FILLETRAD** system variable controls and stores the current fillet radius. The default value of this variable is 0.0000. The prompt sequence that is displayed on invoking the **Fillet** tool is given next.

Select first object or [Undo/Polyline/Radius/Trim/Multiple]: **R** Enter
Specify fillet radius <current>: *Enter a value or press ENTER to accept the current value*

> **Tip**
> *A fillet with a zero radius has sharp corners and is used to clean up lines at corners if they overlap or have a gap.*

Creating Fillets Using the Select First Object Option

This is the default method to fillet two objects. As the name implies, it prompts for the first object required for filleting. The prompt sequence to use this option is given next.

Current Settings: Mode= TRIM, Radius= current value

Select first object or [Undo/Polyline/Radius/Trim/Multiple]: *Specify the first object*
Select second object or shift-select to apply corner or [Radius]: *Select the second object or press the SHIFT key while selecting the object to create sharp corner*

The **Fillet** tool can also be used to cap the ends of two parallel as well as non-parallel lines, see Figure 5-24. The cap is a semicircle whose radius is equal to half the distance between the two parallel lines. The cap distance is calculated automatically when you select the two parallel lines for filleting. You can select lines by using the **Window,Crossing**, or **Last** option, but to avoid unexpected results, select the objects by picking them individually. Also, selection by picking objects is necessary in the case of arcs and circles that have the possibility of more than one fillet. They are filleted closest to the selected points, as shown in Figure 5-25.

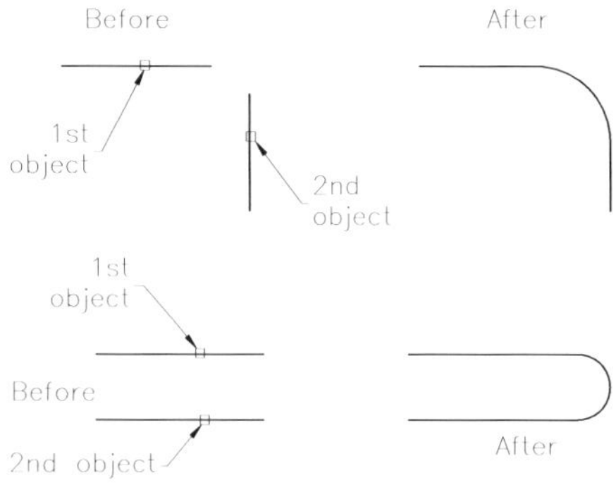

***Figure 5-24** Filleting the parallel and non-parallel lines*

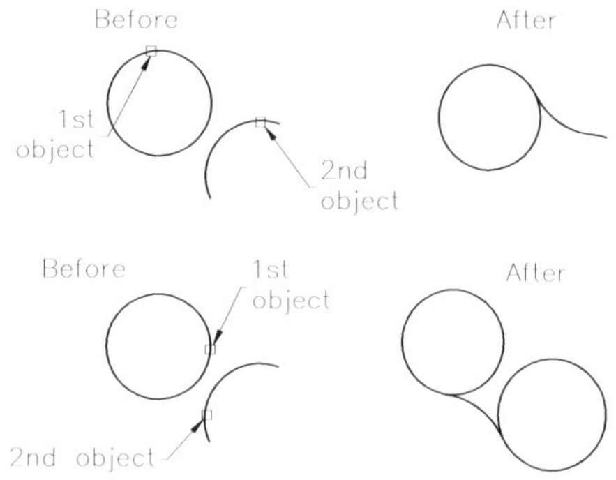

***Figure 5-25** Using the **Fillet** tool on circles and arcs*

Creating Fillets Using the Trim Option

When you create a fillet, an arc is created and the selected objects are either trimmed or extended at the fillet endpoint. This is because the **Trim** mode is set to **Trim**. If it is set to **No Trim**, then the objects are left intact. Figure 5-26 shows a model filleted with the **Trim** mode set to **Trim** and **No Trim**. The prompt sequence is given next.

Select first object or [Undo/Polyline/Radius/Trim/Multiple]: **T** Enter
Specify Trim mode option [Trim/No trim] <current>: *Enter **T** to trim edges, **N** to leave them intact. You can also choose the required option from the dynamic preview*

Creating Fillets Using the Polyline Option

If an object is created by using the **Polyline** or **Rectangle** tool, then the object will be a polyline. You can fillet all the sharp corners in a polyline by using the **Polyline** option of the **Fillet** tool, as shown in Figure 5-27. On selecting this option after specifying the fillet radius, you will be prompted to select a polyline. Select the polyline; all vertices of the polyline will be filleted with the same fillet radius. The prompt sequence for using this option is given next.

Current Settings: Mode= *current*, Radius= *current*
Select first object or [Undo/Polyline/Radius/Trim/Multiple]: **P** Enter
Select 2D polyline: *Select the polyline*

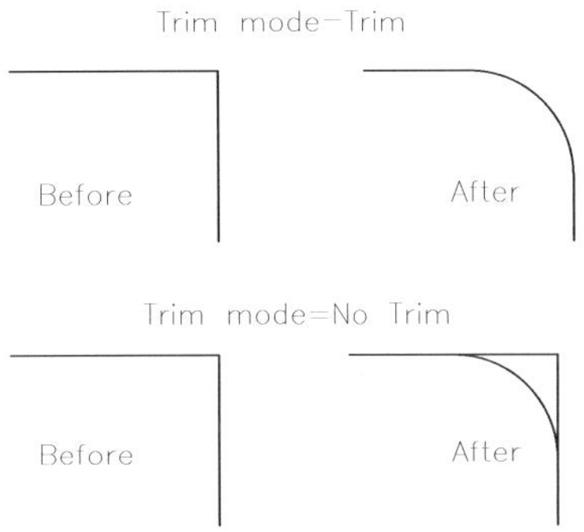

Figure 5-26 *Filleting the lines with the* ***Trim*** *mode set to* ***Trim*** *and* ***No Trim***

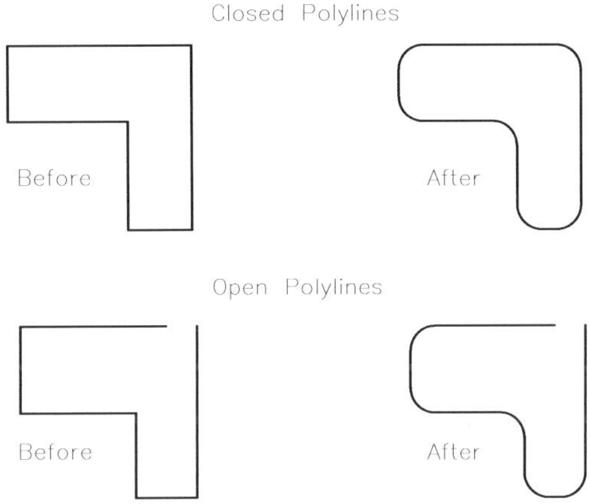

Figure 5-27 *Filleting closed and open polylines*

In AutoCAD LT, you can close an open polyline using the **Fillet** tool. To do so, choose the **Fillet** tool from the **Modify** panel of the **Home** tab and select the two open ends of the polyline; the selected polyline will be closed and form a corner. Figure 5-28 shows an open polyline and Figure 5-29 shows closed polyline after selecting the open entities.

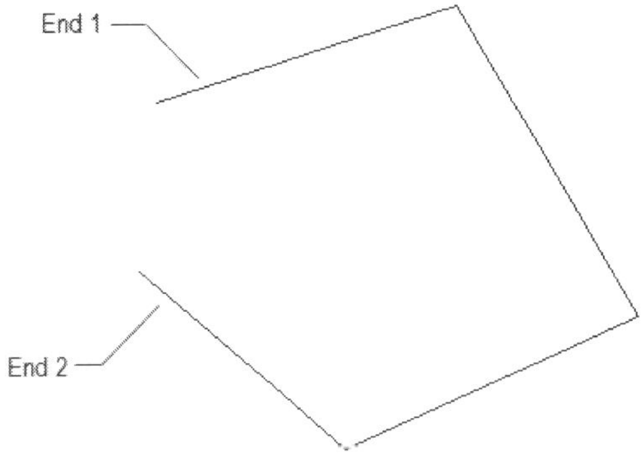

Figure 5-28 *Open polyline with two ends*

Figure 5-29 *Final closed polyline*

Creating Fillets Using the Multiple Option

When you invoke the **Fillet** tool, by default, a fillet is created between a pair of entities only. However, with the help of the **Multiple** option, you can add fillets to more than a pair of entities. On selecting this option, you will be prompted to select the first object and then the second object. On selecting two objects, a fillet will be created between the two entities and again you will be prompted to select the first object and then the second object. This prompt will continue until you press ENTER to terminate the **Fillet** tool. Note that you can use the **Undo** option to undo the fillet created. The prompt sequence to use this option is given next.

Current Settings: Mode= TRIM, Radius= current
Select first object or [Undo/Polyline/Radius/Trim/Multiple]: **M** Enter

Select first object or [Undo/Polyline/Radius/Trim/Multiple]: *Specify the first object of one set*
Select second object or shift-select to apply corner or [Radius]: *Select the second object or press the SHIFT key while selecting the object to create sharp corner*
Select first object or [Undo/Polyline/Radius/Trim/Multiple]: *Specify the first object of the other set*
Select second object or shift-select to apply corner or [Radius]: *Select the second object or press the SHIFT key while selecting the object to create sharp corner*
Select first object or [Undo/Polyline/Radius/Trim/Multiple]: *Specify the first object of the other set or press* Enter

Filleting Objects with a Different UCS

The **Fillet** tool also fillets the objects that are not in the current UCS plane. To create a fillet for these objects, AutoCAD LT automatically changes the UCS transparently so that it can generate a fillet between the selected objects.

Setting the TRIMMODE System Variable

The **TRIMMODE** system variable eliminates any size restriction on the **Fillet** tool. By setting **TRIMMODE** to **0**, you can create a fillet of any size without actually cutting the existing geometry. Also, there is no restriction on the fillet radius. This means that the fillet radius can be larger than one or both objects that are being filleted. The default value of this variable is 1.

Note

TRIMMODE = 0 *Fillet or chamfer without cutting the existing geometry.*
TRIMMODE = 1 *Extend or trim the geometry.*

CHAMFERING THE SKETCHES

Ribbon: Home > Modify > Fillet drop-down > Chamfer
Toolbar: Modify > Chamfer **Command:** CHAMFER (CHA)

Chamfering the sharp corners is another method of reducing the areas of stress concentration in a model. Chamfering is defined as the process by which the sharp edges or corners are beveled. The size of a chamfer depends on its distance from the corner. If a chamfer is equidistant from the corner in both directions, it is a 45-degree chamfer. A chamfer can be drawn between two lines that may or may not intersect. This tool also works on a single polyline. In AutoCAD LT, the chamfers are created by defining two distances or by defining one distance and the chamfer angle.

The prompt sequence that will follow when you choose the **Chamfer** tool from the **Fillet** drop-down in the **Modify** panel is given next.

(TRIM mode) Current chamfer Dist1 = 0.0000, Dist2 = 0.0000
Select first line or [Undo/Polyline/Distance/Angle/Trim/mEthod/Multiple]:

The different options to create chamfers are discussed next.

Creating Chamfers Using the Distance Option

To create a chamfer by entering the distances, enter **D** at the **Select first line or [Undo/Polyline/Distance/Angle/Trim/mEthod/Multiple]** prompt. Next, enter the first and second chamfer distances. The first distance is the distance of the corner calculated along the edge selected first. Similarly, the second distance is calculated along the edge that is selected last. The new chamfer distances remain in effect until you change them. Instead of entering the distance values, you can specify two points to indicate each distance, see Figure 5-30. The prompt sequence is given next.

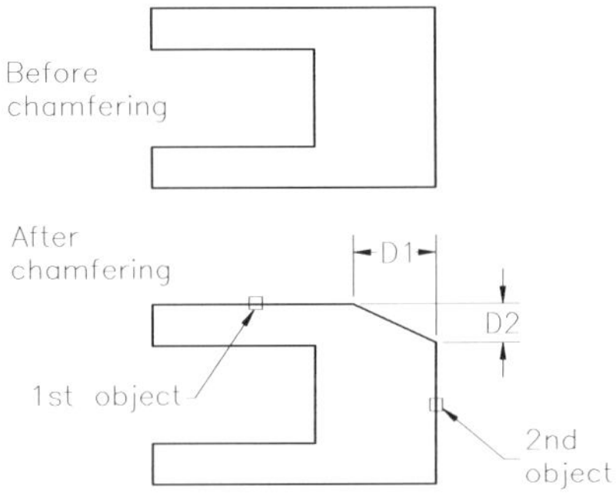

***Figure 5-30** Chamfering the model using the **Distance** option*

Select first line or [Undo/Polyline/Distance/Angle/Trim/mEthod/Multiple]: **D** Enter
Specify first chamfer distance <0.0000>: *Enter a distance value or specify two points*
Specify second chamfer distance <0.0000>: *Enter a distance value or specify two points*

Note

*1. If Dist 1 and Dist 2 are set to zero, the **Chamfer** tool will extend or trim the selected lines such that they end at the same point.*

*2. The first and second chamfer distances are stored in the **CHAMFERA** and **CHAMFERB** system variables. The default value of these variables is 0.0000.*

Creating Chamfers Using the Select First Line Option

In this option, you need to select two nonparallel objects so that they are joined with a beveled line. The size of a chamfer depends on the values of the two distances. The prompt sequence to do so is given next.

(TRIM mode) Current chamfer Dist1 = current, Dist2 = current
Select first line or [Undo/Polyline/Distance/Angle/Trim/mEthod/Multiple]: *Specify the first line*
Select second object or shift-select to apply corner: *Select the second object or press down the SHIFT key while selecting the object to create sharp corner*

Creating Chamfer Using the Polyline Option

Similar to **Fillet** tool, you can chamfer all the sharp corners of a polyline by using the **Polyline** option of the **Chamfer** tool, as shown in Figure 5-31. The prompt sequence to chamfer the polylines is given next.

(TRIM mode) Current chamfer Dist1 = current, Dist2 = current
Select first line or [Undo/Polyline/Distance/Angle/Trim/mEthod/Multiple]: **P** Enter
Select 2D polyline or [Distance/Angle/Method]: *Select the polyline*

Creating Chamfer Using the Angle Option

The other method of creating a chamfer is by specifying the distance and the chamfer angle, as shown in Figure 5-32. The prompt sequence to do so is given next.

(TRIM mode) Current chamfer Dist1 = current, Dist2 = current
Select first line or [Undo/Polyline/Distance/Angle/Trim/mEthod/Multiple]: *A* Enter
Specify chamfer length on the first line <0.0000>: *Enter a distance value or specify two points*
Specify chamfer angle from the first line <0>: *Enter an angle value*
Select first line or [Undo/Polyline/Distance/Angle/Trim/mEthod/Multiple]: *P* Enter
Select 2D polyline or [Distance/Angle/Method]: *Select the polyline*

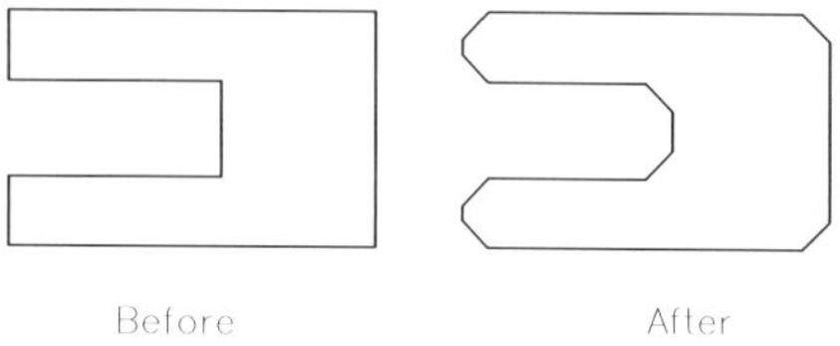

Figure 5-31 *Chamfering using the polyline option*

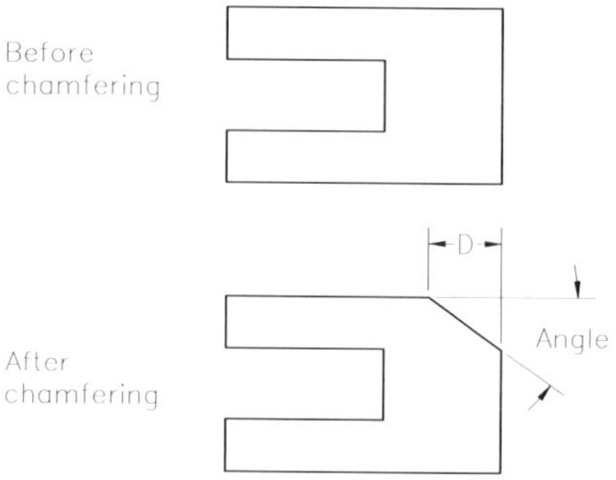

Figure 5-32 *Chamfering using the **Angle** option*

Creating Chamfer Using the Trim Option

On selecting the **Trim** option, the selected objects are either trimmed or extended to the endpoints of the chamfer line or left intact. The prompt sequence to invoke this option is given next.

Select first line or [Undo/Polyline/Distance/Angle/Trim/mEthod/Multiple]: **T** Enter
Enter Trim mode option [Trim/No Trim] <current>:*Enter **T** to trim edges, **N** to leave them intact.*

Creating Chamfer Using the Method Option

On using this option, you can toggle between the **Distance** method and the **Angle** method for creating a chamfer. The current settings of the selected method will be used for creating the chamfer. The prompt sequence to create the chamfer is given next.

Select first line or [Undo/Polyline/Distance/Angle/Trim/mEthod/Multiple]: **E** Enter
Enter trim method [Distance/Angle] <current>: *Enter **D** for the **Distance** option, **A** for the **Angle** option*

Note

*If you set the value of the **TRIMMODE** system variable to **1** (default value), the objects will be trimmed or extended after they are chamfered and filleted. If **TRIMMODE** is set to zero, the objects will be left untrimmed.*

Creating Chamfers Using the Multiple Option

When you invoke the **Chamfer** tool, by default, a chamfer is created only between one pair of entities. However, with the help of the **Multiple** option, you can add chamfers to multiple pairs. On selecting this option, you will be prompted to select first line and then second line. On selecting the two lines, the chamfer will be created. Next, you will again be prompted to select first line and then second line. This prompt will continue until you press ENTER to terminate the **Chamfer** tool. The prompt sequence that follows to create multiple chamfers is given next.

(TRIM mode) Current chamfer Dist1 = current, Dist2= current
Select first line or [Undo/Polyline/Distance/Angle/Trim/mEthod/Multiple]: **M** Enter
Select first line or [Undo/Polyline/Distance/Angle/Trim/mEthod/Multiple]: *Specify the first line of one set*
Select second line or shift-select to apply corner or [Distance Angle Method]: *Select the second object or press the SHIFT key while selecting the object to create sharp corner*
Select first line or [Undo/Polyline/Distance/Angle/Trim/mEthod/Multiple]: *Specify the first line of the other set*
Select second line or shift-select to apply corner or [Distance/Angle/Method]: *Select the second object or press the SHIFT key while selecting the object to create sharp corner*
Select first line or [Undo/Polyline/Distance/Angle/Trim/mEthod/Multiple]: *Specify the first line of the other set or press **ENTER** to terminate the **Chamfer** tool*

Setting the Chamfering System Variables

The chamfer modes, distances, length, and angle can also be set by using the following variables:

CHAMMODE = 0	Distance/Distance (default)
CHAMMODE = 1	Length/Angle
CHAMFERA	Sets first chamfer distance on the first selected line (default = 0.0000)
CHAMFERB	Sets second chamfer distance on the second selected line (default = 0.0000)
CHAMFERC	Sets the chamfer length (default = 0.0000)
CHAMFERD	Sets the chamfer angle from the first line (default = 0)

BLENDING THE CURVES

Ribbon: Home > Modify > Fillet/drop-down > Blend Curves
Command: BLEND

In AutoCAD LT, you can create a smooth or tangent continuous spline between the endpoints of two existing curves. The existing curves can be arcs, lines, helices, open polylines, or open splines. To create a smooth curve between two open curves, choose the **Blend Curves** tool from the **Fillet** drop-down in the **Modify** panel (see Figure 5-23); you will be prompted to select the curves one after the other. Select two curves; a blend curve will be created between the selected curves. The length of the selected curves do not change. The prompt sequence to use this tool is given next.

*Choose the **Blend Curves** tool*
Select first object or [CONtinuity]: *Select the first object*
Select second object: *Select the second object*

This tool provides two options to specify the continuity of the blend curve with the two selected curves: **Tangent** and **Smooth**. By default, the **Tangent** option is chosen. As a result, a tangent continuous curve will be created between the two selected curves. The prompt sequence to use this option has been given earlier in this topic.

You can also blend two curves with a smooth continuity between them. To do so, first enter **CON** at the **Select first object or [CONtinuity]:** Command prompt. Next, enter **S** at the Command prompt and then select the two curves; a smooth curve will be created between the two selected curves. The prompt sequence to use this option is given next.

*Choose the **Blend Curves** tool*
Select first object or [CONtinuity]: **CON** Enter
Enter continuity [Tangent/Smooth] <Smooth>: **S** Enter
Select first object or [CONtinuity]: *Select the first object*
Select second object: *Select the second object*

Figure 5-33 shows the two curves selected and Figure 5-34 shows the resulting tangent and smooth curves as the blend curves.

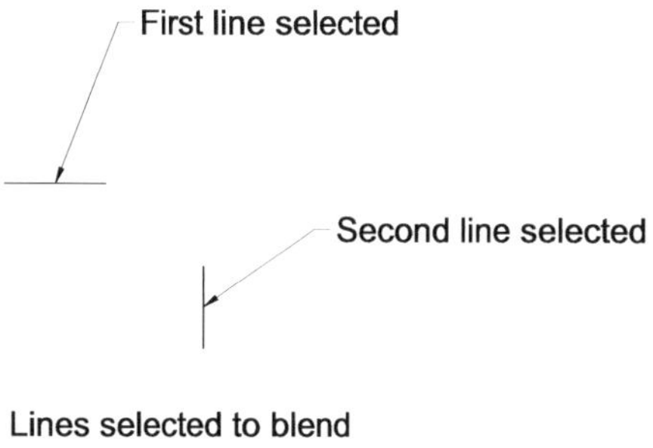

Figure 5-33 *Curves selected to be blended*

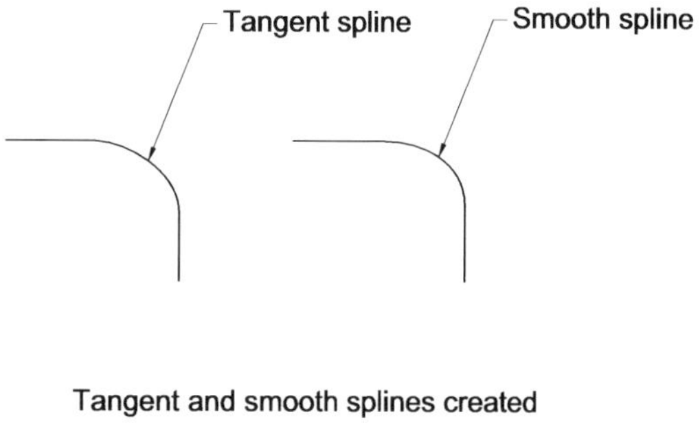

Figure 5-34 *Tangent and smooth blend curves created*

To view the continuity of the spline (blend curve) with the selected curves, select the spline; the control points will be displayed in the form of control vertices. You can change the display of control points from control vertices to fit points. To do so, click on the down-arrow on the spline; a shortcut menu will be displayed. Choose the **Fit** option from the shortcut menu to change the control vertices to fit points. Figure 5-35 shows the control vertices of a tangent continuous spline and a smooth spline created between two open lines. You can change the shape of the splines by dragging its control vertices.

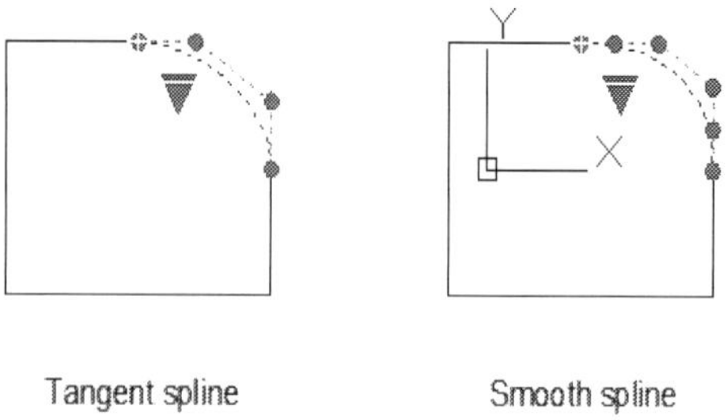

Figure 5-35 *Control vertices of tangent and smooth splines*

TRIMMING THE SKETCHED OBJECTS

Ribbon: Home > Modify > Trim drop-down > Trim
Command: TRIM (TR) **Toolbar:** Modify > Trim

While creating a design, you may need to remove the unwanted and extended edges. Breaking individual objects takes time if you are working on a complex design with many objects. In such cases, you can use the **Trim** tool. This tool is used to trim the objects that extend beyond a required point of intersection. When you invoke this tool from the **Trim** drop-down in the **Modify** panel (Figure 5-36), you will be prompted to select the cutting edges or boundaries. These edges can be lines, polylines, circles, arcs, ellipses, xlines, rays, splines, text, blocks, or even viewports. There can be more than one cutting edge and you can use any selection method to select them. After the cutting edge or edges are selected, you must select each object to be trimmed. An object can be both a cutting edge and an object to be trimmed. You can trim lines, circles, arcs, polylines, splines, ellipses, xlines, and rays. The prompt sequence to trim objects is given next.

Figure 5-36 *Tools in the* ***Trim*** *drop-down*

Current settings: Projection=UCS Edge=None
Select cutting edges...
Select objects or <select all>: *Select the cutting edges* Enter
Select object to trim or shift-select to extend or TRIM [Fence/Crossing/Project/Edge/eRase/Undo]:

Various options used to trim objects are discussed next.

Select object to trim Option

On selecting this option, you have to specify the objects you want to trim and the side from which the objects will be trimmed. This prompt is repeated until you press ENTER. This way you can trim several objects on invoking this tool once. The prompt sequence to use this option is given next.

Current settings: Projection= UCS, Edge= None
Select cutting edges...
Select objects or <select all>: *Select the cutting edges* Enter
Select object to trim or shift-select to extend or **TRIM** [Fence/Crossing/Project/Edge/eRase]: *Select the first object*
Select object to trim or shift-select to extend or **TRIM** [Fence/Crossing/Project/Edge/eRase/Undo]: *Select the second object. Refer to Figure 5-37*
Select object to trim or shift-select to extend or **TRIM** [Fence/Crossing/Project/Edge/eRase/Undo]: Enter

Shift-select to extend Option

This option is used to switch from trim mode to the extend mode. It is used to extend an object instead of trimming. In case the object to be extended does not intersect with the cutting edge, you can press the SHIFT key and then select the object to be extended; the selected edge will be extended taking the cutting edge as the boundary for extension. Note that you need to click near the endpoint that is closest to the cutting edge.

Fence Option

As discussed in earlier chapters, the **Fence** option is used for the selection purpose. Using the **Fence** option, all the objects crossing the selection fence are selected. The prompt sequence for the **Fence** option is given next.

> Select object to trim or shift-select to extend or [Fence/Crossing/Project/Edge/eRase]: **F** Enter
> Specify first fence point: *Specify the first point of the fence*
> Specify next fence point or [Undo]: *Specify the second point of the fence*
> Specify next fence point or [Undo]: *Specify the third point of the fence*
> Specify next fence point or [Undo]: Enter

Crossing Option

The **Crossing** option is used to select the entities by using a crossing window. On using this option, the objects touching the window boundaries or completely enclosing them are selected. The prompt sequence to trim objects using this option is given next.

> Select object to trim or shift-select to extend or [Fence/Crossing/Project/Edge/eRase/Undo]: **C** Enter
> Specify first corner: *Select the first corner of the crossing window*
> Specify opposite corner: *Select the opposite corner of the crossing window*

Project Option

The **Project** option is used to trim those objects that do not intersect the cutting edges in 3D space, but do visually appear to intersect in a particular UCS or the current view. The prompt sequence to invoke this option is given next.

> Select object to trim or shift-select to extend or [Fence/Crossing/Project/Edge/eRase/Undo]: **P** Enter
> Enter a projection option [None/Ucs/View] <current>:

The **None** option is used whenever the objects to be trimmed intersect the cutting edges in 3D space. The **UCS** option is used to project the objects to the *XY* plane of the current UCS, while the **View** option is used to project the objects to the current view direction (trims to their apparent visual intersections).

Edge Option

This option is used to trim those objects that do not intersect the cutting edges, but they intersect if the cutting edges were extended, see Figure 5-38. The prompt sequence is given next.

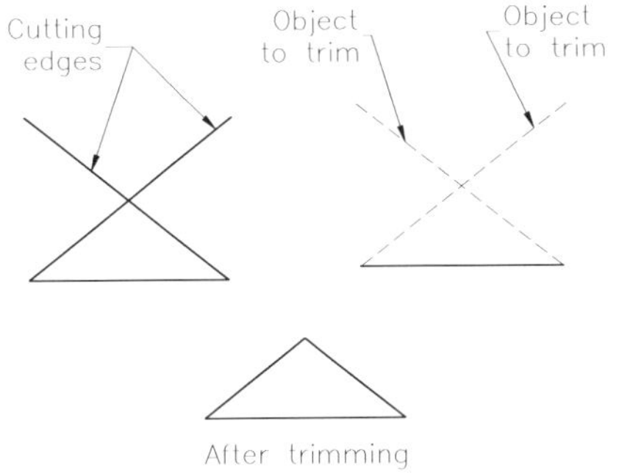

*Figure 5-37 Using the **Trim** tool*

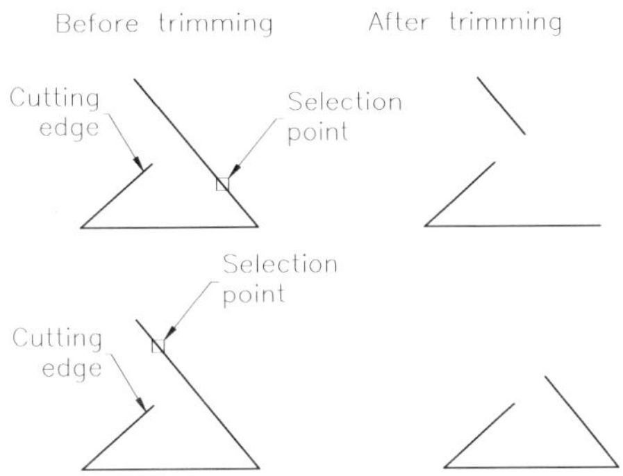

*Figure 5-38 Trimming an object using the **Edge** option (**Extend**)*

Current settings: Projection= UCS Edge= Extend
Select cutting edges...
Select objects: *Select the cutting edge*
Select objects: Enter
Select object to trim or shift-select to extend or [Fence/Crossing/Project/Edge/eRase/Undo]: **E** Enter
Enter an implied edge extension mode [Extend/No extend] <current>: **E** Enter
Select object to trim or shift-select to extend or [Fence/Crossing/Project/Edge/eRase/Undo]: *Select object to trim*

Erase Option

The **Erase** option in the **Trim** tool is used to erase the entities without terminating the **Trim** tool.

Select object to trim or shift-select to extend or [Fence/Crossing/Project/Edge/eRase/Undo]: **R** Enter
Select objects to erase or <exit>: *Select object to erase*
Select objects to erase: *Select object to erase or* Enter
Select objects to erase: Enter

Undo Option

If you want to undo the previous change made by the **Trim** tool, enter **U** at the **Select object to trim or [Fence/Crossing/Project/Edge/eRase/Undo]** prompt.

Note

*You can see the preview of the result in the drawing area. To do so, you need to select the **Command preview** check box available in the **Selection** tab of the **Options** dialog box.*

Exercise 6 — *Fillet, Chamfer, and Trim*

Draw the top illustration shown in Figure 5-39 and then use the **Fillet**, **Chamfer**, and **Trim** tools to obtain the next illustration given in the same figure.

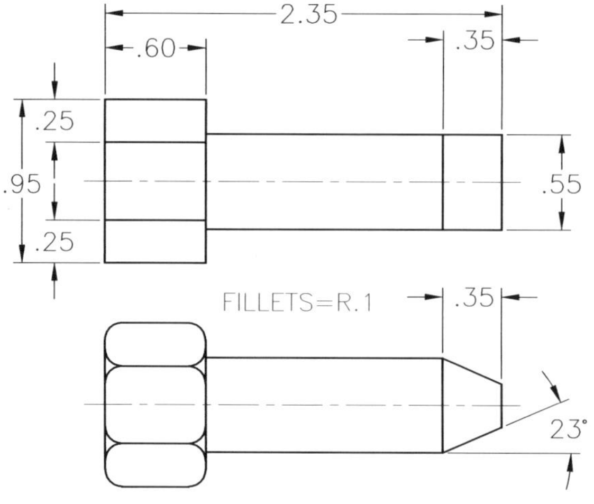

Figure 5-39 *Drawing for Exercise 6*

EXTENDING THE SKETCHED OBJECTS

Ribbon: Home > Modify > Trim drop-down > Extend
Toolbar: Modify > Extend **Command:** EXTEND/EX

The **Extend** tool may be considered as the opposite of the **Trim** tool. You can extend lines, polylines, rays, and arcs to connect to other objects by using the **Extend** tool. However, you cannot extend closed loops. The command prompt of the **Extend** tool is similar to that of the **Trim** tool. You are required to select the boundary edges first. The boundary edges are those objects that the selected lines or arcs extend to meet. These edges can be lines, polylines, circles, arcs, ellipses, xlines, rays, splines, text, blocks, or even viewports. The prompt sequence that will follow when you choose the **Extend** tool is given next.

Current settings: Projection=UCS, Edge=Extend
Select boundary edges ...
Select objects or <select all>: *Select boundary edges* Enter
Select object to extend or shift-select to trim or **EXTEND** [Fence/Crossing/Project/Edge]:

The options used to extend the objects are discussed next.

Select object to extend Option

In this option, you have to specify the object that you want to extend to the selected boundary (Figure 5-40). This prompt is repeated until you press ENTER. Note that you can select a number of objects in a single **Extend** tool.

Shift-select to trim Option

This option is used to switch to the trim mode in the **Extend** tool, if two entities are intersecting. You can press the SHIFT key and then select the object to be trimmed. In this case, the boundary edges are taken as the cutting edges.

Project Option

The **Project** option is used to extend objects in the 3D space. The prompt sequence that will follow when you choose the **Extend** tool is given next.

Current settings: Projection=UCS Edge=Extend
Select boundary edges ...
Select objects or <select all>: *Select boundary edges* Enter
Select object to extend or shift-select to trim or [Fence/Crossing/Project/Edge]: **P** Enter
Enter a projection option [None/UCS/View] <current>:

The **None** option is used whenever the objects to be extended intersect with the boundary edge in 3D space. If you want to extend those objects that do not intersect the boundary edge in 3D space, use the **UCS** or **View** option. The **UCS** option is used to project the objects to the *XY* plane of the current UCS, while the **View** option is used to project the objects to the current view.

Edge Option

You can use this option for extending the objects that do not actually intersect the boundary edge, but would intersect its edge if the boundary edges were extended (Figure 5-41). If you enter **E** at the prompt, the selected object is extended to the implied boundary edge. If you enter **N** at the prompt, only those objects that would actually intersect the real boundary edge are extended (the default). The prompt sequence to use this option is given next.

Current settings: Projection= UCS Edge= Extend
Select boundary edges...
Select objects or <select all>: *Select the boundary edge* Enter
Select object to extend or shift-select to trim or **EXTEND** [Fence/Crossing/Project/ Edge]
: **E** Enter
Enter an implied extension mode [Extend/No extend] <current>: **E** Enter
Select object to extend or shift-select to trim or **EXTEND** [Fence/Crossing/Project/ Edge/ Undo]: *Select the line to extend*

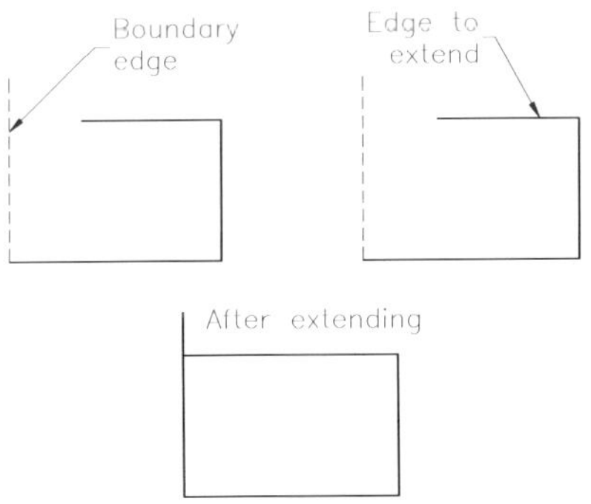

***Figure 5-40** Extending an edge*

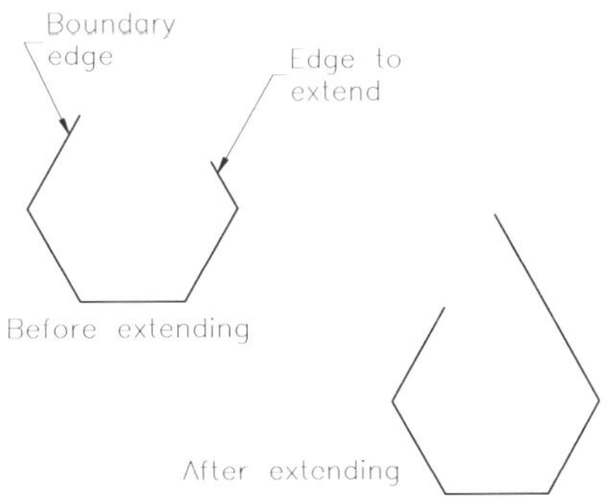

***Figure 5-41** Extending an edge using the **Edge** option (**Extend**)*

Note

*The functions of the **Fence** and **Crossing** options in the **Extend** tool are same as that in the **Trim** tool.*

Undo Option

If you want to remove the previous change created by the **Extend** tool, enter **U** at the **Select object to extend or [Fence/Crossing/Project/Edge/Undo]:** prompt.

Trimming and Extending with Text, Region, or Spline

The **Trim** and **Extend** tools can be used with text, regions, or splines as edges (Figure 5-42). This makes the **Trim** and **Extend** tools the most useful editing tools. The **Trim** and **Extend** tools can also be used with arcs, elliptical arcs, splines, ellipses, 3D Pline, rays, and lines. The system variables **PROJMODE** and **EDGEMODE** determine how the **Trim** and **Extend** tools are executed, see Figure 5-43. The values that can be assigned to these variables are discussed next.

Value	PROJMODE	EDGEMODE
0	True 3D mode	Use regular edge without extension (default)
1	Project to current UCS *XY* plane (default)	Extend or trim the selected object to an imaginary extension of the cutting or boundry edge
2	Project to current view plane	

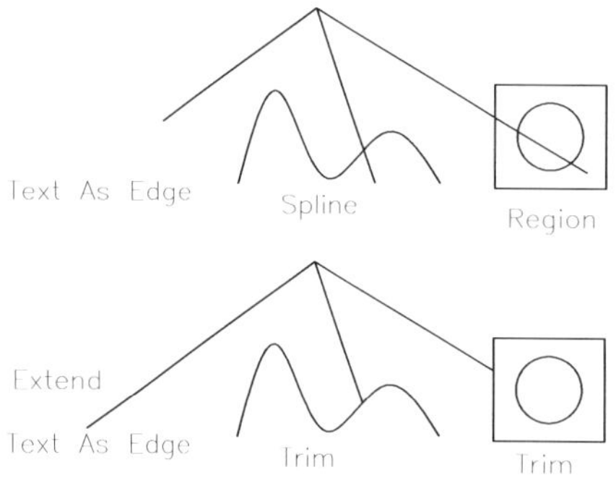

*Figure 5-42 Using the **Trim** and **Extend** tools with text, spline, and region*

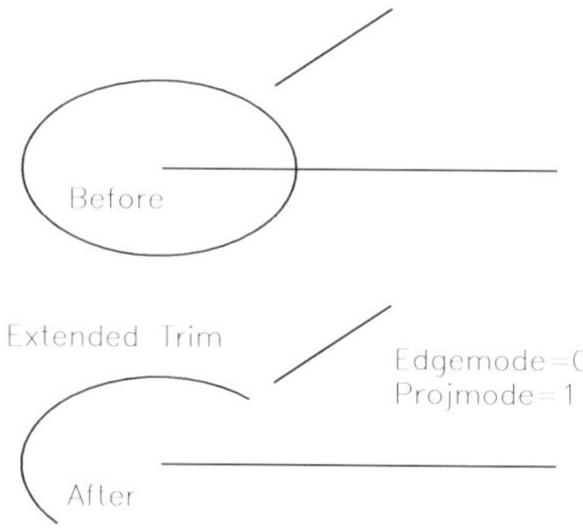

*Figure 5-43 Using the **PROJMODE** and **EDGEMODE** options to trim*

STRETCHING THE SKETCHED OBJECTS

Ribbon: Home > Modify > Stretch **Toolbar:** Modify > Stretch
Command: STRETCH

This tool is used to increase or decrease the length of objects and to alter their shapes also, refer to Figure 5-44. To invoke this tool, choose the **Stretch** tool from the **Modify** panel; you will be prompted to select objects. Use the **Crossing** or **CPolygon** selection method to select the objects to be stretched. After selecting the objects, you will be prompted to specify the base point of displacement. Select the portion of the object that needs to be stretched; you will be prompted to specify the second point of displacement. Specify the new location; the object will lengthen or shorten. Figure 5-44 illustrates the usage of a crossing selection to simultaneously select two angled lines and then stretch their right ends.

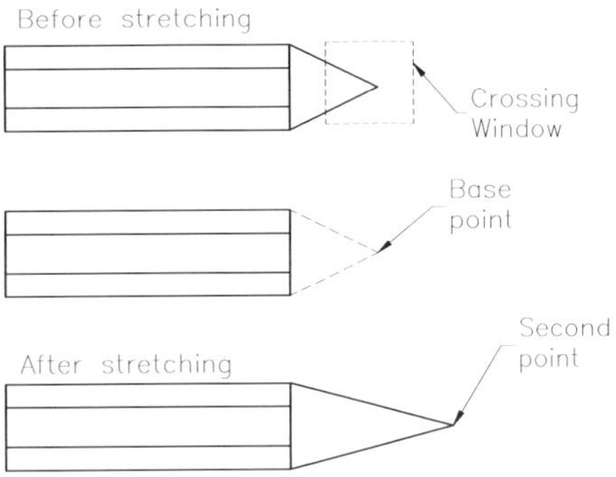

Figure 5-44 Stretching the entities

Note
The regions and solids cannot be stretched. If you select them, they will move instead of getting stretched.

LENGTHENING THE SKETCHED OBJECTS

Ribbon: Home > Modify > Lengthen **Command:** LENGTHEN (LEN)

Like the **Trim** and **Extend** tools, the **Lengthen** tool can also be used to extend or shorten lines, polylines, elliptical arcs, and arcs. This tool has several options that allow you to change the length of objects by dynamically dragging the object endpoint, entering the delta value, entering the percentage value, or entering the total length of the object. This tool also allows the repeated selection of the objects for editing. The prompt that will follow when you invoke the **Lengthen** tool is given next.

Select an object to measure or [DElta/Percent/Total/DYnamic] <current>:

Select an object Option

This is the default selected option. It returns the current length or the included angle of the selected object. If the object is a line, AutoCAD LT returns only the length. However, if the selected object is an arc, AutoCAD LT returns the length and the angle. The same prompt sequence will be displayed, after you select the object.

Delta Option

The **Delta** option is used to increase or decrease the length or angle of an object by defining the distance or angle by which the object will be extended. The delta value can be entered by entering a numerical value or by specifying two points. A positive value will increase (Extend) the length of the selected object; whereas a negative value will decrease it (Trim), see Figure 5-45.

The prompt sequence to change the length of the object after choosing the **Lengthen** tool is given next.

Select an object to measure or [DElta/Percent/Total/DYnamic] <current>: **DE** Enter
Enter delta length or [Angle] <current>: *Specify the delta length*
Select an object to change or [Undo]: *Select the object to be extended* Enter

Percent Option

The **Percent** option is used to extend or trim an object by defining the change as a percentage of the original length or the angle, see Figure 5-45. The current length of the line is taken as 100 percent. If you enter a value more than 100, the length will increase by that amount. Similarly, if you enter a value less than 100, then the length will decrease by that amount. For example, the numerical value150 will increase the length by 50 percent and the numerical value 75 will decrease the length by 25 percent of the original value (negative values are not allowed).

Total Option

The **Total** option is used to extend or trim an object by total length or angle, see Figure 5-45. For example, if you enter a total length of 1.25, AutoCAD LT will automatically increase or decrease the length of the object so that the new length is 1.25. The value can be entered by entering a numerical value or by specifying two points. The object is shortened or lengthened with respect to the endpoint that is closest to the selection point. The selection point is determined from where the object was selected.

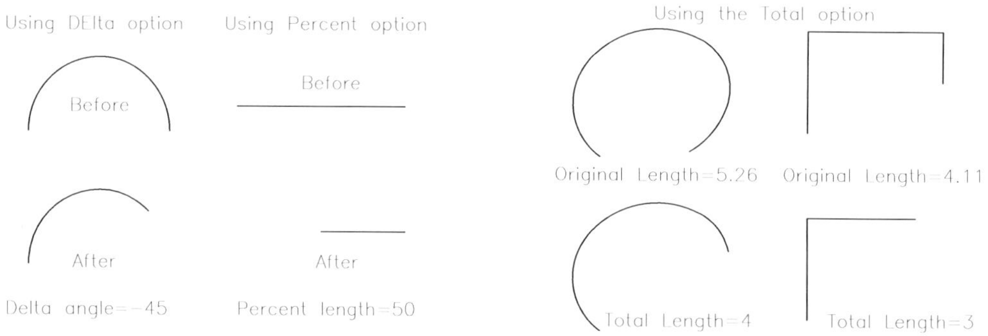

***Figure 5-45** Using the **DElta**, **Percent**, and **Total** options*

Tip

*By default, the **Lengthen** tool is not available in the **Modify** toolbar. To add the **Lengthen** tool in the **Modify** toolbar, right-click on any toolbar to display the shortcut menu. Next, choose **Customize** from the shortcut menu to display the **Customize User Interface** dialog box. Select the **Modify** option in the **Filter the command list by category** drop-down list; all the tools that can be added or are currently available in the **Modify** toolbar will be displayed. Drag the **Lengthen** button from the **Command list** area to the **Modify** toolbar in the drawing area. Choose the **OK** button from the **Customize User Interface** dialog box.*

Dynamic Option

The **Dynamic option** allows you to dynamically change the length or angle of an object by specifying one of the endpoints and dragging it to a new location. The other end of the object remains fixed and unaffected by dragging. The angle of lines, radius of arcs, and shape of elliptical arcs remain unaffected on using this option.

ARRAYING THE SKETCHED OBJECTS

Ribbon: Home > Modify > Array drop-down **Command:** ARRAY (AR)

In some drawings, you may need to create an object multiple times in a rectangular or circular arrangement. This type of arrangement can be obtained by creating an array of objects. An array is defined as the method of creating multiple copies of a selected object and arranging them in a rectangular or circular fashion. This method is more efficient and less time-consuming. In this type of arrangement, each resulting element of the array can be controlled separately. The arrays can be created by using the **Array** drop-down, refer to Figure 5-46. You can use this drop-down to create a rectangular, polar, or path array. The prompt sequence to be followed to create an array of an object after choosing the **Array** drop-down is given next.

Select objects: *Select the object*
Select Objects: 1 found
Select Objects: Enter
Enter array type [Rectangular/PAth/POlar] <Rectangular>:

At the last prompt, you can specify the type of array to be created. The different types of arrays that can be created using the **Array** drop-down are discussed next.

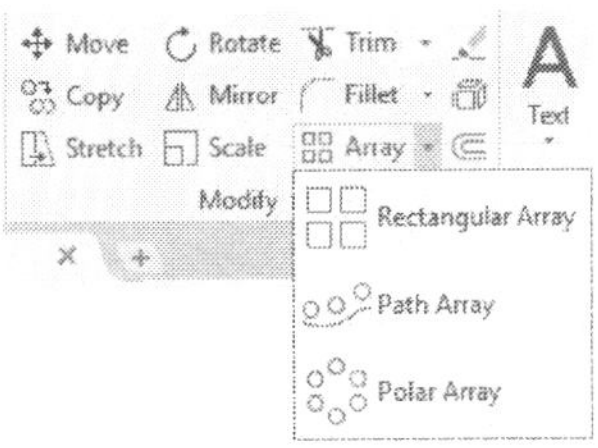

***Figure 5-46** Tools in the **Array** drop-down*

Rectangular Array

Ribbon: Home > Modify > Array drop-down > Rectangular Array
Toolbar: Modify > Array drop-down > Rectangular Array **Command:** ARRAYRECT

A rectangular array is formed by making copies of the selected object along the *X* and *Y* directions of an imaginary rectangle (along rows and columns). To create a rectangular array, choose the **Rectangular Array** tool from the **Modify** panel; you will be prompted to select objects. Select the objects to be arrayed and press ENTER; you will be prompted to select the grip to edit the array. Select the grip and click to specify the spacing for the array, as required. Also, you can enter the value of spacing. Next, press ENTER or X; the array of the selected object will be created, refer to Figure 5-47. This figure also shows the location of the cursor while specifying the opposite corner. The prompt sequence to create the rectangular array of an object after choosing the **Rectangular Array** tool from **Array** drop-down is given next.

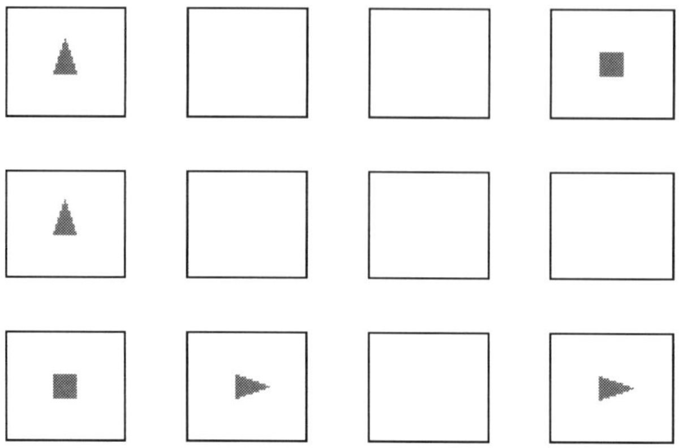

Figure 5-47 *Rectangular array created*

Select objects: *Select the object*
Select objects: 1 found
Select objects: [Enter]
Type = Rectangular Associative = Yes
Select grip to edit array or [ASsociative/Base point/COUnt/Spacings/COLumns/Rows/Levels/eXit]<eXit>: *Press* [Enter] *or* **X**

While specifying the opposite corner, if you move the cursor along the vertical or horizontal direction, the array will be created in the specified direction. Figures 5-48 and 5-49 show the array created in the vertical and horizontal directions, respectively.

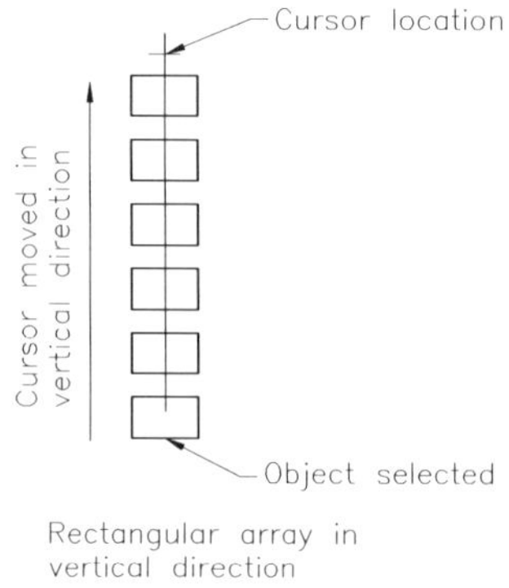

Figure 5-48 *A vertical rectangular array created*

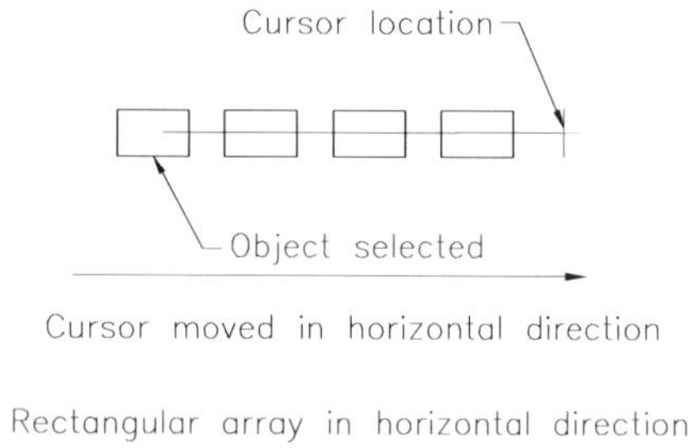

Figure 5-49 *A horizontal rectangular array created*

Rectangular Array Options

To create a rectangular array, you need to specify the options displayed at the **Select grip to edit array or [ASsociative/Base point/COUnt/Spacing/COLumns/Rows/Levels/eXit]<eXit>:** Command prompt. Some of these options are discussed next.

Base point. This option is used to specify the base point of the array to be created. You can specify the base point by selecting a keypoint on the selected object. By default, the centroid is used as the base point for the array. However, you can specify any other point than the centroid of the object as the base point of the array. The prompt sequence that will follow when you invoke the **Base point** option is given next. In this prompt, the **Key point** option has been used.

> Select grip to edit the array or [Associative/Base point/Count/Spacing/Columns/Rows/Levels/eXit] <eXit>: **B** Enter
> Specify base point or [Key point] <centroid> : **K** Enter
> Specify a key point on a source object as the base point: *Select any keypoint on the object*

Level. This option is used to specify the level of the array, refer to Figure 5-50. If you enter **L** at the **Select grip to edit array or [ASsociative/Base point/COUnt/Spacings/COLumns/Rows/Levels/eXit]<eXit>** Command prompt, you will be prompted to enter the number of levels. Enter the required level value and then specify the distance between levels. The prompt sequence that will follow when you invoke the **Level** option is given next.

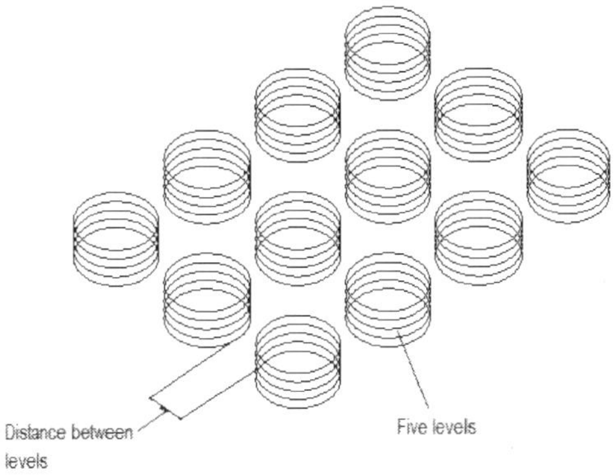

Figure 5-50 *Leveled rectangular array*

> Select grip to edit array or [ASsociative/Base point/COUnt/Spacings/COLumns/Rows/Levels/eXit]<eXit>: L Enter
> Specify number of levels or [Expression] <1>: *Enter the level value* Enter
> Specify the distance between levels or [Total/Expression] <1>: *Click to specify the distance between levels*

Count. This option is used to specify the number of rows and columns in the array. If you enter **COU** at the **Select grip to edit array or [Associative/Base point/COUnt/Spacings/COLumns/Rows/Levels/eXit]<eXit>:** Command prompt, you will be prompted to specify the number of columns. Enter the number of columns in the array and press ENTER; you will be prompted to specify the number of rows in the array. Enter the number of rows and press ENTER.

> Select grip to edit array or [ASsociative/Base point/COUnt/Spacings/COLumns/Rows/Levels/eXit]<eXit>: **COU** Enter
> Enter number of columns or [Expression] <current>: *Specify the number of columns* Enter
> Enter number of rows or [Expression] <current>: *Specify the number of rows* Enter

You can also specify the number of columns and rows by using expressions or mathematical formulae. Figure 5-51 shows a rectangular array of three rows and six columns.

You can also specify the associativity of the objects in the array. Associativity determines whether the objects of the array are dependent upon each other or not. To specify the associativity, enter **ASSOCIATIVE** at the **ARRAYRECT** select grip to edit array or **[ASsociative/Base point/Rows/Columns/Levels/eXit]<eXit>:** Command prompt; you will be prompted to specify whether the objects of the resultant array will be associative or non-associative. Enter **Yes** at the Command prompt to make the objects of the array associative. The associative array behaves as a single block. If you enter **No** at the Command prompt, the objects of the resultant array will be non-associative. If you edit one of the objects in the non-associative array, the other objects in the array will not be affected. After creating the array, press ENTER or X to exit the **Rectangular Array** tool.

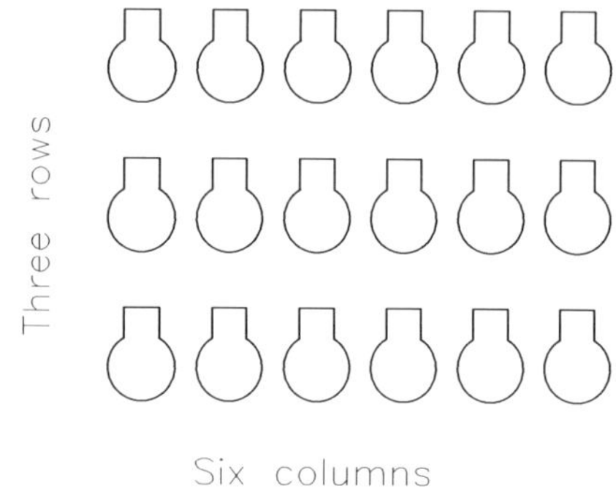

***Figure 5-51** Rectangular array of three rows and six columns*

All aforementioned options for creating a rectangular array are also available at the Dynamic Input, see Figure 5-52, provided you have chosen the **Dynamic Input** button from the Status Bar.

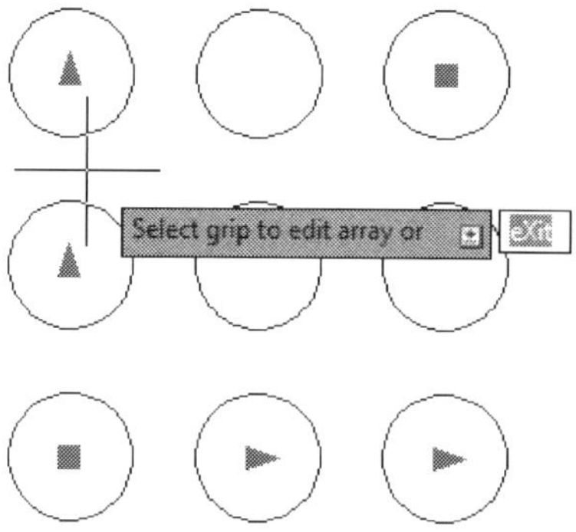

***Figure 5-52** Dynamic input options for rectangular array*

Editing the Associative Rectangular Array with Grips

You can change the number of rows, columns, and the distance between the objects in the associative array dynamically. To do so, select an object from the array; grips will be displayed on it, refer to Figure 5-53. If you hover the cursor over the parent grip of a multiple row and column array, a tooltip with two options, **Move** and **Level Count**, will be displayed, as shown in Figure 5-54. Choose the **Move** option from the tooltip to move the array. If you choose the **Level Count** option from the tooltip, you will be prompted to specify the number of levels. Levels allow you to create a 3D array. Specify the number of levels at the Command prompt or in the **Dynamic Input**; the 3D array will be created. You can view the 3D array in any of the isometric views. The isometric views can be invoked by using the options in the **Named Views** panel of the **View** tab in the **Ribbon**.

If you click on the corner grip of the rectangular array, you will be prompted to specify the number of rows and columns, as shown in Figure 5-55. Specify the number of rows and columns in the edit box displayed or drag the cursor on the screen, preview of the array will be displayed accordingly.

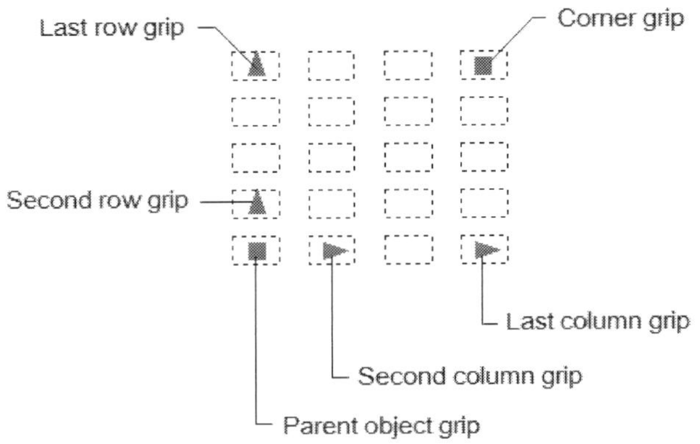

***Figure 5-53** Grips of a rectangular array*

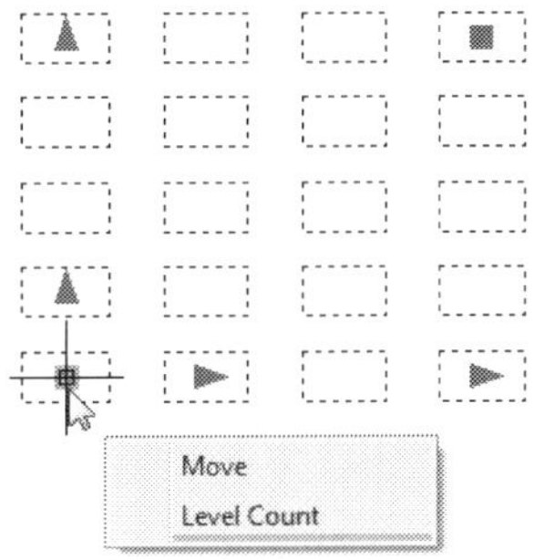

***Figure 5-54** The parent grip tooltip*

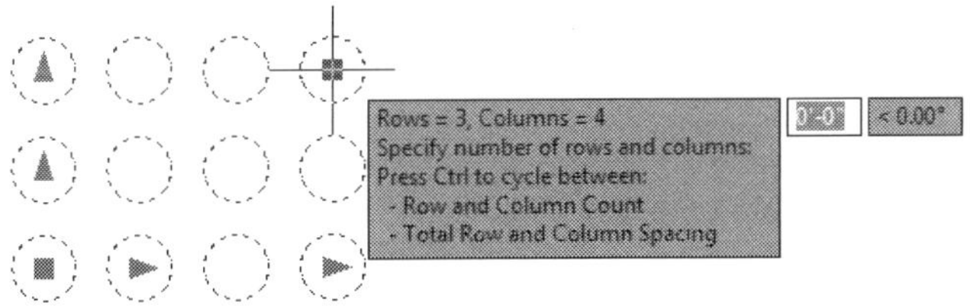

***Figure 5-55** Prompt displayed on clicking on the rectangular array*

You can change the distance between columns of the rectangular array by clicking on second column grip and then dragging the cursor. In this case, if the **Dynamic Input** button is chosen, the value between the two columns will be displayed in the edit box, refer to Figure 5-56. You can also specify the distance between columns in this edit box displayed.

If you want to increase the number of columns, click on the last column grip; you will be prompted to specify the number of columns, as shown in Figure 5-57. Specify the number of columns and press ENTER.

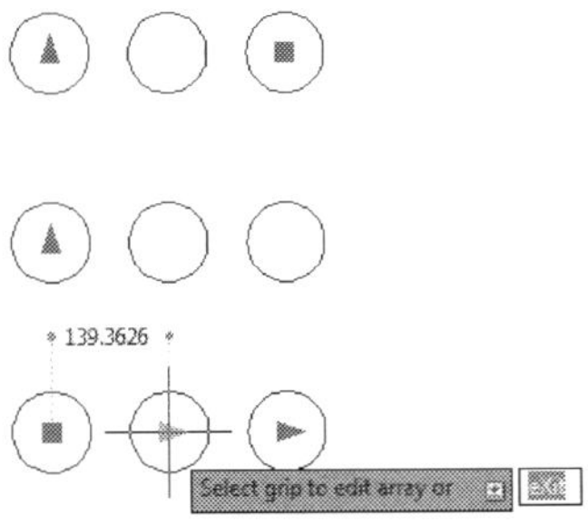

***Figure 5-56** Distance between two columns*

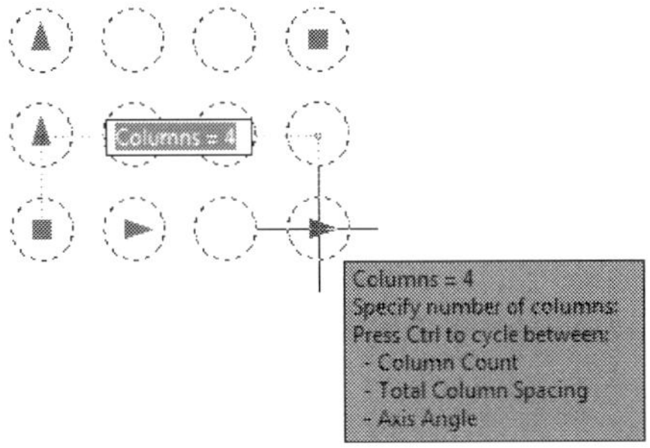

***Figure 5-57** The last column grip tooltip*

Similarly, if you click on the grip on the second row or the last row of the rectangular array, the prompt related to row count will be displayed. Specify the parameters for the rows of the array. Figure 5-58 shows a rectangular array with rows and columns at specified distance.

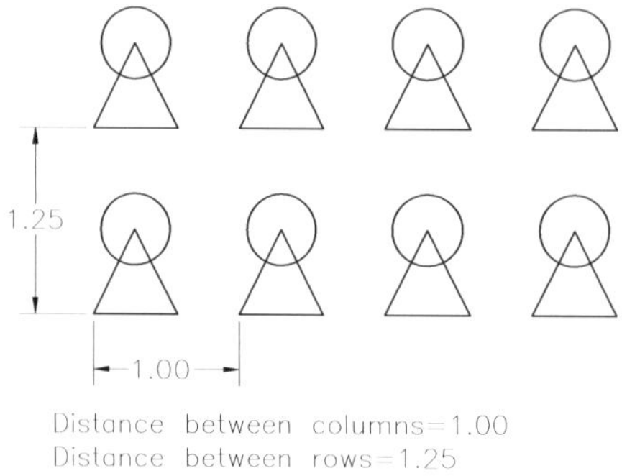

Figure 5-58 A rectangular array with rows and columns at specified distance

Editing the Associative Rectangular Array by Using the Array Contextual Tab

You can also edit the associative rectangular array by using the **Array** contextual tab that will be displayed when you select the rectangular array. The **Array** (Rectangular) contextual tab is shown in Figure 5-59.

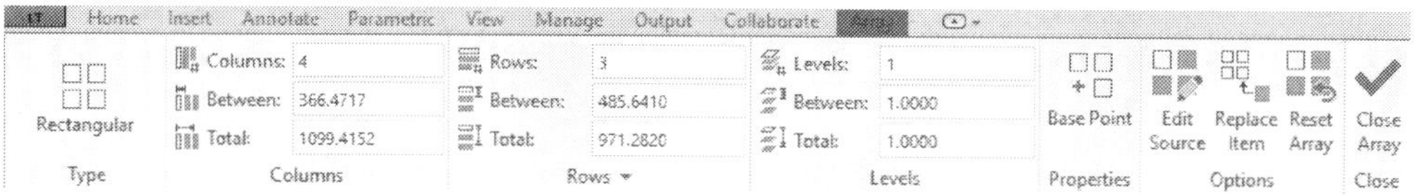

***Figure 5-59** The **Array** (Rectangular) contextual tab*

The different panels and their corresponding options in this tab are discussed next.

Type

This panel displays the type of array to be modified.

Columns

This panel displays three options which are used for changing the number of columns, the distance between two columns, and the total distance between the first and last columns. The description of these options are the same as those discussed in the previous topic.

Rows

This panel displays the options for changing the number of rows, the distance between two rows, and the total distance between the first and last rows. You can also specify the incremental elevation between the rows.

Levels
This panel displays three options for changing the number of levels, the distance between two levels, and the total distance between the first and last levels. The levels allow you to create a 3D array.

Properties
The **Base Point** tool in the **Properties** panel allows you to change the base point of the array.

Options
There are three tools in the **Options** panel: **Edit Source**, **Replace Item**, and **Reset Array**. These options are discussed next.

Edit Source. The **Edit Source** tool is used to edit the source of the array. On choosing this tool, you will be prompted to select an item in the array. Select any object in the array that will act as the source of the array. On selecting an item, the **Array Editing State** message box will be displayed, as shown in Figure 5-60, prompting you either to edit the source object or exit the editing state. Choose **OK** in this message box; the **Edit Array** panel will be added to the **Home** tab of the **Ribbon**, indicating that you are now in the editing mode. Next, modify the source object geometry. On modifying the source object geometry, you will notice that the other items of the array are also modified. Next, choose **Save Changes** from the **Edit Array** panel; the changes made in the array will be saved.

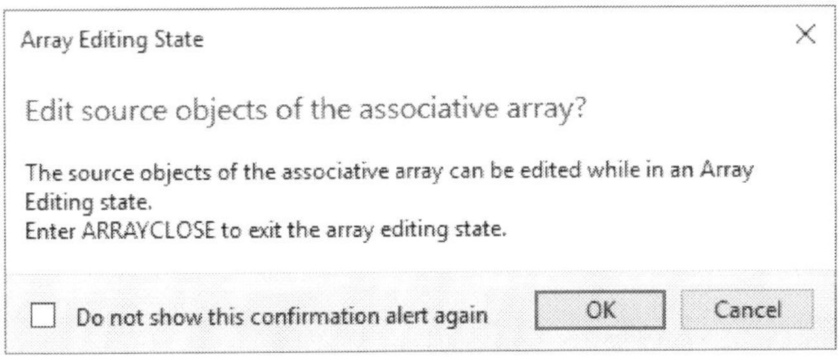

Figure 5-60 *The* ***Array Editing State*** *message box*

Figure 5-61 shows the rectangular array of a triangle and Figure 5-62 shows the source of the array being edited.

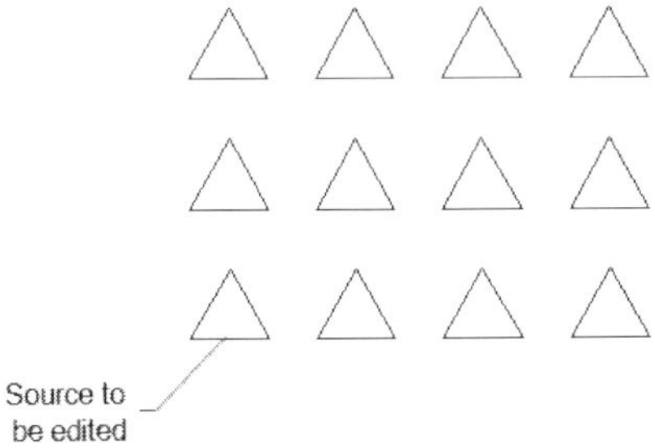

Figure 5-61 *A rectangular array*

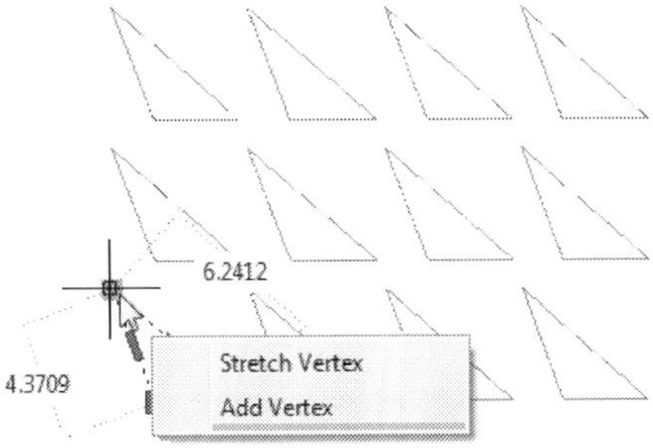

Figure 5-62 *Source of the array being edited*

Replace Item. This tool is used to replace an item in the array with another item. On choosing this tool, you will be prompted to select the replacement object. Select the replacement object and press ENTER; you will be prompted to specify the base point of the replacement object. Click to specify the base point of the replacement object. You can also specify a keypoint as the base point of the replacement object. To do so, enter **K** at the command prompt and then select any keypoint from the array. After specifying the base point, you will be prompted to specify the item to be replaced. Select an item from the array; the selected item will be replaced with the replacement item. You can continue replacing rest of the items in the array by selecting them. Figure 5-63 shows a rectangular array and the replacement object. Figure 5-64 shows the objects of the array after replacing with the selected object.

Reset Array. This tool is used to restore the objects that have been deleted from the array. If you have made any replacements in the array, those replacements can also be reverted by using this tool.

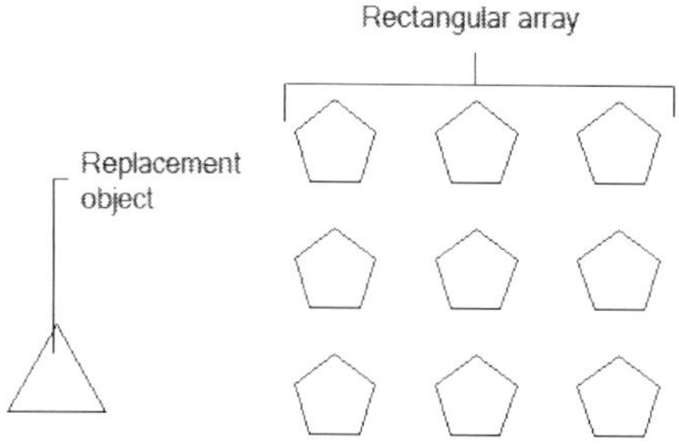

Figure 5-63 *Array with the replacement object*

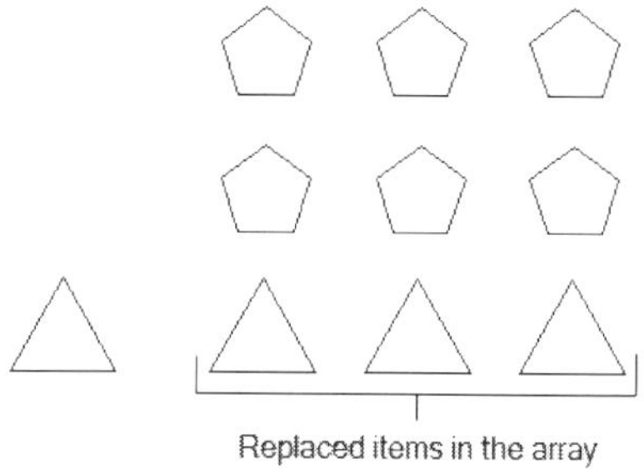

Figure 5-64 *Replaced items in the first row of the array*

Polar Array

Ribbon: Home > Modify > Array drop-down > Polar Array
Toolbar: Modify > Array drop-down > Polar Array **Command:** ARRAYPOLAR

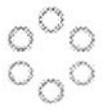

Polar array is an arrangement of objects in circular pattern around a point. A polar array can be created by choosing the **Polar Array** tool from the **Array** drop-down of the **Modify** panel, refer to Figure 5-46. When you choose this tool, you will be prompted to select objects. Select objects to be arrayed; you will be prompted to specify the center point of the array. Select the center point of the array; you will be prompted to select grip to edit array. Press ENTER or X to exit the tool. Figure 5-65 shows a polar array with its center.

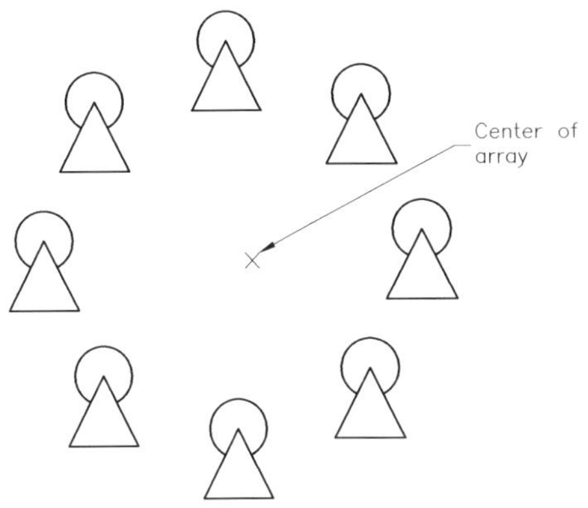

Figure 5-65 *Polar array created*

The prompt sequence to create the polar array of an object after choosing the **Polar Array** tool is given next.

Select objects: *Select the object* Enter
Type = Polar Associative = Yes
Specify center point of array or [Base point/Axis of rotation]: *Click to specify the center point of array*
Select grip to edit array or [ASsociative/Base point/Items/Angle between/Fill angle/ROWs/Levels/ROTate items/eXit] <eXit>: **X** Enter

Polar Array Options

To create a polar array, you need to specify the options displayed at the **Specify center point of array or [Base point/Axis of rotation]:** Command prompt. These options are discussed next.

Base point. This option is used to specify the base point of the polar array. You can specify the base point by clicking on the graphics window or by selecting a keypoint on the selected object. By default, the centroid is used as the base point for the array. You can also click in the drawing window to specify the base point of the array. The prompt sequence followed while using the **Base point** option is given next. In this prompt, the **Key point** option has been used.

Specify center point of array or [Base point/Axis of rotation]: **B** Enter
Specify base point or [Key point] <centroid> : **K** Enter
Specify a key point on the source object as the base point: *Select any keypoint on the object*

Axis of rotation. This option is used to specify the rotation angle of the array, refer to Figure 5-66. If you enter **A** at the **Specify center point of array or [Base point/Axis of rotation]:** Command prompt, you will be prompted to specify the first point on the axis of rotation. Click to specify the first point; you will be prompted to specify the second point on the axis of rotation. Click to specify the second point; the preview of the polar array depending upon the axis of rotation will be displayed. You can also specify the first and second points of the axis of rotation by using the **Dynamic Input**.

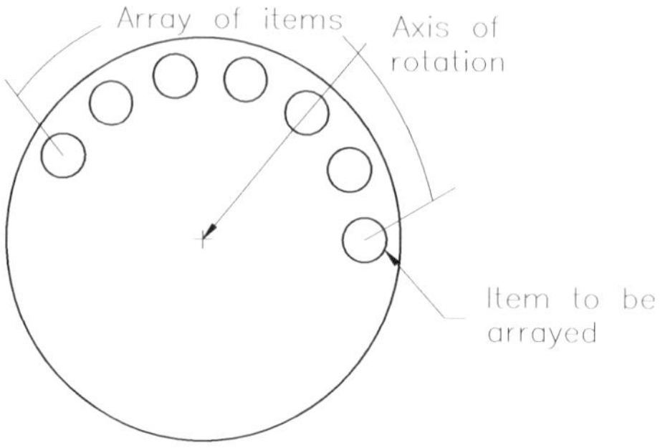

Figure 5-66 *Polar array created around the axis of rotation*

The prompt sequence followed while using the **Axis of rotation** option is given next.

Specify center point of array or [Base point/Axis of rotation]: **A** Enter
Specify first point on axis of rotation: *Click to specify the first point*
Specify second point on axis of rotation: *Click to specify the second point*

After specifying the required polar array option, you will be prompted to enter the number of items to be created. The prompt sequence to enter the number of items in the polar array is given next.

Select grip to edit array or [ASsociative/Base point/Items/Angle between/Fill angle/ROWs/Levels/ROTate items/eXit] <eXit>: **I** Enter
Enter number of items in array or [Expression] <current>:

As evident from the Command prompt, you can specify the number of items in various ways. The first way is that you can enter the number of items directly at the command prompt. The second way to specify the number of items is by entering the number of items directly in the **Array Creation** contextual tab in the **Items** area. You can also change the angle between the items in the polar array. If you enter **ANGLE** or **A** at the Command prompt, you will be prompted to enter the angle between the items. Specify the angle value at the Command prompt and press ENTER. You can also specify the angle by using expressions or mathematical formulae. Another way of specifying the number of items of the polar array is by specifying the fill angle at the **Select grip to edit array or [ASsociative/Base point/Items/Angle between/Fill angle/ROWs/Levels/ROTate items/eXit]<eXit>:** command prompt. This command prompt is displayed when you enter the angle between the items in the polar array. The third method to specify the number of items is to use expressions. The prompt sequence to specify the number of items in the polar array of an object after choosing the **Polar Array** tool is given next. In this prompt sequence, the **Angle between** option is used.

Select objects: *Select the objects to be arrayed*
Select objects: Enter
Type = Polar Associative = Yes
Specify center point of array or [Base point/Axis of rotation]: *Click to specify the center point of the array*

Select grip to edit array or [ASsociative/Base point/Items/Angle between/Fill angle/ROWs/Levels/ROTate items/eXit] <eXit>: **A** Enter
Specify angle between items or [EXpression] <current>: *Enter the angle value*
Select grip to edit array or [ASsociative/Base point/Items/Angle between/Fill angle/ROWs/Levels/ROTate items/eXit] <eXit>: **F** Enter
Specify the angle to fill (+=ccw, -=cw) or EXpression <current>: *Enter the fill angle*
Select grip to edit array or [ASsociative/Base point/Items/Angle between/Fill angle/ROWs/Levels/ROTate items/eXit]<eXit>: **X** Enter

After specifying all the options for the polar array, enter X at the **Select grip to edit array or [ASsociative/Base point/Items/Angle between/Fill angle/ROWs/Levels/ROTate items/eXit]<eXit>:** command prompt to exit the **Polar Array** tool. The **ROWs** option is used to specify the number of items in the radially outward direction, whereas the **Levels** option is used to create a 3D polar array. You can view the 3D polar array in any of the isometric views. Figure 5-67 shows a polar array created by specifying the number or items and the angle between the items. Figure 5-68 shows a polar array created by specifying the number or items and the fill angle.

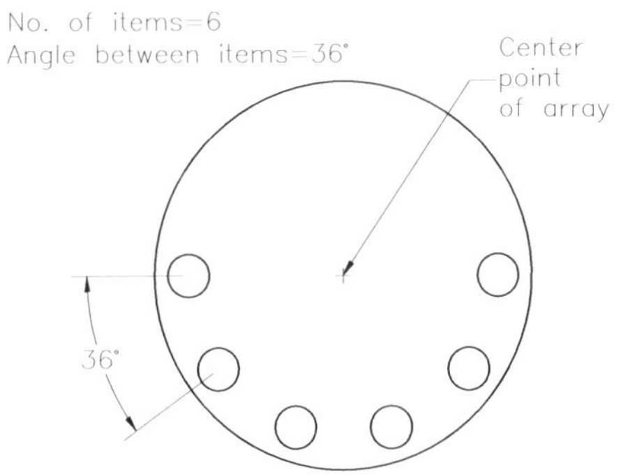

Figure 5-67 *Array created by specifying the number of items and the angle between items*

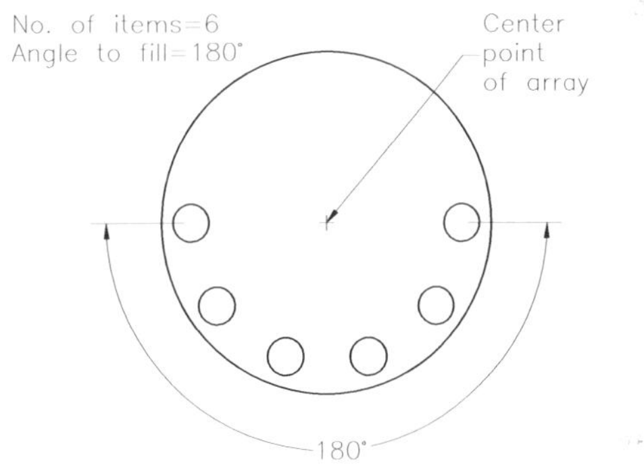

Figure 5-68 *Array created by specifying the number of items and the fill angle*

In an array, you can also make the objects associative. Associativity determines whether the objects of the array will be dependent upon each other or not. To specify the associativity, enter **ASSOCIATIVE** or **AS** at the **Select grip to edit array or [ASsociative/Base point/Items/Angle between/Fill angle/ROWs/Levels/ROtate items/eXit]<eXit>:** command prompt. On doing so, you will be prompted to specify whether the objects of the array created will be associative or non-associative. Enter **Yes** at the Command prompt to make the objects of the array associative. An associative array behaves as a single block. If you enter **No** at the Command prompt, the objects of the array created will be non-associative. If you edit one of the objects in the non-associative array, the other objects in the array will not be affected. After creating the array, press ENTER or X to exit the **Polar Array** tool.

All previously mentioned options for creating the polar array will also be available at the **Dynamic Input**, see Figure 5-69, provided the **Dynamic Input** button is chosen in the Status Bar.

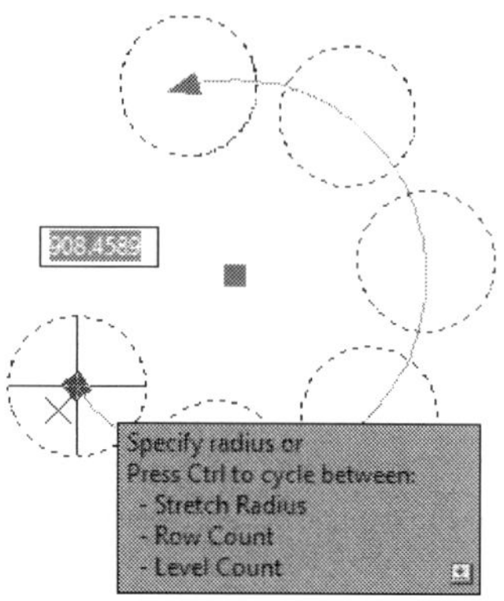

Figure 5-69 Dynamic input options for polar array

Editing the Associative Polar Array with Grips

You can change the number of rows, levels, and the fill angle between the objects in the associative array dynamically. To do so, select an object from the array; the grips will be displayed on the array, as shown in Figure 5-70. If you hover the cursor over the parent grip of a multiple row array, a tooltip with two options, **Stretch Radius** and **Level Count**, will be displayed, as shown in Figure 5-71. Choose the **Stretch Radius** option from the tooltip to change the radius of the array. If you choose **Level Count** from the tooltip, you will be prompted to specify the number of levels. Specify the number of levels at the Command prompt or at the **Dynamic Input**; the 3D array will be created. You can view the 3D array in any of the isometric views. The isometric views can be invoked by using the options in the **Views** panel of the **View** tab in the **Ribbon**.

If you hover the cursor over the second radial grip of the polar array, the angle between the parent item and the second items of the array will be displayed, as shown in Figure 5-72. If you click at this time, an edit box will be displayed and you will be prompted to specify the angle between the items. Enter the desired angle value in this edit box.

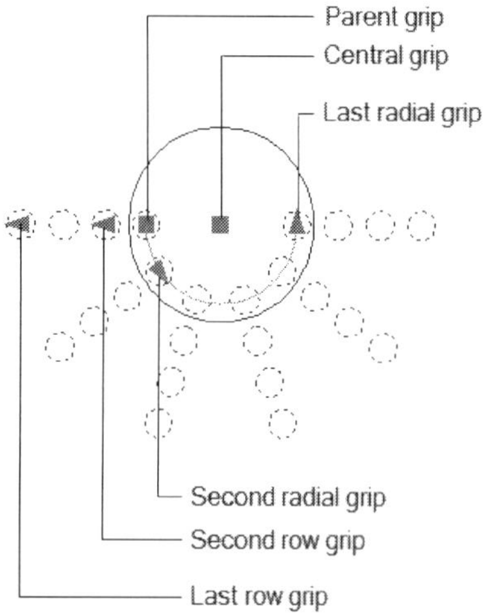

Figure 5-70 Grips of a polar array

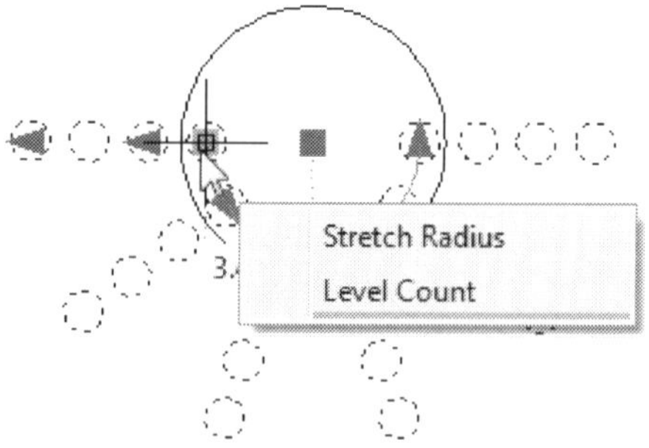

Figure 5-71 The parent grip tooltip

If you hover the cursor over the last grip of the polar array, a tooltip with two options, **Item Count** and **Fill Angle**, will be displayed, as shown in Figure 5-73. If you choose **Item Count** from the tooltip, an edit box will be displayed and you will be prompted to specify the number of items. Enter the number of items in this edit box. If you choose **Fill Angle** from the tooltip, an edit box will be displayed and you will be prompted to specify the fill angle. Enter the fill angle in this edit box.

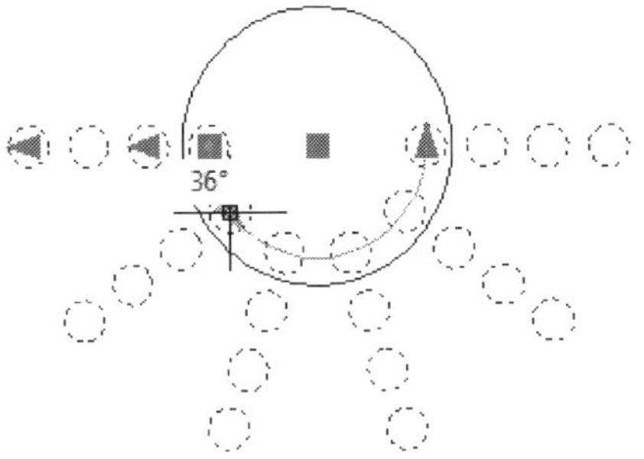

Figure 5-72 *Angle displayed between the parent and second radial grips*

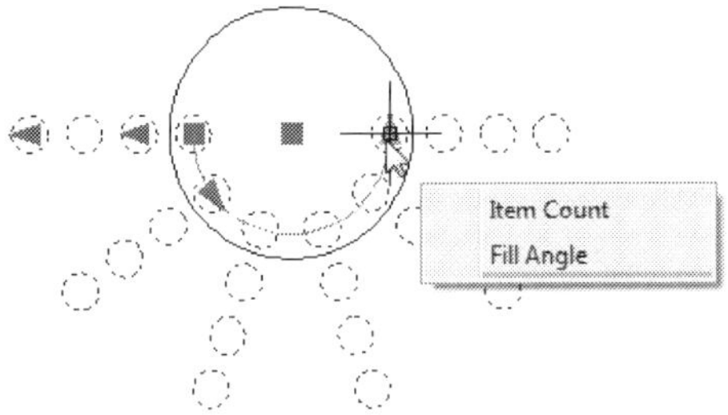

Figure 5-73 *Tooltip displayed on the last radial grip*

If you hover the cursor over the second row grip of the polar array, the current distance between two rows will be displayed, as shown in Figure 5-74. Click on this grip; an edit box will be displayed and you will be prompted to specify the distance between the two rows. Enter the new value in this edit box to specify the distance between the two rows.

If you hover the cursor over the last row grip of the polar array, a tooltip with two options, **Row Count** and **Total Row Spacing**, will be displayed, as shown in Figure 5-75. If you choose **Row Count** from the tooltip, an edit box will be displayed and you will be prompted to specify the number of rows. Specify the number of rows in the edit box to determine the number of rows in the array. If you choose **Total Row Spacing** from the tooltip, an edit box will be displayed and you will be prompted to specify the distance between the first and last row. Enter the desired value in this edit box.

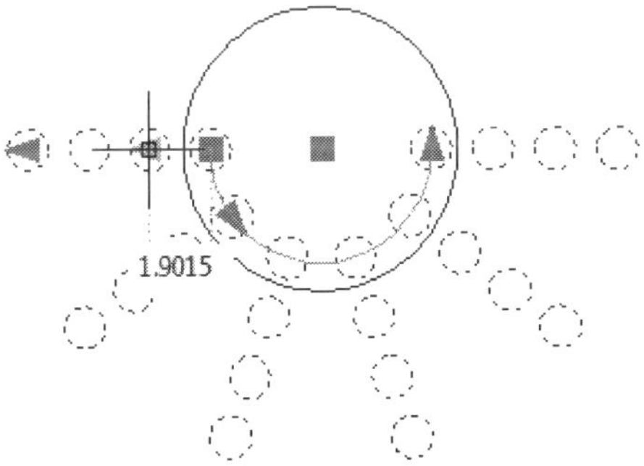

Figure 5-74 *Distance displayed between parent and second row grips*

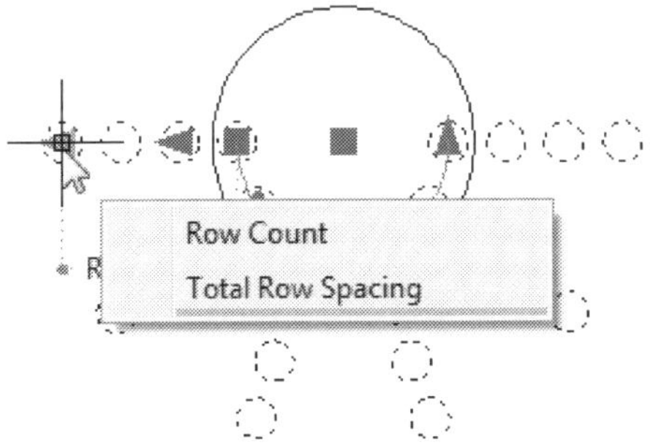

Figure 5-75 *Tooltip displayed on the last row grip*

In case of single row polar array, if you hover the cursor over the parent object, a tooltip with three options, **Stretch Radius, Row Count**, and **Level Count**, will be displayed. You can specify the radius, number of rows, and the number of levels with these options.

Editing the Associative Polar Array Using the Array Contextual Tab

You can also edit the associative polar array by using the **Array** contextual tab that will be displayed when you select the polar array. The **Array** contextual tab is shown in Figure 5-76. Most of the options in the **Array** contextual tab function the same way as those in the rectangular array. The options that are not similar are discussed next.

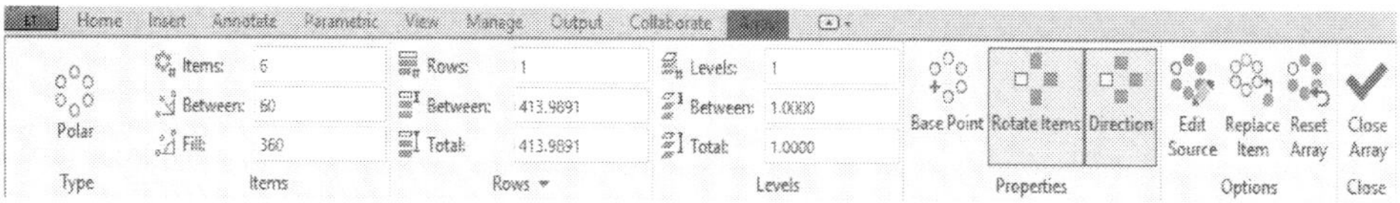

Figure 5-76 *The **Array** (Polar) contextual tab*

Items

This panel displays three options that are used for changing the number of items, angle between two items, and total fill angle between the first and last items. These options are the same as those discussed in the previous topic.

Properties

By default, the **Rotate Items** button is chosen in this panel. As a result, the polar array will be created on rotating the items. Choose the **Base Point** tool if you want to change the base point of the array.

Path Array

Ribbon: Home > Modify > Array drop-down > Path Array
Toolbar: Modify > Array drop-down > Path Array **Command:** ARRAYPATH

In AutoCAD LT, you can create an array of objects along a path called path arrays. The path can be a line, polyline, circle, helix, and so on. To create a path array, choose the **Path Array** tool from the **Modify** panel, see Figure 5-46. On doing so, you will be prompted to select objects. Select the objects to be arrayed and press ENTER; you will be prompted to select the path curve along which the object will be arrayed. Select the path curve; the preview of the path array will be displayed. You will notice that as you move the cursor, the number of items get arranged on the path and you will be prompted to enter the number of items in the array. Enter the desired number at the Command prompt and press ENTER; you will be prompted to specify the distance between the items along the path. You will notice that the spacing between the objects gets adjusted as you move the cursor. Specify the distance at the Command prompt and press ENTER; the array of the selected item will be created along the path and you will be prompted to exit the **Path Array** tool. Press ENTER to accept or X to exit the tool. Figure 5-77 shows the item and the path curve and Figure 5-78 shows the path array created.

The prompt sequence to create the path array of an object after choosing the **Path Array** tool is given next.

Select objects: *Select the object* Enter
Type = Path Associative = Yes
Select path curve: *Select the path*
Select grip to edit array or [ASsociative/Method/Base point/Tangent direction/Items/Rows/Levels/Align items/Z direction/eXit] <eXit>: **I** Enter
Specify the distance between items along path or [Expression] <current>: *Enter the distance value between the items*
Specify number of items or [Fill entire path / Expression] <current>: Enter
Select grip to edit array or [ASsociative/Method/Base point/Tangent direction/Items/Rows/Levels/Align items/Z direction/eXit] <eXit>:X Enter

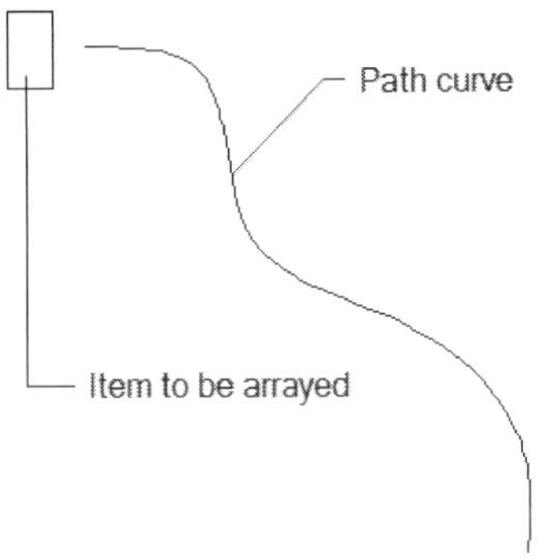

***Figure 5-77** Item and the path curve*

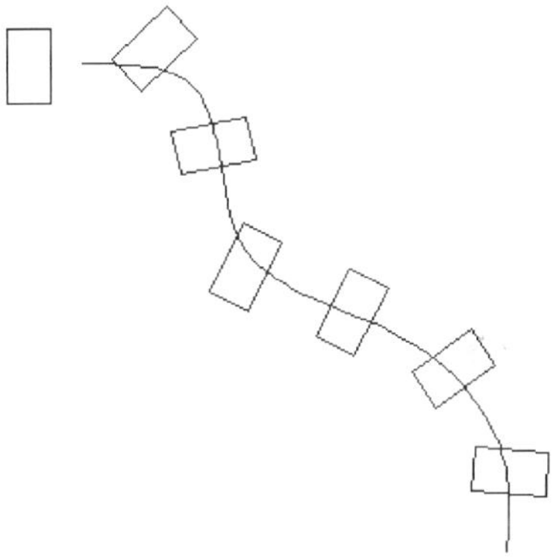

***Figure 5-78** Path array created*

For creating a path array, you need to specify the alignment of the items along the path curve. If you enter **A** at the **Select grip to edit array or [ASsociative/Method/Base point/Tangent direction/Items/Rows/Levels/Align items/Z direction/eXit] <eXit>:** command prompt, you will be prompted to specify whether to align arrayed items to path or not. Enter Y or N; the path array will be created. Figures 5-79 and 5-80 show the path arrays created with the aligned direction and non-aligned orientation of items, respectively.

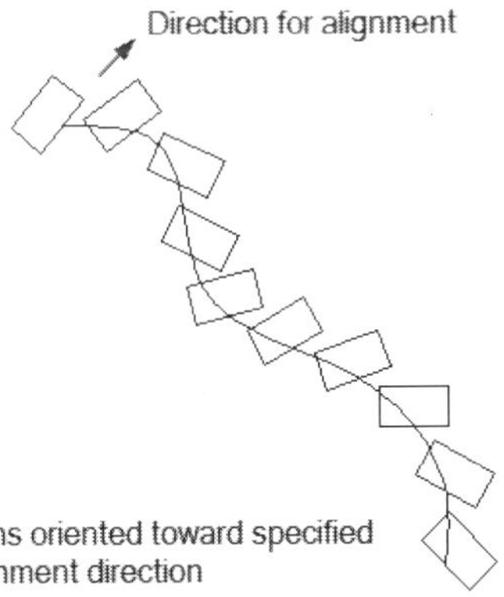

***Figure 5-79** Path array created with aligned direction orientation*

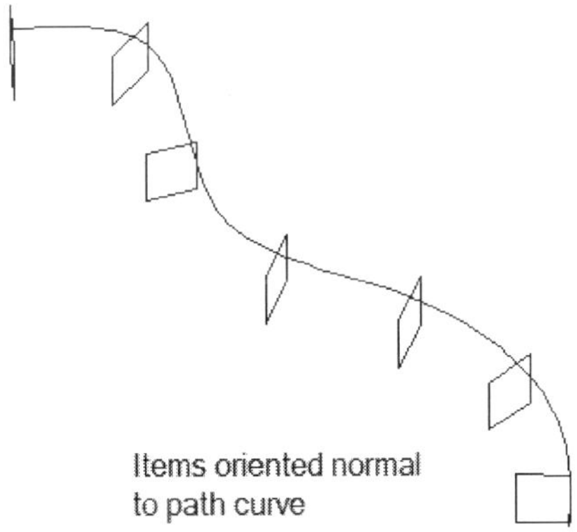

***Figure 5-80** Path array created with non-aligned direction orientation*

After you have specified the number of items to be created, you need to specify the distance between the items. You can specify the number of items in two ways: **Divide** and **Measure**. Select the **Divide** option in the **Measure Method** drop-down of the **Properties** panel and put the values in the edit boxes available in the **Items** panel. Similarly, select the **Measure Method** option of the **Measure** drop-down in the **Properties** panel and put the values in the edit boxes. Figures 5-81 and 5-82 show the path array created by using the **Divide** and **Measure** options, respectively.

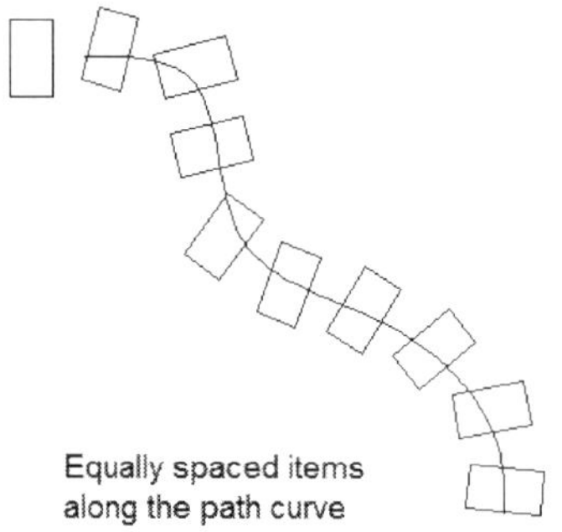

Figure 5-81 Path array created using the ***Divide*** *option*

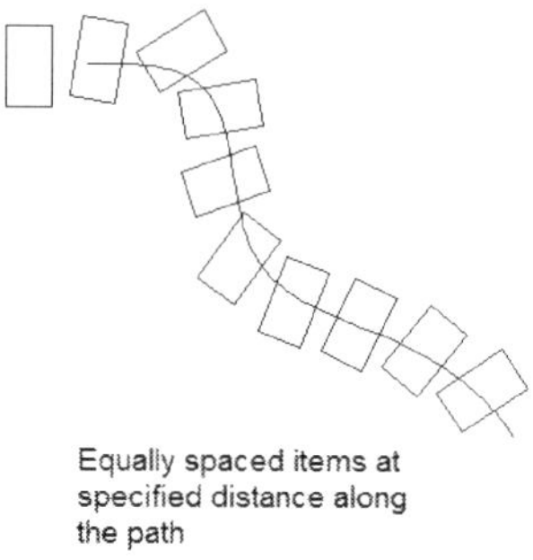

Figure 5-82 Path array created using the ***Measure*** *option*

All the options discussed here for creating the path array are also available at Dynamic Input, see Figure 5-83, which will be available only if the Dynamic Input option is selected from the Status Bar.

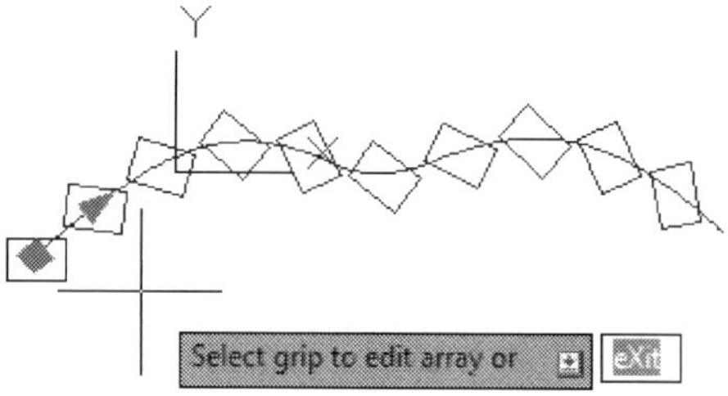

Figure 5-83 Dynamic input options for path array

Editing the Associative Path Array

Like rectangular and polar arrays, you can edit the associative path array by using either the grips or the **Array** contextual tab. The **Array** (Path) contextual tab, as shown in Figure 5-84, will be displayed when you select the path array. Most of the options in the **Array** contextual tab function the same way as those in the rectangular and polar arrays except the options in the **Properties** panel and these options are discussed next.

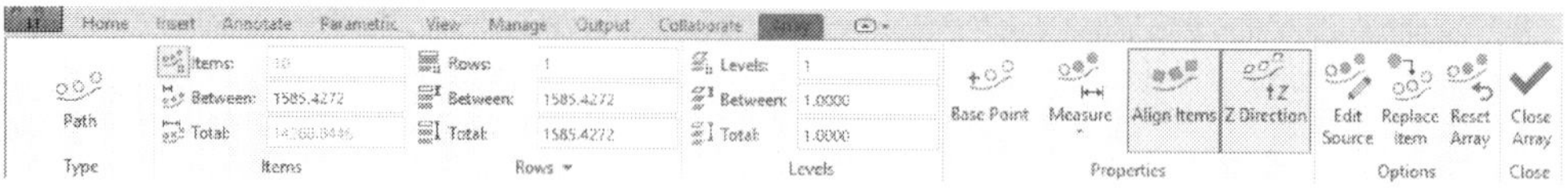

Figure 5-84 The ***Array*** *(Path) contextual tab*

Properties

By default, the **Align Items** and **Z Direction** tools are chosen in this panel. As a result, the path array will be aligned tangent to the path. Also, the original Z direction of the objects will be maintained in case the path is 3-dimensional. You can also use the **Measure** tool to specify the distance between the items of the path array.

MIRRORING THE SKETCHED OBJECTS

Ribbon: Home > Modify > Mirror **Toolbar:** Modify > Mirror
Command: MIRROR/MI

The **Mirror** tool is used to create a mirror copy of the selected objects. The objects can be mirrored at any angle. This tool is helpful in drawing symmetrical figures. On invoking this tool, you will be prompted to select objects. On selecting the objects to be mirrored, you will be prompted to enter the first point of the mirror line and the second point of the mirror line. A mirror line is an imaginary line about which the objects are mirrored. You can specify the endpoints of the mirror line by specifying the points in the drawing area or by entering their coordinates. The mirror line can be specified at any angle. On selecting the first point of the mirror line, a preview of the mirrored objects will be displayed. Next, you need to specify the second endpoint of the mirror line, as shown in Figure 5-85. On selecting the second endpoint, you will be prompted to specify whether you want to delete the source object or not. Enter **Yes** to delete the source object and **No** to retain the source object, see Figure 5-86.

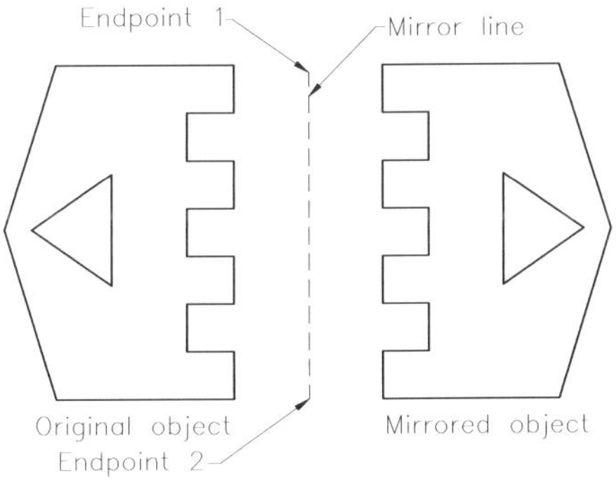

Figure 5-85 *Creating a mirror image of an object by using the **Mirror** tool*

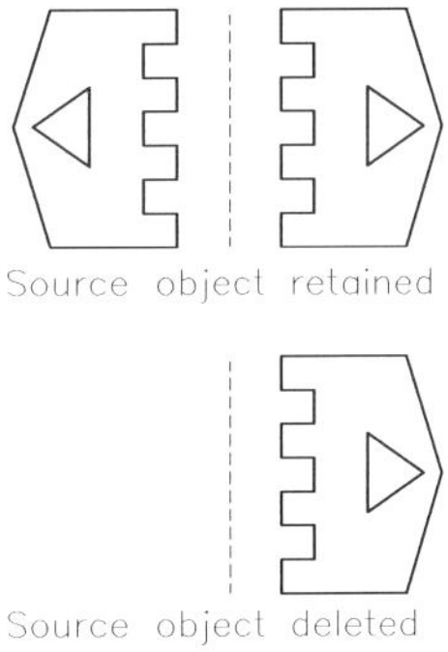

Figure 5-86 *Retaining and deleting old objects after mirroring*

The prompt sequence that will follow when you choose this tool is given next.

Select objects: *Select the objects to be mirrored*
Select objects: Enter
Specify first point of mirror line: *Specify the first endpoint*
Specify second point of mirror line: *Specify the second endpoint*
Erase source objects? [Yes/No] <N>: *Enter **Y** for deletion, **N** for retaining previous objects*

To mirror the objects at some angle, define the mirror line accordingly. For example, to mirror an object such that the mirrored object is placed at an angle of 90 degrees from the original object, define the mirror line at an angle of 45 degrees, see Figure 5-87.

Text Mirroring

By default, the **Mirror** tool reverses all the objects, except the text. But, if you want the text to be mirrored (written backward) then you need to modify the value of the **MIRRTEXT** system variable. This variable has two values that are given next (Figure 5-88).

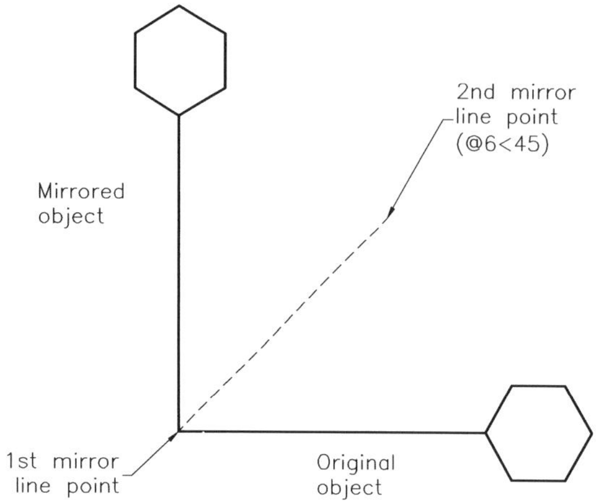

Figure 5-87 Mirroring the object at an angle

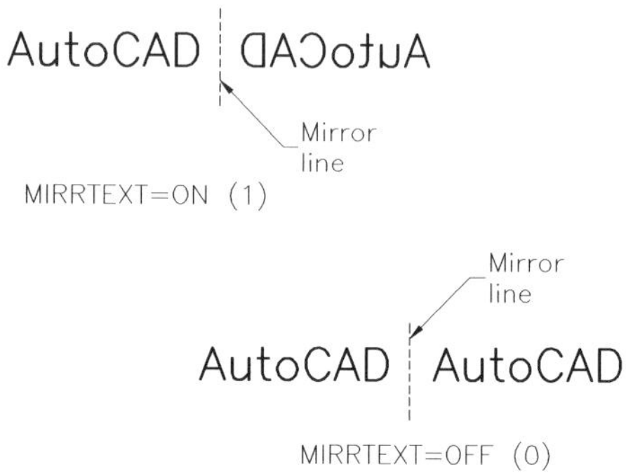

*Figure 5-88 Using the **MIRRTEXT** system variable for mirroring the text*

1 = Text is reversed in relation to the original object.
0 = Restricts the text from being reversed with respect to the original object. This is the default value.

BREAKING THE SKETCHED OBJECTS

Ribbon: Home > Modify > Break at Point, Break **Command:** BREAK/BR
Toolbar: Modify > Break at Point, Break

The **Break** tool breaks an existing object into two parts or erases a portion of an object. This tool can be used to remove a part of the selected objects or to break objects such as lines, arcs, circles, ellipses, xlines, rays, splines, and polylines. You can break the objects using the methods discussed next.

Break at Point

Choose the **Break at Point** tool from the **Modify** panel to break an object into two parts by specifying a breakpoint. On choosing this tool, you will be prompted to select the object to be broken. Once you have selected the object, you will be prompted to specify the first break point. Specify the first break point on the object; the object will be broken.

Break

To break an object by removing a portion of the object between two selected points, choose the **Break** tool from the **Modify** panel; you will be prompted to select the object. Select the object; you will be prompted to select the second break point. Select a point on the object; the portion of the object between the two selected points will be removed. Note that the point at which you select an object becomes the first break point.

The prompt sequence that will follow when you choose this tool is given next.

Select object: *Select the object to be broken*
Specify second break point or [First point]: *Specify the second break point on the object*

The object is broken and the portion in between the broken objects is removed, see Figure 5-89.

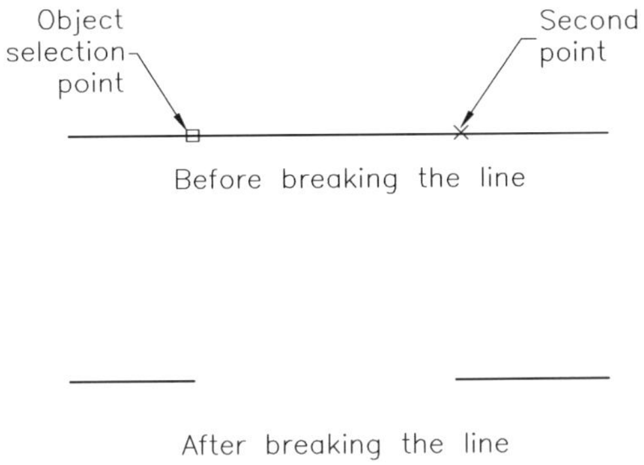

Figure 5-89 *Using the* ***Break*** *option for breaking the line*

You can also specify the first break point after selecting the object. To do so, enter **F** at the **Specify second point or [First point]:** command prompt, refer to Figure 5-90. The prompt sequence that will follow when you choose the **Break** tool is given next.

Select object: *Select the object to be broken*
Specify second break point or [First point]: **F** Enter
Specify first break point: *Specify a new first break point*
Specify second break point: *Specify the second break point on the object*

If you need to work on arcs or circles, make sure that you work in the counterclockwise direction, or you may end up cutting the wrong part. In this case, the second point should be selected in the counterclockwise direction with respect to the first one (Figure 5-91).

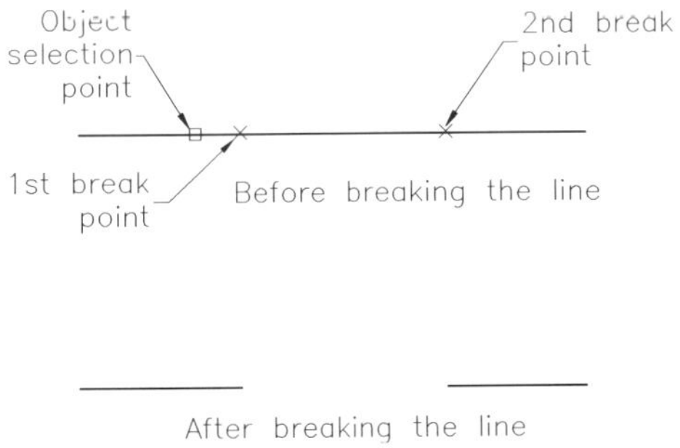

Figure 5-90 *Re-specifying the first break point for breaking the line*

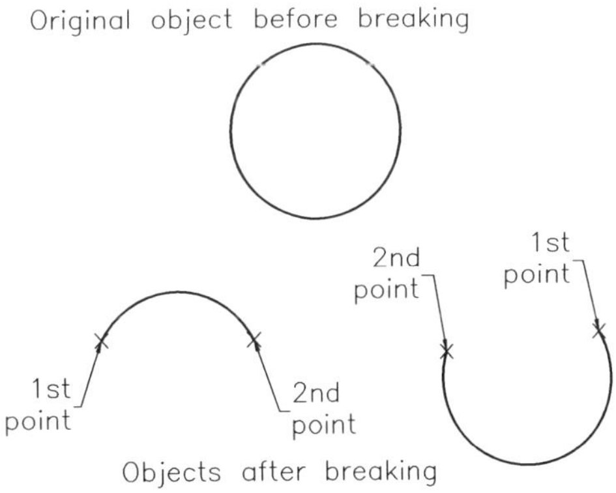

Figure 5-91 *Breaking a circle*

You can use the **Break** tool to break an object into two without removing a portion in between. This can be done by specifying the same point on the object as the first and second break points. If you specify the first break point on a line and the second break point beyond the end of the line, one complete end starting from the first break point will be removed.

Exercise 7 *Break*

Break a line at five different places and then erase the alternate segments. Next, draw a circle and break it into four equal parts.

PLACING POINTS AT SPECIFIED INTERVALS

Ribbon: Home > Draw > Measure **Command:** MEASURE/ME

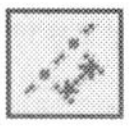

While drawing, you may need to segment an object at fixed distances without actually dividing it. You can use the **Measure** tool to accomplish this task. This tool places points or blocks (nodes) on a given object at a specified distance. The shape of these points is determined by the **PDMODE** system variable and the size is determined by the **PDSIZE** variable. Alternatively, you can also determine the point size and point style by using **Point Style** from the **Utilities** panel of the **Home** tab.

To measure an object, invoke the **Measure** tool from the **Draw** panel and select the object to be measured; you will be prompted to specify the length. Enter the length; the points will be placed at regular intervals of the specified length. Instead of entering a value, you can also select two points that will be taken as distance. The **Measure** tool starts measuring the object from the endpoint that is closest to the object selection point. Note that markers are placed at equal intervals of the specified distance without considering whether the last segment is at the same distance or not.

When a circle is to be measured, an angle from the center is formed that is equal to the Snap rotation angle. This angle becomes the start point of measurement, and markers are placed at equal intervals in the counterclockwise direction.

In Figure 5-92, a line and a circle are measured. The Snap rotation angle is 0 degree. The **PDMODE** variable is set to 3 so that X marks are placed as markers. The prompt sequence that will follow when you invoke this option from the **Draw** menu is given next.

Select object to measure: *Select the object to be measured*
Specify length of segment or [Block]: *Specify the length for measuring the object*

You can also place blocks as markers (Figure 5-93), but the block must already be defined within the drawing. You can align these blocks with the object to be measured. The prompt sequence is given next.

Select object to measure: *Select the object to be measured*
Specify length of segment or [Block]: **B** Enter
Enter name of block to insert: *Enter the name of the block*
Align block with object? [Yes/No] <Y>: *Enter **Y** to align, **N** to not align*
Specify length of segment: *Enter the measuring distance*

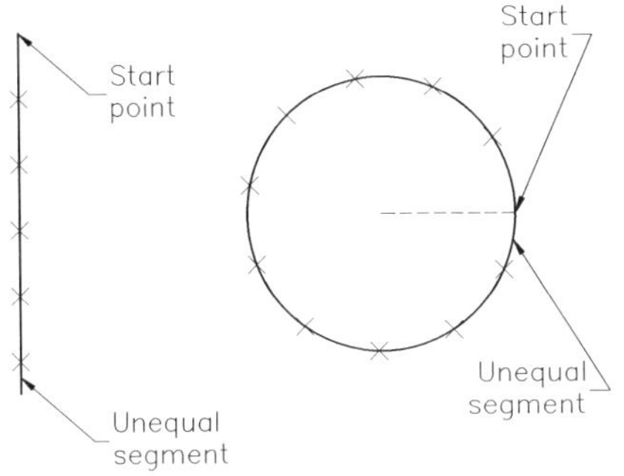

Figure 5-92 Measuring a line and a circle

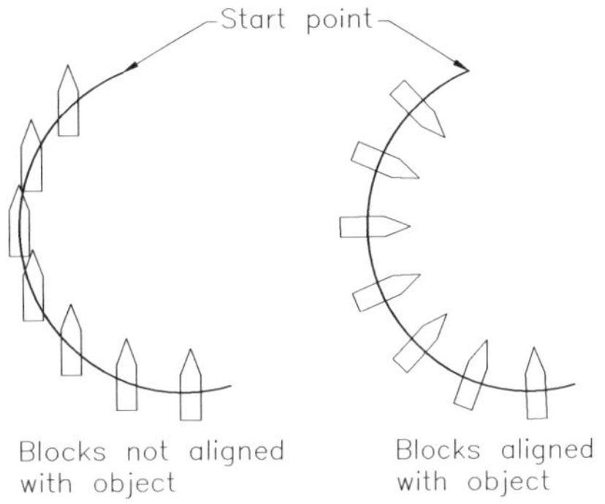

Figure 5-93 Blocks placed as markers

Note
You will learn more about creating and inserting blocks in Chapter 15 (Working with Blocks).

DIVIDING THE SKETCHED OBJECTS

Ribbon: Home > Draw > Divide **Command:** DIVIDE/DIV

The **Divide** tool is used to divide an object into a specified number of equal length segments without actually breaking it. This tool is similar to the **Measure** tool except that here you do not need to specify the distance. The **Divide** tool is used to calculate the total length of an object and place markers at equal intervals. This makes the last interval equal to the rest of the intervals. If you want to divide a line, invoke this tool and select the line, Then, enter the number of divisions or segments. The prompt sequence that will follow when you invoke this tool is given next.

Select object to divide: *Select the object you want to divide*
Enter number of segments or [Block]: *Specify the number of segments*

You can also place blocks as markers, but the blocks must be defined within the drawing. You can then align these blocks with the object to be measured. The prompt sequence to place a block as a marker after choosing the **Divide** tool is given next.

Select object to divide: *Select the object to be measured*
Enter number of segments or [Block]: **B** Enter
Enter name of block to insert: *Enter the name of the block*
Align block with object? [Yes/No] <Y>: *Enter **Y** to align, **N** to not align*
Enter number of segments: *Enter the number of segments*

Figure 5-94 shows a line and a circle divided by using this tool and Figure 5-95 shows the use of blocks for dividing the selected segment.

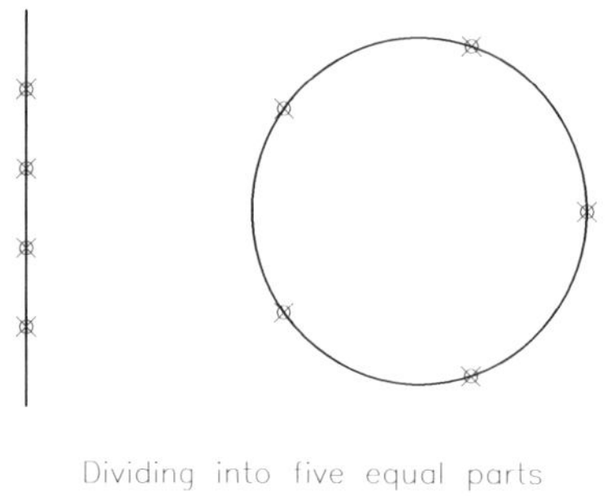

Figure 5-94 Dividing a line and a circle

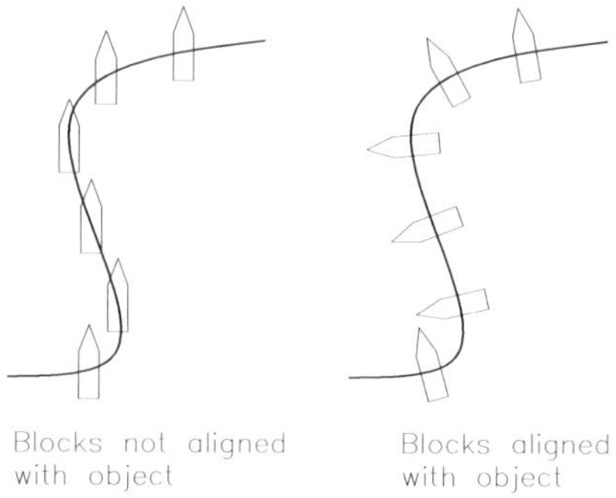

Figure 5-95 Using blocks for dividing the segments

Note

*The size and shape of the points placed by using the **Divide** and **Measure** tools are controlled by the **PDSIZE** and **PDMODE** system variables.*

JOINING THE SKETCHED OBJECTS

Ribbon: Home > Modify > Join **Command:** JOIN/J

The **Join** tool is used to join two or more collinear lines or arcs lying on the same imaginary circle. The lines or arcs can have gap between them. This tool can also be used to join two or more polylines or splines, but they should be on the same plane and should not have any gap between them. Note that this tool can also be used to join the two endpoints of an arc to convert it into a circle. On invoking this tool, you will be prompted to select the source object. The source object is the one with which other objects will be joined. The prompt sequence depends on the type of source object selected. The following prompt sequence is displayed when you invoke this tool:

Select source object or multiple objects to join at once: *Select a sketched entity (line, polyline, arc, elliptical arc, or spline)*
Select object to join: Enter

Joining Collinear Lines

If you have selected a line as the source object, you will be prompted to select lines to join to source. Remember that the lines will be joined only if they are collinear. If there is any gap between the endpoints of lines, the gap will be filled. The prompt sequence for joining two lines with a source line is given next.

Select lines to join to source: *Select the first line to join to the source*
Select lines to join to source: *Select the second line to join to the source*
Select lines to join to source: Enter
2 lines joined to source

Joining Arcs

Disjointed arcs can be joined by using the **Join** tool only if all of them lie on the same imaginary circle. The prompt sequence that follows when you select an arc as the source object is given next.

Select arcs to join to source or [cLose]: *Select the first arc to join to the source*
Select arcs to join to source: *Select the second arc to join to the source or* Enter

After selecting the first arc, enter **L** at the **Select arcs to join to source or [cLose]** prompt to close the arc and convert it into a circle.

Joining Elliptical Arcs

Elliptical arcs can be joined by using the **Join** tool only if they lie on the same imaginary ellipse on which the source elliptical arc lies. The prompt sequence that follows when you select an elliptical arc as the source object is given next.

Select elliptical arcs to join to source or [close]: *Select the first elliptical arc to join to the source*
Select elliptical arcs to join to source: *Select the second elliptical arc to join to the source or* Enter

After selecting an elliptical arc, enter **L** at the **Select arcs to join to source or [cLose]** prompt to close the arc and convert it into an ellipse.

Joining Splines

In this case, you need to select a spline as the source object. On doing so, you will be prompted to select splines to join to the source. The splines will be joined only if they are coplanar and are connected at their ends. The prompt sequence that follows when you select **Spline** as the source object is given next.

Select any open curves to join to source: *Select the first spline to join to the source*
Select any open curves to join to source: *Select the second spline to join to the source or* Enter

Joining Polylines

Only the end-connected polylines can be joined using this tool. The prompt sequence when you select a polyline as the source object is given next.

Select objects to join to source: *Select a polyline/arc/line to join to the source*
Select objects to join to source: *Select a polyline/arc/line to join to the source or* Enter

Example 1 Rectangular and Polar Arrays

In this example, you will create the drawing of an end plate. The dimensions of the end plate are shown in Figure 5-96.

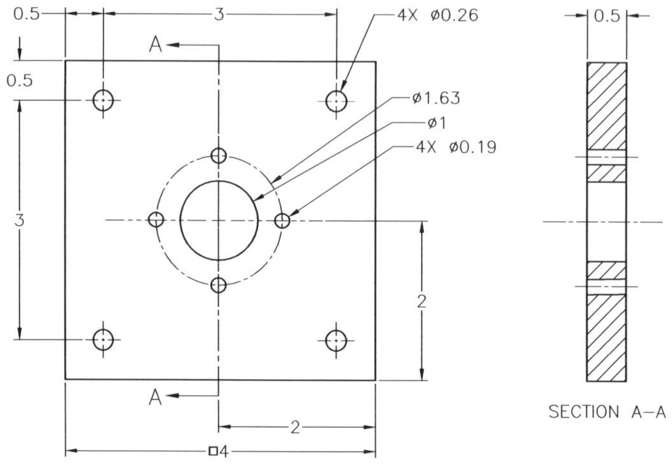

Figure 5-96 *Drawing for Example 1*

First, you need to create a rectangle by using the **Rectangle** tool.

1. Start a new drawing file in the **Drafting & Annotation** workspace.

2. Choose the **Rectangle** tool from **Home > Draw > Rectangle** drop-down and draw a rectangle of **4** units in length and breadth each. The prompt sequence to draw the rectangle is:

   Command: *Choose the **Rectangle** tool from the **Draw** panel*
   Specify first corner point or [Chamfer/Elevation/Fillet/Thickness/Width]: **0,0** Enter
   Specify other corner point or [Area/Dimensions/Rotation]: **@4,4** Enter

After creating the rectangle, you need to create three circles of different radii. These circles can be created by using the **Center, Radius** tool. You need to use the **From** object snap mode to create the third circle.

3. Choose the **Center, Radius** tool from **Home > Draw > Circle** drop-down and draw a circle of diameter **1** unit, as shown in Figure 5-97. The prompt sequence to draw the circle is:

   Command: *Choose the **Center, Radius** tool from the **Draw** panel*
   Specify center point for circle or [3P/2P/Ttr (tan tan radius)]: **2,2** Enter
   Specify radius of circle or [Diameter] <current>: **D** Enter
   Specify diameter of circle <current>: **1** Enter

4. Press ENTER to invoke the **Center, Radius** tool again and draw a circle of diameter **0.26** unit, as shown in Figure 5-98. You can also invoke the **Center, Radius** tool from the **Ribbon**. The prompt sequence to draw the circle is:

   Command: *Choose the **Center, Radius** tool from the **Draw** panel*
   Specify center point for circle or [3P/2P/Ttr (tan tan radius)]: **0.5, 0.5** Enter

Specify radius of circle or [Diameter] <current>: **D** Enter
Specify diameter of circle <current>: **0.26** Enter

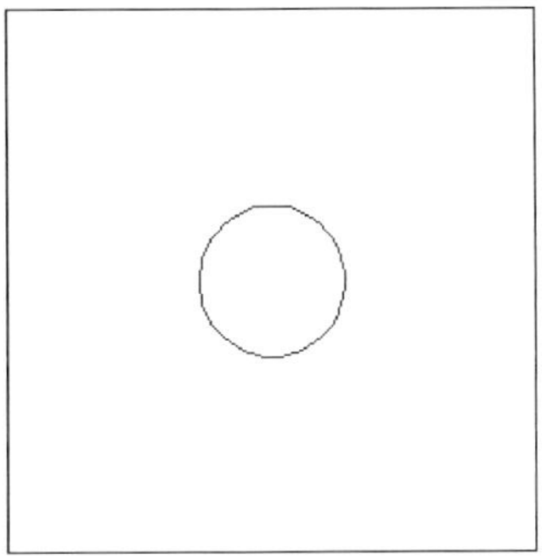

Figure 5-97 *Rectangle and circle created*

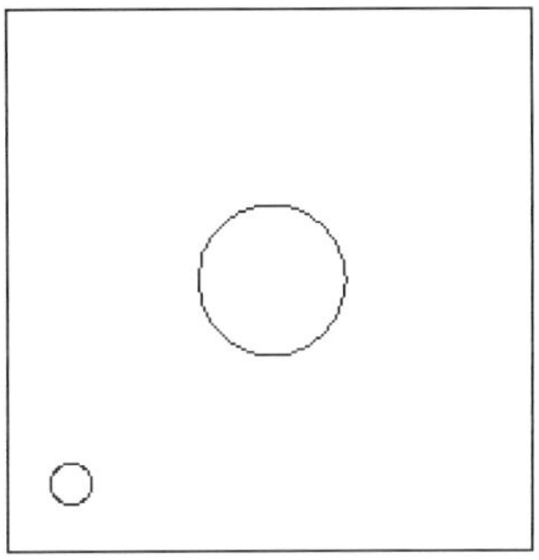

Figure 5-98 *Circle of diameter 0.26 unit created*

5. Again, press ENTER to invoke the **Center, Radius** tool. You can also invoke this tool from the **Draw** panel. Next, press SHIFT and then right-click to invoke a shortcut menu.

6. Choose the **From** option from the shortcut menu and then draw the circle, as shown in Figure 5-99 by following the prompt given next.

*Choose the **Center, Radius** tool from the **Draw** panel*
Specify center point for circle or [3P/2P/Ttr (tan tan radius)]: _from Base point: *Click the center of the circle of diameter 1 unit*
_from Base point: <Offset>: **@-0.8125,0** Enter
Specify radius of circle or [Diameter] <current>: **D**
Specify diameter of circle <0.2600>: **0.19**

After creating all circles, you need to create the pattern of two circles created last. The first array will be a rectangular array and second array will be a polar array. These arrays will be created by using the **Rectangular Array** and **Polar Array** tools.

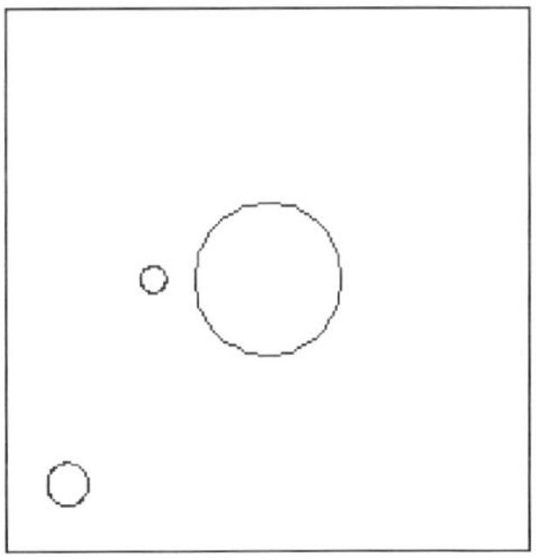

Figure 5-99 *Top view of the model*

7. Choose the **Rectangular Array** tool from **Home > Modify > Array** drop-down and follow the Command prompt given next to create a rectangular array of the circle of diameter **0.26** unit shown in Figure 5-100.

Command: *Choose the **Rectangular Array** tool from the **Modify** panel*
Select objects: *Select the circle of diameter 0.26 unit and press ENTER*
Select objects:
Type = Rectangular Associative = Yes
Select grip to edit array or [ASsociative/Base point/COUnt/Spacing/COLumns/Rows/

Levels/eXit]<eXit>: COU
Enter the number of columns or [Expression] <4>: 2 Enter
Enter the number of rows or [Expression] <3>: 2 Enter
Select grip to edit array or [ASsociative/Base point/COUnt/Spacing/COLumns/Rows/Levels/eXit]<eXit>: S Enter
Specify the distance between columns or [Unit cell]<current>: 3 Enter
Specify the distance between rows <current>: 3 Enter
Select grip to edit array or [ASsociative/Base point/COUnt/Spacing/COLumns/Rows/Levels/eXit]<eXit>: X

8. Next, choose the **Polar Array** tool from **Draw > Modify > Array** drop-down and follow the prompt given next to create a polar array of the circle of diameter **0.19** unit shown in Figure 5-101.

Command: *Choose the **Polar Array** tool from the **Modify** panel*
Select objects: *Select the circle of diameter **0.19** unit and press ENTER*
Select objects:
Type = Polar Associative = Yes
Specify center point of array or [Base point/Axis of rotation]: *Click at the center point of circle of diameter 1 unit*
Select grip to edit array or [ASsociative/Base point/Items/Angle between/Fill angle/ROWs/Levels/ROTate items/eXit]<eXit>: I Enter
Enter number of items or [Expression] <current>: **4** Enter
Select grip to edit array or [ASsociative/Base point/Items/Angle between/Fill angle/ROWs/Levels/ROTate items/eXit]<eXit>: F
Specify the angle to fill (+=ccw, -=cw) or [EXpression] <current>: **360** Enter
Press Enter to accept or [ASsociative/Base point/Items/Angle between/Fill angle/ROWs/Levels/ROTate items/eXit]<eXit>: **X** Enter

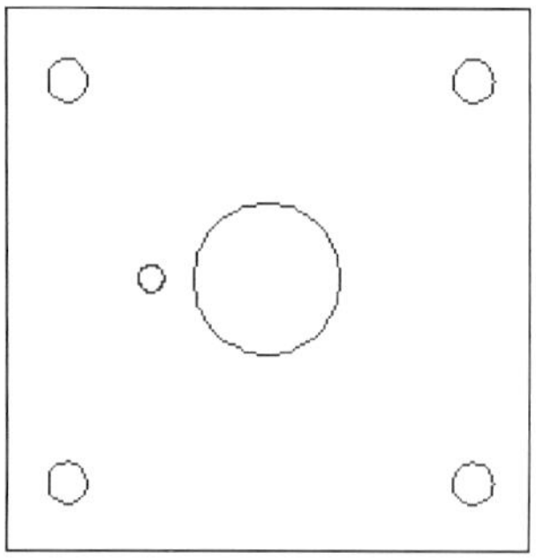

Figure 5-100 *Rectangular array created*

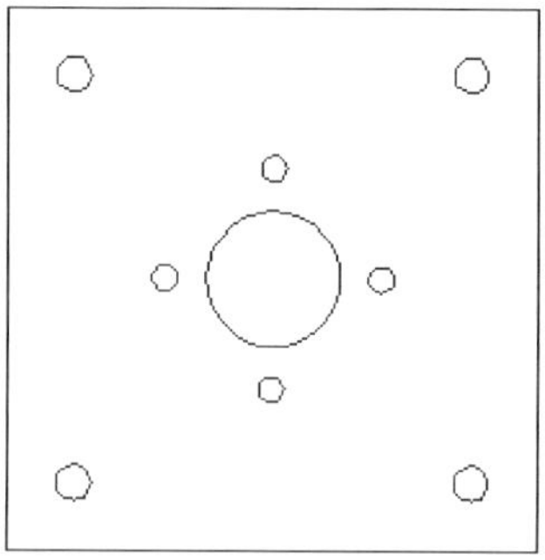

Figure 5-101 *Polar array created*

Self-Evaluation Test

Answer the following questions and then compare them to those given at the end of this chapter:

1. You can create small or large circles, ellipses, and arcs by using the ________ tool, depending on the side to be offset.

2. The ________ tool prunes the objects that extend beyond the required point of intersection.

3. The offset distance is stored in the ________ system variable.

4. Instead of specifying the scale factor, you can use the ________ option to scale an object with reference to another object.

5. If the ________ system variable is set to 1, the mirrored text is not reversed with respect to the original object.

6. There are three types of arrays: ________ , ________ , and ________ .

7. When you shift a group of objects by using the **Move** tool, the size and orientation of those objects change. (T/F)

8. The **Copy** tool is used to make copies of the selected object, leaving the original object intact. (T/F)

9. A fillet cannot be created between two parallel and non-intersecting lines. (T/F)

10. On selecting an object after invoking the **Break** tool, the selection point becomes the first break point. (T/F)

Review Questions

Answer the following questions:

1. Which of the following object selection methods is used to create a polygon that selects all the objects, touching or lying inside it?

   (a) **Last** (b) **WPolygon**
   (c) **CPolygon** (d) **Fence**

2. Which of the following tools is used to enlarge or reduce the size of an object?

   (a) **Trim** (b) **Scaling**
   (c) **Stretch** (d) None of these

3. Which of the following tools is used to change the size of an existing object with respect to an existing entity?

   (a) **Rotate** (b) **Scale**
   (c) **Move** (d) None of these

4. Which of these options of the **Lengthen** tool is used to modify the length of the selected entity such that irrespective of the original length, the entity acquires the specified length?

   (a) **DElta** (b) **DYnamic**
   (c) **Percent** (d) **Total**

5. Which of the following selection options is used to select the most recently drawn entity?

   (a) **Last** (b) **Previous**
   (c) **Add** (d) None of these

6. If a selected object is within a window or crossing specification, the __________ tool works like the **Move** tool.

7. The __________ option of the **Extend** tool is used to extend objects to the implied boundary.

8. If a polyline is not closed then while creating a fillet by using the **Fillet** tool with the **Polyline** option selected, the __________ corner is not filleted.

9. When the chamfer distance is zero, the chamfer created is in the form of a __________.

10. AutoCAD LT saves the previous selection set and allows you select it again by using the __________ selection option.

11. The __________ selection option is used to select objects by creating a section line touching the objects to be selected.

12. In the case of the **Through** option of the **Offset** tool, you do not need to specify a distance; you simply have to specify an offset point. (T/F)

13. Using the **Break** tool, you cannot break an object into two parts without removing a portion in between the two selected points. (T/F)

14. While creating a fillet by using the **Fillet** tool, the extrusion direction of the selected object must be parallel to the Z axis of the UCS. (T/F)

15. In AutoCAD LT, you can rotate a rectangular array. (T/F)

Exercise 8 *Divide*

Create the drawing shown in Figure 5-102. Use the **Divide** tool to divide the circle and use the **NODE** object snap to select the points. Assume the dimensions of the drawing.

Figure 5-102 *Drawing for Exercise 8*

Exercise 9

Create the drawing shown in Figure 5-103 and save it.

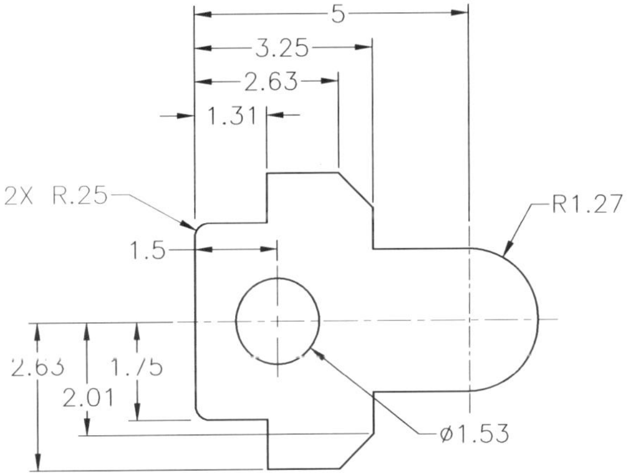

Figure 5-103 *Drawing for Exercise 9*

Exercise 10

Create the drawing shown in Figure 5-104 and save it.

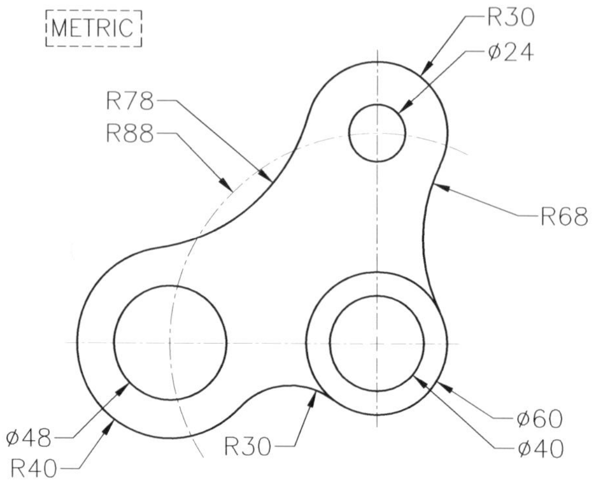

Figure 5-104 Drawing for Exercise 10

Exercise 11

Create the drawing shown in Figure 5-105 and save it.

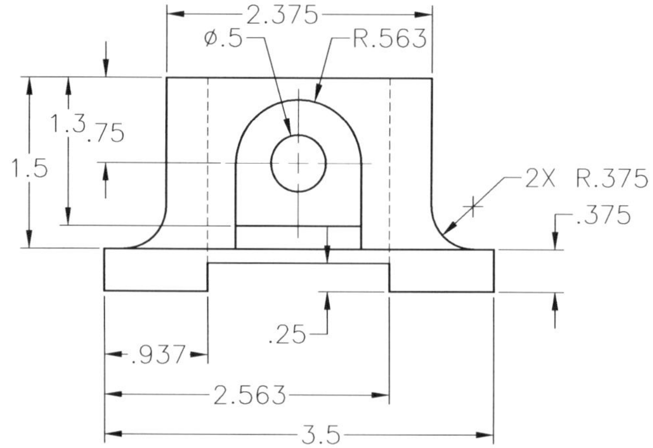

Figure 5-105 Drawing for Exercise 11

Problem-Solving Exercise 1

Create the drawing shown in Figure 5-106 and save it.

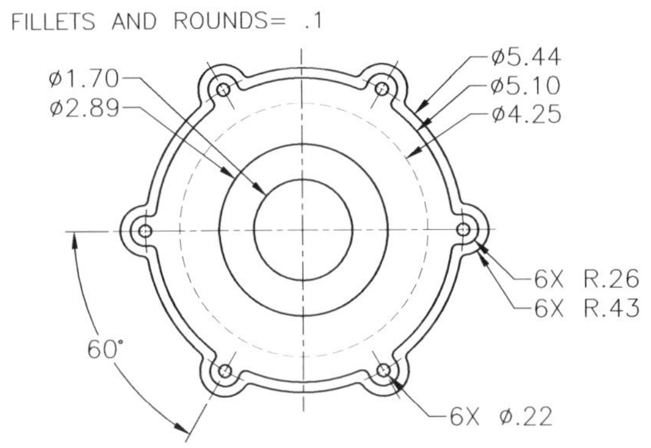

Figure 5-106 *Drawing for Problem-Solving Exercise 1*

Problem-Solving Exercise 2

Create the drawing shown in Figure 5-107 and save it.

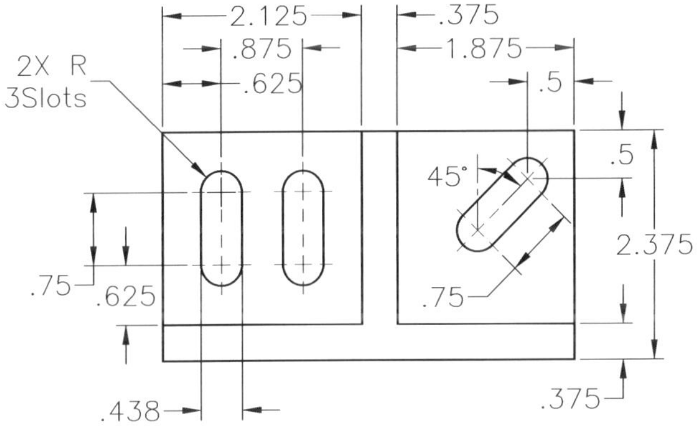

Figure 5-107 *Drawing for Problem-Solving Exercise 2*

Problem-Solving Exercise 3

Draw the dining table with chairs, as shown in Figure 5-108 and save the drawing.

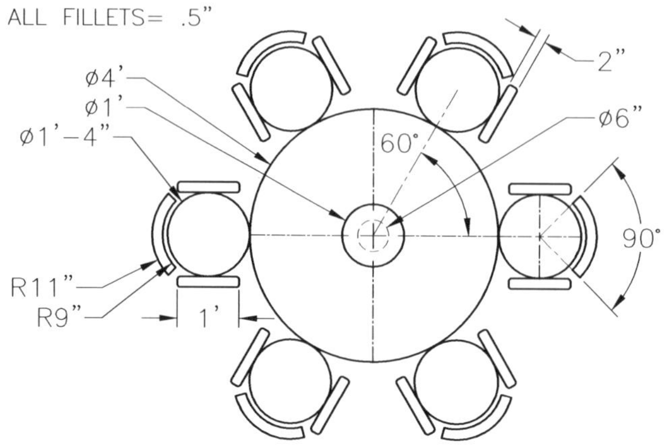

Figure 5-108 *Drawing for Problem-Solving Exercise 3*

Problem-Solving Exercise 4

Draw a reception table with chairs, as shown in Figure 5-109 and save the drawing. The dimensions of the chairs are the same as those used in Problem-Solving Exercise 3.

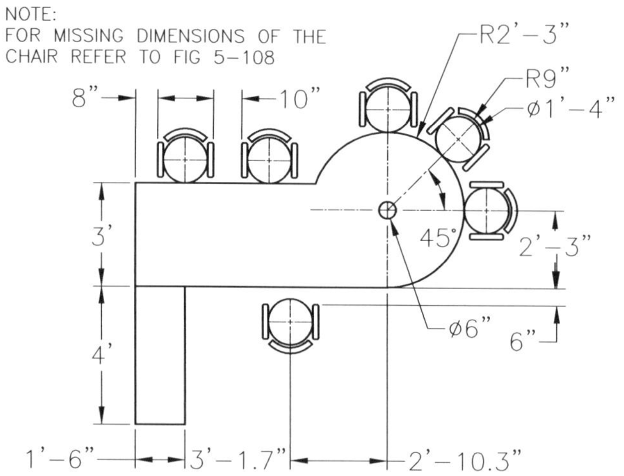

Figure 5-109 *Drawing for Problem-Solving Exercise 4*

Problem-Solving Exercise 5

Draw a center table with chairs, as shown in Figure 5-110, and save the drawing. The dimensions of the chairs are the same as those used in Problem-Solving Exercise 3.

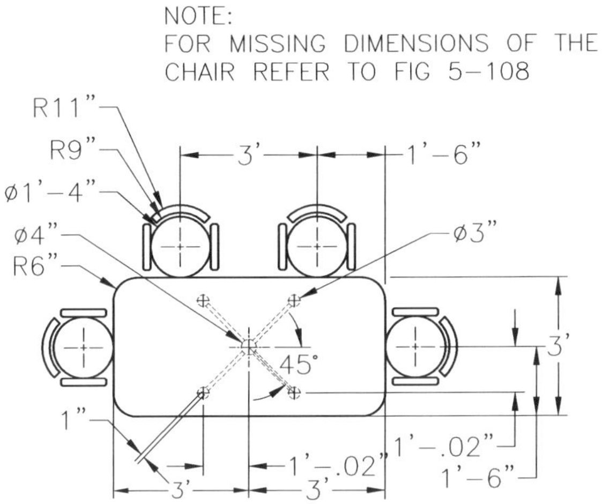

Figure 5-110 Drawing for Problem-Solving Exercise 5

Problem-Solving Exercise 6

Create the drawing shown in Figure 5-111 and save it. Refer to the note given in the drawing to create an arc of radius 30.

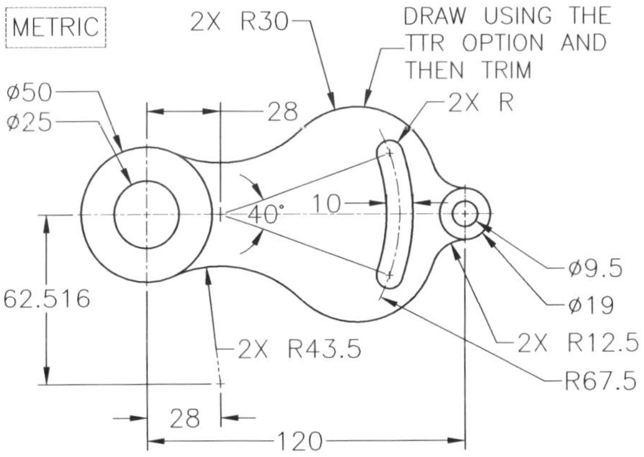

Figure 5-111 Drawing for Problem-Solving Exercise 6

Problem-Solving Exercise 7

Create the drawing shown in Figure 5-112 and save it.

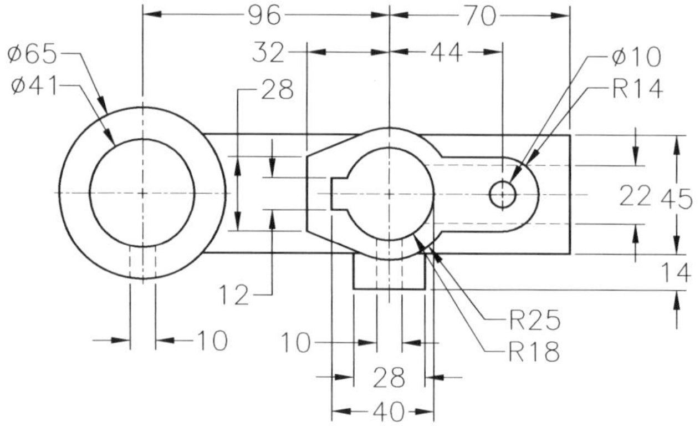

Figure 5-112 Drawing for Problem-Solving Exercise 7

Answers to Self-Evaluation Test

1. OFFSET, **2. TRIM**, **3. OFFSETDIST**, **4. Reference**, **5. MIRRTEXT**, **6. Rectangular**, **Polar**, **Path**, **7.** F, **8.** T, **9.** F, **10.** T

Chapter 6

Editing Sketched Objects-II

Learning Objectives

After completing this chapter, you will be able to:
- *Use grips and adjust their settings*
- *Stretch, move, rotate, scale, and mirror objects with grips*
- *Use the Match Properties tool to match properties of the selected objects*
- *Use the Quick Select tool to select objects*
- *Manage contents using the DesignCenter*
- *Use the Inquiry tools*
- *Use the REDRAW and REGEN commands*
- *Use the Zoom tools and its options*
- *Use the PAN and VIEW commands*
- *Use SHEET SET MANAGER*

Key Terms

- *Grips*
- *Properties Panel*
- *Quick Select*
- *DesignCenter*
- *Area*
- *Distance*
- *Locate Point*
- *List*
- *Time*
- *Status*
- *Regen*
- *Redraw*
- *Zoom*
- *Sheet Set Manager*

INTRODUCTION TO GRIPS

Grips provide a convenient and quick means of editing objects. Grips are small squares that are displayed on the key points of an object on selecting the object, as shown in Figure 6-1. If the grips are not displayed on selecting an object, invoke the **Options** dialog box, choose the **Selection** tab, and select the **Show grips** check box. Using grips you can stretch, move, rotate, scale, and mirror objects, change properties, and load the Web browser. The number of grips depends on the selected object. For example, a line has three grip points and an arc has four grips. Similarly, a circle has five grip points and a dimension (vertical, horizontal, or inclined) has five grips.

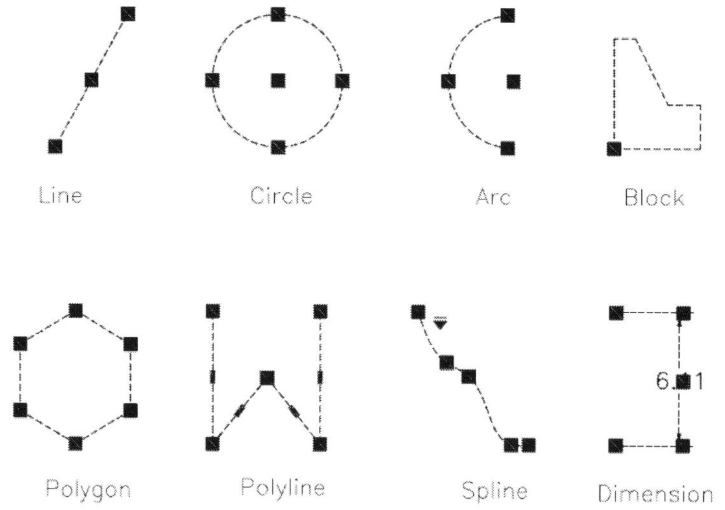

***Figure 6-1** Grips displayed on various objects*

Note

*If grips are not displayed after selecting the objects, refer to Figure 6-1, select the **Show grip tips**, **Show single grip on groups**, and **Show bounding box on groups** check boxes available in the **Grips** area of the **Selection** tab in the **Options** dialog box.*

TYPES OF GRIPS

Grips are classified into three types: unselected grips, hover grips, and selected grips. The selected grips are also called hot grips. When you select an object, the grips are displayed at the definition points of the object and the object is displayed as Neon blue line. These grips are called unselected grips and are displayed in blue. When the cursor is moved over an unselected grip, and paused for a second, the grip will be displayed in orange. These grips are called hover grips. Dimensions corresponding to a hover grip are displayed when you place the cursor on the grip, as shown in Figure 6-2.

If you select a grip, it is displayed in red color and is called as hot grip. Once the grip is hot, the object can be edited. To cancel the grip, press ESC twice. If you press ESC once, the hot grip is converted into an unselected grip.

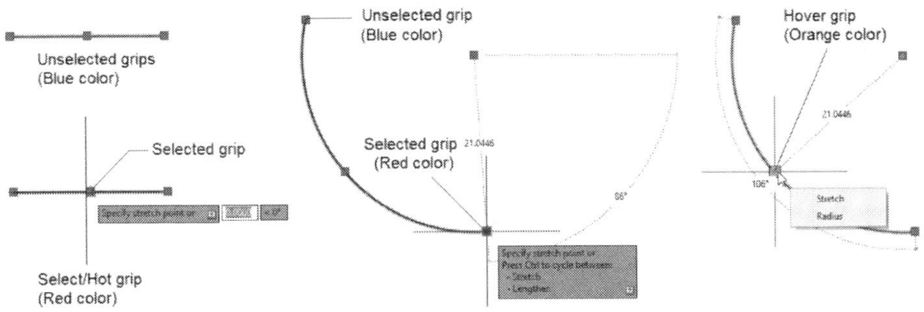

Figure 6-2 *Hover grip type of dimension*

ADJUSTING GRIP SETTINGS

Application Menu: Tools > Options **Command:** OP/OPTIONS

The grip settings can be adjusted by using the options in the **Selection** tab of the **Options** dialog box. This dialog box can also be invoked by choosing **Options** from the shortcut menu displayed upon right-clicking in the drawing area or by choosing the **Options** button from the **Application Menu**.

The options in the **Selection** tab of the **Options** dialog box (Figure 6-3) are discussed next.

Grip size Area

The **Grip size** area of the **Selection** tab of the **Options** dialog box consists of a slider bar and a rectangular box that displays the size of the grip. To adjust the size, move the slider box left or right. The size can also be adjusted by using the **GRIPSIZE** system variable. The **GRIPSIZE** variable is defined in pixels, and its value can range from 1 to 255 pixels.

Grips Area

To assign the color to the unselected grip, selected grip, hover grip, and grip contour, choose the **Grip Colors** button; the **Grip Colors** dialog box will be displayed. Specify the colors in this dialog box. Grip contour is the color applied on the outline of the grip outline. You can also set the grip colors by using the following system variables:

Unselected grip color: GRIPCOLOR
Selected grip color: GRIPHOT
Hover grip color: GRIPHOVER
Grip contour color: GRIPCONTOUR

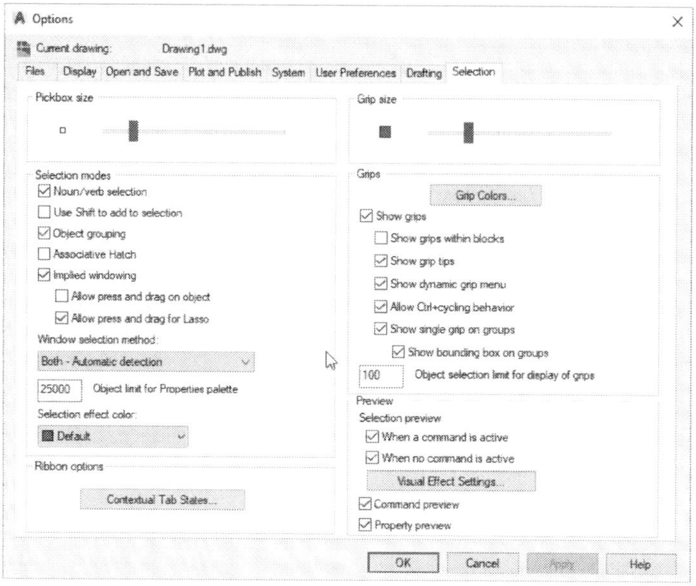

***Figure 6-3** The **Selection** tab of the **Options** dialog box*

The **Grips** area has various check boxes such as **Show grips**, **Show grips within blocks**, and **Show grip tips**, etc. Grips are displayed on selecting an object only if the **Show Grips** check box is selected. They can also be enabled by setting the **GRIPS** system variable to 1. On selecting the **Show grips within blocks** check box, all the grips in the blocks are displayed. You can also enable the grips within a block by setting the value of the **GRIPBLOCK** system variable to 1 (On). If you clear the **Show grips within blocks** check box, only one grip will be displayed at the insertion point of the block. Alternatively, set the **GRIPBLOCK** system variable to 0 (Off), see Figure 6-4. To display the grip tips when the cursor moves over the custom object that supports grip tips, select the **Show grip tips** check box. If you disable this check box, the grip tips are not displayed when the cursor moves over the custom object. You can also enable the grip tips by setting the value of the **GRIPTIPS** system variable to 0 (Off). If **GRIPTIPS** is set to 1 (On), the grip tips for the custom object will be displayed.

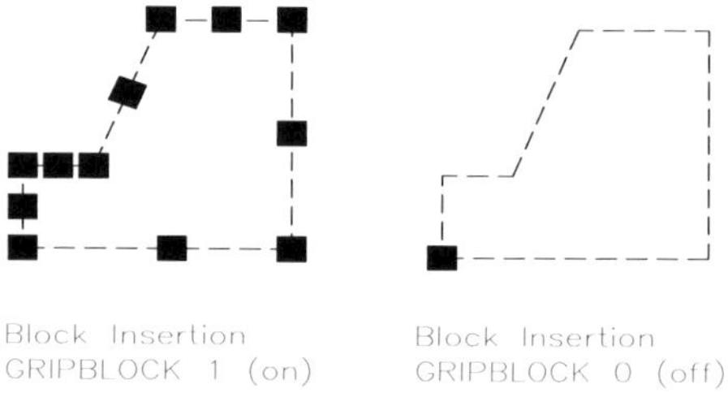

***Figure 6-4** Block insertion with **GRIPBLOCK** set to 1 and 0*

Note

*If a block has a large number of objects, and if **GRIPBLOCK** is set to 1 (On), AutoCAD LT will display grips for every object in the block. Therefore, it is recommended that you set the system variable **GRIPBLOCK** to 0 or clear the **Show grips within blocks** check box in the **Selection** tab of the **Options** dialog box.*

Object selection limit for display of grips

This text box is used to specify the maximum number of objects that can be selected in a single attempt for the display of grips. If using a single selection method you select objects more than the specified limit in the text box, the grips will not be displayed. Note that this limit is set only for those objects that are selected at a single attempt using any of the **Crossing**, **Window**, **Fence**, **All, or Multiple objects selection** options.

EDITING OBJECTS BY USING GRIPS

As mentioned earlier, you can perform different kinds of editing operations using the selected grip. The editing operations are discussed next.

Stretching the Objects by Using Grips (Stretch Mode)

If you select an object, the unselected grips are displayed at the definition points of the object. If you select a grip for editing, you are automatically in the **Stretch** mode. The **Stretch** mode has a function similar to that of the **Stretch** tool. When you select a grip, it acts as a base point and is called a base grip. To select several grips, press and hold the SHIFT key and then select the grips. Now, release the SHIFT key and select one of the hot grips and stretch it; all selected grips will be stretched. The geometry between the selected base grips will not be altered. You can also make copies of the selected objects or define a new base point. When selecting grips on text objects, blocks, midpoints of lines, centers of circles and ellipses, and point objects in the stretch mode, the selected objects are moved to a new location. The following example illustrates the use of the **Stretch** mode and other associated options.

1. Use the **Polyline** tool to draw a W-shaped figure and select the object; grips will be displayed at the endpoints and midpoints of each line, as shown in Figure 6-5(a).

2. Hold the SHIFT key and select the grips on the lower endpoints of the two vertical lines, refer to Figure 6-5(b). The selected grips will become hot grips and their color will change from blue to red.

3. Select one of the selected grips, and drag downwards; the profile will be stretched, refer to Figure 6-5(c). When you select a grip, the following prompt is displayed in the Command prompt area.

   STRETCH
   Specify stretch point or [Base point/Copy/Undo/eXit]:

Note
To select multiple grips, you need to press and hold the SHIFT key before selecting the first grip.

Tip
To stretch a line to some desired length, enter a numerical value in the dimensional input box that will be displayed on selecting a grip of the line.

The Stretch mode has several options: **Base point**, **Copy**, **Undo**, and **eXit**. The **Base point** and **Copy** options can also be invoked from the shortcut menu, as shown in Figure 6-6. The **Base point** option is used to move an object with respect to a base point and the **Copy** option is used to make copies.

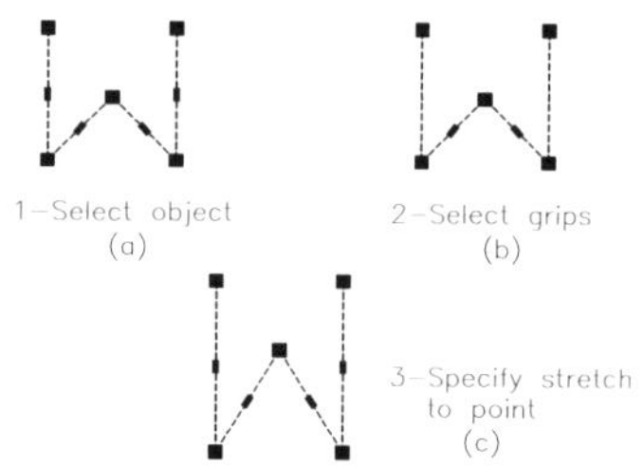

*Figure 6-5 Using the **Stretch** mode to stretch the lines*

4. Select the grip where the two inclined lines intersect, as shown in Figure 6-7(a), and right-click to display a shortcut menu. Choose the **Copy** option and specify a point; the two inclined lines will be copied, as shown in Figure 6-7(b). You can also select a grip, press the CTRL key and specify the point to make multiple copies of the selected object.

5. To move a grip with respect to a base point, select the grip, refer to Figure 6-7(c). Next, choose the **Base Point** option from the shortcut menu and select the base point and then specify the displacement point, as shown in Figure 6-7(d).

6. To terminate the grip editing mode, right-click when the grip is hot to display the shortcut menu and then choose **Exit**. You can also enter **X** at the Command prompt or press ESC to exit.

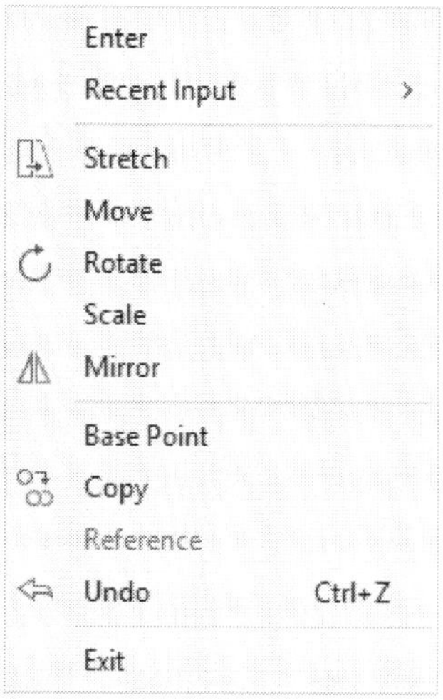

Figure 6-6 Partial view of shortcut menu with editing options

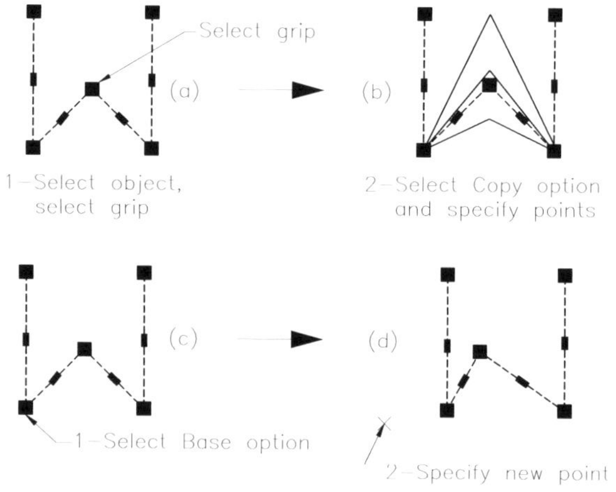

*Figure 6-7 Using the **Copy** and **Base point** options of the **Stretch** mode*

Note

*You can choose an option (**Copy** or **Base Point**) from the shortcut menu that can be invoked by right-clicking your pointing device after selecting a grip. The different modes can also be selected from the shortcut menu. You can also cycle through all the different modes by selecting a grip and pressing the ENTER key or the SPACEBAR.*

Moving the Objects by Using Grips (Move Mode)

The **Move** mode allows you move the selected objects to a new location. When you move objects, their size and angles do not change. You can also use this mode to make the copies of the selected objects or to redefine the base point. The following example illustrates the use of the **Move** mode:

1. Invoke the **Line** tool and draw the shape, as shown in Figure 6-8(a). When you select the objects, grips will be displayed at the definition points and the objects will be highlighted.

2. Select the grip located at the lower left corner, as shown in Figure 6-8(b) and then choose **Move** from the shortcut menu. You can also select a grip and give a null response by pressing the SPACEBAR or ENTER key to invoke the **Move** mode; the following prompt will be displayed at the Command prompt:

   MOVE
   Specify move point or [Base point/Copy/Undo/eXit]:

3. Specify the displacement point. You can also enter coordinates to specify the displacement. If you hold down the CTRL key and then specify the displacement point, the objects will be copied. Also, the distance between the first and the second object defines the snap offset for subsequent copies, refer Figure 6-8(c).

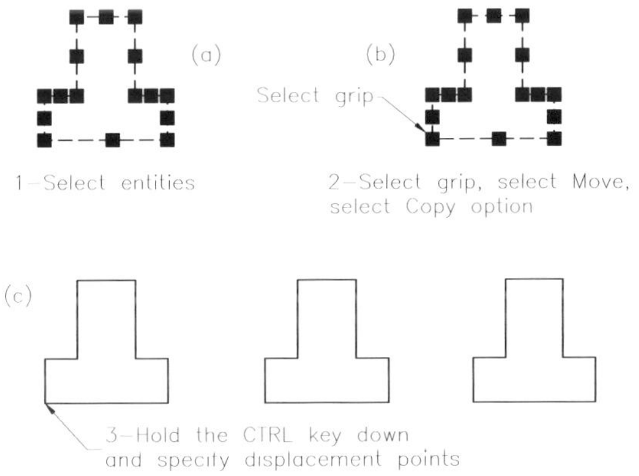

*Figure 6-8 Using the **Move** mode to move and make copies of the selected objects*

Rotating the Objects by Using Grips (Rotate Mode)

The **Rotate** mode allows you to rotate objects around the base point without changing their size. The options of the **Rotate** mode can be used to redefine the base point, specify a reference angle, or make multiple copies that are rotated about the specified base point. You can access the **Rotate** mode by selecting the grip and then choosing **Rotate** from the shortcut menu, or by giving a null response twice by pressing the SPACEBAR or the ENTER key. The following example illustrates the use of the **Rotate** mode:

1. Use the **Line** tool to draw the shape, as shown in Figure 6-9(a). When you select the objects, grips will be displayed at the definition points and the shape will be highlighted.

2. Select the grip located at the lower left corner and then invoke the **Rotate** mode. AutoCAD LT will display the following prompt.

   ROTATE
   Specify a rotation angle or [Base point/Copy/Undo/Reference/eXit]:

3. At this prompt, enter the rotation angle. By default, the rotation angle will be entered through the dimensional input below the cursor in the drawing area. AutoCAD LT will rotate the selected objects by the specified angle [Figure 6-9(b)].

4. To make a copy of the original drawing, as shown in Figure 6-9(c), select the objects, and then select the grip located at its lower left corner. Invoke the **Rotate** mode and then choose the **Copy** option from the shortcut menu or enter **C** (Copy) at the Command prompt or the **Copy** option from the dynamic preview. Enter the rotation angle. AutoCAD LT will rotate the copy of the object through the specified angle [Figure 6-9(d)].

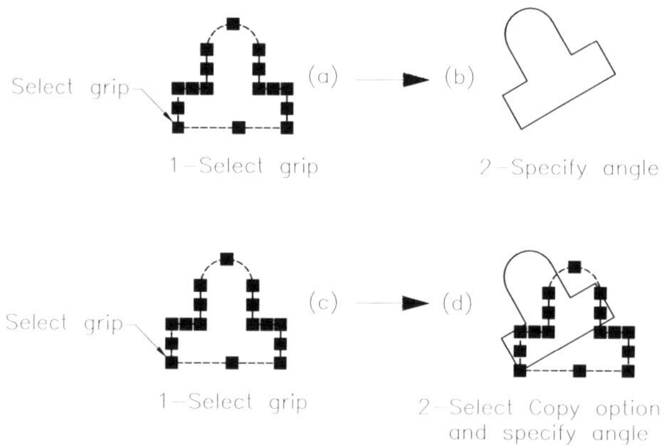

***Figure 6-9** Using the **Rotate** mode to rotate and make the copies of the selected objects*

5. To make another copy of the object, as shown in Figure 6-10(a), select it, and then select the grip at point (P0). Access the **Rotate** mode and the copy option as described earlier. Choose the **Reference** option from the shortcut menu, enter **R** at the prompt sequence, or select the **Reference** option from the dynamic preview, as shown in Figure 6-10(b). The prompt sequence is given next.

   **ROTATE (multiple) **
   Specify Base point: **R**
   Specify reference angle <0>: *Select the grip at (P1).*
   Specify second point: *Select the grip at (P2).*
   Specify new angle or [Base point/Copy/Undo/Reference/eXit]: **45**

In response to the **Specify reference angle <0>:** prompt, select the grips at points (P1) and (P2) to define the reference angle. When you enter a new angle, AutoCAD LT will rotate and insert a copy at the specified angle [Figure 6-10(c)]. For example, if the new angle is 45 degree, the selected objects will be rotated about the base point (P0) so that the line P1P2 makes a 45 degree angle with respect to the positive *X* axis.

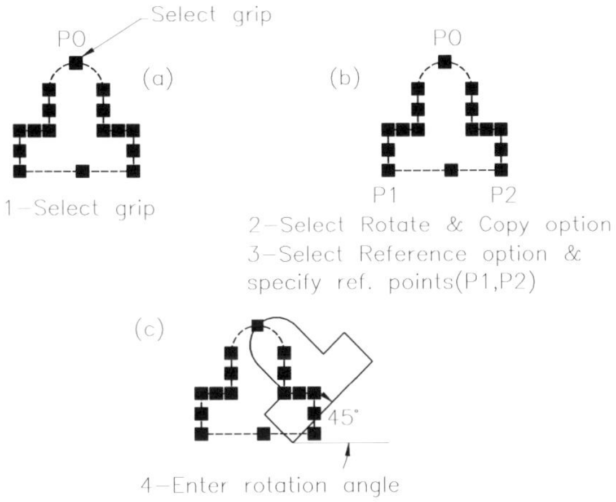

***Figure 6-10** Using the **Rotate** mode to rotate the selected objects by giving a reference angle*

Scaling the Objects by Using Grips (Scale Mode)

The **Scale** mode allows you to scale objects with respect to the base point without changing their orientation. The options of **Scale** mode can be used to redefine the base point, specify a reference length, or make multiple copies that are scaled with respect to the specified base point. You can access the **Scale** mode by selecting the grip and then choosing **Scale** from the shortcut menu, or giving a null response three times by pressing the SPACEBAR or the ENTER key. The following example illustrates the use of the **Scale** mode:

1. Use the **Polyline** tool to draw the shape shown in Figure 6-11(a). Then, select the objects; the grips will be displayed at the definition points.

2. Select the grip located at the lower left corner as the base grip, and then invoke the **Scale** mode. AutoCAD LT will display the following prompt in the Command prompt area.

   SCALE
   Specify scale factor or [Base point/Copy/Undo/Reference/eXit]:

3. At this prompt, enter the scale factor or move the cursor and select a point to specify a new size. AutoCAD LT will scale the selected objects by the specified scale factor [Figure 6-11(b)]. If the scale factor is less than 1 (<1), the objects will be scaled down by the specified factor. If the scale factor is greater than 1 (>1), the objects will be scaled up.

4. To make a copy of the original drawing, as shown in Figure 6-11(c), select the objects, and then select the grip located at their lower left corner. Invoke the **Scale** mode. At the following prompt, enter **C** (Copy), and then enter **B** for the base point.

   **SCALE (multiple) **
   Specify scale factor or [Base point/Copy/Undo/Reference/eXit]: **B**

5. At the **Specify base point** prompt, select the point (P0) as the new base point, and then enter **R** at the following prompt:

   **SCALE (multiple) **
   Specify scale factor or [Base point/Copy/Undo/Reference/eXit]: **R**
   Specify reference length <1.000>: *Select grips at (P1) and (P2).*

After specifying the reference length at the **Specify new length or [Base point/Copy/Undo/Reference/eXit]** prompt, enter the actual length of the line. AutoCAD LT will scale the objects so that the length of the bottom edge is equal to the specified value [Figure 6-11(c)].

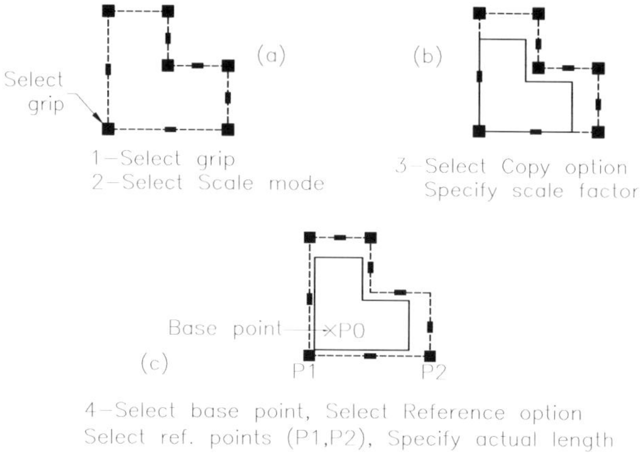

***Figure 6-11** Using the **Scale** mode to scale and make the copies of the selected objects*

Mirroring the Objects by Using Grips (Mirror Mode)

The **Mirror** mode allows you to mirror the objects across the mirror axis without changing their size. The mirror axis is defined by specifying two points. The first point is the base point, and the second point is the point that you select when AutoCAD LT prompts for the second point. The options of the **Mirror** mode can be used to redefine the base point and make a mirror copy of the objects. You can access the **Mirror** mode by selecting a grip and then choosing **Mirror** from the shortcut menu, or giving a null response four times by pressing the SPACEBAR or the ENTER key. The following is the example for the **Mirror** mode.

1. Use the **Polyline** tool to draw the shape shown in Figure 6-12(a). Select the objects; grips will be displayed at the definition points.

2. Select the grip located at the lower right corner (P1), and then invoke the **Mirror** mode. The following prompt will be displayed:

   MIRROR
   Specify second point or [Base point/Copy/Undo/eXit]:

3. At this prompt, specify the second point (P2); the selected objects will be mirrored, with line P1P2 as the mirror axis, as shown in Figure 6-12(b).

4. To make a copy of the original figure, as shown in Figure 6-12(c), select the object, and then select the grip located at its lower right corner (P1). Invoke the **Mirror** mode and then choose the **Copy** option to make a mirror image while retaining the original object. Alternatively, you can also hold down the SHIFT key and make several mirror copies by specifying the second point.

5. Select point (P2) in response to the prompt **Specify second point or [Base point/Copy/Undo/eXit]**. AutoCAD LT will create a mirror image, and the original object will be retained.

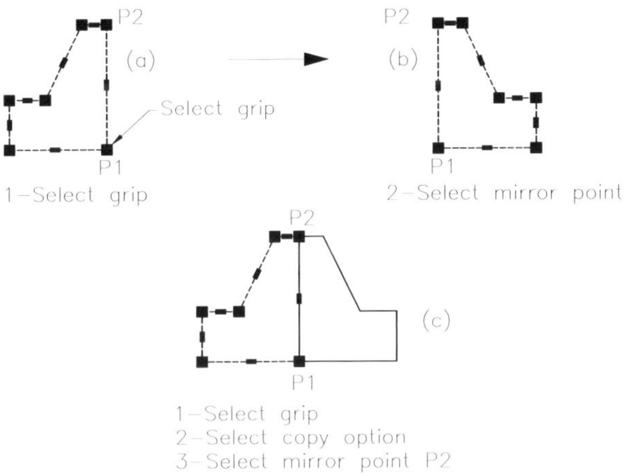

*Figure 6-12 Using the **Mirror** mode to create a mirror image of the selected objects*

Note

*1. You can use some editing tools such as **Erase, Move, Rotate, Scale, Mirror**, and **Copy** on an object with unselected grips. However, this is possible only if the **PICKFIRST** system variable is set to **1** (On).*

2. You cannot select an object when a grip is hot.

3. To remove an object from the selection set displaying grips, press the SHIFT key and then select that object. The object, which is removed from the selection set, will no longer be highlighted.

Editing a Polyline by Using Grips

In AutoCAD LT, when you select a polyline, three grips are displayed in each segment of the polyline. You can edit the polyline by using these grips. To do so, move the cursor on one of the grips and pause for a while; a tooltip will be displayed, as shown in Figure 6-13. To stretch the polyline, choose the **Stretch Vertex** option and specify a new point; the polyline will be stretched. After choosing the **Stretch Vertex** option, you can also invoke the **Base Point** or **Copy** option from the shortcut menu, as discussed earlier.

To add a new vertex, choose the **Add Vertex** option from the tooltip, as shown in Figure 6-14; you will be prompted to specify a new vertex point. Specify a point; a new vertex will be added between the selected vertex and the next vertex, as shown in Figure 6-15. However, if the selected vertex is the last vertex, then a new segment will be added to the last vertex.

To remove a vertex, move the cursor over the vertex to be removed and choose the **Remove Vertex** option from the tooltip displayed.

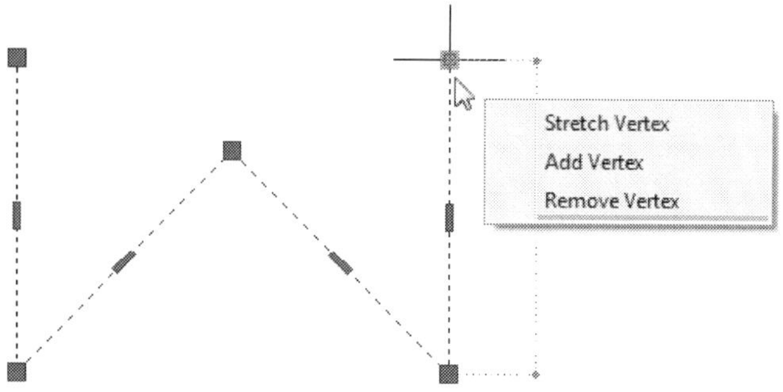

Figure 6-13 *Tooltip displayed near the grip*

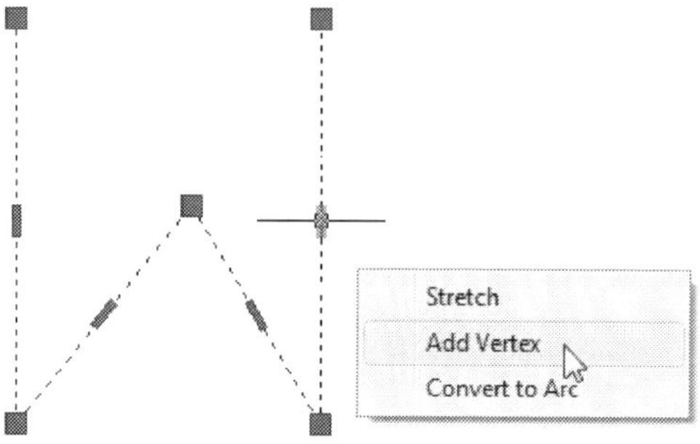

Figure 6-14 *Choosing the* ***Add Vertex*** *option from the tooltip*

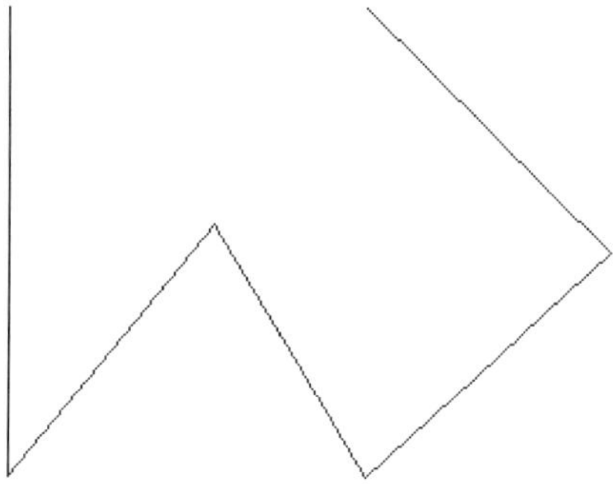

Figure 6-15 *Polyline after adding a new vertex*

If you place the cursor on the middle grip, the tooltip will display the **Convert to Arc** option instead of the **Remove Vertex** option. Choose this option to convert (see Figure 6-16) the selected line to an arc. On choosing this option, you will be prompted to specify the midpoint of the arc. Specify a point on the periphery of the arc; the line will be converted into an arc, as shown in Figure 6-17. If you have drawn an arc using the **Polyline** tool or converted a polyline to an arc, you can convert the arc back to the line by choosing the **Convert to Line** option from the tool tip that is displayed on placing the cursor on the middle grip of the arc.

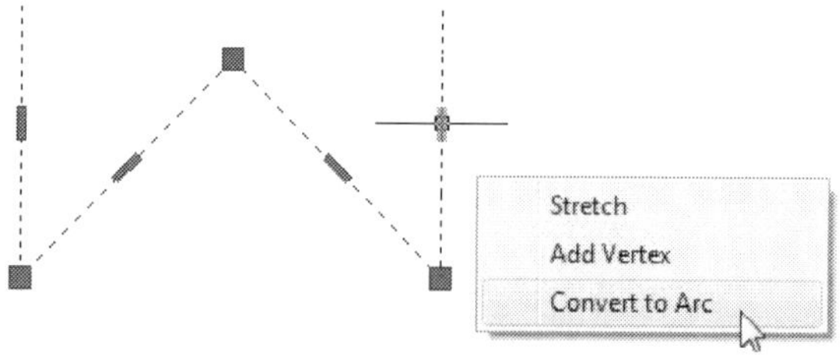

Figure 6-16 *Selecting the* ***Convert to Arc*** *option from the tooltip*

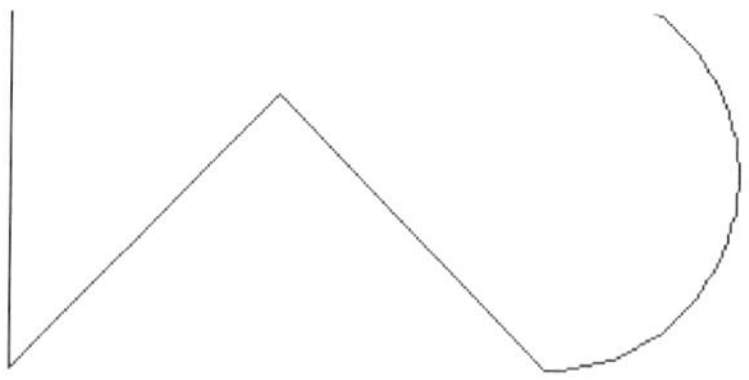

Figure 6-17 *Polyline after converting a line into an arc*

Tip
After choosing an option from the tooltip, you can cycle through the options in the tooltip by pressing the CTRL key .

LOADING HYPERLINKS

If you have already added a hyperlink to an object, you can also use the grips to open a file associated with it. For example, the hyperlink could start a word processor or activate the Web browser and load a Web page that is embedded in the selected object. To launch the Web browser that provides hyperlinks to other Web pages, select the URL-embedded object and then right-click to display the shortcut menu. In the shortcut menu, choose the **Hyperlink > Open** option and AutoCAD LT will automatically load the Web browser. When you move the cursor over or near the object that contains a hyperlink, AutoCAD LT displays the hyperlink information with the cursor.

Note
The process of working with hyperlinks is discussed in the later chapters.

EDITING GRIPPED OBJECTS

You can also edit the properties of the gripped objects by using the **Properties** panel in the **Home** tab, see Figure 6-18. When you select objects without invoking a tool, the grips (rectangular boxes) will be displayed on the selected objects. The gripped objects are highlighted and will display grips (rectangular boxes) at their grip points. For example, to change the color of the gripped objects, select the **Object Color** drop-down list in the **Properties** panel and then select a color from it. The color of the gripped objects will change to the selected color. Similarly, to change the layer, lineweight, or linetype of the gripped objects, select the required linetype, lineweight, or layer from the corresponding drop-down lists. If the gripped objects have different colors, linetypes, or lineweights, the **Object Color**, **Linetype**, and **Lineweight** drop-down lists will appear blank. You can also change the plot style of the selected objects using this panel.

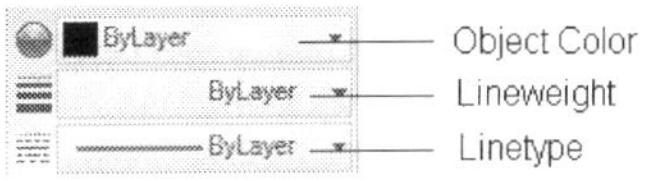

***Figure 6-18** The **Properties** panel*

CHANGING THE PROPERTIES USING THE PROPERTIES PALETTE

Ribbon: View > Palettes > Properties **Toolbar:** Quick Access > Properties
Command: PR/PROPERTIES

As mentioned earlier, each object has properties associated with it such as the color, layer, linetype, line weight, and so on. You can modify these properties by using the **Properties** palette. To view this palette, choose the **Properties** button from the **Palettes** panel in the **View** tab; the **Properties** palette will be displayed, as shown in Figure 6-19. The **Properties** palette can also be displayed when you double-click on the object to be edited. The contents of the **Properties** palette change depending upon the objects selected. For example, if you select a text entity, the related properties such as its height, justification, style, rotation angle, obliquing factor, and so on, will be displayed.

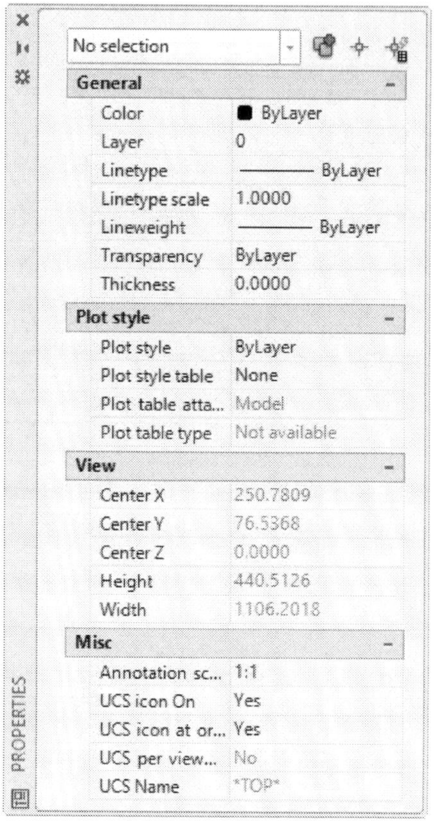

***Figure 6-19** The **PROPERTIES** palette for editing the properties of an entity*

The **PROPERTIES** palette can also be invoked from the shortcut menu. To do so, select an entity and right-click in the drawing area. Choose the **Properties** option from the shortcut menu. If you select more than one entity, the common properties of the selected entities will be displayed in the **PROPERTIES** palette. To change the properties of the selected entities, click in the cell next to the name of the property and change the values manually. Alternatively, you can choose an option from the drop-down list, if available. You can cycle through the options by double-clicking in the property cell.

Note

*Some of the options in the **PROPERTIES** palette have been explained in Chapter 4. Other options are explained in detail in the later chapters.*

MATCHING THE PROPERTIES OF SKETCHED OBJECTS

Ribbon: Home > Properties > Match Properties **Command:** MA/MATCHPROP
Quick Access Toolbar: Match Properties (Customize to Add)

The **Match Properties** tool is used to apply properties like color, layer, linetype, and linetype scale of a source object to the selected objects. On invoking this tool, you will be prompted to select the source object and then the destination objects. The properties of the destination objects will be replaced with the properties of the source object. This is a transparent tool and can be used when another tool is active. The prompt sequence that will follow when you choose the **Match Properties** tool is given next.

> Select source object: *Select the source object.*
> Current active settings: Color Layer Ltype Ltscale Lineweight Transparency Thickness PlotStyle Dim Text Hatch Polyline Viewport Table Material Multileader Center object
> Select destination object(s) or [Settings]:

If you select the destination object in the **Select destination object(s) or [Settings]** prompt, the properties of the source object will be forced on it. If you select the **Settings** option, the **Property Settings** dialog box will be displayed, as shown in Figure 6-20. The properties displayed are those of the source object. You can use this dialog box to edit the properties that are copied from the source to destination objects.

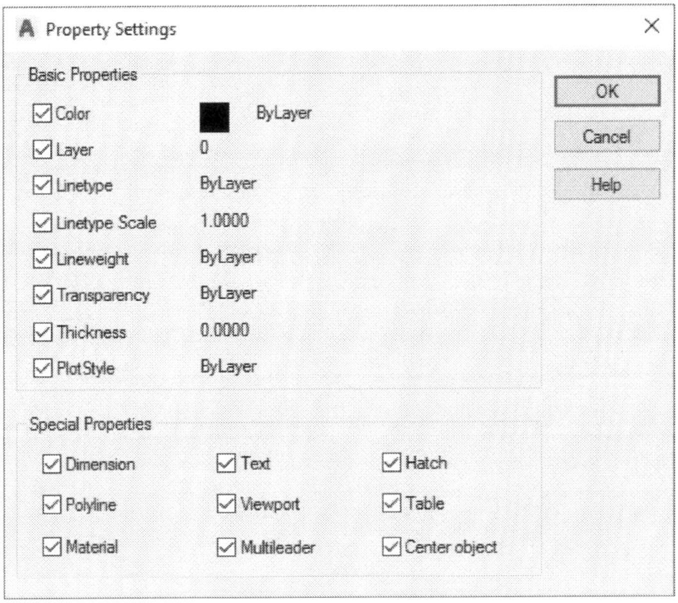

***Figure 6-20** The **Property Settings** dialog box*

QUICK SELECTION OF SKETCHED OBJECTS

Ribbon: Home > Utilities > Quick Select **Command:** QSELECT

The **Quick Select** tool is used to create a new selection set that will either include or exclude all objects whose object type and property criteria match as specified for the selection set. The **Quick Select** tool can be used to select the entities in the entire drawing or in the existing selection set. If a drawing is partially opened, the **Quick Select** tool does not consider the objects that are not loaded. The **Quick Select** tool can be invoked from the **Utilities** panel. You can also choose the **Quick Select** option from the shortcut menu displayed by right clicking in the drawing area. On invoking this tool, the **Quick Select** dialog box will be displayed, see Figure 6-21. The **Quick Select** dialog box is used to specify the object filtering criteria and create a selection set from it.

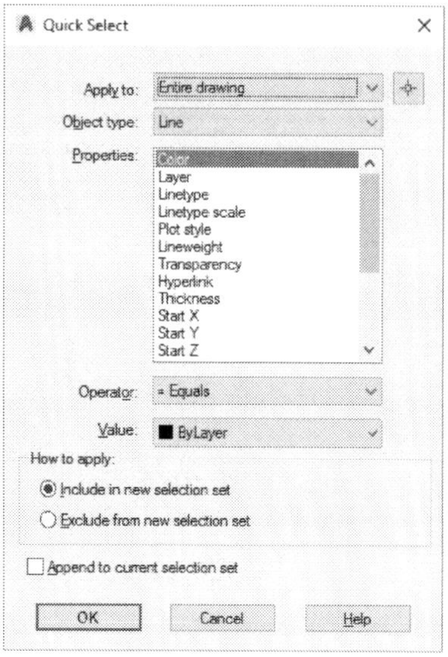

***Figure 6-21** The **Quick Select** dialog box*

Apply to

The **Apply to** drop-down list specifies whether to apply the filtering criteria to the entire drawing or to the current selection set. If there is an existing selection set, the **Current selection** is the default value. Otherwise, the **Entire drawing** is the default value. You can select the objects to create a selection set by choosing the **Select objects** button on the right side of this drop-down list. The **Quick Select** dialog box is temporarily closed when you choose this button and you will be prompted to select the objects. The dialog box will be displayed again once the selection is made.

Object type

This drop-down list specifies the type of object to be filtered. It lists all the available object types and if some objects are selected, it lists all the selected object types. **Multiple** is the default option selected in this drop-down list.

Properties

This list box displays the properties to be filtered. All the properties related to the object type will be displayed in this list box. The property selected from this list box will define the options that will be available in the **Operator** and **Value** drop-down lists.

Operator

This drop-down list is used to specify the range of the filter for the chosen property. The filters that are available are given next.

• Equals	=	• Not Equal	<>
• Greater than	>	• Less than	<>

- Select All
- Wildcard Match (Available only for text objects that can be edited and if you select **Hyperlink** option from the **Properties** list.)

Note
*The **Value** drop-down list will not be available when you select **Select All** from the **Operator** drop-down list.*

Value

This drop-down list is used to specify the property value of the filter. If the values are known, you can select a value. Otherwise, you can enter a value.

How to apply Area

The options under this area are used to specify whether the filtered entities will be included or excluded from the new selection set. This area provides the following two radio buttons:

Include in new selection set

If this radio button is selected, the filtered entities will be included in the new selection set. Also, this radio button creates a new selection set composed only of those objects that conform to the filtering criteria.

Exclude from new selection set

If this radio button is selected, the filtered entities will be excluded from the new selection set. This radio button creates a new selection set of objects that do not conform to the filtering criteria.

Append to current selection set

On selecting this check box, a cumulative selection set is created by using multiple uses of Quick Select. It specifies whether the objects selected using the **Quick Select** tool replace the current selection set or append the current selection set. If you select this check box, then the **Select objects** button available next to **Apply to** drop-down list will be deactivated.

Tip
*Quick Select supports objects and their properties that are created by some other applications. If the objects have properties other than AutoCAD LT then the source application of the object should be running for the properties to be available in the **QSELECT**.*

CYCLING THROUGH SELECTION

In AutoCAD LT, you can cycle through the objects to be selected if they are overlapping or close to other entities. This new feature helps in selecting the entities easily and quickly. To enable this feature, choose the **Selection Cycling** button in the Status Bar. Now, if you move the cursor near an entity that has other entities nearby it then the selection cycling symbol will be displayed, as shown in Figure 6-22. If you select any one of the entities when the selection cycling symbol is displayed, the **Selection** list box with a list of the entities that can be selected will be displayed, as shown in Figure 6-23. You can select the entities from the **Selection** list box.

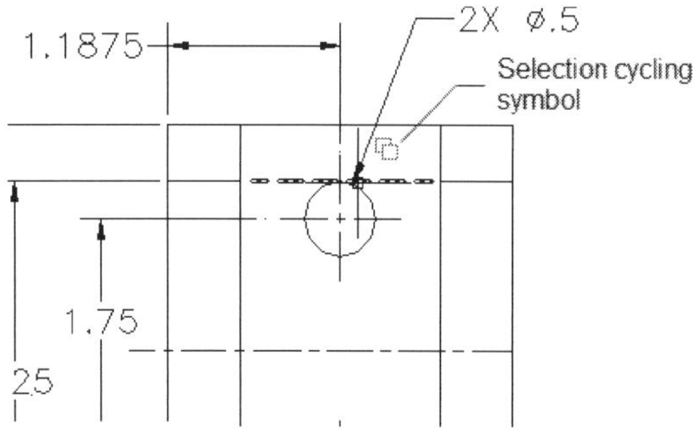

Figure 6-22 The selection cycling symbol displayed

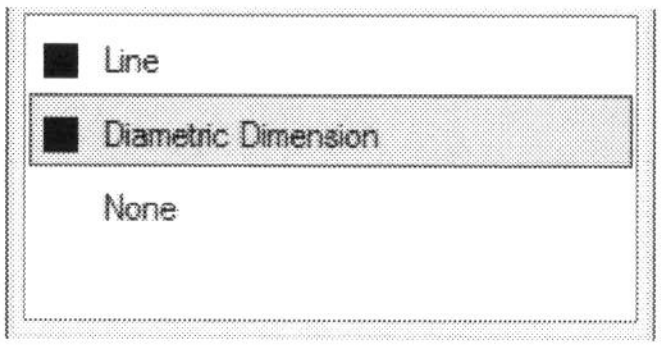

Figure 6-23 *The* ***Selection*** *list box*

MANAGING CONTENTS USING THE DesignCenter

Ribbon: View > Palettes > DesignCenter **Command:** ADC/ADCENTER
Menu Bar: Tools > Palettes > DesignCenter

The **DesignCenter** window is used to locate and organize drawing data, and to insert blocks, layers, external references, and other customized drawing content. These contents can be selected from either your own files, local drives, a network, or the Internet. You can even access and use the contents between the files or from the Internet. You can use the **DesignCenter** to conveniently drag and drop any information that has been previously created into the current drawing. This powerful tool reduces the repetitive tasks of creating information that already exists. To invoke the **DesignCenter** window, choose the **DesignCenter** tool from the **Palettes** panel; the **DesignCenter** window will be displayed, see Figure 6-24.

To move the **DesignCenter**, drag the title bar located on the left of the window. To resize it, click on the borders and drag them to the right or left. Right-clicking on the title bar of the window displays a shortcut menu to move, resize, close, dock, and hide the **DesignCenter** window. The **Auto-Hide** button on the title bar acts as a toggle for hiding and displaying the **DesignCenter**. Also, double-clicking on the title bar of the window docks the **DesignCenter** window. To use this option, make sure that the **Allow Docking** option is selected from the shortcut menu that is displayed on right-clicking on the title bar.

Note

The ***DesignCenter*** *can be turned on and off by pressing the CTRL+2 keys.*

Figure 6-25 shows the buttons in the **DesignCenter** toolbar. When you choose the **Tree View Toggle** button on the **DesignCenter** toolbar, it displays the **Tree View** (Left Pane) with a tree view of the contents of the drives. If the tree view is not displayed, you can also right-click in the window and choose **Tree** from the shortcut menu displayed. Now, the window is divided into two parts, the **Tree View** (left pane) and the **Palette** (right pane). The **Palette** displays folders, files, objects in a drawing, images, Web-based content, and custom content. You can also resize both the **Tree View** and the **Palette** by clicking and dragging the bar between them to the right or the left.

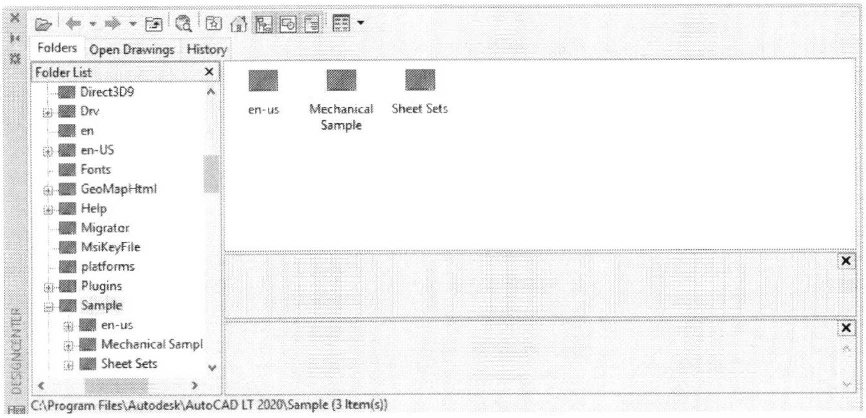

Figure 6-24 *The* ***DesignCenter*** *window*

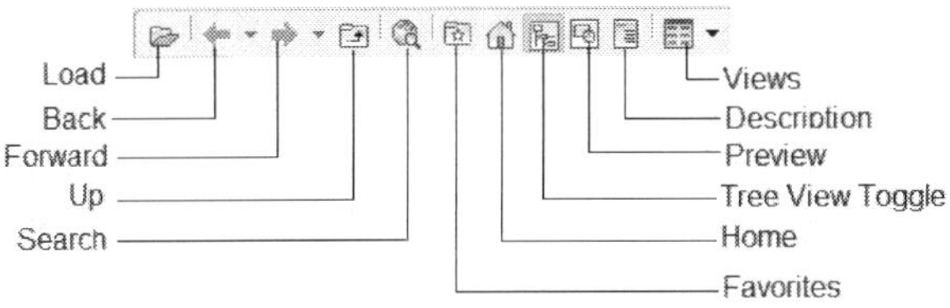

Figure 6-25 *The* ***DesignCenter*** *toolbar*

The **DesignCenter** window has three tabs **Folders**, **Open drawings**, **History**, and a button **Autodesk Seek** on its right. The description of these tabs is given next.

Folders Tab

The **Folders** tab lists all the folders and files in the local and network drives. When this tab is chosen, the **Tree View** displays the tree view of the contents of the drives and the **Palette** displays various folders and files in a drawing, images, and the Web-based content in the selected drive.

In the **Tree View**, you can browse the contents of any folder by clicking on the plus sign (+) adjacent to it to expand the view. Further, expanding the contents of a file displays the categories such as **Blocks**, **Dimstyles**, **Layers**, **Layouts**, **Linetypes**, **Textstyles**, **Xrefs**, etc. Clicking on any one of these categories in the **Tree View** displays the listing under the selected category in the **Palette** (Figure 6-26).

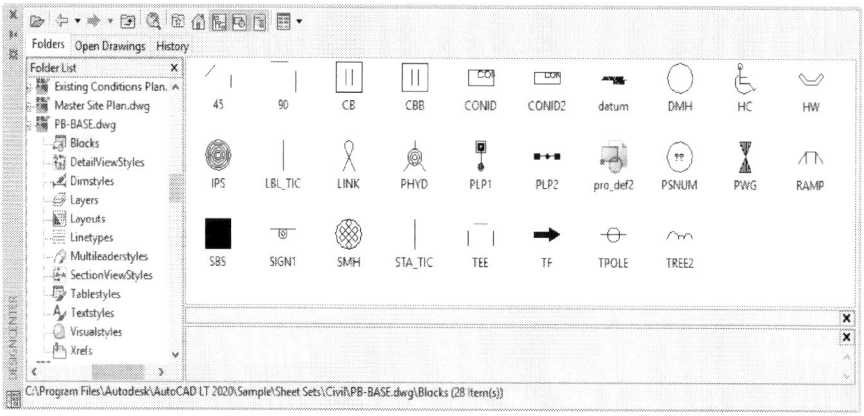

Figure 6-26 *The* ***DesignCenter*** *displaying the* ***Tree pane***, ***Palette***, ***Preview pane***, *and* ***Description box***

You can drag and drop any of the contents into the current drawing, or add them by double-clicking on them. These are then reused as part of the current drawing. When you double-click on specific Xrefs or blocks, AutoCAD LT displays the **External Reference** dialog box and the **Insert** dialog box, respectively. The **External Reference** dialog box helps in attaching the external reference and the **Insert** dialog box helps in inserting the block. If you right-click on a block, the **Insert Block**, **Copy**, or **Create Tool Palette** options will be displayed and similarly, if you right-click the on an **Xref**, the **Attach Xref** or **Copy** option will be displayed in the shortcut menus. Similarly, when you double-click on a layer, text style, dimstyle, layout, or linetype style, they also get added to the current drawing.

If any of these named objects already exist in the current drawing, duplicate definition is ignored and it is not added again. When you right-click on a specific linetype, layer, textstyle, layout, or dimstyle in the palette, a shortcut menu is displayed that gives you an option to **Add** or **Copy**. The **Add** option directly adds the selected named object to the current drawing. The **Copy** option copies the specific named object to the clipboard from where you can paste it into a particular drawing.

Note

You will learn more about inserting blocks in Chapter 15, Working with Blocks.

Right-clicking a particular folder or file in the **Tree View** displays a shortcut menu. The various options in the shortcut menu, besides those discussed earlier, are **Add to Favorites**, **Organize Favorites**, **Create Tool Palette of Blocks** (for folders), **Create Tool Palette** (for drawing files) and **Set as Home**. **Add to Favorites** adds the selected file or folder to the **Favorites** folder, which contains the most often accessed files and folders. **Organize Favorites** allows you to reorganize the contents of the **Favorites** folder. When you select **Organize Favorites** from the shortcut menu, the **Autodesk** folder is opened in a window. **Create Tool Palette** adds the blocks of the selected file or folder to the **Tool Palettes** window, which contains the predefined blocks. **Set as Home** sets the selected file or folder as the **Home** folder. You will notice that when the **Design Center** tool is invoked the next time, the file that was last set will be displayed by default in the DesignCenter.

Open Drawings Tab

The **Open Drawings** tab lists all the drawings that are open, including the current drawing which is being worked on. When you choose this tab, the **Tree View** (left pane) displays the tree view of all the drawings that are currently open and the **Palette** (right pane) displays the various contents in the selected drawing.

History Tab

The **History** tab lists the locations of the most recently accessed files through the **DesignCenter**. When you choose this tab, the **Tree View** (left pane) and the **Palette** (right pane) are replaced by a list box. Right-clicking a particular file displays a shortcut menu. The various options in the shortcut menu are **Explore**, **Search**, **Folders**, **Open Drawings**, **Delete**, **Add to Favorites**, and **Organize Favorites**. The **Explore** option is used to invoke the **Folders** tab of the **DesignCenter** with the file selected in the **Tree View** and the contents of the selected file are displayed in the **Palette View**. The **Folders** option is used to invoke the **Folders** tab of the **DesignCenter**. The **Open Drawings** option is used to invoke the **Open Drawings** tab of the **DesignCenter**. The **Delete** option deletes the selected drawing from the History list. The **Search** option allows you to search for drawings or named objects such as blocks, textstyles, dimstyles, layers, layouts, external references, or linetypes. The **Organize Favorites** option is used to open **Autodesk** folder in a window.

AUTODESK SEEK

The **Autodesk Seek design content** link allows you to download the *.dwg, .dwf, .pdf, .dgn, .gsm, .skp, .rfa* and all other files of various products from the Autodesk online source for product specification and design files. To access the online source, click on the **Autodesk Seek design content** in the **DesignCenter**; a new web page will be displayed. In this page, you can search for the required file type using the **Search** option. Once you get the required files, you can download them to your system.

Choosing the **Back** button in the **DesignCenter** toolbar displays the last item selected in the **DesignCenter**. If you pick the down arrow on the **Back** button, a list of the recently visited items is displayed. You can view the desired item in the **DesignCenter** by selecting it from the list. The **Forward** button is available only if you have chosen the **Back** button once. This button displays the same page as the current page before you choose the **Back** button. The **Up** button moves one level up in the tree structure from the current location. Choosing the **Favorites** button displays shortcuts to files and folders that are accessed frequently by you and are stored in the **Favorites** folder. This reduces the time you take to access these files or folders from their normal location. Choosing the **Tree View Toggle** button in the **DesignCenter** toolbar displays or hides the tree pane with the tree view of the contents displayed in a hierarchical form. Choosing the **Load** button displays the **Load** dialog box, whose options are similar to those of the standard **Select file** dialog box. When you select a file from this dialog box and choose the **Open** button, AutoCAD LT displays the selected file and its contents in the **DesignCenter**.

The **Views** button gives four display format options for the contents of the palette: **Large icons**, **Small icons**, **List**, and **Details**. The **List** option lists the contents in the palette while the **Details** option gives a detailed list of the contents in the palette with the name, file size, and type. Right-clicking in the palette displays a shortcut menu with all the options provided in the **DesignCenter** in addition to the **Add to Favorites**, **Organize favorites**, **Refresh**, and **Create Tool Palette** options. The **Refresh** option refreshes the palette display if you have made any changes to it. The **Create Tool Palette** option adds the drawings of the selected file or folder to the **Tool Palettes**, which contains the predefined blocks. The following example will illustrate how to use the **DesignCenter** to locate a drawing and then use its contents in the current drawing.

Example 1 — DesignCenter

Use the **DesignCenter** to locate and view the contents of the drawing *Kitchens.dwg*. Also, use the **DesignCenter** to insert a block from this drawing and import a layer and a textstyle from the *Blocks and Tables - Imperial.dwg* file located in the **Sample** folder. Use these to make a drawing of a Kitchen plan (*MyKitchen.dwg*) and then add text to it, as shown in Figure 6-27.

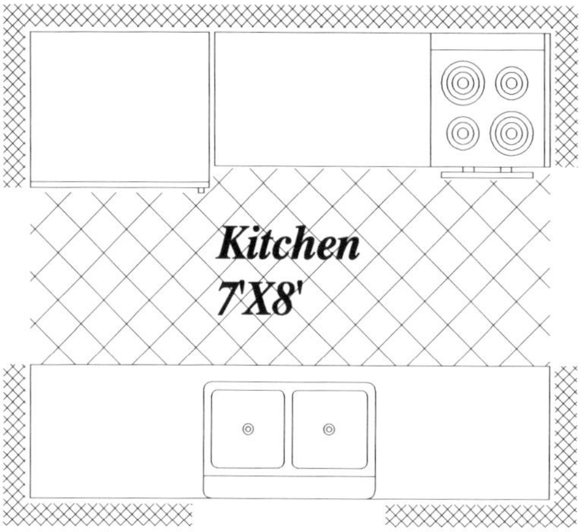

Figure 6-27 *Drawing for Example 1*

1. Open a new drawing using the **Start from Scratch** option. Make sure the **Imperial (feet and inches)** radio button is selected in the **Create New Drawing** dialog box.

2. Change the units to **Architectural** using the **Drawing Units** dialog box. Increase the limits to 10',10'. Use the **Zoom All** tool to increase the drawing display area.

3. Choose the **DesignCenter** tool from the **Palettes** panel in the **View** tab; the **DesignCenter** window is displayed at its default location.

4. In the **DesignCenter** toolbar, choose the **Tree View Toggle** button to display the **Tree View** and the **Palette** (if is not already displayed). Also, choose the **Preview** button, if it is not displayed already. You can resize the window, if needed, to view both the **Tree View** and the **Palette**, conveniently.

5. Choose the **Search** button in the **DesignCenter** to display the **Search** dialog box. Here, select **Drawings** from the **Look for** drop-down list and **C:** (or the drive in which AutoCAD LT 2020 is installed) from the **In** drop-down list. Select the **Search subfolders** check box. In the **Drawings** tab, type **Kitchens** in the **Search for the word(s)** edit box and select **File Name** from the **In the field(s)** drop-down list. Now, choose the **Search Now** button to commence the search. After the drawing has been located, its details and path are displayed in a list box at the bottom of the dialog box.

6. Now, right-click on *Kitchens.dwg* in the list box of the **Search** dialog box and choose **Load into Content Area** from the shortcut menu. You will notice that the drawing and its contents are displayed in the Tree view.

7. Close the **Search** dialog box, if it is still open.

8. Double-click on *Kitchens.dwg* in the Tree View to expand the tree view and display its contents, in case they are not displayed. You can also expand the contents by clicking on the + sign located on the left of the file name in the Tree view.

9. Select **Blocks** in the Tree View to display the list of blocks in the drawing in the **Palette**. Using the left mouse button, drag and drop the block **Kitchen Layout-7x8 ft** in the current drawing.

10. Now, double-click on the *AutoCAD LT Textstyles and Linetypes.dwg* file located in the **DesignCenter** folder in the same directory to display its contents in the **Palette**.

11. Double-click on **Textstyles** to display the list of text styles in the **Palette**. Select **Dutch Bold Italic** in the **Palette** and drag and drop it in the current drawing. You can use this textstyle for adding text to the current drawing.

12. Invoke the **Multiline Text** tool and use the imported textstyle to add the text to the current drawing and complete it, refer to Figure 6-27.

Note

1. To create text which is shown in Figure 6-27, first you need to change the text height.

2. You can import Blocks, Dimstyles, Layers, and so on to the current drawing from any existing drawing.

13. Save the current drawing with the name *MyKitchen.dwg*.

MAKING INQUIRIES ABOUT OBJECTS AND DRAWINGS

When you create a drawing or examine an existing one, you often need some information about the entities in your drawing. The information can be regarding the distance from one location to another, the area of an object like a polygon or circle, coordinates of a location on the drawing, and so on. In manual drafting, you need to measure and calculate manually to get the required information. In AutoCAD LT, you need to use the inquiry tools or commands to obtain information about the selected objects. However, these tools and commands do not affect the drawings in any way. The following is the list of Inquiry tools and commands:

Area	**Distance**	**ID**	**List**	**MASSPROP**
TIME	**DWGPROPS**			

For most of the inquiry tools and commands, you are prompted to select objects. Once the selection is complete, AutoCAD LT switches from the graphics mode to the text mode, and all relevant information about the selected objects is displayed. For some tools and commands, information is displayed in the AutoCAD LT Text Window. The display of the text screen can be tailored to your requirements using a pointing device. Therefore, by moving the text screen to one side, you can view the drawing screen and the text screen simultaneously. If you choose the **minimize** button or the **Close** button, you will return to the graphics screen. You can also return to the graphics screen by entering the **GRAPHSCR** command at the Command prompt. Similarly, you can return to the AutoCAD LT Text Window by entering **TEXTSCR** at the Command prompt.

Measuring Area of Objects

Ribbon: Home > Utilities > Measure drop-down > Area	**Toolbar:** Inquiry > Distance > Area
Menu Bar: Tools > Inquiry > Area	**Command:** Area

Calculating the area of an object manually is time consuming. In AutoCAD LT, the **Area** tool is used to automatically calculate the area of an object in square units. This tool saves time when calculating the area of complicated or irregular shapes. You can use the default option of the **Area** tool to calculate the area and perimeter or circumference of the space enclosed by the sequence of specified points.

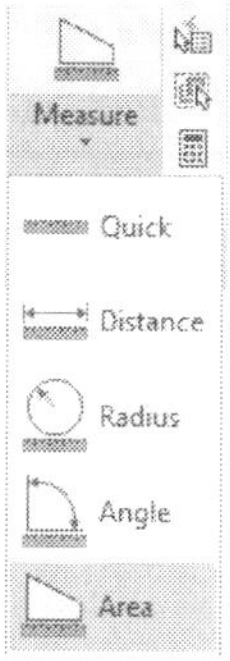

***Figure 6-28** Tools in the **Measure** drop-down*

For example, to find the area of a pentagon created with the help of the **Line** tool, invoke the **Area** tool (Figure 6-28) and select all the vertices of the polygon to define the shape whose area is to be calculated. This is the default method for determining the area of an object. Note that all the points you specify should be in a plane parallel to the *XY* plane of the current UCS. You can use object snaps such as the Endpoint, Intersect, and Tangent, or running Osnaps, to select the vertices quickly and accurately. The prompt sequence that will be displayed on choosing the **Area** tool from the **Utilities** panel is given next.

Specify first corner point or [Object/Add area/Subtract area/eXit] <Object>: *Specify first point.*
Specify next point or [Arc/Length/Undo] : *Specify the second point.*
Specify next point or [Arc/Length/Undo/Total] <Total>: *Continue selecting until all points enclosing the area have been selected.*
Specify next point or [Arc/Length/Undo/Total] <Total>: Enter
Area = X, Perimeter = Y

Here, X represents the numerical value of the area and Y represents the circumference/perimeter.

It is not possible to determine the area of a curved object accurately with the default option of the **Area** tool. However, the approximate area of a curved object can be calculated by specifying several points on the curved entity. If the object whose area you want to find is not closed (formed of independent segments) and has curved lines, you should use the following steps to determine the accurate area of such an object:

1. Convert all the segments in that object into polylines using the **Edit Polyline** tool.

2. Join all the individual polylines into a single polyline. Once you have performed these operations, the object becomes closed and you can then use the **Object** option of the **Area** tool to determine the area.

Object Option

The **Object** option is used to find the area of objects such as polygons, circles, polylines, regions, solids, and splines. If the selected object is a polyline or polygon, the area and perimeter of the polyline will be displayed. In case of open polylines, the area is calculated assuming that the last point is joined to the first point. Additionally, instead of perimeter, the length of this segment is calculated. If the selected object is a circle, ellipse, or planar closed spline curve, information about its area and circumference will be displayed. For a solid, the surface area is displayed. For a 3D polyline, all vertices must lie in a plane parallel to the *XY* plane of the current UCS. The extrusion direction of a 2D polyline whose area you want to determine should be parallel to the *Z* axis of the current UCS. In case of polylines that have a width, the area and length of the polyline are calculated using the centerline. If any of these conditions is violated, an error message is displayed. The prompt sequence for using the **Object** option of the **Area** tool is given below.

Specify first corner point or [Object/Add area/Subtract area/eXit] <Object>: **O** Enter
Select objects: *Select an object.*
Area = (X), Perimeter = (Y)

Here X represents the numerical value of the area and Y represents the circumference/perimeter.

Tip
*The easiest and most accurate way to find the area of a region enclosed by multiple objects is to use the **Boundary** tool to create a polyline and then use the **Object** option. You will learn about the **Boundary** tool in Chapter 11.*

Add area Option

Sometimes you want to add areas of different objects to determine the total area. For example, while drawing the plan of a house, you need to add the areas of all the rooms to get the total floor area. In such cases, you can use the **Add area** option of the **Area** tool. The **Object** option adds the areas and perimeters of selected objects. After choosing this option, specify the first corner point at the **Specify first corner point or [Object/Subtract area/eXit]** prompt. Then continue specifying other corner points and press ENTER; the selected region will be displayed in green color and its area and perimeter will be displayed at the Command prompt. As the **Add area** option is on, you will be prompted to select next corner point again. Keep selecting all corner points to define the area and press ENTER twice to exit the tool; the total area will be displayed. After invoking the **Add area** option, you can also invoke the **Object** option at the **Specify first corner point or [Object/Subtract area/eXit]** prompt to select the objects. On selecting the objects, the regions are displayed in green color, and the area and length of the selected object as well as the combined area will be displayed at the Command prompt. In this manner, you can add areas of different objects. Until the **Add area** mode is active, the string **ADD mode** is displayed along with all subsequent object selection prompts to remind you that the **Add** mode is active.

If the polygon whose area is to be added is not closed, the area and perimeter are calculated assuming that there exists a line that connects the first point to the last point. The length of this imaginary line is added to the perimeter.

Subtract area Option

The **Subtract area** option is used along with the **Add area** option to subtract an area from the previously added area. For example, to calculate the area of the closed profile after subtracting the areas of the circles in Figure 6-29, you need to use the **Subtract area** option. First, invoke the **Area** tool and calculate the area of the closed profile using the **Add area** option; the region will be enclosed in green color area and the total area and the perimeter will be displayed. Give a single null response to exit the **Add area** option. Then, choose the **Subtract area** option and invoke the **Object** option. Now, select both the circles; the circles will be displayed in different colors and their areas will be displayed. Also, the total area will be displayed.

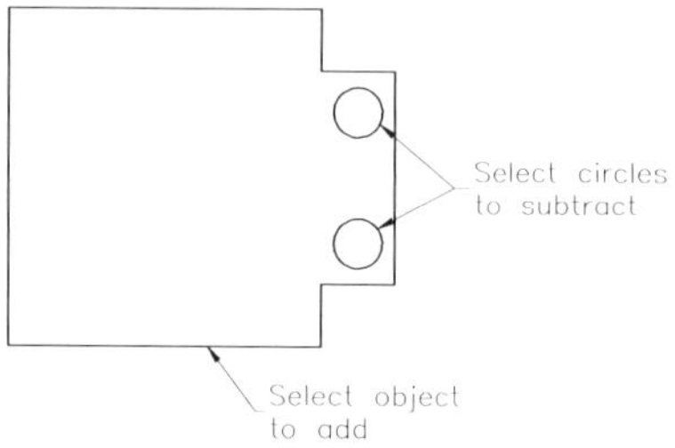

Figure 6-29 *Measuring the area of a sketch using the **Add** and **Subtract area** options*

The prompt sequence for these two modes is given next.

Specify first corner point or [Object/Add area/Subtract area/eXit]<Object>: **A** Enter
Specify first corner point or [Object/Subtract area/eXit]: **O** Enter
(ADD mode) Select objects: *Select the polyline.*
Area = 2.4438, Length = 6.4999
Total area = 2.4438
(ADD mode) Select objects: Enter
Specify first corner point or [Object/Subtract area/eXit]: **S** Enter
Specify first corner point or [Object/Add area/eXit]: **O** Enter
(SUBTRACT mode) Select object: *Select the circle.*
Area = 0.0495, Circumference = 0.7890
Total area = 2.3943
(SUBTRACT mode) Select objects: *Select the second circle.*
Area = 0.0495, Circumference = 0.7890
Total area = 2.3448
(SUBTRACT mode) Select object: Enter
Specify first corner point or [Object/Add area/eXit]: Enter

The **AREA** and **PERIMETER** system variables hold the area and perimeter (or circumference in the case of circles) of the previously selected polyline (or circle). Whenever you use the **Area** tool, the **AREA** variable is reset to zero.

Tip

*If an architect wants to calculate the area of flooring and skirting in a room, the **Area** tool provides you with its area and perimeter. You can use these parameters to calculate the skirting.*

Measuring the Distance between Two Points

Ribbon: Home > Utilities > Measure drop-down > Distance **Toolbar:** Inquiry > Distance
Menu Bar: Tools > Inquiry > Distance **Command:** DI/DIST

The **Distance** tool is used to measure the distance between two selected points, as shown in Figure 6-30. The angles that the selected points make with the *X* axis and the *XY* plane are also displayed. The measurements are displayed in the current units. Additionally, the Delta X (horizontal displacement), Delta Y (vertical displacement), and Delta Z are displayed. The distance computed by the **Distance** tool is saved in the **DISTANCE** variable.

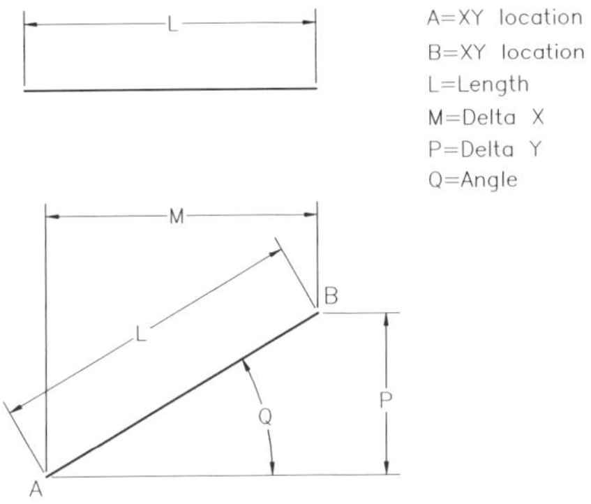

***Figure 6-30** Using the **Distance** tool to measure distance*

The prompt sequence that will follow when you choose the **Distance** tool is given next.

Specify first point: *Specify a point.*
Specify second point or [Multiple points]: *Specify a point.*

AutoCAD LT returns the following information.
Distance = *Calculated distance between the two points.*
Angle in XY plane = *Angle between the two points in the XY plane.*
Angle from XY plane = *Angle the specified points make with the XY plane.*
Delta X = *Change in X*, Delta Y = *Change in Y*, Delta Z = *Change in Z.*

If you give a null response at the **Specify first point** prompt and enter a single number or fraction at the **Specify second point** prompt, AutoCAD LT will convert it into the current unit of measurement and display in the command line. Also, the other values will be calculated with respect to the last used point.

Note
The Z coordinate is used in 3D distances. If you do not specify the Z coordinates of the two points between which you want to know the distance, AutoCAD LT takes the current elevation as the Z coordinate value.

Identifying the Location of a Point

Ribbon: Home > Utilities > ID Point **Toolbar:** Inquiry > Locate Point
Menu Bar: Tools > Inquiry > ID Point **Command:** ID

The **ID Point** tool is used to identify the position of a point in terms of its *X*, *Y*, and *Z* coordinates. The prompt sequence that will follow when you choose the **ID Point** tool from the **Utilities** panel is given next.

Specify point: *Specify the point to be identified.*
X = X coordinate Y = Y coordinate Z = Z coordinate

The current elevation is taken as the *Z* coordinate value. If an **Osnap** mode is used to snap to a 3D object in response to the **Specify point** prompt, the *Z* coordinate displayed will be that of the selected feature of the 3D object. You can also use the **ID Point** tool to identify a location in the drawing area by entering the coordinate values. For example, the following is the prompt sequence to find where the position X = 2.345, Y = 3.674, and Z = 1.0000 is located on the screen.

Specify point: 2.345,3.674,1.00 Enter
X = 2.345 Y = 3.674 Z = 1.0000

The coordinates of the point specified in the **ID Point** tool are saved in the **LASTPOINT** system variable. You can locate a point with respect to the **ID** point by using the relative or polar coordinate system. You can also snap to the last point by typing @ at the **Specify point** prompt.

Listing Information about Objects

Ribbon: Home > Properties > List **Toolbar:** Inquiry > List
Menu Bar: Tools > Inquiry > List **Command:** LI/LIST

The **List** tool displays all the information pertaining to the selected objects. The information is displayed in the **AutoCAD LT Text Window**. The prompt sequence that follows when you invoke the **List** tool from the **Properties** panel is given next.

Select objects: *Select objects whose data you want to list.*
Select objects: Enter

Once you select the objects to be listed, a new **AutoCAD LT Text Window** window will be displayed. The information displayed (listed) varies from object to object. The information about the type of the object, its coordinate position with respect to the current UCS (user coordinate system), the name of the layer on which it is drawn, and whether the object is in model space or paper space is listed for all types of objects. If the color, lineweight, and the linetype are not BYLAYER, they are also listed. Also, if the thickness of the object is greater than 0, it is also displayed. The elevation value is displayed in the form of a *Z* coordinate (in the case of 3D objects). If an object has an extrusion direction different from the *Z* axis of the current UCS, the object's extrusion direction is also provided.

More information based on the objects in the drawing is also provided. For example, the following information is displayed for a line.

1. The coordinates of the endpoints of the line.
2. Its length (in 3D).
3. The angle made by the line with respect to the *X* axis of the current UCS.
4. The angle made by the line with respect to the *XY* plane of the current UCS.
5. Delta X, Delta Y, and Delta Z: this is the change in each of the three coordinates from the start point to the endpoint.
6. The name of the layer in which the line was created.
7. Whether the line is drawn in Paper space or Model space.

For a circle, the center point, radius, true area, and circumference are displayed. For polylines, this tool displays the coordinates. In addition, for a closed polyline, its true area and perimeter are also given. If the polyline is open, AutoCAD LT lists its length and also calculates the area by assuming a segment connecting the start point and endpoint of the polyline. In the case of wide polylines, whole computation is done based on the centerlines of the wide segments. For a selected viewport, the **List** tool displays whether the viewport is on and active, on and inactive, or off. Information is also displayed about the status of Hideplot and the scale relative to paper space. If you use the **List** tool on a polygon mesh, the size of the mesh (in terms of M, X, N), the coordinate values of all the vertices in the mesh, and whether the mesh is closed or open in M and N directions, are all displayed. As mentioned before, if all the information does not fit on a single screen, AutoCAD LT pauses to allow you to press ENTER to continue the listing.

Checking Time-Related Information

Menu Bar: Tools > Inquiry > Time **Command:** TIME

The time and date set in your system are used by AutoCAD LT to provide information about several time factors related to the drawings. Hence, you should be careful about setting the current date and time in your computer. The **TIME** command is used to display information pertaining to time related to a drawing and the drawing session. The display obtained by invoking the **TIME** command is similar to the following:

Command: **TIME**
Current time: Tuesday, April 30, 2019 11:37:04:007 AM
Times for this drawing:
Created: Tuesday, April 30, 2019 11:37:49:777 AM
Last updated: Tuesday, April 30, 2019 11:37:27:354 AM
Total editing time: 0 days 00:02:04:057
Elapsed timer (on): 0 days 00:02:04:055
Next automatic save in: 0 days 00:08:34:178

Enter option [Display/ON/OFF/Reset]: *Enter the required option.*

Displaying Drawing Properties

Application Menu: Drawing Utilities > Drawing Properties **Command:** DWGPROPS

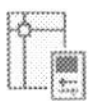

The **DWGPROPS** command is used to display information about drawing properties. Choose **Drawing Utilities > Drawing Properties** from the **Application Menu**; the **Drawing Properties** dialog box will be displayed, as shown in Figure 6-31. This dialog

box has four tabs under which information about the drawing is displayed. This information helps you look for the drawing more easily. These tabs are discussed next.

Figure 6-31 *The **Drawing Properties** dialog box*

General
This tab displays general properties about a drawing like the **Type**, **Size**, and **Location**.

Summary
The **Summary** tab displays predefined properties like the Author, title, and subject. Also this tab is displayed at the last that allows you to specify the information related to the drawing.

Statistics
This tab stores and displays data such as the file, size, and dates about the drawing when they were last saved or modified.

Custom
This tab displays custom file properties including values assigned by you.

BASIC DISPLAY OPTIONS
Drawing in AutoCAD LT is much simpler than manual drafting in many ways. Sometimes while drawing manually, it is very difficult to see and alter minute details. In AutoCAD LT, you can overcome this problem by viewing only a specific portion of the drawing. For example, to display a part of the drawing on a larger area, use the Zoom tools to enlarge or reduce the size of the drawing displayed. Similarly, use the **REGEN** command to regenerate the drawing and **REDRAW**

to refresh the screen. In this chapter, you will learn some of the drawing display commands, such as **REDRAW**, **REGEN**, **PAN**, **ZOOM**, and **VIEW**. These commands can also be used in the transparent mode. It means you can use these commands while another command is in progress.

Redrawing the Screen

Menu Bar: View > Redraw **Command:** REDRAW

The **REDRAW** command is used to redraw the drawing area. It is used to remove the temporary graphics from the drawing area which are left after using the **VSLIDE** command and some other operations. The **REDRAW** command also redraws the objects that are not displayed on the screen as a result of editing some other object. In AutoCAD LT, several commands redraw the screen automatically (for example, when a grid is turned off), but sometimes it is useful to redraw the screen explicitly.

To use the **REDRAW** command in transparent mode, add apostrophe as a prefix. For example, if you are drawing a line after specifying few points, type **'REDRAW** at the Command prompt as given below.

Specify next point or [Close/Undo]: *Specify a point.*
Specify next point or [Close/Undo]: ***'REDRAW***
Resuming LINE command.
Specify next point or [Close/Undo]: *Specify a point.*

In this case, the redrawing process takes place without any prompt for information. The **REDRAW** command affects only the current viewport. If you have more than one viewport, use the **REDRAWALL** command to redraw all the viewports. You can also invoke the **REDRAW** command by selecting the **Redraw** option from the **View** menu.

Regenerating Drawings

Menu Bar: View > Regen **Command:** RE/REGEN

The **REGEN** command is used to regenerate the modified drawing. The need for regeneration usually occurs when you change certain aspects of the drawing. All the objects in the drawing are recalculated and redrawn in the current viewport. One of the advantages of this command is that the drawing is refined by smoothening out circles and arcs. To use this command, type **REGEN** at the Command prompt and press enter; the message **Regenerating model** will be displayed while the system regenerates the drawing. The **REGEN** command affects only the current viewport. If you have more than one viewport, use the **REGENALL** command to regenerate all of them. The **REGEN** command can be aborted by pressing ESC. This saves time if you are going to use another command that causes automatic regeneration.

Note

*Under certain conditions, the **Zoom** and **Pan** tools automatically regenerate the drawing. Some other commands also perform regenerations under certain conditions.*

Zooming Drawings

Ribbon: View > Navigate > Extents **Toolbar:** Zoom
Menu bar: View > Zoom **Command:** Z/ZOOM

Creating drawings in AutoCAD LT would not be of much use if you cannot magnify the drawing view to work on the minute details. The ability to zoom in or magnify has been helpful in creating the minuscule circuits used in the electronics and computer industries. This is performed using the Zoom tools in the **Zoom** drop-down. These are the most frequently used tools. Getting close to or away from the drawing is the function of the Zoom tools. In other words, these tools enlarge or reduce the view of the drawing on the screen, but it does not affect the actual size of the objects. In this way, the Zoom tools function like the zoom lens of a camera. When you magnify the apparent size of a section of the drawing, you see that area in greater detail. On the other hand, if you reduce the apparent size of the drawing, you can see a larger area of the selected environment.

The Zoom tools can also be used in transparent mode. This means that these tools can be used while working with other tools. Various tools in the **Zoom** drop-down are shown in Figure 6-32. You can also invoke these tools by right-clicking in the drawing area and then choosing the **Zoom** option from the shortcut menu even when you are working with some other tool, refer to Figure 6-33. Various tools of the **Zoom** drop-down have been made available in the **Navigation Bar** in the drawing area, as shown in Figure 6-34. The various zoom tools available in the **Navigation Bar** are discussed next.

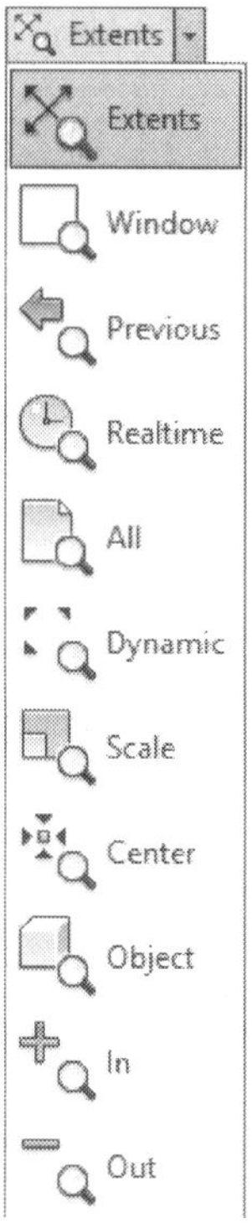

*Figure 6-32 Tools in the **Zoom** drop-down*

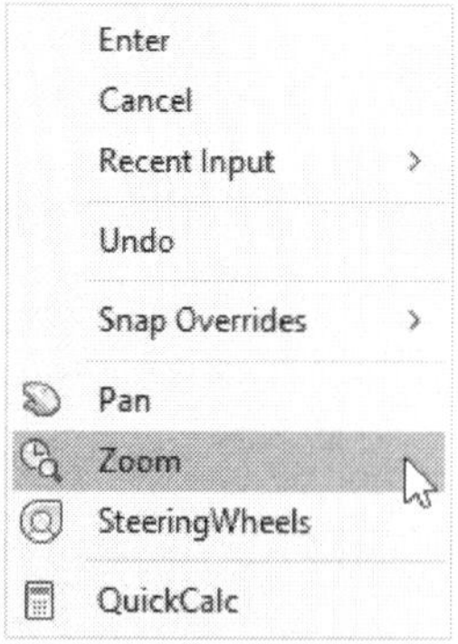

*Figure 6-33 The **Zoom** option in the shortcut menu*

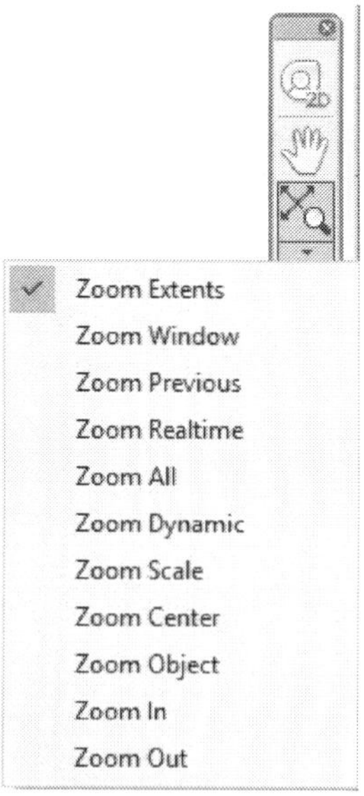

Figure 6-34** The Zoom tools in the **Navigation Bar

Zoom Realtime

You can zoom in or zoom out the drawing by using the **Zoom Realtime** tool available in the **Navigation Bar**. To zoom in, invoke this tool and then hold the pick button down and move the cursor up. If you want to zoom in further, release the pick button and bring the cursor down. Specify a point and move the cursor up again. Similarly, to zoom out, hold the pick button down and move the cursor down. If you move the cursor vertically up from the midpoint of the screen to the top of the window, the drawing will be magnified by 100% (zoom in 2x magnification). Similarly, if you move the cursor vertically down from the midpoint of the screen to the bottom of the window, the drawing display will be reduced to 100% (zoom out 0.5x magnification). Realtime zoom is the default setting for the **Zoom** option. Alternatively, you can invoke the **Zoom Realtime** tool by choosing the **Zoom** option from the shortcut menu displayed by right-clicking in the drawing area.

When you use the realtime zoom, the cursor becomes a magnifying glass and displays a plus sign (+) and a minus sign (–). When you reach the zoom out limit, AutoCAD LT does not display the minus sign (–) while dragging the cursor. Similarly, when you reach the zoom in limit, AutoCAD LT does not display the plus sign (+) while dragging the cursor. To exit the realtime zoom, press ENTER or ESC, or choose **Exit** from the shortcut menu.

Zoom All

This tool is used to adjust the display area on the basis of the drawing limits (Figure 6-35) or extents of an object, whichever is greater. Even if the objects are not within the limits, they are still included in the display. Therefore, with the **Zoom All** option, you can view the entire drawing in the current viewport (Figure 6-36).

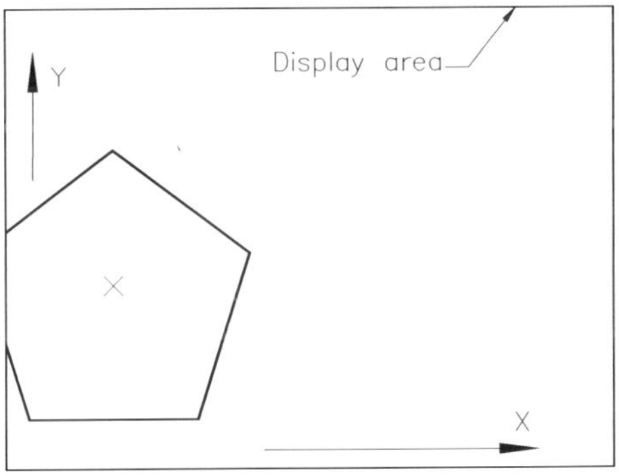

Figure 6-35 *Drawing showing the limits*

Figure 6-36 *Using the **Zoom All** option*

Zoom Center

This tool is used to define a new display window by specifying the center point (Figures 6-37 and 6-38) and magnification or height of the window. Here, you are required to enter the center and the height of the subsequent screen display. If you press ENTER instead of entering a new center point, the center of the view will remain unchanged. Instead of entering a height, you can enter the **magnification factor** by typing a number. If you press ENTER at the height prompt or if the height you enter is the same as the current height, magnification does not take place. For example, if the current height is 2.7645 and you press ENTER at the **Enter magnification or height <current>** prompt, magnification will not take place. The smaller the value, the greater is the enlargement of the image. You can also enter a number followed by **X**. This indicates the change in magnification, not as an absolute value, but as a value relative to the current screen.

The prompt sequence displayed on invoking the **Zoom Center** tool is given next.

Choose the ***Zoom Center*** *tool from the* ***Navigation Bar***
ZOOM Specify center point: *Specify a center point.*
Enter magnification or height <current>: **5X** Enter

In Figure 6-37, the current magnification height is 5X, which magnifies the display five times. If you enter the value **2**, the size (height and width) of the zoom area changes to 2 X 2 around the specified center. In Figure 6-39, if you enter 0.12 as the height after specifying the center point as the circle's center, the circle will zoom to fit in the display area since its diameter is 0.12. The prompt sequence is given next.

Choose the ***Zoom Center*** *tool from the* ***Navigation Bar***
Specify center point: *Select the center of the circle.*
Enter magnification or height <5.0>: **0.12** Enter

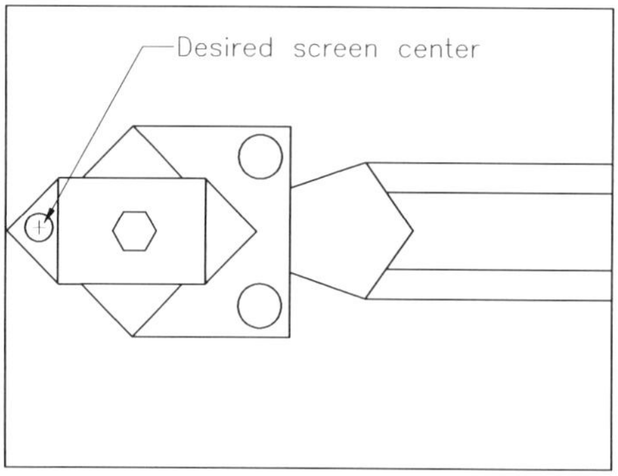

Figure 6-37 *Drawing before using the* ***Zoom Center*** *tool*

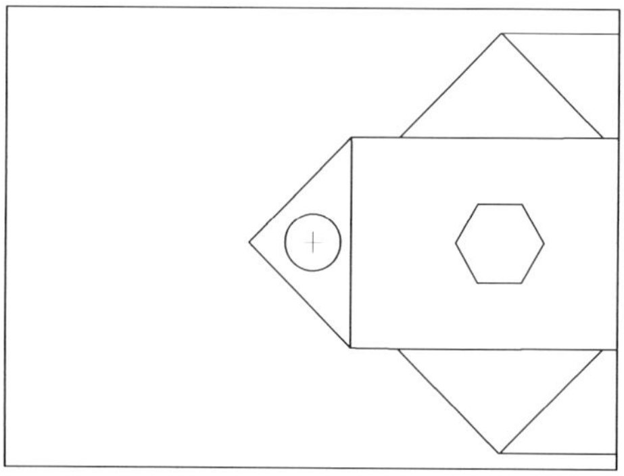

Figure 6-38 *Drawing after using the* ***Zoom Center*** *tool*

Zoom Extents

As the name indicates, this tool is used to zoom to the extents of the biggest object in the drawing. The extents of the drawing comprise the area that has the drawings in it. The rest of the empty area is neglected. On invoking this tool, all the objects in the drawing are magnified to the largest possible display, see Figure 6-40.

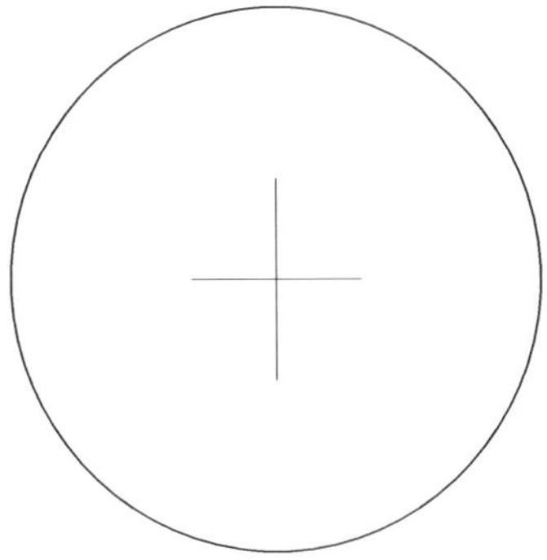

***Figure 6-39** Drawing after using the **Zoom Center** tool*

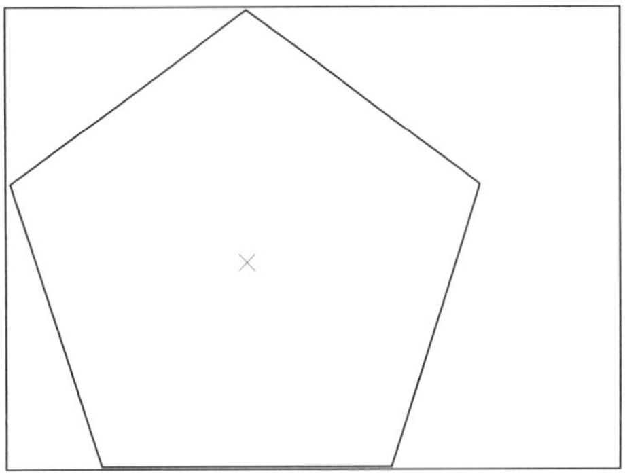

***Figure 6-40** Drawing after using the **Zoom Extents** tool*

Zoom Dynamic

This tool is used to display the portion of a drawing by specifying the area using the view box. To do so, choose this tool from the **Navigation Bar**; a view box will be attached to the cursor and you will be prompted to specify the area to zoom.

Blue dashed box representing drawing extents

Drawing extents are represented by a dashed blue box (Figure 6-41), which constitutes the drawing limits or the actual area occupied by the drawing.

Green dashed box representing the current view

A green dashed box is formed to represent the area of the current viewport (Figure 6-42).

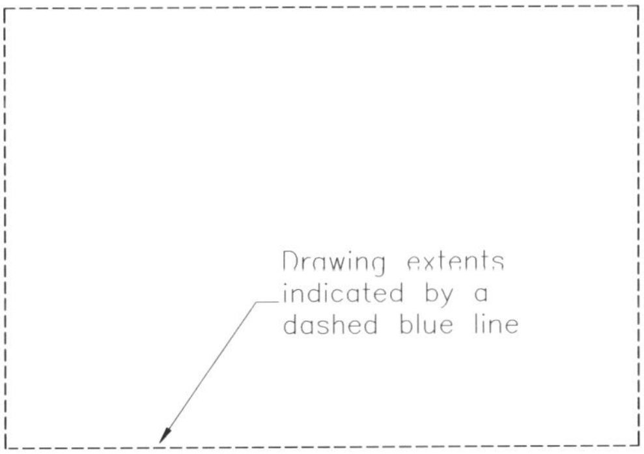

***Figure 6-41** Box representing drawing extents*

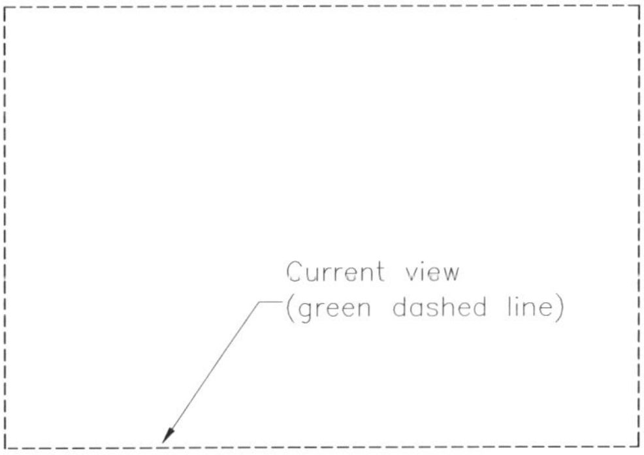

***Figure 6-42** Representation of the current view*

Panning view box (X in the center)

A view box initially of the same size as the current view box is displayed with an X at the center (Figure 6-43). You can move this box with the help of your pointing device. This box is known as the panning view box and it helps you to find the center point of the zoomed display you want. When you have found the center, press the pick button to display the zooming view box.

Zooming view box (arrow on the right side)

On pressing the pick button at the center of the panning view box, the X at the center of the view box is replaced by an arrow pointing at the right edge of the box. This zooming view box (Figure 6-44) indicates the ZOOM mode. You can now increase or decrease the area of this box according to the area you want to zoom into. To shrink the box, move the pointer to the left; to increase it, move the pointer to the right. The top, right, and bottom sides of the zooming view box move as you move the pointer, but the left side remains fixed with the zoom base pointing at the midpoint of the left side. You can slide it up or down along the left side. When you have the zooming view box in the desired size for your zoom display, press ENTER to complete the command and zoom into the desired area of the drawing. Before pressing ENTER, if you want to change the position of the zooming view box, click the pick button of your pointing device to redisplay the panning view box. After repositioning, press ENTER.

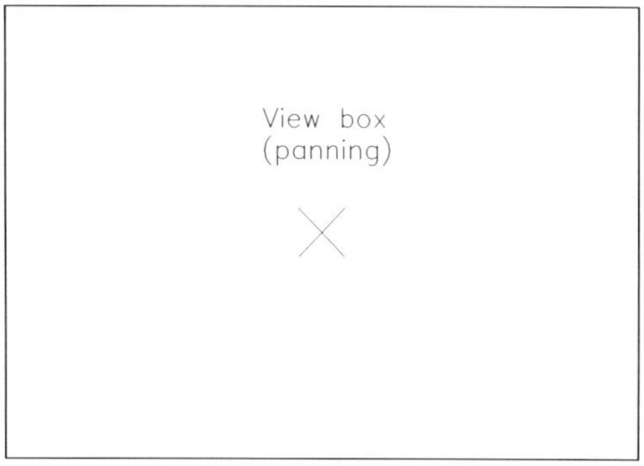

***Figure 6-43** The panning view box*

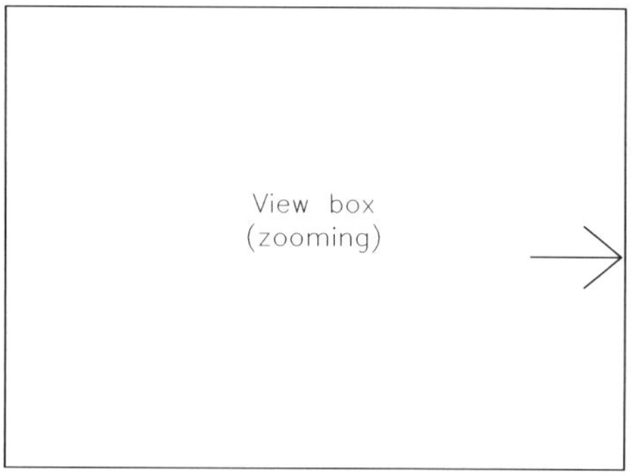

***Figure 6-44** The zooming view box*

Zoom Previous

While working on a complex drawing, you may need to zoom in on a portion of the drawing to edit some minute details. Once the editing is over you may want to return to the previous view. This can be done by choosing the **Zoom Previous** tool from the **Zoom** drop-down in the **Navigation Bar**. Without this tool, it would be very tedious to zoom back to the previous views. AutoCAD LT saves the view specification of the current viewport whenever it is being altered by any of the zoom tools. Up to ten views can be saved for each viewport. To zoom back the last view, choose the **Zoom Previous** tool from the **Navigation Bar**; the view will return to the previous view.

If you erase some objects and then choose the **Zoom Previous** tool, the previous view is restored, but the erased objects are not.

Zoom Window

This is the most commonly used tool of the **Zoom** drop-down. After invoking this tool, you need to specify the area you want to zoom in by specifying two opposite corners of a rectangular window. The center of the specified window becomes the center of the zoomed area. The area inside the window is magnified or reduced in size to fill the display as completely as possible. The points can be specified either by selecting them with the help of the pointing device or by entering their coordinates.

In the **Zoom** drop-down, various options are displayed. Select the **Zoom Window** method from these options. The prompt sequence where you can specify the two corner points of the window is given next.

*Choose the **Zoom Window** tool from the **Navigation Bar***
Specify first corner: *Specify first point.*
Specify opposite corner: *Specify another point.*

This tool can also be invoked by entering **Z** at the command prompt and then entering **W** for window selection. The command sequence in this case is given next.

Zoom [All/Center/Dynamic/Extents/Previous/Scale/Window/Object]<real time>:**W** Enter
Specify first corner: *Specify first point.*
Specify opposite corner: *Specify another point.*

Zoom Scale

The **Zoom Scale** tool of the **Zoom** drop-down is a very versatile option. It can be used in the following ways:

Scale: Zoom Scale: Relative to full view

This option of the **Zoom Scale** tool is used to magnify or reduce the size of a drawing according to a scale factor (Figure 6-45). A scale factor equal to 1 displays an area equal in size to the area defined by the established limits. This may not display the entire drawing if the previous view was not centered on the limits or if you have drawn outside the limits. To get a magnification relative to the full view, you can enter any other number. For example, you can type 4 if you want the displayed image to be enlarged four times. If you want to decrease the magnification relative to the full view, you need to enter a number that is less than 1. In Figure 6-46, the image size is decreased because the scale factor is less than 1. In other words, the image size is half of the full view because the scale factor is 0.5.

The prompt sequence after choosing the **Zoom Scale** tool is given next.

Enter a scale factor (nX or nXP): **0.5** Enter

Scale: Zoom Scale: Relative to current view

The second way to scale is with respect to the current view (Figure 6-47). In this case, instead of entering only a number, enter a number followed by an X. The scale is calculated with reference to the current view. For example, if you enter 0.25X, each object in the drawing will be displayed at one-fourth (1/4) of its current size. The following example shows how to increase the display magnification by a factor of 0.25 relative to its current value (Figure 6-48).

*Choose the **Zoom Scale** tool from the **Navigation Bar***
Enter a scale factor (nX or nXP) : **0.25X** Enter

Figure 6-45 *Drawing before selecting the* ***Zoom Scale*** *tool*

Figure 6-46 *Drawing after selecting the* ***Zoom Scale*** *tool*

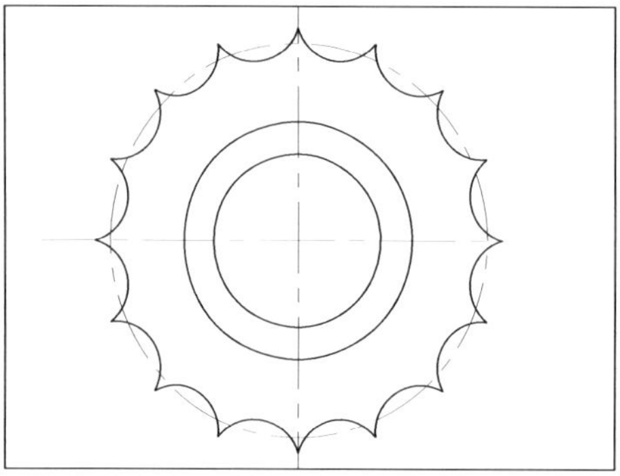

Figure 6-47 *Current view of the drawing*

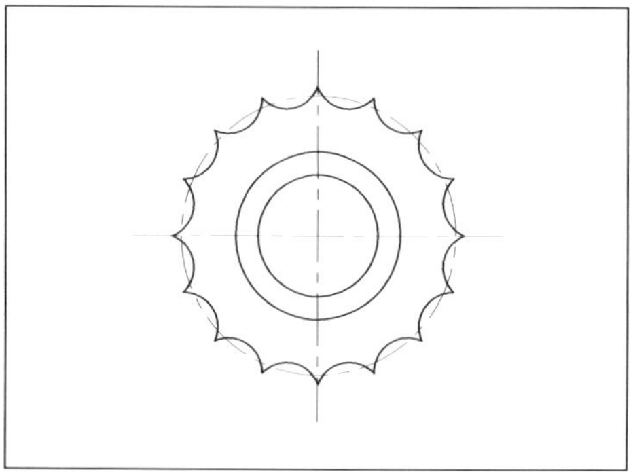

Figure 6-48 *Drawing after applying magnification factor of 0.25X*

Scale: Zoom Scale: Relative to paper space units

The third method of scaling is with respect to paper space. You can use paper space in a variety of ways and for various reasons. For example, you can array and plot various views of your model in the paper space. To scale each view relative to paper space units, you can use the ZOOM XP option. Each view can have an individual scale. The drawing view can be at any scale of your choice in a model space viewport. For example, to display a model space at one-fourth (¼) the size of the paper space units, the prompt sequence is given next.

Choose the ***Zoom Scale*** *tool from the* ***Navigation Bar***
Enter a scale factor (nX or nXP) : **1/4XP** Enter

Note

For better understanding of this topic, refer to "Model Space Viewports, Paper Space Viewports, and Layouts" in Chapter 12.

Zoom Object

This tool is used to select one or more than one objects and display them at the center of the screen in the largest possible size.

Zoom In

This tool is used to zoom into the drawing, which doubles the drawing view size. In this case, the center of the screen is taken as the reference point for enlarging the view of a drawing.

Zoom Out

This tool is used to decrease the size of the drawing view by half. In this case, the center of the screen is taken as the reference point for reducing the view of a drawing.

Exercise 1 — Zoom

Draw the profile shown in Figure 6-49 based on the given dimensions. Use the zoom tools to get a bigger view of the drawing. Do not dimension the drawing.

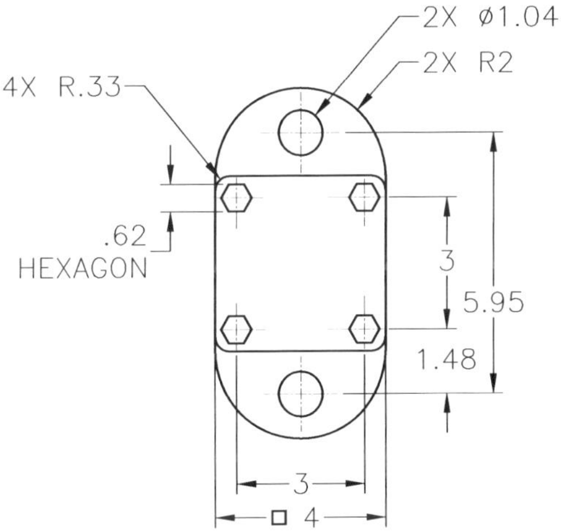

Figure 6-49 *Drawing for Exercise 1*

Panning Drawings

Ribbon: View > Navigate > Pan **Command:** P/PAN
Menu Bar: View > Pan > Realtime

You may want to view or draw on a particular area outside the current display. You can do this by using the **Pan** tool. If done manually, this would be like holding one corner of the drawing and dragging it across the screen. The **Pan** tool allows you to bring into view the portion of the drawing that is outside the current display area. This is done without changing the magnification of the drawing. The effect of this command can be illustrated by imagining that you are looking at a big drawing through a window (display window) that allows you to slide the drawing right, left, up, and down to bring the part you want to view inside this window. You can invoke the **Pan** tool from the shortcut menu also.

Panning in Realtime

You can use the **Realtime Pan** to pan the drawing interactively. To pan a drawing, invoke the tool and then hold the pick button down and move the cursor in any direction. When you select the realtime pan, an image of a hand will be displayed indicating that you are in the **Realtime Pan**. This is the default setting for the **Pan** tool. Choosing the **Pan Realtime** tool in the toolbar or entering **PAN** at the Command prompt automatically invokes the realtime pan. To exit the realtime pan, press ENTER or ESC, or choose **Exit** from the shortcut menu.

The **Pan** tool has various options to pan a drawing in a particular direction. These options can be invoked only from the menu bar, as shown in Figure 6-50. These options are discussed next.

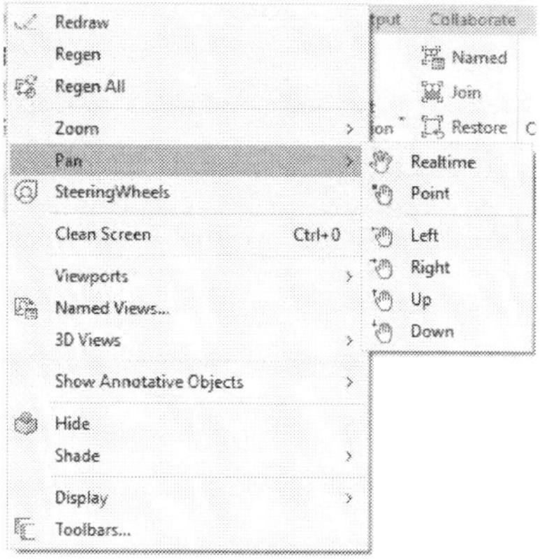

Figure 6-50 *Invoking the* ***Pan*** *options from the* ***View*** *menu*

Point

This option is used to specify the actual displacement. To do this, you need to specify in what direction you want to move the drawing and by what distance. You can give the displacement either by entering the coordinates of the points or by specifying the coordinates by using a pointing device. The coordinates can be entered in two ways. One way is to specify a single coordinate pair. In this case, AutoCAD LT takes it as a relative displacement of the drawing with respect to the screen. For example, in the following case, the **Pan** tool would shift the displayed portion of the drawing 2 units to the right and 2 units up.

Select the ***Point*** *option from the* ***View*** *menu.*
Specify base point or displacement: **2,2** Enter
Specify second point: Enter

In the second case, you can specify two coordinate pairs. AutoCAD LT computes the displacement from the first point to the second. Here, the displacement is calculated between point (3,3) and point (5,5).

Select the ***Point*** *option from the* ***View*** *menu bar.*
Specify base point or displacement: **3,3** Enter *(Or specify a point.)*
Specify second point: **5,5** Enter *(Or specify a point.)*

Left

Moves the drawing to the left so that some of the right portion of the drawing is brought into view.

Right
Moves the drawing to the right so that some of the left portion of the drawing is brought into view.

Up
Moves the drawing up so that some of the bottom portion of the drawing is brought into view.

Down
Moves the drawing down so that some of the top portion of the drawing is brought into view.

> **Tip**
> *You can use the scroll bars to pan the drawing vertically or horizontally. The scroll bars are located at the right side of the drawing area. You can control the display of the scroll bars in the **Display** tab of the **Options** dialog box.*

Creating Views

Ribbon: View > Named Views > View Manager **Command:** VIEW
Menu Bar: View > Named Views

While working on a drawing, you may frequently be working with the **Zoom** and **Pan** tools, and you may need to work on a particular drawing view (some portion of the drawing) more often than others. Instead of wasting time by recalling your zooms and pans and selecting the same area from the screen over and over again, you can store the view under a name and restore it using the name you have given. To do so, choose the **View Manager** button from the **Views** panel; the **View Manager** dialog box will be displayed, as shown in Figure 6-51. This dialog box is used to save the current view with a name so that you can restore (display) it later. It does not save any drawing object data. It stores only the view parameters needed to redisplay that portion of the drawing.

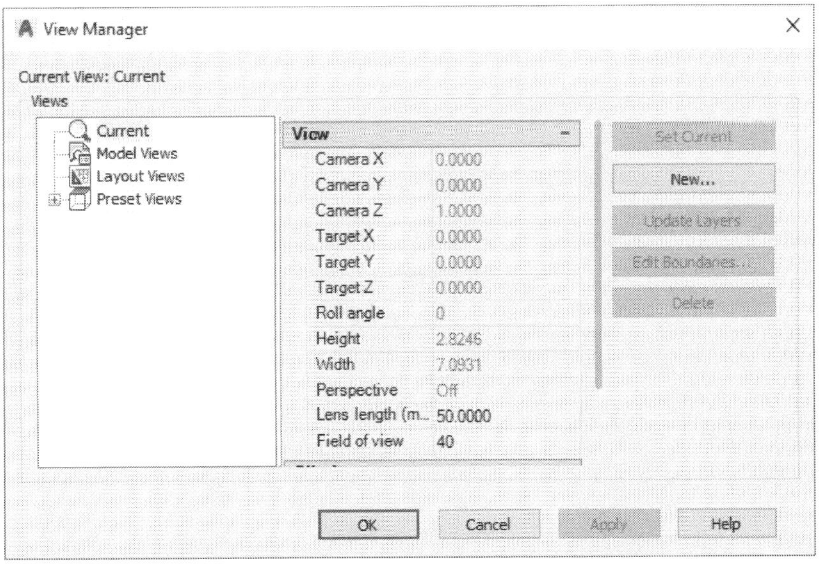

***Figure 6-51** The **View Manager** dialog box*

This dialog box is very useful when you are saving and restoring many views. The **Views** area lists the current view and all the existing named views in the model space and layouts. This area also lists all the preset views such as orthographic and isometric views. As soon as you select a view from the list box, the information about it will be displayed in the **Information** area provided on the right of the list box.

Other options in the **Views** area of the **View Manager** dialog box are discussed next.

Set Current

The **Set Current** button is used to replace the current view by the view you select from the list box in the **Views** area. You can select any predefined view or any preset view to be made current. AutoCAD LT uses the center point and magnification of each saved view and executes a **Zoom Center** with this information when a view is restored.

New

The **New** button is used to create and save a new view by giving it a name. When you choose the **New** button, the **New View** dialog box is displayed, as shown in Figure 6-52. The options in this dialog box are discussed next.

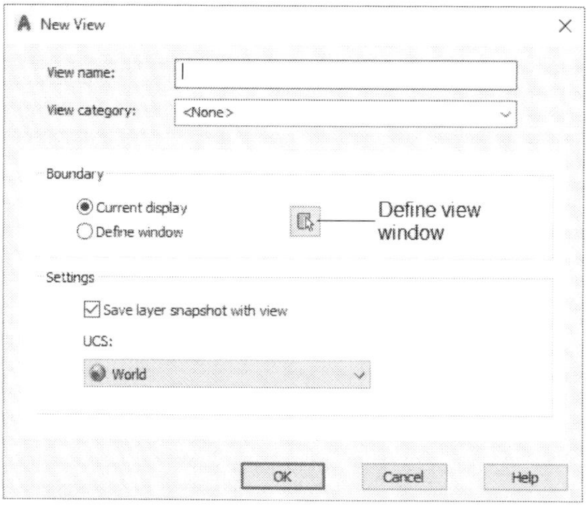

***Figure 6-52** The **New View** dialog box*

View name

You can enter the name for the view in the **View name** edit box.

View category

You can specify the category of the view from the **View category** edit box. The categories include the front view, top view, and so on. If there are some existing categories, you can select them from this drop-down list also.

Boundary Area

This area is used to specify the boundary of the view. To save the current display as the view, select the **Current display** radio button. To define a window that will specify the new view (without first zooming in on that area), select the **Define window** radio button. As soon as you select this radio button, the dialog boxes will be temporarily closed and you will be prompted to define two corners of the window. You can modify the window by choosing the **Define view window** button. You can also enter the *X* and *Y* coordinates in the **Specify first corner** and **Specify other corner** in the command lines.

Settings Area

This area allows you to save the layer visibility and UCS in which you want to visualize the object with the new view. To save the settings of the visibility of the current layers with the view, select the **Save layer snapshot with view** check box. You can select the WCS or the UCS to be saved with the view from the **UCS** drop-down list.

Note

The concept of WCS and UCS will be discussed in later chapters.

Update Layers

The **Update Layers** button is chosen to update the layer information saved with an existing view.

Edit Boundaries

The **Edit Boundaries** button is chosen to edit the boundary that was defined using the **New View Manager** dialog box while creating the new view.

Tip

You can use the shortcut menu to rename or delete any named view in the dialog box. You can also update the layer information or edit the boundary of a view using this shortcut menu.

*The options of the **VIEW** command can be used in the transparent mode by entering **-VIEW** at the Command prompt.*

UNDERSTANDING THE CONCEPT OF SHEET SETS

The sheet sets feature allows you to logically organize a set of multiple drawings as a single unit, called the sheet set. For example, consider a setup in which there are a number of drawings in different folders in the hard drive of a computer. Organizing or archiving these drawings is tedious and time consuming. However, this can be easily and efficiently done by creating sheet sets. In a sheet set, you can import the layouts from an existing drawing or create a new sheet with a new layout and place the views in the new sheet. You can easily plot and publish all the drawings in the sheet set. You can also manage and create sheet sets using the **SHEET SET MANAGER**. To do so, choose the **SHEET SET MANAGER** tool from the **Palettes** panel in the **View** tab or press the CTRL+4 keys.

Creating a Sheet Set

AutoCAD LT allows you to create two different types of sheet sets. The first one is an example sheet set that uses a well organized structure of settings. The second one is used to organize existing drawings. The procedure for creating both these types of sheet sets are discussed next.

Creating an Example Sheet Set

To create an example sheet set, select **New Sheet Set** from the **Open** drop-down list in the **SHEET SET MANAGER** or choose **New > Sheet Set** from the **Application Menu**. You can also enter **NEWSHEETSET** at the Command prompt. When you invoke this command, the **Create Sheet Set** wizard will be displayed with the **Begin** page, as shown in Figure 6-53. In this page, select the **An example sheet set** radio button, if it is not selected by default. Choose the **Next** button; the **Sheet Set Example** page will be displayed, as shown in Figure 6-54.

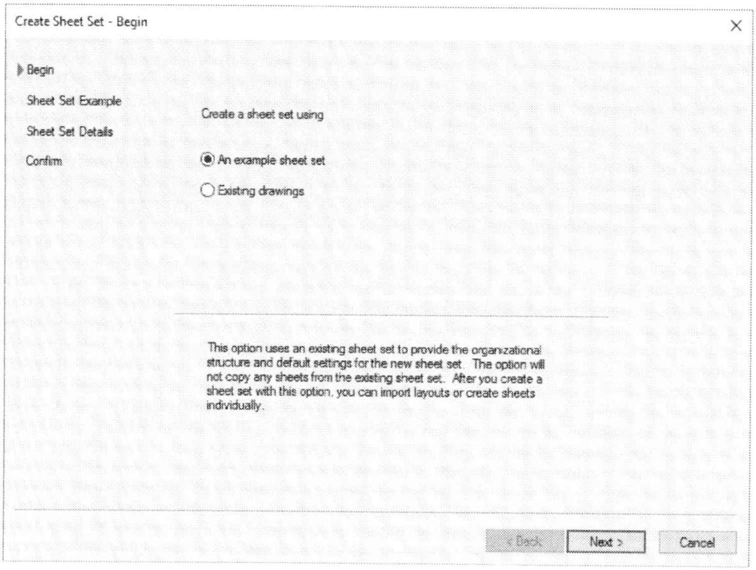

*Figure 6-53 The **Begin** page of the **Create Sheet Set** wizard*

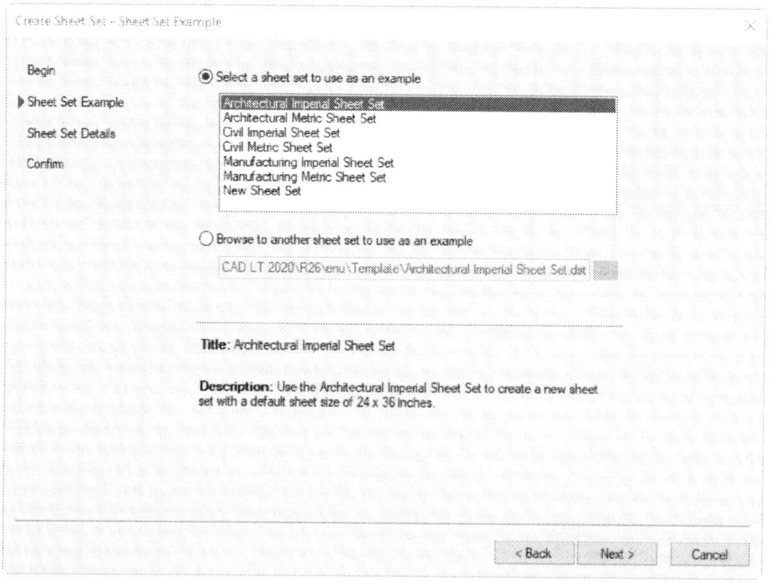

*Figure 6-54 The **Sheet Set Example** page of the **Create Sheet Set** wizard*

By default, the **Select a sheet set to use as an example** radio button is selected in this page. The list box below this radio button displays the list of sheet sets that you can use as an example. Each of these sheet sets has structurally organized settings for the sheets. You can select the required sheet set from this list box. The title and the description related to the selected sheet set are displayed in the lower portion of the dialog box.

You can also select the **Browse to another sheet set to use as an example** radio button to select another sheet set located at a different location. You can enter the location of the sheet set in the edit box below this radio button or choose the **[...]** button to display the **Browse for Sheet Set** dialog box. Using this dialog box, you can locate the sheet set file, which is saved with the *.dst* extension. After selecting the sheet set to use as an example, choose the **Next** button; the **Sheet Set Details** page will be displayed, as shown in Figure 6-55.

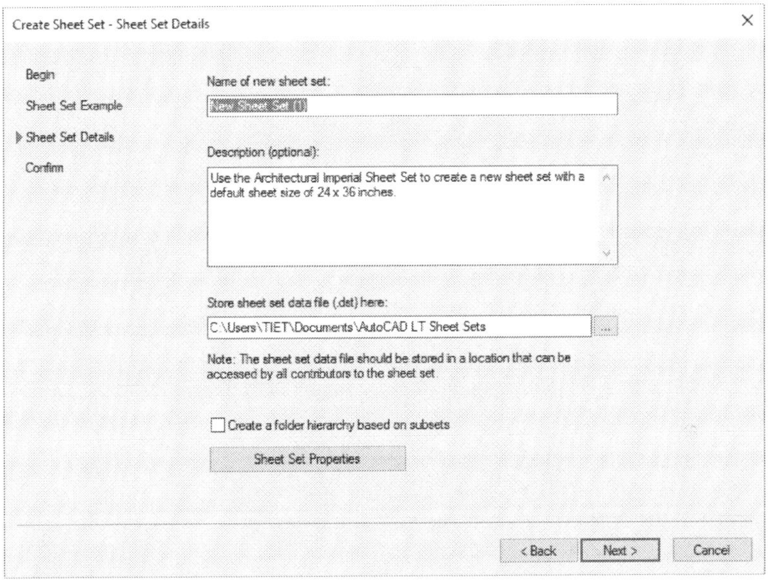

***Figure 6-55** The **Sheet Set Details** page of the **Create Sheet Set** wizard*

Enter the name of the new sheet set in the **Name of new sheet set** edit box. By default, some description is added in the **Description (optional)** area. You can enter additional description in this area. The **Store sheet set data file (.dst) here** edit box displays the default location in which the sheet set data file will be stored. You can modify this location by entering a new location or by selecting the folder using the **Browse for Sheet Set Folder** dialog box which is displayed by choosing the **[...]** button.

You can modify the sheet set properties such as name, storage location, template, description, and so on by choosing the **Sheet Set Properties** button.

Once all the parameters on this page are configured, choose the **Next** button; the **Confirm** page will be displayed, as shown in Figure 6-56. This page shows the detailed structure of the sheet set and also lists its parameters and properties.

After checking all the parameters and properties, choose the **Finish** button; the **SHEET SET MANAGER** will be displayed with the sheet structure in the **Sheets** area and the details of that sheet set in the **Details** area, as shown in Figure 6-57. If the **Details** area is not displayed, right-click in the **SHEET SET MANAGER** and select the **Preview/Details Pane** option from the shortcut menu.

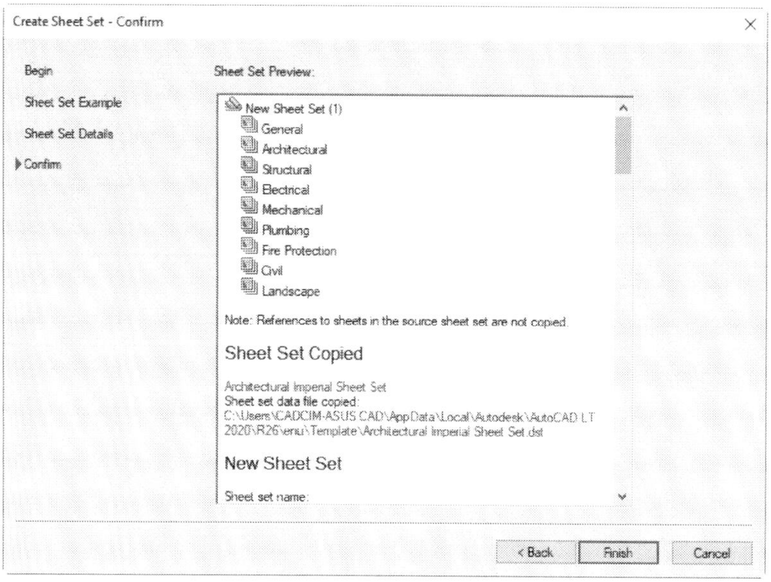

Figure 6-56 *The* ***Confirm*** *page of the* ***Create Sheet Set*** *wizard*

Creating a Sheet Set Using Existing Drawings

As mentioned earlier, this sheet set is used to organize and archive an existing set of drawings. To create this type of sheet set, select the **Existing drawings** radio button from the **Begin** page of the **Create a Sheet Set** wizard and choose **Next**. The **Sheet Set Details** page will be displayed, which is similar to the one shown in Figure 6-54. Enter the name of the sheet set and the description on this page. Note that by default, there will be no description given about the new sheet set. After setting the parameters on this page, choose the **Next** button; the **Choose Layouts** page will be displayed, as shown in Figure 6-58.

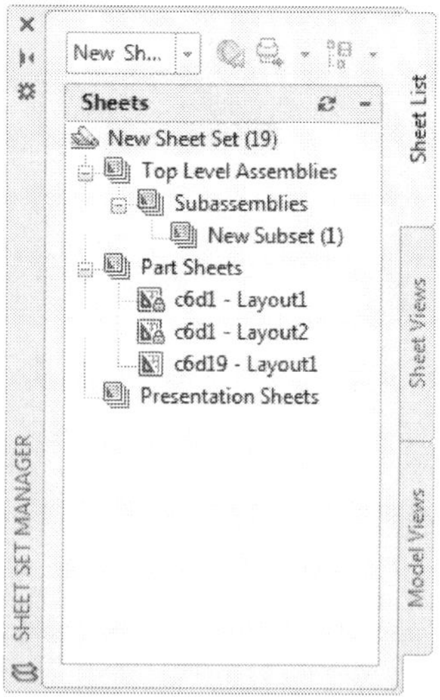

Figure 6-57 *The* ***SHEET SET MANAGER***

Choose the **Browse** button from this page and browse for the folder in which the files to be included in the sheet set are saved. All the drawing files, along with their initialized layouts, are displayed in the list box available below the **Browse** button. You can select as many folders as you want by choosing the **Browse** button.

Tip

You can remove the folders from the list box in the ***Choose Layouts*** *page by selecting them and pressing the DELETE key.*

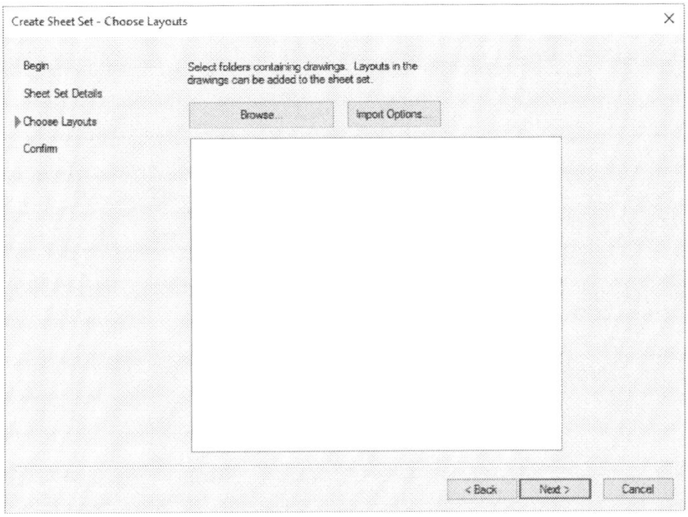

Figure 6-58 *The* ***Choose Layouts*** *page of the* ***Create Sheet Set*** *wizard*

When you select a folder, all the drawings in it and all the initialized layouts in the drawings have a check mark on their left. This suggests that all these drawings and layouts will be included in the sheet set. You can clear the check box of the folder to clear all the check boxes and then select the check boxes of only the required drawings and layouts. You can modify the import options by using the **Import Options** dialog box, which is displayed by choosing the **Import Options** button.

After selecting the layouts to be included, choose the **Next** button to display the **Confirm** page similar to the one shown in Figure 6-56. This page lists all the layouts that will be included in the sheet set. Choose the **Finish** button to complete the process of creating the sheet set.

Adding a Subset to a Sheet Set

For a better and more efficient organization of a sheet set, it is recommended that you add subsets to the sheet set. For example, consider a case where you have created a sheet set called Mechanical Drawings in which you want to store all the mechanical drawings. In this sheet set, you can create subsets such as Bolts, Nuts, Washers, and so on and place the sheets of bolts, nuts, and washers for a more logical organization of the sheet set.

To add a subset to a sheet set, right-click on the sheet set or subset and choose **New Subset** from the shortcut menu. The **Subset Properties** dialog box is displayed, see Figure 6-59.

Enter the name of the subset in the **Subset Name** field. Also, specify the location for saving the DWG file and the template for creating the sheets using this dialog box. If you specify **Yes** in the **Create Folder Hierarchy** field, a new folder will be created under the sheet set. If you specify **Yes** in the **Prompt for template** field, it will prompt you to select the template for the drawings. Choose **OK** after configuring all the parameters; a new subset will be added to the sheet set or the subset that you selected.

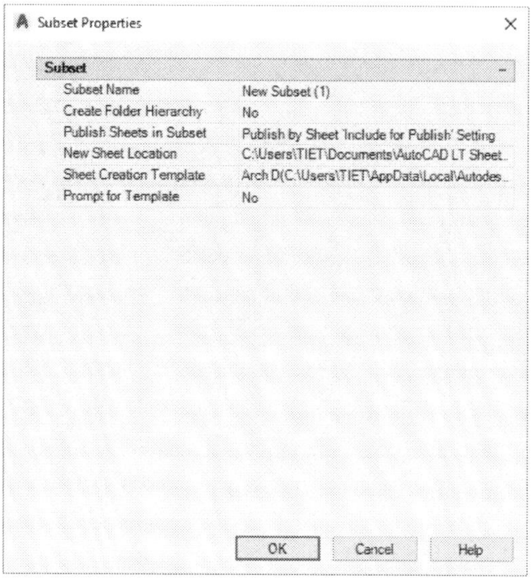

*Figure 6-59 The **Subset Properties** dialog box*

Adding Sheets to a Sheet Set or a Subset

To add a new sheet to a sheet set or a subset, right-click on it in the **SHEET SET MANAGER** window and choose **New Sheet** from the shortcut menu. The **New Sheet** dialog box is displayed. In this dialog box, enter the number and the title of the sheet, along with the file name. You can also set the path of the folder and the sheet template to be used using this dialog box. Choose the **OK** button after configuring all the parameters. A new sheet will be added to the sheet set or the subset that you selected.

Archiving a Sheet Set

AutoCAD LT allows you to archive a sheet set as a zip file, a self-extracting executable file (.exe), or a file folder. All files related to the sheet set are automatically included in the zip file. To archive a sheet set, right-click on its name in the **SHEET SET MANAGER** and choose **Archive** from the shortcut menu. After AutoCAD LT gathers the archive information, the **Archive a Sheet Set** dialog box will be displayed, as shown in Figure 6-60.

Before archiving the sheet set, you can modify the archiving options by using the **Modify Archive Setup** dialog box, as shown in Figure 6-61. This dialog box is displayed when you choose the **Modify Archive Setup** button. Using the **Archive package type** drop-down list, you can specify whether the archived file is a zip file, a self-extracting executable file (*exe*), or a file folder. You can also specify the format in which you want to save the files. You can select the current release format keep existing drawing file formats AutoCAD LT 2018/AutoCAD 2018, AutoCAD LT 2013/AutoCAD 2013, AutoCAD LT 2010/AutoCAD 2010, AutoCAD LT 2007/AutoCAD 2007, AutoCAD LT 2004/AutoCAD 2004, or AutoCAD LT 2000/AutoCAD 2000 formats for archiving the files.

After setting the parameters, choose the **OK** button from the **Archive a Sheet Set** dialog box. The standard save dialog box will be displayed, which can be used to specify the name and the location of the resultant file.

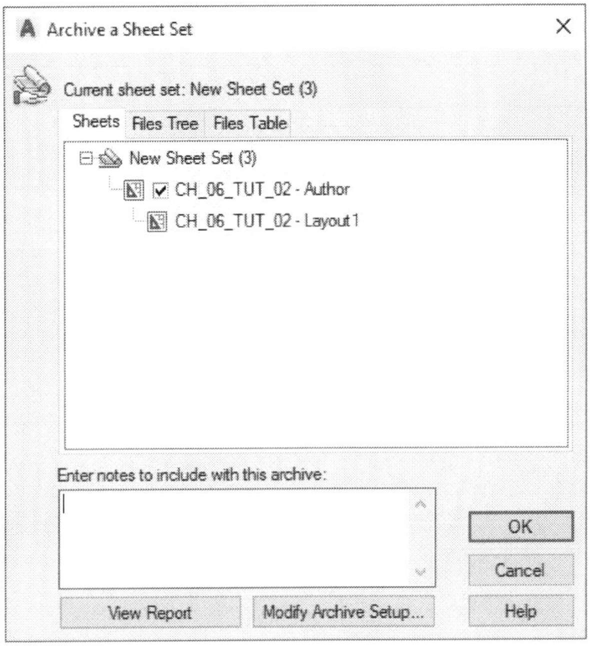

***Figure 6-60** The **Archive a Sheet Set** dialog box*

Resaving All Sheets in a Sheet Set

The **SHEET SET MANAGER** allows you to easily resave all the sheets in a sheet set. To save all the sheets in a sheet set again, right-click on the name of the sheet set in the **SHEET SET MANAGER** and choose **Resave All Sheets** from the shortcut menu, as shown in Figure 6-62. All the sheets in the sheet set will be saved once again.

PLACING VIEWS ON A SHEET OF A SHEET SET

You can place views in the sheets of a sheet set. To place a view on a sheet, open the sheet by double-clicking on it in the **SHEET SET MANAGER**. Next, you need to locate the file from which you want to copy the view. To locate this file, choose the **Model Views** tab of the **SHEET SET MANAGER**. If the location of the file is not already listed in this tab, double-click on **Add New Location** to display the **Browse for Folder** dialog box. Using this dialog box, select the folder in which you have saved the file. All the files of that folder are listed. Click on the plus sign (+) located on the left of the file to display all the views created in that file.

Now, right-click on the view and choose **Place on Sheet** from the shortcut menu, as shown in Figure 6-63; the preview of the view will be attached to the cursor and you will be prompted to specify the insertion point. By default, the view will be placed with 1:1 scale. But, you can change the view scale before placing the view. To change the scale, right-click to display the shortcut menu that has various preset view scales. Choose the desired view scale from this shortcut menu and then place the view. The view will be placed inside the paper space viewport in the layout. Also, the name of the view is displayed below the view in the layout where you placed the view. You can view the list of all the views in the current sheet set by choosing the **Sheet Views** tab.

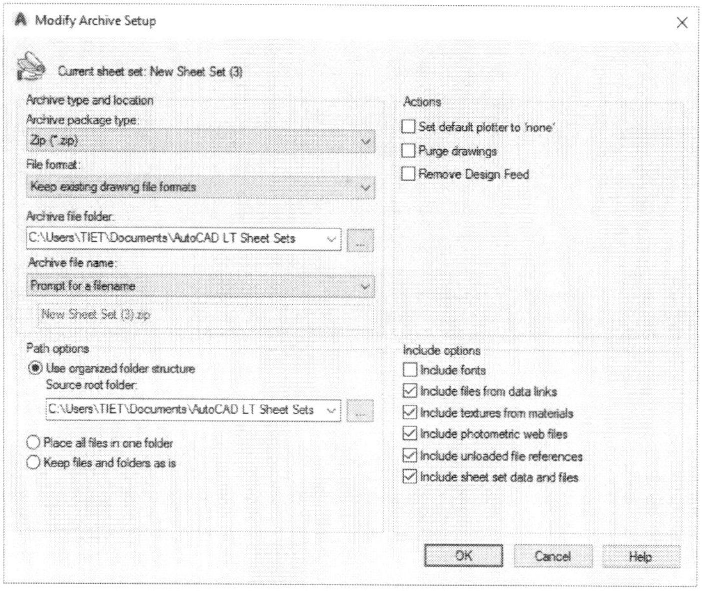

***Figure 6-61** The **Modify Archive Setup** dialog box*

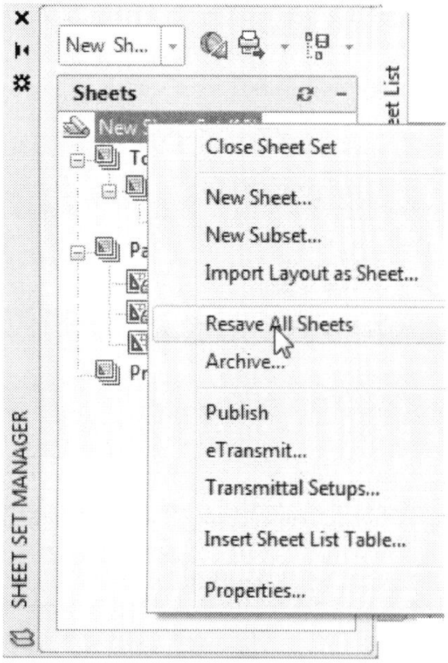

Figure 6-62** Resaving all the sheets in a sheet set using the **SHEET SET MANAGER

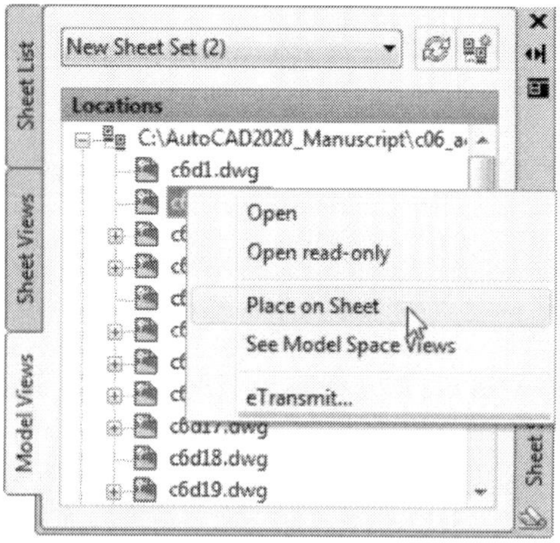

***Figure 6-63** The **Model Views** tab of the **SHEET SET MANAGER** displaying the views in a selected drawing*

Self-Evaluation Test

Answer the following questions and then compare them to those given at the end of this chapter:

1. After selecting a polyline, if you place the cursor on the __________ grip, the **Convert to Arc** option will be displayed in the tooltip.

2. The color of the unselected grips can also be changed by using the __________ system variable.

3. You can access the **Mirror** mode by selecting a grip and then using __________ tool or giving a null response by pressing the SPACEBAR four times.

4. The __________ drop-down list will not be available if you select **Select All** from the **Operator** drop-down list of the **Quick Select** dialog box.

5. The number of grips that will be displayed on an object depends on the object itself. (T/F)

6. You can use the **Options** dialog box to modify grip parameters. (T/F)

7. You need at least one source object while using the **Match Properties** tool. (T/F)

8. You cannot drag and drop entities from the **DesignCenter** window. (T/F)

9. The **Zoom All** tool displays drawing limits or extents, whichever is greater. (T/F)

10. While using the **Zoom Scale** tool with respect to the current view, you need to enter a number followed by **X**. (T/F)

Review Questions

Answer the following questions:

1. Which of these system variables is used to modify the color of a selected grip?

   (a) **GRIPCOLOR** (b) **GRIPHOT**
   (c) **GRIPCOLD** (d) **GRIPBLOCK**

2. Which of these system variables is used to enable the display of grips inside blocks?

   (a) **GRIPCOLOR** (b) **GRIPHOT**
   (c) **GRIPCOLD** (d) **GRIPBLOCK**

3. Which of the following system variables is used to modify the size of grips?

   (a) **GRIPCOLOR** (b) **GRIPSIZE**
   (c) **GRIPCOLD** (d) **GRIPBLOCK**

4. How many views are saved using the **Zoom Previous** tool?

   (a) 6 (b) 8
   (c) 10 (d) 12

5. Which of the following commands recalculates all the objects in a drawing and redraws the current viewport only?

   (a) **REDRAW** (b) **REDRAWALL**
   (c) **REGEN** (d) **REGENALL**

6. You can view the entire drawing (even if it is beyond limits) with the help of the __________ option.

7. The **GRIPSIZE** is defined in pixels, and its value can range from __________ to __________ pixels.

8. The **View Manager** tool does not save any drawing object data. Only the __________ parameters required to redisplay that portion of the drawing are saved.

9. The __________ mode is used to move the selected objects to a new location.

10. The __________ mode allows you to scale objects with respect to the base point without changing their orientation.

11. The **Mirror** mode allows you to mirror objects across the __________ without changing the size of the objects.

12. If you select a grip of an object, the grip becomes a hot grip. (T/F)

13. The **Rotate** mode is used to rotate objects around the base point without affecting their size. (T/F)

14. If you have already added a hyperlink to an object, you can also use the grips to open a file associated with it. (T/F)

15. Using the Zoom tools, the actual size of an object changes. (T/F)

16. The **REDRAW** command can be used as a transparent command. (T/F)

Exercise 2

1. Use the **Line** tool to draw the shape shown in Figure 6-64(a).

2. Use grips (**Stretch** mode) to get the shape shown in Figure 6-64(b).

3. Use the **Rotate** and **Stretch** modes to get the copies shown in Figure 6-64(c).

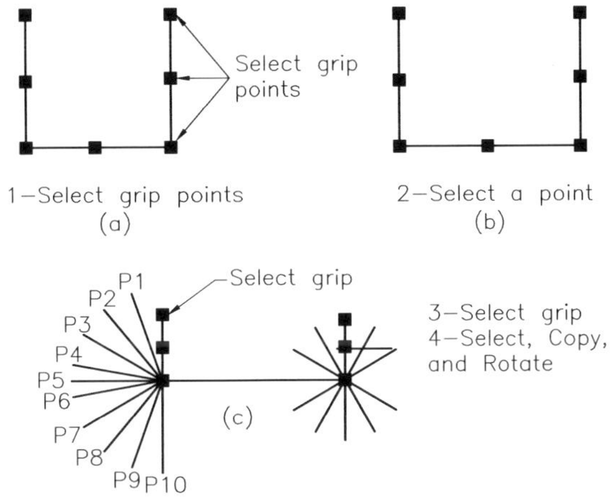

Figure 6-64 Drawing for Exercise 2

Exercise 3

Use the drawing and editing tools to create the sketch shown in Figure 6-65. Use the display tools to facilitate the process.

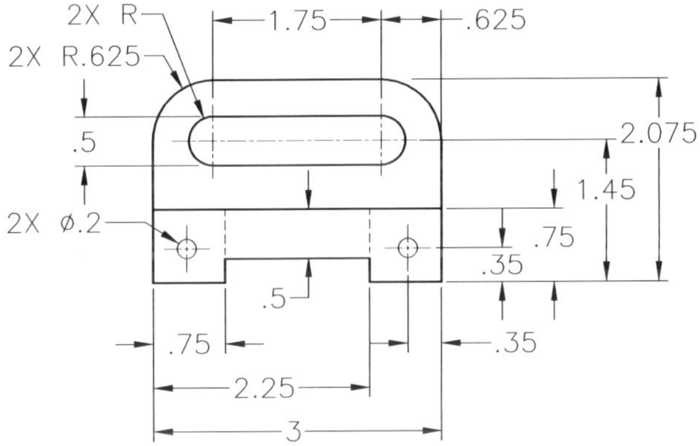

Figure 6-65 Drawing for Exercise 3

Exercise 4

Use the drawing and editing tools to create the sketch shown in Figure 6-66. Use the display tools to facilitate the process.

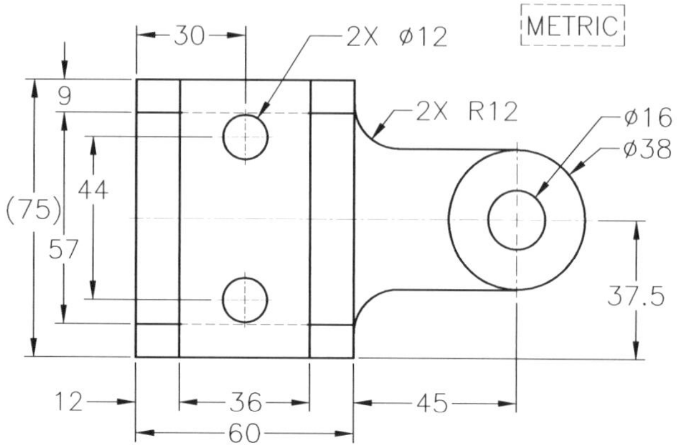

Figure 6-66 *Drawing for Exercise 4*

Problem-Solving Exercise 1

Draw the sketch shown in Figure 6-67 using the draw and edit tools. Use the **Mirror** tool to mirror the shape 9 units across the *Y* axis so that the distance between the two center points is 9 units. Mirror the shape across the *X* axis and then reduce the mirrored shape by 75 percent. Join the two ends to complete the shape of the open end spanner. Save the file. Assume the missing dimensions. Note that this is not a standard size spanner.

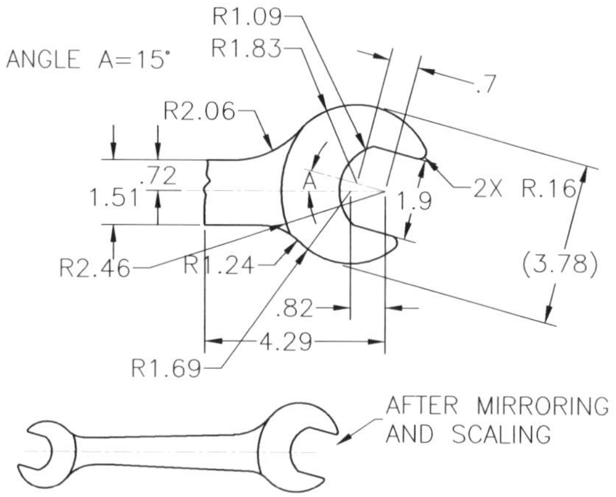

Figure 6-67 *Drawing for Problem-Solving Exercise 1*

Problem-Solving Exercise 2

Use the drawing and editing tools to create the drawing shown in Figure 6-68. Use the display tools to facilitate the process.

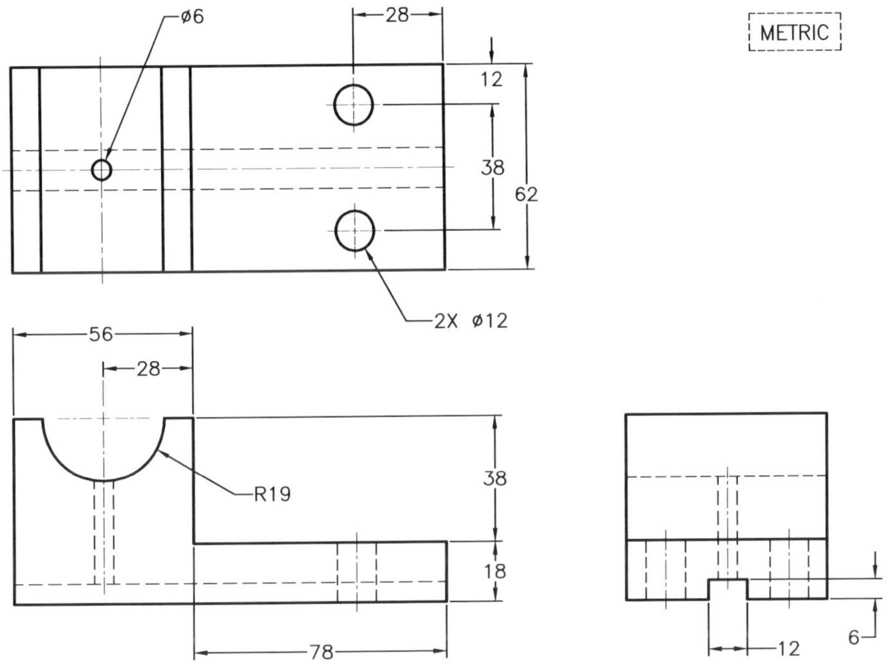

Figure 6-68 Drawing for Problem-Solving Exercise 2

Problem-Solving Exercise 3

Use the drawing and editing tools to create the drawing shown in Figure 6-69. Use the display tools to facilitate the process.

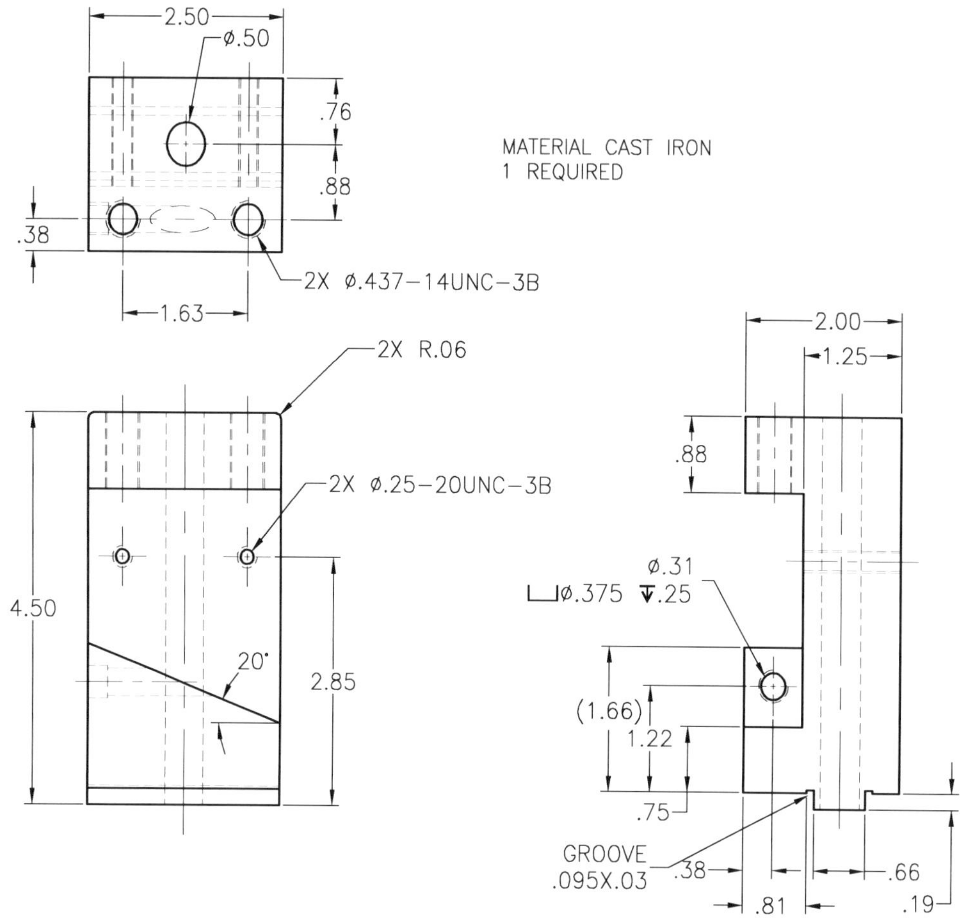

Figure 6-69 *Drawing for Problem-Solving Exercise 3*

Problem-Solving Exercise 4

Draw the reception desk shown in Figure 6-70. To get the dimensions of the chairs, refer to Problem-Solving Exercise 3 of Chapter 5.

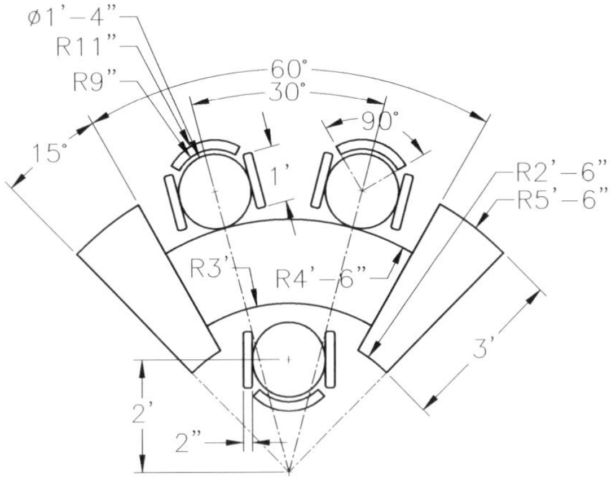

Figure 6-70 Drawing of reception desk for Problem-Solving Exercise 4

Problem-Solving Exercise 5

Draw the views of Vice Body shown in Figure 6-71. The dimensions given in the figure are only for your reference.

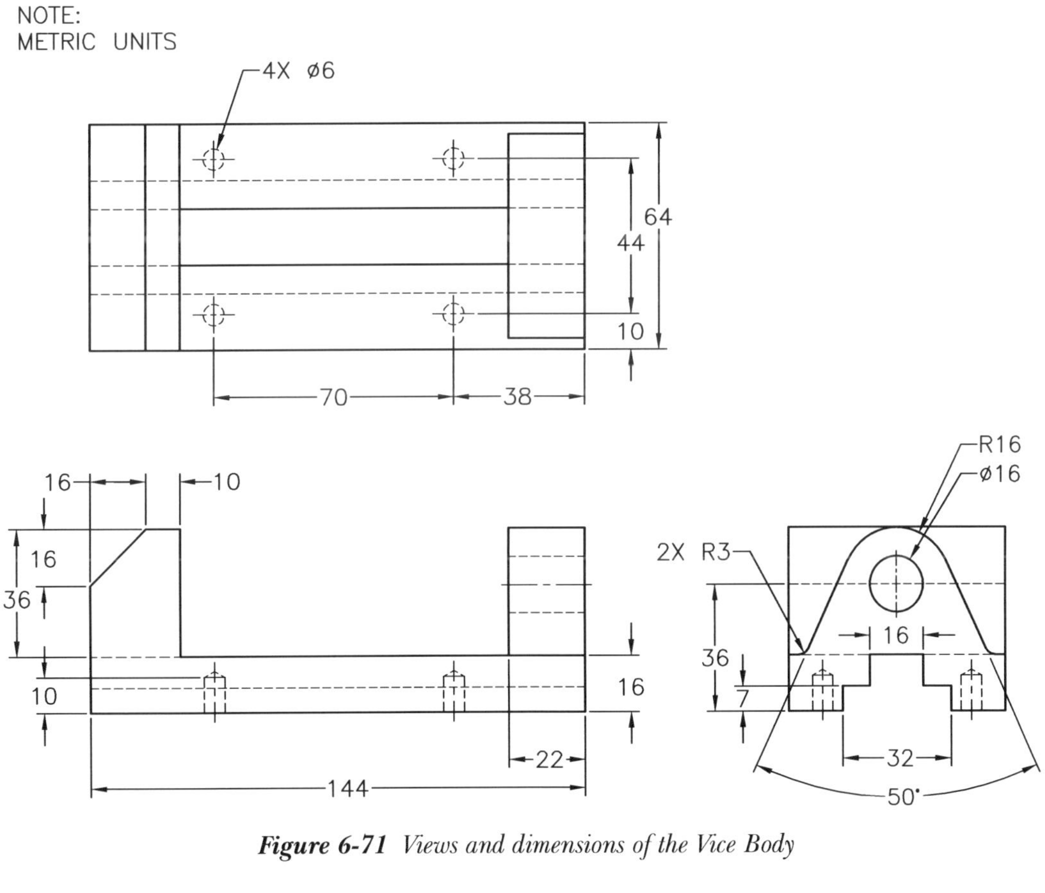

Figure 6-71 Views and dimensions of the Vice Body

Answers to Self-Evaluation Test

1. middle, **2**. **GRIPCOLOR**, **3**. **MIRROR**, **MI**, **4**. **Value**, **5**. T, **6**. T, **7**. T, **8**. F, **9**. T, **10**. T

Chapter 7

Creating Texts and Tables

Learning Objectives

After completing this chapter, you will be able to:

- *Understand the use of annotative objects*
- *Write text using the Single Line and Multi Line Text tools*
- *Edit text using the Edit tool*
- *Create text styles*
- *Draw tables using the Table tool*
- *Create and modify a table style*
- *Use the PROPERTIES palette to change properties*

Key Terms

- *Annotative Objects*
- *Annotation Scale*
- *Text*
- *DDEDIT*
- *Table*
- *Data Link*
- *Text Style*
- *Annotative Text*
- *TEXTALIGN*
- *Sheet Set Table*

ANNOTATIVE OBJECTS

AutoCAD LT provides improved functionality of the drawing annotation that enables you to annotate your drawing easily and efficiently. Annotations are the notes and objects that are inserted into a drawing to add important information to it. The list of annotative objects is given next.

Text	Mtext	Dimensions	Leaders	Blocks
Multileaders	Hatches	Tolerances	Attributes	

All the above mentioned annotative objects have an annotative property. This annotative property allows you to automate the process of display of the drawings at the desired scale on the paper.

ANNOTATION SCALE

Annotation Scale is a feature that allows you to control the size of the annotative objects in model space.

Generally, the formula used to calculate the height of the annotative objects in model space is:

Height of the annotative object in model space = Annotation scale X Height of the annotative object in paper space.

For example, if you need to create an annotative object with a height of 1/4" on paper, and assume that annotation scale is set to 1/2" = 1' (implies 1" = 2', or 1" = 24"),then, the height of the object in model space will be 1/4" x 24"= 6" and the object will be displayed in model space with its height equal to 6".

Note

The above calculation is performed automatically by AutoCAD LT and has been explained to make the concept clear.

Assigning Annotative Property and Annotation Scales

You can assign the annotative properties to objects in many ways. The objects (Mtext, Hatches, Blocks, and Attributes) that are drawn with the help of dialog boxes have the **Annotative** check boxes in their respective dialog box. You can also create the annotative styles, and all the objects created using that style will have the annotative property automatically. The objects that are created using the Command prompt can be converted into annotative after creating them through the **PROPERTIES** palette. You can also override the annotative property of an individual object through the **PROPERTIES** palette, see Figure 7-1.

All annotative objects are indicated with an annotative symbol attached to the cursor. When you move the cursor over an annotative object, the annotative symbol starts rolling on, see Figure 7-2. All annotative styles are indicated with the same annotative symbol displayed next to the cursor. To assign the annotation scale while working in model space, choose the **Annotation Scale** button displayed on the right of the Status Bar; a flyout will be displayed. Select the desired annotation scale from the flyout. This flyout displays 33 commonly used imperial and metric scales, and this list can also be customized. Among these scales, 1:1 annotation scale is selected by default. To change the default annotation scale, enter **CANNOSCALE** in the Command prompt and specify the new annotation scale. To assign the annotation scale while working in viewport, select a viewport first and then assign the annotation scale.

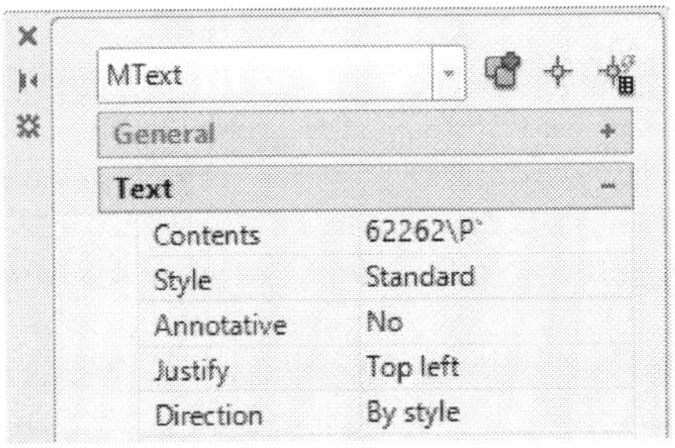

***Figure 7-1** Assigning annotative property through the **PROPERTIES** palette*

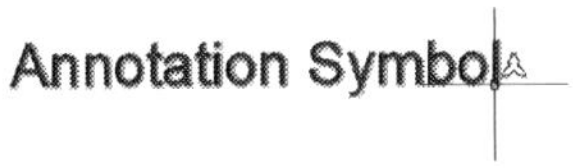

***Figure 7-2** Annotation symbol attached to the cursor*

Customizing Annotation Scale

In any drawing, only few annotation scales are used. Therefore, you can delete the unwanted scales from the list according to your requirement. To customize the **Annotation Scale** list, choose the **Custom** option from the flyout that is displayed when you click on the **Annotation Scale** button in the **Status Bar**; the **Edit Drawing Scales** dialog box will be displayed, as shown in Figure 7-3. With this dialog box, you can add, modify, delete, change the sequence of scales displayed, and restore the default list of scales.

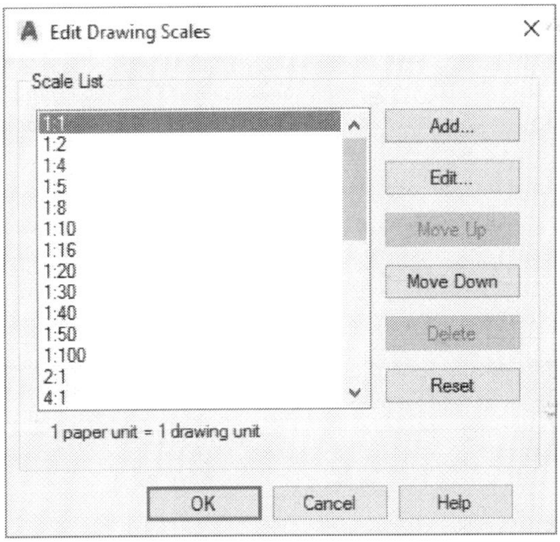

***Figure 7-3** The **Edit Drawing Scales** dialog box*

Note

You cannot delete the annotation scales that have been used to draw any annotative object in the drawing.

MULTIPLE ANNOTATION SCALES

Ribbon: Annotate > Annotation Scaling > Add/Delete Scales **Command:** OBJECTSCALE
Menu Bar: Modify > Annotative Object Scale > Add/Delete Scales

You can assign multiple annotation scales to an annotative object. This enables you to display or print the same annotative object in different sizes. The annotative object is displayed or printed based on the current annotation scale. Assigning multiple annotation scales to annotative objects saves a considerable amount of time that is lost while creating a set of objects with different scales in different layers. You can add multiple annotation scales to objects manually and automatically. Both these methods are discussed next.

Assigning Multiple Annotation Scales Manually

To assign multiple annotation scales manually to an annotative object, invoke the **Add/Delete Scales** tool; you will be prompted to select an annotative object to which you want to add another annotation scale. Select one or more annotation objects and then press ENTER; the **Annotation Object Scale** dialog box will be displayed, see Figure 7-4. Alternatively, select an annotative object and right-click to display the shortcut menu. Now, choose **Annotative Object Scale > Add / Delete Scales** from the shortcut menu to display the **Annotation Object Scale** dialog box. Using this dialog box, you can add annotation scale to an annotative object or delete the annotation scale assigned to the selected annotative object. However, you cannot delete the current annotation scale by using this dialog box. When you place the cursor over an annotative object, all the annotative objects with multiple annotation scales will be indicated with a double-annotation symbol attached to the cursor, see Figure 7-5. You can also control the assigning of multiple annotation scales to annotative objects by using the **Annotation Scaling** panel in the **Annotate** tab, see Figure 7-6.

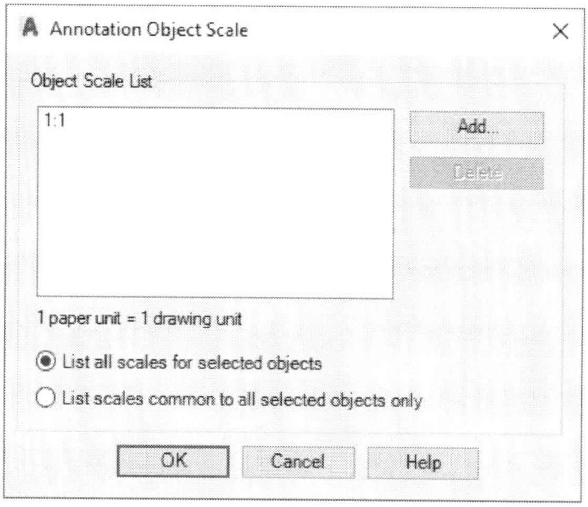

***Figure 7-4** The **Annotation Object Scale** dialog box*

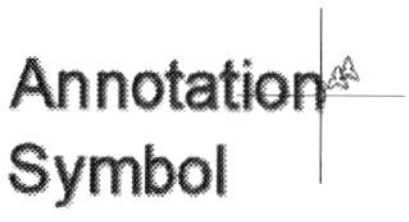

***Figure 7-5** Multiple annotation scale symbol attached to the cursor*

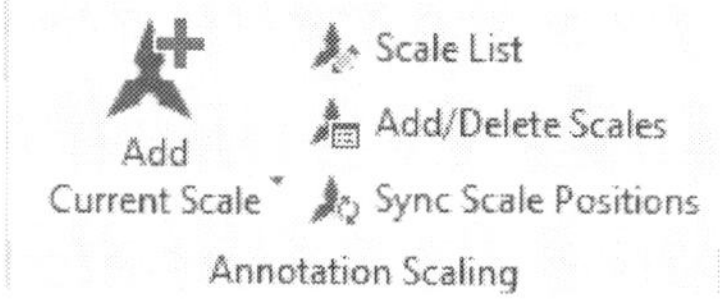

Figure 7-6** The **Annotation Scaling** panel in the **Ribbon

Assigning Multiple Annotation Scales Automatically

The annotation scales that have been set as current can be assigned to annotative objects without invoking the **Annotation Object Scale** dialog box. To do so, choose the **Add scales to annotative objects when the annotation scale changes** button located at the bottom of the Status Bar to activate it. Now onward, all annotation scales that are set as current will be automatically added to the annotation objects.

By default, the annotation scale will be applied to all objects irrespective of their layers. However, you can control the assignment of annotation scale depending upon the layer of the object by using the **ANNOAUTOSCALE** system variable. This system variable can have values ranging from -4 to 4 except 0. The description of these values is given next.

1 = This value assigns the current annotation scale to all annotative objects, except the annotative objects that are in the locked, turned off, frozen, and viewport frozen layers.
2 = This value assigns the current annotation scale to all annotative objects, except the annotative objects that are in the turned off, frozen, and viewport frozen layers.
3 = This value assigns the current annotation scale to all annotative objects, except the ones that are in the locked layers.
4 = This value assigns the current annotation scale to all objects.
-1 = On assigning this value, the **ANNOAUTOSCALE** gets turned off, but when turned on again, it regains the value 1.
-2 = On assigning this value, the **ANNOAUTOSCALE** gets turned off, but when turned on again, it regains the value 2.
-3 = On assigning this value, the **ANNOAUTOSCALE** gets turned off, but when turned on again, it regains the value 3.
-4 = On assigning this value, the **ANNOAUTOSCALE** gets turned off, but when turned on again, it regains the value 4.

CONTROLLING THE DISPLAY OF ANNOTATIVE OBJECTS

After assigning annotation scale to objects, the paper height display scale (in case of plotting) or the viewport scale (in case of viewports) is automatically applied to annotative objects and they are displayed accordingly in the model space or viewport. The annotative objects that do not support the current annotation scale will not be scaled and will be displayed according to the previous annotation scale applied to them.

You can control the display of annotative objects by using the **Annotation Visibility** button in the Status Bar. If this button is turned on, all annotative objects will be displayed in the model space or viewport regardless of the current annotation scale. If this button is turned off, only the annotative objects that have annotation scale equal to that of the current annotation scale will be displayed. Note that the **Annotation Visibility** buttons in the model and layout tabs are independent of each other.

When you select an annotative object, you can observe that the selected annotative object is displayed in all annotative scales assigned to it. The annotation scale that is equal to the current scale is displayed in dark dashed lines, whereas the other scales of the object are displayed in faded dashed lines. You can position the annotation object of different scales at different locations with the help of grips. However, if you need to synchronize the start point of annotative objects of different scale factors with current annotative objects, select the annotative object and then right-click in the drawing area; a shortcut menu will be displayed. Choose **Annotative Object Scale > Synchronize Multiple-scale Positions** from the shortcut menu; the start point of annotative objects will be synchronized. Alternatively, you can also use the **ANNORESET** command to synchronize the start point.

SELECTIONANNODISPLAY system variable is used to control the display of the supported scale representations. If you assign 0 to the system variable, it will stop displaying all the supported scale representations selected; only the representations with the current annotation scale will be displayed. If you assign 1 to this system variable, it will display all the supported scale representations.

Note

*Whenever you create a drawing that involves annotative objects in it, use the **Drafting & Annotation** workspace. This workspace displays the **Ribbon** with drafting and annotation panels visible by default and hides many of the tools. This also makes the drawing and annotating work much more easy. For all examples and exercises given onward and involving annotative objects, you can use this workspace.*

CREATING TEXT

In manual drafting, lettering is accomplished by hand using a lettering device, pen, or pencil. This is a very time-consuming and tedious job. Computer-aided drafting has made this process extremely easy. Engineering drawings invoke certain standards to be followed in connection with the placement of a text in a drawing. In this section, you will learn how a text can be added in a drawing by using the **Single Line** and **Multiline Text** tools.

Writing Single Line Text

Ribbon: Home > Annotation > Text drop-down > Single Line Or
Annotate > Text > Text drop-down > Single Line **Toolbar:** Text > Single Line Text
Menu Bar: Draw > Text > Single Line Text **Command:** TEXT or DTEXT or DT

The **Single Line** tool is used to write text on a drawing. While writing, you can delete the typed text by using the BACKSPACE key. On invoking the **Single Line** tool, you will be prompted to specify the start point. The default and the most commonly used option in the **Single Line** tool is the **Start Point** option. By specifying a start point, the text is left-justified along its baseline. Baseline refers to the line along which their bases lies. After specifying the start point, you need to set the height and the rotation angle of the text.

The **Specify height** prompt determines the distance by which the text extends above the baseline, measured by the capital letters. This distance is specified in drawing units. You can specify the text height by specifying two points or by entering a value. In the case of a null response, the default height, that is, the height used for the previous text drawn in the same style, will be used.

The **Specify rotation angle of text** prompt determines the angle at which the text line will be drawn. The default value of the rotation angle is 0-degree (along east); and in this case, the text is drawn horizontally from the specified start point. The rotation angle is measured in counterclockwise direction. The last angle specified becomes the current rotation angle, and if you give a null response, the last angle specified will be used as default rotation angle. You can also specify the rotation angle by specifying two points. The text will be drawn upside down if a point is specified at a location to the left of the start point.

You can now enter the text in the **Text Editor**. The characters will be displayed as you type them. After entering the text, click outside the **Text Editor**. The prompt sequence displayed on choosing this tool is given next.

Specify start point of text or [Justify/Style]: *Specify the start point.*
Specify height <0.2000>: **0.15** Enter
Specify rotation angle of text <0>: Enter; *the textbox will be displayed. Start typing in it.*

After completing a line, press ENTER; the cursor will automatically be placed at the start of the next line and you can enter the next line of the text. However, if you place the cursor at a new location, a new textbox will be displayed, and you can start typing text at this location with a new start point and the same text parameters. You can enter multiple lines of text at any desired location in the drawing area on invoking the **Single Line** tool once. By pressing BACKSPACE, you can delete one character to the left of the current position of the cursor box. Even if you have entered several lines of text, you can use BACKSPACE to delete the text, until you reach the start point of the first line. To exit the tool, press the ESC key or click outside the text box.

This tool can be used with most of the text alignment modes, although it is most useful in the case of left-justified texts. In the case of aligned texts, this tool is used to assign a height appropriate for the width of the first line to every line of the text. Even if you select the **Justify** option, the text is first left-aligned at the selected point.

Justify Option

AutoCAD LT offers various options to align text. Alignment refers to the layout of a text. The main text alignment modes are **left**, **center**, and **right**. You can align a text by using a combination of modes, for example, top/middle/bottom and left/center/right (Figure 7-7). **Top** refers to a line along which lie the top points of the capital letters. Letters with descenders (such as p, g, and y) dip below the baseline to the bottom. When the **Justify** option is invoked, the user can place the text in one of the fifteen alignment types by selecting the desired alignment option using the Command prompt or the selection preview (Figure 7-8). Note that the selection preview will only be displayed if the **Enable Pointer input** check box is selected in the **Drafting Setting** dialog box. The orientation of the text style determines the command interaction for Text Justify. (Text styles and fonts are discussed later in this chapter). For now, assume that the text style orientation is horizontal.

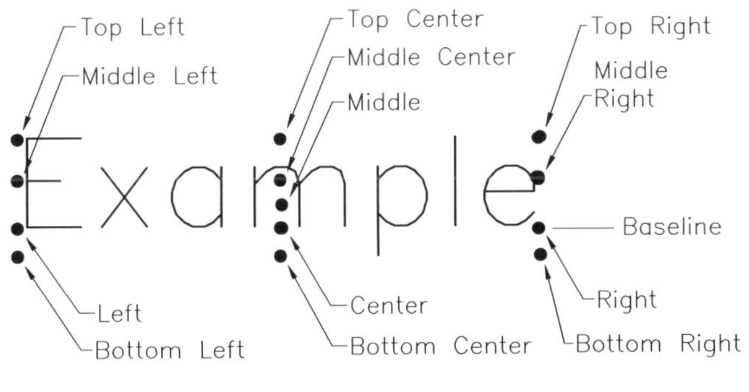

Figure 7-7 Text alignment positions

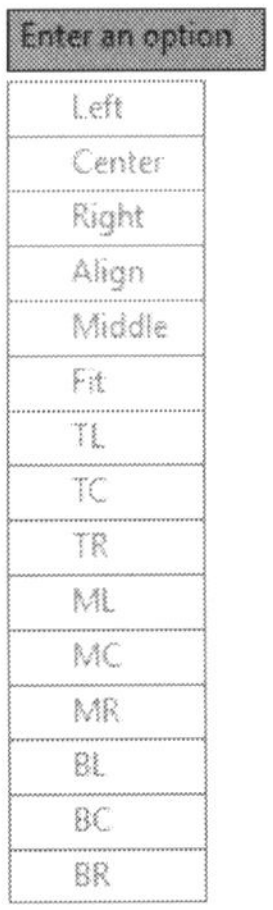

*Figure 7-8 Selection preview for the **Justify** option*

The prompt sequence that will follow when you choose the **Single Line** tool to use this option is given next.

Specify start point of text or [Justify/Style]: **J** Enter
Enter an option [Left/Center/Right/Align/Middle/Fit/TL/TC/TR/ML/MC/MR/BL/BC/BR]: *Select any of these options.*

If the text style is vertically oriented (refer to the "Creating Text Styles" section later in this chapter), only four alignment options are available. The prompt sequence is given next.

Specify start point of text or [Justify/Style]: **J** Enter
Enter an option [Align/Center/Middle/Right]: *You can select the desired alignment option.*

If you know what justification you want, you can enter it directly at the **Specify start point of text or [Justify/Style]** prompt instead of first entering **J** to display the justification prompt. If you need to specify a style as well as a justification, you must specify the style first. The various alignment options are as follows:

Left Option. This option is used to specify the start point as lower left corner of the text, that means, the text is **Left-justified**. The prompt sequence that will follow when you choose this button is given next.

Specify start point of text or [Justify/Style]: **J** Enter
Enter an option [Left/Center/Right/Align/Middle/Fit/TL/TC/TR/ML/MC/MR/BL/BC/BR]: **L** Enter
Specify first endpoint of text baseline: *Specify a point.*
Specify second endpoint of text baseline: *Specify a point.*

Align Option. In this option, the text string is written between two points (Figure 7-9). You must specify the two points that act as the endpoints of the baseline. The two points may be specified horizontally or at an angle. AutoCAD LT adjusts the text width (compresses or expands) so that it fits between the two points. The text height is also changed, depending on the distance between points and the number of letters.

Specify start point of text or [Justify/Style]: **J** Enter
Enter an option [Left/Center/Right/Align/Middle/Fit/TL/TC/TR/ML/MC/MR/BL/BC/BR]: **A** Enter
Specify first endpoint of text baseline: *Specify a point.*
Specify second endpoint of text baseline: *Specify a point.*

Fit Option. This option is very similar to the previous one. The only difference is that in this case, you select the text height, and it does not vary according to the distance between the two points. AutoCAD LT adjusts the letter width to fit the text between the two given points, but the height remains constant (Figure 7-9). The **Fit** option is not accessible for vertically oriented text styles. If you try the **Fit** option on the vertical text style, you will notice that the text string does not appear in the prompt. The prompt sequence is given next.

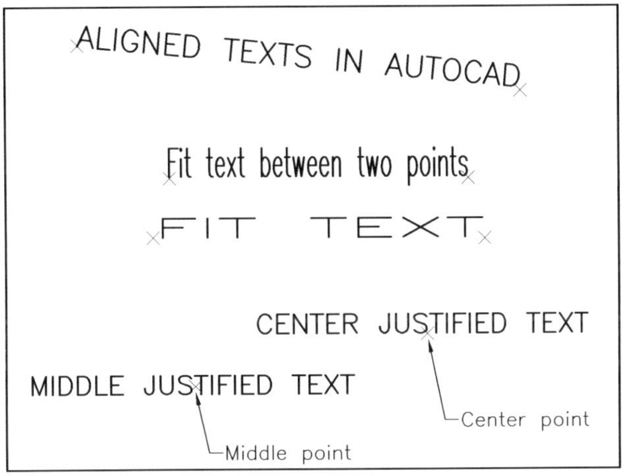

***Figure 7-9** Writing the text using the **Align**, **Fit**, **Center**, and **Middle** options*

Enter an option [Left/Center/Right/Align/Middle/Fit/TL/TC/TR/ML/MC/MR/BL/BC/BR]: **F** Enter
Specify first endpoint of text baseline: *Specify a point.*
Specify second endpoint of text baseline: *Specify a point.*
Specify height<current>: *Enter the height.*

Note
*You do not need to select the **Justify** option (J) for selecting the text justification. You can enter the text justification by directly entering justification when AutoCAD LT prompts "Specify start point of text or [Justify/Style]:"*

Center Option. You can use this option to select the midpoint of the baseline for the text. This option can be invoked by entering **Justify** and then **Center** or **C**. After you select or specify the center point, you must enter the letter height and the rotation angle (Figure 7-9).

Specify start point of text or [Justify/Style]: **C** Enter
Specify center point of text: *Specify a point.*
Specify height<current>: **0.15** Enter
Specify rotation angle of text<0>: Enter

Middle Option. Using this option, you can center text not only horizontally, as with the previous option, but also vertically. In other words, you can specify the middle point of the text string (Figure 7-9). You can alter the text height and the angle of rotation to meet your requirement. The prompt sequence that follows is given next.

Specify start point of text or [Justify/Style]: **M** Enter
Specify middle point of text: *Specify a point.*
Specify height<current>: **0.15** Enter
Specify rotation angle of text<0>: Enter

Right Option. This option is similar to the default left-justified start point option. The only difference is that the text string is aligned to the lower right corner (the endpoint you specify), that is, the text is **Right-justified** (Figure 7-10). The prompt sequence that will follow when you choose this button is given next.

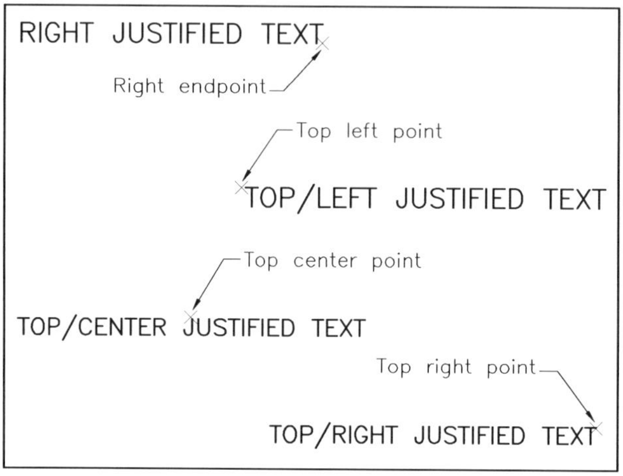

***Figure 7-10** Writing the text using the **Right**, **Top-Left**, **Top-Center**, and **Top-Right** options*

Specify start point of text or [Justify/Style]: **R** Enter
Specify right endpoint of text baseline: *Specify a point.*
Specify height<current>: **0.15** Enter
Specify rotation angle of text<0>: Enter

TL Option. In this option, the text string is justified from top left (Figure 7-10). The prompt sequence is given next.

Specify start point of text or [Justify/Style]: **TL** Enter
Specify top-left point of text: *Specify a point.*
Specify height<current>: **0.15** Enter
Specify rotation angle of text <0>: Enter

Note
The rest of the text alignment options are similar to those already discussed and you can try them on your own. The prompt sequence is almost the same as those given for the previous examples.

Style Option

With this option, you can specify another existing text style. Different text styles can have different text fonts, heights, oblique angles, and other features. This option can be invoked by entering **TEXT** and then **S** at the next prompt. The prompt sequence that will follow when you choose the **Single Line Text** tool for using this option is given next.

Specify start point of text or [Justify/Style]: **S** [Enter]
Enter style name or [?] <Standard>: *Specify the desired style or enter* **?** *to list all styles.*

If you want to work in the previous text style, just press ENTER at the last prompt. If you want to activate another text style, enter the name of the style at the last prompt. You can also choose from a list of available text styles, which can be displayed by entering ?. After you enter ?, the next prompt is given next.

Enter text style(s) to list <*>: *Specify the text styles to list or enter * to list all styles.*

Press ENTER to display the available text style names and the details of the current styles and commands in the **AutoCAD LT Text Window**.

Note
With the help of the ***Style*** *option of the* ***Text*** *tool, you can select a text style from the existing list. If you want to create a new style, use the* ***STYLE*** *command, which is explained later in this chapter.*

ENTERING SPECIAL CHARACTERS

In almost all drafting applications, you need to use special characters (symbols) in the normal text and in the dimension text. For example, you may want to use the degree symbol (°) or the diameter symbol (ø), or you may want to underscore or overscore some text. This can be achieved with the appropriate sequence of control characters (control code). For each symbol, the control sequence starts with a percent sign written twice (%%). The character immediately following the double percent sign depicts the symbol. The control sequences for some of the symbols are given next.

Control sequence	Special character
%%c	Diameter symbol (ø)
%%d	Degree symbol (°)
%%p	Plus/minus tolerance symbol (±)

For example, if you want to write 25° Celsius, you need to enter **25%%dCelsius**. If you want to write 43.0ø, you need to enter **43.0%%c**.

To insert an euro symbol, press and hold the ALT key and enter any numeric value from the numeric keypad and then release the ALT key. Before entering the numbers, make sure that the NUM LOCK is on.

CREATING MULTILINE TEXT

Ribbon: Home > Annotation > Text drop-down > MultilineText
Menu Bar: Draw > Text > Multiline Text
Toolbar: Draw, Text > Multiline Text **Command:** MTEXT/T/MT

The **Multiline Text** tool in the **Text** drop-down of the **Text** panel (see Figure 7-11) is used to write a multiline text whose width is specified by defining two corners of the text boundary or by entering a width using the coordinate entry. The text created by using the **Multiline Text** tool is a single object regardless of the number of lines it contains.

On invoking the **Multiline Text** tool, a sample text "abc" is attached to the cursor and you are prompted to specify the first corner. Specify the first corner and move the pointing device so that a box that shows the location and size of the paragraph text is formed. An arrow is displayed within the boundary indicating the direction of the text flow. Specify the other corner to define the boundary. When you define the text boundary, it does not mean that the text paragraph will fit within the defined boundary. AutoCAD LT only uses the width of the defined boundary as the width of the text paragraph. The height of the text boundary has no effect on the text paragraph.

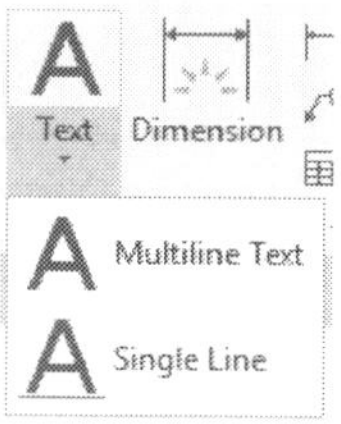

***Figure 7-11** The **Multiline Text** tool in the **Text** drop-down*

Note

*On invoking the **Multiline Text** tool, a sample text "abc" is attached to the cursor. The **MTJIGSTRING** system variable stores the default contents of the sample text. You can specify a string of ten alphanumeric characters as the default sample text.*

The prompt sequence that will be displayed after choosing the **Multiline Text** tool is given next.

Specify first corner: *Select a point to specify first corner.*
Specify opposite corner or [Height/Justify/Line spacing/Rotation/Style/Width/Columns]: *Select an option or select a point to specify other corner. Now, you can write text in this boundary.*

Note

Although the box boundary that you specify controls the width of a paragraph, a single word is not broken to adjust inside the boundary limits. This means that if you write a single word whose width is more than the box boundary specified, AutoCAD LT will write the word irrespective of the box width and therefore, it will exceed the boundary limits.

Once you have defined the boundary of the paragraph text, AutoCAD LT displays the **Text Editor** tab along with the **Text Window**, as shown in Figure 7-12. The **Text Window** and the **Text Editor** tab are discussed next.

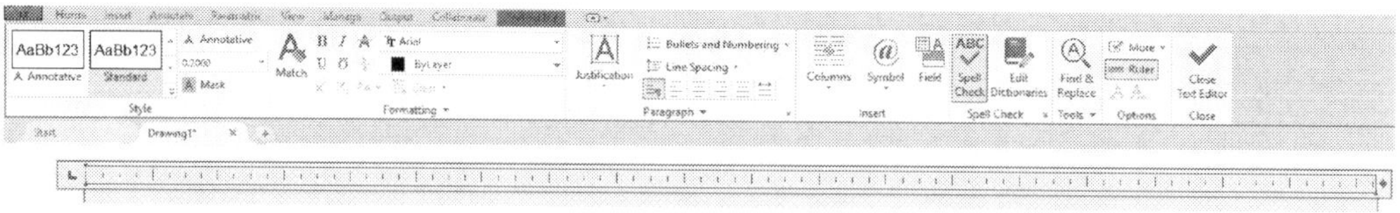

Figure 7-12** The **Text Editor** tab and the **Text Window

Text Window

The **Text Window** is used to enter the multiline text. The width of the active text area is determined by the width of the window that you specify when you invoke the **Multiline Text** tool. You can increase or decrease the size of the text window by dragging the double-headed arrow provided at the top-right and bottom left corner of the text window. You can also move the scroll bar up or down to display the text.

The ruler on the top of the text window is used to specify the indentation of the current paragraph. The top slider of the ruler specifies the indentation of the first line of the paragraph while the bottom slider specifies the indentation of the other lines of the paragraph.

Text Editor Tab

On creating the text window, a contextual tab will be added to the **Ribbon**. The options in this tab are discussed next.

Text Style

The list of available text styles are grouped on the left of the **Style** panel in the **Text Editor** tab. Click the down arrow to scroll down the list of text styles. If you choose the double arrow, a flyout containing text styles created in the current drawing will be displayed. You can select the desired text style from this flyout. You can also create a new text style by using the **STYLE** command, which is explained later in this chapter.

Annotative

The **Annotative** button is used to write the annotative text. The annotative text scales itself according to the current annotative setting. The annotative text also keeps on scaling according to the change in the annotative scale. The annotative texts are defined in the drawing area in terms of the paper height and the current annotation scale setting.

Note

While editing the text, the ***Annotative*** *button is used to convert the non-annotative multiline text into annotative multiline text and vice-versa.*

You can also change the non-annotative text to annotative by setting the text's ***Annotative*** *property to* ***Yes*** *in the* ***PROPERTIES*** *palette. This applies to both single line and multiline text.*

Text Height

The **Text Height** drop-down list is used to specify the text height of the multiline text. The default value in this drop-down list is 0.2000. Once you modify the height, AutoCAD LT retains that value till you change it. Remember that the multiline text height does not affect the height specified for the **TEXT** command.

Bold, Italic, Underline, Overline

You can use the appropriate buttons in the **Formatting** panel to make the selected text bold, italics, underlined, or create overlined text. Bold and italics are not supported by SHX fonts and hence, they will not be available for the particular fonts. These four buttons toggle between on and off.

Font

The **Font** drop-down list in the **Formatting** panel displays all the fonts available in AutoCAD LT. You can select the desired font from this drop-down list, see Figure 7-13. Irrespective of the font assigned to a text style, you can assign a different font to that style for the current multiline text by using the **Font** drop-down list.

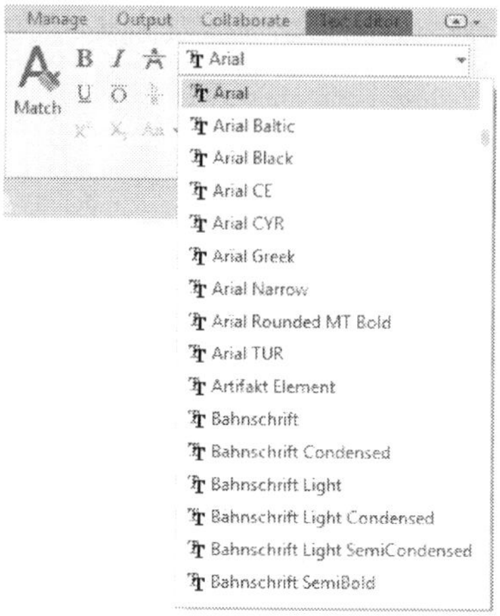

***Figure 7-13** The **Font** drop-down list*

Match

The **Match** tool is used to copy the formatting of a text and then apply it to the other text.

Uppercase

When you select text in the text editor and choose this button, the alphabets written in the lowercase are converted to the uppercase.

Lowercase

When you choose this button, the uppercase text is changed to lowercase text.

Superscript

The **Superscript** button is used to superscribe a text. To do so, select the text and choose the **Superscript** button from the **Formatting** panel of the **Text Editor** contextual tab; the selected text will become a superscript.

Subscript

The **Subscript** button is used to subscribe a text. To subscribe a text, select the text and choose the **Subscript** button from the **Formatting** panel of the **Text Editor** contextual tab; the selected text will become a subscript.

Color

The **Color** drop-down list is used to set the color for the multiline text. You can also select the color from the **Select Color** dialog box that is displayed by selecting **More Colors** in the drop-down list.

Background Mask

The **Mask** option is used for defining background color for multiline text. When you choose this option, the **Background Mask** dialog box will be displayed, as shown in Figure 7-14. To add background mask, select the **Use background mask** check box and select the required color from the drop-down list in the **Fill Color** area. You can set the size of the colored background behind the text using the **Border offset factor** edit box. The previous value of the offset factor is automatically selected in the edit box. The box that defines the background color will be offset from the text by the value you define in this edit box. The value in this edit box is based on the height of the text. If you enter **1** as the value, the height of the colored background will be equal to the height of the text and will extend through the length of the window defined to write the multiline text. Similarly, if you enter **2** as the value, the height of the colored box will be twice the height of the text and will be equally offset above and below the text. However, the length of the colored box will still be equal to the length of the window defined to write the multiline text. You can select the **Use drawing background color** check box in the **Fill Color** area to use the color of the background of the drawing area to add the background mask. The previous color used is automatically selected.

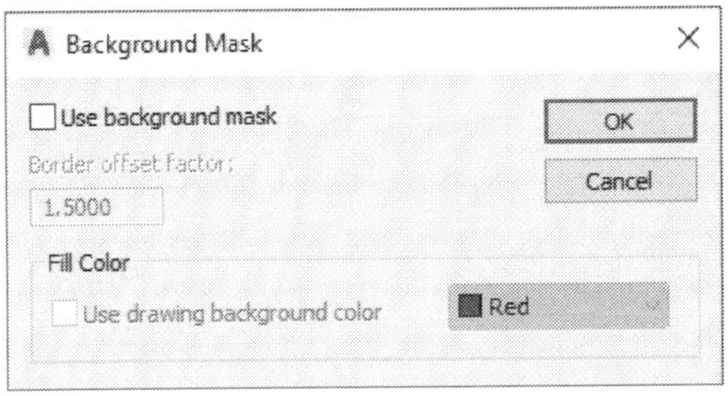

*Figure 7-14 The **Background Mask** dialog box*

Oblique Angle

Expand the **Formatting** panel to view this option. This option is used to specify the slant angle for the text. Enter the angle in the **Oblique Angle** edit box or use spinner to specify the slant angle, which is measured from the positive direction of X-axis in the clockwise direction.

Tracking

Expand the **Formatting** panel to view this option. This option is used to control the spacing between the selected characters. Select the characters and enter the value of the spacing in the **Tracking** edit box. You can also use the **Tracking** spinner to specify this value. The default tracking value is 1.000. You can specify values ranging from 0.7500 to 4.0000.

Width Factor

Expand the **Formatting** panel to view this option. This option is used to control the width of characters. By default, the value is set to 1.000. Select the characters and use the **Width Factor** edit box or the **Width Factor** spinner to specify the width of characters.

Justification

In large complicated technical drawings, the **Justification** option is used to fit the text matter with a specified justification and alignment. For example, if the text justification is bottom-right (BR), the text paragraph will spill to the left and above the insertion point, regardless of how you define the width of the paragraph. When you choose the **Justification** button in the **Paragraph** panel of the **Text Editor** in the **Ribbon**, a cascading menu appears that displays the predefined text justifications. By default, the text is **Top Left** justified. You can choose the new justification from the cascading menu. The various justifications are TL, ML, BL, TC, MC, BC, TR, MR, and BR. Figure 7-15 shows various text justifications for multiline text.

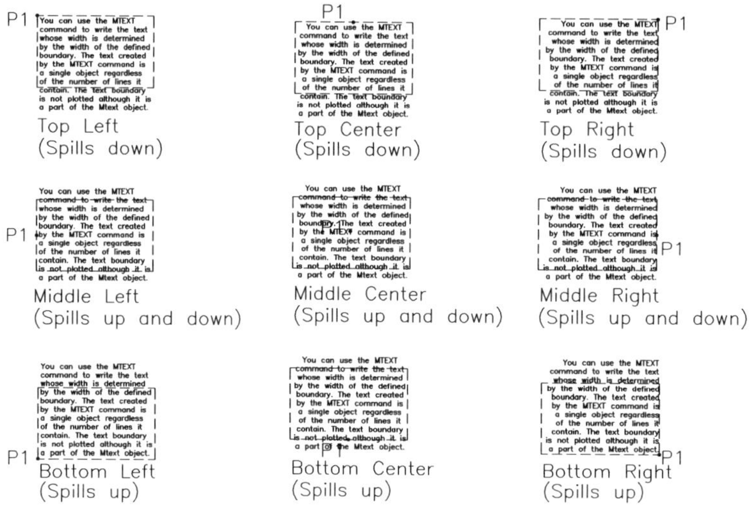

***Figure 7-15** Text justifications for multiline text (P1 is the text insertion point)*

Paragraph

You can control the settings such as tab, indent, alignment, paragraph spacing and line spacing, of a paragraph by using the options in the **Paragraph** dialog box, shown in Figure 7-16. When you click on the small incline arrow at the bottom right of the **Paragraph** panel, the **Paragraph** dialog box is displayed. The options in the **Paragraph** dialog box are discussed next.

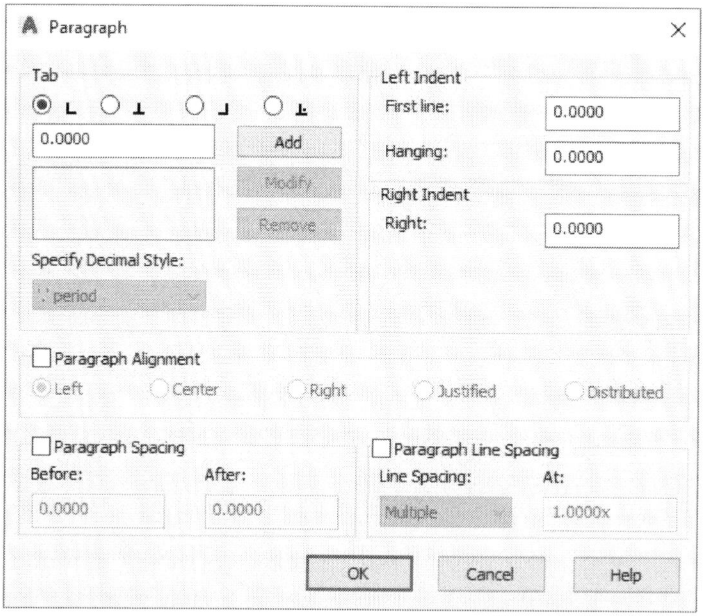

***Figure 7-16** The **Paragraph** dialog box*

Tab. This area is used to specify the tab type by selecting the required radio button. This area is also used to add or remove the additional tab positions up to which the cursor is moved while pressing the TAB key once at the start of a new paragraph for the left, center, right, and decimal justification. This option can also be set by clicking on the ruler of the **In-Place Text** editor.

Left Indent. In this area, you can set the indent of the first line and the following lines of multiline text by entering the values in the **First line** and the **Hanging** edit boxes.

Right Indent. In this area, you can set the right indent of the paragraph of the multiline text by entering the value in the **Right** edit box.

Paragraph Alignment. Select the **Paragraph Alignment** check box to set the alignment for the current or the selected paragraph in the **Text Window**. As you select this check box, the radio buttons available below this check box will be activated. The **Left** radio button is used to left align the text written. The **Center** radio button is used to center align the text. The **Right** radio button is used to right align the text. The **Justify** radio button is used to adjust horizontal spacing so that the text is aligned evenly in between the left and right margins. Justifying the text creates a smooth edge on both sides. The **Distribute** radio button is used to adjust the text evenly throughout the width of the column in the **Text Window**.

Paragraph Spacing. Select the **Paragraph Spacing** check box to set the gap before the start of the paragraph and after the end of the paragraph. According to the gap set by you, AutoCAD LT calculates the gap between the two consecutive paragraphs. This gap is equal to the sum of after paragraph gap for the upper paragraph and the before paragraph gap for the lower paragraph.

Paragraph Line Spacing. Select the **Paragraph Line Spacing** check box to set the gap between the two consecutive lines. Select the **Exactly** option from the **Line Spacing** drop-down list to maintain the gap exactly specified by you in the **At** edit box, irrespective of the text height. On selecting the **At least** option, both the user specified arbitrary value as well as the text height will be considered to determine the gap. If the text height is smaller than the specified value, the line space will be determined by the user specified value. If the text height is larger, the line spacing will be equal to the text height value. By selecting the **Multiple** option, you can specify the spacing according to the text height. When the text height is not equal in a line, the line space will be determined by the largest text height value of that line.

Note
The spaces entered at the end of a line are also considered while justifying a text.

Line Spacing

Line spacing is the distance between two consecutive lines in a multiline text. Choose **Paragraph > Line Spacing** from the **Ribbon** to display a flyout containing options to select some predefined line spacing or for opening the **Paragraph** dialog box, see Figure 7-17. The **1.0x**, **1.5x**, **2x**, **2.5x** options set the line spacing in the multiples of the largest text height value in the same line. The **More** option is chosen to open the **Paragraph** dialog box that has been discussed earlier. The **Clear Line Space** option removes the space setting for the lines of the selected or the current paragraph. As a result, the line spacing will retrieve the default mtext line space setting.

Bullets and Numbering

This option is used to control the settings to display the bullets and numbering in a multiline text. Choose the **Bullets and Numbering** option; a flyout will be displayed, as shown in Figure 7-18. The options in this flyout are discussed next.

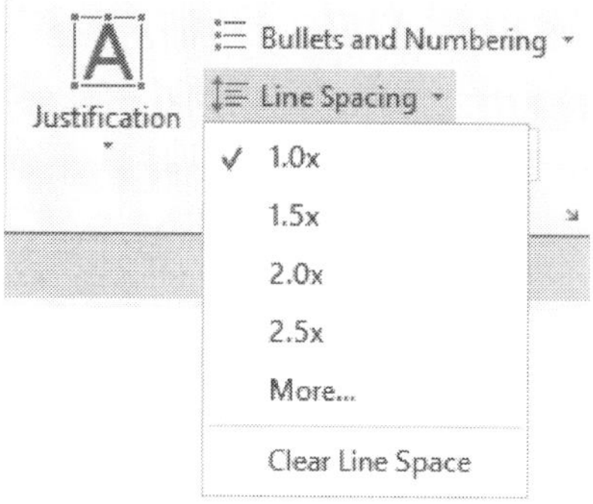

Figure 7-17 Options in the ***Line Spacing*** *flyout*

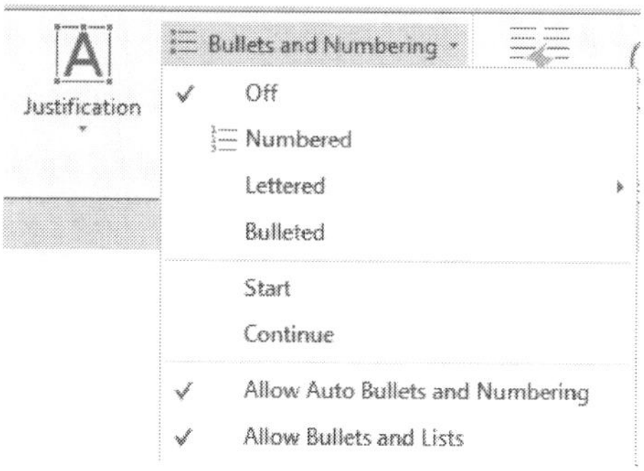

Figure 7-18 *Flyout displayed on choosing the* ***Bullets and Numbering*** *option*

Off. Select this option to remove letters, numbers, and bullets from the selected text.

Numbered. This option inserts numbers for the list formatting.

Lettered. This option inserts the letters for list formatting. You can choose the uppercase letters and lower case letters to be used for the list formatting.

Note

If number of items exceed the number of alphabets, the numbering continues again from the start but by using the double alphabet.

Bulleted. This option inserts bullets for the list formatting.

Start. This option restarts a new letter or a numbering sequence for the list formatting.

Continue. This option adds the selected paragraphs to the last list and continues the sequence.

Allow Auto Bullets and Numbering. Select this option and follow the procedure given below to automatically start the formatting of list.

1. Start a line of text by entering a number.
2. Use period (.), close angle bracket (>), close square bracket (]), close parenthesis ()), or close curly bracket (}) as punctuation after the number.
3. Provide space by pressing the TAB key.
4. Enter the required text.
5. Press the ENTER key to move to the next line; the new line will be automatically listed.
6. Press the SHIFT+ENTER key to add a plain paragraph.
7. To end auto-listing, press the ENTER key twice.

Allow Bullets and Lists. If this option is checked, the list formatting will be applied to the whole text lines in the multiline text area. If you clear this option, any list formatting in the multiline text object will be removed and the items will be converted into the plain text. And, all the **Bullets and Lists** options available on the contextual tab will become unavailable. To make these options available, again right-click in the text window and choose the **Allow Bullets and Lists** sub-option from the **Bullets and Lists** option.

Columns

This button is chosen to create columns in the multiline text. On choosing this button from the **Insert** panel, a flyout will be displayed that has the options to control the number, height, and gap between the columns. These options are shown in Figure 7-19 and are discussed next.

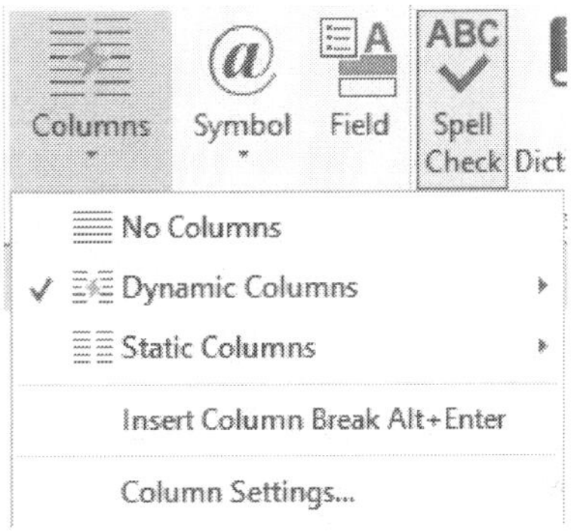

***Figure 7-19** The options in the **Columns** flyout*

No Columns. This option does not create any column. The whole of the multiline text is written in a single column. When you start a multiline text, this option is selected by default.

Dynamic Columns. The dynamic columns are the text driven columns that change according to the quantity of the text. According to the quantity of text written, the columns are added or removed automatically. There are two options to control the height of the dynamic columns, **Auto height** and **Manual height**. The **Auto height** option automatically starts a new column when the text exceeds the range that the preset column can accommodate. The default height of the first column is decided by the height of the window that you create while starting the multiline text. All the other new columns generated are equal in height to the first column. If you change the height of the first column, the height of the remaining columns changes accordingly, in order to be in level with the first one. The **Manual height** option, on the other hand, provides the flexibility to control the height of each column individually. A new column will not start if the text exceeds the range that the present column can accommodate. The text will keep on adding to the same column by increasing the height of that column. Later on, you can add extra columns by adjusting the height of the present column. When you decrease the height of the column in which you have entered the text that does not fit the height of the new column, a new column will start automatically. Similarly, you can add more columns by adjusting the height of the last column.

Static Columns. The **Static Columns** option allows you to specify the number of columns before writing the text. All the generated columns are of the same height and width. You can also change the number of columns after writing the text.

Insert Column Break Alt + Enter. This option is used to start writing the text in a new column manually. When you insert a column break, the cursor automatically moves to the start of the next column. You can also press the ALT+ENTER key to insert a column break.

Column Settings. This option controls the settings to create a column. Choose this option to invoke the **Column Settings** dialog box, see Figure 7-20. The **Column Settings** dialog box has four areas: **Column Type**, **Column Number**, **Height**, and **Width**. The **Column Type** area specifies the type of column you want to create. All options in this area are similar to the options discussed above. In the **Column Number** area, you can specify the number of columns to be generated when you create the manual type of columns. In the **Height** area, you can specify the height of the columns to be generated for **Auto Height Dynamic Columns** and **Static Column** type. The **Width** area controls the width of the columns and the gap between two consecutive columns.

Symbol

This option is used to insert the special characters in the text. When you choose the **Symbol** option from the **Insert** panel of the **Text Editor** tab in the **Ribbon**, a flyout will be displayed with some predefined special characters, see Figure 7-21. You can also choose **Other** from the flyout to display the **Character Map** dialog box. This dialog box has a number of other special characters that you can insert in the multiline text. To insert characters from the dialog box, select the character that you want to copy and then choose the **Select** button. Once you have selected all the required special characters, choose the **Copy** button and then close the dialog box. Now in the text window, position the cursor where you want to insert the special characters and right-click to display the shortcut menu. Choose **Paste** to insert the selected special character in the **Text Editor**.

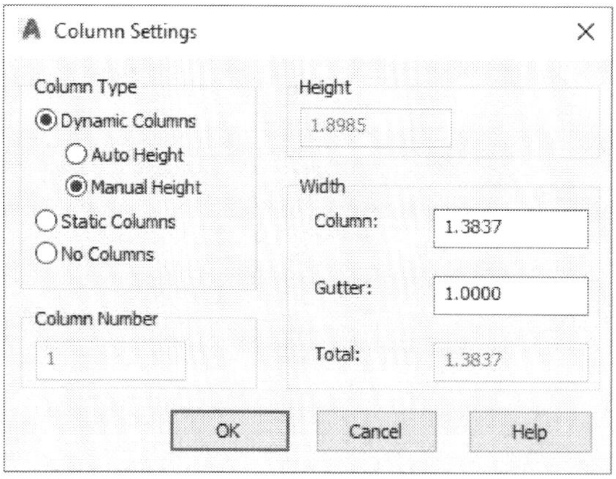

Figure 7-20 *The* ***Column Settings*** *dialog box*

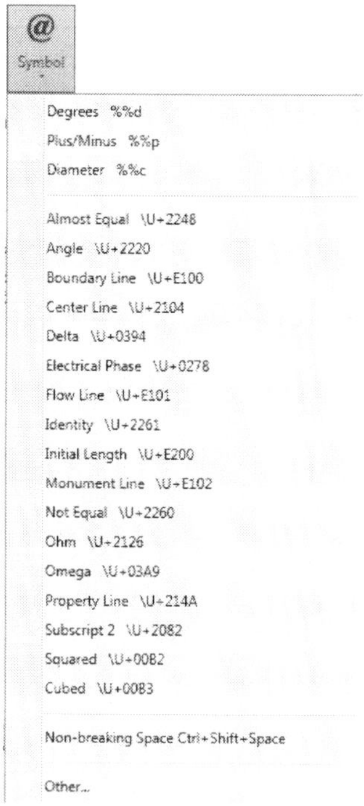

Figure 7-21 *Flyout displayed on choosing the* ***Symbol*** *button from the* ***Insert*** *panel*

Field

AutoCAD LT allows you to insert a field in the multiline text. A field contains data that is associated with the property that defines the field. For example, you can insert a field having the author's name on the current drawing. If you have already defined the author of the current drawing in the **Drawing Properties** dialog box, it will automatically be displayed in the field. If you modify the author and update the field, the changes will automatically be made in the text. When you choose this option, the **Field** dialog box will be displayed, as shown in Figure 7-22.

You can select the field to be added in the **Field names** list box and define the format of the field using the **Format** list box. Choose **OK** after selecting the field and format. If the data in the selected field is already defined, it will be displayed in the **Text** window. If not, the field will display dashes (----).

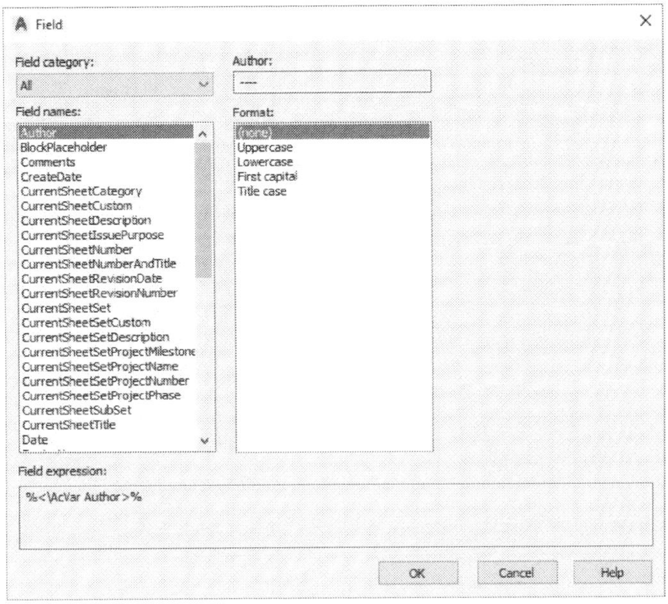

*Figure 7-22 The **Field** dialog box*

Note

*To update a field after the text of that field is modified, double-click on the multiline text to display the **In-Place Text Editor**. Click and select the field in the **Text** window and then right-click to display the shortcut menu. Choose **Update Field** from this menu; the field will be updated. You can also edit the field or convert it into text using the same shortcut menu.*

Spell Check

To check spelling errors, choose the **Spell Check** button; the misspelt words will appear with a red underline. You can specify settings to check spelling errors as per your requirement. To do so, left-click on the inclined arrow in the **Spell Check** panel; the **Check Spelling Settings** dialog box will be displayed. This dialog box is used to specify what to include for spell check such as the dimension text, block attributes, and text in external references.

You can also specify what not to include like capitalized words, mixed cases, uppercase, and words with numbers or punctuation.

Edit Dictionaries

This option is used to match the word with the words in dictionaries while a text is run on spell check. On choosing this option, the **Dictionaries** dialog box will be displayed. This dialog box has two areas, **Main dictionary** and **Custom dictionaries**. In the **Main dictionary** area, you can select the required dictionary from a list of different language dictionaries. And in the **Custom dictionaries** area, you can add the commonly used words to a *.cus* file. You can also import the words from other dictionaries to the current customized *.cus* file.

Find and Replace

When you choose the **Find & Replace** button from the **Tools** panel, the **Find and Replace** dialog box will be displayed, as shown in Figure 7-23. The options that can be chosen from this dialog box are discussed next.

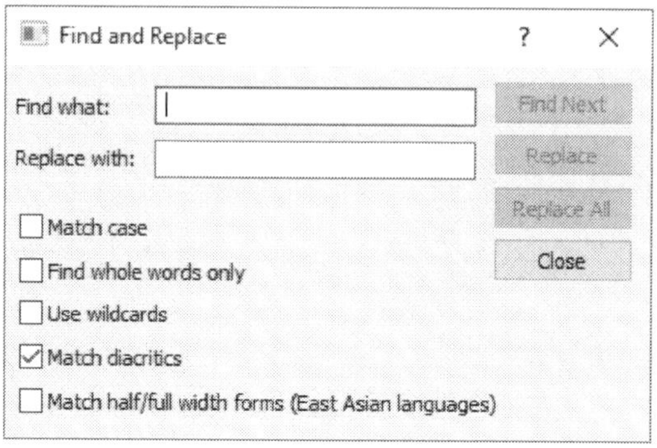

*Figure 7-23 Partial view of the **Find and Replace** dialog box*

Find what. This edit box is used to enter the text or a part of a word or a complete word that you need to find in the drawing.

Replace with. If you want some text to be replaced, enter new text for replacement in this text box.

Match case. If this check box is selected, AutoCAD LT will find out the word only if the case of all characters in the word are identical to the word mentioned in the **Find what** edit box.

Find whole words only. If this check box is selected, AutoCAD LT will match the word in the text only if it is a single word, identical to the one mentioned in the **Find what** text box. For example, if you enter **and** in the **Find what** edit box and select the **Find whole words only** check box, AutoCAD LT will not match the string and in words like sand, land, band, and so on.

Use wildcards. This check box is selected to use the wildcard characters such as * , ?, and so on in the **Find what** edit box and then replace the selected text.

Match diacritics. This check box is selected to match the Latin characters, diacritical marks, or assent in your search.

Match half/full width forms (East Asian languages). If this check box is selected, you can match half or full width characters in your search.

Find Next. Choose this button to continue the search for the text entered in the **Find what** box.

Replace. Choose this button to replace the highlighted text with the text entered in the **Replace with** text box.

Replace All. If you choose this button, all the words in the current multiline text that match the word specified in the **Find what** text box will be replaced with the word entered in the **Replace with** text box.

Import Text

Expand the **Tools** panel to view this option. When you choose this option, AutoCAD LT displays the **Select File** dialog box. In this dialog box, select any text file that you want to import as the multiline text; the imported text will be displayed in the text area. Note that only the ASCII or RTF file is interpreted properly.

ALL CAPS

Expand the **Tools** panel to view this option. If you choose this option, the case of entire written or imported text will be changed to uppercase. However, the case of the text written before choosing this option is not changed.

More

To edit a text, select it and then choose the **More** button from the **Options** panel in the **Text Editor** tab; a flyout will be displayed. The options in the **More** flyout are discussed next.

Character Set. This option is used to define the character set for the current font. You can select the desired character set from the cascading menu that is displayed when you choose this option.

Editor Settings. The **Editor Settings** option has the sub-options to control the display of the **Text Formatting** toolbar. These sub-options are shown in Figure 7-24 and are discussed next.

Always Display as WYSIWYG (What you see is what you get). This option controls the display size and orientation of the text in the **Text Editor**. If you choose this sub-option, the text in the **Text Editor** will be displayed in the **In-Place Text Editor** with its original size, position, and orientation. But if the text is very small, or very large or rotated, then you can deselect this sub-option so that the displayed text is oriented horizontally and is displayed in readable size.

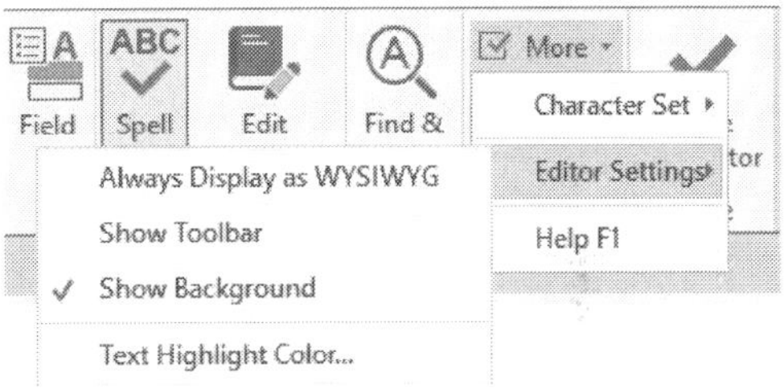

*Figure 7-24 The sub-options of the **Editor Settings** option*

Show Toolbar. This sub-option is used to show or hide the **Text Formatting** toolbar.

Show Background. Choose this sub-option to make the background of the **Text** window opaque. By default, the background is transparent. Invoke the text window over the existing objects/entities in the drawing window to see the effect of the opaque background sub-option.

Text Highlight Color

This sub-option is used to change the highlighted color of the text that appears when you select the text for editing. When you choose this sub-option, the **Select Color** dialog box will be displayed, as shown in Figure 7-25. There are three tabs available in the dialog box: **Index Color**, **True Color**, and **Color Books**. By default, the **True Color** tab is selected. You can set the colors by using the options available in these tabs.

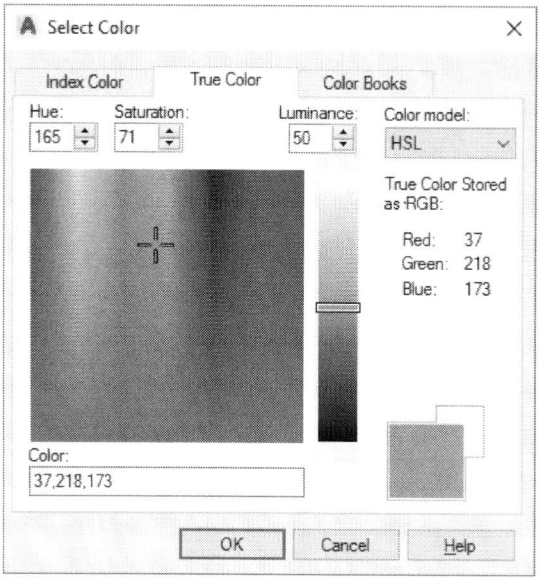

***Figure 7-25** The **Select Color** dialog box*

Note

*You can also remove formatting such as bold, italics, or underline from the selected text. To do so, select the text whose formatting you need to change and then right-click to display a shortcut menu. From the menu, choose the **Remove Formatting** option. Under the sub-headings, you can choose between the Character, Paragraph or All; the formatting of the selected text will be removed.*

Ruler

The **Ruler** button in the **Options** panel is used to toggle the display of ruler in the **Text Window**.

Undo

The **Undo** button allows you to undo the actions in the **In-Place Text Editor**. You can also press the CTRL+Z keys to undo the previous actions.

Redo

The **Redo** button allows you to redo the actions in the **In-Place Text Editor**. You can also press the CTRL+Y keys to redo the previous actions.

The options discussed next are not available in the **Text Editor** tab. However, in the **Text Formatting** toolbar, these options will be displayed on choosing **More > Editor Settings > Show Toolbar** from the **Text Editor** tab.

Stack

To create a fraction text, you must use the stack option with the specialcharacters /, ^, and #. In AutoCAD LT, this option is available in sleep mode in the **Text Editor** tab. When you enter two numbers separated by / or ^ , the stack option becomes active. Alternatively, press ENTER or SPACEBAR after entering two characters; a small yellow icon will be displayed. Click on that icon; a flyout will be displayed, as shown in Figure 7-26. Choose **Stack Properties**; a dialog box will be displayed, as shown in Figure 7-27 .You can use this dialog box to control the Stack properties. The character / stacks the text vertically with a line, and the character ^ stacks the text vertically without a line (tolerance stack). The character # stacks the text with a diagonal line. The stacked text is displayed equal to 70 percent of the actual height. The **Stack** options available in the flyout menu shown in Figure 7-26 are discussed next.

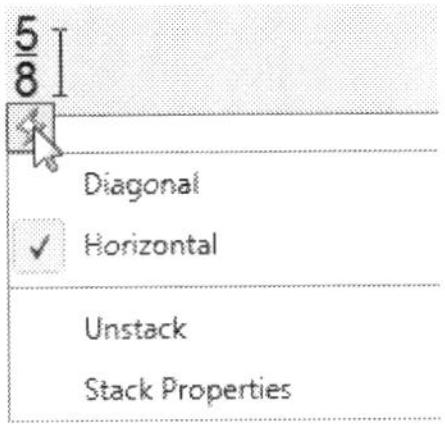

*Figure 7-26 Flyout showing the **Stack** options*

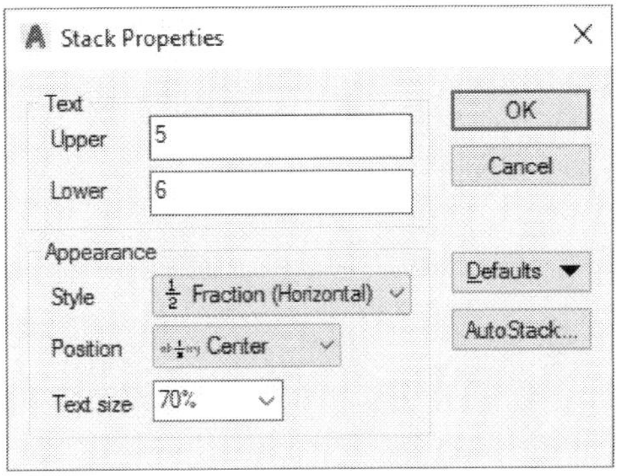

*Figure 7-27 The **Stack Properties** dialog box*

Diagonal. This option stacks the selected text with the first number on top of the second number separated by a diagonal line.

Horizontal. This option stacks the selected text with the first number on top of the second number separated by a horizontal line.

Unstack. This option is used to unstack the selected stacked text.

Stack Properties

When you choose this option, the **Stack Properties** dialog box will be displayed, as shown in Figure 7-27. This dialog box is used to edit the text and the appearance of the selected stacked text. The options in this dialog box are discussed next.

Text Area. You can change the upper and the lower values of the stacked text by entering their values in the **Upper** and **Lower** text boxes, respectively.

Appearance Area. You can change the style, position, and size of the stacked text by entering their values in the **Style**, **Position**, and **Text size** text boxes, respectively.

Defaults. This drop-down list allows you to restore the default values or save the new settings as the default settings for the selected stacked text.

AutoStack. When you choose this button, the **AutoStack Properties** dialog box will be displayed, as shown in Figure 7-28. The options in this dialog box are discussed next.

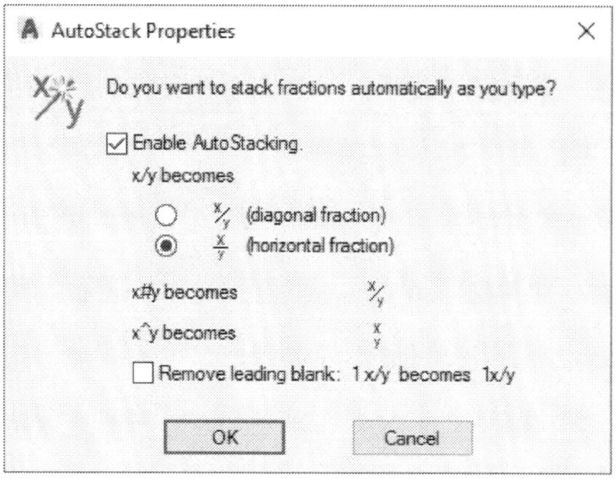

***Figure 7-28** The **AutoStack Properties** dialog box*

Enable AutoStacking. You can enable or disable autostacking by using this check box. You can also choose between the diagonal and horizontal fraction display by selecting the corresponding radio button.

If you clear the **Enable AutoStacking** check box, then the flyout menu showing the stack options, as shown in Figure 7-26, will not be displayed. For invoking the flyout menu, select the fractional text. Next, right-click and choose **Stack** from the shortcut menu.

Remove leading blank. This option removes the gap between a number and a fractional text. For example 1 x/y becomes 1x/y.

Note

*The **Cut** and **Copy** sub-options of the **Edit** option can be used to move or copy the text from the text editor to any other application. Similarly, using the **Paste** sub-option, you can paste text from any windows text-based application to the **Text Editor**.*

Example 1 Multiline Text

In this example, you will use the **Multiline Text** tool to write the following text.

For long, complex entries, create multiline text using the MTEXT option. The angle is 10°, dia = 1/2", and length = 32 1/2".

The font of the text is **Swis721 BT**, text height is 0.20, color is red, and written at an angle of 10-degree with Middle-Left justification. Make the word "multiline" bold, underline the text "multiline text", and make the word "angle" italic. The line spacing type and line spacing between the lines are **At least** and **1.5x**, respectively. Use the symbol for degrees. After writing the text in the **Text window**, replace the word "option" with "command".

1. Choose the **Multiline Text** tool from the **Annotation** panel in the **Home** tab in the **Drafting & Annotation** workspace. After invoking this tool, specify the first corner on the screen to define the first corner of the paragraph text boundary. You need to specify the rotation

angle of the text before specifying the second corner of the paragraph text boundary. The prompt sequence is given next.

Current text style: "Standard" Text height: 0.20 Annotative: No
Specify first corner: *Select a point to specify the first corner.*
Specify opposite corner or [Height/Justify/Line spacing/Rotation/Style/Width/Columns]: **R** Enter
Specify rotation angle <0>: 10. Enter
Specify opposite corner or [Height/Justify/Line spacing/Rotation/Style/Width/Columns]:L Enter
Enter line spacing type [At least/Exactly] <At least>: Enter
Enter line spacing factor or distance <1x>: **1.5x**
Specify opposite corner or [Height/Justify/Line spacing/Rotation/Style/Width/Columns]: *Select another point to specify the other corner.*

The **Text Window** and the **Text Editor** tab are displayed.

2. Select the **Swis721 BT** font from the **Font** drop-down list of the **Formatting** panel in the **Text Editor** tab.

3. Enter **0.20** in the **Text Height** edit box of the **Style** panel, if the value in this edit box is not 0.2.

4. Select **Red** from the **Color** drop-down list in the **Formatting** panel.

5. Now, enter the text in the **Text Window**, as shown in Figure 7-29. To add the degree symbol, choose the **Symbol** button from the **Insert** panel of the **Text Window** tab in the **Ribbon**; a flyout is displayed. Choose **Degrees** from the flyout. When you type 1/2 after Dia = and then press the " key, AutoCAD LT displays a small yellow icon. Click on the icon; a flyout will appear. Choose the **Diagonal** option from the flyout.

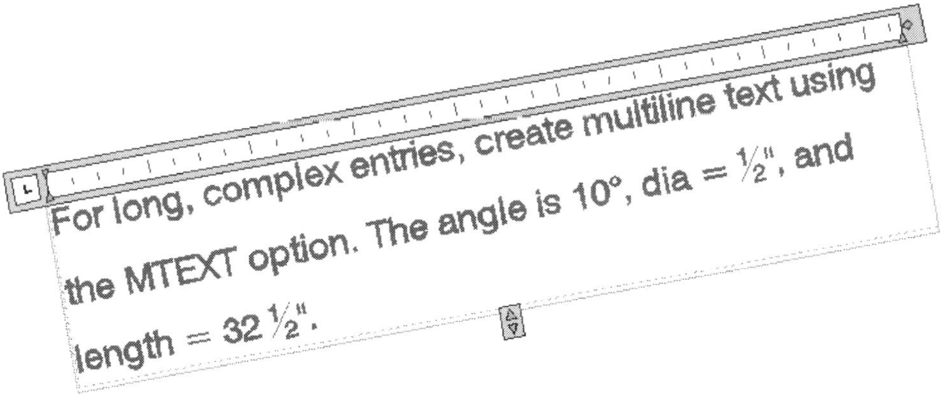

Figure 7-29 *Text entered in the **Text Window***

Similarly, when you type 1/2 after length = 32 and then press the " key, AutoCAD LT displays a small yellow icon. Click on the icon; a flyout will appear. Choose the **Diagonal** option from the flyout.

6. Double-click on the word "multiline" to select it (or click and drag to select the text) and then choose the **B** button to make it boldface and underline the words "multiline text" by using the **U** button from the **Formatting** panel.

7. Highlight the word "angle" by double-clicking on it and then choose the **Italic** button from the **Formatting** panel.

8. Choose the **Middle Left ML** option from the **Justification** drop-down list in the **Paragraph** panel.

9. Choose the **Find & Replace** button from the **Tools** panel in the **Text Editor** tab. Alternatively, right-click on the **Text Window** and choose **Find and Replace** from the shortcut menu. You can also use CTRL+R keys. On doing so, the **Find and Replace** dialog box is displayed.

10. In the **Find what** edit box, enter **option** and in the **Replace with** edit box, enter **command**.

11. Choose the **Find Next** button. AutoCAD LT finds the word "option" and highlights it. Choose the **Replace** button to replace **option** by **command**. The **AutoCAD LT** information box is displayed informing you that AutoCAD LT has finished searching for the word. Choose **OK** to close the information box.

12. Now, choose **Close** to exit the **Find and Replace** dialog box. To exit the editor mode, click outside the **Text Editor**; a text is displayed on the screen, as shown in Figure 7-30.

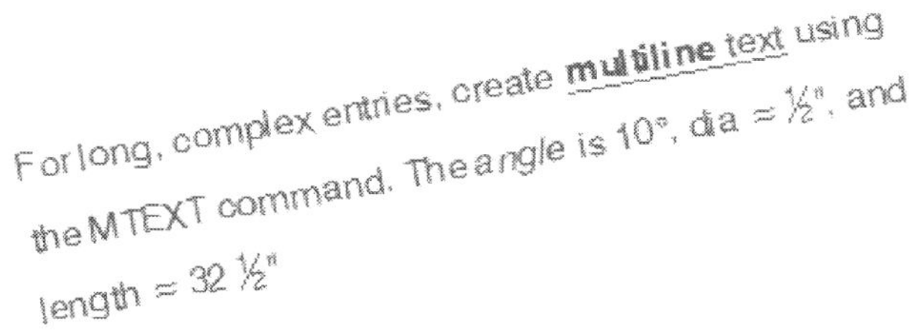

Figure 7-30 *Multiline text for Example 1*

Tip

*The text in the **Text Editor** can be selected by double-clicking on the word, or by triple-clicking on the text to select the entire line or paragraph.*

Exercise 1 — *Single Line & Multiline Text*

Write the text using the **Single Line** and **Multiline Text** tools, as shown in Figures 7-31 and 7-32. Use the special characters and the text justification options shown in the drawing. The text height is 0.1 and 0.15 respectively in Figures 7-31 and 7-32.

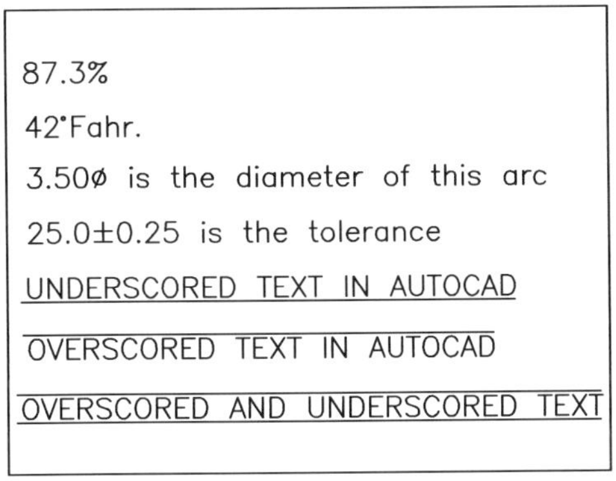

Figure 7-31 Drawing with special characters

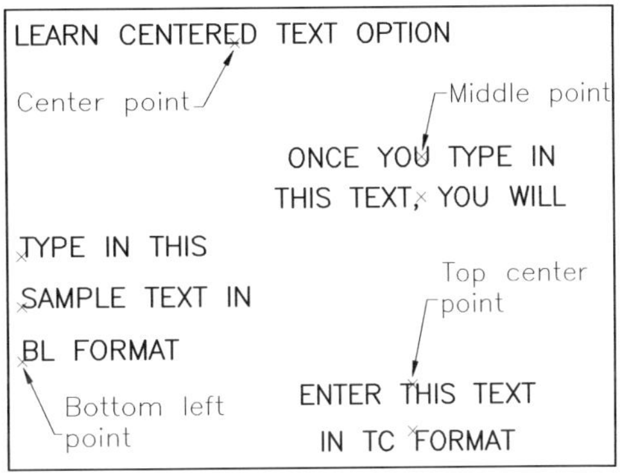

Figure 7-32 Drawing for Exercise 1

EDITING TEXT

The contents of **MTEXT** and **TEXT** object can be edited by using the **DDEDIT** and **Properties** commands. You can also use the AutoCAD LT editing tools such as **Move**, **Erase**, **Rotate**, **Copy**, and **Mirror** with any text object.

In addition to editing, you can also modify the text in AutoCAD LT. The modification that you can perform on the text include changing its scale and justification. The various editing and modifying operations are discussed next.

Editing Text Using the TEXTEDIT (DDEDIT) Command

Menu Bar: Modify > Object > Text > Edit
Toolbar: Text > Edit **Command:** DDEDIT/TEXTEDIT/TEDIT

You can use the **DDEDIT** command to edit text. The most convenient way of invoking this command is by double-clicking on the text. If you double-click on a single line text written by using the **Single Line** tool, AutoCAD LT creates an edit box around the text and highlights it. You can modify the text string in this edit box. The size of the bounding box increases or decreases as you add more text or remove the existing text. Note that for the text object, you cannot modify any of its properties in the bounding box. However, if you double-click on a multiline text written by using the **Multiline Text** tool, the text will be displayed in the **Text Editor**. You can make changes using various options in the editor. Apart from changing the text string, you can also change the properties of a paragraph text.

You can also select the text for editing and then right-click in the drawing area; a shortcut menu is displayed. Depending on the text object you have selected, the **Edit** or **Mtext Edit** options will be available in the shortcut menu. On choosing the appropriate option, the **Text Editor** and the **Text Editor** tab will be displayed.

The prompt sequence to edit a text object using the **TEXTEDIT** command is given next.

Select an annotation object or [Undo/Mode]: **M** Enter
Enter a text edit mode option [Single/Multiple] <Multiple>: M Enter

Edit mode = Multiple
Select an annotation object or [Undo/Mode]: *Select a text object to edit.*

By choosing the **Multiple** option, you can edit multiple text objects at a time without restarting the command.

Editing Text Using the PROPERTIES Palette

Using the **DDEDIT** command with the text object, you can only change the text string, and not its properties such as height, angle, and so on. In this case, you can use the **PROPERTIES** palette for changing the properties. Select the text, right-click to invoke the shortcut menu, and choose the **Properties** option from the shortcut menu; the **PROPERTIES** palette with all properties of the selected text will be displayed, refer to Figure 7-33. In this palette, you can change any value and the text string.

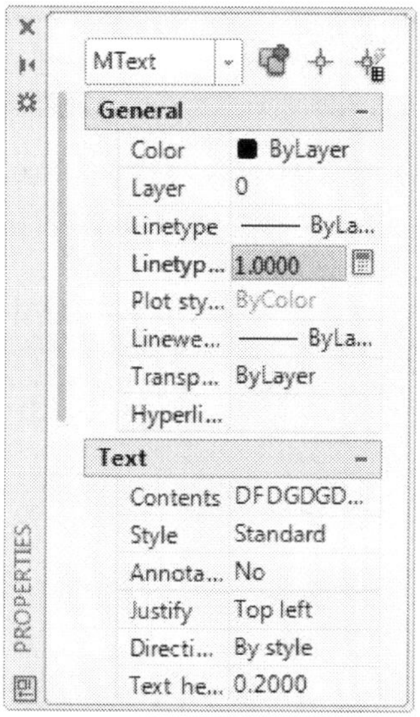

*Figure 7-33 The **PROPERTIES** palette*

You can edit a single line text in the **Contents** edit box. However, to edit a multiline text, you must choose the **Full editor** button in the **Contents** edit box. On doing so, the **Text Editor** will be displayed and you can make the changes.

Modifying the Scale of the Text

Ribbon: Annotate > Text > Scale
Toolbar: Text > Scale
Menu Bar: Modify > Object > Text > Scale
Command: SCALETEXT

You can modify the scale factor of a text by using the **Scale** tool in the extended options of the **Text** panel of the **Annotate** tab. On invoking this tool, you can select the text and specify the base point for scaling the text. AutoCAD LT lists the justification options as the base point to scale the text. Specify the appropriate base point and press ENTER; you will be prompted to specify the new model height or select one of the options. All these options are discussed next.

Paper Height

It scales the text height depending on the annotative properties of a drawing. The **Paper height** option can only be applied to the annotative objects.

Match object

You can use the **Match object** option to select an existing text whose height is used to scale a selected text.

Scale factor

You can use the **Scale factor** option to specify a scale factor to scale a text. You can also use the **Reference** option to specify the scale factor for the text.

Modifying the Justification of the Text

Ribbon: Annotate > Text > Justify	**Toolbar:** Text > Justify
Menu Bar: Modify > Object > Text > Justify	**Command:** JUSTIFYTEXT

You can modify the justification of a text by choosing the **Justify** tool in the extended options of the **Text** panel in the **Annotate** tab; you will be prompted to select the objects. Select the text and press ENTER; AutoCAD LT lists the justification options and you will be prompted to specify the justification. Specify the justification; the justification will be modified. Note that even after modifying the justification using this tool, the location of the text will not be changed. However, you can notice the changed justification location on selecting the text.

Aligning Text

Command: TEXTALIGN

In AutoCAD LT, you can align single, multiple, and attribute texts. To align text, you need to enter **TEXTALIGN** command at the Command prompt. On entering the command, you will be prompted to select the text object to be aligned. Select the text objects and press ENTER; you will be prompted to select the reference text object. Select the object which will act as a reference for the text object to align; you will be prompted to specify the second point for positioning the text to be aligned. While specifying the second point, you can specify spacing and positioning. To do so, choose the **Options** button from the Command prompt; the options will be displayed in the Command prompt and in a flyout. These options are discussed next.

Distribute

The **Distribute** option is used to place the text dynamically.

Set spacing

The **Set spacing** option is used to set uniform spacing around the reference object. After specifying the spacing, the text object can be placed around the reference object with fixed spacing value.

current Vertical

The **current Vertical** option is used to specify the deflection value vertically from the insertion point of the other text.

current Horizontal

The **current Horizontal** option is used to specify the deflection value horizontally from the insertion point of the other text.

Select the required options and specify the second point; the text will got aligned with specified values.

INSERTING TABLE IN THE DRAWING

Ribbon: Home > Annotation > Table Or Annotate > Tables > Table
Menu Bar: Draw > Table
Toolbar: Draw > Table
Tool Palette: Table
Command: TABLE

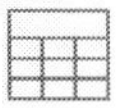

A number of mechanical, architectural, electric, or civil drawings require a table in which some information about the drawing is displayed. For example, the drawing of an assembly needs the Bill of Material, which is a table that provides details such as the number of parts in the drawing, their names, their material, and so on. To enter these information, AutoCAD LT allows you to create tables using the **Table** tool, see Figure 7-34. When you invoke this tool, the **Insert Table** dialog box is displayed, as shown in Figure 7-35. The options in this dialog box are discussed next.

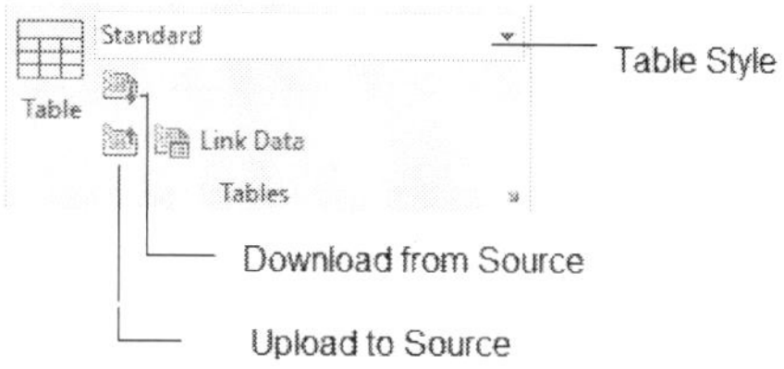

Figure 7-34 Tools in the ***Tables*** *panel of the* ***Annotate*** *tab*

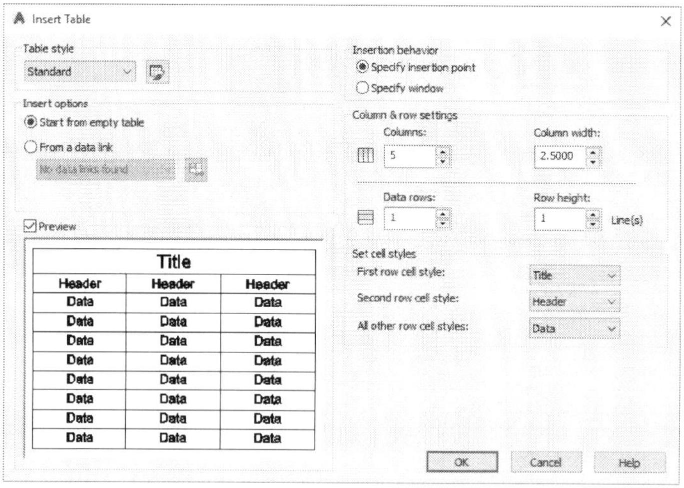

Figure 7-35 The ***Insert Table*** *dialog box*

Table style Area

The drop-down list in this area displays the names of the various table styles in the current drawing. By default, the **Standard** table style is displayed in the drop-down list. Choose the **Launch the Table Style dialog** button on the right of this drop-down list to display the **Table**

Style dialog box. This dialog box can be used to create a new table style, modify, or delete an existing table style. You can also set the selected table style as the current table style. You will learn more about creating a new table style in the next section.

Insert options Area

The options in this area enable you to create tables with different types of data. You can add static data, externally-linked data, or object data to a table. The options in this area are discussed next.

Start from empty table

This option enables you to enter the data manually in the table. An empty table is created in which you have to enter the values manually. This type of table data is known as the static data. This is the default option selected for creating a table.

> **Tip**
> *You can copy an existing excel spreadsheet and paste it on the existing drawing as a table with the static data. To do so, use the* ***Home > Clipboard > Paste*** *drop-down* ***> Paste Special*** *and paste the copied data as AutoCAD LT entity. The resulting table will be similar to the table created using the* ***Start from empty table*** *option.*

From a data link

This option enables you to create a table automatically in AutoCAD LT from an excel sheet. This excel sheet remains linked with the drawing and any changes made in the excel sheet will reflect in the table. From the drop-down list, you can select an already linked excel sheet or you can also attach a new excel sheet to the drawing. To link a new excel file, choose the **Launch the Data Link Manager dialog** button; the **Select a Data Link** dialog box will be displayed, see Figure 7-36. Select the **Create a new Excel Data Link** option; the **Enter Data Link Name** dialog box will be invoked. Enter a name for the new data link that you are creating and choose the **OK** button; the **New Excel Data Link** dialog box will be invoked, see Figure 7-37. Choose the **Browse [...]** button; the **Save As** dialog box will be invoked. Specify the location of the excel file to be linked with the current drawing and choose the **Open** button from the **Save As** dialog box. After choosing the **Open** button, more options will be added in the **New Excel Data Link** dialog box, see Figure 7-38. The options in the modified **New Excel Data Link** dialog box are discussed next.

Choose an Excel file. This drop-down list displays the excel file attached to the current drawing. Choose the **Browse [...]** button to change the excel file to be linked with the current drawing.

Link options Area. In this area, you can specify the part of the excel file to be linked with the drawing. Select the **Link entire sheet** radio button to link the entire worksheet in the form of a table to the drawing. Select the **Link to a named range** radio button to link the already defined name ranges from the excel sheet to the drawing. Select the **Link to range** radio button to enter the range of cells to be included in the data link. Choose the **Preview** button; the preview of the range of cells included in the data link will be displayed. The preview of the attached data from the excel sheet will be displayed in the preview area. Clear the **Preview** check box to disable the preview of the table.

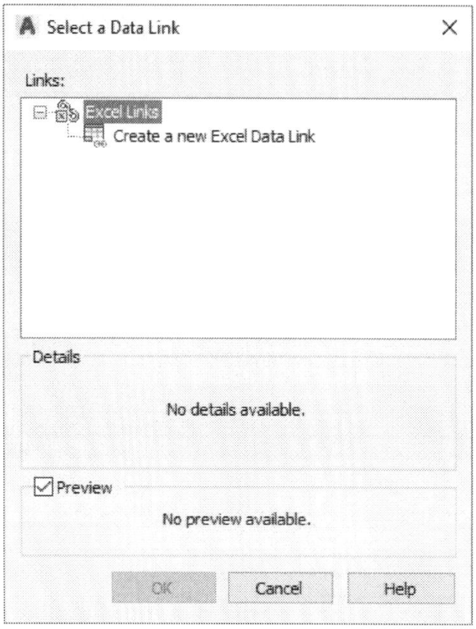

***Figure 7-36** The **Select a Data Link** dialog box*

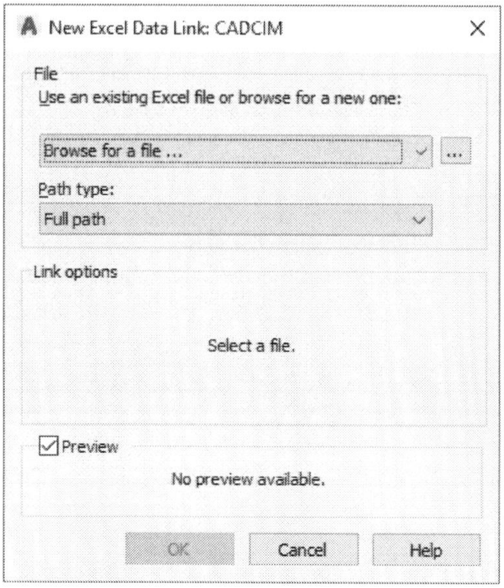

***Figure 7-37** The **New Excel Data Link** dialog box*

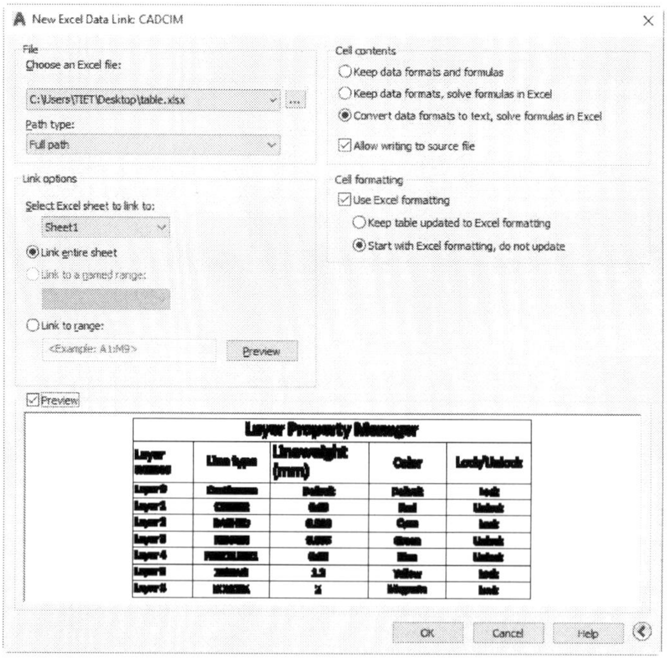

***Figure 7-38** The modified **New Excel Data Link** dialog box*

Cell contents Area. The **Keep data formats and formulas** radio button in this area allows you to link the excel file data along with the supported formulas. The **Keep data formats, solve formulas in Excel** radio button allows you to import data from the excel file, but the calculations made using the formulas are done in Excel. The **Convert data formats to text, solve formulas in Excel** radio button in this area is selected by default and lets you import the data of the excel file as text, and the calculations are done in Excel. The **Allow writing to source file** check box is selected by default. This check box enables you to choose the **Download from Source** button from the **Tables** panel of the **Annotate** tab in the **Ribbon** to update the changes made in the drawing table that is linked to the excel sheet.

Cell formatting Area. Select the **Use Excel formatting** check box to import any formatting settings if specified in the excel sheet. Other options in this area will be available only when the **Use Excel formatting** check box is selected. The **Keep table updated to Excel formatting** radio button allows you to update the drawing table according to the changes made in the excel sheet. If you select the **Start with Excel formatting, do not update** radio button, any formatting changes specified in the excel sheet will be imported to the table, but the changes made in the excel sheet after importing will not be updated in the drawing table. Choose the **OK** button twice to display the **Insert Table** dialog box.

Tip

*If you have made any changes in the drawing table, choose the **Upload to Source** tool from the **Tables** panel in the **Annotate** tab; the changes made in the drawing file will be reflected in the excel sheet that is linked to the drawing table. Similarly, if you have made any changes in the excel file after uploading, choose the **Download from Source** tool from the **Tables** panel in the **Annotate** tab; the changes made in the excel file will be reflected in the drawing file.*

Insertion behavior Area

The options in this area are used to specify the method of placing the table in the drawing. These options are discussed next.

Specify insertion point

This radio button is selected to place the table using the upper left corner of the table. If this radio button is selected and you choose **OK** from the **Insert Table** dialog box, you will be prompted to select the insertion point, which is by default the upper left corner of the table. By creating a different table style, you can change the point using which the table is inserted.

Specify window

If this radio button is selected and you choose **OK** from the **Insert Table** dialog box, you will be prompted to specify two corners for placing the table. The number of rows and columns in the table will depend on the size of the window you define.

Column & row settings Area

The options in this area are used to specify the number and size of rows and columns. The availability of these options depends on the option selected from the **Insert options** and **Insertion behavior** areas. These options are discussed next.

Columns

This spinner is used to specify the number of columns in the table.

Column width
This spinner is used to specify the width of columns in the table.

Data rows
This spinner is used to specify the number of rows in the table.

Row height
This spinner is used to specify the height of rows in the table. The height is defined in terms of lines and the minimum value is one line.

Set cell styles Area
The options in this area are used to assign different cell styles for the rows in the new table. You can assign different cell styles to all the rows of a table. The options in this area are discussed next.

First row cell style
This drop-down list is used to specify a cell style for the first row of the table. By default, the **Title** cell style is selected for the first row of the table.

Second row cell style
This drop-down list is used to specify a cell style for the second row of the table. By default, the **Header** cell style is selected for the second row of the table.

All other row cell styles
This drop-down list is used to specify a cell style for all the other rows of the table. By default, the **Data** cell style is selected for the remaining rows of the table.

After setting the parameters in the **Insert Table** dialog box, choose the **OK** button. Depending on the type of insertion behavior selected, you will be prompted to insert the table. As soon as you complete the insertion procedure, the in-place **Text editor** is displayed and you are allowed to enter the parameters in the first row of the table. By default, the first row is the title of the table. After entering the data, press ENTER. The first field of the first column is highlighted, which is the column head, and you are allowed to enter the data in it.

AutoCAD LT allows you to use the arrow keys on the keyboard to move to the other cells in the table. You can enter the data in the field and then press the arrow key to move to the other cells in the table. After entering the data in all the fields, press ENTER to exit the **Text Editor** toolbar.

Tip
*You can also right-click while entering the data in the table to display the shortcut menu. This shortcut menu is similar to that shown in the in-place **Text Editor** and can be used to insert field, symbols, text, and so on.*

CREATING A NEW TABLE STYLE

Ribbon: Home > Annotation > Table Style	**Toolbar:** Styles > Table Style
Menu Bar: Format > Table Style	**Command:** TABLESTYLE

To create a new table style, choose **Table Style** from the extended options of the **Annotation** panel in the **Home** tab; the **Table Style** dialog box will be displayed, as shown in Figure 7-39. You can also invoke this dialog box by choosing the inclined arrow of the **Tables** panel in the **Annotate** tab.

To create a new table style, choose the **New** button from the **Table Style** dialog box; the **Create New Table Style** dialog box will be displayed, as shown in Figure 7-40.

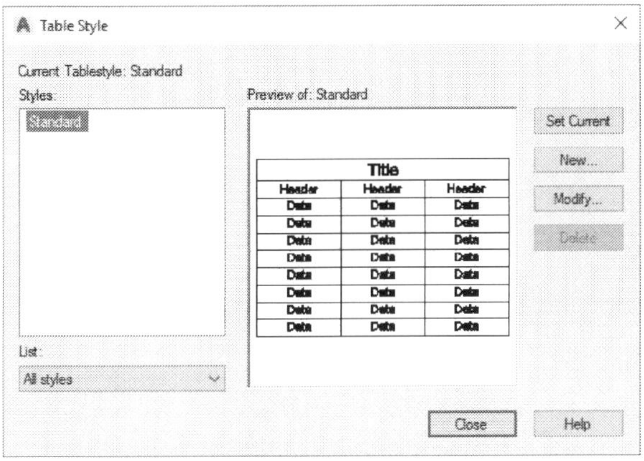

*Figure 7-39 The **Table Style** dialog box*

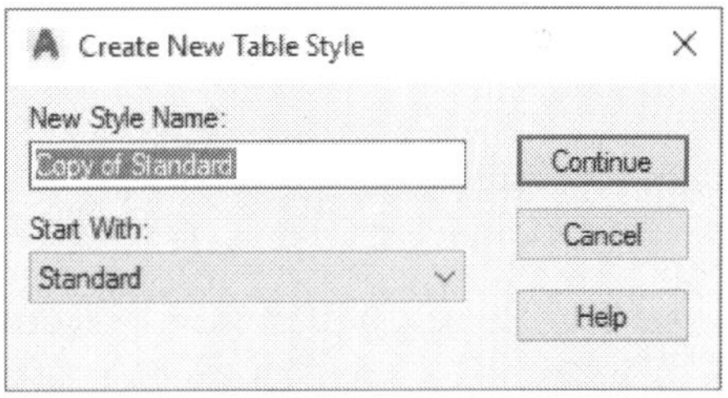

*Figure 7-40 The **Create New Table Style** dialog box*

Enter the name of the table style in the **New Style Name** edit box. Select the style on which you want to base the new style from the **Start With** drop-down list. By default, this drop-down list shows only the **Standard** table style. After specifying the settings, choose the **Continue** button from the **Create New Table Style** dialog box; the **New Table Style** dialog box will be displayed, see Figure 7-41. The options in this dialog box are discussed next.

Starting table Area

The options in this area enable you to select a table in your drawing to be used as reference for formatting the current table style. Once the table is selected, the table style associated with that table gets copied to the current table style and then you can modify it according to your requirement. The **Remove the starting table from this table style** button allows you to remove the initial table style from the current table style. This button is highlighted only when a table style is attached to the current one.

General Area

The **Table direction** drop-down list from the **General** area is used to specify the direction of the table. By default, this direction is down. As a result, the title and headers will be at the top and the data fields will be below them. If you select **Up** from the **Table direction** drop-down list, the title and headers will be at the bottom of this table and the data fields will be on the top of the table.

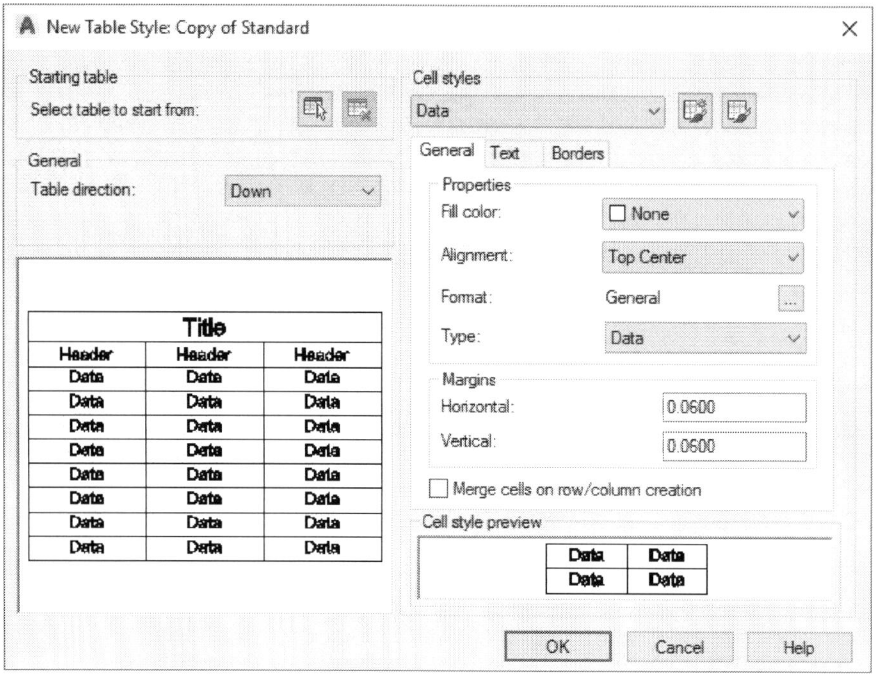

*Figure 7-41 The **New Table Style** dialog box*

Cell styles Area

This area has the options to define a new cell style or to modify the existing ones. The **Cell styles** drop-down list displays the existing cell styles within the table. It also displays the options to create a new cell style or to manage the existing ones. These options are discussed next.

Create new cell style

To create a new cell style, select this option from the **Cell styles** drop-down list. Alternatively, you can choose the **Create a new cell style** button on the right of the **Cell styles** drop-down list. On choosing this button, the **Create New Cell Style** dialog box will be invoked. Next, enter a style name for the new cell style. Select the existing cell style from the **Start With** drop-down list; the settings from the existing style will be used as a reference for the new one to be created. Next, choose the **Continue** button; the new cell style will get added to the **Cell style** drop-down list. Next, you can modify this new cell style by modifying the options in the **General**, **Text**, and **Borders** tab of the **New Table Style** dialog box.

General Tab

The options in this tab are used to control the general appearance, alignment, and formatting of the table cells. These options are shown in Figure 7-42 and are discussed next.

Fill color. This drop-down list is used to specify the fill color for the cells.

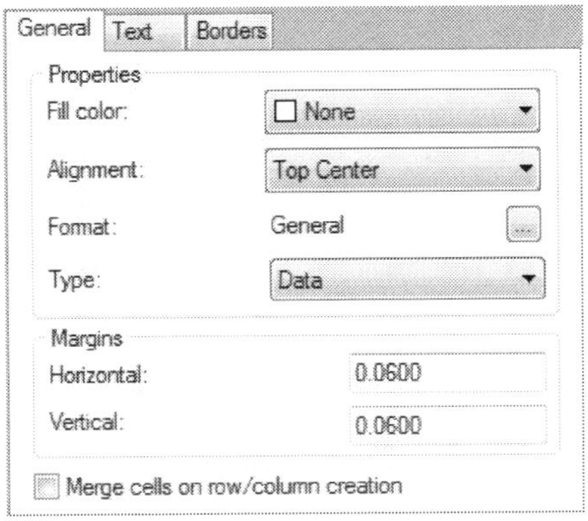

*Figure 7-42 The **General** tab of the **New Table Style** dialog box*

Alignment. This drop-down list is used to specify the alignment of the text entered in the cells. The default alignment is top center.

Format. If you choose the **Browse** [...] button available on the right of **Format**, the **Table Cell Format** dialog box will be displayed. This dialog box is used to specify the data type and format of the data type to be entered in the table. While creating the table, once the data type and format are specified, you cannot enter any other type of data or format without changing or modifying the table style. The default data type is **General**. In this data type, you can enter any alphanumeric characters.

Type. This drop-down list is used to specify the cell style either as a **Label** or **Data**.

Horizontal. This edit box is used to specify the minimum spacing between the data entered in the cells and the left and right border lines of the cells.

Vertical. This edit box is used to specify the minimum spacing between the data entered in the cells and the top and bottom border lines of the cells.

Merge cells on row/column creation. This check box is selected to merge all the new rows and columns created by using this cell style into one cell.

Text Tab

The options in this tab are used to control the display of the text to be written in the cells. These options are shown in Figure 7-43 and are discussed next.

Text style. This drop-down list is used to select the text style that is used for entering the text in the cells. By default, it shows only **Standard**, which is the default text style. You will learn to create more text styles later in this chapter.

Text height. This edit box is used to specify the height of the text to be entered in the cells.

Text color. This drop-down list is used to specify the color of the text that will be entered in the cells. If you select the **Select Color** option, the **Select Color** dialog box will be displayed. You can select the required color from the **True Color**, **Index Color**, or **Color Book** in this dialog box.

Text angle. This edit box is used to specify the slant angle of the text to be entered in the cell.

Borders Tab

The options in this tab are used to set the properties of the border of the table, see Figure 7-44. The line weight and color settings that you specify using this tab will be applied to all borders, outside borders, inside borders, bottom border, left border, top border, right border, or without border depending on which button is chosen from this tab. Select the **Double line** check box to display the borders with double lines. You can also control the spacing between the double lines by entering the gap value in the **Spacing** edit box.

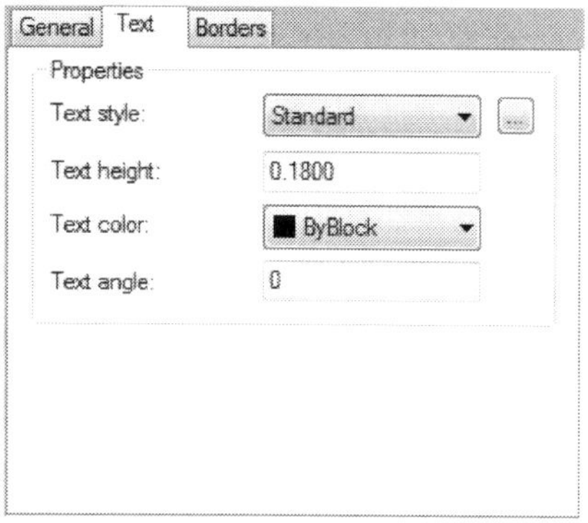

Figure 7-43 The ***Text*** *tab of the* ***New Table Style*** *dialog box*

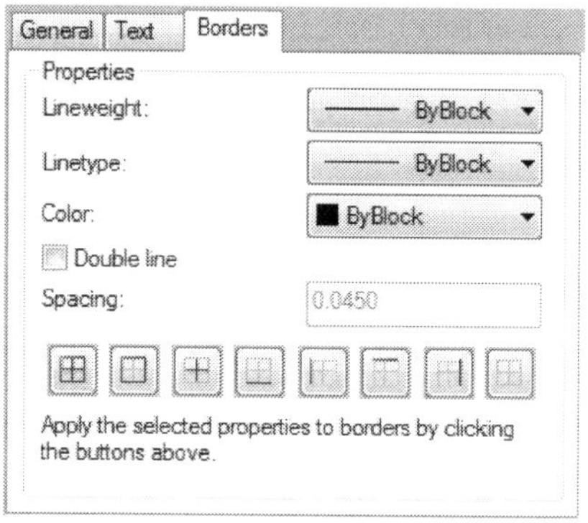

Figure 7-44 The ***Borders*** *tab of the* ***New Table Style*** *dialog box*

Manage cell styles

To create a new cell style, select this option from the **Cell style** drop-down list. Alternatively, choose the **Manage Cell Styles dialog** button on the right of the **Cell styles** drop-down list; the **Manage Cell Styles** dialog box will be invoked, see Figure 7-45. This dialog box displays all cell styles in the current table. You can also create a new cell style, delete, or rename an existing cell style. Note that the cell styles Title, Header, and Data are the default table styles provided in AutoCAD LT, and they cannot be deleted or renamed.

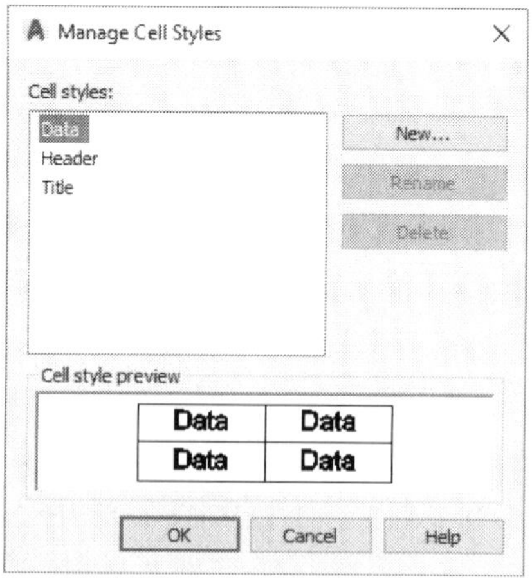

Figure 7-45 The ***Manage Cell Styles*** *dialog box*

SETTING A TABLE STYLE AS CURRENT

To set a table style as the current style for creating all the new tables, invoke the **Table Style** dialog box by choosing **Table Style** from the extended options of the **Annotation** panel in the **Home** tab. Next, select the table style from the **Styles** list box in the **Table Style** dialog box and choose the **Set Current** button. You can also set a table style current by selecting it from the **Table Style** drop-down list in the **Tables** panel. This is a convenient method of setting a table style current.

MODIFYING A TABLE STYLE

To modify a table style, choose **Table Style** in the extended options of the **Annotation** panel in the **Home** tab; the **Table Style** dialog box will be displayed. Select the table style from the **Styles** list box in the **Table Style** dialog box and choose the **Modify** button; the **Modify Table Style** dialog box is displayed. This dialog box is similar to the **New Table Style** dialog box. Modify the options in the various tabs and areas of this dialog box and then choose **OK** to exit the **Modify Table Style** dialog box.

MODIFYING TABLES

Select any cell in the table; the **Table Cell** tab will be added to the **Ribbon**, as shown in Figure 7-46. The options in the **Table Cell** tab are used to modify the table, insert block, add formulas, and perform other operations.

*Figure 7-46 The **Table Cell** tab added to the **Ribbon***

Modifying Rows

To insert a row above a cell, select a cell and choose the **Insert Above** tool from the **Rows** panel in the **Table Cell** tab. To insert a row below a cell, select a cell and choose the **Insert Below** tool from the **Rows** panel in the **Table Cell** tab. To delete the selected row, choose the **Delete Row(s)** tool from the **Rows** panel in the **Table Cell** tab. You can also add more than one row by selecting more than one row in the table.

Modifying Columns

This option is used to modify columns. To add a column to the left of a cell, select the cell and choose the **Insert Left** tool from the **Columns** panel in the **Table Cell** tab. To add a column to the right of a cell, select a cell and choose the **Insert Right** tool from the **Columns** panel in the **Table Cell** tab. To delete the selected column, choose the **Delete Column(s)** tool from the **Columns** panel in the **Table Cell** tab. You can also add more than one column by selecting more than one row in the table.

Merge Cells

This button is used to merge cells. Choose this button; the **Merge Cells** drop-down is displayed. There are three options available in the drop-down. Select multiple cells using the **SHIFT** key and then choose **Merge All** from the drop-down to merge all the selected cells. To merge all the cells in the row of the selected cell, choose the **Merge By Row** button from the drop-down. Similarly, to merge all cells in the column of the selected cell, select the **Merge By Column** tool from the drop-down. You can also divide the merged cells by choosing the **Unmerge Cells** button from the **Merge** panel.

Match Cell

This button is used to inherit the properties of one cell into the other. For example, if you have specified **Top Left Cell Alignment** in the source cell, then using the **Match Cell** button, you can inherit this property to the destination cell. This option is useful if you have assigned a number of properties to one cell, and you want to inherit these properties in some specified number of cells. Choose **Match Cell** from the **Cell Styles** panel in the **Table Cell** tab; the cursor is changed to the match properties cursor and you are prompted to choose the destination cell. Choose the cells to which you want the properties to be inherited and then press ENTER.

Table Cell Styles

This drop-down list displays the pre-existing cell styles or options to modify the existing ones. Select the desired cell style to be assigned to the selected cell. The **Cell Styles** drop-down list also has the options to create a new cell style or manage the existing ones. These options have been discussed earlier in the **Creating a New Table Style** topic.

Edit Borders

Choose the **Edit Borders** button from the **Table Cell** tab; the **Cell Border Properties** dialog box will be displayed, as shown in Figure 7-47. The options in this dialog box are similar to those in the **Border** tab of the **New Table Style** dialog box.

Text Alignment

The down arrow with the **Middle-Center** button of the **Cell Styles** panel in the **Ribbon** is used to align the text written in cells with respect to the cell boundary. Choose this button; the **Text Alignment** drop-down will be displayed. Select the desired text alignment from this drop-down; the text of the selected cell will get aligned accordingly.

Cell Locking

This button is used to lock the cells so that they cannot be edited by accident. Select a cell and choose **Cell Locking** from the **Cell Format** panel in the **Table Cell** tab; the **Cell Locking** drop-down list will be displayed. Four options are available in the drop-down list. The **Unlocked** option is chosen by default. Choose the **Content Locked** option to prevent the modification in the selected content of the text, but you can modify the formatting of the text. Choose the **Format Locked** option to prevent the modification in the formatting of the text, but in this case, you can modify the content of the text. Select the **Content and Format Locked** option to prevent the modification of both formatting and content of the text.

Data Format

The display of the text in the cell depends on the format type selected. Choose **Cell Format** to change the format of the text in the cell. On doing so, the **Data Format** drop-down list is displayed. Choose the required format from it. You can also select the **Custom Table Cell Format** option and choose the required format from the **Data type** list box in the **Table Cell Format** dialog box and then choose the **OK** button.

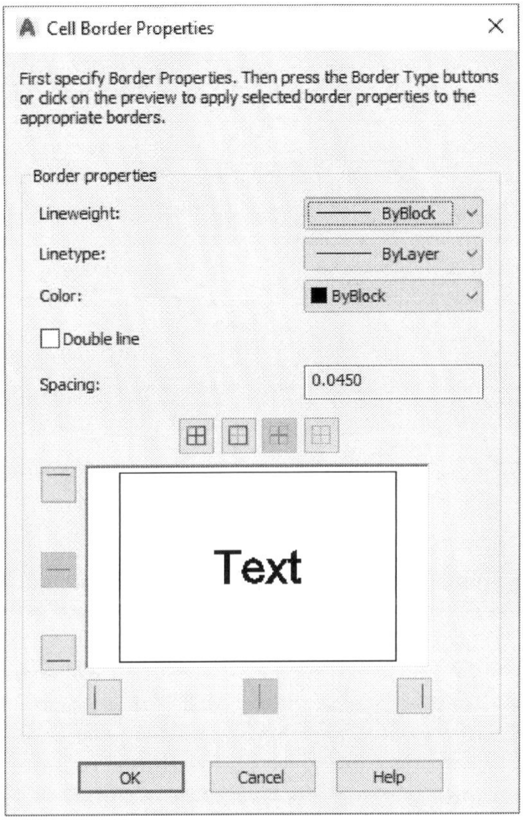

*Figure 7-47 The **Cell Border Properties** dialog box*

Block

Block tool is used to insert a block inside the selected cell. Choose the **Block** tool from the **Insert** panel; the **Insert a Block in a Table Cell** dialog box will be displayed, refer to Figure 7-48. Enter the name of the block in the **Name** edit box or choose the **Browse** button to locate the destination file of the block. If you have browsed the file path, it will be displayed in the **Path** area. The options available in the **Insert a Block in a Table Cell** dialog box are discussed next.

Properties Area

The options in this area are discussed next.

Scale. This edit box is used to specify the scale of the block. By default, this edit box is not available because the **AutoFit** check box is selected below this drop-down list. Selecting the **AutoFit** check box ensures that the block is scaled such that it fits in the selected cell.

Rotation angle. The **Rotation angle** edit box is used to specify the angle by which the block will be rotated before being placed in the cell.

Overall cell alignment. This drop-down list is used to define the block alignment in the selected cell.

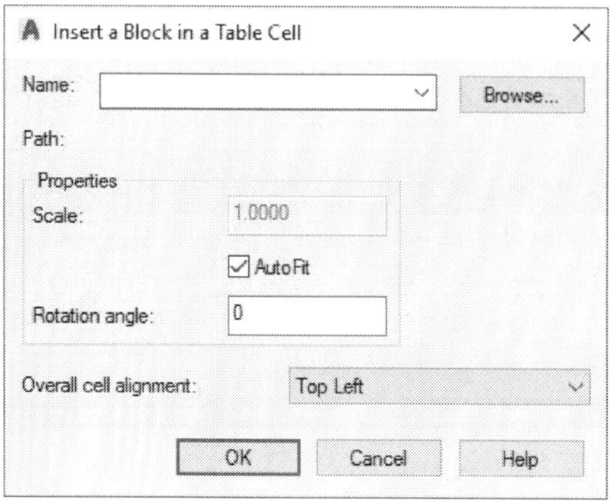

*Figure 7-48 The **Insert a Block in a Table Cell** dialog box*

Field

You can also insert a field in the cell. The field contains the data that is associative to the property that defines the field. For example, you can insert a field that has the name of the author of the current drawing. If you have already defined the author of the current drawing in the **Drawing Properties** dialog box, it will automatically be displayed in the field. If you modify the author name and update the field, the changes will automatically be made in the text. When you choose the **Field** button from the **Insert** panel, the **Field** dialog box will be displayed. You can select the field to be added from the **Field names** list box and select the format of the field from the **Format** list box. Choose **OK** after selecting the field and format. If the data in the selected field is already defined, it will be displayed in the **Text window**. If not, the field will display dashes (----).

Formula

Choose **Formula** from the **Insert** panel; a drop-down list is displayed. This drop-down list contains the formulas that can be applied to a given cell. The formula calculates the values for that cell using the values of other cell. In a table, the columns are named with letters (like A, B, C, ...) and rows are named with numbers (like 1, 2, 3, ...). The **TABLEINDICATOR** system variable controls the display of column letters and row numbers. By default, the **TABLEINDICATOR** system variable is set to 1, which means the row numbers and column letters will be displayed when **Text Editor** is invoked. Set the system variable to zero to turn off the visibility of row numbers and column letters. The nomenclature of cells is done using the column letters and row numbers. For example, the cell corresponding to column A and row 2 is A2. For a better understanding, some of the cells have been labeled accordingly in Figure 7-49.

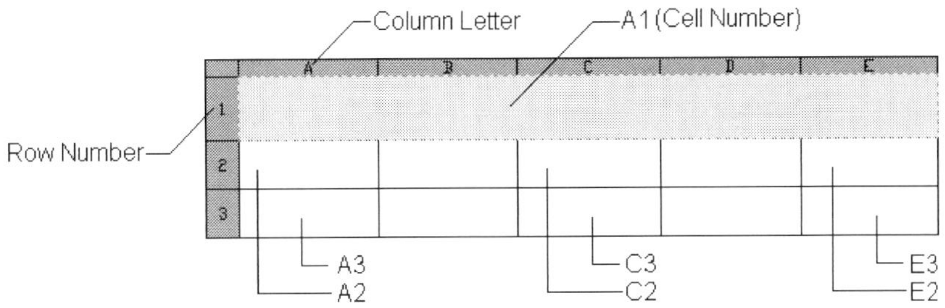

***Figure 7-49** The **Table** showing nomenclature for Columns, Rows, and Cells*

Formulas are defined by the range of cells. The range of cells is specified by specifying the name of first and the last cell of the range, separated by a colon (:). The range takes all the cells falling between specified rows/columns. For example, if you write A2 : C3, this means all the cells falling in 2nd and 3rd rows, Column A and B will be taken into account. To insert a formula, double click on the cell; **Text Editor** is invoked. You can now write the syntax of the formula in the cell. The syntax for different formulas are discussed later while explaining different formulas. Formulas can also be inserted by using the **Formula** drop-down list. Different formulas available in the **Formula** drop-down list are discussed next.

Sum

The **Sum** option gives output for a given cell as the sum of the numerical values entered in a specified range of cells. Choose the **Sum** option from the **Table Cell > Insert > Formula** drop-down; you will be prompted to select the first corner of the table cell range and then the second corner. The sum of values of all the cells that fall between the selected range will be displayed as the output. As soon as you specify the second corner, the **Text Editor** is displayed and also the formula is displayed in the cell. In addition to the formula, you can also write multiline text in the cell. Choose **Close Text Editor** from the **Close** panel to exit the editor. When you exit the text editor, the formula is replaced by a hash (#). Now, if you enter numerical values in the cells included in the range, the hash (#) is replaced according to the addition of those numerical values. The prompt sequence, when you select the **Sum** option, is given next.

Select first corner of table cell range: *Specify a point in the first cell of the cell range.*
Select second corner of table cell range: *Specify a point in the last cell of the cell range.*

Note
*The syntax for the **Sum** option is: =Sum{Number of the first cell of cell range (for example: A2): Number of the last cell of the cell range (for example: C5)}*

Average

This option is used to insert a formula that calculates the average of values of the cells falling in the cell range. The prompt sequence for this option is the same as for the **Sum** option.

Note
*The syntax for the **Average** option is: =Average{Number of the first cell of the cell range (for example: A2): Number of the last cell of the cell range (for example: C5)}*

Count

This option is used to insert a formula that calculates the number of cells falling under the cell range. The prompt sequence for this option is the same as for the **Sum** option.

Note

*The syntax for the **Count** option is: =Count{Number of the first cell of cell range (for example: A2): Number of the last cell of cell range (for example: C5)}*

Cell

This option equates the current cell with a selected cell. Whenever there is a change in the value of the selected cell, the change is automatically updated in the other cell. To do so, choose the **Cell** option from **Table Cell > Insert > Formula** drop-down; you will be prompted to select a table cell. Select the cell with which you want to equate the current cell. The prompt sequence for the **Cell** option is given next.

Select table cell: *Select a cell to equate with the current cell.*

Note

*The syntax for the **Cell** option is: =Number of the cell.*

Equation

Using this option, you can manually write equations. The syntax for writing the equations should be the same as explained earlier.

Manage Cell Content

The **Manage Cell Contents** button is used to control the sequence of the display of blocks in the cell, if there are more than one block in a cell. Choose **Manage Cell Contents** from the **Insert** panel; the **Manage Cell Content** dialog box will be displayed, see Figure 7-50. The options in the **Manage Cell Content** dialog box are discussed next.

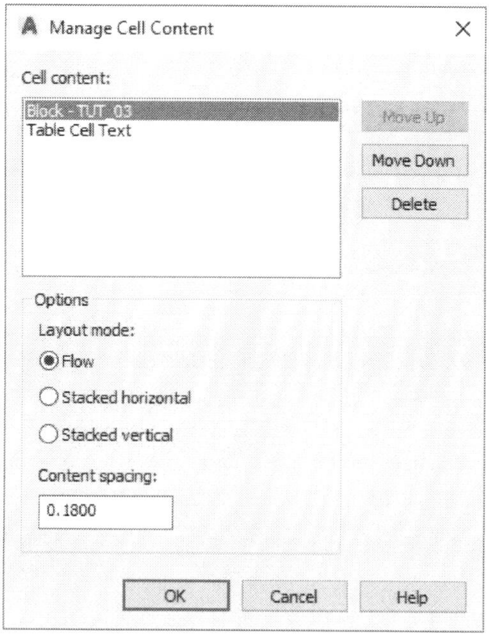

***Figure 7-50** The **Manage Cell Content** dialog box*

Cell content Area

This area lists all blocks entered in the cell according to the order of their insertion sequence.

Move Up

This button is used to move the selected block one level up in the display order.

Move Down

This button is used to move the selected block one level down in the display order.

Delete

This button is used to delete the selected block from the table cell.

Options Area

The options in this area are used to control the direction in which the inserted block is placed in the cell. If you select the **Flow** radio button, the direction of placement of the blocks in the cell will depend on the width of the cell. Select the **Stacked horizontal** radio button to place the inserted blocks horizontally. Similarly, select the **Stacked vertical** radio button to place the inserted blocks vertically. You can also specify the gap to be maintained between the two consecutive blocks by entering the desired gap value in the **Content spacing** edit box.

Link Cell

To insert data from an excel into the selected table, choose **Data > Link Cell** from the **Table Cell** tab; the **Select a Data Link** dialog box will be displayed. The options in this dialog box are similar to the **Select a Data Link** dialog box that has been discussed earlier in the "**Inserting Table in the Drawing**" topic of this chapter.

Download from source

If the contents of the attached excel spreadsheet are changed after linking it to a cell, you can update these changes in the table by choosing this button. AutoCAD LT will inform you about the changes in the content of the attached excel sheet by displaying an information bubble at the lower-right corner of the screen.

Tip

*The **Cut** and **Copy** options can be used to move or copy the content from one cell to another. Using the **Paste** option, you can paste the content that you have cut or copied from one cell to another. Place the cursor on the **Recent Input** option; a flyout containing the recent command inputs will be displayed. Choose the **Remove All Property Overrides** option to restore all the default properties of the table.*

Note

*The options in the **Table Cell** tab are also available in the shortcut menu that is displayed when you select any cell in the table and then right-click on it.*

CREATING TEXT STYLES

Ribbon: Annotate > Text > Text Style (Inclined arrow) or Home > Annotation > Text Style
Toolbar: Text > Text Style or Styles > Text Style
Menu Bar: Format > Text Style **Command:** STYLE/ST

By default, the text in AutoCAD LT is written using the default text style which is called **Standard**. This text style is assigned a default text font (*txt.shx*). Another default text style that is available is **Annotative**. This text style is also assigned a default text font (*txt.shx*). If you need to write a text using some other fonts and other parameters, you need to use the **Text Editor**. This is because you can change the formatting and font of the text only by using this command.

However, it is a tedious job to use the **Text Editor** every time to write the text and change its properties. That is why, AutoCAD LT provides you with an option for modifying the default text style or creating a new text style. After creating a new text, you can make it current. All the texts written after making the new style current will use this style. To create a new text style or modify the default style, left click on the inclined arrow in the **Text** panel of the **Annotate** tab; the **Text Style** dialog box will be displayed, as shown in Figure 7-51.

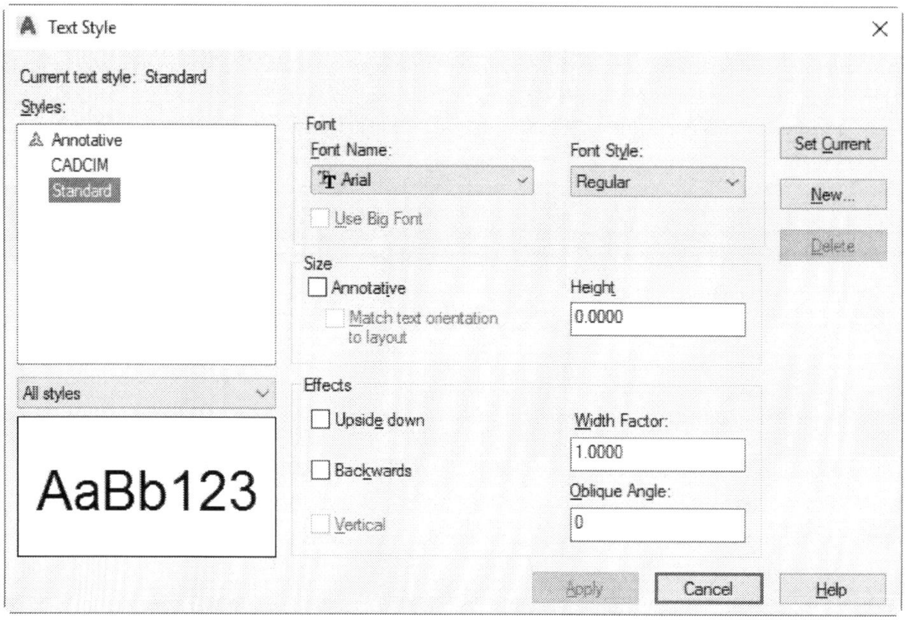

***Figure 7-51** The **Text Style** dialog box*

The **Styles** area displays the styles present in the drawing along with the current style highlighted in blue. An annotative symbol is displayed in front of the annotative text styles. The **Style List Filter** drop-down list below the **Styles** area is used to specify whether all styles will be displayed or only the styles that have been used in the drawing will be displayed. To create a new style, choose the **New** button from the **Text Style** dialog box; the **New Text Style** dialog box will be displayed, as shown in Figure 7-52. Choose the **OK** button from the dialog box.

A new style having the entered name and the properties present in the **Text Style** dialog box will be created. To modify this style, select the style name from the list box and then change the different settings by entering new values in the appropriate boxes. You can change the font by selecting a new font from the **Font Name** drop-down list. Similarly, you can change the text height, width, and oblique angle.

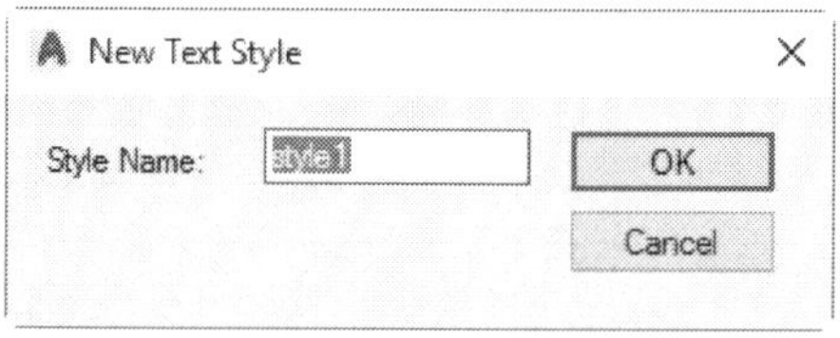

***Figure 7-52** The **New Text Style** dialog box*

Remember that if you have already specified the height of the text in the **Text Style** dialog box, AutoCAD LT will not prompt you to enter the text height while writing the text using the **Single Line** tool. The text will be created using the height specified in the text style. If you want AutoCAD LT to prompt you for the text height, specify 0 text height in the dialog box. Select the **Annotative** check box to automate the process of scaling the text height. Annotative texts are defined according to the height of the text to be displayed on the paper. According to the annotation scale set for the spaces, the text will be displayed in the viewports and the model space. Select the **Match text orientation to layout** check box to match the orientation of the text in the paper space viewport with the orientation of the layout.

For **Width Factor**, 1 is the default value. If you want the letters expanded, enter a width factor greater than 1. For compressed letters, enter a width factor less than 1. Similarly, for the **Oblique Angle**, 0 is the default value. If you want the slant of the letters toward the right, the value should be greater than 0; to slant the letters toward the left, the value should be less than 0. You can also force the text to be written upside down, backwards, and vertically by checking their respective check boxes. As you make the changes, you can see their effect in the **Preview** box. After making the desired changes, choose the **Apply** button and then the **Close** button to exit the dialog box. Figure 7-53 shows the text objects with all these settings.

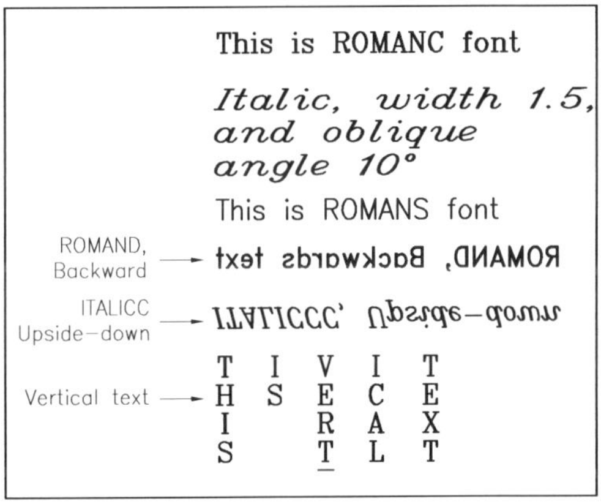

***Figure 7-53** Specifying different features to text style files*

CREATING ANNOTATIVE TEXT

In AutoCAD LT is now you do not need to calculate the text height in advance. While creating the annotative text, if you decide the text height to be displayed on the paper, the current annotation scale will automatically decide the display size of the text in the model space or the paper space viewport. For example, if you want the text to be displayed at a height of 1/4" on the paper, you can define a text style having a **Paper Text Height** of 1/4". When you add text to a viewport having a scale of 1/4"=1'0", the current annotation scale, which is set as the same scale as of the viewport, automatically scales the text to display appropriately at 12". You can create annotative text by assigning the annotative text style that has been explained earlier.

To write a single line annotative text, choose an annotative type text style from the **Text Style** dialog box and set it as the current text style. The annotative type text style will be displayed with an annotative symbol on its side. Next, enter the text in the drawing using the **Single Line** tool in the Command prompt. To write multiline annotative text, enter the **Multiline Text** tool at the Command prompt and specify the two opposite corners of the box denoting the width of the multiline text; the **Text Editor** will be displayed on the screen. You can also select an existing annotative text style from **Text Style** option in the **Text Editor** tab or choose **Annotative** button in the **Style** panel **Text Editor** tab to create the annotative multiline text.

The existing non-annotative texts whether it is single line or multiline can also be converted into the annotative text. To do so, select the text object and right-click on it to choose the **Properties** option from the shortcut menu. In the **PROPERTIES** palette below the **Text** area, click on the **Annotative** edit box and select the **Yes** option from the drop-down list.

CHECKING SPELLING

Ribbon: Annotate > Text > Check Spelling	**Toolbar:** Text > Spell Check
Menu Bar: Tools > Spelling	**Command:** SPELL/SP

You can check the spelling of the text in a drawing. The text that can be checked for spelling by using the **Check Spelling** tool are: single line or multiline text, dimension text, text in external references, and block attribute text. To check the spelling in a given text, choose the **Check Spelling** tool from the **Text** panel in the **Annotate** tab; the **Check Spelling** dialog box will be displayed, see Figure 7-54. To start the spell check, choose the **Start** button from the **Check Spelling** dialog box. If there is no spelling mistake in the drawing, the **AutoCAD LT Message** dialog box with the message '**Spelling check complete**' will be displayed. Choose the **OK** button from the **AutoCAD LT Message** dialog box to close it. If any spelling error is found in the drawing, AutoCAD LT will highlight the word and zoom it according to the size of the window so that it is easily visible. The options in the **Check Spelling** dialog box are discussed next.

The **Where to check** drop-down list displays three options to specify the portion of the drawing to be Spell checked during the spelling check. These options are: **Entire drawing**, **Current space/layout**, and **Selected objects**. If you select the **Selected objects** option, the **Select text objects** button will be highlighted to enable you to select the text in the drawing to be checked. The **Not in dictionary** box displays the text that is found to be misspelled. The correct spelled alternate words are listed in the **Suggestions** box. The **Main dictionary** drop-down list displays the language options in which you want to check the text.

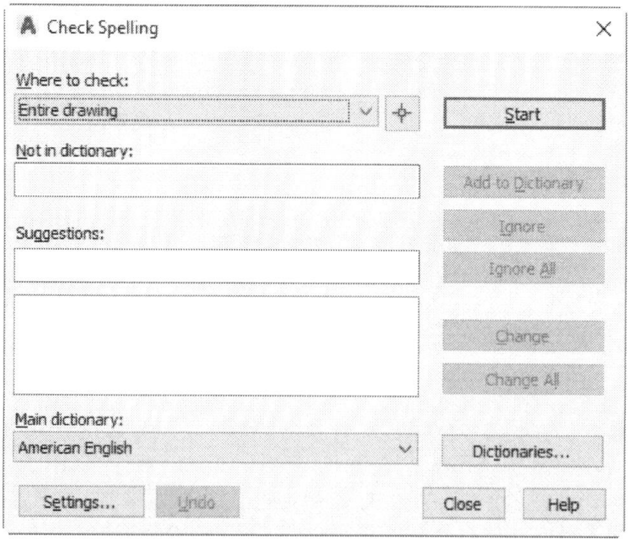

Figure 7-54 *The* ***Check Spelling*** *dialog box*

The **Add to Dictionary** button is used to add the identified misspelled word to the dictionary. The **Ignore** button leaves the identified misspelled words intact. The **Ignore All** button leaves all the identified misspelled words intact. The **Change** button substitutes the present word with the word suggested in the **Suggestions** box. The **Change All** button substitutes all the words that are similar to the currently selected word with the word suggested in the **Suggestions** box. You can also use the MS Word dictionary or any other dictionary for checking spellings. Choose the **Dictionaries** button; the **Dictionaries** dialog box will be displayed, see Figure 7-55. Next, select the **Manage custom dictionaries** option from the **Current custom dictionary** drop-down list; the **Manage Custom Dictionaries** dialog box will be displayed, see Figure 7-56. From this dialog box, you can create a new dictionary, add an existing dictionary, or delete a dictionary from the **Custom dictionaries list**. To add the words listed in the custom dictionary, choose the **Add** button from the **Dictionaries** dialog box. The **Settings** button in the **Check Spelling** dialog box is used to specify the type of text to be checked for spelling in your drawing.

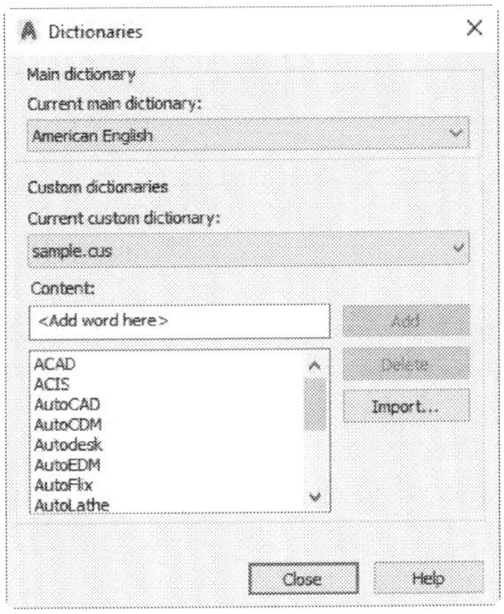

*Figure 7-55 The **Dictionaries** dialog box*

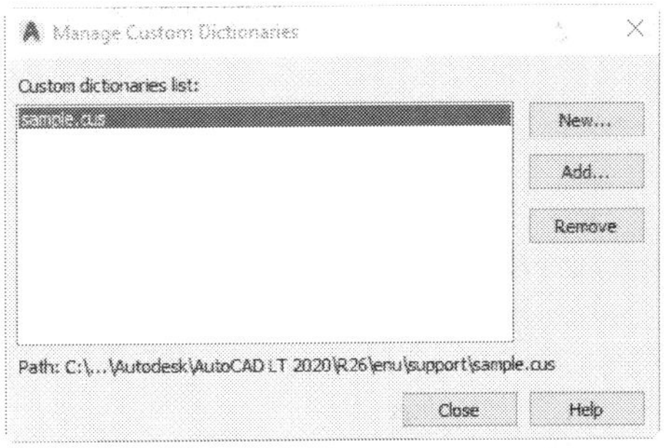

*Figure 7-56 The **Manage Custom Dictionaries** dialog box*

Note

*The dictionaries can also be changed by specifying the name in the **DCTMAIN** or **DCTCUST** system variable.*

TEXT QUALITY AND TEXT FILL

AutoCAD LT supports **TrueType fonts**. You can use your own **TrueType fonts** by adding them to the Fonts directory. You can also keep your fonts in a separate directory, in that case you must specify the location of your fonts directory in the AutoCAD LT search path.

The resolution and text fill of the **TrueType font** text is controlled by the **TEXTFILL** and **TEXTQLTY** system variables. If **TEXTFILL** is set to 1, the text will be filled. If the value is set to 0, the text will not be filled. On the screen the text will appear filled, but when it is plotted the text will not be filled. The **TEXTQLTY** variable controls the quality of the **TrueType font** text. The value of this variable can range from 0 to 100. The default value is 50, which gives a resolution of 300 dpi (dots per inch). If the value is set to 100, the text will be drawn at 600 dpi. The higher the resolution, the more time it takes to regenerate or plot the drawing.

FINDING AND REPLACING TEXT

Ribbon: Annotate > Text > Find Text **Toolbar:** Text > Find
Menu Bar: Edit > Find **Command:** FIND

You can use the **Find Text** search box to find and replace a text. The text can be a line text created by the **Single Line** tool, paragraph text created by the **Multiline Text** tool, dimension annotation text, block attribute value, hyperlinks, or hyperlink description. To find a text, enter the text in the **Find Text** search box in the **Text** panel and press ENTER; the **Find and Replace** dialog box will be displayed, as shown in Figure 7-57. You can use this dialog box to perform the following functions:

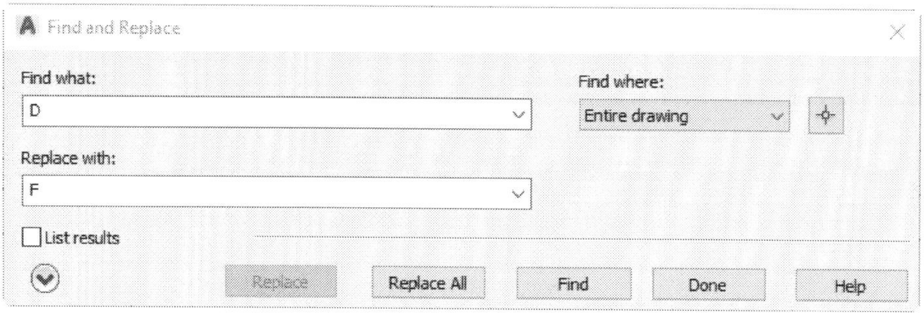

*Figure 7-57 The **Find and Replace** dialog box*

Finding Text

To find a text, enter the text that you want to find in the **Find what** edit box. You can search the entire drawing or confine your search to the selected text. To select the text, choose the **Select objects** button available to the right of the **Find where** drop-down list. The **Find and Replace** dialog box will temporarily be closed and AutoCAD LT switches to the drawing window. Once you have selected the text, the **Find and Replace** dialog box is displayed again. In the **Find where** drop-down list, you can specify if you need to search the entire drawing or the current selection. Choose the **More Options (Alt+ Shift +>)** button available at the bottom left corner of the **Find and Replace** dialog box; the **Find and Replace** dialog box gets expanded, as shown in Figure 7-58. In this dialog box, you can specify whether to find the whole word and whether to match the case of the specified text. To find the text, choose the **Find** button. The text found along with the surrounding text will be displayed in the **Text String** column of the **List results** area, provided the **List results** check box is selected. To find the next occurrence of the text, choose the **Find** button again.

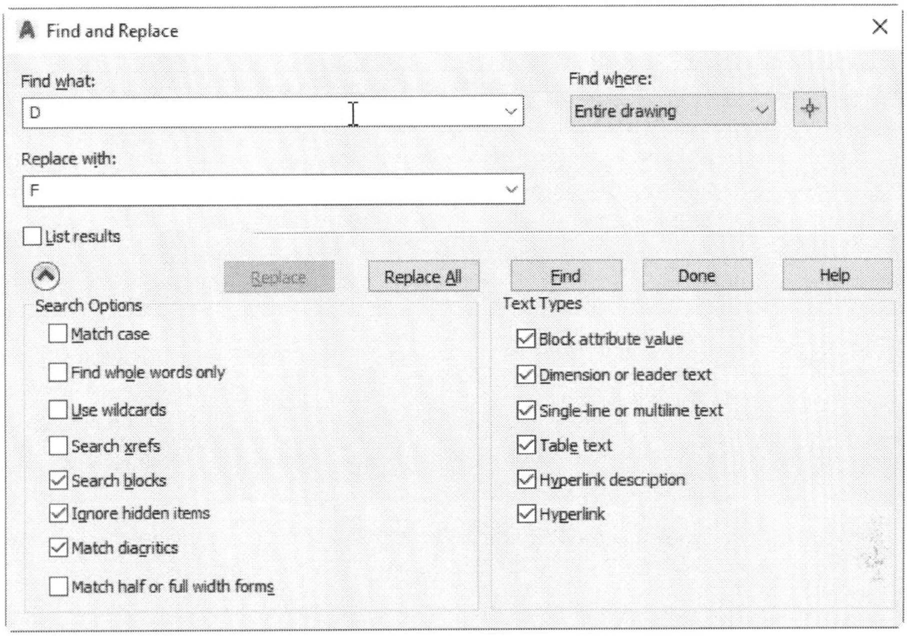

*Figure 7-58 The expanded **Find and Replace** dialog box*

Replacing Text

If you want to replace the specified text with the new text, enter the new text in the **Replace with** edit box. Now, if you choose the **Replace** button, only the found text will be replaced. If you choose the **Replace All** button, all occurrences of the specified text will be replaced with the new text.

CREATING TITLE SHEET TABLE IN A SHEET SET

While working with a sheet set, it is recommended that you create a title sheet that has the details about the sheets in the sheet set. You can enter the details about the sheets in the table. The advantage of using a table is that the information in it can be automatically updated if there is a change in the sheet number or name. Also, if a sheet is removed from the current sheet set, you can easily update the table to reflect the change in the sheet set.

To create a table in a sheet set, double-click on any one of the layouts added to the sheet set. Remember that this layout will be the title sheet.

Tip

*If the title sheet is displayed at the bottom of the list in the **SHEET SET MANAGER**, you can drag and move it to the top, below the name of the sheet set. Hold the left mouse button down on the title sheet and drag the cursor upward. Next, release the left mouse button below the name of the sheet set.*

When the title sheet is opened, right-click on the name of the sheet set in the **SHEET SET MANAGER**, and then choose the **Insert Sheet List Table** option from the shortcut menu, as shown in Figure 7-59. Note that this option will not be available, if the model tab is active or if the layout is not from the current sheet set. On choosing the **Insert Sheet List Table** option, the **Sheet List Table** dialog box will be displayed, as shown in Figure 7-60.

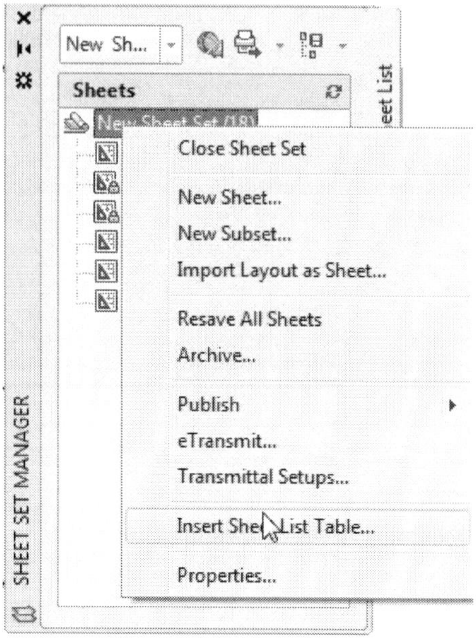

Figure 7-59** Inserting table in the title sheet using the **SHEET SET MANAGER

Enter the title of the table in the **Title Text** text box in the **Table Data** area. By default, two rows will be displayed for each subset in the table. This is because there are only two rows displayed in the **Column Settings** area. You can add additional rows by choosing the **Add** button. To change the data type of a row, click on the field in the **Data type** column. The field will be changed into a drop-down list. Select the required data type from this drop-down list. After specifying all the parameters, choose **OK** from the **Insert Sheet List Table** dialog box. The table will be attached to the cursor and you will be prompted to specify the insertion point. Specify the insertion point for the table. The table will be inserted and based on the parameters selected, the sheets are displayed in the table. Figure 7-61 shows a sheet list table inserted in a title sheet.

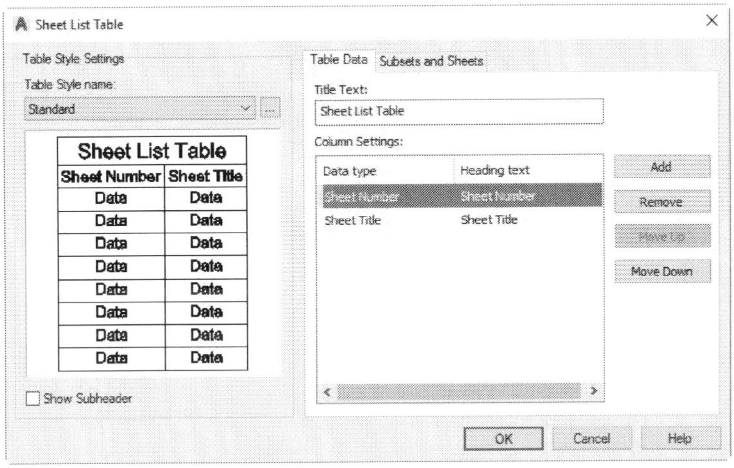

*Figure 7-60 The **Sheet List Table** dialog box*

Sheet List Table	
1	Title Sheet
Main Parts	
2	Base Part
3	Brasses
4	Cap
Fastners	
5	Bolt
6	Nut
7	Washer

Figure 7-61 Sheet list table

If any changes are made in the sheet set numbering or any other property of the sheets in the sheet set, you can easily highlight those changes in the sheet list table by updating it. To update the sheet list table, right-click on it and choose **Sheet List Table > Update Sheet List Table** from the shortcut menu. The sheet list table is automatically updated.

Self-Evaluation Test

Answer the following questions and then compare them to those given at the end of this chapter:

1. Multiple lines of text can be entered at any desired location in the drawing area by using the __________ tool.

2. With the __________ justification option of the **Single Line** tool, AutoCAD LT adjusts the letter width to fit the text between the two given points, but the height remains constant.

3. While writing a text by using the **Multiline Text** tool, the height specified in the **Text Editor** does not affect the __________ system variable.

4. You can change the text string in the edit box by using the __________ tool to edit a single line text. However, to edit a multiline text, you must choose the full editor button in the **Contents** edit box of the **PROPERTIES** palette.

5. You can use the __________ system variable to specify the new font mapping file.

6. Tables in AutoCAD LT are created using the **Tablet** tool. (T/F)

7. An annotative text automatically gets scaled according to the viewport's scale. (T/F)

8. You can insert a block into a table cell. (T/F)

9. The **Standard** text style cannot be used for creating annotative text. (T/F)

10. You can control the height of an individual column separately by choosing the **Manual height** sub-option from **Text Editor > Insert > Columns > Dynamic Columns** of the **Ribbon**. (T/F)

Review Questions

Answer the following questions:

1. Which of the following buttons in the **Table** toolbar is used to inherit the properties from one cell to another?

   (a) **Cell Styles** (b) **Match Cells**
   (c) **Link Cells** (d) **Manage Cell Content**

2. Which of the following text styles is not present in AutoCAD LT by default?

   (a) **Standard** (b) **Annotative**
   (c) **Auto text** (d) None of these

3. If you want the text to be displayed at a height of 1/4" on the paper, you can define a text style having a paper height of 1/4". When you add a text to a viewport having a scale of 1/4"=1'0", the current annotation scale, which is set to the same scale as the viewport, automatically scales the text to display approximately at __________.

   (a) 0.1875" (b) 0.375"
   (c) 2.66" (d) 4.8"

4. Which of the following characters in the **Text Editor** tab is used to stack the text with a diagonal line without using the **Autostack Properties** dialog box?

(a) ^ (b) /
(c) # (d) @

5. Which of the following commands can be used to create a new text style and modify the existing ones?

(a) **TEXT** (b) **MTEXT**
(c) **STYLE** (d) **SPELL**

6. The __________ sub-option in the **Formula** flyout of the **Insert** panel in the **Table** tab is used to equate the current cell with the selected cell.

7. The four main text alignment modes are __________, __________, __________, and __________.

8. You can use the __________ tool to write a paragraph text whose width can be specified by defining the __________ of the text boundary.

9. When the **Justify** option is invoked, the user can place the text in one of the __________ various types of alignment by choosing the desired alignment option.

10. A text created by using the __________ tool is a single object irrespective of the number of lines it contains.

11. Using the **Multiline Text** tool, the character __________ stacks a text vertically without a line (tolerance stack).

12. If you want to edit text, select it and then right-click such that various editing options __________ in the menu are available.

13. The __________ tool is used to check the spelling of all the texts written in the current drawing.

14. You cannot insert a field by using the **Multiline Text** tool. (T/F)

15. You can add or delete rows and columns from a table by using the **Table** toolbar. (T/F)

16. The **Single Line** tool does not allow you to see the text on the screen as you type it. (T/F)

Exercise 2 *Text*

Write the text, shown in Figure 7-62, on the screen. Use the text justification that will produce the text as shown in the drawing. Assume a value for text height. Use the **PROPERTIES** palette to change the text, as shown in Figure 7-63.

Figure 7-62 *Drawing for Exercise 2*

Figure 7-63 *Drawing after changing the text*

Exercise 3 — Text Style

Write the text on the screen, as shown in Figure 7-64. First, you must define new text styles by using the **STYLE** command with the attributes, as shown in the figure. The text height is 0.25 units.

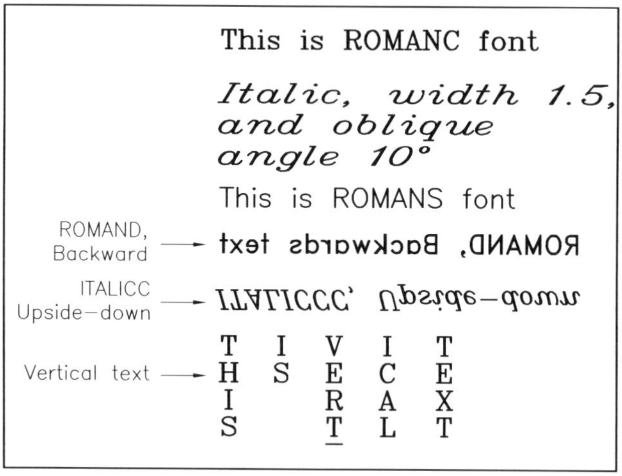

Figure 7-64 *Drawing for Exercise 3*

Exercise 4

Draw the sketch shown in Figure 7-65 using the draw, edit, and display commands. Do not dimension the drawing.

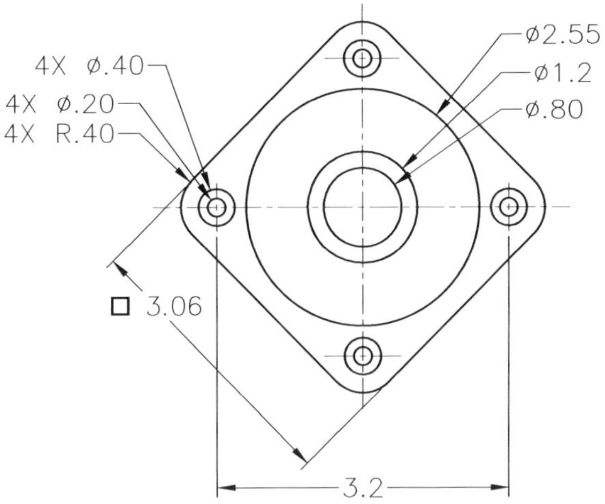

Figure 7-65 Drawing for Exercise 4

Exercise 5 — *Mirror*

Draw the sketches shown in Figures 7-66 and 7-67. Use the **Mirror** tool to duplicate the features that are identical. Do not dimension the drawing.

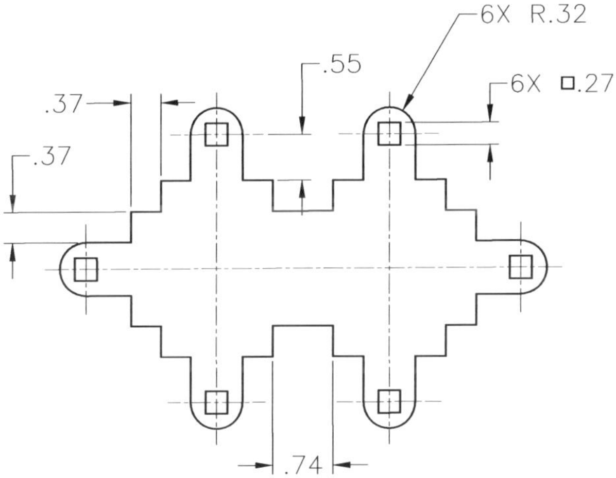

Figure 7-66 Drawing for Exercise 5

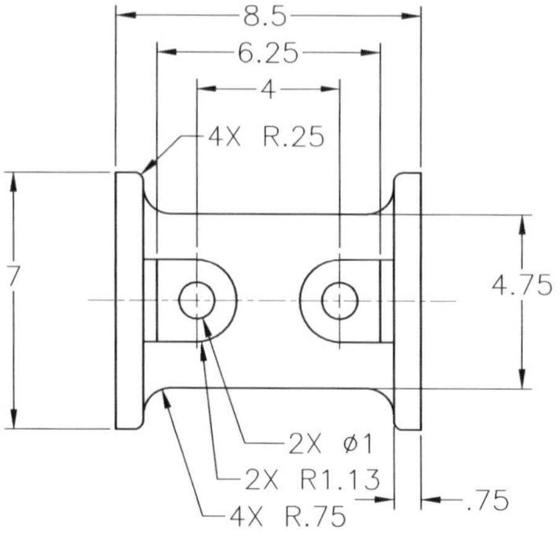

Figure 7-67 Drawing for Exercise 5

Exercise 6

Draw Figure 7-68. Do not dimension the drawing.

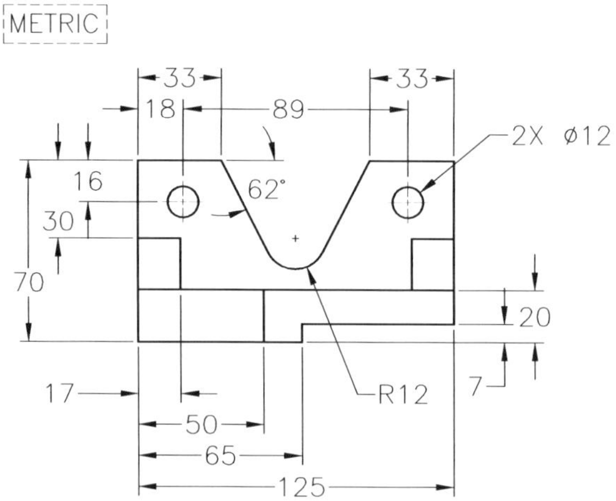

Figure 7-68 Drawing for Exercise 6

Problem-Solving Exercise 1

Draw the sketch shown in Figure 7-69 using the draw, edit, and display commands. Assume the missing dimensions. Do not dimension the drawing.

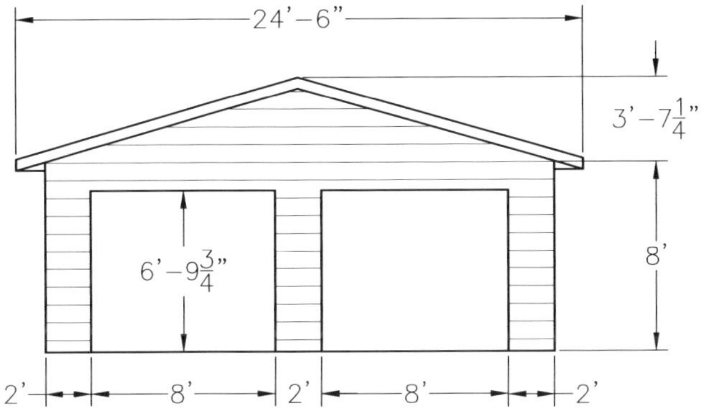

Figure 7-69 *Drawing for Problem-Solving Exercise 1*

Problem-Solving Exercise 2

Draw Figure 7-70 using the drawing, editing, and displaying tools of AutoCAD LT. Also, add text to the drawing. Assume the missing dimensions. Do not dimension the drawing.

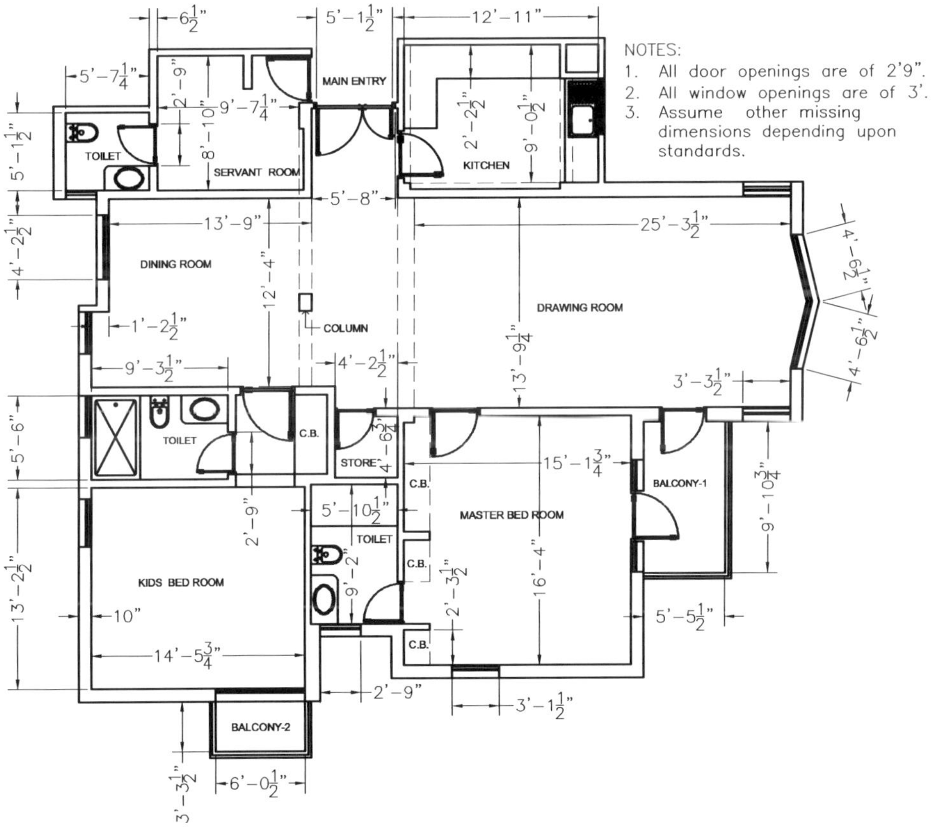

Figure 7-70 *Drawing for Problem-Solving Exercise 2*

Answers to Self-Evaluation Test

1. Single Line, **2.** Fit, **3.** TEXTSIZE, **4.** Edit, **5.** FONTMAP, **6.** F, **7.** T, **8.** T, **9.** F, **10.** T

Chapter 8

Basic Dimensioning, Geometric Dimensioning, and Tolerancing

Learning Objectives

After completing this chapter, you will be able to:

- *Understand the need of dimensioning in drawings*
- *Understand fundamental dimensioning terms*
- *Apply the associative and annotative dimensioning*
- *Use the Quick Dimension option for quick dimensioning*
- *Create various types of dimensions in a drawing*
- *Create center marks and centerlines*
- *Attach leaders to objects*
- *Attach and modify multileaders*
- *Use geometric tolerancing, feature control frames, and characteristic symbols*
- *Combine geometric characteristics and create composite position tolerancing*
- *Use the projected tolerance zone*
- *Use feature control frames with leaders*

Key Terms

- *Associative Dimensions*
- *Definition Points*
- *Annotative Dimensions*
- *Dimension Break*
- *Center Marks and Centerlines*
- *Inspection Dimensions*
- *Leaders*
- *Multileaders*
- *Geometric Tolerance*
- *Complex Feature Control Frames*
- *Projected Tolerance Zone*

NEED FOR DIMENSIONING

To make designs more informative and practical, a drawing must convey more than just the graphic picture of a product. To manufacture an object, the drawing of that object must contain size descriptions such as the length, width, height, angle, radius, diameter, and location of features. These informations are added to the drawing by dimensioning. Some drawings also require information about tolerances with the size of features. The information conveyed through dimensioning are vital and often as important as the drawing itself. With the advances in computer-aided design/drafting and computer-aided manufacturing, it has become mandatory to draw part to actual size so that dimensions reflect the actual size of features. At times, it may not be necessary to draw the object of the same size as the actual object would be, but it is absolutely essential that the dimensions be accurate. Incorrect dimensions will lead to manufacturing errors.

By dimensioning, you not only give the size of a part, but also give a series of instructions to a machinist, an engineer, or an architect. The way the part is positioned in a machine, the sequence of machining operations, and the location of various features of the part depend on how you dimension the part. For example, the number of decimal places in a dimension (2.000) determines the type of machine that will be used to do that machining operation. The machining cost of such an operation is significantly higher than for a dimension that has only one digit after the decimal (2.0). Similarly, whether a part is to be forged or cast, the radii of the edges, and the tolerance you provide to these dimensions determine the cost of the product, the number of defective parts, and the number of parts you get from a single die.

DIMENSIONING IN AutoCAD LT

The objects that can be dimensioned in AutoCAD LT range from straight lines to arcs. The dimensioning tools provided by AutoCAD LT can be classified into four categories:

Dimension Drawing tools
Dimension Editing tools
Dimension Style tools
Dimension Utility tools

While dimensioning an object, AutoCAD LT automatically calculates the length of the object or the distance between two specified points. Also, settings such as the gap between the dimension text and the dimension line, the space between two consecutive dimension lines, arrow size, and text size are maintained and used when the dimensions are being generated for a particular drawing. The generation of arrows, lines (dimension lines, extension lines), and other objects that form a dimension is automatically performed by AutoCAD LT to save the user's time. This also results in uniform drawings. However, you can override the default measurements computed by AutoCAD LT and change the settings of various standard values. The modification of dimensioning standards can be achieved through the dimension variables.

The dimensioning functions offered by AutoCAD LT provide you with extreme flexibility in dimensioning by letting you dimension various objects in a variety of ways. This is of great help because different industries, such as architectural, mechanical, civil, or electrical have different standards for the placement of dimensions.

FUNDAMENTAL DIMENSIONING TERMS

Before studying AutoCAD LT's dimensioning tools, it is important to know and understand various dimensioning terms that are common to linear, angular, radius, diameter, and ordinate dimensioning. Figures 8-1 and 8-2 show various dimensioning parameters.

Dimension Line

The dimension line indicates the distance or the angle being measured. Usually, this line has arrows at both ends, and the dimension text is placed along the dimension line. By default, the dimension line is drawn between the extension lines (Figure 8-1 and Figure 8-2). If the dimension line does not fit inside, two short lines with arrows pointing inward are drawn outside the extension lines. The dimension line for angular dimensions (which are used to dimension angles) is an arc. You can control the positioning and various other features of the dimension lines by setting the parameters in the dimension styles. (The dimension styles are discussed in Chapter 10.)

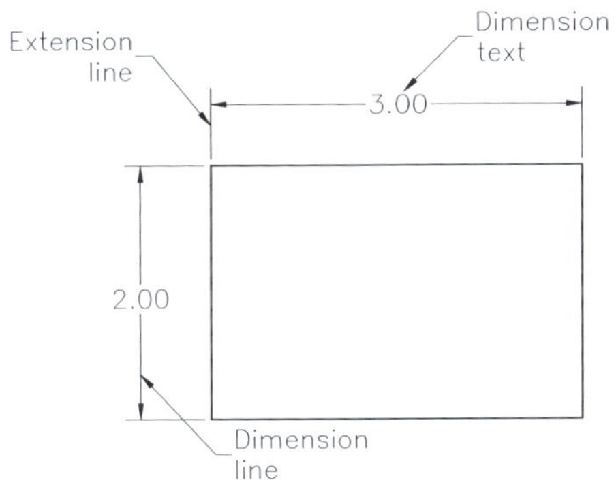

***Figure 8-1** Various dimensioning parameters*

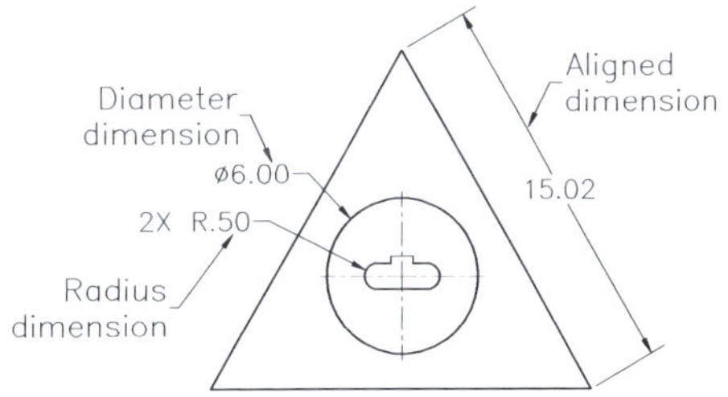

***Figure 8-2** Various dimensioning parameters*

Dimension Text

The dimension text is a text string that reflects the actual measurement (dimension value) between the selected points as calculated by AutoCAD LT. You can accept the value that AutoCAD LT returns or enter your own value. In case you use the default text, AutoCAD LT can be supplied with instructions to append the tolerances to it. Also, you can attach prefixes or suffixes of your choice to the dimension text.

Arrowheads

An arrowhead is a symbol used at the end of a dimension line (where dimension lines meet the extension lines). Arrowheads are also called terminators because they signify the end of the dimension line. Since drafting standards differ from company to company, AutoCAD LT allows you to draw arrows, oblique, closed arrows, open arrows, dots, right angle arrows, or user-defined blocks (Figure 8-3). The user-defined blocks at the two ends of the dimension line can be customized to your requirements. The size of the arrows, tick oblique marks, user blocks, and so on can be regulated by using the dimension variables.

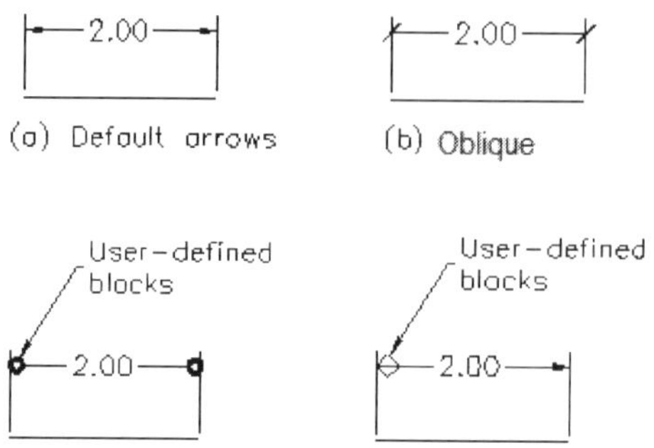

Figure 8-3 Using arrows, oblique marks, and user-defined blocks

Extension Lines

Extension lines are drawn from the object measured to the dimension line (Figure 8-4). These lines are also called witness lines. Extension lines are used in linear and angular dimensioning. Generally, extension lines are drawn perpendicular to the dimension line. However, you can make extension lines inclined at an angle by choosing the **Oblique** tool from the **Dimensions** panel of the **Annotate** tab. Alternatively, you can choose the **Dimension Edit** tool from the **Dimension** toolbar. AutoCAD LT also allows you to suppress either one or both extension lines in a dimension (Figure 8-5). You can insert breaks in a dimension or an extension line, in case they intersect other geometric objects or dimension entities. You can also control various other features of the extension lines by setting parameters in dimension styles. (Dimension styles are discussed in Chapter 10.)

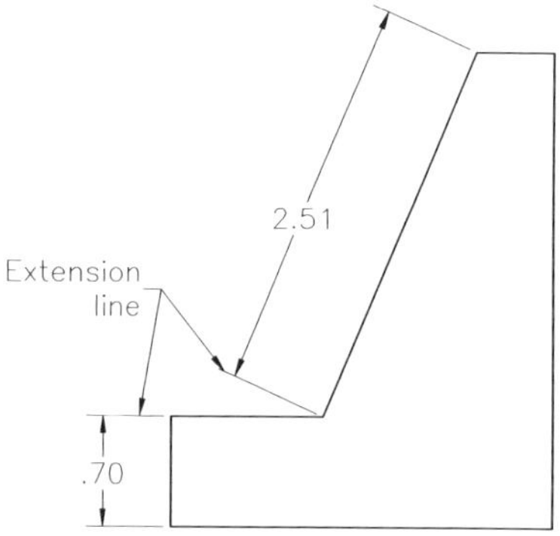

Figure 8-4 Extension lines

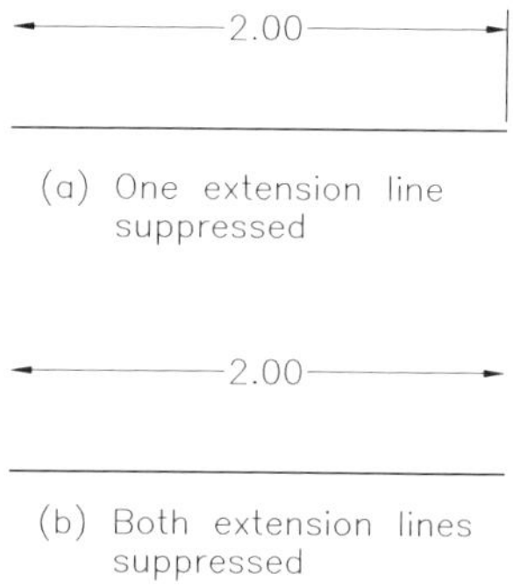

Figure 8-5 Extension line suppressed

Leader

A leader is a line that stretches from the dimension text to the object being dimensioned. Sometimes the text for dimensioning and other annotations do not adjust properly near the object. In such cases, you can use a leader and place the text at the end of the leader line. For example, the circle shown in Figure 8-6 has a keyway slot that is too small to be dimensioned. In this situation, a leader can be drawn from the text to the keyway feature. Also, a leader can be used to attach annotations such as part numbers, notes, and instructions to an object. You can also draw multileaders that are used to connect one note to different places or many notes to one place.

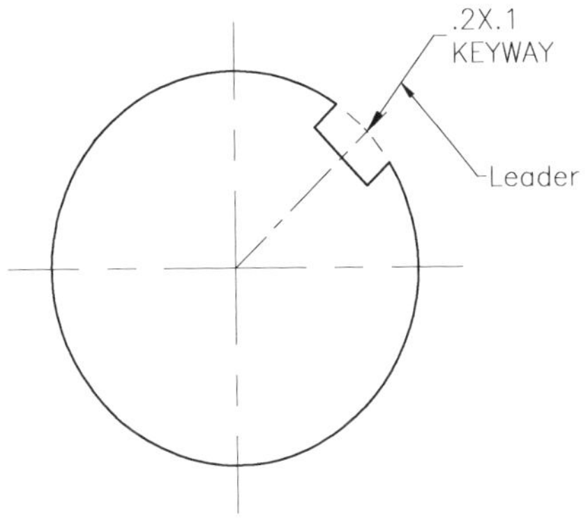

Figure 8-6 *Leader used to attach annotation*

Center Mark and Centerlines

The center mark is a cross mark that represents the center point of a circle or an arc. Centerlines are mutually perpendicular lines that pass through the center of a circle/arc and intersect the circumference of the circle/arc. A center mark or a centerline is automatically drawn when you dimension a circle or an arc (see Figure 8-7). The length of center mark and the extension of centerline beyond the circumference of circle are determined by the value assigned to the **DIMCEN** dimension variable. You can toggle between the center mark and the centerlines by entering a positive and a negative value respectively for the **DIMCEN** variable. Alternatively, you can use the **Dimension Style Manager** dialog box to toggle between the center mark and the centerlines. This will be discussed in detail in Chapter 10.

Alternate Units

With the help of alternate units, you can generate dimensions for two systems of measurement at the same time (Figure 8-8). For example, if the dimensions are in inches, you can use the alternate units dimensioning facility to append metric dimensions to the dimensions (the process of controlling the alternate units through the dimension variables is discussed in Chapter 10).

Tolerances

Tolerance is the amount by which the actual dimension can vary (Figure 8-9). AutoCAD LT can attach the plus/minus tolerances to the dimension text (actual measurement computed by AutoCAD LT). This is also known as deviation tolerance. The plus and minus tolerances that you specify can be same or different. You can use the dimension variables to control the tolerance feature (these variables are discussed in Chapter 10).

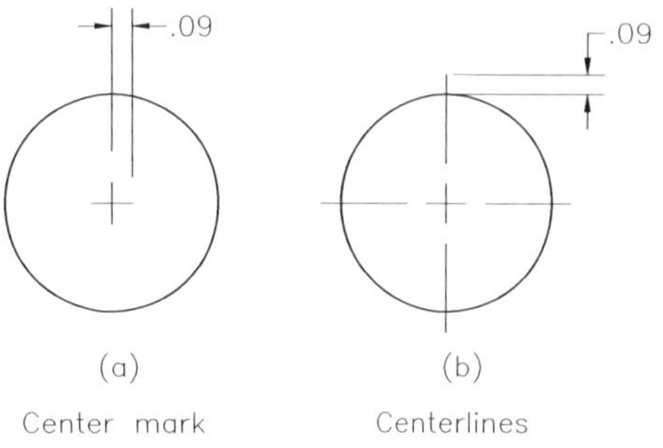

Figure 8-7 Center mark and centerlines

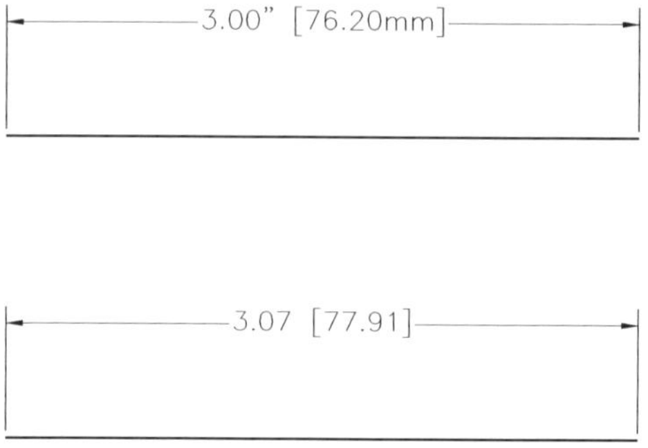

Figure 8-8 Using alternate units for dimensioning

Limits

Instead of appending tolerances to dimension text, you can apply tolerances to the measurement itself (Figure 8-10). Once you define tolerances, AutoCAD LT automatically calculates the upper and lower limit values of the dimension. These values are then displayed as a dimension text.

For example, if the actual dimension as computed by AutoCAD LT is 2.6105 units and the tolerance values are +0.025 and -0.015, the upper and lower limits will be 2.6355 and 2.5955. After calculating the limits, AutoCAD LT will display them as a dimension text, as shown in Figure 8-10. The dimension variables that control the limits are discussed in Chapter 10.

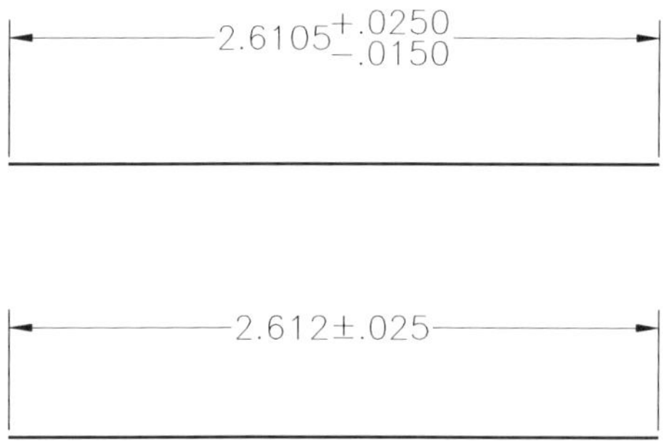

Figure 8-9 *Using tolerances with dimensions*

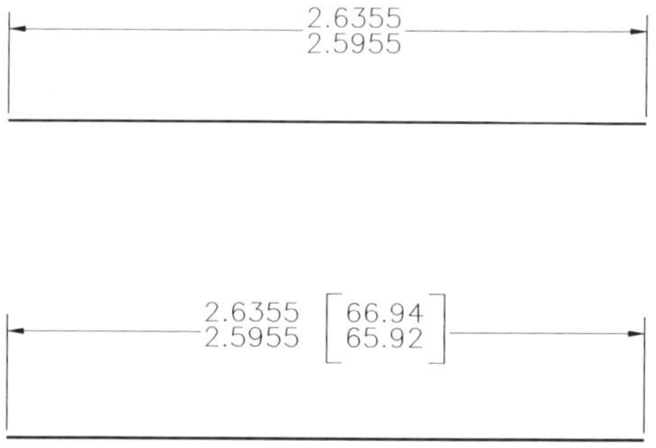

Figure 8-10 *Using limits with dimensions*

ASSOCIATIVE DIMENSIONS

The Associative dimensioning is a method of dimensioning, in which the dimension is associated with the object that is dimensioned. In other words, the dimension is influenced by the changes in the size of the object. In the earlier releases of AutoCAD LT, the dimensions were not truly associative, but were related to the objects being dimensioned by definition points on the DEFPOINTS layer. To cause the dimension to be associatively modified, these definition points had to be adjusted along with the object being changed. If you select the object and its defpoints (using the Crossing selection method), then the dimension will be modified. If the dimensions are associated to the object and the object changes its size, the dimensions will also change automatically. With the introduction of the true associative dimensions, there is no need to select the definition points along with the object. This eliminates the use of definition points for updating the dimensions.

The values and location of the associative dimensions are updated automatically if the value or location of the object is modified. For example, if you edit an object using simple editing operations such as breaking an object using the **Break** tool, then the true associative dimension will be modified automatically. The dimensions can be converted into the true associative dimensions using the **Reassociate** tool in the **Dimensions** panel of the **Annotate** tab to reassociate the dimension. The association of the dimensions with the objects can be removed using the **DIMDISASSOCIATE** command. Both these commands will be discussed later in this chapter.

The dimensioning variable **DIMASSOC** controls the associativity of dimensions. The default value of this variable is **2**, which means the dimensions are associative. When the value is **1**, the dimensions placed are non-associative. When the **DIMASSOC** is turned off (value of this variable is **0**), then the dimension will be placed in the exploded format. This means that the dimensions will now be placed as a combination of individual arrowheads, dimension lines, extension lines, and text. Also note that the exploded dimensions cannot be associated to any object.

DEFINITION POINTS

Definition points are the points drawn at the positions used to generate a dimension object. The definition points are used by the dimensions to control their updating and rescaling. AutoCAD LT draws these points on a special layer called **DEFPOINTS**. These points are not plotted by the plotter because AutoCAD LT does not plot any object on the **DEFPOINTS** layer. If you explode a dimension (which is as good as turning **DIMASSOC** off), the definition points are converted into point objects on the **DEFPOINTS** layer. In Figure 8-11, the small circles indicate the definition points for different objects.

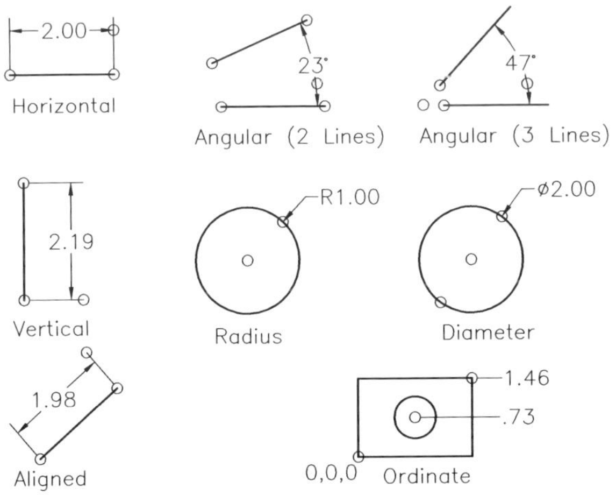

***Figure 8-11** Definition points of linear, radial, angular, and ordinate dimensions*

The definition points for linear dimensions are the points used to specify the extension lines and the point of intersection of the first extension line and the dimension line. The definition points for the angular dimension are the endpoints of the lines used to specify the dimension and the point used to specify the dimension line arc. For example, for a three-point angular dimension, the definition points are the extension line endpoints, angle vertex, and the point used to specify the dimension line arc.

The definition points for the radius dimension are the center point of the circle or arc, and the point where the arrow touches the object. The definition points for the diameter dimension are the points where the arrows touch the circle. The definition points for the ordinate dimension are the UCS origin, feature location, and leader endpoint.

Note

In addition to the definition points just mentioned, the middle point of the dimension text serves as the definition point for all types of dimensions.

ANNOTATIVE DIMENSIONS

When all the elements of a dimension such as text, spacing, and arrows get scaled according to the specified annotation scale, it is known as Annotative Dimension. They are created in the drawing by assigning annotative dimension styles to them. You can also change the non-annotative dimensions to annotative by changing their **Annotative** property to **Yes** in the **PROPERTIES** palette.

SELECTING DIMENSIONING TOOLS

AutoCAD LT provides the following fundamental dimensioning types:

Quick dimensioning	**Linear dimensioning**	**Diameter dimensioning**
Radius dimensioning	**Angular dimensioning**	**Ordinate dimensioning**
Arc Length dimensioning	**Aligned dimensioning**	**Jogged dimensioning**

Figures 8-12 and 8-13 show various fundamental dimension types.

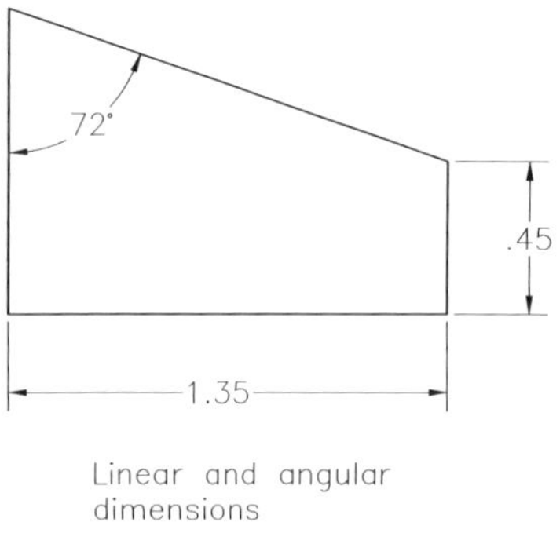

Figure 8-12 Linear and angular dimensions

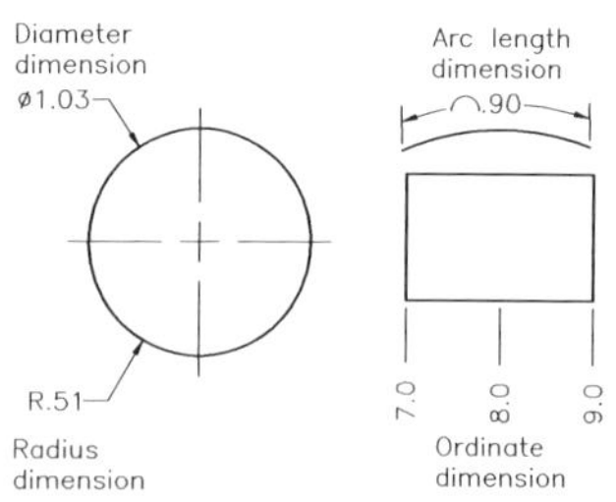

Figure 8-13 Radius, diameter, arc length, and ordinate dimensions

You can select the requisite tool from the menu bar, toolbar, and Ribbon to apply dimensions. You can also use the Command prompt to work with the dimensions. The procedure to invoke the dimensioning tool is discussed next.

Using the Ribbon and the Toolbar

You can select the dimensioning tools from the **Dimensions** panel of the **Annotate** tab (Figure 8-14) or from the **Dimension** toolbar (Figure 8-15). The **Dimension** toolbar can be displayed by choosing **Tools > Toolbars > AutoCAD LT > Dimension** from the menu bar, if the menu bar is displayed.

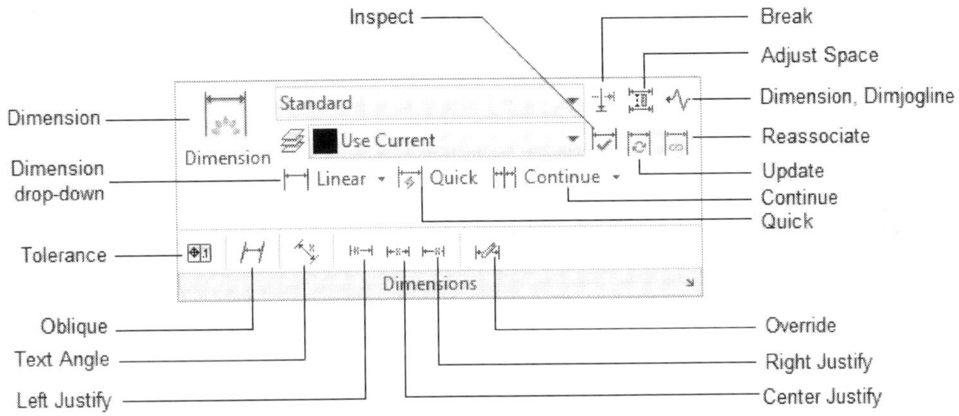

*Figure 8-14 The **Dimensions** panel*

*Figure 8-15 The **Dimension** toolbar*

Note

*The **DIMDEC** variable sets the number of decimal places for the value of primary dimension and the **DIMADEC** variable for angular dimensions. For example, if **DIMDEC** is set to 3, AutoCAD LT will display the decimal dimension up to three decimal places (2.037).*

DIMENSIONING A NUMBER OF OBJECTS TOGETHER

Ribbon: Annotate > Dimensions > Quick	**Command:** QDIM
Menu Bar: Dimension > Quick Dimension	**Toolbar:** Dimension > Quick Dimension

The **Quick Dimension** tool is used to dimension a number of objects at the same time. It also helps you to quickly edit dimension arrangements already existing in the drawing and also create new dimension arrangements. It is especially useful while creating a series of baseline or continuous dimensions. It also allows you to dimension multiple arcs and circles at the same time. When you are using the **Quick Dimension** tool, you can relocate the datum base point for baseline and ordinate dimensions. The prompt sequence that will follow when you choose this tool is given next.

Select geometry to dimension: *Select the objects to be dimensioned and press ENTER.*
Specify dimension line position, or [Continuous/Staggered/Baseline/Ordinate/Radius/Diameter/datumPoint/Edit/seTtings] <Continuous>: *Press ENTER to accept the default dimension arrangement and specify dimension line location or enter new dimension arrangement or edit the existing dimension arrangement.*

For example, you can dimension all circles in a drawing (Figure 8-16) by using the quick dimensioning as follows:

Associative dimension priority = Endpoint.
Select geometry to dimension: *Select all circles.*
Select geometry to dimension: Enter
Specify dimension line position, or
[Continuous/Staggered/Baseline/Ordinate/Radius/Diameter/datumPoint/Edit/seTtings] <Continuous>: *Press D for diameter dimensioning and select a point where you want to position the radial dimension.*

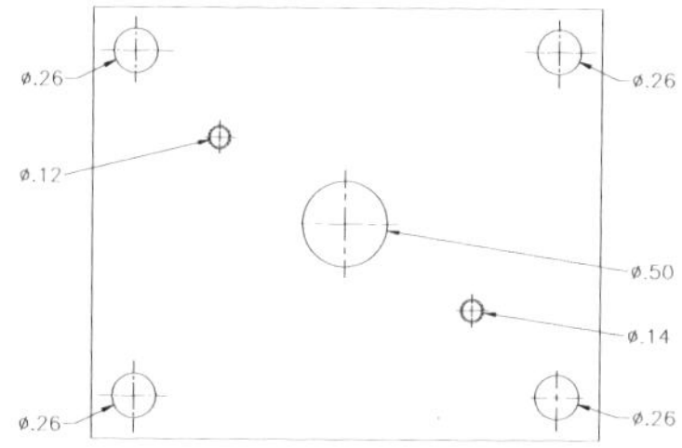

Figure 8-16 *Using the **Quick Dimension** tool to dimension multiple circles*

CREATING LINEAR DIMENSIONS

Ribbon: Annotate > Dimensions > Dimension drop-down > Linear
Menu Bar: Dimension > Linear **Toolbar:** Dimension > Linear
Command: DIMLIN or DIMLINEAR

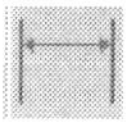

Linear dimensioning is used to measure the shortest distance between two points. You can directly select the object to dimension or select two points. The points can be any two points in the space, endpoints of an arc or line, or any set of points that can be identified. To achieve accuracy, points must be selected with the help of object snaps or by selecting an object to dimension. In case the object selected is aligned, then the linear dimensions will add the **Horizontal** or **Vertical** dimension to the object. The prompt sequence that will follow when you choose the **Linear** tool is given next.

Specify first extension line origin or <select object>: Enter
Select object to dimension: *Select the object.*
Specify dimension line location or
[Mtext/Text/Angle/Horizontal/Vertical/Rotated]: *Select a point to locate the position of the dimension.*

Instead of selecting the object, you can also select the two endpoints of the line that you want to dimension (Figure 8-17). Usually the points on the object are selected by using the object snaps (endpoints, intersection, center, and so on). The prompt sequence is as follows.

> Specify first extension line origin or <select object>: *Select a point.*
> Specify second extension line origin: *Select second point.*
> Specify dimension line location or [Mtext/Text/Angle/Horizontal/Vertical/Rotated]: *Select a point to locate the position of the dimension.*

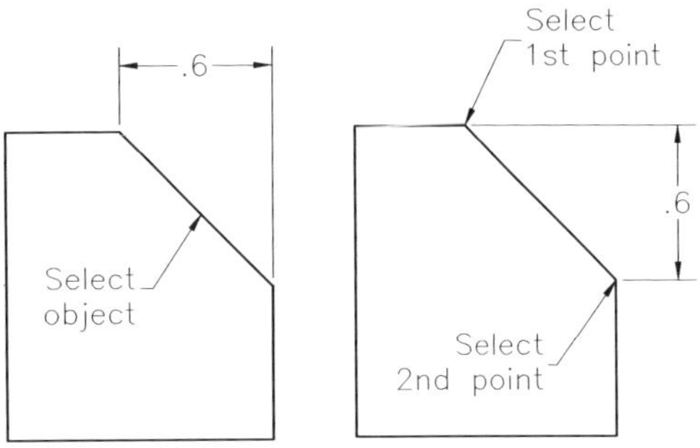

Figure 8-17 *Drawing linear dimensions*

Using the **Linear** tool, you can obtain the horizontal or vertical dimension by simply defining the appropriate dimension location point. If you select a point above or below the dimension, AutoCAD LT creates a horizontal dimension. If you select a point that is on the left or right of the dimension, AutoCAD LT creates a vertical dimension through that point.

Linear Tool Options

The options displayed after choosing the **Linear** tool are discussed next.

Mtext Option

The **Mtext** option is used to override the default dimension text and also change the font, height, and so on by using the **Text Editor**. When you enter **M** at the **Specify dimension line location or [Mtext/Text/Angle/Horizontal/Vertical/Rotated]** prompt, the **Text Editor** is displayed. You can change the text by entering a new text. You can also use various options of the **Text Editor** (explained in Chapter 7). Choose the **Close Text Editor** button. However, if you override the default dimensions, the dimensional associativity of the dimension text is lost. This means that if you modify the object using the definition points, AutoCAD LT will not recalculate the dimension text. Even if the dimension is a true associative dimension, the text will not be recalculated when the object is modified. The prompt sequence to invoke this option is given next.

> Specify first extension line origin or <select object>: *Specify a point.*
> Specify second extension line origin: *Specify the second point.*
> Specify dimension line location or
> [Mtext/Text/Angle/Horizontal/Vertical/Rotated]: **M** Enter *(Enter the dimension text in the* ***Text Editor*** *and then click outside the text editor to accept the changes.)*
> Specify dimension line location or
> [Mtext/Text/Angle/Horizontal/Vertical/Rotated]: *Specify the dimension location.*

Text Option

This option also allows you to override the default dimension. However, this option will prompt you to specify the new text value in the Command prompt itself, see Figure 8-18. The prompt sequence to invoke this option is given next.

Specify first extension line origin or <select object>: *Select a point.*
Specify second extension line origin: *Select second point.*
Specify dimension line location or
[Mtext/Text/Angle/Horizontal/Vertical/Rotated]: **T** Enter
Enter dimension text <Current>: *Enter new text.* Enter
Specify dimension line location or
[Mtext/Text/Angle/Horizontal/Vertical/Rotated]: *Specify the dimension location.*

Angle Option

This option allows you to change the angle of the dimension text, see Figure 8-18.

Rotated Option

This option allows you to create a dimension that is rotated at a specified angle, see Figure 8-18.

Horizontal Option

This option allows you to create a horizontal dimension regardless of where you specify the dimension location, see Figure 8-19.

Vertical Option

This option allows you to create a vertical dimension regardless of where you specify the dimension location, see Figure 8-19.

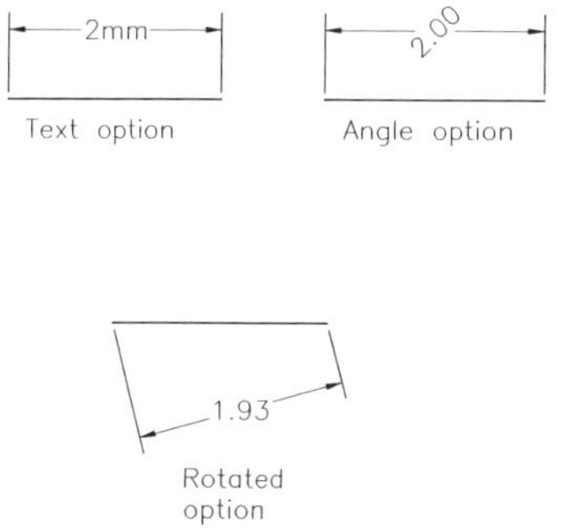

Figure 8-18 *The **Text**, **Angle**, and **Rotated** options*

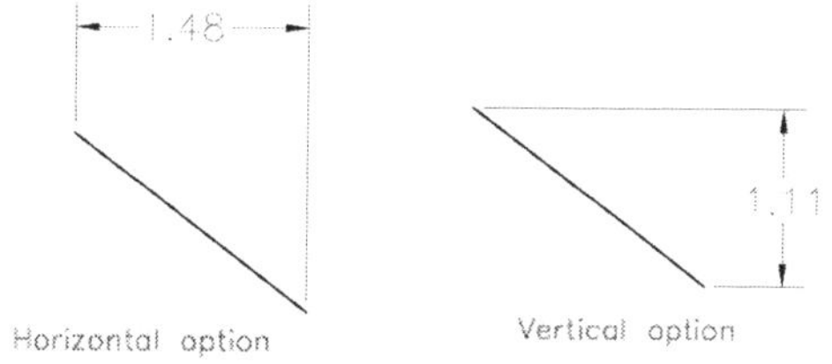

Figure 8-19 *The **Horizontal** and **Vertical** options*

Note

If you override the default dimensions, the dimensional associativity of the dimension text is lost and AutoCAD LT will not recalculate the dimension when the object is scaled.

Example 1 Horizontal Dimension

In this example, you will use linear dimensioning to dimension a horizontal line of 4 units length. The dimensioning will be done first by selecting the object and later on by specifying the first and second extension line origins. Using the **Text Editor** tab, modify the default text such that the dimension is underlined.

Selecting the Object

1. Start a new file in the **Drafting & Annotation** workspace and draw a line of 4 units length.

2. Choose the **Linear** tool from **Annotate > Dimensions > Dimension** drop-down; you will be prompted to specify the extension line origin or the object. The prompt sequence to apply the linear dimension is as follows:

   Specify first extension line origin or <select object>: Enter
   Select object to dimension: *Select the line.*
   Specify dimension line location or
   [Mtext/Text/Angle/Horizontal/Vertical/Rotated]: **M** Enter

   *The **Text Editor** tab will be displayed, as shown in Figure 8-20. Select the default dimension value and then choose the **Underline** button from the **Formatting** panel of the **Text Editor** tab of the **Ribbon** to underline the text. Click anywhere in the drawing area to exit the **Text Editor** tab.*

   Specify dimension line location or
   [Mtext/Text/Angle/Horizontal/Vertical/Rotated]: *Place the dimension.*
   Dimension text = 4.0000

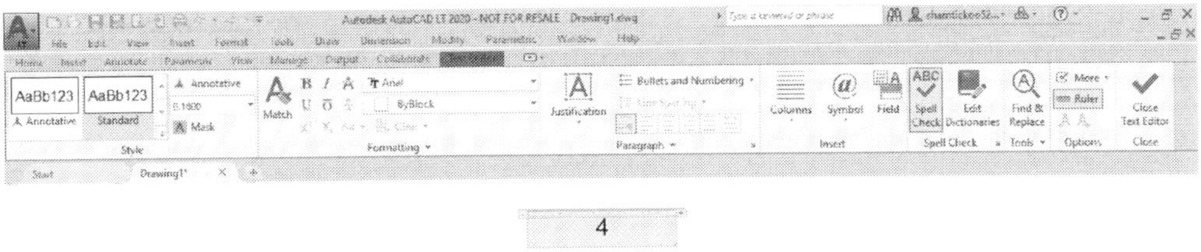

Figure 8-20 *The **Text Editor** tab*

Specifying Extension Line Origins

1. Choose the **Linear** tool from **Annotate > Dimensions > Dimension** drop-down. The prompt sequence is as follows:

   Specify first extension line origin or <select object>: *Select the first endpoint of the line using the **Endpoint** object snap, see Figure 8-21.*

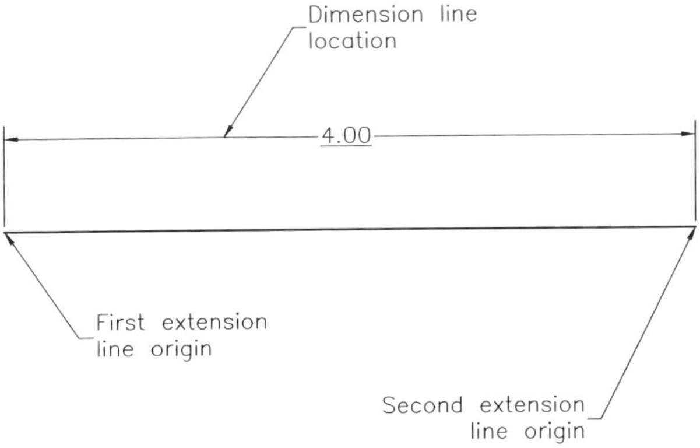

Figure 8-21 *Line for Example 1*

Specify second extension line origin: *Select the second endpoint of the line using the* ***Endpoint*** *object snap, see Figure 8-21.*
Specify dimension line location or
[Mtext/Text/Angle/Horizontal/Vertical/Rotated]: **M** Enter
Select the text and then choose the ***Underline*** *button from the* ***Formatting Panel*** *the* ***Ribbon*** *to underline the text in the* ***Text Editor Tab****. Click anywhere in the drawing area.*
Specify dimension line location or
[Mtext/Text/Angle/Horizontal/Vertical/Rotated]: *Place the dimension.*
Dimension text = 4.00

CREATING ALIGNED DIMENSIONS

Ribbon: Annotate > Dimensions > Dimension drop-down > Aligned
Menu Bar: Dimension > Aligned **Toolbar:** Dimension > Aligned
Command: DIMALI / DIMALIGNED

Generally, the drawing consists of various objects that are neither parallel to the *X* axis nor to the *Y* axis. Dimensioning of such objects can be done using aligned dimensioning.

In horizontal or vertical dimensioning, you can only measure the shortest distance from the first extension line origin to the second extension line origin along the horizontal or vertical axis, respectively whereas with the help of aligned dimensioning, you can measure the true aligned distance between the two points. The function of the **Aligned** tool is similar to that of the other linear dimensioning tools. The dimension created with the **Aligned** tool is parallel to the object being dimensioned. The prompt sequence that will follow when you choose this tool is given next.

Specify first extension line origin or <select object>: *Specify the first point or press ENTER.*
Specify second extension line origin: *Specify second point.*
Specify dimension line location or [Mtext/Text/Angle]: *Specify the location for the dimension line.*
Dimension text = Current

The options in this tool are similar to those of the **Linear** tool. Figure 8-22 illustrates the aligned dimensioning.

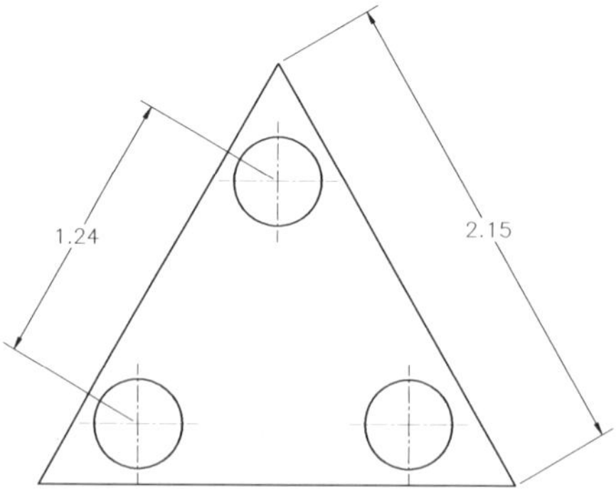

Figure 8-22 *The aligned dimensioning*

Exercise 1 — Aligned Dimension

Draw the object shown in Figure 8-23 and then use linear and aligned dimensioning to dimension the part. The distance between the dotted lines is 0.5 units. The dimensions should be up to 2 decimal places. To get dimensions up to 2 decimal places, enter DIMDEC at the Command prompt and then enter 2. (There will be more information about dimension variable in Chapter 10.)

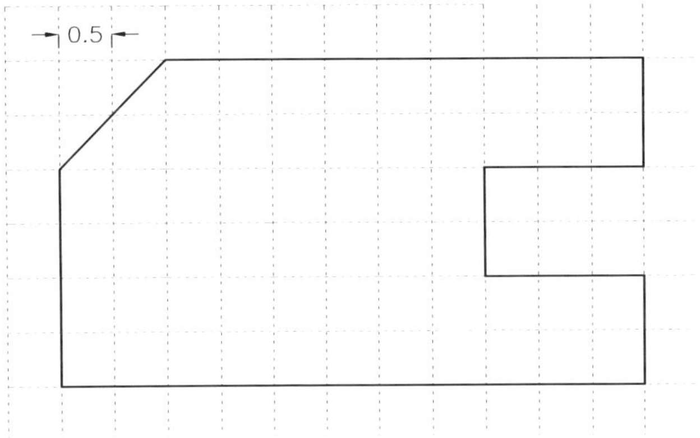

Figure 8-23 *Drawing for Exercise 1*

CREATING ARC LENGTH DIMENSIONS

Ribbon: Annotate > Dimensions > Dimension drop-down > Arc Length
Menu Bar: Dimension > Arc Length **Toolbar:** Dimension > Arc Length
Command: DIMARC

The Arc Length dimensioning is used to dimension the length of an arc or the polyline arc segment. You are required to select an arc or a polyline arc segment and the dimension location. Figure 8-24 shows the Arc Length dimensioning of an arc. Choose the **Arc Length** tool in the **Dimensions** panel. The prompt sequence that will follow after choosing this tool is given next.

Select arc or polyline arc segment: *Select arc or polyline arc segment to dimension.*
Specify arc length dimension location, or [Mtext/Text/Angle/Partial/Leader]: *Specify the location for the dimension line.*
Dimension text = *Current.*

Using the **Partial** option, you can dimension a selected portion of the arc, as shown in Figure 8-25. The prompt sequence for the **Partial** option is given next.

Select arc or polyline arc segment: *Select arc or polyline arc segment to dimension.*
Specify arc length dimension location, or [Mtext/Text/Angle/Partial]: **P** Enter
Specify first point for arc length dimension: *Specify the first point on arc.*
Specify second point for arc length dimension: *Specify the second point on arc.*
Specify arc length dimension location, or [Mtext/Text/Angle/Partial]: *Specify the location for the dimension line.*
Dimension text = *Current*

Using the **Leader** option, you can attach a leader to the dimension text, starting from its circumference. This leader is drawn radial to the arc, as shown in Figure 8-26.

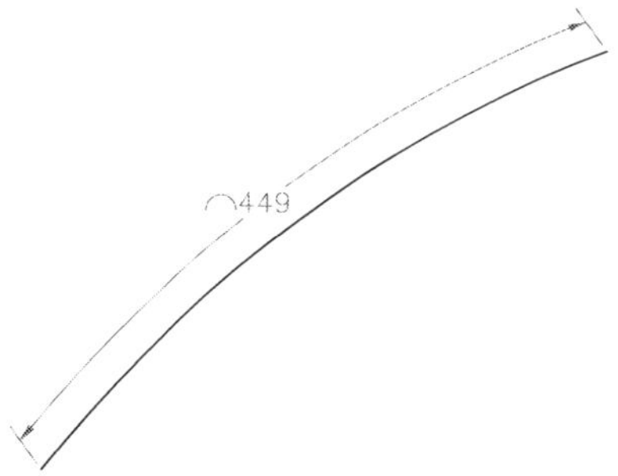

Figure 8-24 *Arc Length dimensioning*

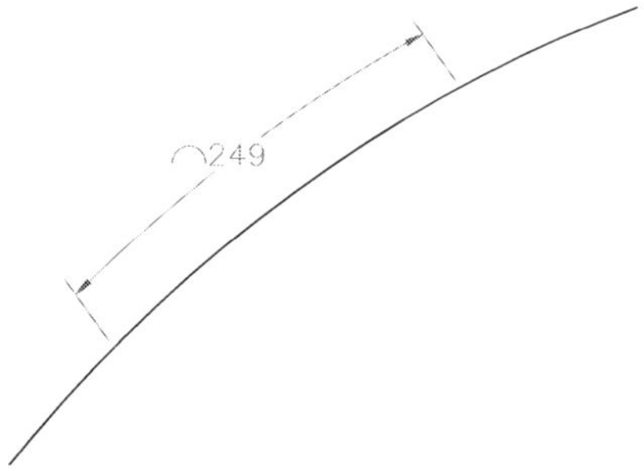

Figure 8-25 *Partial Arc Length dimensioning*

Note

*The **Leader** option is displayed only when the arc subtends an included angle greater than 90 degrees at its centre.*

CREATING ROTATED DIMENSIONS

Rotated dimensioning is used when you want to place the dimension line at an angle (if you do not want to align the dimension line with the selected extension line origins), as shown in Figure 8-27. You can invoke this option by entering **ROTATED** at the command line after choosing the **Linear** tool from the **Dimensions** panel. The **ROTATED** dimension option will prompt you to specify the dimension line angle. The prompt sequence is given next.

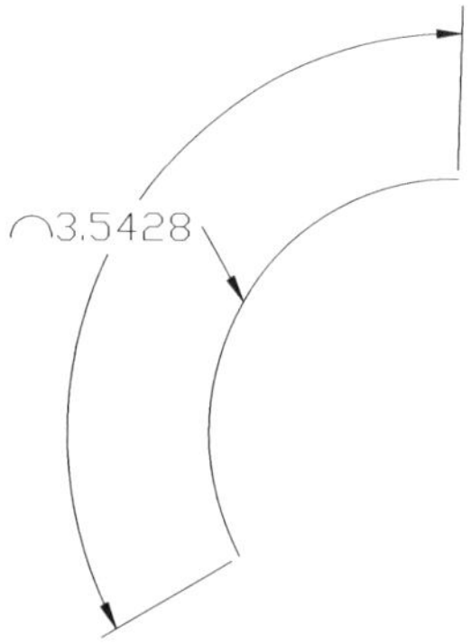

Figure 8-26 *Leader Arc Length dimensioning*

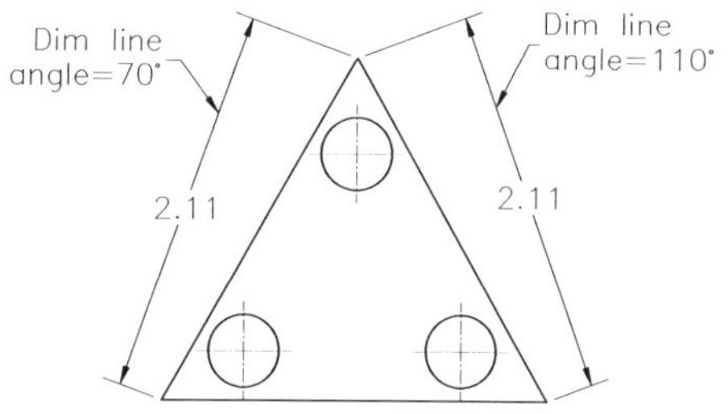

Figure 8-27 *Rotated dimensioning*

Specify first extension line origin or <select object>: *Select the origin of the first extension line.*
Specify second extension line origin: *Select the origin of the second extension line.*
Specify dimension line location or
[Mtext/Text/Angle/Horizontal/Vertical/Rotated]: **R** Enter
Specify angle of dimension line <0>: **110** Enter
Specify dimension line location or [Mtext/Text/Angle/Horizontal/Vertical/Rotated]: *Select the location for the dimension line.*
Dimension text = current

Note
You can draw horizontal and vertical dimensioning by specifying the rotation angle of 0 degree for horizontal dimensioning and 90 degree for vertical dimensioning.

CREATING BASELINE DIMENSIONS

Ribbon: Annotate > Dimensions > Continue drop-down > Baseline
Menu Bar: Dimension > Baseline **Toolbar:** Dimension > Baseline
Command: DIMBASE or DIMBASELINE

Sometimes in manufacturing, you may want to locate different points and features of a part with reference to a fixed point (base point or reference point). This can be accomplished by using the Baseline dimensioning (Figure 8-28). To invoke the Baseline dimension, choose the **Baseline** tool from the **Dimensions** panel. Using this tool, you can continue a linear dimension from the first extension line origin of the first dimension to the dimension point. The new dimension line is automatically offset by a fixed amount to avoid overlapping of the dimension lines. This has to be kept in mind that there must already exist a linear, ordinate, or angular associative dimension to use the Baseline dimensions. When you choose the **Baseline** tool, the last linear, ordinate, or angular dimension created will be selected and used as the baseline. The prompt sequence that will follow when you choose this tool is given next.

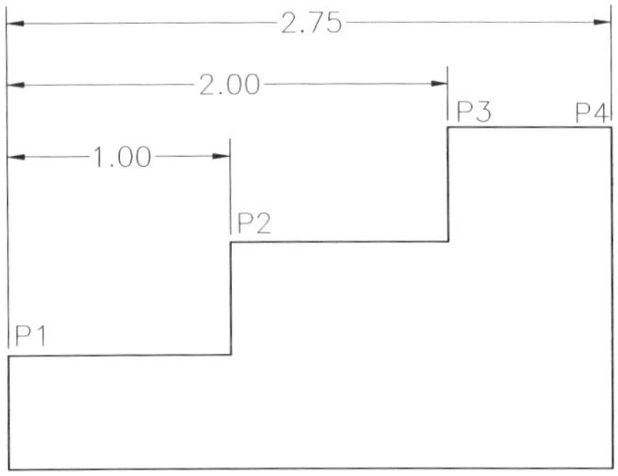

Figure 8-28 *Baseline dimensioning*

Specify a second extension line origin or [Select/Undo] <Select>: *Select the origin of the second extension line.*
Dimension text = current
Specify a second extension line origin or [Select Undo] <Select>: *Select the origin of the second extension line.*
Dimension text = current
Specify a second extension line origin or [Select Undo] <Select>: *Select the origin of the second extension line or press ENTER.*
Select base dimension: Enter

When you use the **Baseline** tool, you cannot change the default dimension text. However, the **DIM** command allows you to override the default dimension text.

Command: **DIM**
Select objects or specify first extension line origin or [Angular/Baseline/Continue/Ordinate/aliGn/Distribute/Layer/Undo]:
Specify second extension line origin or [Undo]:
Specify dimension line location or second line for angle [Mtext/Text/text aNgle/Undo]:T
Enter dimension text: 1 Enter

Specify dimension line location or second line for angle [Mtext/Text/text aNgle/Undo]:
Select objects or specify first extension line origin or [Angular/Baseline/Continue/Ordinate/aliGn/Distribute/Layer/Undo]:B
Specify first extension line origin as baseline or [Offset]:
Specify second extension line origin or [Select/Offset/Undo] <Select>: Enter Enter
Select objects or specify first extension line origin or [Angular/Baseline/Continue/Ordinate/aliGn/Distribute/Layer/Undo]:

The next dimension line is automatically spaced and drawn by AutoCAD LT. Note that in AutoCAD LT if the value of **DIMCONTINUEMODE** system variable is set to 0, the dimensions created by using the **Baseline** tool will be based on the current dimension style. Whereas, if you set the value to 1 then the dimensions will be created based upon the selected dimension.

CREATING CONTINUED DIMENSIONS

Ribbon: Annotate > Dimensions > Continue drop-down > Continue
Menu Bar: Dimension > Continue **Toolbar:** Dimension > Continue
Command: DIMCONT or DIMCONTINUE

Using the **Continue** tool, you can continue a linear dimension from the second extension line of the previous dimension. This is also called as Chained or Incremental dimensioning. Note that there must exist linear, ordinate, or angular associative dimension to use the Continue dimensions. The prompt sequence that will follow when you choose this tool is given next.

Specify second extension line origin or [Select/Undo] <Select>: *Specify the point on the origin of the second extension line.*
Dimension text = current
Specify second extension line origin or [Select/Undo] <Select>: *Specify the point on the origin of the second extension line.*
Dimension text = current
Specify second extension line origin or [Select/Undo] <Select>: Enter
Select continued dimension: Enter

Also, in this case, the **DIM** command should be used if you want to change the default dimension text.

Command: **DIM**
Select objects or specify first extension line origin or [Angular/Baseline/Continue/Ordinate/aliGn/Distribute/Layer/Undo]:(P1,see Figure 8-29).
Specify second extension line origin or [Undo]:
Specify dimension line location or second line for angle [Mtext/Text/text aNgle/Undo]:T Enter
Enter dimension text <8478.5>: 0.75 Enter
Specify dimension line location or second line for angle [Mtext/Text/text aNgle/Undo]:
Select objects or specify first extension line origin or [Angular/Baseline/Continue/Ordinate/aliGn/Distribute/Layer/Undo]:C
Specify first extension line origin to continue:
Specify second extension line origin or [Select/Undo] <Select>:
Specify second extension line origin or [Select/Undo] <Select>:

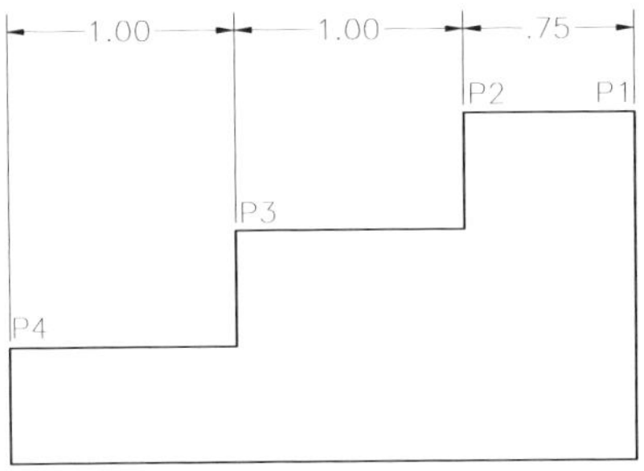

Figure 8-29 *Continue dimensioning*

The default base (first extension line) for the dimensions created with the **Continue** tool is the previous dimension's second extension line. You can override the default extension by pressing ENTER at the **Specify second extension line origin or [Select/Undo] <Select>** prompt, and then specifying the other dimension. The extension line origin nearest to the selection point is used as the origin for the first extension line. Note that, in AutoCAD LT, if the value of **DIMCONTINUEMODE** system variable is set to 0, the dimensions created by using the **Continue** tool will be based on the current dimension style. Whereas, if you set the value to 1 then the dimensions will be created based upon the selected dimension.

Tip

*You can use the **Select** option of the **Baseline** and **Continue** tools to select any other existing dimension to be used as the baseline or continuous dimension.*

Exercise 2 — Baseline Dimension

Draw the object shown in Figure 8-30 and then use baseline dimensioning to dimension the top half and continue dimensioning to dimension the bottom half. The distance between the dotted lines is 0.5 unit.

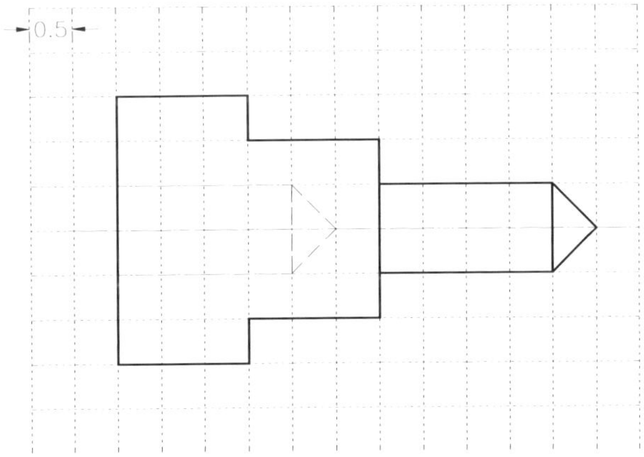

Figure 8-30 *Drawing for Exercise 2*

CREATING ANGULAR DIMENSIONS

Ribbon: Annotate > Dimensions > Dimension drop-down > Angular
Menu Bar: Dimension > Angular **Toolbar:** Dimension > Angular
Command: DIMANG or DIMANGULAR

The Angular dimensioning is used for applying angular dimension to an entity. The **Angular** tool is used to generate a dimension arc (dimension line in the shape of an arc with arrowheads at both ends) to indicate the angle between two nonparallel lines. This tool can also be used to dimension the vertex and two other points, a circle with another point, or the angle of an arc. For every set of points, there exists one acute angle and one obtuse angle (inner and outer angles). If you specify the dimension arc location between the two points, you will get the acute angle; if you specify it outside the two points, you will get the obtuse angle. Figure 8-31 shows the four ways to dimension two nonparallel lines. The prompt sequence that will follow when you choose this tool is given next:

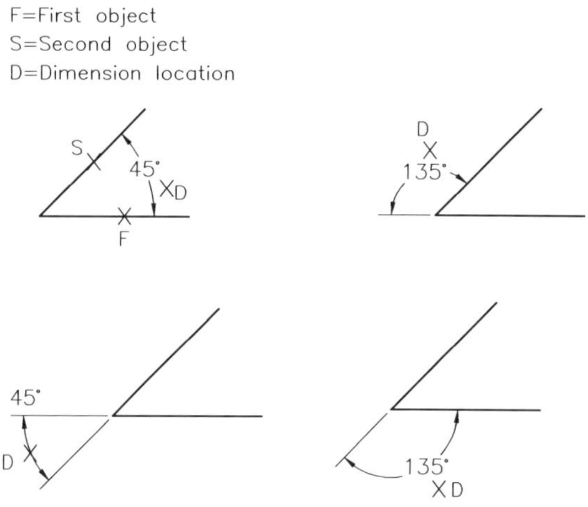

Figure 8-31 *Angular dimensioning between two nonparallel lines*

Select arc, circle, line, or <specify vertex>: *Select the object or press ENTER to select a vertex point where two segments meet.*
Select second line: *Select the second object.*
Specify dimension arc line location or [Mtext/Text/Angle/Quadrant]: *Place the dimension or select an option.*
Dimension text = current

If you want to override the default angular value, use the **Mtext** or **Text** option. Use the %%d control sequence after the number at the text prompt. For example, for 45°, type 45%%d and then press ENTER.

The methods of dimensioning various entities using this tool are discussed next.

Dimensioning the Angle between Two Nonparallel Lines

The angle between two nonparallel lines or two straight line segments of a polyline can be dimensioned using the **Angular** tool. The vertex of the angle is taken as the point of intersection of the two lines.

The following example illustrates the dimensioning of two nonparallel lines by choosing the **Angular** tool from the **Dimension** drop-down in the **Dimensions** panel. You can also apply the angular dimension by using the **DIMANGULAR** command.

Select arc, circle, line, or <specify vertex>: *Select the first line.*
Select second line: *Select the second line.*
Specify dimension arc line location or [Mtext/Text/Angle/Quadrant]: **M** Enter *(Enter the new value in the **Text Editor** and click anywhere in the drawing area.*
Specify dimension arc line location or [Mtext/Text/Angle/Quadrant]: *Specify the dimension arc location or select an option.*

The location of the extension lines and the dimension arc is determined by the placement of the dimension arc. In AutoCAD LT, you can place the dimension text outside the quadrant in which you measure the angle by extending the dimension arc. Choose the **Quadrant** option from the shortcut menu or from the **Specify dimension arc line location or [Mtext/Text/Angle/Quadrant]** prompt. Next, you will be prompted to specify the quadrant in which you want to measure the angle. Then, specify the quadrant with mouse. If the dimension arc line is lying outside the quadrant that is being measured, the dimension arc will be extended up to that location with the help of extension line. Figure 8-32(a) shows a dimension created without using the **Quadrant** option and Figure 8-32(b) shows the same dimension created by using the **Quadrant** option.

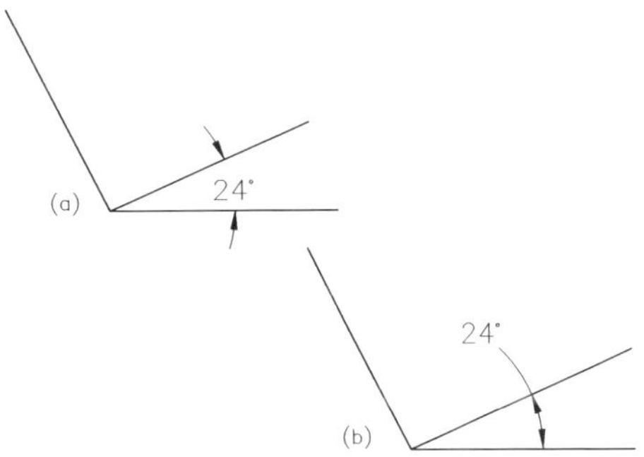

***Figure 8-32** The angular dimension created with and without choosing the **Quadrant** option*

Dimensioning the Angle of an Arc

Angular dimensioning can also be used to dimension the angle of an arc. In this case, the center point of the arc is taken as the vertex and the two endpoints of the arc are used as the extension line origin points for the extension lines (Figure 8-33). The following example illustrates the dimensioning of an arc by using the **Angular** tool:

Select arc, circle, line, or <specify vertex>: *Select the arc.*
Specify dimension arc line location or [Mtext/Text/Angle/Quadrant]: *Specify a location for the arc line or select an option.*

Angular Dimensioning of Circles

The angular feature associated with the circle can be dimensioned by selecting a circle object at the **Select arc, circle, line, or <specify vertex>** prompt. The center of the selected circle is used as the vertex of the angle. The first point selected (when the circle is selected for angular dimensioning) is used as the origin of the first extension line. In similar manner, the second point selected is taken as the origin of the second extension line (Figure 8-34). The following is the prompt sequence for dimensioning a circle:

Select arc, circle, line, or <specify vertex>: *Select the circle at the point where you want the first extension line.*
Specify second angle endpoint: *Select the second point on or away from the circle.*
Specify dimension arc line location or [Mtext/Text/Angle/Quadrant]: *Select the location for the dimension line.*

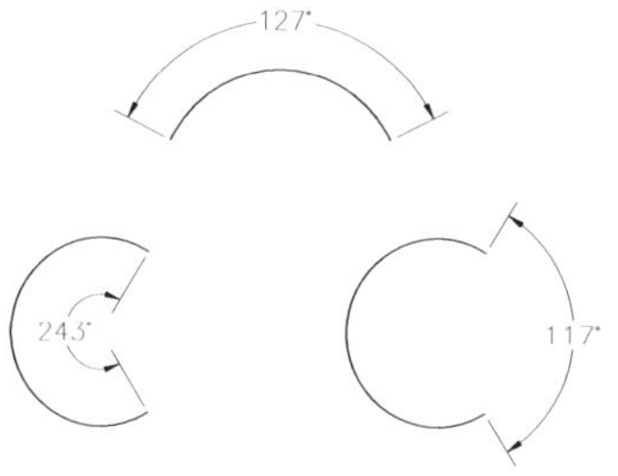

Figure 8-33 *Angular dimensioning of arcs*

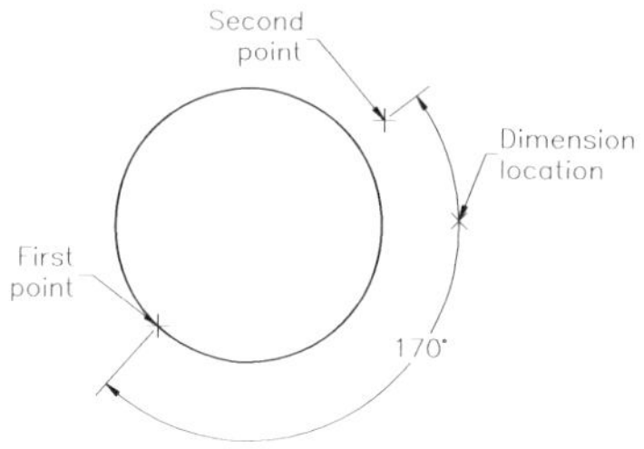

Figure 8-34 *Angular dimensioning of a circle*

Angular Dimensioning based on Three Points

If you press ENTER at the **Select arc, circle, line, or <specify vertex>** prompt, AutoCAD LT allows you to select three points to create an angular dimension. The first point is the vertex point, and the other two points are the first and second angle endpoints of the angle (Figure 8-35). The coordinate specifications of the first and the second angle endpoints must not be identical. However, the angle vertex coordinates and one of the angle endpoint coordinates can be identical. The following example illustrates angular dimensioning by defining three points:

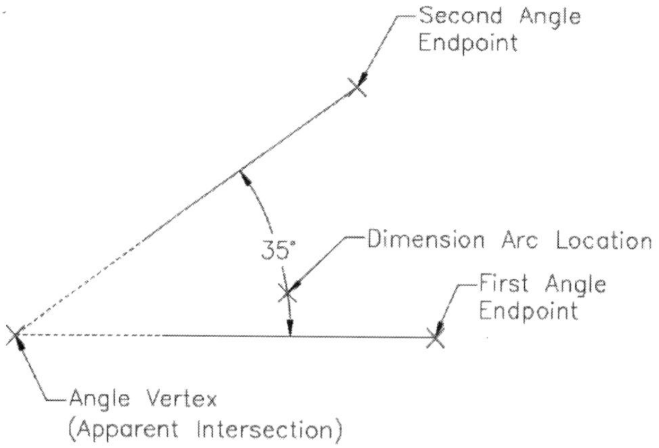

Figure 8-35 *Angular dimensioning using 3 points*

Select arc, circle, line, or <specify vertex>: Enter
Specify angle vertex: *Specify the first point vertex. This is the point where two segments meet. If the two segments do not meet, use the **Apparent Intersection** object snap.*

Specify first angle endpoint: *Specify the second point. This point will be the origin of the first extension line.*
Specify second angle endpoint: *Specify the third point. This point will be the origin of the second extension line.*
Specify dimension arc line location or [Mtext/Text/Angle/Quadrant]: *Select the location for the dimension line.*
Dimension text = current

Exercise 3 Angular Dimension

Draw the profile, as shown in Figure 8-36 and then use angular dimensioning to dimension all angles of the part. The distance between the dotted lines is 0.5 unit.

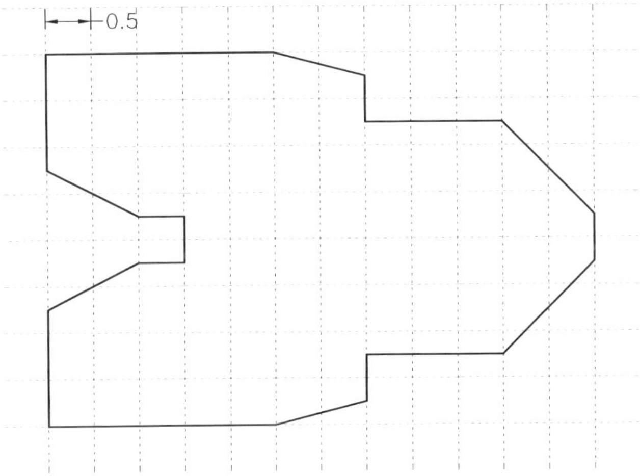

Figure 8-36 *Drawing for Exercise 3*

CREATING DIAMETER DIMENSIONS

Ribbon: Annotate > Dimensions > Dimension drop-down > Diameter
Menu Bar: Dimension > Diameter **Toolbar:** Dimension > Diameter
Command: DIMDIA

Diameter dimensioning is used to dimension a circle or an arc. Here, the measurement is done between two diametrically opposite points on the circumference of the circle or the arc (Figure 8-37). The dimension text generated by AutoCAD LT begins with the ø symbol to indicate a diameter dimension. The prompt sequence that will follow when you choose the **Diameter** tool in the **Dimensions** panel is given next.

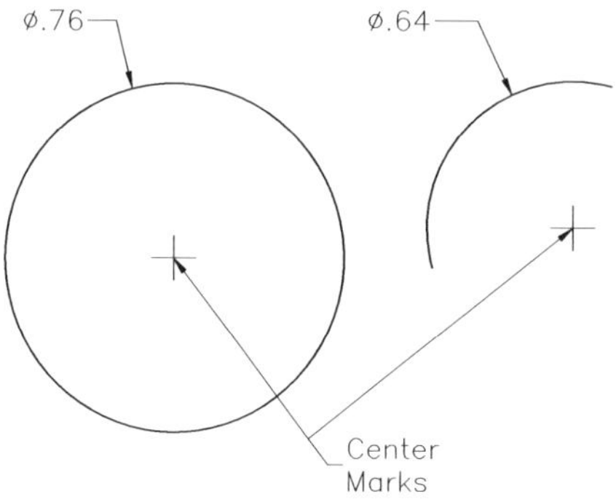

Figure 8-37 *Diameter dimensioning*

Select arc or circle: *Select an arc or circle by selecting a point anywhere on its circumference.*
Dimension text = Current
Specify dimension line location or [Mtext/Text/Angle]: *Specify a point to position the dimension.*

If you want to override the default value of the dimension text, use the **Mtext** or the **Text** option. The control sequence %%C is used to obtain the diameter symbol ø. It is followed by the dimension text that should appear in the diameter dimension. For example, if you want to write a text that displays a value ø20, then enter %%c20 at the text prompt.

CREATING JOGGED DIMENSIONS

Ribbon: Annotate > Dimensions > Dimension drop-down > Jogged
Menu Bar: Dimension > Jogged **Toolbar:** Dimension > Jogged
Command: DIMJOGGED

The necessity of the Jogged dimension arises because of the space constraint. Also, the Jogged dimension is used when you want to avoid the merging of the dimension line with other dimensions. Also, there are instances when it is not possible to show the center of the circle in the sheet. In such situations, the jogged dimensions are used, as shown in Figure 8-38. The jogged dimensions can be added using the **Jogged** tool. Note that with this tool, you can add only jogged radius dimensions. To add jogged dimensions, invoke the **Jogged** tool from the **Dimensions** panel and select an arc or a circle from the drawing area; you will be prompted to select the center location override. Specify a new location to override the existing center. This point will also become the start point of the dimension line. Next, specify the location of the dimension line and the jog. The Command prompt that will follow when you invoke the **Jogged** tool is given next.

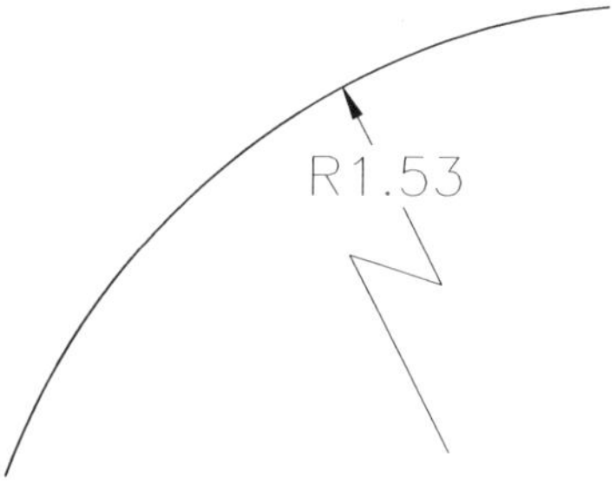

Figure 8-38 *Jogged dimensioning*

Select arc or circle: *Select arc or circle to be dimensioned.*
Specify center location override: *Specify a point which will currently override the actual center point location.*

Dimension text = *Current*
Specify dimension line location or [Mtext/Text/Angle]: *Specify a point to position dimension line.*
Specify jog location: *Specify a point for the positioning of jog.*

CREATING RADIUS DIMENSIONS

Ribbon: Annotate > Dimensions > Dimension drop-down > Radius
Menu Bar: Dimension > Radius **Toolbar**: Dimension > Radius
Command: DIMRAD

The Radius dimensioning is used to dimension a circle or an arc as shown in Figure 8-39. Radius and diameter dimensioning are similar; the only difference is that instead of the diameter line, a radius line is drawn (half of the diameter line), which is measured from the center to any point on the circumference. The dimension text generated by AutoCAD LT is preceded by the letter R to indicate a radius dimension. If you want to use the default dimension text (dimension text generated automatically by AutoCAD LT), simply specify a point to position the dimension at the Specify dimension line location or [Mtext/Text/Angle] prompt. You can also enter a new value or specify a prefix or suffix, or suppress the entire text by entering a blank space following the Enter dimension text <current> prompt. A center mark for the circle/arc is drawn automatically, provided the center mark value controlled by the DIMCEN variable is not 0. The prompt sequence that will follow when you choose this button is given next.

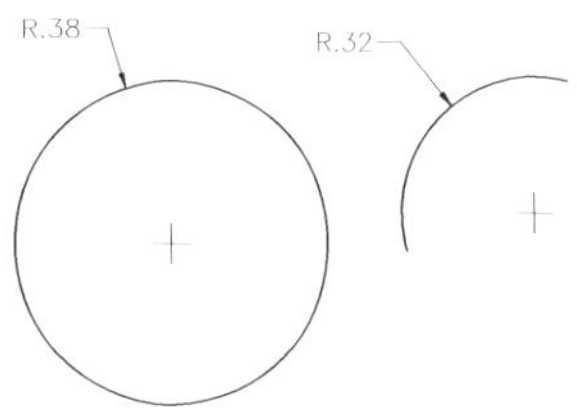

Figure 8-39 *Radius dimensioning*

Select arc or circle: *Select the object that you want to dimension.*
Dimension text = Current
Specify dimension line location or [Mtext/Text/Angle]: Specify the dimension location.

If you want to override the default value of the dimension text, use the **Text** or the **Mtext** option. You can also enter the required value at the text prompt.

Note
In case of diametric, radial, and jogged radial dimensions, you can extend the dimension line beyond the endpoints of the arc by creating the arc extension line beyond the endpoints. These arc extension lines are similar to the other extension lines. The system variables ***DIMSE1*** *and* ***DIMSE2*** *allow the display of the first and the second extension lines, respectively. These variables should be* ***ON*** *in order to suppress the respective extension line.*

CREATING JOGGED LINEAR DIMENSIONS

Ribbon: Annotate > Dimensions > Dimension, Dimjogline
Menu Bar: Dimension > Jogged Linear
Toolbar: Dimension > Jogged Linear **Command:** DIMJOGLINE

The **Dimension, Dimjogline** tool is used to add or remove a jog in the existing dimensions. This kind of dimensioning technique is generally used to dimension the components that have a high length to width ratio, see Figure 8-40. To add a jog to a linear dimension, choose the **Dimjogline** tool from the **Dimensions** panel and select the dimension to which you want to add a jog. Next, pick a point along the dimension line to specify the location of the jog placement. Alternatively, you can press the ENTER key to place the jog automatically. To remove a jog, invoke the **Dimjogline** tool and choose **Remove** from the shortcut menu. Next, specify the dimension line from which you want to remove the jog. You can modify the location of the jog symbol with the help of grips. Note that you can add a jog only to the linear or aligned dimensions with this tool.

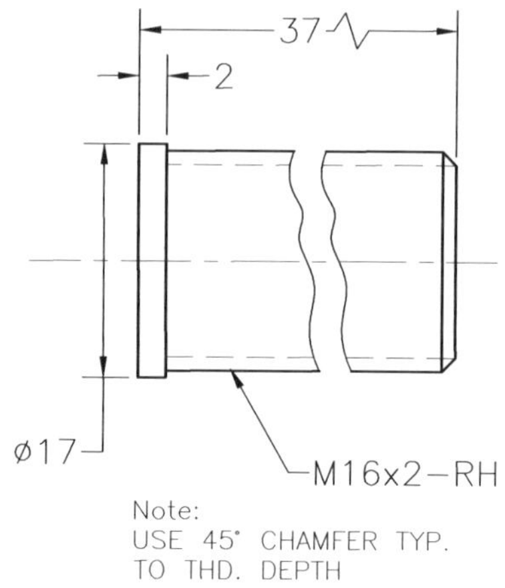

Figure 8-40 Jogged linear dimensioning

Note

*The height of jog symbol can be changed by varying the **Jog height factor** in the **Lines & Arrows** rollout of the **PROPERTIES** palette.*

GENERATING CENTER MARKS AND CENTERLINES

Toolbar: Dimension > Center Mark **Command:** DIMCENTER
Menu bar: Dimension > Center Mark

When circles or arcs are dimensioned with the **Radius** or **Diameter** tool, a small mark known as center mark or a line known as centerline may be drawn at the center of the circle/arc. Sometimes, you need to mark the center of a circle or an arc without using these dimensioning tools. This can be achieved with the help of the **Center Mark** tool. You can invoke this tool by entering **DIMCENTER** at the Command prompt. When you invoke this tool, you are prompted to select the arc or the circle. The result of this tool will depend upon the value of the **DIMCEN** variable. If the value of this variable is positive, center marks are drawn, see Figure 8-41 and if the value is negative, centerlines are drawn, see Figure 8-42.

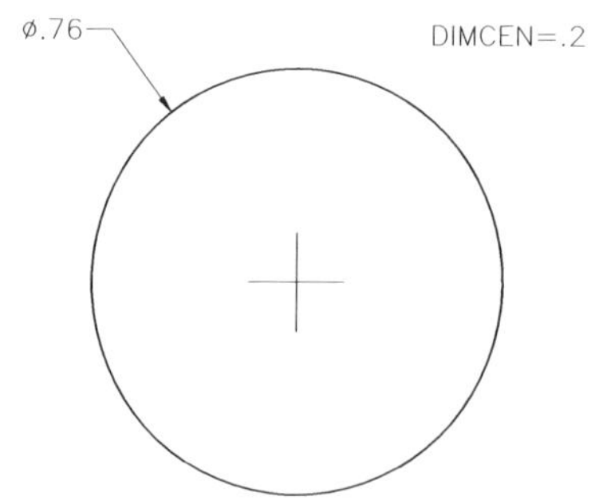

***Figure 8-41** Using a positive value for the **DIMCEN** variable*

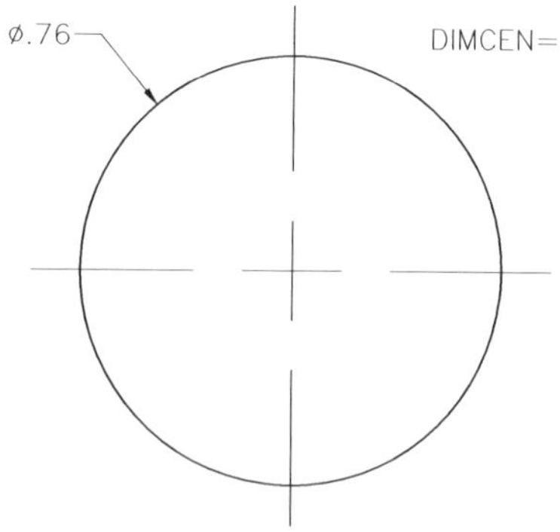

***Figure 8-42** Using a negative value for the **DIMCEN** variable*

Note

*The center marks created by using the **Center Mark** tool are lines and not associative dimensioning objects. These center marks have an explicit linetype.*

CREATING ASSOCIATIVE CENTERMARK

Ribbon: Annotate > Centerlines > Center Mark **Command:** CENTERMARK

The **Center Mark** tool is used to create an associative center mark at the center of a selected circle, arc, or polygonal arc. A center mark is a combination of two elements, center cross and extension lines. The center marks created using the **Center Mark** tool are associated with the selected object. If the dimension or position of the object is updated, the center mark also get automatically updated. On invoking this tool, you are prompted to select a circle or an arc to add the center mark. Select a circle or an arc to create an associated center mark, as shown in Figure 8-43. You can add a center mark to one or more circles at a time as the **CENTERMARK** command automatically repeats after selecting a circle or an arc. You can change the properties of the center mark by using the **PROPERTIES** palette, as shown in Figure 8-44. The appearance of the center mark can be controlled by using the system variables like CENTEREXE, CENTERMARKEXE, CENTERLAYER, CENTERLTYPE, CENTERCROSSSIZE, AND CENTERCROSSGAP.

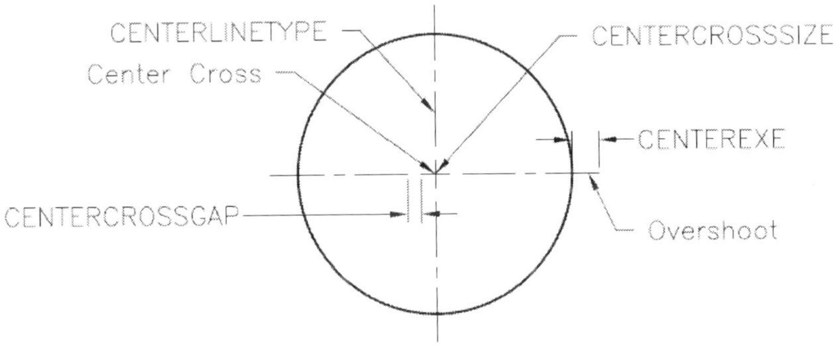

Figure 8-43 *Circle with the associative center mark*

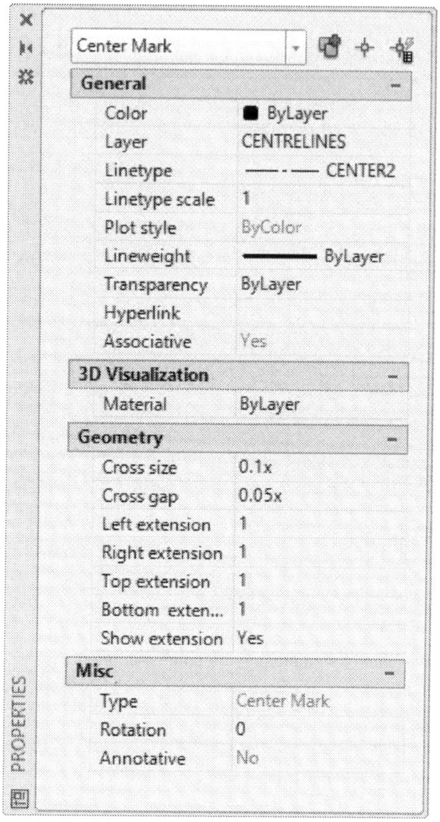

Figure 8-44 *The center mark* ***PROPERTIES*** *palette*

CREATING ASSOCIATIVE CENTERLINES

Ribbon: Annotate > Centerlines > Centerline **Command:** CENTERLINE

The **Centerline** tool is used to create centerline geometry for a specified linetype and is associated with selected lines and polylines. This tool creats a centerline between the apparent midpoint of the start and endpoints of any two selected lines. If the lines are nonparallel lines, the centerline will be drawn between the imaginary intersection point and the endpoint of the selected lines. To create a centerline between two lines or polylines, choose the **Centerline** tool from the **Centerlines** panel in the **Annotate** tab; you will be prompted to select the first line. Select the first line; you will be prompted to select the second line. Select the second line, centerline will be created, as shown in Figure 8-45 and Figure 8-46.

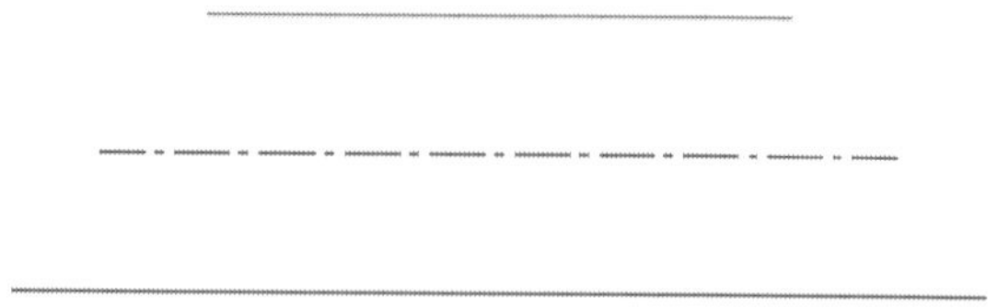

Figure 8-45 *Centerline created between two parallel lines*

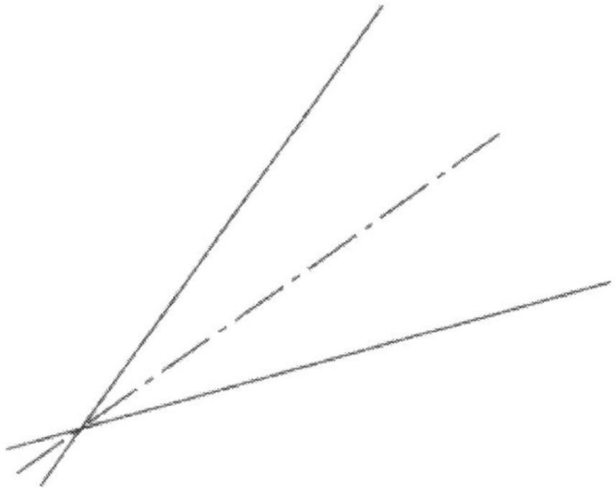

Figure 8-46 Centerline created between two nonparallel lines

You can change the appearance of the centerlines by using system variables like CENTEREXE, CENTERLAYER, CENTERLTYPE as the system variables are valid for both centerlines and center marks.

Note

*1. You can disassociate centerlines and center marks from objects using the **CENTERDISASSOCIATE** command.*

*2. You can reassociate centerlines and center marks with the selected objects using the **CENTERREASSOCIATE** command.*

CREATING ORDINATE DIMENSIONS

Ribbon: Annotate > Dimensions > Dimension drop-down > Ordinate
Menu Bar: Dimension > Ordinate **Toolbar:** Dimension > Ordinate
Command: DIMORDINATE

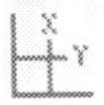

Ordinate dimensioning is used to dimension the X and Y coordinates of the selected point. This type of dimensioning is also known as arrowless dimensioning because no arrowheads are drawn in it. Ordinate dimensioning is also called datum dimensioning because all dimensions are related to a common base point. The current UCS (user coordinate system) origin becomes the reference or the base point for ordinate dimensioning. With ordinate dimensioning, you can determine the X or Y displacement of a selected point from the current UCS origin.

Dimension text (*X* or *Y* coordinate value) and the leader line along the *X* or *Y* axis are automatically placed using Ordinate dimensioning (Figure 8-47). Since ordinate dimensioning pertains to either the *X* coordinate or the *Y* coordinate, you should keep ORTHO on. When ORTHO is off, the leader line is automatically given a bend when you select the second leader line point that is offset from the first point. This allows you to generate offsets and avoid overlapping text on closely spaced dimensions. In ordinate dimensioning, only one extension line (leader line) is drawn.

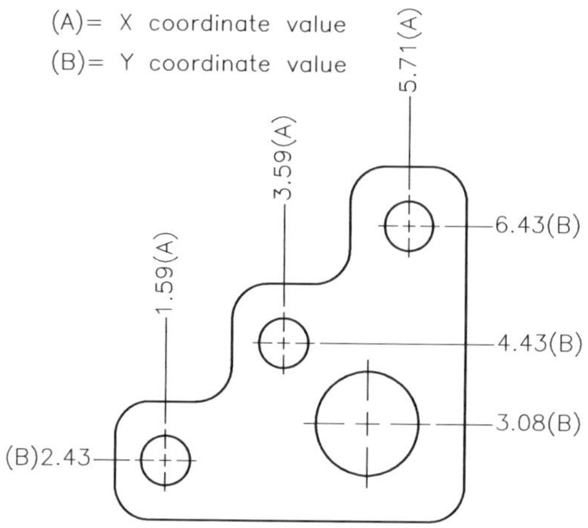

***Figure 8-47** Ordinate dimensioning*

The leader line for an *X* coordinate value will be drawn perpendicular to the *X* axis, and the leader line for a *Y* coordinate value will be drawn perpendicular to the *Y* axis. Since you cannot override this, the leader line drawn perpendicular to the *X* axis will have the dimension text aligned with the leader line. The dimension text is the X datum of the selected point. The leader line drawn perpendicular to the *Y* axis will have the dimension text, which is the Y datum of the selected point, aligned with the leader line. Any other alignment specification for the dimension text is nullified. Hence, changes in the Text Alignment in the **Dimension Style Manager** dialog box (**DIMTIH** and **DIMTOH** variables) have no effect on the alignment of the dimension text. You can specify the coordinate value that you want to dimension at the **Specify leader endpoint or [Xdatum/Ydatum/MText/Text/Angle]** prompt.

If you select or enter a point, AutoCAD LT checks the difference between the feature location and the leader endpoint. If the difference between the *X* coordinates is greater, the dimension measures the *Y* coordinate; otherwise, the *X* coordinate is measured. In this manner, AutoCAD LT determines whether it is an X or Y type of ordinate dimension. However, if you enter Y instead of specifying a point, AutoCAD LT will dimension the *Y* coordinate of the selected feature. Similarly, if you enter X, AutoCAD LT will dimension the *X* coordinate of the selected point. The prompt sequence that follows when you choose this tool is given next.

Specify feature location: *Select a point on an object.*
Specify leader endpoint or [Xdatum/Ydatum/Mtext/Text/Angle]: *Enter the endpoint of the leader.*

You can override the default text with the help of the **Mtext** or **Text** option. If you use the **Mtext** option, the **Text Editor Tab** will be displayed. If you use the **Text** option, you will be prompted to specify the new text in the Command line itself.

Exercise 4 — Ordinate Dimension

Draw the model shown in Figure 8-48 and then use ordinate dimensioning to dimension the part. The distance between the dotted lines is 0.5 unit.

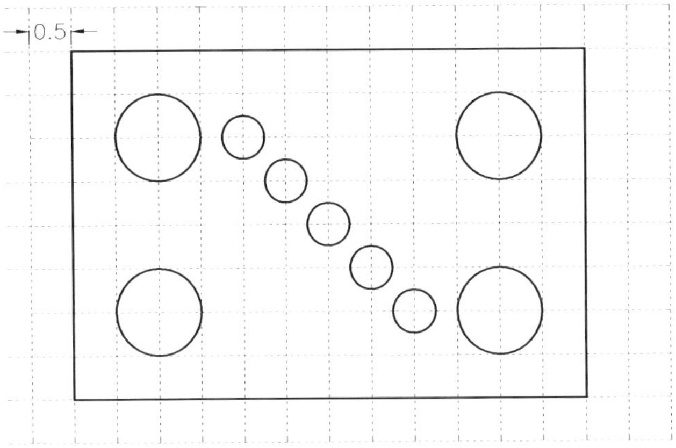

Figure 8-48 *Drawing for Exercise 4*

MAINTAINING EQUAL SPACING BETWEEN DIMENSIONS

Ribbon: Annotate > Dimensions > Adjust Space **Toolbar:** Dimension > Dimension Space
Menu Bar: Dimension > Dimension Space **Command:** DIMSPACE

The **Adjust Space** tool is used to equally space the overlapping or the unequally spaced linear and angular dimensions. Maintaining equal spacing between the dimension lines increases the clarity of the drawing display. Figure 8-49 shows a drawing with unequally spaced dimensions, and Figure 8-50 shows the same drawing with equally spaced dimensions after the use of the **Adjust Space** tool. Figure 8-51 shows a drawing with its angular dimensions equally spaced.

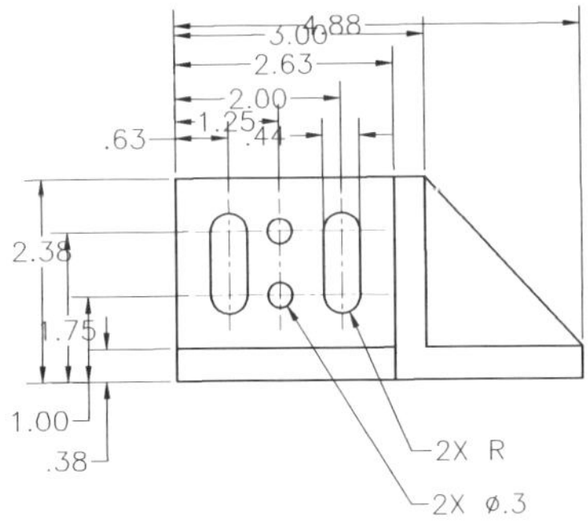

Figure 8-49 *Drawing with its linear dimensions unequally spaced*

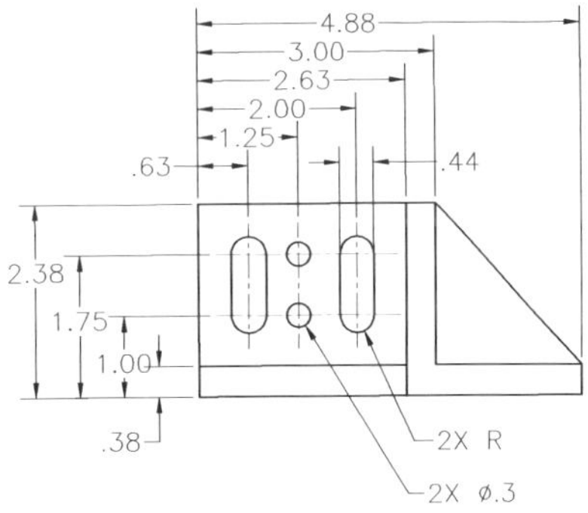

Figure 8-50 *Drawing with its linear dimensions equally spaced*

The prompt sequence that will follow when you choose the **Adjust Space** tool is given next.

Select base dimension: *Select a linear or an angular dimension with respect to which all other dimensions will get spaced.*

Select dimensions to space: *Select the dimensions that you want to be equally spaced from the specified base dimension.*
Select dimensions to space: *Select more similar dimensions or press* Enter
Enter value or [Auto] <Auto>: *Enter a value to specify the spacing between the selected dimensions or enter A to automatically calculate the gap between the dimensions.*

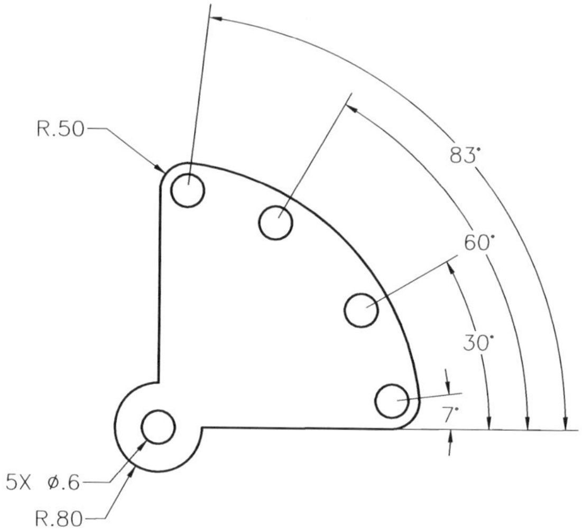

Figure 8-51 *Drawing with its angular dimensions equally spaced*

Enter **0** in the above prompt to align all the selected dimensions in a single line. With the **Auto** option selected, AutoCAD LT will calculate the space value on the basis of the dimension text height. The spacing is automatically maintained to a value that is double of the dimension text height.

CREATING DIMENSION BREAKS

Ribbon: Annotate > Dimensions > Break
Menu Bar: Dimension > Dimension Break
Toolbar: Dimension > Dimension Break
Command: DIMBREAK

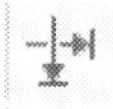

The **Break** tool is used to create a break in the dimension line, extension line, or multileaders at the point where they intersect with other drawing entities or annotations. Inserting dimension breaks will keep annotative objects separate from the main drawing, which increases the clarity of the drawing, see Figure 8-52. The prompt sequence that will follow when you choose this tool is given next.

Select dimension to add/remove break or [Multiple]: *Select a dimension in which you want to insert a break.*
Select object to break dimension or [Auto/Manual/Remove] <Auto>: *Select objects or dimensions that intersect the above selected dimension, enter an option or press* Enter *to choose the* ***Auto*** *option.*

The options in the **Break** tool are discussed next.

Multiple

This option allows you to select more than one dimension for adding or removing a break. The prompt sequence that will follow is given next.

Select dimensions: *Select the dimensions by any object selection method and press* Enter
Select object to break dimensions or [Auto/Remove] <Auto>: *Enter an option or press* Enter

The **Auto** option, available in the above prompt, creates breaks automatically at the intersections of the selected dimensions with the other drawing and annotation entities. Also, if the selected dimensions are self-intersecting, then the **Auto** option, if chosen, creates a break at the point of intersection. The **Remove** option removes all the dimension breaks that exist in the selected dimensions.

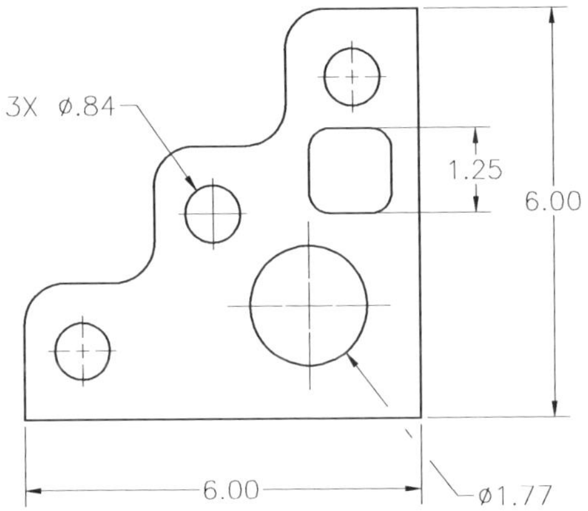

Figure 8-52 *Drawing with dimension breaks*

Auto

This option creates the break automatically at the intersection of the selected dimension with the other drawing and annotation entities.

Note

All dimension breaks created by using the ***Multiple*** *and* ***Auto*** *options update automatically when you modify the broken dimension or the intersecting objects. However, the new objects that are created over the broken dimension do not have any effect on the display of the broken dimension. For example, the dimension that has already been broken will not be further broken with respect to newly created objects even if the object(s) interfere with the dimension. To break the newly created dimension, you need to use the* ***Break*** *tool again.*

Remove

This option removes all the dimension breaks from the selected dimension.

Manual

This option is used to create a break in the dimension manually. You have to specify two points between which you want to break the dimension or the extension line. You can also create the dimension break at only one location with this option.

Note

The dimension breaks created by the ***Manual*** *option do not update automatically when you modify the broken dimension or the intersecting objects. For updating the dimension break, you need to remove the dimension and then again add the dimension break.*

CREATING INSPECTION DIMENSIONS

Ribbon: Annotate > Dimensions > Inspect **Toolbar:** Dimension > Inspection
Menu Bar: Dimension > Inspection **Command:** DIMINSPECT

A drawing sheet provides every minute information about the dimension of the product, including the inspection rate. The **Inspect** tool in AutoCAD LT is used to describe Inspection Rate of critical dimension of the product to ensure its quality. The inspection rate is used to specify how frequently the dimensions are to be checked to ensure that the variations in the dimensions are within the range. Select a dimension from the drawing and choose the **Inspect** tool from the **Dimensions** panel; the **Inspection Dimension** dialog box will be displayed, as shown in Figure 8-53. Choose the **OK** button; the selected dimension will change into the inspection dimension that consists of three fields (see Figure 8-54), which are discussed next.

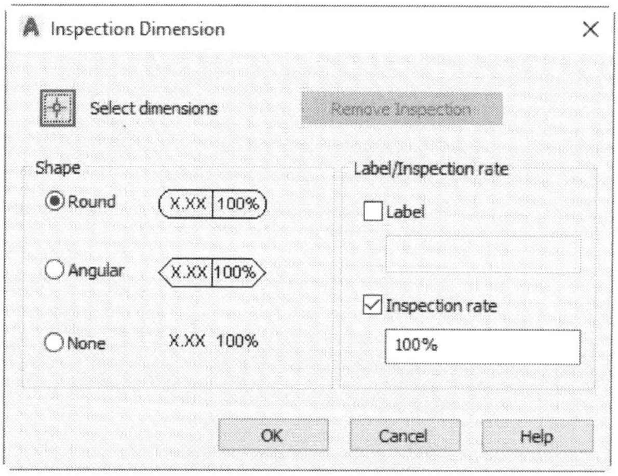

Figure 8-53 *The* ***Inspection Dimension*** *dialog box*

Label

The label is located at the extreme left of the inspection dimension and is used to specify the particular inspection dimension, see Figure 8-54.

Dimension Value

The dimension value is located in the middle of the inspection dimension and is used to display the value of the dimension to be maintained, see Figure 8-54.

Inspection Rate

The inspection rate is located at the right-end of the inspection dimension. It is used to specify the frequency of carrying out inspections, see Figure 8-54. The frequency of inspection is specified in terms of percentage value. The value 100% signifies that you need to check the dimension each time you inspect a component. Similarly, if the value is 50 % then you need to check the dimension for every second component.

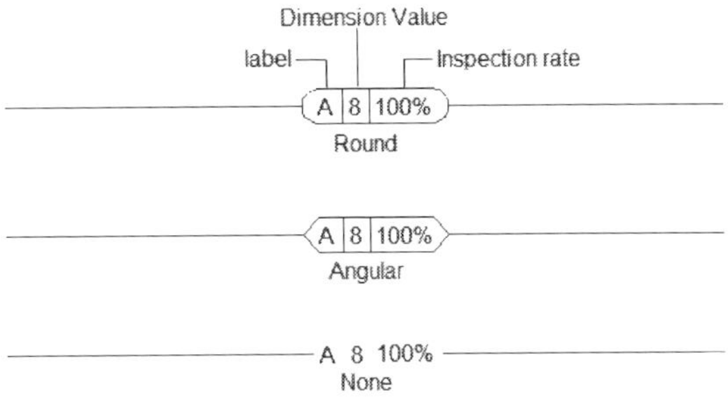

Figure 8-54 *Shapes and components of inspection dimension*

If you have not selected the dimension before invoking the **Inspect** tool, choose the **Select dimensions** button from the **Inspection Dimension** dialog box (refer to Figure 8-53); the dialog box will temporarily disappear from the screen, thereby enabling you to select the dimension that you want to convert into the inspection dimension. Select the dimensions and press the ENTER key; the **Inspection Dimension** dialog box will be displayed again. All the selected dimensions will display the same value of the label and inspection dimension. Next, specify the shape of the boundary around the inspection dimension from the **Shape** area. Figure 8-50 displays the shapes available in the **Inspection Dimension** dialog box. Next, enter the values for the label and inspection rate in their respective edit boxes in the **Label/Inspection rate** area and choose the **OK** button. You can also control the display of label and inspection rate in the inspection dimension by clearing or selecting the **Label** and **Inspection rate** check boxes respectively. To remove the inspection dimension of the selected dimension, choose the **Remove Inspection** button from the **Inspection Dimension** dialog box and then choose the **OK** button.

WORKING WITH TRUE ASSOCIATIVE DIMENSIONS

The true associative dimensions are the dimensions that are automatically modified when the objects to which they are associated are modified. By default, all dimensions in AutoCAD LT are true associative dimensions. If the dimension attached to the object is true associative, then it will be modified automatically when the object is modified. In this case, you do not have to select the definition points of the dimensions. Any dimension in AutoCAD LT can be converted into a disassociated dimension and then converted back to the true associative dimension. The procedure to do so is discussed next.

Removing the Dimension Associativity

Command: DIMDISASSOCIATE

The **DIMDISASSOCIATE** command is used to remove the associativity of the dimensions from the object to which they are associated. When you invoke this command, you will be prompted to select the dimensions to be disassociated. The true association of the selected dimensions is automatically removed once you exit this command. The number of dimensions disassociated is displayed in the Command prompt.

Converting a Dimension into a True Associative Dimension

Ribbon: Annotate > Dimensions > Reassociate **Command:** DIMREASSOCIATE
Menu Bar: Dimension > Reassociate Dimensions

The **Reassociate** tool is used to create a true associative dimension by associating the selected dimension to the specified object. When you invoke this tool, you will be prompted to select the objects. These objects are the dimensions to be associated. Select the dimensions to be associated and press ENTER; a cross is displayed and you are prompted to select the feature location. This cross implies that the dimension is not associated. You can define a new association point for the dimensions by selecting the objects or by using the object snaps. If you select a dimension that has already been associated to an object, the cross will be displayed inside a box. The prompt sequence that is displayed varies depending upon the type of dimension selected. In case of linear, aligned, radius, and diameter dimensions, you can directly select the object to associate the dimension. If the arcs or circles are assigned angular dimensions using three points, then also you can select these arcs or circles directly for associating the dimensions. For rest of the dimension types, you can use the object snaps to specify the point to associate the dimensions.

Note

*If you have edited a dimension by using the **Mtext** or **Text** option, then on using the **Reassociate** tool, the overridden value will be replaced by the original value.*

Exercise 5

Draw and dimension the object, as shown in Figure 8-55. Assume the missing dimensions.

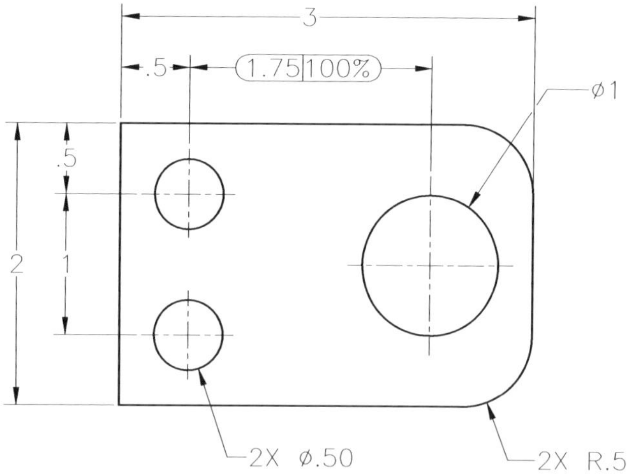

Figure 8-55 *Drawing for Exercise 5*

DRAWING LEADERS

Command: QLEADER

The leader line is used to attach annotations to an object or when the user wants to show a dimension without using another dimensioning tool. Sometimes, leaders of the dimensions of circles or arcs are so complicated that you need to construct a leader of your own. The leaders can be created using the **QLEADER** command. The leaders drawn by using this command create the arrow and the leader lines as a single object. The text is created as a separate object. This command can create multiline annotations and offer several options such as copying existing annotations and so on. You can customize the leader and annotation by selecting the **Settings** option at the **Specify first leader point, or [Settings] <Settings>** prompt. The prompt sequence that will follow when you use this command is given next.

Specify first leader point, or [Settings] <Settings>: *Specify the start point of the leader.*
Specify next point: *Specify the endpoint of the leader.*
Specify next point: *Specify the next point.*
Specify text width <current>: *Enter the text width of multiline text.* Enter
Enter first line of annotation text <Mtext>: *Press ENTER; AutoCAD LT displays the **Text Editor**. Enter text in it and then choose **Close Text Editor** to exit from the **Ribbon.***

If you press ENTER at the **Specify first leader point, or [Settings] <Settings>** prompt, then the **Leader Settings** dialog box is displayed. The **Leader Settings** dialog box gives you a number of options for the leader line and the text attached to it. It has the following tabs:

Annotation Tab

This tab provides you with various options to control annotation features, see Figure 8-56.

Annotation Type Area

The options in **Annotation Type** area and their usage are discussed next.

MText. When this radio button is selected, AutoCAD LT uses the **Text Editor** to create an annotation. Therefore, on selecting this radio button, the options in the **MText options** area become available.

Copy an Object. This radio button allows you to copy an existing annotation object (like multiline text, single line text, tolerance, or block) and attach it at the end of the leader. For example, if you have a text string in the drawing that you want to place at the end of the leader, you can use the **Copy an Object** radio button to place it at the end of the leader.

Tolerance. Select the **Tolerance** radio button and choose the **OK** button to exit from the **Leader Settings** dialog box. Then, specify the next point to complete the leader line; AutoCAD LT will display the **Geometric Tolerance** dialog box. In this dialog box, specify the tolerance and choose **OK** to exit it. AutoCAD LT will place the specified geometric tolerance with the feature control frame at the end of the leader (Figure 8-57).

Block Reference. The **Block Reference** radio button allows you to insert a predefined block at the end of the leader. When you select this option, AutoCAD LT will prompt you to enter the block name and insertion point.

None. This radio button creates a leader without placing any annotation at the end of the leader.

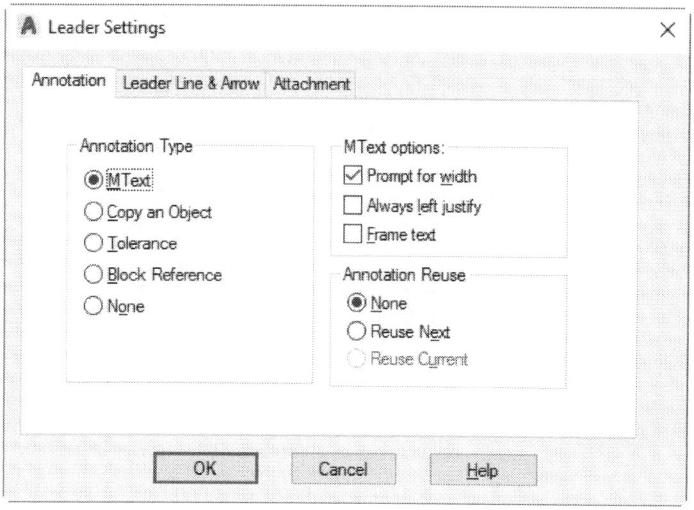

*Figure 8-56 The **Annotation** tab of the **Leader Settings** dialog box*

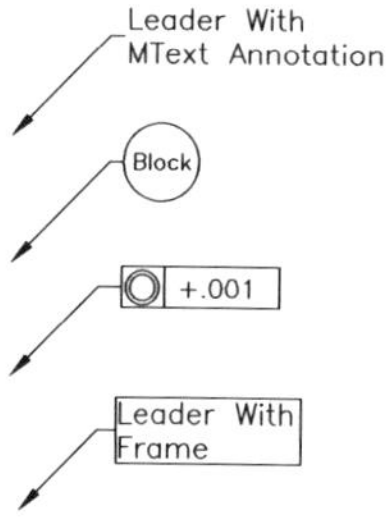

Figure 8-57 Leaders with different annotation types

MText options Area

The options under this area will be available only if the **MText** radio button is selected from the **Annotation Type** area. This area provides you with the following options.

Prompt for width. Selecting this check box allows you to specify the width of the multiline text annotation.

Always left justify. Select this check box to left justify the multiline text annotation in all situations. Selecting this check box makes the prompt for the width option unavailable.

Frame text. Selecting this check box draws a box around the multiline text annotation.

Annotation Reuse Area

The options under this area allow you to reuse the annotation.

None. When selected, AutoCAD LT does not reuse the leader annotation.

Reuse Next. This radio button is used to reuse the annotation that you are going to create next for all subsequent leaders.

Reuse Current. This radio button allows you to reuse the current annotation for all subsequent leaders.

Leader Line & Arrow Tab

The options in the **Leader Line & Arrow** tab are related to the leader parameters, see Figure 8-58.

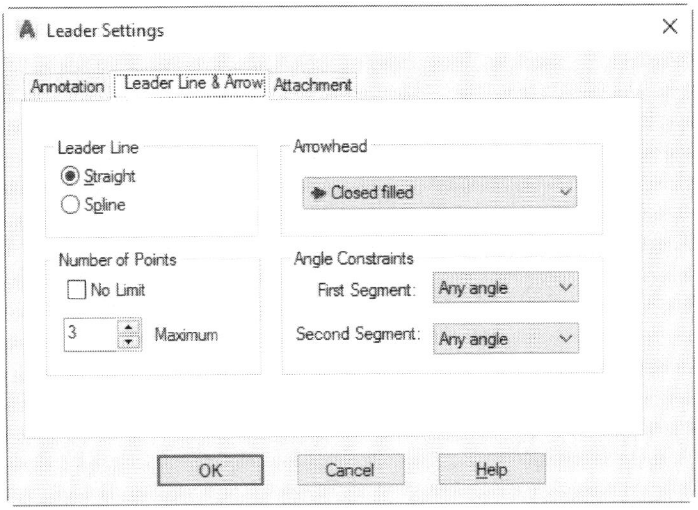

*Figure 8-58 The **Leader Line & Arrow** tab of the **Leader Settings** dialog box*

Leader Line Area

This area has the options for the leader line type such as straight or spline. The **Spline** option draws a spline through the specified leader points and the **Straight** option draws straight lines. Figure 8-59 shows the straight and splined leader lines.

Number of Points Area

The options provided under this area are used to specify the number of points in the leader.

No Limit. If this check box is selected, you can define as many numbers of points as you want in the leader line. AutoCAD LT will keep prompting you for the next point, until you press ENTER at this prompt.

Maximum. This spinner is used to specify the maximum number of points on the leader line. The default value in this spinner is 3; as a result, there will be only three points in the leader line. You can specify the number of points by using this spinner to control the shape of the leader. This has to be kept in mind that the start point of the leader is the first leader point. This spinner will be available only if the **No Limit** check box is clear. Figure 8-59 shows a leader line with five points.

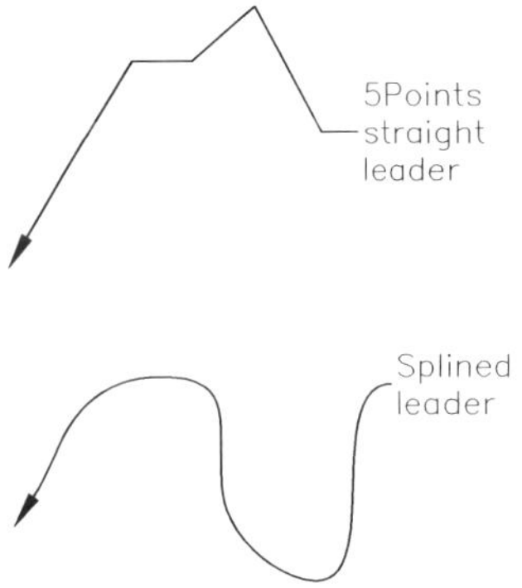

Figure 8-59 Straight and splined leader lines

Arrowhead Area

The options in the drop-down list under this area allow you to define a leader arrowhead. The arrowhead is the same as the one for dimensioning. You can also use the user-defined arrows by selecting **User Arrow** from the drop-down list.

Angle Constraints Area

The options provided under this area are used to define the angle for the segments of the leader lines.

First Segment. This drop-down list is used to specify the angle at which the first leader line segment will be drawn. You can select the predefined values from this drop-down list.

Second Segment. This drop-down list is used to specify the angle at which the second leader line segment will be drawn.

Attachment Tab

The **Attachment** tab (Figure 8-60) will be available only if you have selected **MText** from the **Annotation Type** area of the **Annotation** tab. The options in this tab are used to attach the multiline text to the leader. It has two columns: **Text on left side** and **Text on right side**. Both these columns have five radio buttons below them. You can select the required radio button corresponding to the options for attaching the multiline text. If you draw a leader from the right to the left, AutoCAD LT uses the settings under **Text on left side**. Similarly, if you draw a leader from the left to the right, AutoCAD LT uses the settings as specified under **Text on right side**. This area also provides you with the **Underline bottom line** check box. If this check box is selected, then the last line of the multiline text will be underlined.

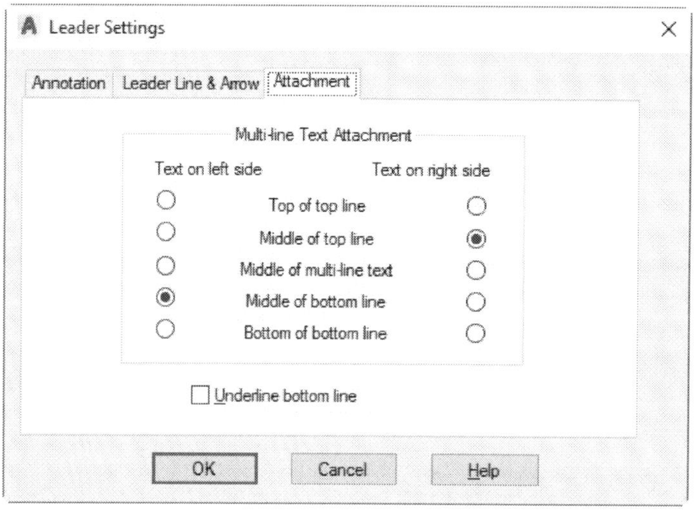

***Figure 8-60** The **Attachment** tab of the **Leader Settings** dialog box*

Note

*You can use the Command Line to create leaders with the help of the **LEADER** command. The options under this command are similar to those under the **QLEADER** command. The only difference is that the **LEADER** command uses the Command Line.*

Exercise 6 — Qleader

Make the drawing shown in Figure 8-61 and then use the **QLEADER** command to dimension the part accordingly. The distance between the dotted lines is 0.5 units.

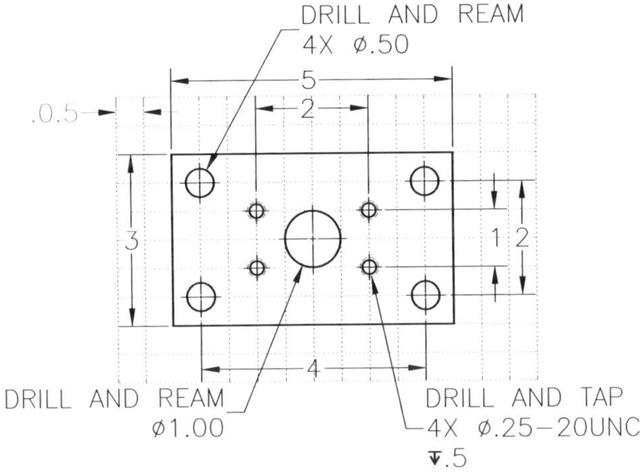

***Figure 8-61** Drawing for Exercise 6*

MULTILEADERS

Ribbon: Annotate > Leaders > Multileader **Toolbar:** Multileader > Multileader
Command: MLEADER/MLD

Multileaders are the enhanced leaders, wherein the leader and its content are part of the same object. A Multileader provides you enough flexibility so that you can create either the arrowhead or the tail end first. Alternatively, you can specify the content of the leader first and then draw the leader. Multileaders can have more than one leader so that a single comment can be pointed at more than one location. Besides this, multiple notes can be attached to a single leader so that more than one comment can be pointed at a single location. You can add or remove leaders from the previously created multileaders. You can also control and modify the appearance of the multileaders.

DRAWING MULTILEADERS

To draw a multileader, choose the **Multileader** tool from the **Leaders** panel. The prompt sequence after choosing this tool is given next.

Specify leader arrowhead location or [leader Landing first/Content first/Options] <Options>: *Specify the location for the arrowhead from where the leader will start.*
Specify leader landing location: *Specify the leader landing location, see Figure 8-62.*

AutoCAD LT displays the **Text Editor**. Enter the text in it and click outside the editor to accept and exit the tool. If you click outside the editor without entering any text and exit the tool, no text will be attached to the multileader.

The other options in the **Multileader** tool are discussed next.

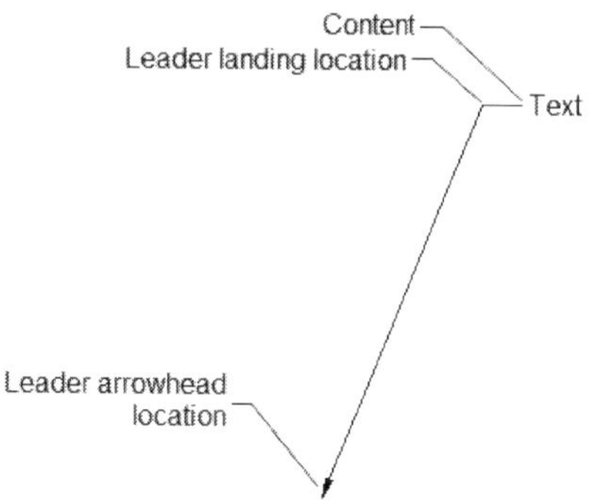

***Figure 8-62** Image displaying the options to locate the leader start point*

leader Landing first

This option is used to locate the leader landing line first. Choose the **leader Landing first** option from the shortcut menu at the **Specify leader arrowhead location or [leader Landing first/Content first/ Options] <Options>** prompt to invoke this option. Alternatively, if the **Dynamic Input** button is turned on in the Status Bar, then you can choose this option from the dynamic input box associated with the cursor. On doing so, you will be prompted to specify a point where the leader landing should be placed. Specify the leader landing location; you will be prompted to specify the leader arrowhead location. The leader landing will automatically adjust itself to the leader landing point, depending upon the direction in which you create the leader. For example, if you create the leader to the left of the leader landing location, the landing will automatically be created to the right of the leader landing location.

Content first

This option is used to specify the content (multiline text or block) of the leader first. Choose the **Content first** option from the shortcut menu or from the **Specify leader arrowhead location or [leader Landing first/Content first/Options] <Options>** prompt to invoke this option. Alternatively, if the **Dynamic Input** button is turned on in the Status Bar, you can choose this option from the dynamic input box associated with the cursor. After specifying the content to be attached with the leader, a horizontal leader landing will automatically be attached to the content and then you can specify the leader arrowhead location.

Note

If you have drawn a multileader earlier by using any one of the above-mentioned options, then the succeeding multileaders will be created by using previous option only, until otherwise modified.

Options

The sub options within this option are used to control the leader type, content to be attached with the leader, size of the leader landing, and so on. These suboptions are discussed next.

Leader type

This option provides the suboptions for the leader line type such as straight, spline, or none. The **Spline** suboption draws a spline through the specified leader points and the **Straight** option draws the straight lines. Figure 8-59 shows the straight and spline leader lines. The **None** option enables you to draw the content of the leader without drawing the leader itself.

leader landing

This option provides you the suboptions to control the display of the horizontal landing line. The **No** suboption will create a leader with no horizontal landing and the **Yes** suboption will create a leader with the horizontal landing. If you choose the **Yes** suboption, then you will be prompted to specify the length of the horizontal landing. The new leader will be created with the specified landing length. Figure 8-63 shows the leaders created by using various suboptions of the **leader landing**.

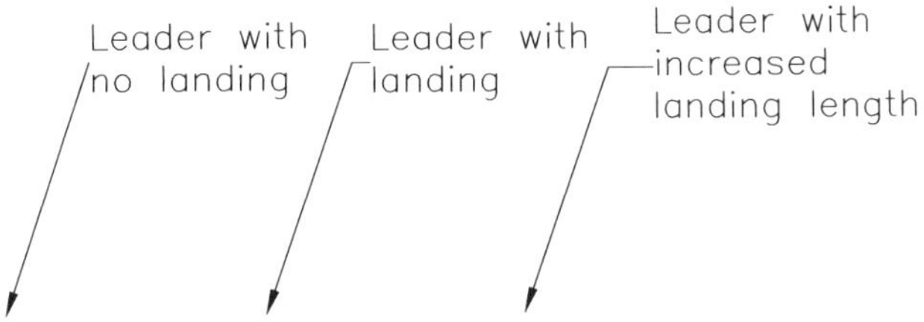

Figure 8-63 *Leaders drawn by using various types of landing suboptions*

Content type

This option is used to specify the type of content to be attached with the leader. The **Mtext** suboption uses the AutoCAD LT **Text Editor** to create the content. The **Block** suboption allows you to insert a predefined block at the end of the leader. When you select this option, AutoCAD LT will prompt you to enter the block name and the specified block will be attached to the new leader. The **None** suboption creates a leader without placing any content at the end of the leader.

Maxpoints

This option is used to specify the maximum number of points on the leader line. The default value is 2, which means there will be only two points on the leader line. You can specify the maximum number of points by entering the new value. This has to be kept in mind that the start point of the leader is the first leader point.

First angle

This option is used to constrain the angle of the first leader line to a fixed value. You can only specify a value which is the natural number multiple of 15 degrees.

Second angle

This option is used to constrain the angle of the second leader line with respect to the end point of the first leader line. You can only specify a value which is the natural number multiple of 15degrees.

eXit options

This option will return you back to the main options of the multileader.

Note

All settings specified in the ***Options*** *heading of the multileader will last only for that particular leader and the next leader will be created with the default settings. You can also change the default settings of the multileader from the* ***Multileader Style Manager*** *dialog box that will be discussed in detail in Chapter 10.*

ADDING LEADERS TO EXISTING MULTILEADER

Ribbon: Annotate > Leaders > Add Leader **Toolbar:** Multileader > Add Leader
Command: MLEADEREDIT/MLE

The **Add Leader** tool is used to add leaders to an existing multileader, so that you can point a single content to more than one location. To do so, choose the **Add Leaders** tool in the **Leaders** panel; you will be prompted to select the multileader to which you want to attach the new leader. After selecting the desired multileader, a new leader will branch out from the landing location of the existing multileader. Next, you will be prompted to specify the location of the arrowhead of the new leader. Next, you can attach any number of leaders to the selected multileader. To exit this tool, press the ENTER key.

REMOVING LEADERS FROM EXISTING MULTILEADER

Ribbon: Annotate > Leaders > Remove Leader **Toolbar:** Multileader > Remove Leader
Command: MLEADEREDIT/MLE

The **Remove Leader** tool is used to remove leaders from an existing multileader. To remove a leader, choose the **Remove Leader** tool from the **Leaders** panel; you will be prompted to select the multileader from which you want to remove leaders. Select the multileader; you will be prompted to select the leaders to be removed from the selected multileader. Select the leaders and then press the ENTER key. You can also select all the leaders of the specified multileader. But, in such cases, all multileaders will get deleted from the drawing area.

ALIGNING MULTILEADERS

Ribbon: Annotate > Leaders > Align **Toolbar:** Multileaders > Align Multileaders
Command: MLEADERALIGN/MLA

The **Align** tool is used to arrange the selected multileaders by aligning them about a line or making them parallel or by maintaining the spacing between the horizontal landing of the leaders. To do so, choose the **Align** tool from the **Leaders** panel; you will be prompted to select the multileaders to be aligned. After selecting the multileaders, press the ENTER key. Next, you will be prompted to select one of the multileaders with respect to which all other multileaders will get aligned. Also, you can choose the alignment type from the different options available at the Command prompt. The prompt sequence after choosing the **Align** tool is given next.

Select multileaders: *Select the multileaders to be aligned and* Enter.
Current mode: *Use current spacing.*
All further prompt sequences will vary with the alignment type used in aligning the leaders. The alignment type used previously will become the default alignment type for the current tool.

Select multileader to align to or [Options]: *Enter **O** to choose the type of alignment.*
Enter an option [Distribute/make leader segments Parallel/specify Spacing/Use current spacing] <Use current spacing>: *Specify an option and* Enter.

The options in the above prompt sequence are discussed next.

Distribute

This option is used to accommodate all the selected multileaders at constant spacing between the two specified points. The prompt sequence that will be followed is given next.

Enter an option [Distribute/make leader segments Parallel/specify Spacing/Use current spacing] <Distribute>: **D** Enter.
Specify first point or [Options]: *Specify the location of the first point.*
Specify second point: *Specify the location of the second point and its orientation with respect to the first point.*

The tail end of all the selected leaders landing will get aligned with equal spacing along the line joining the first and the second specified point. Figure 8-64 shows a drawing with its multileaders nonaligned. Figure 8-65 displays the same drawing with its multileaders aligned along an imaginary vertical line by using the **Distribute** option.

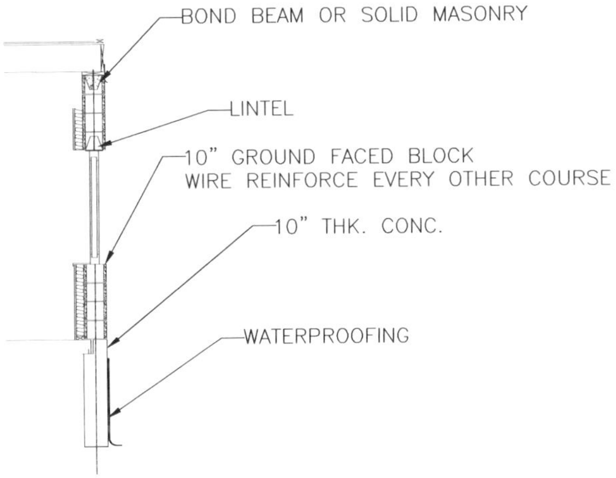

Figure 8-64 *Drawing with non-aligned multileaders*

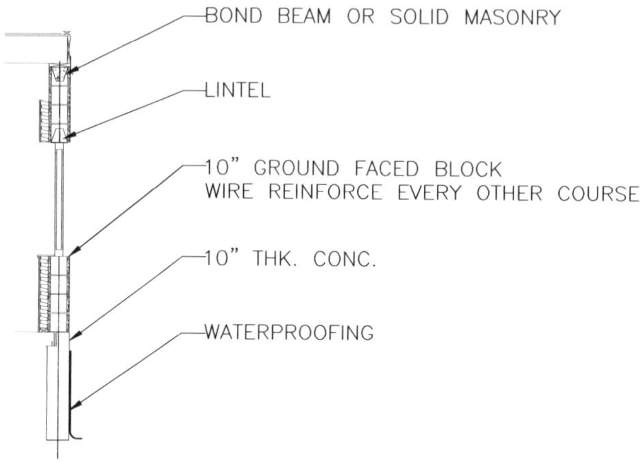

Figure 8-65 *Drawing with multileaders aligned using the* ***Distribute*** *option*

make leader segments Parallel

This option is used to make all the selected multileaders parallel to one of the leaders selected as reference. The prompt sequence that will be followed is given next.

> Enter an option [Distribute/make leader segments Parallel/specify Spacing/Use current spacing] <current>: **P** Enter.
> Select multileader to align to or [Options]: *Select the leader with which you want to make all other selected multileaders parallel.*

Figure 8-66 shows the drawing with its leader aligned parallel to the lowest leader of the drawing.

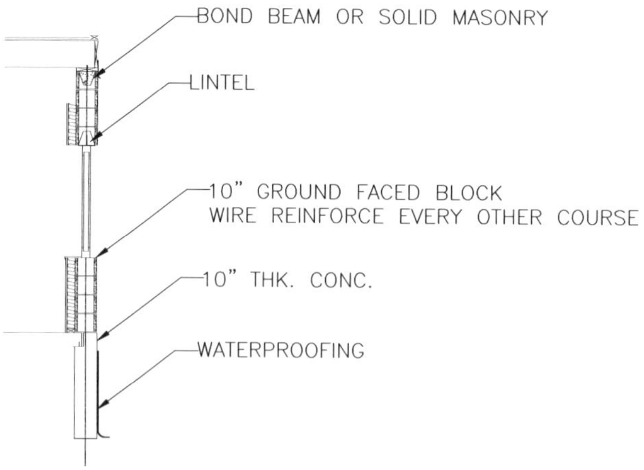

Figure 8-66 *Drawing with multileaders aligned using the* ***make leader segments Parallel*** *option*

specify Spacing

This option is used to align the selected multileaders in the specified direction, and also maintains a constant spacing between the landing lines. You need to specify one reference leader, with respect to which the specified interval and direction will be measured. The prompt sequence that will be followed is given next.

Enter an option [Distribute/make leader segments Parallel/specify Spacing/Use current spacing] <current>: **S** Enter.
Specify spacing <current>: *Enter the distance value to be maintained between the two consecutive leader landing lines.*
Select multileader to align to or [Options]: *Select one of the leaders with respect to which the specified distance will be measured.*
Specify direction: *Specify the desired direction in the drawing area for the alignment of multileaders.*

When you select a multileader to align with other multileaders, an imaginary line will be displayed in the drawing area. This line allows you to specify the direction of alignment. All the multileaders will get aligned to the selected multileader at the specified distance and direction. Figure 8-67 shows the drawing with its multileaders aligned vertical using the **specify Spacing** option.

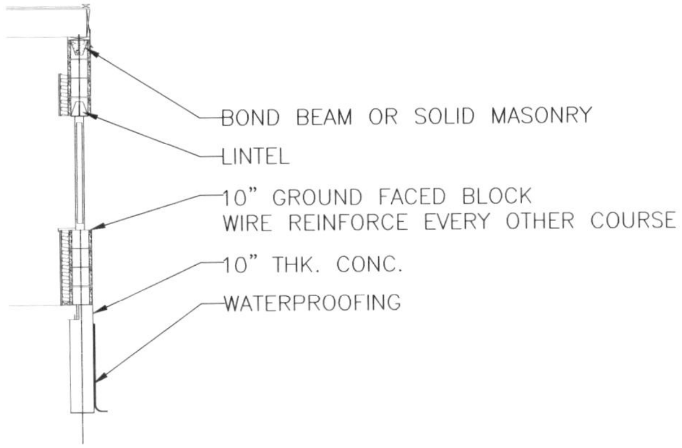

Figure 8-67 *Drawing with multileaders aligned using the **specify Spacing** option*

Use current spacing

This option is used to align the selected multileaders in the specified direction and also to retain the distance between the landing lines intact. You need to specify one reference leader with respect to which the distance will be measured in the specified direction. The prompt sequence that will be followed is given next.

Enter an option [Distribute/make leader segments Parallel/specify Spacing/Use current spacing] <specify Spacing>: **U** Enter.
Select multileader to align to or [Options]: *Select one of the leaders with respect to which the direction to be specified is maintained.*
Specify direction: *Specify the desired direction in the drawing area for the alignment of the multileaders.*

COLLECTING MULTIPLE LEADERS

Ribbon: Annotate > Leaders > Collect **Toolbar:** Multileader > Collect Multileader
Command: MLEADERCOLLECT/MLC

The **Collect** tool is used to collect the content of the selected multileaders and attach them to a single leader landing. Note that only the multileaders having predefined blocks as content can be collected by this tool. To collect the multileaders, choose the **Collect** tool from the **Leaders** panel. Select the multileaders in the order in which you want them to be collected and press ENTER. The content of the last selected multileader will be retained to its landing position and the content of all other multileaders will move to the last multileader. Next, specify a point in the drawing area where the upper left-corner of the collected content of the multileaders will be placed. You can collect the content horizontally or vertically by placing the content one after another, or by specifying the space between which the contents will be placed, and the content exceeding the specified distance will be sent to the next row. The prompt sequence after choosing the **Collect** tool is given next.

Select multileaders: *Select the multileaders in the order in which you want to collect the content of these multileaders and press* Enter.
Specify collected multileader location or [Vertical/Horizontal/Wrap] <current>: *Specify a point in the drawing area where the upper left-corner of the collected content will be placed or choose an option from command prompt.*

If you choose **Horizontal** from the shortcut menu or from the **Specify collected multileader location or [Vertical/Horizontal/Wrap] <current>** prompt sequence, the contents of the selected multileaders will get collected horizontally. Figure 8-68 shows the multileaders prior to the collection and Figure 8-69(a) shows the same leaders after the horizontal alignment. If you choose **Vertical** from the shortcut menu or from the **Specify collected multileader location or [Vertical/Horizontal/Wrap] <current>** prompt sequence, the contents of the selected multileaders will get collected vertically, see Figure 8-69(b).

If you choose the **Wrap** option from the shortcut menu displayed by right-clicking at the **Specify collected multileader location or [Vertical/Horizontal/Wrap] <current>** prompt sequence, you will be prompted to enter a value for the wrap width. The contents of the selected multileaders will be placed side by side and the contents that could not be accommodated into the specified wrap width will be sent to the next row. In Figure 8-69(c), three blocks get accommodated into the specified wrap width and the remaining one is sent to the next row. Alternatively, you can also enter the number of blocks to be accommodated into one row and the remaining content will automatically be sent to the next row. Choose **Number** from the shortcut menu displayed by right-clicking or you can select this option from the **Specify wrap width or [Number]** prompt sequence. Next, enter the number of blocks to be accommodated into each row. In Figure 8-69(d), only two blocks are specified to be accommodated into each row, so the remaining two blocks have been sent to the second row.

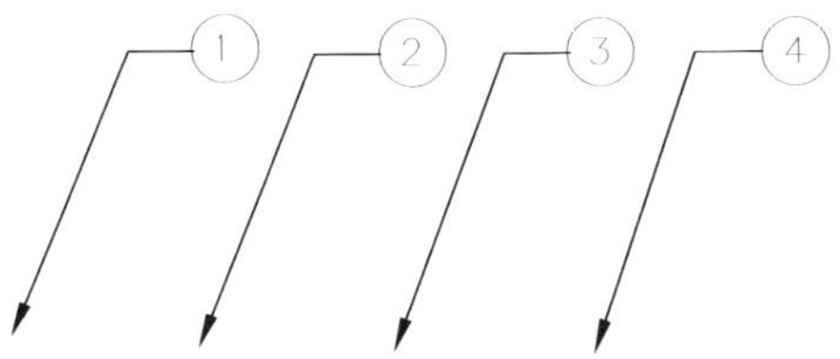

Figure 8-68 Multileaders prior to the collection

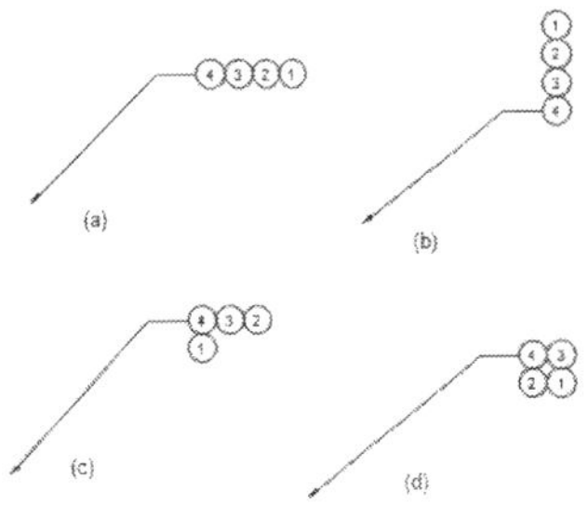

Figure 8-69 Contents of the multileaders after being collected

GEOMETRIC DIMENSIONING AND TOLERANCING

One of the most important parts of the design process is assigning the dimensions and tolerances to parts, since every part is manufactured from the dimensions given in the drawing. Therefore, every designer must understand and have a thorough knowledge of the standard practices used in the industry to make sure that the information given on the drawing is correct and can be understood by other people. Tolerancing is equally important, especially in the assembled parts. Tolerances and fits determine how the parts will fit. Incorrect tolerances could result in a product that is not usable. In addition to dimensioning and tolerancing, the function and the relationship that exists between the mating parts is important if the part is to perform the way it was designed. This aspect of the design process is addressed by geometric dimensioning and tolerancing, generally known as GD & T.

Geometric dimensioning and tolerancing is a means to design and manufacture parts with respect to the actual function and relationship that exists between different features of the same part or the features of the mating parts. Therefore, a good design is not achieved by just giving dimensions and tolerances. The designer has to go beyond dimensioning and think of the intended function of the part and how the features of the part are going to affect its function. For example, Figure 8-70 shows a part with the required dimensions and tolerances. In this drawing, there is no mention of the relationship between the pin and the plate. Is the pin perpendicular to the plate? If it is, to what degree should it be perpendicular? Also, it does not mention on which surface the perpendicularity of the pin is to be measured. A design like this is open to individual interpretation based on intuition and experience. This is where geometric dimensioning and tolerancing play an important part in the product design process.

Figure 8-71 has been dimensioned using geometric dimensioning and tolerancing. The feature symbols define the datum (reference plane) and the permissible deviation in the perpendicularity of the pin with respect to the bottom surface. In a drawing like this, chances of making a mistake are minimized.

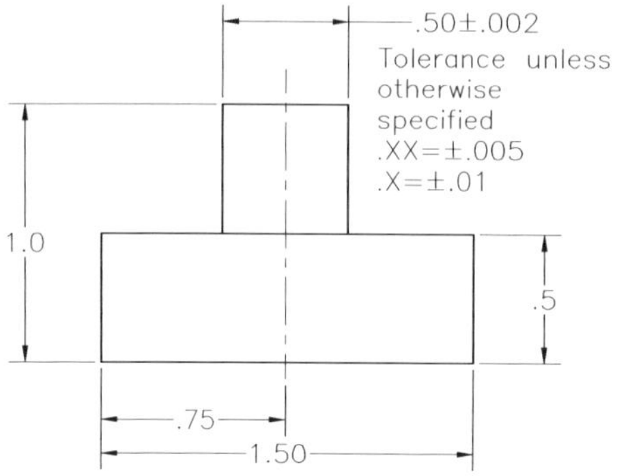

Figure 8-70 Traditional dimensioning and tolerancing technique

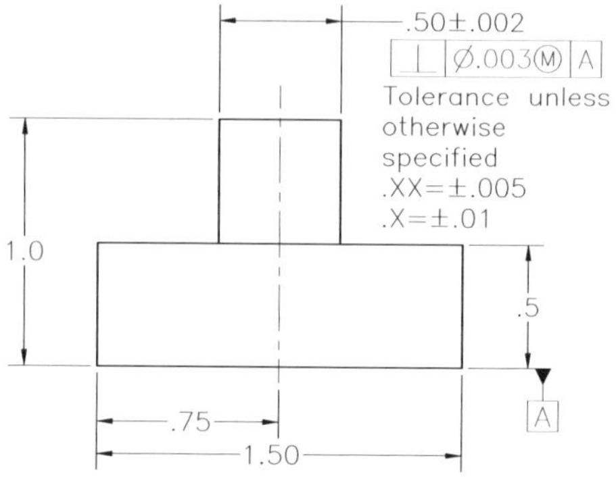

Figure 8-71 Geometric dimensioning and tolerancing

Geometric Characteristics and Symbols

Before discussing the application of AutoCAD LT tools in geometric dimensioning and tolerancing, you need to understand the following feature symbols and tolerancing components. Figure 8-72 shows the geometric characteristics and symbols used in geometric dimensioning and tolerancing.

Kind of feature	Type of feature	Characteristics	
Related	Location	Position	⌖
		Concentricity or Coaxiality	◎
		Symmetry	⌯
	Orientation	Parallelism	//
		Perpendicularity	⊥
		Angularity	∠
Individual	Form	Cylindricity	⌭
		Flatness	⏥
		Circularity or Roundness	○
		Straightness	—
Individual or related	Profile	Surface Profile	⌓
		Line Profile	⌒
Related	Runout	Circular Runout	↗
		Total Runout	⌰

Figure 8-72 Characteristics and symbols used in geometric tolerancing

Note

Symbols used in geometric dimensioning and tolerancing are the building blocks of geometric dimensioning and tolerancing.

ADDING GEOMETRIC TOLERANCE

Ribbon: Annotate > Dimensions > Tolerance **Toolbar:** Dimension > Tolerance
Menu Bar: Dimension > Tolerance **Command:** TOL/TOLERANCE

Geometric tolerance displays the deviations of profile, orientation, form, location, and runout of a feature. In AutoCAD LT, geometrical tolerancing is displayed by feature control frames. The frames contain all information about tolerances for a single dimension. To display feature control frames with various tolerancing parameters, you need to enter specifications in the **Geometric Tolerance** dialog box (Figure 8-73). You can invoke the **Geometric Tolerance** dialog box by choosing the **Tolerance** tool from the **Dimensions** panel.

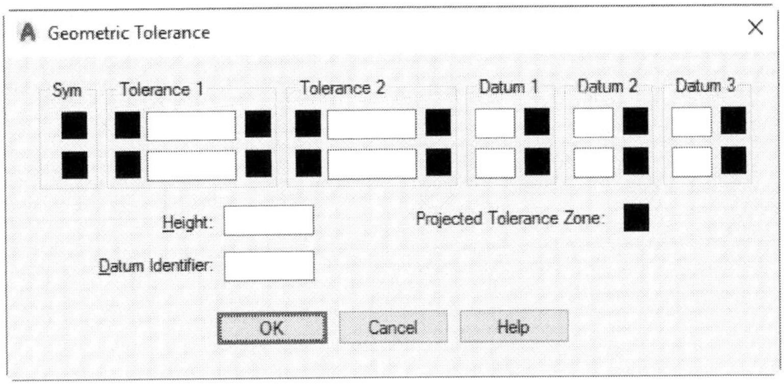

Figure 8-73 *The* ***Geometric Tolerance*** *dialog box*

Various components that constitute geometric tolerancing (GTOL) are shown in Figures 8-74 and 8-75.

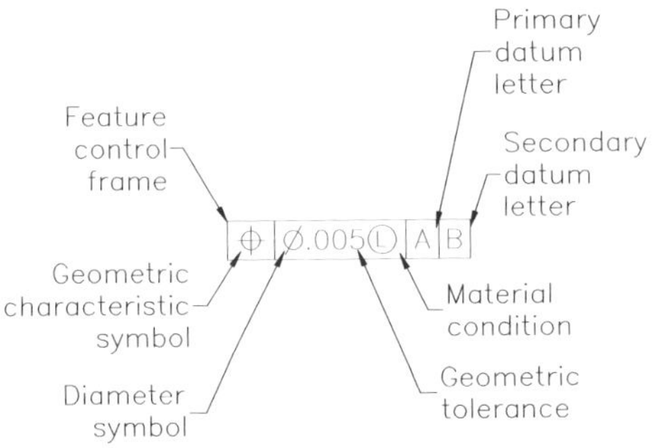

Figure 8-74 *Components of GTOL*

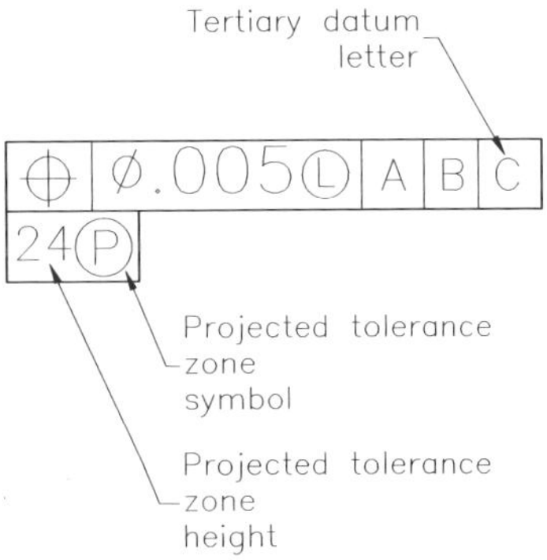

Figure 8-75 *Components of GTOL*

Feature Control Frame

The feature control frame is a rectangular box that contains the geometric characteristics symbols and tolerance definition. The box is automatically drawn to standard specifications; you do not need to specify its size. You can copy, move, erase, rotate, and scale the feature control frame. You can also snap to them using various Object snap modes. You can edit feature control frames using the **DDEDIT** command or you can also edit them using grips. The system variable **DIMCLRD** controls the color of the feature control frame.

Geometric Characteristics Symbol

The geometric characteristics symbols indicate the characteristics such as straightness, flatness, perpendicularity, and so on of a feature. You can select the required symbol from the **Symbol** dialog box (Figure 8-76). This dialog box is displayed by selecting the box provided in the **Sym** area of the **Geometric Tolerance** dialog box. To select the required symbol, just pick the symbol using the left mouse button. The symbol will now be displayed in the box under the **Sym** area.

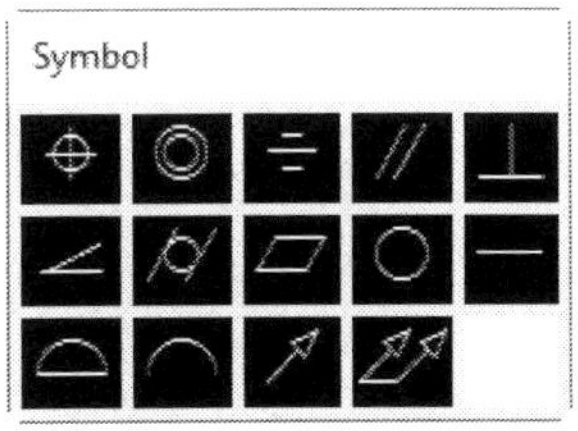

Figure 8-76 *The* ***Symbol*** *dialog box*

Tolerance Value

The tolerance value specifies the tolerance on the feature. For example, a value of .003 indicates that the feature must be within a 0.003 tolerance zone. Similarly, .003 indicates that this feature must be located at a true position within a 0.003 diameter. The tolerance value can be entered in the edit box provided under the **Tolerance 1** or the **Tolerance 2** area of the **Geometric Tolerance** dialog box. The system variable **DIMCLRT** controls the color of the tolerance text, variable **DIMTXT** controls the tolerance text size, and variable **DIMTXSTY** controls the style of the tolerance text. On using the **Projected Tolerance Zone**, the projected tolerance zone symbol, which is an encircled P will be inserted after the projected tolerance zone value.

Material Condition Modifier

The material condition modifier specifies the material condition when the tolerance value takes effect. For example, .003(M) indicates that this feature must be located at a true position within a 0.003 diameter at maximum material condition (MMC). The material condition modifier symbol can be selected from the **Material Condition** dialog box (Figure 8-77). This dialog box can be invoked by selecting the boxes located on the right side of the edit boxes under the **Tolerance 1**, **Tolerance 2**, **Datum 1**, **Datum 2**, and **Datum 3** areas of the **Geometric Tolerance** dialog box.

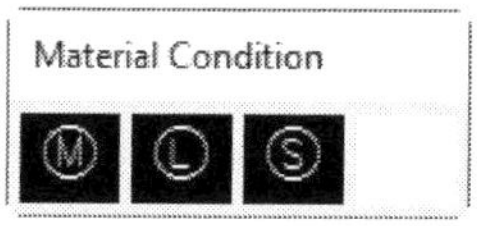

Figure 8-77 *The* ***Material Condition*** *dialog box*

Datum

The datum is the origin, surface, or feature from which the measurements are made. The datum is also used to establish the geometric characteristics of a feature. The datum feature symbol consists of a reference character enclosed in a feature control frame. You can create the datum feature symbol by entering characters (like -A-) in the **Datum Identifier** edit box in the **Geometric Tolerance** dialog box and then selecting a point where you want to establish this datum.

You can also combine datum references with geometric characteristics. AutoCAD LT automatically positions the datum references on the right end of the feature control frame.

Note

In AutoCAD LT, you can change the specifications of ***Geometric Tolerance*** *by double-clicking on* ***Geometric Tolerance****; the* ***Geometric Tolerance*** *dialog box will be displayed. In the dialog box, you can change the specifications as required.*

COMPLEX FEATURE CONTROL FRAMES

Combining Geometric Characteristics

Sometimes, it is not possible to specify all geometric characteristics in one frame. For example, Figure 8-78 shows the drawing of a plate with a hole in the center.

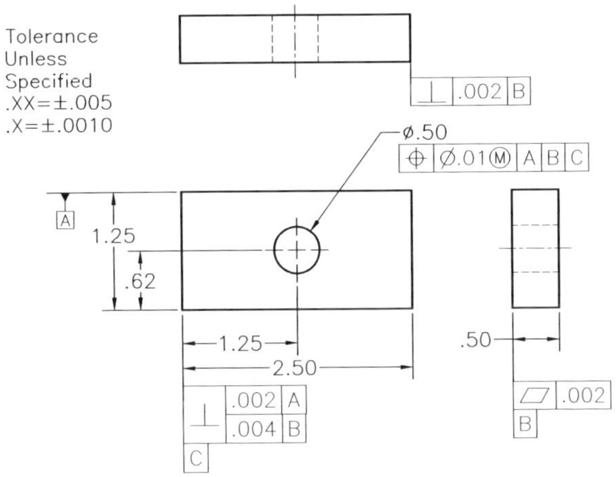

Figure 8-78 *Combining feature control frames*

In this part, it is determined that surface C must be perpendicular to surfaces A and B within 0.002 and 0.004, respectively. Therefore, we need two frames to specify the geometric characteristics of surface C. The first frame specifies the allowable deviation in perpendicularity of surface C with respect to surface A. The second frame specifies the allowable deviation in perpendicularity of surface C with respect to surface B. In addition to these two frames, we need a third frame that identifies datum surface C.

All the three feature control frames can be defined in one instance of the **Tolerance** tool.

1. Choose the **Tolerance** tool to invoke the **Geometric Tolerance** dialog box. Select the box under the **Sym** area to display the **Symbol** dialog box. Select the **Perpendicular** symbol. AutoCAD LT will display the selected symbol in the first row of the **Sym** area.

2. Enter **.002** in the edit box under the **Tolerance 1** area of the first row and enter **A** in the first row edit box under the **Datum 1** area.

3. Select the second row box under the **Sym** area to display the **Symbol** dialog box. Select the **Perpendicular** symbol. AutoCAD LT will display the selected symbol in the second row box of the **Sym** area.

4. Enter **.004** in the second row edit box under the **Tolerance 1** area and enter **B** in the second row edit box under the **Datum 1** area.

5. In the **Datum Identifier** edit box, enter **C** and then choose the **OK** button to exit the dialog box.

6. In the graphics screen, select the position to place the frame. Similarly, create the remaining feature control frames.

Composite Position Tolerancing

Sometimes the accuracy required within a pattern is more important than the location of the pattern with respect to the datum surfaces. To specify such a condition, composite position tolerancing may be used. For example, Figure 8-79 shows four holes (pattern) of diameter 0.15. The design allows a maximum tolerance of 0.025 with respect to datum A, B, and C at the maximum material condition (holes are smallest). The designer wants to maintain a closer positional tolerance (0.010 at MMC) between the holes within the pattern. To specify this requirement, the designer must insert the second frame. This is generally known as composite position tolerancing. AutoCAD LT provides the facility to create two composite position tolerance frames by means of the **Geometric Tolerance** dialog box. The composite tolerance frames can be created as follows:

1. Invoke the **Tolerance** tool to display the **Geometric Tolerance** dialog box. Select the box under the **Sym** area to display the **Symbol** dialog box. Select the **Position** symbol. AutoCAD LT will display the selected symbol in the first row of the **Sym** area.

2. In the first row of the **Geometric Tolerance** dialog box, enter the geometric characteristics and the datum references required for the first position tolerance frame.

3. Next, select the box under the **Sym** area from the second row to display the **Symbol** dialog box. Select the **Position** symbol; AutoCAD LT will display the selected symbol in the second row of the **Sym** area.

4. In the second row of the **Geometric Tolerance** dialog box, enter the geometric characteristics and the datum references required for the second position tolerance frame.

5. When you have finished entering the values, choose the **OK** button in the **Geometric Tolerance** dialog box, and then select the point where you want to insert the frames. AutoCAD LT will create two frames and automatically align them with the common position symbol, as shown in Figure 8-79.

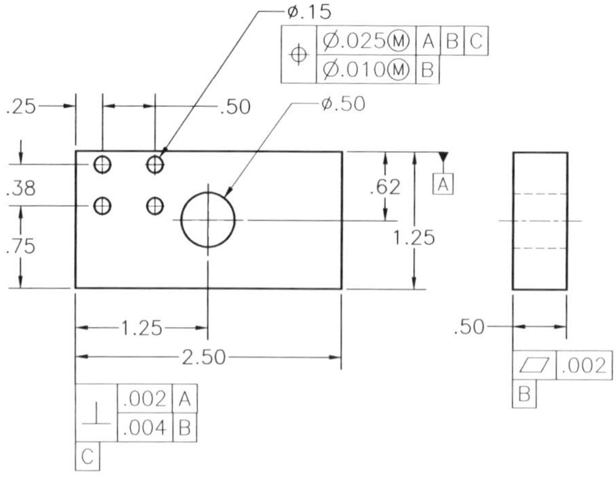

***Figure 8-79** Composite position tolerancing*

USING FEATURE CONTROL FRAMES WITH LEADERS

The **Leader Settings** dialog box that is invoked by using the **QLEADER** command has the **Tolerance** option which allows you to create feature control frame and attach it to the end of the leader extension line, see Figure 8-80. The following is the prompt sequence for using the **QLEADER** command with the **Tolerance** option:

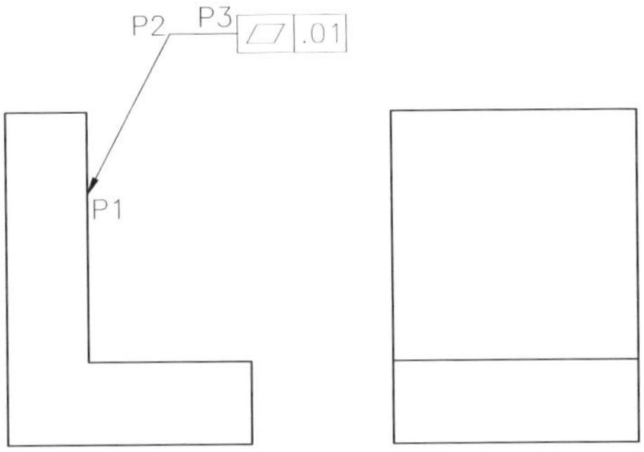

Figure 8-80 *Using the feature control frame with leader*

Specify first leader point, or [Settings] <Settings>: *Press ENTER to display the **Leader Settings** dialog box. Choose the **Annotation** tab. Now, select the **Tolerance** radio button from the **Annotation Type** area. Choose **OK**.*
Specify first leader point, or [Settings] <Settings>: *Specify the start point of the leader line.*
Specify next point: *Specify the second point.*
Specify next point: *Specify the third point to display the **Geometric Tolerance** dialog box.*

Now, specify the tolerance value and choose the **OK** button; the feature control frame will be displayed with leader.

PROJECTED TOLERANCE ZONE

Figure 8-81 shows two parts joined with a bolt. The lower part is threaded, and the top part has a drilled hole. When these two parts are joined, the bolt that is threaded in the lower part will have the orientation error that exists in the threaded hole. In other words, the error in the threaded hole will extend beyond the part thickness, which might cause interference, and the parts may not assemble. To avoid this problem, projected tolerance is used. The projected tolerance establishes a tolerance zone that extends above the surface. In Figure 8-81, the position tolerance for the threaded hole is 0.010 which extends 0.1 above the surface (datum A). By using the projected tolerance, you can ensure that the bolt is within the tolerance zone up to the specified distance, refer to Figure 8-81.

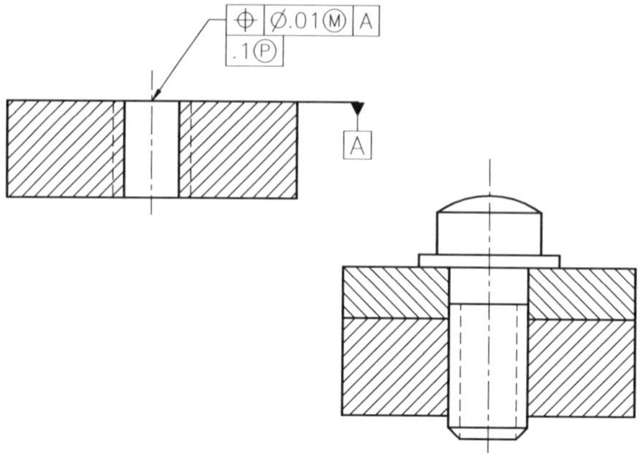

Figure 8-81 *Projected tolerance zone*

You can use the AutoCAD LT GD & T feature to create feature control frames for the projected tolerance zone as discussed next.

1. Invoke the **QLEADER** command and then press ENTER at the **Specify first leader point, or [Settings] <Settings>** prompt to display the **Leader Settings** dialog box.

2. Choose the **Annotation** tab and then select the **Tolerance** radio button from the **Annotation Type** area. Choose **OK** to return to the command line. Specify the first, the second, and the third leader points, refer to Figure 8-81. On specifying the third point, the **Geometric Tolerance** dialog box will be displayed. Click once in the **Sym** area in the first row; the **Symbol** dialog box will be displayed. Choose the **Position** symbol from the **Symbol** dialog box.

3. In the first row of the **Geometric Tolerance** dialog box, enter the geometric characteristics and the datum references required for the first position tolerance frame.

4. In the **Height** edit box, enter the height of the tolerance zone (.1 for the given drawing) and select the box on the right of **Projected Tolerance Zone**. The projected tolerance zone symbol will be displayed in the box.

5. Choose the **OK** button in the **Geometric Tolerance** dialog box. AutoCAD LT will create two frames and automatically align them, refer to Figure 8-81.

Example 2 — *Tolerance*

In this example, you will create a feature control frame to define the perpendicularity specification, see Figure 8-82.

1. Choose the **Tolerance** tool from the **Dimensions** panel of the **Annotate** tab to display the **Geometric Tolerance** dialog box. Choose the upper box from the **Sym** area to display the **Symbol** dialog box. Select the **Perpendicularity** symbol. This symbol will be displayed in the **Sym** area.

2. Select the box on the left of the upper edit box under the **Tolerance 1** area; the diameter symbol will appear to denote a cylindrical tolerance zone.

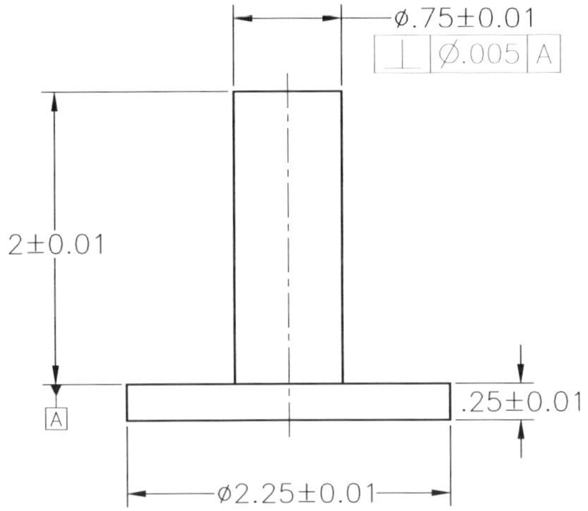

Figure 8-82 *Drawing for Example 2*

3. Enter **.005** in the upper edit box under the **Tolerance 1** area in the **Geometric Tolerance** dialog box.

4. Enter **A** in the edit box under the **Datum 1** area. Choose the **OK** button to accept the changes made in the **Geometric Tolerance** dialog box.

5. The **Enter tolerance location** prompt is displayed in the Command line area and the **Feature Control Frame** is attached to the cursor at its middle left point. Select a point to insert the frame.

6. To attach the datum symbol, invoke the **Leader Settings** dialog box and select the **Tolerance** radio button as explained in step 1.

7. Choose the **Leader Linc & Arrow** tab and select the **Datum triangle filled** option from the drop-down list in the **Arrowhead** area.

8. Set the number of points in the leader to **2** in the **Number of Points** spinner.

9. Choose **OK** to return to the command line. Specify the first and second leader points, refer to Figure 8-82. On specifying the second point, the **Geometric Tolerance** dialog box will be displayed.

10. Enter **A** in the **Datum Identifier** edit box. Choose **OK** to exit the **Geometric Tolerance** dialog box. On doing so, the datum symbol will be displayed, refer to Figure 8-82.

Example 3 *Tolerance*

In this example, you will create a leader with combination feature control frames to control runout and cylindricity, see Figure 8-83.

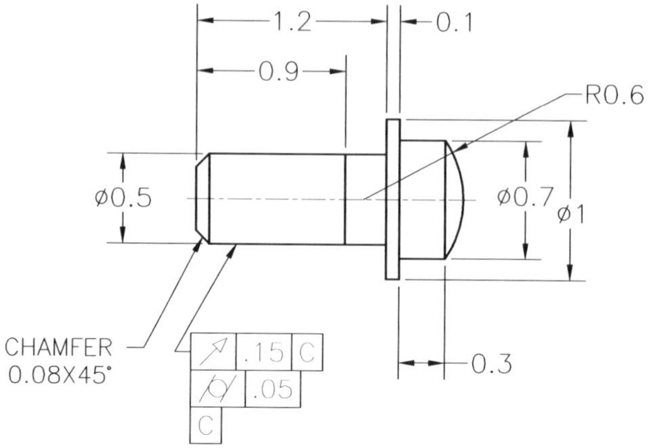

Figure 8-83 *Drawing for Example 3*

1. Enter the **QLEADER** command and follow the prompt sequence given below.

   Specify first leader point, or [Settings] <Settings>: *Press ENTER to display the **Leader Settings** dialog box. Choose the **Annotation** tab. Select the **Tolerance** radio button from the **Annotation Type** area. Choose **OK**.*
   Specify first leader point, or [Settings] <Settings>: *Specify the leader start point, as shown in Figure 8-83.*
   Specify next point: *Specify the second point of the leader.*
   Specify next point: *Specify the third point of the leader line to display the **Geometric Tolerance** dialog box.*

2. Choose the **Runout** symbol from the **Symbol** dialog box; the **Runout** symbol will be displayed on the first row of the **Sym** area. Enter **.15** in the first row edit box under the **Tolerance 1** area.

3. Enter **C** in the edit box under the **Datum 1** area.

4. Select the edit box on the second row of the **Sym** area and select the **Cylindricity** symbol; the **Cylindricity** symbol will be displayed in the second row of the **Sym** area.

5. Enter **.05** in the second row edit box of the **Tolerance 1** area.

6. Enter **C** in the **Datum Identifier** edit box.

7. Choose the **OK** button to accept the changes in the **Geometric Tolerance** dialog box; the control frames will be automatically attached at the end of the leader.

CREATING ANNOTATIVE DIMENSIONS, TOLERANCES, LEADERS, AND MULTILEADERS

Annotative dimensions are drawn in the drawing by assigning annotative dimension style to the current drawing. To assign annotative dimension, select the **Dimension Style** (inclined arrow) from the **Dimensions** panel or from the **Dimension** toolbar. Note that the dimension style selected should have an annotative symbol next to it. You can also change the non-annotative dimensions to annotative by changing the dimension's **Annotative** property to **Yes** in the **PROPERTIES** palette.

For drawing the annotative geometric tolerances and leaders, you first need to add the simple tolerances to the drawing and then select all tolerances. Next, you need to modify the **Annotative** property under the **Misc** area of the **PROPERTIES** palette to **Yes**.

The annotative leaders are drawn by assigning annotative dimension style, whereas the annotative multileaders are drawn by assigning annotative multileader style. The leaders are created with two components: the leader and its content. Therefore, drawing annotative leaders does not ensure that the content attached to the leader will also be annotative. But, the multileaders are drawn as a single component, so the multileaders drawn with annotative style will have annotative content also.

Note

The procedure of creating and modifying dimension styles and multileader styles will be discussed in detail in Chapter 10.

Self-Evaluation Test

Answer the following questions and then compare them to those given at the end of this chapter:

1. The __________ tool is used to dimension either the *X* coordinate or the Y coordinate of a selected object.

2. The __________ symbols are the building blocks of geometric dimensioning and tolerances.

3. In the __________ dimensioning, the dimension text is aligned by default with the object being dimensioned.

4. The __________ are automatically updated when the object to which they are assigned is modified.

5. The __________ point is taken as the vertex point of the angular dimensions while dimensioning an arc or a circle.

6. Extra leaders can be added or removed from existing multileaders by using the __________ tool.

7. You can specify dimension text or accept the measured value computed by AutoCAD LT. (T/F)

8. The **Adjust Space** tool is used to maintain equal spacing between linear dimensions or angular dimensions. (T/F)

9. The leaders drawn by using the **Leader** tool create arrow, leader lines, and text as a single object. (T/F)

10. You cannot combine **Geometric Tolerance** with leaders. (T/F)

Review Questions

Answer the following questions:

1. Which of the following tools can be used to convert dimensions into true associative dimensions?

   (a) **Reassociate** (b) **Associate**
   (c) **Disassociate** (d) None of these

2. Which of the following tools can be used to dimension more than one object in a single effort?

   (a) **Linear** (b) **Angular**
   (c) **Quick Dimension** (d) None of these

3. Which of the following tools is used to dimension different points and features of a part with reference to a fixed point?

   (a) **Baseline** (b) **Angular**
   (c) **Radius** (d) **Aligned**

4. Which of the following tools can be used to add geometric dimensions and tolerance to the current drawing?

   (a) **Geometric Tolerance** (b) **Tolerance**
   (c) **Single Line** (d) None of these

5. Which of the following options of the **Align** tool can be used to maintain a constant spacing between the selected multileader landing lines?

   (a) **Distribute** (b) **make leader segments Parallel**
   (c) **Specify Spacing** (d) **Use current spacing**

6. Geometric dimensioning and tolerancing is generally known as __________.

7. Give three examples of geometric characteristics that indicate the characteristics of a feature __________.

8. The three ways to return to the Command prompt from the **Dim:** prompt (dimensioning mode) are __________, ___________, and __________.

9. The six fundamental dimensioning types which are provided by AutoCAD LT to dimension an object are _________.

10. Horizontal dimensions measure displacement along the _________.

11. Using the **Multileader** tool, you can specify the content of a multileader before drawing the leader itself. (T/F)

12. Only inner angles (acute angles) can be dimensioned with angular dimensioning. (T/F)

13. In addition to the most recently drawn dimension (the default base dimension), you can use any other linear dimension as the base dimension. (T/F)

14. In the continued dimensions, the base point for the successive continued dimensions is the base dimension's first extension line. (T/F)

15. You cannot add dimension break to straight multileaders. (T/F)

Exercise 7

Draw the object shown in Figure 8-84 and then dimension it. Save the drawing as *DIMEXR7*.

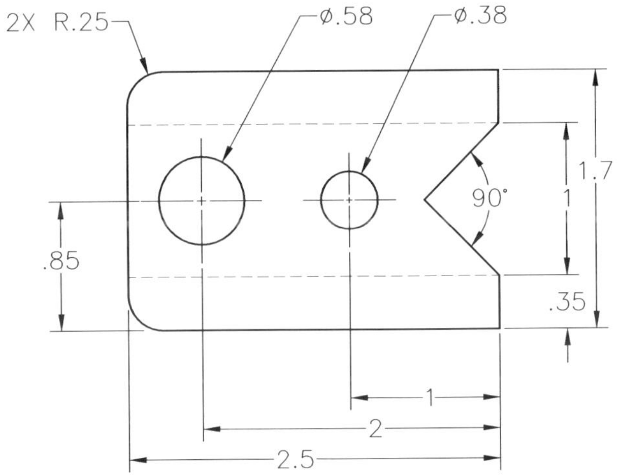

Figure 8-84 *Drawing for Exercise 7*

Exercise 8

Draw and dimension the object shown in Figure 8-85. Save the drawing as *DIMEXR8*.

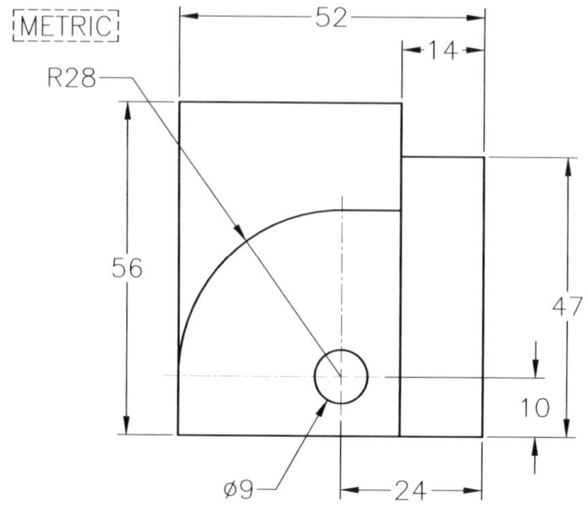

Figure 8-85 Drawing for Exercise 8

Exercise 9

Draw the object shown in Figure 8-86 and then dimension it. Save the drawing as *DIMEXR9*.

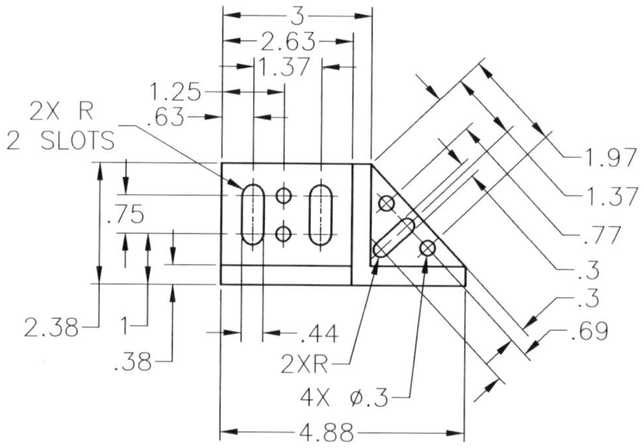

Figure 8-86 Drawing for Exercise 9

Exercise 10

Draw the object shown in Figure 8-87 and then dimension it. Save the drawing as *DIMEXR10*.

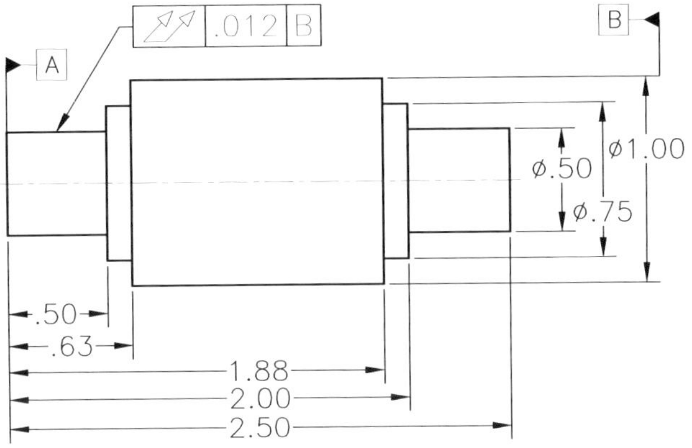

Figure 8-87 *Drawing for Exercise 10*

Exercise 11

Draw the object shown in Figure 8-88 and then dimension it. Save the drawing as *DIMEXR11*.

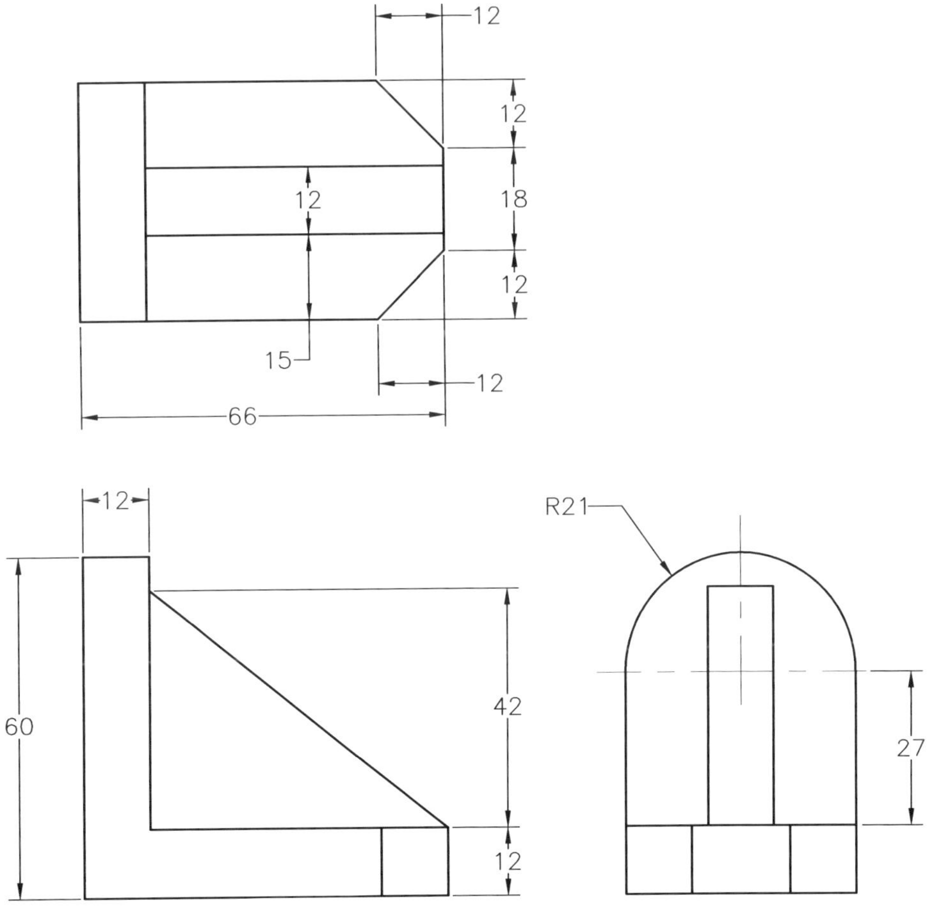

Figure 8-88 *Drawing for Exercise 11*

Exercise 12

Draw the object shown in Figure 8-89 and then dimension it. Save the drawing as *DIMEXR12*.

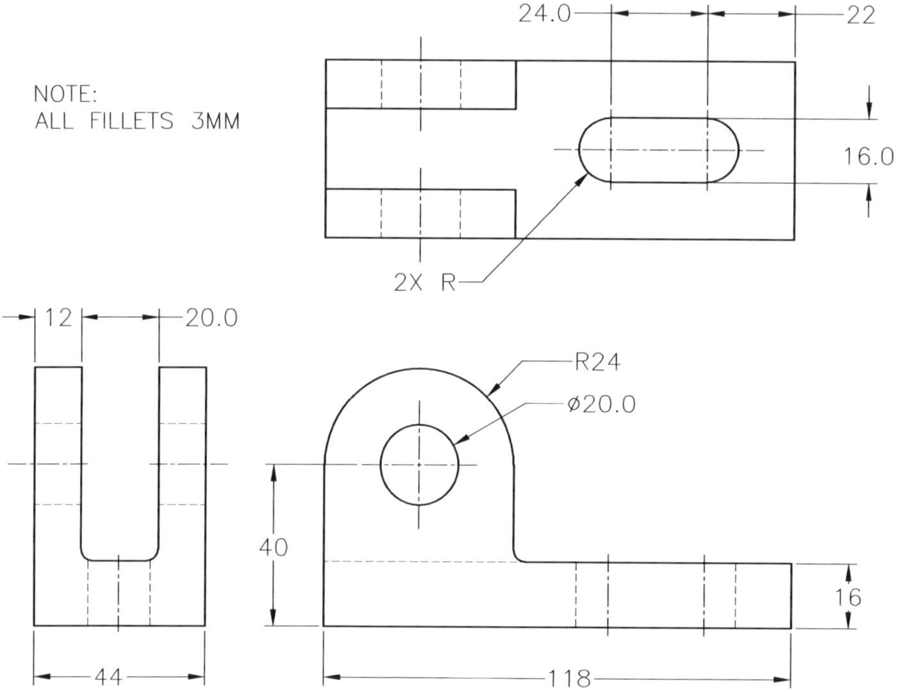

Figure 8-89 *Drawing for Exercise 12*

Exercise 13

Draw the object shown in Figure 8-90 and then dimension it. Save the drawing as *DIMEXR13*.

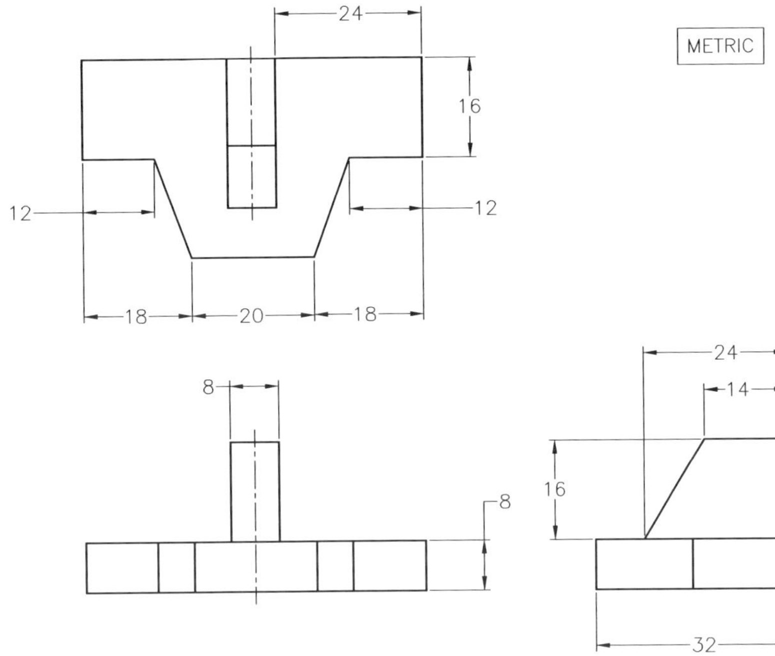

Figure 8-90 *Drawing for Exercise 13*

Problem-Solving Exercise 1

Draw the object shown in Figure 8-91 and dimension it, as shown in the drawing. Save the drawing as *DIMPSE1*.

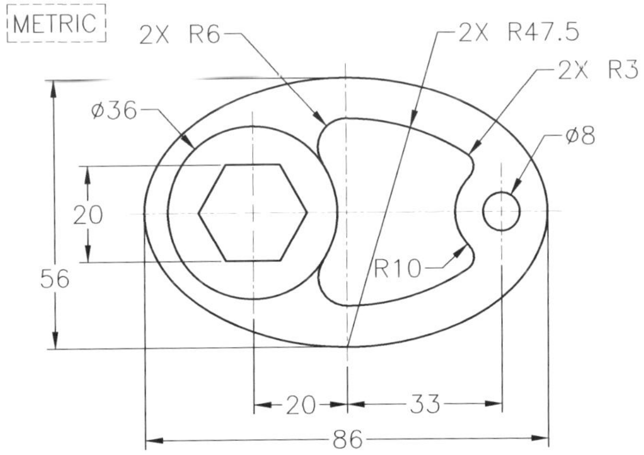

Figure 8-91 *Drawing for Problem-Solving Exercise 1*

Problem-Solving Exercise 2

Draw Figure 8-92 and then dimension it, as shown in the drawing. Save the drawing as *DIMPSE2*.

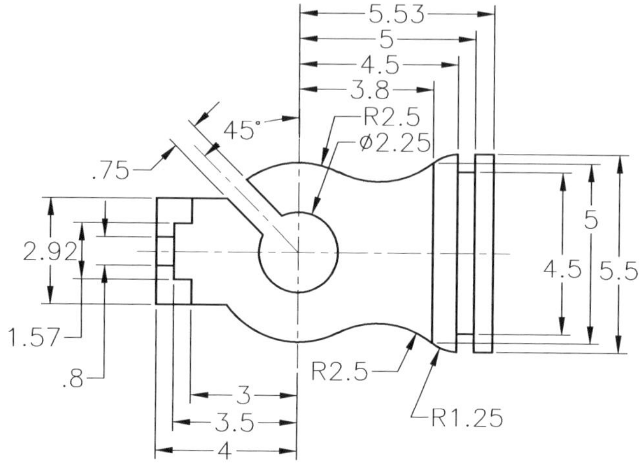

Figure 8-92 *Drawing for Problem-Solving Exercise 2*

Problem-Solving Exercise 3

Draw Figure 8-93 and then dimension it, as shown in the drawing. Save the drawing as *DIMPSE3*.

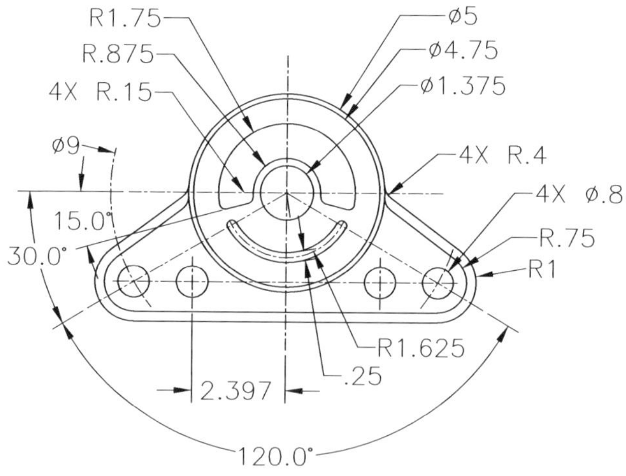

Figure 8-93 *Drawing for Problem-Solving Exercise 3*

Answers to Self-Evaluation Test

1. Ordinate, **2.** geometric characteristics, **3.** aligned, **4.** true associative dimensions, **5.** center, **6. Remove Leader**, **7.** T, **8.** T, **9.** F, **10.** F

Chapter 9

Editing Dimensions

Learning Objectives

After completing this chapter, you will be able to:

- *Edit dimensions*
- *Stretch, extend, and trim dimensions*
- *Use the Oblique and Text Angle command options to edit dimensions*
- *Update dimensions using the Update command*
- *Use the PROPERTIES palette to edit dimensions*
- *Dimension in model space and paper space*
- *Control the display of constraints*
- *Convert a dimensional constraint into an annotational constraint*

Key Terms

- *Dimension editing tools*
- *Stretch*
- *Trim*
- *Extend*
- *Edit Dimension Text*
- *Update*
- *Dimension PROPERTIES Palette*
- *Multileader PROPERTIES Palette*
- *Model Space Dimension*
- *Paper Space Dimension*
- *Fully-Defined Sketch*
- *Under-Defined Sketch*
- *Over-Defined Sketch*

EDITING DIMENSIONS USING EDITING TOOLS

For editing dimensions, AutoCAD LT has provided some special editing tools that work with dimensions. These editing tools can be used to define new dimension text, return to the home text, create oblique dimensions, and rotate and update the dimension text. You can also use the **Trim**, **Stretch**, and **Extend** tools to edit the dimensions. In case the dimension assigned to an object is a true associative dimension, it will be automatically updated if the object is modified. However, if the dimension is not true associative dimension, you will have to include the dimension along with the object in the edit selection set. The properties of the dimensioned objects can also be changed using the **PROPERTIES** palette or the **Dimension Style Manager**.

Editing Dimensions by Stretching

You can edit a dimension by stretching it. However, to stretch a dimension, appropriate definition points must be included in the selection crossing or window. As the middle point of the dimension text is a definition point for all types of dimensions, you can easily stretch and move the dimension text to any location you want. When you stretch the dimension text, the gap in the dimension line gets filled automatically. While editing, the definition points of the dimension being edited must be included in the selection crossing box. The dimension is automatically calculated when you stretch the dimension.

Note

Dimension type remains the same after stretching. For example, vertical dimension maintains itself as a vertical dimension and measures only the vertical distance even after the line it dimensions is modified and converted into an inclined line. The following example illustrates the stretching of object lines and dimensions.

Example 1 — Edit by Stretching

In this example, you will stretch the objects and dimensions shown in Figure 9-1 using grips. The new location of the lines and dimensions is at a distance of 0.5 unit in the positive *Y* axis direction, see Figure 9-2.

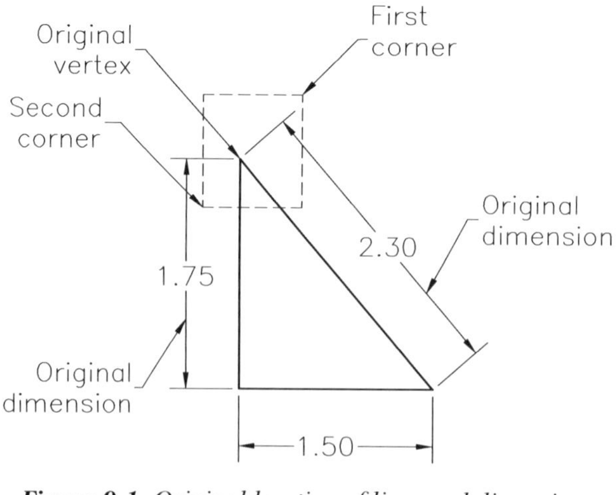

Figure 9-1 *Original location of lines and dimensions*

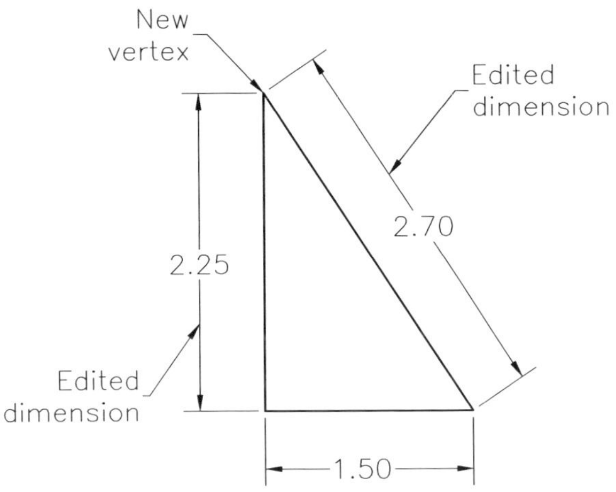

Figure 9-2 *New location of lines and dimensions*

1. Choose the **Stretch** tool from the **Modify** panel of the **Home** tab. The prompt sequence after choosing this tool is given below:

   Select objects to stretch by crossing-window or crossing-polygon
   Select objects: Specify opposite corner: *Define a crossing window using the first and second corners, as shown in Figure 9-1.*
   Select objects: Enter
   Specify base point or [Displacement]<Displacement>: *Select original vertex using the osnap as the base point.*
   Specify second point or <use first point as displacement>: **@0.5<90**

2. The selected entities will be stretched to new location. The dimension that was initially 1.75 will become 2.25 and the dimension that was initially 2.30 will become 2.70, see Figure 9-2. Press ESC to remove the grip points from the objects.

Exercise 1

The two dimensions given in Figure 9-3(a) are too close. Fix the drawing by stretching the dimension, as shown in Figure 9-3(b).

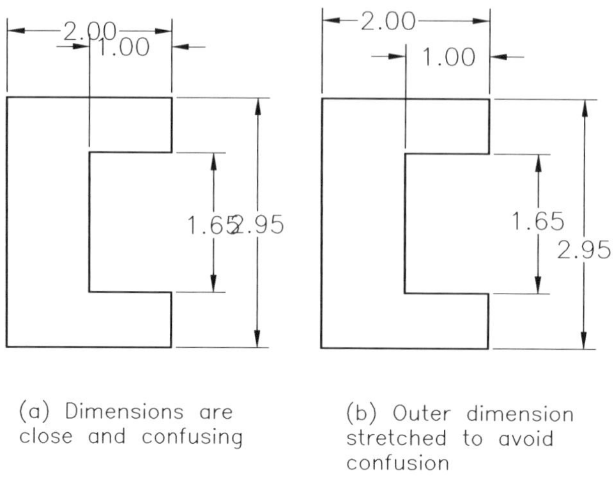

Figure 9-3 *Drawing for Exercise 1, stretching dimensions*

1. Stretch the outer dimension to the right so that there is some distance between the two dimensions.

2. Stretch the dimension text of the outer dimension so that the dimension text is staggered (lower than the first dimension).

Editing Dimensions by Trimming and Extending

Trimming and extending operations can be carried out with all types of linear dimensions (horizontal, vertical, aligned, and rotated) and the ordinate dimension. Even if the dimensions are true associative, you can trim and extend them (see Figures 9-4 and 9-5). AutoCAD LT trims or extends a linear dimension between the extension line definition points and the object used as a boundary or trimming edge. To extend or trim an ordinate dimension, AutoCAD LT moves the feature location (location of the dimensioned coordinate) to the boundary edge. To retain the original ordinate value, the boundary edge to which the feature location point is moved should be orthogonal to the measured ordinate. In both cases, the imaginary line drawn between the two extension line definition points is trimmed or extended by AutoCAD LT, and the dimension is adjusted automatically.

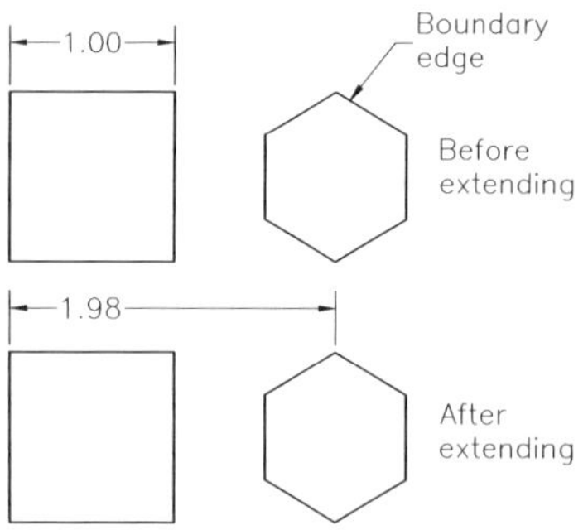

Figure 9-4 *Dimensions edited by extending*

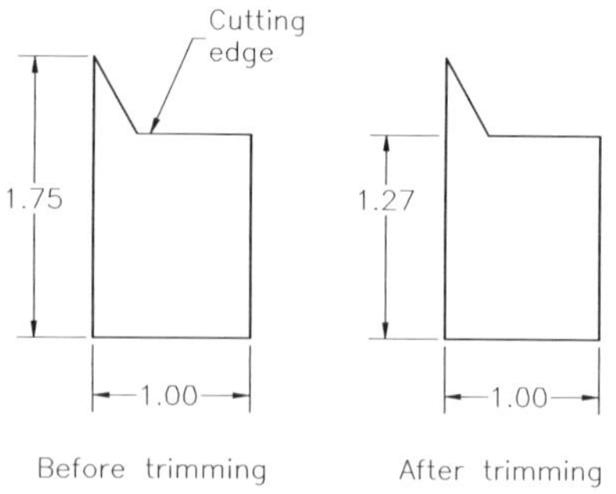

Figure 9-5 *Edge mode extended trimming*

Exercise 2

Use the **Edge > Extend** option of the **Trim** tool to trim the dimension given in Figure 9-6(a), so that it looks like Figure 9-6(b).

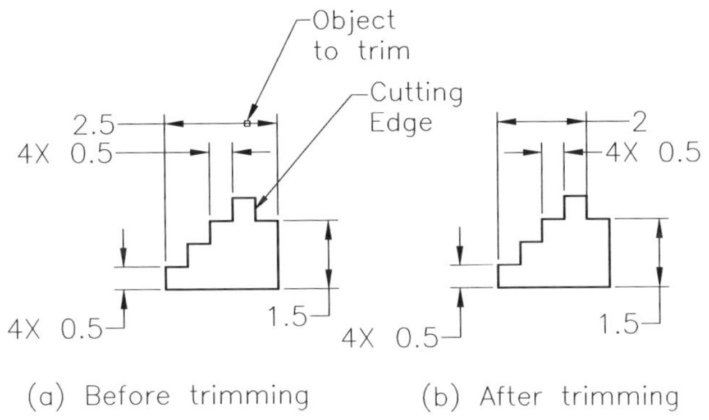

Figure 9-6 *Drawing for Exercise 2*

1. Make the drawing and dimension it, as shown in Figure 9-6(a).

2. Trim the dimensions by using the **Edge > Extend** option of the **Trim** tool.

Flipping Dimension Arrow

You can flip the arrowheads individually. To flip the arrow, select the dimension. Place the cursor on the grip corresponding to the arrowhead that you want to flip. When the color of the grip turns red, a shortcut menu will be invoked. Now, choose the **Flip Arrow** option from the shortcut menu.

MODIFYING THE DIMENSIONS

Toolbar: Dimension > Dimension Edit **Command:** DIMEDIT

The dimensions can be modified by choosing the **Dimension Edit** tool from the **Dimension** toolbar (Figure 9-7). Alternatively, you can use the **DIMEDIT** command to modify the dimensions. This command has four options: **New**, **Rotate**, **Home**, and **Oblique**. The prompt sequence that will follow when you choose this tool is given below:

Enter type of dimension editing (Home/New/Rotate/Oblique) <Home>: *Enter an option.*

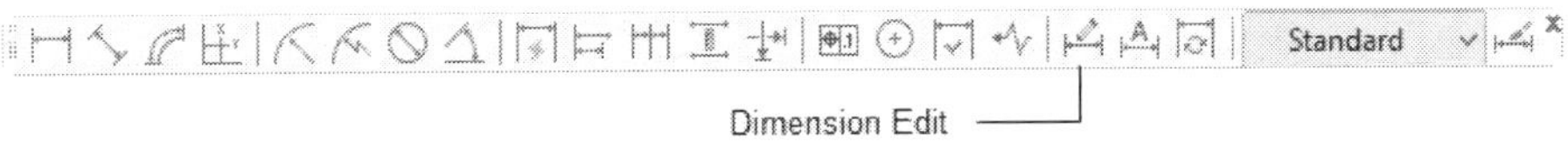

Figure 9-7 *The **Dimension Edit** tool from the **Dimension** toolbar*

Home

The **Home** option restores the text of a dimension to its original (home/default) location if the position of the text has been changed by stretching or editing, see Figure 9-8.

New

The **New** option is used to replace the existing dimension with a new text string. When you invoke this option, the **Text Editor** will be displayed. By default, 0.0000 will be displayed. Using the **Text Editor**, enter the dimension or write the text string with which you want to replace the existing dimension. Once you have entered a new dimension in the editor and exit the **Text Editor**, you will be prompted to select the dimension to be replaced. Select the dimension and press ENTER; it will be replaced by a new dimension, see Figure 9-8.

Rotate

The **Rotate** option is used to position the dimension text at the specified angle. With this option, you can change the orientation (angle) of the dimension text of any number of associative dimensions. The angle can be specified by entering a value at the **Specify angle for dimension text** prompt or by specifying two points at the required angle. Once you have specified the angle, you will be prompted to select the dimension text to be rotated. Select the dimension and press ENTER; the text will rotate about its middle point, see Figure 9-8. You can also invoke this option by choosing the **Text Angle** tool from the **Dimensions** panel.

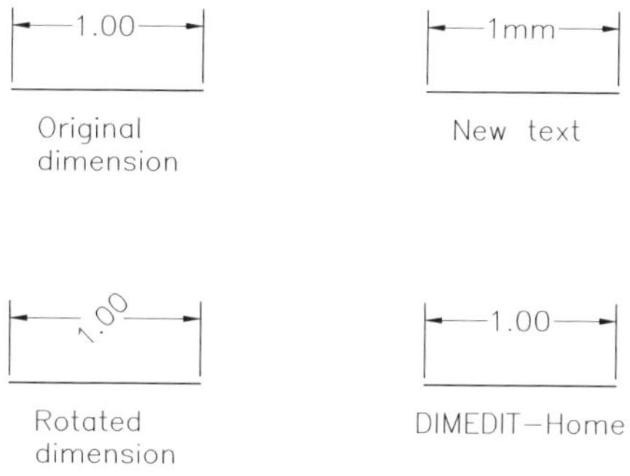

***Figure 9-8** Using the **Dimension Edit** tool to edit dimensions*

Oblique

In linear dimensions, extension lines are drawn perpendicular to the dimension line. The **Oblique** option bends the linear dimensions. It draws extension lines at an oblique angle (Figure 9-9). This option is particularly important to create isometric dimensions and can be used to resolve conflicting situations due to the overlapping of extension lines with other objects. Making an existing dimension oblique by specifying an angle oblique to it does not affect the generation of new linear dimensions. The oblique angle is maintained even after performing most editing operations. When you invoke this option, you will be prompted to select the dimension to be edited. After selecting it, you will be prompted to specify the oblique angle. The extensions lines will be bent at the angle specified. You can also invoke this option by choosing the **Oblique** tool from the **Dimensions** panel.

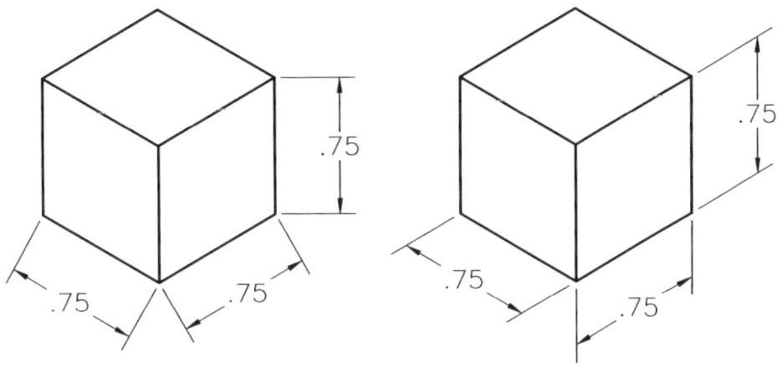

Figure 9-9 *Using the **Oblique** option to edit dimensions*

EDITING THE DIMENSION TEXT

Toolbar: Dimension > Dimension Text Edit   **Command:** DIMTEDIT
Menu Bar: Dimension > Align Text

The dimension text can be edited by using the **Dimension Text Edit** tool from the **Dimension** toolbar. This tool is used to edit the placement and orientation of a single existing dimension. You can use this tool in cases where dimension texts of two or more dimensions are too close together. In such cases, the **Dimension Text Edit** tool is invoked to move the dimension text to some other location so that there is no confusion. The prompt sequence that will follow when you choose the **Dimension Text Edit** tool is given next.

Select dimension: *Select the dimension to modify.*
Specify new location for dimension text or [Left/Right/Center/Home/Angle]:

Left

Using this option, you can left-justify the dimension text along the dimension line. The vertical placement setting determines the position of the dimension text. In this setting, the horizontally aligned text is moved to the left and the vertically aligned text is moved down, see Figure 9-10. This option can be used only with the linear, diameter, or radial dimensions. You can also invoke this option by choosing the **Left Justify** tool from the **Dimensions** panel.

Right

Using this option, you can right-justify the dimension text along the dimension line. Similar to the Left option, the vertical placement setting determines the position of the dimension text. The horizontally aligned text is moved to the right, and the vertically aligned text is moved up, see Figure 9-10. This option can be used only with linear diameter and radius dimensions. You can also invoke this option by choosing the **Right Justify** tool from the **Dimensions** panel.

Center

Using this option, you can center-justify the dimension text for linear and aligned dimensions, see Figure 9-10. The vertical setting controls the vertical position of the dimension text. You can also invoke this option by choosing the **Center Justify** tool from the **Dimensions** panel.

Home

The **Home** option is used to restore (move) the text of a dimension to its original (home/default) location, if the position of the text has changed, see Figure 9-10.

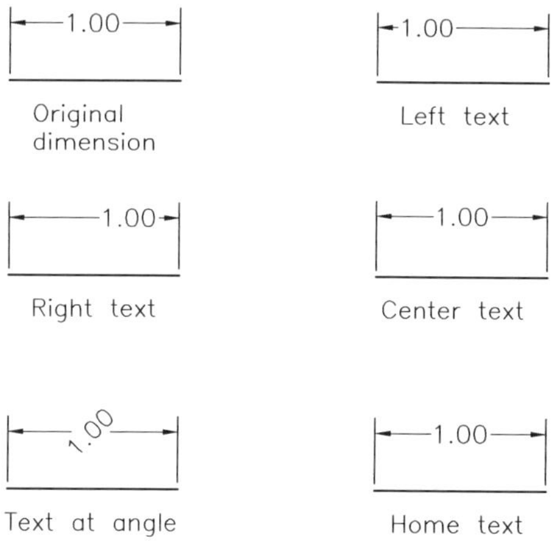

*Figure 9-10 Using the **Dimension Text Edit** tool to edit dimensions*

Angle

Using the **Angle** option, you can position the dimension text at the angle you specify, see Figure 9-10. The angle can be specified by entering its value at the **Specify angle for dimension text** prompt or by specifying two points at the required angle. You will notice that the text rotates around its middle point. If the dimension text alignment is set to Orient Text Horizontally, the dimension text is aligned with the dimension line. If the information about the dimension style is available on the selected dimension, AutoCAD LT uses it to redraw the dimension, or the prevailing dimension variable settings are used for the redrawing process. Entering 0-degree angle changes the text to its default orientation.

UPDATING DIMENSIONS

Ribbon: Annotate > Dimensions > Update **Toolbar:** Dimension > Dimension Update
Menu Bar: Dimension > Update

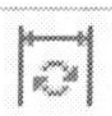

The **Update** tool is used to regenerate and update the prevailing dimension entities (such as arrows heads and text height) using the current settings for the dimension variables, dimension style, text style, and units. On choosing this tool, you will be prompted to select the dimensions to be updated. You can select all the dimensions or specify those that are to be updated.

EDITING DIMENSIONS WITH GRIPS

You can also edit dimensions by using the GRIP editing modes. GRIP editing is the easiest and quickest way to edit dimensions. You can perform the following operations with GRIPS.

1. Position the text anywhere along the dimension line. Note that you cannot move the text and position it above or below the dimension line.
2. Stretch a dimension to change the spacing between the dimension line and the object line.
3. Stretch the dimension along the length.
4. Move, rotate, copy, mirror, or scale the dimensions.
5. Relocate the dimension origin.
6. Load Web browser (if any *Universal Resource Locator* is associated with the object).

EDITING DIMENSIONS USING THE PROPERTIES PALETTE

Ribbon: View > Palettes > Properties **Toolbar:** Standard > Properties
Menu Bar: Modify > Properties **Command:** PROPERTIES/PR/MO/CH

You can also modify a dimension or leader by using the **PROPERTIES** palette. The **PROPERTIES** palette is displayed when you choose the **Properties** button from the **Palettes** panel. Alternatively, you can invoke the **PROPERTIES** palette by choosing the **Properties** option from the **Palettes** cascade in the **Tools** menu. All the properties of the selected object are displayed in the **PROPERTIES** palette (see Figure 9-11). Select the dimension before invoking the **PROPERTIES** palette, otherwise it would not give the description of the dimension.

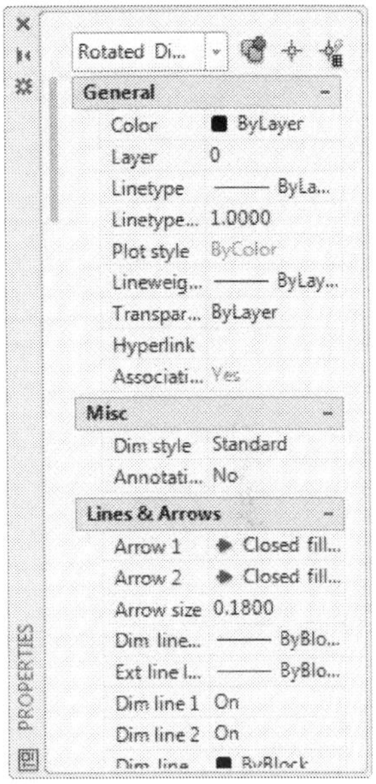

Figure 9-11 The PROPERTIES palette for dimensions

PROPERTIES Palette (Dimension)

You can use the **PROPERTIES** palette (Figure 9-11) to change the properties, the dimension text style, or geometry, format, and annotation-related features of the selected dimension. The changes take place dynamically in the drawing. The **PROPERTIES** palette provides the following categories for the modification of dimensions.

General

In the **General** category, the **Color**, **Layer**, **Linetype**, **Linetype scale**, **Plot style**, **Lineweight**, **Transperancy**, **Hyperlink**, and **Associative** parameters are available with their current values. To change the color of the selected object, select the **Color** property and then select the required color from the drop-down list. Similarly, the properties such as layer, plot style, linetype, and lineweight can be changed from the respective drop-down lists. The linetype scale can be changed manually in the corresponding cell.

Misc

This category displays the dimension style by name (for the **DIMSTYLE** system variable, use **SETVAR**) and also specifies whether the dimension text will be annotative or not. You can change the dimension style and the annotative property of the text from the respective drop-down lists of the selected dimension.

Lines & Arrows

The various parameters of the lines and arrows in the dimension such as arrowhead size, type, arrow lineweight, and so on can be changed in this category.

Text

The various parameters that control the text in the dimension object such as text color, text height, vertical position text offset, and so on can be changed in this category.

Fit

In the **Fit** category, the **Dim line forced**, **Dim line inside**, **Dim scale overall**, **Fit**, **Text inside**, and **Text movement** parameters are available. All parameters can be changed in the drop-down list, except **Dim scale overall** (which can be changed manually).

Primary Units

In the Primary Units category, the **Decimal separator**, **Dim prefix**, **Dim suffix, Dim sub-units suffix, Dim roundoff**, **Dim scale linear**, **Dim sub-units scale, Dim units**, **Suppress leading zeros**, **Suppress trailing zeros**, **Suppress zero feet**, **Suppress zero inches**, and **Precision** parameters are available. Among these parameters, **Dim units**, **Suppress leading zeros**, **Suppress trailing zeros**, **Suppress zero feet**, **Suppress zero inches**, and **Precision** can be changed with the help of corresponding drop-down lists. The other parameters can be changed manually.

Alternate Units

Alternate units are required when a drawing is to be read in two different units. For example, if an architectural drawing is to be read in both metric and feet-inches, you can turn the alternate units on. The primary units can be set to metric and the alternate units to architectural. As a result, the dimensions of the drawing will be displayed in metric units as well as in engineering. In the alternate unit category, there are various parameters for the alternate units. They can be changed only if the **Alt enabled** parameter is **on**. The parameters such as **Alt format**, **Alt precision**, **Alt suppress leading zeros**, **Alt suppress trailing zeros**, **Alt suppress zero feet**, and **Alt suppress zero inches** can be changed from the respective drop-down lists and others can be changed manually.

Tolerances

The parameters of this category can be changed only if the **Tolerances** display parameter has some mode of the tolerance selected. The parameters listed in this rollout depend on the mode of tolerance selected.

PROPERTIES Palette (Multileader)

The **PROPERTIES** palette for **Multileader** can be invoked by selecting a Leader and then choosing the **Properties** option from the **Palettes** panel. You can also invoke the **PROPERTIES** palette (Figure 9-12) from the shortcut menu by right-clicking in the drawing area and then choosing **Properties**. Various properties under the **PROPERTIES** palette (Multileader) are described next.

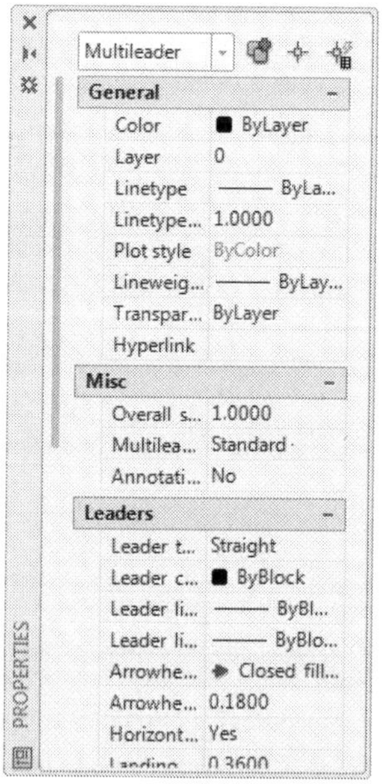

*Figure 9-12 The **PROPERTIES** palette for modifying multileaders*

General

The parameters in the **General** category are same as those discussed in the previous section (**PROPERTIES** palette for dimensions).

Misc

This category displays the **Overall scale**, **Multileader style**, **Annotative**, and **Annotative scale** of the **Multileader**. You can change the style, annotative property, and annotation scale of the Multileader by using the respective drop-down lists.

Leaders

This category controls the display of certain elements such as lines, arrowheads, landing distance, and so on. The **Multileader** is composed of these elements.

Text

This category displays the properties that are used to control the text appearance and location of the **Multileader** text. These properties can be changed by selecting the desired option from the respective drop-down lists. Now, you can modify the dimension text by double-clicking on the required dimension.

Example 2 — Modify Dimensions

In this example, you will modify the dimensions given in Figure 9-13 so that they match the dimensions given in Figure 9-14.

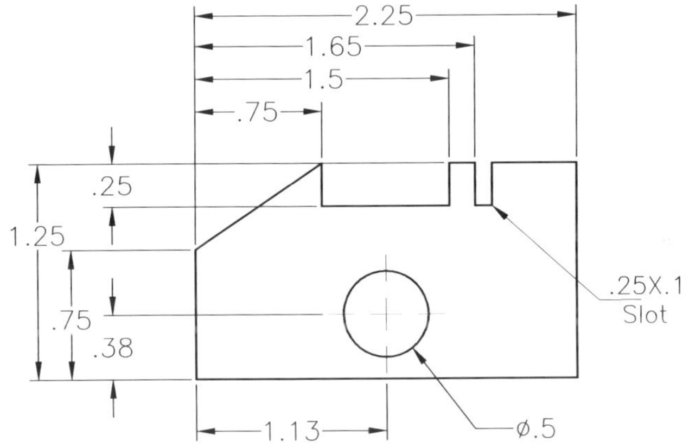

***Figure 9-13** Drawing for Example 2*

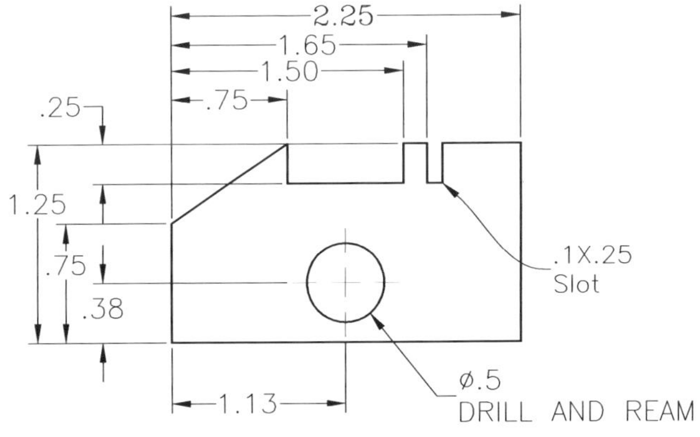

***Figure 9-14** Drawing after editing the dimensions*

1. Choose the **Text Style** (inclined arrow) tool from the **Text** panel of the **Annotate** tab and create a style with the name **ROMANC**. Select **romanc.shx** as the font for the style.

2. Select the dimension **2.25** and enter **PROP** at the Command prompt to display the **PROPERTIES** palette.

3. In the **Text** category, select the **Text style** drop-down list and then select the **ROMANC** style from this drop-down list; the changes will take place dynamically.

4. Select **0.0000** from the **Precision** drop-down list in the **Primary Units** area.

5. Once all the required changes are made in the linear dimension, choose the **Select Objects** button in the **PROPERTIES** palette; you will be prompted to select the object. Select the leader line and then press ENTER.

6. The **PROPERTIES** palette will display the leader options. Select **Spline** from the **Leader type** drop-down list in the **Leaders** category; the straight line will be dynamically converted into a spline with an arrow.

7. Close the **PROPERTIES** palette.

8. Choose the **Dimension Edit** tool from the **Dimension** toolbar. Enter **N** in the prompt sequence to display the **Text Editor**.

9. Enter **%%C.5 DRILL AND REAM** in the **Text Editor** and then click outside it to accept the changes. You will be prompted to select the object to be changed.

10. Select the diameter dimension and then press ENTER; the diameter dimension will be modified to the new value.

MODEL SPACE AND PAPER SPACE DIMENSIONING

Dimensioning objects can be drawn in the model space or paper space. If the drawings are in model space, associative dimensions should also be created in them. If the drawings are in the model space and the associative dimensions are in the paper space, the dimensions will not change when you perform editing operations such as stretching, trimming, and extending, or display operations such as zoom and pan in the model space viewport. The definition points of a dimension are located in the space where the drawing is drawn. Enter **DIMSTYLE** to invoke the **Dimension Style Manager** dialog box. Depending on whether you want to modify the present style or you want to create a new style, you can choose the **Modify**, **New**, or **Override** button to invoke the corresponding **Dimension Style** dialog box. You can select the **Scale dimensions to layout** radio button in the **Fit** tab (see Figure 9-15) to scale the dimensions according to paper space. Choose **OK** and then **Close** to exit the dialog boxes. AutoCAD LT calculates a scale factor that is compatible with the model space and the paper space viewports. Now, choose the **Update** tool from the **Dimension** toolbar and select the dimension objects for updating.

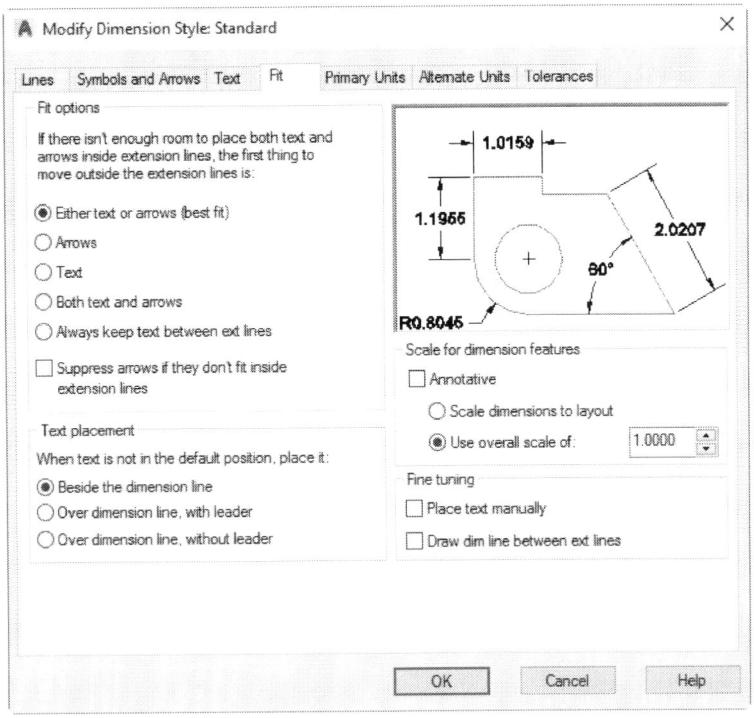

*Figure 9-15 Selecting paper space scaling in the **Modify Dimension Style** dialog box*

The drawing shown in Figure 9-16 uses paper space scaling. The main drawing and detail drawings are located in different floating viewports (paper space). The zoom scale factors for these viewports are different: 0.3XP, 1.0XP, and 0.5XP. When you use paper scaling, AutoCAD LT automatically calculates the scale factor for dimensioning so that the dimensions are uniform in all the floating viewports (model space viewports).

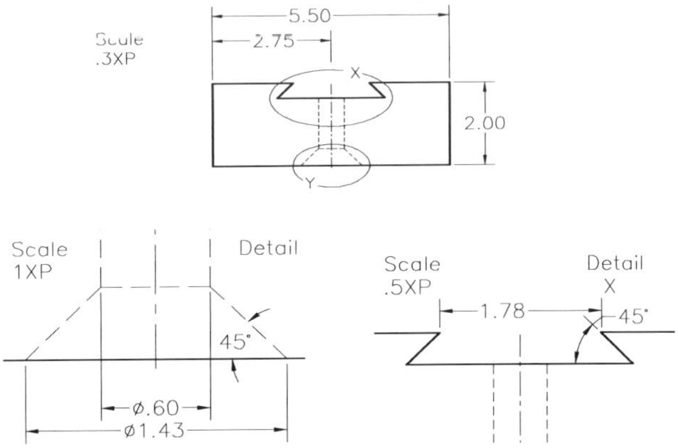

*Figure 9-16 Dimensioning in paper model space viewports using paper space scaling or setting **DIMSCALE** to 0*

CONTROLLING THE DISPLAY OF CONSTRAINTS

To control the display of the constraints, click on the inclined arrow in the **Geometric** panel of the **Parametric** tab; the **Constraint Settings** dialog box is displayed, as shown in Figure 9-17. In this dialog box, the **Geometric** tab will be chosen and the check boxes corresponding to all constraints will be selected. You can control the transparency of the constraint bar by entering a value in the edit box under the **Constraint bar transparency** area or by adjusting the slider near the edit box in the **Constraint bar transparency** area of the **Constraint Settings** dialog box. After specifying the parameters, choose **OK**.

On moving the cursor over a constraint bar, the constraint symbol and entities on which the constraint was applied will be highlighted. If multiple constraints are displayed in a sketch, it causes confusion. Therefore, you need to hide or display the constraint symbols. To hide a particular constraint, move the cursor over that constraint; the constraint bar will be highlighted and a cross-mark will be displayed on it. Click on the cross-mark to hide that constraint. To hide all constraints, choose the **Hide All** button in the **Geometric** panel of the **Parametric** tab. To display all hidden constraints, choose the **Show All** button from the **Geometric** panel. If you want to display constraints of a particular entity, choose the **Show/Hide** button from the **Geometric** panel; you will be prompted to select an entity. Select the entity from the drawing area and press ENTER; a shortcut menu will be displayed and you will be prompted to select an option. Choose the **Show** option; the constraints to that particular entity will be displayed. Remember that hiding a constraint does not delete that constraint. To delete a constraint, move the cursor over the constraint bar and press the DELETE key. If you want to delete multiple applied constraints, choose the **Delete Constraints** button in the **Manage** panel of the **Parametric** tab of the **Ribbon**; you will be prompted to select entities. Select the entities individually or by using the selection box, and then press ENTER; the constraints applied on the selected entities will be deleted.

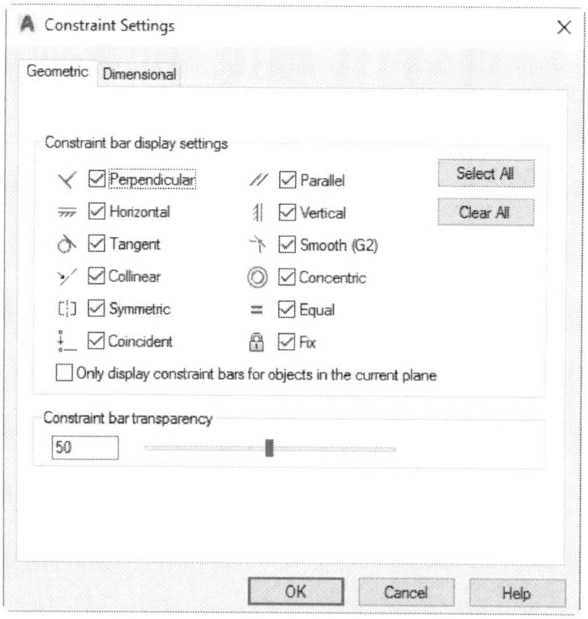

*Figure 9-17 The **Constraint Settings** dialog box*

Tip

If you move the cursor over the constraint bar and right-click, a shortcut menu will be displayed. Choose the option corresponding to the constraint to be deleted or hidden. Also, you can choose the ***Constraint Bar Settings*** *option to display the* ***Constraint Settings*** *dialog box.*

Note

In AutoCAD LT, you can't add geometrical constraints or dimensional constraints. If you open a file which contains geometrical and dimensional constraints then you can manage them by changing their visibility. The visibility can be managed by deleting geometrical constraints and by editing dimensional constraints.

CONCEPT OF A FULLY-DEFINED SKETCH

It is important for you to understand the concept of fully-defined sketches. If you have created a sketch at the design stage, you need to add required geometrical and dimensional constraints to the sketch to constrain its degrees of freedom with respect to the surrounding. After applying the required constraints, the sketch may exist in any of the following three states:

1. Under-defined
2. Fully-defined
3. Over-defined

Under-defined

An under-defined sketch is the one in which some of the geometrical constraints or dimensional constraints are not defined. As a result, the degrees of freedom of the sketch are not fully constrained, and therefore, the entities may move or change their size unexpectedly. So, you need to add some geometrical constraints or dimensional constraints to it to make it fully-defined.

Fully-defined

A fully-defined sketch is one in which all the entities and their positions are fully-defined by geometrical constraints, dimensional constraints, or both. In a fully-defined sketch, all degrees of freedom of a sketch are constrained, and therefore the sketched entities cannot move or change their size and location unexpectedly.

Over-defined

An over-defined sketch is one in which some of the geometrical constraints, dimensional constraints, or both are conflicting. Also, if the geometrical constraints or the dimensional constraints in a sketch exceed the required number, the sketch will be over-defined.

CONTROLLING THE DISPLAY OF THE DIMENSIONAL CONSTRAINT

On applying a dimensional constraint to an entity, a value will be displayed along with a name. You can hide the selected dimensional constraints of an object by using the **Show/Hide** button. To do so, choose the **Show/Hide** button and select the respective constraint. Next, right-click in the drawing area; a shortcut menu will be displayed. Choose the **Hide** option from it; the selected constraint will be hidden.

To display all the dimensional constraints in the drawing, choose the **Show All** button from the **Dimensional** panel of the **Parametric** tab. To hide the annotational constraint, turn off the corresponding layer from the **Layer Properties Manager**.

In AutoCAD LT when you apply a dimensional constraint to an entity, a default name and a lock symbol will be displayed along with the value. Now open that file in AutoCAD LT and if you need to display only the value, click on the inclined arrow on the **Dimensional** panel of the **Parametric** tab; the **Constraint Settings** dialog box will be displayed with the **Dimensional** tab chosen, as shown in Figure 9-18. Specify the format of the dimensional constraint to be displayed in the **Dimension name format** drop-down list available in the **Dimensional constraint format** area of this dialog box.

If you convert a dimensional constraint into an annotational constraint, a lock symbol will be displayed. If you do not need the lock symbol to be displayed for an annotational constraint, clear the **Show lock icon for annotational constraints** check box from the **Constraint Settings** dialog box. In case, you want to view the dynamic constraints of an entity whose dimensional constraints are hidden by choosing the **Show Dynamic Constraints** button, select the **Show hidden dynamic constraints for selected objects** check box in the **Constraint Settings** dialog box.

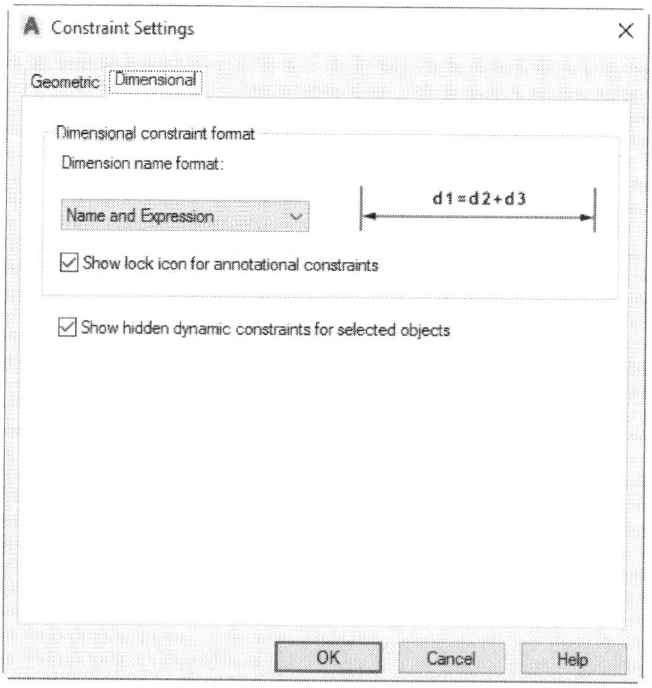

Figure 9-18 *The* ***Constraint Settings*** *dialog box*

WORKING WITH EQUATIONS

Equations are mathematical relations between dimensions. Consider the sketch of a bolt. All the dimensions of a bolt are driven by the base diameter. In AutoCAD LT, you can't create equations but can change them. To edit these equations, first you will create a file in AutoCAD then open it in AutoCAD LT. But if most of the dimensions need to be represented as equations, then you need to use the **Parameters Manager**.

Self-Evaluation Test

Answer the following questions and then compare them to those given at the end of this chapter:

1. Which state of the sketch does not have all its constraints defined?

   (a) Under-defined (b) Fully-defined
   (c) Over-defined (d) All of these

2. The __________ option of the **Dimension Text Edit** tool is used to justify the dimension text toward the left side.

3. The __________ option of the **Dimension Text Edit** tool is used to justify the dimension text to the center of the dimension.

4. The __________ option of the **Dimension Text Edit** tool is used to create a new text string.

5. The __________ option of the **Dimension Text Edit** tool is used to bend the extension lines through the specified angle.

6. The __________ tool from the **Dimension** panel is used to update the dimensions.

7. In associative dimensioning, the items constituting a dimension (such as dimension lines, arrows, leaders, extension lines, and dimension text) are drawn as a single object. (T/F)

8. You can add equations to dimensions using the **PROPERTIES** palette. (T/F)

9. You cannot edit dimensions using grips. (T/F)

10. The true associative dimensions cannot be trimmed or extended. (T/F)

Review Questions

Answer the following questions:

1. With the __________ tool, you can edit the dimension text.

2. The __________ tool is particularly important for creating isometric dimensions and is applicable in resolving conflicting situations arising due to the overlapping of extension lines with other objects.

3. The __________ tool is used to edit the placement and orientation of a single existing dimension.

4. The __________ tool regenerates (updates) prevailing associative dimension objects (like arrows and text height) using the current settings for the dimension variables, dimension style, text style, and units.

5. Explain when to use the **Extend** tool and how it works with dimensions.

6. Explain the use and working of the **PROPERTIES** palette for editing dimensions.

7. The horizontal, vertical, aligned, and rotated dimensions cannot be edited using grips. (T/F)

8. Trimming and extending operations can be carried out with all types of linear (horizontal, vertical, aligned, and rotated) dimensions and with the ordinate dimension. (T/F)

9. To extend or trim an ordinate dimension, AutoCAD LT moves the feature location (location of the dimensioned coordinate) to the boundary edge. (T/F)

10. Once moved from the original location, the dimension text cannot be restored to its original position. (T/F)

Exercise 3 — Edit Dimensions

1. Create and dimension the drawing shown in Figure 9-19. Assume the dimensions where necessary.
2. Edit the dimensions so that they match the dimensions shown in Figure 9-20.

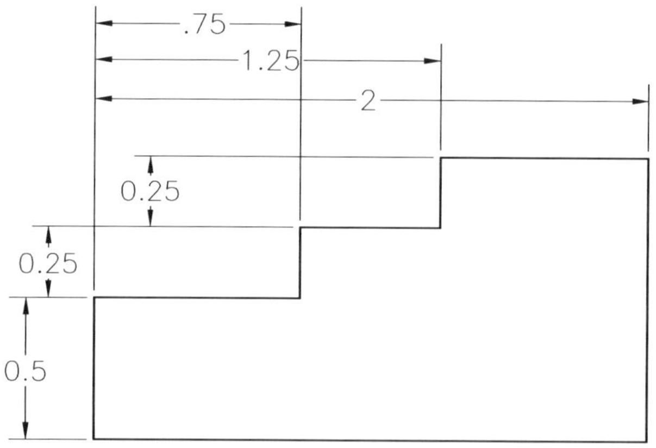

Figure 9-19 *Drawing for Exercise 3 before editing dimensions*

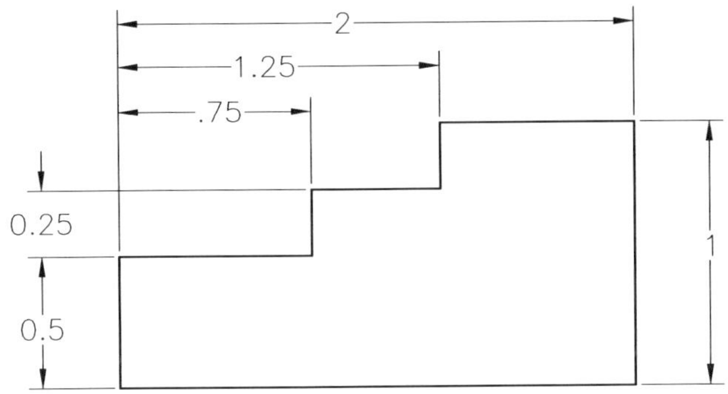

Figure 9-20 *Drawing for Exercise 3 after editing dimensions*

Exercise 4 **Edit Dimensions**

1. Draw the object shown in Figure 9-21(a). Assume the dimensions where necessary.
2. Dimension the drawing, as shown in Figure 9-21(a).
3. Edit the dimensions so that they match the dimensions shown in Figure 9-21(b).

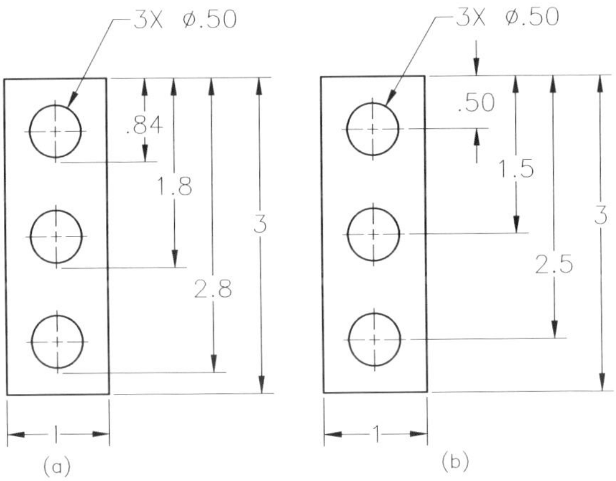

Figure 9-21 *Drawings for Exercise 4*

Problem-Solving Exercise 1

Create the drawing shown in Figure 9-22 and then dimension it. Edit the dimensions so that they are positioned as shown in the drawing. You can change the dimension text height and arrow size to 0.08 unit.

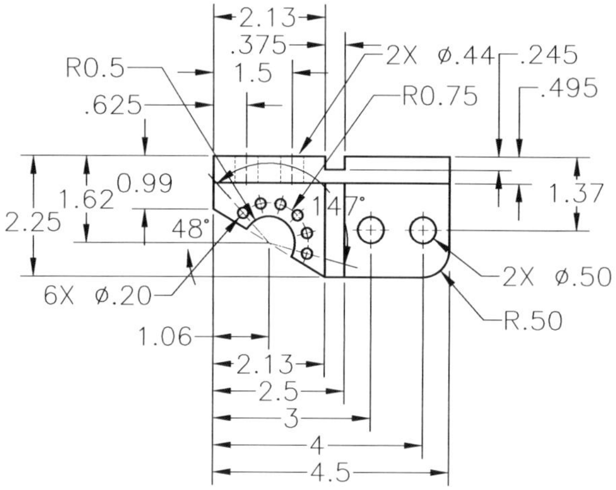

Figure 9-22 *Drawing for Problem-Solving Exercise 1*

Problem-Solving Exercise 2

Draw the front and side view of an object shown in Figure 9-23 and then dimension the two views. Edit the dimensions so that they are positioned as shown in the drawing. You can change the dimension text height and arrow size to 0.08 units.

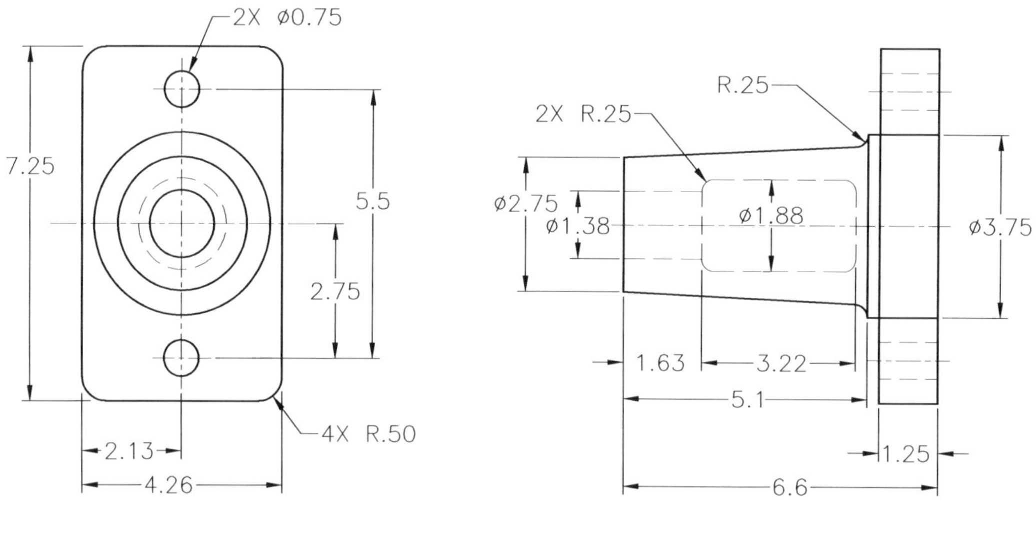

Figure 9-23 *Drawing for Problem-Solving Exercise 2*

Problem-Solving Exercise 3

Create the drawing of the floor plan shown in Figure 9-24 and then apply dimensions to it. Edit the dimensions, if needed so that they are positioned as shown in the drawing.

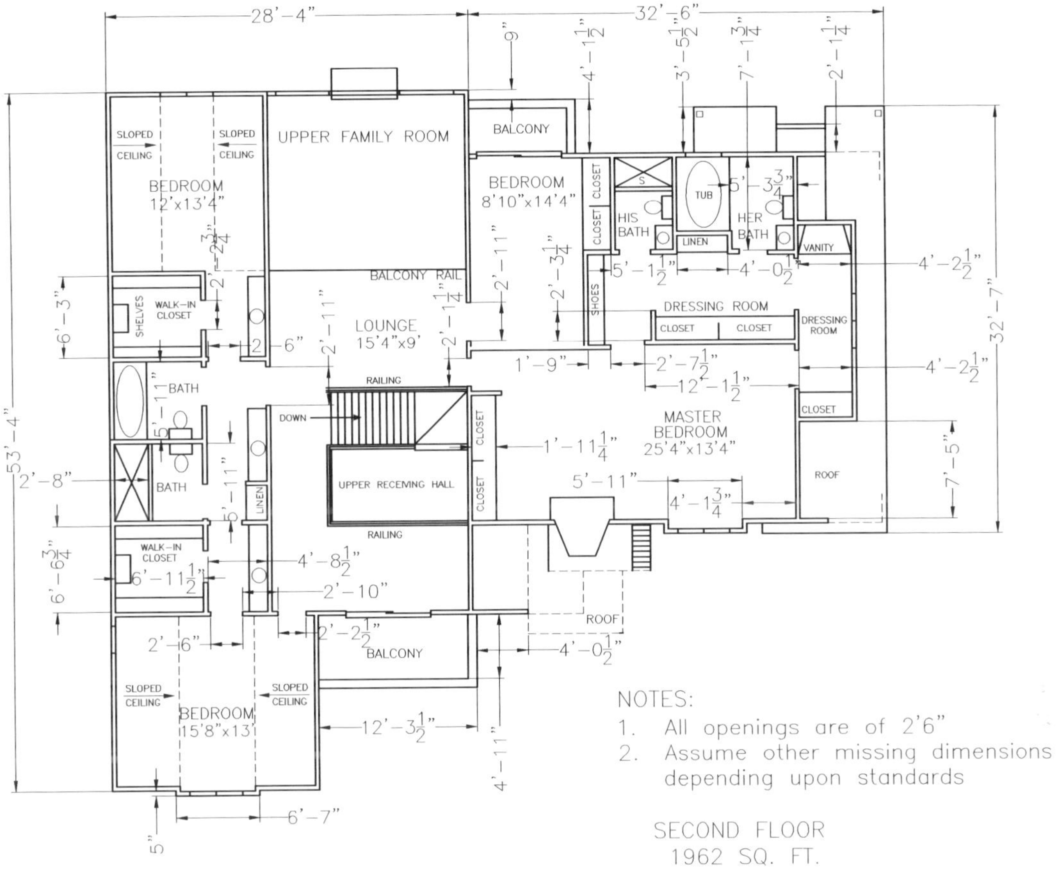

***Figure 9-24** Drawing for Problem-Solving Exercise 3*

Answers to Self-Evaluation Test

1. a, **2. Left**, **3. Center**, **4. New**, **5. Oblique**, **6. Update**, **7.** T, **8.** F, **9.** F, **10.** F

Chapter 10

Dimension Styles, Multileader Styles, and System Variables

Learning Objectives

After completing this chapter, you will be able to:

- *Use styles and variables to control dimensions*
- *Create dimension styles*
- *Set dimension variables*
- *Use dimension style overrides*
- *Compare and list dimension styles*
- *Import externally referenced dimension styles*
- *Create, restore, and modify multileader styles*

Key Terms

- *DIMSTYLE*
- *DIMCEN*
- *Dimension Style Families*
- *Dimension Styles Overrides*
- *MLEADERSTYLE*

USING STYLES AND VARIABLES TO CONTROL DIMENSIONS

In AutoCAD LT, the appearance of dimensions in the drawing area and the manner in which the dimensions are saved in the drawing database are controlled by a set of dimension variables. The dimensioning tools use these variables as arguments. The variables that control the appearance of dimensions can be managed using dimension styles. You can use the **Dimension Style Manager** dialog box to control the dimension styles and dimension variables through a set of dialog boxes.

CREATING AND RESTORING DIMENSION STYLES

Ribbon: Annotate > Dimensions > Dimension Style drop-down > Manage Dimension Style
Toolbar: Dimension > Dimension Style or Styles > Dimension Style
Menu Bar: Dimension > Dimension Style **Command:** DIMSTYLE/D

The dimension styles control the appearance and positioning of dimensions and leaders in the drawing. If the default dimensioning style (Standard or Annotative) does not meet your requirements, you can select another existing dimensioning style or create a new one. The default names of the dimension style file are **Standard** and **Annotative**. Dimension styles can be created by using the **Dimension Style Manager** dialog box. Left-click on the inclined arrow in the **Dimensions** panel of the **Annotate** tab to invoke the **Dimension Style Manager** dialog box (Figure 10-1).

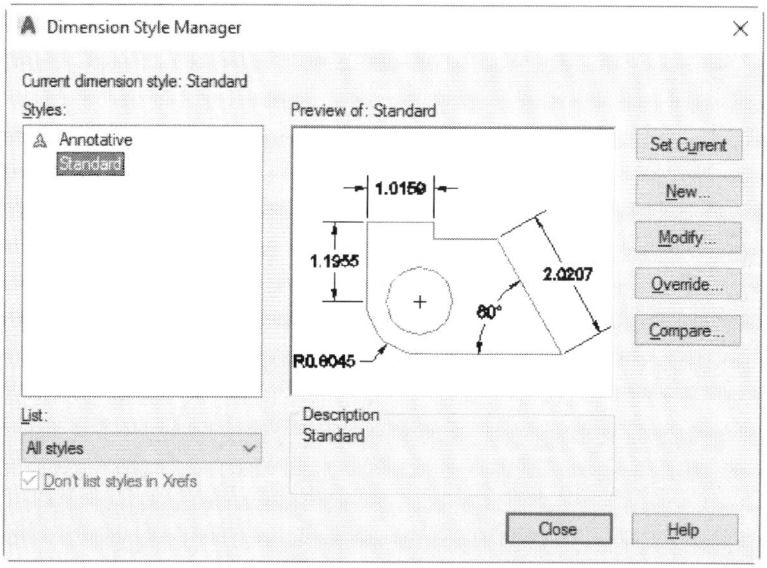

*Figure 10-1 The **Dimension Style Manager** dialog box*

In the **Dimension Style Manager** dialog box, choose the **New** button to display the **Create New Dimension Style** dialog box (Figure 10-2). Enter the dimension style name in the **New Style Name** text box and then select the required style that you want to be the basis of your style from the **Start With** drop-down list. Select the **Annotative** check box to make the new dimension style annotative. Choose the **Help** button to get the help and information about the annotative objects. The **Use for** drop-down list allows you to select the dimension type to which you want to apply the new dimension style. For example, if you wish to use the new style only for the diameter dimension, select **Diameter dimensions** from the **Use for** drop-down list. Choose the **Continue** button to display the **New Dimension Style** dialog box. The parameters of the **New Dimension Style** dialog box will be discussed later. After specifying the parameters of the new dimension style in the **New Dimension Style** dialog box, choose **OK**; the **Dimension Style Manager** dialog box will be displayed again. The options in this dialog box are discussed next.

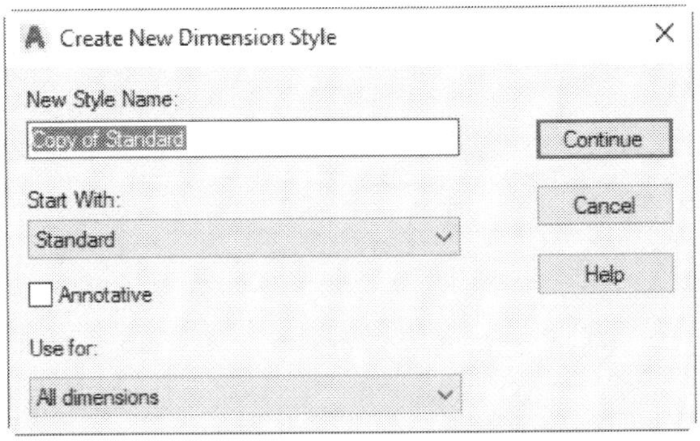

Figure 10-2 *The* ***Create New Dimension Style*** *dialog box*

In the **Dimension Style Manager** dialog box, the current dimension style name is shown in front of **Current dimension style** and is also shown highlighted in the **Styles** list box. A brief description of the current style (its differences from the default settings) is also displayed in the **Description** area. The **Dimension Style Manager** dialog box also has the **Preview of** window that displays the preview of the current dimension style. A style can be made current (restored) by selecting the name of the dimension style you want to make current from the list of defined dimension styles and choosing the **Set Current** button. You can also make a style current by double-clicking on the style name in the **Styles** list box. The list of dimension styles displayed in the **Styles** list box is dependent on the option selected from the **List** drop down-list. If you select the **Styles in use** option, only the dimension styles in use will be listed in the **Style** list box. If you right-click on a style in the **Styles** list box, a shortcut menu is displayed that provides you with the options to **Set current**, **Rename**, or **Delete** a dimension style. Selecting the **Don't list styles in Xrefs** check box does not list the names of Xref styles in the **Styles** list box. Choosing the **Modify** button displays the **Modify Dimension Style** dialog box which can be used to modify the existing style. Choosing the **Override** button displays the **Override Current Style** dialog box where you can define overrides to an existing style (discussed later in this chapter). Both these dialog boxes along with the **New Dimension Style** dialog box have identical options. Choosing the **Compare** button displays the **Compare Dimension Styles** dialog box (also discussed later in this chapter) that allows you to compare two existing dimension styles.

Note

The ***Dimension Style*** *drop-down list in the* ***Dimensions*** *panel under the* ***Annotate*** *tab also displays the dimension styles. Selecting a dimension style from this list will also make the style as current.*

NEW DIMENSION STYLE DIALOG BOX

The **New Dimension Style** dialog box can be used to specify the dimensioning attributes (variables) that affect various properties of the dimensions. The various tabs provided under the **New Dimension Style** dialog box are discussed next.

Lines Tab

The options in the **Lines** tab (Figure 10-3) of the **New Dimension Style** dialog box are used to specify the dimensioning attributes (variables) that affect the format of the dimension lines. For example, the appearance and behavior of the dimension lines and extension lines can be changed with this tab. If the settings of the dimension variables have not been altered in the current editing session, the settings displayed in the dialog box are the default settings.

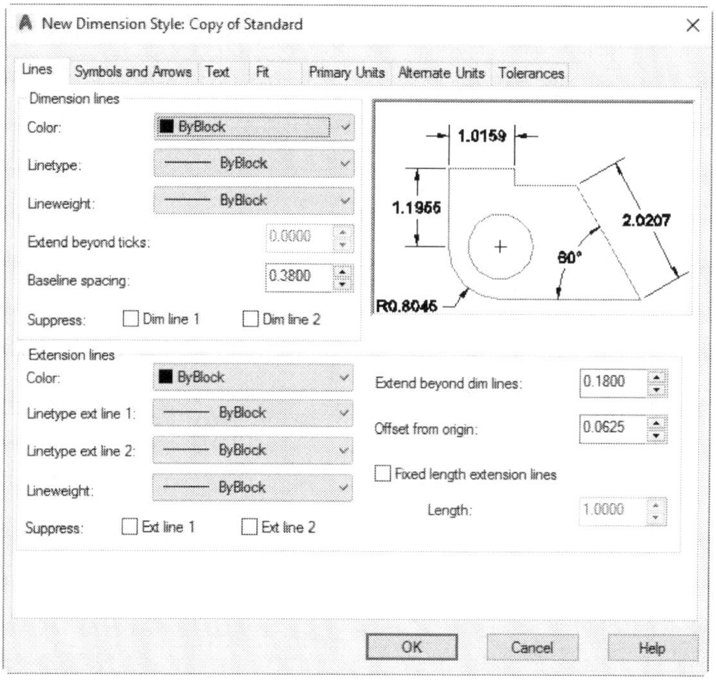

***Figure 10-3** The **Lines** tab of the **New Dimension Style** dialog box*

Dimension lines Area

This area provides you with the options for controlling the display of the dimension lines and leader lines. These options are discussed next.

Color. This drop-down list is used to set the colors for the dimension lines and arrowheads. Its dimension arrowheads have the same color as the dimension line because arrows constitute a part of the dimension line. The color you set here will also be assigned to the leader lines and arrows. The default color for the dimension lines and arrows is ByBlock. You can specify the color of the dimension line by selecting it from the **Color** drop-down list. You can also select **Select Color** from the **Color** drop-down list to display the **Select Color** dialog box where you can choose a specific color. The color number or the special color label is stored in the **DIMCLRD** variable; the default value of this variable is 0.

Linetype. This drop-down list is used to set the linetype for the dimension lines.

Lineweight. This drop-down list is used to specify the lineweight for the dimension line. You can select the required lineweight by selecting the corresponding option from this drop-down list. This value is also stored in the **DIMLWD** variable. The default value is ByBlock(-2). The other values for assigning lineweight to dimension lines are By Layer (-1). Remember that you cannot assign lineweight to the arrowheads using this drop-down list.

Extend beyond ticks. The **Extend beyond ticks** spinner will be available only when you select the oblique, Architectural tick, or any such arrowhead type in the **First** and **Second** drop-down lists in the **Arrowheads** area from the **Symbols and Arrows** tab. This spinner is used to specify the distance by which the dimension line will extend beyond the extension line. The extension value entered in the **Extend beyond ticks** edit box gets stored in the **DIMDLE** variable. By default, this edit box is disabled because the oblique arrowhead type is not selected.

Baseline spacing. The **Baseline spacing** (baseline increment) spinner is used to control the spacing between successive dimension lines drawn using the baseline dimensioning, see Figure 10-4. You can specify the dimension line increment as per your requirement by specifying the desired value using the **Baseline spacing** spinner. The default value displayed in the **Baseline spacing** spinner is 0.3800 unit.

Suppress. There are two suppress check boxes. These check boxes are used to control the display of the first and second dimension lines. By default, both dimension lines will be drawn. You can suppress one or both the dimension lines by selecting their corresponding check boxes.

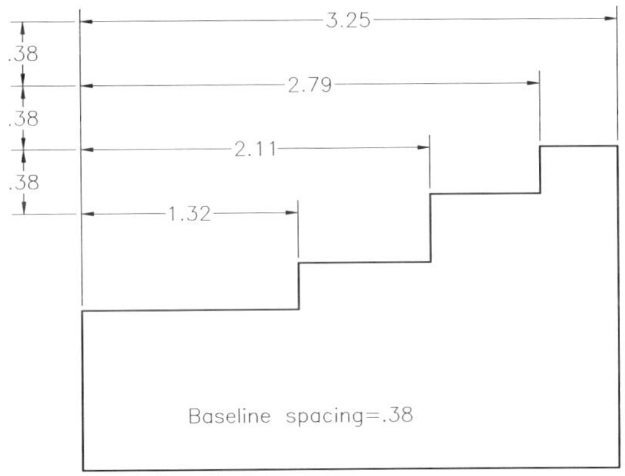

Figure 10-4 *Baseline spacing*

Note

The first and second dimension lines are determined by how you select the extension line origins. If the first extension line origin is on the right, the first dimension line will also be on the right.

Extension lines Area

The options in this area are discussed next.

Color. This drop-down list is used to control the color of the extension lines. The default extension line color is ByBlock. You can assign a new color to the extension lines by selecting it from this drop-down list.

Linetype ext line 1. The options in this drop-down list are used to specify the linetype of extension line 1. By default, the line type for the extension line 1 is set to ByBlock. You can change the linetype by selecting a new value of linetype from the drop-down list.

Linetype ext line 2. The options in this drop-down list are same as for the Linetype ext line 1. The options are used to specify the line type of extension line 2.

Note

*You can specify different linetypes for the dimensions and the extensions lines. Use the **Linetype** drop-down list in the **Dimension Lines** area to specify the linetype for dimensions. Use the **Linetype ext line 1** and **Linetype ext line 2** drop-down lists to specify the linetype for the extension lines.*

Lineweight. This drop-down list is used to modify the lineweight of the extension lines. The default value is ByBlock. You can change the lineweight value by selecting a new value from this drop-down list.

Extend beyond dim lines. It is the distance by which the extension lines extend past the dimension lines, see Figure 10-5. You can change the extension line offset using the **Extend beyond dim lines** spinner. The default value for the extension distance is 0.1800 units.

Offset from origin. It is the distance by which the extension line is offset from the point you specify as the origin of the extension line, see Figure 10-6. You may need to override this setting for specific dimensions while dimensioning curves and angled lines. You can specify an offset distance of your choice using this spinner. AutoCAD LT stores this value in the DIMEXO variable. The default value for this distance is 0.0625.

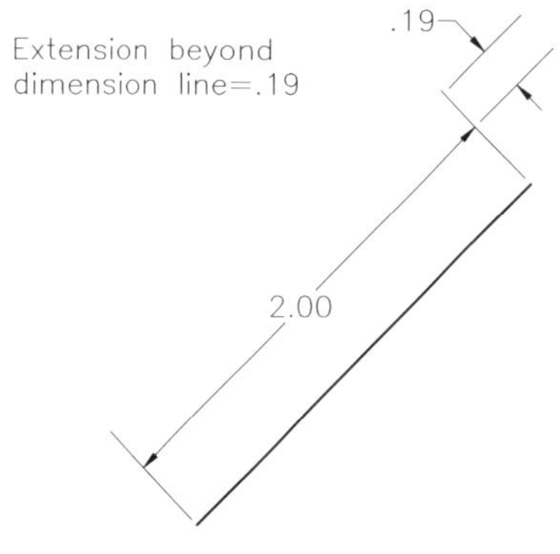

***Figure 10-5** Extension beyond dimension lines*

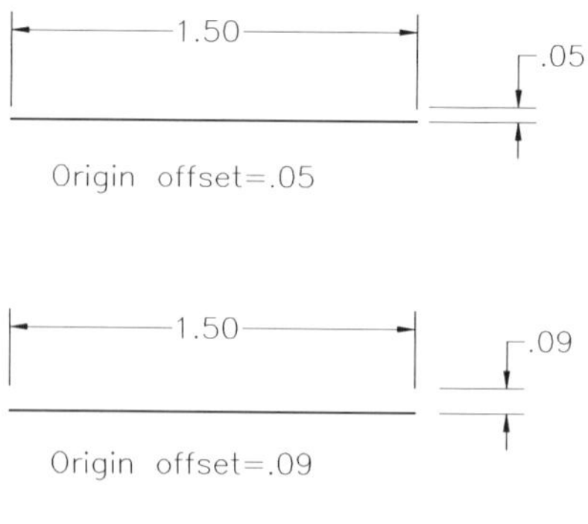

***Figure 10-6** The offset from origin*

Fixed length extension lines. With the selection of the **Fixed length extension lines** check box, you can specify a fixed length (starting from the dimension line to the origin) for the extension lines in the **Length** edit box. By default, the check box is cleared and the length spinner is not available. Once the check box is selected, you can specify the length of the extension line either by entering a numerical value in the **Length** edit box or using a spinner. Figure 10-7 displays a drawing with full length extension lines and Figure 10-8 displays the same drawing with fixed length extension lines.

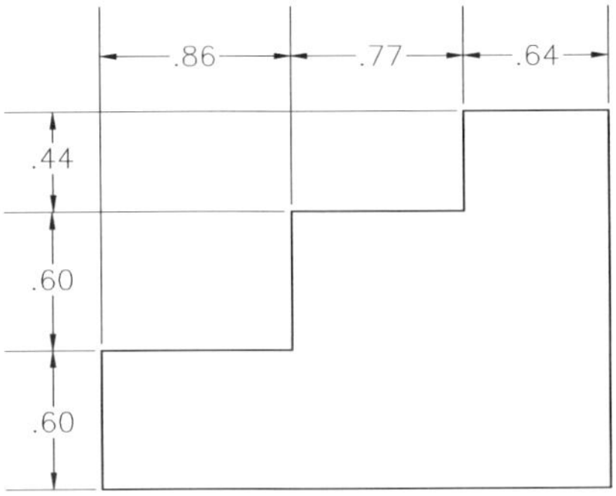

Figure 10-7 Drawings with full length extension lines

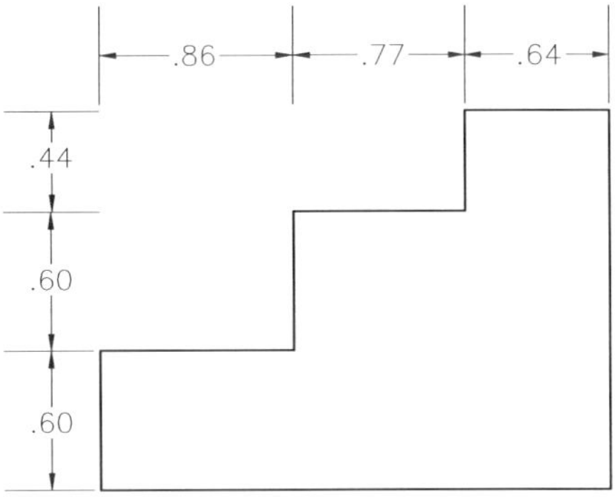

Figure 10-8 Drawing with fixed length extension lines

Suppress. These check boxes are used to control the display of the extension lines. By default, both extension lines will be drawn. You can suppress one or both of them by selecting the corresponding check boxes (Figure 10-9).

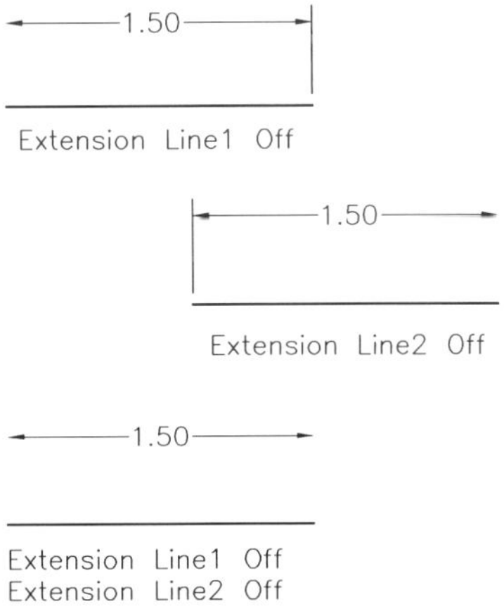

Figure 10-9 Suppressing the extension lines

Symbols and Arrows Tab

The options in the **Symbols and Arrows** tab (Figure 10-10) of the **New Dimension Style** dialog box are used to specify the variables and attributes that affect the format of the symbols and arrows. You can change the appearance of symbols and arrows as per your requirement.

Note

The first and second extension lines are determined by how you select the extension line origins. If the first extension line origin is on the right, the first extension line will also be on the right.

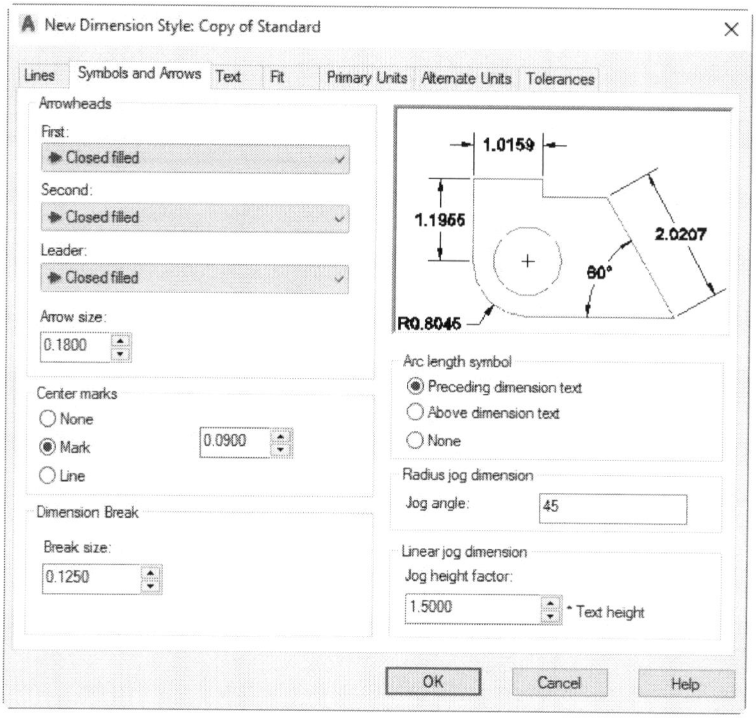

*Figure 10-10 The **Symbols and Arrows** tab of the **New Dimension Style** dialog box*

Arrowheads Area

The options in this area are used to specify the arrowheads and they are discussed next.

First/Second. When you create a dimension, AutoCAD LT draws the terminator symbols at the two ends of the dimension line. These terminator symbols, generally referred to as **Arrowheads**, represent the beginning and the end of a dimension. AutoCAD LT has provided nineteen standard termination symbols that you can apply at each end of the dimension line. In addition to these, you can create your own arrows or terminator symbols. By default, the same arrowhead type is applied at both ends of the dimension line. If you select the first arrowhead, it is automatically applied to the second end by default. However, if you want to specify a different arrowhead at the second dimension line endpoint, you must select the desired arrowhead type from the **Second** drop-down list. The first endpoint of the dimension line is the intersection point of the first extension line and the dimension line. The first extension line is determined by the first extension line origin. However, in angular dimensioning, the second endpoint is located in a counterclockwise direction from the first point, regardless of how the points were selected when creating the angular dimension. The specified arrowhead types are selected from the **First** and **Second** drop-down lists.

AutoCAD LT provides you with an option of specifying a user-defined arrowhead. To define a user-defined arrow, you must create one as a block. (Refer to Chapter 15 for more information regarding blocks.) Now, from the **First** or the **Second** drop-down list, select **User Arrow**; the **Select Custom Arrow Block** dialog box will be displayed, see Figure 10-11.

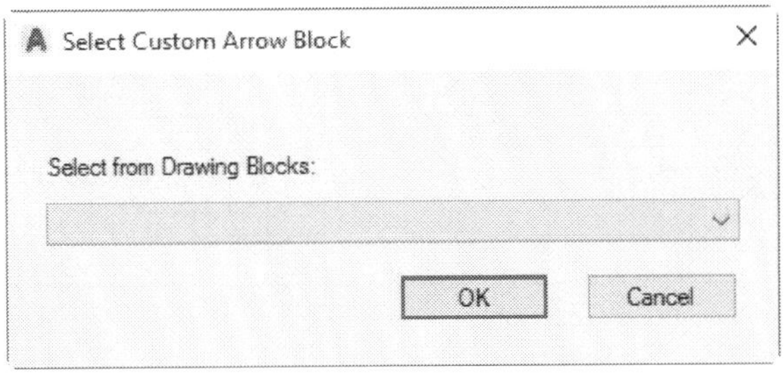

***Figure 10-11** The **Select Custom Arrow Block** dialog box*

All the blocks in the current drawing will be available in the **Select from Drawing Blocks** drop-down list. You can select the desired block and it will become the current arrowhead.

Creating an Arrowhead Block

1. To create a block for an arrowhead, you will use a 1 x 1 box, refer to Figure 10-12. AutoCAD LT automatically scales the X and Y scale factors of the block to the arrowhead size multiplied by the overall scale. You can specify the arrow size in the **Arrow size** spinner. The **DIMASZ** variable controls the length of the arrowhead. For example, if **DIMASZ** is set to 0.25, the length of the arrow will be 0.25 units. Also, if the length of the arrow is not 1 unit, it will leave a gap between the dimension line and the arrowhead block.

2. The arrowhead must be drawn as it would appear on the right side of the dimension line. Choose the **Create** tool from **Block** panel in the **Home** tab to convert it into a block.

3. The insertion point of the arrowhead block must be the point that will coincide with the extension line, see Figure 10-12.

Leader. The **Leader** drop-down list displays the arrowhead types for the Leader arrow. Here, also, you can either select the standard arrowheads from the drop-down list or select **User Arrow** that allows you to define and use a user-defined arrowhead type.

Arrow size. This spinner is used to define the size of the arrowhead, see Figure 10-13. The default value is 0.1800 unit, which is stored in the **DIMASZ** system variable.

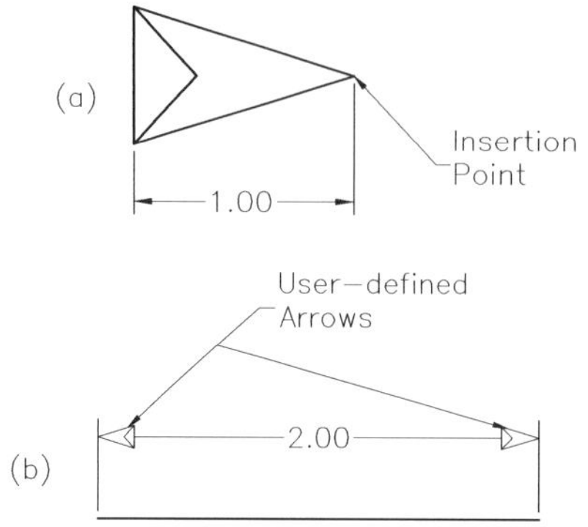

Figure 10-12 Creating user-defined arrows

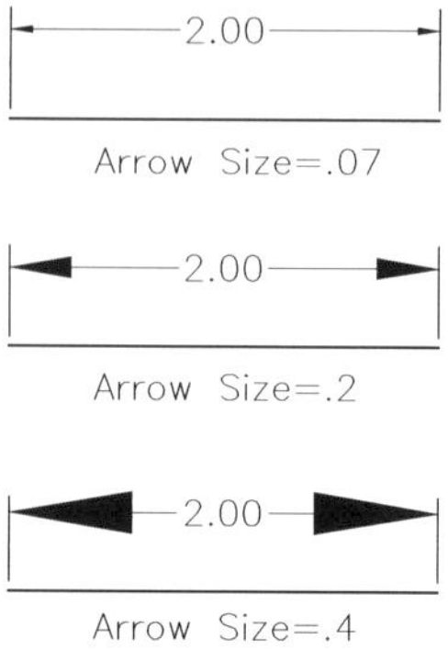

Figure 10-13 Defining arrow sizes

Center marks Area

This area deals with the options that control the appearance of the center marks and centerlines in the radius and diameter dimensioning. However, keep in mind that the center marks or the centerlines will be drawn only when dimensions are placed outside the circle.

None. If you select the **None** radio button, no mark or line will be drawn at the center of the circle.

Mark. If you select the **Mark** radio button, a mark will be drawn at the center of the circle.

Line. If you select the **Line** radio button, the centerlines will be drawn at the center of the circles.

The spinner in the **Center marks** area is used to set the size of the center marks or centerlines. This value is stored in the **DIMCEN** variable. The default value of this variable is 0.0900.

Note

*If you use the **DIMCEN** command, a positive value will create a center mark whereas a negative value will create a centerline. If the value is 0, AutoCAD LT does not create center marks or centerlines.*

Dimension Break Area

The **Break size** spinner in this area is used to control the default break length in the dimension while applying the break dimensions. The default value of this spinner is 0.1250. Figure 10-14 shows a drawing with dimensioning breaks.

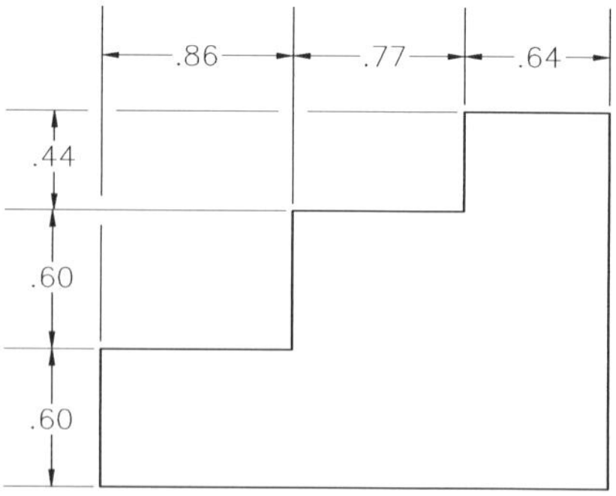

Figure 10-14 Drawing with dimension breaks

Arc length symbol Area

The radio buttons in this area are used to specify the position of arc while applying the arc length dimension.

Preceding dimension text. If you select the **Preceding dimension text** radio button, the arc symbol will appear before the dimension text while applying the arc length dimension.

Above dimension text. With the **Above dimension text** radio button selected, the arc symbol in the arc length dimension will appear above the dimension text.

None. Select the **None** radio button, if you do not want the arc symbol to appear with the arc length dimension.

Radius jog dimension Area

The **Jog angle** edit box in this area is used to specify the angle of jog that appears while applying the jogged radius dimension. By default, its value is 45-degree.

Linear jog dimension Area

The option in this area is used to control the height of the jog (vertical height from the vertex of one jog angle to another) that appears while applying the jogged linear dimension. The jog height is always maintained with respect to the text height of the dimension. The **Jog height factor** spinner is used to change the factor that will be multiplied with the text height to calculate the linear jog height.

Exercise 1

Draw and dimension the drawing, as shown in Figure 10-15.

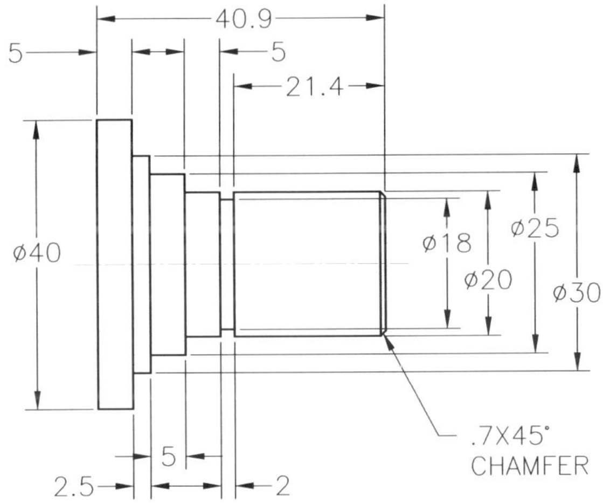

Figure 10-15 *Drawing for Exercise 1*

CONTROLLING THE DIMENSION TEXT FORMAT

Text Tab

You can control the dimension text format through the **Text** tab of the **New Dimension Style** dialog box (Figure 10-16). In the **Text** tab, you can control the parameters such as the placement, appearance, horizontal and vertical alignment of the dimension text, and so on. For example, you can force AutoCAD LT to align the dimension text along the dimension line. You can also force the dimension text to be displayed at the top of the dimension line. You can save the settings in a dimension style file for future use. The **New Dimension Style** dialog box has the **Preview** window that updates dynamically to display the text placement as the settings are changed. Individual items of the **Text** tab and the related dimension variables are described next.

Text appearance Area

The options in this area are discussed next.

Text style. The **Text style** drop-down list displays the names of the predefined text styles. From this list, you can select the style name that you want to use for dimensioning. You must define the text style before you can use it in dimensioning (see "Creating Text Styles" in Chapter 7). Choosing the **[...]** button displays the **Text Style** dialog box that allows you to create a new or modify an existing text style. The change in the dimension text style does not affect the text style you are using to draw the other text in the drawing.

Text color. This drop-down list is used to modify the color of the dimension text. The default color is **ByBlock**. If you choose the **Select Color** option from the **Text color** drop-down list, the **Select Color** dialog box is displayed, where you can choose a specific color.

Fill color. This drop-down list is used to set the fill color of the dimension text. A box of the selected color will be placed around the dimension text.

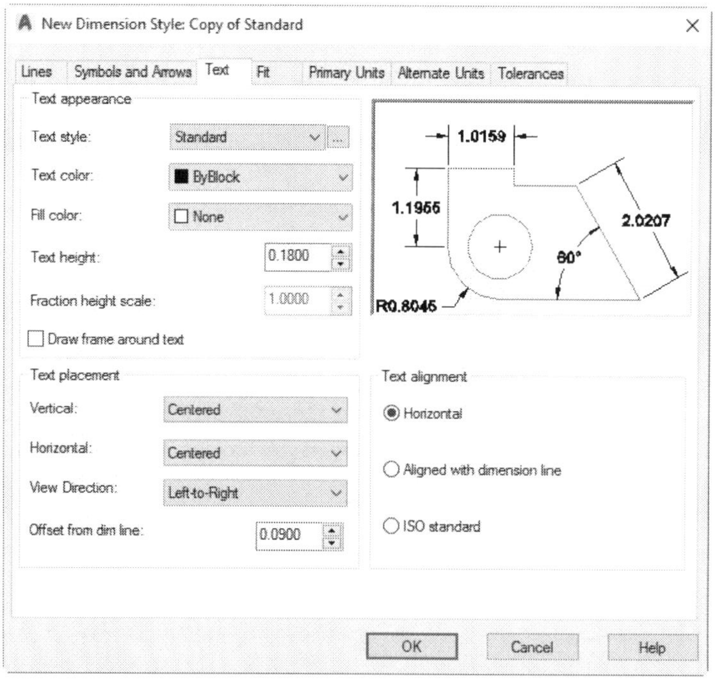

Figure 10-16 *The **Text** tab of the **New Dimension Style** dialog box*

Text height. This spinner is used to modify the height of the dimension text, see Figure 10-17. You can change the dimension text height only when the current text style does not have a fixed height. In other words, the text height specified in the **STYLE** command should be zero. This is because a predefined text height (specified in the **STYLE** command) overrides any other setting for the dimension text height. This value is stored in the **DIMTXT** variable. The default text height is 0.1800 units.

Fraction height scale. This spinner is used to set the scale of the fractional units in relation to the dimension text height. This spinner will be available only when you select a format for the primary units, in which you can define the values in fractions, such as architectural or fractional.

Draw frame around text. Select this check box to draw a frame around the dimension text, see Figure 10-18.

Text placement Area

The options in this area are discussed next.

Vertical. The **Vertical** drop-down list displays the options that control the vertical placement of the dimension text. The current setting is highlighted. Controlling the vertical placement of the dimension text is possible only when the dimension text is drawn in its normal (default) location. This setting is stored in the **DIMTAD** system variable. The options in this drop-down list are discussed next.

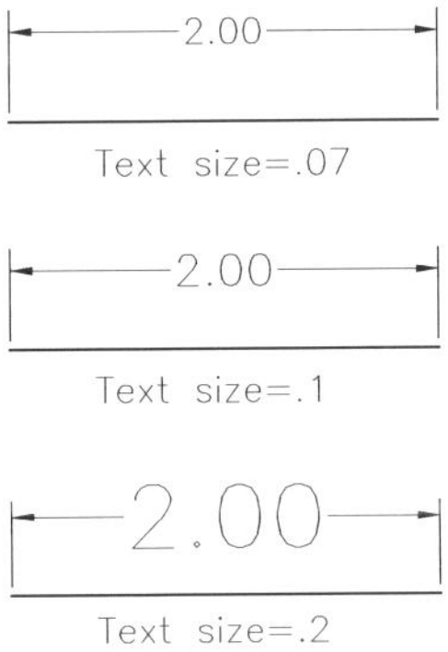

Figure 10-17 Changing the dimension height

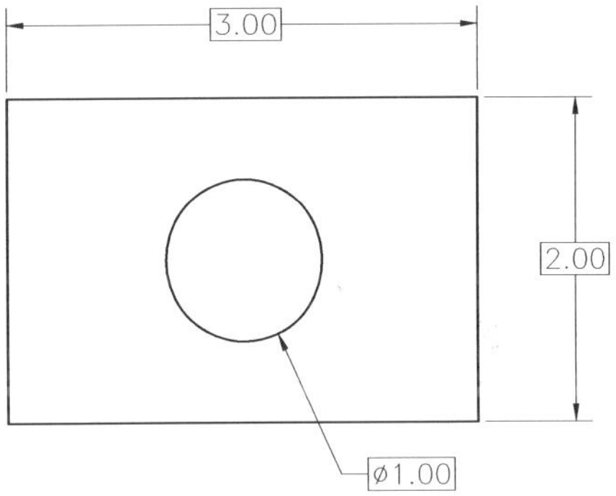

Figure 10-18 Dimension text inside the frame

Centered. If this option is selected, the dimension text gets positioned on the dimension line in such a way that the dimension line splits to allow the placement of the text, see Figure 10-19. If the **1st** or **2nd Extension Line** option is selected in the **Horizontal** drop-down list, then the text will be positioned on the extension line, not on the dimension line. The value stored in the **DIMTAD** system variable for **Center** is 0.

Above. If this option is selected, the dimension text is placed above the dimension line, except when the dimension line is not horizontal and the dimension text inside the extension lines is horizontal. The distance of the dimension text from the dimension line is controlled by the **DIMGAP** variable. This results in an unbroken solid dimension line under the dimension text, see Figure 10-19. The value stored in the **DIMTAD** system variable for **Above** is 1.

Outside. This option places the dimension text on the side of the dimension line. The value stored in the **DIMTAD** system variable for **Outside** is 2.

JIS. This option lets you place the dimension text to conform to the **JIS** (Japanese Industrial Standards) representation. The value stored in the **DIMTAD** system variable for **JIS** is 3.

Below. This option places the dimension text below the dimension line. The value stored in the **DIMTAD** system variable for **Below** is 4.

Note

The selected horizontal and vertical placement options are reflected in the dimensions shown in the ***Preview*** *window.*

Horizontal. This drop-down list is used to control the horizontal placement of the dimension text. You can select the required horizontal placement from this list. However, remember that these options will be useful only when the **Place text manually** check box in the **Fine Tuning** area of the **Fit** tab is cleared. The options in this drop-down list are discussed next.

Centered. This option is used to place the dimension text between the extension lines. This is the default option.

At Ext Line 1. This option is used to place the text near the first extension line along the dimension line, see Figure 10-20.

At Ext Line 2. This option is selected to place the text near the second extension line along the dimension line, see Figure 10-20.

Over Ext Line 1. This option is selected to place the text over the first extension line and also along the first extension line, see Figure 10-20.

Over Ext Line 2. This option is selected to place the text over the second extension line and also along the second extension line, see Figure 10-20.

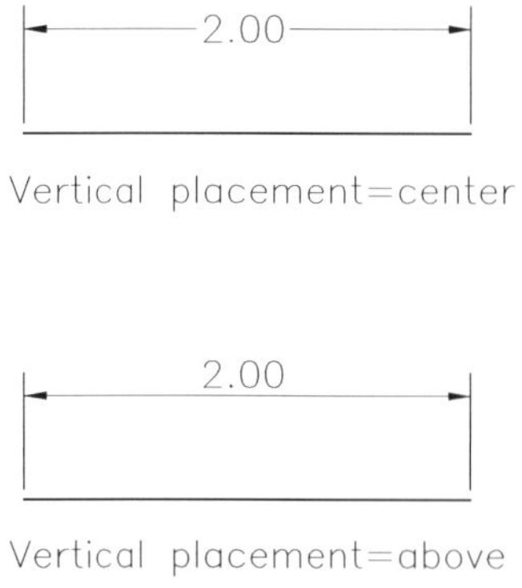

Figure 10-19 Vertical text placement

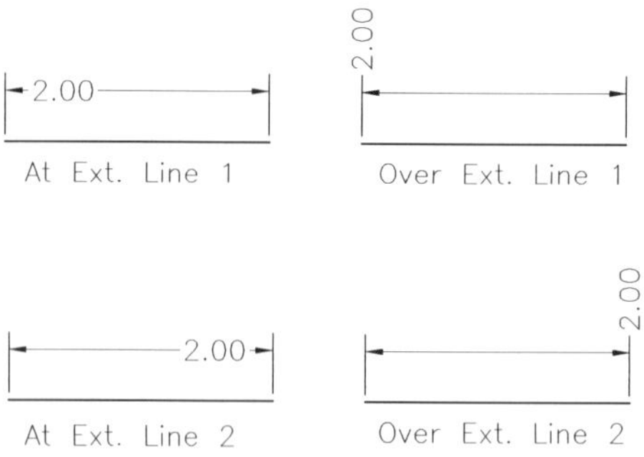

Figure 10-20 Horizontal text placement

View Direction. The options in this drop-down list are used to change the viewing direction of the dimensions either from Left-to-Right or Right-to-Left. Figures 10-21 and 10-22 show the dimensions applied to the entities using the **Left-to Right** and **Right-to-Left** options, respectively.

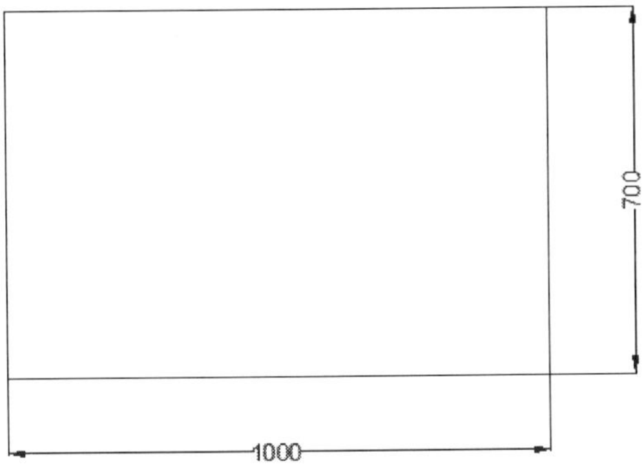

*Figure 10-21 Dimensioning the entity using the **Left-to-Right** option*

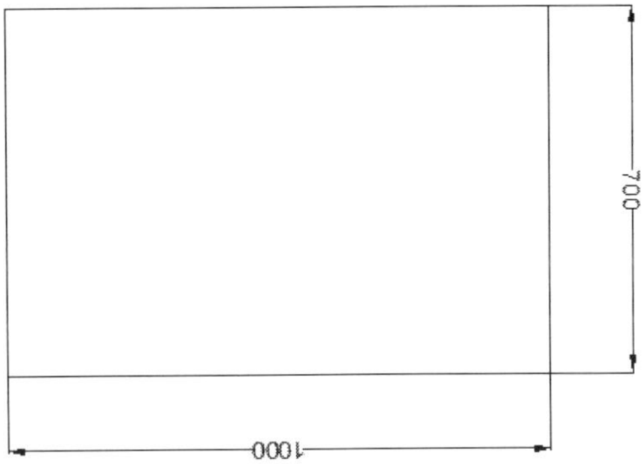

*Figure 10-22 Dimensioning the entity using the **Right-to-Left** option*

Offset from dimline. This spinner is used to specify the distance between the dimension line and the dimension text (Figure 10-23). You can also set the text gap in this spinner. The text gap value is also used as the measure of minimum length for the segments of the dimension line and in basic tolerance. The default value specified in this box is 0.09 units. The value of this setting is stored in the **DIMGAP** system variable.

Text alignment Area

The options in this area are discussed next.

Horizontal. This is the default option and if selected, the dimension text is drawn horizontally with respect to the current UCS (user coordinate system). The alignment of the dimension line does not affect the text alignment. Selecting this radio button turns both the **DIMTIH** and **DIMTOH** system variables on. The text is drawn horizontally even if the dimension line is at an angle.

Aligned with dimension line. If this radio button is selected then the text aligns with the dimension line (Figure 10-24) and both the system variables **DIMTIH** and **DIMTOH** are turned off.

ISO standard. If you select the **ISO standard** radio button, the dimension text is aligned with the dimension line, only when the dimension text is inside the extension lines. Selecting this option turns the system variable **DIMTOH** on. This means the dimension text outside the extension line is horizontal regardless of the angle of the dimension line.

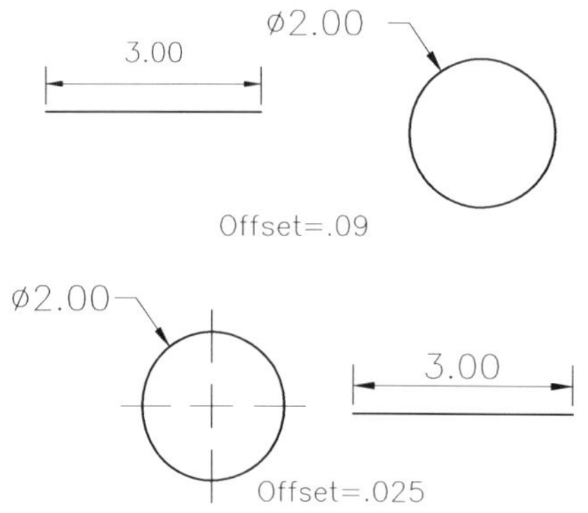

Figure 10-23 *Offset from the dimension line*

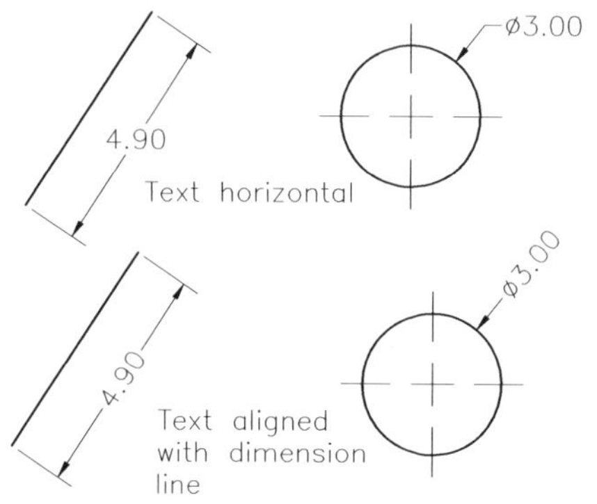

Figure 10-24 *Specifying the text alignment*

Exercise 2

Draw Figure 10-25 and then set the values in the **Lines**, **Symbols and Arrows**, and **Text** tabs of the **New Dimension Style** dialog box to dimension the drawing, as shown in the figure. (Baseline spacing = 0.25, Extension beyond dimension lines = 0.10, Offset from origin = 0.05, Arrow size = 0.09, Text height = 0.08.)

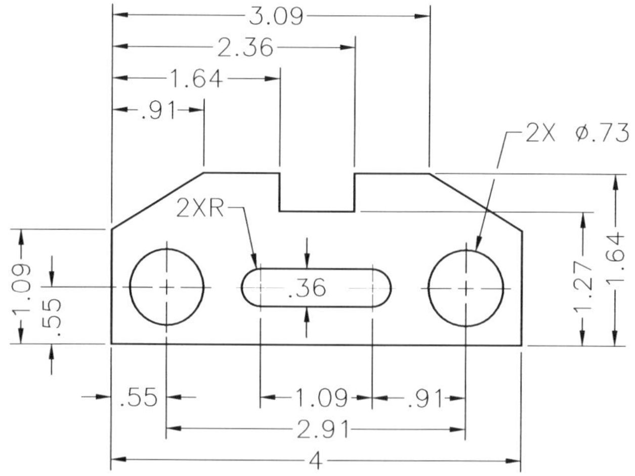

Figure 10-25 *Drawing for Exercise 2*

FITTING DIMENSION TEXT AND ARROWHEADS

Fit Tab

The **Fit** tab provides you with the options that are used to control the placement of dimension lines, arrowheads, leader lines, text, and the overall dimension scale (Figure 10-26). The options in this tab are discussed next.

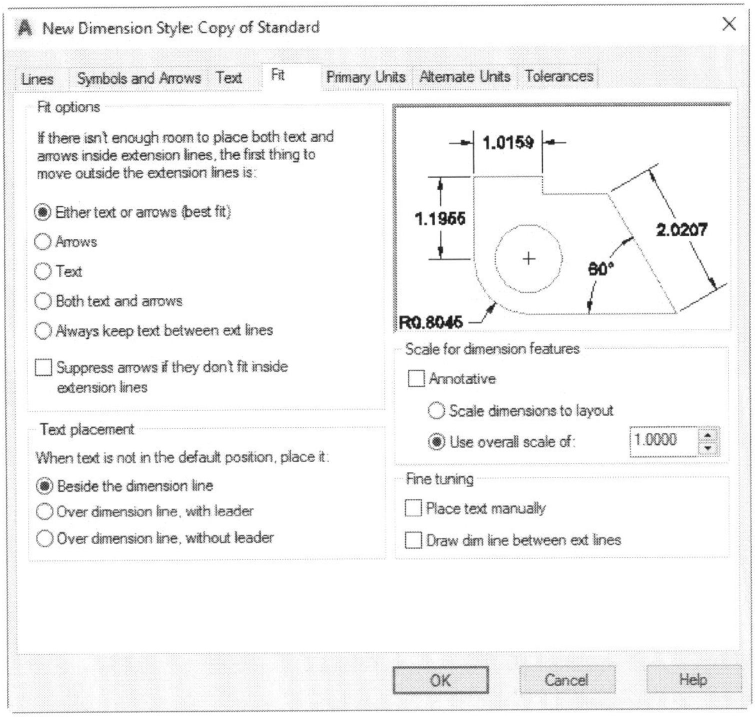

*Figure 10-26 The **Fit** tab of the **New Dimension Style** dialog box*

Fit options Area

These options are used to set the priorities for moving the text and arrowheads outside the extension lines if the space between the extension lines is not enough to fit both of them.

Either text or arrows (best fit). This is the default option. In this option, AutoCAD LT places the dimension where it fits best between the extension lines.

Arrows. When you select this option, AutoCAD LT places the text and arrowheads inside the extension lines if there is enough space to fit the both. If the space is not available, the arrows are moved outside the extension lines. If there is not enough space for text, both text and arrowheads are placed outside the extension lines.

Text. When you select this option, AutoCAD LT places the text and arrowheads inside the extension lines, if there is enough space to fit both. If there is enough space to fit the arrows, the arrows will be placed inside and the dimension text moves outside the extension lines. However, if there is not enough space for either the text or the arrowheads, both are placed outside the extension lines.

Both text and arrows. If you select this option, AutoCAD LT will place the arrows and dimension text between the extension lines, if there is enough space available to fit both. Otherwise, both the text and arrowheads are placed outside the extension lines.

Always keep text between ext lines. This option always keeps the text between the extension lines even in cases where AutoCAD LT would not do so. Selecting this radio button does not affect the radius and diameter dimensions.

Suppress arrows if they don't fit inside the extension lines. If you select this check box, the arrowheads are suppressed if the space between the extension lines is not enough to adjust them.

Text placement Area

This area provides you with the options to position the dimension text when it is moved from the default position. The options in this area are discussed next.

Beside the dimension line. This option places the dimension text beside the dimension line.

Over dimension line, with leader. Selecting this option places the dimension text away from the dimension line and a leader line is created, which connects the text to the dimension line. But if the dimension line is too close to the text, a leader is not drawn. The Horizontal placement decides whether the text is placed to the right or left of the leader.

Over dimension line, without leader. In this option, AutoCAD LT does not create a leader line, if there is insufficient space to fit the dimension text between the extension lines. The dimension text can be moved freely, independent of the dimension line.

Scale for dimension features Area

The options under this area are used to set the value for the overall dimension scale or scaling to the paper space.

Annotative. This check box is used to specify that the selected dimension style is annotative. With this option, you can also convert an existing non-annotative dimension style to annotative and vice-versa. If you select the **Annotative** check box from the **Create New Dimension Style** dialog box, then the **Annotative** check box will also be selected by default.

Use overall scale of. The current general scaling factor that pertains to all the size-related dimension variables, such as text size, center mark size, and arrowhead size, is displayed in the **Use overall scale of** spinner. You can alter the scaling factor to your requirement by entering the scaling factor of your choice in this spinner. Altering the contents of this box alters the value of the **DIMSCALE** variable as the current scaling factor is stored in it. The overall scale (**DIMSCALE**) is not applied to the measured lengths, coordinates, angles, or tolerance. The default value for this variable is 1.0. In this condition, the dimensioning variables assume their preset values and the drawing is plotted at full scale. The scale factor is the reciprocal of the drawing size and so the drawing is to be plotted at the half size. The overall scale factor (**DIMSCALE**) will be the reciprocal of ½, which is 2.

Note

*If you are in the middle of the dimensioning process and you change the **DIMSCALE** value and save the changed setting in a dimension style file, the dimensions with that style will be updated.*

Tip

*When you increase the limits of the drawing, you need to increase the overall scale of the drawing using the **Use overall scale of** spinner before dimensioning. This will save the time required in changing the individual scale factors of all the dimension parameters.*

Scale dimensions to layout. If you select the **Scale dimensions to layout** radio button, the scale factor between the current model space viewport and the floating viewport is computed automatically. Also, on selecting this radio button, the **Use overall scale of** spinner is disabled (it is disabled in the dialog box) and the overall scale factor is set to 0. When the overall scale factor is assigned a value of 0, AutoCAD LT calculates an acceptable default value based on the scaling between the current model space viewport and the paper space. If you are in the paper space (**TILEMODE=0**), or are not using the **Scale dimensions to layout** feature, AutoCAD LT sets the overall scale factor to 1; otherwise, AutoCAD LT calculates a scale factor that makes it possible to plot text sizes, arrow sizes, and other scaled distances at the values, in which they have been previously set. (For further details regarding model space and layouts, refer to Chapter 12.)

Fine tuning Area

The **Fine tuning** area provides additional options governing placement of the dimension text. The options in this area are discussed next.

Place text manually. When you dimension a text, AutoCAD LT places the dimension text in the middle of the dimension line (if there is enough space). If you select the **Place text manually** check box, you can position the dimension text anywhere along the dimension line. You will also notice that when you select this check box, the **Horizontal Justification** is ignored. The default value of this variable is **off**. Selecting this check box enables you to position the dimension text anywhere along the dimension line.

Draw dim line between ext lines. This check box is selected when you want the dimension line to appear between the extension lines, even if the text and dimension lines are placed outside the extension lines. When you select this option in the radius and diameter dimensions (when default text placement is horizontal), the dimension line and arrows are drawn inside the circle or arc, and the text and leader are drawn outside.

FORMATTING PRIMARY DIMENSION UNITS

Primary Units Tab

You can use the **Primary Units** tab of the **New Dimension Style** dialog box to control the dimension text format and precision values (Figure 10-27). You can use the options under this tab to control Units, Dimension Precision, and Zero Suppression for dimension measurements. AutoCAD LT lets you attach a user-defined prefix or suffix to the dimension text. For example, you can define the diameter symbol as a prefix by entering %%C in the **Prefix** edit box; AutoCAD LT will automatically attach the diameter symbol in front of the dimension text. Similarly, you can define a unit type, such as **mm**, as a suffix; AutoCAD LT will then attach **mm** at the end of every dimension text. This tab also enables you to define zero suppression, precision, and dimension text format.

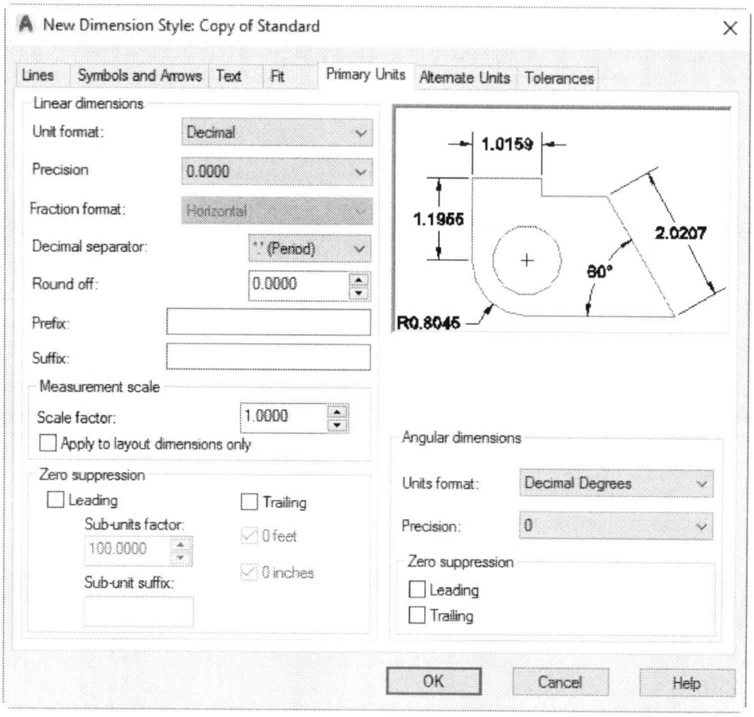

*Figure 10-27 The **Primary Units** tab of the **New Dimension Style** dialog box*

Linear dimensions Area

The options in this area are discussed next.

Unit format. This drop-down list provides you with the options of specifying the units for the primary dimensions. The formats include **Scientific, Decimal**, **Engineering**, **Architectural**, **Fractional**, and **Windows Desktop**. Remember that by selecting a dimension unit format, the drawing units (which you might have selected by using the **Units** tool from the **Format** menu bar) are not affected. The unit setting for linear dimensions is stored in the **DIMLUNIT** system variable. The values for system variable stored for **Scientific**, **Decimal**, **Engineering**, **Architectural**, **Fractional**, and **Windows Desktop** are 1, 2, 3, 4, 5, and 6.

Precision. This drop-down list is used to control the number of decimal places for the primary units. The settings for precision (number of decimal places) are saved in the **DIMDEC** variable and depend upon the units and angle format you have selected.

Fraction format. This drop-down list is used to set the fraction format. The options are **Diagonal**, **Horizontal**, and **Not Stacked**. This drop-down list will be available only when you select **Architectural** or **Fractional** from the **Unit format** drop-down list. The value is stored in the **DIMFRAC** variable.

Decimal separator. This drop-down list is used to select an option that will be used as the decimal separator. For example, Period [.], Comma [,] or Space [ ]. If you have selected Windows desktop units in the **Unit format** drop-down list, AutoCAD LT uses the Decimal symbol settings.

Round off. The **Round off** spinner is used to set the value for rounding off the dimension values. The number of decimal places of the round off value should always be less than or equal to the value in the **Precision** edit box. For example, if the **Round off** spinner is set to 0.05, all dimensions will be rounded off to the nearest 0.05 unit. Therefore, the value 1.06 will round off to 1.05 and the value 1.09 will round off to 1.10, see Figure 10-28. The value is stored in the **DIMRND** variable and the default value in the **Round off** edit box is 0.

Prefix. You can append a prefix to the dimension measurement by entering it in this edit box. The dimension text is converted into **Prefix<dimension measurement>** format. For example, if you enter the text "Abs" in the **Prefix** edit box, "Abs" will be placed in front of the dimension text (Figure 10-29). The prefix string is saved in the **DIMPOST** system variable.

Note
*Once you specify a prefix, default prefixes such as **R** in radius dimensioning and Ø in diameter dimensioning are cancelled.*

Suffix. Just like appending a prefix, you can append a suffix to the dimension measurement by entering the desired suffix in this edit box. For example, if you enter the text **mm** in the **Suffix** edit box, the dimension text will have <dimension measurement>mm format, see Figure 10-29. AutoCAD LT stores the suffix string in the **DIMPOST** variable.

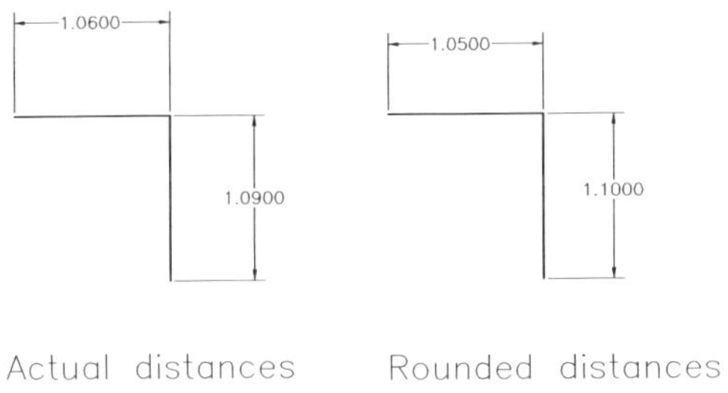

Figure 10-28 Rounding off the dimension measurements

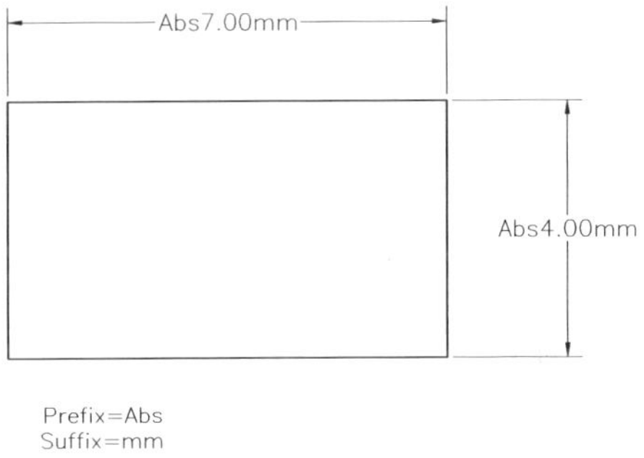

Figure 10-29 Adding prefix and suffix to the dimensions

Tip
*The **DIMPOST** variable is used to append both prefix and suffix to the dimension text. This variable takes string value as its argument. For example, if you want to have a suffix for centimeters, set **DIMPOST** to **cm**. To add a prefix to a dimension text, type the prefix text string and then "<>".*

Measurement scale Area

The options in this area are discussed next.

Scale factor. You can specify a global scale factor for the linear dimension measurements by setting the desired scale factor in the **Scale factor** spinner. All the linear distances measured by dimensions, which include radii, diameters, and coordinates, are multiplied by the existing value in this spinner. For example, if the value of the **Scale factor** spinner is set to 2, two unit segments will be dimensioned as 4 units (2 x 2). However, the angular dimensions are not affected. In this manner, the value of the linear scaling factor affects the contents of the default (original) dimension text (Figure 10-30). The default value for linear scaling is 1. With the default value, the dimension text generated is the actual measurement of the object being dimensioned. The linear scaling value is saved in the **DIMLFAC** variable.

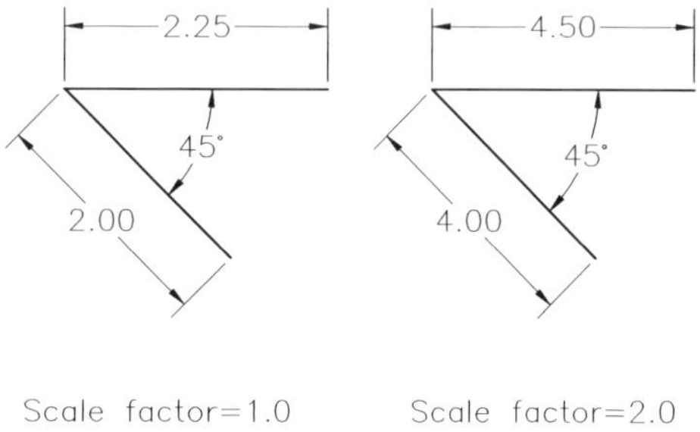

Figure 10-30 *Identical figures dimensioned using different scale factors*

Note

The linear scaling value is not exercised on rounding a value, or on plus or minus tolerance value. Therefore, changing the linear scaling factor will not affect the tolerance values.

Apply to layout dimensions only. When you select the **Apply to layout dimensions only** check box, the scale factor value is applied only to the dimensions in the layout. The value is stored as a negative value in the **DIMLFAC** variable. If you change the **DIMLFAC** variable from the **Dim:** prompt, AutoCAD LT displays the viewport option to calculate the **DIMLFAC** variable. First, set the **TILEMODE** to 0 (paper space), and then invoke the **MVIEW** command to get the **Viewport** option. Now set **TILEMODE** to 1; the paper space is disabled and the model space is set to current.

Zero suppression Area

The options in this area are used to suppress the leading or trailing zeros in the dimensioning. This area provides you with four check boxes. These check boxes can be selected to suppress the leading or trailing zeros or zeros in the feet and inches. The **0 feet** and the **0 inches** check boxes will be available only when you select **Engineering** or **Architectural** from the **Unit format** drop-down list. When the Architectural units are being used, the **Leading** and **Trailing** check boxes are disabled. For example, if you select the **0 feet** check box, the dimension text 0'-8 ¾" becomes 8 ¾". By default, the 0 feet and 0 inches values are suppressed. If you want to suppress the inches part of a feet-and-inches dimension when the distance in the feet portion is an integer value and the inches portion is zero, select the **0 inches** check box. For example, if you select the **0 inches** check box, the dimension text 3'-0" becomes 3'. Similarly, if you select the **Leading** check box, the dimension that was initially 0.53 will become .53. If you select the **Trailing** check box, the dimension that was initially 2.0 will become 2.

Sub-units factor and Sub-unit suffix

The **Sub-units factor** option is used to set the value from sub-units into a single unit and the **Sub-unit suffix** option is used to add a suffix after the single unit. For example, assume an entity having dimension 0.05 unit. After selecting the **Leading** and **Trailing** check boxes from the **Zero suppression** area in the **Primary Units** tab of the **New Dimension Style** dialog box (Figure 10-27), if you set **Sub-units factor** as 100 (by typing manually or using spinner) and enter "**m**" in **Sub-unit suffix** then AutoCAD LT will display dimension as **5m** on the screen.

Angular dimensions Area

This area provides you with the options to control the units format, precision, and zero suppression for the Angular units.

Units format. The **Units format** drop-down list displays a list of unit formats for the angular dimensions. The default value in which the angular dimensions are displayed is **Decimal Degrees**. The value for angular dimensions is stored in the **DIMAUNIT** variable.

Precision. You can select the number of decimal places for the angular dimensions from this drop-down list. This value is stored in the **DIMADEC** variable.

Zero suppression Area. Similar to the linear dimensions, you can suppress the **Leading** and **Trailing** or both zeros in the angular dimensions by selecting the respective check boxes in the area.

FORMATTING ALTERNATE DIMENSION UNITS

Alternate Units Tab

By default, the options in the **Alternate Units** tab of the **New Dimension Style** dialog box are disabled. If you want to perform alternate units dimensioning, select the **Display alternate units** check box. By doing so, AutoCAD LT activates various options in this area (Figure 10-31). This tab sets the format, precision, angles, placement, scale, and so on for the alternate units in use. In this tab, you can specify the values that will be applied to the alternate dimensions.

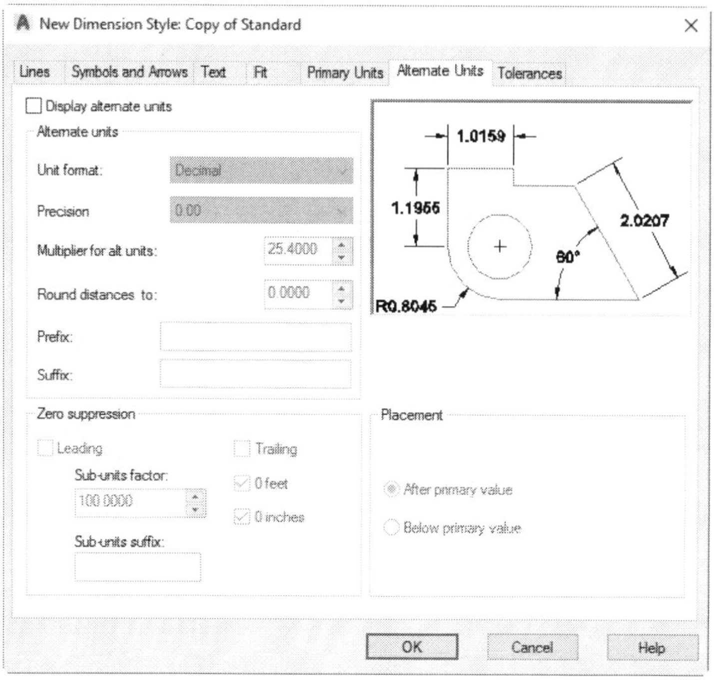

*Figure 10-31 The **Alternate Units** tab of the **New Dimension Style** dialog box*

Alternate units Area

The options in this area are identical to those under the **Linear dimensions** area of the **Primary Units** tab. This area provides you with the options to set the format for all dimension types.

Unit format. You can select a unit format from this drop-down list to apply to the alternate dimensions. The options under this drop-down list include **Scientific**, **Decimal**, **Engineering**, **Architectural Stacked**, **Fractional Stacked**, **Architectural**, **Fractional**, and **Windows Desktop**.

Precision. You can select the number of decimal places for the alternate units from the **Precision** drop-down list.

Multiplier for alt units. To generate a value in the alternate system of measurement, you need a factor with which all the linear dimensions will be multiplied. The value for this factor can be set using the **Multiplier for alt units** spinner. The default value of **Multiplier for alt units** is 25.4.

Round distances to. This spinner is used to set a value to which you want all your measurements (made in alternate units) to be rounded off. For example, if you set the value of the **Round distances to** spinner to 0.25, all the alternate dimensions get rounded off to the nearest .25 unit.

Prefix/Suffix. The **Prefix** and **Suffix** edit boxes are similar to the edit boxes in the **Linear dimensions** area of the **Primary Units** tab. You can enter the text or symbols that you want to precede or follow the alternate dimension text. You can also use control codes and special characters to display special symbols.

Zero suppression Area

This area allows you to suppress the leading or trailing zeros in decimal unit dimensions by selecting either both, or none of the **Trailing** and **Leading** check boxes. Similarly, selecting the **0 feet** check box suppresses the zeros in the feet area of the dimension, when the dimension value is less than a foot. Selecting the **0 inches** check box suppresses the zeros in the inches area of the dimension. For example, 1'-0" becomes 1'.

Sub-units factor and Sub-unit suffix

The **Sub-units factor** sets the value from sub-units into a single unit and **Sub-unit suffix** adds a suffix after the single unit. For example, assume an entity having dimension 0.05 unit. After choosing the **Leading** and **Trailing** check boxes under the **Zero suppression** area in the **Alternate Units** tab of the **New Dimension Style** dialog box (Figure 10-31), if you set **Sub-units factor** as 100 (by typing manually or using spinner) and enter **m** in **Sub-unit suffix** then AutoCAD LT will display the dimension as **5m** on the screen.

Placement Area

This area provides the options that control the positioning of the Alternate units.

After primary value. Selecting the **After primary value** radio button places the alternate units dimension text after the primary units. This is the default option, see Figure 10-32.

Below primary value. Selecting the **Below primary value** radio button places the alternate units dimension text below the primary units, see Figure 10-32.

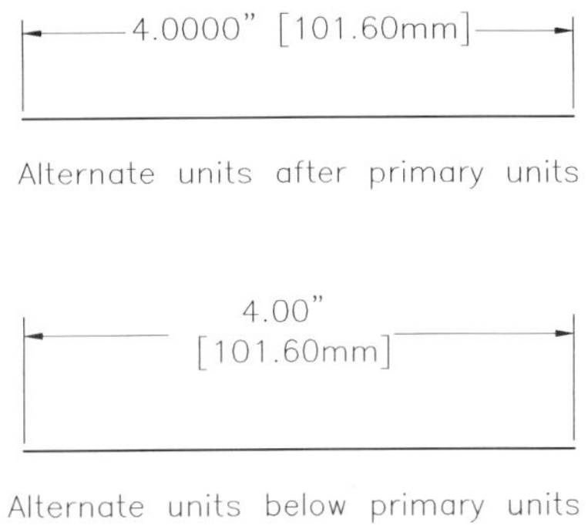

***Figure 10-32** Placement of alternate units*

FORMATTING THE TOLERANCES

Tolerances Tab

The **Tolerances** tab (Figure 10-33) allows you to set the parameters for options that control the format and display of the tolerance dimension text. These include the alternate unit tolerance dimension text.

Tolerance format Area

The **Tolerance format** area of the **Tolerances** tab (Figure 10-33) is used to specify the tolerance method, tolerance value, position of tolerance text, and precision and height of the tolerance text. For example, if you do not want a dimension to deviate more than plus 0.01 and minus 0.02, you can specify this by selecting **Deviation** from the **Method** drop-down list and then specifying the plus and minus deviation in the **Upper Value** and the **Lower Value** edit boxes. When you dimension, AutoCAD LT will automatically append the tolerance to it. The **DIMTP** variable sets the maximum (or upper) tolerance limit for the dimension text and **DIMTM** variable sets the minimum (or lower) tolerance limit for the dimension text. Different settings and their effects on relevant dimension variables are explained in the following sections.

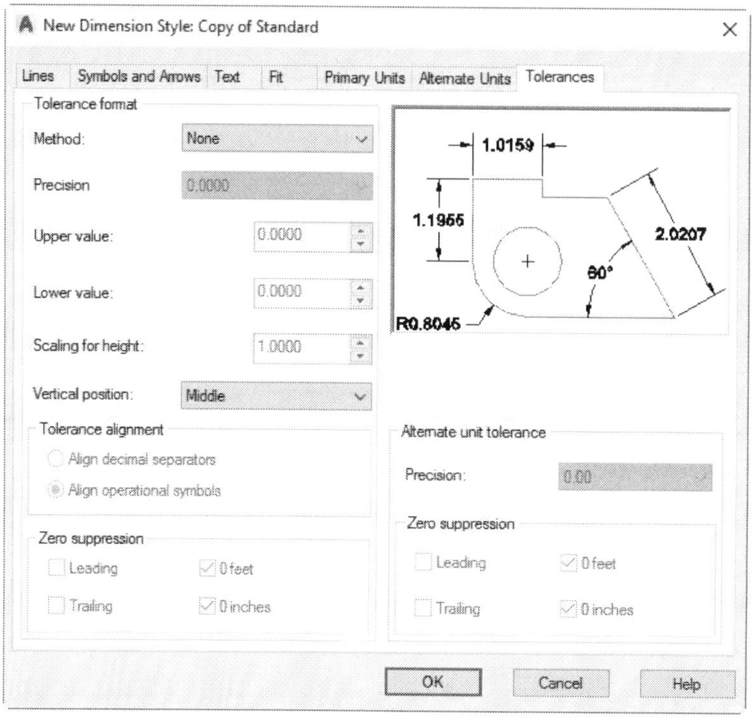

*Figure 10-33 The **Tolerances** tab of the **New Dimension Style** dialog box*

Method. The **Method** drop-down list lets you select the tolerance method. The tolerance methods supported by AutoCAD LT are **Symmetrical**, **Deviation**, **Limits**, and **Basic**. These tolerance methods are described next.

None. Selecting the **None** option sets the **DIMTOL** variable to 0 and does not add tolerance values to the dimension text, that is, the **Tolerances** tab is disabled.

Symmetrical. This option is used to specify the symmetrical tolerances. When you select this option, the **Lower Value** spinner is disabled and the value specified in the **Upper Value** spinner is applied to both plus and minus tolerances. For example, if the value specified in the **Upper Value** spinner is 0.05, the tolerance appended to the dimension text is ±0.05, see Figure 10-34. The value of **DIMTOL** is set to 1 and the value of **DIMLIM** is set to 0.

Deviation. If you select the **Deviation** tolerance method, the values in the **Upper Value** and **Lower Value** spinners will be displayed as plus and minus dimension tolerances. If you enter values for the plus and minus tolerances, AutoCAD LT appends a plus sign (+) to the positive values of the tolerance and a negative sign (–) to the negative values of the tolerance. For example, if the upper value of the tolerance is 0.005 and the lower value of the tolerance is 0.002, the resulting dimension text generated will have a positive tolerance of 0.005 and a negative tolerance of 0.002 (Figure 10-34). Even if one of the tolerance values is 0, a sign is appended to it. On specifying the deviation tolerance, AutoCAD LT sets the **DIMTOL** variable value to 1 and the **DIMLIM** variable value to 0. The values in the **Upper Value** and **Lower Value** edit boxes are saved in the **DIMTP** and **DIMTM** system variables, respectively.

Limits. If you select the **Limits** tolerance method from the **Method** drop-down list, AutoCAD LT adds the upper value (contents of the **Upper Value** spinner) to the dimension text (actual measurement) and subtracts the lower value (contents of the **Lower Value** spinner) from the dimension text. The resulting values are displayed as the dimension text, see Figure 10-34. Selecting the **Limits** tolerance method results in setting the **DIMLIM** variable value to 1 and the **DIMTOL** variable value to 0. The numerical values in the **Upper Value** and **Lower Value** edit boxes are saved in the **DIMTP** and **DIMTM** system variables, respectively.

Basic. A basic dimension text is a dimension text with a box drawn around it (Figure 10-34). The basic dimension is also called a reference dimension. Reference dimensions are used primarily in geometric dimensioning and tolerances. The basic dimension can be realized by selecting the basic tolerance method. The distance provided around the dimension text (distance between dimension text and the rectangular box) is stored as a negative value in the **DIMGAP** variable. The negative value signifies the basic dimension. The default setting is off, resulting in the generation of dimensions without the box around the dimension text.

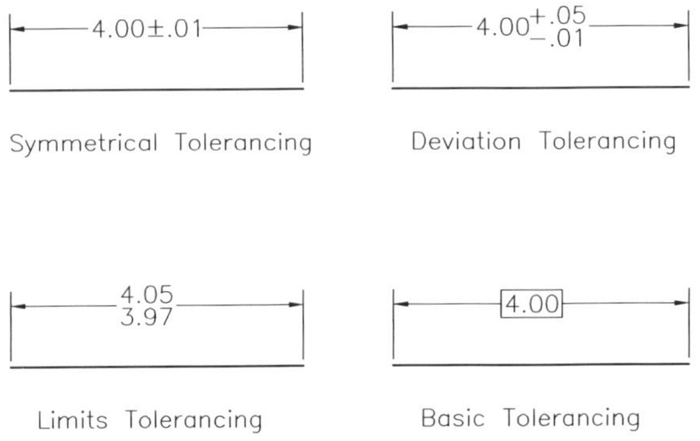

Figure 10-34 Specifying tolerance using various tolerancing methods

Precision. The **Precision** drop-down list is used to select the number of decimal places for the tolerance dimension text. The value is stored in **DIMTDEC** variable.

Upper value/Lower value. In the **Upper value** spinner, the positive upper or maximum value is specified. If the method of tolerances is symmetrical, the same value is used as the lower value also. The value is stored in the **DIMTP** variable. In the **Lower** spinner, the lower or minimum value is specified. The value is stored in the **DIMTM** variable.

Scaling for height. The **Scaling for height** spinner is used to specify the height of the dimension tolerance text relative to the dimension text height. The default value is 1, which means the height of the tolerance text is the same as the dimension text height. If you want the tolerance text to be 75 percent of the dimension height text, enter **0.75** in the **Scaling for height** edit box. The ratio of the tolerance height to the dimension text height is calculated by AutoCAD LT and then stored in the **DIMTFAC** variable. **DIMTFAC = Tolerance Height/Text Height.**

Vertical position. This drop-down list allows you to specify the location of the tolerance text for deviation and symmetrical methods only. The three alignments are possible with the bottom, middle, or top of the main dimension text. The settings are saved in the **DIMTOLJ** system variable (Bottom=0, Middle=1, and Top=2).

Tolerance alignment Area

The options in this area are used to control the alignment of the tolerance value text when they are placed in stacked condition. These options get highlighted only when you select the **Deviation** or **Limits** option from the **Method** drop-down list. Select the **Align decimal separators** radio button to align the tolerance text vertically along the decimal point, see Figure 10-35(a). Select the **Align operational symbols** radio button to align the tolerance text vertically along the plus sign (+) and negative sign(-), see Figure 10-35(b).

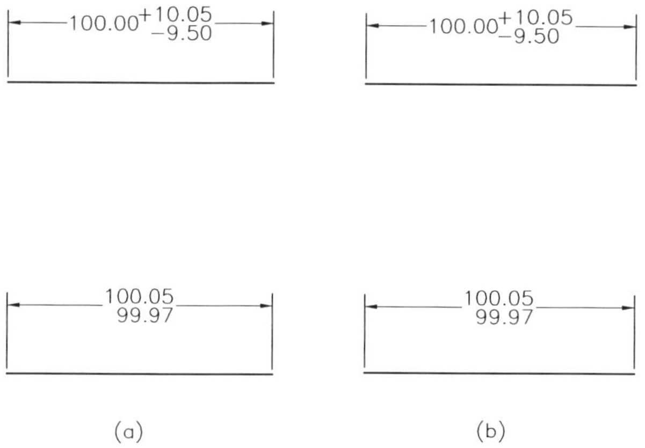

Figure 10-35 Various tolerance alignment options

Zero suppression Area

This area controls the zero suppression in the tolerance text depending on which one of the check boxes is selected. Selecting the **Leading** check box suppresses the leading zeros in all the decimal tolerance text. For example, 0.2000 becomes .2000. Selecting the **Trailing** check box suppresses the trailing zeros in all the decimal tolerance text. For example, 0.5000 becomes 0.5. Similarly, selecting both the boxes suppresses both the trailing and leading zeros and selecting none, suppresses none. If you select the **0 feet** check box, the zeros in the feet portion of the tolerance dimension text are suppressed if the dimension value is less than one foot. Similarly, selecting the **0 inches** check box suppresses the zeros in the inches portion of the dimension text.

Alternate unit tolerance Area

The options in this area define the precision and zero suppression settings for the alternate unit tolerance values. The options under this area will be available only when you display the alternate units along with the primary units.

Precision. This drop-down list is used to set the number of decimal places to be displayed in the tolerance text of the alternate dimensions.

Zero suppression Area

Selecting the respective check boxes controls the suppression of the **Leading** and **Trailing** zeros in decimal values and the suppression of zeros in the Feet and Inches portions for dimensions in the feet and inches format.

Exercise 3 — Dimension Style

Draw Figure 10-36 and then dimension it by setting the values in various tabs of the **New Dimension Style** dialog box to dimension it, as shown. (Baseline spacing = 0.25, Extension beyond dim lines = 0.10, Offset from origin = 0.05, Arrowhead size =0.07, Text height = 0.08.)

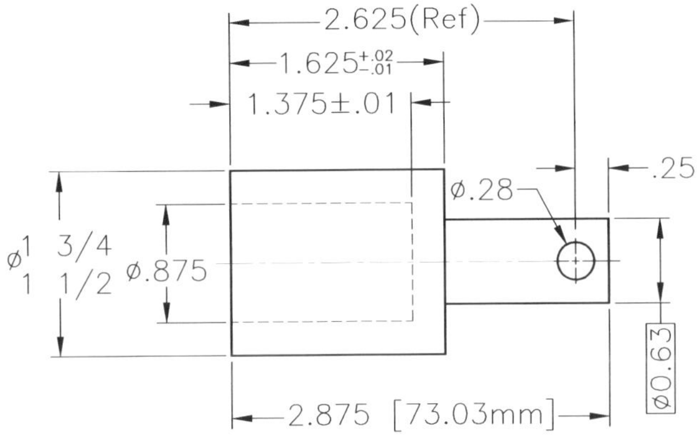

Figure 10-36 *Drawing for Exercise 3*

DIMENSION STYLE FAMILIES

The dimension style feature of AutoCAD LT lets the user define a dimension style with values that are common to all dimensions. For example, the arrow size, dimension text height, and color of the dimension line are generally the same in all types of dimensioning such as linear, radial, diameter, and angular. These dimensioning types belong to the same family because they have some characteristics in common. In AutoCAD LT, this is called a dimension style family, and the values assigned to the family are called dimension style family values.

After you have defined the dimension style family values, you can specify variations on it for other types of dimensions such as radial and diameter. For example, if you want to limit the number of decimal places to two in radial dimensioning, you can specify that value for radial dimensioning. The other values will stay the same as the family values to which this dimension type belongs. When you use the radial dimension, AutoCAD LT automatically uses the style that was defined for radial dimensioning; otherwise, it creates a radial dimension with the values as defined for the family. After you have created a dimension style family, any changes in the parent style are applied to family members, if the particular property is same to the parent dimension style. Special suffix codes are appended to the dimension style family names that correspond to different dimension types. For example, if the dimension style family name is MYSTYLE and you define a diameter type of dimension, AutoCAD LT will append $4 at the end of the dimension style family name. The name of the diameter type of dimension will be MYSTYLE$4. The following are the suffix codes for different types of dimensioning.

Suffix Code	Dimension Type	Suffix Code	Dimension Type
0	Linear	2	Angular
3	Radius	4	Diameter
6	Ordinate	7	Leader

Example 1 — Dimension Style Family

The following example illustrates the concepts of dimension style families, refer to Figure 10-37.

1. Specify the values for the dimension style family.
2. Specify the values for the linear dimensions.
3. Specify the values for the diameter and radius dimensions.
4. After creating the dimension style, use it to dimension the given drawing.

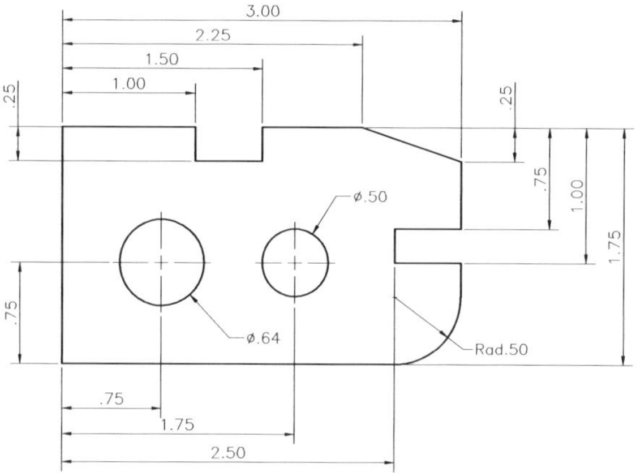

Figure 10-37 *Drawing for Example 1*

1. Start a new file in the **Drafting & Annotation** workspace and draw an object, refer to Figure 10-37.

2. Left-click on the inclined arrow in the **Dimensions** panel of the **Annotate** tab; the **Dimension Style Manager** dialog box is displayed.

3. Choose the **New** button to display the **Create New Dimension Style** dialog box. In this dialog box, enter **MyStyle** in the **New Style Name** edit box. Select **Annotative** from the **Start With** drop-down list. Also, select **All dimensions** from the **Use for** drop-down list.

   Now, choose the **Continue** button to display the **New Dimension Style: MyStyle** dialog box. In this dialog box, first choose the **Lines** tab and then enter the following values in their respective options. Next, choose the **Symbols and Arrows** tab and enter the following values:

   Lines tab
   Baseline Spacing: 0.15

   Symbols and Arrows tab
   Arrow size: 0.09

Offset from origin: 0.03
Extend beyond dim lines: 0.07

Center marks: Select the **Line** radio button
Enter **0.05** in the spinner in the **Center marks** area

4. Choose the **Text** tab and change the following values:

   Text Height: 0.09   Offset from dim line: 0.03

5. Choose the **Fit** tab and make sure the **Annotative** check box is selected.

6. After entering the values, choose the **OK** button to return to the **Dimension Style Manager** dialog box. This dimension style contains the values that are common to all dimension types.

7. Now, choose the **New** button again in the **Dimension Style Manager** dialog box to display the **Create New Dimension Style** dialog box. AutoCAD LT displays **Copy of MyStyle** in the **New Style Name** edit box. Select **MyStyle** from the **Start With** drop-down list if it is not already selected. From the **Use for** drop-down list, select **Linear dimensions**. Choose the **Continue** button to display the **New Dimension Style: MyStyle: Linear** dialog box and set the following values in the **Text** tab:

   a. Select the **Aligned with dimension line** radio button in the **Text alignment** area.
   b. In the **Text placement** area, select **Above** from the **Vertical** drop-down list.

8. In the **Primary Units** tab, set the precision to two decimal places. Select the **Leading** check box in the **Zero suppression** area. Next, choose the **OK** button to return to the **Dimension Style Manager** dialog box.

9. Choose the **New** button again to display the **Create New Dimension Style** dialog box. Select **MyStyle** from the **Start With** drop-down list and the **Diameter dimensions** type from the **Use for** drop-down list. Next, choose the **Continue** button; the **New dimension Style: MyStyle: Diameter** dialog box is displayed.

10. Choose the **Text** tab and select the **Centered** option from the **Vertical** drop-down list in the **Text placement** area, if it is not selected by default. Then, select the **Horizontal** radio button from the **Text alignment** area.

11. Choose the **Primary Units** tab and then set the **Precision** to two decimal places. Select the **Leading** check box in the **Zero suppression** area. Next, choose the **OK** button to return to the **Dimension Style Manager** dialog box.

12. In this dialog box, again choose the **New** button to display the **Create New Dimension Style** dialog box. Select **MyStyle** from the **Start With** drop-down list and **Radius dimensions** from the **Use for** drop-down list. Choose the **Continue** button to display the **New Dimension Style: MyStyle: Radial** dialog box.

13. Choose the **Primary Units** tab and then set the precision to two decimal places. Select the **Leading** check box in the **Zero suppression** area. Next, enter **Rad** in the **Prefix** edit box.

14. In the **Fit** tab, select the **Text** radio button in the **Fit options** area. Next, choose the **OK** button to return to the **Dimension Style Manager** dialog box.

15. Select **MyStyle** from the **Styles** list box in the **Dimension Style Manager** dialog box and choose the **Set Current** button. Choose the **Close** button to exit the dialog box.

16. Choose the **Linear** button from the **Dimensions** panel; the **Select Annotation Scale** dialog box is displayed. Select the **1:1** option from the drop-down list and choose the **OK** button.

17. Use the linear and baseline dimensions to draw the linear dimensions, refer to Figure 10-37. While entering linear dimensions, you will notice that AutoCAD LT automatically uses the values that were defined for linear type of dimensioning.

18. Use the diameter dimensioning to dimension the circles, refer to Figure 10-37. Again, notice that the dimensions are drawn based on the values specified for the diameter type of dimensioning.

19. Now, use the radius dimensioning to dimension the fillet, refer to Figure 10-37.

USING DIMENSION STYLE OVERRIDES

Most of the dimension characteristics are common in a production drawing. The values that are common to different dimensioning types can be defined in the dimension style family. However, at times, you might have different dimensions. For example, you may need two types of linear dimensioning: one with tolerance and one without tolerance. One way to draw these dimensions is to create two dimensioning styles. You can also use the dimension variable overrides to override the existing values. For example, you can define a dimension style (**MyStyle**) that draws dimensions without tolerance. Now, to draw a dimension with tolerance or update an existing dimension, you can override the previously defined value through the **Dimension Style Manager** dialog box or by setting the variable values at the Command prompt. Now, you can remove style override of any selected dimension by choosing the **Remove Style Overrides** option from the shortcut menu displayed on right clicking. The following example illustrates how to use the dimension style overrides.

Example 2 — *Dimension Style Override*

In this example, you will update the overall dimension (3.00) so that the tolerance is displayed with the dimension. You will also add linear dimensions, as shown in Figure 10-38.

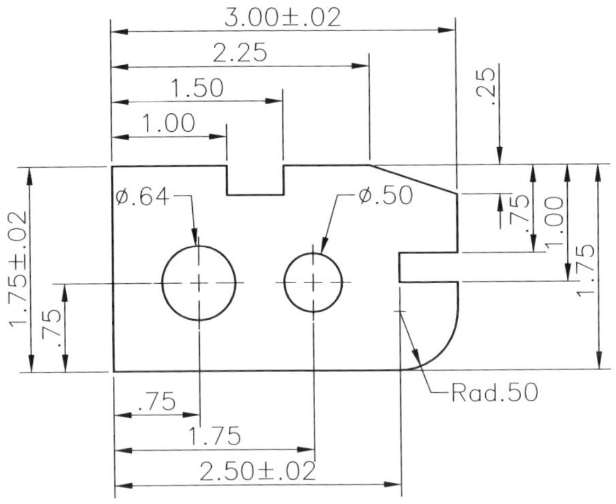

***Figure 10-38** Drawing for Example 2*

This problem can be solved by using dimension style overrides as well as by using the **PROPERTIES** palette. However, here only the dimension style overrides method is discussed.

1. Invoke the **Dimension Style Manager** dialog box. Select **MyStyle** from the **Styles** list box and choose the **Override** button to display the **Override Current Style: MyStyle** dialog box. The options in this dialog box are same to the **New Dimension Style** dialog box discussed earlier in this chapter.

2. Choose the **Tolerances** tab and select **Symmetrical** from the **Method** drop-down list.

3. Set the value of the **Precision** spinner to two decimal places. Set the value of the **Upper value** spinner to **0.02** and select the **Leading** check box in the **Zero suppression** area. Next, choose the **OK** button to exit the dialog box (this does not save the style). On doing so, you will notice that **<style overrides>** is displayed under **MyStyle** in the **Styles** list box, indicating that the style overrides the **MyStyle** dimension style.

4. The **<style overrides>** is displayed until you save it under a new name or under the style it is displayed in, or until you delete it. Select **<style overrides>** and right-click to display the shortcut menu. Choose the **Save to current style** option from the shortcut menu to save the overrides to the current style.

5. Choose the **Update** tool from the **Dimension** panel in the **Annotate** tab and select the dimension that measures **3.00**. The dimension now displays the symmetrical tolerance.

6. Draw the remaining two linear dimensions. They will automatically appear with the tolerances, see Figure 10-38.

Tip

*You can also use the **Override** tool from the **Dimension** panel of the **Annotate** tab to apply change to the existing dimensions.*

COMPARING AND LISTING DIMENSION STYLES

Choosing the **Compare** button in the **Dimension Style Manager** dialog box displays the **Compare Dimension Styles** dialog box where you can compare the settings of two dimensions styles or list all the settings of one of them (Figure 10-39).

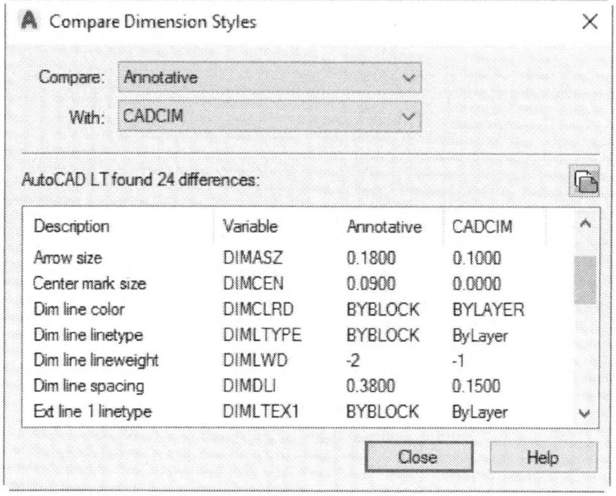

Figure 10-39 *The* ***Compare Dimension Styles*** *dialog box*

The **Compare** and the **With** drop-down lists display the dimension styles in the current drawing. Selecting the dimension style from the respective list compares the two styles. In the **With** drop-down list, if you select **<none>** or the same style as selected from the **Compare** drop-down list, all the properties of the selected style are displayed. The comparison results are displayed under different headings: **Description** of the Dimension Style property, the **System variable** controlling a particular setting, and the values of the variable for both the dimension styles which differ in the two styles in comparison. The number of differences between the selected dimension styles are displayed below the **With** drop-down list. The button (at the right side in the middle) provided in this dialog box prints the comparison results to the Windows clipboard from where they can be pasted to other Windows applications.

USING EXTERNALLY REFERENCED DIMENSION STYLES

The externally referenced dimensions cannot be used directly in the current drawing. When you Xref a drawing, the drawing name is appended to the style name and the two are separated by the (0) symbol. It uses the same syntax as the other externally dependent symbols. For example, if the drawing (FLOOR) has a dimension style called DIM1 and you Xref this drawing in the current drawing, AutoCAD LT will rename the dimension style to FLOOR0DIM1. You cannot make this dimension style current, nor can you modify or override it. However, you can use it as a template to create a new style. To accomplish this task, invoke the **Dimension Style Manager** dialog box. If the **Don't list styles in Xrefs** check box is selected, the styles in the Xref are not displayed. Clear this check box to display the Xref dimension styles and choose the **New** button. In the **New Style Name** edit box of the **Create New Dimension Style** dialog box, as shown in Figure 10-40, enter the name of the dimension style. AutoCAD LT will create a new dimension style with the same values as those of the externally referenced dimension style (FLOOR0DIM1).

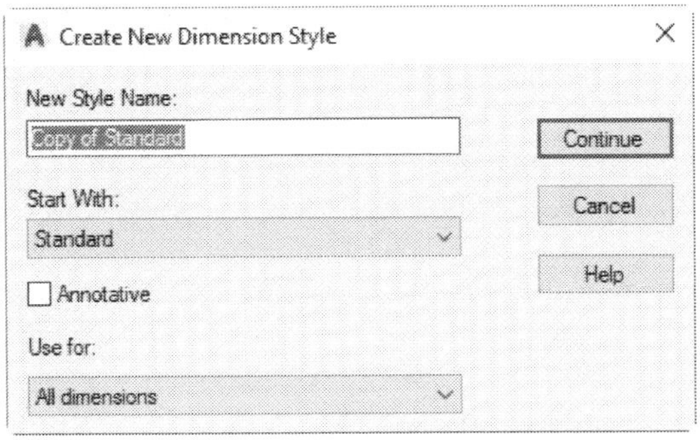

Figure 10-40 The ***Create New Dimension Style*** *dialog box*

Note
You will learn more about External References in Chapter 17.

CREATING AND RESTORING MULTILEADER STYLES

Ribbon: Annotate > Leaders > Multileader Style Manager (Inclined arrow)
Toolbar: Multileader > Multileader Style or Styles > Multileader Style
Command: MLEADERSTYLE/MLS

The multileader styles control the appearance and positioning of multileaders in the drawing. If the default multileader styles (**Standard** and **Annotative**) do not meet your requirement, you can select any other existing multileader style as per your requirement. The default multileader style file names are **Standard** and **Annotative**. Left-click on the inclined arrow in the **Leaders** panel of the **Annotate** tab; the **Multileader Style Manager** dialog box will be displayed, as shown in Figure 10-41(A).

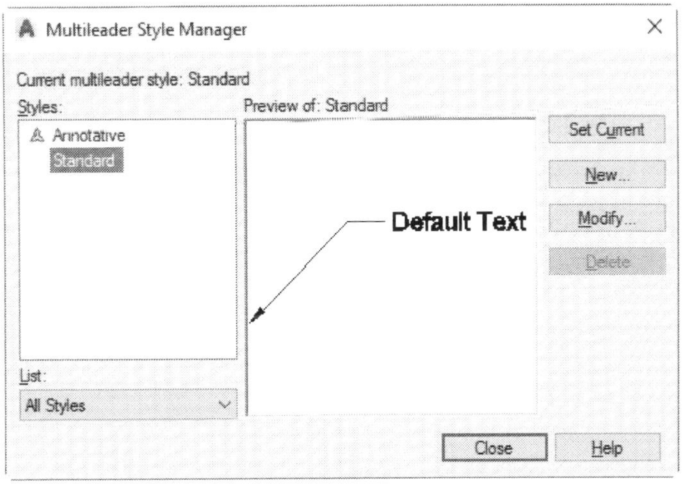

Figure 10-41(A) The ***Multileader Style Manager*** *dialog box*

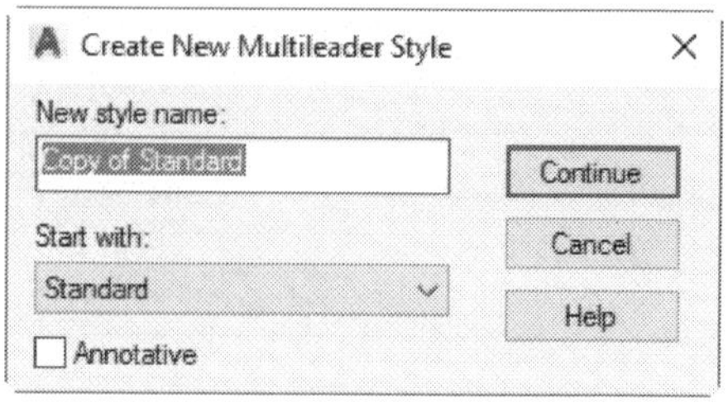

Figure 10-41(B) *The* ***Create New Multileader Style*** *dialog box*

From the **Multileader Style Manager** dialog box, choose the **New** button to display the **Create New Multileader Style** dialog box, see Figure 10-41(B). Enter the multileader style name in the **New style name** text box and then select a style from the **Start with** drop-down list on which you want to base your current style. Select the **Annotative** check box to specify that the new dimension style should be annotative. Choose the **Help** button to get the help and information about the annotative objects. Choose the **Continue** button to display the **Modify Multileader Style** dialog box in which you can define the new style. After defining the new style, choose the **OK** button. The parameters of the **New Multileader Style** dialog box are discussed in the next section.

In the **Multileader Style Manager** dialog box, the current multileader style name is shown in front of the **Current multileader style** option and is also highlighted in the **Styles** list box. The **Multileader Style Manager** dialog box also has a **Preview of** window that displays a preview of the current multileader style. A style can be made current (restored) by selecting the name of the multileader style that you want to make current from the list of defined multileader styles and choosing the **Set Current** button. You can also make a style current by double-clicking on the style name in the **Styles** list box. The **Multileader Style Control** drop-down list in the **Multileaders** panel also displays the multileader styles. Select the required multileader style from this list to set it as current. The list of multileader styles displayed in the **Styles** list box depends on the option selected from the **List** drop down-list. If you select the **Styles in use** option, only the multileader styles in use will be listed in the **Styles** list box. If you right-click on a style in the **Styles** list box, a shortcut menu will be displayed to provide you with the options such as **Set current**, **Modify, Rename**, and **Delete**. Choose the **Modify** button to display the **Modify Multileader Style** dialog box in which you can modify an existing style. Choose the **Delete** button to delete the selected multileader style that has not been used in the drawing.

MODIFY MULTILEADER STYLE DIALOG BOX

The **Modify Multileader Style** dialog box can be used to specify the multileader attributes (variables) that affect various properties of the multileader. The various tabs provided in the **Modify Multileader Style** dialog box are discussed next.

Leader Format Tab

The options in the **Leader Format** tab (Figure 10-42) of the **Modify Multileader Style** dialog box are used to specify the multileader attributes that affect the format of the multileader lines. For example, the appearance and behavior of the multileader lines and the arrow head can be changed with this tab.

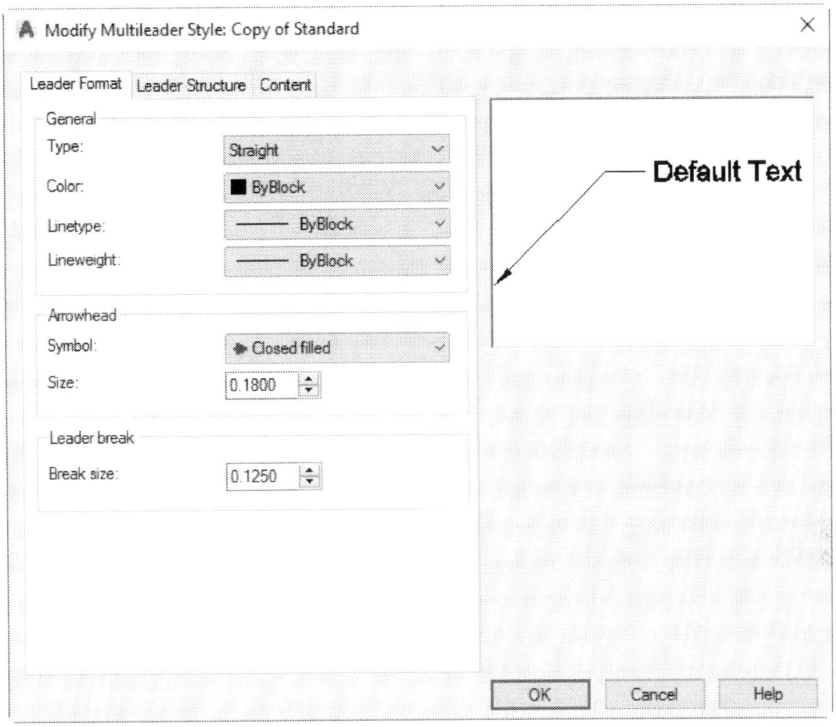

*Figure 10-42 The **Leader Format** tab of the **Modify Multileader Style** dialog box*

General Area

This area provides you the options for controlling the display of the multileader lines. These options are discussed next.

Type. This option is used to specify the type of lines to be used for creating the multileaders. You can select the **Straight**, **Spline**, or **None** option from the **Type** drop-down list. Select the **None** option to create the multileader with no leader lines. You will only be able to draw the content of that multileader. The default line type for the multileaders is **Straight**.

Color. This drop-down list is used to set the colors for the leader lines and arrowheads. The multileader arrowheads have the same color as the multileader lines because the arrows are a part of the multileader lines. The default color for the multileader lines and arrows is **ByBlock**. Select the **Select Color** option from the **Color** drop-down list to display the **Select Color** dialog box from where you can choose a specific color.

Linetype. This drop-down list is used to set the linetype for the multileader lines.

Lineweight. This drop-down list is used to specify the lineweight for the multileader lines. You can select the required lineweight from this drop-down list. The default value is **ByBlock**. Note that you cannot assign the lineweight to the arrowheads using this drop-down list.

Arrowhead Area

This area provides you the options for controlling the shape and size of the arrowhead. The options in this area are discussed next.

Symbol. When you create a multileader, AutoCAD LT draws the terminator symbol at the starting point of the multileader line. This terminator symbol is generally referred to as the arrowhead, and it represents the beginning of the multileader. AutoCAD LT provides you with nineteen standard termination symbols that can be selected from the **Symbol** drop-down list of the **Arrowhead** area. In addition to this, you can create your own arrows or terminator symbols.

Size. This spinner is used to specify the size of the arrowhead.

Leader break Area

The **Break size** spinner in this area is used to specify the break length in the multileader while applying the dimension breaks. The default value of **Break size** is 0.1250.

Leader Structure Tab

The options in the **Leader Structure** tab (Figure 10-43) of the **Modify Multileader Style** dialog box are used to specify the dimensioning attributes that affect the structure of the multileader lines. The attributes that can be controlled by using the **Leader Structure** tab are the number of lines to be drawn before adding the content, adding landing before the content, length of the landing line, multiline to be annotative or not, and so on.

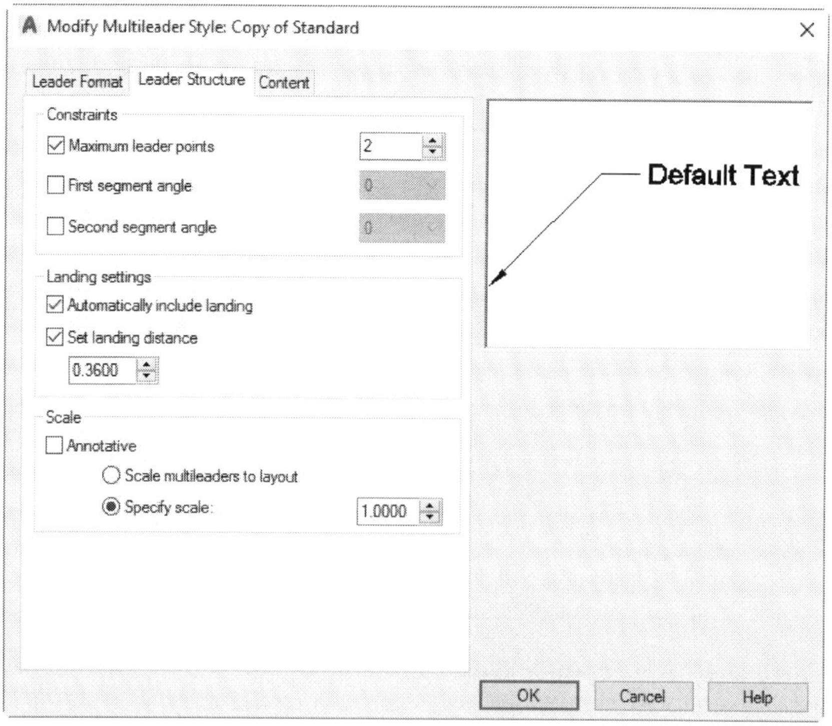

*Figure 10-43 The **Leader Structure** tab of the **Modify Multileader Style** dialog box*

Constraints Area

This area provides you the options to control the number of multileader points and the direction of the multileader.

Maximum leader points. This check box is used to specify the maximum number of points in the multileader line. The default value is 2, which means that there will be only two points in the leader line. Select the check box to specify the maximum number of points. You can change the value of the maximum leader points in the spinner in front of this option. Note that the start point of the multileader is the first multileader point and it should also be included in the counting.

First segment angle. This check box is used to specify the angle of the first multileader line from the horizontal. Select this check box to specify a value in the drop-down list displayed in front of it.

Second segment angle. This check box is used to specify the angle of the second multileader line from the horizontal. Select this check box to specify a value in the drop-down list displayed in front of it.

Note

*The **First** and **Second segment angle** values can be in multiples of the angle value specified in the respective spinners.*

Landing settings Area

This area provides you the options to control the inclusion of landing line and its length.

Automatically include landing. Select this check box to attach a landing line to the multileader. By default, this check box is selected and is used to attach the landing line to the multileaders.

Set landing distance. By default, this check box is selected and used to specify the length of the landing line to be attached with the multileader. You can specify the value in the spinner that is below this check box. This spinner gets highlighted only when you select the **Set landing distance** check box. The default value of the landing length is set to 0.36.

Scale Area

The options under this area are used to set the value for the overall multileader scale or the scale of the multileader in the paper space.

Annotative. This check box is used to set the selected multileader style to annotative. With this option, you can also convert an existing non-annotative multileader style to annotative and vice-versa. If you select the **Annotative** check box from the **Create New Multileader Style** dialog box, then the **Annotative** check box in the **Modify Multileader Style** dialog box will also be selected by default.

Scale multileaders to layout. If you select the **Scale multileaders to layout** radio button, the scale factor between the current model space viewport and the floating viewport (paper space) will be computed automatically. Also, you can disable the **Specify scale** spinner (it is disabled in the dialog box) and the overall scale factor is set to 0 by selecting this radio button. When the overall scale factor is assigned a value of 0, AutoCAD LT calculates an acceptable default value based on the scaling between the current model space viewport and the paper space. AutoCAD LT sets the overall scale factor to 1 if you are in the paper space or not using the **Scale multileaders to layout** feature. Otherwise, AutoCAD LT calculates a scale factor that makes it possible to plot the multileaders at the values in which they have been previously set. For further details regarding the model space and layouts, refer to Chapter 12.

Specify scale. All the current multileaders are scaled with a value specified in the **Specify scale** spinner. You can alter the scaling factor as per your requirement by entering the scaling factor of your choice in this spinner. The default value for this variable is **1.0**. With this value, AutoCAD LT assumes its preset value and the drawing is plotted in a full scale. The scale factor is the reciprocal of the drawing size. So, for plotting the drawing at the one-fourth size, the overall scale factor will be 4.

Content Tab

The options in the **Content** tab (Figure 10-44) of the **Modify Multileader Style** dialog box are used to specify the multileader attributes that affect the content and the format of the text or block to be attached with the multileader.

You can attach the multiline text or block to the multileader. You can also attach nothing as a content to the multileader. Select the desired multileader type from the **Multileader type** drop-down list; the other options in the **Content** tab of the **Modify Multileader Style** dialog box will vary with the change in the multileader type. Figure 10-44 displays the options in the **Modify Multileader Style** dialog box for the **Mtext** multileader type and these options are discussed next.

Text options Area

The options in this area are discussed next.

Default text. This option is used to specify the default text to be attached with the multileader. Choose the **[...]** button; the **In-Place Text Editor** will be displayed. Enter the text that you want to display with the multileader by default and then click outside the text editor window; the preview window in the **Content** tab will display the multileader with the default text attached to it. While creating a new multileader, AutoCAD LT prompts you to specify whether you want to retain the default text or overwrite it with a new text.

Text style. This drop-down list is used to select the text style to be used for writing the content of the multileader. Only the predefined and default text styles are displayed in the drop-down list.

Text angle. This drop-down list is used to control the rotation of the multiline text with respect to the landing line.

Text color. This drop-down list is used to select the color to be used for writing the content of the multileader.

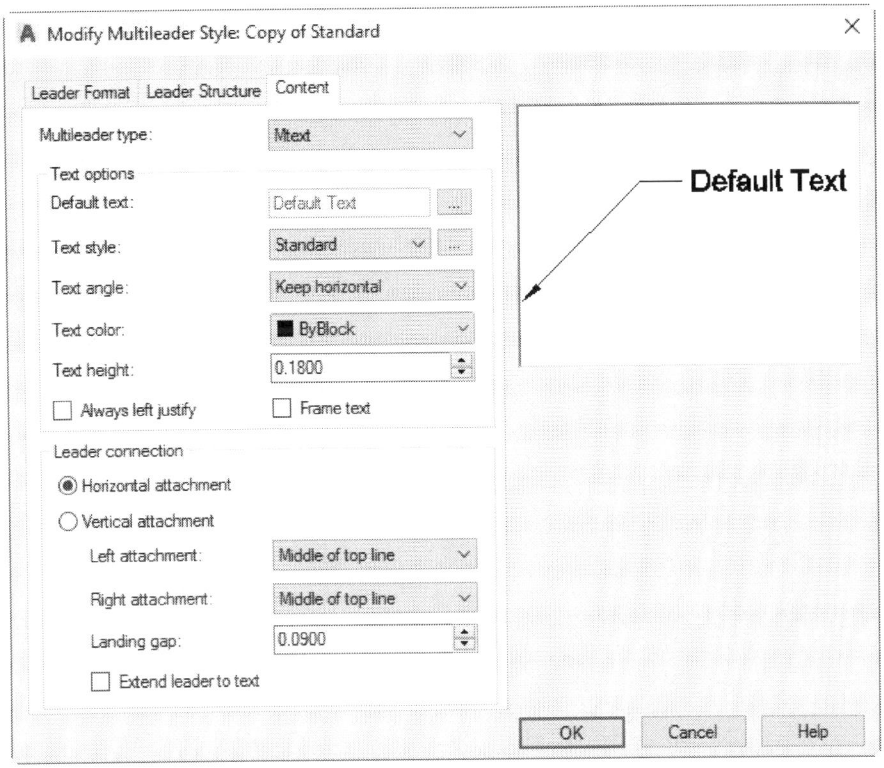

*Figure 10-44 The **Content** tab of the **Modify Multileader Style** dialog box*

Text height. This spinner is used to specify the height of the multiline text to be attached with the multileader.

Always left justify. Select this check box to left justify the text attached to the multileader. On clearing the **Always left justify** check box, a multileader with the multileader style shown in Figure 10-45 (a) is displayed. On selecting this check box, a multileader with the multileader style as shown in Figure 10-45 (b) is displayed.

Frame text. Select this check box, it will enable you to draw a rectangular frame around the multiline text to be attached with the multileader, see Figure 10-46.

Leader connection Area

The options provided in this area are used for controlling the attachment of the multiline text to the multileader.

Horizontal attachment. Select this radio button to place the leader at the right or left of the text. If you select this radio button, you need to select an appropriate option from the **Left Attachment** and **Right attachment** drop-down lists to attach the multiline text to the landing line.

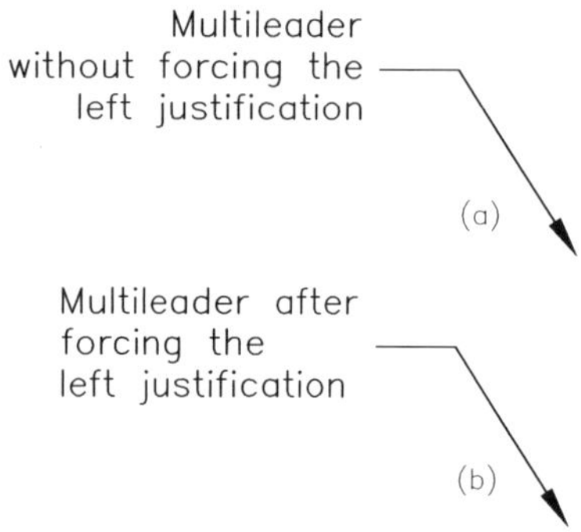

*Figure 10-45 Multileaders displaying the effect of the **Always left justify** option*

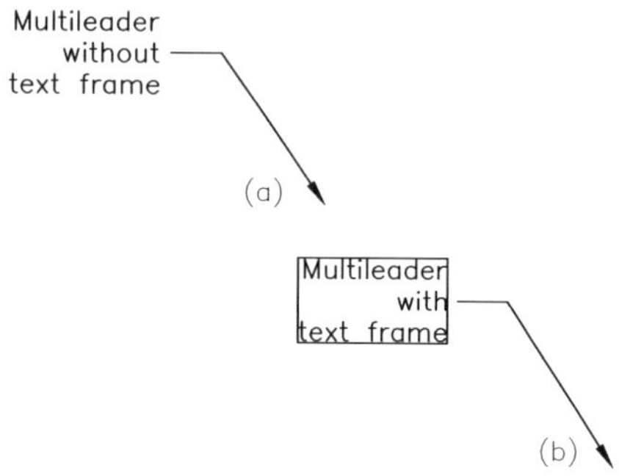

*Figure 10-46 Multileaders displaying the effect of the **Frame text** option*

Vertical attachment. Select this radio button to place the leader at the top or bottom of the text. If you select this radio button, you need to select an appropriate option from the **Top attachment** and **Bottom attachment** drop-down lists to attach the multiline text with the landing line.

Landing gap. This spinner is used to specify the gap between the landing line and the multiline text at the point of attachment. It is available in both the cases; Horizontal attachment or Vertical attachment. The default value in the spinner is 0.09.

Extend leader to text. Select this check box to extend the leader line to text. If you deselect it then the leader can be extended upto the frame only.

If you select **Block** from the **Multileader type** drop-down list, the options will change accordingly. Figure 10-47 displays the options in the **Modify Multileader Style** dialog box for the **Block** option of the **Multileader type** drop-down list and these options are discussed next.

Block options Area

Source block. This drop-down list is used to select the block to be attached with the multileader as content. You can attach the standard block listed in the drop-down list or attach the user defined blocks to the multileader by selecting **User Block** from the drop-down list. Six standard shapes of block are available in this drop-down list with their previews on the side of the block name. While creating the multileader, if you select the **Detail Callout** option from the **Source block** drop-down list, you will be prompted to specify the **View number** and **Sheet number** to be displayed within the block in stacked form. For the other remaining standard blocks, you will be prompted to specify the **Tag number** only to be displayed within the block. To attach the user-defined block to the multileader, select **User Block** from the **Source block** drop-down list; the **Select Custom Content Block** dialog box will be displayed with the list of all the blocks defined in the current drawing under the **Select from Drawing Blocks** drop-down list. Select the desired block and choose the **OK** button; the selected block will be added to the **Source block** drop-down list for the current drawing. Also, it will be attached to the multileader as content.

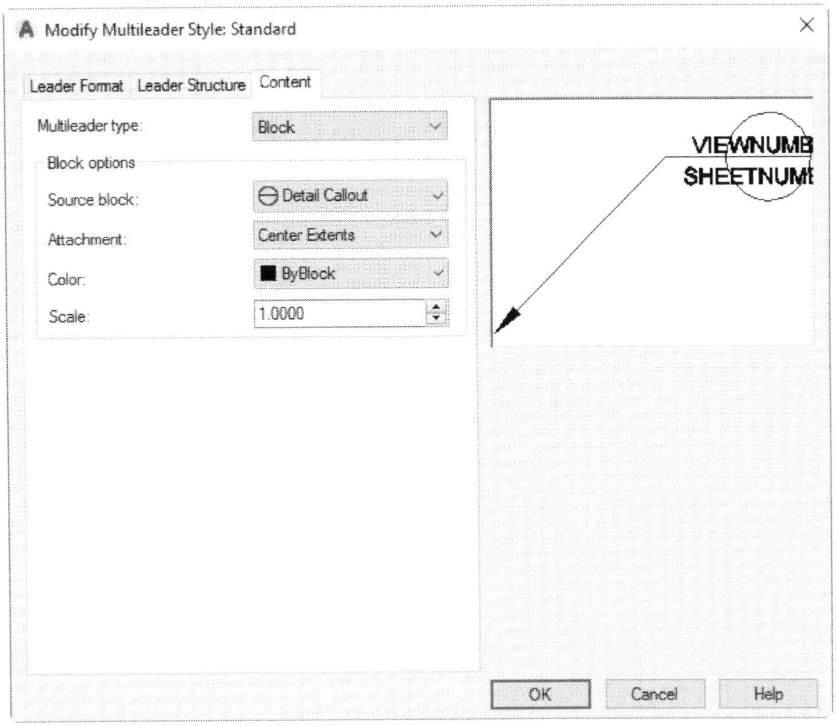

Figure 10-47 The ***Content*** *tab of the* ***Modify Multileader Style*** *dialog box for the* ***Block*** *option of the* ***Multileader type*** *drop-down list*

Attachment. This drop-down list is used to specify the point of attachment of the block to the leader. Select **Center Extents** from the drop-down list to attach the leader landing line in the middle of the outer boundary of the block. Select **Insertion point** to attach the leader landing line to the insertion point specified while defining the block.

Color. This drop-down list is used to specify the color of the block to be attached with the leader landing line.

Scale. This spinner is used to specify the scale of the block to be inserted. For example, if the block is 1 square inch and the scale specified is 0.5000, then the block inserted will be 1/2 inch square.

Self-Evaluation Test

Answer the following questions and then compare them to those given at the end of this chapter:

1. The **DIMTVP** variable is used to control the __________ position of the dimension text.

2. You can attach the multiline text or __________ to the multileader.

3. A basic dimension text is the dimension text with a __________ drawn around it.

4. The **Suppress** check boxes in the **Dimension Lines** area are used to control the display of __________ and __________.

5. You can specify the tolerance using __________ methods.

6. The __________ button in the **Dimension Style Manager** dialog box is used to override the current dimension style.

7. You can invoke the **Dimension Style Manager** dialog box using both the **Annotate** and **Home** tabs. (T/F)

8. The size of the arrow block is determined by the value specified in the **Arrow size** edit box. (T/F)

9. A block can be set as default content to be attached with the multileader. (T/F)

10. The size of the tolerance text with respect to dimensions can be defined. (T/F)

Review Questions

Answer the following questions:

1. Which of the following buttons can be used to make a dimension style active for dimensioning?

   (a) **Set Current** (b) **New**
   (c) **Override** (d) **Modify**

2. Which of the following tabs in the **Dimension Style Manager** dialog box is used to add the suffix **mm** to dimensions?

   (a) **Fit** (b) **Text**
   (c) **Primary Units** (d) **Alternate Units**

3. Which of the following tabs of the **Dimension Style Manager** dialog box will be used if you want to place the dimension text manually every time you create a dimension?

   (a) **Fit** (b) **Text**
   (c) **Primary Units** (d) **Alternate Units**

4. The size of the __________ is determined by the value stored in the **Arrow size** edit box.

5. When **DIMSCALE** is assigned the value __________, AutoCAD LT calculates an acceptable default value based on the scaling between the current model space viewport and the paper space.

6. If you use the **DIMCEN** command, a positive value will create a center mark, whereas a negative value will create a __________.

7. If you select the __________ check box, you can position the dimension text anywhere along the dimension line.

8. You can append a prefix to the dimension measurement by entering the desired prefix in the **Prefix** edit box of the __________ dialog box.

9. If you select the **Limits** option from the **Method** drop-down list, AutoCAD LT__________ the upper value to the dimension and __________ the lower value from the dimension text.

10. You can use the __________ tool to override a dimension value.

11. You cannot replace the default arrowheads at the end of dimension lines. (T/F)

12. When the **DIMTVP** variable has a negative value, the dimension text is placed below the dimension line. (T/F)

13. The length of a multileader landing line cannot be changed. (T/F)

14. The named dimension style associated with the dimension being updated by overriding is not updated. (T/F)

Exercises 4 Through 9

Create the drawings shown in Figures 10-48 through 10-53. You must create dimension style and multileader style files and specify the values for different dimension types such as linear, radial, diameter, and ordinate.

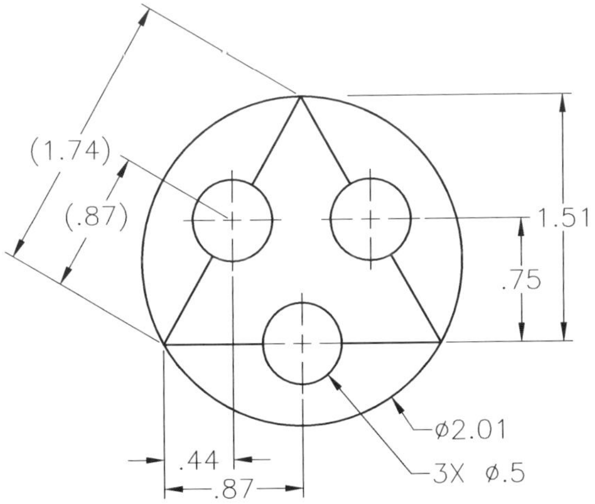

***Figure 10-48** Drawing for Exercise 4*

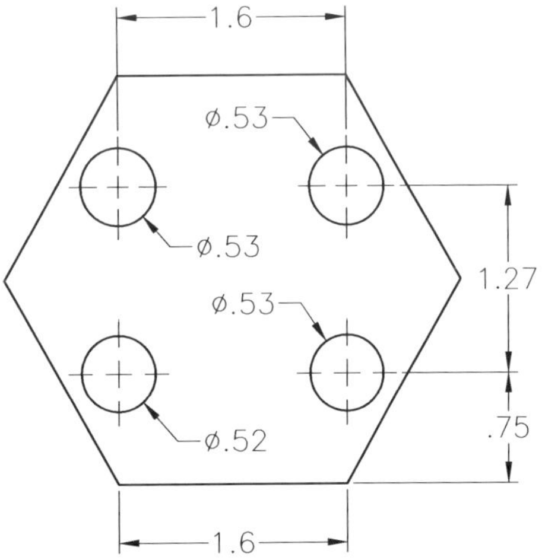

***Figure 10-49** Drawing for Exercise 5*

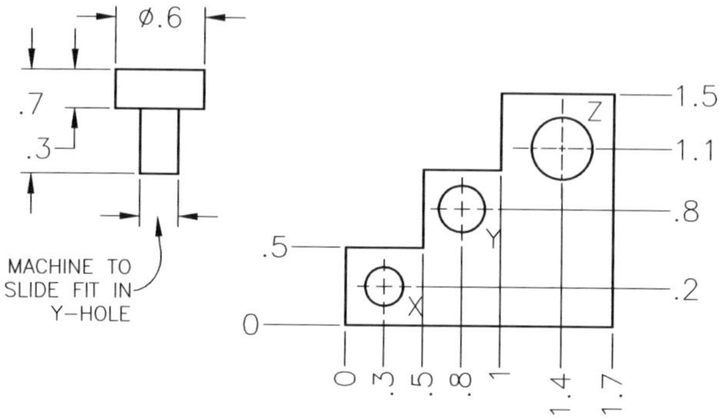

HOLE	X	Y	Z
DIA.	.25	.3H7	.40

Figure 10-50 Drawing for Exercise 6

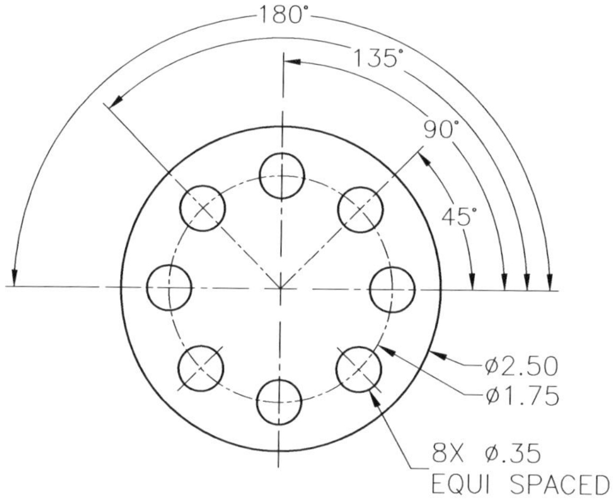

Figure 10-51 Drawing for Exercise 7

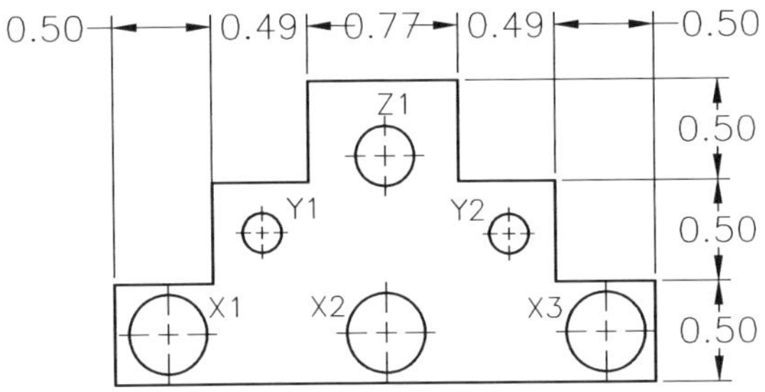

HOLE	X1	X2	X3	Y1	Y2	Z1
DIM.	R.2	R.2	R.2	R.1	R.1	R.15
QTY.	1	1	1	1	1	1
X	.25	1.375	2.50	.75	2.0	1.375
Y	.25	.25	.25	.75	.75	1.125
Z	THRU	THRU	THRU	1.0	1.0	THRU

Figure 10-52 *Drawing for Exercise 8*

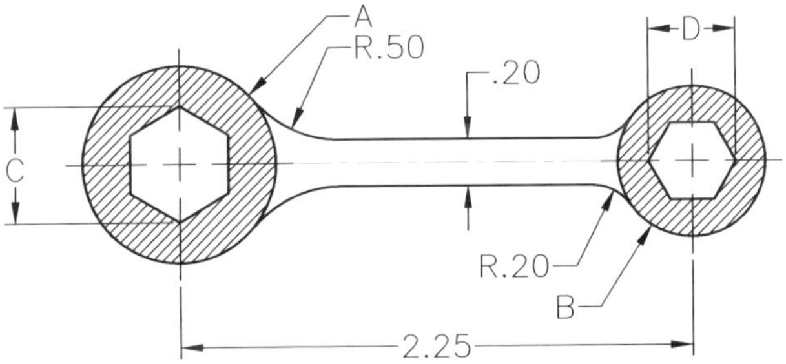

SPANNER NO.	A	B	C	D
S1	.85	.65	.50	.38
S2	1.00	.75	.59	.44
S3	1.15	.88	.67	.52
S4	1.25	.95	.74	.56

Figure 10-53 *Drawing for Exercise 9*

Exercise 10

Draw the sketch shown in Figure 10-54. You must create the dimension style and multileader style. Specify different dimensioning parameters. Also, suppress the leading and trailing zeros in the dimension style.

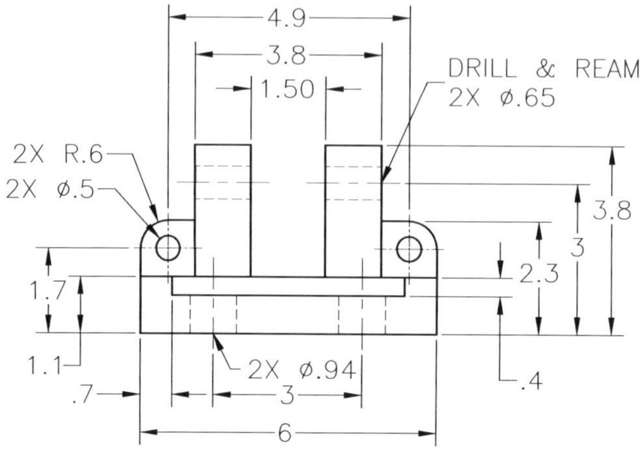

Figure 10-54 *Drawing for Exercise 10*

Exercise 11

Draw the sketch shown in Figure 10-55. You must create the dimension style and specify different dimensioning parameters in the dimension style.

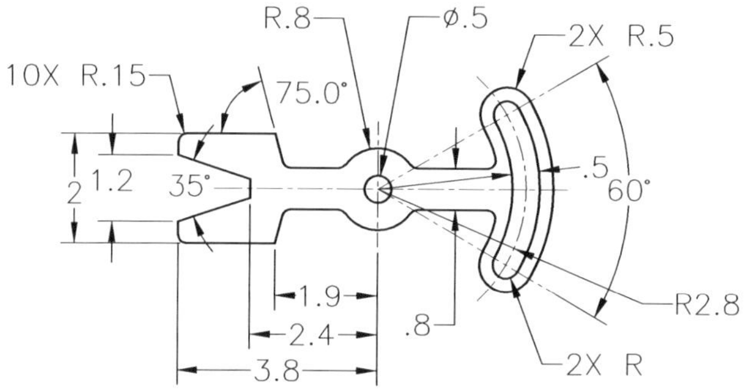

Figure 10-55 *Drawing for Exercise 11*

Exercise 12 **Dimension Style**

Draw the sketch shown in Figure 10-56. You must create the dimension style and specify different dimensioning parameters in the dimension style.

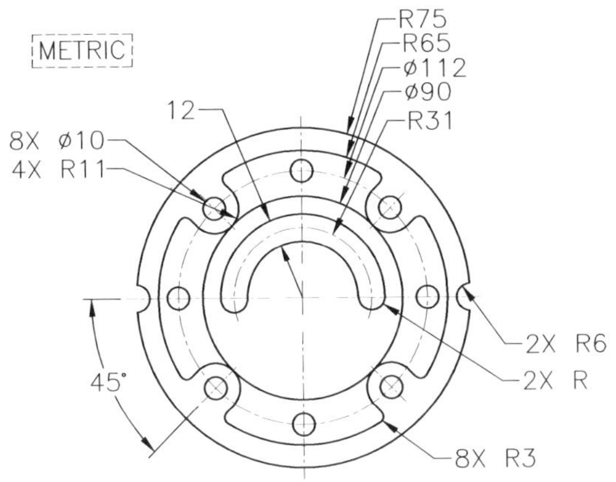

Figure 10-56 Drawing for Exercise 12

Problem-Solving Exercise 1 — *Dimension Style*

Create the drawing shown in Figure 10-57. You must create the dimension style and specify different dimensioning parameters in the dimension style. Also, suppress the leading and trailing zeros in the dimension style.

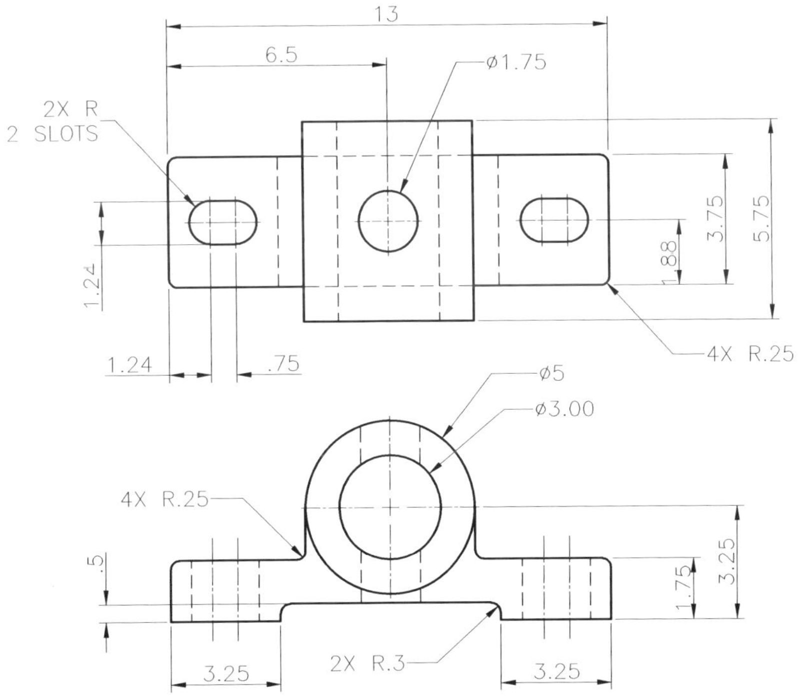

Figure 10-57 Drawing for Problem-Solving Exercise 1

Problem-Solving Exercise 2 — Dimension Style

Draw the shaft shown in Figure 10-58. You must create the dimension style and specify the dimensioning parameters based on the given drawing.

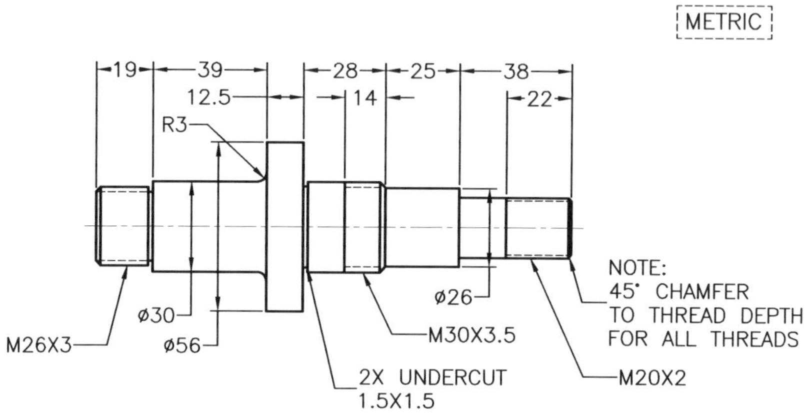

Figure 10-58 Drawing for Problem-Solving Exercise 2

Problem-Solving Exercise 3 — Dimension Style

Draw the connecting rod shown in Figure 10-59. You must create the dimension style and specify the dimensioning parameters based on the given drawing.

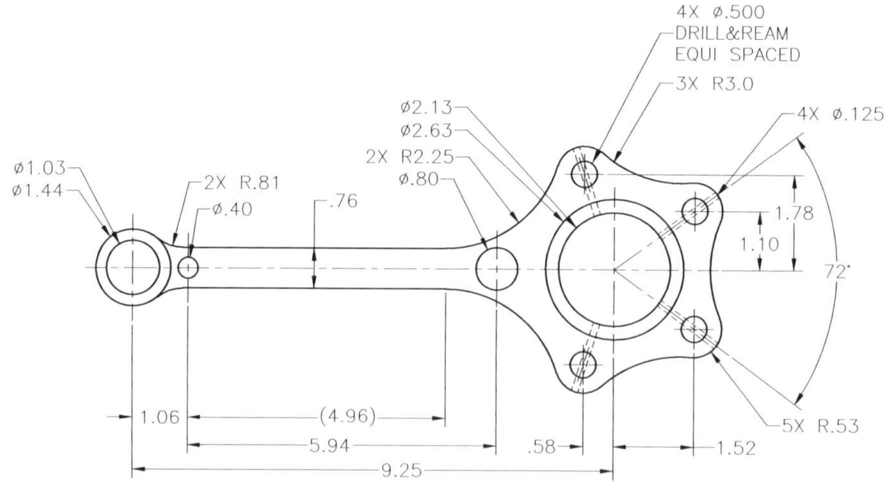

Figure 10-59 Drawing for Problem-Solving Exercise 3

Problem-Solving Exercise 4

Create the drawing shown in Figure 10-60.

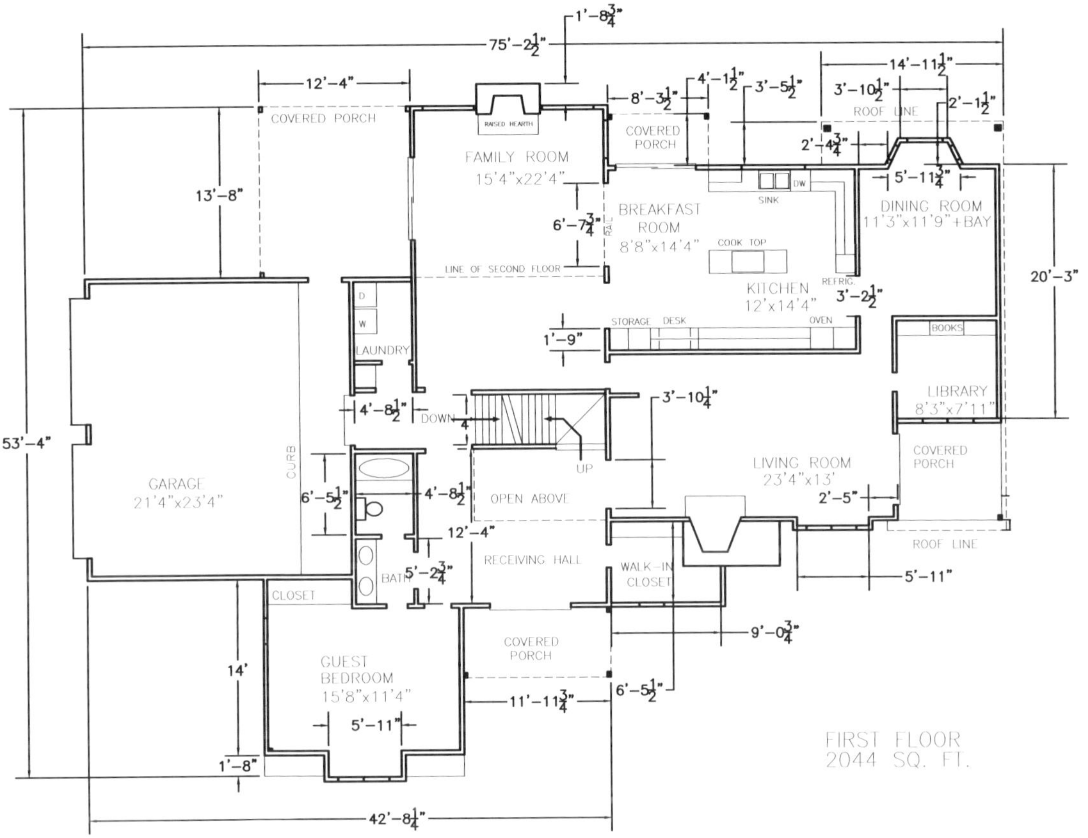

Figure 10-60 *Drawing for Problem-Solving Exercise 4*

Problem-Solving Exercise 5

Create the drawing shown in Figure 10-61.

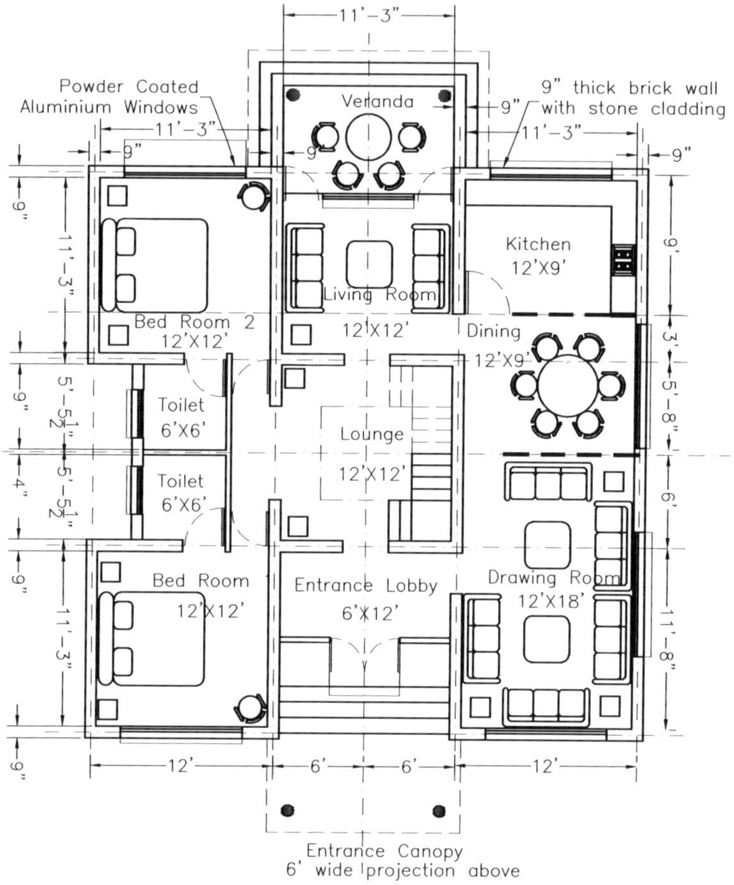

Figure 10-61 Drawing for Problem-Solving Exercise 5

Answers to Self-Evaluation Test

1. vertical, **2.** block, **3.** frame, **4.** first, second dimension lines, **5.** four, **6. Override, 7.** T, **8.** T, **9.** T, **10.** T

Chapter 11

Hatching Drawings

Learning Objectives

After completing this chapter, you will be able to:

- *Hatch an area by using the Hatch tool*
- *Use boundary hatch with Pre-defined, User-defined, and Custom hatch patterns as options*
- *Specify pattern properties*
- *Preview and apply hatching*
- *Create annotative hatching*
- *Edit associative hatch and hatch boundary*
- *Hatch inserted blocks*
- *Align hatch lines in adjacent hatch areas*

Key Terms

- *Hatching*
- *Pattern*
- *Gradient*
- *Boundaries*
- *Islands*
- *Edit Hatch*

HATCHING

In many drawings, such as sections of solids, the sectioned area needs to be filled with some pattern. Different filling patterns make it possible to distinguish between different parts or components of an object. Also, the material of which an object is made can be indicated by the filling pattern. You can also use these filling patterns in graphics for rendering architectural elevations of buildings, or indicating different levels in terrain and contour maps. Filling objects with a pattern is known as hatching (Figure 11-1). This hatching process can be accomplished by using the **Hatch** tool in the **Draw** panel of the **Home** tab or the **Tool Palettes**.

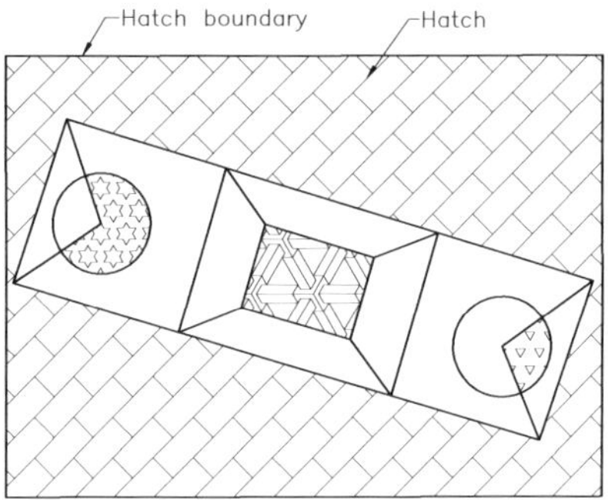

Figure 11-1 *Illustration of hatching*

Before using the **Hatch** tool, you need to understand the terminology related to hatching. Some of the terms are explained next.

Hatch Patterns

AutoCAD LT supports a variety of hatch patterns (Figure 11-2). Every hatch pattern consists of one or more hatch lines or a solid fill. The lines are placed at specified angles and spacing. You can change the angle and the spacing between the hatch lines. These lines may be broken into dots and dashes, or may be continuous, as required. The hatch pattern is trimmed or repeated, as required, to fill the specified area exactly. The lines comprising the hatch are drawn in the current drawing plane. The basic mechanism behind hatching is that the line objects of the pattern you have specified are generated and incorporated in the desired area in the drawing. Although a hatch can contain many lines, AutoCAD LT normally groups them together into an internally generated object and uses them for all practical purposes. For example, if you want to perform an editing operation, such as erasing the hatch, all you need to do is select any point on the hatch and press ENTER; the entire pattern gets deleted. If you want to break a pattern into individual lines to edit them, you can use the **Explode** tool from the **Modify** panel of the **Home** tab.

Hatch Boundary

Hatching can be used on parts of a drawing enclosed by a boundary. This boundary may be lines, circles, arcs, polylines, 3D faces, or other objects, and at least part of each bounding object must be displayed within the active viewport.

Figure 11-2 *Example of some hatch patterns*

HATCHING DRAWINGS USING THE HATCH TOOL

Ribbon: Draw > Hatch **Toolbar:** Draw > Hatch
Menu Bar: Draw > Hatch **Command:** HATCH/H

The **Hatch** tool is used to hatch a region enclosed within a boundary (closed area) by selecting a point inside the boundary or by selecting the objects to be hatched. This tool automatically designates a boundary and ignores other objects (whole or partial) that may not be a part of this boundary. When you choose the **Hatch** tool, the **Hatch Creation** tab will be displayed, as shown in Figure 11-3. Also, you will be prompted to pick internal point. Select the type of hatch pattern from the **Pattern** panel of the **Hatch Creation** tab, set the properties of the hatch pattern in the **Properties** panel, and move the cursor inside a closed profile; preview of the hatch pattern will be displayed. Now, pick internal point; the hatch will be applied. Alternatively, when you are prompted to pick an internal point, select the type of hatch pattern in the **Pattern** panel, set the properties of the hatch pattern in the **Properties** panel, and then pick an internal point; the hatch will be applied.

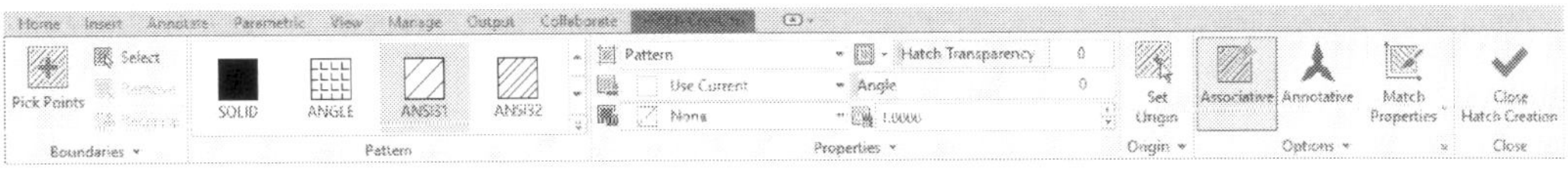

Figure 11-3 *The **Hatch Creation** tab*

Example 1 *Hatch*

In this example, you will hatch a circle using the default hatch settings. Later, in the chapter, you will learn to change the settings to get the desired hatch pattern.

1. Create a circle and then choose the **Hatch** tool from the **Draw** panel; the **Hatch Creation** tab is displayed and you are prompted to pick an internal point. Move the cursor inside the circular region; the preview of the hatch pattern is displayed.

2. Select a point inside the circle (P1) (Figure 11-4) and press ENTER; a hatch is applied, as shown in Figure 11-5.

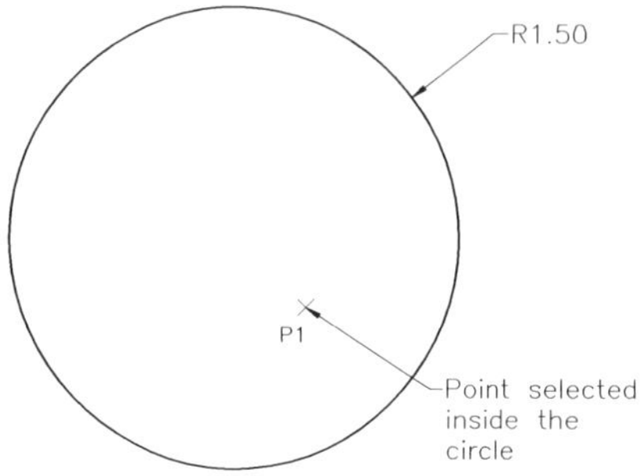

Figure 11-4 Specifying a point to hatch the circle

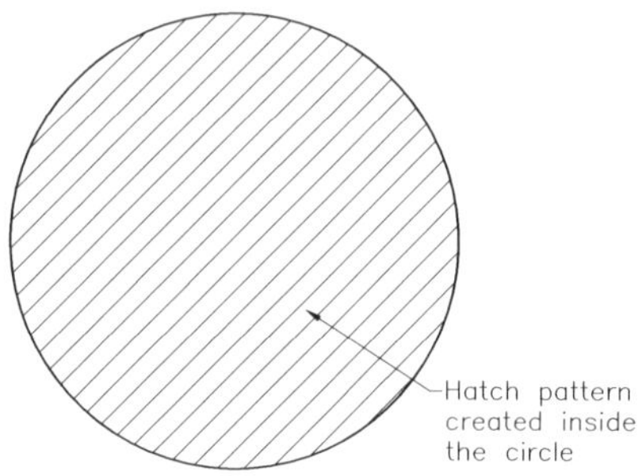

Figure 11-5 Drawing after hatching

Tip

*The **FILLMODE** system variable is set to On by default (value of the variable is 1) and hence the hatch patterns are displayed. In case of large hatching areas, you can set the **FILLMODE** to Off (value of the variable is 0) so that the hatch pattern is not displayed and the regeneration time is saved.*

PANELS IN THE HATCH CREATION TAB

Before or after specifying the pick points, you can change the parameters of a hatch pattern using various options in the panels of the **Hatch Creation** tab. These panels and their options are discussed next.

Boundaries Panel

The options in the **Boundaries** panel are used to define the hatch boundary. This is done by selecting a point inside a closed area to be hatched or by selecting the objects. You can also remove islands, create hatch boundary, and define the boundary set by using the options in this panel, as discussed next.

Pick Points

This option is chosen by default and used to define a boundary from the objects that form a closed area. After invoking the **Hatch** tool, move the cursor over a closed region; preview of the hatch will be displayed. Click inside the closed object; a boundary will be defined around the selected point and the hatch will be applied, as shown in Figure 11-6. The following prompts appear when you click inside the closed object.

Pick internal point or [Select objects/Undo/seTtings]: *Select a point inside the object to hatch.*
Selecting everything visible...
Analyzing the selected data...
Analyzing internal islands...
Pick internal point or [Select objects/Undo/seTtings]: *Select another internal point or press* Enter *to end selection.*

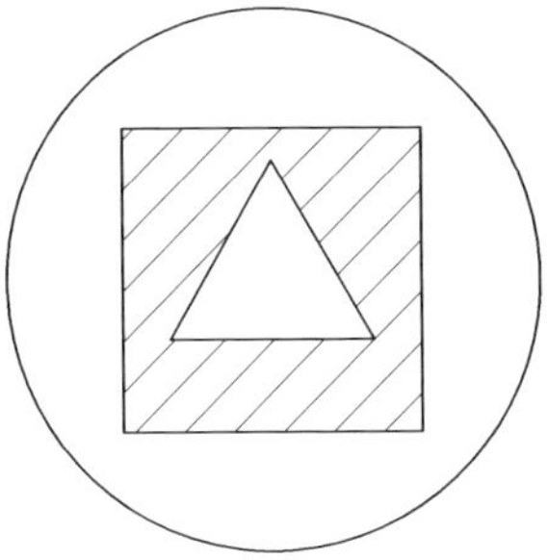

***Figure 11-6** Defining multiple hatch boundaries by selecting a point*

Tip

*You can enter **U** or select **Undo** at the Command prompt to undo the last selection made. You can also undo a hatch pattern that you have already applied to an area by entering **Undo** at the Command prompt.*

Boundary Definition Error. Sometimes, while selecting the boundary to be hatched, AutoCAD LT displays an error. This error may occur due to various reasons. AutoCAD LT displays different types of **Boundary Definition Error** message boxes depending on the kind of error occurring while selecting the boundary. For example, if you pick a point inside any boundary that is not closed, a message box will be displayed, as shown in Figure 11-7, informing that the hatch boundary is not valid. Choose the **Close** button and then create a closed sketch as boundary. You can also specify the gap tolerance value in the **Gap Tolerance** edit box in the **Options** panel so that hatch can be created if the gap is within the permissible limit. If the **Gap Tolerance** value is within the permissible limit, then while creating the hatch pattern, the **Hatch-Open Boundary** message box will be displayed informing that the hatch boundary is not closed. You can continue or stop hatching by choosing the corresponding option from the message box or you can close the message box by clicking on the **Close** button.

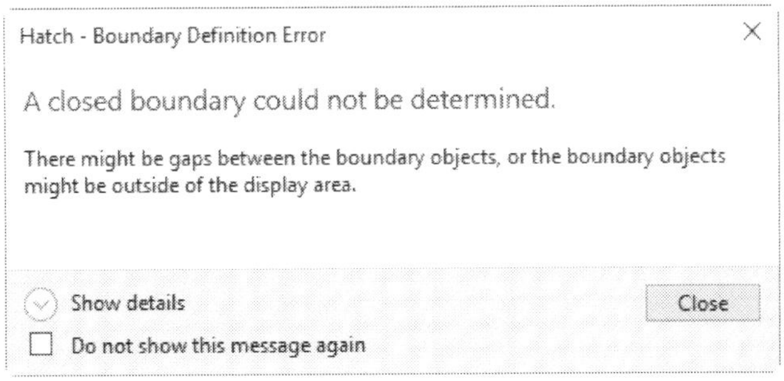

***Figure 11-7** The **Boundary Definition Error** message box*

Select

This option lets you select objects that form the boundary for hatching. It is useful when you have to hatch an object and disregard objects that lie inside it or intersect with it. When you select this option, AutoCAD LT will prompt you to select objects. You can select the objects individually or use the other object selection methods. In Figure 11-8, the **Select** option is used to select the triangle. It uses the triangle as the hatch boundary, and everything inside it is hatched. The text inside the triangle, in this case, also gets hatched. To avoid hatching of such internal objects, select them at the next **Select objects** prompt. In Figure 11-9, the text is selected to exclude it from hatching. While using the **Pick Points** option, the text automatically gets selected to be excluded from the hatching.

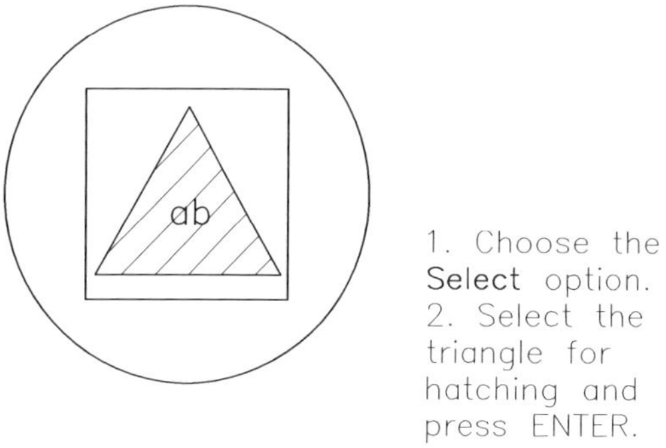

***Figure 11-8** Using the **Select** option to specify the hatching boundary*

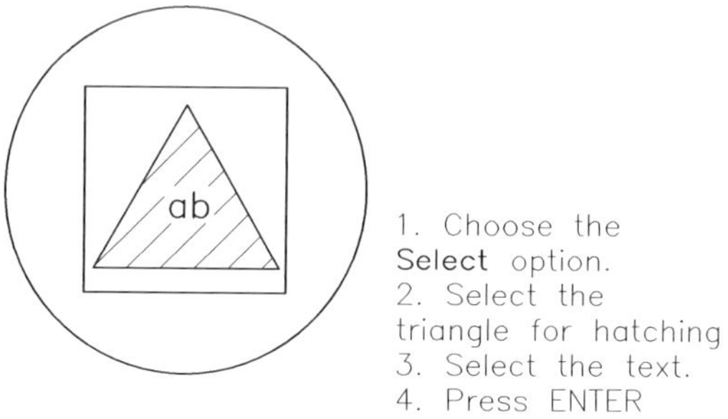

***Figure 11-9** Using the **Select** option to exclude the text from hatching*

Tip

1. If an area with many intersecting objects is to be hatched then select the entire object to be hatched rather than choosing the internal points within each of the smaller regions created by the intersection.

2. The layers containing text or lines that make the selection of hatch boundaries difficult can be turned off.

Remove

This option is used to remove boundaries and islands from the hatching area. Boundaries inside another boundary are known as islands. If you choose the **Pick Points** option to hatch an area, the inside boundaries, which are known as islands, will not be hatched by default. But if you want to hatch the islands, you can choose the **Select** option and then the **Remove** option in the **Boundaries** panel. For example, if you have a rectangle with circles in it, as shown in Figure 11-10, you can use the **Pick points** option to select a point inside the rectangle. On choosing this option, AutoCAD LT will select both the circles and the rectangle. To remove the circles (islands), you can use the **Remove** option. When you select this option, AutoCAD LT will prompt you to select the islands to be removed. Select the islands to be removed and press ENTER to return to the dialog box. Similarly, you can remove boundaries.

Tip

*It may be a good idea to use the **Select Objects** option to select the object containing islands if you want to remove the islands from the hatching area.*

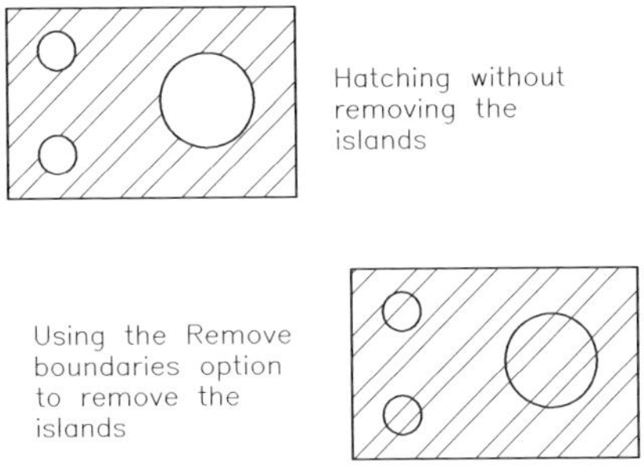

Figure 11-10 *Using the* ***Remove Boundary*** *option to remove islands from the hatch area*

Recreate

This option is available while editing a hatch and is used to recreate boundaries around the existing hatch pattern. On choosing this option, you will be prompted to specify whether you want to recreate boundaries as a region or as a polyline. You can also associate the hatch to the new boundary.

Retain Boundary Objects Drop-down List

When you select an internal point in a region to be hatched, a boundary is created around it. By default, this boundary will be removed as soon as the hatch pattern is applied. The **Retain Boundary Objects** drop-down list (see Figure 11-11) provides options to specify whether the boundary is to be retained as object or not. You can also specify the type of object either as a polyline or a region.

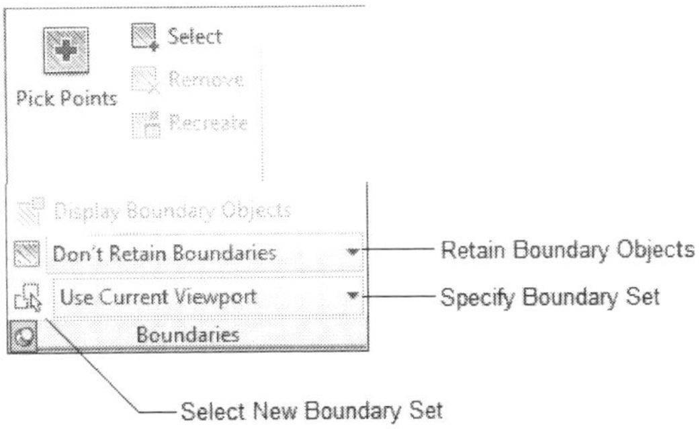

Figure 11-11 *Options in the expanded* ***Boundaries*** *panel*

Select the **Don't Retain Boundaries** option, if you do not need the boundary to be saved. In case, you need to retain the boundary, you can retain it as a polyline or region. If you select the **Retain Boundaries - Polyline** option, the boundary created around the hatch area will be a polyline. Similarly, when you select **Retain Boundaries - Region**, the boundary of the hatch area will become a region. Region is a two-dimensional area that can be created from closed shapes or loops.

Display Boundary Objects Drop-down List

If you have chosen any one of the **Retain Boundaries** option then you can choose this option to display the resulting boundary, while editing. However, the boundary will merge with the profile of the drawing object. You can use the **Move** command to view the resulting hatch boundary.

Defining Boundary Set Area

If you invoke the **Hatch** tool without forming a boundary set, then only the **Use Current Viewport** option will be available in the **Specify Boundary Set** drop-down list (see Figure 11-11). The benefit of creating a selection set is that when you select a point or select the objects to define the hatch boundary, AutoCAD LT will search only for the objects that are in the selection set.

The default boundary set is **Use Current Viewport**, which comprises everything that is visible in the current viewport. Hatching is made faster by specifying a boundary set because, in this case, AutoCAD LT does not have to examine everything on screen. This option allows you to define a boundary area so that only a specific portion of the drawing is considered for hatching. You use this option to create a new boundary set.

When you choose the **Select New Boundary Set** button, you are prompted to select the objects to be included in the new boundary set. While constructing the boundary set, AutoCAD LT uses only those objects that you select and that are hatchable. If a boundary set already exists, it is replaced by the new one. If you do not select any hatchable objects, no new boundary set is created. AutoCAD LT retains the current set, if there is any. Once you have selected the objects to form the boundary set, press ENTER; you will notice that **Use Boundary Set** gets added to the drop-down list.

Remember that by confining the search to the objects in the selection set, the hatching process is faster. If you select an object that is not a part of the selection set, AutoCAD LT ignores it. When a boundary set is formed, it becomes the default for hatching until you exit the **Hatch** tool or select the **Use Current Viewport** option from the **Specify Boundary Set** drop-down list.

Tip

To improve the hatching speed and to define the boundary to be hatched easily in large drawings, you should zoom in the area to be hatched. Since AutoCAD LT does not have to search the entire drawing to find hatch boundaries, the hatch process gets faster.

Pattern Panel

The **Pattern** panel displays all predefined patterns available in AutoCAD LT. However, the list depends upon the option selected in the **Hatch Type** drop-down list in the **Properties** panel. By default, the **Pattern** option is selected in this drop-down list and the predefined patterns are listed in the **Pattern** panel. A predefined pattern consists of **ANSI**, **ISO**, and other pattern types. The hatch pattern selected in this panel will be applied to the object. The selected pattern will be stored in the **HPNAME** system variable. **ANSI31** is the default pattern in the **HPNAME** system variable. If you need to hatch a solid by using a solid color, then choose the **Solid** option and specify the color in the **Hatch Color** option in the **Properties** panel. Similarly, if you need to create a user-defined pattern, choose the **USER** option from the **Pattern** panel and set the properties.

Properties Panel

The options in this panel (see Figure 11-12) are used to set the properties of the pattern selected in the **Pattern** panel. The different options are discussed next.

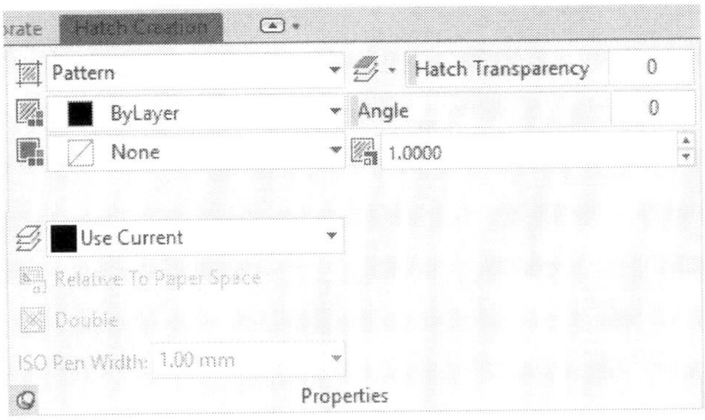

*Figure 11-12 Options in the **Properties** panel*

Hatch Type

The **Hatch Type** drop-down list displays the types of patterns that can be used for hatching drawing objects. The four types of hatch patterns available are **Solid**, **Gradient**, **Pattern**, and **User defined**. The predefined type of patterns come with AutoCAD LT and are stored in the *acad.pat* and *acadiso.pat* files. The **Pattern** type of hatch pattern is the default type. If you select the **Gradient** option from this drop-down list, the corresponding options will be listed in the **Hatch Creation** tab. These options are discussed later.

Hatch Color

Specify the color of the hatch in this drop-down list. On selecting the **Use Current** option, the color set in the **Properties** panel of the **Home** tab will be applied to the hatch.

Background Color

If you need to apply a background color to a hatch, then set a color in the **Background Color** drop-down list.

Hatch Transparency

If you need a hatch to be displayed in the transparent mode, set the transparency value in this edit box. You can also set the value by using the slider or by double-clicking in the edit box. By default, it uses the transparency value set in the **Properties** panel of the **Home** tab. If you need to change the value, then select the required option in the **Hatch Transparency** edit box. The options available in this list are **Use Current**, **ByLayer Transparency**, **ByBlock Transparency**, and **Transparency Value**.

Hatch Angle

The **Hatch Angle** slider is used to set the angle by which you can rotate the hatch pattern with respect to the *X* axis of the current UCS. The angle value is stored in the **HPANG** system variable. The angle of hatch lines of a particular hatch pattern is governed by the values specified in the hatch definition. For example, in the **ANSI31** hatch pattern definition, the specified angle of hatch lines is 45-degree. If you select an angle of 0, the angle of hatch lines will be 45-degree. If you enter an angle of 45-degree, the angle of the hatch lines will be 90-degree.

Hatch Pattern Scale

The **Hatch Pattern Scale** drop-down list is used to set the scale factors by which you can expand or contract the selected hatch pattern. You can enter the scale factor of your choice in the edit box by double-clicking in it. The scale value is stored in the **HPSCALE** system variable. The value 1 does not mean that the distance between the hatch lines is 1 unit. The distance between the hatch lines and other parameters of a hatch pattern is governed by the values specified in the hatch definition. For example, in the **ANSI31** hatch pattern definition, the specified distance between the hatch lines is 0.125. If you select a scale factor of 1, the distance between the lines will be 0.125. If you enter a scale factor of 0.5, the distance between the hatch lines will be 0.5 X 0.125 = 0.0625.

Double

This option is available only for user-defined patterns. When you choose this option, AutoCAD LT doubles the original pattern by drawing a second set of lines at right angle to the original lines in the hatch pattern. For example, if you have a parallel set of lines as a user-defined pattern and if you select the **Double** option, the resulting pattern will have two sets of lines intersecting at 90-degree. You can notice different hatching types created using the **Double** option in Figure 11-13. If the **Double** option is selected, the **HPDOUBLE** system variable is set to 1.

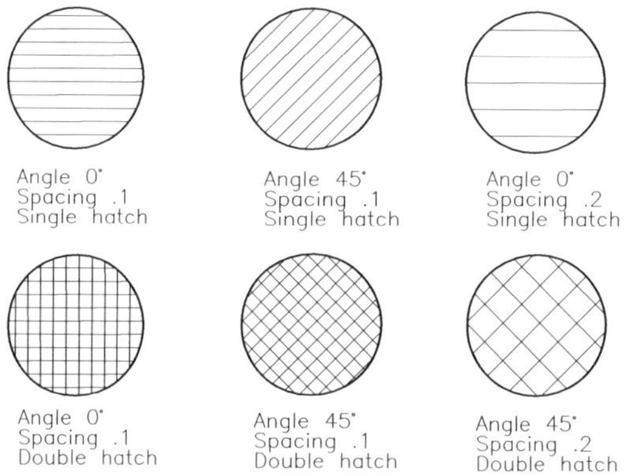

*Figure 11-13 Different hatching types created using the **Double** option*

Relative To Paper Space

This option is available only in a layout. If this option is selected, then AutoCAD LT will automatically scale the hatched pattern relative to the paper space units. This option can be used to display the hatch pattern at a scale that is appropriate for your layout.

ISO Pen Width

The **ISO Pen Width** drop-down list is available only for ISO hatch patterns. You can select the desired pen width value from the **ISO Pen Width** drop-down list. The value selected specifies the ISO-related pattern scaling.

Origin Panel

Hatch pattern alignment is an important feature of hatching, as on many occasions, you need to hatch adjacent areas with similar or sometimes identical hatch patterns while keeping the adjacent hatch patterns properly aligned. Proper alignment of hatch patterns is taken care of automatically by generating all lines of every hatch pattern from the same reference point. The reference point is normally at the origin point (0,0). Figure 11-14 shows two adjacent hatch areas. The area on the right is hatched using the pattern **ANSI32** at an angle of 0-degree and the area on the left is hatched using the same pattern at an angle of 90-degree. When you hatch these areas, the hatch lines may not be aligned, as shown in Figure 11-14(a). The options in the **Origin** panel allow you to specify the origin of hatch so that they get properly aligned, as shown in Figure 11-14(b). The options in this panel are discussed next.

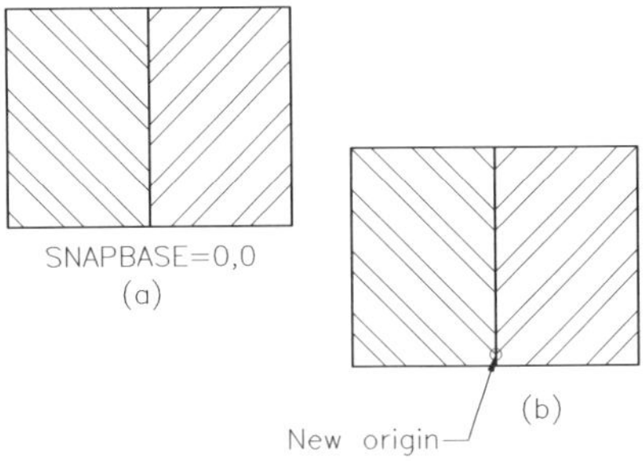

Figure 11-14 *Aligning hatch patterns using the* ***SNAPBASE*** *variable*

By default, the **Use Current Origin** button is chosen. This implies that the origin of the hatch pattern to be created is the origin of the current drawing. On choosing **Set Origin**, you need to specify the origin point for the hatch pattern in the drawing area.

You can also choose the other buttons to set the origin. For example, if you choose the **Bottom Left** button from this panel, the origin of the hatch pattern will be at the bottom left corner of the boundary. Choose the **Store as Default Origin** button to store the origin just selected as the default origin for all the hatch patterns to be created now onwards.

Note
The reference point for hatching can also be changed using the ***SNAPBASE*** *system variable.*

Options Panel

The options in this panel allow you to specify the draw order and some commonly used properties of the hatch pattern.

Associative

This button is chosen by default, therefore when you modify the boundary of a hatch object, the hatch patterns will be automatically updated to fill up the new area. But, if the hatch boundary is a region, you cannot edit the shape of the hatch boundary. One of the major advantages with the associative hatch feature is that you can edit the hatch pattern or edit the geometry that is hatched without having to modify the associated pattern or boundary separately. After editing, AutoCAD LT automatically regenerates the hatch and the hatch geometry to reflect the changes. To edit the hatch boundary, select it and edit it by using grips.

Annotative

Choose this button to create an annotative hatch. An annotative hatch is defined relative to the paper space size. The scale of the annotative hatch objects changes in the viewport or layout according to the annotation scale assigned to the hatch objects and the annotation scale specified for that particular layout or viewport.

Gap Tolerance

The **Gap Tolerance** edit box is used to set the value up to which the open area will be considered closed when selected for hatching using the **Pick Points** method. The default value of the gap tolerance is 0. As a result, an open area will not be selected for hatching. You can set the value of the gap tolerance using the **Gap Tolerance** edit box. If the gap in the open area is less than the value specified in this edit box, the area will be considered closed and will be selected for hatching.

Create Separate Hatches

If you hatch multiple closed areas that are not nested together, then on selecting this option, a separate hatch will be created for each closed area. As a result, you can edit the hatches separately. If this option is not selected, the hatch created in all the selected closed areas will be treated as single entity.

Island Detection Style

The drop-down list below the **Create Separate Hatches** option is used to select the style of the island detection during hatching. There are four styles available in this drop-down list. The effect of using a particular style is displayed in the form of an illustration in the image tile placed before the name and is also shown in Figure 11-15. To set a particular style, select the corresponding option. The four styles available in this drop-down list are discussed next.

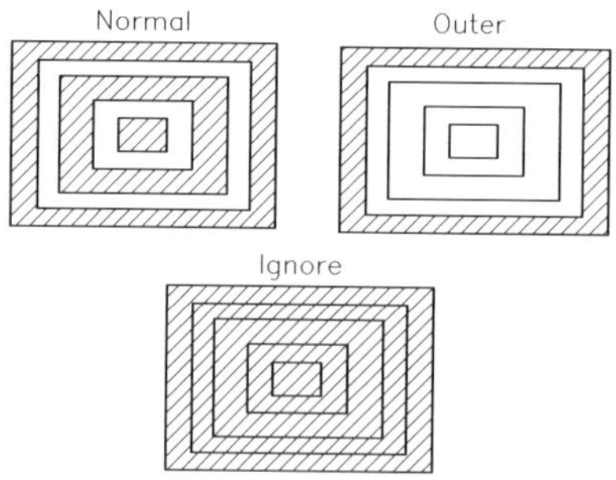

Figure 11-15 *Using hatching styles*

Note

The selection of an island detection style carries meaning only if the objects to be hatched are nested (that is, one or more selected boundaries are within another boundary).

Normal Island Detection. This style is selected by default. This style hatches inward starting at the outermost boundary. If it encounters an internal boundary, it turns off the hatching. An internal boundary causes the hatching to turn off until another boundary is encountered. In this manner, alternate areas of the selected object are hatched, starting with the outermost area. Thus, areas separated from the outside of the hatched area by an odd number of boundaries are hatched, while those separated by an even number of boundaries are not.

Outer Island Detection. This particular option also lets you hatch inward from an outermost boundary, but the hatching is turned off if an internal boundary is encountered. Unlike the previous case, it does not turn on the hatching again. The hatching process, in this case, starts from both ends of each hatch line; only the outermost level of the structure is hatched.

Ignore Island Detection. In this option, all areas bounded by the outermost boundary are hatched. The option ignores any hatch boundaries that are within the outer boundary. All islands are completely ignored and everything within the selected boundary is hatched.

No Island Detection. In this option, even if the object is nested, the individual closed boundary is hatched separately.

Tip

It is also possible to set the pattern and the island detection style at the same time by using the ***HPNAME*** *system variable. AutoCAD LT stores the Normal style code by adding* ***N*** *to the pattern name. Similarly,* ***O*** *is added for the Outer style, and* ***I*** *for the Ignore style to the value of the* ***HPNAME*** *system variable. For example, if you want to apply the BOX pattern using the outer style of island detection, you should enter the* ***HPNAME*** *value to the* ***BOX, O****. Now, when you apply the hatch pattern, the BOX pattern is applied using the outer style of hatching.*

Match Properties

The **Match Properties** drop-down list is used to hatch the specified boundaries using the properties of an existing hatch. This drop-down list has two options. By default, the **Use current origin** option is selected. As a result, the current origin will be taken as the hatch origin. If you select the **Use source hatch origin** option, the hatch pattern will accept the origin of the source hatch as the origin of the current hatch pattern.

On selecting any one of the options, the following command sequence appears. Note that you must have applied hatch to an object before invoking this option.

Select hatch object: *Select the object from which you have to inherit the hatch pattern*
Pick internal point or [Select objects/Undo/seTtings]: *Pick a point inside the object to hatch.*
Pick internal point or [Select objects/Undo/seTtings]: Enter *(The selected pattern now becomes the current hatch pattern. Hatch properties such as angle or scale of the pattern can be adjusted.)*

Specifying the Draw Order

The drop-down list below the **Island detection** drop-down list in the expanded **Options** panel is used to assign a draw order to the hatch. If you want to send the hatch behind all the entities, select the **Send to Back** option. Similarly, if you want to place the hatch in front of all the entities, select the **Bring to Front** option. If you want to place the hatch behind the hatch boundary, select **Send Behind Boundary**. Similarly, if you want to place the hatch in front of the boundary, select **Bring in Front of Boundary**. You can also select the **Do Not Assign** option, if you do not want to assign the draw order to the hatch.

Hatch Settings

You can also set the parameters discussed above using the **Hatch and Gradient** dialog box, as shown in Figure 11-16. To invoke this dialog box, choose the inclined arrow in the **Options** panel of the **Hatch Creation** tab or after choosing the **Hatch** tool from the **Draw** panel of the **Home** tab, type **T** and press ENTER when you are prompted to pick internal point. The default appearance of the **Hatch and Gradient** dialog box is slightly different from the one shown in Figure 11-16. This is because options like **Islands** and **Boundary retention** are not visible by default. To make such options visible, choose the **More Options** button available at the lower right corner of the **Hatch and Gradient** dialog box.

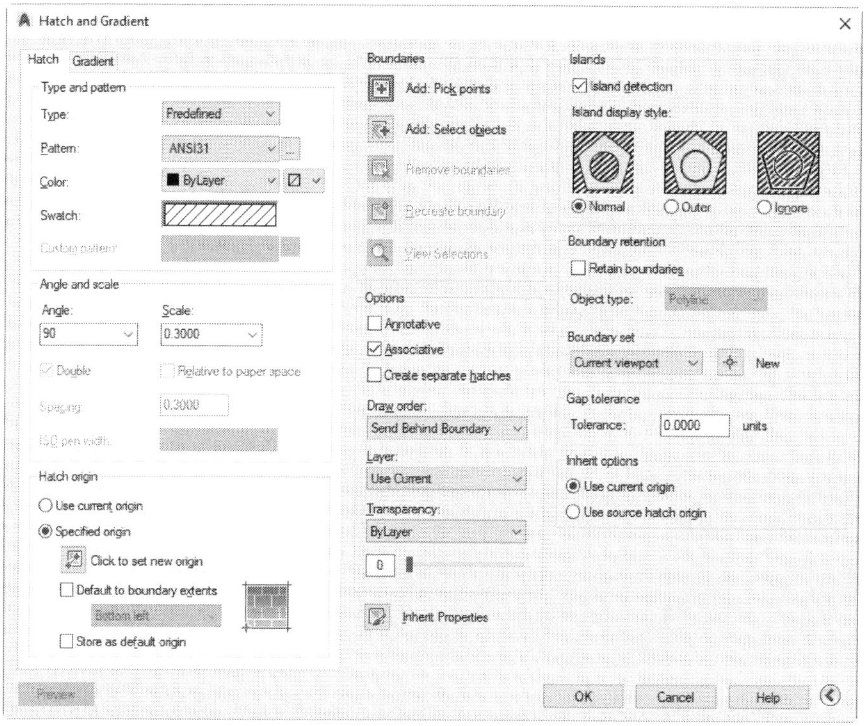

*Figure 11-16 The **Hatch and Gradient** dialog box*

Close

Choose the **Close Hatch Creation** button to close the **Hatch Creation** tab. You can also click once in the drawing area after completing the hatching process to exit the **Hatch Creation** tab.

Exercise 1 *Hatch Scale & Hatch Angle*

In this exercise, you will hatch the given drawing using the hatch pattern named **STEEL**. Set the scale and the angle to match the drawing shown in Figure 11-17.

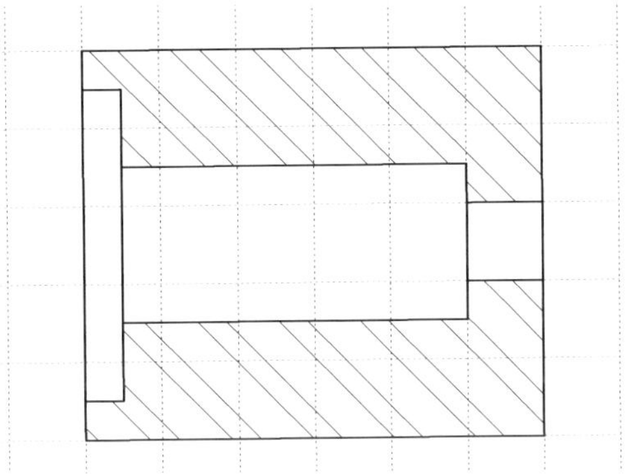

Figure 11-17 Drawing for Exercise 1

Exercise 2 Hatch Pattern

In this exercise, you will hatch the front section view of the drawing in Figure 11-18 using the hatch pattern for brass. Two views, top, and front are shown. In the top view, the cutting plane indicates how the section is cut and the front view shows the full section view of the object. The section lines must be drawn only where the material is actually cut.

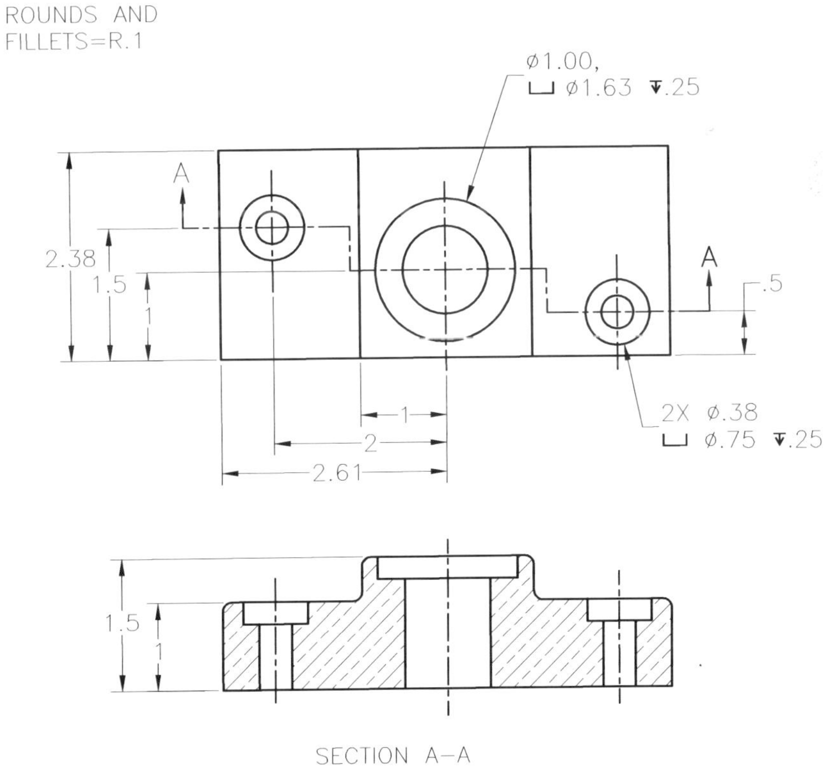

Figure 11-18 Drawing for Exercise 2

Exercise 3 — Align Hatch

In this exercise, you will hatch the given drawing using the hatch pattern **ANSI31**. Align the hatch lines, as shown in the drawing (Figure 11-19).

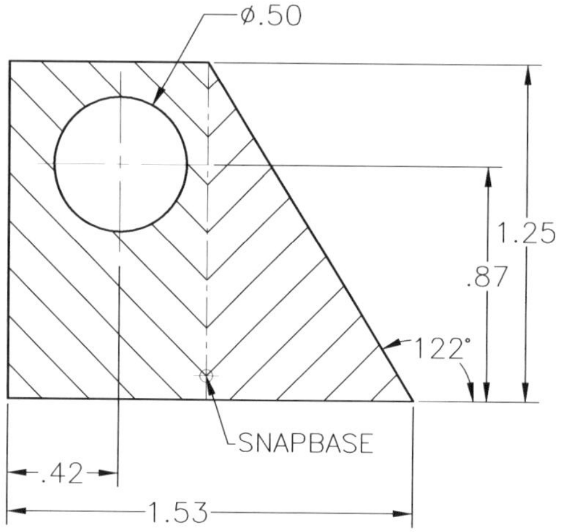

Figure 11-19 *Drawing for Exercise 3*

Setting the Parameters for Gradient Pattern

During hatching, you can select the **Gradient** option in the **Hatch Type** drop-down list to fill the boundary in a set pattern of colors. On selecting the **Gradient** option from the **Hatch Type** drop-down list, nine fixed patterns will be listed in the **Pattern** panel and their corresponding option will be displayed in the **Hatch Creation** tab, as shown in Figure 11-20. You can select the required gradient or specify the gradient pattern by entering its value in the **GFNAME** system variable. The default value of this variable is 1. As a result, the first gradient pattern is selected.

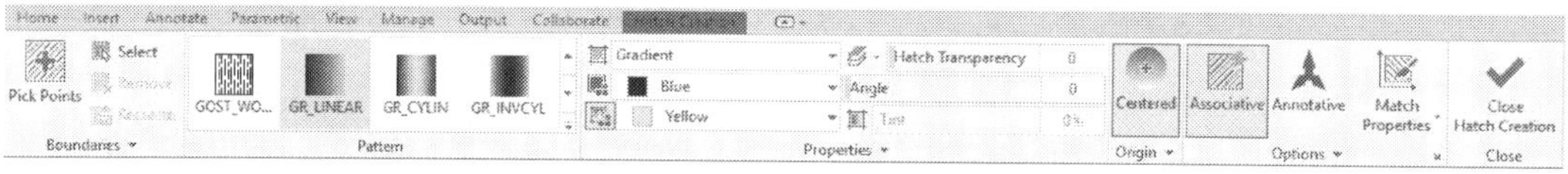

Figure 11-20 *The* ***Hatch Creation*** *tab with the options for the* ***Gradient*** *pattern*

You can set two colors for the gradient from the **Gradient Color 1** and **Gradient Color 2** drop-down lists available in the **Properties** panel of the **Hatch Creation** tab. By default, you can not set color tint for the gradient. If you need to set color tint then choose the **Gradient Colors** button available on the left of the **Gradient Color 2** drop-down list. On doing so, the **Gradient Color 2** drop-down list will be disabled. Now, you can set the color tint by using the **Gradient Tint and Shade** slider. You can set the angle of the color by using the **Gradient Angle** slider.

Using the **Gradient Angle** slider, you can set the angle for rotating the pattern of the gradient fill with respect to the *X* axis of the current UCS. You can select any angle from this slider or you can also double-click and enter an angle of your choice in the edit box. The angle value is stored in the **GFANG** system variable.

The symmetric condition of the gradient is set by choosing the **Centered** button in the **Origin** panel. If this button is not chosen, then the gradient fill is moved up and to the left.

The other options are same as discussed earlier.

Tip
To snap the hatch objects, set the ***OSOPTIONS*** *system variable to* ***1****. You can also invoke the* ***Options*** *dialog box and choose the* ***Drafting*** *tab. Then, clear the* ***Ignore hatch objects*** *check box from the* ***Object Snap Options*** *area.*

CREATING ANNOTATIVE HATCH

You can create annotative hatch having similar annotative properties like text and dimensions. The annotative hatch are defined relative to the viewport scaling; you only have to specify the hatch scale according to its display on the sheet. The display size of the hatch in the model space will be controlled by the current annotation scale multiplied by the paper space height.

To create an annotative hatch, choose the **Hatch** tool from the **Draw** panel; the **Hatch Creation** tab will be displayed. Choose the **Select** tool from the **Boundaries** panel, select the objects that you want to hatch, and enter **T** (for setting); the **Hatch and Gradient** dialog box will be displayed. In the **Options** area of this dialog box, select the **Annotative** check box and choose the **OK** button. You can also convert the existing non-annotative hatch into the annotative hatch. To do so, select the non-annotative hatch in the drawing and select **Yes** from the **Annotative** drop-down list in the **Pattern** list of the **PROPERTIES** palette.

Note
While creating the annotative hatch, pattern will only be displayed in the drawing area for the annotative scale that is set as current. To display the hatch pattern at any other annotative scale, you have to add that scale to the selected hatch using the ***OBJECTSCALE*** *command.*

HATCHING THE DRAWING USING THE TOOL PALETTES

Ribbon: View > Palettes > Tool Palettes **Command:** TOOLPALETTES
Toolbar: Standard Annotation > Tool Palettes Window
Menu Bar: Tools > Palette > Tool Palettes

You can use the **Tool Palettes** shown in Figure 11-21 to insert predefined hatch patterns and blocks in the drawings. A number of tabs such as **Command Tool Samples**, **Hatches and Fills**, **Civil, Structural, Electrical**, and so on are available in this window. In this chapter, you will learn to insert **Imperial Hatches**, **ISO Hatches** and **Gradient Samples** in the **Hatches and Fills** tab of the **Tool Palettes**. The **Imperial Hatches** list provides the options to insert the hatch patterns that are created using the Imperial units. The **ISO Hatches** list provides the options to insert the hatch patterns that are created using the Metric units. You will notice that the hatch patterns provided in both these lists are similar. The basic difference between the two lists is their scale factor. The **Gradient Samples** list provides options to add the color gradients to objects as hatch.

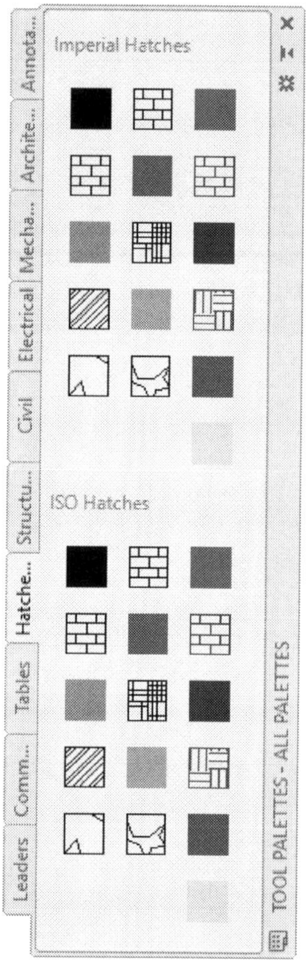

*Figure 11-21 The **Hatches and Fills** tab of the **TOOL PALETTES** window*

Tip
*The **Tool Palettes** can be turned on and off by pressing the CTRL+3 keys.*

AutoCAD LT provides two methods to insert the predefined hatchpatterns from the **Tool Palettes**: **Drag and Drop** method and **Select and Place** method. Both these methods are discussed next.

Drag and Drop Method

To insert the predefined hatch pattern from the **TOOL PALETTES** using this method, move the cursor over the desired predefined pattern in the **TOOL PALETTES**. You will notice that as you move the cursor over the hatch pattern, the hatch icon gets converted into a 3D icon. Also, a tool tip is displayed that shows the name of the hatch pattern. Press and hold the left mouse button and drag the cursor within the area to be hatched. Release the left mouse button, and you will notice that the selected predefined hatch pattern is added to the drawing.

Select and Place Method

You can also add the predefined hatch patterns to the drawings using the this method. To add the hatch pattern, move the cursor over the desired pattern in the **TOOL PALETTES** and click the left mouse button; the selected hatch pattern will be attached to the cursor and you will be prompted to specify the insertion point of the hatch pattern. Now, move the cursor within the area to be hatched and click the left mouse button; the selected hatch pattern will be inserted at the specified location.

Modifying the Properties of the Predefined Patterns available in Tool Palettes

To modify the properties of the predefined hatch patterns, move the cursor over the hatch pattern in the **TOOL PALETTES** and right-click on it to display the shortcut menu. Using the options available in this shortcut menu, you can cut or copy the desired hatch pattern available in one tab of **TOOL PALETTES** and paste it on the other tab. You can also delete and rename a selected hatch pattern using the **Delete** and **Rename** options, respectively. To update and change the image displayed on the selected hatch pattern, choose the **Update tool image** or **Specify image** option. To modify the properties of the selected hatch pattern, choose **Properties** from the shortcut menu, as shown in Figure 11-22; the **Tool Properties** dialog box will be displayed, as shown in Figure 11-23.

In the **Tool Properties** dialog box, the name of the selected hatch pattern is displayed in the **Name** edit box. You can also rename the hatch pattern by entering a new name in the **Name** edit box. The **Image** area available on the left of the **Name** edit box displays the image of the selected hatch pattern. You can change the displayed image by choosing the **Specify image** option from the shortcut menu that will be displayed when you right-click on the image. If you enter a description of the hatch pattern in the **Description** text box, it is stored with the hatch definition in the **TOOL PALETTES**. Now, when you move the cursor over the hatch pattern in **TOOL PALETTES** and pause for a second, the description of the hatch pattern appears along with its name in the tooltip. The **Tool Properties** dialog box displays the properties of the selected hatch pattern under the following categories.

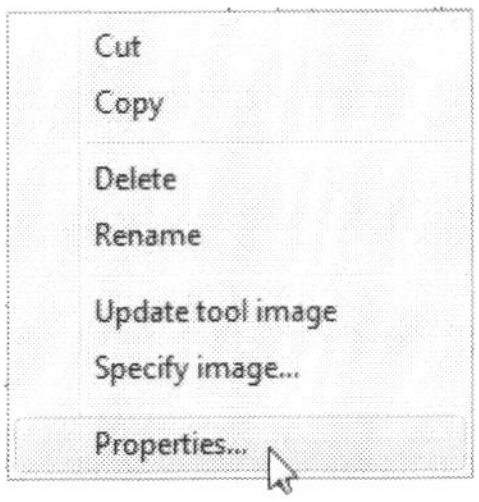

***Figure 11-22** Choosing **Properties** from the shortcut menu*

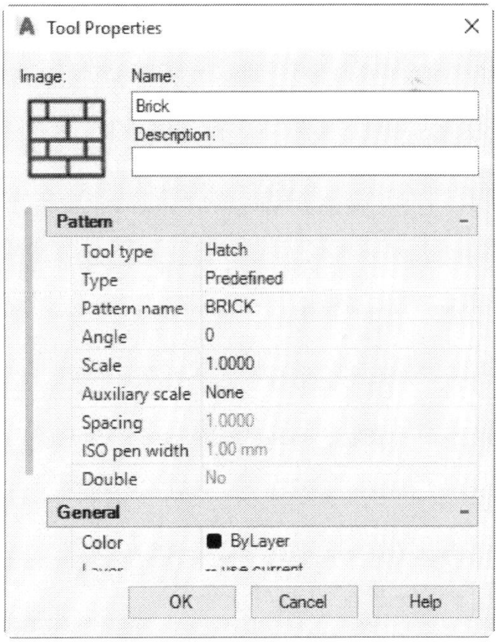

***Figure 11-23** The **Tool Properties** dialog box*

Pattern
In this category, you can change the pattern type, pattern name, angle, and scale of the selected pattern. You can modify the spacing of the **User defined** patterns in the **Spacing** text box. Also, the ISO pen width of the ISO patterns can be redefined in the **ISO pen width** text box. The **Double** drop-down list is available only for the **User-defined** hatch patterns. You can select **Yes** or **No** from the **Double** drop-down list to determine the hatch pattern to be doubled at right angles to the original pattern or not. When you choose the button in the **Type** property field, AutoCAD LT displays the **Hatch Pattern Type** dialog box. You can select the type of hatch pattern from the **Pattern Type** drop-down list. If the **Predefined** pattern type is selected, you can specify the pattern name by either selecting it from the **Pattern** drop-down list or from the **Hatch Pattern Palette** dialog box displayed on choosing the **Pattern** button. Similarly, if you select the **Custom** pattern type, you can enter the name of the custom pattern in the **Custom Pattern** edit box. If you select the **User defined** pattern type, both the **Pattern** drop-down list and the **Custom Pattern** edit box are not available.

General
In this category, you can specify the general properties of the hatch pattern such as color, layer, linetype, plot style, transparency, and line weight for the selected hatch pattern. The properties of a particular field can be modified from the drop-down list available on selecting that field. Choose **OK** to apply the changes and close the dialog box.

HATCHING AROUND TEXT, DIMENSIONS, AND ATTRIBUTES
When you select a point within a boundary to be hatched and if it contains text, dimensions, and attributes then, by default, the hatch lines do not pass through the text, dimensions, and attributes present in the object being hatched by default. AutoCAD LT places an imaginary box around these objects that does not allow the hatch lines to pass through it. Remember that if you are using the select objects option to select objects to hatch, you must select the text/attribute/shape along with the object in which it is placed when defining the hatch boundary. If multiple line text is to be written, the **Multiline Text** tool is used. You can also select both the boundary and the text when using the window selection method. Figure 11-24 shows you how hatching takes place around multiline text, attributes, and dimensions.

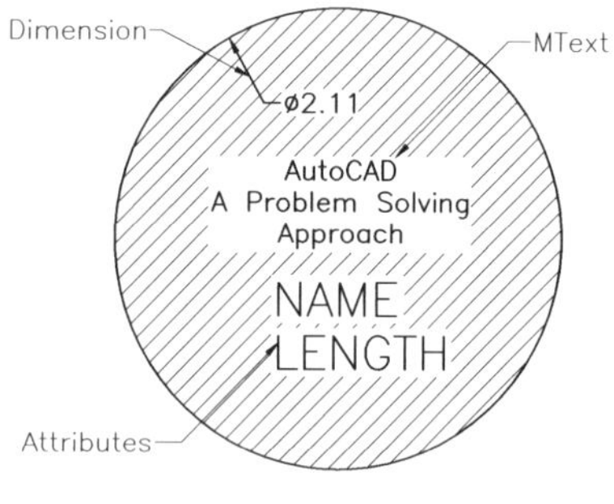

***Figure 11-24** Hatching around dimensions, multiline text, and attributes*

EDITING HATCH PATTERNS
Using the Hatch Editor Tab
On selecting a hatch pattern, the **Hatch Editor** tab will be displayed in the **Ribbon**, as shown in Figure 11-25. The panels and their options in this tab are similar to that of the **Hatch Creation** tab. Change the parameters of the hatch pattern in the corresponding panels; the hatch pattern will be modified instantaneously. Press ESC to exit the **Hatch Editor** tab.

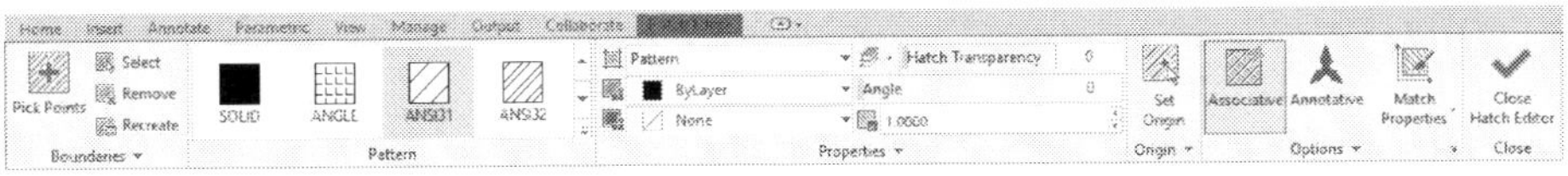

*Figure 11-25 The **Hatch Editor** tab with the options for the **Hatch** pattern*

Using the Edit Hatch Tool

Ribbon: Home > Modify > Edit Hatch **Toolbar:** Modify II > Edit Hatch
Command: HATCHEDIT/HE

The **Edit Hatch** tool is used to edit a hatch pattern. When you invoke this tool and select the hatch for editing, the **Hatch Edit** dialog box will be displayed, as shown in Figure 11-26.

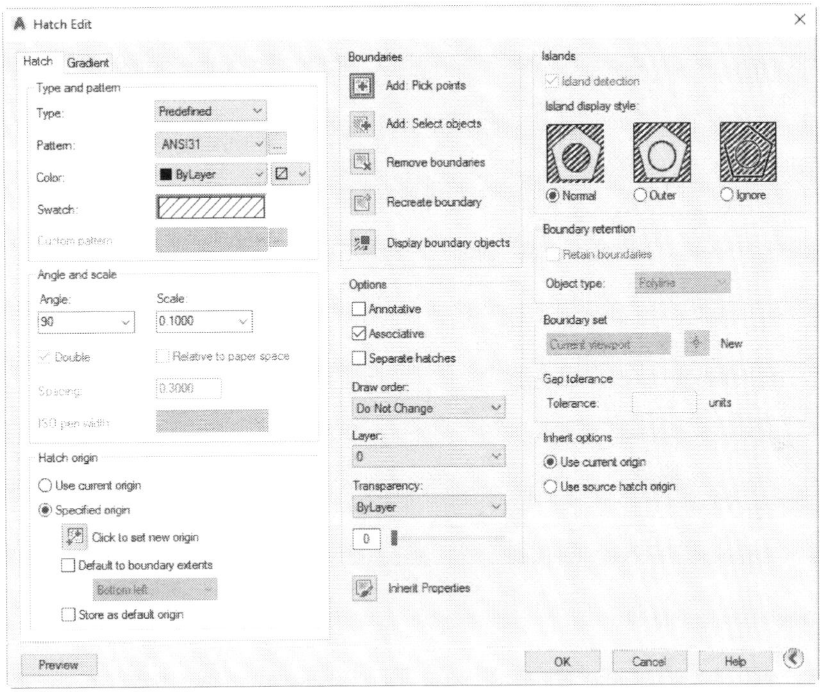

*Figure 11-26 The **Hatch** tab of the **Hatch Edit** dialog box*

The **Hatch Edit** dialog box is used to change or modify a hatch pattern. This dialog box is the same as the **Hatch and Gradient** dialog box, except that only the options that control the hatch pattern are available. The available options work in the same way as they do in the **Hatch and Gradient** dialog box.

The **Hatch Edit** dialog box has two tabs, **Hatch** and **Gradient**. In the **Hatch** tab, you can redefine the type of hatch pattern by selecting another type from the **Type** drop-down list. If you are using the **Predefined** pattern, you can select a new hatch pattern name from the **Pattern** drop-down list. You can also change the scale or angle by entering new values in the **Scale** or **Angle** edit box. While using the **User defined** pattern, you can redefine the spacing between the lines in the hatch pattern by entering a new value in the **Spacing** edit box. If you are using the **Custom** pattern type, you can select another pattern from the **Custom pattern** drop-down list. You can also redefine the island detection style by selecting either of the **Normal**, **Outer**, or **Ignore** styles from the **Islands** area of the dialog box. You can also convert a non-annotative hatch into an annotative hatch and vice-versa. If you want to copy the properties from an existing hatch pattern, choose the **Inherit Properties** button and then select the hatch whose properties you want to be inherited. You can also change the draw order of the hatch pattern using the options available in the **Draw order** area. If the **Associative** radio button in the **Options** area of the dialog box is selected, the pattern is associative. This implies that whenever you modify the hatch boundary, the hatch pattern is automatically updated. The appearance of the gradient fill can be specified using the **Gradient** tab of the dialog box. You can specify the gradient fill comprising different shades and tints of a single color or double colors by selecting the **One color** and **Two color** radio buttons, respectively. You can also specify the color of the gradient fill or the shade and tint of a single color using the color swatch and the **Shade and Tint** Slider. If the **Centered** button is selected, AutoCAD LT will apply a symmetrical gradient fill. Also, AutoCAD LT provides you with an option to select the desired display pattern of the gradient fill by selecting any one of the nine fixed patterns for the gradient fill.

Note

If a hatch pattern is associative, the hatch boundary can be edited using grips and editing tools and the associated pattern is modified accordingly. This is discussed later.

In Figure 11-27, the object is hatched using the **ANSI31** hatch pattern. Using the **Edit Hatch** tool from the **Modify** panel of the **Home** tab, you can edit the hatch using the **Hatch Edit** dialog box, refer to Figure 11-28. You can also edit an existing hatch through the command line by entering **-HATCHEDIT** at the Command prompt.

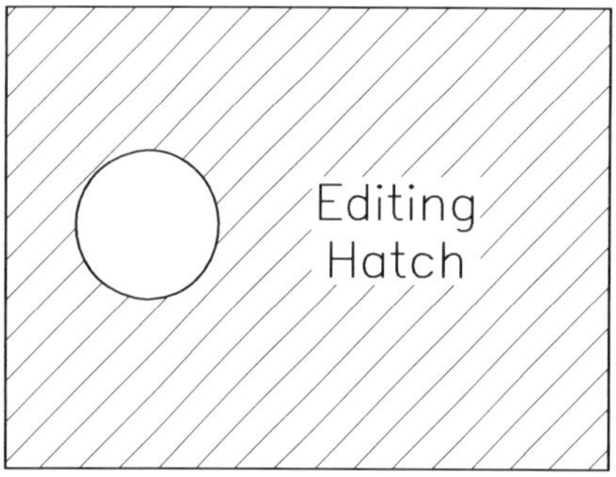

Figure 11-27 ***ANSI31*** *hatch pattern*

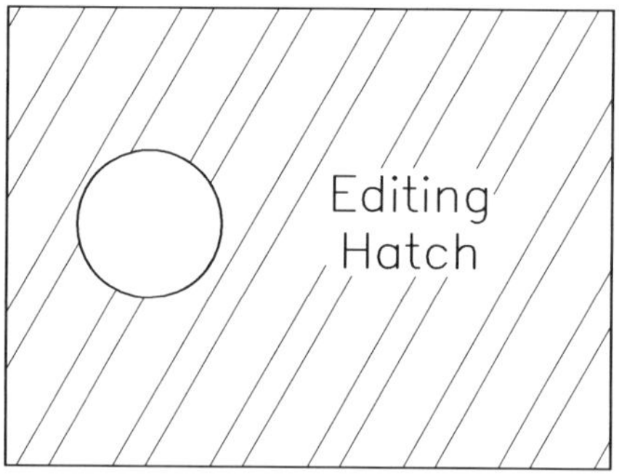

Figure 11-28 *The modified hatch pattern using the* ***Edit Hatch*** *tool*

Using the Properties Tool

Ribbon: View > Palettes > Properties **Command:** PROPERTIES/PR
Menu Bar: Modify > Properties
Quick Access Toolbar: Properties (*Customize to Add*)

You can use the **Properties** tool to edit a hatch pattern. When you select a hatch pattern for editing, and invoke the **Properties** tool, AutoCAD LT displays the **PROPERTIES** palette for the hatch, see Figure 11-29. You can also invoke the **PROPERTIES** palette by selecting the hatch pattern and right-clicking to display a shortcut menu. Choose the **Properties** option from the shortcut menu; the **PROPERTIES** palette is displayed. This palette displays the properties of the selected pattern under the following categories.

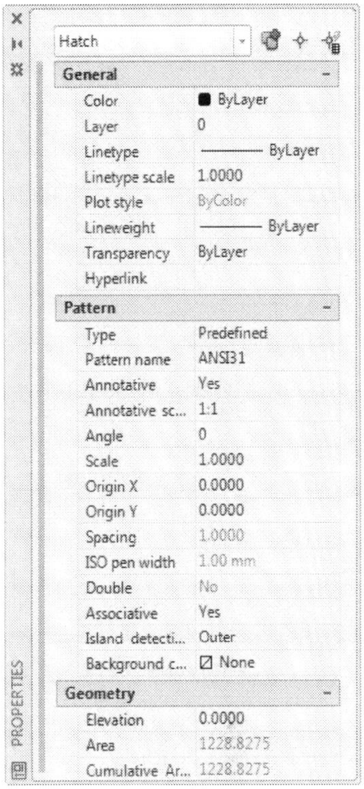

*Figure 11-29 The **PROPERTIES** palette (Hatch)*

General

In this category, you can change the general pattern properties like color, layer, linetype, linetype scale, lineweight, and so on. When you click on the field corresponding to a particular property, a drop-down list is displayed from where you can select an option or value. Whenever a drop-down list does not get displayed, you can enter a value in the field.

Pattern

In this category, you can change the pattern type, pattern name, annotative property, annotation scale (will be displayed when you choose **Yes** for annotative property), angle, scale, spacing, associativity, and island detection style properties of the pattern. In the case of ISO patterns, you can redefine the ISO pen width of the pattern modify the spacing of the **User defined** patterns. You can also determine whether you want to have a **User defined** pattern as double or not. When you choose the button in the **Type** property field, AutoCAD LT displays the **Hatch Pattern Type** dialog box, see Figure 11-30. Here, you can select the type of hatch pattern from the **Pattern Type** drop-down list. If you have selected a **Predefined** pattern type, you can select a pattern name from the **Pattern** drop-down list or choose the **Pattern** button to display the **Hatch Pattern Palette** dialog box. You can then select a pattern here in one of the tabs and then choose **OK** to exit the dialog box. Now, choose **OK** in the **Hatch Pattern Type** dialog box to return to the **PROPERTIES** palette. You will notice that the pattern name you have selected is displayed in the **Pattern** name field.

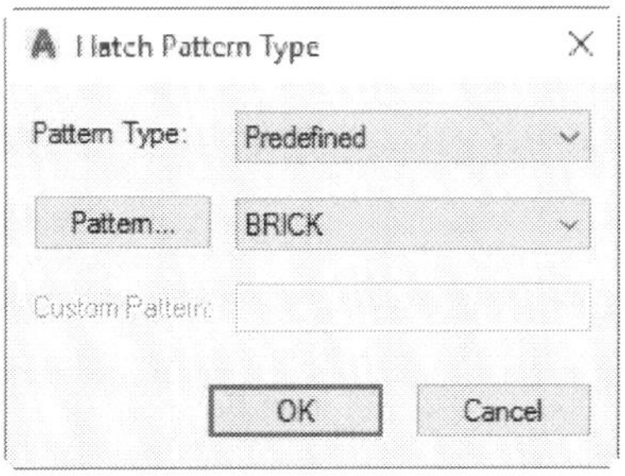

*Figure 11-30 The **Hatch Pattern Type** dialog box*

Similarly, if you select the **Custom** pattern type, you can enter the name of the custom pattern in the **Custom Pattern** edit box. If you select a **User defined** pattern type, both the **Pattern Type** drop-down list and the **Custom Pattern** edit box will not be available. When you click in the **Pattern name** property field, the button is displayed. When you choose the button, the **Hatch Pattern Palette** dialog box is displayed with the ANSI31 pattern selected. Select the **Yes** or **No** option from the **Annotative** drop-down list to convert the existing hatch into annotative or non-annotative respectively. When you click on the **Annotation scale** property field, the button will be displayed. On choosing the button, the **Annotation Object Scale** dialog box will be invoked. You can add other annotation scales to the selected hatch with the help of this dialog box. The values of the angle, scale, and spacing properties can be entered in the corresponding fields. A value for the ISO pen width can be selected from the **ISO pen width** drop-down list. For the user-defined hatch patterns, you can select **Yes** or **No** from the **Double** drop-down list to specify if you want the hatch pattern to double at right angle to the original pattern or not. You can also select **Yes** or **No** from the **Associative** drop-down list to determine if a pattern is associative or not. Similarly, you can select an island detection style from the **Island detection style** drop-down list.

Tip
*It is convenient to choose the button in the **Pattern Type** edit box to display the **Hatch Pattern Type** dialog box and enter both the type and name of the pattern at the same time.*

Geometry

In this category, the elevation of the hatch pattern can be changed. A new value of elevation for the hatch pattern can be entered in the **Elevation** field. This category also displays the area and the cumulative area of the hatch.

EDITING THE HATCH BOUNDARY

Using Grips

One of the ways you can edit the hatch boundary is by using grips. You can select the hatch pattern or hatch boundaries. If you select the hatch pattern, the hatch highlights and a grip is displayed at the centroid of the hatch. A centroid for a region that is coplanar with the *XY* plane is the center of that particular area. However, if you select an object that defines the hatch boundary, the object grips are displayed at the defining points of the selected object. Once you change the boundary definition, and if the hatch pattern is associative, AutoCAD LT will re-evaluate the hatch boundary and then hatch the new area. When you edit the hatch boundary, make sure that there are no open spaces in it. AutoCAD LT will not create a hatch if the outer boundary is not closed. Figure 11-31 shows the result of moving the circle and text, and shortening the bottom edge of the hatch boundary of the object shown in Figure 11-28. The objects were edited by using grips and since the pattern is associative, when modifications are made to the boundary object, the pattern automatically fills up the new area. If you select the hatch pattern, AutoCAD LT will display the hatch object grip at the centroid of the hatch. You can select the grip to make it hot and then edit the hatch object. You can stretch, move, scale, mirror, or rotate the hatch pattern. Once an editing operation takes place on the hatch pattern then, the associativity is lost and AutoCAD LT displays the message: "**Hatch boundary associativity removed**" in the prompt window.

While creating the hatch, the **Don't Retain Boundaries** option is selected in the **Retain Boundary Objects** drop-down list of the **Hatch Creation** panel. Therefore, all objects selected or found by the selection or point selection processes during hatch creation are associated with the hatch as boundary objects. And, editing any of them may affect the hatch. If, however, the **Retain Boundaries - Polyline** or the **Retain Boundaries-Region** check boxes was selected when the hatch was created, only the retained polyline boundary created by **HATCH** is associated with the hatch as its boundary object. Editing it will affect the hatch, and editing the objects selected or found by selection or point selection processes during the hatch created will have no effect on the hatch. You can of course select and simultaneously edit the objects selected or found by the selection or point selection processes as well as the retained polyline boundary created by the **Hatch** tool.

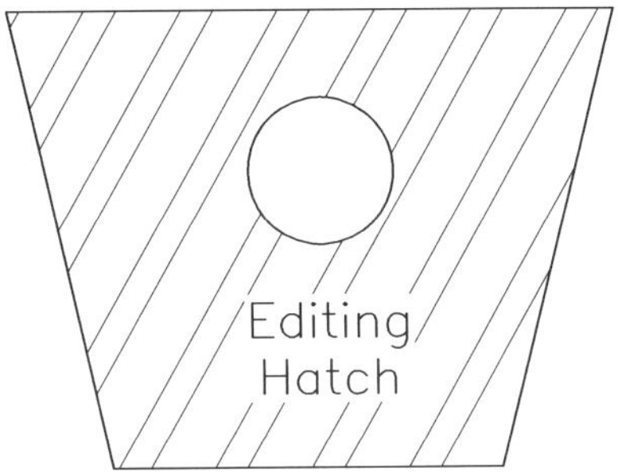

***Figure 11-31** The result of using grips to edit the hatch boundary of the object shown in Figure 11-28*

Trimming the Hatch Patterns

You can trim the hatch patterns by using a cutting edge. For example, Figure 11-32 shows a drawing before trimming the hatch. In this drawing, the outer loop was selected as the object to be hatched. This is the reason the space between the two vertical lines on the right is also hatched. Figure 11-33 shows the same drawing after trimming the hatch using vertical lines as the cutting edge. You will notice that even after trimming some of the portions of the hatch, it remains a single entity.

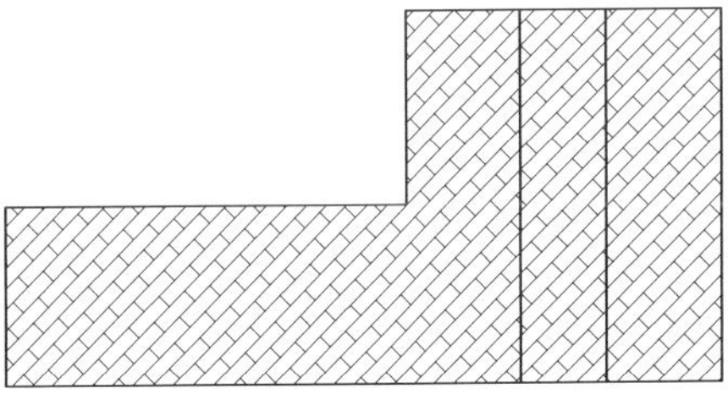

***Figure 11-32** Before trimming the hatch*

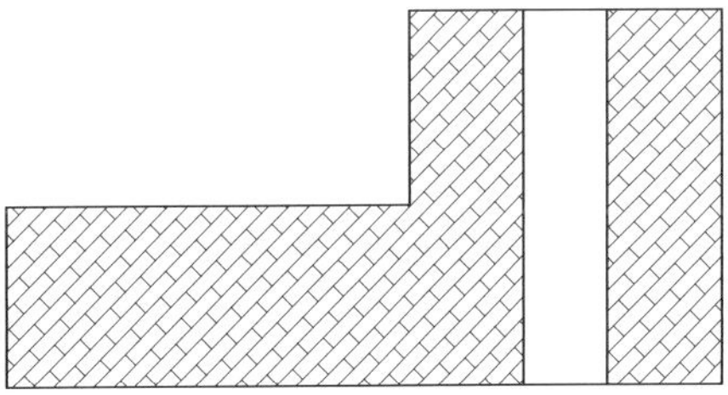

***Figure 11-33** After trimming the hatch by using vertical lines as the cutting edge*

Example 2 *Hatch*

In this example, you will hatch the drawing, as shown in the Figure 11-34, using various hatch patterns.

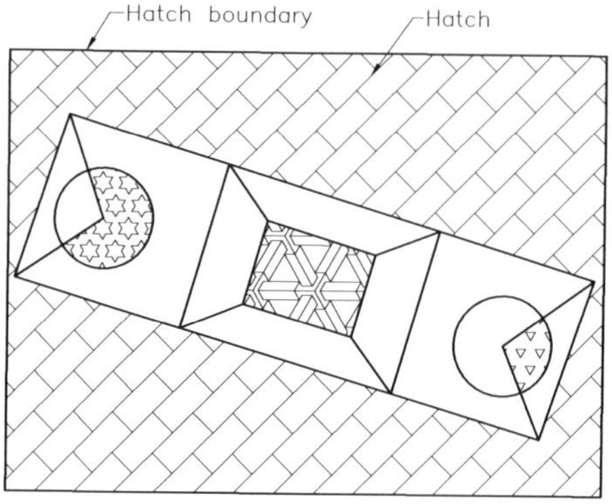

Figure 11-34 *Example 2 for Hatching*

1. Make a drawing, refer to Figure 11-34.

2. Choose the **Hatch** tool from the **Draw** panel in the **Home** tab; the **Hatch Creation** tab is displayed.

3. Select the **AR-BRSTD** pattern from the **Pattern** panel and click inside the outer rectangle's boundary to select the internal pick point.

4. Next, you need to change the angle of the hatch pattern to 45°. To do so, drag the **Angle** slider in the **Properties** panel. Also, adjust the **Hatch Pattern Scale** using the **Hatch Pattern Scale** spinner.

5. Select the **Outer Island Detection** option from the **Island Detection** drop-down list in the **Options** panel, if it is not selected by default.

6. Exit the **Hatch Creation** tab by pressing ENTER.

7. Again, choose the **Hatch** tool and select the **STARS** pattern from the **Pattern** panel; you are prompted to pick an internal point in the object. Select a point in the right section of the left circle, refer to Figure 11-34; preview of the pattern is displayed. You have to specify the values of the **Hatch Angle** and **Hatch Pattern Scale** options. After making the required changes, exit the **Hatch Creation** tab.

8. Choose the **Hatch** tool and select the **ESCHER** pattern from the **Pattern** panel; you are prompted to pick an internal point in the object. Select a point in the innermost rectangle in the middle, refer to Figure 11-34; a preview will be displayed. Adjust the scale of the hatch pattern, if required and then exit.

9. Invoke the **Hatch** tool once again and select **TRIANG** from the **Pattern** panel; you are prompted to pick an internal point in the object. Select a point in the right section of the

right circle, refer to Figure 11-34; preview of the pattern is displayed. Set the desired values for **Hatch Angle** and **Hatch Pattern Scale** and then exit.

Example 3 Hatch

In this example, you will hatch the drawing as shown in Figure 11-35. But, the hatching should be in two entities.

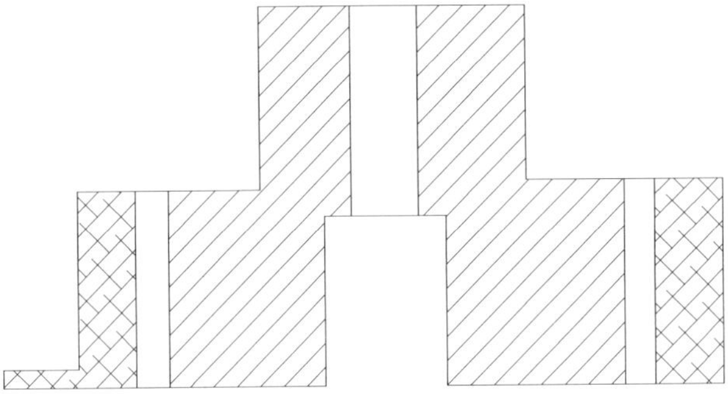

Figure 11-35 *Example 3 for hatching*

To create this kind of hatching, you have to follow the steps given below:

1. Make a drawing, refer to Figure 11-35.
2. Choose the **Hatch** tool from the **Draw** panel in the **Home** tab; the **Hatch Creation** tab is displayed. Make sure that the entities having different hatch patterns are drawn as different entities.
3. Select **ANSI38** from the **Pattern** panel; you will be prompted to pick an internal point. Select any internal point of the two outermost entities. Set the scale of the pattern, if required.
4. Press SPACEBAR to exit the tool.
5. Choose the **Hatch** tool and select the **ANSI31** pattern from the **Pattern** panel; you will be prompted to pick an internal point in the object.
6. Select the internal points of the remaining two entities; a preview is displayed. Set the scale of the pattern, if required. After making the required adjustments, exit the tool by choosing the **Close Hatch Creation** button in the **Close** panel.

Using AutoCAD LT Editing Tools

When you use the editing tools such as **Move**, **Rotate**, **Scale**, and **Stretch**, associativity is maintained, provided all objects that define the boundary are selected for editing. If any of the boundary-defining objects is missing, the associativity will be lost and AutoCAD LT will display the message **Hatch boundary associativity removed**. When you rotate or scale an associative hatch, the new rotation angle and the scale factor are saved with the hatch object data. This data is then used to update the hatch. When using the **Array**, **Copy**, and **Mirror** tools, you can array, copy, or mirror just the hatch boundary, without the hatch pattern. Similarly, you can just erase the hatch boundary using the **Erase** tool and associativity is removed. If you explode an associative hatch pattern, the associativity between the hatch pattern and the defining boundary is removed. Also, when the hatch object is exploded, each line in the hatch pattern becomes a separate object.

When the original boundary objects are being edited, the associated hatch gets updated, but the new boundary objects do not have any effect. For example, when you have a square island within a circular boundary and then you erase the square, the hatch pattern is updated to fill up the entire circle. But, once the island is removed, another island cannot be added, since it was not calculated as a part of the original set of boundary objects.

HATCHING BLOCKS AND XREF DRAWINGS

When you apply hatching to inserted blocks and xref drawings, their internal structure is treated as if the block or xref drawing were composed of independent objects. This means that if you have inserted a block that consists of a circle within a rectangle and you want the internal circle to be hatched, you need to invoke the **Hatch** tool and then specify a point within the circle to generate the hatch, refer to Figure 11-36. However, if you choose the **Select** option from the **Boundaries** panel of the **Hatch Creation** tab, you will be prompted to select an object. Select an object; the entire block will be selected and a hatch will be created, as shown in Figure 11-36.

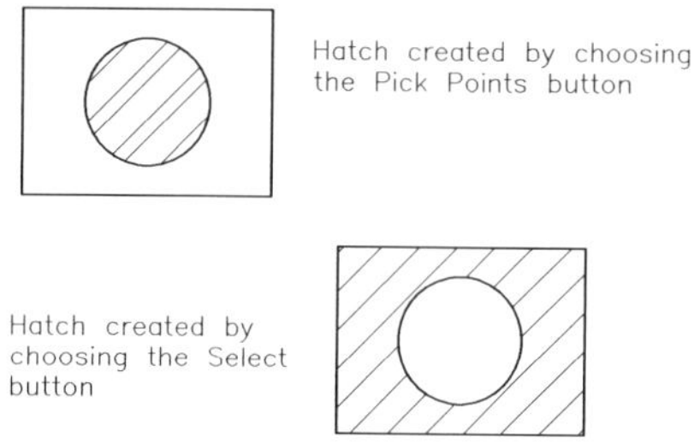

Figure 11-36 *Hatching inserted blocks*

When you xref a drawing, you can hatch any part of the drawing that is visible. Also, if you hatch an xref drawing and then use the **XCLIP** command to clip it, the hatch pattern is not clipped, although the hatch boundary associativity is removed. Similarly, when you detach the xref drawing, the hatch pattern and its boundaries are not detached, although the hatch boundary associativity is removed.

CREATING A BOUNDARY USING CLOSED LOOPS

Ribbon: Home > Draw > Boundary **Command:** BOUNDARY/BO
Menu Bar: Draw > Boundary

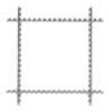

The **Boundary** tool is used to create a polyline or region around a selected point within a closed area, in a manner similar to the one used for defining a hatch boundary. When this tool is invoked, AutoCAD LT displays the **Boundary Creation** dialog box, as shown in Figure 11-37.

The options in the **Boundary Creation** dialog box are similar to those in the **Boundaries** panel of the **Hatch Creation** tab discussed earlier. Although, only the options related to boundary selections are available, the **Pick Points** button in the **Boundary Creation** dialog box is used to create a boundary by selecting a point inside the object, whose boundary you want to create.

When you choose the **Pick Points** button, the dialog box disappears temporarily and you are prompted to select the internal point. Select a point that lies within the boundary of the object.

Once you select an internal point, a polyline or a region will be formed around the boundary (Figure 11-38). To end this process, press ENTER or right-click at the **Pick internal point** prompt. Whether the boundary created is a polyline or a region is determined by the option you have selected from the **Object type** drop-down list in the **Boundary retention** area. **Polyline** is the default option. You can edit the boundary that has been created with the editing tools. The boundary is selected by using the **Last** object selection option.

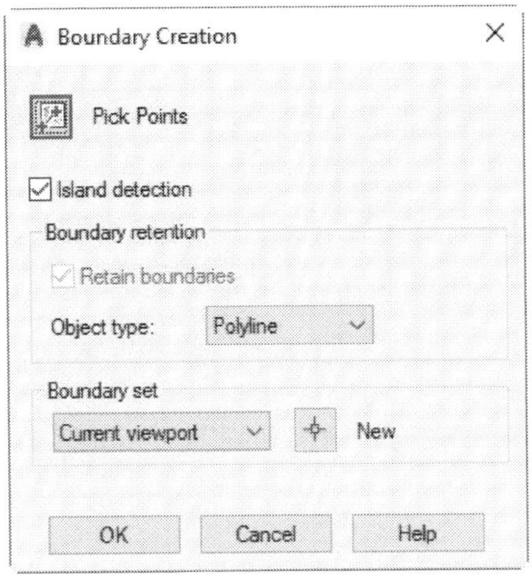

Figure 11-37 The ***Boundary Creation*** *dialog box*

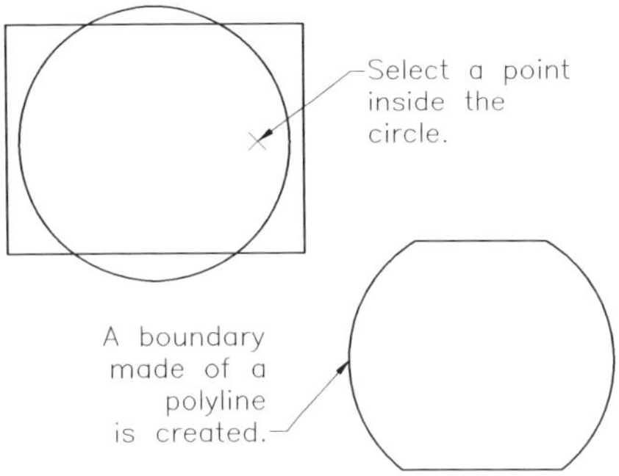

Figure 11-38 Using the ***Boundary*** *tool to create a polyline boundary*

Similar to the **Hatch** tool, you can also define a boundary set here by choosing the **New** button in the **Boundary set** area of the dialog box. The dialog box will temporarily close to allow you to select objects to be used to create a boundary. The default boundary set is current viewport, which means everything visible in the current viewport consists of the boundary set. As discussed earlier, the boundary set option is especially useful when you are working with large and complex drawings, where examining everything on the screen becomes a time-consuming process.

The **Boundary Creation** dialog box also provides you the option of determining the island detection method. The **Island detection** check box is available below the **Pick Points** button and it is selected by default. As a result, the Island detection method is Flood type and islands are included as boundary objects. If you clear this check box, the Ray casting method of island detection is enabled, where rays shall be cast from the selected internal point in all directions (by default, using the dialog box). The nearest closed object it encounters is used for boundary creation. If the selected point does not lie within the encountered boundary, a **Boundary Definition Error** dialog box is displayed and you have to select another internal point.

Note

The ***HPBOUND*** *system variable controls the type of boundary object created using the* ***Boundary*** *tool. If its value is 1, the object created is a polyline and if its value is 0, the object created is a region.*

OTHER FEATURES OF HATCHING

1. In AutoCAD LT, the hatch patterns are separate objects. The objects store the information about the hatch pattern boundary with reference to the geometry that defines the pattern for each hatch object.

2. When you save a drawing, the hatch patterns are stored with the drawing. Therefore, the hatch patterns can be updated even if the hatch pattern file that contains the definitions of hatch patterns is not available.

3. If the system variable **FILLMODE** is 0 (Off), the hatch patterns are not displayed. To see the effect of a changed **FILLMODE** value, you must use the **REGEN** command to regenerate the drawing after the value has been changed.

4. You can edit the boundary of a hatch pattern even when the hatch pattern is not visible (**FILLMODE**=0).

5. When you save an AutoCAD LT drawing in Release 12 format (DXF), the hatch objects are automatically converted to Release 12 hatch blocks.

6. You can use the **CONVERT** command to change the pre-release hatch patterns to AutoCAD LT 2020 objects. You can also use this command to change the pre-Release 16 polylines to AutoCAD LT optimized format to save memory and disk space.

Exercise 4 — *Boundary*

See Figure 11-39 and then create the drawing shown in Figure 11-40 using the **Boundary** tool to create a hatch boundary. Copy the boundary from the drawing shown in Figure 11-40, and then hatch.

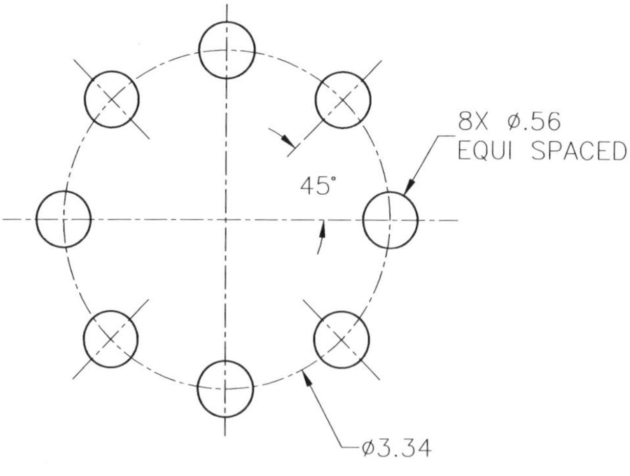

Figure 11-39 *Drawing for Exercise 4*

Figure 11-40 *Final drawing for Exercise 4*

Self-Evaluation Test

Answer the following questions and then compare them to those given at the end of this chapter:

1. If you need to hatch a drawing that has a gap, then specify the gap value in the __________ edit box in the **Hatch Creation** tab.

2. One of the ways to specify a hatch pattern from the group of stored hatch patterns is by selecting an option from the __________ drop-down list.

3. The value that you enter in the __________ edit box lets you rotate a hatch pattern with respect to the *X* axis of the current UCS.

4. The __________ option in the **Hatch Creation** tab lets you select the objects that form a boundary for hatching.

5. While hatching, you can select the __________ option from the **Hatch Type** drop-down list to fill the boundary in a set pattern of colors.

6. The **ISO Pen Width** drop-down list is available in the **Hatch Creation** tab only for the __________ patterns.

7. Different filling patterns make it possible to distinguish between different parts or components of an object. (T/F)

8. If AutoCAD LT does not find the entered pattern in the *acad.pat* file, it searches for it in a file with the same name as the pattern. (T/F)

9. When a boundary set is formed, it does not become the default boundary set for hatching. (T/F)

10. You can edit the hatch boundary and the associated hatch pattern by using grips. (T/F)

Review Questions

Answer the following questions:

1. Which of the following system variables has to be set to 1 if the **Double** hatch box is selected?

   (a) **HPSPACE** (b) **HPDOUBLE**
   (c) **HPANG** (d) **HPSCALE**

2. For which of the following hatch patterns will the **ISO pen width** drop-down list be available?

   (a) **ANSI** (b) **Predefined**
   (c) **Custom** (d) **ISO**

3. Which of the following options should be chosen if you want to have the same hatching pattern, style, and properties as that of the existing hatch?

   (a) **Match Properties** (b) **Select**
   (c) **Pick points** (d) **Inherit Properties**

4. Which of the following variables can be used to align the hatches in adjacent hatch areas?

   (a) **SNAPBASE** (b) **FILLMODE**
   (c) **SNAPANG** (d) **HPANG**

5. In which of the following system variables will the specified hatch spacing value be stored?

   (a) **HPDOUBLE** (b) **HPANG**
   (c) **HPSCALE** (d) **HPSPACE**

6. One of the advantages of using the _________ tool is that you don't have to select each object comprising the boundary of the area you want to hatch, as in the case of the _________ tool.

7. To select a custom hatch pattern, first select **Custom** from the **Type** drop-down list and then select the name of a previously stored hatch pattern from the _________ drop-down list.

8. There are three hatching styles available in AutoCAD LT. They are solid, _________, and _________.

9. If you select the _________ options from the **Islands** area, all the areas bounded by the outermost boundary are hatched, ignoring any hatch boundaries that lie within the outer boundary.

10. The **Hatch** tool does not allow you to hatch a region enclosed within a boundary (closed area) by selecting a point inside the boundary. (T/F)

11. The **Boundary Definition Error** message box is displayed if AutoCAD LT finds that the selected point is not inside the boundary or that the boundary is not closed. (T/F)

12. The **Tolerance** edit box is used to set the value up to which the open area will be considered closed when selected for hatching using the **Pick Points** method. (T/F)

13. When you use editing tools such as **Move**, **Scale**, **Stretch**, and **Rotate**, the associativity is lost even if all the boundary objects are selected. (T/F)

14. The hatching procedure in AutoCAD LT does not work on inserted blocks. (T/F)

15. Patterns drawn using the **Hatch** tool are associative. (T/F)

Exercise 5 Hatch Pattern

Hatch the drawings shown in Figures 11-41 and 11-42 using the hatch pattern to match.

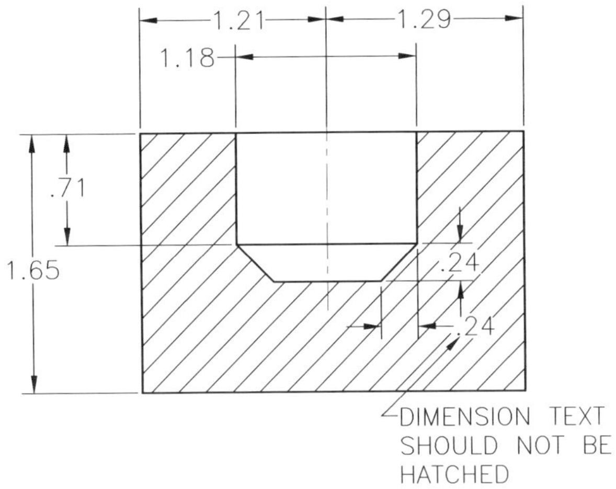

Figure 11-41 Drawing for Exercise 5

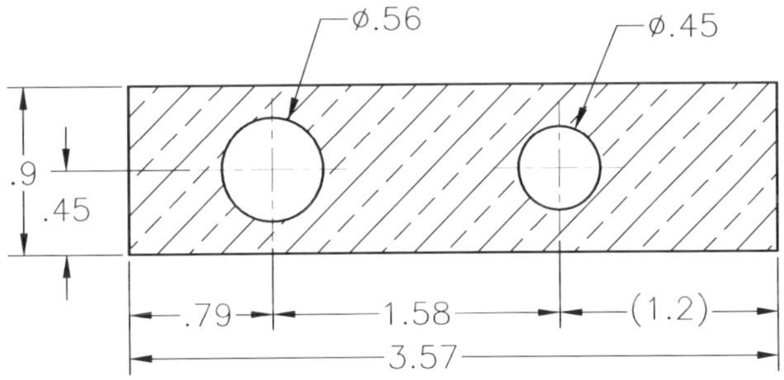

Figure 11-42 Drawing for Exercise 5

Exercise 6 Hatch Align

Hatch the drawing, as shown in Figure 11-43, using the hatch pattern **ANSI31**. Use the **SNAPBASE** variable to align the hatch lines, as shown in the drawing.

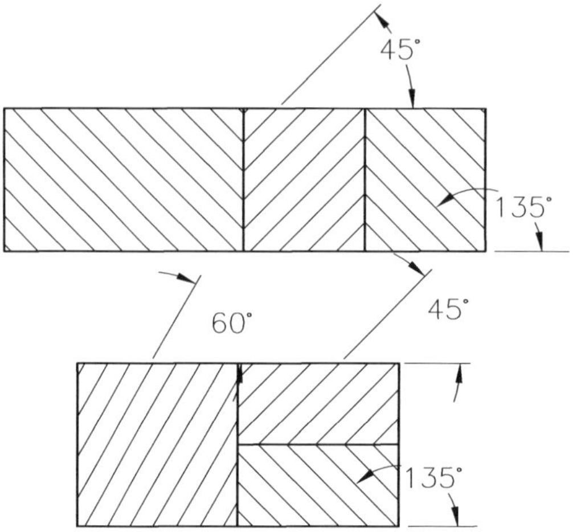

***Figure 11-43** Drawing for Exercise 6*

Exercise 7 — Hatch

Figure 11-44 shows the top and front views of an object. It also shows the cutting plane line. Based on the cutting plane line, hatch the front views in section. Use the hatch pattern of your choice.

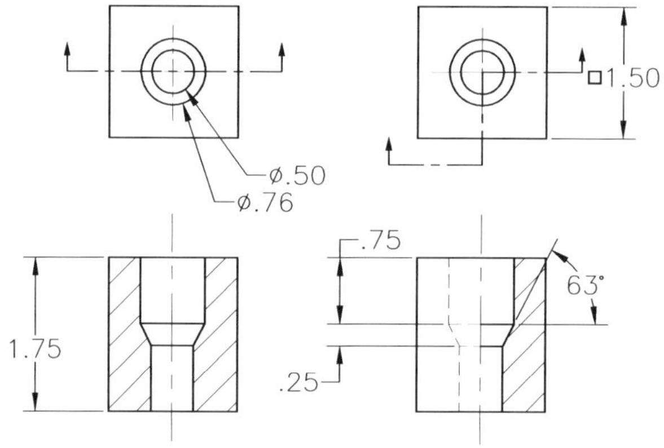

***Figure 11-44** Drawing for Exercise 7*

Exercise 8 — Hatch

Figure 11-45 shows the top and front views of an object. Hatch the front view in full section. Use the hatch pattern of your choice.

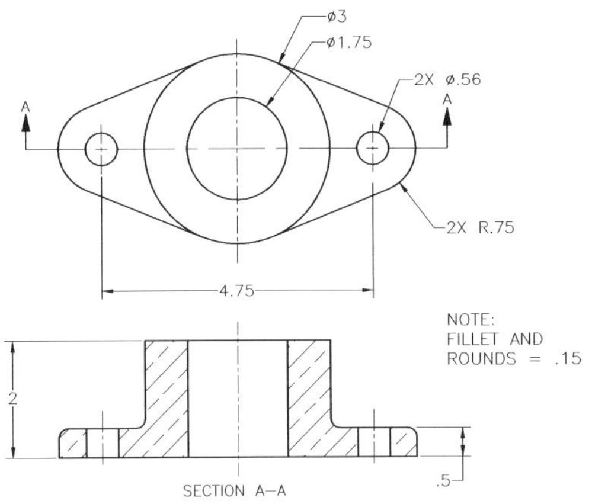

Figure 11-45 Drawing for Exercise 8

Exercise 9 **Hatch**

Figure 11-46 shows the front and side views of an object. Hatch the side view in half section. Use the hatch pattern of your choice.

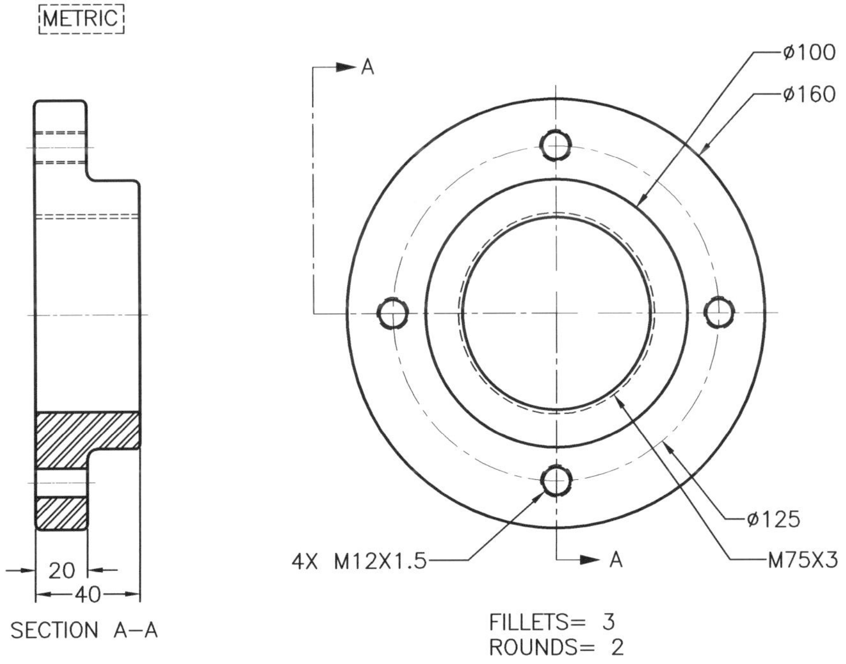

Figure 11-46 Drawing for Exercise 9

Exercise 10 Hatch

Figure 11-47 shows the front view with the broken section and top views of an object. Hatch the front view as shown. Use the hatch pattern of your choice.

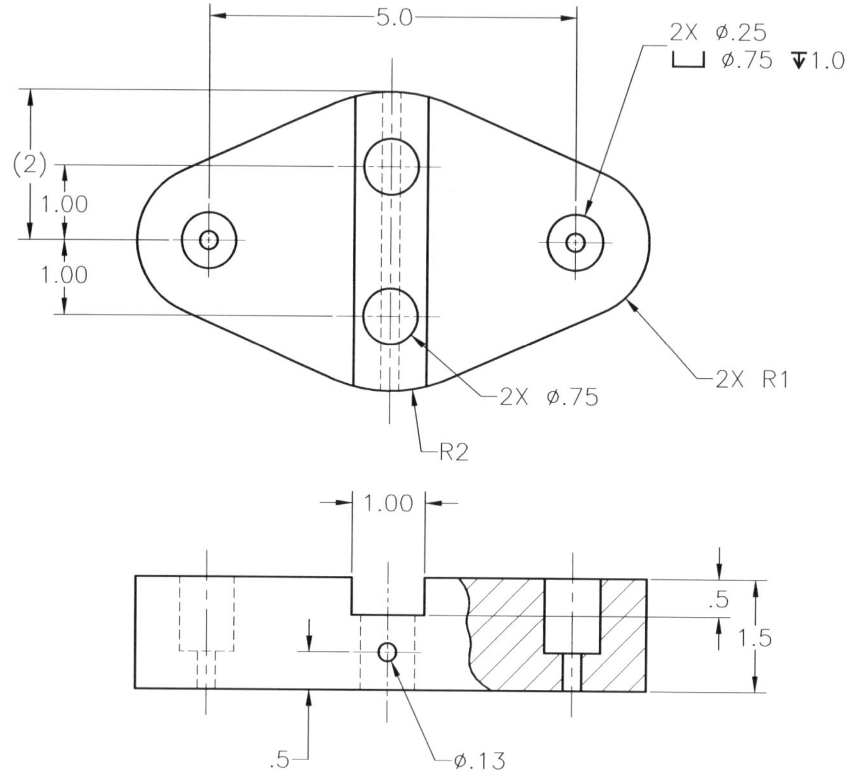

Figure 11-47 *Drawing for Exercise 10*

Exercise 11 *Hatch*

Figure 11-48 shows the front, top, and side views of an object. Hatch the side view in section using the hatch pattern of your choice.

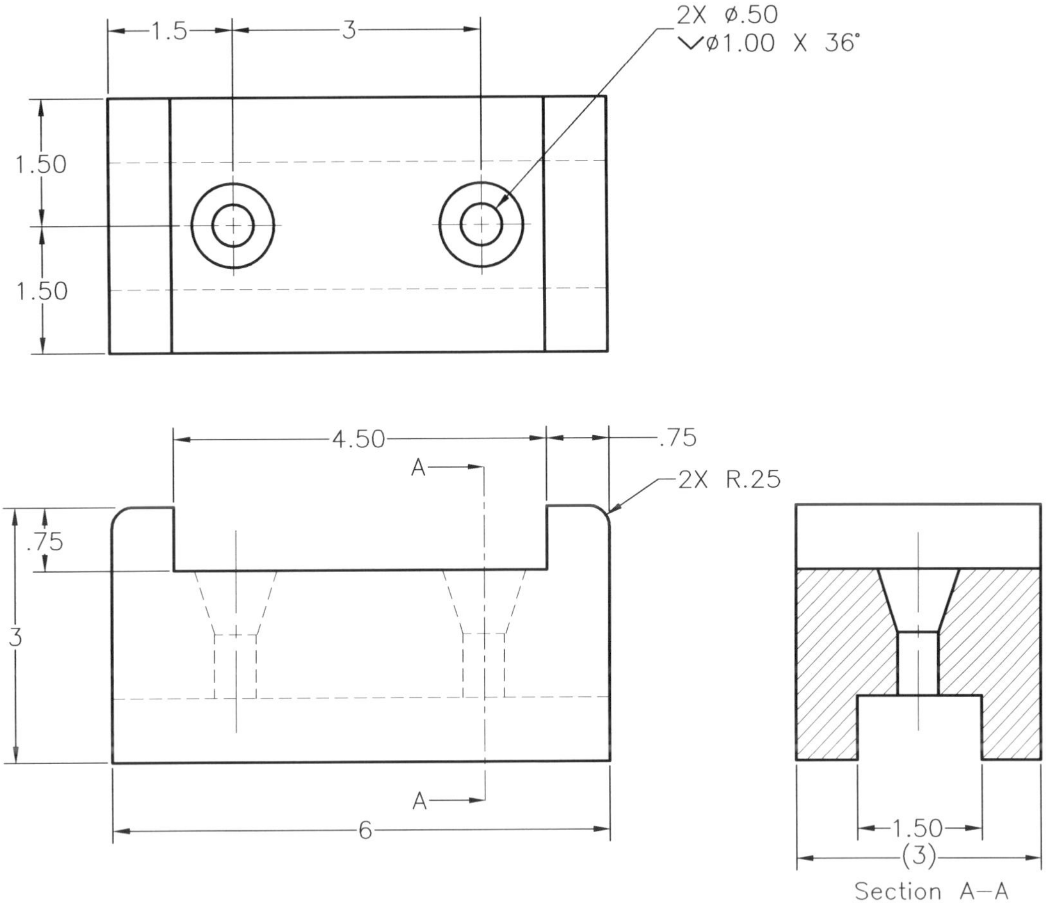

Figure 11-48 *Drawing for Exercise 11*

Problem-Solving Exercise 1

Figure 11-49 shows an object with front and side views with aligned section. Hatch the side view using the hatch pattern of your choice.

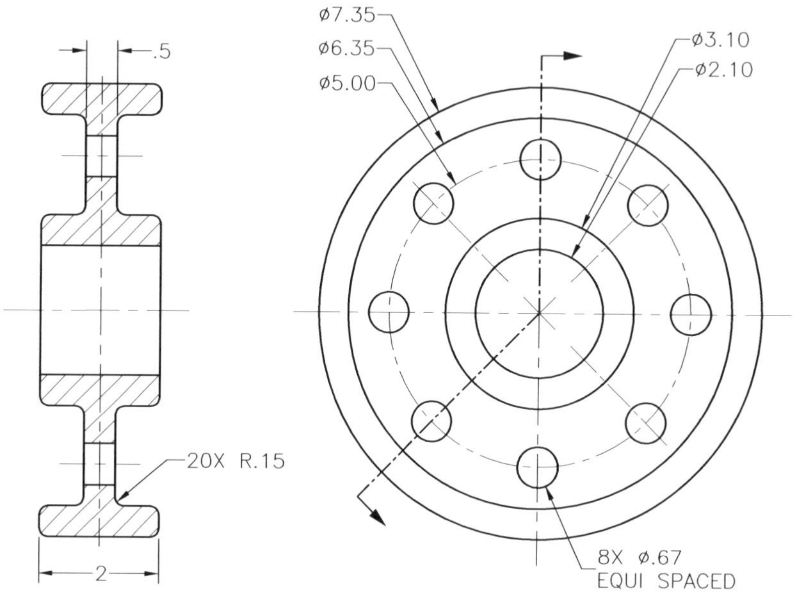

Figure 11-49 *Drawing for Problem-Solving Exercise 1*

Problem-Solving Exercise 2

Figure 11-50 shows the front view, side view, and the detail "A" of an object. Hatch the side view and draw the detail drawing as shown.

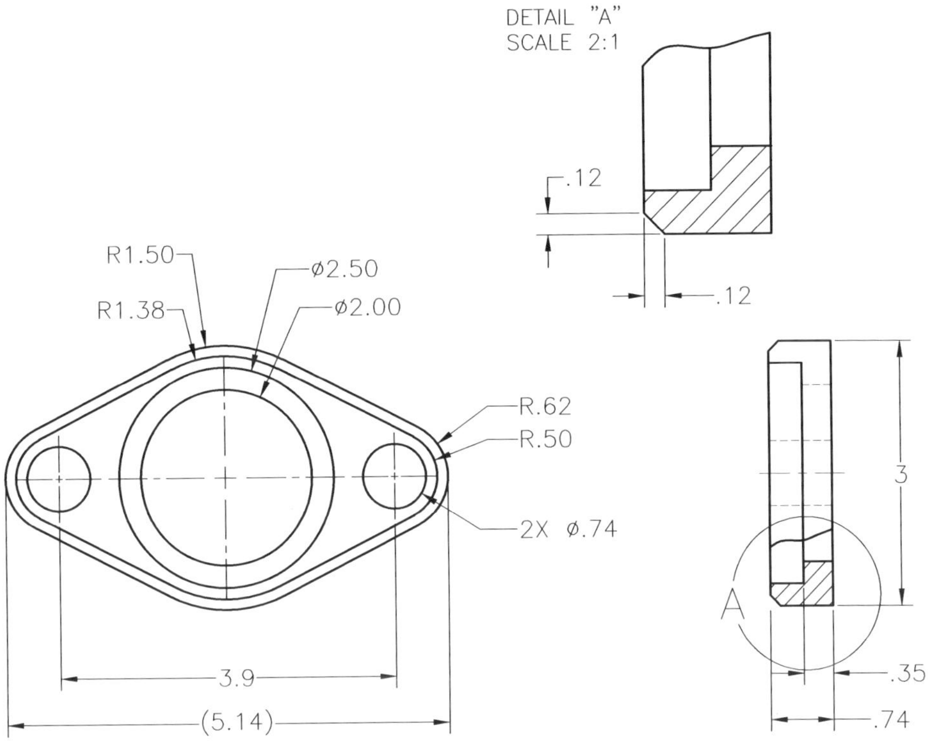

Figure 11-50 Drawing for Problem-Solving Exercise 2

Problem-Solving Exercise 3

Create the drawing shown in Figure 11-51.

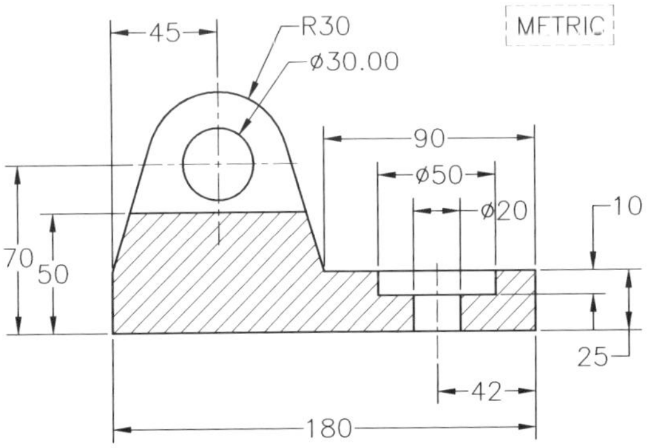

Figure 11-51 Drawing for Problem-Solving Exercise 3

Problem-Solving Exercise 4

Create the drawing shown in Figure 11-52.

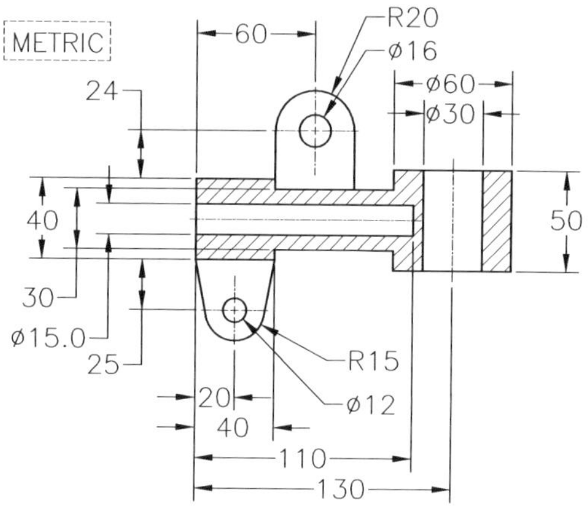

Figure 11-52 *Drawing for Problem-Solving Exercise 4*

Problem-Solving Exercise 5

Draw a detail drawing whose top, side, and section views are given in Figure 11-53. Then, hatch the section view.

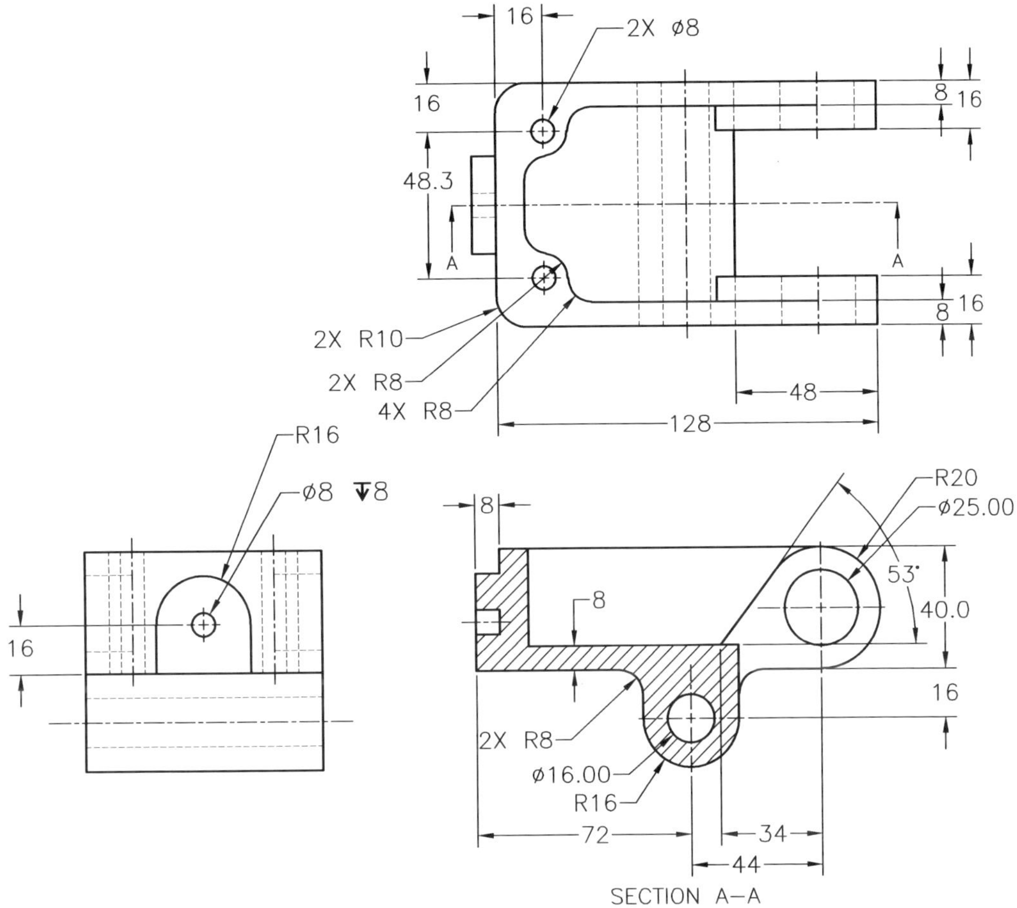

Figure 11-53 *Views and dimensions of the drawing for Problem-Solving Exercise 5*

Answers to Self-Evaluation Test

1. Gap Tolerance, 2. Pattern, **3. Angle**, **4. Select Boundary Objects**, **5. Gradient**, **6.** ISO hatch, **7.** T, **8.** T, **9.** F, **10.** T

Chapter 12

Model Space Viewports, Paper Space Viewports, and Layouts

Learning Objectives

After completing this chapter, you will be able to:

- *Understand the concepts of model space and paper space*
- *Create tiled viewports in the model space*
- *Create floating viewports*
- *Control the visibility of viewport layers*
- *Set the linetype scaling in paper space*
- *Control the display of annotative objects in viewports*

Key Terms

- *Viewports*
- *Model Space*
- *Paper Space*
- *Tiled Viewport*
- *Temporary Model Space*
- *Rectangular Viewport*
- *Polygonal Viewport*
- *Maximize Viewport*
- *MVIEW*
- *VPLAYER*
- *PAGESETUP*
- *MVSETUP*
- *SPACETRANS*

MODEL SPACE AND PAPER SPACE/LAYOUTS

For ease in designing, AutoCAD LT provides two different types of environments, model space and paper space. The paper space is also called layout. The model space is basically used for designing or drafting work. This is the default environment that is active when you start AutoCAD LT. Almost the entire design is created in the model space. The paper space is used for plotting drawings or generating drawing views for the solid models. A layout can be considered a sheet of paper on which you can place the design created in the model space and then print it. You can also assign different plotting parameters to these layouts for plotting. Almost all the commands of the model space also work in the layouts. Note that you cannot select the drawing objects created in model space when they are displayed in the viewports in layouts. However, you can snap on to the different points of the drawing objects such as the endpoints, midpoints, center points, and so on using the **OSNAP** options.

You can shift from one environment to the other by choosing the **Model** tab or the **Layout1/ Layout2** tabs at the bottom of the drawing area. If these tabs are not available by default, then to display these tabs, select the **Layout Tabs** option from the **Interface** panel of the **View** tab of the **Ribbon**.

You can also shift from one environment to the other using the **TILEMODE** system variable. The default value of this variable is **1**. If the value of this system variable is set to **0**, you will be shifted to the layouts and if its value is set to **1**, you will be shifted to model space. The viewports created in the model space are called tiled viewports and viewports in layouts are called floating viewports.

MODEL SPACE VIEWPORTS (TILED VIEWPORTS)

Ribbon: View > Model Viewports > Viewport Configuration Drop-down
Toolbar: Viewports > Display Viewports Dialog
Menu Bar: View > Viewports > New Viewports **Command:** VPORTS

A viewport in the model space is defined as a rectangular area of the drawing window in which you can create the design. When you start AutoCAD LT, only one viewport is displayed in the model space. You can create multiple non-overlapping viewports in the model space to display different views of the same object, see Figure 12-1. Each of these viewports will act as individual drawing area. This is generally used while creating solid models. You can view the same solid model from different positions by creating the tiled viewports and defining the distinct coordinate system configuration for each viewport. You can also use the **Pan** or **Zoom** tool to display different portions or different levels of the detail of the drawing in each viewport. The tiled viewports can be created using the **Named** tool available in the **Model Viewports** panel of the **View** tab.

Creating Tiled Viewports

As mentioned earlier, the display screen in the model space can be divided into multiple non-overlapping tiled viewports. All these viewports are created only in rectangular shape. This number depends on the equipment and the operating system on which AutoCAD LT is running.

Each tiled viewport contains a view of the drawing. The tiled viewports touch each other at the edges without overlapping. While using tiled viewports, you are not allowed to edit, rearrange, or turn individual viewports on or off. These viewports are created using the **Named** tool when the system variable **TILEMODE** is set to 1 or the **Model** tab is active. When you choose the **Named** button from the **Model Viewports** panel in the **View Tab**, the **Viewports** dialog box is displayed. You can use this dialog box to create new viewport configurations and save them. The options under both the tabs of the **Viewports** dialog box are discussed next.

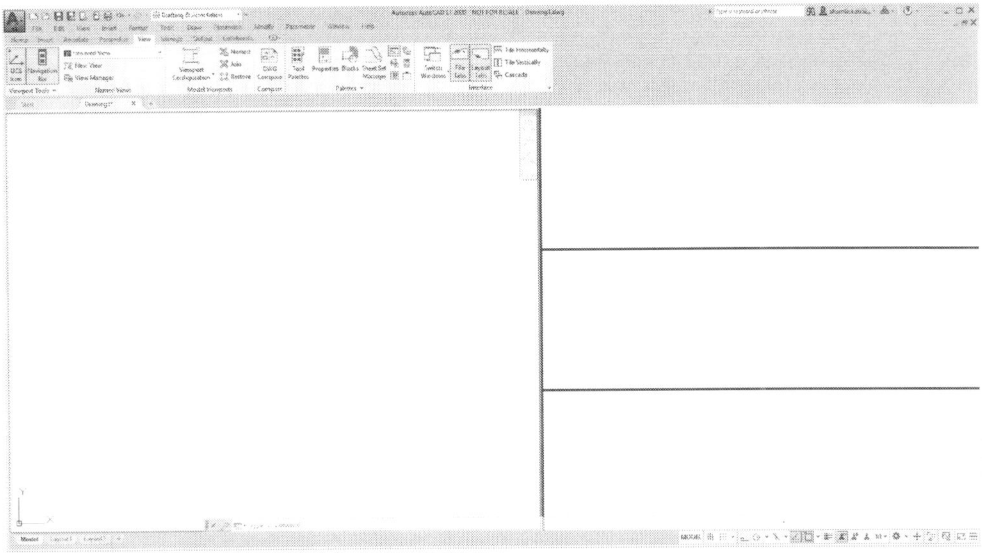

***Figure 12-1** Screen display with multiple tiled viewports*

New Viewports Tab

The **New Viewports** tab of the **Viewports** dialog box (Figure 12-2) provides the options related to standard viewport configurations. You can also save a user-defined configuration using this tab. The name for the new viewport configuration can be specified in the **New name** edit box. If you do not enter a name in this edit box, the viewport configuration you create is not saved and, therefore, cannot be used later. A list of standard viewport configurations is listed in the **Standard viewports** list box. This list also contains the ***Active Model Configuration***, which is the current viewport configuration. From the **Standard viewports** list, you can select and apply any one of the listed standard viewport configurations. A preview image of the selected configuration is displayed in the **Preview** window. The **Apply to** drop-down list has the **Display** and **Current viewport** options. Selecting the **Display** option applies the selected viewport configuration to the entire display and selecting the **Current viewport** option applies the selected viewport configuration to only the current viewport. With this option, you can create more viewports inside the existing viewports. The changes will be applied to the current viewport and the new viewports will be created inside the current viewport.

From the **Setup** drop-down list, you can select **2D** or **3D**. When you select the **2D** option, it creates the new viewport configuration with the current view of the drawing in all the viewports initially. Using the **3D** option, you can apply the standard orthogonal and isometric views to the viewports. For example, if a configuration has four viewports, they are assigned the **Top**, **Front**, **Right**, and **SE Isometric** views, respectively. You can also modify these standard orthogonal and isometric views by selecting from the **Change view to** drop-down list and replacing the existing view in the selected viewport. For example, you can select the viewport that is assigned the **Top** view and then select the **Bottom** view from the **Change view to** drop-down list to replace it. The preview image in the **Preview** window reflects the changes you make. If you use the **2D** option, you can select a named viewport configuration to replace the selected one. Choose **OK** to exit the dialog box and apply the created or selected configuration to the current display in the drawing. When you save a new viewport configuration, it saves the information about the number and position of viewports, the viewing direction and zoom factor, and the grid, snap, coordinate system, and UCS icon settings.

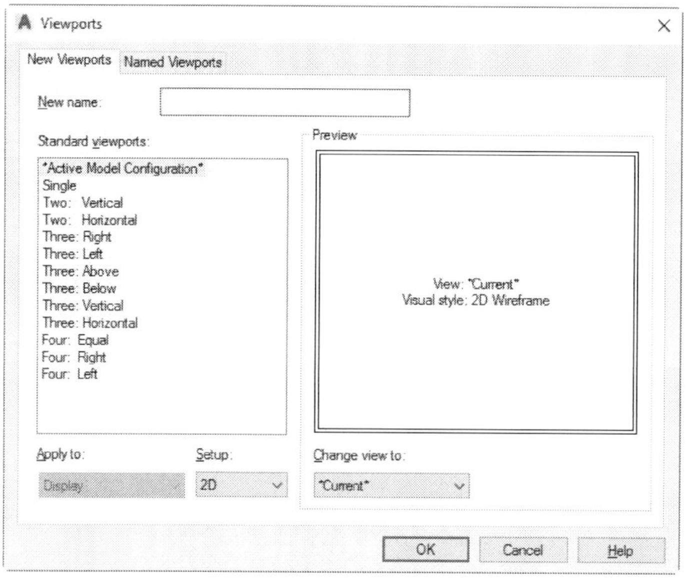

Figure 12-2 *The* ***New Viewports*** *tab of the* ***Viewports*** *dialog box*

Named Viewports Tab

The **Named Viewports** tab of the **Viewports** dialog box (Figure 12-3) displays the name of the current viewport corresponding to **Current name**. The names of all the saved viewport configurations in a drawing are displayed in the **Named viewports** list box. You can select any one of the named viewport configurations and apply it to the current display. A preview image of the selected configuration is displayed in the **Preview** window. In the **Named viewports** list box, you can select a name and right-click to display a shortcut menu. On choosing the **Delete** option, the selected viewport configuration will be deleted and on choosing the **Rename** option, you can rename the selected viewport configuration. Choose **OK** to exit the dialog box and apply the selected viewport configuration to the current display.

MAKING A VIEWPORT CURRENT

The viewport you are currently working in is called the current viewport. You can display several model space viewports on the screen, but you can work in only one of them at a time. You can switch from one viewport to another even when you are in the middle of a command. For example, you can specify the start point of the line in one viewport and the endpoint of the line in the other viewport. The current viewport is indicated by a border that is heavy compared to the borders of the other viewports. Also, the graphics cursor appears as a drawing cursor (screen crosshairs) only when it is within the current viewport. Outside the current viewport this cursor appears as an arrow cursor. You can enter points and select objects only from the current viewport. To make a viewport current, you can select it with the pointing device. Another method of making a viewport current is by assigning its identification number to the **CVPORT** system variable. The identification numbers of the named viewport configurations are not listed in the display.

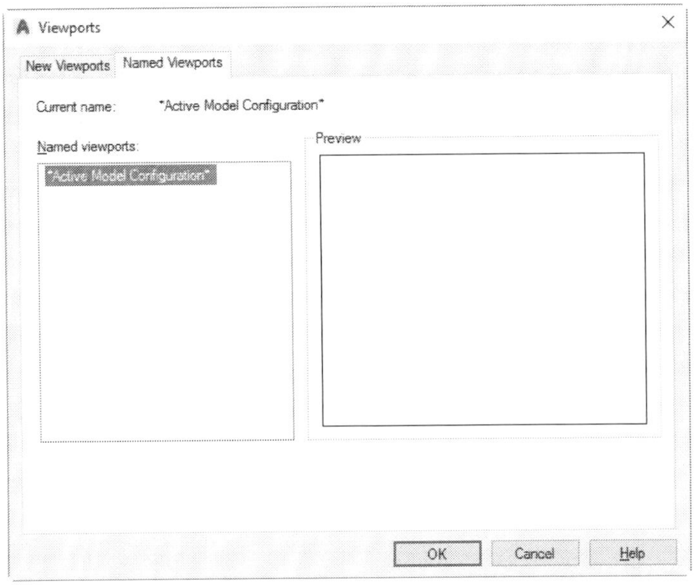

***Figure 12-3** The **Named Viewports** tab of the **Viewports** dialog box*

JOINING TWO ADJACENT VIEWPORTS

AutoCAD LT provides you with an option of joining two adjacent viewports. However, remember that the viewports you wish to join should result in a rectangular-shaped viewport only. As mentioned earlier, the viewports in the model space can only be in rectangular shape. Therefore, you will not be able to join two viewports, in case they do not result in a rectangular shape. The viewports can be joined by using the **Join Viewports** tool available in the **Model Viewports** panel. On invoking this tool, you will be prompted to select the dominant viewport. A dominant viewport is the one whose display will be retained after joining. After selecting the dominant viewport, you will be prompted to select the viewport to be joined. Figure 12-4 shows the viewport configuration before joining and Figure 12-5 shows the viewport configuration after joining.

***Figure 12-4** Selecting the dominant viewport and the viewport to be joined*

***Figure 12-5** Viewports after joining*

Note

*You can also use the **-VPORTS** Command to save, restore, delete, or join the viewport configurations.*

SPLITTING AND RESIZING VIEWPORTS IN MODEL SPACE

In AutoCAD LT 2020, you can split the viewports in the model space. To do so, enter the **-VPORTS** command; the **Enter an option [Save/Restore/Delete/Join/Single/?/2/3/4/Toggle/MOde] <3>:** prompt will be displayed. Next, enter 2, 3, or 4 at the command prompt to split a viewport in 2, 3, or 4 viewports, respectively.

Also, you can resize the viewports in model space using the horizontal and vertical splitting lines. To resize a viewport, hold down the left mouse button on the horizontal or vertical splitting line and drag the cursor in a direction; the viewport will be resized in the specified direction. You can also resize all the viewports at a time. To do so, hold down the cursor at the intersection point of horizontal and vertical splitting line and drag the cursor in a direction; all the viewports will be resized according to the specified direction.

PAPER SPACE VIEWPORTS (FLOATING VIEWPORTS)

As mentioned earlier, the viewports created in the layouts are called floating viewports. This is because unlike in model space, the viewports in the layouts can be overlapping and of any shape without any restriction. You can even convert a closed object into a viewport in the layouts. Figure 12-6 shows a layout with floating viewports. The methods of creating floating viewports are discussed next.

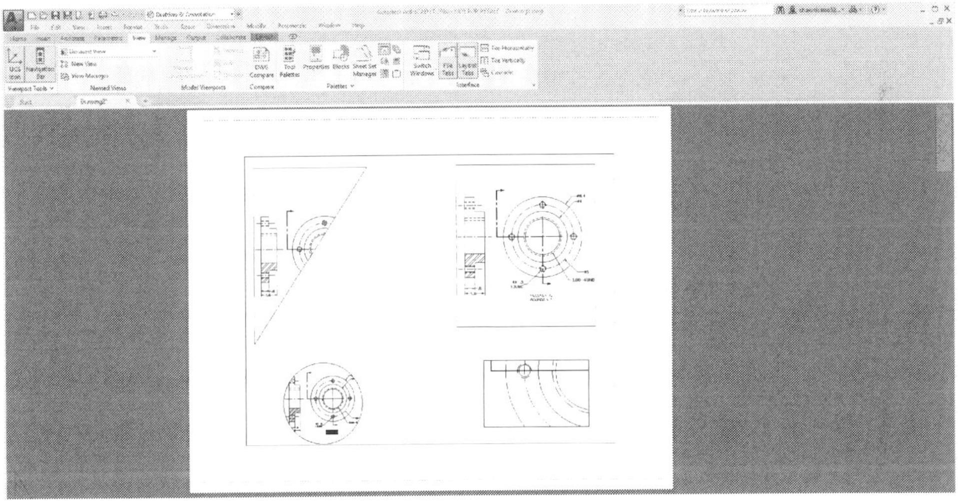

Figure 12-6 *Screen display with multiple floating viewports*

Creating Floating Viewports

Ribbon: View > Model Viewports > Named
Toolbar: Viewports > Display Viewports Dialog
Menu Bar: View > Viewports > New Viewports **Command:** VPORTS

This tool is used to create the floating viewports in layouts. However, when you invoke this tool in the layouts, the dialog box displayed is slightly modified. Instead of the **Apply to** drop-down list in the **New Viewports** tab, the **Viewport Spacing** spinner is displayed, refer to Figure 12-7. This spinner is used to set the spacing between the adjacent viewports. The rest of the options in both the **New Viewports** and the **Named Viewports** tabs of the **Viewports** dialog box are the same as those discussed under the tiled viewports. When you select a viewport configuration and choose **OK**, you will be prompted to specify the first and the second corner of a box that will act as a reference for placing the viewports. You will also be given an option of **Fit**. This option fits the configuration of viewports such that they fit exactly in the current display.

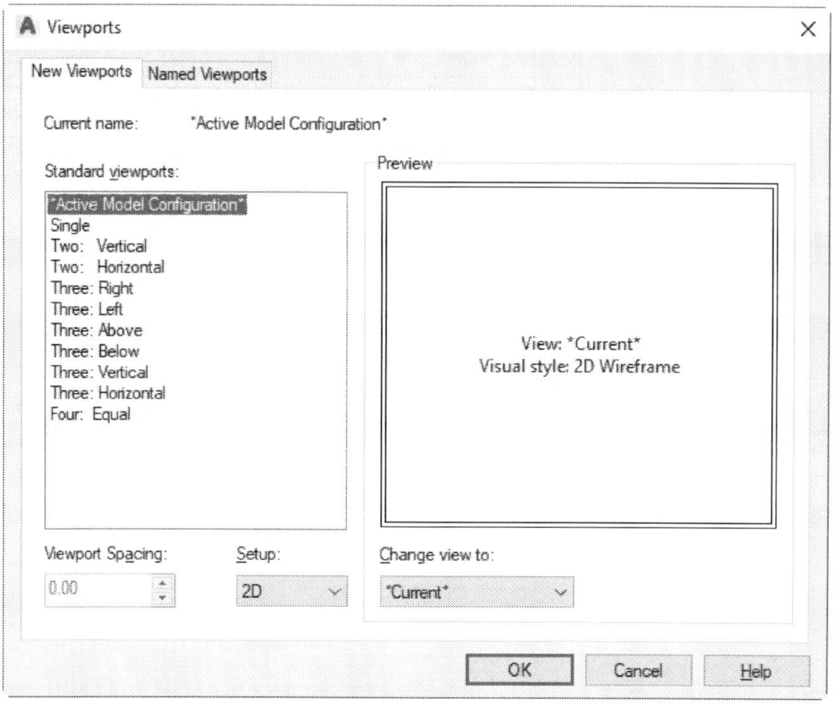

***Figure 12-7** The **New Viewports** tab of the **Viewports** dialog box displayed in layouts*

Note

*You can also use the **+VPORTS** command to display the **Viewports** dialog box. When you invoke this command, you will be prompted to specify the **Tab Index**. Enter **0** to display the **New Viewports** tab and enter **1** to display the **Named Viewports** tab.*

Creating Rectangular Viewports

Ribbon: Layout contextual tab > Layout Viewports > Viewports drop-down > Rectangular
Menu Bar: View > Viewports > New Viewports
Toolbar: Viewports > Single Viewport **Command:** -VPORTS

To create a rectangular viewport, choose the **Rectangular** tool from **Layout > Layout Viewports > Viewports** drop-down (See Figure 12-8) in the **Ribbon**. The prompt sequence that will follow is given next.

Specify corner of viewport or
[ON/OFF/Fit/Shadeplot/Lock/NEw/NAmed/Object/Polygonal/Restore/LAyer/2/3/4] <Fit>: *Specify the start point of the viewport.*
Specify opposite corner: *Specify the end point of the viewport.*

You can also create 2, 3 or 4 viewports in one go by entering 2, 3 or 4 at the prompt **Specify corner of viewport or [ON/OFF/Fit/Shadeplot/Lock/NEw/NAmed/Object/Polygonal/Restore/LAyer/2/3/4] <Fit>**.

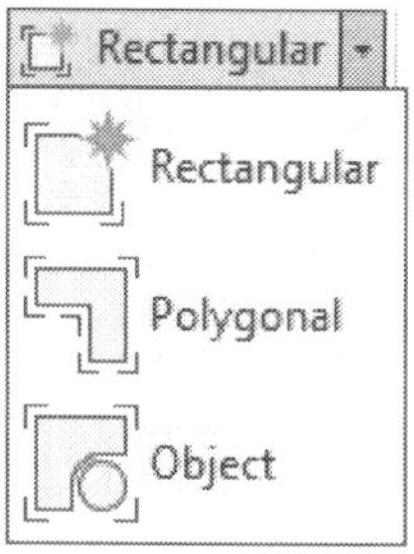

***Figure 12-8** Tools in the **Viewports** drop-down*

The viewports automatically fit in the drawn rectangular area.

The prompt sequence for the 2 Viewports option is given next.

Command: **-VPORTS**
Specify corner of viewport or
[ON/OFF/Fit/Shadeplot/Lock/NEw/NAmed/Object/Polygonal/Restore/LAyer/2/3/4] <Fit>: 2 Enter
Enter viewport arrangement [Horizontal/Vertical] <Vertical>: *Specify the orientation of the viewport.*
Specify first corner or [Fit] <Fit>: *Specify the start point of the viewport.*
Specify opposite corner: *Specify the end point of the viewport.*

The prompt sequence for creating 3 viewports is given next.

Command: **-VPORTS**
[ON/OFF/Fit/Shadeplot/Lock/NEw/NAmed/Object/Polygonal/Restore/LAyer/2/3/4] <Fit>: 3 Enter
Enter viewport arrangement
[Horizontal/Vertical/Above/Below/Left/Right] <Right>: *Specify the orientation of the viewport using Horizontal or Vertical option. You can also specify the position of the largest viewport among the three using Above, Below, Left, or Right option.*
Specify first corner or [Fit] <Fit>: *Specify the start point of the viewport.*
Specify opposite corner: *Specify the end point of the viewport.*

The prompt sequence for creating 4 viewports is given next.

Command: **-VPORTS**
[ON/OFF/Fit/Shadeplot/Lock/NEw/NAmed/Object/Polygonal/Restore/LAyer/2/3/4] <Fit>: 4 Enter
Specify first corner or [Fit] <Fit>: *Specify the start point of the viewport.*
Specify opposite corner: *Specify the end point of the viewport.*

Creating Polygonal Viewports

Ribbon: Layout contextual tab > Layout Viewports > Viewports drop-down > Polygonal
Menu Bar: View > Viewports > Polygonal Viewports
Toolbar: Viewports > Polygonal Viewport **Command:** -VPORTS

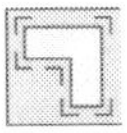

As mentioned earlier, you can create floating viewports of any closed shape. The viewports thus created can even be self-intersecting in shape. To create a polygonal viewport, choose the **Polygonal** tool from **Layout > Layout Viewports > Viewports** drop-down (refer to Figure 12-8). The prompt sequence that will follow when you choose this tool is given next.

Command: **-VPORTS**
Specify corner of viewport or
[ON/OFF/Fit/Shadeplot/Lock/NEw/NAmed/Object/Polygonal/Restore/LAyer/2/3/4] <Fit>:
P Enter
Specify start point: *Specify the start point of the viewport.*
Specify next point or [Arc/Length/Undo]: *Specify the next point or select an option.*
Specify next point or [Arc/Close/Length/Undo]: *Specify the next point or select an option.*

Various options in the prompt sequence are discussed next.

Arc

This option is used to switch to the arc mode for creating the viewports. When you invoke this option, the options for creating the arcs will be displayed. You can switch back to the line mode by choosing the **Line** option.

Close

This option is used to close the polygon and create the viewport. The last entity that will be used to close the polygon will depend upon whether you were in the arc mode or in the line mode. If you were in the line mode, the last entity will be a line. If you were in the arc mode, the last entity will be an arc.

Length

This option is used to specify the length of the next line of the viewport. The line will be drawn in the direction of the last drawn line segment. In case the last drawn segment was an arc, the line will be drawn tangent to it.

Undo

This option is used to undo the last drawn segment of the polygonal viewport.

Figure 12-9 shows the polygonal viewport created using a combination of lines and arcs.

Figure 12-9 *Object viewport*

Converting an Existing Closed Object into a Viewport

Ribbon: Layout contextual tab > Layout Viewports > Viewports drop-down > Object
Toolbar: Viewports > Convert Object to Viewport **Command:** -VPORTS > O

This tool allows you to convert an existing closed object into a viewport. However, remember that the object selected should be a single entity. The objects that can be converted into a viewport include polygons drawn using the **Polygon** tool, rectangles drawn using the **Rectangle** tool, polylines (last segment closed using the **Close** option), circles, ellipses, closed splines, or regions. To convert any of these objects into a viewport, choose the **Object** tool from the **Layout Viewports** panel. You will be prompted to select the object that needs to be converted into a viewport. Figure 12-10 shows a viewport created using a polygon of nine sides and Figure 12-11 shows a viewport created using a closed spline.

Note

*When you shift to the layouts, the **Page Setup** dialog box is displayed for printing and a rectangular viewport is created that fits the drawing area. If you want, you can retain or delete this viewport using the **Erase** tool.*

Figure 12-10 *A viewport created using a polygon of nine sides*

Figure 12-11 *A viewport created using a closed spline*

TEMPORARY MODEL SPACE

Sometimes when you create a floating viewport in the layout, the drawing is not displayed completely inside it, see Figures 12-10 and 12-11. In such cases, you need to zoom or pan the drawings to fit them in the viewport. But when you invoke any of the **Zoom** or the **Pan** tools in the layouts, the display of the entire layout is modified instead of the display inside of the viewport. Now, to change the display of the viewports, you will have to switch to the temporary model space. The temporary model space is defined as a state when the model space is activated in the layouts. The temporary model space is exactly similar to the actual model space and you can make any kind of modifications in the drawing from temporary model space. Therefore, the main reason for invoking the temporary model space is that you can modify the display of the drawing. The temporary model space can be invoked by choosing the **PAPER** button from the Status Bar. You can also switch to the temporary model space by double-clicking inside the viewports. You will see that the model space UCS icon is automatically displayed when you switch to the temporary model space. Also, the extents of the viewport become the extents of the drawing. You can use the **Zoom** and **Pan** tools to fit the model inside the viewport. The temporary model space can also be invoked using the **MSPACE** command.

Once you have modified the display of the drawing in the temporary model space, you have to switch back to the paper space. This is done by choosing the **MODEL** button from the Status Bar. You can also switch back to the paper space by double-clicking anywhere in the layout outside the viewport, or by using the **PSPACE** command.

Example 1 Create Viewports

In this example, you will draw the object shown in Figure 12-12 and then create a floating viewport of the shape shown in Figure 12-13 to display the object in the layout. The dimensions of the viewport are in the paper space. Do not dimension the object.

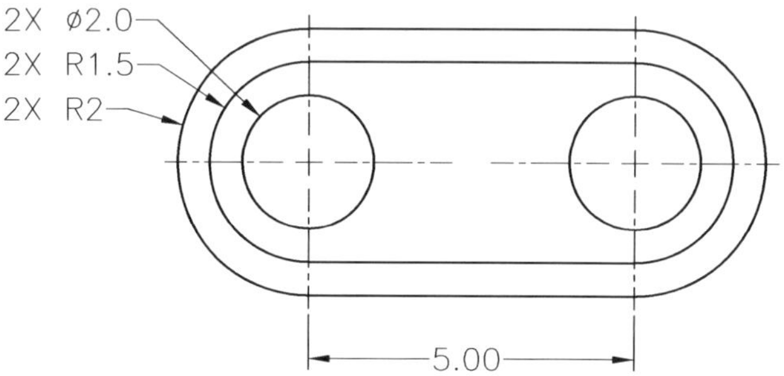

Figure 12-12 *Model for Example 1*

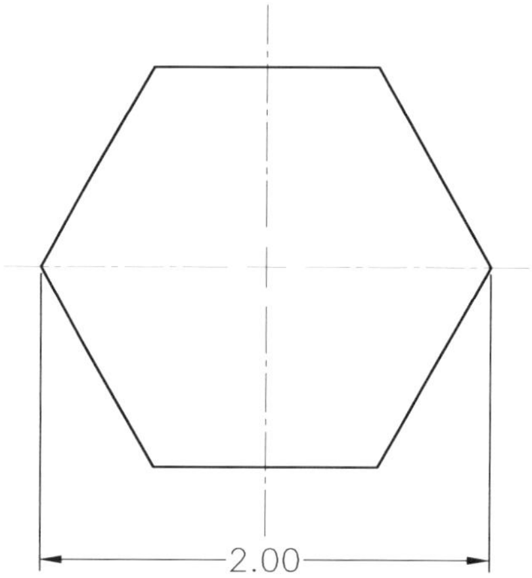

Figure 12-13 *Shape of the floating viewport*

1. Start a new drawing and then draw the object shown in Figure 12-12.
2. Choose the **Layout1** tab to switch to the layout; a rectangular viewport will be displayed in this layout.
3. Choose the **Erase** tool from the **Modify** panel in the **Home** tab; you will be prompted to select the object. Type **L** in the command prompt and press ENTER to delete the last object. In this case, the last object is viewport so it will be deleted.
4. Choose the **Polygon** tool from the **Draw** panel in the **Home** tab and create the required hexagon, refer to Figure 12-13.
5. Choose the **Object** tool from **Layout > Layout Viewports > Viewports** drop-down; you will be prompted to select an object. Select the hexagon; it will be converted into a viewport.

You will see that the complete object is not displayed inside the viewport. Therefore, you need to modify its display.

6. Double-click inside the viewport to switch to the temporary model space. The border of the viewport will become thick, indicating that you have switched to the temporary model space.

7. Now, using the **Zoom** and the **Pan** tools, fit the drawing inside the viewport.

8. Choose the **MODEL** button from the Status Bar to switchback to the paper space. The drawing will be displayed fully inside the viewport, see Figure 12-14.

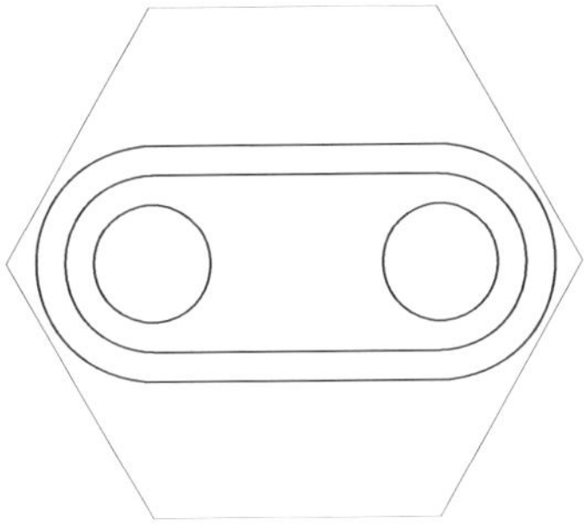

Figure 12-14 *Displaying the drawing inside the polygonal viewport*

EDITING VIEWPORTS

You can perform various editing operations on the viewports. For example, you can control the visibility of the objects in the viewports, lock their display, clip the existing viewports using an object, and so on. All these editing operations are discussed next.

Controlling the Display of Objects in Viewports

The display of the objects in the viewports can be turned on or off. If the display is turned off, the objects will not be displayed in the viewport. However, the object in the model space is not affected by this editing operation. To control the display of the objects, select the viewport entity in the layout and right-click to display the shortcut menu. In this menu, choose **Display Viewport Objects > No**. If there is only one viewport, you will be prompted to confirm whether you really want to turn off all active viewports. Enter **Y** to turn off the display. However, if there are more than one viewports, the visibility of the selected viewports will be automatically turned off when you choose **Display Viewport Objects > No** from the shortcut menu. Similarly, you can again turn on the display of the objects by choosing **Display Viewport Objects > Yes** from the shortcut menu. This shortcut menu is displayed on selecting the viewport and right-clicking. This editing operation can also be done using the **OFF** option of the **MVIEW** or the **-VPORTS** command.

Locking the Display of Objects in Viewports

To avoid accidental modification in the display of objects in the viewports, you can lock their display. If the display of a viewport is locked, the tools such as **Zoom** and **Pan** do not work in it. Also, you cannot modify the view in the locked viewport. For example, if the display of a viewport is locked, you cannot zoom or pan the display or change the view in that viewport even if you switch to the temporary model space. To lock the display of the viewports, select it and right-click on it to display the shortcut menu. In this menu, choose **Display Locked > Yes**. Now, the display of this viewport will not be modified. However, you can draw objects or delete objects in this viewport by switching to the temporary model space. Similarly, you can unlock the display of the objects in the viewports by choosing **Display Locked > No** from the shortcut menu. You can also lock or unlock the display of the viewports using the **Lock** option of the **MVIEW** command or the **-VPORTS** command.

Controlling the Display of Hidden Lines in Viewports

While working with three-dimensional solid or surface models, there are a number of occasions where you have to plot the solid models such that the hidden lines are not displayed. Plotting solid models in the model space (Tilemode=1) can be easily done by selecting the **Hidden** option from the **Shade plot** drop-down list. This drop-down list is available in the **Shaded viewport options** area in the **Plot** dialog box. If this area is not available by default, you need to choose the **More Options** button in the dialog box. This option is not available in layouts. In this case, you will have to control the display of the hidden lines in the viewports. To control the display of the hidden lines, select the viewport and right-click to display the shortcut menu. In this menu, choose **Shade plot > Hidden**. Although the hidden lines will be displayed in the viewports, now they will not be displayed in the printouts. The display of the hidden lines can also be controlled using the **Shadeplot** option of the **MVIEW** command or the **-VPORTS** command.

Note

*You can also use the other options in the **Shade plot** drop-down list. These options are explained in detail in Chapter 13 (Plotting Drawings).*

Tip

Apart from the previously mentioned editing operations, you can also move, copy, rotate, stretch, scale, or trim the viewports using the respective commands. You can also use the grips to edit the viewports.

Clipping Existing Viewports

Ribbon: Layout contextual tab > Layout Viewports > Clip
Menu Bar: Modify > Clip > Viewport
Toolbar: Viewports > Clip existing Viewport **Command:** VPCLIP

You can modify the shape of the existing viewport by clipping it using an object or by defining the clipping boundary. The viewports can be clipped by choosing the **Clip** tool from the **Layout Viewports** panel in the **Layout** tab. This command can also be invoked by using the **VPCLIP** command. The prompt sequence that will follow when you invoke this tool is given next.

Select viewport to clip: *Select the viewport to be clipped.*
Select clipping object or [Polygonal] <Polygonal>: *Select an object for clipping the viewport or specify an option.*

Select Clipping Object Option

This option is used to clip the viewport using a selected closed loop. The objects that can be used for clipping the viewports include circles, ellipses, closed polylines, closed splines, and regions. As soon as you select the clipping object, the original viewport will be deleted and the selected object will be converted into a viewport. The portion of the display that was common to both the original viewport and the object selected will be displayed. You can, however, change the display of the viewport using the **Zoom** tool or the **Pan** tool. Figure 12-15 shows a viewport and an object that will be used to clip the viewport and Figure 12-16 shows the new viewport created after clipping.

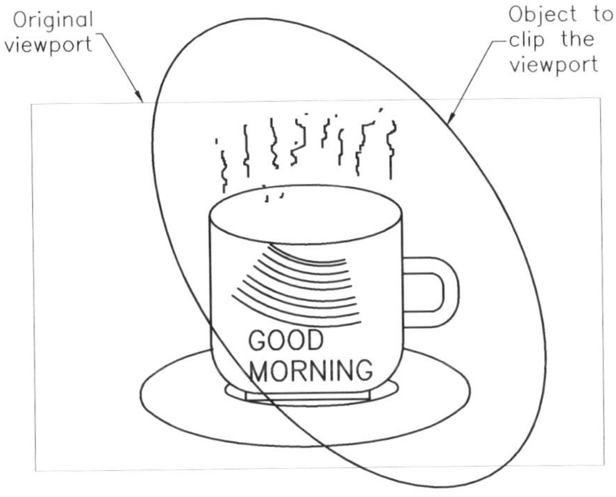

***Figure 12-15** Selecting the object for clipping the viewport*

***Figure 12-16** New viewport created after clipping*

Polygonal

This option is used to create a polygonal boundary for clipping the viewports. When you invoke this option, the options for creating a polygonal boundary will be displayed. You can draw a polygonal boundary for clipping the viewport using these options.

Delete

This option is used to delete the new clipping boundary created using an object or using the **Polygonal** option. The original viewport is restored when you invoke this option, which will be available only if the viewport has been clipped at least once. If the viewport is clipped more than once, you can restore only the last viewport clipping boundary.

Maximizing Viewports

Status Bar: Maximize Viewport

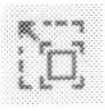

While working with floating viewports, you may need to invoke the temporary model space to modify the drawing. One of the options is that you double-click inside the viewport to invoke the temporary model space and make the changes in the drawing. But in this case, the shape and size of the floating viewport will control the area of the temporary model space. If the viewport is polygonal and small in size, you may have to zoom and pan the drawing a number of times. To avoid this, AutoCAD LT allows you to maximize a viewport on the screen. This provides you all the space in the drawing area to make the changes in the drawing.

To maximize a floating viewport, choose the **Maximize Viewport** button from the Status Bar. The viewport is automatically maximized in the drawing area and the **Maximize Viewport** button is replaced by the **Minimize Viewport** button. If there are more than one floating viewports, two arrows will be displayed on either side of the **Minimize Viewport** button. These arrows can be used to switch to the display in the other floating viewports. After making the changes in the drawing, choose the **Minimize Viewport** button to restore the original display of the layout. When you do so, the view and the magnification in all the viewports is the same as that before maximizing them. Also, the visibility of the layers remains the same as that before maximizing the viewport.

CONTROLLING THE PROPERTIES OF VIEWPORT LAYERS

Command: VPLAYER

You can control the properties of layers inside a floating viewport using the **VPLAYER** command or by using the **Layer Properties Manager**. The **VPLAYER** command is used to control the visibility of layers in individual floating viewports. For example, you can use the **VPLAYER** command to freeze a layer in the selected viewport. The contents of this layer will not be displayed in the selected viewport, although in the other viewports, they will be displayed. This command can be used from either temporary model space or paper space. The only restriction is that **TILEMODE** is set to 0 (Off); that is, you can use this command only in the **Layout** tab.

Command: **VPLAYER** Enter
Enter an option [?/Color/Ltype/LWeight/TRansparency/Freeze/Thaw/Reset/reMoveoverrides/Newfrz/Vpvisdflt]:

? Option

You can use this option to obtain a listing of the frozen layers in the selected viewport. When you enter ?, you will be prompted to select the viewport. Select the viewport; **AutoCAD LT text window** will be displayed showing all the layers that are frozen in the current layer. On invoking this command in temporary model space, AutoCAD LT will temporarily shift you to the paper space to let you select the viewport.

Color Option

The **Color** option is used to assign a color to a layer (or layers) in the viewports. You can either use True colors or you can specify a Color book, if you have previously installed any. The changes can be applied on the current, selected, or all the viewports.

Ltype Option

You can use this option to specify any linetype to a layer (or layers) in the current, selected, or all the viewports.

LWeight Option

The **LWeight** option is used to specify a line width to a particular layer or layers. You can specify the width between 0.00 mm to 2.11 mm. Then you are prompted to specify the name(s) of the layer(s) to assign the line width. In this case also, you can apply the changes to the current, selected, or all the viewports.

TRansparency Option

The **TRansparency** option is used to set the transparency level of a layer (or layers) in one or more viewports. When you select this option, you will be prompted to specify the transparency level. Specify the transparency level; you will be prompted to specify the layer for which you need to set the transparency level. If you want to specify more than one layer, the names of the layers must be separated by commas. If you are working on a temporary model space, you can also select an object whose layer you want to set the transparency level. On specifying the name of the layer(s), AutoCAD LT will prompt you to select the viewport(s) to change the transparency. Select one or all viewports; the transparency level will be applied to the specified layers in the viewport after you exit this command.

Freeze Option

The **Freeze** option is used to freeze a layer (or layers) in one or more viewports. When you select this option, you will be prompted to specify the name(s) of the layer(s) you want to freeze. If you want to specify more than one layer, the layer names must be separated by commas. You can also select an object whose layer you want to freeze. Once you have specified the name of the layer(s), AutoCAD LT prompts you to select the viewport(s), to freeze the specified layer(s). You can select one or all the viewports. The layers will be frozen after you exit this command.

Thaw Option

With this option, you can thaw the layers that have been frozen in the viewports. Layers that have been frozen, thawed, turned on, or turned off globally are not affected by **VPLAYER** Thaw. For example, if a layer has been frozen, the objects on it are not regenerated on any viewport, even if **VPLAYER** Thaw is used to thaw that layer in any viewport. If you want to thaw more than one layer, they must be separated by commas. You can thaw the specified layers in the current, selected, or all the viewports.

Reset Option

With the **Reset** option, you can set the visibility of the layer(s) in the specified viewports to their current default setting. The visibility defaults of a layer can be set by using the **Vpvisdflt** option of the **VPLAYER** command. When you invoke the **Reset** option, you will be prompted to specify the names of the layers to be reset. You can reset the layers in the current viewport, in selected viewports, or in all the viewports.

Newfrz (New Freeze) Option

With this option, you can create new layers that are frozen in all the viewports. This option is used mainly where you need a layer that is visible only in one viewport. This can be accomplished by creating the layer with the **Newfrz** option and then thawing it in the viewport where you want to make the layer visible. On invoking this option, you will be prompted to specify the name(s) of the new layer(s) that will be frozen in all the viewports. To specify more than one layer, separate the layer names with commas. After you specify the name(s) of the layer(s), AutoCAD LT creates frozen layers in all viewports. Also, the default visibility setting of the new layer(s) is set to Frozen; therefore, if you create any new viewports, the layers created with **VPLAYER Newfrz** are also frozen in them.

Vpvisdflt (Viewport Visibility Default) Option

With this option, you can set a default for the visibility of the layer(s) in the subsequent new viewports. When a new viewport is created, the frozen/thawed status of any layer depends on the **Vpvisdflt** setting for that particular layer. When you invoke this option, you will be prompted to specify the names of the layer(s) whose visibility is to be changed. After specifying the name(s), you will be prompted to specify whether the layers should be frozen or thawed in the new viewports.

CONTROLLING THE LAYERS IN VIEWPORTS USING THE LAYER PROPERTIES MANAGER DIALOG BOX

You can use the **LAYER PROPERTIES MANAGER** dialog box to control the layer display properties in viewports. To invoke the **LAYER PROPERTIES MANAGER** dialog box, choose the **Layers Properties** button from the **Layers** panel in the **Home** tab. When you invoke this dialog box, some additional properties are added to it, see Figure 12-17. These properties are used to override the global property of the layer in a particular viewport, while retaining the global layer properties in other floating viewports and the model space. To set properties of a viewport, double-click inside it to activate the temporary model space and then set the properties. The properties are discussed next.

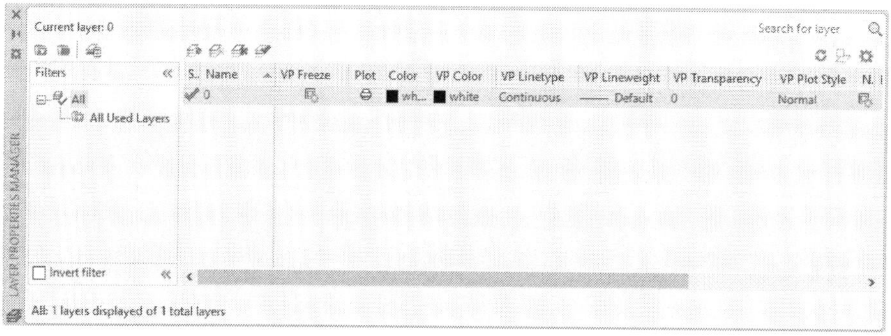

***Figure 12-17** The **LAYER PROPERTIES MANAGER** dialog box with added properties*

VP Freeze

When the **TILEMODE** option is turned off, you can freeze or thaw the selected layers in the current floating viewport by selecting the **VP Freeze** option. You can freeze a layer in the current floating viewport if it is thawed in the model space but you cannot thaw a layer in the current viewport if it is frozen in the model space. The frozen layers still remain visible in other viewports.

VP Color

The swatch under the **VP Color** column is used to change the display color of the objects in the selected layer in the current floating viewport. In all other floating viewports and model space, the color of the objects remains unaffected.

VP Linetype

The field under the **VP Linetype** column is used to change the linetype defined for the selected layer in the active floating viewport. In all other floating viewports and model space, the linetype remains unaffected.

VP Lineweight

The field under the **VP Lineweight** column is used to override the lineweight defined for the selected layer in the active floating viewport. In all other floating viewports and the model space, the lineweight remains unaffected.

VP Transparency

The field under the **VP Transparency** column is used to override the transparency defined for the layer selected in the active floating viewport. In all other floating viewports and the model space, the transparency remains unaffected.

VP Plot Style

The field under the **VP Plot Style** column is used to override the plot style settings assigned to the selected layer in the active floating viewport. The plot style for all other floating viewports and model space remains unaffected. You cannot override the plot styles for the color dependent plot styles. The override for the plot style also does not affect the plot if the visual style is set to **Realistic** or **Conceptual**.

Note

By default, all the overrides that you have defined for the current active viewport will get highlighted in light blue color in the ***LAYER PROPERTIES MANAGER*** *dialog box. Also, the icon of the selected layer under the* ***Status*** *column will change to inform you that some of the properties of the selected layer have been overridden by the new one.*

Removing Viewport Overrides

To remove the viewport overrides defined for the active viewports, open the **LAYER PROPERTIES MANAGER** dialog box in the active viewport and right-click on the layer property from which you want to remove the viewport override; a shortcut menu will be displayed. Next, choose the **Remove Viewport Overrides for** option from the shortcut menu to display the cascading menu. You can make a choice to remove the override for a single property / all properties of the selected layer / all layers in the current viewport / all viewports, see Figure 12-18. Choose the required option from the cascading menu to remove the viewport overrides. You can also remove the layer property overrides for all layers of the selected viewports from the paper space. To do so, make the paper space current; select the boundaries of the viewports for which you want to remove the override and choose the **Remove Viewport Overrides for All Layers** option from the shortcut menu.

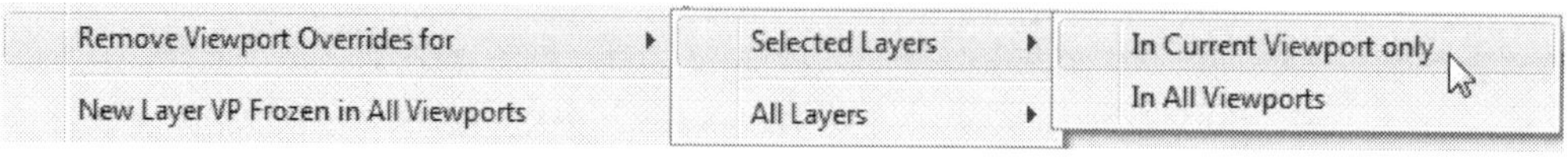

Figure 12-18 Cascading menu displayed for the ***Remove Viewport Overrides for*** *option of the* ***Layer*** *shortcut menu*

Note

For more information about the ***LAYER PROPERTIES MANAGER*** *dialog box, see Chapter 4.*

PAPER SPACE LINETYPE SCALING (PSLTSCALE SYSTEM VARIABLE)

By default, the linetype scaling is controlled by the **LTSCALE** system variable. Therefore, the display size of the dashes depends on the **LTSCALE** factor, on the drawing limits, or on the drawing units. If you have different viewports with different zoom (XP) factors, the size of the dashes will be different for these viewports. Figure 12-19 shows three viewports with different sizes and different zoom (XP) factors. You will notice that the dash length is different in each of these three viewports.

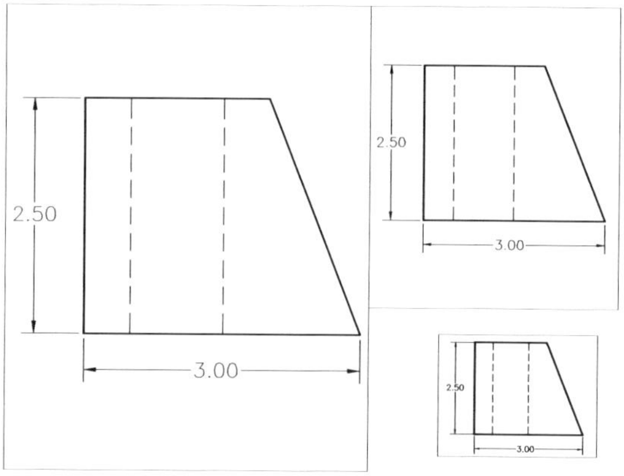

Figure 12-19 Varying sizes of the dashed lines with ***PSLTSCALE*** *= 0*

Generally, it is desirable to have identical line spacing in all viewports. This can be achieved with the **PSLTSCALE** system variable. If you set the **PSLTSCALE** to 0, the size of the dashes will depend on the **LTSCALE** system variable and on the zoom (XP) factor of the viewport where the objects have been drawn. If you set **PSLTSCALE** to **1** and **TILEMODE** to **0**, the size of the dashes for objects in the model space are scaled to match the **LTSCALE** of objects in the paper space viewport, regardless of their zoom scale. In other words, if **PSLTSCALE** is set to 1, even if the viewports are zoomed to different sizes, the length of the dashes will be identical in all viewports. Figure 12-20 shows three viewports with different sizes. Notice that the dash length is identical in all the three viewports.

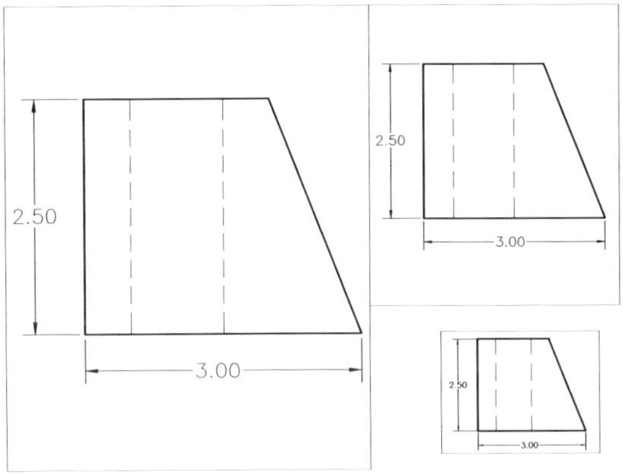

Figure 12-20 Identical sizes of the dashed lines with PSLTSCALE = 1

Tip
*You can control the scale factor for displaying the objects in the viewports using the **Viewport Scale Control** drop-down list. This drop-down list is available in the **Viewports** toolbar.*

INSERTING LAYOUTS

Ribbon: Layout contextual tab > Layout > Layout drop down > New Layout
Toolbar: Layouts > New Layout
Menu Bar: Insert > Layout > New Layout **Command:** LAYOUT

The **New Layout** tool, available in the **Layout** drop-down of the **Layout** panel in the **Layout** tab of the **Ribbon**, is used to create new layouts. The **LAYOUT** command can also be used to create a new layout. This command also allows you to rename, copy, save, and delete existing layouts. A drawing designed in the **Model** tab can be composed for plotting in the **Layout** tab. The prompt sequence is as follows.

Enter layout option [Copy/Delete/New/Template/Rename/SAveas/Set/?]<Set>:

The options in the prompt sequence are discussed next.

Copy Option

This option is used to copy a layout. When you invoke this option, you will be prompted to specify the layout that has to be copied. Upon specifying the layout, you will be prompted to specify the name of the new layout. If you do not enter a name, the name of the copied layout is assumed with an incremental number in the brackets next to it. For example, Layout 1 is copied as Layout1 (2). The name of the new layout appears as a new tab next to the copied layout tab. Alternatively, you can right-click on the **Model** or **Layout** tab and then choose **Move or Copy** from the shortcut menu to move or copy the selected layout; the **Move or Copy** dialog box will be displayed, see Figure 12-21. Select the layout from the **Before layout** area to move it above the previous layout and then choose the **OK** button. For example, if you want to move the Layout 2 before Layout 1, then select Layout 2 from the **Move or Copy** dialog box; the Layout 2 will be moved before Layout 1. To create a copy of the selected layout, select the **Create a copy** check box.

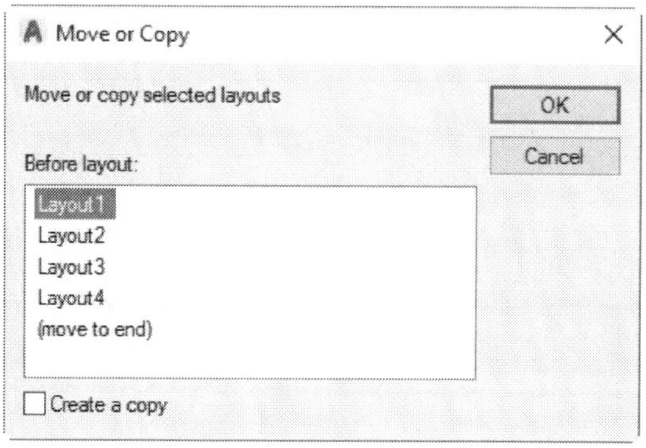

Figure 12-21 *The* ***Move or Copy*** *dialog box*

Tip
You can also drag and drop layouts to move them. To create copies of the selected layouts, press the CTRL key as you drag and drop the layouts.

Delete Option

This option is used to delete an existing layout. On invoking this option, you will be prompted to specify the name of the layout to be deleted. The current layout is the default layout for deleting. You can also right-click on the **Model** or the **Layout** tab and choose **Delete** from the shortcut menu; the AutoCAD LT alert window will be displayed. Choose the **OK** button to delete the selected layout. Note that the **Model** tab cannot be deleted.

New Option

This option is used to create a new layout. On choosing this option, you will be prompted to specify the name of the new layout. A new tab with the new layout name will appear in the drawing. Alternatively, you can right-click on the **Model** or the **Layout** tab and choose **New Layout** from the shortcut menu to add a new layout. The new layout tab will be added at the end of the existing layout tabs with the default name **Layout N**, where **N** is a natural number starting from one and acquires an ascending value that has not been used in the layout names of the current drawing.

Template Option

This option is used to create a new template based on existing layout template in the *.dwg*, *.dwt*, or *.dxf* files. This option invokes the **Select Template From File** dialog box, see Figure 12-22. You can also invoke this dialog box by right-clicking on the **Model** tab, the **Layout** tab, and then choosing the **From template** option from the shortcut menu.

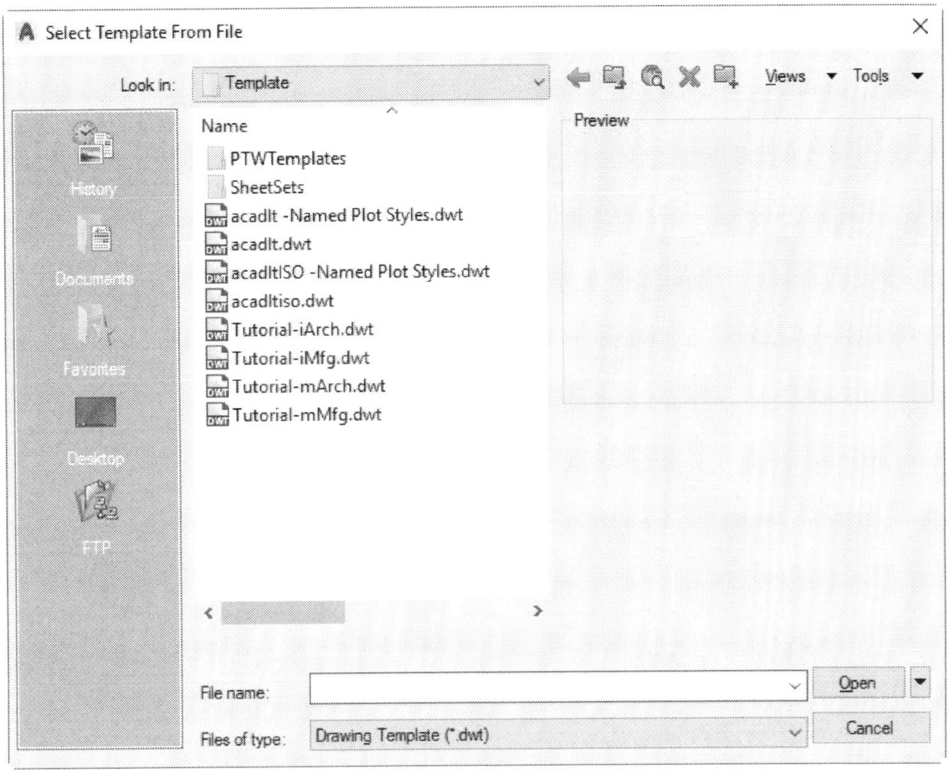

Figure 12-22 *The* ***Select Template From File*** *dialog box*

The layout and geometry from the specified template or drawing file is inserted into the current drawing. After the *dwt*, *dwg*, or *dxf* file is selected, the **Insert Layout(s)** dialog box is displayed, as shown in Figure 12-23.

Choose the **Layout from Template** button from the **Layouts** toolbar to create a layout using an existing template or a drawing file.

Note

If you insert a template that has a title block, it will be inserted as a block and all the text in the title block will be inserted as attributes. You will learn more about blocks and attributes in later chapters.

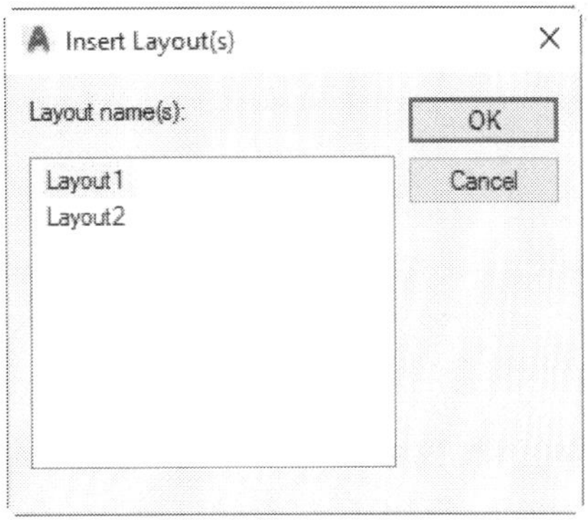

Figure 12-23 *The* ***Insert Layout(s)*** *dialog box*

Rename Option

This option allows you to rename a layout. On choosing this option, you will be prompted to specify the name of the layout to be renamed. On specifying the name, you will be prompted to specify the new name of the layout. The layout names have to be unique and can contain up to 255 characters, out of which only 32 are displayed in the tab. The characters in the name are not case-sensitive. You can also right-click on the **Model** or the **Layout** tab and choose **Rename** from the shortcut menu to rename the selected layout.

Tip
*You can also double-click on the **Layout** tab to rename it.*

SAveas Option

This option is used to save a layout in the drawing template file. On choosing this option, you will be prompted to specify the layout that has to be saved. If you specify the name of the layout to be saved, the **Create Drawing File** dialog box will be displayed. In this dialog box, you can enter the name of the template in the **File name** edit box. The layout templates can be saved in the *.dwg*, *.dwt*, or the *.dxf* format.

Set Option

This option is used to set a layout as the current layout. When you invoke this option, you will be prompted to specify the name of the layout that has to be made current.

? Option

This option is used to list all the layouts available in the current drawing. The list is displayed in the Command line. You can open the **AutoCAD LT Text Window** to view the list by pressing the F2 key.

IMPORTING LAYOUTS TO SHEET SETS

To add a layout to the current sheet set, right-click on the **Layout** tab and then choose the **Import Layout as Sheet** option from the shortcut menu; the **Import Layout as Sheet** dialog box will be invoked. This dialog box displays all the layouts available in the selected drawing. Select the check box on the left of the drawing file name under the **Drawing Name** column and choose the **Import Checked** button to import the selected layouts into the current sheet set.

Note
A layout can be imported to only one sheet set. If a layout already belongs to a sheet set, you have to create a copy of the drawing to import its layout to another sheet set.

Tip
You can also drag and drop the layout from a drawing to add it to the sheet set. But make sure that you save the drawing file before you drag and drop the layout.

INSERTING A LAYOUT USING THE WIZARD

Command: LAYOUTWIZARD

This command displays the **Create Layout Wizard** that guides you step-by-step through the process of creating a new layout.

DEFINING PAGE SETTINGS

Ribbon: Output > Plot > Page Setup Manager **Command:** PAGESETUP
Toolbar: Layouts > Page Setup Manager

The **Page Setup Manager** tool is used to specify the layout and plot device settings for each new layout. You can also right-click on the current **Layout** tab and choose the **Page Setup Manager** option from the shortcut menu to invoke this tool. When you invoke this tool, the **Page Setup Manager** dialog box is displayed, which will be discussed in Chapter 13.

Example 2

In this example, you will create a drawing in the model space and then use the paper space to plot the drawing. The drawing to be plotted is shown in Figure 12-24.

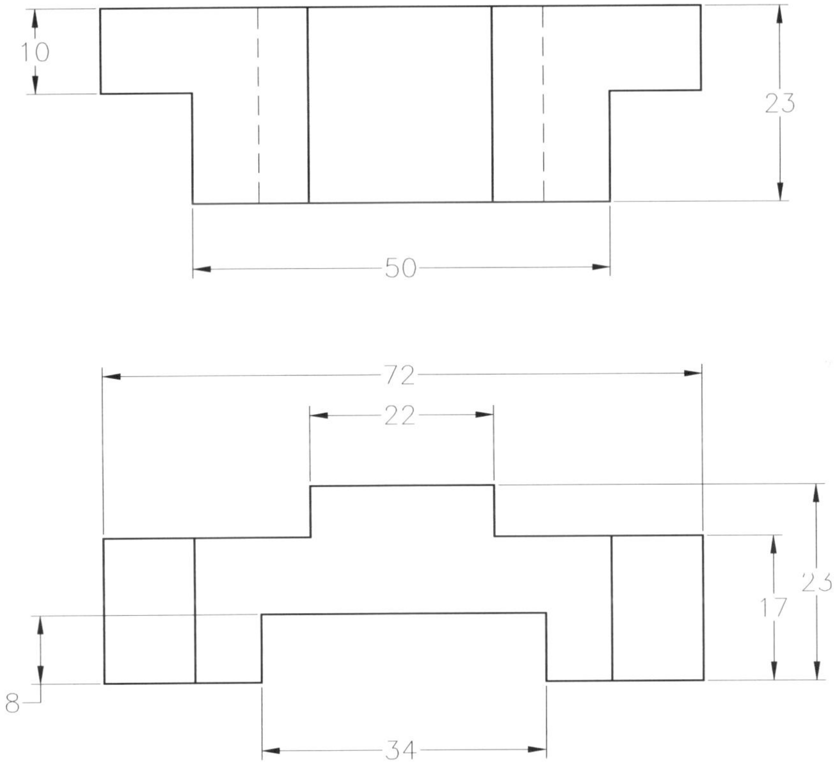

***Figure 12-24** Drawing for Example 2*

1. Increase the limits to 75, 75 and then draw the sketch shown in Figure 12-24.

2. Choose the **Layout1** tab; AutoCAD LT displays **Layout1** with the default viewport. Delete this viewport. Right-click on the **Layout1** tab and then choose **Page Setup Manager** option from the shortcut menu to display the **Page Setup Manager** dialog box. **Layout1** is automatically selected in the **Current page setup** list box.

3. Choose the **Modify** button to display the **Page Setup - Layout1** dialog box. Select the printer or plotter from the **Name** drop-down list in the **Printer/plotter** area. In this example, **HP Lasejet4000** is used. From the drop-down list in the **Paper size** area, select the paper size that is supported by your plotting device. In this example, the paper size is **ISO full bleed A4 (210 x 297 MM)**. Choose the **OK** button to accept the settings and exit the dialog box. Close the **Page Setup Manager** dialog box by choosing the **Close** button.

4. Choose the **Rectangular** tool from the **Viewports** drop-down in the **Layout Viewports** panel of the **Layout** tab in the **Ribbon**; you are prompted to specify the start point of the viewport. The prompt sequence is as follows:

   Specify corner of viewport or [ON/OFF/Fit/Shadeplot/Lock/Object/Polygonal/Restore/LAyer/2/3/4] <Fit>: **F** Enter
   Regenerating model.

5. Choose the **Extents** tool from the **Zoom** drop-down in the **Navigate** panel of the **View** tab in the **Ribbon** to zoom to the extents of the viewport.

6. Double-click in the viewport to switch to the temporary model space and repeat the previous step.

7. Create a dimension style with a text height of 1.5 and a arrowhead height of 1.25. Define all the other parameters based on the text and arrowhead heights and then select the **Annotative** check box from the **Scale for dimension features** area of the **Fit** tab in the **New Dimension Style** dialog box.

8. Using the new dimension style, dimension the drawing. Repeat step 5.

9. Double-click in the paper space to switch back to the paper space. Choose the **Plot** tool from the **Quick Access Toolbar**, the **Batch Plot** message box is displayed. Select the **Continue to**
   plot a single sheet option from this message box to display the **Plot - Layout1** dialog box.

10. Select the **Window** option from the **What to plot** drop-down list in the **Plot area**; the dialog box will be closed temporarily and you will be prompted to specify the first and second corners of the window. Define a window close to the boundary of the viewport.

11. As soon as you define both the corners of the window, the **Plot** dialog box will be redisplayed on the screen. Select the **Fit to paper** check box from the **Plot scale** area.

12. Select the **Center the plot** check box from the **Plot offset (origin set to printable area)** area.

13. Choose the **Preview** button to display the plot preview. You can make any adjustments, if required, by redefining the window.

14. After you are satisfied with the preview, right-click and choose **Plot** from the shortcut menu; the drawing will get printed. Save this drawing with the name *Example2.dwg*.

CONVERTING THE DISTANCE BETWEEN MODEL SPACE AND PAPER SPACE

Toolbar: Text > Convert distance between spaces **Command:** SPACETRANS

While working with drawings in layouts, you may need to find a distance value that is equivalent to a specific distance in the model space. For example, you may need to write text whose height should be equal to a similar text written in the model space. To convert these distances between the model space and layouts, AutoCAD LT provides the **SPACETRANS** command. Note that this command does not work in the model space. This command works only in layouts or in the temporary model space invoked from the layouts, but there should be at least one viewport in the drawing. When you invoke this command in the paper space, AutoCAD LT prompts you to select the viewport. After selecting the viewport, AutoCAD LT prompts you to specify the model space distance. Enter the original distance value that was measured in the model space; AutoCAD LT displays the paper space equivalent to the specified distance.

Similarly, when you invoke this command in the temporary model space, AutoCAD LT prompts you to specify the paper space distance. Enter the distance value measured in the paper space. AutoCAD LT displays the model space equivalent to the specified distance.

CONTROLLING THE DISPLAY OF ANNOTATIVE OBJECTS IN VIEWPORTS

Some new buttons need to be added to the Status Bar to control the annotation scale in viewports and model space separately. When you activate a floating viewport, a new **Viewport Scale** button is added to the Status Bar. The **Viewport Scale** button lists the same set of scales as the **Annotation Scale**. You can set an annotation display scale either from the **Viewport Scale** button or the **Annotation Scale** button, and the other scales will be updated accordingly. The viewport will zoom to an appropriate scale so that the annotation objects can be displayed at the specified scale.

Also, when you activate a floating viewport,the **Viewport Lock** button is added to the Status Bar. With the help of this button, you can toggle between the lock and unlock states of the viewport. The **Viewport Scale** and **Annotation Scale** buttons are not accessible when the viewport is locked. If the viewport is unlocked and you zoom the drawing instead of specifying the viewport scale, the annotation scale will not be changed and the current scale representation will remain intact and visible. But, the viewport scale will be changed to display the actual scale of the viewport.

The example given next will explain various concepts related to creating and controlling the display of annotations in viewports.

Note

When the paper space is active, the annotation scale is always 1:1 and it cannot be modified.

Example 3 Annotative Text

In this example, you will draw the object, as shown in Figure 12-25, and create the floating viewports, as shown in Figure 12-26. The left viewport has a scale of 3/8”=1’-0” and the right viewport has a scale of 1-1/2”=1’-0”. All the annotations that are created in the model space should be displayed with a text height of 0.08” on the sheet even if the same annotation appears in multiple viewports.

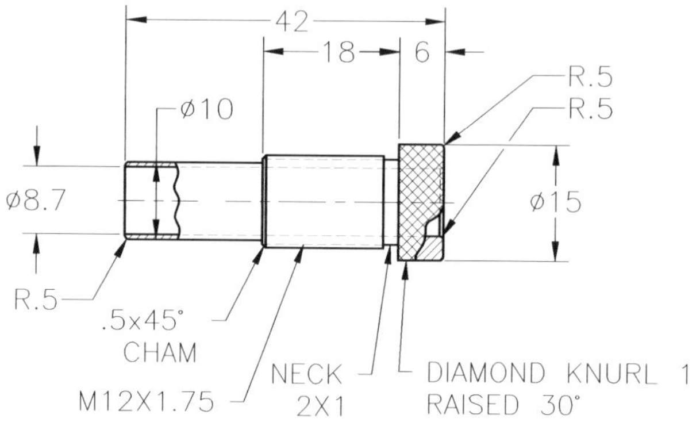

***Figure 12-25** Model for Example 3*

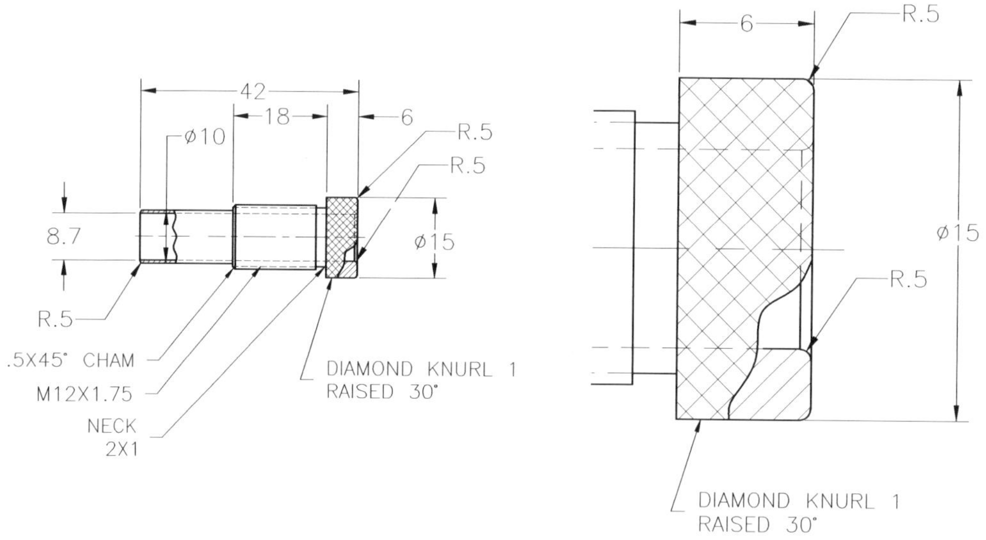

***Figure 12-26** Displaying the drawing in two viewports*

1. Start a new file in the **Drafting & Annotation** workspace and draw the object, as shown in Figure 12-25.

2. Set the **Annotation Scale** to 3/8”=1’-0” in the Status Bar.

3. Create an annotative text style with the **Paper Text Height** equal to **0.08**.

4. Create an annotative dimension style with the values given next and create the dimensions, refer to Figure 12-25.
   Arrow size = **0.07**
   Text height = **0.08**

5. Create an annotative multileader style with the values given next and draw the multileaders, refer to Figure 12-25.

   Landing distance = **0.075**
   Arrowhead size = **0.07**
   Text height = **0.08**

6. Change the annotation scale to 1-1/2”=1’-0”, select all the dimensions from the right of the object, and then choose the **Add Current Scale** tool from the **Annotation Scaling** panel of the **Annotate** tab; the annotation scale of 1-1/2”=1’-0” is added to the selected dimensions. You will notice that the selected dimensions and multileaders appear smaller than the other annotations because they reflect the current annotation scale of 1-1/2”=1’-0”.

7. Turn the **Annotation Visibility** button off. Now you can see the annotations that support a scale of 1-1/2”=1’-0”. This helps you to find out the dimensions to which the scale of 1-1/2”=1’-0” has been assigned.

8. Select the annotations from the right of the object and adjust their locations with the help of grips, such that the placement of dimensions remains similar to the one shown in Figure 12-25. Notice that when you select the annotation object, its different scale representations are displayed with faded dashed lines.

9. From the Status Bar, set the annotation scale to 3/8”=1’-0” and then change it back to 1-1/2”=1’-0”. Now you will notice that the same annotation objects not only change the size, but also change the location.

10. Choose the **Layout1** tab to switch to the layouts.

11. A rectangular viewport is automatically created in this layout. Choose the **Erase** tool from the **Modify** panel of the **Home** tab; you will be prompted to select the object. Enter **L** in this prompt to delete the last object, which in this case is the viewport.

12. Draw two rectangles of dimensions **3’X3.5’** and **2.25’X3.5’** side-by-side, refer to Figure 12-26.

13. Choose the **Object** tool from **Layout > Layout Viewports > Viewports drop-down > Object Viewports** of the **Ribbon**; you will be prompted to select the object. Select one of the rectangles; it will be converted into a viewport. Similarly, convert the second rectangle into a viewport.

14. Activate the viewport on the left and set its annotation scale to 3/8”=1’-0” in the Status Bar.

15. Similarly, activate the viewport on the right and set its annotation scale to 1-1/2”=1’-0”. Pan the view so that it looks similar to Figure 12-26.

Self-Evaluation Test

Answer the following questions and then compare them to those given at the end of this chapter:

1. The __________ tool is used to create tiled viewports.

2. The viewports in layouts are called __________ viewports.

3. The two working environments provided by AutoCAD LT are __________ and __________.

4. By default, the linetype scaling is controlled by the __________ system variable.

5. When you join two adjacent viewports, the resultant viewport is __________ in shape.

6. The default viewport that is created in a new layout is __________ in shape.

7. Viewports in the model space can be of any shape. (T/F)

8. Viewports in the model space can overlap each other. (T/F)

9. You can join two different tiled viewports. (T/F)

10. You cannot insert any additional layout in the current drawing. (T/F)

Review Questions

Answer the following questions:

1. Which of the following commands can be used to control the display of objects in viewports?

   (a) **MVIEW** (b) **DVIEW**
   (c) **LAYOUT** (d) **MSPACE**

2. Which of the following tools can be used to switch to the temporary model space?

   (a) **Quick View Drawings** (b) **Named**
   (c) **Quick View Layouts** (d) **Model or Paper space**

3. Which of the following options in the paper space can be used to hide the hidden lines of solid models in printing?

   (a) **Hide** (b) **Shadeplot**
   (c) **Create** (d) **None**

4. Which of the following tools can be used to clip an existing floating viewport?

(a) **View Manager** (b) **Join**
(c) **Clip** (d) **Restore**

5. Which of the following options of the **VPLAYER** command is used to create a layer that will be frozen in all viewports?

(a) **Freeze** (b) **Thaw**
(c) **Newfrz** (d) **Reset**

6. You can work only in the __________ tiled viewport.

7. The __________ tool can be used to set similar linetype scale for all the viewports.

8. The __________ tool is used to switch back to the paper space from the temporary model space.

9. The __________ dialog box is used to save a viewport configuration in the model space.

10. Layers that have been frozen, thawed, switched on, or switched off globally are not affected by the __________ tool.

11. Only the viewports that are created in layouts can be polygonal in shape. (T/F)

12. You cannot lock the display of a floating viewport. (T/F)

13. An existing closed loop can be converted into a viewport in the model space. (T/F)

14. You can create an array of viewports using the **Named** tool in the model space. (T/F)

15. By Default, PSLTSCALE is set to 0. (T/F)

Exercise 1 — *Tiled Viewport*

In this exercise, you will perform the following operations:

a. In the model space, make the drawing of the shaft shown in Figure 12-27.
b. Create three tiled viewports in the model space and then display the drawing in all the three tiled viewports.
c. Create a new layout with the name **Title Block** and insert a title block of ANSI A size in this layout.
d. Create two viewports, one for the drawing and one for the detail "A". See Figure 12-27 for the approximate size and location. The dimensions in detail "A" viewport must not be shown in the other viewport. Also, adjust the LTSCALE factor for hidden and center lines.
e. Plot the drawing.

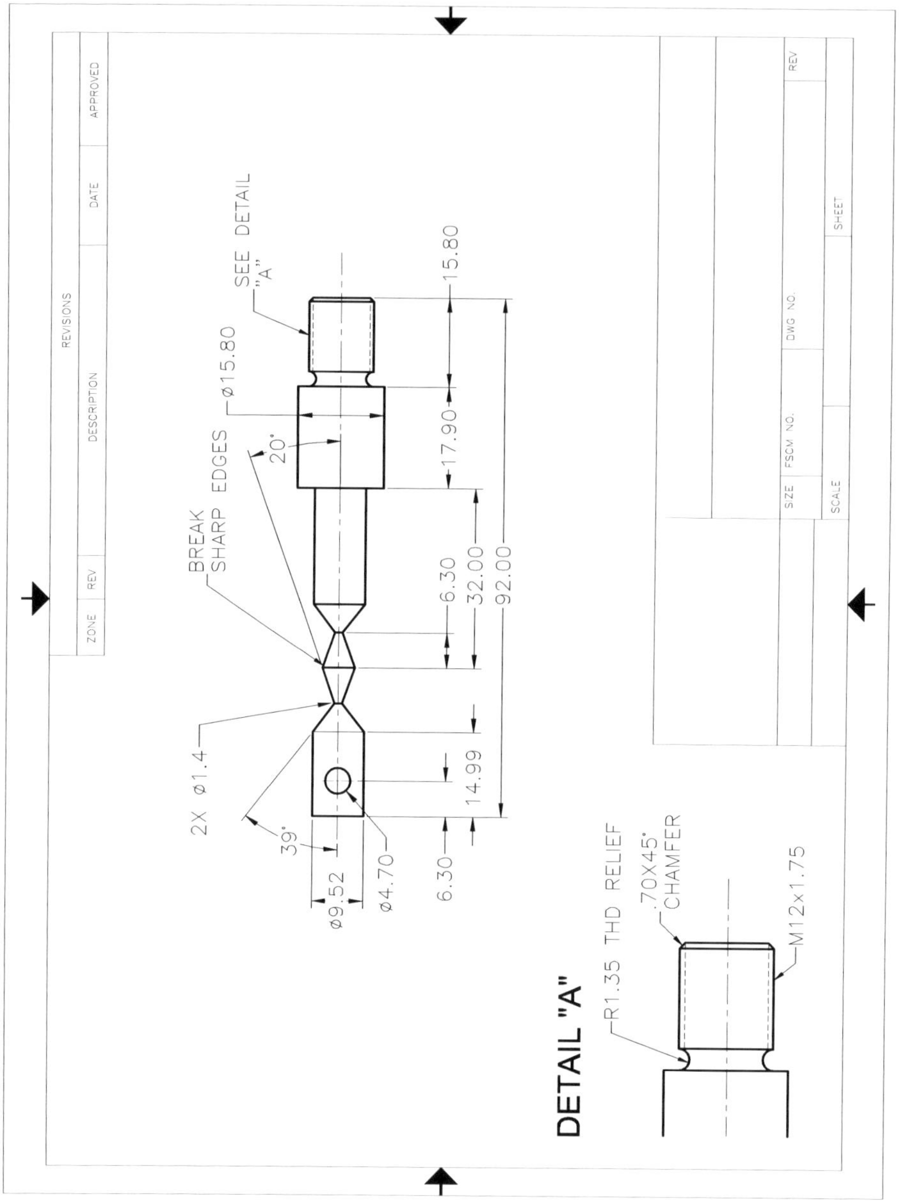

Figure 12-27 Drawing for Exercise 1

Answers to Self-Evaluation Test

1. VPORTS, **2.** floating, **3.** model space, paper space/layouts, **4. LTSCALE**, **5.** rectangular, **6.** rectangular, **7.** F, **8.** F, **9.** T, **10.** F

Chapter 13

Plotting Drawings

Learning Objectives

After completing this chapter, you will be able to:

- *Set plotter specifications and plot drawings*
- *Configure plotters and edit their configuration files*
- *Create, use, and modify plot styles and plot style tables*
- *Plot sheets in a sheet set*

Key Terms

- *Plot*
- *Page Setup*
- *Plot Style*
- *Plotter Manager*
- *Named Plot Style*
- *Styles Manager*
- *Color Dependent Plot Style*
- *Plot Style Table Editor*

PLOTTING DRAWINGS IN AutoCAD LT

After you have completed a drawing, you can store it on the computer storage device such as the hard drive or diskette. However, to get its hard copy, you should plot the drawing on a sheet of paper using a plotter or printer. A hard copy is a handy reference for professionals working on site. With pen plotters, you can obtain a high-resolution drawing. Basic plotting has already been discussed in Chapter 2, Getting Started with AutoCAD LT. You can plot drawings in the **Model** tab or any of the layout tabs. A drawing has a **Model** and two layout tabs (**Layout1**, **Layout2**) by default. Each of these tabs has its own settings and can be used to create different plots. You can also create new layout tabs using the **New Layout** tool. This is discussed in Chapter 12.

PLOTTING DRAWINGS USING THE PLOT DIALOG BOX

Quick Access Toolbar: Plot **Toolbar:** Standard > Plot **Command:** PLOT/Ctrl+P
Application Menu: Print > Plot **Ribbon:** Output > Plot > Plot

The **Plot** tool is used to plot a drawing. When you choose this tool, the **Plot** dialog box is displayed. This dialog box can also be invoked by right-clicking on the **Model** tab or any of the **Layout** tabs and then choosing the **Plot** option from the shortcut menu displayed. Figure 13-1 shows the expanded **Plot** dialog box.

In this dialog box, some values are set while configuring AutoCAD LT for the first time. You can examine those values and if they conform to your requirements, you can start plotting directly. Otherwise, you can alter them to define plot specifications by using the options in the **Plot** dialog box. The available plot options are discussed next.

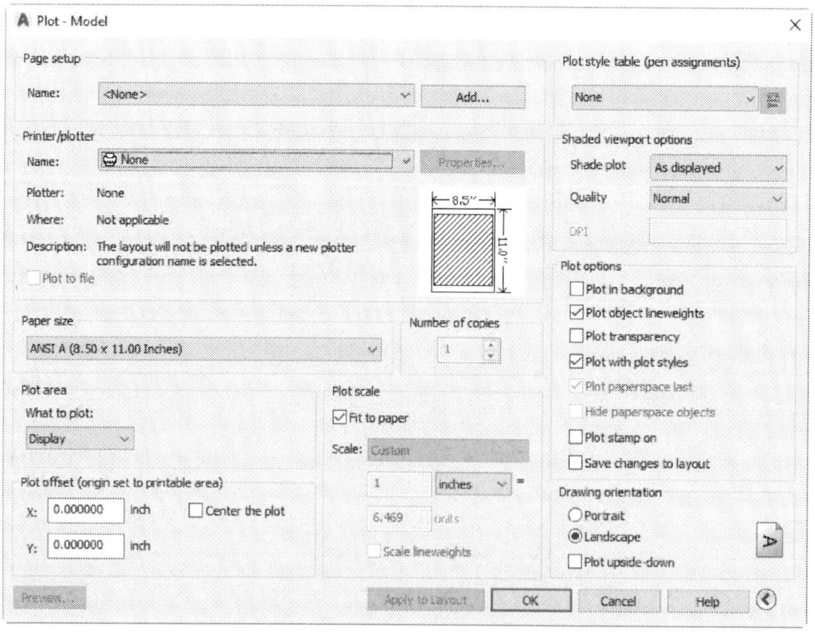

*Figure 13-1 The expanded **Plot-Model** dialog box*

Page setup Area

The **Name** drop-down list in this area displays all the saved and named page setups. A page setup contains the settings required to plot a drawing on a sheet of paper to create a layout. It consists of all the settings related to the plotting of a drawing such as the scale, pen settings, and so on. These settings can be saved as a named page setup, which can be later selected from this drop-down list and used for plotting a drawing. If you select **Previous plot** from the drop-down list, the settings used for the last drawing plotted are applied to the current drawing. You can also import the existing page setup from the other files by selecting the **Import** option from the drop-down list. The page setup can be imported from any drawing file(*.dwg*), from a template file(*.dwt*), or from a drawing interchange format file(*.dxf*). You can choose the base for the page setup on a named page setup, or you can add a new named page setup by choosing the **Add** button, which is located next to the drop-down list. When you choose this button, AutoCAD LT displays the **Add Page Setup** dialog box, as shown in Figure 13-2.

Enter the name of the new page setup in this dialog box and choose **OK**, all settings that you configure in the current **Plot** dialog box will be saved under this page setup.

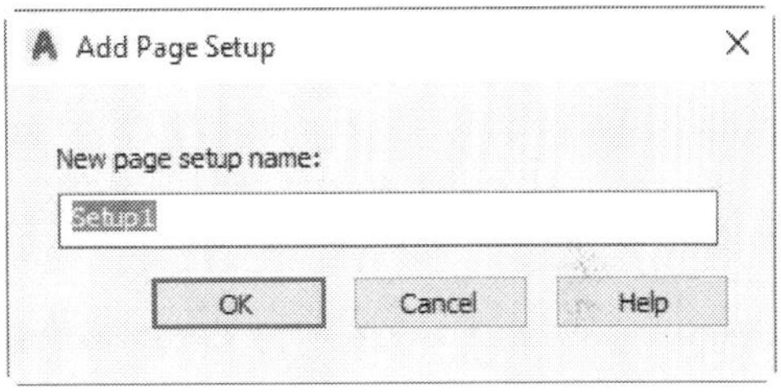

***Figure 13-2** The **Add Page Setup** dialog box*

> **Tip**
> *To create a new page setup based on the existing one, select the existing page setup from the **Name** drop-down list and make modifications in it. Next, choose the **Add** button; the modified page setup will be saved.*

Printer/plotter Area

This area displays all the information about the printer and plotter currently selected in the **Name** drop-down list. It displays information of the plotter driver and the printer port being used. It also displays the physical location and some description text about the selected plotter or printer. All the currently configured plotters are displayed in the **Name** drop-down list.

> **Note**
> *To add plotters and printers to the **Name** drop-down list, choose the **Plotter Manager** tool from the **Plot** panel in the **Output** tab; a window will be displayed. Double-click on the **Add-A-Plotter Wizard** icon in this window to display the **Add Plotter** wizard. You can use this wizard to add a plotter to the list of configured plotters. Once the plotter is added, the plotter configuration file (PC3) for the plotter will be created. This file consists of all the settings needed by the specific plotter to plot the drawing. (The **Plotters** window will be discussed later in this chapter in the section "Adding Plotters").*

Properties

To check information about a configured printer or plotter, choose the **Properties** button. When you choose this button, the **Plotter Configuration Editor** dialog box will be displayed. This dialog box lists all the details of the selected plotter under three tabs: **General**, **Ports**, and

Device and Document Settings. The **Plotter Configuration Editor** dialog box will be discussed later in the "Editing Plotter Configuration" section of this chapter.

Plot to file

If you select this check box, AutoCAD LT plots the output to a file rather than to the plotter. Depending on the plotter selected, the file can be plotted in the *.dwf*, *.plt*, *.jpg*, or *.png* format. On selecting this check box and choosing **OK** from the **Plot** dialog box, the **Browse for Plot File** dialog box will be displayed. Specify the file name and its location in this dialog box.

Partial Preview Window

The window displayed below the **Properties** button is called the Partial Preview window. The preview in this window dynamically changes as you modify the parameters in the **Plot** dialog box. The outer rectangle in this window is the paper you selected. It also shows the size of the paper. The inner hatched rectangle is the section of the paper that is used by the image. If the image extends beyond the paper, a red border is displayed around the paper.

Paper size Area

The drop-down list in this area displays all standard paper sizes for the selected plotting device. You can select any size from the list to make it current. If **None** has been selected currently from the **Name** drop-down list in the **Printer/plotter** area, AutoCAD LT will display the list of all standard paper sizes.

Number of copies Area

You can use the spinner available in this area to specify the number of copies that you want to plot. If multiple layouts and copies are selected and some of the layouts are set for plotting to a file or AutoSpool, they will produce a single plot. AutoSpool allows you to send a file for plotting while you are working on another program.

Plot area Area

Using the **What to plot** drop-down list provided in this area, you can specify the portion of the drawing to be plotted. You can also control the way plotting will be carried out. The options in the **What to plot** drop-down list are described next.

Display

If you select this option, the portion of the drawing that is currently being displayed on the screen is plotted.

Extents

This option resembles the **Extents** tool of the **Zoom** drop-down and prints the drawing to the extents of the objects. If you add more objects to drawing, they are also included in the plot and the extents of the drawing are recalculated. If you reduce the drawing extents by erasing, moving, or scaling the objects, the extents of the drawing are again recalculated. You can use the **Extents** tool to determine which objects shall be plotted.

Limits

This option is available only if you plot from the **Model** tab. Selecting this option plots the complete area defined within the drawing limits.

Window

On selecting this option, you need to specify the section of the drawing to be plotted by defining a window. To define a window, select the **Window** option from the **What to plot** drop-down list. On doing so, the **Plot** dialog box will be temporarily closed and you will be prompted to specify two points on the screen that define a window. Specify the points; the area within this window will be plotted. Once you have defined the window, the **Plot** dialog box is displayed again on the screen. You will notice that the **Window<** button is now displayed on the right of the **What to plot** drop-down list. To again select the area to be plotted, choose the **Window** button. If the **Model** tab is chosen, you will notice that the previously selected area is displayed in white and the remaining area is displayed in gray. After selecting the area to be plotted, you can choose the **OK** button in the dialog box to plot the drawing.

View

Selecting the **View** option enables you to plot a view that was created with the **View Manager** dialog box. The view must be defined in the current drawing. If no view has been created, the **View** option is not displayed. When you select this option, a drop-down list is displayed in this area. You can select a view for plotting from this drop-down list and then choose **OK** button in the **Plot** dialog box. While using the **View** option, the specifications of the plot will depend upon the specifications of the named view.

Layout

This option is available only when you are plotting from the layout. This option prints the entire content of the drawing that lies inside the printable area of the paper selected from the drop-down list in the **Paper size** area.

Plot offset (origin set to printable area) Area

This area allows you to specify an offset of the plotting area from the lower left corner of the paper. The lower left corner of the specified plot area is positioned at the lower left margin of the paper by default. If you select the **Center the plot** check box, AutoCAD LT automatically centers the plot on the paper by calculating the *X* and *Y* offset values. You can specify an offset from the origin by entering positive or negative values in the **X** and **Y** edit boxes. For example, if you want the drawing to be plotted 4 units to the right and 4 units above the origin point, enter **4** in both the **X** and **Y** edit boxes. Depending on the units you have specified in the **Paper size** area of the dialog box, the offset values are either in inches, in millimeters, or in pixels.

Plot scale Area

This area controls the drawing scale of the plot area. Apart from the **Custom** option, the **Scale** drop-down list has thirty-three architectural and decimal scales by default. The default scale setting is **1:1** when you are plotting a layout. However, if you are plotting in the **Model** tab, the **Fit to paper** check box is selected. The **Fit to paper** option allows you to automatically fit the entire drawing on the paper. It is useful when you have to print a large drawing using a printer that uses a smaller size paper.

Whenever you select a standard scale from the drop-down list, the scale is displayed in the edit boxes as a ratio of the plotted units to the drawing units. You can also change the scale factor manually in these edit boxes. When you do so, the **Scale** edit box displays **Custom**. For example, for an architectural drawing, which is to be plotted at the scale 1/4"=1'-0", you can enter either 1/4"=1'-0" or 1=48 in the edit boxes.

Note

*The **PSLTSCALE** system variable controls the paper space linetype scaling and has a default value of 1. This implies that irrespective of the zoom scale of the viewports, the linetype scale of the objects in the viewports remains the same. If you want the linetype scale of the objects in different viewports with different magnification factors to appear different, you should set the value of the **PSLTSCALE** variable to 0. This has been discussed in detail in Chapter 12 (Model Space Viewports, Paper Space Viewports, and Layouts).*

The **Scale lineweights** check box is available only if you are plotting in a layout. This option is not available in the **Model** tab. If you select the **Scale lineweights** check box, you can scale lineweights in proportion to the plot scale. Lineweights generally specify the linewidth of the printable objects and are plotted with the original lineweight size, regardless of the plot scale.

Note

*You can save the custom scales that you use during plotting or in layouts in the **Edit Drawing Scales** dialog box. To invoke the **Edit Drawing Scales** dialog box, choose the **Scale List** tool from the **Annotation Scaling** panel in the **Annotate** tab. The **Scale List** area lists the default scales in AutoCAD LT. Choose the **Add** button to invoke the **Add Scale** dialog box. Enter a name for the custom scale in the **Name appearing in the scale list** edit box. Next, enter the scale in the **Scale properties** area and choose the **OK** button; the name specified for the custom scale will be listed in the **Scale List** area. In this way, you can keep a track of the custom scales used.*

Plot style table (pen assignments) Area

This area will be available when you expand the **Plot** dialog box. This area allows you to view and select a plot style table, edit the current plot style table, or create a new plot style table. A plot style table is a collection of plot styles. A plot style is a group of pen settings that are assigned to an object or layer and that determines the color, linetype, thickness, line ending, line joining and the fill style of the drawing objects when they are plotted. It is a named file that allows you to control the pen settings for a plotted drawing.

You can select the required plot style from the drop-down list in this area. Whenever you select a plot style, AutoCAD LT displays the **Question** message box prompting you to specify whether the selected plot style should be assigned to all layouts or not. If you choose **Yes**, the selected plot style will be used to plot from all layouts. You can also select **None** from the drop-down list to plot a drawing without using any plot styles. You can assign different plot style tables to a drawing and plot the same drawing differently each time. The use of plot styles will be discussed later in this chapter.

You can also select **New** from the drop-down list to create a new plot style. When you select this option, a wizard will be started that will guide you through the process of creating a new plot style.

Edit

Using this button, you can edit the plot style table selected from the **Plot style table** drop-down list. This button is not available if you have selected **None** from the drop-down list. When you choose the **Edit** button, AutoCAD LT displays the **Plot Style Table Editor**, where you can edit the selected plot style table. This dialog box has three tabs: **General**, **Table View**, and **Form View**. The **Plot Style Table Editor** will be discussed later in the "Using Plot Styles" section of this chapter.

Shaded viewport options Area

The options in this area are used to print a shaded or a rendered image and are discussed next.

Shade plot

This drop-down list is used to select a technique that will be used for plotting the drawings. This drop-down list will be available only while plotting from the model space. If you select **As displayed** from this drop-down list, the drawing will be plotted as it is displayed on the screen. If you select the **Legacy wireframe** option, the model will be plotted in wireframe mode displaying all hidden geometries, even if it is shaded in the drawing. If you select the **Legacy hidden** option, then the line will be plotted with hidden lines suppressed. On selecting the **Hidden**, **Wireframe**, **Conceptual**, **Realistic**, **Shaded**, **Shaded with edges**, **Shades of Gray**, **Sketchy**, and **X-Ray** options, the drawing will be plotted in the corresponding visual style, even if the model is displayed in some other visual styles. Similarly, selecting the **Rendered** option will plot the rendered image of the drawing. The other options in the drop-down list are used to specify the quality for plotting the shaded and rendered model. But if you are plotting a drawing from the paper space, the display settings of the viewport will be used for plotting it. To set the display settings of a viewport, select the viewport and right-click; a shortcut menu will be displayed. Choose the **Shade plot** option from the shortcut menu and then select the desired shading option.

Quality

This drop-down list is used to select printing quality in terms of dots per inch (dpi) for the printed drawing. The **Draft** option prints the drawing with 0 dpi which results in wireframe printout. The **Preview** option prints the drawing at 150 dpi, the **Normal** option prints the drawing at 300 dpi, the **Presentation** option prints the drawing at 600 dpi, the **Maximum** option prints the drawing at the maximum dpi of the selected plotting device. You can also specify a custom dpi by selecting the **Custom** option from this drop-down list. The custom value of dpi can be specified in the **DPI** drop-down list, which is enabled below the **Quality** drop-down list on selecting the **Custom** option.

Plot options Area

This area displays various check boxes that can be selected as per the plot requirements. They are described next.

Plot in background

Select this check box to perform the printing and plotting operation in the background. While plotting in the background, you can return immediately to your drawing without waiting for the printing or plotting operation to finish. By default, the background plotting is turned off for plotting and it is turned on for publishing. The **BACKGROUNDPLOT** system variable is used to control the default settings for background plotting.

Plot object lineweights

Select this check box, if you need to plot the drawing with specified lineweights.

Plot transparency

When you select this check box, AutoCAD LT will plot drawing using the transparency applied to the objects.

Plot with plot styles

When you select the **Plot with plot styles** check box, AutoCAD LT plots using the plot styles applied to the objects in the drawing and defined in the plot style table. The different property characteristics associated with the different style definitions are stored in the plot style tables and can be easily attached to the geometry.

Plot paperspace last

This check box is not available when you are in the **Model** tab because no paper space objects are present in the **Model** tab. This option is available when you are working in the layout tab. By selecting the **Plot paperspace last** check box, you can plot the model space geometry before paper space objects. Usually the paper space geometry is plotted before the model space geometry. This option is also useful when there are multiple tabs selected for plotting and you want to plot the model space geometry before the layout tabs.

Hide paperspace objects

This check box is available in the **Layout** tab only and is used to specify whether or not the objects drawn in layouts will be hidden while plotting. If this check box is selected, the objects created in layouts will be hidden.

Plot stamp on

This check box is selected to turn the plot stamp on. The plot stamp is a user-defined information that will be displayed on the sheet while plotting. You can set the plot stamp information when you select this check box. When you select this check box, the **Plot Stamp Settings** button is displayed on the right of this check box. You can choose this button to display the **Plot Stamp** dialog box to set the parameters for the plot stamp.

Save changes to layout

This check box is selected to save the changes made using the **Plot** dialog box.

Drawing orientation Area

This area provides options to specify the orientation of the drawing on the paper. You can change the drawing orientation by selecting the **Portrait** or **Landscape** radio button with or without selecting the **Plot upside-down** check box. The paper icon displayed on the right side of this area indicates the orientation of the selected paper and the letter icon (A) on it indicates the orientation of the drawing on the page. The **Landscape** radio button is selected by default for AutoCAD LT drawings and orients the length of the paper along the *X* axis. If we assume this orientation to be at a rotation angle of 0 degree, then while selecting the **Portrait** radio button, the plot is oriented with the width along the *X* axis, which is equivalent to the plot being rotated through a rotation angle of 90 degrees. Similarly, if you select both the **Landscape** radio button and the **Plot upside-down** check box at the same time, the plot gets rotated through a rotation angle of 180-degree and if you select both the **Portrait** radio button and the **Plot upside-down** check box at the same time, the plot gets rotated through a rotation angle of 270 degrees. The AutoCAD LT screen conforms to the landscape orientation by default.

Preview

When you choose the **Preview** button, AutoCAD LT displays the drawing on the screen just as it would be plotted on the paper. Once the regeneration is performed, the dialog boxes on the screen disappear, and an outline of the paper size is shown. In the plot preview (Figure 13-3), the cursor is replaced by the **Zoom Realtime** icon. This icon can be used to zoom in and out interactively by pressing and moving the left mouse button. You can right-click to display a shortcut menu and then choose **Exit** to exit the preview or press the ENTER or ESC key to return to the dialog box. You can also choose **Plot** to plot the drawing right away or choose the other zooming options available.

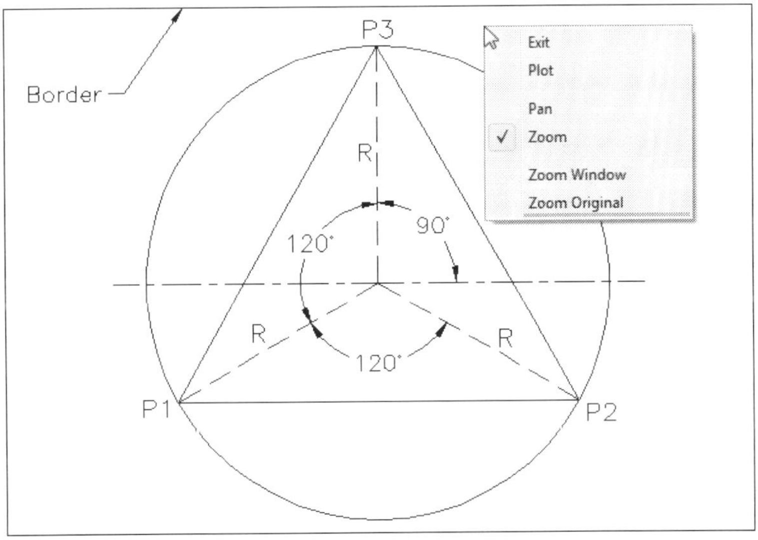

***Figure 13-3** Full plot preview with the shortcut menu*

After setting all the parameters, if you choose the **OK** button in the **Plot** dialog box, AutoCAD LT starts plotting the drawing in the file or plotters as specified. Also, the **Plot Job Progress** dialog box, where you can view the progress of plotting will be displayed.

ADDING PLOTTERS

Application Menu: Print > Manage Plotters
Command: PLOTTERMANAGER **Ribbon:** Output > Plot > Plotter Manager

In AutoCAD LT, the plotters are added using the **Plotter Manager** tool. This tool is discussed next.

The Plotter Manager Tool

When you invoke the **Plotter Manager** tool, AutoCAD LT will display the **Plotters** window, see Figure 13-4.

The **Plotters** window is basically a Windows Explorer window. It displays all the configured plotters and the **Add-A-Plotter Wizard** icon. You can right-click on any one of the icons belonging to the plotters that have already been configured to display a shortcut menu. You can choose **Delete** from the shortcut menu to remove a plotter from the list. You can also choose **Rename** from the shortcut menu to rename the plotter configuration file or choose the **Properties** option to view the properties of the configured device.

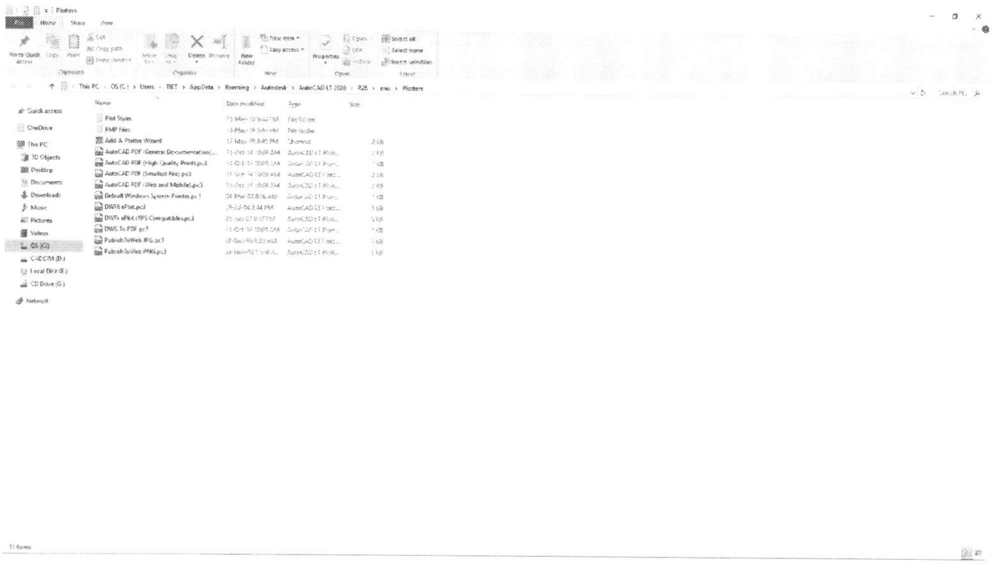

Figure 13-4 *The **Plotters** window*

Add-A-Plotter Wizard

If you double-click on the **Add-A-Plotter Wizard** icon in the **Plotters** window, AutoCAD LT guides you to configure a nonsystem plotter for plotting your drawing files. AutoCAD LT stores all the information of a configured plotter in configured plot (PC3) files. The PC3 files are stored at the location *C:\Users\<owner>\AppData\Roaming\Autodesk\AutoCAD LT 2020\R20.1\enu\Plotters* by default. You can add your own folder to store information of a configured plotter. To do so, add path of the folder in the **Support Files Search Path** given in the **Files** tab of the **Options** dialog box. The steps for configuring a new plotter using the **Add-A-Plotter Wizard** are given next.

1. Open the **Plotters** window by choosing the **Plotter Manager** tool from the **Plot** panel and double-click on the **Add-A-Plotter Wizard** icon, the **Add Plotter - Introduction Page** will be displayed.
2. In the **Add Plotter - Introduction Page**, read the introduction carefully, and then choose the **Next** button to move to the **Add Plotter - Begin** page.
3. On the **Add Plotter - Begin** page, the **My Computer** radio button is selected by default. Choose the **Next** button; the **Add Plotter - Plotter Model** page is displayed.
4. On this page, select a manufacturer and model of required plotter from the **Manufacturers**

and **Models** list boxes, respectively. If your plotter is not present in the list of available plotters, and you have a driver disk for your plotter, choose the **Have Disk** button to locate the *.hif* file from the driver disk, and install the driver supplied with your plotter. Now, choose the **Next** button; the **Add Plotter - Import Pcp or Pc2** page is displayed.

5. In the **Add Plotter - Import Pcp or Pc2** page, if you want to import configuring information from a PCP or a PC2 file created with a previous version of AutoCAD LT, you can choose the **Import File** button and select the file. Otherwise, simply choose the **Next** button to advance to the next page.
6. On the **Add Plotter - Ports** page, select the port from the list to be used while plotting, and choose the **Next** button.
7. On the **Add Plotter - Plotter Name** page, you can specify the name of the currently configured plotter or the default name will be entered automatically. Choose the **Next** button.
8. When you reach the **Add Plotter - Finish** page, you can choose the **Finish** button to exit the **Add Plotter Wizard**.

   You can also choose the **Edit Plotter Configuration** button to display the **Plotter Configuration Editor** dialog box where you can edit the current plotter's configuration. Also, in this page, you can choose the **Calibrate Plotter** button to display the **Calibrate Plotter** wizard. This wizard allows you to calibrate your plotter by setting up a test measurement. After test plotting, it compares the plot measurements with the actual measurements and computes a correction factor.

Once you have chosen **Finish** to exit the wizard, a PC3 file for the newly configured plotter will be displayed in the **Plotters** window. This PC3 file contains all the settings needed by the plotter to plot. Also, the newly configured plotter name is added to the **Name** drop-down list in the **Printer/plotter** area in the **Plot** dialog box. You can now use the plotter for plotting.

EDITING THE PLOTTER CONFIGURATION

You can modify the properties of the selected plot device by using the **Plotter Configuration Editor** dialog box. This dialog box can be invoked in several ways. As discussed earlier, while using the **Plot** or **Page Setup** dialog box, you can choose the **Properties** button in the **Printer/plotter** area to display the **Plotter Configuration Editor** dialog box, see Figure 13-5. You can modify the default settings of a plotter while configuring it by choosing the **Edit Plotter Configuration** button on the **Add Plotter - Finish** page of the **Add Plotter** wizard. You can also select the PC3 file for editing in the **Plotters** window by using Windows Explorer (by default, PC3 files are stored in *\Documents and Settings\<owner>\Application Data\Roaming\Autodesk\AutoCAD LT 2020\R20.1\enu\Plotters*) and double-click on the file. The three tabs in the **Plotter Configuration Editor** dialog box are discussed next.

General Tab

This tab contains basic information about the configured plotter or the PC3 file. You can make changes only in the **Description** area. The rest of the information in the tab is read only. This tab contains information on the configured plotter file name, plotter driver type, HDI driver file version number, name of the system printer (if any), and the location and name of the PMP file (if any calibration file is attached to the PC3 file).

Ports Tab

This tab contains information about the communication between the plotting device and your computer. You can choose between a serial (local), parallel (local), or network port. The default settings for parallel and serial ports are **LPT1** and **COM1**, respectively. You can also change the port name, if your device is connected to a different port. You can also select the **Plot to File** radio button, if you want to save the plot as a file. You can select **AutoSpool**, if you want plotting to occur automatically, while you continue to work on another application.

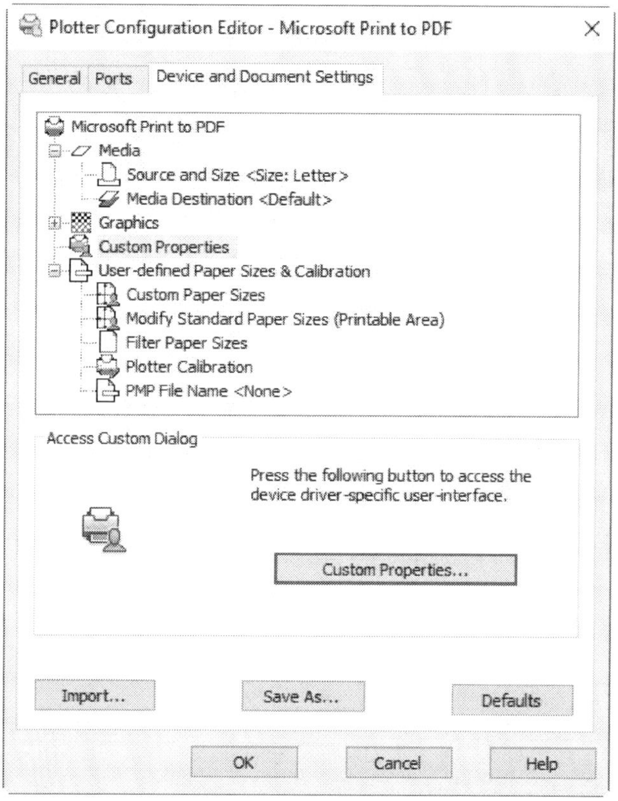

***Figure 13-5** The **Plotter Configuration Editor** dialog box*

Device and Document Settings Tab

This tab contains the plotting options specific to the selected plotter. These options are displayed as a tree view in the window. For example, if you configure a plotter, you have the option to modify the pen characteristics. You can select any plotter properties from the tree view displayed in the window to change the values as required. Whenever you select an icon from the tree view in the window, the corresponding information is displayed in an area below it. For example, if you select **PMP File Name <None>** in the tree view of the window, the **PMP file** area is displayed below. This area contains the current settings and the options to modify it. The information that is displayed within brackets (< >) can be modified. By default, **Custom properties** is displayed as highlighted in the window because it contains the properties that are modified commonly. The **Access Custom Dialog** area is displayed below the window. On choosing the **Custom Properties** button in this area, a dialog box specific to the selected plotter will be displayed. This dialog box has several properties of the selected plotter grouped and displayed under various areas and can be modified here.

Once you have made the desired changes, choose **Save As** in the **Plotter Configuration Editor** dialog box to save the changes you just made to the PC3 file.

Tip
It is better to create a new PC3 file for a plotter and keep the original file as it is so that you encounter no error while using the specific printer later. The PC3 files determine the proper functioning of a plotter and any modifications may lead to errors.

IMPORTING PCP/PC2 CONFIGURATION FILES

If you want to import a PCP or PC2 configuration file or plot settings created by previous releases of AutoCAD LT into the **Model** tab or the current layout for the drawing, you can use the **PCINWIZARD** command to display the **Import PCP or PC2 Plot Settings** wizard. All information from a PCP or PC2 file regarding plot area, plot offset, paper size, plot scale, and plot origin can be imported. Read the **Introduction** page of the wizard that is displayed carefully and then choose the **Next** button. The **Browse File name** page is displayed. Here, you can either enter the name of the PCP or PC2 file directly in the **PC2 or PCP file name** edit box or choose the **Browse** button to display the **Import** dialog box where you can select the file to be imported. After you specify the file for importing, choose **Open** to return to the wizard. Choose the **Next** button to display the **Finish** page. After importing the files, you can modify the rest of the plot settings for the current layout.

SETTING PLOT PARAMETERS

Before starting with the drawing, you can set various plotting parameters in the **Model** tab or in the Layouts. The plot parameters that can be set include the plotter to be used, for example, plot style table, the paper size, units, and so on. All these parameters can be set using the **Page Setup Manager** tool as discussed next.

Working with Page Setups

Toolbar: Layouts > Page Setup Manager
Application Menu: Print > Page Setup
Ribbon: Output > Plot > Page Setup Manager **Command:** PAGESETUP

As discussed earlier, a page setup contains the settings required to plot a drawing. Each layout as well as the **Model** tab can have a unique page setup attached to it. You can use the **Page Setup Manager** tool to create named page setups that can be used later. A page setup consists of specifications for the layout page, plotting device, paper size, and settings for the layouts to be plotted. This tool can also be invoked by choosing the **Page Setup Manager** option from the shortcut menu displayed on right-clicking on the current **Model** or **Layout** tab. Remember that the **Page Setup Manager** option will be available in the shortcut menu only for the current **Model** or **Layout** tab.

When you invoke the **Page Setup Manager** tool, AutoCAD LT displays the **Page Setup Manager** dialog box. The names of the tabs displayed in the **Current page setup** list box of the **Page**

setups area depend on the tab (**Model or Layout**) from which you invoke this dialog box. For example, if you invoke this dialog box from the **Model** tab, it displays only **Model** in this list box. However, if you invoke this dialog box from the **Layout** tab, it displays the list of all the layouts that are invoked at least once. Figure 13-6 shows the **Page Setup Manager** dialog box invoked from the **Layout1** tab. In this case, only the **Layout1** was activated at least once. You can use this dialog box to create a new page setup, modify the existing page setup, or import a page setup from an existing file.

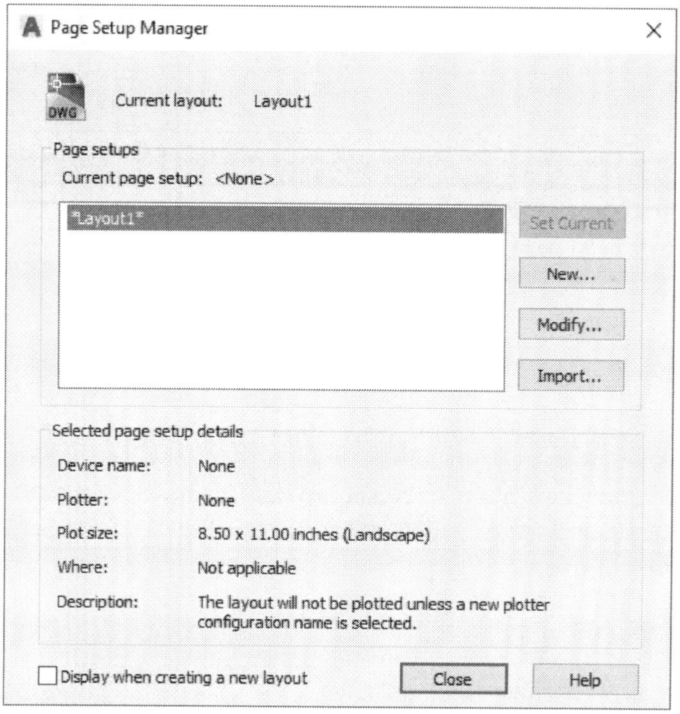

***Figure 13-6** The **Page Setup Manager** dialog box invoked from the **Layout1** tab*

Creating a New Page Setup

To create a new page setup, choose the **New** button from the **Page Setup Manager** dialog box. The **New Page Setup** dialog box will be displayed, as shown in Figure 13-7. Enter the name of the new page setup in the **New page setup name** text box. The existing page setups with which you can start working are shown in the **Start with** area. You can select any of the page setups listed in this area and choose **OK** to proceed.

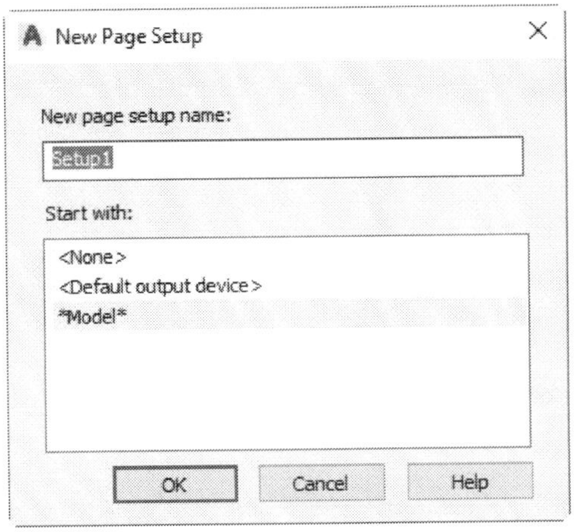

Figure 13-7 *The* ***New Page Setup*** *dialog box*

When you choose **OK**, the **Page Setup** dialog box will be displayed. This dialog box is similar to the **Plot** dialog box, see Figure 13-8.

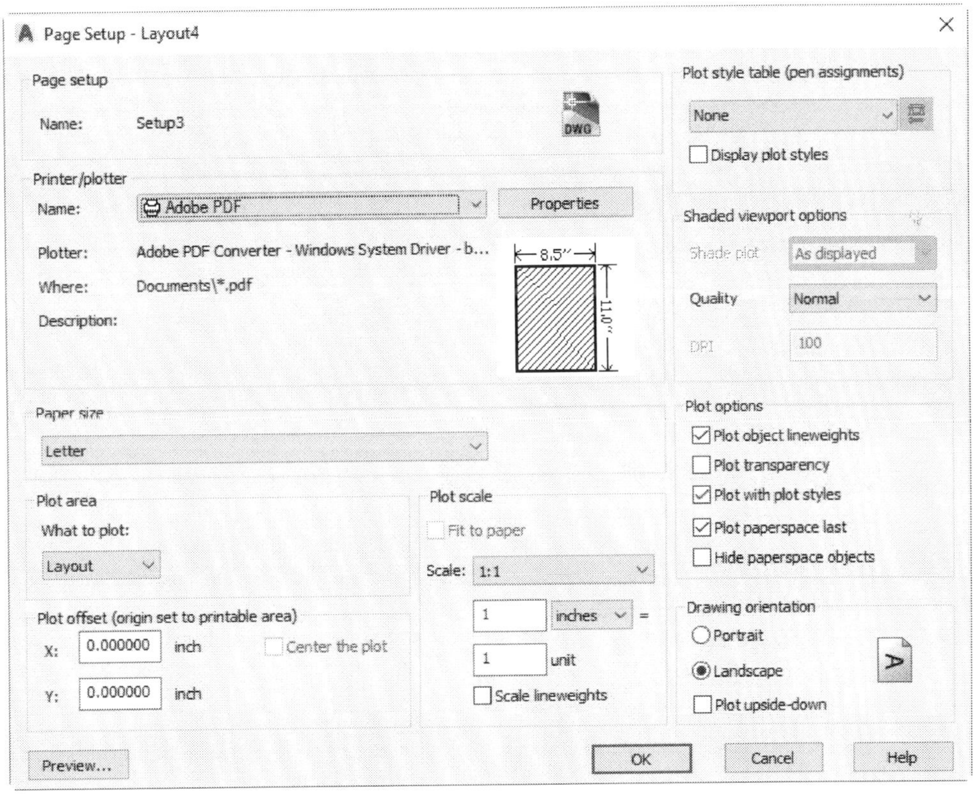

Figure 13-8 *The* ***Page Setup*** *dialog box*

Modifying the Page Setup

To modify the page setup, select the page setup from the **Current page setup** list box and choose the **Modify** button. The **Page Setup** dialog box will be displayed. Modify the parameters in this dialog box and exit.

Note

*If the **Display when creating a new layout** check box is selected in the **Page Setup Manager** dialog box then each time you invoke a new layout, the **Page Setup Manager** dialog box will be displayed.*

Importing a Page Setup

Command: PSETUPIN

AutoCAD LT allows you to import a user-defined page setup from an existing drawing and use it in the current drawing or base the current page setup for the drawing on it. This option is available on choosing the **Import** button from the **Page Setup Manager** dialog box. It is also possible to bypass this dialog box and directly import a page setup from an existing drawing into a new drawing layout by using the **PSETUPIN** command. This command facilitates importing a saved and named page setup from a drawing into a new drawing. The settings of the named page setup can be applied to layouts in the new drawing. When you choose the **Import** button from the **Page Setup Manager** dialog box or invoke the **PSETUPIN** command, the **Select Page Setup From File** dialog box is displayed, as shown in Figure 13-9. You can use this dialog box to locate a *.dwg*, *.dwt*, or *.dwf* file whose page setups have to be imported. After you select the file, AutoCAD LT displays the **Import Page Setups** dialog box, as shown in Figure 13-10. You can also enter **-PSETUPIN** at the Command prompt to display prompts at the command line.

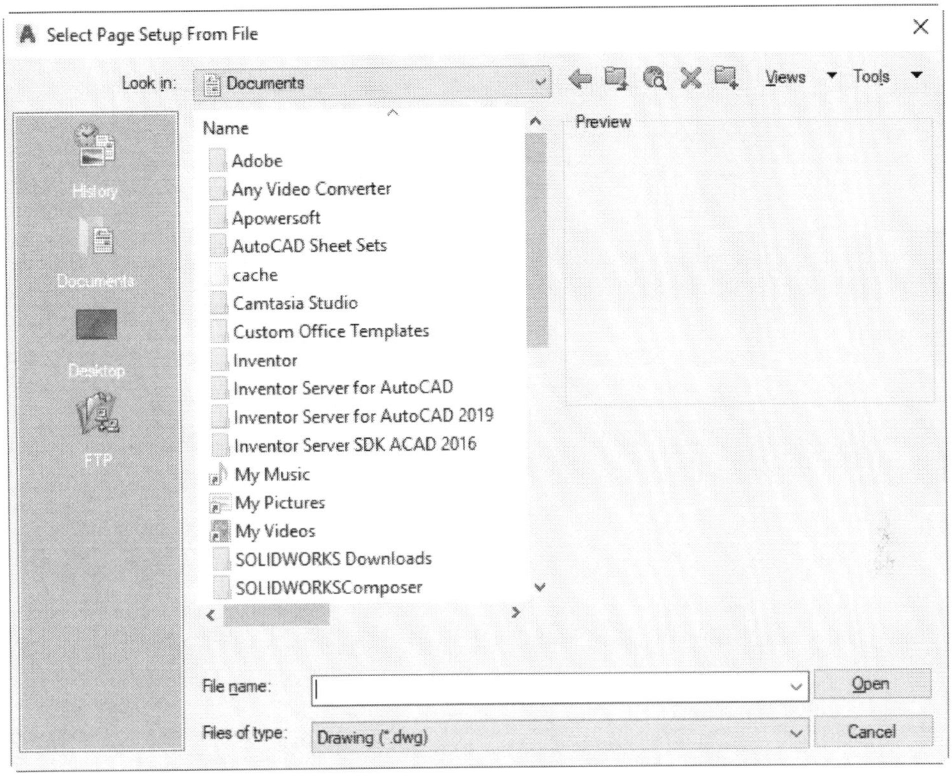

***Figure 13-9** The **Select Page Setup From File** dialog box*

Note

*If a page setup with the same name already exists in the current file, the **Question** message box will be displayed informing you that " A layout page setup has already been defined. Would you like to redefine it?" If you choose **Yes** in this message box, the current page setup will be redefined.*

USING PLOT STYLES

The plot styles can change the complete look of a plotted drawing. You can use this feature to override the color, linetype, and lineweight of a drawing. For example, if an object is drawn on a layer that is assigned red color and no plot style is assigned to it, the object will be plotted as red. However, if you have assigned a plot style to the object with the color blue, the object will be plotted as blue irrespective of the layer color it was drawn on. Similarly, you can change the Linetype, Lineweight, end, join, and fill styles of the drawing, and also change the output effects such as dithering, grayscales, pen assignments, and screening. Basically, you can use **Plot Styles** effectively to plot the same drawing in various ways.

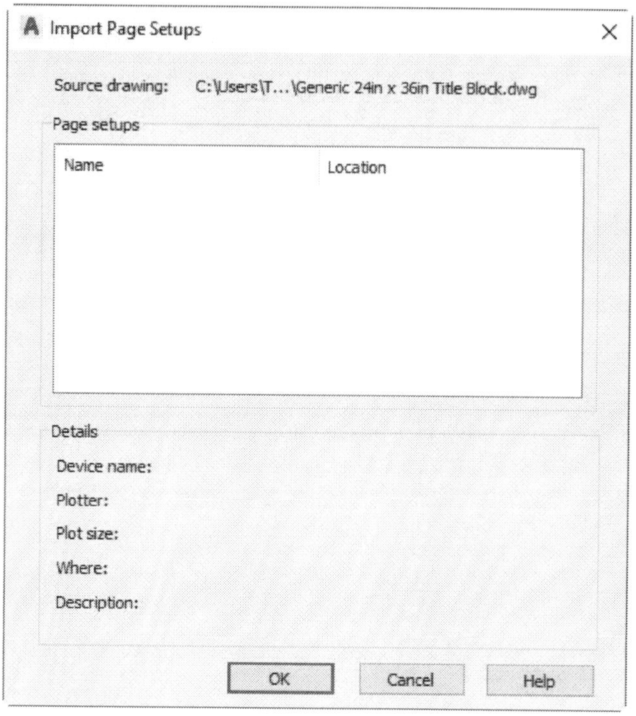

*Figure 13-10 The **Import Page Setups** dialog box*

Every object and layer in the drawing has a plot style property. The plot style characteristics are defined in the plot style tables attached to the **Model** tab, layouts, and viewports within the layouts. You can attach and detach different plot style tables to get different looks for your plots. Generally, there are two plot style modes. They are **Color-dependent** and **Named**. The **Color-dependent** plot styles are based on object color and there are **255** color-dependent plot styles. It is possible to assign each color in the plot style a value for the different plotting properties and these settings are then saved in a color-dependent plot style table file that has a *.ctb* extension. Similarly, **Named** plot styles are independent of the object color and you can assign any plot style to any object regardless of that object's color. These settings are saved in a named plot style table file that has *.stb* extension. Every drawing in AutoCAD LT is in either of the plot style modes.

Adding a Plot Style

Application Menu: Print > Manage Plot Styles
Command: STYLESMANAGER

All plot styles are saved in the *C:\Users <owner>\AppData\Roaming\Autodesk\AutoCAD LT 2020\R20.1\enu\Plotters\Plot Styles* folder. On choosing **Print > Manage Plot Styles** from the **Application Menu**, the **Plot Styles** window will be displayed, see Figure 13-11. This window displays icons for all the available plot styles in addition to the **Add-A-Plot Style Table Wizard** icon. You can double-click on any of the plot style icons to display the **Plot Style Table Editor** dialog box and edit the selected plot style. When you double-click on the **Add-A-Plot Style Table Wizard** icon, the **Add Plot Style Table** wizard is displayed and you can use it to create a new plot style.

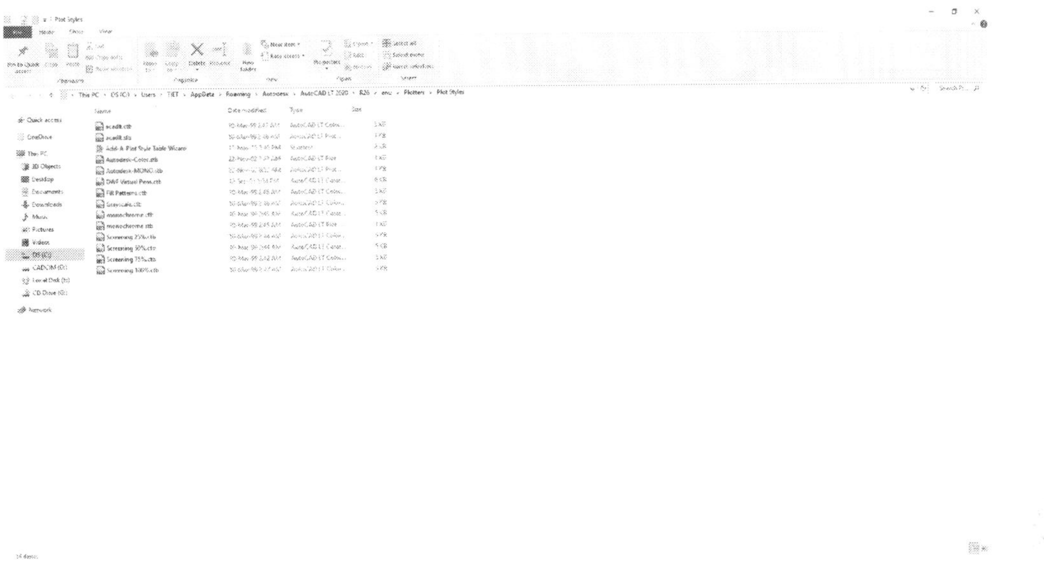

*Figure 13-11 The **Plot Styles** window*

Add-A-Plot Style Table Wizard

If you want to add a new plot style table to your drawing, double-click on the **Add-A-Plot Style Table Wizard** in the **Plot Styles** window to display the **Add Plot Style Table** wizard. The following steps are required for creating a new plot style table using the wizard.

1. Read the introduction page carefully and choose the **Next** button.

2. In the **Begin** page, select the **Start from scratch** radio button and choose **Next**. On selecting this option, a new plot style table is created. Therefore, the **Browse File** page is not available.

   In addition to the **Start from scratch** option, this page has three more options: **Use an existing plot style table**, **Use My R14 Plotter Configuration (CFG)**, and **Use a PCP or PC2 file**. When you use the **Use an existing plot style table** option, an existing plot style table is used as a base for the new plot style table you are creating. In such a situation, the **Table Type** page of the wizard is not available and is not displayed because the table type will be based on the existing plot style table you are using to create a new one. With the **Use My R14 Plotter Configuration (CFG)** option, the pen assignments from the Release 14 *acad.cfg* file are used as a base for the new table you are creating. If you are using the **Use a PCP or PC2** option, the pen assignments saved earlier in the Release 14 PCP or PC2 file are used to create the new plot style.

3. The **Pick Plot Style Table** page allows you to select the **Color-Dependent Plot Style Table** or the **Named Plot Style Table** according to your requirement. Select the **Color-Dependent Plot Style Table** radio button and then choose the **Next** button.

4. Since you have selected the **Start from scratch** radio button in the **Begin** page, the **Browse File** page is not available and the **File name** page is displayed. However, if you had selected

any of the other three options on the **Begin** page, the **Browse File name** page would have been displayed. You can select an existing file from the drop-down list available in this page or choose the **Browse** button to display the **Select File** dialog box. You can then browse and select a file from a specific folder and choose **Open** to return to the wizard. You can also enter the name of the existing plot style table on which you want to base the new plot style table, directly in the edit box. After you have specified the file name, choose **Next** to display the **File name** page of the wizard. In the **File name** page, enter a file name for the new plot style table and choose **Next**. The **Finish** page is displayed.

Note

*If you are using the pen assignments from Release 14 acad.cfg file to define the new plot style table, you also have to specify the printer or plotter to use from the drop-down list available in the **Browse File** page of the wizard.*

5. The **Finish** page gives you the option of choosing the **Plot Style Table Editor** button to display the **Plot Style Table Editor** and then edit the plot style table you have created. If you select the **Use this plot style table for new and pre-AutoCAD LT 2020-English drawings** check box in this page of the wizard, the plot style table that you have created will become the default plot style table for all the drawings you create. This check box is available only if the plot style mode you have selected in the wizard is the same as the default plot style mode specified by you in the **Default plot style behavior for new drawings** area of the **Plot Style Table Settings** dialog box. This dialog box can be invoked by choosing the **Plot Style Table Settings** button from the **Plot and Publish** tab of the **Options** dialog box. Choose the **Finish** button in the **Finish** page of the wizard to exit the wizard. A new plot style table gets added to the **Plot Styles** window and can be used for plotting.

Note

*You can also choose **Add Plot Style Table/ Add Color-Dependent Plot Style Table** from the **Tools > Wizards** menu to display wizards that are similar to the **Add Plot Style Table** wizard. However, in the **Begin** page, the **Use an existing plot style table** option is not available. Also, the **Table Type** page is not available and the **Finish** page has an additional option to use the new plot style table for the current drawing.*

Plot Style Table Editor

When you double-click on any of the plot style table icons in the **Plot Styles** window, the **Plot Style Table Editor** is displayed, where you can edit the particular plot style table. You can also choose the **Plot Style Table Editor** button in the **Finish** page to display the **Plot Style Table Editor**. Alternatively, expand the **Plot** dialog box and choose the button adjacent to the drop-down list in the **Plot style table (pen assignments)** area to display the **Plot Style Table Editor** dialog box.

The **Plot Style Table Editor** has three tabs: **General**, **Table View**, and **Form View**. You can edit all properties of an existing plot style table using these tabs. The description of the tabs is as follows;

General Tab

This tab provides information about the file name, location of the file, version, and scale factor. All information except the description is read only. You can enter a description about the plot style table in the **Description** text box here. If you select the **Apply global scale factor to non-ISO linetypes** check box, all the non-ISO linetypes in a drawing are scaled by the scale factor specified in the **Scale factor** edit box below the check box. If this check box is cleared, the **Scale factor** edit box is not available.

Table View Tab

This tab displays all plot styles along with their properties in a tabular form and they can be edited individually in the table, see Figure 13-12.

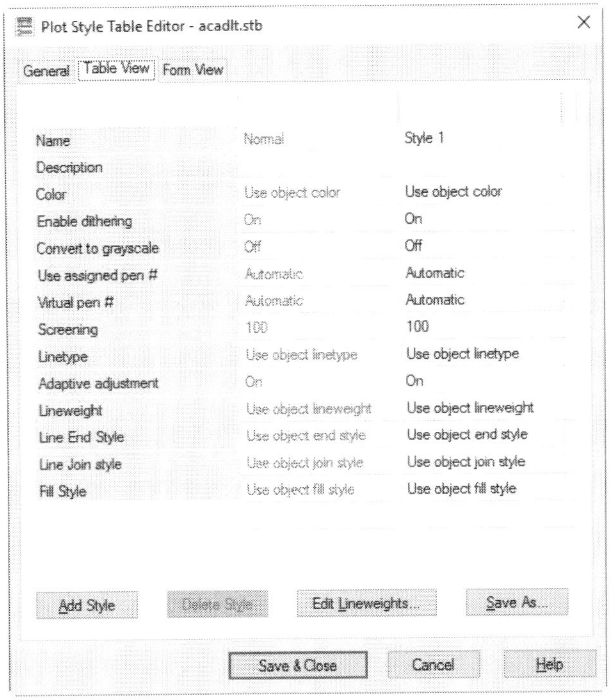

*Figure 13-12 The **Plot Style Table Editor** with the **Table View** tab chosen*

If you use **acad-Named Plot Style.dwt** template, you can edit existing styles or add new styles by choosing the **Add Style** button. On doing so, a new column with the default style name **Style1** will be added in the table. You can change the style name if you want. To edit various properties in the table, select the particular value to be modified; the corresponding drop-down list will be displayed. You can select a value from this drop-down list. The **Normal** plot style table is not available, and therefore, it cannot be edited. This plot style is assigned to layers by default.

You can select a particular plot style by clicking on the white area above the column and the entire column gets highlighted. You can select several plot styles by pressing the SHIFT key and selecting more plot styles. All the plot styles that are selected are highlighted. If you choose the **Delete Style** button now, the selected plot styles are removed from the table except the Normal Style which can not be deleted.

On choosing the **Edit Lineweights** button, the **Edit Lineweights** dialog box will be displayed. You can select the units for specifying the lineweights in the **Units for Listing** area of the dialog box, and can use either **Millimeters (mm)** or **Inches (in)** for specifying units. You can also edit the value of a lineweight by selecting it in the **Lineweights** list box and choosing the **Edit**

Lineweight button. After you have edited the lineweights, choose the **Sort Lineweights** button to rearrange the lineweight values in the list box. Choose **OK** to exit the **Edit Lineweights** dialog box and return to **Plot Style Table Editor**.

With a color-dependent plot style table, the **Table View** tab displays all 255 plot styles, one for each color, and the properties can be edited in the table in the same way as discussed for named plot styles. The only difference is that you cannot add a new plot style or delete an existing one, and therefore, the **Delete Style** and **Add Style** buttons are not available. The properties that can be defined in a plot style are discussed next.

Name. This field displays the name of the color in the case of the color-dependent plot styles and the name of the style in the case of the named plot styles.

Description. You can enter the description about the plot style in this field.

Color. The color you assign to the plot style overrides the color of the object in the drawing. The default value is Use object color.

Enable dithering. Dithering is described as a mixing of various colored dots to produce a new color. You can enable or disable this property by selecting from the drop-down list that is available in this field. Dithering is enabled by default and is independent of the color selected.

Convert to grayscale. If you are using a plotter that supports grayscaling, selecting **On** from the drop-down list in this field applies a grayscale to the objects color. By default, **Off** is selected and the object's color is used.

Use assigned pen #. This property is applied only to pen plotters. The pens range from 1 to 32. The default value is Automatic, which implies that the pen used will be based on the plotter configuration.

Virtual pen #. Other plotters can also behave like pen plotters using virtual pens. The value of this property lies between 1 and 255. The default value is Automatic. This implies that AutoCAD LT will assign a virtual pen automatically from the AutoCAD LT Color Index (ACI).

Screening. This property of a plot style indicates the amount of ink used while plotting. The value ranges between 0 and 100. The default value is 100, which creates the plot in its full intensity. Similarly, a value of 0 produces white color. This may be useful when plotting on a colored background.

Linetype. Like the property of color, the linetype assigned to a plotstyle overrides the object linetype on plotting. The default value is Use object linetype.

Adaptive adjustment. This property is applied by default and implies that the linetype scale of a linetype is applied such that on plotting, the linetype pattern will be completed.

Lineweight. The lineweight value assigned here overrides the value of the object lineweight on plotting. The default value is Use object lineweight.

Line End Style. This determines the manner in which a plotted line ends. The effect of this property is more noticeable when the thickness of the line is substantial. The line can end in a **Butt**, **Square**, **Round**, or **Diamond** shape. The default value is Use object end style.

Line Join style. You can select the manner in which two lines join in a plotted drawing. The available options are **Miter**, **Bevel**, **Round**, and **Diamond**. The default value is Use object join style.

Fill Style. The fill style assigned to a plot style overrides the objects fill style, when plotted. The available options are **Solid**, **Checkerboard**, **Crosshatch**, **Diamonds**, **Horizontal Bars**, **Slant Left**, **Slant Right**, **Square Dots**, and **Vertical Bars**.

Form View Tab

This tab displays all properties in one form, see Figure 13-13. Also, it displays all available plot styles in the **Plot styles** list box. You can select any style from the list box and then edit its properties in the **Properties** area.

If you want to add a new plot style to the named plot style table, choose the **Add Style** button when the **Form View** tab is chosen; the **Add Plot Style** dialog box with the default plot style name **Style 2** will be displayed. You can change the name of a plot style in the **Plot style** edit box, see Figure 13-14. Now, when you choose the **OK** button, the new style will be added in the **Plot styles** list box and you can select it for editing. If you want to delete a style, select it and then choose the **Delete Style** button. With color-dependent plot styles, the **Form View** tab also does not provide options that allow you to add or delete plot styles.

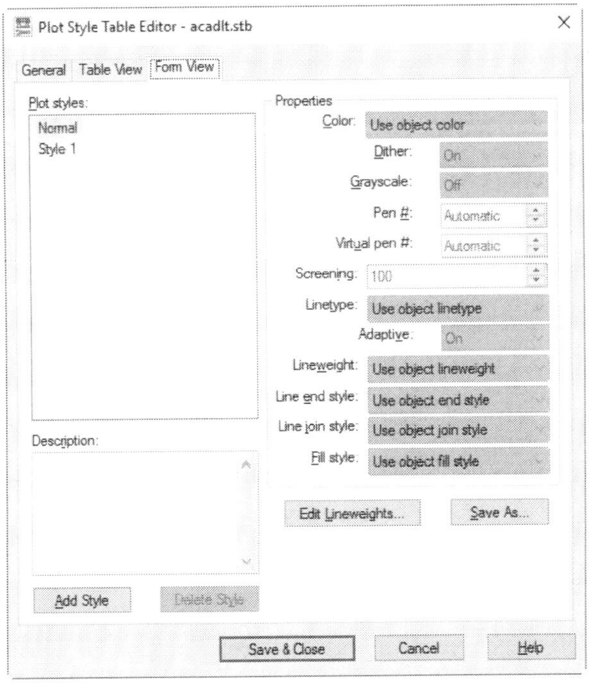

*Figure 13-13 The **Plot Style Table Editor** with the **Form View** tab chosen*

After editing, choose the **Save & Close** button to save and return to the **Plot Styles** window. You can also choose the **Save As** button to display the **Save As** dialog box and save a plot style table with another name. To remove the changes you made to a plot style table, choose the **Cancel** button.

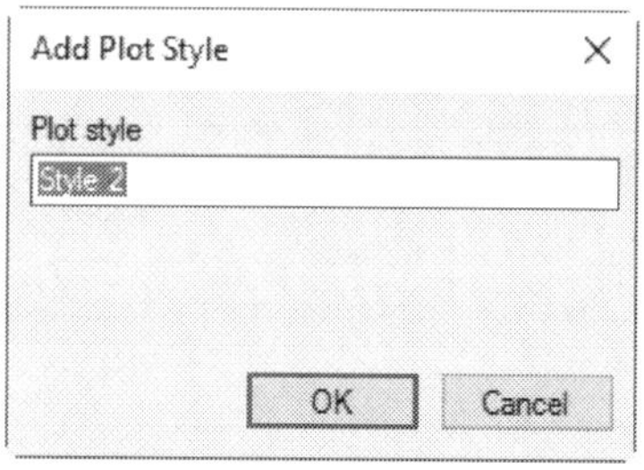

*Figure 13-14 The **Add Plot Style** dialog box*

Applying Plot Styles

You can select a plot style table that you want to use as a default for drawings from the **Current plot style table settings** area of the **Plot Style Table Settings** dialog box. To display the **Plot Style Table Settings** dialog box, choose the down arrow in the right of the **Plot** panel in the **Output** tab; the **Options** dialog box will be displayed with the **Plot and Publish** tab chosen. Choose the **Plot Style Table Settings** button; the **Plot Style Table Settings** dialog box will be displayed. If the **None** option is selected in the **Default Plot Style Table** drop-down list, the drawing will be plotted with the object properties as displayed on the screen. When you select the **Use named plot styles** radio button from the **Default plot style behavior for new drawings** area of the **Plot Style Table Settings** dialog box, the **Default plot style for layer 0** and **Default plot style for objects** drop-down lists will be available. You can select the default plot styles that you want to assign to Layer 0 and to the objects in a drawing from these drop-down lists, respectively. If you choose the **Add or Edit Plot Style Tables** button from the **Plot Style Table Settings** dialog box, the **Plot Styles** window will be displayed. Here, you can double-click on any plot style table icon available and edit it using the **Plot Style Table Editor** that is displayed.

To change the plot style table for a current layout, you have to invoke the **Page Setup** or **Plot** dialog box and then select a plot style table from the **Plot styles** drop-down list in the **Plot style table (pen assignments)** area of the dialog box. A color-dependent plot style table can be selected and applied to a tab only if the default plot style mode has already been set to color dependent. Similarly, to apply a named plot style table to a tab, select the **Use named plot styles** radio button from the **Plot Style Table Settings** dialog box.

A color-dependent plot style cannot be applied to objects or layers therefore the **Plot Style Control** drop-down list is not available in the **Properties** toolbar when a drawing has a color-dependent plot style mode. The plot styles also appear grayed out in the **LAYER PROPERTIES MANAGER** and cannot be selected and changed. However, named plot styles can be applied to objects and layers. A plot style applied to an object overrides the plot style applied to the layer on which the object is drawn. To apply a plot style to a layer, invoke the **LAYER PROPERTIES MANAGER** where all the layers in the selected tab are displayed. Select a layer to which you want to apply a plot style and select the default plot style (Normal) currently applied to the layer; the **Select Plot Style** dialog box will be displayed, see Figure 13-15. The **Plot styles** list box in this dialog box displays all the plot styles present in the plot style table attached to the current tab. You can select another plot style table to be attached to the current tab from the **Active plot style table** drop-down list. You will notice that all the plot styles in the selected plot style table are displayed in the list box now. You can also choose the **Editor** button to display the **Plot Style Table Editor** to edit plot style tables, as discussed earlier. The **Select Plot Style** dialog box also displays the name of the original plot style assigned to the object adjacent to **Original**. Also, the new plot style to be assigned to the selected object is displayed next to **New**.

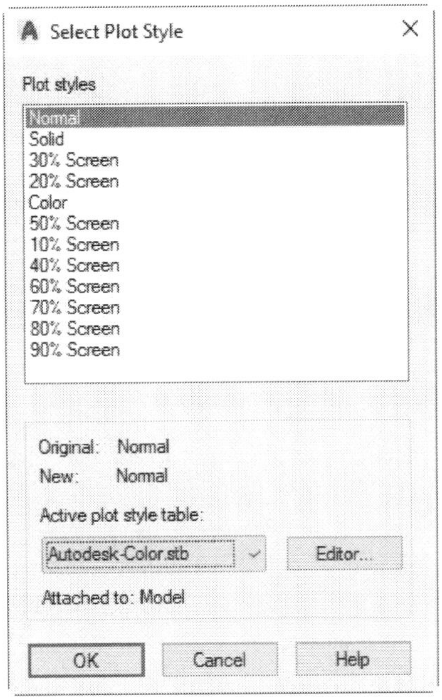

***Figure 13-15** The **Select Plot Style** dialog box*

You can apply a named plot style to an object using the **Plot Style Control** drop-down list in the **Properties** toolbar or the **PROPERTIES** palette. The process is the same as that applied for layers, colors, linetypes, and lineweights. This named plot style is applied to an object irrespective of the tab on which it is drawn. If the plot style assigned to an object is present in the plot style table of the tab in which it is present, the object is plotted with the specified plot style. However, if the plot style assigned to the object is not present in the plot style table assigned to the tab on which it is drawn, the object will be plotted with the properties that are displayed on the screen. The default plot style assigned to an object is **Normal** and the default plot style assigned to a layer is **ByLayer**.

Setting the Current Plot Style

You can use the **PLOTSTYLE** command to set the current plot style of new objects or of the selected object. You can set the current plot styles by choosing **Print > Edit Plot Style Tables** from the **Application Menu**, and if no object has been selected in the drawing, AutoCAD LT displays the **Current Plot Style** dialog box, see Figure 13-16. You can select a plot style from the list box and choose **OK** to assign it to the selected objects in the drawing. All the plot styles present in the current plot style table that are assigned to the current tab are displayed in the list box in the **Current Plot Style** dialog box. You can select any one of these plot styles and choose **OK**. Now, if you create new objects, they will have the plot style that you had set current in the **Current Plot Style** dialog box. The parameters of this dialog box are described next.

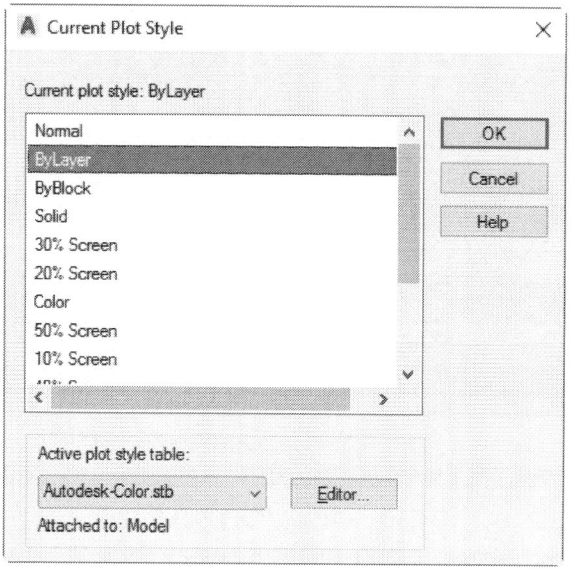

*Figure 13-16 The **Current Plot Style** dialog box*

Current plot style

The name of the current plot style is displayed adjacent to this label.

Plot style list box

This list box lists all the available plot styles that can be assigned to an object, including the default plot style, **Normal**.

Active plot style table

This drop-down list displays the names of all the available plot style tables. The current plot style table attached to the current layout or viewport is displayed in the edit box.

Editor

If you choose the **Editor** button adjacent to the **Active plot style table** drop-down list, AutoCAD LT displays the **Plot Style Table Editor** to edit the selected plot style table.

Attached to

The tab to which the selected plot style table is attached, such as **Model** or any one of the layout tabs, is displayed next to this label.

Example 1 — *Plot Style*

Create the drawing shown in Figure 13-17. Next, create a named plot style with the name *My First Table.stb* with a plot style having the following parameters:

1. Screening : 65%
2. Object line weight : 0.6000 mm

3. Line Type : ISO Dash
4. Object Color : Blue (5)

Additionally, plot the drawing using the **Date and Time** and **Paper size** stamps.

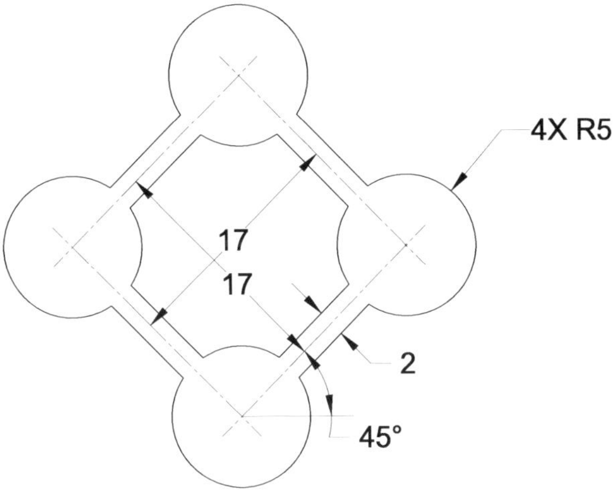

Figure 13-17 *Drawing for Example 1*

1. Create the drawing, as shown in Figure 13-17. You can create the drawing by making an octagon and then converting its alternate edge into an arc with the given radius.

2. Choose the **Print > Manage Plot Styles** from the **Application Menu**; a window will be displayed with all the plot styles available. Double-click on the **Add-A-Plot Style Table Wizard** shortcut icon; the **Add Plot Style Table** wizard will be displayed. Choose the **Next** button; the **Begin** page will be displayed.

3. Select the **Start from scratch** radio button and choose the **Next** button; the **Pick Plot Style Table** page will be displayed. Now, select the **Named Plot Style Table** radio button and then choose the **Next** button; a window will be displayed prompting for the file name. Enter **My First Table** in the **File name** text box and then choose the **Next** button, the **Add Plot Style Table - Finish** window is displayed.

4. In the **Add Plot Style Table - Finish** window, select **Plot Style Table Editor** button; a window named **Plot Style Table Editor - My First Table.stb** is displayed with the **Table View** tab chosen by default.

5. Choose the **Add Style** button at the bottom left of the window; a new column named **Style 1** will be added in the **Add Style** area. Now, enter the following values in the database:

Row	**Value**
• Screening	65
• Lineweight	0.6000 mm
• Linetype	ISO Dash
• Color	Blue

Next, choose the **Save & Close** button and then choose the **Finish** button in the displayed window.

6. Now, enter the PLOTSTYLE command to invoke the **Current Plot Style** dialog box. Next, select the **My First Table.stb** plot style from the drop-down list under the **Active plot style table** area of this dialog box. Choose the **OK** button.

7. Open the **LAYER PROPERTIES MANAGER** and click under the **Plot Style** column to invoke the **Select Plot Style** dialog box. Select **Style 1** from the **Plot styles** area and choose the **OK** button.

8. Now, choose the **Plot** tool from the **Quick Access Toolbar**; the **Plot** dialog box is displayed. Next, select the **Plot stamp on** check box; the **Plot Stamp Settings** button will be displayed on the right of the check box. Choose this button; the **Plot Stamp** dialog box will be displayed. In this dialog box, select the **Date and Time** and **Paper size** check boxes. Next, clear all other check boxes. Choose the **OK** button to exit the dialog box, and then choose the **Preview** button from the **Plot-Model** dialog box to preview the plot. If the plot seems to be fine, right-click to invoke the shortcut menu. Choose the **Plot** option from the shortcut menu to take print.

Exercise 1 — Plot Style

Create the drawing shown in Figure 13-18. Create a named plot style table *My Named Table.stb* with three plot styles: Style 1, Style 2, and Style 3, in addition to the Normal plot style. The Normal plot style is used for plotting the object lines. These three styles have the following specifications:

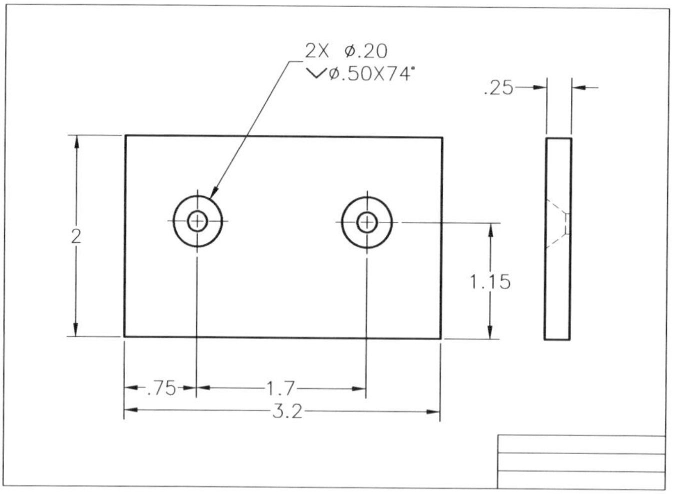

Figure 13-18 *Drawing for Exercise 1*

Style 1. This style has a value of Screening = 50. The dimensions, dimension lines, and the text in the drawing must be plotted with this style.

Style 2. This style has a value of Lineweight = 0.800. The border and title block must be plotted with this style.

Style 3. This style has a linetype of Medium Dash. The centerlines must be plotted with this plot style.

PLOTTING SHEETS IN A SHEET SET

Using the **Sheet Set Manager**, you can easily plot all the sheets available in a sheet set. However, before plotting the sheets in a sheet set, you need to make sure that you have selected the required printer in the page setup of all the sheets in the sheet set. This is because the printer set in the page setup of the sheet will be automatically selected to plot the sheet.

To print the sheets after setting the page setup, right-click on the name of the sheet set in the **Sheet Set Manager** and choose **Publish > Publish to Plotter** from the shortcut menu. If the value of the **BACKGROUNDPLOT** system variable is set to **2**, which is the default value, all the sheets will be automatically plotted in the background and you can continue working on the drawings.

Self-Evaluation Test

Answer the following questions and then compare them to those given at the end of this chapter:

1. The size of a plot can be specified by selecting any paper size from the __________ drop-down list in the **Plot** dialog box.
2. If you want to store a plot in a file and not have it printed directly on a plotter, select the __________ check box in the **Printer/plotter** area.
3. The scale for a plot can be specified in the __________ edit box in the **Plot** dialog box.
4. If you select the __________ option from the **What to plot** drop-down list, the portion of the drawing that is in the current display is plotted.
5. Before you plot sheets in the sheet set, it is important that you set the __________ for the individual sheets in their page setups.
6. You can set the quality of a plot using the __________ drop-down list in the **Shaded viewport options** area.
7. All the settings of a plotter are saved in the *.PC3* file. (T/F)
8. Different objects in the same drawing can be plotted in different colors with different linetypes and line widths. (T/F)
9. You can partially or fully preview a drawing before plotting. (T/F)
10. The **PSLTSCALE** system variable controls the paper space linetype scaling and has a default value of 1. (T/F)

Review Questions

Answer the following questions:

1. Which of the following check boxes will not available in the **Plot options** area of the **Plot** dialog box, while plotting in a **Layout** tab?

   (a) **Plot paperspace last** (b) **Hide objects**
   (c) **Plot with plot styles** (d) None of these

2. On invoking which of the following tools, the **Plotters** window will be displayed?

   (a) **Plot** (b) **Manage Plotters**
   (c) **Plot Style** (d) None of these

3. With which command is it possible to bypass the **Plot/Page Setup** dialog box and directly import a page setup from an existing drawing into a new drawing layout?

   (a) **PSETUPIN** (b) **PLOTTERMANAGER**
   (c) **PLOTSTYLE** (d) None of these

4. Which of the following tools is used to create a new plot style?

   (a) **Style** (b) **Manage Plot Styles**
   (c) **Plot Style** (d) None of these

5. Which of the following commands can be used to import a PCP file or PC2 files?

   (a) **PCINWIZARD** (b) **PCIN**
   (c) **PLOTSTYLE** (d) None of these

6. You can view a plot on the specified paper size before actually plotting it by choosing the __________ button from the **Plot** dialog box.

7. The **Page Setup Manager** dialog box is displayed when you invoke the **Page Setup Manager** tool. (T/F)

8. By selecting the **View** option from the **What to plot** drop-down list in the **Plot** area, you can plot a view that was created by using the **View Manager** tool in the current drawing. (T/F)

9. If you do not want the hidden lines of a 3D object created in the **Model** tab, you can select the **Hidden** option from the **Shade plot** drop-down list in the **Shaded viewport options**area. (T/F)

10. The orientation of a drawing can be changed using the **Plot** dialog box. (T/F)

11. The **BACKGROUNDPLOT** system variable is used to control the default setting for background plotting. (T/F)

Exercise 2

Create the drawing shown in Figure 13-19 and plot it according to the following specifications. Also, create and use a plot style table with the specified plot styles.

1. The drawing is to be plotted on 10 x 8 inch paper.
2. The object lines must be plotted with a plot style Style 1. Style 1 must have a lineweight = 0.800 mm.
3. The dimension lines must be plotted with plot style Style 2. Style 2 must have a value of screening = 50.
4. The centerlines must be plotted with plot style Style 3. Style 3 must have a linetype of Medium Dash and screening = 50.
5. The border and title block must be plotted with plot style Style 4. The value of the lineweight should be =0.25 mm.

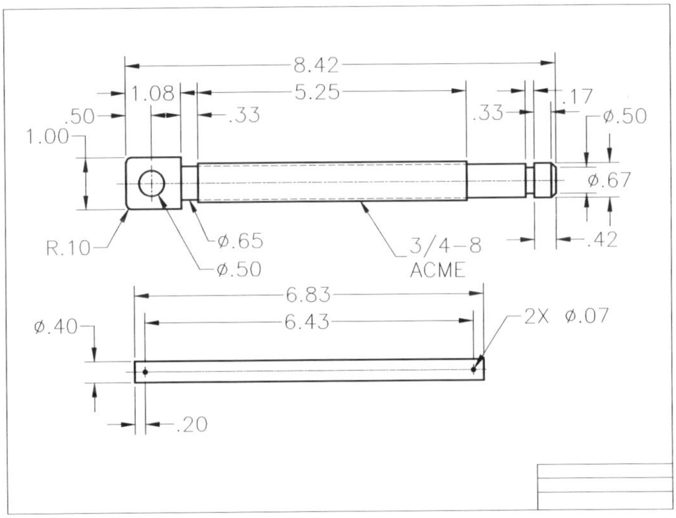

Figure 13-19 Drawing for Exercise 2

Exercise 3

Create the drawing shown in Figure 13-20 and then plot it according to your specifications.

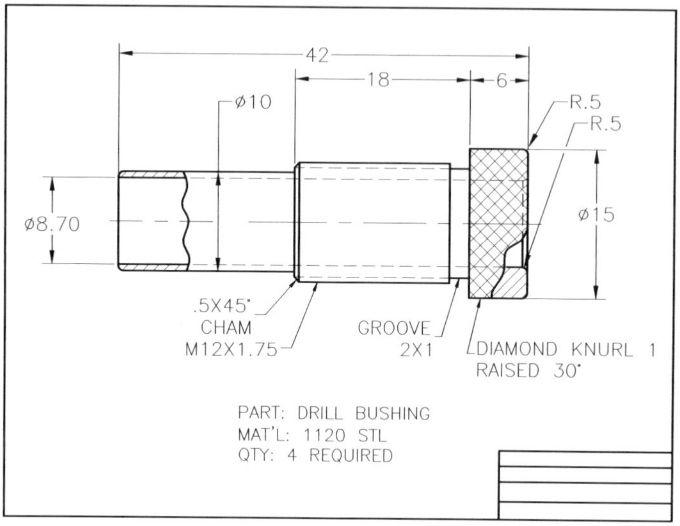

Figure 13-20 Drawing for Exercise 3

Problem-Solving Exercise 1

Make the drawing shown in Figure 13-21 and plot it according to your specifications.

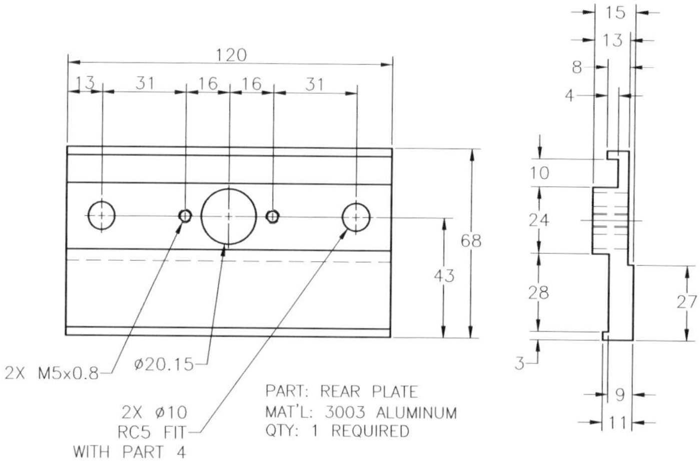

Figure 13-21 Drawing for Problem-Solving Exercise 1

Answers to Self-Evaluation Test

1. **Paper size**, **2**. **Plot to file**, **3**. **Custom**, **4**. **Display**, **5**. **Paper size**, **6**. **Quality**, **7**. T, **8**. T, **9**. T, **10**. T

Chapter 14

Template Drawings

Learning Objectives

After completing this chapter, you will be able to:

- *Create template drawings*
- *Load template drawings using dialog boxes and Command line*
- *Customize drawings with layers and dimensioning specifications*
- *Customize drawings with layouts, viewports, and paper space*

Key Terms

- *Template*
- *Plot Size*
- *Layout*
- *Template Files (*.dwt)*
- *LTSCALE*
- *Viewport*
- *Drawing Scale*
- *DIMSCALE*
- *STARTUP*
- *TEXTSIZE*

CREATING TEMPLATE DRAWINGS

One way to customize AutoCAD LT is to create template drawings that contain initial drawing setup information and if desired, visible objects and text. When the user starts a new drawing, the settings associated with the template drawing are automatically loaded. If you start a new drawing from the scratch, AutoCAD LT loads default setup values. For example, the default limits are (0.0,0.0), (12.0,9.0) and the default layer is 0 with white color and a continuous linetype. Generally, these default parameters need to be reset before generating a drawing on the computer using AutoCAD LT. A considerable amount of time is required to set up the layers, colors, linetypes, lineweights, limits, snaps, units, text height, dimensioning variables, and other parameters. Sometimes, border lines and a title block may also be needed.

In production drawings, most of the drawing setup values remain the same. For example, the company title block, border, layers, linetypes, dimension variables, text height, LTSCALE, and other drawing setup values do not change. You will save considerable time if you save these values and reload them when starting a new drawing. You can do this by creating template drawings that contain the initial drawing setup information configured according to the company specifications. They can also contain a border, title block, tolerance table, block definitions, floating viewports in the paper space, and perhaps some notes and instructions that are common to all drawings.

STANDARD TEMPLATE DRAWINGS

AutoCAD LT comes with standard template drawings like *Acadlt.dwt*, *Acadltiso.dwt*, *Acadlt-named plot styles.dwt*, *Acadltiso-named plot styles.dwt*, and so on. The iso template drawings are based on the drawing standards developed by ISO (International Organization for Standardization). When you start a new drawing with **STARTUP** system variable set to 1, the **Create New Drawing** dialog box will be displayed. To load the template drawing, choose the **Use a Template** button; the list of standard template drawings is displayed. From this list, you can select any template drawing according to your requirements. If you want to start a drawing with the default settings, choose the **Start from Scratch** button in the **Create New Drawing** dialog box. The following are some of the system variables, with the default values that are assigned to the new drawing.

System variable Name	Default Value
CHAMFERA	0.0000
CHAMFERB	0.0000
COLOR	Bylayer
DIMALT	OFF
DIMALTD	2
DIMALTF	25.4000
DIMPOST	None
DIMASO	ON
DIMASZ	0.1800
FILLETRAD	0.0000
GRID	0.5000
GRIDMODE	0
ISOPLANE	Top
LIMMIN	0.0000,0.0000
LIMMAX	12.0000,9.0000
LTSCALE	1.0000

MIRRTEXT	0 (Text not mirrored like other objects)
TILEMODE	1 (OFF)

Example 1 Advance Setup Wizard

Create a drawing template using the **Use a Wizard** button of the **Advanced Setup** wizard with the following specifications and save it with the name *proto1.dwt.*

Units	Engineering with precision 0'-0.00"
Angle	Decimal degrees with precision 0
Angle Direction	Counterclockwise
Area	144'x96'

Step 1: Setting the STARTUP system variable

Set the value of the **STARTUP** system variable to 1. Choose the **New** tool from the **Quick Access Toolbar** to display the **Create New Drawing** dialog box. Choose the **Use a Wizard** button and then select the **Advanced Setup** option, as shown in Figure 14-1. Next, choose the **OK** button; the **Units** page of the **Advanced Setup** wizard is displayed, as shown in Figure 14-2.

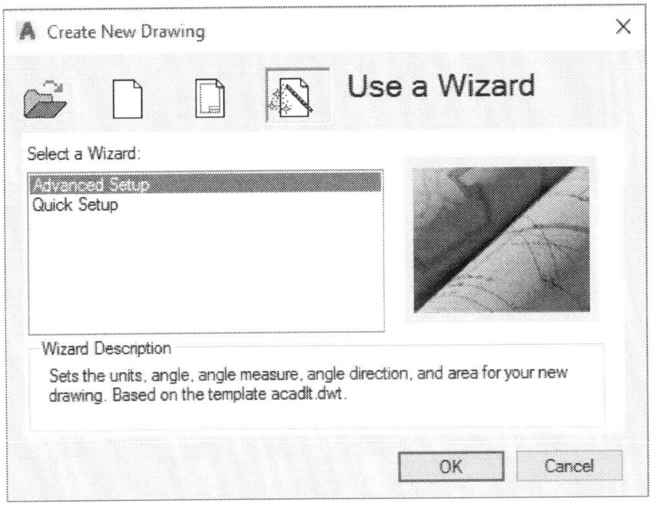

*Figure 14-1 The **Advanced Setup** wizard in the **Create New Drawing** dialog box*

Step 2: Setting the units of the drawing file

Select the **Engineering** radio button. Next, select **0'-0.00"** precision from the **Precision** drop-down list, refer to Figure 14-2, and then choose the **Next** button; the **Angle** page of the **Advanced Setup** dialog box is displayed.

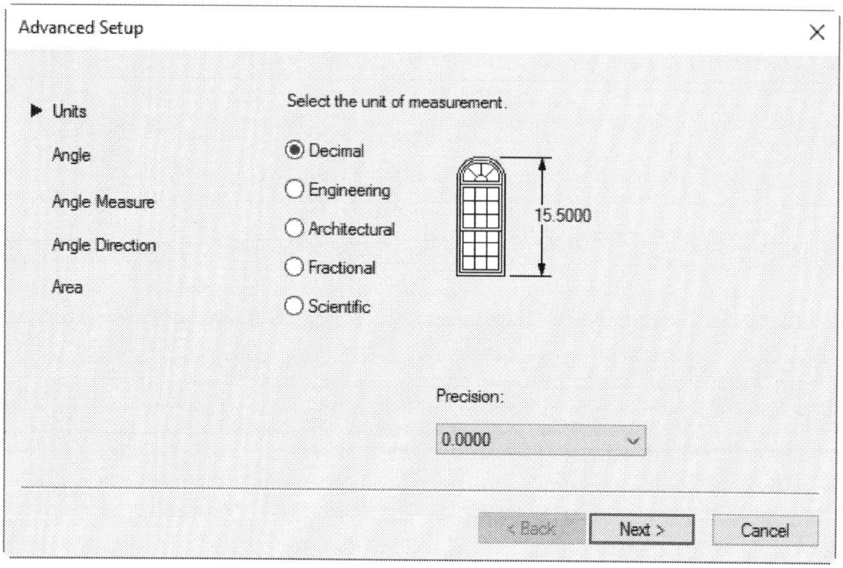

*Figure 14-2 The **Units** page of the **Advanced Setup** Wizard*

Step 3: Setting the angle measurement system

In the **Angle** page, select the **Decimal Degrees** radio button and select **0** from the **Precision** drop-down list, as shown in Figure 14-3. Choose the **Next** button; the **Angle Measure** page of the **Advanced Setup** dialog box is displayed.

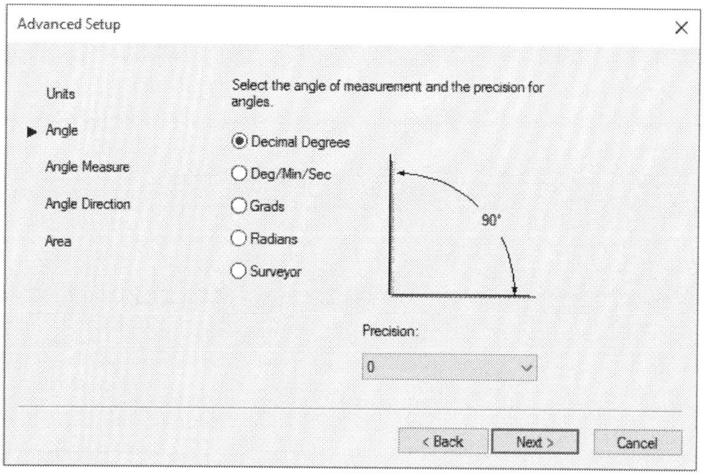

*Figure 14-3 The **Angle** page of the **Advanced Setup** Wizard*

Step 4: Setting the horizontal axis for angle measurement

In the **Angle Measure** page, select the **East** radio button. Choose the **Next** button to display the **Angle Direction** page.

Step 5: Setting the angle measurement direction and drawing area

Select the **Counter-Clockwise** radio button and then choose the **Next** button; the **Area** page is displayed. Specify the area as 144' and 96' by entering the value of the width and length as

144' and **96'** in the **Width** and **Length** edit boxes and then choose the **Finish** button. Use the **All** option of the Zoom tools to display new limits on the screen.

Step 6: Saving the drawing as template file

Now, save the drawing as *proto1.dwt* using the **Save** tool from the **Quick Access Toolbar**. You need to select **AutoCAD LT Drawing Template (*dwt)** from the **Files of type** drop-down list and enter **proto1** in the **File name** edit box in the **Save Drawing As** dialog box. Next, choose the **Save** button; the **Template Options** dialog box will be displayed on the screen, as shown in Figure 14-4. Enter the description about the template in the **Description** edit box and choose the **OK** button. Now, the drawing will be saved as *proto1.dwt* on the default drive.

Note

To customize only the units and area, you can use the ***Quick Setup*** *option in the* ***Create New Drawing*** *dialog box.*

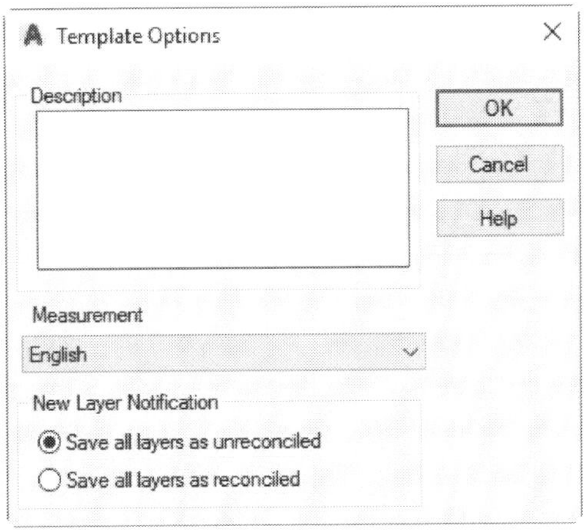

Figure 14-4 *The* ***Template Options*** *dialog box*

Example 2 — Start from Scratch Option

Create a drawing template using the following specifications. The template should be saved with the name *proto2.dwt*.

Limits	18.0,12.0
Snap	0.25
Grid	0.50
Text height	0.125
Units	3 digits to the right of decimal point
	Decimal degrees
	2 digits to the right of decimal point
	0 angle along positive *X* axis (east)
	Angle positive if measured counterclockwise

Step 1: Starting a new drawing

Start AutoCAD LT and choose the **Start from Scratch** button from the **Create New Drawing** dialog box. From the **Default Settings** area, select the **Imperial (feet and inches)** radio button, as shown in Figure 14-5. Choose **OK** to open a new file.

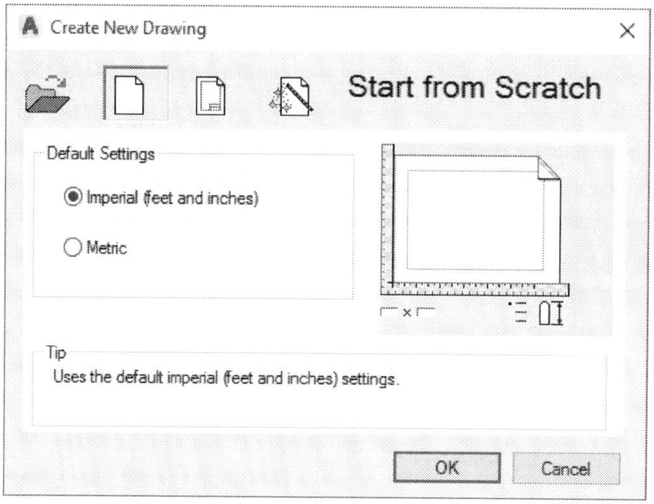

***Figure 14-5** The default unit settings specified in the **Create New Drawing** dialog box*

Step 2: Setting limits, snap, grid, and text size

The **LIMITS** command can be invoked by entering **LIMITS** at the Command prompt.

Command: **LIMITS**
Reset Model space limits:
Specify lower left corner or [ON/OFF] <0.0000,0.0000>: Enter
Specify upper right corner <12.0000,9.0000>: **18,12** Enter

After setting the limits, the next step is to expand the drawing display area. Choose the **All** tool from the **Zoom** drop-down to display new limits on the screen.

Now, right-click on the **Grid Display** button in the Status Bar to display a shortcut menu. Choose the **Settings** option from the shortcut menu to display the **Drafting Settings** dialog box. Choose the **Snap and Grid** tab. Enter **0.25** in the **Snap X spacing** and **Snap Y spacing** edit boxes in the **Snap spacing** area, respectively. Enter **0.5** in the **Grid X spacing** and **Grid Y spacing** edit boxes. Then, choose the **OK** button.

Note
*You can also use the **SNAP** and **GRID** commands to set these values.*

The size of the text can be changed by entering **TEXTSIZE** at the Command prompt.

Command: **TEXTSIZE**

Enter new value for TEXTSIZE <0.2000>: **0.125**

Step 3: Setting units

Choose the **Units** tool from **Application Menu > Drawing Utilities** or enter **UNITS** at the Command prompt to invoke the **Drawing Units** dialog box, as shown in Figure 14-6. In the **Length** area, select **0.000** from the **Precision** drop-down list. In the **Angle** area, select **Decimal Degrees** from the **Type** drop-down list and **0.00** from the **Precision** drop-down list. Also, make sure the **Clockwise** check box in the **Angle** area is not selected.

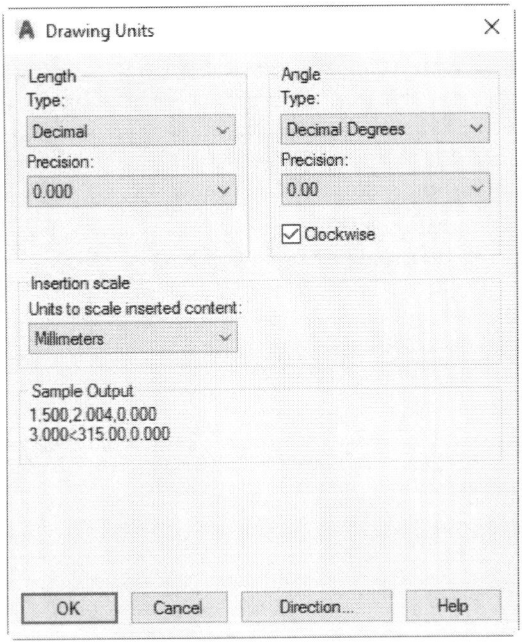

Figure 14-6 The ***Drawing Units*** *dialog box*

Choose the **Direction** button from the **Drawing Units** dialog box to display the **Direction Control** dialog box (Figure 14-7) and then select the **East** radio button. Exit both the dialog boxes.

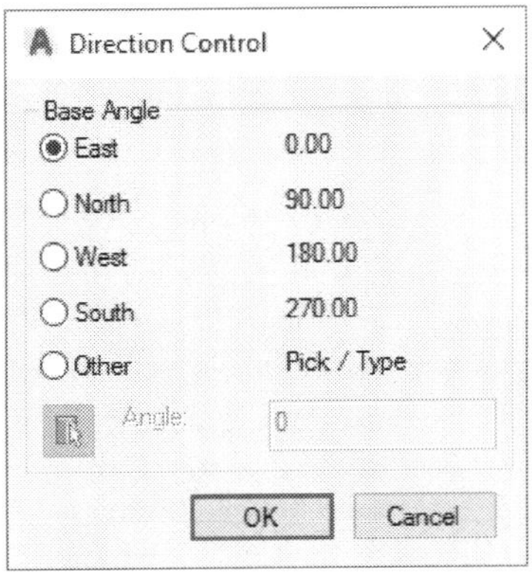

Figure 14-7 The ***Direction Control*** *dialog box*

Step 4: Saving the drawing as template file

Now, save the drawing as *proto2.dwt* using the **Save** tool from the **Quick Access** toolbar. You need to select **AutoCAD LT Drawing Template (*dwt)** from the **Files of type** drop-down list and enter **proto2** in the **File name** edit box in the **Save Drawing As** dialog box. Next, choose the **Save** button; the **Template Options** dialog box will be displayed on the screen. Enter the description about the template in the **Description** edit box and choose the **OK** button; the drawing will be saved as *proto2.dwt* on the default drive. You can also save this drawing to some other location by specifying other location from the **Save in** drop-down list of the **Save Drawing As** dialog box.

LOADING A TEMPLATE DRAWING

You can use the template drawing to start a new drawing file. To use the preset values of the template drawing, restart AutoCAD LT or choose the **New** tool from the **Quick Access Toolbar**. The dialog box that appears will depend on whether you have set the **STARTUP** system variable to **1** or **0**. If you have set this value as **1**, the **Create New Drawing** dialog box will appear. Choose the **Use a Template** option. All templates that are saved in the default **Template** directory will be shown in the **Select a Template** list box, see Figure 14-8. If you have saved the template in any other location, choose the **Browse** button. On doing so, the **Select a template file** dialog box will be displayed. You can use this dialog box to browse the directory in which the template file is saved.

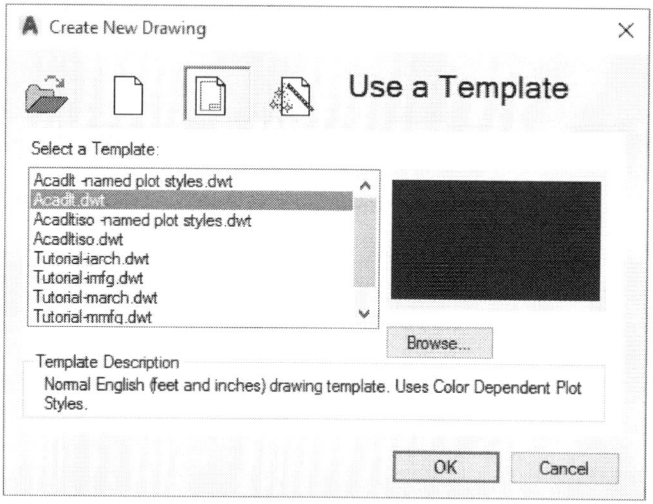

Figure 14-8 *Default templates in the* ***Create New Drawing*** *dialog box*

If you have set the **STARTUP** system variable to 0, the **Select template** dialog box appears when you choose the **New** tool. This dialog box also displays the default **Template** folder and all template files saved in it, see Figure 14-9. You can use this dialog box to select the template file that you want to open.

Using any of the previously mentioned dialog boxes, select the *proto1.dwt* template drawing. AutoCAD LT will start a new drawing that will have the same setup as that of the template drawing *proto1.dwt*.

You can have several template drawings, each with a different setup. For example, **PROTOB** for a 18" x 12" drawing, **PROTOC** for a 24" x 18" drawing. Each template drawing can be created according to user-defined specifications. You can then load any of these template drawings, as discussed previously.

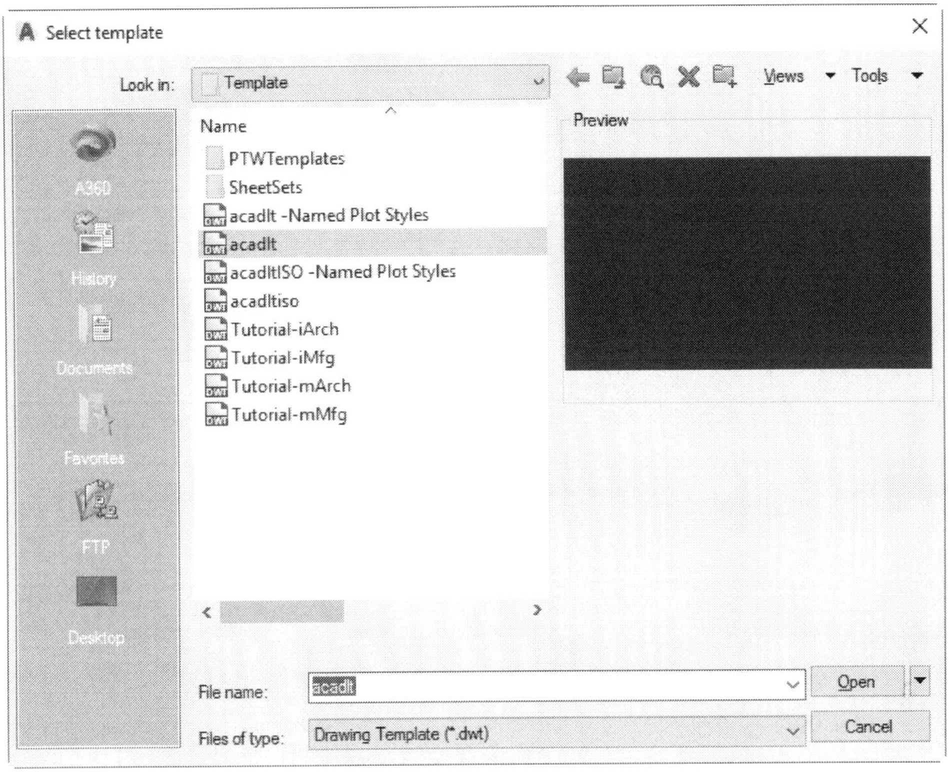

Figure 14-9 The ***Select template*** *dialog box that appears while starting a new drawing file, when the value of* ***STARTUP*** *variable is set to* ***0***

CUSTOMIZING DRAWINGS WITH LAYERS AND DIMENSIONING SPECIFICATIONS

Most production drawings need multiple layers for different groups of objects. In addition to layers, it is a good practice to assign different colors to different layers to control the line width at the time of plotting. You can generate a template drawing that contains the desired number of layers with linetypes and colors according to your company specifications. You can then use this template drawing to make a new drawing. The next example illustrates the procedure used for customizing a drawing with layers, linetypes, and colors.

Example 3 *Template with Title Block & Layers*

Create a template drawing *proto3.dwt* that has a border and the company's title block, as shown in Figure 14-10.

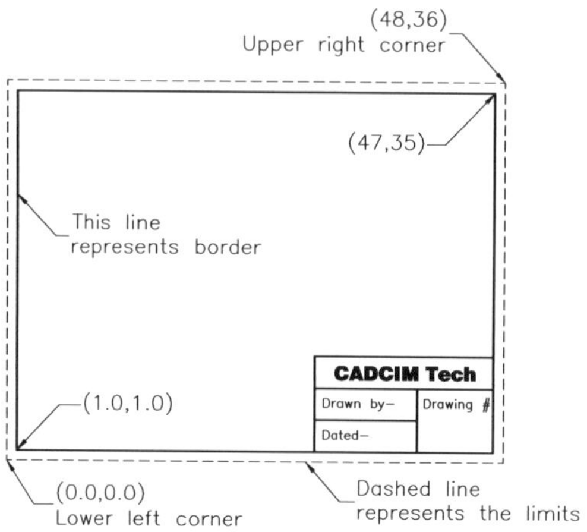

Figure 14-10 *The template drawing for Example 3*

This template drawing will have the following initial drawing setup:

Limits	48.0,36.0
Text height	0.25
Border line lineweight	0.012"
Ltscale	4.0

DIMENSIONS

Overall dimension scale factor 4.0
Dimension text above the extension line
Dimension text aligned with dimension line

LAYERS

Layer Name	Line Type	Color
0	Continuous	White
OBJ	Continuous	Red
CEN	Center	Yellow
HID	Hidden	Blue
DIM	Continuous	Green
BOR	Continuous	Magenta

Step 1: Setting limits, text size, polyline width, polyline, and linetype scaling

Start a new drawing with default parameters by selecting the **Start from Scratch** option in the **Create New Drawings** dialog box. In the new drawing file, use the AutoCAD LT tools to set up the values as given for this example. Also, draw a border and a title block, as shown in Figure 14-10. In this figure, the hidden lines indicate drawing limits. The border lines are 1.0 units inside the drawing limits. For border lines, increase the lineweight to a value of 0.012".

Use the following procedure to produce the prototype drawing for Example 3:

1. Invoke the **LIMITS** command by entering **LIMITS** at the Command prompt. The prompt sequence is given next.

   Command: **LIMITS**
   Reset Model space limits:
   Specify lower left corner or [ON/OFF] <0.0000,0.0000>: Enter
   Specify upper right corner <12.0000,9.0000>: **48,36** Enter

2. Increase the drawing display area by selecting the **All** option from the **Zoom** drop-down list.

3. Enter **TEXTSIZE** at the Command prompt to change the text size.

   Command: **TEXTSIZE**
   Enter new value for TEXTSIZE <0.2000>: **0.25** Enter

4. Next, draw the border using the **Rectangle** tool. The prompt sequence to draw the rectangle is:

   Command: **RECTANGLE**
   Specify first corner point or [Chamfer/Elevation/Fillet/Thickness/Width]: **1.0,1.0** Enter
   Specify other corner point or [Area/Dimensions/Rotation]: **47.0,35.0** Enter

5. Now, select the rectangle and change its lineweight to **0.012"**. Make sure that the **Show/ Hide Lineweight** button is chosen in the Status Bar.

6. Enter **LTSCALE** at the Command prompt to change the linetype scale.

   Command: **LTSCALE**
   Enter new linetype scale factor<Current>: **4.0** Enter

Step 2: Setting dimensioning parameters

You can use the **Dimension Style Manager** dialog box to set the dimension variables. Click the inclined arrow displayed on the **Dimensions** panel title bar in the **Annotate** tab; the **Dimension Style Manager** dialog box will be displayed, as shown in Figure 14-11.

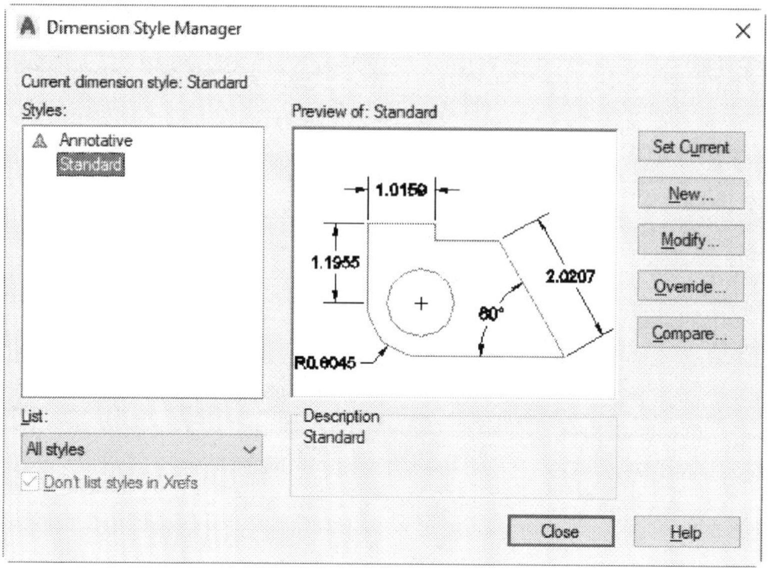

*Figure 14-11 The **Dimension Style Manager** dialog box*

You can also invoke this dialog box by entering **DIMSTYLE** at the Command prompt. Choose the **New** button from the **Dimension Style Manager** dialog box; the **Create New Dimension Style** dialog box will be displayed. Specify the new style name as **MYDIM1** in the **New Style Name** edit box, as shown in the Figure 14-12, and then choose the **Continue** button; the **New Dimension Style:MYDIM1** dialog box is displayed.

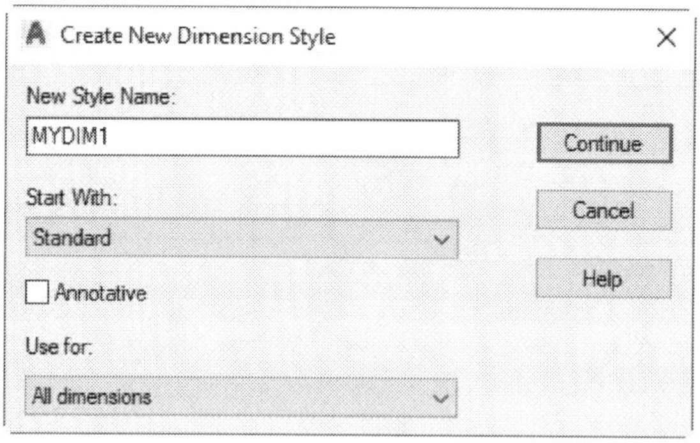

*Figure 14-12 The **Create New Dimension Style** dialog box*

Specifying overall dimension scale factor

To specify a dimension scale factor, choose the **Fit** tab in the **New Dimension Style: MYDIM1** dialog box. Next, select the **Use overall scale of** radio button in the **Scale for dimension features** area, as shown in Figure 14-13; the edit box corresponding to it will be activated. Enter **4** in this edit box.

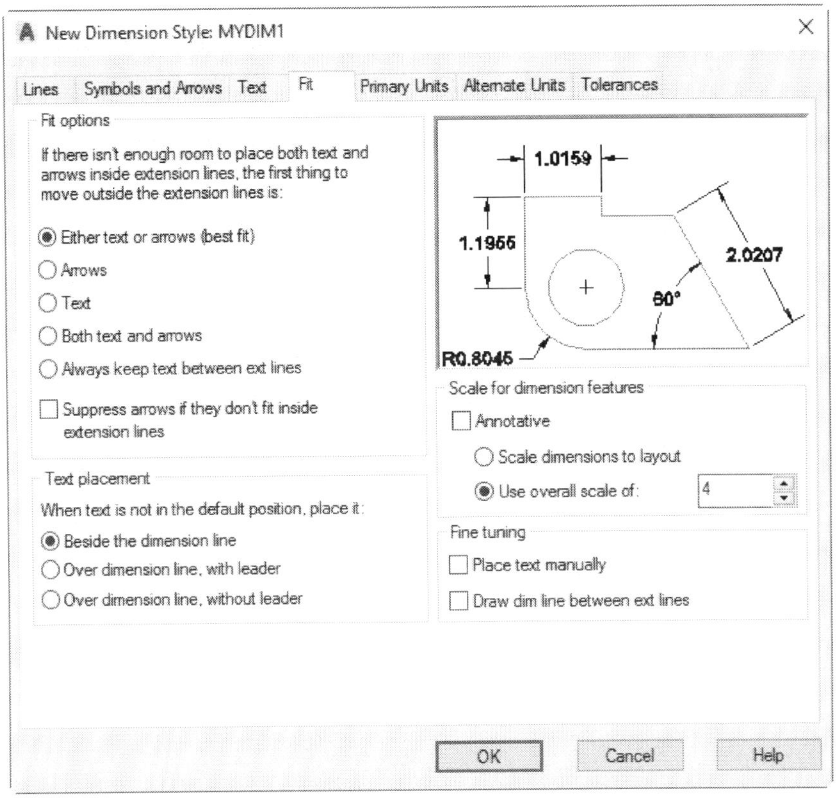

Figure 14-13 The ***Fit*** *tab of the* ***New Dimension Style: MYDIM1*** *dialog box*

Placing the dimension text over the dimension line

In the **Fit** tab of the **New Dimension Style: MYDIM1** dialog box. Select the **Over dimension line, with leader** radio button from the **Text placement** area.

Dimensioning text aligned with the dimension line

In the **Text alignment** area of the **Text** tab of the **New Dimension Style: MYDIM1** dialog box, select the **Aligned with dimension line** radio button and then choose the **OK** button.

Setting the new dimension style to current

A new dimension style with the name **MYDIM1** is shown in the **Styles** area of the **Dimension Style Manager** dialog box. Select this dimension style and then choose the **Set Current** button to make it the current dimension style. Choose the **Close** button to exit this dialog box.

Step 3: Setting layers

Choose the **Layer Properties** tool from the **Layers** panel or choose the **Layer** tool from the **Format** menu bar to invoke the **LAYER PROPERTIES MANAGER**. Choose the **New Layer** button in the **LAYER PROPERTIES MANAGER** and rename **Layer1** as **OBJ**. Choose the color swatch of the OBJ layer to display the **Select Color** dialog box. Select the **Red** color and choose **OK**; the red color is assigned to the OBJ layer. Again, choose the **New Layer** button in the **LAYER PROPERTIES MANAGER** and rename the **Layer1** as **CEN**. Choose the linetype swatch to display the **Select Linetype** dialog box.

If different linetypes are not already loaded, choose the **Load** button to display the **Load or Reload Linetypes** dialog box. Select the **CENTER** linetype from the **Available Linetypes** area and choose the **OK** button; the **Select Linetype** dialog box will reappear. Select the **CENTER** linetype from the **Loaded linetypes** area and choose **OK**. Choose the color swatch to display the **Select Color** dialog box. Select the **yellow** color and choose **OK**; the color yellow and linetype center will be assigned to the layer CEN.

Similarly, different linetypes and different colors can be set for different layers mentioned in the statement of this example, as shown in Figure 14-14.

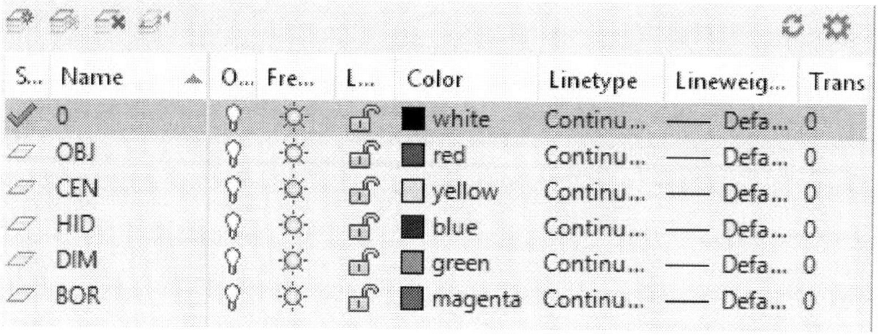

Figure 14-14** Partial view of the **LAYER PROPERTIES MANAGER

Step 4: Adding title block

Next, add the title block and the text, as shown in Figure 14-10. After completing the drawing, save it as *proto3.dwt*. You have created a template drawing (proto3) that contains all the information given in Example 3.

CUSTOMIZING A DRAWING WITH LAYOUT

The Layout (paper space) provides a convenient way to plot multiple views of a three-dimensional (3D) drawing or multiple views of a regular two-dimensional (2D) drawing. It takes quite some time to set up the viewports in the model space with different vpoints and scale factors. You can create prototype drawings that contain predefined viewport settings, with vpoint and the other desired information. If you create a new drawing or insert a drawing, the views are automatically generated. The following example illustrates the procedure for generating a prototype drawing with paper space and model space viewports:

Example 4 — Template with Layouts

Create a drawing template, as shown in Figure 14-15, with four views in Layout3 (Paper space) that display front, top, side, and 3D views of the object. The plot size is 10.5 by 8 inches. The plot scale is 0.5 or 1/2" = 1". The paper space viewports should have the following vpoint settings:

Viewports	Vpoint	View
Top right	1,-1,1	3D view
Top left	0,0,1	Top view
Lower right	1,0,0	Right side view
Lower left	0,-1,0	Front view

Figure 14-15 Paper space with four viewports

Start AutoCAD LT and create a new drawing. Use the following commands and options to set various parameters:

Step 1: Creating a new layout

First, choose the **New Layout** button in Layout Tabs; a new layout is automatically added with the default name as Layout3.

Note

You can also use the ***LAYOUT*** *command to create a new layout.*

Step 2: Specifying the page setup for the new layout

Next, choose the new layout (**Layout3**) tab; the new layout (**Layout3**) will be displayed with the default viewport. Delete this existing viewport. To invoke the **Page Setup Manager** dialog box, right-click on the layout in the Layout Tabs; a shortcut menu will be displayed. Choose **Page Setup Manager** from the shortcut menu; the **Page Setup Manager** dialog box will be displayed. Choose the **Modify** button to modify the default page setup. In the **Page Setup - Layout3** dialog box, select the required printer from the **Printer/plotter** area. In this example, **Microsoft XPS Document Writer** has been used.

Now, from the **Paper size** area, select the paper size that is supported by the selected plotting device. In this example, the paper size is A4. Choose the **OK** button to accept the settings and return to the **Page Setup Manager** dialog box. Choose the **Close** button to close the **Page Setup Manager** dialog box.

Step 3: Creating new layer for the viewports object

Next, you need to set up a layer with the name VIEW for viewports object and assign it green color. Invoke the **LAYER PROPERTIES MANAGER**. Choose the **New Layer** button and rename the Layer1 as VIEW. Choose the color swatch of the VIEW layer to display the **Select Color** dialog box. Select the color **Green** and choose the **OK** button. This color will be assigned to VIEW layer. Also, make the VIEW layer current and then exit the **LAYER PROPERTIES MANAGER**.

Step 4: Creating viewports

To create four viewports, choose the small inclined arrow at the lower-right corner from **Layout > Layout Viewports** in the **Ribbon**; the **Viewports** dialog box is displayed. Choose the **New Viewports** tab and then select the **Four: Equal** option from the **Standard Viewports** list box. Next, choose the **OK** button from the dialog box; you will be prompted to specify the starting point of the viewports. The following is the prompt sequence that follows after choosing the **OK** button.

Specify first corner or [Fit] <Fit>: **0.25,0.25** Enter
Specify opposite corner: **10.25,7.75** Enter

Step 5: Setting the required viewpoint in all layers

Choose the **PAPER** button in the Status Bar to activate the model space or enter **MSPACE** at the Command prompt.

Command: **MSPACE** (or **MS**)

Make the lower left viewport active by clicking on it. Next, you need to change the viewpoints of different paper space viewports by using the **Viewpoint** tool. To invoke this tool, choose the **Viewpoint** tool from **View > 3D Views** in the menu bar or enter **-VPOINT** at the Command prompt. The viewpoint values for different viewports are given in the statement of Example 4. To set the view point for the lower left viewport, the Command prompt sequence is given next.

*Choose the **Viewpoint** tool from **View > 3D Views** in the menu bar*
Current view direction: VIEWDIR= 0.0000,0.0000,1.0000 Enter
Specify a view point or [Rotate] <display compass and tripod>: **0,-1,0** Enter

Similarly, use the **Viewpoint** tool to set the viewpoint of the other viewports.

Make the top left viewport active by selecting a point in the viewport and then use the **Scale** tool to specify the paper space scale factor to 0.5. The **Scale** tool can be invoked by choosing **View > Zoom > Scale** from the menubar or by entering **ZOOM** at the Command prompt. The Command prompt sequence is given next.

Command: **ZOOM**
Specify corner of window, enter a scale factor (nX or nXP), or
[All/Center/Dynamic/Extents/Previous/Scale/Window/Object] <real time>: **0.5XP** Enter

Now, make the next viewport active and specify the zoom scale factor. Do the same for the remaining viewports.

Step 6: Creating border line

Use the **Model** button in the Status Bar to switch to model space environment and then set a new layer PBORDER with yellow color. Make the PBORDER layer current, draw a border, and if needed, a title block using the **Polyline** tool. You can also switch to paper space environment by entering **PSPACE** at the Command prompt.

The **Polyline** tool can be invoked by choosing the **Polyline** tool from the **Draw** menu or by choosing the **Polyline** tool from the **Draw** panel. The **Polyline** tool can also be invoked by entering **PLINE** at the Command prompt. While specifying the coordinate values for the **PLINE** command, make sure that the **Dynamic Input** button is turned off in the Status Bar.

Command: *Choose the **Polyline** tool from the **Draw** panel*
Specify start point: **0,0** Enter
Current line-width is 0.0000
Specify next point or [Arc/Halfwidth/Length/Undo/Width]: **0,8.0** Enter
Specify next point or [Arc/Close/Halfwidth/Length/Undo/Width]: **10.5,8.0** Enter
Specify next point or [Arc/Close/Halfwidth/Length/Undo/Width]: **10.5,0** Enter
Specify next point or [Arc/Close/Halfwidth/Length/Undo/Width]: **C** Enter

Step 7: Creating a wireframe model

Choose the **SW Isometric** from the **3D Views > Views > Menu Bar** and draw the wireframe model as shown in Figure 14-16. The prompt sequence for doing so is given next.

Command: *Choose the **Line** tool from the **Draw** panel*
Specify start point: **0,0,0** Enter
Specify next point: **0,2.25,0** Enter
Specify next point: **0,2.25,2.81** Enter
Specify next point: **0,1.5,2.81** Enter
Specify next point: **0,0,0** Enter
Specify next point: **1.5,0,0** Enter
Specify next point: **1.5,2.25,0** Enter
Specify next point: **1.5,2.25,2.81** Enter
Specify next point: **1.5,1.5,2.81** Enter
Specify next point: **1.5,0,0** Enter Enter

Command: *Choose the **Line** tool from the **Draw** panel*
Specify start point: **0,2.25,2.81** Enter
Specify next point: **1.5,2.25,2.81** Enter Enter

Command: *Choose the **Line** tool from the **Draw** panel*
Specify start point: **0,2.25,0** Enter
Specify next point: **1.5,2.25,0** Enter Enter

Command: *Choose the **Line** tool from the **Draw** panel*
Specify start point: **0,1.5,2.81** Enter
Specify next point: **1.5,1.5,2.81** Enter Enter

Step 8: Saving and testing the template file

The last step is to choose the **Model** tab (or change the **TILEMODE** to 1), if not already active and save the prototype drawing as template. To test the layout that you just created, make the 3D drawing, as shown in previous step. Switch to the **Layout 3** tab; you will find four different views of the object (Figure 14-17). If the object views do not

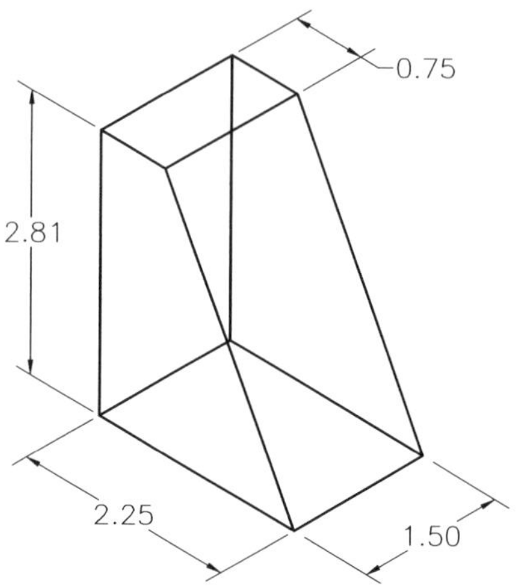

Figure 14-16 *3D tapered block*

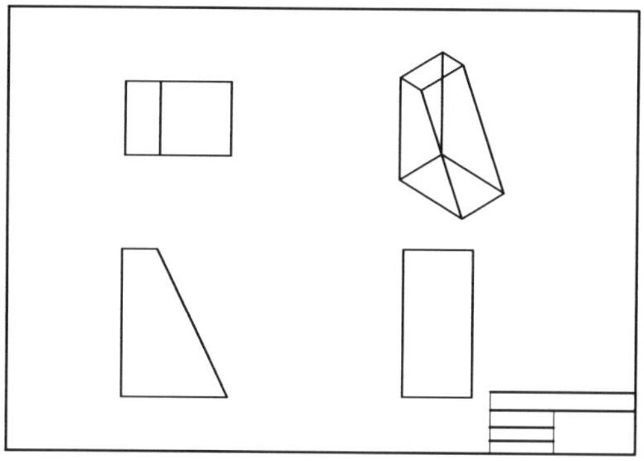

Figure 14-17 *Four views of a 3D object in paper space*

appear in the viewports, use the **PAN** commands to position the views in the viewports. You can freeze the VIEW layer so that the viewports do not appear on the drawing. You can plot this drawing from the Layout3 with a plot scale factor of 1:1 and the size of the plot will be exactly as specified.

CUSTOMIZING DRAWINGS WITH VIEWPORTS

In certain applications, you may need multiple model space viewport configurations to display different views of an object. This involves setting up the desired viewports and then changing the viewpoint for different viewports. You can create a prototype drawing that contains a required number of viewports and the viewpoint information. If you insert a 3D object in one of the viewports of the prototype drawing, you will automatically get different views of the object without setting viewports or viewpoints. The following example illustrates the procedure for creating a prototype drawing with a standard number (four) of viewports and viewpoints.

Example 5 — Template with Viewports

Create a prototype drawing with four viewports, as shown in Figure 14-18. The viewports should have the following viewpoints:

Viewports	Vpoint	View
Top right	1,-1,1	3D view
Top left	0,0,1	Top view
Lower right	1,0,0	Right side view
Lower left	0,-1,0	Front view

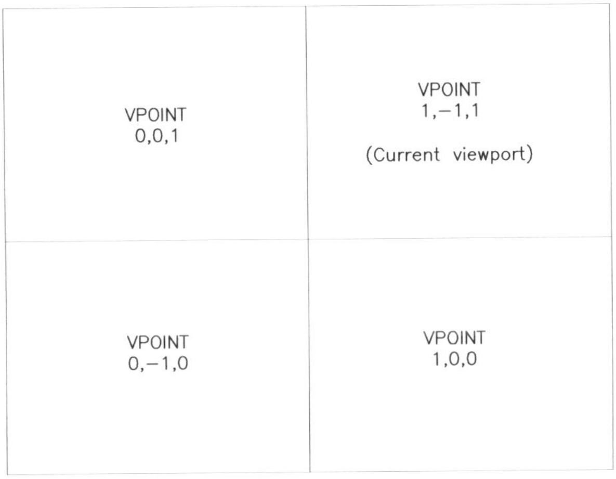

Figure 14-18 *Viewports with different viewpoints*

Step 1

Start AutoCAD LT and create a new drawing from scratch.

Step 2

Setting viewports in Model tab

Viewports and corresponding viewpoints can be set with the **VPORTS** command. You can also choose the **New Viewports** tool from **View > Viewports** in the menu bar; the **Viewports** dialog box, as shown in Figure 14-19. Select **Four: Equal** from the **Standard viewports** area. In the **Preview** area, four equal viewports are displayed. Select **3D** from the **Setup** drop-down list. The four viewports with the different viewpoints will be displayed in the **Preview** area as Top, Front, Right and SE Isometric. **Top** represents the viewpoints as (0,0,1), **Front** represents the viewpoints as (0,-1,0), **Right** represents the viewpoints as (1,0,0) and **SE Isometric**, represents the viewpoints as (1,-1,1) respectively. Choose the **OK** button. Save the drawing as *proto5.dwt*.

Viewports and viewpoints can also be set by entering **-VPORTS** and **VPOINT** at the Command prompt, respectively.

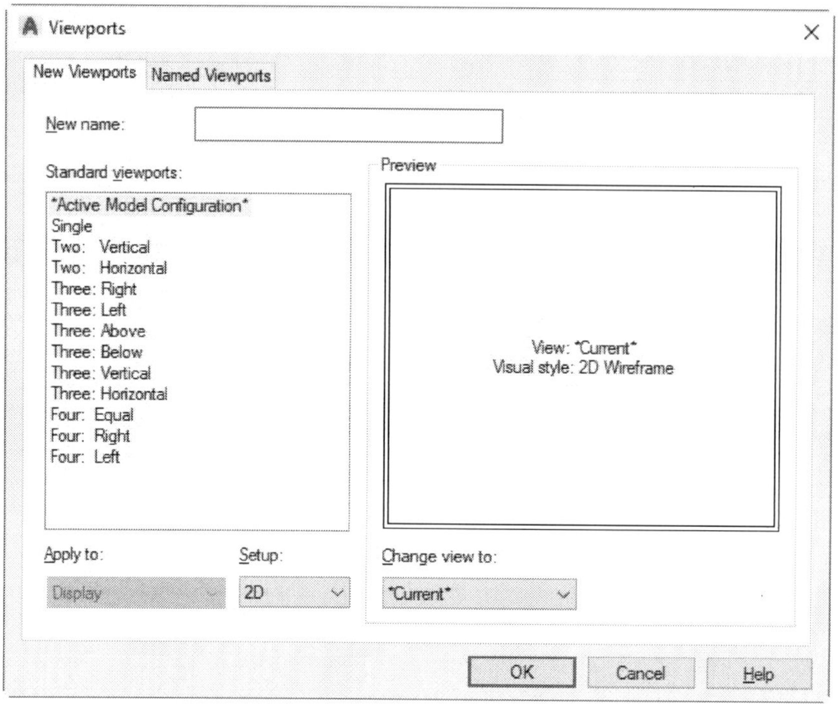

Figure 14-19 *The* ***Viewports*** *dialog box*

Step 3

Open the drawing of 3D tapered block, as shown in Figure 14-16.

Step 4

Again, start a new drawing, TEST, using the prototype drawing *proto5.dwt*. Make the top right viewport current and then insert or create a drawing, refer to Figure 14-16. Four different views will be automatically displayed on the screen, as shown in Figure 14-20.

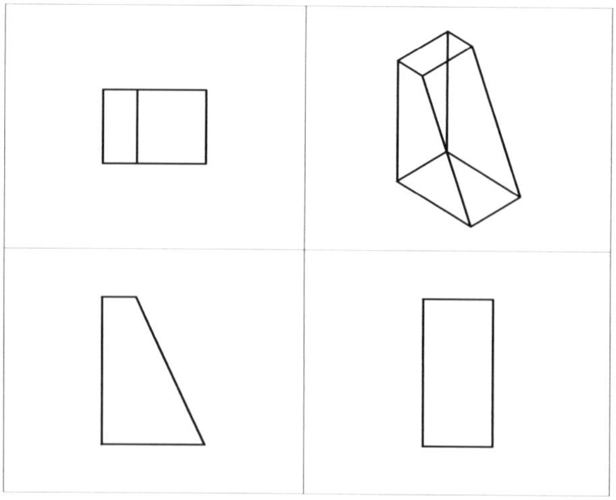

Figure 14-20 *Different views of a 3D tapered block*

CUSTOMIZING DRAWINGS ACCORDING TO PLOT SIZE AND DRAWING SCALE

For controlling the plot area, it is recommended to use layouts. You can make the drawing of any size, use the layout to specify the sheet size, and then draw the border and title block. However, you can also plot a drawing in the model space and set up the system variables so that the plotted drawing is according to your specifications. You can generate a template drawing according to plot size and scale. For example, if the scale is 1/16" = 1' and the drawing is to be plotted on a 36" by 24" area, you can calculate drawing parameters like limits, **DIMSCALE**, and **LTSCALE** and save them in a template drawing. This will save considerable time in the initial drawing setup and provide uniformity in the drawings. The next example explains the procedure involved in customizing a drawing according to a certain plot size and scale.

Note

You can also use the paper space to specify the paper size and scale.

Example 6 Template with Plot Size and Drawing Scale

Create a drawing template (PROTO6) with the following specifications:

Plotted sheet size	36" by 24" (Figure 14-21)
Scale	1/8" = 1.0'
Snap	3'
Grid	6'
Text height	1/4" on plotted drawing
Linetype scale	Calculate
Dimscale factor	Calculate
Units	Architectural
	Precision, 16-denominator of the smallest fraction
	Angle in degrees/minutes/seconds
	Precision, 0d00'
	Direction control, base angle, east
	Angle positive, if measured counterclockwise
Border	Border should be 1" inside the edges of the plotted drawing sheet, using PLINE 1/32" wide when plotted (Figure 14-21)

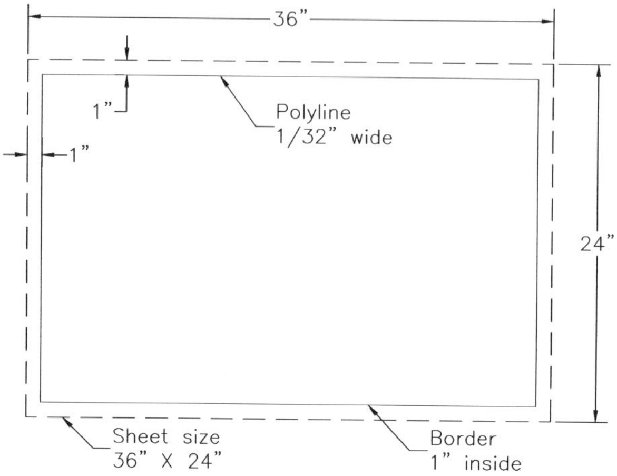

Figure 14-21 Border of the template drawing

Step 1: Calculating limits, text height, linetype scale, dimension scale, and polyline width

In this example, you need to calculate some values before you set the parameters. The limits of the drawing depend on the plotted size of the drawing and its scale. Similarly, **LTSCALE** and **DIMSCALE** depend on the plot scale of the drawing. The following calculations explain the procedure for finding the values of limits, ltscale, dimscale, and text height.

Limits

Given:
Sheet size 36" x 24"
Scale 1/8" = 1'
or 1" = 8'

Calculate:
X Limit
Y Limit
Since sheet size is 36" x 24" and scale is 1/8"=1'
Therefore, X Limit = 36 x 8' = 288'
Y Limit = 24 x 8' = 192'

Text height

Given:
Text height when plotted = 1/4"
Scale 1/8" = 1'

Calculate:
Text height
Since scale is 1/8" = 1'
or 1/8" = 12"
or 1" = 96"
Therefore, scale factor = 96
Text height = 1/4" x 96
= 24" = 2'

Linetype scale and dimension scale

Known:
Since scale is 1/8" = 1'
or 1/8" = 12"
or 1" = 96"

Calculate:
LTSCALE and DIMSCALE
Since scale factor = 96
Therefore, LTSCALE = Scale factor = 96
Similarly, DIMSCALE = 96
(All dimension variables, like DIMTXT and DIMASZ, will be multiplied by 96.)

Polyline Width

Given:
Scale is 1/8" = 1'

Calculate:
PLINE width
Since scale is 1/8" = 1'
or 1" = 8'
or 1" = 96"

Therefore,
PLINE width = 1/32 x 96
= 3"

After calculating the parameters, use the following AutoCAD LT commands to set up the drawing and save the drawing as *proto6.dwt.*

Step 2: Setting units

Start a new drawing and enter **UNITS** at the Command prompt to display the **Drawing Units** dialog box. Select **Architectural** from the **Type** drop-down list in the **Length** area. Select **0'-01/16"** from the **Precision** drop-down list. Make sure the **Clockwise** check box in the **Angle** area is not selected. Select **Deg/Min/Sec** from the **Type** drop-down list and select **0d00'** from the **Precision** drop-down list in the **Angle** area. Now, choose the **Direction** button to display the **Directional Control** dialog box. Select the **East** radio button, if it is not selected, in the **Base Angle** area and then choose the **OK** button twice to close both the dialog boxes.

Step 3: Setting limits, snap and grid, textsize, linetype scale, dimension scale, dimension style and pline

To set limits, enter **LIMITS** at the Command prompt.

Command: **LIMITS**
Specify lower left corner or [ON/OFF] <0'-0",0'-0">:**0,0** Enter
Specify upper right corner <1'-0",0'-9">: **288',192'** Enter

Choose the **All** tool of the **ZOOM** drop-down to increase the drawing display area.

Right-click on the **Snap Mode** or **Grid Display** button in the Status Bar to invoke the shortcut menu. In the shortcut menu, choose **Settings** to display the **Drafting Settings** dialog box. In this dialog box, enter **3'** and **3'** in the **Snap X spacing** and **Snap Y spacing** edit boxes, respectively. Similarly, enter **6'** and **6'** in the **Grid X spacing** and **Grid Y spacing** edit boxes, respectively. Then, choose the **OK** button.

You can also set these values by entering **SNAP** and **GRID** at the Command prompt.

The size of the text can be changed by entering **TEXTSIZE** at the Command prompt.

Command: **TEXTSIZE**
Enter new value for TEXTSIZE <current>: **2'** Enter

To set the **LTSCALE**, choose the **Other** option from **Home > Properties > Linetype** drop-down list, or choose the **Linetype** option from the **Format** menu bar, or enter **LINETYPE** at the Command prompt; the **Linetype Manager** dialog box will be invoked. Choose the **Show details** button; the **Linetype Manager** dialog box will be expanded. Now, specify the **Global scale factor** as **96** in the **Global scale factor** edit box. Choose the **OK** button to accept the changes and exit the **Linetype Manager** dialog box.

You can also change the scale of the linetype by entering **LTSCALE** at the Command prompt.

Choose the inclined arrow displayed on the **Dimensions** panel title bar in the **Annotate** tab to invoke the **Dimension Style Manager** dialog box, refer to Figure 14-11. Next, choose the **New** button from the **Dimension Style Manager** dialog box to invoke the **Create New Dimension Style** dialog box. Specify the new style name as **MYDIM2** in the **New Style Name** edit box and then choose the **Continue** button. The **New Dimension Style: MYDIM2** dialog box will be displayed. Choose the **Fit** tab and set the value in the **Use overall scale of** spinner to **96** in the **Scale for dimension features** area. Now, choose the **OK** button to again display the **Dimension Style Manager** dialog box. Choose the **Close** button to exit the dialog box.

You can invoke the **PLINE** command by choosing the **Polyline** tool from the **Draw** panel or entering **PLINE** at the Command prompt. While specifying the coordinate values for the **PLINE** command, make sure that the **Dynamic Input** button is turned off in the Status Bar.

Command: *Choose the **Polyline** tool from the **Draw** panel*
Specify start point: **8',8'** Enter
Current line-width is 0'-0"
Specify next point or [Arc/Halfwidth/Length/Undo/Width]: **W** Enter
Specify starting width<0'-00">: **3** Enter
Specify ending width<0'-3">: Enter
Specify next point or [Arc/Halfwidth/Length/Undo/Width]: **@280,0** Enter
Specify next point or [Arc/Close/Halfwidth/Length/Undo/Width]: **@0,184** Enter
Specify next point or [Arc/Close/Halfwidth/Length/Undo/Width]: **@-280,0** Enter
Specify next point or [Arc/Close/Halfwidth/Length/Undo/Width]: **C** Enter

Now, save the drawing as *proto6.dwt*.

Self-Evaluation Test

Answer the following questions and then compare them to those given at the end of this chapter:

1. The template drawings are saved in the __________ format.

2. To use a template file, select the __________ option in the **Create New Drawing** dialog box.

3. To start a drawing with the default setup, select the __________ option in the **Create New Drawing** dialog box.

4. If the plot size is 36" x 24", and the scale is 1/2" = 1', then X Limit = __________ and Y Limit = __________.

5. You can use the __________ tool to set up a viewport in the paper space.

6. You can use the __________ tool to switch to model space.

7. The values that can be assigned to **TILEMODE** are __________ and __________.

Review Questions

Answer the following questions:

1. The default value of **DIMSCALE** is __________.

2. The default value of **DIMTXT** is __________.

3. The default value of **SNAP** is __________.

4. Architectural units can be selected by using the __________ command or the __________ command.

5. Name three standard template drawings that come with AutoCAD LT software __________, __________, and __________.

6. If the plot size is 24" x 18", and the scale is 1:20, the X Limit = __________ and Y Limit = __________.

7. If the plot size is 200 x 150 and limits are (0.00,0.00) and (600.00,450.00), the **LTSCALE** factor = __________.

8. __________ provides a convenient way to plot multiple views of a 3D drawing or multiple views of a regular 2D drawing.

9. You can use the __________ tool to switch to paper space.

10. In the model space, if you want to reduce the display size by half, the scale factor you enter for the **Scale** tool is __________.

Exercise 1 — Template with Limits

Create a drawing template (*protoe1.dwt*) with the following specifications:

Units	Architectural with precision 0'-0 1/16
Angle	Decimal Degrees with precision 0
Base angle	East
Angle direction	Counterclockwise
Limits	48' x 36'

Exercise 2 — Template with Limits, Text Height, & Units

Create a drawing template (*protoe2.dwt*) with the following specifications:

Limits	36.0,24.0
Snap	0.5
Grid	1.0
Text height	0.25
Units	Decimal
	Precision 0.00
	Decimal degrees
	Precision 0
	Base angle, East
	Angle positive if measured counterclockwise

Exercise 3 — Template with Layers, LTSCALE, & DIMSCALE

Create a drawing template (*protoe3.dwt*) with the following specifications:

Limits	48.0,36.0
Text height	0.25
PLINE width	0.03
LTSCALE	4.0
DIMSCALE	4.0
Plot size	10.5 x 8

LAYERS

Layer Name	Line Type	Color
0	Continuous	White
OBJECT	Continuous	Green
CENTER	Center	Magenta
HIDDEN	Hidden	Blue
DIM	Continuous	Red
BORDER	Continuous	Cyan

Exercise 4 Relative Rectangular & Absolute Coordinates

Create a prototype drawing (*protoe4.dwt*) with the following specifications:

Limits	36.0,24,0
Border	35.0,23.0
Grid	1.0
Snap	0.5
Text height	0.15
Units	Decimal (up to 2 places)
LTSCALE	1
Current layer	Object

LAYERS

Layer Name	Linetype	Color
0	Continuous	White
Object	Continuous	Red
Hidden	Hidden	Yellow
Center	Center	Green
Dim	Continuous	Blue
Border	Continuous	Magenta
Notes	Continuous	White

This prototype drawing should have a border line and a title block as shown in Figure 14-22.

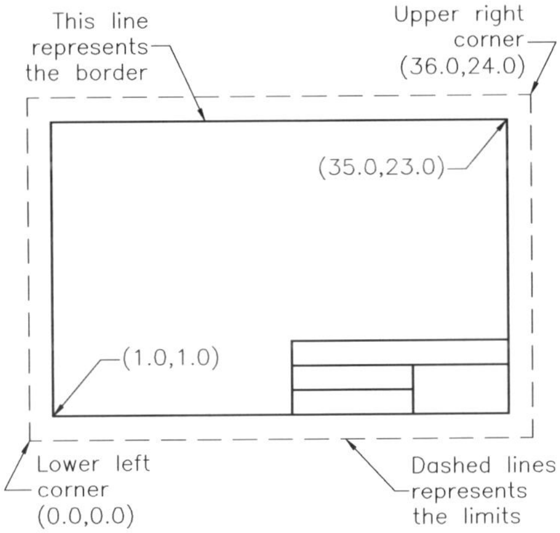

Figure 14-22 *Prototype drawing*

Exercise 5 Template with Plot Sheet Size & Title Block

Create a template drawing shown in Figure 14-23 with the following specifications and save it with the name *protoe5.dwt*:

Plotted sheet size	36" x 24" (Figure 14-23)
Scale	1/2" = 1.0'
Text height	1/4" on plotted drawing
LTSCALE	24
DIMSCALE	24
Units	Architectural 32-denominator of smallest fraction to display Angle in degrees/minutes/seconds Precision 0d00"00" Angle positive if measured counterclockwise
Border	Border is 1-1/2" inside the edges of the plotted drawing sheet, using the PLINE 1/32" wide when plotted.

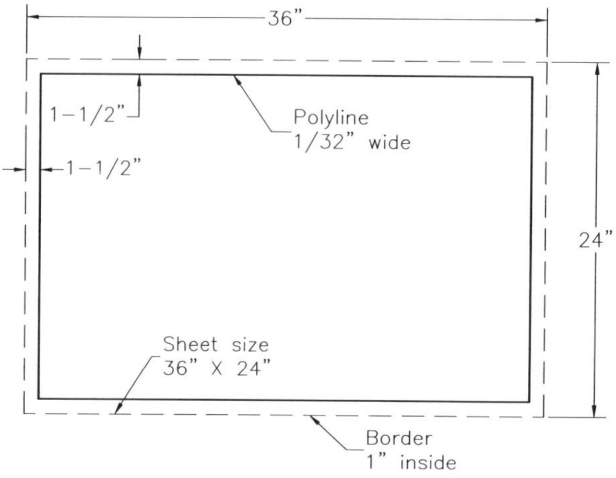

***Figure 14-23** Drawing for Exercise 5*

Exercise 6 Template with Title Block & Dimension Style

Create a prototype drawing, as shown in Figure 14-24 with the following specifications (the name of the drawing is *protoe6.dwt*):

Plotted sheet size	24" x 18" (Figure 14-24)
Scale	1/2"=1.0'
Border	The border is 1" inside the edges of the plotted drawing sheet, using the PLINE 0.05" wide when plotted (Figure 14-24)

Dimension text over the dimension line
Dimensions aligned with the dimension line

Calculate overall dimension scale factor
Enable the display of alternate units
Dimensions to be associative.

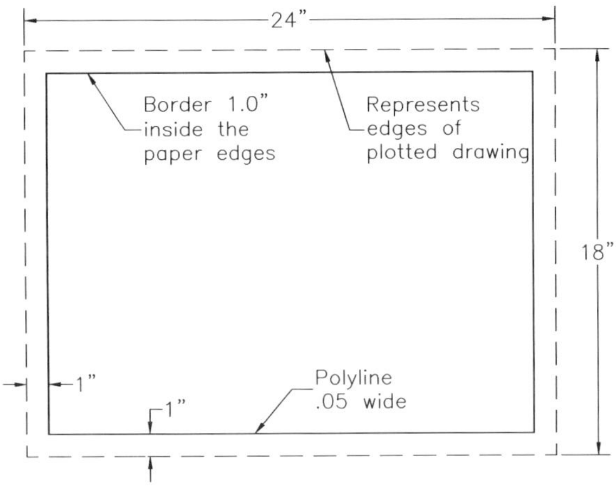

Figure 14-24 *Prototype drawing*

Exercise 7 *Creating & Using Template for Generating Drawing*

Create a template with the necessary specifications to draw the Articulated Rod shown in Figure 14-25, with the following specifications.

Limits	36.0,24,0
Border	35.0,23.0
Grid	1.0
Snap	0.5
Text height	0.15
Units	Decimal (up to 2 places)
LTSCALE	1
Current layer	Object

LAYERS

Layer Name	Linetype	Color
0	Continuous	White
Object	Continuous	Red
Hidden	Hidden	Yellow
Center	Center	Green
Dim	Continuous	Blue
Border	Continuous	Magenta
Notes	Continuous	White

Also, use this template and the layers created in it to draw the views of the Articulated Rod.

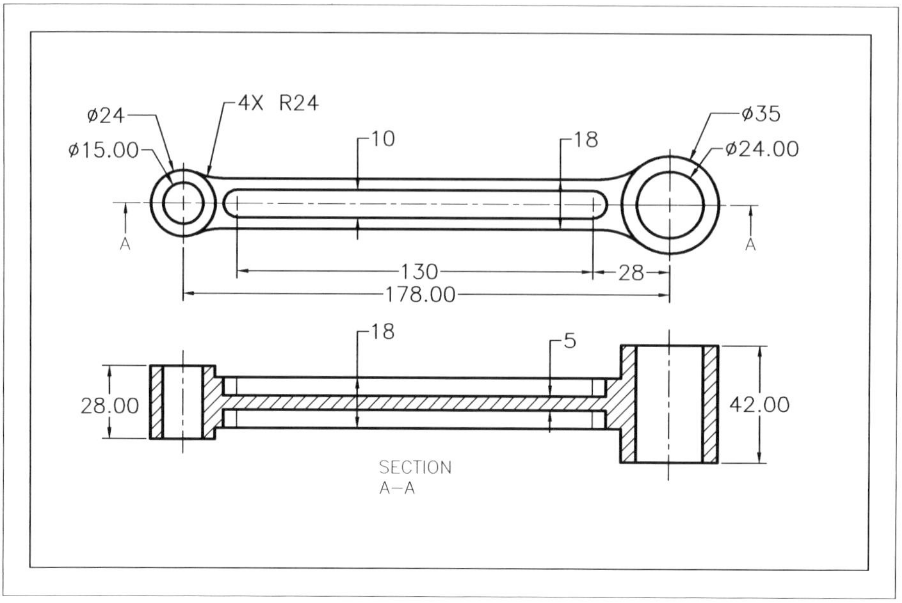

Figure 14-25 *Views and dimensions of the Articulated Rod*

Answers to Self-Evaluation Test

1. *.dwt*, **2. Use a Template**, **3. Start from Scratch**, **4.** 72',48', **5. Named**, **6. Quick View Layouts**, **7. 0, 1**

Chapter 15

Working with Blocks

Learning Objectives

After completing this chapter, you will be able to:

- *Create and insert blocks*
- *Add parameters and assign actions to the blocks to make them dynamic blocks*
- *Create drawing files by using the Write Block dialog box*
- *Use the DESIGNCENTER to locate, preview, copy, or insert blocks and existing drawings*
- *Use the Tool Palettes to insert blocks*
- *Edit blocks*
- *Split a block*
- *Rename blocks and delete unused blocks*

Key Terms

- *Blocks*
- *Annotative Blocks*
- *Dynamic Blocks*
- *Parameters*
- *Actions*
- *Nesting of Blocks*
- *Write Block*
- *XPLODE*
- *Constraints to Blocks*

THE CONCEPT OF BLOCKS

The ability to store parts of a drawing or the entire drawing such that they need not be redrawn when required in the same drawing or another drawing is a great benefit to the user. These parts of a drawing, entire drawings, or symbols (also known as **blocks**) can be placed (inserted) in a drawing at the location of your choice with the desired orientation and scale factor. A block is given a name (block name) and is referenced (inserted) by its name. All objects within a block are treated as a single object. You can move, erase, or list the block as a single object, that is, you can select the entire block simply by checking anywhere on it. As for the edit and inquiry commands, the internal structure of a block is immaterial, since a block is treated as a primitive object, like a polygon. If a block definition is changed, all references to the block in the drawing are updated to incorporate the changes.

A block is created by using the **Create Block** tool in the **Block Definition** panel of the **Insert** tab in the **Ribbon**. You can also save objects in a drawing, or an entire drawing as a drawing file using the **Write Block** tool. The main difference between the two is that a wblock can be inserted in any other drawing, but a block can be inserted only in the drawing file in which it was created.

One of the important features of AutoCAD LT is the annotative blocks that can be used as symbol to annotate your drawing. The annotative blocks are defined in terms of paper space height. The annotative blocks are displayed in floating viewports and their respective size in model space is calculated by multiplying the current annotation scale set for those spaces and the paper space height of the block.

Another feature of AutoCAD LT is that instead of inserting a symbol as a block (which results in the addition of the content of the referenced drawing to the drawing in which it is inserted), you can reference the other drawings (Xref) in the current file. This means that the contents of the referenced drawing are not added to the current drawing file, although they become part of that drawing on the screen. This is explained in detail in Chapter 17.

CONVERTING ENTITIES INTO A BLOCK

Ribbon: Insert > Block Definition > Create Block **Command:** BLOCK/B
Toolbar: Draw > Make Block

You can convert the entities in the drawing window into a block by using the **BLOCK** command or by choosing the **Create Block** tool from the **Block Definition** panel in the **Insert** tab or the **Home** tab. Alternatively, you can do so by choosing the **Make Block** tool from the **Draw** toolbar. When you invoke this tool, the **Block Definition** dialog box will be displayed, as shown in Figure 15-1. You can use the **Block Definition** dialog box to save any object or objects as a block.

In the **Name** edit box of the **Block Definition** dialog box, enter the name of the block you want to create. All the block names present in the current drawing are displayed in the **Name** drop-down list in an alphabetical and numerical order. This way you can verify whether a block you have defined has been saved. By default, the block name can have up to 255 characters. Also, it can contain letters, digits, blank spaces as well as any special characters including the $ (dollar sign), - (hyphen), and _ (underscore), provided they are not being used for any other purpose by AutoCAD LT or Windows.

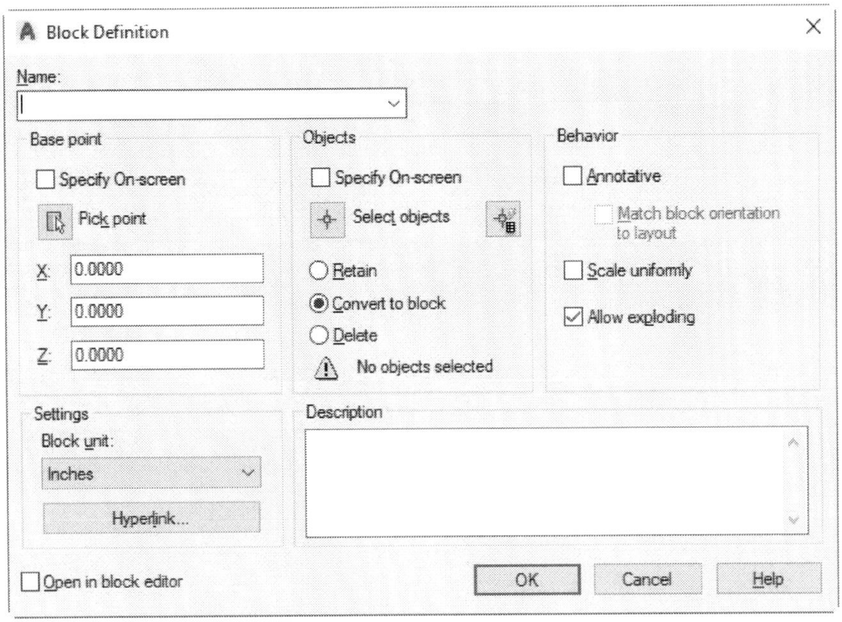

Figure 15-1 *The* ***Block Definition*** *dialog box*

Note

The block name is controlled by the ***EXTNAMES*** *system variable and its default value is 1. If the value is set to 0, the block name will be only thirty-one characters long and will not include spaces or any other special characters, apart from a $ (dollar sign), - (hyphen), or _ (underscore).*

If a block already exists, with the block name that you have specified in the **Name** edit box, and you choose **OK** in the **Block Definition** dialog box, the **Block - Redefine Block** message box will be displayed informing you that the block with this name is already defined. It will also prompt you to specify if you want to redefine the block or not. In this dialog box, you can either redefine the existing block by choosing the **Redefine** button or you can exit it by choosing the **No** button. You can then use another name for the block in the dialog box.

After you have specified a block name, you are required to specify the insertion base point, which will be used as a reference point to insert the block. Usually, either the center or the lower left corner of the block is defined as the insertion base point. Later on, when you insert the block, you will notice that it appears at the insertion point, and you can insert it with reference to this point. The point you specify as the insertion base point is taken as the origin point of the block's coordinate system. You can specify the insertion point by choosing the **Pick point** button in the **Base point** area of the dialog box. The dialog box is temporarily removed, and you can select a base point on the screen. Alternatively, you can also enter the coordinates in the **X**, **Y**, and **Z** edit boxes. Once the insertion base point is specified, the dialog box reappears and the *X*, *Y*, and *Z* coordinates of the insertion base point are displayed in the **X**, **Y**, and **Z** edit boxes respectively. If no insertion base point is selected, AutoCAD LT assumes the insertion point coordinates to be 0,0,0 which are the default coordinates.

After specifying the insertion base point, you are required to select the objects that will constitute the block. Until the objects are selected, AutoCAD LT displays a warning: **No objects selected**, at the bottom of the **Objects** area. Choose the **Select objects** button; the warning disappears. You can select the objects on the screen using any selection method. After completing the selection process, right-click or press the ENTER key to return to the dialog box. The number of objects selected is displayed at the bottom of the **Objects** area of the dialog box.

The **Objects** area of the **Block Definition** dialog box also has a **QuickSelect** button. On choosing this button, the **Quick Select** dialog box is displayed, which allows you to define a selection set based on the properties of objects. **Quick Select** is used in cases where the drawings are very large and complex. The **Quick Select** dialog box has been discussed earlier in Chapter 6, Editing Sketched Objects-II.

In the **Objects** area, if you select the **Retain** radio button, the selected objects that form the block, are retained on the screen as individual objects. If you select the **Convert to block** radio button, the selected objects are converted into a block and will not be displayed on the screen after the block has been defined. Rather, the created block will be displayed in place of the original objects. If you select the **Delete** radio button, the selected objects will be deleted from the drawing, after the block has been defined.

If you select the **Annotative** check box in the **Behavior** area, the block created will become annotative. The block will now acquire annotative properties like text, dimension, hatch, and so on. On selecting the **Annotative** check box, the **Match block orientation to layout** check box will get highlighted. If you select the **Match block orientation to layout** check box, the orientation of the block in paper space viewport will always remain aligned to the orientation of the layout, while inserting the block. If you select the **Scale uniformly** check box, the block can only be scaled uniformly in all directions, while inserting the block in drawing area. In such cases, if you create an annotative block, you can scale it only uniformly, while inserting the block in drawing area. The **Scale uniformly** check box is selected by default and will remain unavailable for modification when you select the **Annotative** check box. If you select the **Allow exploding** check box, the block can be exploded into separate entities using the **Explode** tool, whenever required.

In the **Settings** Area, the **Block unit** drop-down list displays the units that will be used while inserting the current block. For example, if the block is created with inches as the units and you select **Feet** from the **Block unit** drop-down list, the block will be scaled to feet. You can also invoke the **Insert Hyperlink** dialog box by choosing the **Hyperlink** button in the **Settings** Area. This dialog box allows you to link any specific files, websites, or named views with the current drawing. You can also link the drawing to a default email address or you can select one from the recently used email addresses.

The **Open in block editor** check box is available at the bottom of the **Block Definition** dialog box. If this check box is selected, the **Block Editor** will open as soon as you close the **Block Definition** dialog box. Also, the entities of the block will be displayed in the authoring area of the block editor. You will learn more about the **Block Editor** in the next section.

After setting all parameters in the **Block Definition** dialog box, choose the **OK** button to complete defining the block.

Exercise 1 — Block

Draw a circle of 1 unit radius and then draw multiple circles inside it, as shown in Figure 15-2. Next, convert them into a block and name the entity as CIRCLE. Refer to the following figure for details.

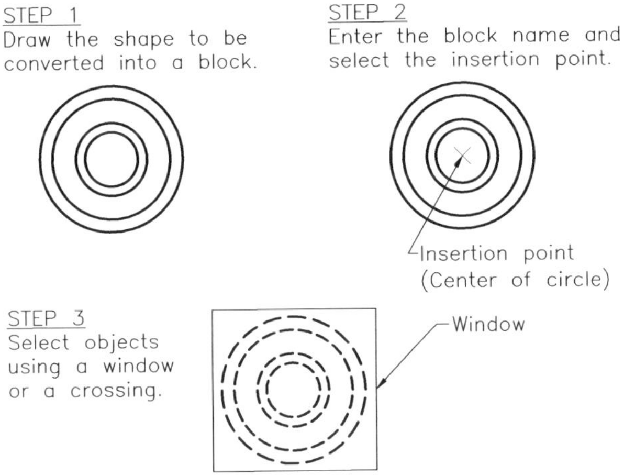

Figure 15-2 Block created from multiple circles

INSERTING BLOCKS

Ribbon: Insert > Block > Insert **Command:** INSERT/I
Toolbar: Insert > Insert Block or Draw > Insert Block
Menubar: Insert > Block

The blocks created in the current drawing are inserted using the **Insert** tool. An inserted block is called a block reference. You should determine the layer and location to insert the block, and also the angle by which you want the block to be rotated prior to its insertion. If the layer on which you want to insert the block is not the current layer, select the appropriate option from the **Layer** drop-down list in the **Layers** panel of the **Home** tab or choose the **Set Current** button in the **LAYER PROPERTIES PALETTE** to make it current.

To insert a block, choose the **Insert Block** tool; a flyout will be displayed. In the flyout, the blocks available in the drawing are displayed. Click on the required block; the selected block will be attached to the cursor. Specify the required location to insert the block; the block will be inserted in the drawing. Note that if the block is not available in the drawing, type **INSERT** in the command line; the **BLOCKS** palette will be invoked, as shown in Figure 15-3. You can specify different parameters of the block or external files to be inserted in the **BLOCKS** palette. The options in the **BLOCKS** palette are discussed next.

Filter

This search box is used to search the name of the block to be inserted. All blocks are displayed in the **Recent Blocks** area. The browse button(...) next to this search box is used to insert external files. When you choose this button, the **Select Drawing File** dialog box will be displayed, as shown in Figure 15-4.

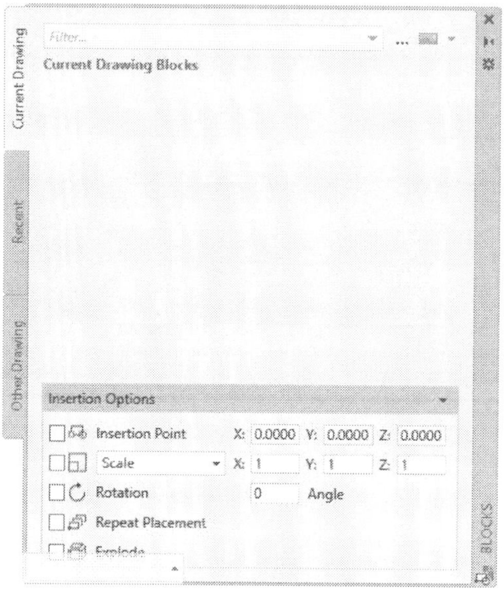

Figure 15-3 BLOCKS palette

This dialog box is similar to the standard **Select File** dialog box discussed in Chapter 1. You can select a drawing file from the files listed in the current directory. You can also change the directory by selecting the desired directory from the **Look in** drop-down list. When you select the drawing file and choose the **Open** button, the drawing file preview is displayed in the **Other** drawing tab of the **Blocks** palette. The **Path** option displays the path of the external file selected to be inserted.

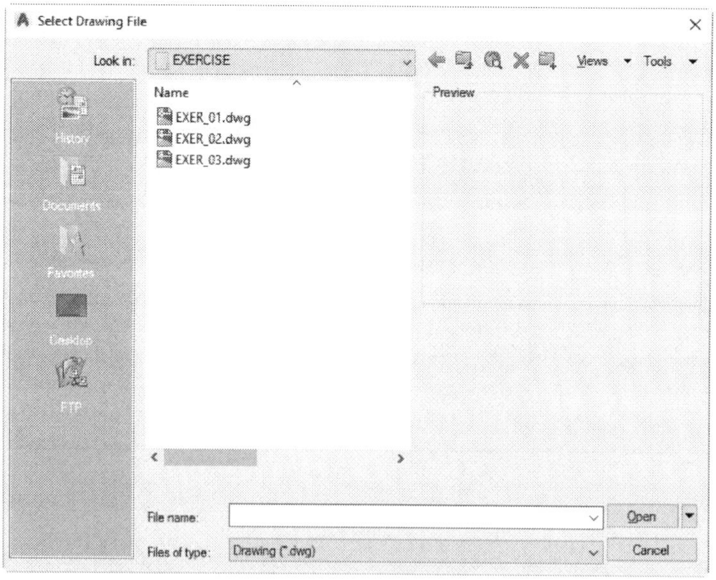

Figure 15-4 *The* ***Select Drawing File*** *dialog box*

Note

*1. If the name you have specified in the **Filter** edit box does not exist as a block in the current drawing, AutoCAD LT will search the drives and directories on the path (specified in the **Options** dialog box) for a drawing of the same name. If the block is found, it will be inserted.*

*2. Also, suppose you have inserted a block in a drawing and then you want to insert a drawing with the same name as the block, AutoCAD LT will display a message saying that XX is already defined as a block and prompts you to define the action you want to perform. If you choose **Redefine**, the block in the drawing will get replaced by the drawing with the same name, that is, the block gets redefined.*

*3. To change the name of a block, invoke the **Rename** dialog box by typing Rename in the command prompt. Next, in the **Named Objects** area, select the block whose name you want to change; its current name will be displayed in the **Old Name** edit box. Enter a new name in the **Rename To** edit box to change the name.*

Tip

*You can create a block in the current drawing from an existing drawing file. This saves the time by avoiding redrawing the object as a block. Locate and select an existing drawing file using the **Browse** button in the **Block** palette. Next, choose the **Open** button after selecting the existing drawing; the drawing will be added to the **Other Drawing** tab of the **Blocks** palette. Click on this drawing, you will be prompted to specify the insertion point. Now, instead of specifying the insertion point, press the ESC key; the selected file will be converted into a block, but will not be inserted into the drawing.*

Insertion point Check Box

When a block is inserted, its coordinate system is aligned parallel to the current UCS. In the Insertion point area, you can specify the **X**, **Y**, and **Z** coordinate locations of the block insertion point in the **X**, **Y**, and **Z** edit boxes, respectively. If you select the **Insertion point** check box, the **X**, **Y**, and **Z** edit boxes will not be available. By default, the **Insertion point** check box is selected, therefore, you can specify the insertion point directly on the screen.

Scale Check Box

In this area, you can specify the X, Y, and Z scale factors of the block to be inserted in the **X**, **Y**, and **Z** edit boxes, respectively. By selecting the **Scale** check box, you can specify the scale factors of the block in the edit boxes. The **Scale** check box is cleared by default and the block is inserted with a scale factor value of 1 along the three axes. Also, if **Uniform Scale** is selected in the **Scale** drop-down list, the value entered in the edit box will get uniformly applied to the X, Y, and Z scale factors. The X and Y scale factors allow you to stretch or compress a block along the X and Y axes, respectively. You can also insert 3D objects into a drawing by specifying the third scale factor (since 3D objects have three dimensions), the Z scale factor. Figure 15-5 shows a block inserted with different X and Y scale factors.

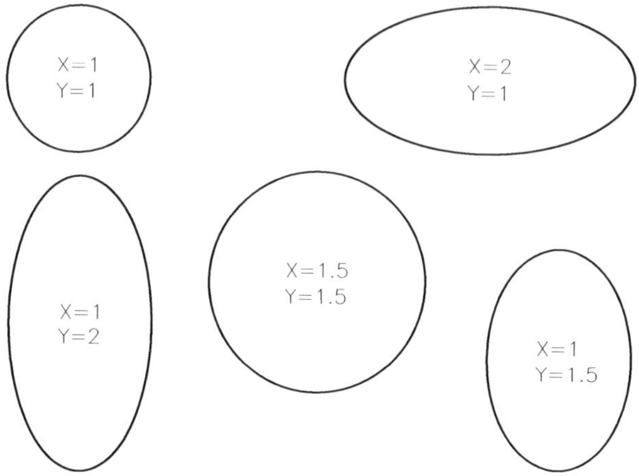

***Figure 15-5** Block inserted with different scale factors*

Tip

1. By specifying negative scale factors, you can insert a mirror image of a block along a particular axis. A negative scale factor for both the X and Y axes is the same as rotating the block reference through 180 degrees, since it mirrors the block reference in the opposite quadrant of the coordinate system. The effect of the negative scale factor on the block (DOOR) can be marked by a change in position of the insertion point marked with an (X), as shown in Figure 15-6.

2. Also, specifying a scale factor of less than 1 inserts the block reference smaller than the original size. A scale factor greater than 1 inserts the block reference larger than its original size.

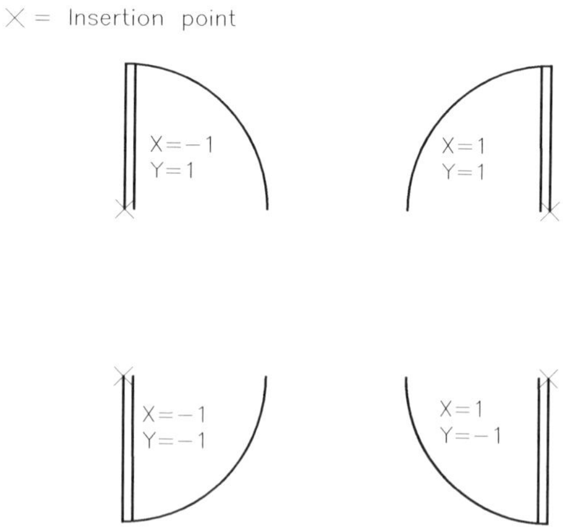

***Figure 15-6** Block inserted using negative scale factors*

Rotation Check Box

You can enter the angle of rotation for the block to be inserted in the **Angle** edit box. The insertion point is taken as the location about which the rotation takes place. Selecting the **Rotation** check box enables you to specify the angle of rotation on the screen. This check box is cleared by default and, therefore, the block is inserted at an angle of 0 degree.

Repeat Placement

This check box is used to insert another block at the previous insertion point.

Note

You can control the units for the insertion of the block through the ***INSUNITS*** *system variable. While doing so, the* ***Factor*** *information displayed in the* ***Block Unit*** *area will change accordingly.*

Explode Check Box

By selecting this check box, the block is inserted as a collection of individual objects. The function of the **Explode** check box is identical to that of the **Explode** tool. Once a block is exploded, the X, Y, and Z scale factors become identical. Therefore, you are provided access to only one scale factor edit box (**X** edit box), the **Y** and **Z** edit boxes are not available, and the **Uniform Scale** check box also gets selected. The X scale factor is assigned to the Y and Z scale factors too. You must enter a positive scale factor value.

Note

If you select the ***Explode*** *check box before insertion, the block reference will be exploded and the objects will be inserted with their original properties such as layer, color, and linetype.*

Once you have entered the relevant information in the Block Palette, choose the Close button to exit the Block Palette.If you have selected the insertion check boxes, you can specify the insertion point, scale, and angle of rotation with a pointing device. Whenever the insertion point is to be specified on the screen (by default), you can specify the scale factors and rotation angle values. These values will override the values specified in the dialog box by using the command line. Before specifying the insertion point on the screen, you can right-click to display the shortcut menu, which has all the options available through the command line. You can choose the options for insertion from the dynamic preview. On being prompted to specify the insertion point, press the down arrow key to see the options in the dynamic preview. However, if you have already specified an insertion point in the **Blocks** palette and have selected the **Scale** or **Rotation** check box of the **Blocks** palette, you are allowed to specify only the scale factors or the rotation angle at the command line. The following command prompt will be displayed when all the three check boxes are selected:

Specify insertion point or [Basepoint/Scale/X/Y/Z/Rotate]: *Specify an insertion point on the screen.*
Enter X scale factor, specify opposite corner, or [Corner/XYZ] <1>: *Specify scale factor in X- axis or select an option or press ENTER to accept the default scale factor of 1.*
Enter Y scale factor <use X scale factor>: *Specify Y scale factor.*
Specify rotation angle <0>: *Specify the angle of rotation of the inserted block.*

Tip

Using the Command prompt, you can override scale factors and rotation angles already specified in the dialog box.

The Command prompt options are discussed next.

Basepoint

If you enter **B** at the **Specify insertion point** prompt or select the option from the dynamic preview, you are again prompted to specify the base point. Specify the base point by clicking the cursor at the desired location. This point will now act as the insertion point. All prompts are also displayed at the cursor input so there is no need to always take a look on the command prompt. The prompt sequence for this option is given next.

Specify insertion point or [Basepoint/Scale/X/Y/Z/Rotate]: **B** Enter
Specify base point: *Specify base point.*
Specify base point: Specify insertion point: or [Basepoint/Scale/X/Y/Z/Rotate]: *Specify insertion point.*

Scale

On entering **S** at the **Specify insertion point** prompt, you are prompted to enter the scale factor. After entering it, the block assumes the specified scale factor, and AutoCAD LT lets you drag the block until you locate the insertion point on the screen. The *X*, *Y*, and *Z* axes are uniformly scaled by the specified scale factor. The prompt sequence for this option is given next.

Specify insertion point or [Basepoint/Scale/X/Y/Z/Rotate]: **S** Enter
Specify scale factor for XYZ axes<1>: *Enter a value to preset general scale factor.*
Specify insertion point or [Basepoint/Scale/X/Y/Z/Rotate]: *Specify insertion point.*

X, Y, Z

After entering **X**, **Y**, or **Z** at the Specify insertion point or [Basepoint/Scale/X/Y/Z/Rotate] prompt, you can specify the scale factor along that axis. These options in the command prompt are only available when **Scale** is selected from the **Scale** drop-down list in the **Insertion Option** area of the **BLOCKS** palette. The prompt sequence when you use the X option is given next.

Specify insertion point or [Basepoint/Scale/X/Y/Z/Rotate]: **X** Enter
Specify X scale factor<1>: *Enter a value for the X scale factor.*
Specify insertion point or [Basepoint/Scale/X/Y/Z/Rotate]: *Select the insertion point.*
Specify rotation angle <0>: *Specify angle of rotation.*

Rotate

On entering **R** at the **Specify insertion point** prompt, you are asked to specify the rotation angle. You can enter the angle of rotation or specify it by specifying two points on the screen. Dragging is resumed only when you specify the angle. Also, the block assumes the specified rotation angle. The prompt sequence for this option is given next.

Specify insertion point or [Basepoint/Scale/X,Y,Z/Rotate]: **R**
Specify rotation angle<0>: *Enter a value for the rotation angle.*
Specify insertion point or [Basepoint/Scale/Rotate]: *Select the insertion point.*

Exercise 2 — *Basepoint Insertion*

Create a block with the name SQUARE at the insertion base point 1,2. Insert this block in the drawing. The X scale factor is 2 units, the Y scale factor is 2 units, and the angle of rotation is 35-degree. It is assumed that the block SQUARE is already defined in the current drawing.

Exercise 3 — *Scaled Insertion*

a. Insert the block CIRCLE created in Exercise 1. Use different X and Y scale factors to get different shapes after inserting this block.
b. Insert the block CIRCLE created in Exercise 1. Use the **Corner** option to specify the scale factor.

Exercise 4 — *Scaled Insertion*

a. Construct a triangle and form a block of it. Name the block as TRIANGLE. Now, set the Y scale factor of the inserted block as 2.
b. Insert the block TRIANGLE with a rotation angle of 45 degrees. After defining the insertion point, enter the X and Y scale factor of 2.

CREATING AND INSERTING ANNOTATIVE BLOCKS

You can create an annotative block by selecting the **Annotative** check box from the **Behavior** area of the **Block Definition** dialog box. The annotative block acquires the annotative properties like text, dimension, hatch, and so on. To convert an existing non-annotative block into an annotative one, choose the **Create Block** tool from the **Create Block** drop-down in the **Block Definition** panel of the **Insert** tab; the **Block Definition** dialog box will be displayed. Select the block to be converted to annotative from the **Name** drop-down list of the **Block Definition** dialog box. Select the **Annotative** check box from the **Behavior** area and then choose the **OK** button. AutoCAD LT will display a message box stating that the selected block is already defined as a block. If you want to redefine the block, choose the **Redefine** button; the specified block will be converted to annotative.

The annotative blocks are indicated by an annotative symbol attached to the block in the preview displayed in the **Insert** dialog box. While inserting the annotative block in the AutoCAD LT session for the first time, the **Select Annotation Scale** dialog box will be displayed on the screen, see Figure 15-7. Select the annotation scale from the drop-down list and then choose the **OK** button; the block will be inserted at the specified annotation scale. The Annotative blocks are inserted at a scale value decided by the multiplication of the current annotation scale and the block scale specified in the **Scale** area of the **Insert** dialog box.

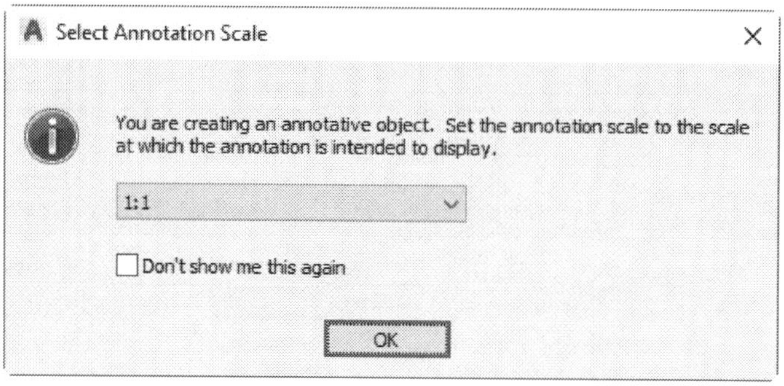

Figure 15-7 *The* ***Select Annotation Scale*** *dialog box*

Note

While inserting the annotative blocks, the settings specified for the ***INSUNITS*** *system variable are ignored. Also, the* ***Block Unit*** *area of the* ***Insert*** *dialog box will display no change in the factor value.*

Example 1 — Annotative Block

In this example, you will draw the object shown in Figure 15-8 and convert it into an annotative block, named NOR Gate. Next, you will insert the NOR Gate block into the drawing at the annotation scales of 1:1, 1:2, and 1:8 and notice the changes in the size of the annotative blocks inserted in the drawing.

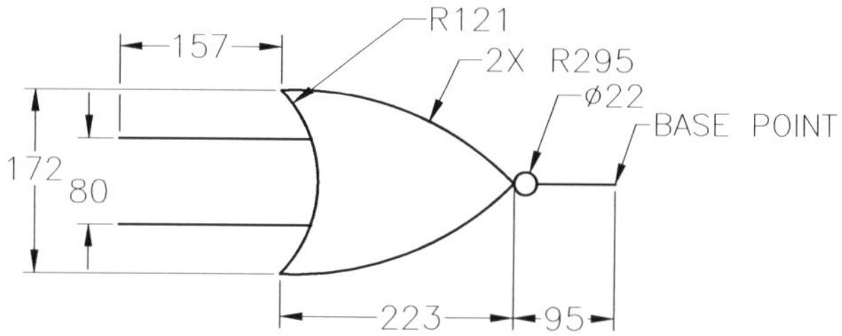

Figure 15-8 *Drawing of block for Example 1*

1. Start a new file in the **Drafting & Annotation** workspace and draw the object, refer to Figure 15-8.

2. Invoke the **Block Definition** dialog box by choosing the **Create Block** tool from the **Block Definition** panel in the **Insert** tab.

3. Enter **NOR Gate** as the name of the block in the **Name** edit box. Next, choose the **Select objects** button from the **Objects** area; the **Block Definition** dialog box will disappear. Select the object drawn and press the ENTER key; the **Block Definition** dialog box will appear. Next, select the **Delete** radio button from the **Objects** area.

4. Choose the **Pick point** button from the **Base point** area; the **Block Definition** dialog box will disappear from the screen. Specify the base point, as shown in Figure 15-8.

5. Select the **Annotative** check box from the **Behavior** area. Next, choose the **OK** button from the **Block Definition** dialog box; the selected objects disappear from the screen and an annotative block is defined with the name **NOR Gate**.

   Before proceeding further, ensure that the automatically **Add scales to annotative objects when the annotation scale changes** button is chosen in the Status Bar. Now, you need to change the annotation scale of the drawing to 1:8.

6. Click on the down-arrow on the right of the **Annotation Scale** button in the Status Bar, and choose the scale **1:8** from the flyout displayed.

7. To insert the block into the drawing at the annotation scale of 1:8, choose the **Insert Block** tool from the **Block** panel in the **Insert** tab.

8. Select the **NOR Gate** block from the **Name** drop-down list. Select the **Specify On-screen** check box from the **Insertion point** area and choose the **OK** button.

9. Specify the insertion point for the block by clicking on the screen; the block is inserted into the drawing at an annotation scale of 1:8.

10. Similarly, set the annotation scale to **1:2** in the Status Bar and insert the block. Next, set the annotation scale to **1:1** and insert the block.

11. Notice the difference in the sizes of the inserted blocks, see Figure 15-9. This automated variation in the size occurs due to annotative blocks. You will notice that the **Annotation Visibility** button on the right of the **Annotation Scale** button is on.

12. Now, set the current annotation scale to **1:8**. Choose the **Add/Delete Scales** tool from the **Annotation Scaling** panel in the **Annotate** tab. Select the block displayed at the annotation scale of 1:8 and press ENTER; the **Annotation Object Scale** dialog box is displayed. Choose the **Add** button; the **Add Scales to Object** dialog box is displayed. Press and hold the CTRL key and select the scale of 1:2 and 1:1 from the **Scale List** area.

13. Next, choose **OK**; the selected annotation scales get associated with the selected block. In this way, you can associate different annotation scales to a single annotative block.

14. Select the block to which you had added the annotation scales; the preview of the block with all annotation scales associated to the block is displayed, as shown in Figure 15-10. The bigger block with the current annotation (1:8) scale is displayed with dark dotted lines and the smaller blocks with other annotation scales (1:1, 1:2) are displayed with the faded dashed lines.

15. To move the block with the current annotation scale (1:8) to the other locations, select the blue grip displayed at the insertion point and move the block to the desired location. In this way, you can place the block with different annotation scales to any desired location.

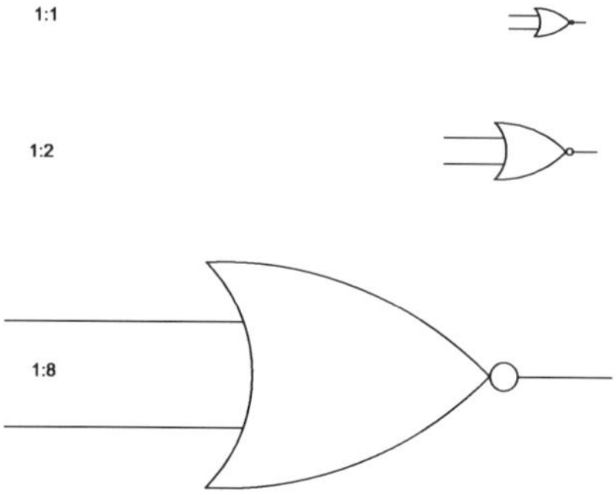

Figure 15-9 Annotative blocks inserted at different annotation scales

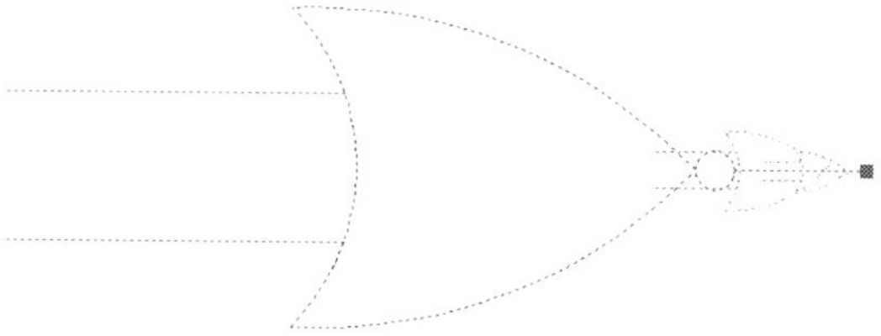

Figure 15-10 Different annotation scales associated to a single block

Block Editor

Ribbon: Insert > Block Definition > Block Editor **Command:** BEDIT/BE
Toolbar: Standard > Block Editor
Menubar: Tools > Block Editor

This application is used to edit existing blocks or create new blocks. To invoke the **Block Editor**, choose the **Block Editor** tool from the **Block Definition** panel of the **Insert** tab or enter **BE** (shortcut for the **BEDIT** command) at the Command line. You can also double-click on the existing block to edit the block. On doing so, the **Edit Block Definition** dialog box will be displayed, as shown in Figure 15-11.

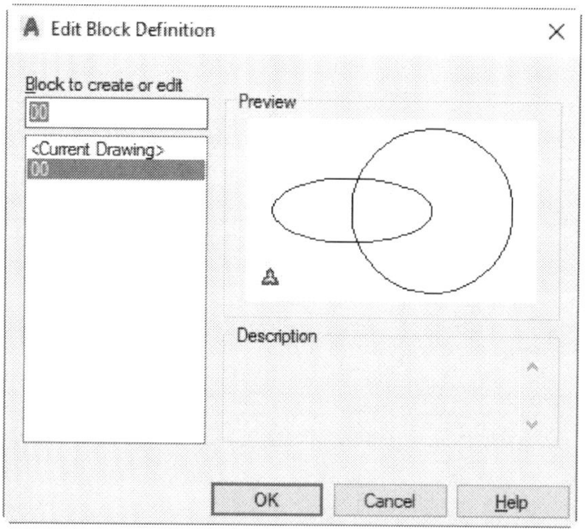

*Figure 15-11 The **Edit Block Definition** dialog box*

If you want to create a new block, enter its name in the **Block to create or edit** text box and choose **OK**; the **Block Editor** will be invoked where you can draw the entities in the new block. Similarly, if you want to edit a block, select it from the list box provided in this dialog box; its preview will be displayed in the **Preview** area. Also, its related description, if any, will be displayed in the **Description** area. Choose the **OK** button; the **Block Editor** is invoked.

The default appearance of the **Block Editor** is shown in Figure 15-12. The drawing area of the **Block Editor** has a dull background and is known as the authoring area. You can edit existing entities or add new ones to the block in the authoring area.

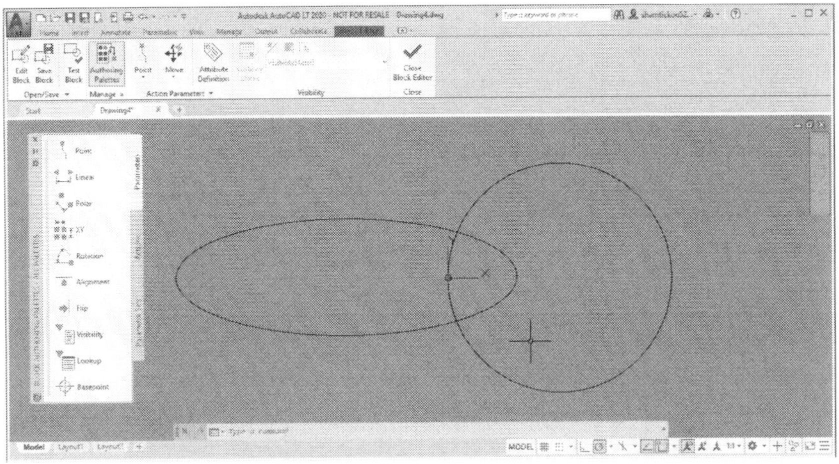

*Figure 15-12 Default appearance of the **Block Editor***

In addition to the authoring area, the **Block Editor** tab and **BLOCK AUTHORING PALETTES** are provided in the **Block Editor** that contain tools to create dynamic blocks. This will be discussed in detail later in this chapter. Now, you can edit a block using any tool, as you did in the drawing. When you are finished with the editing, choose the **Save Block** tool in the **Open/Save** panel of the **Block Editor** tab to save the changes. Choose the **Close Block Editor** button from the **Close** panel to return to the drawing again. In this way, you can edit the block at any time of your design process.

DYNAMIC BLOCKS

The concept of dynamic blocks is new in AutoCAD LT. It provides you the flexibility of modifying the geometry of the inserted blocks dynamically or using the **PROPERTIES** palette. You can create dynamic blocks by adding **Parameters** and **Actions** to existing blocks using the **Action Parameters** panel in the **Block Editor** tab (see Figure 15-13) or the **BLOCK AUTHORING PALETTES**.

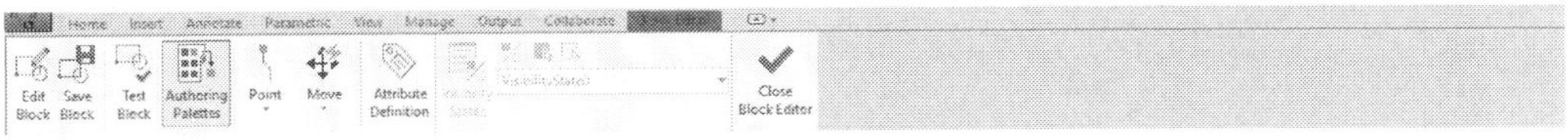

*Figure 15-13 The **Block Editor** tab*

Block Editor Tab

The **Block Editor** tab, refer to Figure 15-13, provides the tools to create and modify dynamic blocks. Additionally, you can create visibility states for dynamic blocks using the **Visibility** panel of the **Block Editor** tab. All these tools are discussed next.

Edit Block

If there are multiple blocks to be edited, choose this tool to display the **Edit Block Definition** dialog box. Note that if you have modified the current block using the tools in the **Block Editor**, you will be prompted to specify whether you want to save the changes in the current block. On saving the changes, the **Edit Block Definition** dialog box will be displayed. You can select another block to edit or enter the name of the new block that you want to create. Next, proceed to the **Block Editor** to edit the block.

Save Block

This tool is chosen to save the changes that you have made to the block in the **Block Editor**.

Save Block As

This tool is used to save a block with a different name. Expand the **Open/Save** panel and choose this tool; the **Save Block As** dialog box will be displayed, as shown in Figure 15-14. Enter the name with which you want to save the current block in the **Block Name** edit box and then choose the **OK** button; the block will be saved with the specified name and it will become the current block in the **Block Editor**.

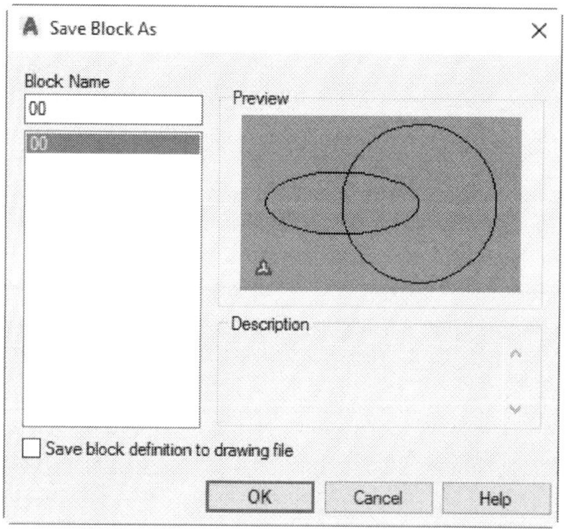

*Figure 15-14 The **Save Block As** dialog box*

Test Block

On choosing this button, the **Test Block Window** will be displayed.If you have made any changes to the block in the **Block Editor**, you can check them in this window without saving the block. After testing the block, choose the **Close Test Block** button to close the **Test Block Window**.

Authoring Palettes

The **Authoring Palettes** button is chosen from the **Manage** panel to toggle on/off the display of the **BLOCK AUTHORING PALETTES** in the authoring area. The **BLOCK AUTHORING PALETTES** contain the tools for creating dynamic blocks.

Parameters

You can set parameters for the blocks to enable them to react dynamically. To add parameters to the existing blocks, choose a tool from the **Parameter** drop-down and then choose one of the buttons from the flyout displayed, as shown in Figure 15-15. You can also enter **BPARAMETER** at the Command prompt when the **Dynamic Input** button is chosen, all parameters will be listed in the dynamic preview. These parameters are discussed later in this chapter.

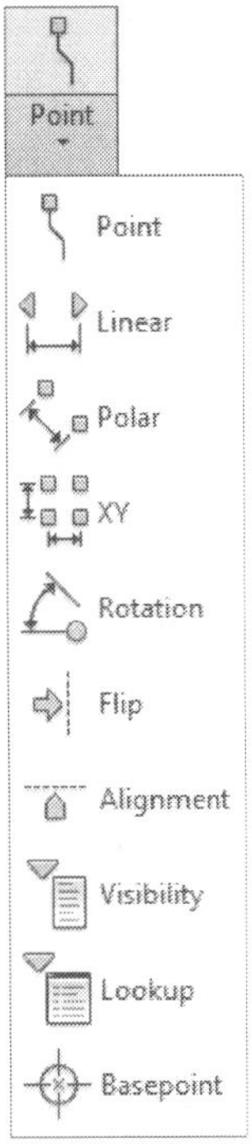

*Figure 15-15 Tools in the **Parameter** drop-down*

Actions

You can choose a tool from the **Actions** drop-down to assign actions to the parameters added to the dynamic blocks. Depending on the type of parameter selected, the possible actions are displayed in the dynamic preview. The types of actions in the **Block Editor** are discussed later in this chapter.

Attribute Definition

Choose the **Attribute Definition** tool from the **Action Parameters** panel of the **Block Editor** tab to invoke the **Attribute Definition** dialog box to assign attributes to the block. Attributes are discussed in detail in Chapter 16.

Note

*Choose the **Update Fields** tool from the **Data** panel in the **Insert** tab to regenerate the dynamic block such that the text size of the parameters and actions are updated.*

Close Block Editor

When you choose this button, the **Block Editor** tab is closed and you return to the drawing environment. If this button is chosen before saving the changes in the current block, the **Block - Changes not saved** message box will be displayed, as shown in Figure 15-16, and you will be prompted to specify whether or not you want to save changes in the current block.

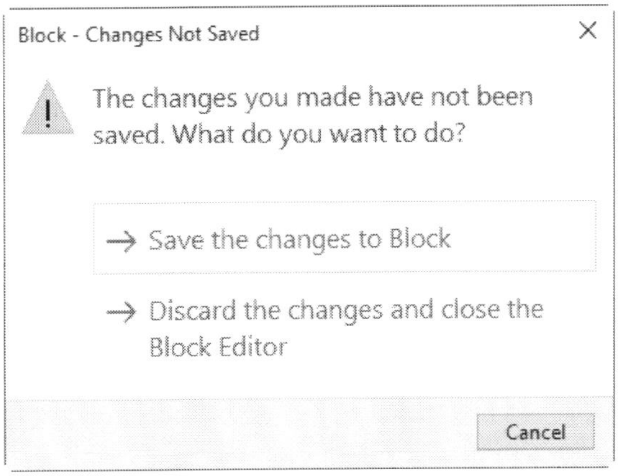

*Figure 15-16 The **Block - Save Parameter Changes?** message box*

Adding Parameters and Assigning Actions to Dynamic Blocks (BLOCK AUTHORING PALETTES)

The **BLOCK AUTHORING PALETTES**, shown in Figure 15-17, contains the tools to add parameters and actions to the dynamic blocks. You can also invoke these tools from the **Parameters** drop-down in the **Action Parameters** panel of the **Block Editor** tab, refer to Figure 15-15. On doing so, different types of parameters and actions will be displayed at the pointer input or the Command prompt. The command sequence will be the same in both the cases. The types of parameters and actions that can be added to dynamic blocks are discussed next.

Point Parameter

The **Point** parameter is used to assign the **Stretch** or **Move** action to a dynamic block. A grip point will be displayed at the location where you place the **Point** parameter. This grip point will be used as the base point when you assign an action to the **Point** parameter.

To assign a **Point** parameter, invoke the **Point** tool from the **Parameters** tab of the **BLOCK AUTHORING PALETTES**. The following prompt sequence will be displayed when you invoke this parameter from the **Parameters** tab:

Specify parameter location or [Name/Label/Chain/Description/Palette]: *Select a keypoint on the block to add the **Point** parameter.*
Specify label location: *Specify a point to place the label.*

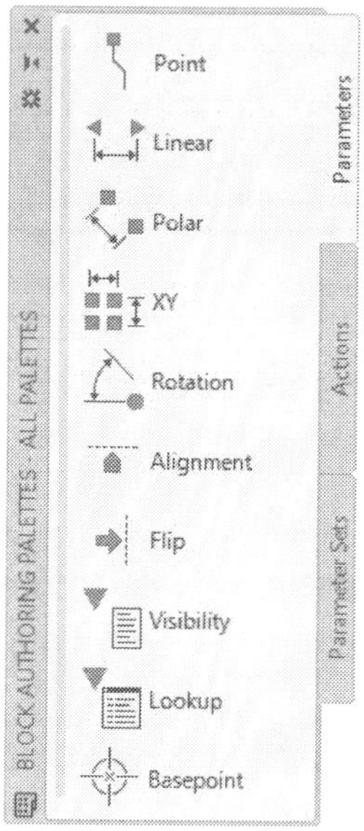

Figure 15-17** The **Parameters** tab of the **BLOCK AUTHORING PALETTES

The options available at the Command prompt are discussed next.

Name. The name of a parameter is displayed in the **PROPERTIES** palette when you select the **Point** parameter in the **Block Editor**. The default name for the point parameter is Point. However, you can change the name of the parameter using this option. The prompt sequence to modify the name of a parameter is given next.

Specify parameter location or [Name/Label/Chain/Description/Palette]: **N** Enter
Enter parameter name <Point>: *Enter new name for the parameter.*
Specify parameter location or [Name/Label/Chain/Description/Palette]: *Specify a location for the parameter.*

Tip

*You can double-click on the label to find out the actions that are assigned to that parameter. For example, if you double-click on the **Point** parameter, you can perform the move and stretch actions.*

Label. Labels of a parameter are displayed in the authoring area, as shown in Figure 15-18. The default label of a point parameter is Position. Using the **Label** option, you can modify the label of the point parameter. The prompt sequence for modifying the label is as follows:

Specify parameter location or [Name/Label/Chain/Description/Palette]: **L** Enter
Enter position property label <Position>: *Enter the new label for the **Point** parameter*
Specify parameter location or [Name/Label/Chain/Description/Palette]: *Specify a location for the parameter*

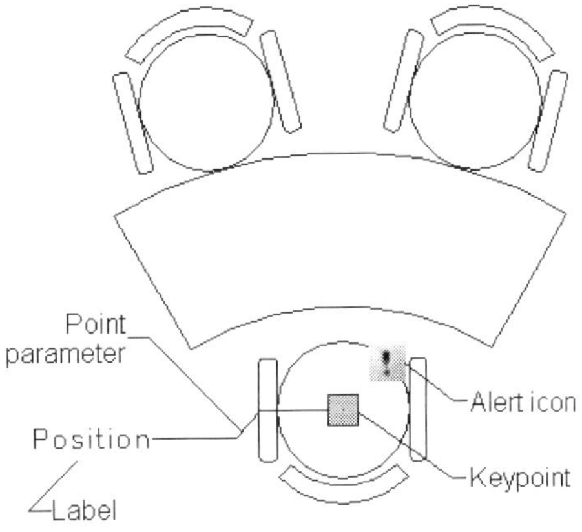

Figure 15-18** Labels of the **Point Parameter

Chain. This option is used when the current point parameter is assigned an action, which is also associated with other parameters. In this case, if the **Chain** option is set to **Yes** and the other parameters are edited, the point parameter is also edited with them. If this option is set to **No**, the point parameter is not edited, when the other parameters are edited.

Description. This option allows you to enter the description about a parameter. This description is displayed in the **PROPERTIES** palette in the **Block Editor**.

Palette. This option is used to specify whether or not the base X and base Y coordinate values of the keypoint where the parameter label is placed will be displayed in the **PROPERTIES** palette when you select the block outside the **Block Editor**.

Assigning the Move Action to the Point Parameter

To assign the move action to the **Point** parameter, double-click on the label and select the **Move** option from the dynamic preview or from the Command line. You can also choose the **Move** tool from the **Action Parameters** panel. Alternatively, you can choose the **Move** tool from the **Actions** tab of the **BLOCK AUTHORING PALETTES**. The prompt sequence that will follow when you invoke it from the **BLOCK AUTHORING PALETTES** is given next.

Select parameter: *Select the point parameter.*
Specify selection set for action
Select objects: *Select objects on which action will be applied.*
Select objects: Enter

You need to specify the distance multiplier and angle offset properties to the actions using the **PROPERTIES** palette. The **Move** action will not work until these options are set.

Distance Multiplier. This option is used during the dynamic modification of the blocks, using grips of the parameters. Using this option, you can specify the distance by which the selected entities of the dynamic block will move with respect to the one unit movement of the cursor, while dragging the cursor using the grips. To set the distance multiplier, select the action parameter and invoke the **PARAMETERS** palette. Now, enter the required multiplier value in the **Distance multiplier** field in the **Overrides** rollout of the **PROPERTIES** palette. By default, the value of the distance multiplier factor is 1. As a result, the entities will move by the same distance as moved by the cursor. If you set this value to 0.5, the entities will move half the distance moved by the cursor, refer to Figure 15-19.

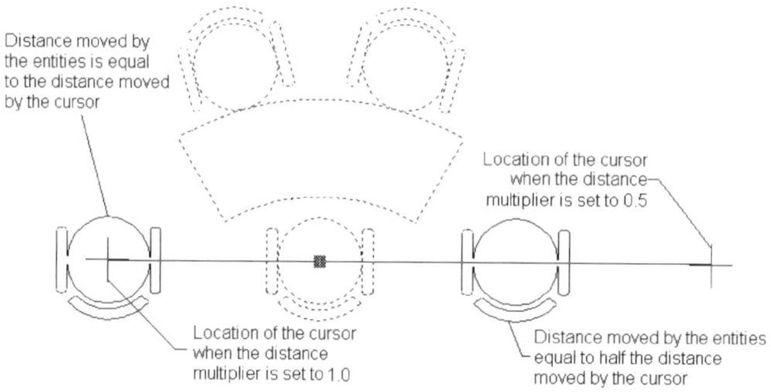

***Figure 15-19** Results of different values of the distance multiplier*

Note

*You can test the action parameters by invoking the **Test Block Window** and moving the block.*

Angle Offset. This option is used to specify the angular offset for the selected entities of the dynamic block. The angle offset works when the entities are dragged using the parameter grip. To set the angle offset, select the action parameter and invoke the **PARAMETERS** palette. Now, enter the required value in the **Angle offset** field in the **Overrides** rollout of the **PROPERTIES** palette. By setting this value, you can ensure that the entities move at an angle from the trace line. For example, if you set the value of the angle offset to 30, the entities will be moved at an angle of 30 degrees with respect to the trace line, which is displayed while dragging the entities using the parameter grips. Figure 15-20 shows the manipulation of entities in the drawing with the default angle offset of 0 degree and an angle offset of 30 degrees.

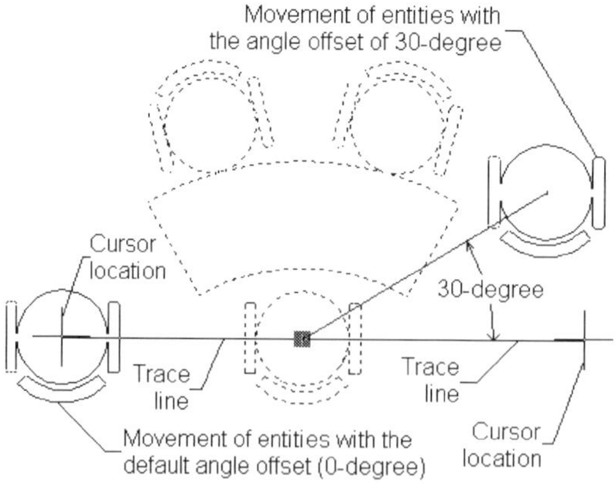

***Figure 15-20** Result of the angle offset during the dynamic manipulation*

Assigning the Stretch Action to the Point Parameter

You can invoke the **Stretch** action by double-clicking on the parameter or by choosing it from the **BLOCK AUTHORING PALETTES**. On invoking this action and selecting the parameter, you are prompted to specify the stretch frame. The entities lying inside the stretch frame will be moved during the dynamic manipulation. The entities that are crossed by the stretch frame will be stretched. The following prompt sequence will be displayed on invoking this action:

Select parameter: *Select the parameter to associate the action.*
Specify first corner of stretch frame or [CPolygon]: *Specify the first corner of stretch frame or enter CP to define a crossing polygon for specifying the stretch frame.*
Specify opposite corner: *Specify opposite corner of stretch frame.*
Specify objects to stretch
Select objects: *Select objects for stretching.*
Select objects: Enter

Figure 15-21(a) shows the stretch frame and the entities selected for the stretch action and Figure 15-21(b) shows the preview of the entities during dynamic manipulation.

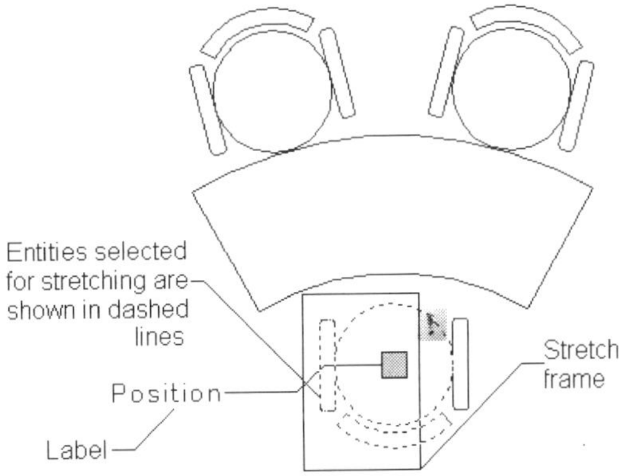

Figure 15-21(a) *Selecting entities for the **Stretch** action*

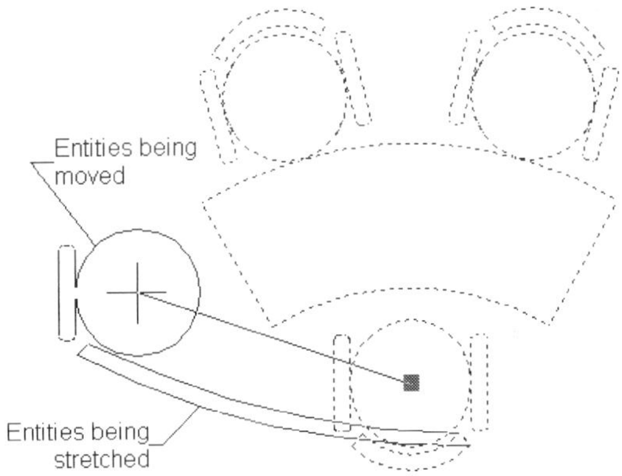

Figure 15-21(b) *Dynamically stretching the entities of a block*

Linear Parameter

The linear parameter is displayed as the distance between two keypoints and is similar to a linear or an aligned dimension. This parameter can be associated with the Array, Move, Stretch, or Scale actions. Figure 15-22 shows a block with a linear parameter added to it. To add this parameter, choose the **Linear** tool from the **BLOCK AUTHORING PALETTES**; the following prompt sequence will be displayed:

Specify start point or [Name/Label/Chain/Description/Base/Palette/Value set]: *Specify start point for the parameter.*

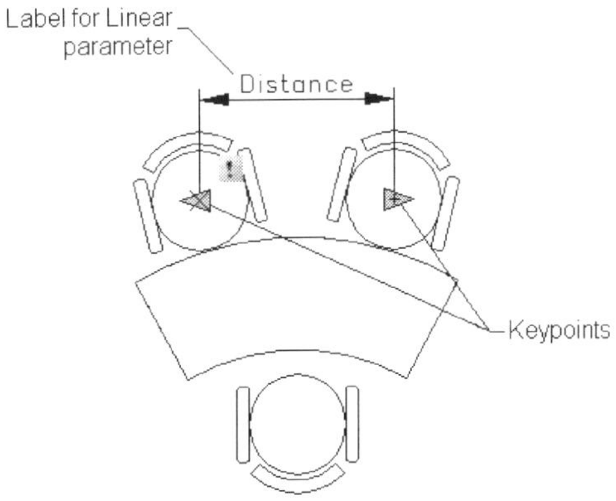

Figure 15-22 *The **Linear** parameter added to a block*

Specify endpoint: *Specify endpoint for the parameter.*
Specify label location: *Specify a point where the label will be placed.*

You can specify the base of the parameter and the distance within which the entities are to be moved at the Command prompt when you are prompted to specify the start point. Some of the options that will be available when you invoke the **Linear Parameter** tool have already been discussed in the **Point** parameter. The remaining options are discussed next.

Base. This option lets you to specify the base of the parameter. This base point will be stationary while editing the endpoint of the block. You can specify the option of keeping the start point or the midpoint stationary while using the **Base** option.

Value set. This option allows you specify a set of values for parameters such that the manipulation will be in accordance with these specified values. The values for the parameter can be specified by providing a list or by specifying the increment and range. If there is a specified value set for a parameter, small vertical grey lines are displayed at those values in the **Block Editor**. These vertical grey lines are also displayed in the drawing when you select the parameter grip to manipulate the block.

Note
*You can also set the **Base** and **Value Set** options in the **Misc** and **Value set** rollouts of the **PROPERTIES** palette of a **Linear Parameter**, respectively.*

After adding the **Linear** parameter, you can perform the array, move, scale, and stretch actions. Assign the **Move** or **Stretch** action as discussed earlier.

Assigning the Scale Action to the Linear Parameter

Invoke the **Scale** action tool from the **Actions** tab of **BLOCK AUTHORING PALETTES**, or double-click on the linear parameter and select the **Scale** option. The prompt sequence that follows when you assign the **Scale** action is as follows:

Select parameter: *Select the linear parameter to associate the action.*
Specify selection set for action
Select objects: *Select the objects for scaling.*
Select objects: Enter

You can scale the blocks by using a property called **Base type**. To specify the **Base type** property, display the **PROPERTIES** palette for the **Scale** action. Next, specify the base type in the **Overrides** rollout. There are two types of base type, dependent and independent. The base type can be dependent on the original base point of the parameter to which the scale action is assigned. You can also make the base type independent so that the entities can be scaled based on the specified base point and the second point.

To test the action, choose the **Test Block** tool from the **Open/Save** panel and then select the block; the **Linear** parameter grips will be displayed. Click on a grip to select it; the **Specify point location or [Base Point/Undo/Exit]** prompt will be displayed. Specify the new base point, if needed. Moving the cursor in the second or third quadrant scales the entities by a factor more than 1, as shown in Figure 15-23. If you move the cursor in the first or fourth quadrant, the entities will be scaled by a factor less than 1.

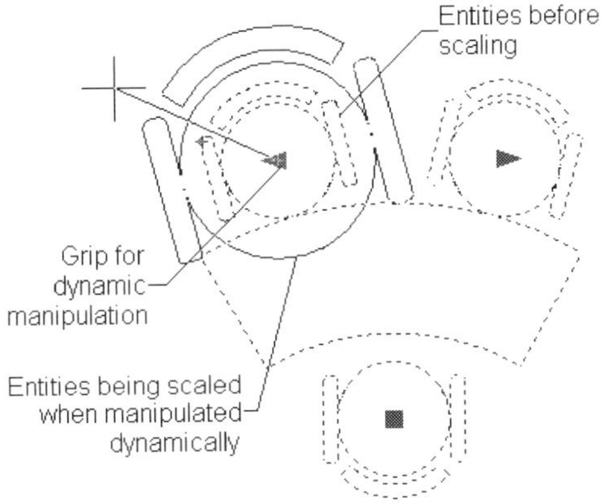

Figure 15-23 *Entities being scaled by using dynamic manipulation*

Assigning the Array Action to the Linear Parameter

By adding array action to the entities in the block,you can create the array dynamically by using grips. Invoke the **Array** action tool from **BLOCK AUTHORING PALETTES** or double-click on the linear parameter and select the **Array** option; you will be prompted to select the objects to create the array. Next, select the object; you will be prompted to enter the distance between the columns. The number of instances in the array will depend on the distance by which you move the cursor after selecting the parameter grip. Figure 15-24 shows the preview of an array being created dynamically using the **Array** action.

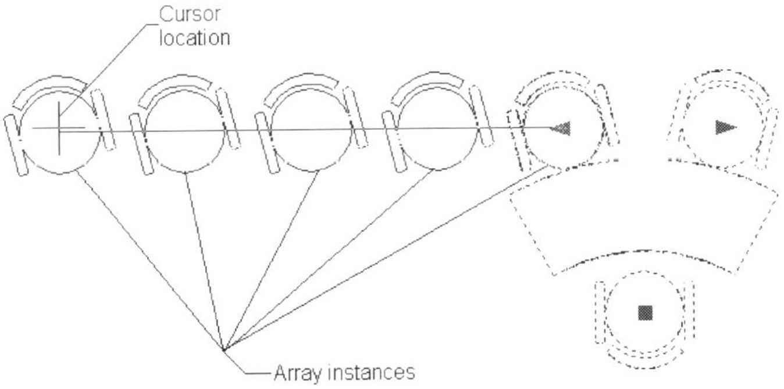

Figure 15-24 *Creating an array dynamically using the **Array** action*

Polar Parameter

The **Polar** parameter is defined by the distance between the two keypoints and an angle. The **Move**, **Scale**, **Stretch**, **Polar Stretch**, or **Array** actions can be associated with the **Polar** parameter. To add a polar parameter, choose **Point > Polar** from the **Action Parameters** panel of the **Block Editor**. The following prompt sequence will be displayed:

Specify base point or [Name/Label/Chain/Description/Palette/Value set]: *Specify start point for the parameter.*
Specify endpoint: *Specify endpoint for the parameter.*
Specify label location: *Specify a point where Label will be placed.*

Note that the working of the **Value set** option is different in case of the **Polar** parameter. You can invoke the **PROPERTIES** palette for the **Polar** parameter and change the value sets in the **Value Set** parameters, or specify them when you are prompted to specify the base point. The prompt sequence for this option is given next.

Specify base point or [Name/Label/Chain/Description/Palette/Value set]: **V** Enter
Enter distance value set type [None/List/Increment] <None>: **L** Enter
Enter list of distance values (separated by commas): *Specify list of values for the* ***Distance*** Enter
Enter angle value set type [None/List/Increment] <None>: **L** Enter
Enter list of angle values (separated by commas): *Specify list of values for the* ***Angle*** *parameter.*
Specify base point or [Name/Label/Chain/Description/Palette/Value set]:

Similarly, you can use the **Increment** option to specify the increment and range for the distance and angle parameters.

Assigning the Polar Stretch Action to the Polar Parameter

By specifying the polar stretch action, you can stretch the entities and at the same time rotate them. As you move the cursor, the entities specified for rotation will rotate by the same angle that has been moved by the cursor. Remember that the polar stretch action can only be applied to the polar parameter. To add this action, choose the **Polar Stretch** action from the **BLOCK AUTHORING PALETTES** or double-click on the parameter and select the polar stretch option. The following is the prompt sequence:

Select parameter: *Select the parameter to associate the action.*
Specify parameter point to associate with action or enter [sTart point/Second point] <Second>: *Specify the point that will be associated with the action.*
Specify first corner of stretch frame or [CPolygon]: *Specify the first corner of stretch frame.*
Specify opposite corner: *Specify opposite corner of stretch frame.*
Specify objects to stretch
Select objects: *Select the object to stretch, refer to Figure 15-25.*
Select objects: Enter
Specify objects to rotate only
Select objects: *Select the object that needs to be rotated only, refer to Figure 15-25.*
Select objects: Enter

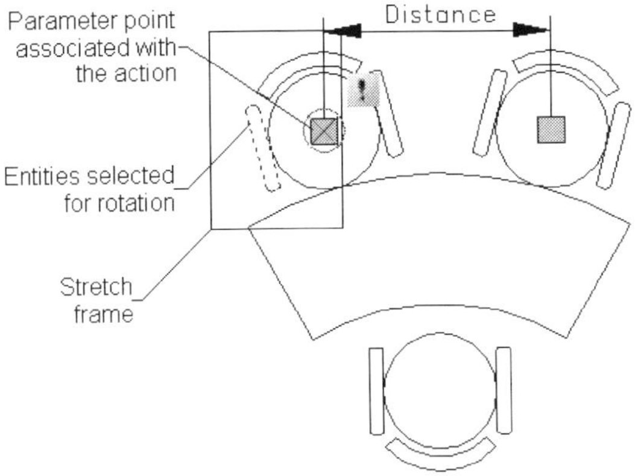

Figure 15-25 Selecting the entities to assign the polar stretch action

Set the **Distance multiplier** and **Angle offset** in the **PROPERTIES** palette, as discussed earlier. Next, invoke the **Test Block Window** and select the block; the polar parameter grips will be displayed.

Click on the grip to select it; you will be prompted to specify the point location. Specify the new point; some of the entities will stretch, whereas the others will rotate, as shown in Figure 15-26. Exit the **Test Block Window** by choosing the **Close Test Block Window** button.

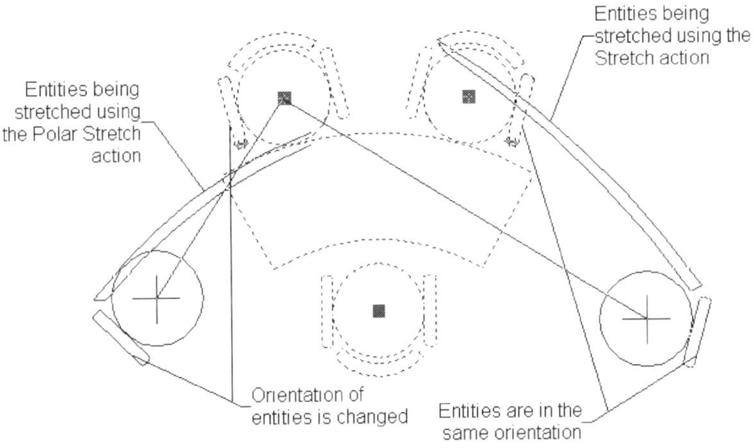

Figure 15-26 Difference between the stretch action and the polar stretch action

> **Tip**
> *While assigning different actions and parameters to the block entities in the* ***Block Editor****, there is no need to exit the block editor and check the actions. Choose the* ***Test Block*** *tool in the* ***Open/Save*** *panel in the* ***Block Editor****; a new test window will be displayed. In this window, you can check the changes applied to the block. To exit this window, choose the* ***Close Test Block Window*** *button from the* ***Close*** *panel.*

XY Parameter

The XY parameter is used to define the X and Y distances between a specified base point and an endpoint in the dynamic block. You can assign the array, move, scale, and stretch actions to the XY parameter. To add this parameter, choose the **XY** parameters tool from the **BLOCK AUTHORING PALETTES**. The prompt sequence that will be displayed is given next.

Specify base point or [Name/Label/Chain/Description/Palette/Value set]: *Specify the base point from where the X and Y distance will be measured.*
Specify endpoint: *Specify endpoint up to which the distances will be measured.*

Figure 15-27 shows the XY parameter. Double-click on the parameter to display the dynamic preview. The dynamic preview lists the actions that can be assigned to this parameter.

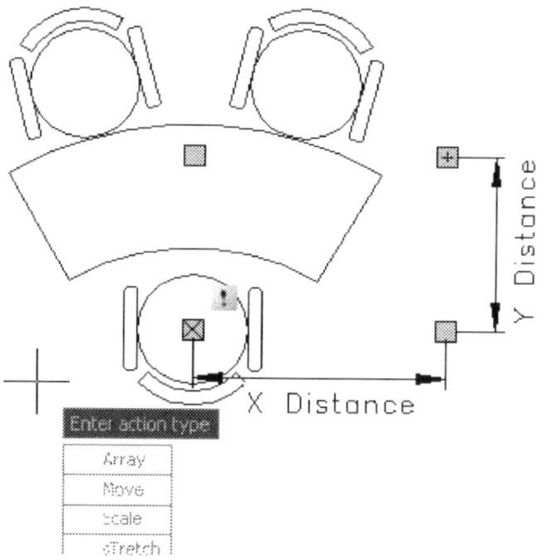

***Figure 15-27** XY parameter assigned to a point and the actions that can be assigned to this parameter*

Rotation Parameter

The rotation parameter is used to define an angular variation for the selected entities of the dynamic block. You can assign the rotate action to this parameter, which ensures that the selected entities of the dynamic block can be rotated around a predefined base point. To add this parameter, choose the **Rotation** parameter from the **BLOCK AUTHORING PALETTES**. The prompt sequence that will be displayed is as follows:

Specify base point or [Name/Label/Chain/Description/Palette/Value set]: *Specify base point around which the selected entities of the dynamic block will be rotated.*
Specify radius of parameter: *Specify the radius, which defines the imaginary circle along the circumference of which the entities will be rotated.*
Specify default rotation angle or [Base angle] <0>: *Specify default rotation angle at which the grip point will be placed for rotating the entities dynamically.*
Specify label location: *Specify a point where the label will be placed.*

When you specify the radius of the parameter, you will be prompted to specify the default rotation angle or base angle. The base angle defines the datum for measuring the rotation angle. By default, this value is 0-degree, which means that the angles will be measured from the positive X-axis. You can also modify the base angle to any other value, such that the angles are measured from the new base angle. For example, if you modify the base angle value to 30-degree, the default rotation angle will be measured from an axis defined at 30-degree from the X-axis, as shown in Figure 15-28.

Assigning the Rotate Action to the Rotation Parameter

The **Rotate** action can only be assigned to the **Rotation** parameter. This action allows you to rotate the selected components of the dynamic block using grips, as shown in Figure 15-29. To add the **Rotate** action, double-click on the **Rotation** parameter. The following prompt sequence will be displayed:

Specify selection set for action
Select objects: *Select the entities to be rotated.*
Select objects: Enter

Next, invoke the **Test Block Window** and select the block; the **Rotation** parameter grips will be displayed on the block. Click on a grip to select it; you will be prompted to specify the rotation angle. Specify the angle; the entities will rotate as specified. Exit the **Test Block Window** by choosing the **Close Test Block Window** button.

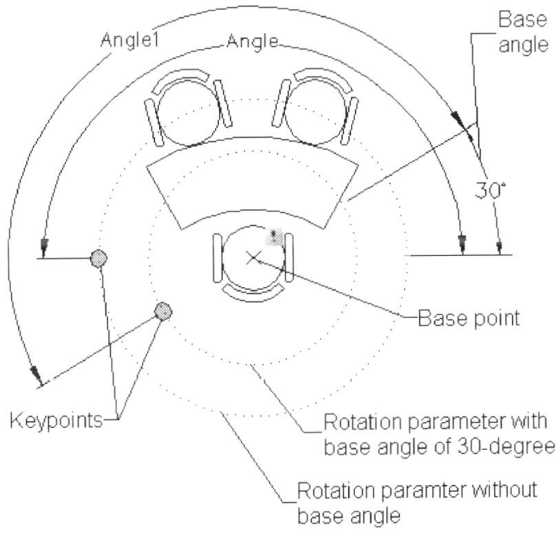

*Figure 15-28 The **Rotation** parameters with and without the base angle*

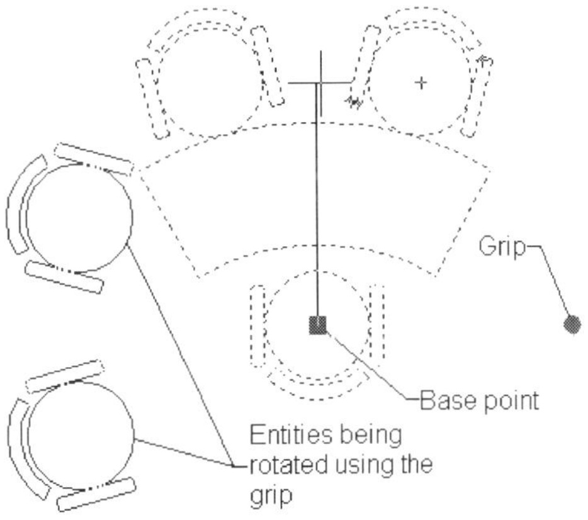

*Figure 15-29 The **Dynamic** manipulation of entities after adding the **Rotate** action*

Alignment Parameter

The **Alignment** parameter is used to align the entire dynamic block with the other entities in the drawing. The alignment is defined using the base point at which the dynamic block grip is created. The block is rotated and moved while aligning. Remember that because the entire block is aligned using this parameter, you do not need to assign any action to this parameter. When you invoke this parameter, the following prompt sequence is displayed:

Specify base point of alignment or [Name]: *Specify the base point to align the dynamic block.*
Alignment type = Perpendicular
Specify alignment direction or alignment type [Type] <Type>: *Specify the alignment direction by defining another point in the drawing window.*

Remember that the dynamic block will be aligned at the angle that is defined while defining the alignment direction in the **Specify alignment direction or alignment type [Type] <Type>** prompt.

Type. Enter **T** at the **Specify alignment direction or alignment type [Type] <Type>** prompt to specify the type of alignment. The types of alignment are discussed next.

Perpendicular. This alignment type ensures that the dynamic block is aligned perpendicular to the entities in the drawing.

Tangent. This alignment type ensures that the dynamic block is aligned tangent to the entities in the drawing.

After adding the alignment parameter, invoke the **Test Block Window** and select the block; the dynamic block grip is displayed at the base point of the alignment parameter. Select the grip and then move the dynamic block close to an existing entity in the drawing. The dynamic block aligns itself to the entity and the alignment angle depends on the alignment direction that you defined. Exit the **Test Block Window** by choosing the **Close Test Block Window** button.

Flip Parameter

The **Flip** parameter is used to add a flip action to the dynamic block. The flip action reverses the orientation of the dynamic block. Thus in simple terms, the flip parameter is used to create a mirrored image of the dynamic block and remove the original block. The mirror line is defined by the reflection line, which you specify while defining the flip parameter, see Figure 15-30. Remember that depending on the location of the reflection axis, the location of the flipped entities also changes. When you add the flip action, an arrow is displayed at the base point. You can click on this arrow to flip the orientation of the selected entities of the dynamic block. The following prompt sequence will be displayed when you invoke the **Flip** parameter tool from the **BLOCK AUTHORING PALETTES**:

Specify base point of reflection line or [Name/Label/Description/Palette]: *Specify the base point from where the reflection line will start.*
Specify endpoint of reflection line: *Specify the endpoint of the reflection line, thus defining its orientation.*
Specify label location: *Specify location for label of the parameter.*

Assigning the Flip Action to the Flip Parameter

As mentioned earlier, you can assign the **Flip** action to the **Flip** parameter so as to reverse the orientation of the selected entities of the block. To assign the **Flip** action, double-click on the **Flip** parameter; you will be prompted to select the objects to be flipped. Select the objects and press ENTER; the flip action will be applied. Figure 15-31 shows the orientation and location of the selected entities before and after flipping.

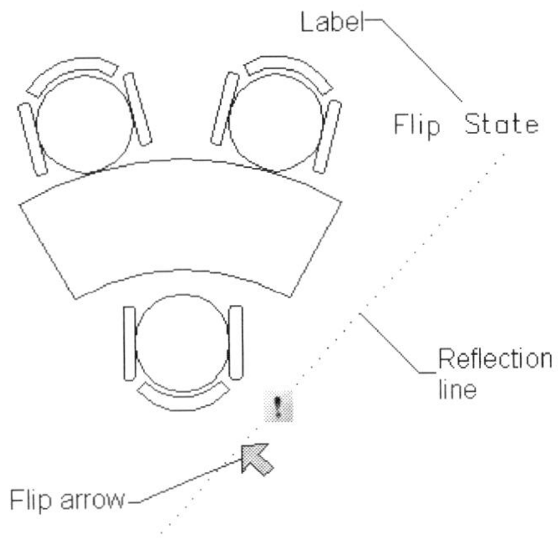

*Figure 15-30 Defining the **Flip** parameter*

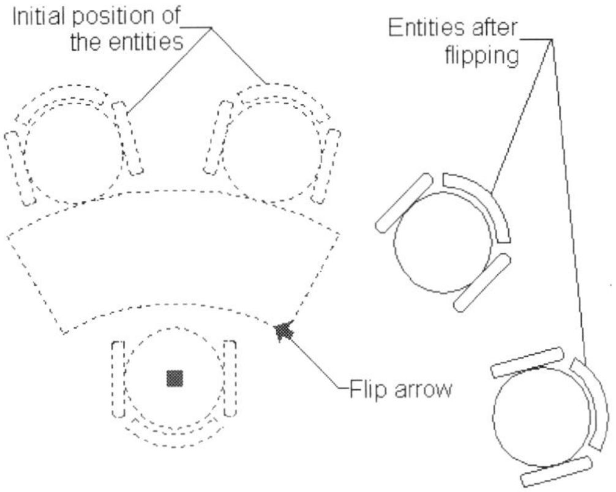

Figure 15-31 Dynamically flipping the entities of the dynamic block

Visibility Parameter

The visibility parameter is used to create visibility states of a dynamic block. Using the visibility states, you can control the display of entities in the dynamic block and specify whether they would be visible or hidden. When you invoke this tool, you will be prompted to specify the location of the parameter. As soon as the visibility parameter is added, the following options will be available in the **Visibility** panel of the **Block Editor**.

Visibility Mode. This button toggles the value of the **Visibility Mode** in between 0 and 1. The default value of this mode is set to 0 and therefore, the entities that have been made invisible will not be shown in the authoring area. If the value of this mode is set to 1, the entities that you make invisible will also be displayed in gray color in the authoring area.

Make Invisible. This tool is used to make some of the entities invisible in the current visibility state. When you choose this tool, you are prompted to select the entities to be hidden.

Make Visible. This tool is chosen to make the entities visible that were made invisible in the current visibility state using the **Make Invisible** tool. When you choose this tool, all the entities that were hidden are displayed in the authoring area, even if the **Visibility Mode** is set to 0. Select the entities that you want to make visible; the selected entities will be made visible after you exit the **Make Visible** tool.

Visibility States. This tool is used to create an additional visibility state. On choosing this tool, the **Visibility States** dialog box will be displayed, as shown in Figure 15-32. By default, **VisibilityState0** is available and listed in the **Visibility states** area. To create a new visibility state, choose the **New** button; the **New Visibility State** dialog box will be displayed, as shown in Figure 15-33. The options in this dialog box are discussed next.

Visibility state name. Specify the name of the new visibility state in this edit box.

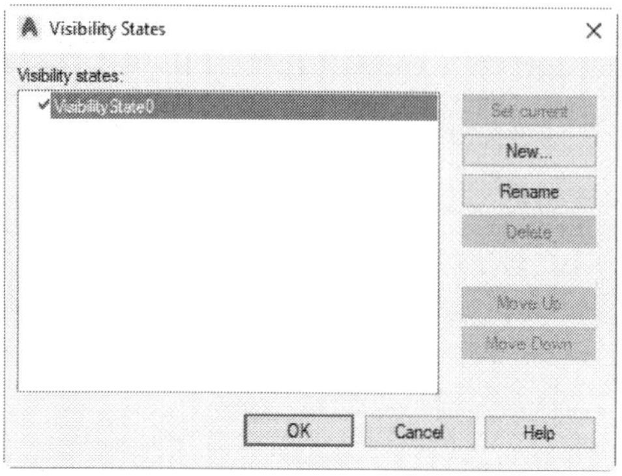

Figure 15-32 The ***Visibility States*** *dialog box*

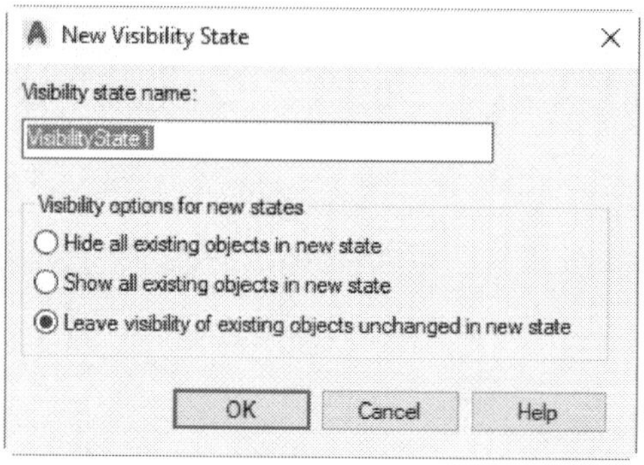

Figure 15-33 The ***New Visibility State*** *dialog box*

Visibility options for new states. The options in this area are used to control the visibility of the new visibility state. By default, the **Leave visibility of existing objects unchanged in new state** radio button is selected, implying that the visibility of entities in the new state will be similar to the visibility of the objects in the current state. If you select the **Hide all existing objects in new state** radio button, all entities will be hidden in the new visibility state. If you select the **Show all existing objects in new state** radio button, all objects will be visible in the new visibility state.

The current visibility state is displayed in the drop-down list in the **Visibility** panel of the **Block Editor** tab. To make any other visibility state as the current visibility state, select it in the drop-down list. To rename an existing visibility state, select its name from the **Visibility states** list box available in the **Visibility states** dialog box and choose the **Rename** button.

After defining the visibility states, exit the **Block Editor**. Now, you can hide or show the entities as per the requirements of the drawing. When you select the dynamic block for which the visibility state has been defined, the lookup grip will be displayed, which resembles an arrow head. If you click on the lookup grip, a shortcut menu will be displayed, listing all available visibility states. In the list, the current visibility state is displayed with a check mark on its left. In Figure 15-34, **Visibility State0** is the current visibility state. Figure 15-35 shows the drawing in which the **Visibility State2** has been made as the current visibility state and therefore, the table is hidden in it.

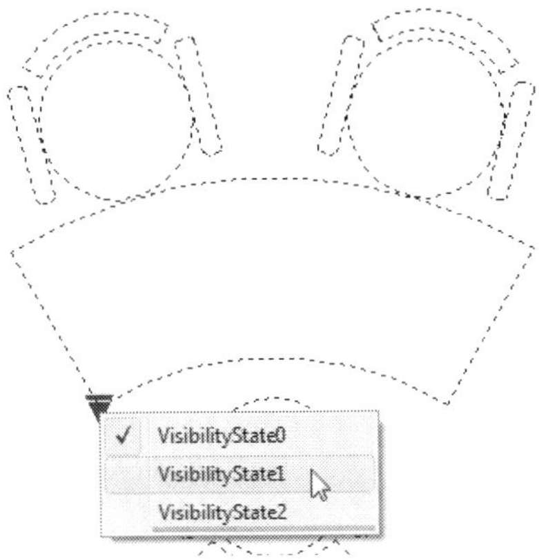

Figure 15-34 Shortcut menu displayed on clicking the lookup grip

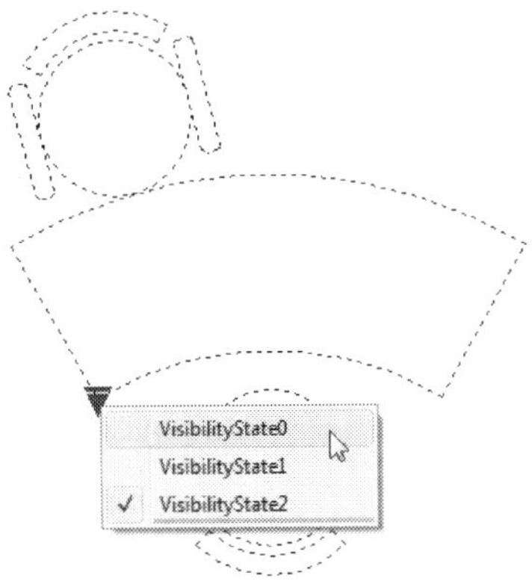

Figure 15-35 Changing the visibility state using the shortcut menu

Lookup Parameter

The **Lookup** parameter is added to assign a lookup action to the dynamic block. Using the lookup action, you can control the values of the parameters assigned to the dynamic block. To add this parameter, choose **Lookup** tool from the **BLOCK AUTHORING PALETTES** and specify the location of the parameter.

Assigning the Lookup Action to the Lookup Parameter

To assign the lookup action to the lookup parameter, double-click on it; you will be prompted to specify the action location. On specifying it, the **Property Lookup Table** dialog box will be displayed, as shown in Figure 15-36.

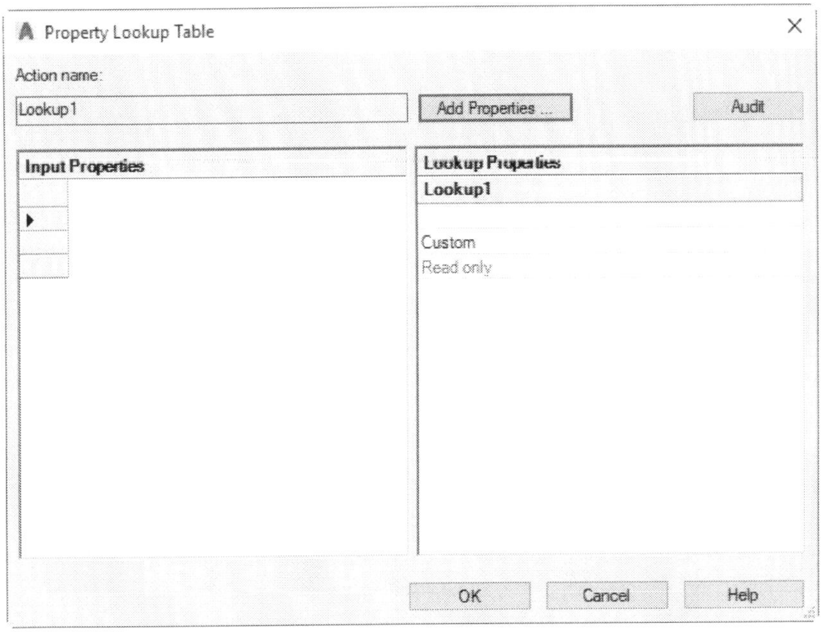

*Figure 15-36 The **Property Lookup Table** dialog box*

To add a lookup property, choose the **Add Properties** tool; the **Add Parameter Properties** dialog box will be displayed, as shown in Figure 15-37. This dialog box displays the parameters assigned to the current dynamic block. Select single or multiple properties and choose **OK**; all properties will be added as rows in the **Input Properties** area of the **Properties Lookup Table** dialog box. Save the changes and close the **Block Editor**. Next, select the block; the lookup grips will be displayed. Select a lookup grip; a shortcut menu listing all property values will be displayed. Select the required values and perform the action.

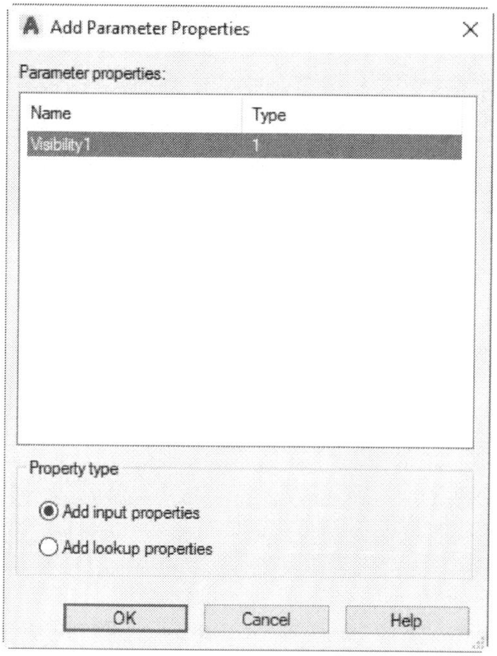

Figure 15-37 The ***Add Parameter Properties*** *dialog box*

Base Point Parameter

The **Base Point** parameter is used to create a base point for the block, which will be used as the insertion base point while inserting this block. Note that the blocks that are inserted are also modified, depending on the new base point that you specify using this parameter. To add this parameter, choose the **Base Point** tool from the **BLOCK AUTHORING PALETTES** and select the point that you want to use as the base point.

ADDING PARAMETER AND ACTION SIMULTANEOUSLY USING PARAMETER SETS

In the previous section, you learned how to add a parameter and then assign an action to it. AutoCAD LT also allows you to add parameters and actions simultaneously using the **Parameters Sets** tab of the **BLOCK AUTHORING PALETTES**, see Figure 15-38. Various parameter-action combinations that can be defined for a dynamic block are available in this tab as individual sets. However, note that the entities that will be affected by the specified action are not automatically defined using the parameter sets. You need to double-click on the action to select the objects. For example, instead of first applying the **Point** parameter and then adding the move action to it, you can directly apply the **Point Move** set. After you specify the parameter and the action, double-click on **Move** in the authoring area and select the entities of the dynamic block that will be moved using this action.

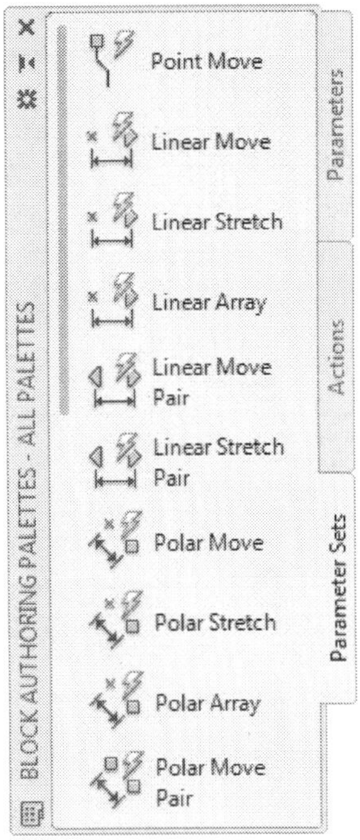

Figure 15-38** The **Parameter Sets** tab of the **BLOCK AUTHORING PALETTES

> **Tip**
> *To delete any action applied to a parameter, right-click on the action bar displayed on the parameter. Next, choose the **Delete** option from the shortcut menu displayed. You can also create a new selection set or modify the existing selection set by choosing the **Action Selection Set** option. To rename an action, choose the **Rename Action** option from the shortcut menu.*

INSERTING BLOCKS USING THE DESIGNCENTER

You can use the **DESIGNCENTER** to locate, preview, copy, or insert blocks or existing drawings into the current drawing. To insert a block, choose the **DESIGNCENTER** button from the **Palettes** panel in the **View** tab to display the **DESIGNCENTER** window. By default, the tree pane is displayed. Choose the **Tree View Toggle** button to display the tree pane on the left side, if it is not already displayed. Expand **Computer** to display *C:\Program Files\Autodesk\AutoCAD LT 2020\Sample\en-us\DesignCenter* folder by clicking on the plus (+) signs on the left of the respective folders. Click on the plus sign adjacent to the folder to display its contents. Select a drawing file you wish to use to insert blocks from and then click on the plus sign adjacent to the drawing again. All the icons depicting the components such as blocks, dimension styles, layers, linetypes, text styles, and so on, in the selected drawing are displayed. Select **Blocks** by clicking on it in the **tree pane**; the blocks in the drawing are displayed in the palette. Select the block you wish to insert and drag and drop it into the current drawing. Later, you can move it in the drawing to the desired location. You can also right-click on the block name to display the shortcut menu, as shown in Figure 15-39.

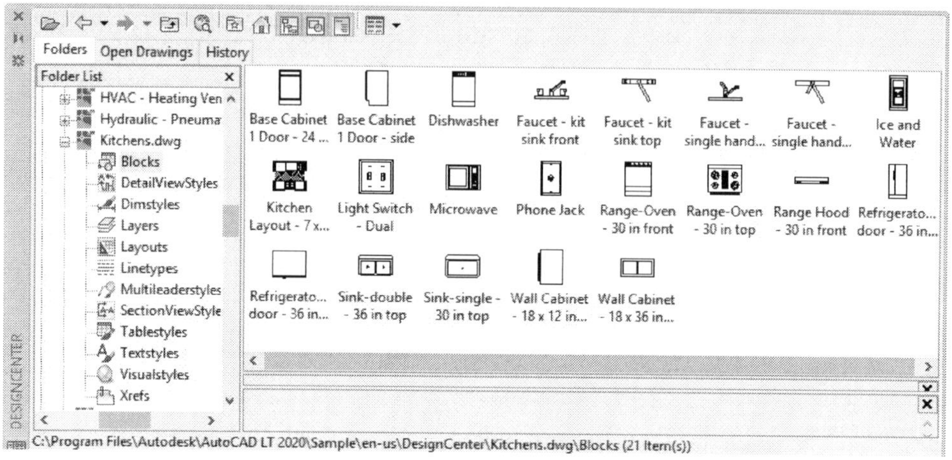

Figure 15-39 *Using the **DESIGNCENTER** to insert blocks*

Choose **Insert Block** from the shortcut menu; the **Insert** dialog box is displayed. Here, you can specify the insertion point, scale, and rotation angle in the respective edit boxes. On selecting the **Specify On-screen** check box in the **Insert** dialog box, you will be allowed to specify these parameters on the screen. The selected block is inserted into the current drawing. You can also choose **Copy** from the shortcut menu; the selected block will be copied to the clipboard. Now, you can right-click in the drawing area to display a shortcut menu and choose **Paste**; the preview of the selected block will be attached to the cursor and as you move the cursor, the block also moves with it. You can now select a point to paste the block. The advantage of this option over drag and drop is that you can select an insertion point at the time of pasting. In the case of a drag and drop operation, you need to move the inserted block to a specific point after it has been dropped on the screen.

USING TOOL PALETTES TO INSERT BLOCKS

You can use the **TOOL PALETTES** (see Figure 15-40) to insert predefined blocks in the current drawing. The **TOOL PALETTES** has many tabs. You can view the complete list of tabs by clicking on stacks of the tabs available at the end of the list of tabs. In this chapter, you will learn how to insert blocks using the options in the **TOOL PALETTES**.

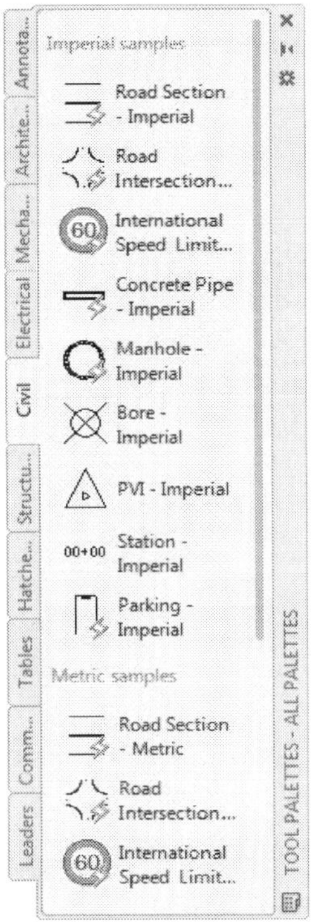

Figure 15-40 The TOOL PALETTES

Inserting Blocks in the Drawing

AutoCAD LT provides two methods to insert blocks from the **TOOL PALETTES**, Drag and Drop method and Select and Place method. Both these methods of inserting blocks using the **TOOL PALETTES** are discussed next.

Drag and Drop Method

To insert blocks from the **TOOL PALETTES** in the drawing using this method, move the cursor over the desired predefined block in the **TOOL PALETTES**. You will notice that as you move the cursor over the block, the block icon gets converted into an icon. Also, a tooltip is displayed that shows the name and description of the block. Press and hold the left mouse button and drag the cursor to the drawing area. Release the left mouse button, and you will notice that the selected block is inserted in the drawing. You may need to modify thedrawing display area to view the block. Remember that when a block is inserted from the **TOOL PALETTES** using the drag and drop method, you are not prompted to specify its rotation angle or scale. The blocks are automatically inserted with their default scale factor and rotation angle.

Select and Place Method

You can also insert the desired block in the drawings using the select and place method. To insert the block using this method, move the cursor over the desired block in the **TOOL PALETTES**; the block icon is changed to an icon. Press the left mouse button; the selected block is attached to the cursor and the **Specify insertion point or [Basepoint/Scale/X/Y/Z/Rotate]** prompt is displayed. Modify any parameter using the prompt sequence and then move the cursor to the required location in the drawing area. Click on the left mouse button; the selected block is inserted at the specified location.

Modifying Properties of the Blocks in the Tool Palettes

To modify the properties of a block, move the cursor over it in the **TOOL PALETTES** and right-click to display the shortcut menu. Using the options in this shortcut menu, you can cut or copy the desired block available in one tab of **TOOL PALETTES** and paste it on the other tab. You can also delete and rename the selected block using the **Delete** and **Rename** options, respectively. To modify the properties of the block, choose **Properties** from the shortcut menu; the **Tool Properties** dialog box is displayed, as shown in Figure 15-41.

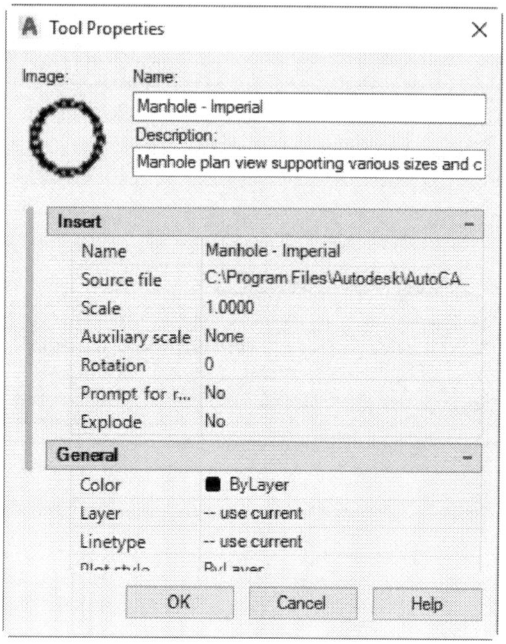

***Figure 15-41** The **Tool Properties** dialog box*

In the **Tool Properties** dialog box, the name of the selected block is displayed in the **Name** edit box. You can rename the block by entering a new name in the **Name** edit box. The **Image** area on the left of the **Name** edit box displays the image of the selected block. If you enter a description of the block in the **Description** text box, it is stored with the block definition in the **TOOL PALETTES**. Now, when you move the cursor over the block in **TOOL PALETTES** and pause for a second, the description along with its name appears in the tooltip. The **Tool Properties** dialog box displays the properties of the selected block under the following categories.

Insert

In this category, you can specify the insertion properties of the selected block such as its name, original location of the block file, scale, and rotation angle. The **Name** edit box specifies the name of the block. The **Source file** edit box displays the location of the file, in which the selected block is created. When you choose the **[...]** button in the **Source file** edit box, AutoCAD LT displays the location of the file in the **Select Linked Drawing** dialog box. The **Scale** edit box is used to specify the scale factor of the block. The block will be inserted in the drawing according to the scale factor specified in this edit box. You can enter the angle of rotation in the **Rotation** edit box. The **Explode** edit box is used to specify whether the block will be exploded while inserting or will be inserted as a single entity.

General

In this category, you can specify the general properties of the block such as the **Color**, **Layer**, **Linetype**, **Plot style**, **Lineweight** and **Transparency** for the selected block. The properties of a particular field can be modified from the drop-down list available on selecting that field.

Custom

In this category, you can specify the custom properties of the block, such as the dimensions and related parameters.

ADDING BLOCKS IN TOOL PALETTES

By default, the **TOOL PALETTES** window displays the predefined blocks in AutoCAD LT. You can also add the desired block and the drawing file to the **TOOL PALETTES** window. This is done using the **DESIGNCENTER**. AutoCAD LT provides two methods for adding blocks from the **DESIGNCENTER** to the **TOOL PALETTES**; Drag and Drop method and Shortcut menu. These two methods are discussed next.

Drag and Drop Method

To add blocks from the **DESIGNCENTER** in the **TOOL PALETTES**, move the cursor over the desired block in the **DESIGNCENTER**. Press and hold the left mouse button on the block and drag the cursor to the **TOOL PALETTES** window. You will notice that a box with a + sign is attached to the cursor and a black line appears on the **TOOL PALETTES** window, as shown in Figure 15-42. If you move the cursor up and down in the **TOOL PALETTES**, the black line also moves between the two consecutive blocks. This line is used to define the position of the block to be inserted in the **TOOL PALETTES** window. Release the left mouse button and you will notice that the selected block is added to the location specified by the black line in the **TOOL PALETTES**.

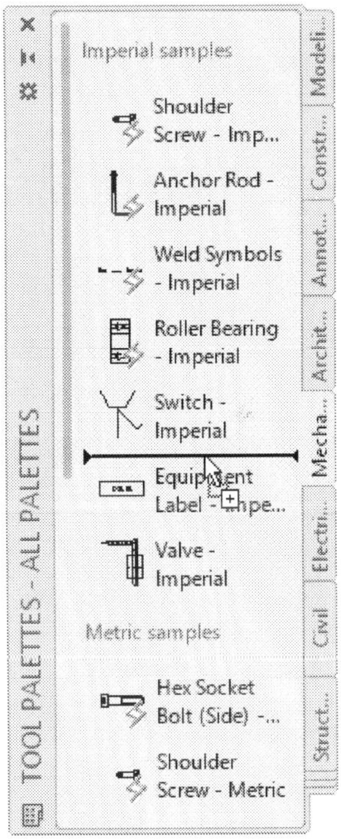

Figure 15-42 Specifying the location for inserting a block in the TOOL PALETTES window

Shortcut Menu

You can also add the desired block from the **DESIGNCENTER**to the **TOOL PALETTES** using the shortcut menu. To add the block, move the cursor over the desired block in the **DESIGNCENTER** and right-click on it to display a shortcut menu. Choose **Create Tool Palette** from it. You will notice that a new tab with the name **New Palette** is added to the **TOOL PALETTES**. And, the block is added in the new tab of the **TOOL PALETTES**. Also, a text box appears that displays the current name of the tab. You can change its name by entering a new one in this text box.

You can also add a number of blocks in a drawing to the **Tool Palettes** using the following two methods:

Select the **Blocks** folder of any drawing in the **DESIGNCENTER** and right-click in the **Tree View** area of the **DESIGNCENTER**; a shortcut menu will be displayed. Choose **Create Tool Palette** from the shortcut menu; a new tab will be added to the **TOOL PALETTES** with the same name as that of the drawing file selected in the **DESIGNCENTER**. This new tab contains all blocks which were in the folder that you selected from the **DESIGNCENTER**.

You can also add all the blocks in a drawing by right-clicking on the drawing in the **tree view** of the **DESIGNCENTER**; a shortcut menu is displayed. Choose **Create Tool Palette** from it; you will notice that a new tab is added to the **TOOL PALETTES** which contains all the blocks that were available in the selected drawing. You will also notice that the new tab has the same name as that of the selected drawing.

MODIFYING EXISTING BLOCKS IN THE TOOL PALETTES

If you modify an existing block that was added to the **TOOL PALETTES** and then insert it using the **TOOL PALETTES** in the same or a new drawing, you will notice that the modified block is inserted and not the original block. However, if you insert the modified block from the **TOOL PALETTES** in the drawing in which the original block was already inserted, AutoCAD LT inserts the original block and not the modified one. This is because the file already has a block of the same name in its memory.

To insert the modified block, you first need to delete the original block from the current drawing using the **Erase** tool. Next, you need to delete the block from the memory of the current drawing. The unused block can be deleted from the memory of the current drawing using the **PURGE** command. To invoke this command, enter **PURGE** at the command window. The **Purge** dialog box is displayed. Choose the (+) sign located on the left of **Blocks** in the tree view available in the **Items not used in drawing** area. You will notice that a list of blocks in the drawing is shown. Select the original block to be deleted from the memory of the current drawing and then choose the **Purge** button. The **Confirm Purge** dialog box is displayed, which confirms the purging of the selected item. Choose **Yes** in it and then choose the **Close** button to exit the **Purge** dialog box. Next, when you insert the block using the **TOOL PALETTES**, the modified block is inserted in the drawing.

LAYERS, COLORS, LINETYPES, AND LINEWEIGHTS FOR BLOCKS

A block possesses the properties of the layer on which it is drawn. The block may be composed of objects drawn on several different layers, with different colors, linetypes, and lineweights. All this information is preserved in the block. At the time of insertion, each object in the block is drawn on its original layer with the original linetype, lineweight, and color, irrespective of the current drawing layer, object color, object linetype, and object lineweights. You may want all instances of a block to have identical layers, linetype properties, lineweight, and color. This can be achieved by allocating all the properties explicitly to the objects forming the block. On the other hand, if you want the linetype and color of each instance of a block to be set according to the linetype and color of the layer on which it is inserted, draw all the objects forming the block on layer 0 and set the color, lineweight, and linetype to **By Layer**. Objects with a **By Layer** color, linetype, and lineweight can have their colors, linetypes, and lineweights changed after insertion by changing the layer settings. If you want the linetype, lineweight, and color of each instance of a block to be set according to the current explicit linetype, lineweight, and color at the time of insertion, set the color, lineweight, and linetype of its objects to **By Block**. You can use the **PROPERTIES** palette to change some of the characteristics associated with a block (such as layer).

For example, assume block B1 includes a square and a triangle that were originally drawn on layer X and layer Y, respectively. Let the color assigned to the layer X be red and to layer Y be green. Also, let the linetype assigned to layer X be continuous and for layer Y be hidden. Now, if we insert B1 on layer L1 with color yellow and linetype dot, block B1 will be on layer L1, but the square will be drawn on layer X with color red and linetype continuous. The triangle will be drawn on layer Y with the color green and the linetype hidden.

The **By Layer** option instructs AutoCAD LT to assign objects within the block the color and linetype of the layers on which they were created. There are three exceptions:

1. If objects are drawn on a special layer (layer 0), they are inserted on the current layer. These objects assume the characteristics of the current layer (the layer on which the block is inserted) at the time of insertion, and can be modified after insertion by changing that layer's settings.
2. Objects created with the special color **By Block** are generated with the color that is current at the time of insertion of the block. This color may be explicit or **By Layer**. You are thus allowed to construct blocks that assume the current object color.
3. Objects created with the special linetype **By Block** are generated with the linetype that is prevalent at the time the block is inserted. Blocks are thus constructed with the current object linetype, which may be **By Layer** or explicit.

Note

If a block is created on a layer that is frozen at the time of insertion, it is not shown on the screen.

Tip

*If you provide drawing files to others for their use, then **BYLAYER** settings applied on the drawing files provide the greatest compatibility with varying office standards for layer/color/linetype/lineweight. This is because they can be changed more easily after insertion.*

NESTING OF BLOCKS

The concept of having one block within another block is known as the nesting of blocks. For example, you can insert several blocks by selecting them and then with the **Create Block** tool, create another block. Similarly, if you use the **Insert** tool to insert a drawing containing several blocks into the current drawing, it creates a block containing nested blocks in the current drawing. There is no limit to the degree of nesting. The only limitation in nesting of blocks is that blocks that reference themselves cannot be inserted. The nested blocks must have different block names. Nesting of blocks affects layers, colors, and linetypes. The general rule is given next.

If an inner block has objects on layer 0, or objects with linetype or color **By Block**, these objects may said to behave like fluids. They "float up" through the nested block structure until they find an outer block with fixed color, layer, or linetype. These objects then assume the characteristics of the fixed layer. If a fixed layer is not found in the outer blocks then the objects with color or linetype **By Block** are formed, which means the objects will assume the color white and linetype CONTINUOUS.

To understand the concept of nested blocks, let us do the following example.

Example 2 — Nested Blocks

1. Draw a rectangle on layer 0, and form a block with the named X using this block.
2. Change the current layer to OBJ, set its color to red, and linetype to hidden.
3. Draw a circle on OBJ layer.
4. Insert the block X in the OBJ layer.
5. Combine the circle with the block X (rectangle) to form a block Y.
6. Now, insert block Y in any layer (say, layer CEN) with the color green and linetype continuous.

You will notice that block Y is generated in red and its linetype is hidden. However, the block X, which is nested in block Y and created on layer 0, is not generated in the color (green) and linetype (continuous) of the layer CEN. This is because the object (rectangle) on layer 0 floated up through the nested block structure and assumed the color and linetype of the first outer block (Y) with a fixed color (red), layer (OBJ), and linetype (hidden). If both the blocks (X and Y) were on layer 0, the objects in the block Y would assume the color and linetype of the layer on which the block was inserted.

Example 3 — Nested Block

1. Change the color of layer 0 to red.
2. Draw a circle with color **By Block** and then form its block, B1. It appears black because its color is set to **By Block** (Figure 15-43).
3. Set the color to **By Layer** and draw a square. The color of the square is red.
4. Insert block B1. Notice that the block B1 (circle) assumes red color.
5. Create another block B2 consisting of the Block B1 (circle) and square.
6. Create a layer L1 with green color and hidden linetype. Make it current. Insert block B2 in layer L1.
7. Explode block B2. Notice the change.
8. Explode block B1, circle. You will notice that the color of the circle changes to black because it was drawn with the color set to **By Block** .

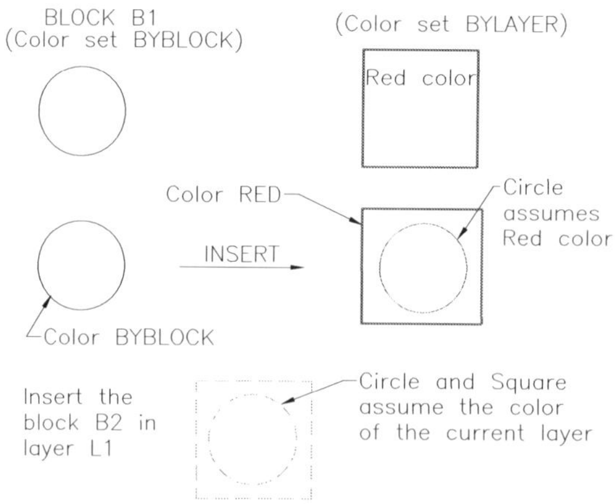

Figure 15-43 Blocks with different layers and colors

Example 4 Nested Block

Part A

1. Draw a unit square on layer 0 and make it a block named B1.
2. Draw a circle of radius 0.5 and change it into a block named B2.
3. Insert block B1 into the drawing with a X scale factor of 3 and a Y scale factor of 4.
4. Now, insert the block B2 in the drawing and position it at the top of B1.
5. Make a block of the entire drawing and name it Plate.
6. Insert the block **Plate** in the current layer.
7. Create a new layer with different colors and linetypes and insert blocks B1, B2, and Plate. Keep in mind the layers on which the individual blocks and the inserted block were made.

Part B

Try nesting the blocks drawn on different layers and with different linetypes.

Part C

Change the layers and colors of the different blocks you have drawn so far.

CREATING DRAWING FILES USING THE WRITE BLOCK DIALOG BOX

Ribbon: Insert > Block Definition > Create Block > Write Block
Command: WBLOCK

The blocks are symbols created by the **Create Block** tool and can be used only in the drawing, in which they were created. This is a shortcoming because you may need to use a particular block in different drawings. The **Write Block** tool is used to export symbols by writing them to new drawing files that can then be inserted in any drawing. With the **Write Block** tool, you can create a drawing file (*.dwg* extension) of the specified blocks, selected objects in the current drawing, or the entire drawing. All the used named objects (linetypes, layers, styles, and system variables) of the current drawing are inherited by the new drawing created with the **Write Block** tool. This block can then be inserted in any drawing.

When you invoke the **Write Block** tool, the **Write Block** dialog box is displayed, as shown in Figure 15-44. This dialog box converts the blocks into drawing files and also saves objects as drawing files. You can also save the entire current drawing as a new drawing file.

The **Write Block** dialog box has two main areas: **Source** and **Destination**. The **Source** area allows you to select objects and blocks, specify insertion base points, and convert them into drawing files. In this area of the dialog box, different default settings are displayed, depending upon the selection you make. By default, the **Objects** radio button is selected. In the **Destination** area, the **File name and path** edit box displays *new block.dwg* as the new file name and its location. The **Block** drop-down list is also not available. Now, you can select objects in a drawing and save them as a wblock, and can enter a name and a path for the file. Sometimes the current drawing consists of blocks. To save a block as a wblock, you can select the **Block** radio button. When the **Block** radio button is selected, the **Block** drop-down list is available. The **Block** drop-down list displays all the block names in the current drawing and you can select a block name to convert it into a wblock. The **Base point** and **Objects** areas are not available, since the insertion points and objects have already been saved with the block definition. Also, you will notice that in the **Destination** area, by default, the **File name and path** edit box displays the name of the selected block. This means that you can keep the name of the wblock the same as the selected block or you can change it.On selecting the **Entire drawing** radio button, the current drawing will be selected as a block and saves it as a new file. When you use this option, the **Base point** and **Objects** areas are not available.

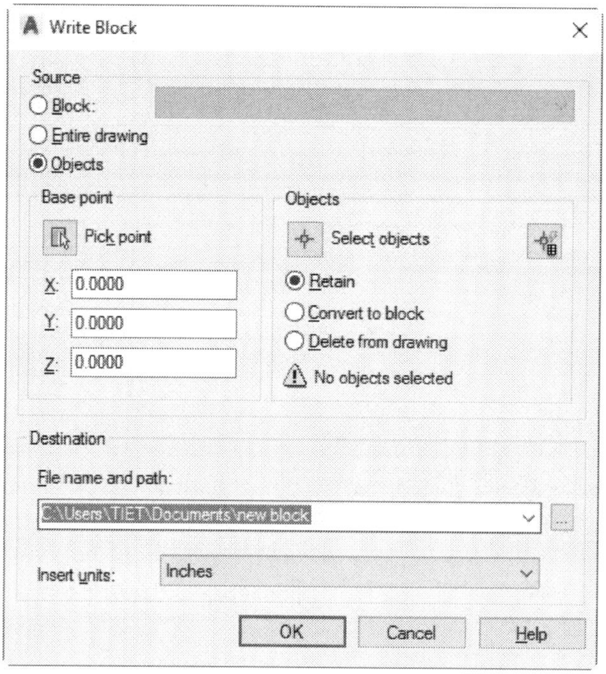

***Figure 15-44** The **Write Block** dialog box*

The **Base point** area allows you to specify the base point of a wblock, which is used as an insertion point. You can either enter values in the **X**, **Y**, and **Z** edit boxes or choose the **Pick point** button to select it on the screen. The default value is 0, 0, 0. The **Objects** area allows you to select objects to save as a file. You can use the **Select objects** button to select objects or use the **QuickSelect** button to set parameters in the **Quick Select** dialog box to select objects in the current drawing. The number of objects selected is displayed at the bottom of the **Objects** area. If the **Retain** radio button is selected in the **Objects** area, the selected objects in the current drawing are kept as such, after they have been saved as a new file. If the **Convert to block** radio button is selected, the selected objects in the current drawing will be converted into a block with the same name as the new file, after being saved as a new file. On selecting the **Delete from drawing** radio button, it deletes the selected objects from the current drawing after they have been saved as a file.

Note

*Both the **Base point** and **Objects** areas will be available in the **Write Block** dialog box only when the **Objects** radio button is selected in the **Source** area of the dialog box.*

The **Destination** area sets the file name, location and units of the new file in which the selected objects are saved. In the **File name and path** edit box, you can specify the file name and the path of the block or the selected objects. You can choose the **[...]** button to display the **Browse for Drawing File** dialog box, where you can specify the path where the new file will be saved. From the **Insert units** drop-down list, you can select the units which will be applied to the new file when inserted as a block. The settings for units are stored in the **INSUNITS** system variable and the default option Inches has a value of 1. After specifying the required information in the dialog box, choose **OK**. The objects or the block is saved as a new file in the path specified by you. A **WBLOCK Preview** window with the new file contents is displayed. This preview image is stored and displayed in the **DESIGNCENTER**, when using it to insert drawings and blocks.

Tip

By using the ***Entire drawing*** *radio button in the* ***Write Block*** *dialog box, you can save the current drawing as a new drawing. It is a recommended method to reduce the file size of the drawing. This is because all unused blocks, layers, linetypes, text styles, dimension styles, multiline styles, shapes, and so on are removed from the drawing. The new drawing does not contain any information that is no longer needed. The* ***Entire drawing*** *option is faster than the* ***-PURGE*** *command (which also removes unused named objects from a drawing file) and can be used whenever you have completed a drawing and want to save it. The* ***-PURGE*** *command has been discussed later in this chapter.*

Note

Whenever a drawing is inserted into the current drawing, it acts as a single object. It cannot be edited unless exploded.

DEFINING THE INSERTION BASE POINT

Ribbon: Insert > Block Definition > Set Base Point
Command: BASE

The **Set Base Point** tool lets you set the insertion base point for a drawing, just as you set the base insertion point using the **Create Block** tool. This base point is defined that when you insert the drawing into some other drawings, the specified base point is placed on the insertion point. By default, the base point is at the origin (0,0,0). When a drawing is inserted on a current layer, it does not inherit the color, linetype, or thickness properties of the current layer. On invoking the **Set Base Point** tool, following prompt sequence is displayed.

Enter base point <0.0000,0.0000,0.0000>: *Specify a base point or press ENTER to accept the default value.*

Exercise 5 — *WBLOCK*

1. Create a drawing file named CHAIR using the **Write Block** tool. Make a listing of your *.dwg* files and make sure that *CHAIR.dwg* is listed. Quit the drawing editor.
2. Begin a new drawing and insert the drawing file into it. Save the drawing.

EDITING BLOCKS

Ribbon: Insert > Reference > Edit Reference **Command:** REFEDIT
Toolbar: Refedit > Edit reference In place
Menubar: Tools > Xref and Block In-place Edit > Edit Reference Inplace

You can edit blocks by breaking them into parts and then making modifications and redefining them or by editing them in place. Both these methods have been discussed here.

Editing Blocks in Place

You can edit blocks in the current drawing by using the **Edit Reference** tool, referred to as the in-place reference editing. This feature of AutoCAD LT allows you to make minor changes to blocks, wblocks, or drawings that have been inserted in the current drawing without breaking them up into component parts or opening the original drawing and redefining them. This command saves valuable time of going back and forth between drawings and redefining blocks.

You can invoke the **Edit Reference** tool from the **Reference** panel in the **Insert** tab or by entering **REFEDIT** at the Command prompt. On doing so, the **Reference Edit** dialog box will be displayed. Alternatively, select the block, right-click on any block reference and then choose the **Edit Block In-Place** option from the shortcut menu displayed. When you invoke the **REFEDIT** command, the following prompt is displayed.

Select reference: *Select the block to edit.*

Once you have selected the block reference to be edited, the **Reference Edit** dialog box is displayed. The **Reference Edit** dialog box has two tabs: **Identify Reference** and **Settings**. The description of these tabs is as follows:

Identify Reference Tab

The **Identify Reference** tab, as shown in Figure 15-45, provides information for identifying the reference edit, selecting, and editing the references.

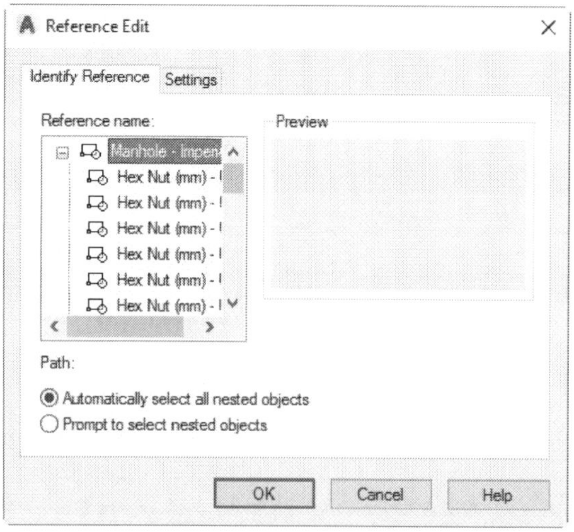

***Figure 15-45** The **Identify Reference** tab in the **Reference Edit** dialog box*

Reference name. The **Reference name** list box displays the name of the selected reference. A plus sign (+) next to the name implies that the selected block reference contains nested references. When you click on the plus sign, the nested reference is displayed in a tree view. If a block does not contain any nested blocks, this plus sign is not displayed next to the reference name in the list box. In the figure, the block Valve-2 contains a nested block Valve. An image of the selected block is displayed in the **Preview** box. If you want to see a preview of the nested block, select its name in the list box; the corresponding preview image is displayed in the **Preview** area.

Path. It displays the location of the selected reference. Note that if the selected reference is a block, no path is displayed.

The **Automatically select all nested objects** radio button is selected by default and allows you to automatically include all the selected objects in the reference editing session. The selected objects also include the nested objects.

The **Prompt to select nested objects** radio button, when selected, allows you to individually select the nested objects in the reference editing session. If this radio button is selected and you choose the **OK** button, the **Reference Edit** dialog box is closed. You are prompted to select the nested objects in the reference that you want to edit.

Settings Tab

The **Settings** tab, as shown in Figure 15-46, provides options for editing references. The **Create unique layer, style, and block names** check box is selected by default and allows you to control the layer and symbol names of the objects that are extracted from the selected reference. If you clear this check box, the names of the layers remain the same as in the reference drawing. Similarly, the **Display attribute definitions for editing** check box, when selected, allows you to edit attributes and attribute definitions associated with the block references. The modified attribute definitions are effective for future insertions, and no changes are made in the current insertions. Attributes are explained in detail in the next chapter. The **Lock objects not in working set** check box, when selected, allows you to lock all the objects that are not in the working set.

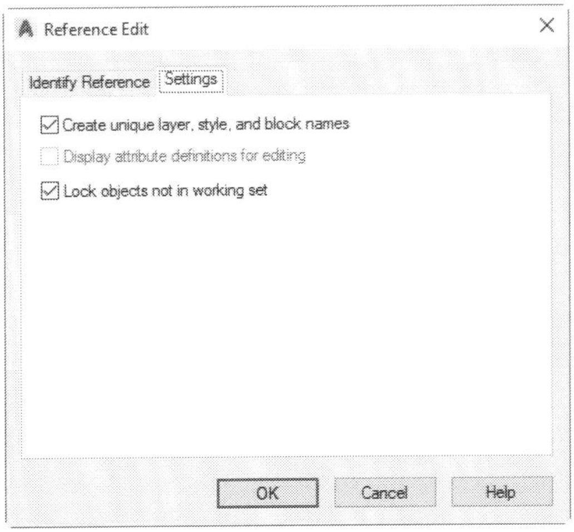

*Figure 15-46 The **Settings** tab of the **Reference Edit** dialog box*

After selecting the required block to edit, choose **OK** to exit the dialog box. If you have selected the **Prompt to select nested objects** radio button, the following prompt sequence will be displayed:

Select nested objects: *Select objects within the block that you want to modify.*
n entities added
Select nested objects: Enter
n items selected
Use **REFCLOSE** or the **Refedit** toolbar to end reference editing session.

Once you have selected the objects to be edited and pressed ENTER, the total number of selected objects will be displayed. Also, you will notice that the **Edit Reference** panel has been added to the **Ribbon** and the objects, except the selected ones have faded out. You can control the fading intensity of the objects by using the options from the **Fade control** area of the **Display** tab in the **Options** dialog box, see Figure 15-47. In this area, you can use the slider bar to increase or decrease the fading intensity or you can enter a value in the edit box. You can also control the fading intensity of other objects at the time of editing by using the **XFADECTL** variable. By default, the fading intensity value is set to 70.

The objects that have been selected for editing are referred to as the working set. You can use any drawing and editing command to modify this working set. Sometimes, you may need to add an external object from the current drawing to the block. To do so, choose the **Add to Working Set** button in the **Edit Reference** panel, see Figure 15-48. Next, select the objects to be added to the working set and press ENTER; these objects will then get deleted from the current drawing and added to the current working set. Similarly, to remove objects from a working set, choose the **Remove from Working set** button from the **Edit Reference** panel. You are prompted to select the objects from the working set that you want to remove. On completing the selection, press ENTER. The objects that have been removed from the working set appear faded and are added back to the current drawing. You can also use the **REFSET** command to add or remove objects from a working set. But this command can be used only when a reference has already been selected using the **REFEDIT** command.

*Figure 15-47 The **Fade control** area of the **Display** tab in the **Options** dialog box*

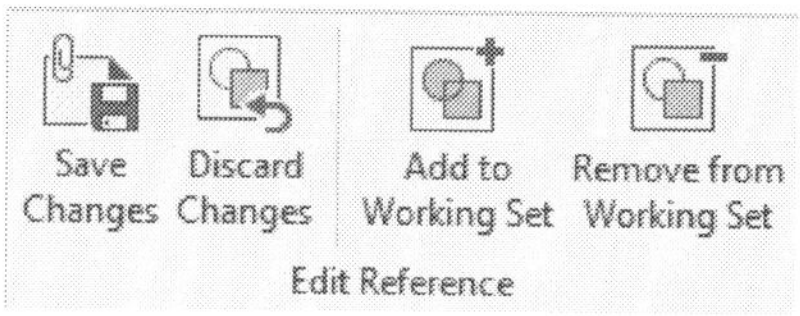

*Figure 15-48 The **Edit Reference** panel*

After adding or removing objects from the existing set, choose the **Save Changes** tool in the **Edit Reference** panel to save the changes; the **AutoCAD LT** information box will be displayed informing that all reference edits will be saved. This information box also prompts you to specify whether you want to continue saving or cancel the command. Choose **OK** to save the modifications or choose **Cancel** to cancel the command. If you choose **OK**, the modifications are applied to the current block as well as to all future insertions.

Note
The Automatic Save feature of AutoCAD LT is disabled during reference editing.

To exit reference editing without saving any changes in the block reference, choose the **Discard Changes** button from the **Edit Reference** panel; the **AutoCAD LT** information box will be displayed, as shown in Figure 15-49, informing that all changes that have been made in the object will be discarded. To continue, choose **OK**, and to get back to reference editing, choose **Cancel**.

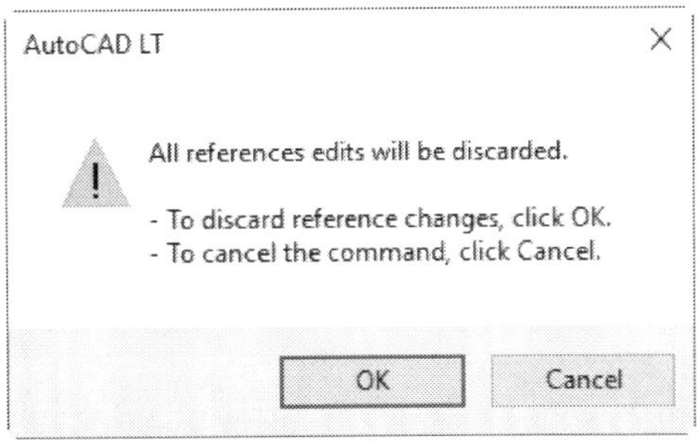

Figure 15-49 *The* ***AutoCAD LT*** *information box*

Exploding Blocks Using the XPLODE Command

Command: XPLODE/X

With the **XPLODE** command, you can explode ablock or blocks into component objects and simultaneously control their properties such as layer, linetype, color, and lineweight. The scale factor of the object to be exploded should be equal. Note that if the scale factor of the objects to be exploded is not equal, you need to change the value of the **EXPLMODE** system variable to 1. Note that if the **Allow exploding** check box in the **Behavior** area of the **Block Definition** dialog box was cleared while creating the block, you will not be able to explode the block. The command prompts for this command are as follows:

Command: **XPLODE**
Select objects to XPlode
Select objects: *Using any object selection method, select objects, and then press ENTER.*

On pressing ENTER, AutoCAD LT reports the total number of objects selected and also the number of objects that cannot be exploded. If you select multiple objects to explode, AutoCAD LT further prompts you to specify whether the changes in the properties of the component objects should be made individually or globally. The prompt is given next.

XPlode Individually/<Globally>: *Enter i, g, or press ENTER to accept the default option.*

If you enter **i** at the above prompt, AutoCAD LT will modify each object individually, one at a time. The next prompt is given below.

Enter an option [All/Color/LAyer/LType/LWeight/Inherit from parent block/Explode] <Explode>: *Select an option.*

The options available at the Command line are discussed next.

All

This option sets all the properties such as color, layer, linetype, and lineweight of the selected objects, after exploding them. AutoCAD LT prompts you to enter new color, linetype, lineweight, and layer name for the exploded component objects.

Color
This option sets the color of the exploded objects. The prompt is given next.

New color [Truecolor/COlorbook]<BYLAYER>: *Enter a color option or press ENTER.*

When you enter **BYLAYER**, the component objects take on the color of the exploded object's layer and when you enter **BYBLOCK**, they take on the color of the exploded object.

LAyer
This option sets the layer of the exploded objects. By default current layer will be inherited. The command prompt is as follows.

Enter new layer name for exploded objects <current>: *Enter an existing layer name or press ENTER.*

LType
This option sets the linetype of the components of the exploded object. The command prompt is given next.

Enter new linetype name for exploded objects <ByLayer>: *Enter a linetype name or press ENTER to accept the default options.*

LWeight
This option sets the lineweight of the components of the exploded object. The command prompt is given next.

Enter new lineweight: *Enter a lineweight or press ENTER to accept the default option.*

Inherit from parent block
This option sets the properties of the component objects to that of the exploded parent object, provided the component objects are drawn on layer 0 and the color, lineweight, and linetype are **BYBLOCK**.

Explode
This option explodes the selected object exactly as in the **EXPLODE** command.
On selecting the **Globally** option, the changes will be applied to all the selected objects. The options are similar to the ones discussed in the **Individually** option.

RENAMING BLOCKS

Command: RENAME

Blocks can be renamed using the **RENAME** command. To rename a block, enter **RENAME** at the Command prompt and press ENTER; the **Rename** dialog box will be displayed, see Figure 15-50.

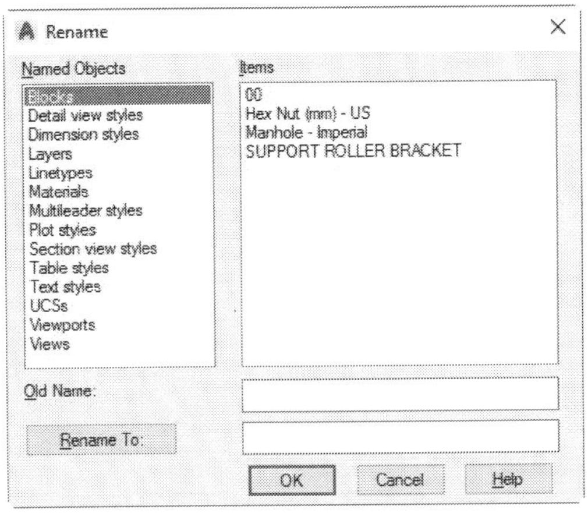

Figure 15-50 *The **Rename** dialog box*

In this dialog box, the **Named Objects** list box displays the categories of object types that can be renamed, such as blocks, layers, dimension styles, linetypes, Multileader styles, material, table styles and text styles, UCSs, views, and viewports. You can rename all of these objects except layer 0 and continuous linetype. When you select **Blocks** from the **Named Objects** list, the **Items** list box displays all the block names in the current drawing. When you select a block name to rename from the **Items** list box, it is displayed in the **Old Name** edit box. Enter the new name to be assigned to the block in the **Rename To** edit box. Choosing the **Rename To** button applies the change in name to the old name. Choose **OK** to exit the dialog box. For example, to rename a block named Bracket to **Valve-3**, select **Bracket** from the **Items** list box; it is displayed in the **Old Name** edit box. Enter **Valve-3** in the **Rename To** edit box and choose the **Rename To** button; the **Valve-3** block appears in the **Items** list box. Now, choose **OK** to exit the dialog box.

Note

*The layer 0 and Continuous linetype cannot be renamed and therefore, they do not appear in the **Items** list box, when **Layers** and **Linetypes** are selected in the **Named Objects** list box. To rename a block, enter **-RENAME** or **-REN** at the Command window.*

DELETING UNUSED BLOCKS

Sometimes after completing a drawing, you may notice that the drawing contains several named objects, such as dimstyles, textstyles, layers, blocks, and so on that are not being used. Since these unused named objects unnecessarily occupy disk space, you may want to remove them. Unused blocks can be deleted with the **-PURGE** command. For example, to delete an unused block named Drawing2, the prompt sequence is given next.

Command: **-PURGE**
Enter type of unused objects to purge
[Blocks/DEtailviewstyles/Dimstyles/Groups/LAyers/LTypes/MAterials/MUltileaderstyles/Plotstyles/SHapes/textSTyles/Mlinestyles/SEctionviewstyles/Tablestyles/Visualstyles/Regapps/Zero-length geometry/Empty text objects/Orphaned data/All]: **B**
Enter name(s) to purge <*>: **Drawing2**
Verify each name to be purged? [Yes/No] <Y>: Enter
Purge block "Drawing2"? <N>: **Y**

If there are no objects to be removed, AutoCAD LT displays a message "No unreferenced blocks found".

Self-Evaluation Test

Answer the following questions and then compare them to those given at the end of this chapter:

1. The ____________ command lets you create a drawing file (*.dwg* extension) of a block defined in the current drawing.

2. The ____________ command can be used to change the name of a block.

3. The _________ tool is used to place an existing block in a drawing.

4. You can delete the unreferenced blocks using the _________ command.

5. You can use the _________ to locate, preview, copy, and insert blocks or existing drawings into the current drawing.

6. The _________ command is used for in-place reference editing.

7. Individual objects in a block cannot be erased using the **Block Editor**. (T/F)

8. A block can be mirrored by providing a scale factor of -1 for X. (T/F)

9. Blocks created by using the **Create Block** tool in the **Block** panel can be used in any drawing. (T/F)

10. You cannot redefine any existing block. (T/F)

Review Questions

Answer the following questions:

1. Which one of the following actions cannot be assigned to the **Point** parameter?

   (a) **Move** (b) **Array**
   (c) **Stretch** (d) None of these

2. Which of the following commands is used to get back the objects that consist of a block and have been removed from the drawing?

   (a) **OOPS** (b) **BLIPS**
   (c) **BLOCK** (d) **UNDO**

3. By what amount is a block rotated, if the value of both the X and Y scale factors is -1?

   (a) 90 (b) 180
   (c) 270 (d) 360

4. When you insert a drawing into the current drawing, how many blocks belonging to the inserted drawing are brought into the current drawing?

   (a) 1 (b) 2
   (c) All (d) None

5. The __________ command is used to create a rectangular array of a block.

6. The __________ tab of the **BLOCK AUTHORING PALETTES** allows you to insert a parameter set.

7. The automatic save feature is __________ during in-place reference editing.

8. You cannot use the **REFEDIT** command on blocks inserted using the __________ command.

9. The Layer 0 and the Continuous linetype __________ can be renamed using the **RENAME** command.

10. An entire drawing can be converted into a block. (T/F)

11. The objects in a block inherit the properties of the layer on which they are drawn, such as color and linetype. (T/F)

12. If the objects forming a block are drawn with linetype **BYLAYER**, then at the time of the insertion, each object that makes up a block is drawn with the linetype **BYLAYER**. (T/F)

13. Objects created with the special color **BYBLOCK** are generated with the color that was current at the time the block was inserted. (T/F)

14. In the array generated with the **MINSERT** command, there is no way to change the number of rows or columns or the spacing between them after insertion. (T/F)

15. The **Entire drawing** option of the **Write Block** tool has the same effect as the **PURGE** command. (T/F)

Exercise 6 *Block*

Draw part (a) of Figure 15-51 and define it as a block named B. Next, using the relevant insertion method, generate the pattern as shown in the same figure. Note that the pattern is rotated at 30 degrees.

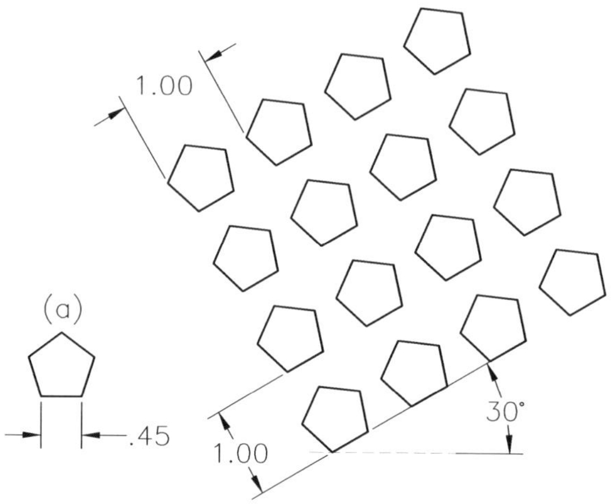

Figure 15-51 *Drawing for Exercise 6*

Exercise 7 — *Block*

Draw Block A of Figure 15-52 and define it as a block named Chair. The dimensions of the chair can be referred from the Problem Solving Exercise 3 of Chapter 5. Next, using the block insert command, insert the chair around the table as shown in the same figure.

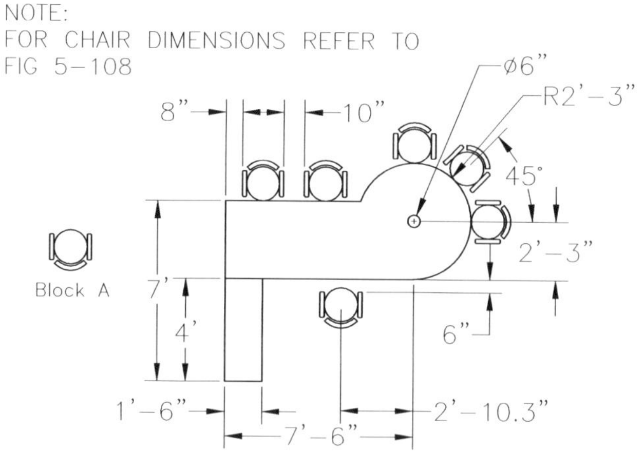

Figure 15-52 *Drawing for Exercise 7*

Answers to Self-Evaluation Test

1. **WBLOCK**, **2.** **RENAME**, **3.** **Insert**, **4.** **PURGE**, **5.** **DESIGNCENTER**, **6.** **REFEDIT**, **7.** F, **8.** T, **9.** F, **10.** F

Chapter 16

Defining Block Attributes

Learning Objectives

After completing this chapter, you will be able to:
- *Understand block attributes*
- *Create annotative block attributes*
- *Edit attribute tag names*
- *Insert blocks with attributes and assign values to attributes*
- *Extract attribute values from inserted blocks*
- *Control attribute visibility*
- *Edit attributes*

Key Terms

- *Attribute Definition*
- *Block Attribute Manager*
- *ATTDISP*
- *EATTEDIT*
- *-ATTEDIT*
- *REFEDIT*

UNDERSTANDING ATTRIBUTES

In AutoCAD LT, you can attach information to blocks. This information can then be retrieved and processed by other programs for various purposes. For example, you can use this information to create a bill of material for a project, find the total number of computers in a building, or determine the location of each block in a drawing. Attributes can also be used to create blocks (such as title blocks) with prompted or preformatted text, to control text placement. The information associated with a block is known as attribute value or attribute. AutoCAD LT references the attributes with a block through tag names.

Before assigning attributes to a block, you must create an attribute definition by using the **Define Attributes** tool. The attribute definition describes the characteristics of the attribute. You can define several attribute definitions (tags) and include them in the block definition. Each time you insert a block, AutoCAD LT will prompt you to enter the value of the attribute. The attribute value automatically replaces the attribute tag name. The information (attribute values) assigned to a block can be extracted and written to a file by using the **Extract Data** tool. This file can then be inserted in the drawing as a table or processed by other programs to analyze the data. The attribute values can be edited by using the tools in the **Edit Attribute** drop-down.

DEFINING ATTRIBUTES

Ribbon: Insert > Block Definition > Define Attributes **Command:** ATT/ATTDEF

When you invoke the **Define Attributes** tool, the **Attribute Definition** dialog box will be displayed, refer to Figure 16-1. The block attributes can be defined using this dialog box. When creating an attribute definition, you must define the mode, attributes, insertion point, and text information for each attribute. All these information can be entered in the dialog box. The following is the description of each area of the **Attribute Definition** dialog box:

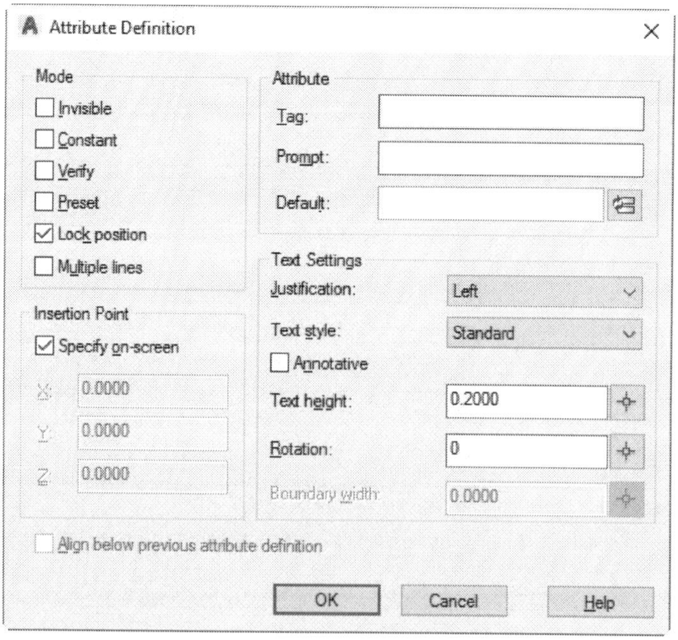

*Figure 16-1 The **Attribute Definition** dialog box*

Mode Area

The **Mode** area of the **Attribute Definition** dialog box has six check boxes: **Invisible**, **Constant**, **Verify**, **Preset**, **Lock position**, and **Multiple lines**. These check boxes determine the display and edit features of the block attributes. For example, if you select the **Invisible** check box, the attribute becomes invisible which means, it is not displayed on the screen. Similarly, if the **Constant** check box is selected, the attribute becomes constant. This means that its value is predefined and cannot be changed. These options are described next.

Invisible

This option allows you to create an attribute that is not visible on the screen, by default. Select this check box if you want the attribute to be invisible.

Constant

This option allows you to create an attribute that has a fixed value and cannot be changed after block insertion.

Verify

This option allows you to verify the specified attribute value while inserting a block by asking you twice for the data to verify the value of attribute.

Preset

This option allows you to create an attribute that is automatically set to the default value. When you insert a block the default values are used, not the attribute values. But unlike a constant attribute, the preset attribute value can be edited later.

Lock position

This check box is selected by default and it is used to lock the position of the attributes with respect to the block object. In case of non-dynamic blocks, if the attributes are created with the **Lock position** check box cleared, then a separate grip will be displayed on that attribute. This grip can be used to modify the location of the attribute. When the dynamic blocks are created with the **Lock position** check box cleared, the separate grip does not get displayed on the attribute. Besides this, the attribute cannot be manipulated by the parameters and action.

Multiple lines

Select this check box to specify that the default value of the attribute may be a single-line or multiple line text.

Attribute Area

The **Attribute** area (Figure 16-2) of the **Attribute Definition** dialog box has three edit boxes: **Tag**, **Prompt**, and **Default**, where you can enter values. You can enter up to 256 characters in each of these edit boxes. If the first character to be entered in any one of these edit boxes is a space, you should start with a backslash (\). But if the first character is a backslash (\), you should start the value to be entered with two backslashes (\\). The three edit boxes have been described next.

***Figure 16-2** The **Attribute** area of the **Attribute Definition** dialog box*

Tag

This is like a label that is used to identify an attribute. For example, the tag name COMPUTER can be used to identify an item. The tag names specified in lowercase letters are automatically converted into uppercase when displayed. The tag name cannot be null. Also, it must not contain any blank spaces.

Prompt

The text that you enter in the **Prompt** edit box is used as a prompt when you insert a block that contains the defined attribute. For example, if COMPUTER is the tag, you can enter WHAT IS THE MEMORY? or ENTER MEMORY: in the **Prompt** edit box. AutoCAD LT will then prompt you with this same statement when you insert the block with which the attribute is defined. If you have selected the **Constant** check box in the **Mode** area, the **Prompt** edit box is not available because no prompt is required if the attribute is constant. If you do not enter anything in the **Prompt** edit box, the entry specified in the **Tag** edit box is used as the prompt.

Default

The entry in the **Default** edit box defines the default value of the specified attribute. If you do not enter a value, the attribute takes the value entered in the **Tag** edit box. The entry of a value is optional.

Insert Field

This button is used to insert a field as the value of the attribute. When you choose this button, the **Field** dialog box is displayed that can be used to insert the required field.

Multiline Editor

This button is displayed in place of the **Insert Field** button when the **Multiple lines** check box is selected from the **Mode** area. Choose this button to invoke the **Text Formatting** window on the screen. You can enter the text that you want to assign as the default value of the attribute in the text window.

Note

*The **Text Formatting** toolbar displayed here has some commonly used options only. The full **Text Formatting** toolbar can be displayed by changing the value of the **ATTIPE** system variable to 1.*

Insertion Point Area

The **Insertion Point** area of the **Attribute Definition** dialog box (Figure 16-3) allows you to define the insertion point for the block attribute text. You can define the insertion point by entering the values in the **X**, **Y**, and **Z** edit boxes or by specifying it on the screen. To specify the insertion point on the screen, select the **Specify on-screen** check box. Now, set the parameters in all the other fields and areas and then choose **OK**. You will be prompted to select the start point of the attribute.

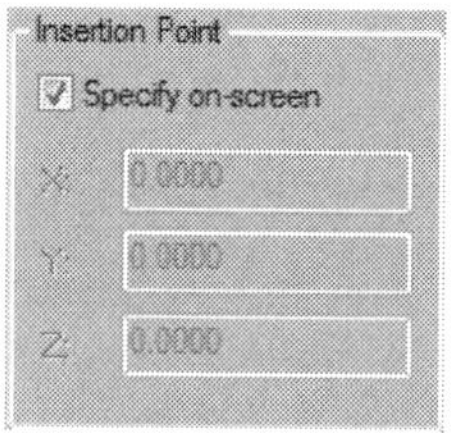

***Figure 16-3** The **Insertion Point** area*

Just below the **Insertion Point** area of the **Attribute Definition** dialog box, a check box labeled **Align below previous attribute definition** is displayed. This check box will not be available when you use the **Attribute Definition** dialog box for the first time. After you have defined an attribute and when you press ENTER to display the **Attribute Definition** dialog box again, this check box becomes available. You can select this check box to place the subsequent attribute text just below the previously defined attribute automatically. When you select this check box, the **Insertion Point** area and the **Text Settings** area of the dialog box will not be available and AutoCAD LT will assume previously defined values for text such as text height, text style, text justification, and text rotation. The text will be automatically placed on the following line.

Text Settings Area

The **Text Settings** area of the **Attribute Definition** dialog box (Figure 16-4) allows you to control the justification, text style, annotation property, height, rotation, and boundary width of the attribute text. To set the text justification, select a justification type from the **Justification** drop-down list. The default option is **Left** for the single line text and **Top left** for the multiline text. Similarly, you can use the **Text style** drop-down list to select a text style. All the text styles defined in the current drawing are displayed in the **Text style** drop-down list. The default text style is **Standard**. To write annotative attributes, select the **Annotative** text style from the **Text style** drop-down list. Select the **Annotative** check box to assign the annotative property to the attribute text. The annotative attributes can be attached to both the annotative or non-annotative blocks. You can specify the text height and text rotation in the **Text height** and **Rotation** edit boxes, respectively. You can also define the text height by choosing the **Text Height** button. When you choose this button, AutoCAD LT temporarily exits the **Attribute Definition** dialog box and allows you to enter the height value by selecting points on the screen or from the Command prompt. Once the height on the screen is defined, the **Attribute Definition** dialog box will reappear and the defined text height will be displayed in the edit box. Similarly, you can define the text rotation by choosing the **Rotation** button and then selecting points on the screen or by entering the rotation angle at the Command prompt. The **Boundary width** edit box is used to specify the maximum width for the multiline text. If the width of the text line is more than this value, the text will automatically go to the second line. This edit box will be available only when you select the **Multiple lines** check box from the **Mode** area.

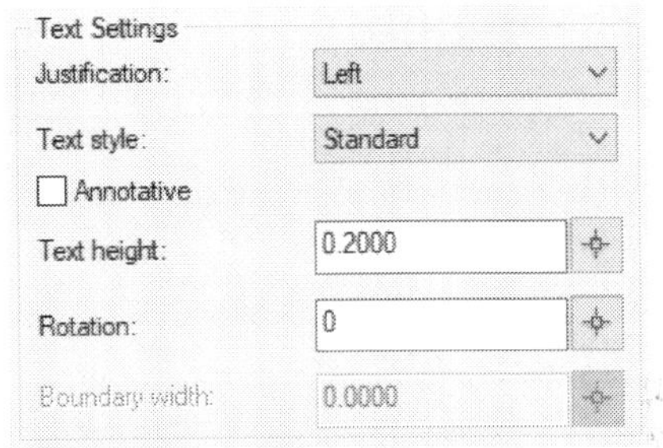

*Figure 16-4 The **Text Settings** area of the **Attribute Definition** dialog box*

Note

1. The text style must be defined before it can be used to specify the text.

*2. If you select a style that has the predefined height, AutoCAD LT automatically disables the **Text height** edit box.*

*3. If you have selected the **Align** option from the **Justification** drop-down list, the **Insertion Point** area and the **Text height** and **Rotation** edit boxes in the **Text Settings** area will be disabled.*

*4. If you have selected the **Fit** option from the **Justification** drop-down list, the **Insertion Point** area and the **Rotation** edit box are disabled. To specify the location of the attribute, choose **OK** from the dialog box; you will be prompted to specify the first and second endpoints of the text baseline. Specify the point; the text will fit between the two endpoints that you specify.*

After you complete the settings in the **Attribute Definition** dialog box and choose **OK**, the attribute tag text is inserted in the drawing at the specified insertion point. Now, you can use the **Create Block** tool to select all the objects and attributes to define a block.

Note

*You can use the **-ATTDEF** command to display the dynamic prompt in the drawing area. The options in the **Attribute Definition** dialog box are available through the dynamic prompt too. Refer to Figure 16-5.*

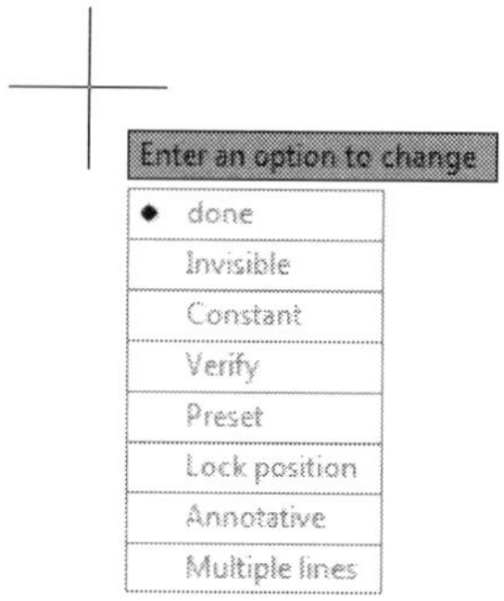

***Figure 16-5** Dynamic prompt for the **-ATTDEF** command*

Example 1 — Attribute Definition

In this example, you will define the following attributes for a computer and then create a block using the **Create Block** tool. The name of the block is COMP.

Mode	Tag name	Prompt	Default value
Constant	ITEM		Computer
Preset, Verify	MAKE	Enter make:	CAD-CIM
Verify	PROCESSOR	Enter processor type:	Unknown
Verify	HD	Enter Hard-Drive size:	40 GB
Invisible, Verify	RAM	Enter RAM:	256 MB

1. Draw the sketch of a computer, as shown in Figure 16-6. Assume the dimensions or measure the dimensions of the computer you are using for AutoCAD LT.

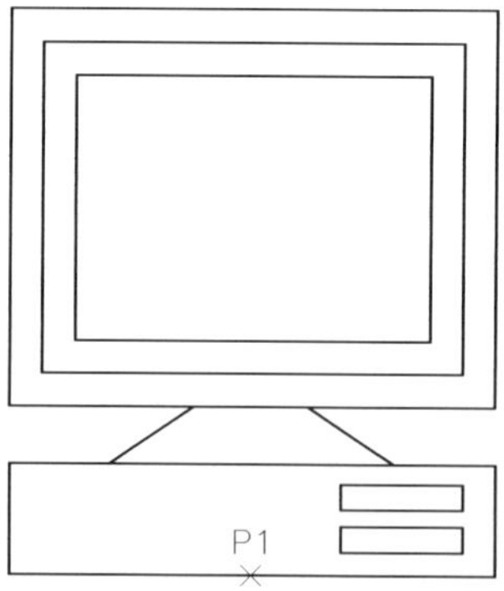

***Figure 16-6** Drawing for Example 1*

2. Choose the **Define Attributes** tool from the **Block Definition** panel in the **Insert** tab; the **Attribute Definition** dialog box is displayed.

3. Define the first attribute shown in the preceding table. Select the **Constant** check box in the **Mode** area because the mode of the first attribute is constant. In the **Tag** edit box, enter the tag name, **ITEM**. Similarly, enter **COMPUTER** in the **Default** edit box. Note that the **Prompt** edit box will not be available because the mode is constant.

4. In the **Insertion Point** area, select the **Specify on-screen** check box to define the text insertion point.

5. In the **Text Settings** area, specify the justification, style, annotative property, height, and rotation of the text.

6. Choose the **OK** button once you have entered information in the **Attribute Definition** dialog box. Select a point below the insertion base point (P1) of the computer to place the text.

7. Press ENTER to invoke the **Attribute Definition** dialog box again. Enter the mode and attribute information for the second attribute as shown in the table at the beginning of Example 1. You need not define the insertion point and text options again. Select the **Align below previous attribute definition** check box that is located just below the **Insertion Point** area. You will notice that when you select this check box, the **Insertion Point** and **Text Settings** areas are not available. Now, choose the **OK** button. AutoCAD LT places the attribute text just below the previous attribute text.

8. Similarly, define the remaining attributes also (Figure 16-7).

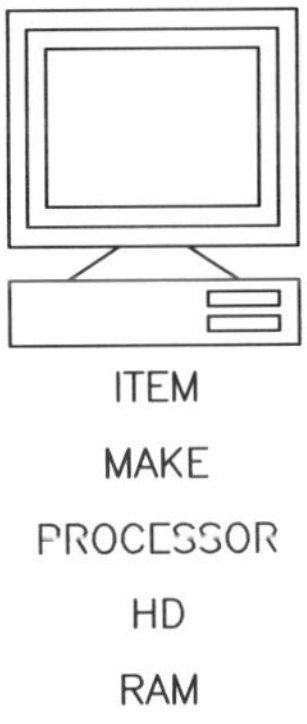

Figure 16-7 *Attributes defined below the computer drawing*

9. Now, use the **Create Block** tool to create a block. Make sure that the **Retain** radio button is selected in the **Objects** area. The name of the block is **COMP**, and the insertion point of the block is P1, midpoint of the base. When you select objects for the block, make sure you also select attributes.

10. Insert the block created. You will notice that the order of prompts is the same as the order of attributes selection.

EDITING ATTRIBUTE DEFINITION

Menu Bar: Modify > Object > Text > Edit **Command:** DDEDIT

You can edit the text and attribute definitions before you define a block, using the **Edit** tool from the **Modify > Object > Text** menu. After invoking this tool, AutoCAD LT will prompt you to **Select an annotation object or [Undo/Mode]**. If you select an attribute created using the **Attribute Definition** dialog box, the **Edit Attribute Definition** dialog box is displayed (Figure 16-8).

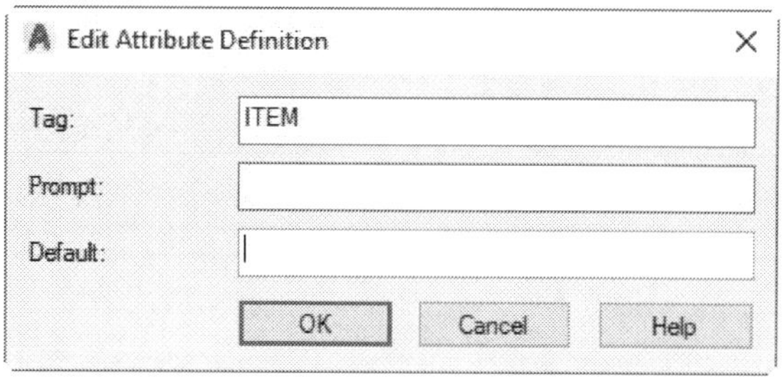

***Figure 16-8** The **Edit Attribute Definition** dialog box*

You can also invoke the **Edit Attribute Definition** dialog box by double-clicking on the attribute definition. You can enter the new values in the respective edit boxes. Once you have entered the changed values, choose the **OK** button in the dialog box. After you exit the dialog box, AutoCAD LT will continue to prompt you to select another text or attribute object (Attribute tag). If you have finished editing and do not want to select another attribute object to edit, press ENTER to exit the command.

Using the PROPERTIES Palette

The **Properties** tool has been already discussed in Chapter 4. It can also be used to edit defined attributes. Select the attribute to be modified and right-click to display a shortcut menu. Next, choose **Properties** from the shortcut menu; the **PROPERTIES** palette will be displayed, refer to Figure 16-9. You will notice that **Attribute Definition** is displayed in the text box located at the top of the palette. Also, you will find that all properties of the selected attribute are displayed under four headings. They are **General**, **3D Visualization**, **Text**, and **Misc**. You can change these values in their corresponding fields. For example, you can modify the color, layer, linetype, thickness, linetype scale, and so on, of the selected attribute under the **General** head. Similarly, you can modify the tag name, prompt, and value of the selected attribute in the **Tag**, **Prompt**, and **Value** fields under the **Text** heading. Under the **Text** head, you can also modify the text style, justification, annotation scale, text height, rotation angle, width factor, and make the angle values of the selected attribute oblique.

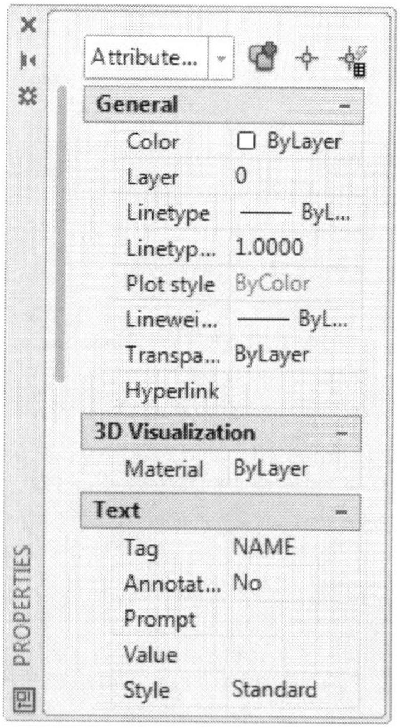

***Figure 16-9** The **PROPERTIES** palette to modify attributes*

You can also determine if you want the attribute text to appear upside down or backwards or not under the **Misc** heading.

Here, you can also modify the attribute modes, which have been already defined. When you select a particular mode, for example **Invisible**, a drop-down list is available in the corresponding field. This list displays two options, **Yes** and **No**. If you select **Yes**, the attribute becomes invisible and if you select **No**, the attribute becomes visible. To select a particular mode, you should choose **Yes** from their corresponding drop-down lists.

INSERTING BLOCKS WITH ATTRIBUTES

The value of the attributes can be specified during block insertion, either at the Command prompt or in the **Edit Attributes** dialog box, if the system variable **ATTDIA** is set to **1**. When you use the **Insert** tool or the **-INSERT** command to insert a block in a drawing (discussed earlier in Chapter 15, Working with Blocks), and after you have specified the insertion point, scale factors, and rotation angle, the **Edit Attributes** dialog box (Figure 16-10) will be displayed.

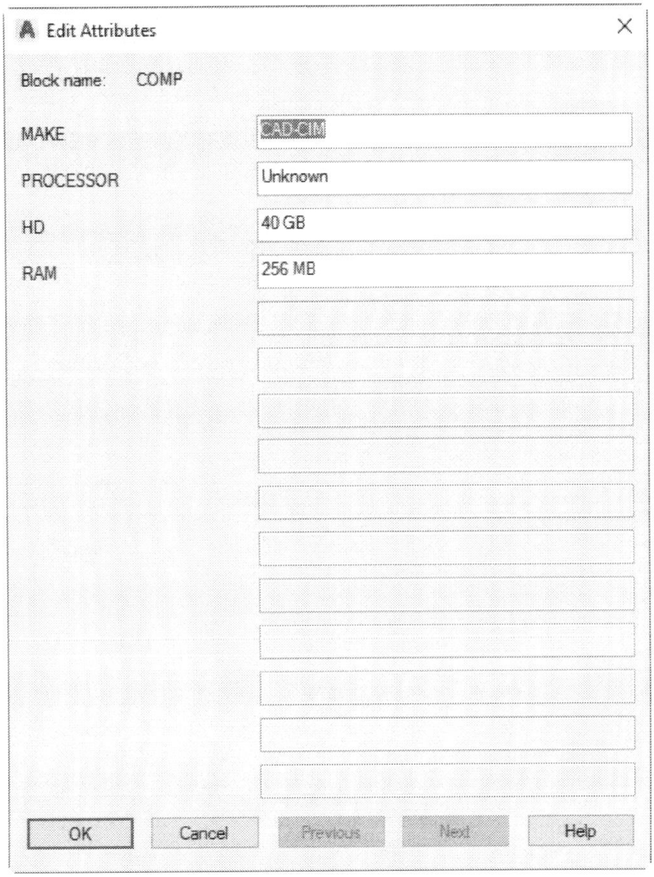

*Figure 16-10 The **Edit Attributes** dialog box*

If the value of the system variable **ATTDIA** is set to **0**, the **Edit Attributes** dialog box will be disabled and the prompts and their default values which you had specified with the attribute definition, are then displayed at the Command prompt after you have specified the insertion point, scale, and rotation angle for the block to be inserted.

In the **Edit Attributes** dialog box, the prompts that were entered while specifying attribute definition in the dialog box are displayed with their default values in the corresponding fields. The **Edit Attributes** dialog box will display 15 attributes this time as compared to 8 attributes in the previous release of AutoCAD LT. If an attribute has been defined with the **Constant** mode, it is not displayed in the dialog box because a constant attribute value cannot be edited. You can enter the attribute values in the fields located next to the attribute prompt. If no new values are specified, the default values are displayed. Eight attribute values are displayed at a time in the dialog box. If there are more attributes, they can be accessed by using the **Next** or **Previous** button. The block name is displayed at the top of the dialog box. After entering the new attribute values, choose the **OK** button. AutoCAD LT will place these attribute values at the specified location.

Tip

*1. It is convenient to use the **Edit Attributes** dialog box because you can view all the attribute values at a glance and can correct them before placing. Therefore, it is a good idea to set the **ATTDIA** value to 1, if not already set by default, before you insert a block with attributes.*

*2. Attributes can also be defined from the Command prompt by setting the system variable **ATTDIA** to 0. Now, when you choose the **Insert** tool, AutoCAD LT does not display the **Edit Attributes** dialog box. Instead, AutoCAD LT prompts you to enter the attribute values for various attributes that have been defined in the block at the pointer input.*

Example 2

In this example, you will insert the block (COMP) that was defined in Example 1. The following is the list of the attribute values for computers:

ITEM	MAKE	PROCESSOR	HD	RAM
Computer	Gateway	486-60	150 MB	16 MB
Computer	Zenith	486-30	100 MB	32 MB
Computer	IBM	386-30	80 MB	8 MB
Computer	Dell	586-60	450 MB	64 MB
Computer	CAD-CIM	Pentium-90	100 Min	32 MB
Computer	CAD-CIM	Unknown	600 MB	Standard

1. Draw the floor plan shown in Figure 16-11 (assume the dimensions).

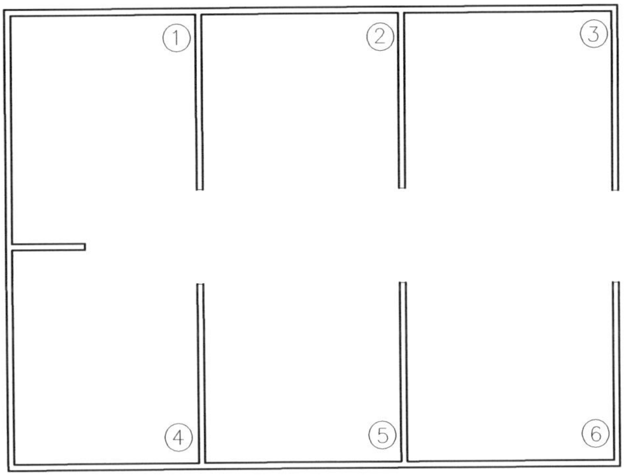

Figure 16-11 Floor plan drawing for Example 2

2. Set the system variable **ATTDIA** to 1. Type INSERT in command line to invoke the **BLOCKS** palette. Enter COMP in the **Filter** area. Now select the block and specify an insertion point on the screen. After you specify the insertion point, the **Edit Attributes** dialog box is displayed. In this dialog box, you can specify the attribute values in respective edit boxes.

3. Similarly, Insert other blocks and define their attribute values, as shown in Figure 16-12.

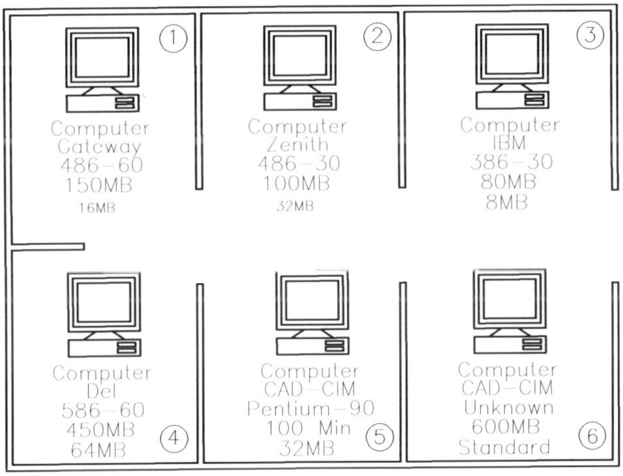

Figure 16-12 The floor plan after inserting blocks and defining their attributes

4. Save the drawing for further use.

MANAGING ATTRIBUTES

Ribbon: Insert > Block Definition > Manage Attributes **Command:** BATTMAN
Menu Bar: Modify > Object > Attribute > Block Attribute Manager

The **Manage Attributes** tool allows you to manage attribute definitions for blocks in the current drawing through the **Block Attribute Manager** dialog box. This dialog box is shown in Figure 16-13. If the attribute that is edited is in the **Constant** mode, then changes in the default value of the attribute in the existing drawing can only be seen upon regeneration. If the mode is other than **Constant**, the changes in the attribute can only be seen for new block insertions.

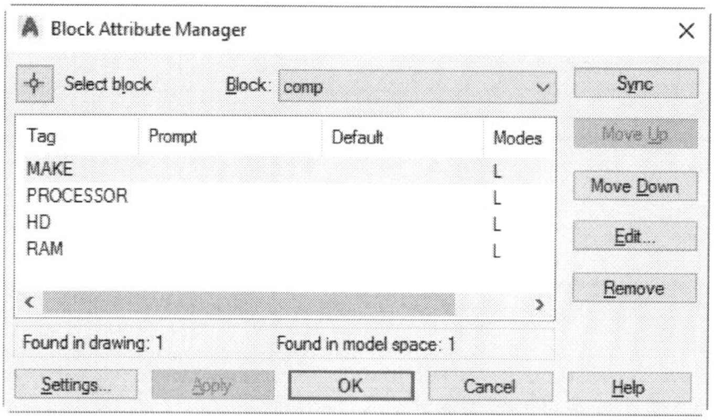

*Figure 16-13 The **Block Attribute Manager** dialog box*

When you invoke this tool, AutoCAD LT displays the number of blocks that exist in the current drawing below the list box in the dialog box. The block can be in the model space or in the layout. The names of the existing blocks in the current drawing are displayed in the **Block** drop-down list. Attributes of the selected block are displayed in the attribute list. By default, the **Tag**, **Prompt**, **Default**, **Modes**, and **Annotative** attribute properties are displayed in the attribute list. You can edit the attribute definitions in blocks, remove attributes from blocks, and change the order in which you were prompted for attribute values while inserting the block.

Select block

This button allows you to select a block from the drawing area whose attributes you want to edit. When you choose the **Select block** button, the dialog box closes temporarily until you select block from the drawing or cancel by pressing ESC. Once you have selected the block, the dialog box is displayed again. The name of the block you have selected is displayed in the **Block** drop-down list. If you modify the attributes of a block and then select a new block before saving the attribute changes, you will be prompted to save the changes before selecting another block through an alert message box (Figure 16-14).

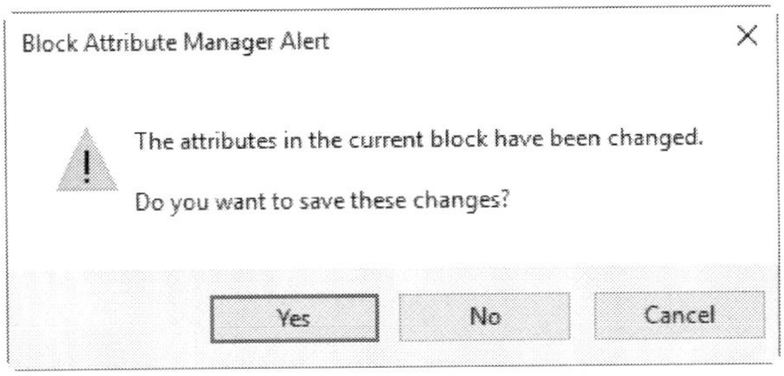

*Figure 16-14 The **Block Attribute Manager Alert** message box*

Block Drop-down List

This drop-down list in the **Block Attribute Manager** dialog box allows you to choose the block whose attributes you want to modify. It lists all the blocks in the current drawing that have attributes.

Sync

This button of the **Block Attribute Manager** dialog box allows you to update all instances of the selected block with the attribute properties currently defined. This does not affect any of the values assigned to attributes in each block when attributes were defined. On choosing this button, you can update attributes in all block references in the current drawing with the changes you made to the block definition. For example, you may have used the **Block Attribute Manager** dialog box to modify attribute properties of several block definitions in your drawing. But you do not want it to automatically update the existing block references when you made the changes. Now, when you are satisfied with the attribute changes you made, you can apply those changes to all blocks in the current drawing by using the **Sync** button.

You can also use the **Synchronize** tool in the **Block Definition** panel to update attribute properties in block references to match their block definition. This tool can also be invoked by entering **ATTSYNC** at the Command prompt or by choosing the **Synchronize Attributes** tool from the **Modify II** toolbar.

Note

*Changing the attribute properties of an existing block does not affect the values assigned to the block. For example, in a block containing an attribute whose **Tag** is Cost and default value is 200, the default value 200 remains unaffected, if the **Tag** is changed to UnitCost.*

Move Up

This button moves the selected attribute tag earlier in the prompt sequence. Now, when you insert the block, the attribute you have just moved up will appear earlier in the prompt sequence. The **Move Up** button will not be available if a constant attribute is selected and when the attribute is at the topmost position in the attribute list.

Move Down

This button moves the selected attribute tag later in the prompt sequence. The **Move Down** button will not be available if a constant attribute is selected and when the attribute is at the bottom position in the attribute list.

Edit

This button allows you to modify the attribute properties. To edit the attribute definition in blocks, select the attribute and then choose **Edit** from the dialog box; the **Edit Attribute** dialog box will be displayed. In the dialog box, **Active Block** displays the name of the block that you have selected and whose properties have to be edited.

Note

To edit an attribute, you can also double-click on the attribute or choose the ***Single*** *tool from* ***Insert > Block > Edit Attribute*** *drop-down. Then, select the attribute to display the* ***Enhanced Attribute Editor*** *dialog box.*

The options in the **Edit Attribute** dialog box are discussed next.

Attribute Tab

The options under the **Attribute** tab of the **Edit Attribute** dialog box are used to modify the mode and data of attributes (refer to Figure 16-15). The options under the **Mode** area can be selected for the block. The **Data** area of the dialog box has three edit boxes: **Tag**, **Prompt**, and **Default**, where you can enter the data to be changed.

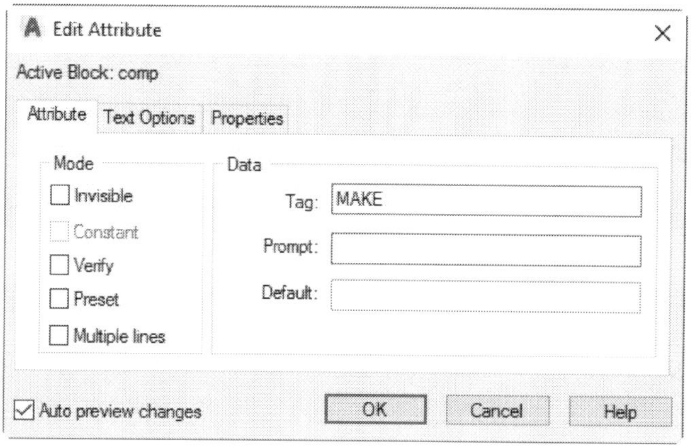

***Figure 16-15** The **Attribute** tab of the **Edit Attribute** dialog box*

Text Options Tab

The options under this tab (Figure 16-16) are used to set the properties that define the way an attribute's text is displayed in the drawing. The options in this tab are discussed next.

Text Style. The options in this drop-down list are used to specify the text style for attribute text. Default values for this text style are assigned to the text properties displayed in this dialog box.

Justification. Options in this drop-down list are used to specify how attribute text is justified.

Height. This edit box is used to specify the height of the attribute text. If the height is defined in the current text style, this edit box is not available.

Rotation. This edit box is used to specify the rotation angle of the attribute text.

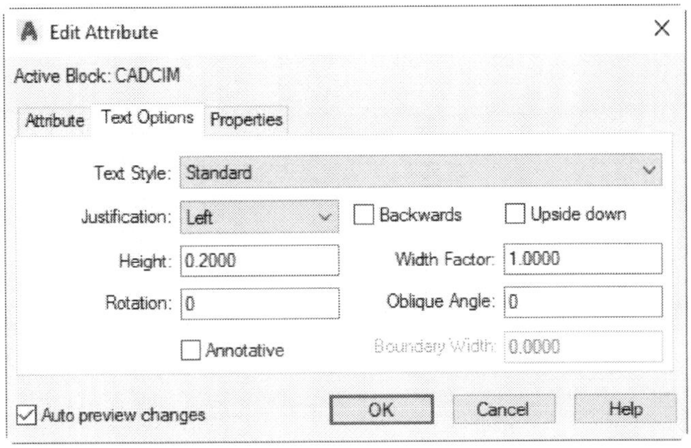

***Figure 16-16** The **Text Options** tab of the **Edit Attribute** dialog box*

Backwards. This check box is used to specify whether or not the text is displayed backwards. Select this box to display the text backwards.

Upside down. This check box is used to specify whether or not the text is displayed upside down. Select this box to display the text upside down.

Width Factor. This edit box is used to set the character spacing for attribute text. Entering a value less than 1.0 condenses the text and a value greater than 1.0 expands it.

Oblique Angle. This edit box is used to specify the angle at which the attribute text is slanted away from its vertical axis.

Annotative. This check box is used to convert the non-annotative attribute to the annotative attribute and vice-versa.

Boundary Width. This edit box sets the width of the boundary that will be displayed while writing the multiline text for the attributes' default value. The value specified here is the relative scale value. If you specify a value less than 1, it will decrease the boundary width. Whereas, if you specify a value more than 1, it will increase the boundary width. Accordingly, the paragraph width for the multiline text will increase or decrease. You can modify the value of the boundary width only when you select the **Multiple lines** check box from the **Mode** area of the **Attribute Definition** dialog box.

Properties Tab

The options under this tab of the **Edit Attribute** dialog box (Figure 16-17) are used to define the layer, color, lineweight, and linetype for the attribute. Also, if the drawing uses plot styles, you can assign a plot style to the attribute. The options of the **Properties** tab are discussed next.

Layer. The layer(s) on which the attribute was defined is displayed in this drop-down list.

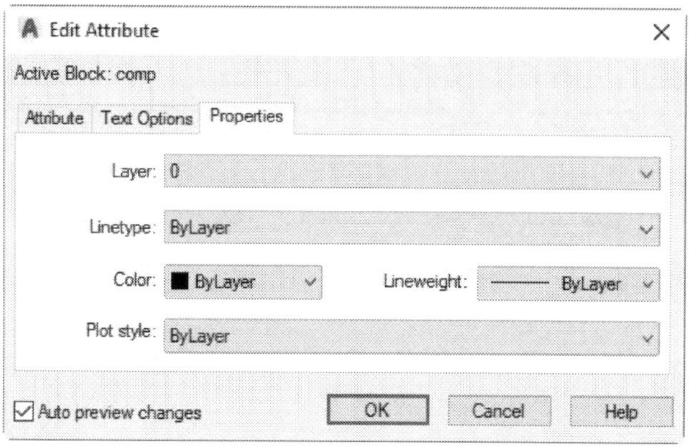

Figure 16-17 The ***Properties*** *tab of the* ***Edit Attribute*** *dialog box*

Linetype. The options in this drop-down list are used to specify the linetype of attribute text.

Color. The options in this drop-down list are used to specify the attribute's text color.

Lineweight. The options in this drop-down list are used to specify the lineweight of attribute text. The changes you made to this option will not come into effect if the **LWDISPLAY** system variable is off.

Plot style. The options in this drop-down list are used to specify the plot style of the attribute. If the current drawing uses color-dependent plot styles, the **Plot style** list in this dialog box will not be available.

Auto preview changes

This check box controls whether or not the drawing area is immediately updated to display any visible changes you make in an attribute. If the **Auto preview changes** check box is selected, changes are immediately visible. If this check box is cleared, changes are not immediately visible.

Tip

The buttons such as ***Move Up****,* ***Move Down****,* ***Edit****,* ***Remove****, and* ***Settings*** *can also be invoked by using the shortcut menu, which appears by right-clicking on the attributes in the attribute list of the* ***Block Attribute Manager*** *dialog box.*

Settings

Choosing this button of the **Block Attribute Manager** opens the **Block Attribute Settings** dialog box (Figure 16-18), where you can customize how attribute information is listed in the **Block Attribute Manager**.

Display in list

You can specify the attribute properties you want to be displayed in the list by selecting the check boxes available in this area of the **Block Attribute Settings** dialog box. This area shows the check boxes of all the properties that are displayed in the attribute list. Only the check boxes of the properties selected are displayed in the attribute list. These properties can be viewed in the attribute list by scrolling it. The **Tag** check box is always selected by default.

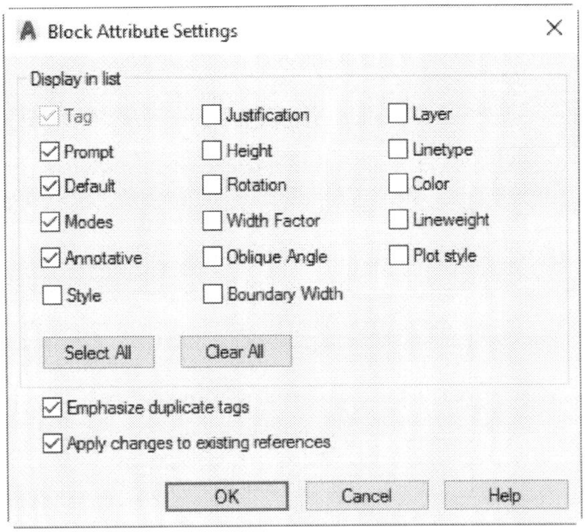

***Figure 16-18** The **Block Attribute Settings** dialog box*

This area of the dialog box has two buttons, **Select All** and **Clear All**, which select and clear all the check boxes, respectively.

Emphasize duplicate tags

This check box turns duplicate tag emphasis on and off. If this check box is selected, duplicate attribute tags are displayed in red type in the attribute list. For example, if a block has PRICE as a tag more than once, the attribute PRICE will be displayed in red in the attribute list. If this check box is cleared, duplicate tags are not emphasized in the attribute list.

Apply changes to existing references

This check box is used to specify whether or not to update all existing instances of the block whose attributes you are modifying. Therefore, if this check box is selected, all instances of the block with the new attribute definitions are updated. If this check box is cleared, only new insertions of the block with the new attribute definitions will be displayed.

Use **Sync** in the **Block Attribute Manager** to apply changes immediately to existing block instances. This temporarily overrides the **Apply changes to existing references** option.

Tip

*If constant attributes or nested attribute blocks are affected by your changes, use the **REGEN** command to update the display of those blocks in the drawing area.*

Remove

This button removes the selected attribute from the block definition. If the **Apply changes to existing references** check box is selected in the **Block Attribute Settings** dialog box before you choose the **Remove** button, the attribute is removed from all instances of the block in the current drawing. If this check box is cleared before choosing the **Remove** button, the attribute is removed only from the attribute list and the blocks that will be inserted henceforth. You can remove attributes from block definitions and from all existing block references in the current drawing. Attributes removed from existing block references do not disappear in the drawing area until you regenerate the drawing using the **REGEN** command. You cannot remove all attributes from the block, at least one attribute should remain. However, if you want to remove all the attributes, you have to redefine the block.

Note that the **Remove** button will not be available for the blocks with only one attribute.

THE ATTEXT COMMAND FOR ATTRIBUTE EXTRACTION

Command: ATTEXT **Menubar:** Tools > Attribute Extraction

The **ATTEXT** command allows you to use the **Attribute Extraction** dialog box (Figure 16-19) for extracting attributes. The information about the **File Format**, **Template File**, and **Output File** must be entered in the dialog box to extract the defined attribute. Also, you must select the blocks whose attribute values you want to extract. If you do not specify a particular block, all the blocks in the drawing are used.

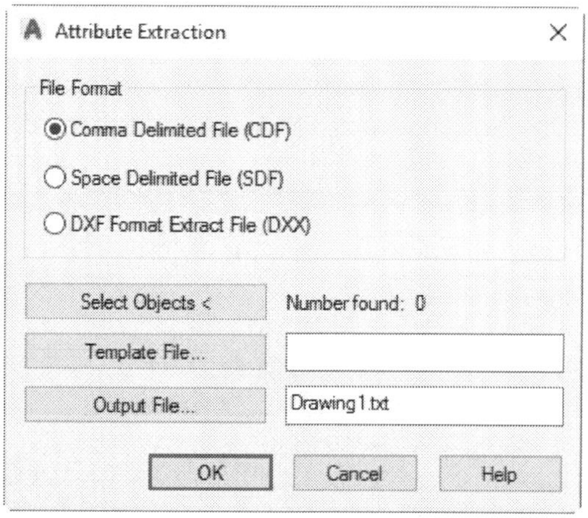

*Figure 16-19 The **Attribute Extraction** dialog box*

File Format Area

This area of the dialog box allows you to select the file format. You can select either of the three radio buttons available in this area as per your requirement. The format selection is determined by the application that you plan to use to process data. Both CDF and SDF formats can be used with the database software. All of these formats are printable.

Comma Delimited File (CDF)

When you select this radio button, the extracted attribute information is displayed in a CDF format. Here, each character field is enclosed in single quote, and the records are separated by a delimiter (comma by default). A CDF file is a text file with the extension *.txt*. Of the three formats available, this is the most cumbersome.

Space Delimited File (SDF)

In SDF format, the records are of fixed width as specified in the template file. The records are separated by spaces and the character fields are not enclosed in single quote. The SDF file is a text file with the extension *.txt*. This file format is the most convenient and easy to use.

DXF Format Extract File (DXX)

If you select this file format, you will notice that the **Template File** button and template name edit box in the **Attribute Extraction** dialog box are not available. This is because extraction in this file format does not require any template. The file created by this option contains only block references, attribute values, and end-of-sequence objects. This is the most complex of the three file formats available and is related to programming. The extension of these files is *.dxx*.

Select Objects

Select the blocks with attributes whose attribute information you want to extract. You can use any object selection method. Once you have selected the blocks that you want to use for attribute extraction, right-click or press ENTER. The **Attribute Extraction** dialog box is redisplayed and the number of objects you have selected are displayed adjacent to **Number found**.

Template File

When you choose the **Template File** button, the **Template File** dialog box is displayed, where you are allowed to select a template file that has been defined already. After you have selected a template file, choose the **Open** button to return to the **Attribute Extraction** dialog box. The name of the selected file is displayed in the **Template File** edit box. The template file is saved with the extension of the file as *.txt*. The following are the fields that you can specify in a template file (the comments given on the right are for explanation only; they must not be entered with the field description):

BL:LEVEL	Nwww000	(Block nesting level)
BL:NAME	Cwww000	(Block name)
BL:X	Nwwwddd	(X coordinate of block insertion point)
BL:Y	Nwwwddd	(Y coordinate of block insertion point)
BL:Z	Nwwwddd	(Z coordinate of block insertion point)
BL:NUMBER	Nwww000	(Block counter)
BL:HANDLE	Cwww000	(Block's handle)
BL:LAYER	Cwww000	(Block insertion layer name)
BL:ORIENT	Nwwwddd	(Block rotation angle)
BL:XSCALE	Nwwwddd	(X scale factor of block)
BL:YSCALE	Nwwwddd	(Y scale factor of block)
BL:ZSCALE	Nwwwddd	(Z scale factor of block)
BL:XEXTRUDE	Nwwwddd	(X component of block's extrusion direction)
BL:YEXTRUDE	Nwwwddd	(Y component of block's extrusion direction)
BL:ZEXTRUDE	Nwwwddd	(Z component of block's extrusion direction)
Attribute tag		(The tag name of the block attribute)

The extract file may contain several fields. For example, the first field might be the item name and the second field might be the price of the item. Each line in the template file specifies one field in the extract file. A line in a template file consists of the name of the field, the width of the field in characters, and its numerical precision (if applicable). For example, consider the case given next.

ITEM N015002
BL:NAME C015000

Where **BL:NAME** --Field name
Blankspaces ---Blank spaces (must not include the tab character)
C ------------------Designates a character field
N ------------------Designates a numerical field
015 ---------------Width of field in characters
002 ---------------Numerical precision

BL:NAME or **ITEM** Indicates the field names; can be of any length.

C Designates a character field; that is, the field contains characters or it starts with characters. If the file contains numbers or starts with numbers, then C will be replaced by N. For example, **N015002**.

015 Designates a field that is fifteen characters long.

002 Designates the numerical precision. In this example, the numerical precision is 2, or two places following the decimal. The decimal point and the two digits following the decimal are **included in the field width**. In the next example, the numerical precision (000) is not applicable because the field does not have any numerical value (the field contains letters only).

After creating a template file, when you choose the **Template File** button, the **Template File** dialog box is displayed where you can browse and select a template file (Figure 16-20).

Note

1. You can put any number of spaces between the field name and the character C or N (ITEM N015002). However, you must not use the tab characters. Any alignment in the fields must be done by inserting spaces after the field name.

2. In the template file, a field name must not appear more than once. The template file name and the output file name must be different.

The template file must contain at least one field with an attribute tag name because the tag names determine which attribute values are to be extracted and from which blocks. If several blocks have different block names but the same attribute tag, AutoCAD LT will extract attribute values from all the selected blocks. For example, if there are two blocks in the drawing with the attribute tag PRICE, then when you extract the attribute values, AutoCAD LT will extract the value from both blocks (if both blocks were selected). To extract the value of an attribute, the tag name must match the field name specified in the template file. AutoCAD LT automatically converts the tag names and the field names to uppercase letters before making a comparison.

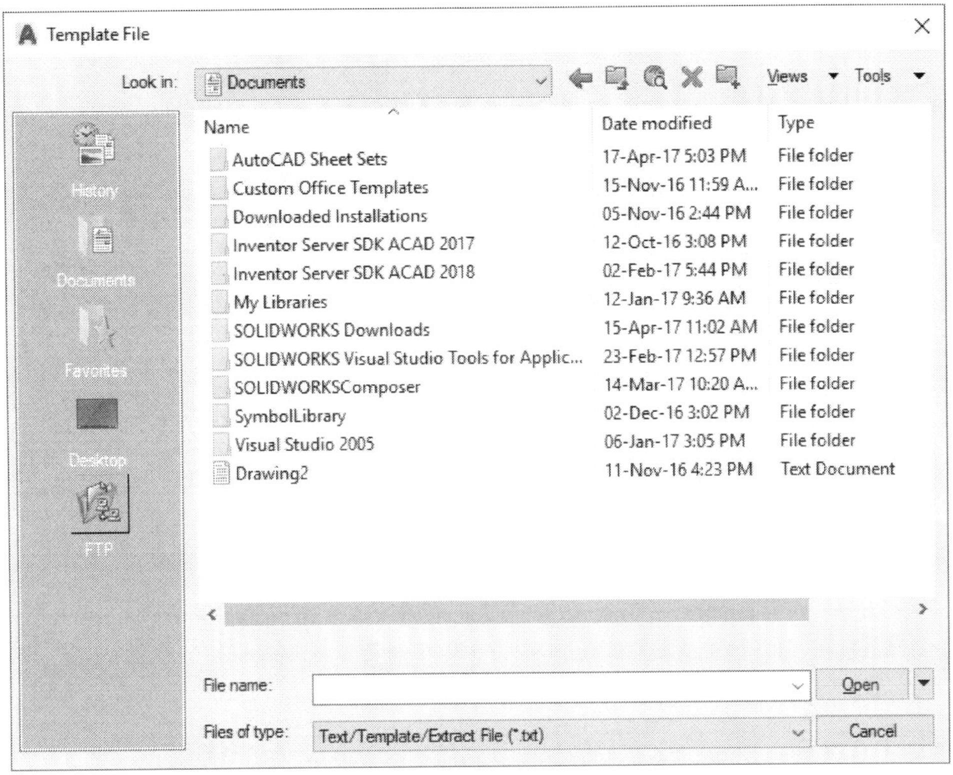

*Figure 16-20 The **Template File** dialog box to select a template file*

Output File

When you choose the **Output File** button, the **Output File** dialog box is displayed. You can select an existing file from the dialog box, if you want the extracted or output file to be saved as an existing file. You can enter a name in the **File name** edit box in the **Output File** dialog box (Figure 16-21) and then choose the **Save** button, if you want to save the output file as a new file. By default, the output file has the same name as the drawing name. For example, a drawing named *Drawing1.dwg* will have an output file by the name *Drawing1.txt* by default. Once a name for the output file is specified, it is displayed in the **Output File** edit box in the **Attribute Extraction** dialog box. You can also enter the file name in this edit box. As discussed earlier, AutoCAD LT appends *.txt* file extension for CDF or SDF files and *.dxx* file extension for DXF files.

Note

*You can also use the **-ATTEXT** command to extract attributes using the Command prompt. Here, you are prompted to specify a file format for the extract information and you can also select specific blocks to extract their attribute information. You can specify a template file using the **Select Template File** dialog box and an extract file using the **Create extract file** dialog box.*

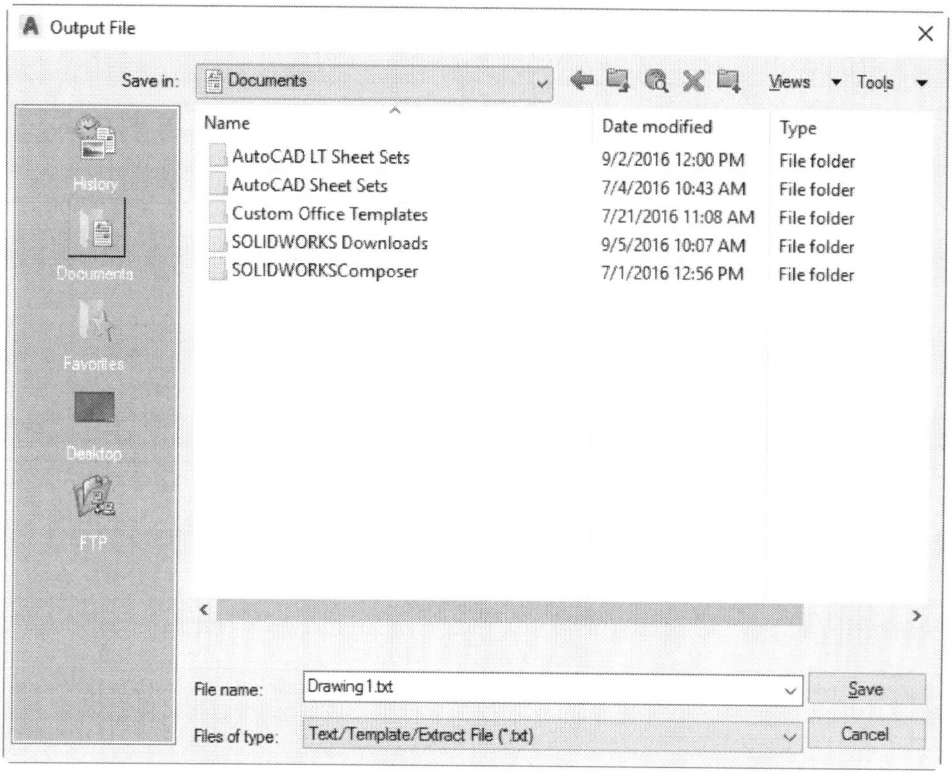

*Figure 16-21 The **Output File** dialog box to save an output file*

CONTROLLING ATTRIBUTE VISIBILITY

Ribbon: Home > Block > Retain Attribute Display drop-down > Retain Attribute Display/ Display All Attributes/Hide All Attributes **Command:** ATTDISP

The options to change the display of attributes are available in **Retain Attribute Display** drop-down of the **Block** panel in the **Home** tab of the **Ribbon**. Generally, the attributes are visible, unless they are defined invisible by using the **Invisible** mode. The invisible attributes are not displayed, but they are the part of the block definition. The tools to toggle the display of attributes are **Retain Attribute Display**, **Display All Attributes**, and **Hide All Attributes** available in the **Retain Attribute Display** drop-down.

The **Retain Attribute Display** tool is used to display the attributes as they were set while creation. For example, the attributes created using the **Invisible** mode will not be displayed.

If you choose the **Hide All Attributes** tool, all attributes will become invisible.

If you choose the **Display All Attributes** tool, all attributes will be displayed in the drawing area.

In Example 2 of this chapter, the RAM attribute was defined with the **Invisible** mode. If you choose the **Retain Attribute Display** tool, the RAM values will not be displayed with the block, refer to Figure 16-22. If you want to make the RAM attribute values visible, choose the **Display All Attributes** tool from the **Block** panel.

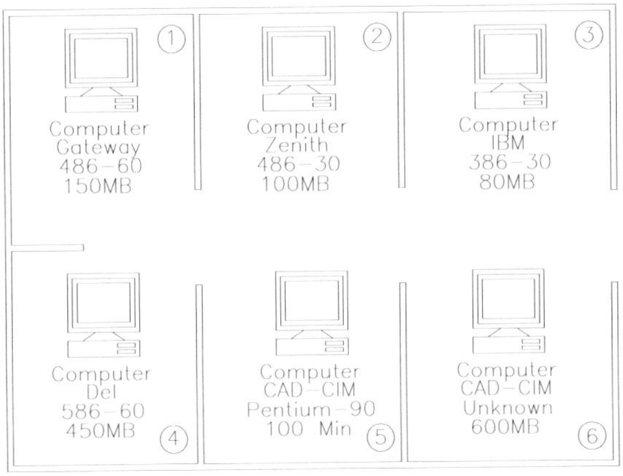

Figure 16-22 *The drawing of Example 2 after choosing the* ***Retain Attribute Display*** *tool*

> **Tip**
> *After you have defined the attribute values and saved them with the block definition, it is recommended to hide all the attributes. By doing this, the drawing is simplified and also the regeneration time is reduced.*

EDITING BLOCK ATTRIBUTES

Ribbon: Insert > Block > Edit Attribute drop-down > Single / Multiple
Command: EATTEDIT **Toolbar:** Modify II > Edit Attribute

The block attributes can be edited by using various methods. These methods are discussed next.

Editing Attributes Using the Enhanced Attribute Editor

Choose the **Single** tool from the **Edit Attribute** drop-down in the **Block** panel to edit the block attribute values. When you invoke this tool, AutoCAD LT prompts you to select the block whose values you want to edit. After selecting the block, the **Enhanced Attribute Editor** dialog box is displayed (Figure 16-23). This dialog box allows you to change the **Attribute**, **Text Options**, and **Properties** of the block attribute. This dialog box can also be invoked by double-clicking on the block or the attribute in the current drawing. The **Enhanced Attribute Editor** dialog box displays all the attributes of the selected block and their properties. You can change the properties of the attribute you want. If an attribute has been defined with the **Constant** mode, it is not displayed in the dialog box because a constant attribute value cannot be edited. The dialog box displays the following tabs.

Attribute Tab

The options under this tab are used to change the value of the attribute. Also, here the **Mode** of the attribute is not displayed. The other attributes of the block such as **Tag**, **Prompt**, and **Value** are displayed, as shown in Figure 16-23.

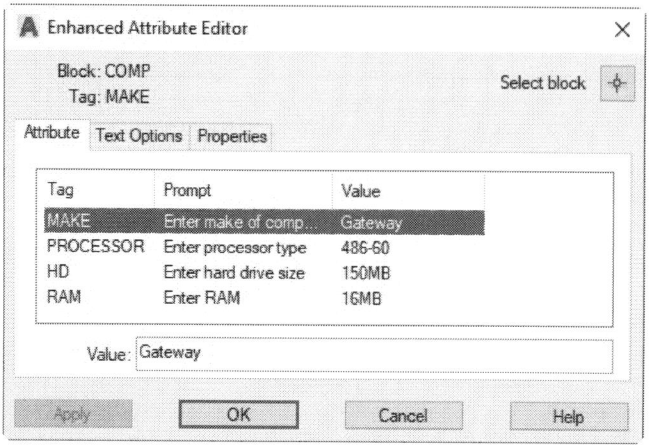

*Figure 16-23 The **Attribute** tab of the **Enhanced Attribute Editor** dialog box*

Text Options Tab

Under this tab, the options related to the text of attributes can be modified. This includes **Text Style**, **Justification**, **Height**, **Rotation**, **Backwards**, **Upside down**, **Width Factor**, **Oblique Angle**, **Annotative**, and **Boundary width**, as shown in Figure 16-24.

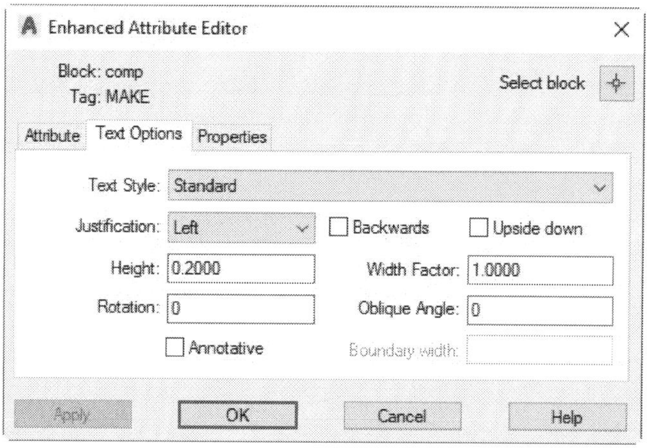

*Figure 16-24 The **Text Options** tab of the **Enhanced Attribute Editor** dialog box*

Properties Tab

This tab is used to edit the properties of attributes such as **Layer**, **Linetype**, **Color**, **Lineweight**, and **Plot style**. Choose the **Properties** tab of **Enhanced Attribute Editor** to display the dialog box, as shown in Figure 16-25.

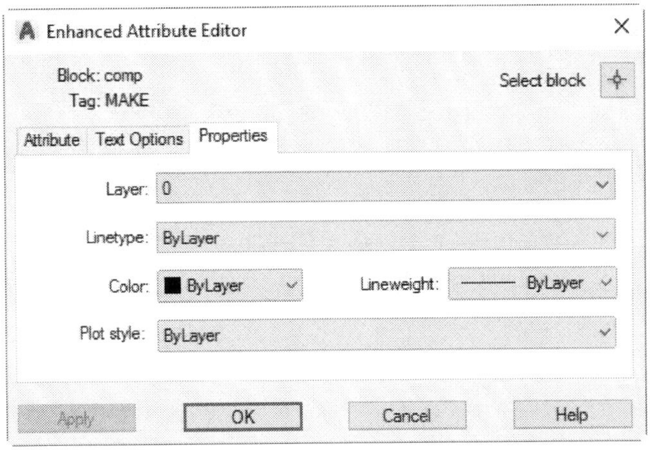

*Figure 16-25 The **Properties** tab of the **Enhanced Attribute Editor** dialog box*

Editing Attributes Using the Edit Attributes Dialog Box

The **ATTEDIT** command is used to edit the block attribute values through the **Edit Attributes** dialog box. Invoke this command; AutoCAD LT prompts you to select the block whose values are to be edited. After selecting the block, the **Edit Attributes** dialog box is displayed (Figure 16-26).

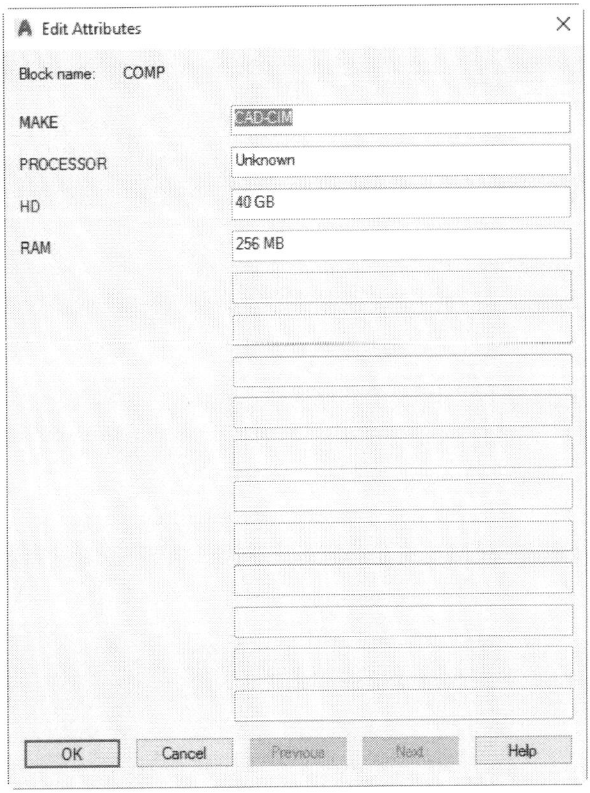

*Figure 16-26 The **Edit Attributes** dialog box*

The dialog box is similar to the **Attribute Definition** dialog box and shows the prompts and the attribute values of the selected block. If an attribute has been defined with the **Constant** mode, it is not displayed in the dialog box because a constant attribute value cannot be edited. To make any changes, select the existing value and enter a new value in the corresponding edit box. After you have made the modifications, choose the **OK** button. The attribute values are updated in the selected block.

If a selected block has no attributes, AutoCAD LT will display the alert message **That block has no editable attributes**. Similarly, if the selected object is not a block, AutoCAD LT again displays the alert message **That object is not a block**.

Note

*You cannot use the **ATTEDIT** command to perform the global editing of attribute values or to modify the position, height, or style of the attribute value. The global editing can be performed using the **-ATTEDIT** command, which is discussed in the next section.*

Example 3

In this example, you will choose the **Single** tool from the **Edit Attribute** drop-down in the **Block** panel to change the attribute of the first computer (150 MB to 2.1 GB), which is located in Room-1.

1. Open the drawing created in Example 2. The drawing has six blocks with attributes. The name of the block is **COMP** and it has five defined attributes, one of them is invisible. Zoom in the drawing so that the first computer is displayed on the screen (Figure 16-27).

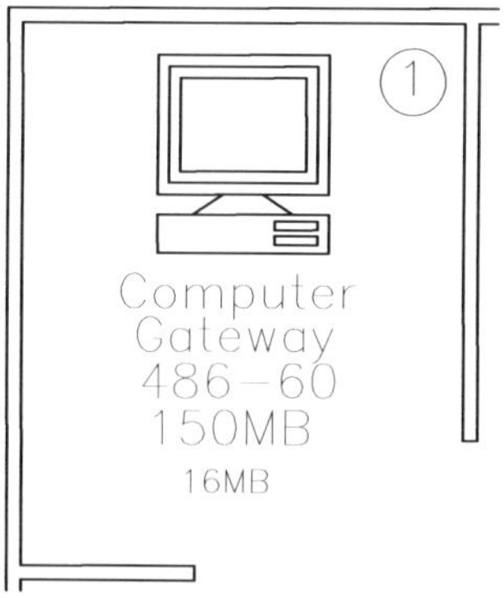

Figure 16-27 *Zoomed view of the first computer*

2. Choose the **Single** tool from **Insert > Block > Edit Attribute** drop-down; you are prompted to select a block. Select the computer located in Room-1. The **Enhanced Attribute Editor** dialog box showing the attribute prompts and values will be displayed, refer to Figure 16-23.

3. Edit the values, choose **Apply**, and then the **OK** button in the dialog box. When you exit the dialog box, the attribute values are updated.

Tip

*You can also replace the attributes with the **FIND** command. This command can be invoked by entering **FIND** at the pointer input. When you invoke this command, the **Find and Replace** dialog box is displayed.*

Global Editing of Attributes

Ribbon: Insert > Block > Edit Attribute drop-down > Multiple **Command:** -ATTEDIT

Choose the **Multiple** tool from the **Edit Attribute** drop-down in the **Block** panel to edit the attribute values independently of the blocks that contain the attribute reference. For example, if there are two blocks, COMPUTER and TABLE, with the attribute value PRICE, you can globally edit this value (PRICE) independently of the block that references these values. You can also edit the attribute values one at a time. For example, you can edit the attribute value (PRICE) of the block TABLE without affecting the value of the other block, COMPUTER. On choosing the **Multiple** tool from the **Edit Attribute** drop-down, AutoCAD LT displays the following prompt:

Edit attributes one at a time? [Yes/No]<Y>: **N**
Performing global editing of attribute values

If you enter **N** at this prompt, it means that you want to do the global editing of the attributes. However, you can restrict the editing of attributes by block names, tag names, attribute values, and visibility of attributes on the screen.

Editing Visible Attributes Only

After you select global editing, AutoCAD LT will display the following prompt:

Edit only attributes visible on screen? [Yes/No] <Y>: **Y**

If you enter **Y** at this prompt, AutoCAD LT will edit only those attributes that are visible and displayed on the screen. The attributes might not have been defined with the **Invisible** mode, but if they are not displayed on the screen, they are not visible for editing. For example, if you zoom in, some of the attributes may not be displayed on the screen. Since the attributes are not displayed on the screen, they are invisible and cannot be selected for editing.

Editing All Attributes

If you enter **N** at the previously mentioned prompt, AutoCAD LT flips from graphics to text screen and displays the message stating: '**Drawing must be regenerated afterwards**'.

Now, AutoCAD LT will edit all attributes even if they are not visible or displayed on the screen. Also, changes that you make in the attribute values are not reflected immediately. Instead, the attribute values are updated and the drawing is regenerated after you are done with the command.

Editing Specific Blocks

Although you have selected global editing, you can confine the editing of attributes to specific blocks by entering the block name at the prompt. For example,

Enter block name specification <*>: **COMP**

When you enter the name of the block, AutoCAD LT will edit the attributes that have the given block (COMP) reference. You can also use the wild-card characters to specify the block names. If you want to edit attributes in all blocks that have attributes defined, press ENTER.

Editing Attributes with Specific Attribute Tag Names

Like blocks, you can confine attribute editing to those attribute values that have the specified tag name. For example, if you want to edit the attribute values that have the tag name MAKE, enter the tag name at the following AutoCAD LT prompt:

Enter attribute tag specification <*>: **MAKE**

When you specify the tag name, AutoCAD LT will not edit attributes that have a different tag name, even if the values being edited are the same. You can also use the wild-card characters to specify the tag names. If you want to edit attributes with any tag name, press ENTER.

Editing Attributes with a Specific Attribute Value

Like blocks and attribute tag names, you can confine attribute editing to a specified attribute value. For example, if you want to edit the attribute values that have the value 100 MB, enter the value at the following AutoCAD LT prompt:

Enter attribute value specification <*>: **100MB**

When you specify the attribute value, AutoCAD LT will not edit attributes that have a different value, even if the tag name and block specification are the same. You can also use the wild-card characters to specify the attribute value. If you want to edit attributes with any value, press ENTER.

Sometimes the value of an attribute is null, and these values are not visible. If you want to select the null values for editing, make sure you have not restricted the global editing to visible attributes. To edit the null attributes, enter \ at the following prompt:

Enter attribute value specification <*>: \

After you enter this information, AutoCAD LT will prompt you to select the attributes. You can select the attributes by selecting individual attributes or by using one of the object selection options (Window, Crossing, or individually).

Select Attributes: *Select the attribute values parallel to the current UCS only.*

After you select the attributes, AutoCAD LT will prompt you to enter the string you want to change and the new string. A string is a sequence of consecutive characters. It could also be a portion of the text. AutoCAD LT will retrieve the attribute information, edit it, and then update the attribute values.

Enter string to change: *Enter the value to be modified.*
Enter new string: *Enter the new value.*

The following is the complete command prompt sequence after choosing the **Multiple** tool. It is assumed that the editing is global and for visible attributes only.

Edit attributes one at a time? [Yes/No] <Y>: **N**
Performing global editing of attribute values.
Edit only attributes visible on screen? [Yes/No] <Y>: **N**
Drawing must be regenerated afterwards.
Enter block name specification <*>: Enter
Enter attribute tag specification <*>: Enter
Enter attribute value specification <*>: Enter
n attributes selected.
Enter string to change: *Enter the value to be modified.*
Enter new string: *Enter the new value.*

Note

AutoCAD LT regenerates the drawing at the end of the command automatically unless the system variable ***REGENMODE*** *is off, which controls automatic regeneration of the drawing.*

If you select an attribute defined with the ***Constant*** *mode using the* ***Multiple*** *tool, the prompt displays 0 found, since attributes with the* ***Constant*** *mode are not editable.*

Example 4

In this example, you will use the drawing from Example 2 to edit the attribute values that are highlighted in the following table. The tag names are given at the top of the table (ITEM, MAKE, PROCESSOR, HD, RAM). The RAM values are invisible in the drawing.

	ITEM	MAKE	PROCESSOR	HD	RAM
COMP	Computer	Gateway	486-60	150 MB	**16 MB**
COMP	Computer	Zenith	486-30	100 MB	**32 MB**
COMP	Computer	IBM	386-30	80 MB	**8 MB**
COMP	Computer	Del	586-60	450 MB	**64 MB**
COMP	Computer	**CAD-CIM**	Pentium-90	100 Min	**32 MB**
COMP	Computer	**CAD-CIM**	**Unknown**	600 MB	Standard

Make the following changes in the highlighted attribute values shown in the above table.

1. Change Unknown to Pentium.
2. Change CAD-CIM to Compaq.
3. Change MB to Meg for all attribute values that have the tag name RAM. (No changes should be made to the values that have the tag name HD.)

The following steps are required to change the attribute value from **Unknown** to **Pentium**.

1. Choose the **Multiple** tool from **Insert > Block > Edit Attribute** drop-down and enter **N** at the next prompt and press ENTER as given below.

   Edit attributes one at a time? [Yes/No] <Y>: **N**
   Performing global editing of attribute values.

2. You need to edit only those attributes that are visible on the screen, so press ENTER at the following prompt:

   Edit only attributes visible on screen? [Yes/No] <Y>: Enter

3. As shown in the table, the attributes belong to a single block, COMP. A drawing may have more blocks. To confine the attribute editing to the COMP block only, enter the name of the block (COMP) at the next prompt.

   Enter block name specification <*>: **COMP** Enter

4. At the next two prompts, enter the attribute tag name and the attribute value specification. When you enter these two values, only those attributes that have the specified tag name and attribute value will be edited.

   Enter attribute tag specification<*>: **Processor** Enter
   Enter attribute value specification<*>: **Unknown** Enter

   On entering these values, AutoCAD LT will prompt you to select attributes. Use any object selection option to select all the blocks. AutoCAD LT will search for the attributes that satisfy the given criteria (attributes belong to the block COMP, the attributes have the tag name Processor, and the attribute value is Unknown). Once AutoCAD LT locates such attributes, they are highlighted.

5. At the next two prompts, enter the string that you want to change, and then enter the new string.

   Enter string to change: **Unknown** Enter
   Enter new string: **Pentium** Enter

6. The following is the Command prompt sequence to change the make of the computer from **CAD-CIM** to **Compaq**:

   *Choose the **Multiple** tool.*
   Edit attributes one at a time? [Yes/No] <Y>: **N** Enter
   Performing global editing of attribute values.
   Edit only attributes visible on screen? [Yes/No] <Y>: Enter
   Enter block name specification <*>: **COMP** Enter
   Enter attribute tag specification <*>: **MAKE** Enter
   Enter attribute value specification <*>: Enter
   Select Attributes: *Use any selection method to select the attributes.*
   n attributes selected.
   Select Attributes: Enter

Enter string to change: **CAD-CIM**
Enter new string: **Compaq**

7. The following is the Command prompt sequence to change **MB** to **Meg**:

*Choose the **Multiple** tool.*
Edit attributes one at a time? [Yes/No] <Y>: **N**
Performing global editing of attribute values.
At the next prompt, you must enter **N** because the attributes you want to edit (tag name, RAM) are not visible on the screen.

Edit only attributes visible on screen? [Yes/No] <Y>: **N**
Drawing must be regenerated afterwards.
Enter block name specification <*>: **COMP**

At the next prompt, about the tag specification, you must specify the tag name because the text string MB also appears in the hard drive size (tag name, HD). If you do not enter the tag name, AutoCAD LT will change all MB attribute values to Meg.

Enter attribute tag specification <*>: **RAM**
Enter attribute value specification <*>:
n Attributes selected
Enter string to change: **MB**
Enter new string: **Meg**

8. Choose the **Display All Attributes** tool from the **Block** panel to display the invisible attributes.

Note

*You can also use the **-ATTEDIT** command to edit the attribute values individually. Attribute value, position, height, angle, style, layer, and color can be changed using this command.*

Example 5

In this example, you will use the drawing of Example 4 to edit attributes individually (Figure 16-28). Make the following changes in the attribute values:

a. Change the attribute value 100 Min to 100 MB.

b. Change the height of all attributes with the tag name RAM to 0.075 units.

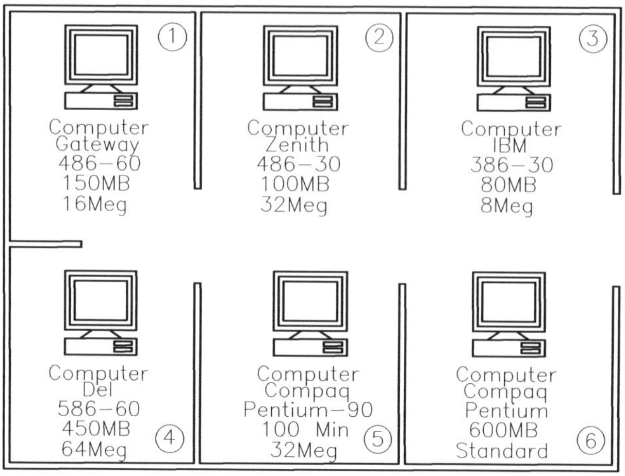

***Figure 16-28** The attribute values to be changed individually*

1. Load the drawing that you have saved in Example 4.

2. Double-click on the **100 Min** attribute value in the drawing; the **Enhanced Attribute Editor** dialog box is displayed.

3. In the **Value** edit box, change **100 Min** to **100 MB**. Choose **Apply** and then choose **OK**.

4. To change the height of attribute text, double-click on the value of **RAM** in the drawing; the **Enhanced Attribute Editor** dialog box is displayed.

5. In the dialog box, choose the **Text Options** tab and change the height to **0.075** in the **Height** edit box.

6. Choose **Apply** and then **OK**.

7. Change the height of the other attribute values using the process followed in Steps 5 and 6.

In-place Editing of Blocks with Attributes

Ribbon: Insert > Reference > Edit Reference **Command:** REFEDIT
Toolbar: Refedit > Edit Reference In-Place

The **Edit Reference** tool has already been discussed in Chapter 15, Working with Blocks. This tool can also be used for in-place editing of blocks with attributes. After invoking the **Edit Reference** tool, select a block with attributes that you want to edit. The **Reference Edit** dialog box is displayed with the name of the block in the **Reference name** list box. To be able to edit attributes, you should select the **Display attribute definitions for editing** check box in the **Settings** tab of the dialog box and then choose **OK** to exit. When you select this check box, it displays the attributes and makes them available for editing. At the next prompt, **Select nested objects**, you can select any part of the block with attributes that need to be edited and press ENTER. If you want to edit some other objects that are part of the block, you can select them too. All the selected objects become a part of the working set. You will notice that when you select the block with attributes, the tags replace the assigned attribute values and objects in the drawing that were not selected appear faded.

You can now edit the block geometry or edit only the attributes. To edit an attribute, double-click on it; the respective **Edit Attribute Definition** dialog box will be displayed, refer to Figure 16-29. Using the options in this dialog box, you can change the value of the attribute.

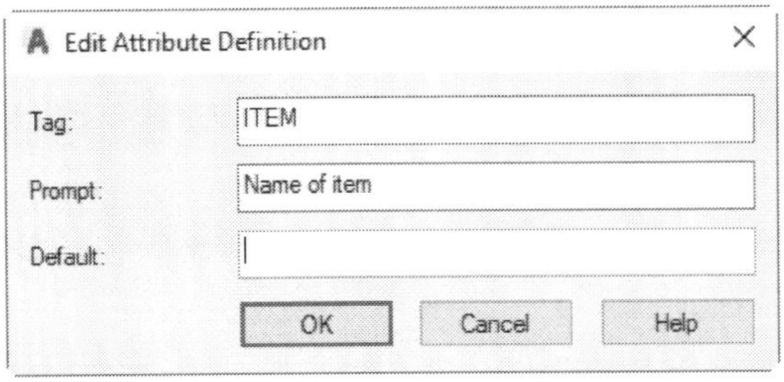

*Figure 16-29 The **Edit Attribute Definition** dialog box*

INSERTING TEXT FILES IN THE DRAWING

Ribbon: Annotate > Text > Text drop-down > Multiline Text **Command:** MTEXT
Menu Bar: Draw > Text > Multiline Text

You can insert a text file in a drawing by using the **Import Text** option that is displayed when you right-click in the text window of the **Text Editor**. The **Text Editor** is displayed on using the **Multiline Text** tool.

On invoking the **Multiline Text** tool, AutoCAD LT prompts you to enter the insertion point and other corner of the paragraph text box, within which the text file will be placed. After you specify these points, the **Text Editor** is displayed. To insert the text file *TEST.txt*, right-click in the text window of the **Text Editor** to display the shortcut menu. In this shortcut menu, choose **Import Text**. AutoCAD LT displays the **Select File** dialog box.

In the **Select File** dialog box, you can select the text file **TEST** from the list box and then choose the **Open** button. The imported text is displayed in the text window of the **Text Editor** (Figure 16-30). Note that only the ASCII files are properly interpreted. Now, click on the screen, outside the text editor to get the imported text in the selected area on the screen (Figure 16-31).

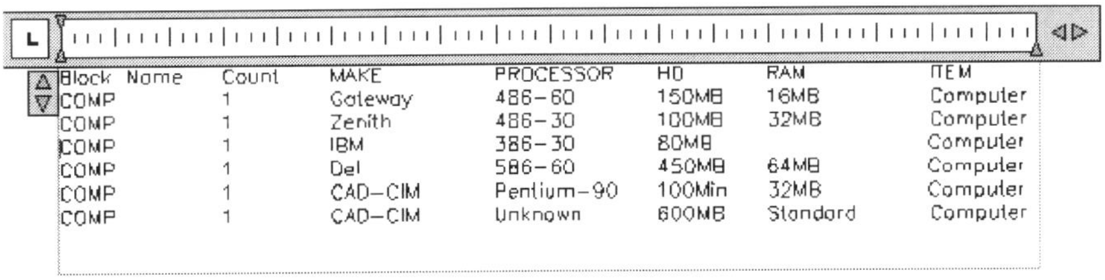

*Figure 16-30 The **Text Editor** displaying the imported text*

You can also use the **Multiline Text** tool to change the text style, height, direction, width, rotation, line spacing, and attachment.

Block Name	Count	MAKE	PROCESSOR	HD	RAM	ITEM
COMP	1	Gateway	486-60	150MB	16MB	Computer
COMP	1	Zenith	486-30	100MB	32MB	Computer
COMP	1	IBM	386-30	80MB8MB		Computer
COMP	1	Del	586-60	450MB	64MB	Computer
COMP	1	CAD-CIM	Pentium-90	100Min	32MB	Computer
COMP	1	CAD-CIM	Unknown	600MB	Standard	Computer

Figure 16-31 *The imported text file on the screen*

Self-Evaluation Test

Answer the following questions and then compare them to those given at the end of this chapter:

1. The entry in the **Value** edit box of the **Attribute Definition** dialog box defines the __________ of the specified attribute.

2. If you have selected the **Align** option from the **Justification** drop-down list in the **Text Options** tab of the **Enhanced Attribute Editor** dialog box, the **Height** and **Rotation** edit boxes will be __________.

3. You can use the __________ tool of the **Edit Attribute** drop-down in the __________ panel of the **Insert** tab to edit attribute definitions.

4. If the value of the **ATTDIA** variable is __________, it disables the **Edit Attributes** dialog box.

5. In the __________ file, the records are not separated by a comma and the character fields are not enclosed with a single quote.

6. The __________ tool is used to redefine an existing block with attributes in a drawing.

7. Like the **Constant** attribute, the **Preset** attribute cannot be edited. (T/F)

8. In case of tag names, any lowercase letter is automatically converted into an uppercase letter. (T/F)

9. You can choose the **Single** tool from the **Edit Attribute** drop-down in the **Block** panel to modify the justification, height, or style of an attribute value. (T/F)

10. If you select the **Display All Attribute** option in the **Attribute Display** drop-down list of the **Block** panel, then even the attributes defined with the **Invisible** mode are displayed. (T/F)

Review Questions

Answer the following questions:

1. Not selecting any of the check boxes in the **Mode** area of the **Attribute Definition** dialog box displays all the prompts at the Command prompt and the values will be visible on the screen. This mode is also referred to as

   (a) Formal (b) Normal
   (c) Abnormal (d) None of these

2. Which of the following system variables when set to 0 will suppress the display of prompts for the new values?

   (a) **ATTDIA** (b) **ATTREQ**
   (c) **ATTMODE** (d) **ATTDEF**

3. Which of the following tools is used to invoke the **Block Attribute Manager** dialog box?

   (a) **Define Attributes** (b) **Manage Attributes**
   (c) **Block Editor** (d) **Edit Reference**

4. Which of the following tools is used to update the selected block after making changes in the block?

   (a) **Create Block** (b) **Edit Reference**
   (c) **Synchronize** (d) **Edit Attribute**

5. Which of the following characters starts with character string for leading blank space in the string to be changed?

   (a) space ( ) (b) backslash (\)
   (c) asterisk (*) (d) colon (:)

6. You can insert the text file in the drawing by choosing the __________ button in the **In-Place Text Editor** dialog box displayed while using the **Multi Line Text** tool.

7. The function of the **Preset** option is ______________.

8. If you select the __________ check box in the **Mode** area of the **Attribute Definition** dialog box, the **Prompt** edit box will be disabled.

9. You should select the __________ check box in the **Attribute Definition** dialog box to automatically place the subsequent attribute text just below the previously defined attribute.

10. The attribute extract file is saved as a __________ file.

11. If you do not enter anything in the **Prompt** edit box, the entry made in the **Tag** edit box will be displayed as prompt. (T/F)

12. You can also use the **Find and Replace** dialog box to modify attribute values. (T/F)

13. When using the **Edit Reference** tool for in-place editing of attributes, the existing blocks in a drawing do not get updated. Only the subsequent insertions display the modified block. (T/F)

14. You can use ? and * in the string value. When these characters are used in string value, AutoCAD LT does not interpret them as wild-card characters. (T/F)

15. The template file name and the output file name can be the same. (T/F)

Exercise 1 — Attribute Definition

In this exercise, you will define the following attributes for a resistor and then create a block using the **Create Block** tool. The name of the block is **RESIS**. The distance between the dotted lines is 0.5 units.

Mode	**Tag name**	**Prompt**	**Default value**
Verify	RNAME	Enter name	RX
Verify	RVALUE	Enter resistance	XX
Verify, Invisible	RPRICE	Enter price	00

1. Draw the resistor, as shown in Figure 16-32.

2. Choose the **Define Attributes** tool to invoke the **Attribute Definition** dialog box.

3. Define the attributes, as shown in the preceding table and position the attribute text. Refer to Figure 16-32.

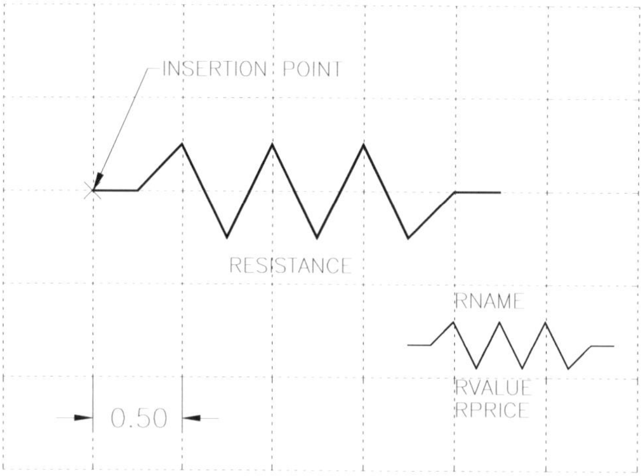

***Figure 16-32** Drawing of a resistor for Exercise 1*

4. Use the **BLOCK** command to create a block. The name of the block is **RESIS**, and the insertion point of the block is at the left end of the resistor. When you select the objects for the block, make sure you also select the attributes.

Exercise 2

In this exercise, you will use the **Insert** tool to insert the block that was defined in Exercise 1 (RESIS). The following table shows the attribute values for the resistances in the electric circuit:

RNAME	RVALUE	RPRICE
R1	35	.32
R2	27	.25
R3	52	.40
R4	8	.21
RX	10	.21

1. Draw the electric circuit diagram, as shown in Figure 16-33 (assume the dimensions).

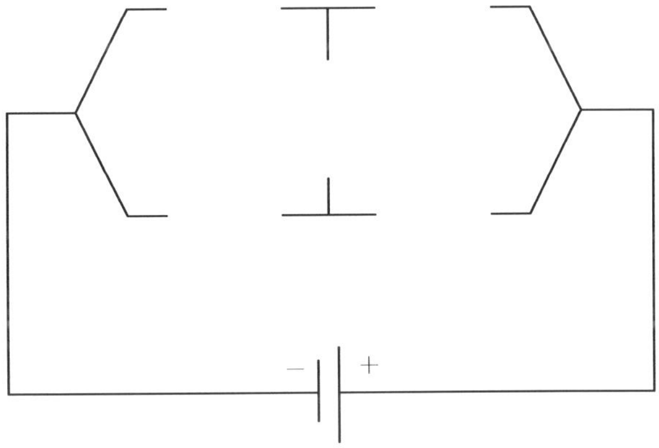

Figure 16-33 *Electric circuit diagram without resistors for Exercise 2*

2. Set the system variable **ATTDIA** to **1**. Use the **Insert** tool to insert the blocks and define the attribute values in the **Attribute Definition** dialog box.

3. Repeat the **Insert** tool to insert other blocks and define their attribute values as given in the table. Save the drawing as *attexr2.dwg* (Figure 16-34).

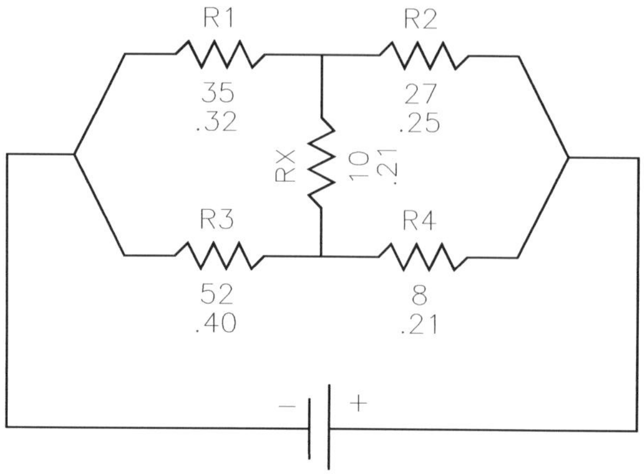

Figure 16-34 Electric circuit diagram with resistors for Exercise 2

Exercise 3 — *Edit Attribute*

In this exercise, you will use the **EATTEDIT** command to change the attributes of the resistances that are highlighted in the following table. You will also extract the attribute values and insert the text file in the drawing.

1. Load the drawing **ATTEXR2** that was created in Exercise 2. The drawing has five resistances with attributes. The name of the block is RESIS and it has three defined attributes, one of them is invisible.

2. Double click on the block to edit the values that are highlighted in the following table.

RESIS	R1	**40**	.32
RESIS	R2	**29**	.25
RESIS	R3	52	**.45**
RESIS	R4	8	**.25**
RESIS	**R5**	10	.21

3. Extract the attribute values and write values to a text file.

4. Use the **Multiline Text** tool to insert the text file in the drawing.

Exercise 4 — *Attribute Data Extraction*

In this exercise, you will create the blocks with required attributes. Next, draw the circuit diagram shown in Figure 16-35 and then extract the attributes to create the Bill of Materials.

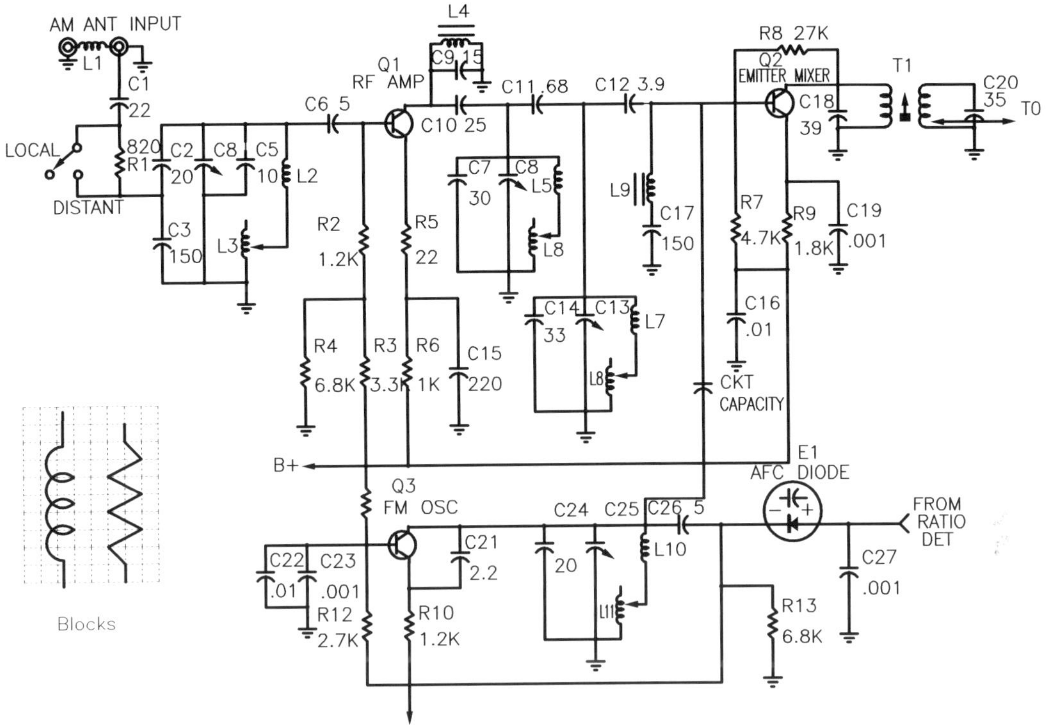

Blocks

Figure 16-35 Drawing of the circuit diagram for Exercise 4

Answers to Self-Evaluation Test

1. default value, **2**. disabled, **3**. **Single**, **Block**, **4**. 0, **5**. Space Delimited, **6**. **Edit Reference**, **7**. F, **8**. T, **9**. T, **10**. T

Chapter 17

Understanding External References

Learning Objectives

After completing this chapter, you will be able to:

- *Understand external references and their applications*
- *Understand dependent symbols*
- *Use the External References Palette*
- *Use the Attach, Unload, Reload, Detach, and Bind options*
- *Edit the path of an xref*
- *Understand the difference between the Overlay and Attachment options*
- *Work with Underlays*
- *Attach Files to a Drawing*
- *Use the DesignCenter to attach a drawing as an xref*
- *Use the Bind tool to add dependent symbols*
- *Use the Clip tool to clip xref drawings*
- *Use the Edit Reference tool for in-place editing*

Key Terms

- *XRef*
- *Attach*
- *Reload*
- *Detach*
- *Unload*
- *Bind*
- *Overlay*
- *Underlay*
- *Frame*
- *Clip*

EXTERNAL REFERENCES

The external reference feature allows you to reference an external drawing without making that drawing a permanent part of the existing drawing. For example, assume that we have an assembly drawing ASSEM1 that consists of two parts, SHAFT and BEARING. The SHAFT and BEARING are separate drawings created by two CAD operators or provided by two different vendors. We want to create an assembly drawing from these two parts. One way to create an assembly drawing is to insert these two drawings as blocks by using the **Insert** tool in the **Block** panel. Now assume that the design of BEARING has changed due to customer or product requirements. To update the assembly drawing, you have to make sure that you insert the BEARING drawing after the changes have been made. If you forget to update the assembly drawing, then the assembly drawing will not reflect the changes made in the piece part drawing. In the production environment, this could have serious consequences.

You can solve this problem by using the **external reference** facility which lets you link the piece part drawings with the assembly drawing. If the xref drawings (piece part) get updated, the changes are automatically reflected in the assembly drawing. This way, the assembly drawing stays updated, no matter when the changes were made in the piece part drawings. There is no limit to the number of drawings that you can reference. You can also have **nested references**. For example, the piece part drawing BEARING could be referenced in the SHAFT drawing, and the SHAFT drawing could be referenced in the assembly drawing ASSEM1. When you open or plot the assembly drawing, AutoCAD LT automatically loads the referenced drawing SHAFT and the nested drawing BEARING. While using External References, several people working on the same project can reference the same drawing and all the changes made are displayed everywhere the particular drawing is being used.

If you use the **Insert** tool to insert the piece parts, the piece parts become a permanent part of the drawing, and therefore, the drawing file size increases. However, if you use the external reference feature to link the drawings, the piece part drawings are not saved with the assembly drawing. AutoCAD LT only saves the reference information with the assembly drawing; therefore, the size of the drawing is minimized. Like blocks, the xref drawings can be scaled, rotated, or positioned at any desired location, but they cannot be exploded. You can also use only a part of the Xref by making clipped boundary of Xrefs.

Tip

External referenced drawings are useful for creating parts or subassemblies and then putting them together in one drawing to create the main assembly. You can also use the overlays for laying out the content of a drawing with multiple views before plotting.

DEPENDENT SYMBOLS

When you use the **Insert** tool to insert a drawing, the information about the named objects is lost, if names are duplicated. However, if they are unique, they are imported. The named objects are entries such as blocks, text styles and layers. For example, if the assembly drawing has a layer Hidden of green color and HIDDEN linetype and the piece part Bearing has also a layer Hidden of blue color and HIDDEN2 linetype, the values set in the assembly drawing will override the values of the inserted drawing when the Bearing drawing is inserted in the assembly drawing (Figure 17-1). As a result, in the assembly drawing, the layer Hidden will retain green color and

HIDDEN linetype, ignoring the layer settings of the inserted drawing. Only those layers that have the same names are affected. The remaining layers that have different layer names are added to the current drawing.

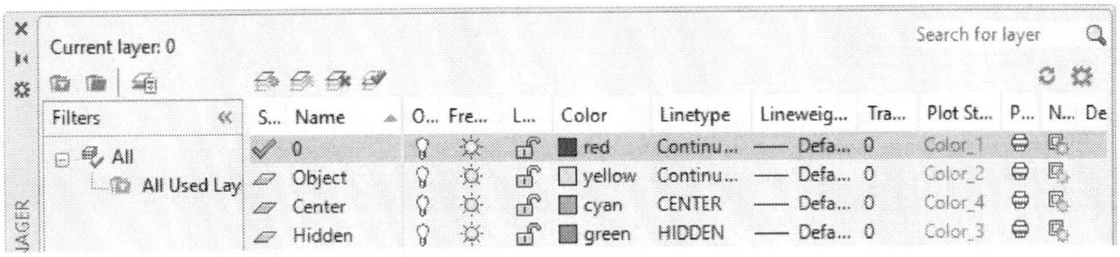

Figure 17-1 Partial view of the layer settings of the current drawing in the ***LAYER PROPERTIES MANAGER*** *dialog box*

In the xref drawings, the information about the named objects is not lost because AutoCAD LT will create additional named objects such as specified layer settings, as shown in Figure 17-2. For xref drawings, these named objects become dependent symbols (features such as layers, linetypes, object color, text style, and so on).

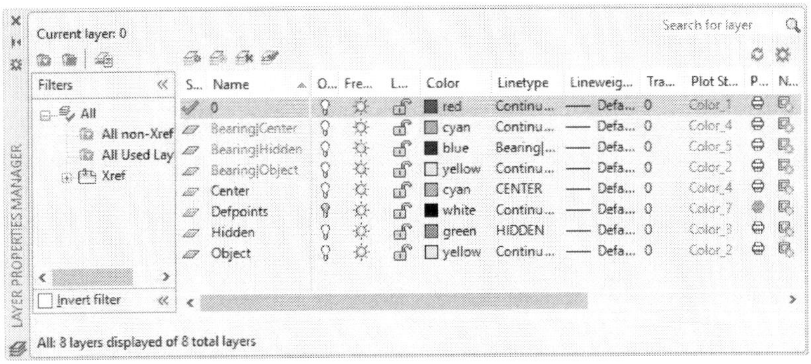

Figure 17-2 *Xref creates additional layers*

The layer Hidden of the xref drawing (Bearing) is apspended with the name of the xref drawing Bearing, and the two are separated by the vertical bar symbol (|). The names of these layers appear in light gray color in the **LAYER PROPERTIES MANAGER** or **Layer** drop-down list of the **Layers** panel in the **Home** tab. These layers can neither be selected nor be made current. The layer name Border changes to Bearing|Border. Similarly, CEN is renamed as Bearing|CEN and OBJ is renamed as Bearing|OBJ (Figure 17-2). The information added to the current drawing is not permanent. It is added only when the xref drawing is loaded. If you detach the xref drawing, the dependent symbols are automatically erased from the current drawing.

When you xref a drawing, AutoCAD LT does not let you reference the symbols directly. For example, you cannot make the dependent layer, Bearing|Border, as current layer. Therefore, you cannot add any objects to that layer. However, you can change the color, linetype, lineweight, plotstyle, or visibility (on/off, freeze/thaw) of the layer in the current drawing.

Note

You cannot make the xref-dependent layers current in a drawing. When the xref drawing is bound to the current drawing by using the ***Xbind*** *tool, only then you can make the xref-dependent layers a permanent part of the current drawing and use them. The* ***Xbind*** *tool will be discussed later in this chapter.*

MANAGING EXTERNAL REFERENCES IN A DRAWING

Ribbon: View > Palettes > External References Palette
Menu Bar: Insert > External References **Command:** XREF

When you choose the **External References Palette** button from the **Palettes** panel (Figure 17-3), AutoCAD LT displays the **EXTERNAL REFERENCES** palette (Figure 17-4).

Figure 17-3 *The* ***Palettes*** *panel*

The **EXTERNAL REFERENCES** palette displays the status of each Xref in the current drawing and the relation between the various Xrefs. It allows you to attach a new xref, detach, unload, load an existing one, change an attachment to an overlay, or an overlay to an attachment. You can also open a reference drawing for editing from this palette. Additionally, it allows you to edit an xref's path and bind the xref definition to the drawing.

Apart from the methods mentioned in the command box, you can also invoke the **EXTERNAL REFERENCES** palette by selecting an Xref in the current drawing and then right-clicking in the drawing area to display a shortcut menu. Next, choose **External References** from the shortcut menu; the **EXTERNAL REFERENCES** palette will be displayed. The upper right corner of the palette has two buttons: **List View** and **Tree View**.

Figure 17-4 *The* ***EXTERNAL REFERENCES*** *palette*

List View

Choosing the **List View** button displays the xrefs present in the drawing in alphabetical order. This is the default view. The list view displays information about xrefs in the current drawing under the following headings:

Reference Name

This column lists the name of all the existing references in the current drawing.

Status

This column lists the current status of each xref in the drawing. It lists whether an xref is loaded, unloaded, unreferenced, not found, orphaned, unresolved, or marked to be reloaded. A loaded xref implies that the xref is attached to the current drawing. You can then unload it and then reload it using the options in the dialog box (this will be discussed later). An xref selected to be unloaded or reloaded displays **Unload** and **Reload**, respectively, under the **Status** column. If the xref has nested references that cannot be found, the status is **Unreferenced**, and if the parent of the nested reference gets unloaded, or cannot be found, its status is described as **Orphaned**. An unreferenced xref will not be displayed. If the xref is not found in the search paths defined, its status is **Not Found**. A missing xref or one that cannot be found is **Unresolved**.

Size

The file size of each xref is listed here.

Type

This column lists whether the xref is an attachment or overlay.

Date

This column lists the date on which the xref drawing was last saved.

Saved Path

This column lists the path of the xref, that is, the route taken to locate the particular referenced drawing.

Choose any of these headings; AutoCAD LT sorts and lists the Xrefs in the current drawing according to that particular title. For example, on choosing **Reference Name**, the xrefs are sorted and listed as per the name. The column widths can be increased or decreased as per your requirements. When you place your cursor at the edge of a column title button, the cursor changes into a horizontal resizing cursor. Now, press the pick button of your mouse and drag the column edge to increase or decrease its width. After you increase the column widths, it is possible that the width of the columns extend beyond the list box width. In such a case, a horizontal scroll bar appears at the bottom of the list box. You can use the scroll bar to view the columns that extend beyond the width of the list box.

On choosing the **Tree View** button available in the right side of the **File References** title bar, the xrefs are displayed in a hierarchical tree view in the **EXTERNAL REFERENCES** palette. The palette displays information on nested xrefs and their relationship with one another. Xrefs are indicated by an icon of a paper with a paper clip. This icon appears with a cross mark when the xref gets unloaded, and if there is a missing xref, the"!" sign appears. Similarly, the upward arrow indicates that the xref was reloaded and the arrow pointing downward indicates that the xref is unloaded. You can also choose **List View** and **Tree View** by pressing the F3 and F4 keys, respectively.

Attaching an Xref Drawing (Attach Option)

The **Attach** button is available at the upper left corner of the **EXTERNAL REFERENCES** palette. If you choose the down arrow on this button, a flyout will be displayed. Choose the **Attach DWG** option from the flyout to attach an xref drawing to the current drawing. This option can also be invoked by right-clicking on the **File References** area. The following examples illustrate the process of attaching an xref to the current drawing. In this example, it is assumed that there are two drawings, SHAFT and BEARING. SHAFT is the current drawing that is loaded on the screen (Figure 17-5) and the BEARING drawing is saved on the disk. If you want to xref the BEARING drawing in the SHAFT drawing, you need to follow the steps given below:

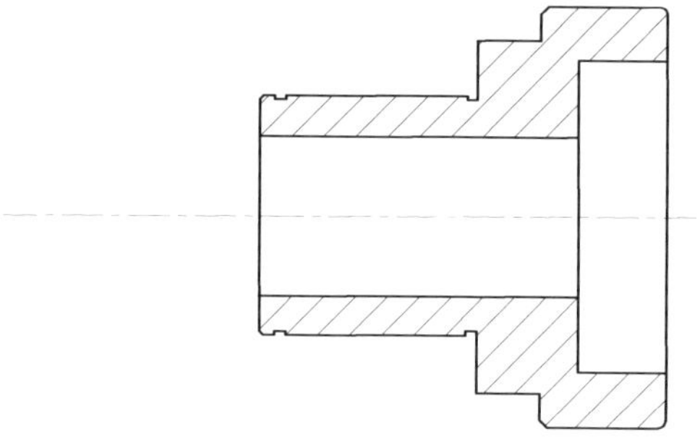

Figure 17-5 *Current drawing SHAFT*

1. The first step is to make sure that the SHAFT drawing is on the screen (draw the shaft drawing with assumed dimensions).

Tip

No drawing needs to be on the screen. You could attach both drawings, BEARING and SHAFT to an existing drawing, even if it is a blank drawing.

2. Choose the **External References Palette** button from the **Palettes** panel to display the **EXTERNAL REFERENCES** palette. In this palette, choose the **Attach DWG** button; the **Select Reference File** dialog box will be displayed.

   Select the drawing that you want to attach (BEARING) and then choose the **Open** button; the **Attach External Reference** dialog box will be displayed on the screen (Figure 17-6). In this dialog box (Figure 17-6), the name of the file that you have selected to be attached to the current drawing as an xref is displayed in the **Name** edit box. You can also specify the name of the file to be attached from the **Name** drop-down list.

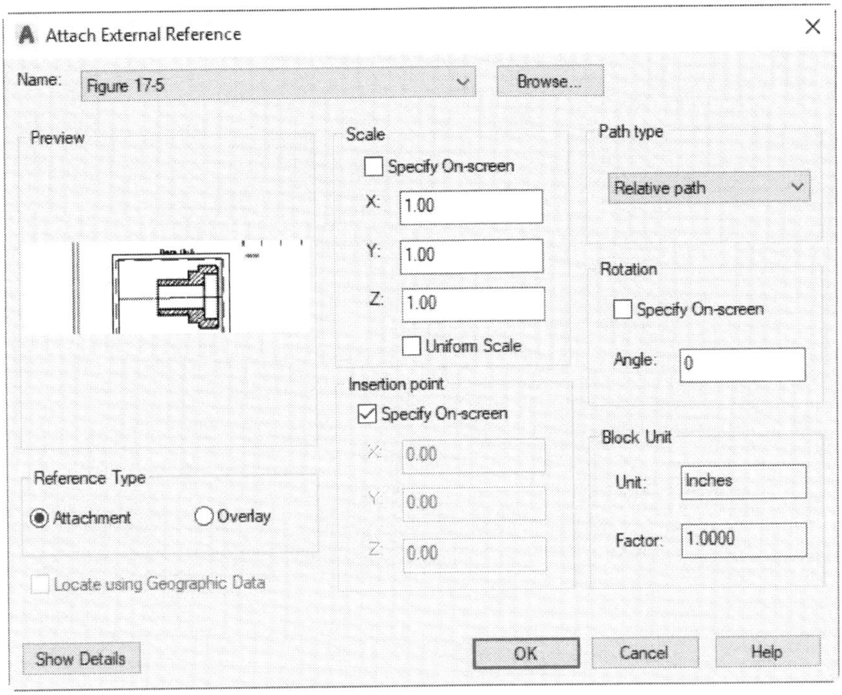

*Figure 17-6 The **Attach External Reference** dialog box*

In the **Reference Type** area, select the **Attachment** radio button, if it is not already selected (default option). The **Overlay** option is discussed later in this chapter. The **Path type** drop-down list is used to specify whether you want to attach a drawing with full path, relative path, or no path. If you select the **Full path** option, the precise location of the xreffed drawing is saved. If you select the **Relative path** option, the position of the xreffed drawing with reference to the host drawing is saved. If you select the **No path** option, AutoCAD LT will search for the xreffed drawing in only that folder in which the host drawing is saved. You can either specify the insertion point, scale factors, and rotation angle in the respective **X**, **Y**, **Z**, and **Angle** edit boxes or select the **Specify On-screen** check boxes to use the pointing device to specify them on the screen. By default, the scale factors in **X**, **Y**, and **Z** edit boxes is 1 and the rotation angle is 0. The **Block Unit** area provides information regarding the units of the inserted block. The **Unit** edit box displays the unit of the block. The **Factor** edit box displays the scale factor depending on the unit of the block and that of the current drawing. If you choose the **Show Details** button, the path of the file is displayed adjacent to **Found in**. Also, the saved path of the file is displayed adjacent to **Saved path**. Choose the **OK** button from the **Attach External Reference** dialog box to accept the default values and exit the dialog box. Specify the insertion point; the drawing is attached to the current drawing, but it appears faded. After attaching the BEARING drawing as an xref, save the current drawing with the file name SHAFT (Figure 17-7). You can control the fading intensity of the attached objects by using the options from the **Fade Control** area of the **Display** tab in the **Options** dialog box. In this area, you can either use the slider bar to increase or decrease the fading intensity or you can enter a value in the edit box. You can also use the

XFADECTL variable to control the fading intensity of other objects while editing them. By default, the fading intensity value is set to 70.

3. Open the BEARING drawing and make the changes shown in Figure 17-8 (draw polylines on the sides). Now, save the drawing with the file name BEARING.

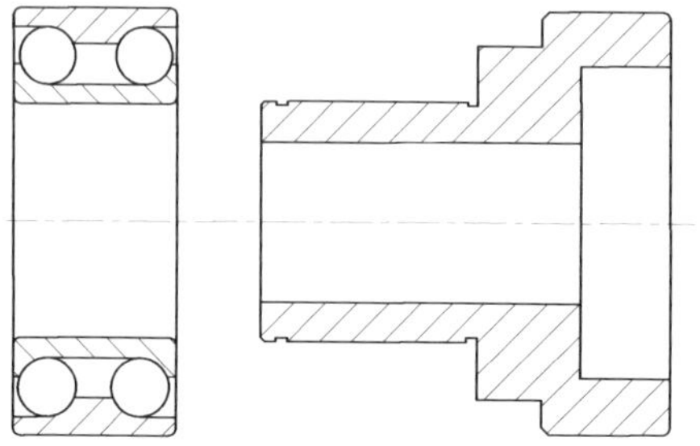

Figure 17-7 Attaching the BEARING drawing as an xref

4. Open the SHAFT drawing. In the **EXTERNAL REFERENCES** palette, you will notice that the message **Needs reloading** is displayed in the **Status** column of the BEARING drawing. Right-click on the BEARING and choose **Reload**; the modified BEARING drawing is automatically updated (Figure 17-9). This is the most useful feature of external reference. You could also have inserted the BEARING drawing as a block, but if you had updated the BEARING drawing, the drawing in which it was inserted would not have been updated automatically.

Figure 17-8 The modified xref BEARING drawing

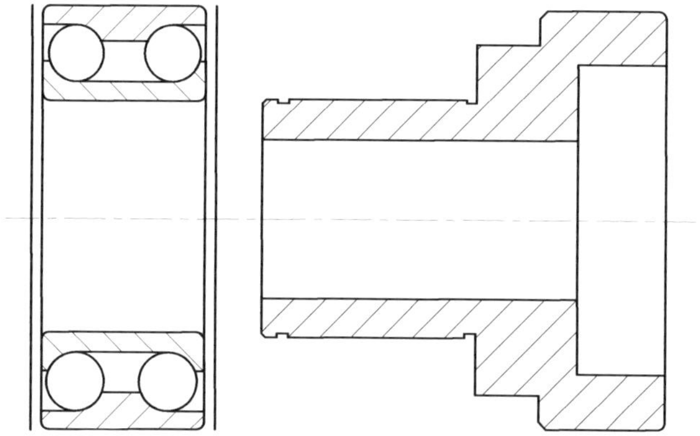

Figure 17-9 BEARING drawing automatically updated after loading the SHAFT drawing

When you attach an xref drawing, AutoCAD LT remembers the name of the attached drawing. If you xref the drawing again, AutoCAD LT displays a message as given next.
Xref "BEARING" has already been defined.
Using existing definition.
Specify insertion point or [Scale/X/Y/Z/Rotate/PScale/PX/PY/PZ/PRotate]: *Specify the location to place another copy of the xref.*

Note

If the external reference drawing that you want to attach is currently being edited, AutoCAD LT will attach the drawing that was last saved through the ***Save, Write Block,*** *or* ***Exit Autodesk AutoCAD LT 2020*** *button.*

Points to Remember about Xref

1. When you enter the name of the xref drawing, AutoCAD LT checks for block names and xref names. If a block exists with the same name as the name of the xref drawing in the current drawing, the **ATTACH** tool is terminated and an error message is displayed.

2. When you xref a drawing, the objects that are in the model space are attached. Any objects that are in the paper space are not attached to the current drawing.

3. The layer 0, DEFPOINTS, and the linetype CONTINUOUS are treated differently. The current drawing layers 0, DEFPOINTS, and linetype CONTINUOUS will override the layers and linetypes of the xref drawing. For example, if the layer 0 of the current drawing is white and the layer 0 of the xref drawing is red, the white color will override the red.

4. The xref drawings can be nested. For example, if the BEARING drawing contains the reference INRACE and you xref the BEARING drawing to the current drawing, the INRACE drawing is automatically attached to the current drawing. If you detach the BEARING drawing, the INRACE drawing gets detached automatically.

5. You can rename an xref under the **File References** column name in the list box of the **EXTERNAL REFERENCES** palette by highlighting the xref and then clicking on it again. You can now enter a new name. An AutoCAD LT warning is displayed: **Caution! "XXXX" is an externally referenced block. Renaming it will also rename its dependent symbols**.

6. When you xref a drawing, AutoCAD LT stores the name and path of the drawing by default. If the name of the xref drawing or the path where the drawing was originally stored has changed or you cannot find it in the path specified in the **Options** dialog box, AutoCAD LT cannot load the drawing, plot it, or use the **Reload** option of the **EXTERNAL REFERENCES** palette.

Detaching an Xref Drawing (Detach Option)

The **Detach** option can be used to detach or remove the xref drawings. If there are any nested xref drawings defined with the xref drawings, they are also detached. Once a drawing is detached, it is erased from the screen. To detach an xref drawing, select the file name in the **EXTERNAL REFERENCES** palette list box to highlight it and then right-click on it to select the **Detach** option. After selecting the **Detach** option, the xref is completely removed from the current drawing.

Updating an Xref Drawing (Reload Option)

When you load a drawing, AutoCAD LT automatically loads the referenced drawings. The **Reload** option of the **EXTERNAL REFERENCES** palette lets you update the xref drawings and nested xref drawings at any time. You do not need to exit the drawing editor and then reload the drawing. To reload the xref drawings, invoke the **EXTERNAL REFERENCES** palette, select the xreffed drawing in the list box, and then right-click on it to choose the **Reload** option from the shortcut menu. AutoCAD LT will scan for the referenced drawings and the nested xref drawings and load the most recently saved version of the drawing.

You can reload all the attached xref drawings at one time by selecting **Reload All References** from the drop-down list of the **Refresh** button on the upper left corner of the **EXTERNAL REFERENCES** palette.

The **Reload** option is generally used when the xref drawings are currently being edited and you want to load the updated drawings. The xref drawings are updated based on what is saved on the disk. Therefore, before reloading an xref drawing, you should make sure that the xref drawings that are being edited have been saved. If AutoCAD LT encounters an error while loading the referenced drawings, the **External References** tool is terminated, and the entire reload operation is canceled.

Unloading an Xref Drawing (Unload Option)

The **Unload** option allows you to temporarily remove the definition of an xref drawing from the current drawing. However, AutoCAD LT retains the pointer to the xref drawings. When you unload the xref drawings, the drawings are not displayed on the screen. You can reload the xref drawings by using the **Reload** option.

> **Tip**
> *It is recommended that you unload the referenced drawings if they are not being used. After unloading the xref drawings, the drawings load much faster and need lesser memory.*

Adding an Xref Drawing (Bind Option)

The **Bind** option lets you convert the xref drawings to blocks in the current drawing. The bound drawings, including the nested xref drawings (that are no longer xrefs), become a permanent part of the current drawing. The bound drawing cannot be detached or reloaded. You can use this option when you want to send a copy of your drawing to a customer for review. Because the xref drawings are a part of the existing drawing, you do not need to include the xref drawings or the path information. You can also use this option to safeguard the master drawing from accidental editing of the piece parts. To bind the xref drawings, select the file names in the **EXTERNAL REFERENCES** palette and then right-click and choose the **Bind** option from the shortcut menu; the **Bind Xrefs/DGN underlays** dialog box (Figure 17-10) is displayed. AutoCAD LT provides two methods to bind the xref drawing in the **Bind Type** area of the dialog box. These methods are discussed next.

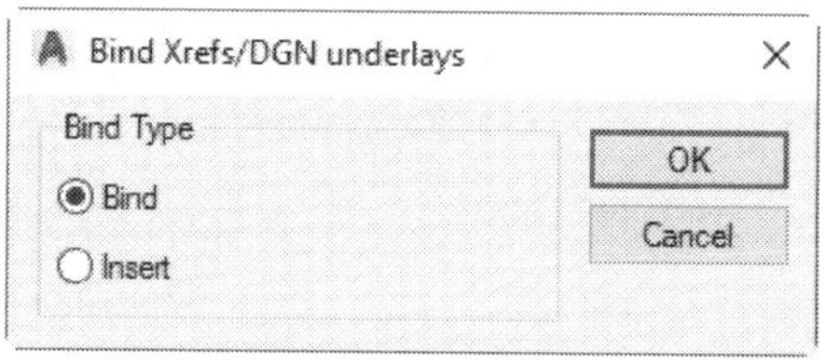

***Figure 17-10** The **Bind Xrefs/DGN underlays** dialog box*

Bind

When you use the **Bind** radio button, AutoCAD LT binds the selected xref definition to the current drawing. All the xrefs are converted to blocks and the named objects are renamed. For example, if you xref the drawing BEARING with a layer named OBJECT, a new layer BEARING|OBJECT is created in the current drawing. When you bind this drawing, the xref dependent layer BEARING|OBJECT will become a locally defined layer BEARING\$0\$OBJECT (Figure 17-11). If the BEARING\$0\$OBJECT layer already exits, AutoCAD LT will automatically increment the number, and the layer name becomes BEARING\$1\$OBJECT.

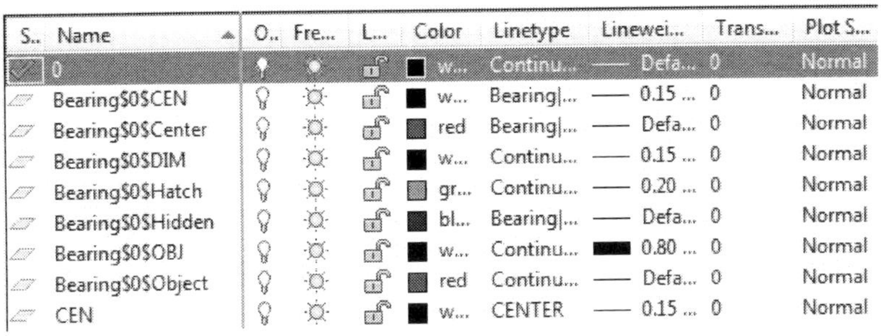

Figure 17-11 *Partial view of the* ***Layer Properties Manager*** *dialog box*

Insert

When you use the **Insert** option, AutoCAD LT inserts the xref drawing. The xrefs get converted into blocks. For example, if you xref the drawing SHAFT with a layer named OBJECT, a new layer SHAFT|OBJECT is created in the current drawing. If you use the **Insert** option to bind the xref drawing, the layer name SHAFT|OBJECT is renamed as OBJECT. If the object layer already exists, then the values set in the current drawing override the values of the inserted drawing.

Editing an XREF's Path

By default, AutoCAD LT saves the path of the referenced drawing and displays it in the **Saved Path** column in the **EXTERNAL REFERENCES** palette. As mentioned earlier, when AutoCAD LT loads the drawing containing a referenced file, and if it is not able to find the file at the location specified in the **Saved Path** column of the **EXTERNAL REFERENCES** palette, it searches for the file in the current directory and in the **Support File Search Path** locations specified in the **Files** tab of the **Options** dialog box. If a file with the same name is found, it is loaded. Now, when you invoke the **EXTERNAL REFERENCES** palette, you will notice that if you select an xref name in the list box to highlight it, the path displayed in the **Saved Path** column for the xref file is different from the one displayed in the **Found At** edit box. To update the path of the xref file, choose the **Save Path** button. The new path is saved and displayed in the **Saved Path** column.

If AutoCAD LT cannot locate the specified file even in the directories specified in the **Files** tab of the **Options** dialog box, it will display an error message saying that it cannot find the specified file. The path of the file is displayed as marker text in the current drawing. Now, when you invoke the **EXTERNAL REFERENCES** palette, the status of the drawing is shown as **Not Found**. To specify a new path for the xref file, click in the **Saved Path** field; the path will be highlighted and the **Browse** button will be displayed next to the path. Click on this button; the **Select new path** dialog box will be displayed. Using this dialog box, you can locate the drawing to be used as xref. Once you have found the file, choose the **Open** button to return to the **EXTERNAL REFERENCES** palette. The new path is displayed in the **Saved Path** column and the **Found At** edit box. The specified xref file is reloaded and replaces the marker text in the drawing, when you choose the **OK** button in the **EXTERNAL REFERENCES** palette. If you remember the new location of the xref file, you can also enter it in the **Found At** edit box. For example, if a drawing, which was originally in the C:\CAD\Proj1 subdirectory, has been moved to C:\Parts directory, the path must be edited so that AutoCAD LT is able to load the xref drawing.

THE OVERLAY OPTION

As discussed earlier, when you attach an xref to a drawing, the **Attach External References** dialog box is displayed. The **Reference Type** area of this dialog box has two radio buttons, **Attachment** and **Overlay**. You can select any of these radio buttons to xref a drawing. The **Attachment** radio button is selected by default. The advantage of selecting the **Overlay** radio button is that you can access the desired drawing instead of the drawing along with its xreffed attachments. For example, consider three people working on three different drawings that are a part of the same project. The first designer is working on the layout of walls of a room, the second designer is working on the furniture layout of the room, and the third on the electrical layout of that room. The names of the drawings are WALLS, FURNITURE, and ELECTRICAL, respectively. Assume that the designer working on the walls layout selects the **Attachment** radio button to xref the FURNITURE drawing so that he or she can check the furniture layout according to the wall structure. After insertion, the WALLS drawing will comprise the wall structure (current drawing) along with the furniture layout (xreffed drawing). Now, if the designer working on the electrical layout xrefs the WALLS drawing to check the location of electrical fittings with respect to the walls, he/she will get the drawing that has the furniture layout as well as the wall layout. This is because the FURNITURE drawing was xreffed in the WALLS drawing by selecting the **Attachment** radio button.

In the above example, the designer working on the ELECTRICAL drawing may not require the FURNITURE drawing. This is because at this stage, he/she is more interested in checking the electrical fittings with respect to the wall structure. So the furniture layout that is xreffed with the wall structure needs to be avoided. This can be done by selecting the **Overlay** radio button while X-referencing the FURNITURE drawing in the WALLS drawing. This means that the designer working on the wall structure needs to xref the furniture layout by selecting the **Overlay** radio button. Now, if the wall structure is xreffed in some other drawing, the furniture layout will not appear.

One of the problems of using the **Attachment** option is that you cannot have a circular reference. For example, assume you are designing the plant layout of a manufacturing unit. One person is working on the floor plan (see Figure 17-12), and the other person is working on the furniture layout in the offices (Figure 17-13). The names of the two drawings are FLOORPLN and OFFICES, respectively. The person working on the office layout uses the **Attachment** option to insert the FLOORPLN drawing so that he or she has the latest floor plan drawing. The person who is working on the floor plan wants to reference the OFFICES drawing.

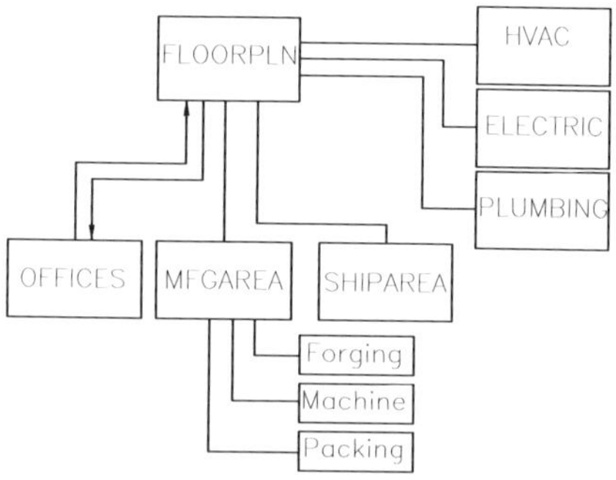

***Figure 17-12** Hierarchy of FLOORPLAN drawing*

Now, if the **Attachment** option is used to reference the drawings, AutoCAD LT displays an error message. This is because by attaching the OFFICES drawing, a circular reference is created. The AutoCAD LT message displayed is "**Circular references detected. Continue?**" (Figure 17-14). If you choose the **No** button, the **External References Palette** tool is canceled and no drawing is referenced. But if you choose the **Yes** button, the following message is displayed **Breaking**

circular reference from "offices" to "current drawing" and the particular file you wanted to reference is referenced.

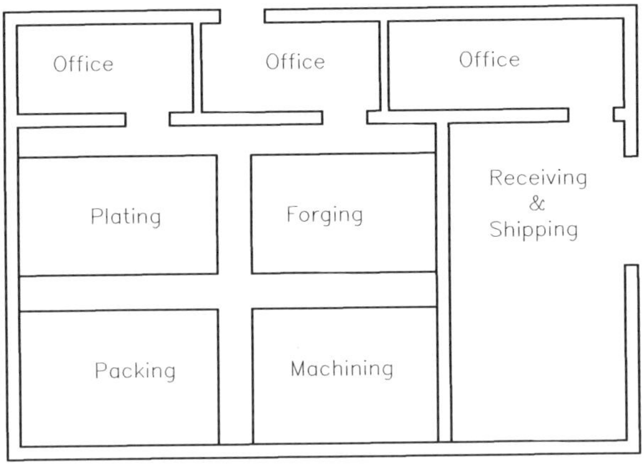

Figure 17-13 Hierarchy of OFFICES drawing

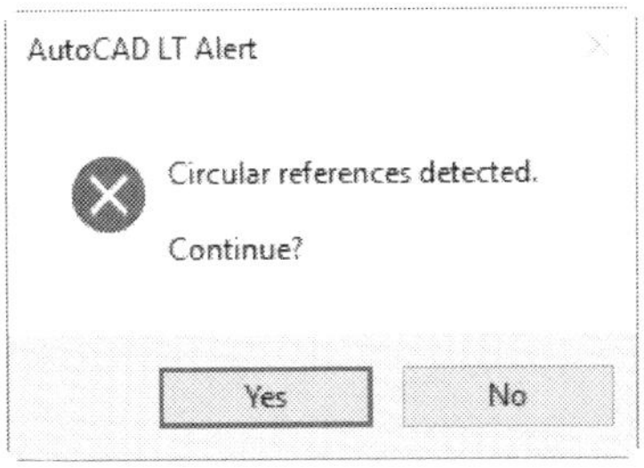

*Figure 17-14 The **AutoCAD LT Alert** message box*

However, to overcome this problem of circular reference, you can use the **Overlay** option to overlay the OFFICES drawing. This is a very useful option because the **Overlay** option lets different operators avoid circular reference and share the drawing data without affecting the drawing. Overlaying allows you to view a referenced drawing without having to attach it to the current drawing. This option can be invoked by selecting the **Overlay** radio button in the **Attach External References** dialog box, which is displayed after you have selected a drawing to reference. Also, when a drawing that has a nested overlay is overlaid, the nested overlay is not visible in the current drawing. This is another difference between attaching an xref and overlaying an xref to a drawing. This feature is especially useful when you want to reference a drawing that another user who is referencing your drawing does not need. Although the attachment will reference the nested reference too, the overlay option ignores nested references.

In AutoCAD LT, you can change an external referenced file from attachment to overlay and vice-versa. To do so, select the file from the **EXTERNAL REFERENCES** palette and right-click on it; a shortcut menu will be displayed, refer to Figure 17-15. Hover the cursor on the **Xref Type** option in the shortcut menu; two options are displayed, **Attach** and **Overlay**. Select the option as per requirement. The selected file will become attachment or overlay as per the option selected. You can change the type of multiple reference files by selecting all of them and then right-clicking on them.

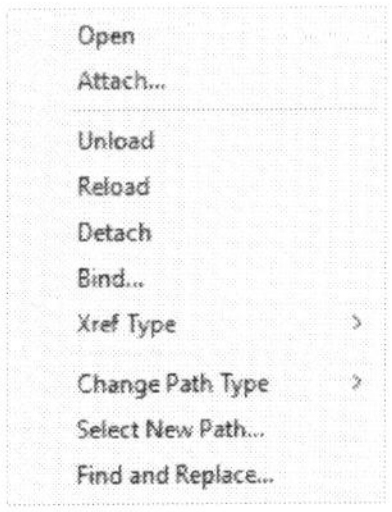

Figure 17-15 The shortcut menu

Example 1 Attachment and Overlay

In this example, you will use the **Attachment** and **Overlay** options to attach and reference the drawings. Two drawings, PLAN and PLANFORG are given. The PLAN drawing (Figure 17-16) consists of the floor plan layout, and the PLANFORG drawing (Figure 17-17) has the details of the forging section only. The CAD operator who is working on the PLANFORG drawing wants to xref the PLAN drawing for reference. Also, the CAD operator working on the PLAN drawing should be able to xref the PLANFORG drawing to complete the project. The following steps illustrate how to accomplish the defined task without creating a circular reference.

Download these files from *https://www.cadcim.com*. The path of the file is as follows: *Textbooks > CAD/CAM > AutoCAD > AutoCAD 2020: A Problem-Solving Approach, Basic and Intermediate > Input Files.*

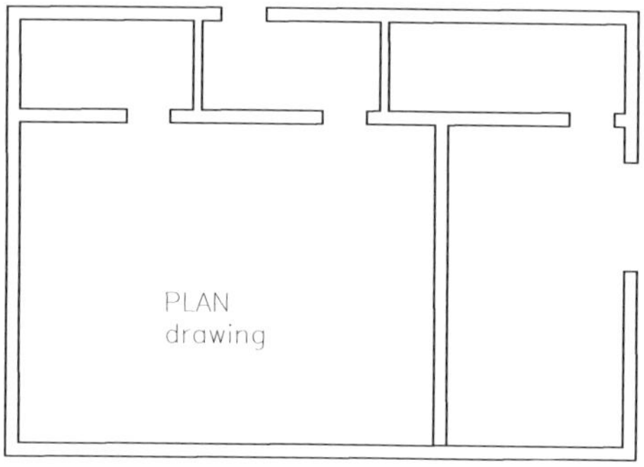

Figure 17-16 *The PLAN drawing*

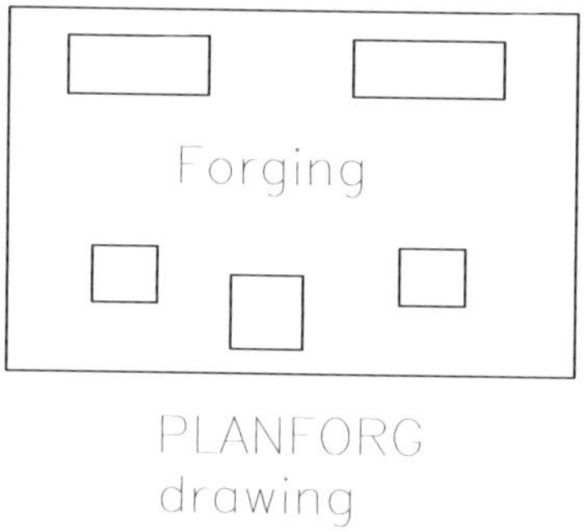

Figure 17-17 *The PLANFORG drawing*

How circular reference is caused?

1. Open the drawing PLANFORG, and then choose the **External References** tool from the **Palettes** panel in the **View** tab. Next, choose the **Attach DWG** button from the **EXTERNAL REFERENCES** palette; the **Select Reference File** dialog box is displayed. Select the PLAN drawing from the list box of the **Select Reference File** dialog box and choose the **Open** button; the **Attach External Reference** dialog box is displayed. In this dialog box, the name of the PLAN drawing is displayed in the **Name** edit box, and the **Attachment** radio button is selected by default in the **Reference Type** area. Choose **OK** to exit the dialog box and specify an insertion point on the screen. Now, the drawing consists of the PLANFORG and PLAN. Save the drawing.

2. Open the drawing file PLAN. Next, choose the **External References Palette** button and attach the PLANFORG drawing to the PLAN drawing using the same steps as described in Step 1. AutoCAD LT will display the message that the circular reference has been detected and will ask you if you want to continue. If you choose **Yes** in the AutoCAD LT message box, the circular reference is broken and you are allowed to reference the specific drawing.

   The possible solution for the operator working on the PLANFORG drawing is to detach the PLAN drawing. This way the PLANFORG drawing does not contain any reference to the PLAN drawing and would not cause any circular reference. The other solution is to use the **Overlay** option, as follows :

How to prevent circular reference?

3. Open the PLANFORG drawing (Figure 17-18) and select the **Overlay** radio button in the **Attach External References** dialog box, which is displayed after you have selected the PLAN drawing to reference. The PLAN drawing is overlaid on the PLANFORG drawing (Figure 17-19).

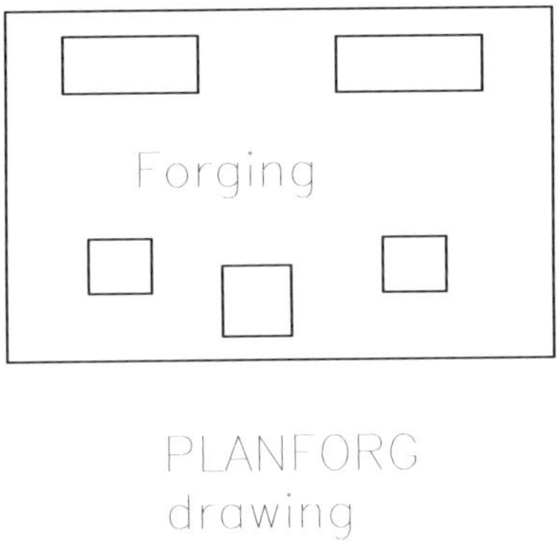

Figure 17-18 *The PLANFORG drawing*

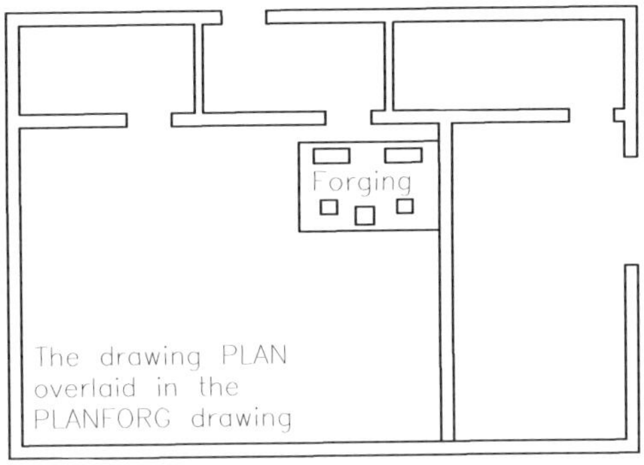

Figure 17-19 *The PLANFORG drawing after overlaying the PLAN drawing*

4. Open the drawing file PLAN (Figure 17-20), and select the **Attachment** radio button in the **Attach External Reference** dialog box which is displayed when you select the PLANFORG drawing in the **Select Reference File** dialog box to attach it as an xref to the PLAN drawing. You will notice that only the PLANFORG drawing is attached (Figure 17-21). The drawing that was overlaid in the PLANFORG drawing (PLAN) does not appear in the current drawing. This way, the CAD operator working on the PLANFORG drawing can overlay the PLAN drawing, and the CAD operator working on the PLAN drawing can attach the PLANFORG drawing, without causing a circular reference.

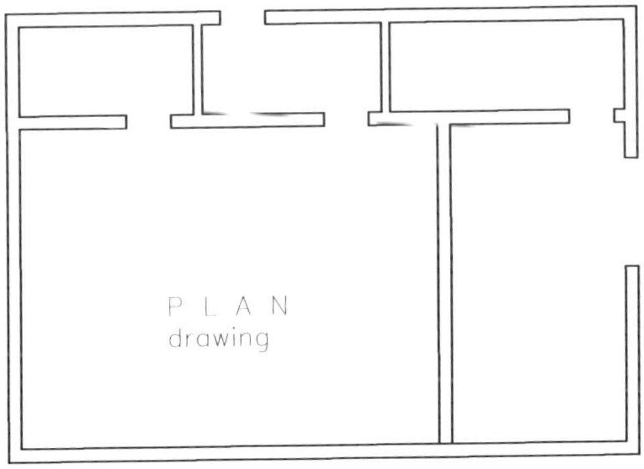

Figure 17-20 *The PLAN drawing*

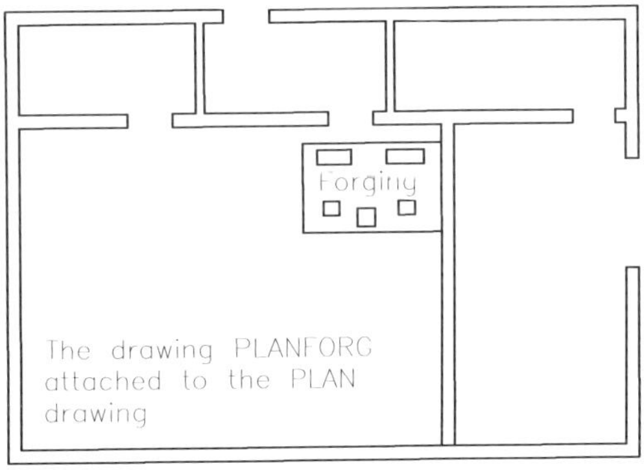

Figure 17-21 *The PLAN drawing after attaching the PLANFORG drawing*

ATTACHING FILES TO A DRAWING

Ribbon: Insert > Reference > Attach **Command:** ATTACH

You can use the **Attach** tool in the **Reference** panel (Figure 17-22) to attach a DWG, DGN, DWF, PDF, or image file without invoking the **EXTERNAL REFERENCES** palette. Using this tool, you can attach a drawing file easily since most of the xref operations involve simply attaching a drawing file. When you invoke this tool, AutoCAD LT` displays the **Select Reference File** dialog box. To attach a *.dwg, .dgn, .pcg, .isd, .dwf, .pdf,* or image file, specify it in the **Files of type** drop-down list in the **Select Reference** dialog box; the corresponding files will be listed in the dialog box. Select the drawing file to be attached and choose the **Open** button; the **Attach External Reference** dialog box is displayed. Select the **Attachment** radio button under the **Reference Type** area. You can specify the insertion point, scale, and rotation angle on screen or in the respective edit boxes.

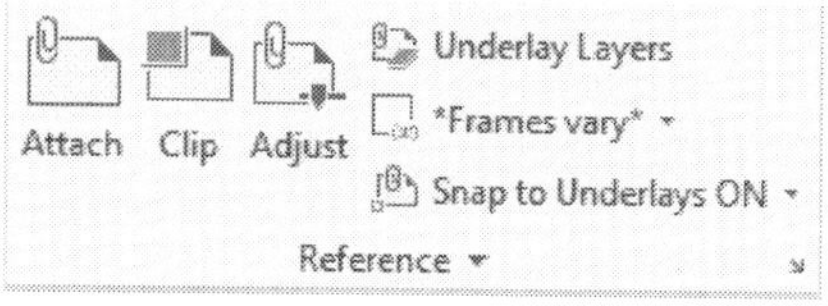

***Figure 17-22** The **Attach** tool in the **Reference** panel*

Note

*1. To select a .dgn, .dwf, .pdf, or image file, specify the file type in the **Files of type** drop-down list in the **Select Reference File** dialog box; the files will be attached as an underlay. Underlays are discussed in the next section.*

*2. AutoCAD LT maintains a log file (.xlg) for xref drawings if the **XREFCTL** system variable is set to 1. This file lists information about the date and time of loading and other xref operations to be completed. This .xlg file is saved in the current drawing with the same name as the current drawing and is updated each time the drawing is loaded or any xref operations are carried out.*

WORKING WITH UNDERLAYS

You can attach a DWF, DGN, or PDF file as an underlay to the current drawing file. The underlay files are not a part of the original drawing files. Therefore, if you add a file as an underlay, it does not increase the file size of the current drawing. The procedure to add a file as an underlay is similar to attaching a drawing file using the **Attach** tool. After you select the file to attach, the **Attach <XXXX> Underlay** dialog box will be displayed, where <XXXX> is the file type. Figure 17-23 shows the **Attach PDF Underlay** dialog box that is displayed on selecting a pdf file from the **Select Reference File** dialog box.

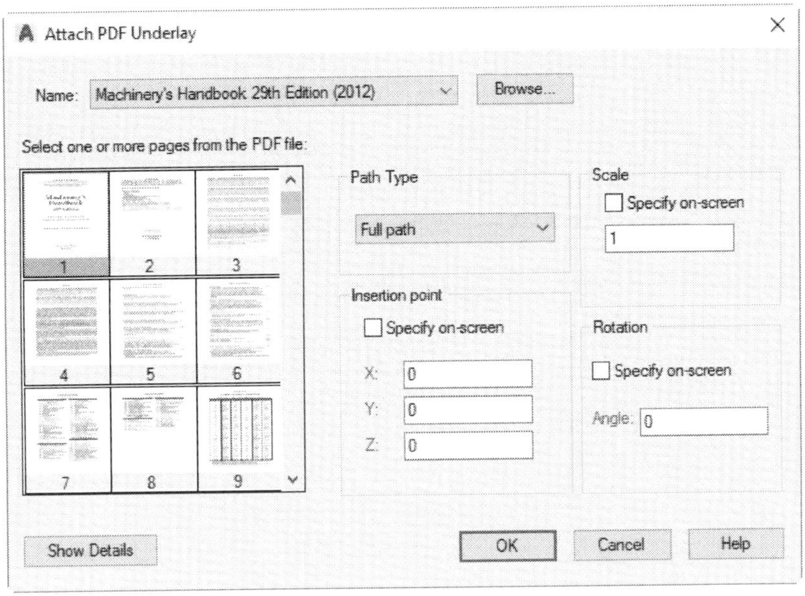

*Figure 17-23 The **Attach PDF Underlay** dialog box*

If the selected *.pdf* file has multiple pages, all pages of the pdf file are listed in the **Select one or more pages from the PDF file** area. Select the pages to be attached from this area. If you have selected multiple pages as well as the **Specify on-screen** check box from the **Insertion point** area, then you are prompted to specify different insertion points for different pages.

The files attached as an underlay behave like blocks. The general modify commands like move, copy, rotate, mirror, and so on can be applied on them. However, you cannot bind a file that is attached as an underlay or modify the attached file in the current drawing file.

Editing an Underlay

As discussed earlier, you cannot edit a file that is attached as an underlay. However, you can control the appearance of the underlay by adjusting the contrast, fade, and monochrome display. To do so, select the attached object; a contextual tab will be displayed. Figure 17-24 shows the **PDF Underlay** tab that is displayed on selecting a PDF file.

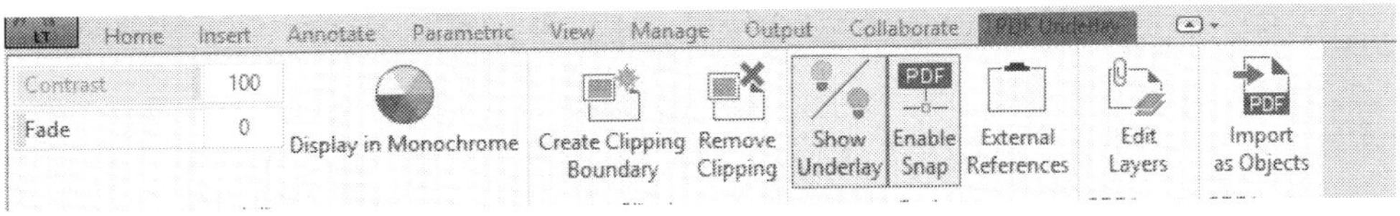

*Figure 17-24 The **PDF Underlay** tab*

You can use the options in this contextual tab to adjust the fade, contrast, and monochrome display of the underlay. You can create a new clipping boundary similar to that of an attached drawing. By default, the **Enable Snap** button is chosen in the **Options** panel. Therefore, you can snap entities in the underlaid object. If you deselect this button, you cannot snap entities in the underlaid objects. You can use the **Show Underlay** button from the **Options** panel to display/hide the underlaid objects. Both **Enable Snap** and **Show Underlay** are toggle buttons. If the attached underlay has layers, you can hide/display the selected layers. To do so, choose the **Edit Layers** button from the contextual tab; the **Underlay Layers** dialog box will be displayed, as shown in Figure 17-25. If multiple drawings are attached as an underlay, all file names will be listed in the **Reference Name** drop-down list. Select the file from the **Reference Name** drop-down list for which you need to hide the layers; the corresponding layers will be listed in the list box. Click on the bulb icon of the layer to be hidden. Alternatively, select the layer from the list box and right-click; a shortcut menu will be displayed. Choose the **Layer(s) Off** option to hide the selected layer. To hide multiple layers, press the CTRL key and select the layers to be hidden. Next, choose **Layer(s) Off**. Then, press ESC to exit the editing mode; the contextual tab will disappear.

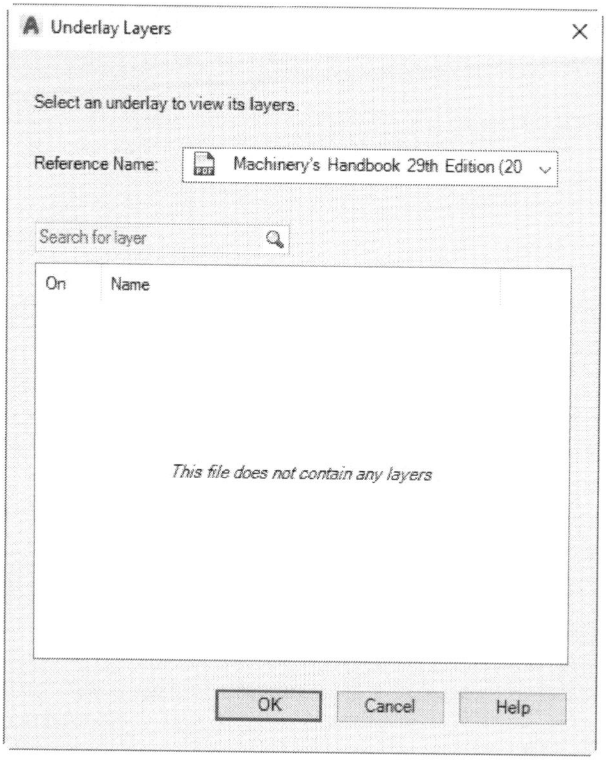

***Figure 17-25** The **Underlay Layers** dialog box*

If you have attached a file as an underlay, you can invoke the **Underlay Layers** dialog box without invoking the contextual tab by choosing the **Underlay Layers** tool from the **Reference** panel in the **Insert** tab. Similarly, you can switch on/off the OSNAP settings for the drawing that are underlaid by choosing the **Snap to Underlays ON / Snap to Underlays OFF** button respectively from the **Snap to Underlays** drop-down in the **Reference** panel. You can import geometry, fills and hatches, raster images, and True Type text objects from a specified PDF file by choosing the **Import as objects** button from the **PDF Import** panel of the **PDF Underlay** contextual tab.

Note

*If there are more underlays of different file types and you have set different osnap setting for each file type, then the **Underlay Osnaps Vary** button will be displayed in the **Snap to Underlays*** *drop-down in the* ***Reference*** *panel. However, if you choose the* ***Snap to Underlays ON / Snap to Underlays OFF*** *button, the corresponding osnap setting will be applied to all underlays.*

OPENING AN XREFFED OBJECT IN A SEPARATE WINDOW

If you are in the host drawing and you want to open a selected xreffed object in a separate window without using the **Select File** dialog box, you can use the **Open Reference** tool available in the **External Reference** contextual tab which is displayed on selecting an external reference. When you invoke this tool, you are prompted to select the xref. Select the xreffed object that you want to open in a separate window. When you select the desired xref, AutoCAD LT opens the DWG file of the xreffed object in a separate window. You can now make the desired changes in the DWG file of the xreffed object. Save the changes and then close the drawing. When you open the host drawing, you will notice that the **Communication Center** displays a message that the external reference file has changed and the xreffed drawing needs to be reloaded. Reload the xreffed drawing using the **EXTERNAL REFERENCES** palette and you will notice that the host drawing is updated.

USING THE DesignCenter TO ATTACH A DRAWING AS AN XREF

The **DesignCenter** can also be used to attach an xref to a drawing. To do so, choose the **DesignCenter** button from the **Palettes** panel in the **View** tab; the **DESIGNCENTER** will be displayed. In the **DESIGNCENTER**, choose the **Tree View Toggle** button, if it is not already chosen to display the tree pane. Expand the **Tree view** and double-click on the folder whose contents you want to view. The content of the selected folder is displayed in the palette. To attach a drawing as an Xref, right click on the corresponding thumbnail on the right in the palette; a shortcut menu is displayed, refer to Figure 17-26. Choose **Attach as Xref** from the shortcut menu; the **Attach External Reference** dialog box will be displayed. Alternatively, you can also use the right mouse button to drag and drop the drawing into the current drawing; a shortcut menu will be displayed again. Choose **Create Xref**; and attach it by using **External Reference** pallete.

In the **Attach External Reference** dialog box, the **Name** edit box displays the name of the selected file to be inserted as an xref. Select the **Attachment** radio button in the **Reference type** area, if not already selected. Specify the insertion point, scale, and rotation in the respective edit boxes or select the **Specify On-screen** check boxes to specify this information on the screen. Choose **OK** to exit the dialog box; the selected object is attached as an xref to the current drawing.

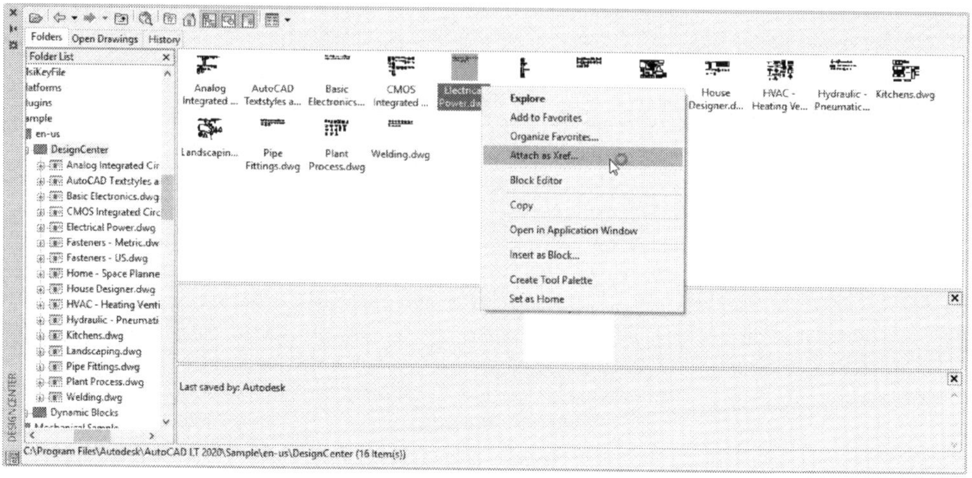

Figure 17-26 The DESIGNCENTER

ADDING XREF DEPENDENT NAMED OBJECTS

Menu Bar: Modify > Object > External Reference > Bind
Toolbar: Reference > Xbind **Command:** XB/XBIND

You can use the **Xbind** tool (Figure 17-27) to add the selected named objects such as blocks, dimension styles, layers, line types, and text styles of the xref drawing to the current drawing. The following example describes the use of this command.

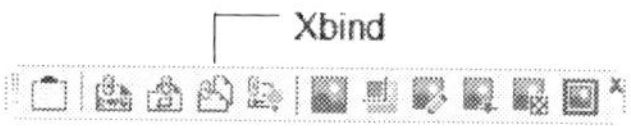

*Figure 17-27 The **Xbind** tool in the **Reference** toolbar*

1. Load the drawing Bearing that was created earlier. Make sure the drawing has the following layer setup. Otherwise, create the following layers using the **Layer Properties Manager** dialog box.

Layer Name	Color	Linetype
0	White	Continuous
Object	Red	Continuous
Hidden	Blue	Hidden2
Center	White	Center2
Hatch	Green	Continuous

2. Draw a circle and create it as a block with the name SIDE. Save the drawing as BEARING.

3. Start a new drawing with the following layer setup:

Layer Name	Color	Linetype
0	White	Continuous
Object	Red	Continuous
Hidden	Green	Hidden

4. Use the **Attach** tool in the **Reference** panel to attach the Bearing drawing to the current drawing. When you xref the drawing, the layers will be added to the current drawing as discussed earlier in this chapter.

5. Now, invoke the **Xbind** tool; the **Xbind** dialog box is displayed. This dialog box has two areas with list boxes. They are **Xrefs** and **Definitions to Bind**. If you want to bind the blocks defined in the xref drawing Bearing, first click on the plus sign adjacent to the xref Bearing; the icons for the named objects in the drawing are displayed in a tree view (Figure 17-28). Click on the plus sign next to the Block icon. AutoCAD LT lists the blocks defined in the xref drawing (Bearing). Select the block Bearing|SIDE and then choose the **Add** button. The block name will be added to the **Definitions to Bind** list box. Choose **OK** to exit the dialog box. AutoCAD LT will bind the block with the current drawing and a message is displayed at the Command prompt: **1 Block(s) bound**. The name of the block will change to Bearing0SIDE. You can invoke the **Block Definition** dialog box by choosing the **Create Block** tool in the **Block Definition** panel and check the **Name** drop-down list to see if the block with the name Bearing0SIDE has been added to the drawing. If you want to insert the block, you must enter the new block name (Bearing0SIDE). You can also rename the block to another name that is easier to use.

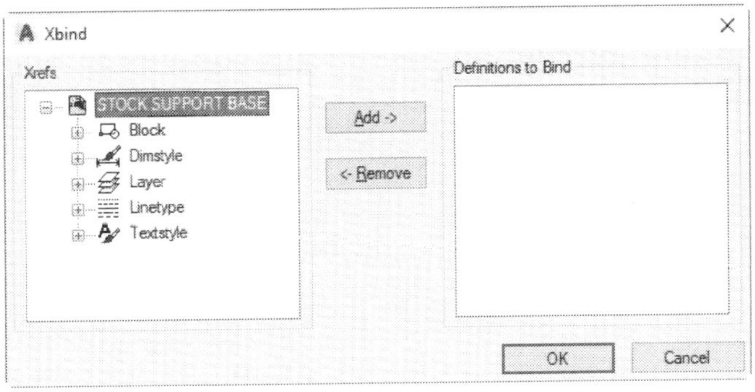

Figure 17-28 *The* ***Xbind*** *dialog box*

If the block contains a reference to another xref drawing, AutoCAD LT binds that xref drawing and all its dependent symbols to the current drawing. Once you bind the dependent symbols, AutoCAD LT does not delete them not even when the xref drawing is detached. For example, the block Bearing0SIDE will not be deleted even when you detach the xref drawing or end the drawing session.

You can also use the **-XBIND** command to bind the selected dependent symbols of the xref drawing using the Command prompt.

6. Similarly, you can bind the dependent symbols, Bearing|STANDARD (textstyle), Bearing|Hidden, and Bearing|Object layers of the xref drawing. Click on the plus signs adjacent to the respective icons to display the contents and then select the layer or textstyle you want to bind and choose the **Add** button. The selected named objects are displayed in the **Definitions to Bind** list box. If you have selected a named object that you do not want to bind, select it in the **Definitions to Bind** list box and choose the **Remove** button. Once you have finished selecting the named objects that you want to bind to the current drawing, choose **OK**. A message indicating the number of named objects that are bound to the current drawing is displayed at the Command prompt.

   Once bound, the layer names will change to Bearing0Hidden and Bearing0Object. If the layer name Bearing0Hidden was already there, the layer will be named Bearing1Hidden. These two layers become a permanent part of the current drawing. Even if the xref drawing is detached or the current drawing session is closed, the layers are not discarded.

CLIPPING EXTERNAL REFERENCES

Ribbon: Insert > Reference > Clip **Command:** CLIP

The **Clip** tool (Figure 17-29) is used to trim an xref after it has been attached to a drawing to display only a portion of the drawing (Figure 17-30). However, clipping xref does not in any way modify the referenced drawing. On invoking the **Clip** tool, you are prompted to select an object to clip. Select a DWG, DGN, IMAGE, or PDF; the respective clipping options will be displayed.

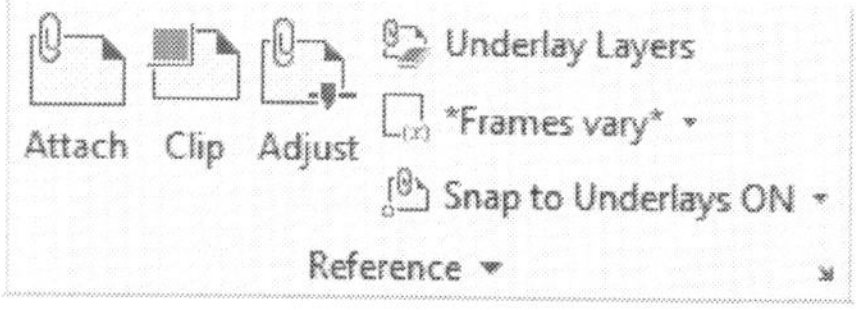

***Figure 17-29** The **Clip** tool in the **Reference** panel*

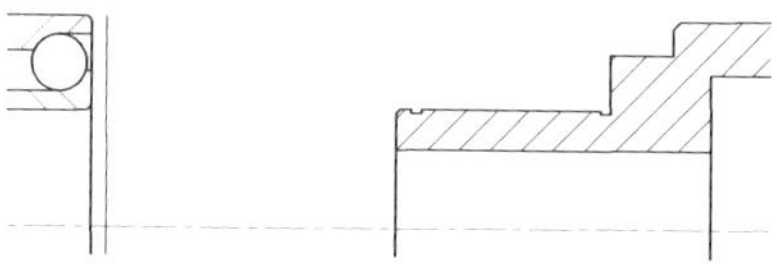

***Figure 17-30** Using the **Clip** tool to clip*

You can also invoke the **Clip** tool by selecting an xref and then right-clicking in the drawing area to display a shortcut menu. Next, choose the corresponding clip command from it. For example, to clip an attached *.dwg* file, select the attached *.dwg* file, right-click, and choose the **Clip Xref** option; the following prompt sequence will be displayed.

CLIP Select object to clip: Enter clipping option
[ON/OFF/Clipdepth/Delete/generate Polyline/New boundary] <New>: *Press ENTER to specify a new clip boundary or enter an option.*
[Select polyline/Polygonal/Rectangular/Invert clip] <Rectangular>: *Press ENTER to select the **Rectangular** option, and then specify two corners of the rectangular boundary.*

You can also right-click in the drawing area at the **Enter clipping option** prompt to display a shortcut menu. This shortcut menu displays all the options available at the Command prompt that can be selected here. All the clipping options available are discussed next.

New boundary

The clipping boundary can be specified by using the **Rectangular**, **Polygonal**, or **Select polyline** option. The **Rectangular** option generates a rectangular boundary and the **Polygonal** option allows you to specify a boundary of any shape. You can draw a boundary using the **Polyline** tool or the **Polygon** tool and then, use the **Select polyline** option to select this polyline as the clipping boundary. The **Invert clip** option inverts the direction of the clipping. For example, if the objects outside the clipping boundary are hidden, by default, the **Invert clip** option will hide the objects inside the clipping boundary and display the objects outside the boundary. After selecting the **Invert clip** option, you need to redefine the clipping boundary using any one of the options discussed above. The **Invert clip** option can only be used with the 2D Wireframe visual style. If a boundary already exists, AutoCAD LT will ask you if the old boundary should be deleted. You can enter **YES** if you want to delete the old boundary and define a new one. If you enter **NO**, the old boundary is retained and the **Clip Xref** tool exits.

ON/OFF

The **ON/OFF** option allows you to specify whether to display the clipped portion or not. When the clipping boundary is off, you can see the complete xref drawing and when it is on, the drawing that is within the clipping polygon is displayed.

Delete

The **Delete** option completely deletes the predefined clipping boundary and the entire xref gets displayed. The **Erase** tool cannot be used to delete the clipping boundary.

generate Polyline

If you have a clipped boundary, select this option to create a polyline coinciding with the boundary of the clipped xref drawing. You can edit the polyline boundary without affecting the clipped drawing. For example, if you stretch the boundary, it does not affect the xref drawing. The edited boundary can be used later to specify a new clipping boundary.

Clipdepth

This option sets the front and back cliping planes on an xref or block. Objects outside the volume defined by the boundary and the specified depth are not displayed. Regardless of the current UCS, the clip depth is applied parallel to the clipping boundary. If you use the **Clipdepth** option, it prompts you to specify a front clip point and a back clip point. Specifying these points, creates a clipping frame passing through them and parallel to the clipping boundary. If the front clipping plane is specified behind the back clipping plane, AutoCAD LT displays an error message and the clipdepth is also not applied. The **Distance** option for specifying the front or back clip points creates a clipping plane at a specified distance from the clipping boundary parallel to it. The **Remove** option removes both the front and back clipping planes and the entire object becomes visible.

Similarly, you can clip the other underlaid xrefs. The options available for clipping the underlaid Xrefs are **ON**, **OFF**, **Delete**, and **New Boundary**. These options are the same as discussed above.

DISPLAYING CLIPPING FRAME

You can select the appropriate option from the **Frames** drop-down list in the **Reference** panel of the **Insert** tab (Figure 17-31) to turn on or off the display of clipping boundary of all the clipped Xrefs. If there are multiple underlays of different file types and you have set different frame settings for each file type, then the **Frames Vary** button will be displayed in the **Reference** panel of the **Insert** tab. You can also use the **FRAME** system variable to turn on or off the display of clipping boundary of all clipped Xrefs. When the value of **FRAME** system variable is 0 (default), the clipping boundary will not be displayed. When it is 1, the clipping boundary will be displayed and plotted. When it is 2, the clipping boundary will be displayed, but not plotted. To control the display of frames of individual attached Xrefs, you need to invoke the individual system variables like **XCLIPFRAME**, **DGNFRAME**, **PDFFRAME**, and **IMAGEFRAME**.

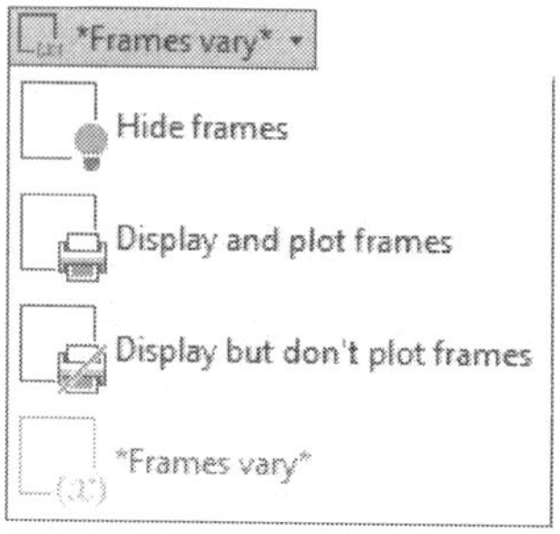

*Figure 17-31 Options in the **Frames settings vary** drop-down list*

DEMAND LOADING

The demand loading feature loads only that part of the referenced drawing that is required in the existing drawing. For example, demand loading provides a mechanism by which objects on frozen layers are not loaded. Also, only the clipped portion of the referenced drawing can be loaded. This makes the xref operation more efficient since less disk space is used, especially when the drawing is reopened. Demand loading is enabled by default. You can modify its settings in the **External References (Xrefs)** area of the **Open and Save** tab of the **Options** dialog box (Figure 17-32). You can select any of the three options available in the **Demand load Xrefs** drop-down list in this dialog box. These options are **Disabled**, **Enabled**, and **Enabled with copy**. These options correspond to a value of **0**, **1**, and **2** of the **XLOADCTL** system variable, respectively, and are discussed next in the table.

Setting	Value of XLOADCTL	Features
Disabled	0	1. Turns off demand loading. 2. Loads entire xref drawing file. 3. The file is available on the server and other users can edit the xref drawing.
Enabled	1	1. Turns on demand loading. 2. The referenced file is kept open. 3. Makes the referenced file read-only for other users.
Enabled with copy	2	1. Turns on demand loading with the copy option. 2. A copy of a referenced drawing is opened. 3. Other users can access and edit the original referenced drawing file.

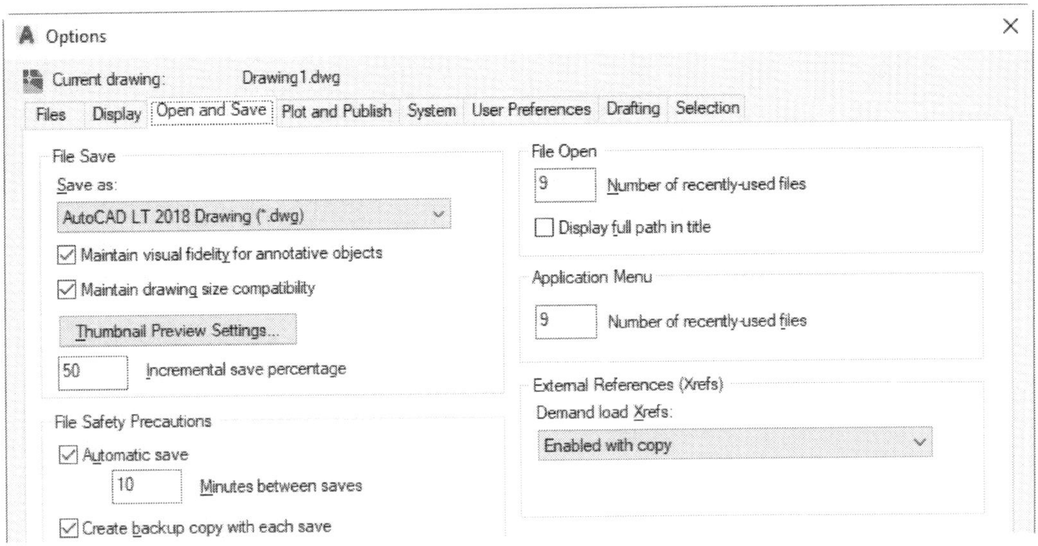

***Figure 17-32** Partial view of the **Open and Save** tab of the **Options** dialog box*

You can also set the value of **XLOADCTL** at the Command prompt. When you are using the **Enabled with copy** option of demand loading, the temporary copies of the xref are saved in the AutoCAD LT temporary files directory (defined in the **Temporary External Reference File Location** folder in the **Files** tab of the **Options** dialog box) or in a user-specified directory. The **XLOADPATH** system variable creates a temporary path to store demand loaded Xrefs.

EDITING REFERENCES IN-PLACE

Ribbon: Insert > Reference > Edit Reference **Command:** REFEDIT
Toolbar: Refedit > Edit Reference In-Place

Often you have to make minor changes in the xref drawing if you want to save yourself from the trouble of going back and forth between drawings. In this situation, you can use in-place reference editing to select the xref, modify it, and then save it after modifications. This feature of AutoCAD LT has already been discussed in detail with reference to blocks in Chapter 15, Working with Blocks. The following steps explain the referencing editing process.

1. To edit in-place, select an external referenced object; the **External Reference** contextual tab will be added to the **Ribbon**. Choose the **Edit Reference In-Place** tool from the **Edit** panel; the **Reference Edit** dialog box will be displayed. After selecting the external referenced object, you can also invoke the shortcut menu and choose the **Edit Xref In-place** option from it to invoke the **Reference Edit** dialog box.

2. In the **Reference name** list box of the **Reference Edit** dialog box, the selected reference and its nested references are listed. Select the specific xref you wish to edit from the list.

3. In the **Settings** tab of the dialog box, select both the **Create unique layer, style, and block names** and the **Lock objects not in working set** check boxes. The **Display attribute**

definitions for editing check box is disabled by default. In the **Identify Reference** tab of the dialog box, select the **Prompt to select nested objects** radio button. Choose **OK** to return to the current drawing. At the **Select nested objects:** prompt, select the objects you want to modify and press ENTER; the **Edit Reference** drop-down will be added to the **Ribbon** (Figure 17-33), and the objects that have not been selected for modifications will become faded. The fading is controlled by the **XFADECTL** system variable or by using the **Xref display** slider bar in the **Display** tab of the **Options** dialog box. You can add or remove objects to the working set by choosing the respective tools in the **Edit Reference** drop-down in the **Insert** tab or by using the **REFSET** command. Once you have defined a working set, all the standard AutoCAD LT commands can be used to modify them.

Figure 17-33** The **External Reference** contextual tab added to the **Ribbon

4. When you choose the **Save Changes** tool in the **Edit Reference** drop-down, AutoCAD LT displays a message: **All reference edits will be saved**. Choose **OK** to return to the drawing area. The modifications made are saved in the drawing as well as in the current drawing as a reference. On choosing the **Discard Changes** button in the **Edit Reference** drop-down, the changes made will not be saved and the current drawing is redisplayed.

Note

*In the **External References (Xrefs)** area of the **Open and Save** tab of the **Options** dialog box, if you select the **Allow other users to Refedit current drawing** check box, the current drawing can be edited in-place by other users even when it is open and is being referenced by another file. This option is selected by default and can also be controlled by the **XEDIT** system variable. The default value of **XEDIT** is 1 and can be changed using the Command prompt.*

Self-Evaluation Test

Answer the following questions and then compare them to those given at the end of this chapter:

1. The __________ are entries such as blocks, layers, and text styles.

2. When you use the **Insert** tool to insert a drawing, the information about the named objects is lost if the names are ____________, and if the names are ___________, the drawing will be imported.

3. The ___________ button of the **EXTERNAL REFERENCES** palette is used to attach an xref drawing to the current drawing.

4. The ________________ feature loads only that part of the referenced drawing that is required in the existing drawing.

5. The _________ option can be used to overcome the problem of circular reference.

6. If the **Retain changes to Xref layers** check box is _________ in the **External References (Xrefs)** area of the **Open and Save** tab of the **Options** dialog box, the layer settings such as color, linetype, on/off, and freeze/thaw are retained.

7. If an assembly drawing has been created by inserting a drawing, the assembly drawing will be updated automatically when a change is made in the inserted drawing. (T/F)

8. The external reference facility helps you keep a drawing updated. (T/F)

9. Objects can be added to a dependent layer. (T/F)

10. While referencing a drawing, if you use the **Attachment** option, the drawing will reference the nested references too. (T/F).

Review Questions

Answer the following questions:

1. Which of the following features lets you reference an external drawing without making this drawing a permanent part of the existing drawing?

   (a) demand loading (b) external reference
   (c) external clipping (d) insert drawing

2. If an xref has nested references that cannot be found, which of the following will be displayed under the status heading of the **List View** button in the **EXTERNAL REFERENCES** palette?

   (a) **Orphaned** (b) **Not found**
   (c) **Unreferenced** (d) **Unresolved**

3. Which of the following system variables, when set to 1, will allow AutoCAD LT to maintain a log file (*.xlg*) for xref drawings?

   (a) **XLOADCTL** (b) **XLOADPATH**
   (c) **XREFCTL** (d) **INDEXCTL**

4. Which of the following system variables, when set to 0, will not allow the clipping boundary to be displayed?

   (a) **XCLIPFRAME** (b) **XLOADCTL**
   (c) **INDEXCTL** (d) **XREFCTL**

5. In the _________ drawings, the information regarding dependent symbols is not lost.

6. AutoCAD LT maintains a log file for xref drawings, if the _________ variable is set to 1.

7. It is possible to edit xrefs in-place using the _________ tool.

8. You can use the __________ tool to add selected dependent symbols from the xref drawing to the current drawing.

9. You can use the __________ system variable to turn on or off the display of clipping boundary of all clipped Xrefs.

10. If the xref drawings get updated, changes are not automatically reflected in the assembly drawing when you open an assembly drawing. (T/F)

11. There is a limit to the number of drawings you can reference. (T/F)

12. It is not possible to have nested references. (T/F)

13. Like blocks, the xref drawings can be scaled, rotated, or positioned at any desired location. (T/F)

14. You can change the color, linetype, or visibility (on/off, freeze/thaw) of a dependent layer. (T/F)

Exercise 1 — *Bind Xref*

In this exercise, you will start a new drawing and xref the drawings as Part-1 and Part-2, refer to Figure 17-34 and Figure 17-35. For assembly, refer to Figure 17-36. You will also edit one of the piece parts to correct the size and use the **Bind Xref** option to bind some of the dependent symbols to the current drawing. The parameters of layers for Part-1, Part-2 and ASSEM1 are as follows:

For Part-1, set up the following layers:

Layer Name	Color	Linetype
0	White	Continuous
Object	Red	Continuous
Hidden	Blue	Hidden2
Center	White	Center2
Dim-Part1	Green	Continuous

For Part-2, set up the following layers:

Layer Name	Color	Linetype
0	White	Continuous
Object	Red	Continuous
Hidden	Blue	Hidden
Center	White	Center
Dim-Part2	Green	Continuous
Hatch	Magenta	Continuous

For ASSEM1, set up the following layers:

Layer Name	Color	Linetype
0	White	Continuous
Object	Blue	Continuous
Hidden	Yellow	Hidden

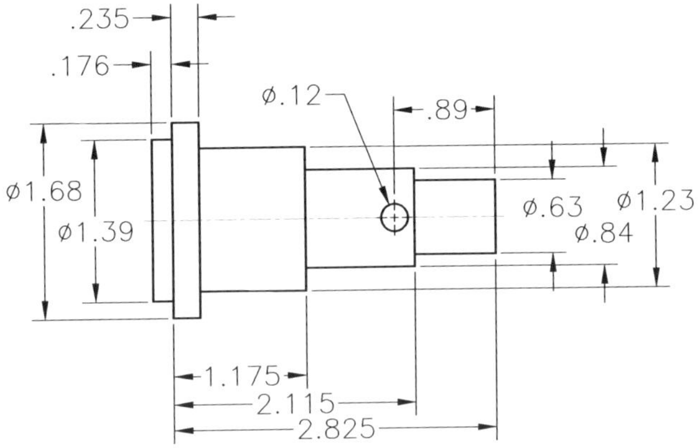

Figure 17-34 *Drawing of Part-1*

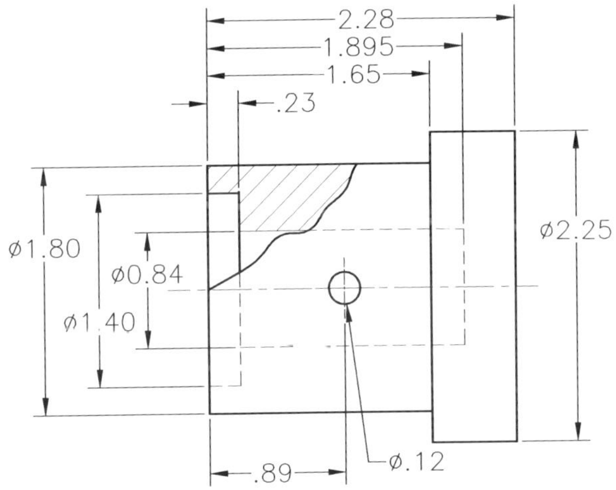

Figure 17-35 *Drawing of Part-2*

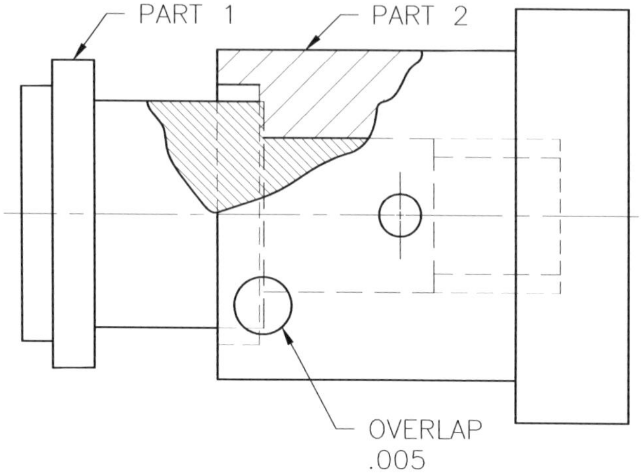

Figure 17-36 *Assembly drawing after attaching Part-1 and Part-2*

Answers to Self-Evaluation Test

1. named objects, **2.** duplicated, unique, **3. Attach**, **4.** demand loading, **5. Overlay**, **6.** selected, **7.** F, **8.** T, **9.** F, **10.** T

Index

C

D

E

F

G

H

I

J

K

L

M

N

O

P

Q

R

U

V

W

X

Z

Other Publications by CADCIM Technologies

The following is the list of some of the publications by CADCIM Technologies. Please visit *www.cadcim.com* for the complete listing.

AutoCAD Textbooks

- AutoCAD 2020: A Problem-Solving Approach, Basic and Intermediate, 26th Edition
- AutoCAD 2019: A Problem-Solving Approach, Basic and Intermediate, 25th Edition
- AutoCAD 2018: A Problem-Solving Approach, Basic and Intermediate, 24th Edition
- Advanced AutoCAD 2018: A Problem-Solving Approach, 3D and Advanced, 24th Edition
- Customizing AutoCAD 2020, 13th Edition

Autodesk Inventor Textbooks

- Autodesk Inventor Professional 2020 for Designers, 20th Edition
- Autodesk Inventor Professional 2019 for Designers, 19th Edition

AutoCAD MEP Textbooks

- AutoCAD MEP 2020 for Designers, 5th Edition
- AutoCAD MEP 2018 for Designers, 4th Edition
- AutoCAD MEP 2016 for Designers, 3rd Edition

AutoCAD Plant 3D Textbooks

- AutoCAD Plant 3D 2018 for Designers, 4th Edition
- AutoCAD Plant 3D 2016 for Designers, 3rd Edition

Autodesk Fusion 360 Textbook

- Autodesk Fusion 360: A Tutorial Approach

Solid Edge Textbooks

- Solid Edge 2019 for Designers, 16th Edition
- Solid Edge ST10 for Designers, 15th Edition

NX Textbooks

- Siemens NX 2019 for Designers,12th Edition
- NX 12.0 for Designers, 11th Edition

NX Mold Textbook

- Mold Design Using NX 11.0: A Tutorial Approach

NX Nastran Textbook

- NX Nastran 9.0 for Designers

SolidWorks Textbooks

- SOLIDWORKS 2019 for Designers, 17th Edition
- Learning SOLIDWORKS 2018: A Project Based Approach
- SOLIDWORKS 2018: A Tutorial Approach

SolidWorks Simulation Textbooks

- SOLIDWORKS Simulation 2018: A Tutorial Approach
- SOLIDWORKS Simulation 2016: A Tutorial Approach

CATIA Textbooks

- CATIA V5-6R2018 for Designers, 16th Edition
- CATIA V5-6R2017 for Designers, 15th Edition

Creo Parametric Textbooks

- Creo Parametric 5.0 for Designers, 5th Edition
- Creo Parametric 4.0 for Designers, 4th Edition

ANSYS Textbooks

- ANSYS Workbench 14.0: A Tutorial Approach
- ANSYS 11.0 for Designers

Creo Direct Textbook

- Creo Direct 2.0 and Beyond for Designers

Autodesk Alias Textbooks

- Learning Autodesk Alias Design 2016, 5th Edition
- Learning Autodesk Alias Design 2015, 4th Edition

AutoCAD LT Textbooks

- AutoCAD LT 2017 for Designers, 12th Edition

EdgeCAM Textbooks

- EdgeCAM 11.0 for Manufacturers
- EdgeCAM 10.0 for Manufacturers

Autodesk Revit MEP Textbooks

- Exploring Autodesk Revit 2019 for MEP, 6th Edition
- Exploring Autodesk Revit 2018 for MEP, 5th Edition

AutoCAD Civil 3D Textbooks

- Exploring AutoCAD Civil 3D 2019, 9th Edition
- Exploring AutoCAD Civil 3D 2018, 8th Edition
- Exploring AutoCAD Civil 3D 2017, 7th Edition

AutoCAD Map 3D Textbooks
- Exploring AutoCAD Map 3D 2018, 8th Edition
- Exploring AutoCAD Map 3D 2017, 7th Edition

RISA-3D Textbook
- Exploring RISA-3D 14.0

Autodesk Navisworks Textbooks
- Exploring Autodesk Navisworks 2019, 5th Edition
- Exploring Autodesk Navisworks 2017, 4th Edition
- Exploring Autodesk Navisworks 2016, 3rd Edition

AutoCAD Raster Design Textbooks
- Exploring AutoCAD Raster Design 2017
- Exploring AutoCAD Raster Design 2016

Bentley STAAD.Pro Textbooks
- Exploring Bentley STAAD.Pro (CONNECT Edition)
- Exploring Bentley STAAD.Pro V8i (SELECTseries 6)

Autodesk 3ds Max Design Textbooks
- Autodesk 3ds Max Design 2015: A Tutorial Approach, 15th Edition
- Autodesk 3ds Max Design 2014: A Tutorial Approach

Autodesk 3ds Max Textbooks
- Autodesk 3ds Max 2019: A Comprehensive Guide, 19th Edition
- Autodesk 3ds Max 2018: A Comprehensive Guide, 18th Edition
- Autodesk 3ds Max 2019 for Beginners: A Tutorial Approach, 19th Edition

Autodesk Maya Textbooks
- Autodesk Maya 2019: A Comprehensive Guide, 11th Edition
- Character Animation: A Tutorial Approach

Pixologic ZBrush Textbooks
- Pixologic ZBrush 4R8: A Comprehensive Guide, 4th Edition
- Pixologic ZBrush 4R7: A Comprehensive Guide, 3rd Edition
- Pixologic ZBrush 4R6: A Comprehensive Guide

Fusion Textbooks
- Blackmagic Design Fusion 7 Studio: A Tutorial Approach, 3rd Edition
- The eyeon Fusion 6.3: A Tutorial Approach

Flash Textbooks
- Adobe Flash Professional CC 2015: A Tutorial Approach, 3rd Edition
- Adobe Flash Professional CC: A Tutorial Approach
- Adobe Flash Professional CS6: A Tutorial Approach

Computer Programming Textbooks
- Introducing PHP 7/MySQL
- Introduction to C^{++} programming, 2nd Edition
- Learning Oracle 12c - A PL/SQL Approach
- Learning ASP.NET AJAX
- Introduction to Java Programming, 2nd Edition
- Learning Visual Basic.NET 2008

MAXON CINEMA 4D Textbooks
- MAXON CINEMA 4D R20 Studio: A Tutorial Approach, 7th Edition
- MAXON CINEMA 4D R19 Studio: A Tutorial Approach, 6th Edition
- MAXON CINEMA 4D R18 Studio: A Tutorial Approach, 5th Edition

Oracle Primavera Textbooks
- Exploring Oracle Primavera P6 Professional 18, 3rd Edition
- Exploring Oracle Primavera P6 v8.4

AutoCAD Textbooks Authored by Prof. Sham Tickoo and Published by Autodesk Press
- AutoCAD: A Problem-Solving Approach: 2013 and Beyond
- AutoCAD 2012: A Problem-Solving Approach
- AutoCAD 2011: A Problem-Solving Approach
- AutoCAD 2010: A Problem-Solving Approach
- Customizing AutoCAD 2010
- AutoCAD 2009: A Problem-Solving Approach

Coming Soon from CADCIM Technologies
- SolidCAM 2019: A Tutorial Approach
- Project Management Using Microsoft Project 2016 for Project Managers
- AutoCAD Electrical 2020: A Tutorial Approach
- Exploring ETabs

Made in the USA
Las Vegas, NV
22 June 2021

25209106R00448